The Reader's Adviser

The Reader's Adviser
A Layman's Guide to Literature
13th EDITION
Barbara A. Chernow and George A. Vallasi, Series Editors

Volume 1
The Best in American and British Fiction, Poetry, Essays, Literary Biography, Bibliography, and Reference
Edited by Fred Kaplan

Books about Books • Bibliography • Reference Books: Literature • Broad Studies and General Anthologies • British Poetry: Early to Romantic • British Poetry: Middle Period • Modern British and Irish Poetry • American Poetry: Early Period • Modern American Poetry • British Fiction: Early Period • British Fiction: Middle Period • Modern British Fiction • American Fiction: Early Period • Modern American Fiction • Commonwealth Literature • Essays and Criticism • Literary Biography and Autobiography

Volume 2
The Best in American and British Drama and World Literature in English Translation
Edited by Maurice Charney

The Drama • British Drama: Early to Eighteenth Century • Shakespeare • Modern British and Irish Drama • American Drama • World Literature • Greek Literature • Latin Literature • French Literature • Italian Literature • Spanish Literature • Portuguese Literature • German and Netherlandic Literature • Scandinavian Literature • Russian Literature • East European Literatures • Yiddish Literature • Hebrew Literature • Spanish American Literature • African Literature • Middle Eastern Literature • Literature of the Indian Subcontinent • Chinese Literature • Japanese Literature • Southeast Asian and Korean Literature

Volume 3
The Best in General Reference Literature, the Social Sciences, History, and the Arts
Edited by Paula T. Kaufman

Reference Books: General • Dictionaries • General Biography and Autobiography • The Social Sciences • Education • Ancient History • United States History • Western Hemisphere: Canada and Latin America • British History • World History • Music and Dance • Art and Architecture • The Mass Media • Folklore and Humor • Travel and Exploration

Volume 4
The Best in the Literature of Philosophy and World Religions
Edited by William L. Reese

General Philosophy • Greek and Roman Philosophy • Medieval Philosophy •
Renaissance Philosophy • Modern Philosophy • Twentieth-Century Philosophy •
Ancient Religion and Philosophy • Eastern Religion and Philosophy • Judaism •
Early Christianity • Late Christianity • Bibles • Minority Religions

Volume 5
The Best in the Literature of Science, Technology, and Medicine
Edited by Paul T. Durbin

General Science • History of Science, Technology, and Medicine • Philosophy of
Science and Pseudoscience • Mathematics • Statistics and Probability • Information
and Communication Science • Astronomy and Space Science • Earth Sciences •
Physics • Chemistry • Biology • Ecology and Environmental Science • Genetics •
Medicine and Health • Illness and Disease • Clinical Psychology and Psychiatry •
Engineering and Technology • Energy • Ethics of Science, Technology,
and Medicine • Science and Society

THE
Reader's Adviser

A Layman's Guide to Literature
13th EDITION

Volume 1

The Best in American and British Fiction, Poetry, Essays, Literary Biography, Bibliography, and Reference

Edited by Fred Kaplan

Barbara A. Chernow and George A. Vallasi, Series Editors

R. R. BOWKER COMPANY
New York & London, 1986

Published by R. R. Bowker Company,
a division of Reed Publishing USA
245 West 17th Street, New York, NY 10011
Copyright © 1986 by Reed Publishing USA,
a division of Reed Holdings, Inc.

International Standard Book Numbers
0-8352-2145-8 (Volume 1)
0-8352-2146-6 (Volume 2)
0-8352-2147-4 (Volume 3)
0-8352-2148-2 (Volume 4)
0-8352-2149-0 (Volume 5)
0-8352-2315-9 (Volume 6)
International Standard Serial Number 0094-5943
Library of Congress Catalog Card Number 57-13277

The paper used in this publication meets the minimum
requirements of American National Standard for
Information Sciences—Permanence of Papers for
Printed Library Materials, ANSI Z39.48-1984.

Contents

Preface

Over its thirteen editions, and since its first publication in 1921, chapters of *The Reader's Adviser* have been expanded and reorganized and new topics have been introduced, thus better to serve the needs of a growing and more diversified population. The first edition, entitled *The Bookman's Manual,* was based on Bessie Graham's course on book salesmanship given at the William Penn Evening High School in Philadelphia. Graham organized the book so that the chapters corresponded to the general classifications familiar to booksellers and, by providing publishers and prices in her text, she simplified book ordering for the bookseller. Since 1921, however, the book industry has experienced significant changes—comparatively few independent book dealers exist, information on titles is available from a wide variety of printed and computerized sources, and publishers are taking fewer risks by printing just enough copies of a title to meet immediate demands. At the same time that these changes were occurring, *The Reader's Adviser* was finding a broader audience; although still used by booksellers, the librarians, general readers, and high school and college students found that the topical organization of the volume with its annotated bibliographies also met their needs. For the nonspecialist who is interested in reading about a particular subject, *The Reader's Adviser* is a perfect starting point. The six-volume set provides annotated bibliographies arranged by subject, with brief biographies of authors, creative artists, and scientists worthy of special mention; in addition, it informs the reader of a book's availability, price, and purchasing source. Since the set is kept up to date by regular revisions, the volumes also serve as a reflection of the current state of the best available literature in print in the United States.

As a result of the growth of new fields of interest to the reading public and the continuing increase in the number of titles published, *The Reader's Adviser* has expanded with each succeeding edition. For this thirteenth edition, it has grown from three to six volumes. The first three volumes will appear simultaneously in 1986; the final three in 1988. The organization of the first two volumes is similar to that in the twelfth edition: Volume 1 covers mainly American and British fiction and poetry and Volume 2 covers drama, Shakespeare, and world literature in English translation. Volume 3, which covers the best in general reference literature, the social sciences, history, and the arts, has experienced the most significant changes—most chapters have been expanded, virtually new chapters have been created for the arts, and several chapters have been moved to form the nuclei of Volumes 4 and 5. Volume 4 covers the Bible, world religions, and philosophy; Volume 5 is devoted to science, technology, and medicine. Except for Volume 6, containing indexes to the entire set, each of the volumes has been edited by a specialist in the field, the whole project having been coordinated by the series editors.

Although the thirteenth edition of *The Reader's Adviser* retains the essential format and basic structure of the earlier editions, the editors and publisher have made a number of improvements designed to enhance the appearance and usefulness of the volumes. First, the design has been modified to increase readability and provide a more open look. The typeface is easier to read, biographies are printed in a larger face, and the titles in the "books about" sections following the biographies are in alphabetical order according to the authors' surnames. Finally, the authors and anonymous sagas that form the main headings in *The Reader's Adviser* are listed in alphabetical order within the chapters rather than the chronological order of previous editions. In the front matter of each volume, a Chronology of these individuals and works provides the reader with an overview of the development of a particular genre. For each chapter, the editors chose an eminent scholar or librarian with particular expertise in the subject area, so that the selection of bibliographies and main listings would reflect the best-informed judgment of a specialist in the field.

The greatest challenge was that of selection—which titles and authors to include. Since *The Reader's Adviser* is not a research tool for students and scholars, but rather a reference work designed for the nonspecialist, the editors' goal was to include those books generally available to an intelligent reader through the facilities of the library system of a moderately sized municipality. Books must be currently available in English from a publisher or distributor in the United States. Out-of-print titles are included for those major works which, because of their importance in the field, could not be excluded from the list. If a book is not presently available in English or cannot be purchased in the United States, it is considered out of print (o.p.) by the editors. In some disciplines, such as modern American poetry, publishers allow titles to go out of print quickly and the available literature was found to be surprisingly thin. The reader will also note that Volume 2 (the comparative literature volume) reveals how little of the world's non-English literature has been translated into English.

In selecting authors for main entries, contributing editors weighed a number of criteria—historical importance, current popularity as determined by the number of in-print titles, and space limitations. Particularly in American and British fiction, U.S. and world history, and the social sciences chapters, the necessity of adding new authors sometimes required eliminating authors who were previously the subjects of main entries in earlier editions of *The Reader's Adviser*. Most major authors are represented; other authors were selected as examples of particular movements or styles. The latter category is subjective; although these choices are valid, someone else's choices might have been equally valid. The constraints of space impose their own compromises.

The organization of each volume and of each chapter is designed to move the reader from the general to the specific, from reference books, books of history and criticism, and anthologies to specific authors, scientists, and creative artists. Each chapter opens with a brief introduction that provides a framework for the literature of a particular period or discipline, followed by general reading lists and then, with few exceptions, the main entries. In chapters covering more than one area of study, such as the social sciences, or more than one country, such as Southeast Asia, this pattern repeats itself for each major division. Each author selected as a main entry receives a brief biography followed by bibliographies of books by and about him or her. Wherever possible, the date of first publication follows the title of a work mentioned in the short biography or will instead appear, when available, as the first date in the "Books by. . ." entries below. In addition to *Books in Print, The New Columbia Encyclopedia* (1975) has served as the authority in verifying dates. The bibliographies of books by an author are mainly composed of collections of works and in-print titles of individual works in the particular genre covered by the chapter. Other titles may be mentioned in the biography, but only those works relevant to the genre under discussion appear in the bibliographies.

The bibliographic entries are so designed that the reader will be able both to locate a book in a library and to know where it is available for purchase and at what price. The editors have included the following information available or applicable for each title: author; title (translated titles or original titles are given in parentheses following the title); editor; series title; translator; authors of prefaces, introductions, and forewords; edition; number of volumes; reprint data; publisher (if more than one, publishers are listed alphabetically); date of publication; and price. The reader should be cautioned that the accuracy and completeness of information depends in large part on the information publishers supply to the *Books in Print* database and the information listed in individual publishers' catalogs.

If a date is listed directly after a title, this indicates the date of the publication of the first edition, regardless of whether that edition is still in print. For reprints, the date of the particular edition from which it was reprinted is given. If a title consists of more than one volume, and is listed with only one price, this is the price of the entire set. As book pricing changes so rapidly, some prices listed in *The Reader's Adviser* may have already changed. Although the editors considered the possibility of deleting prices from *The Reader's Adviser*, it was decided to retain them as an indication to the reader of the general price category into which an individual title falls and to assist the librarian in acquisition. Finally, the reader should be aware that not all in-print editions of a work are necessarily listed, but rather those selected by the editors because of their quality or special features.

To guide the reader through the volumes, *The Reader's Adviser* includes cross-references in three forms. The "see" reference leads the reader to the appropriate volume and chapter for information on a specific author or topic. "See also" refers the reader to additional information in another chapter or volume. Within any introductory narrative portions, the name of an author who appears as a main listing in another chapter or volume is printed in large and small capital letters. In each case, if the chapter cross-referenced is in a different volume from that being consulted, the volume number is also provided.

Each volume of *The Reader's Adviser* has three indexes—one for names, one for book titles, and one for general subjects. The Name Index includes all authors, editors, compilers, composers, directors, actors, artists, philosophers, and scientists cited in *The Reader's Adviser*. If a name appears as a main listing in the text, the name as well as the first page number of the main listing appear in boldface type. The Title Index includes book titles with two exceptions: collected works or generic titles by authors who receive main listings (e.g., *Selected Prose of T. S. Eliot*) and "books about" titles that follow the main listings and include the name of the main-entry author (e.g., *Booker T. Washington* by Louis R. Harlan). (This does not hold true in the case of Chapter 3, "Shakespeare," in Volume 2, where all works by and about him are included.) Therefore, to ensure locating all titles by and about a main-entry author, the user should look up that author in the Name Index to locate the primary listing.

In preparing the thirteenth edition of *The Reader's Adviser*, the series editors are indebted to a great many people for assistance and advice. We are especially grateful to the many people at R. R. Bowker who have worked with us; in particular, to Olga S. Weber, who provided encouragement, support, and a critical eye in reading manuscripts; to Kathy Kleibacker, for her constant faith in the project; and to Marion Sader, Julia Raymunt, Iris Topel, and Nancy Bucenec for their attention to detail and concern for quality in editing and production. We were fortunate in our choice of volume editors. Fred Kaplan, general editor of Volume 1, The Best in American and British Fiction, Poetry, Essays, Literary Biography, Bibliography, and Reference, is Professor of English at Queens College and at the Graduate Center, City University of New York; he is a distinguished Dickens and Carlyle scholar, the editor of *Dickens Studies Annual*, a member of the board of the Carlyle Papers, and is currently writing a biography of Dickens. The general editor of Volume 2, The Best in American and British Drama and World Literature in English Translation, is Maurice Charney, Distinguished Professor at Rutgers University in the department of English. His published works include *How to Read Shakespeare* and a biography of Joe Orton. Paula T. Kaufman, who served as general editor of Volume 3, The Best in General Reference Literature, the Social Sciences, History, and the Arts, is director of the academic information services group, Columbia University Libraries. Volume 4, The Best in the Literature of Philosophy and World Religions, was developed under the general editorship of William L. Reese. He is Professor of Philosophy at the State University of New York, Albany. His publications include the *Dictionary of Philosophy and Religion*. Paul T. Durbin is general editor of

Volume 5, The Best in the Literature of Science, Technology, and Medicine. He is Professor of Philosophy at the University of Delaware and editor of *A Guide to the Culture of Science, Technology, and Medicine.* All made invaluable suggestions for organizing their volumes, recommended contributing editors, and reviewed each chapter for substantive content. The editors also wish to thank the following individuals for their help in the preparation of *The Reader's Adviser:* Hilda H. Golden, University of Massachusetts, Amherst; Jill Levenson, University of Toronto; J. Hillis Miller, Yale University; Susan Morgan, New York Public Library, Jefferson Market Branch; Margaret Renald, Queens College of the City University of New York; Paul Schmidt, New York Public Library, Jefferson Market Branch. Finally, a special thanks to David B. Biesel, who first brought the project to us, and to Antoinette Boone and Frank Van Orman Brown, who keyboarded all of the chapters, assisted in verifying bibliographic data, and coded material for the indexes.

In the 65 years since *The Reader's Adviser* first appeared, it has grown from a tool for booksellers to a standard reference work. In addition to bibliographic information, the introductions and biographies are enjoyable reading for someone just browsing through the volumes. *The Reader's Adviser* has a distinguished history; it is hoped that these latest volumes will continue in that tradition.

Barbara A. Chernow
George A. Vallasi

Contributing Editors

Robert Balay, BROAD STUDIES AND GENERAL ANTHOLOGIES: LITERATURE
Reference Editor, *Choice*

Maurice Beebe, MODERN AMERICAN FICTION
Editor of the *Journal of Modern Literature*, Temple University

George Bornstein, MODERN BRITISH AND IRISH POETRY
Professor of English at the University of Michigan, Ann Arbor, and author of
Transformations of Romanticism in Yeats, Eliot and Stevens and *Yeats and Shelley*,
as well as editor of *Romantic Modern Reevaluations of Literary Tradition*

James M. Cox, AMERICAN POETRY: EARLY PERIOD
Professor of English at Dartmouth College, author of *Mark Twain: The Fate of
Humor*, and editor of *Robert Frost: A Collection of Critical Essays*

Alan Warren Friedman, MODERN BRITISH FICTION
Professor of English at the University of Texas, Austin, and author of *William
Faulkner*

Norman Fruman, BRITISH POETRY: MODERN TO ROMANTIC
Professor of English at the University of Minnesota and author of *Coleridge: The
Damaged Archangel*, and numerous articles in eighteenth-century and Romantic
studies

Morris Golden, BRITISH FICTION: EARLY TO ROMANTIC
Professor of English at the University of Massachusetts, Amherst, and author of
Fielding's Moral Psychology and *The Self Observed: Swift, Johnson, Wordsworth*

Chandler Grannis, BOOKS ABOUT BOOKS
Contributing Editor, *Publishers Weekly*

Catherine Griffiths, COMMONWEALTH LITERATURE
Doctoral Candidate, Department of English, University of Toronto

Fred Kaplan, BRITISH FICTION: MIDDLE PERIOD
Professor of English at Queens College and at the Graduate Center, City University
of New York; distinguished Dickens and Carlyle scholar; the editor of *Dickens
Studies Annual;* member of the board of the Carlyle Papers; and currently writing
a biography of Dickens

Frederick R. Karl, LITERARY BIOGRAPHY AND AUTOBIOGRAPHY
Professor of English, New York University

Kathleen Bonann Marshall, ESSAYS AND CRITICISM
Adjunct Lecturer in English, University of Iowa

Donald G. Marshall, ESSAYS AND CRITICISM
Professor of English, University of Iowa

Charles Molesworth, MODERN AMERICAN POETRY
Professor of English at Queens College and at the Graduate Center, City University
of New York; and author of *The Fierce Embrace: A Study of Contemporary American
Poetry; Gary Snyder's Vision;* and *Donald Barthelme's Fiction*

Jean Peters, BIBLIOGRAPHY
Manager, Information Resources, R. R. Bowker Company

Hartley S. Spatt, BRITISH POETRY: MIDDLE PERIOD
Associate Professor of English at the State University of New York, Maritime
College

William J. Stuckey, AMERICAN FICTION: EARLY PERIOD
Professor of English at Purdue University

Barbara Turman Wilkie, REFERENCE BOOKS: LITERATURE
Information Research Specialist, Investment Library, CIGNA Corp., West
Hartford, Connecticut

Abbreviations

abr.	abridged	ltd. ed.	limited edition
AHR	*American Historical Review*	MLA	Modern Language Association
Amer.	America(n)	Mod.	Modern
annot.	annotated	*N.Y. Herald Tribune*	*New York Herald Tribune*
bd.	bound	*N.Y. Times*	*New York Times*
bdg.	binding	o.p.	out-of-print
Bk(s).	Book(s)	orig.	original
Class.	Classic(s)	pap.	paperback
coll.	collected	Pr.	Press
coll. ed.	collector's ed.	pref.	preface
comp.	compiled, compiler	pt(s).	parts
corr.	corrected	*PW*	*Publishers Weekly*
Ctr.	Center	repr.	reprint
ed.	edited, editor, edition	rev. ed.	revised edition
Eng.	English	*SB*	*Studies in Bibliography*
enl. ed.	enlarged edition	sel.	selected
fl.	flourished	Ser.	Series
fwd.	foreword	*SR*	*Saturday Review*
gen. ed(s).	general editor(s)	Stand.	Standard
ill.	illustrated	Supp.	Supplement
imit. lea.	imitation leather	*TLS*	*Times Literary Supplement*
intro.	introduction		
lea.	leather	trans.	translated, translator, translation
lg.-type ed.	large-type edition		
Lib.	Library	Univ.	University
lib. bdg.	library binding	Vol(s).	Volume(s)
Lit.	Literature		
LJ	*Library Journal*		

Chronology

Main author entries appear here chronologically by year of birth. Within each chapter, main author entries are arranged alphabetically by surname.

Stevens, Wallace. 1879–1955
Williams, William Carlos. 1883–1963
Pound, Ezra. 1885–1972
H. D. 1886–1961
Jeffers, Robinson. 1887–1962
Moore, Marianne. 1887–1972
Ransom, John Crowe. 1888–1974
Aiken, Conrad. 1889–1973
MacLeish, Archibald. 1892–1982
Millay, Edna St. Vincent. 1892–1950
Cummings, E. E. 1894–1962
Reznikoff, Charles. 1894–1976
Bogan, Louise. 1897–1970
Benét, Stephen Vincent. 1898–1943
Crane, Hart. 1899–1932
Tate, Allen. 1899–1979
Riding, Laura. 1901–
Hughes, Langston. 1902–1967
Cullen, Countee. 1903–1946
Rakosi, Carl. 1903–
Eberhart, Richard. 1904–
Zukofsky, Louis. 1904–1978
Kunitz, Stanley. 1905–
Rexroth, Kenneth. 1905–1983
Warren, Robert Penn. 1905–
Oppen, George. 1908–1984
Roethke, Theodore. 1908–1963
Olson, Charles. 1910–1970
Bishop, Elizabeth. 1911–1979
Patchen, Kenneth. 1911–1972
Schwartz, Delmore. 1913–1966
Shapiro, Karl. 1913–
Berryman, John. 1914–1972
Ignatow, David. 1914–
Jarrell, Randall. 1914–1965
Stafford, William. 1914–
Brooks, Gwendolyn. 1917–
Lowell, Robert. 1917–1977
Duncan, Robert. 1919–
Swenson, May. 1919–

Bukowski, Charles. 1920–
Nemerov, Howard. 1920–
Carruth, Hayden. 1921–
Wilbur, Richard. 1921–
Dickey, James. 1923–
Dugan, Alan. 1923–
Hugo, Richard. 1923–1982
Levertov, Denise. 1923–
Logan, John. 1923–
Simpson, Louis. 1923–
Justice, Donald. 1925–
Koch, Kenneth. 1925–
Merrill, James. 1925–
Ammons, A. R. 1926–
Bly, Robert. 1926–
Creeley, Robert. 1926–
Ginsberg, Allen. 1926–
O'Hara, Frank. 1926–1966
Snodgrass, W. D. 1926–
Ashbery, John. 1927–
Kinnell, Galway. 1927–
Merwin, W. S. 1927–
Wright, James. 1927–1980
Hall, Donald. 1928–
Sexton, Anne. 1928–1977
Dorn, Edward. 1929–
Howard, Richard. 1929–
Rich, Adrienne. 1929–
Corso, Gregory. 1930–
Snyder, Gary. 1930–
McClure, Michael. 1932–
Plath, Sylvia. 1932–1963
Baraka, Imamu Amiri. 1934–
Strand, Mark. 1934–
Wright, Charles. 1935–
Williams, C. K. 1936–
Wakoski, Diane. 1937–
Simic, Charles. 1938–
Pinsky, Robert. 1940–
Hass, Robert. 1941–
Smith, Dave. 1942–
Glück, Louise. 1943–

10. British Fiction: Early Period
Malory, Sir Thomas. fl. 1470
More, Sir Thomas, St. 1478–1535
Bunyan, John. 1628–1688
Defoe, Daniel. 1661–1731
Swift, Jonathan. 1667–1745
Richardson, Samuel. 1689–1761
Fielding, Henry. 1707–1754
Sterne, Laurence. 1713–1768
Smollett, Tobias George. 1721–1771
Goldsmith, Oliver. 1728–1774
Burney, Fanny. 1752–1840

11. British Fiction: Middle Period
Radcliffe, Ann. 1764–1823
Edgeworth, Maria. 1767–1849
Scott, Sir Walter. 1771–1832
Austen, Jane. 1775–1817
Peacock, Thomas Love. 1785–1866
Marryat, Captain Frederick. 1792–1848
Shelley, Mary Wollstonecraft. 1797–1851
Bulwer-Lytton. 1803–1873
Disraeli, Benjamin. 1804–1881
Gaskell, Elizabeth Cleghorn. 1810–1865
Thackeray, William Makepeace. 1811–1863
Dickens, Charles. 1812–1870
Reade, Charles. 1814–1884
Trollope, Anthony. 1815–1882
Brontë, Charlotte. 1816–1855
Brontë, Emily Jane. 1818–1848
Eliot, George. 1819–1880
Kingsley, Charles. 1819–1875
Brontë, Anne. 1820–1849
Collins, Wilkie. 1824–1889
Meredith, George. 1828–1909
Carroll, Lewis. 1832–1898
Du Maurier, George. 1834–1896
Butler, Samuel. 1835–1902

Hardy, Thomas. 1840–1928
Hudson, William Henry. 1841–1922
Stevenson, Robert Louis. 1850–1894
Moore, George. 1852–1933
Conrad, Joseph. 1857–1924
Gissing, George. 1857–1903
Doyle, Sir Arthur Conan. 1859–1930
Barrie, Sir J. M. 1860–1937
Kipling, Rudyard. 1865–1936

12. Modern British Fiction
Wells, H. G. 1866–1946
Bennett, Arnold. 1867–1931
Galsworthy, John. 1867–1933
Douglas, Norman. 1868–1952
Munro, H. H. 1870–1916
Ford, Ford Madox. 1873–1939
Richardson, Dorothy. 1873?–1957
Maugham, W. Somerset. 1874–1965
Forster, E. M. 1879–1970
Joyce, James. 1881–1941
Woolf, Virginia. 1882–1941
Lewis, Wyndham. 1884–1957
Swinnerton, Frank. 1884–1982
Lawrence, D. H. 1885–1930
Firbank, Ronald. 1886–1926
Cary, Joyce. 1888–1957
Compton-Burnett, Dame Ivy. 1892–1969
Sackville-West, Victoria. 1892–1962
Tolkien, J. R. R. 1892–1973
West, Dame Rebecca. 1892–1983
Huxley, Aldous. 1894–1963
Rhys, Jean. 1894–1979
Hartley, L. P. 1895–1972
Lewis, C. S. 1898–1963
Bowen, Elizabeth. 1899–1973
Hughes, Richard. 1900–1976
O'Faolain, Sean. 1900–

Pritchett, V. S. 1900–

O'Connor, Frank. 1903–1966

Orwell, George. 1903–1950

Waugh, Evelyn. 1903–1966

Greene, Graham. 1904–

Isherwood, Christopher. 1904–1986

Green, Henry. 1905–1974

Koestler, Arthur. 1905–1983

Powell, Anthony. 1905–

Snow, Sir C. P. 1905–1980

White, T. H. 1906–1964

Golding, William. 1911–

O'Brien, Flann. 1911–1966

Durrell, Lawrence. 1912–

Pym, Barbara. 1913–1980

Wilson, Angus. 1913–

Burgess, Anthony. 1917–

Spark, Muriel. 1918–

Lessing, Doris. 1919–

Murdoch, Iris. 1919–

Scott, Paul. 1920–1978

Amis, Kingsley. 1922–

Braine, John. 1922–

Fowles, John. 1926–

Sillitoe, Alan. 1928–

Bradbury, Malcolm. 1932–

Wilson, Colin. 1932–

Lodge, David. 1935–

Thomas, D. M. 1935–

Bragg, Melvyn. 1939–

Drabble, Margaret. 1939–

Carter, Angela. 1940–

13. American Fiction: Early Period

Brown, Charles Brockden. 1771–1810

Irving, Washington. 1783–1859

Cooper, James Fenimore. 1789–1851

Hawthorne, Nathaniel. 1804–1864

Poe, Edgar Allan. 1809–1849

Stowe, Harriet Beecher. 1811–1896

Melville, Herman. 1819–1891

Wallace, Lewis. 1827–1905

Twain, Mark. 1835–1910

Harte, Bret. 1836?–1902

Howells, William Dean. 1837–1920

Bierce, Ambrose. 1842–1914?

James, Henry. 1843–1916

Cable, George Washington. 1844–1925

Harris, Joel Chandler. 1848–1908

Jewett, Sarah Orne. 1849–1909

Bellamy, Edward. 1850–1898

Chopin, Kate. 1851–1904

Garland, Hamlin. 1860–1940

Wister, Owen. 1860–1938

Henry, O. 1862–1910

14. Modern American Fiction

Wharton, Edith. 1862–1937

Norris, Frank. 1870–1902

Crane, Stephen. 1871–1900

Dreiser, Theodore. 1871–1945

Glasgow, Ellen. 1874–1945

Stein, Gertrude. 1874–1946

Anderson, Sherwood. 1876–1941

Cather, Willa. 1876–1947

London, Jack. 1876–1916

Sinclair, Upton. 1878–1968

Lardner, Ring. 1885–1933

Lewis, Sinclair. 1885–1951

Miller, Henry. 1891–1980

Barnes, Djuna. 1892–1982

Parker, Dorothy. 1893–1967

Porter, Katherine Anne. 1894–1980

Gordon, Caroline. 1895–1981

Dos Passos, John. 1896–1970

Fitzgerald, F. Scott. 1896–1940

Faulkner, William. 1897–1962

Wilder, Thornton. 1897–1975

Hemingway, Ernest. 1899–1961

Wolfe, Thomas. 1900–1938

Steinbeck, John. 1902–1968

Caldwell, Erskine. 1903–
Cozzens, James Gould. 1903–1978
Nin, Anaïs. 1903–1977
Farrell, James T. 1904–1979
West, Nathanael. 1904–1940
O'Hara, John. 1905–1970
Warren, Robert Penn. 1905–
Wright, Richard. 1908–1960
Agee, James. 1909–1955
Welty, Eudora. 1909–
Morris, Wright. 1910–
Cheever, John. 1912–1982
McCarthy, Mary. 1912–
Burroughs, William S. 1914–
Ellison, Ralph. 1914–
Malamud, Bernard. 1914–1986
Bellow, Saul. 1915–
Percy, Walker. 1916–
Auchincloss, Louis. 1917–
McCullers, Carson. 1917–1967
Powers, J. F. 1917–
Jackson, Shirley. 1919–1965
Salinger, J. D. 1919–
Jones, James. 1921–1977
Gaddis, William. 1922–
Kerouac, Jack. 1922–1969
Vonnegut, Kurt, Jr. 1922–
Mailer, Norman. 1923–
Purdy, James. 1923–
Baldwin, James. 1924–
Berger, Thomas. 1924–
Capote, Truman. 1924–1984
Gass, William. 1924–
Hawkes, John. 1925–
O'Connor, Flannery. 1925–1965
Styron, William. 1925–
Vidal, Gore. 1925–
Kennedy, William. 1928–
Barth, John. 1930–
Elkin, Stanley. 1930–
Barthelme, Donald. 1931–
Doctorow, E. L. 1931–

Morrison, Toni. 1931–
Coover, Robert. 1932–
Heller, Joseph. 1932–
Updike, John. 1932–
Gardner, John. 1933–1982
Kosinski, Jerzy. 1933–
Roth, Philip. 1933–
Kesey, Ken. 1935–
Pynchon, Thomas. 1937–
Oates, Joyce Carol. 1938–
Irving, John. 1942–

15. Commonwealth Literature

Haliburton, Thomas Chandler. 1796–1865
Moodie, Susanna. 1803–1885
Furphy, Joseph. 1843–1912
Roberts, Charles G. 1860–1943
Carman, Bliss. 1861–1929
Scott, Duncan Campbell. 1862–1947
Leacock, Stephen. 1869–1944
Brennan, Christopher. 1870–1932
Richardson, Henry Handel. 1870–1946
Service, Robert W. 1874–1958
Franklin, Miles. 1879–1954
Lindsay, Norman. 1879–1969
Mansfield, Katherine. 1883–1923
Pratt, E. J. 1883–1964
Shute, Nevil. 1899–1960
Slessor, Kenneth. 1901–1971
Stead, Christina. 1902–1983
Callaghan, Morley. 1903–
Sargeson, Frank. 1903–1982
Birney, Earle. 1904–
Hope, A. D. 1907–
Ross, Sinclair. 1908–
Brasch, Charles Orwell. 1909–1973
Klein, A. M. 1909–1972
Porter, Hal. 1911–
Layton, Irving. 1912–
White, Patrick. 1912–

Davies, Robertson. 1913–
Davin, Daniel Marcus. 1913–
Stewart, Douglas. 1913–
Wright, Judith. 1915–
McAuley, James. 1917–1976
Waddington, Miriam. 1917–
Gallant, Mavis. 1922–
Morrieson, Ronald Hugh. 1922–
1972
Jolley, Elizabeth. 1923–
Frame, Janet. 1924–
Astley, Thea. 1925–
Baxter, James Keir. 1926–1972
Laurence, Margaret. 1926–
Kroetsch, Robert. 1927–
Beaver, Bruce. 1928–
Hood, Hugh. 1928–
Findley, Timothy. 1930–
Jones, Evan. 1931–
Macpherson, Jay. 1931–
Munro, Alice. 1931–
Richler, Mordecai. 1931–
Cohen, Leonard. 1934–
Hall, Rodney. 1935–
Keneally, Thomas. 1935–
Shapcott, Thomas W. 1935–
Stow, Randolph. 1935–
Hine, Daryl. 1936–
Grace, Patricia. 1937–
Murray, Les A. 1938–
Atwood, Margaret. 1939–
Hanrahan, Barbara. 1939–
Ondaatje, Michael. 1943–

16. Essays and Criticism
Bacon, Francis. 1516–1626
Sidney, Sir Philip. 1554–1586
Burton, Robert. 1577–1640
Browne, Sir Thomas. 1605–1682
Addison, Joseph. 1672–1719
Steele, Sir Richard. 1672–1729
Lamb, Charles. 1775–1834

Hazlitt, William. 1778–1830
De Quincey, Thomas. 1785–1859
Carlyle, Thomas. 1795–1881
Macaulay, Thomas Babington, 1st
Baron. 1800–1859
Emerson, Ralph Waldo. 1803–1882
Holmes, Oliver Wendell. 1809–1894
Thoreau, Henry David. 1817–1862
Arnold, Matthew. 1822–1888
Pater, Walter. 1839–1894
James, Henry. 1843–1916
Stevenson, Robert Louis. 1850–
1894
Quiller-Couch, Sir Arthur. 1863–
1944
Smith, Logan Pearsall. 1865–1946
Belloc, Hilaire. 1870–1953
Beerbohm, Sir Max. 1872–1956
Chesterton, G. K. 1874–1936
Mencken, H. L. 1880–1956
Eliot, T. S. 1888–1965
Thurber, James. 1894–1961
Wilson, Edmund. 1895–1972
Burke, Kenneth. 1897–
Cowley, Malcolm. 1898–
Tate, Allen. 1899–1979
White, E. B. 1899–1985
Blackmur, R. P. 1904–1965
Perelman, S. J. 1904–1979
Trilling, Lionel. 1905–1975
MacDonald, Dwight. 1906–1982
Barzun, Jacques. 1907–
Fisher, M. F. K. 1908–
Frye, Northrop. 1912–
Ong, Walter J. 1912–
Thomas, Lewis. 1913–
Kazin, Alfred. 1915–
Fiedler, Leslie A. 1917–
De Man, Paul. 1919–1983
Kermode, Frank. 1919–
Howe, Irving. 1920–
Williams, Raymond. 1921–

Introduction

While there is no end to the making of reference books, this new edition of Volume 1 of *The Reader's Adviser* warrants a prefatory pause for comment on its distinctive features. To the many merits of the twelfth edition, which this replaces, the thirteenth has added one new chapter on "Commonwealth Literature."

Some of the distinguished contributors to the twelfth edition have given way to equally distinguished contributors to the thirteenth. Death, time, and changing inclinations take their toll and have their effect. Indeed, one of the contributors, Maurice Beebe, has died since the completion of his chapter in the present work. If there is no end of reference works, there are reference works that seem, to their editors at any rate, to have no end.

The editor feels fortunate to have persuaded Norman Fruman to do the chapter on the Romantics, Hartley S. Spatt on Victorian poetry, George Bornstein on modern British poetry, Charles Molesworth on modern American poetry, Allan Warren Friedman on modern British fiction, Catherine Griffiths on Commonwealth literature, Donald G. Marshall and Kathleen Bonann Marshall on essays and criticism, Barbara Turman Wilkie on reference books, Robert Balay on anthologies, and Frederick R. Karl on biography. And also fortunate to have retained from among the contributors to the twelfth edition Chandler Grannis, Jean Peters, James M. Cox, Morris Golden, William J. Stuckey, and Maurice Beebe.

The problems each contributing editor faced were both generic and distinctive. The readers of this volume can feel assured that the advice that they are getting is from experts, each of great and widely recognized distinction in his or her field. They have all struggled admirably to find effective, intelligent ways to select from huge bodies of material an appropriate, representative, selectively comprehensive, and above all useful list of primary and secondary materials to present to our readers as a basic guide to the field. The choices were often difficult to make. In the chapters dealing with "contemporary" literature, the difficulty was compounded by the fact that not only had the secondary literature grown considerably since the twelfth edition, but that the primary literature, naturally, had also been growing. And in the chapter on "Essays and Criticism" the contributing editors were faced with the formidable challenge of making a representative selection from a field whose very definition has been changing in the last decade. That change has produced an explosion of prose in areas of "criticism" that did not exist ten years ago. In a sense, then, this volume not only provides maps to the separate areas, but, interestingly, traces the overall pattern of what has been happening in recent years in our literature and in our evaluation of literature.

Fred Kaplan

The Reader's Adviser

CHAPTER 1

Books about Books

Chandler Grannis

Care has been taken that the art of printing should be encouraged, and that it should be easy and cheap and safe for any person to communicate his thoughts to the public.
—JOHN ADAMS, *Dissertation on the Canon and the Feudal Law*

The ever-growing literature about the world of books reflects the fascination experienced by those who work in that world. The histories, analyses, memoirs, and biographies related to books are usually entertaining, often both witty and wise. But they are also instructive. Taken together, they offer an extraordinary store of guidance and experience for the contemporary person whose life is in some way concerned with books. The how-to books about bookselling, bookmaking, and other aspects of the industry have, in many cases, equal charm, together with functional value.

BOOK INDUSTRY HISTORY: GENERAL AND BRITISH

Bennett, Henry S. *English Books and Readers.* Cambridge Univ. Pr. 3 vols. 1952 ea. $49.50–$69.50 set $150.00. History of books from Caxton to the eve of the Civil War.

Bonham-Carter, Victor. *Authors by Profession.* Kaufmann 2 vols. 1978–84 ea. $14.95–$16.95. Called "the most readable and current economic history of authorship."

Briggs, Asa, ed. *Essays in the History of Publishing: In Celebration of the 250th Anniversary of the House of Longman.* Longman 1974 $15.00. A handsome work; valuable historical articles, plus assessments of the future.

Carpenter, Kenneth E., ed. *Books and Society in History.* Bowker 1983 $29.95. Eleven papers on different periods in history, European and American, exploring the role of the book. Given at the Association of College and Research Libraries preconference in June 1980.

Curwen, Henry. *A History of Booksellers: The Old and the New.* 1873. Gale 1968 $44.50. A seminal study of British bookselling.

Darnton, Robert. *The Business of the Enlightenment: A Publishing History of the "Encyclopédie," 1775–1800.* Harvard Univ. Pr. 1979 $20.00. Archives found by the author made possible a massive study of the renowned French encyclopedia.

———. *The Literary Underground of the Old Regime.* Harvard Univ. Pr. 1982 $16.50. A

leading scholar of French publishing and printing history presents studies of pre-
revolutionary antiestablishment publishing, underground and in exile.

Darton, F. J. Harvey. *Children's Books in England: Five Centuries of Social Life*. 1932.
Ed. by Brian Anderson, Cambridge Univ. Pr. 1982 $27.95. Illustrated scholarly
material on John Newbery, Thomas Day, Peter Parley, and others.

Davenport, Cyril. *The Book: Its History and Development*. 1930. Gale 1977 $45.00.
The story prior to film composition and electronic data processing.

Diringer, David. *The Book before Printing: Ancient, Medieval, and Oriental*. Dover pap.
$10.00; Peter Smith repr. of 1953 ed. 1983 $16.25. Long a standard work.

Fitch, Noel R. *Sylvia Beach and the Lost Generation: A History of Literary Paris in the
Twenties and Thirties*. Norton 1983 $25.00. A comprehensive account of the per-
sonalities of the era and of Beach's shop, Shakespeare and Company.

Ford, Hugh D. *Published in Paris: American and British Writers, Printers and Publishers in Paris, 1920–1939*. Pushcart Pr. 1980 pap. $14.95. The many aspects of a leg-
endary era.

Kenney, E. J. *The Classical Text: Aspects of Editing in the Age of the Printed Book*.
Univ. of California Pr. 1974 $22.50. Converting scribal editions of classical texts
into printed form raised new editorial questions.

Kenyon, Frederic G. *Books and Readers in Ancient Greece and Rome*. Folcroft 2d ed.
1951 $20.00; Ares 1980 $12.50. Bookmaking and early publishing methods from
the time of Homer, c.850 B.C., to 400 A.D.

Lehmann-Haupt, Hellmut. *The Life of the Book*. Greenwood repr. of 1957 ed. 1975
$17.00. Addressed to young readers, but of general value.

Levarie, Norma. *The Art and History of Books*. Da Capo 1982 pap. $18.95. Some em-
phasis on the book arts.

Norrie, Ian, ed. *Mumby's Publishing and Bookselling in the 20th Century*. Bowker
(Bell & Hyman) 6th ed. 1982 $35.00. Revised and enlarged from Edward A.
Mumby's classic work, updating the story of the book trade (primarily British)
from Roman times to 1980.

Rostenberg, Leona. *English Publishers in the Graphic Arts, 1599–1700*. Burt Franklin
1963 $23.50

———. *Literary, Political, Scientific, Religious and Legal Publishing, Printing and Bookselling in England, 1551–1700*. Burt Franklin 2 vols. 1963 o.p.

Taubert, Sigfred, ed. *The Book Trade of the World*. Bowker 4 vols. 1972–84 ea. $70.00;
Saur 4 vols. lib. bdg. $280.00. Country-by-country survey of bookselling and pub-
lishing today, reported by leading figures in the book industry.

Taylor, Isaac. *History of the Transmission of Ancient Books to Modern Times*. 1875.
Haskell 1971 $49.95. A century-old piece of scholarship, still valued.

Thompson, James Westfall, trans. and ed. *The Frankfort Book Fair (1574)*. Burt
Franklin 1968 $29.00; by Henry Estienne, Schram 1970 $23.50. Reprint of the
Caxton Club's (Chicago) edition of 1911; fully and heavily illustrated account of
the fair and its meaning in book trade history.

Thwaite, Mary F. *From Primer to Pleasure in Reading*. Horn Bk. 1972 $14.00. History
of children's books in England from the invention of printing to 1914, with an
outline of developments in Australia, North America, and Western Europe.

Winship, George Parker. *The Cambridge Press, 1638–1692*. 1945. *Essay Index Repr.
Ser*. Ayer repr. of 1945 ed. $22.50. A scholarly account of the beginnings of print-
ing and bookmaking in Massachusetts.

Winterich, John T. *Early American Books and Printing*. Dover 1981 pap. $4.95. Win-
terich was always painstaking in his scholarship—and irrepressible in his humor and his love of the illuminating fact.

Woodfield, Denis B. *Surreptitious Printing in England, 1550–1640*. Bibliographical Society of Amer. 1973 $17.50. Unauthorized, though not necessarily "underground," publishing of works in English, French, Italian, Spanish, and Dutch.

BOOK INDUSTRY HISTORY: NORTH AMERICAN

Bader, Barbara. *American Picture Books: From Noah's Ark to the Beast Within*. Macmillan 1976 $45.00. Beautifully color-reproduced pages of hundreds of children's books, with accounts of the significant writers, illustrators, and publishers of these books during a decisive 80-year period.

Belok, Michael V. *Forming the American Minds: Early School Books and Their Compilers, 1783–1837*. Heinemann 1973 $12.50. Aims, contents, and editor-authors of school textbooks in the early U.S. Republic.

Bonn, Thomas L. *Under Cover: An Illustrated History of American Mass Market Paperbacks*. Penguin 1982 pap. $12.95. Almost 200 illustrations, more than 100 in full color; relation of packaging to editorial and marketing decisions; roles of artist, art director; notes on top firms.

Charvat, William. *Literary Publishing in America, 1790–1850*. Univ. of Pennsylvania Pr. 1959 o.p. Includes relation of publishing to early U.S. geography and transport.

Cole, John Y., ed. *Books in Action: The Armed Services Editions*. Lib. of Congress 1984 pap. $4.95. Historical review of the World War II project in which publishers cooperated in issuing soft-cover editions of hundreds of current and standard titles, distributed free to service people.

Davis, Kenneth C. *Two-Bit Culture: The Paperbacking of America*. Houghton Mifflin 1984 $18.95 pap. $9.95. Broad study of the mass-market paperback revolution, its origins, personalities, methods, and relation to authorship and reading.

Dennison, Sally. *Alternative Publishing: Five Modern Histories*. Univ. of Iowa Pr. 1984 $12.95 pap. $9.95. How "small press" publishing established Eliot, Woolf, Joyce, Nin, and Nabokov.

Ford, Worthington. *The Boston Book Market, 1679–1700*. Burt Franklin repr. of 1917 ed. 1973 $21.00. A significant part of the story of early bookselling in the United States.

Lehmann-Haupt, Hellmut, Lawrence C. Wroth, and Rollo G. Silver. *The Book in America: A History of the Making and Selling of Books in the United States*. 1939. Bowker rev. ed. 1951 o.p. The most detailed, comprehensive single volume on the subject.

Madison, Charles A. *Book Publishing in America*. McGraw-Hill 1966 o.p. Leading companies and personalities from 1630 to 1965.

———. *Irving to Irving: Author-Publisher Relations 1800–1974*. Bowker 1974 o.p. The love-hate relations between some U.S. writers and their publishers.

———. *Jewish Publishing in America*. Hebrew Publishing 1976 $11.95. History of leading companies, personalities, trends.

Meckler, Alan Marshall. *Micropublishing: A History of Scholarly Micropublishing in America, 1938–1980*. Greenwood 1982 $23.95. One aspect of publishing in the new age; an answer to the "knowledge explosion" and its deluge of paper.

Schick, Frank L. *The Paperbound Book in America*. Bowker 1958 o.p. A history up to the late 1950s; highly detailed; includes European backgrounds.

Sheehan, Donald. *This Was Publishing*. Indiana Univ. Pr. 1952 o.p. How U.S. publishing was conducted in "old line" houses, 1865–1915.

Stern, Madeleine B. *Books and Book People in 19th-Century America*. Bowker 1978 $29.95. Includes a 75-year history of *Publishers Weekly*, 1872–1947; also many episodes and personalities in the book world.

——. *Imprints on History: Book Publishing and American Frontiers*. AMS Pr. repr. of 1956 ed. 1976 $31.50. Accounts of 16 publishing houses of different kinds, with notes on approximately 200 others.

——, ed. *Publishers for Mass Entertainment in Nineteenth-Century America*. G. K. Hall 1980 $29.50. Accounts of almost 50 firms, their chief publications, personnel, changes in location, ownership, and programs.

Tebbel, John. *A History of Book Publishing in the United States*. Bowker 4 vols. 1972–81 ea. $35.00–$39.95. Era-by-era (1630–1980), highly detailed, readable; the publishers, the unfolding developments, the economic and social environments, and the other parts of the book industry.

Winterich, John T. *Early American Books and Printing*. Dover repr. of 1935 ed. 1981 pap. $4.95. Author was a bibliophile, historian, journalist, and a coeditor of the *Colophon*.

BOOK INDUSTRY BIOGRAPHIES:
PERSONS, COMPANIES, AND ORGANIZATIONS

A great many of the biographies of people or units in the book industry are printed in short-run scholarly editions, or in editions for special circulation, or in small trade editions that sell out and are not reprinted. Hence, many valuable titles are soon out of print. However, we include some of these out-of-print titles in this section for the benefit of those interested in such biographies.

ABINGDON PRESS

Pilkington, James Penn. *The Methodist Publishing House: A History*. Abingdon 1968 vol. 1 $7.50. This volume covers the first 100 years (to 1870) of the Methodist publishing enterprises in the United States.

AMERICAN BOOKSELLERS ASSOCIATION

Anderson, Charles B., ed. *Bookselling in America and the World*. Times Bks. 1975 o.p. History of the ABA, 1900–1975; lists and chronologies; articles on world bookselling; American bookselling history to 1900.

D. APPLETON CO.

Wolfe, Gerard R. *The House of Appleton*. Scarecrow Pr. 1981 $20.00. History of a once prominent publisher, now a merged imprint.

ASSOCIATION OF BOOK TRAVELERS

Chaney, Beverley D., ed. *The First Hundred Years: Association of Book Travelers, 1884–1984*. Association of Bk. Travelers and Chaney 1984. History and memoirs of the publishers' traveling representatives to the book trade in the United States.

BANTAM BOOKS

Petersen, Clarence. *The Bantam Story: Twenty-Five Years of Paperback Publishing.* Bantam 1970 pap. o.p. A narrative that emphasizes Bantam, but places the firm in context; title list.

BEACH, SYLVIA

Beach, Sylvia. *Shakespeare and Company.* Harcourt 1959 o.p. The author's American bookshop in Paris was the first publisher of *Ulysses* and a literary center of the 1920s. (See also Noel R. Fitch and Hugh D. Ford in the first section of this chapter.)

BLACKWELLS

Norrington, A. L. P. *Blackwell's, 1879–1979: The History of a Family Firm.* Blackwell 1984 $20.00. The English companies—retailers, exporters, publishers—that evolved from the famous antiquarian bookshop in Oxford, England.

R. R. BOWKER CO.

Fleming, E. McClung. *R. R. Bowker: Militant Liberal.* Bowker 1952 o.p. Life of the versatile journalist, New York political reformer, entrepreneur, and publisher, co-founder of *Publishers Weekly* (1872) and associated publications, who guided the firm until 1933.

CAMBRIDGE UNIVERSITY PRESS

Black, Michael H. *Cambridge University Press, 1584–1984.* Cambridge Univ. Pr. 1984 $19.95. Concise account of the evolution, through stresses and successes, of the first formally chartered university press (charter 1534, continuous publishing since 1584).

CANFIELD, CASS

Canfield, Cass. *Up and Down and Around: A Publisher Recollects the Time of His Life.* Harper's Magazine Pr. 1971 o.p. The author's career in book publishing; the statesmen, other public figures, and writers he knew; leadership at Harper.

CAPE, JONATHAN

Howard, Michael S. *Jonathan Cape: Publisher.* Merrimack 1980 $18.95. A leading twentieth-century British publisher with close ties to the United States.

CAREY, MATTHEW

Bradsher, Earl L. *Matthew Carey, Editor, Author and Publisher.* AMS Pr. repr. of 1912 ed. $12.00. Basic study of the U.S. book trade pioneer in the early years of the Republic.

CERF, BENNETT A.

Cerf, Bennett A. *At Random: The Reminiscences of Bennett Cerf.* Random 1977 $12.95. Edited by the late publisher's wife and associates; colorful memoirs from written and oral records.

COCKERELL, SIR SYDNEY CARLYLE

Blunt, Wilfrid. *Cockerell.* Knopf 1965 o.p. Cockerell (1867–1962) was associated with famous literary and artistic figures, worked with William Morris, Emery

Walker, and others in the important private presses—Kelmscott, Doves, and
Ashendene.

COLUMBIA UNIVERSITY PRESS

Wiggins, Henry H. *Columbia University Press, 1893–1983.* Columbia Univ. Pr. 1983
o.p. History and analysis of one of the two or three largest university presses in
the United States.

COMMINS, SAXE

Commins, Dorothy. *What Is an Editor? Saxe Commins at Work.* Univ. of Chicago Pr.
1978 pap. $5.95. How the great Random House editor worked with O'Neill,
Faulkner, Irwin Shaw, and others.

DAIGH, RALPH

Daigh, Ralph. *Maybe You Should Write a Book.* Prentice-Hall 1977 $8.95 1979 pap.
$3.95. Cheerfully scrappy memoirs of mass-market publishing and advice on au-
thorship.

DELL PUBLISHING COMPANY

Lyles, William H. *Putting Dell on the Map: A History of Dell Paperbacks.* Greenwood
1983 $27.95. One of the most successful mass-market publishers.

DORAN, GEORGE H.

Doran, George H. *Chronicles of Barabbas, 1884–1934.* Holt 2d ed. 1952 o.p. The well-
told story of the pains and pleasures of publishing, full of interesting anecdotes
of a brilliant period.

GOLLANCZ, VICTOR

Hodge, Sheila. *Gollancz: The Story of a Publishing House, 1928–1978.* Random 1978
o.p. The brilliant, innovative, left liberal Victor Gollancz and his successful career in British publishing.

GOODSPEED, CHARLES E.

Goodspeed, Charles E. *Yankee Bookseller.* Greenwood repr. of 1937 ed. 1974 $20.00. A
legend in modern times: Goodspeed's Bookshop, Boston, and its proprietor.

HALDEMAN, E. JULIUS

Haldeman, E. Julius. *The First Hundred Million.* Ayer repr. 1975 $24.00. The maver-
ick publishing effort that produced hundreds of titles in vest-pocket-sized, cen-
ter-stapled "Little Blue Books."

HARLEQUIN BOOKS

Harlequin's 30th Anniversary, 1949–1979. Harlequin 1979 pap. $1.25. House history;
a mass-market paperback publisher's shift from general books to an all-out romance publishing program.

HARPER & ROW

Exman, Eugene. *The Brothers Harper, 1817–1853.* Harper 1965 $7.95. How the Harp-
ers established their famous house; methods of promotion and sale; relations
with U.S. and British writers; printing practices; business ventures and profits.

————. *The House of Harper: One Hundred and Fifty Years of Publishing.* Harper 1967 o.p. A broad portrait of the firm and its people, candid about failures and foibles, entertainingly written. (See also Cass Canfield, above.)

HAYDN, HIRAM

Haydn, Hiram. *Words and Faces.* Harcourt 1974 $8.95. Outspoken memoirs of the author and editor at Bobbs-Merrill, Harcourt, and Atheneum.

THE HOGARTH PRESS

Woolf, Leonard. *Beginning Again.* Harcourt 1975 pap. $3.45
————. *Downhill All the Way: An Autobiography, 1919–1939.* Harcourt 1975 $3.45. The writer describes the private press operated by himself and his wife, the essayist and novelist Virginia Woolf; their life together; his work as publisher, editor, writer, and political worker; and the Woolfs' literary and artistic circle.

HOLT, RINEHART & WINSTON

Madison, Charles A. *The Owl among Colophons: Henry Holt as Publisher and Editor.* Holt 1966 o.p. A short account by a former head of Holt's college department.

HOUGHTON MIFFLIN COMPANY

Ballou, Ellen B. *The Building of the House: Houghton Mifflin's First Half Century.* Houghton Mifflin 1970 $12.50. Achievements and failures of a major publishing firm up to 1921; includes printing plant and design development, mergers, trade publishing, and the *Atlantic Monthly.*

HUBBARD, ELBERT

Champney, Freeman. *Art and Glory: The Story of Elbert Hubbard.* Crown 1968 o.p. Life of the turn-of-the-century publisher, populist, and arts-and-crafts proponent.

JOHNSTON, EDWARD

Johnston, Priscilla. *Edward Johnston.* Pentalic 1976 pap. $6.95. A full-scale personal and artistic biography of the great English calligrapher, type designer, and teacher, by one of his daughters.

KNOPF, ALFRED A.

Portrait of a Publisher, 1915–1965. Ed. by Paul A. Bennett, Knopf 2 vols. 1965 o.p. Essays by dozens of well-known book people; many fine photos. Worth seeking out.

KRAUS, HANS PETER

Kraus, Hans Peter. *A Rare Book Saga: The Autobiography of H. P. Kraus.* Putnam 1978 $15.00. Kraus, a refugee from Nazi Vienna, founded in New York an outstanding book and manuscript business that is also involved in related services and publishing.

LANE, ALLEN

Morpurgo, J. E. *Allen Lane, King Penguin: A Biography.* Methuen 1980 $25.00. More than any other individual, Lane showed what could be done with pocket-sized paperback reprints of quality; scholarly and witty career of a modern pioneer.

LIVERIGHT, HORACE

Gilmer, Walker. *Horace Liveright: Publisher of the Twenties.* David Lewis 1970 o.p. The short, brilliant career of a publisher who brought out important new writers.

LUSTY, ROBERT

Lusty, Robert. *Bound to Be Read.* Doubleday 1976 $14.95. Memoirs of a leading contemporary English publisher, executive with Hutchinson and Michael Joseph, with close ties to the United States.

MASSEE, MAY

Hodowanec, George V., ed. *The May Massee Collection: Creative Publishing for Children, 1923–1963.* Emporia State Univ. Pr. 1979 $25.00. The famous Viking Press editor's complete files are on view and form the center of a research collection at Emporia.

McGRAW-HILL

Burlingame, Roger. *Endless Frontiers: The Story of McGraw-Hill.* McGraw-Hill 1959 o.p. A detailed record of the firm's role in the expansion of U.S. scientific and technical book publishing.

MEYNELL, SIR FRANCIS: THE NONESUCH PRESS

Dreyfus, John. *A History of the Nonesuch Press: With an Introduction by Geoffrey Keynes and a Descriptive Catalogue by David McKittrick, Susan Randall, and John Dreyfuss.* Nonesuch 1981 $250.00. Meynell's distinguished, commercial, fine press.
Meynell, Francis. *My Lives.* Random 1971 o.p. A twentieth-century Renaissance man—poet, journalist, publisher, industrialist, radical, book designer, founder of the Nonesuch Press in London.

OXFORD UNIVERSITY PRESS

Barker, Nicolas. *The Oxford University Press and the Spread of Learning: An Illustrated History.* Oxford Univ. Pr. 1978 $35.00. Oversize; 64-page historical review, 236 pages of plates. Issued in connection with the five-hundredth anniversary of printing in Oxford.
Sutcliffe, Peter. *The Oxford University Press: An Informal History.* Oxford 1978 $22.50. Pleasant reading, but detailed; reviews struggles from the first press in the city of Oxford in 1478, but concentrates on the university press itself since 1860.

PERKINS, MAXWELL E.

Berg, A. Scott. *Maxwell Perkins: Editor of Genius.* Dutton 1978 $15.00; Pocket Bks. 1979 pap. $5.95. The famed Scribner editor of Wolfe, Fitzgerald, Hemingway, and others.

PRINCETON UNIVERSITY PRESS

Darrow, Whitney, and Herbert S. Bailey, Jr. *Princeton University Press, 1905–1980.* Princeton Univ. Pr. 1980. Founding and growth of one of the leading scholarly presses.

REGNERY, HENRY

Regnery, Henry. *Memoirs of a Dissident Publisher.* Regnery-Gateway 1979 $12.95. Experiences and views of a general publisher and political conservative.

REYNOLDS, PAUL R.

Reynolds, Paul R. *Middle Man: The Adventures of a Literary Agent.* Morrow 1972 pap. $6.95. The author represented many of the recent era's outstanding authors.

ROSENBACH, A. S. W.

Wolf, Edwin, II, and John F. Fleming. *Rosenbach: A Biography.* World Publishing 1960 o.p. Founded in 1903, the firm gave new status to the entire rare book and manuscript business as an aid to important collections and literary scholarship.

SCHOLASTIC

Lippert, Jack E. *Scholastic: A Publishing Adventure.* Scholastic 1978. Maurice ("Robbie") Robinson and the innovative educational program of schoolroom periodicals, books, and other materials that he built; by his partner.

CHARLES SCRIBNER'S SONS

Burlingame, Roger. *Of Making Many Books: A Hundred Years of Writing and Publishing.* Scribner repr. of 1948 ed. 1971 $10.00. A great publisher and his role in U.S. literature; correspondence with authors. (See also Maxwell E. Perkins, on preceding page.)

SIMON & SCHUSTER

Schwed, Peter. *Turning the Pages: An Insider's Story of Simon & Schuster, 1924–1984.* Macmillan 1984 $17.95. Cheerful, candid account of perhaps the most colorful and successful of the publishing houses that grew out of the turbulent 1920s into the corporate 1980s.

STELOFF, FRANCES

Rogers, W. G. *Wise Men Fish Here: The Story of Frances Steloff and the Gotham Book Mart.* Harcourt 1965 o.p. Still regarded by many as the prototype of "a real bookshop," Frances Steloff's enterprise has been identified with the forward trends in U.S. writing since 1920.

TARG, WILLIAM

Targ, William. *Indecent Pleasures.* Macmillan 1975 o.p. A leading trade book editor, publisher, and bibliophile offers short, incisive pieces on books.

THOMAS, ISAIAH

Nichols, Charles Lemuel. *Isaiah Thomas: Printer, Writer and Collector.* Burt Franklin repr. of 1912 ed. 1971 $21.50. Work of the leading U.S. bookman of the revolutionary period and after; includes a bibliography of books he produced. First issued by Boston's Club of Odd Volumes.

TICKNOR & FIELDS

Tryon, Warren S. *Parnassus Corner: A Life of James T. Fields, Publisher to the Victorians.* Houghton Mifflin 1963 o.p. Account of one of the most outstanding New England publishers in the decades after 1854.

UNIVERSITY OF CALIFORNIA PRESS

Frugé, August. *A. F.: Reflections from a Publishing Career—Prepared by His Staff and Friends.* . . . Univ. of California Pr. 1977. Made up mostly of 89 pages of writings on scholarly publishing by the director of the press on the occasion of his retirement.

UNIVERSITY OF NORTH CAROLINA PRESS

A Statesman of the Republic of Books. Univ. of North Carolina Pr. 1970. Prepared by the staff of the press; includes statements by and in honor of Lambert Davis upon his retirement as director.

THE UNWINS

Unwin, Philip. *The Publishing Unwins.* Heinemann 1972 o.p. Saga of the English publishing family and its leading members since early in the nineteenth century.
Unwin, Sir Stanley. *The Truth about a Publisher.* Bowker 1960 o.p. The sprightly English bookman was active until he died at 83. His autobiography gives a lively picture of his youth and his long professional career, the writers and other publishers he encountered, and his battles for copyright and the book trade.

THE WARD RITCHIE PRESS

Ritchie, Ward. *The Ward Ritchie Press and Anderson, Ritchie & Simon.* Ward Ritchie 1961 o.p. Outstanding among the fine commercial printers and publishers for which California is known.

WARNE, FREDERICK K.

King, Arthur, and A. R. Stuart. *The House of Warne: One Hundred Years of Publishing.* Warne 1965 o.p. Publisher of Kate Greenaway, Randolph Caldecott, Beatrix Potter, and many more makers of children's books.

WEYBRIGHT, VICTOR

Weybright, Victor. *The Making of a Publisher: A Life in the 20th-Century Book Revolution.* Morrow 1967 o.p. The beginning of the New American Library, growth and conflict; founding of Weybright & Talley.

JOHN WILEY & SONS

Moore, John Hammond. *Wiley: 175 Years of Publishing.* Wiley 1982. The growth of a leading publisher of science, technology, business, and college books; authors, company leaders, world connections.

H. W. WILSON CO.

Lawler, John Lawrence. *H. W. Wilson Company: Half a Century of Bibliographic Publishing.* 1950. Ed. by Lee Ash, Gregg 1972 o.p. Ingenious and persistent, Wilson systematically built a complex of major services for libraries, schools, and the book industry.

BOOK INDUSTRY: EDUCATION AND OPERATIONS

American Booksellers Association, ed. *A Manual on Bookselling: How to Open and Run Your Own Bookstore.* Crown 3d ed. 1980 $15.95 pap. $8.95. The definitive how-to book.

Andersen, Arthur, and Company. *Book Distribution in the United States: Issues and Perspectives.* Book Industry Study Group 1982 pap. $60.00. Tables, analysis.

Appelbaum, Judith, and Nancy Evans. *How to Get Happily Published: A Complete and Candid Guide.* Harper 1978 $13.41; New Amer. Lib. 1972 pap. $6.95. Practical guide for the author, about publishers and about successful relations with them.

Association of American Publishers. *AAP Industry Statistics.* Association of Amer. Publishers annual. For members of the AAP.

———. *Professional and Reference Books: A Guide for Booksellers.* Association of Amer. Publishers 1983 pap. free. Prepared by the Marketing Committee of the AAP's Professional and Scholarly Publishing Division. Includes advice on stocking and selling books in these areas.

———. *Survey of Compensation and Personnel Practices in the Publishing Industry.* Association of Amer. Publishers 1984 $195.00. Available only to AAP members.

Association of American University Presses, ed. *One Book, Five Ways: Procedures of Five University Presses.* Kaufmann 1978 $19.95 pap. $11.95. The memos, forms, and specifications that each one of five publishers would use in the process of publishing the same book, from manuscript to sales plan.

An Author's Primer to Word Processing. Association of Amer. Publishers 1984 pap. $2.95. New technology and the writer.

Bailey, Herbert S., Jr. *The Art and Science of Book Publishing.* 1970. Univ. of Texas Pr. 1980 pap. $8.95. By the director of Princeton University Press. Financial management for a creative industry; addressed to students and actual or aspiring managers.

Belkin, Gary S. *Getting Published: A Guide for Business People and Other Professionals.* Wiley 1983 $14.95 pap. $8.95. Includes special problems of special fields.

Bermont, Hubert. *The Handbook of Association Publishing.* Bermont 1978 $30.00. Publishing for institutional purposes, more than for general commercial reasons.

Blissett, William, ed. *Editing Illustrated Books.* Garland 1981 $20.00. Scholarly papers on historical and current practice, given at a conference at the University of Toronto in 1979.

Bliven, Bruce, Jr. *Book Traveler.* Dodd 1975 o.p. The daily work of George Scheer, well-known publishers' sales representative to booksellers. A *New Yorker* profile.

Bodian, Nat G. *The Book Marketing Handbook.* Bowker 2 vols. 1980–83 ea. $59.95. Hundreds of short segments on techniques of promoting and selling scientific, technical, and other professional books and journals by many channels.

———. *Copywriter's Handbook.* ISI Pr. 1984 $29.95 pap. $19.95. Writing the advertising and sales promotion material for scholarly and other specialized books and journals.

Cain, Michael Scott. *An Intelligence Guide to Book Distribution.* Dustbooks 1981 $12.50. Especially pertinent to small operations.

Carter, Robert A., ed. *Trade Book Marketing.* Bowker 1983 $29.95 pap. $19.95. Comprehensive, including the marketing environment, relations with editors, retailing of hardcover and paperback books, rights, advertisements, publicity, and more.

Children's Book Council Staff. *Illustrating Children's Books.* Children's Bk. Council 10 copies for $3.75. Including a selection of related titles.

―――. *Writing Books for Children and Young People.* Children's Bk. Council 10 copies for $3.75. Including selective lists of other sources.

Congrat-Butlar, Stefan, comp. *Translation and Translators.* Bowker 1979 $35.00. Background and growth of translated books, the structure of the field, and lists of translators and their markets.

Curtis, Richard. *How to Be Your Own Literary Agent.* Houghton Mifflin 1984 $12.95 pap. $7.95. A subject not often covered at length.

Dessauer, John P. *Book Industry Trends.* Bowker 1985 pap. $150.00. Analysis and voluminous tabulations of book publishing data; includes charts, graphs, and tables that publishers, librarians, and so on, can use to forecast their future growth.

―――. *Book Publishing: What It Is, What It Does.* Bowker 2d ed. 1981 $29.95 pap. $15.95. Concise but full instruction on every step in book publishing and each of its major divisions.

DuBoff, Leonard D. *Book Publishers' Legal Guide.* Butterworth 1983 $50.00. Important basic information.

Duke, Judith S. *Religious Publishing and Communication.* Knowledge Industry 1980 $29.95. One of several area surveys; books are included.

―――. *The Technical, Scientific and Medical Publishing Market.* Knowledge Industry 1984 $29.95. Survey of a vast field that is actually not one field, but many.

Geiser, Elizabeth, and Arnold Dolin. *The Business of Book Publishing.* Westview Pr. 1985 $46.00. Chapters by 31 contributors describe the successive functions and the different areas of the industry.

Glenn, Peggy. *Publicity for Books and Authors: A Do-It-Yourself Manual for Small Publishing Firms and Enterprising Authors.* Aames-Allen 1984 $16.95 pap. $12.95. A comprehensive review.

Grannis, Chandler B., ed. *What Happens in Book Publishing.* Columbia Univ. Pr. 2d ed. 1967 $32.00. Twenty chapters by specialists, on the functions and principal branches of publishing.

Greenfeld, Howard. *Books: From Writer to Reader.* Crown 1976 pap. $4.95. The successive steps in general book publishing, with useful illustrations; for young and adult readers.

Guidelines for Bias-Free Publishing. McGraw-Hill 1983 pap. $2.00. For editors, writers, and others.

Harman, Eleanor, and Ian Montagnes. *The Thesis and the Book.* Univ. of Toronto Pr. 1976 pap. $8.50. Describes the work required to make a publishable book out of a thesis.

Henderson, Bill, ed. *The Publish-It-Yourself Handbook: Literary Tradition and How-To.* Pushcart Pr. 1979 $12.50. Accounts by writers who have produced and sold their own books without resorting to vanity publishers. Some literary history.

Hill, Mary, and Wendell Cochran. *Into Print: A Practical Guide to Writing, Illustrating, and Publishing.* Kaufmann 1977 pap. $7.95. Relations among author, publisher, and illustrator.

Holt, Robert Lawrence. *Publishing: A Complete Guide for Schools, Small Presses and Entrepreneurs.* California Health 1982 $25.95 pap. $19.95. Writing, editing, design, producing, selling, with an antivanity emphasis.

Horn, David. *Boards and Buckram.* Univ. Pr. of New England 1980 $10.00. Entertaining but seriously intended essays on the operations, author relations, and markets of the scholarly press.

Huenefeld, John. *The Huenefeld Guide to Book Publishing.* Huenefeld 1978 loose-leaf bdg. $88.00. The author and his firm are leading advisers and producers of business information for new and small publishers.

Huenefeld, John, and Virginia Wiley. *Planning and Control Guides and Forms: For Small Book Publishers*. Huenefeld pap. $44.00. Management tools.

Hyde, Sidney T., ed. *Selling the Book: A Bookshop Promotion Manual*. Shoe String 1977 $10.50. A variety of materials.

Meyer, Carol. *Writer's Survival Manual: The Complete Guide to Getting Your Book Published Right*. Bantam pap. $3.95; Crown 1982 $13.95. Comprehensive.

Poets and Writers Newsletter (CODA), eds. *The Writing Business: A Poets and Writers Handbook*. Pushcart Pr. 1984 pap. $17.95. Details about book contracts, small press publishing, and earning by writing.

Poynter, Dan. *The Self-Publishing Manual: How to Write, Print and Sell Your Own Book*. Para 1984 $14.95. Covers a lot of ground.

Reynolds, Paul R. *The Writing and Selling of Fiction*. Morrow 1980 rev. ed. $9.95 pap. $4.95. A famous literary agent's experience regarding relations among agent, author, and publisher.

Seuling, Barbara. *How to Write a Children's Book and Get It Published*. Scribner 1984 $14.95. A successful author and editor describes the writing, illustrating, placing, and publishing of children's books.

Smith, Datus C., Jr. *Economics of Book Publishing in Developing Countries*. Unipub 1977 pap. $5.00. Problems and prospects, incisively summed up by the former head of Franklin Book Programs, a technical assistance agency.

Smith, Roger H. *Paperback Parnassus*. Westview Pr. 1976 o.p. Details of the mass-market paperback industry and its intricate distribution system.

Stainton, Elsie Meyers. *Author and Editor at Work: Making a Better Book*. Univ. of Toronto Pr. 1981 pap. $4.95. Advice to authors and editors about their own crafts and their relations with each other.

To Be a Publisher: A Handbook on Some Principles and Programs of Book Publishing Education. Association of Amer. Publishers 1979. Organizing education for, in, and about book publishing. Prepared by the AAP's former Education for Publishing Committee.

Ward, Audrey, and Philip Ward. *The Small Publisher: A Manual and Case Histories*. State Mutual Bk. 1979 $25.00. One of the service guides for the small press movement.

White, Ken. *Bookstore Planning and Design*. McGraw-Hill 1982 $44.50. White, architect and designer for business, has specialized in bookstores.

The World of Translations. Pen Amer. Ctr. 1971 $2.00. Thirty-nine conference papers on world problems of translating literary manuscripts and materials.

BOOK INDUSTRY: TRENDS, ISSUES, COMMENTARY

Altbach, Philip G., and Sheila McVey, eds. *Perspectives on Publishing*. Lexington Bks. 1976 o.p. A full issue of the *Annals of the American Academy of Political and Social Sciences*. U.S. and world trends in book publishing.

Altbach, Philip G., and Eva Marie Rathgeber. *Publishing in the Third World: Trend Report and Bibliography*. Praeger 1980 $33.95. The varied status of publishing in the different countries of Africa, Asia, and Latin America.

Benjamin, Curtis G. *A Candid Critique of Book Publishing*. Bowker 1977 o.p. Provocative views and recommendations on book industry practice by the late head of McGraw-Hill.

————. *U.S. Books Abroad: Neglected Ambassadors.* Lib. of Congress 1982 pap. free. U.S. book export trends, previous aid programs, proposals for improvement, and growth. Has influenced policy.

Bernstein, Robert, and others. *Book Publishing in the U.S.S.R.: Reports of the Delegations of U.S. Book Publishers Visiting the U.S.S.R., 1962 and 1970.* Harvard Univ. Pr. 2d ed. enl. 1972 pap. $5.95. After these discussions, the U.S.S.R. acceded to international copyright and began paying royalties directly to foreigners.

Book Industry Study Group Special Reports:

Lambert, Douglas M. *Physical Distribution: A Profit Opportunity for Printers, Publishers, and Their Customers.* Bowker 1982 $30.00.

Noble, J. Kendrick, Jr. *Trends in Textbook Markets 1984.* Bowker 1984 $50.00.

Boorstin, Daniel. *Books in Our Future: A Report from the Librarian of Congress to the Congress.* U.S. Government Printing Office 1984 pap. $2.50. Analysis of the present condition of reading and books, and recommendations to combat illiteracy and aliteracy.

Bowker Lectures on Book Publishing. Bowker 1957 o.p. Memorial series of 17 lectures from 1934–57.

Bowker (R. R.) Memorial Lectures. Bowker 2d series 1973–82 pap. ea. $3.00. Contains the following individual titles: Harriet F. Pilpel, *Obscenity and the Constitution;* Barbara A. Ringer, *The Demonology of Copyright;* Frances E. Henne, *The Library World and the Publishing of Children's Books;* Samuel S. Vaughan, *Medium Rare: A Look at the Book and Its People;* Herbert S. Bailey, Jr., *The Traditional Book in the Electronic Age;* Peter Mayer, *The Spirit of the Enterprise;* Richard De Gennaro, *Research Libraries Enter the Information Age;* Oscar Dystel, *Mass-Market Publishing;* Robert Giroux, *The Education of an Editor;* Lowell A. Martin, *The Public Library: Middle-Age Crisis or Old Age.*

Cheney, O. H. *Economic Survey of the Book Industry 1930–1931.* 1931. Intro. by Robert W. Frase, Bowker 1960 o.p. Still cited.

Cole, John Y., ed. *The Audience for Children's Books. Viewpoint Ser.* Lib. of Congress 1980 pap. free. Symposium on ways and means of bringing books to children.

————. *The International Flow of Information: A Trans-Pacific Perspective. Viewpoint Ser.* Lib. of Congress 1981 free. Record of a useful symposium.

————. *Responsibilities of the American Book Community.* Lib. of Congress 1981 pap. $7.95. Papers from two seminars on financial concentration and related issues in publishing and bookselling.

————. *Television, the Book, and the Classroom.* Lib. of Congress 1978 pap. $4.95. Papers by Mortimer J. Adler, Frank Stanton, and other experts.

Cole, John Y., and Thomas G. Sticht, eds. *The Textbook in American Society.* Lib. of Congress 1982 pap. $5.95. Papers by 18 educators, writers, critics, and publishers.

Coser, Lewis A., Charles Kadushin, and Walter Powell. *Books: The Culture and Commerce of Publishing.* Basic Bks. 1982 $19.00; Univ. of Chicago Pr. 1985 pap. $12.50. Three sociologists deeply probe social and business forces affecting trade, college, and scholarly publishing. Lively and provocative.

Davison, Peter, and others, eds. *Bookselling, Reviewing and Reading.* Chadwyck-Healey 1978 $47.00. Selections on the book trade and its customers.

Fitzgerald, Frances. *America Revised: History Schoolbooks in the Twentieth Century.* Little, Brown 1979 $11.95; Random (Vintage) 1980 pap. $3.95. Analysis and strong criticism of bland, inadequate contemporary texts and the policies that produce them.

Graubard, Stephen, ed. *Reading in the 1980s.* Bowker 1983 $19.95. The state of reading, the book industry, technology, criticism, and prospects for change: 18 essays, all but one from the winter 1983 issue of *Daedalus* (American Academy of Arts and Sciences). (See also Roger H. Smith, below.)

Gross, Gerald, ed. *Editors on Editing.* Grosset & Dunlap 1962 pap. o.p. Still valuable; 25 pieces by editors in different fields.

——. *Publishers on Publishing.* Grosset & Dunlap 1961 o.p. In all, 36 selections from publishers' writings.

Henderson, Bill, ed. *The Art of Literary Publishing: Editors on Their Craft.* Pushcart Pr. 1980 $15.00. Articles and statements by distinguished contemporary book editors.

Jovanovich, William. *Now Barabbas.* Harper 1964 pap. o.p. Essays on publishers' and editors' relations with authors and others.

Kazin, Alfred, Dan M. Lacy, and Ernest L. Boyer. *The State of the Book World. Viewpoint Ser.* Lib. of Congress 1981 pap. free. Papers on criticism, books in the future, books and schools.

Kefauver, Weldon A. *Scholars and Their Publishers.* MLA 1977 pap. $5.00. A report by a university press director.

Kerr, Chester. *A Report on American University Presses.* 1949. Association of Amer. Univ. Presses pap. o.p. A landmark study, still consulted. Worth seeking out.

Kujoth, Jean S., ed. *Publishing: Inside Views.* Scarecrow Pr. 1981 o.p. Fifty articles by expert observers on issues and trends of the 1960s.

L'Engle, Madeleine. *Dare to Be Creative.* Lib. of Congress. 1984 pap. free. Lecture co-sponsored by the library's Center for the Book and Children's Literature Center. Eloquent plea for integrity and freedom in the writing and publishing of children's books.

Machlup, Fritz, and Kenneth W. Leeson. *Information through the Printed Word: The Dissemination of Scholarly, Scientific and Intellectual Knowledge.* Praeger 4 vols. 1978 ea. $37.95–$39.95. Massive research, facts, and figures.

National Enquiry into Scholarly Communication. *Scholarly Communication: The Report of the National Enquiry.* Johns Hopkins Univ. Pr. 1979 pap. $6.95. Result of a major collaboration among leading scholarly, library, and publishing groups concerning the dissemination of the great masses of scholarly work now being produced. Includes recommendations.

Nemeyer, Carol A. *Scholarly Reprint Publishing in the United States.* Bowker 1972 o.p. Description and analysis of a major publishing phenomenon, now past its peak, but still important.

Shatzkin, Leonard. *In Cold Type: Overcoming the Book Crisis.* Houghton Mifflin 1983 $17.95 pap. $8.95. Analyses and exhortations on the marketing and other functions of book publishers.

Smith, Roger H., ed. *The American Reading Public: What It Reads, Why It Reads.* Bowker 1963 o.p. The publishers' markets, how they are reached, how readers respond. The winter 1961 issue of *Daedalus*, with additional essays.

Sutherland, Zena, and May Hill Arbuthnot. *Children and Books.* Scott, Foresman 6th ed. 1981 $29.95. Wide-ranging work on children's reading, books, and authors.

Turow, Joseph G. *Getting Books to Children: An Exploration of Publisher-Market Relations.* Amer. Lib. Association 1979 $10.00. Insightful. Heavy sociological language at times.

Unwin, Stanley, and Philip Unwin. *The Truth about Publishing.* Academy Chicago 1982 pap. $6.95; Allen & Unwin 8th ed. 1976 $16.50. An outspoken, lively classic on the fundamentals of book publishing by a great English publisher. Updated by his son.

Van Nostrand, Albert. *The Denatured Novel*. Greenwood repr. of 1960 ed. 1973
$15.00. Critique of presumed effect of market policies on writing.

Walter, G. *Soviet Book Publishing Policy*. Cambridge Univ. Pr. 1978 $29.95. An exten-
sive updating of information, which, however, continues to change.

Whiteside, Thomas. *The Blockbuster Complex: Conglomerates, Show Business and
Book Publishing*. Wesleyan Univ. Pr. 1981 $16.95. A *New Yorker* series on the
state of popular publishing. It aroused furious controversy.

Bestsellers

Bestseller lists are provided weekly and annually by trade, specialized, and general media. *Publishers Weekly* reports fiction, nonfiction, and paperback bestsellers
weekly, with major cumulations, statistical reviews, and analysis in the annual summary number, usually an early March issue of the magazine. Current and annual
lists are provided by leading news media and special-interest periodicals. Annual
bestseller listings and analyses published in Bowker periodicals are reprinted each
year in the *Bowker Annual of Library and Book Trade Information* and the *Book Publishing Annual*. For additional information, see the section "Book Industry: Trends,
Issues, Commentary," above.

Hackett, Alice Payne, and James Henry Burke. *80 Years of Best Sellers, 1895–1975*.
Bowker 1977 o.p. Bestsellers, year by year, all-time lists, lists by major subjects,
historical notes.

Hart, James D. *The Popular Book: A History of America's Literary Taste*. Greenwood
repr. of 1950 ed. 1976 $27.75; Univ. of California Pr. pap. $4.95. Books for "popular" reading: their authors, publishers, history, and place in U.S. culture.

Kujoth, Jean S. *Best-Selling Children's Books*. Scarecrow Pr. 1973 $16.00. Overall re-
view.

Mott, Frank Luther. *Golden Multitudes: The Story of Best Sellers in the United States*.
1947. Bowker 1960 o.p. Important and readable literary, economic, and cultural
history; still cited.

Book Industry References

This section includes some of the most widely used reference materials needed by
people who work in the book industry. Several statistical sources are included in the
section "Book Industry: Education and Operations," above. Bibliographies are listed
in Chapter 2, and books needed in editing manuscripts, in Chapter 3.

AB Bookman's Yearbook. Antiquarian Bookman annual $15.00. Free with a subscrip-
tion to *AB Bookman's Weekly*. Review and forecast for the out-of-print and specialized book trade, with principal *AB* articles of the past year reprinted.

An Advertiser's Guide to Scholarly Publishing. Amer. Univ. Pr. Services 1985 in progress. Hundreds of journals with full data desired by advertisers. Cross-references.

American Book Trade Directory. Bowker biennial 31st ed. 1985 $119.95. State and lo-
cal listing of more than 24,000 U.S. and Canadian book outlets showing principal stock, specialties, contacts. Also includes appraisers, auctioneers, private
book clubs, foreign-language and other specialties.

American Library Directory. Bowker annual 38th ed. 1985 $119.95. Detailed listing of
approximately 34,000 U.S. and Canadian libraries above high school level, including geographical arrangement, with top personnel, departments, and statistics for each library.

American National Standard for Compiling Book Publishing Statistics. Amer. National Standards Institute 1977. Compiled by Committee Z-39, a cooperative group dealing with book industry standards of all kinds.

Basic Book List. Amer. Booksellers Association biennial 1984 $9.00 to members, $15.00 to nonmembers. Basic lists for bookstore stock, both hardcover and paperback.

Book Buyer's Handbook. Amer. Booksellers Association 1984 loose-leaf free to members, $150.00 to associate members. Comprehensive directory, continuously updated, of publishers' terms and policies, wholesalers and other suppliers, and data useful to booksellers. Essential for store operation, valuable as data source.

Bowker Annual of Library and Book Trade Information. Bowker annual 1986 $69.95. Compendium of yearly information and trend analysis on publishing and the library world. Many statistical tables. Reviews of legislation, funding, education, salaries, research, reference sources. Directories of library and book trade organizations.

Brownstone, David M., and Irene M. Franck. *The Dictionary of Publishing.* Van Nostrand 1982 $18.95. Legal, financial, business, and technical terms related to the special language of book, newspaper, or magazine publishing.

Cassell's and Publishers Association Directory of Publishing in Great Britain, the Commonwealth, Ireland, South Africa and Pakistan. International Pubns. triennial 1983 pap. $32.50

Children's Books: Awards and Prizes. Children's Bk. Council rev. ed. 1985 $50.00. Approximately 120 U.S., British Commonwealth, and other international awards, including the history of each award and the names of winners up to 1984–85.

Directory of Literary Magazines, 1985. Coordinating Council of Literary Magazines annual 1985 pap. $5.00. Describes more than 350 member magazines.

Glaister, Geoffrey. *Glaister's Glossary of the Book: Terms Used in Paper-Making, Printing, Bookbinding, and Publishing.* Univ. of California Pr. 2d ed. 1979 $75.00. Far more than a glossary; virtually an encyclopedic dictionary.

Gottlieb, Robin. *Publishing Children's Books in America, 1919–1976.* Children's Bk. Council 1978 $15.00. Fully annotated listings of books, articles, and other materials covering children's book publishing houses, leaders and editors, and specialized bookstores, starting with the first *Children's Book Week.*

Graphic Designer's Production Handbook. Hastings 2d ed. 1983 pap. $9.95. Concise, practical.

IMS/Ayer Directory of Publications. IMS Pr. 116th ed. 1984 $99.00. A famous old standby. Details publications in the United States and other markets; includes demographic data and maps.

Index Translationum. Unipub annual, various prices. International bibliography of translations from and into the principal languages. Breakdowns are by nation, world area, language, topic, etc.

International Directory of Little Magazines and Small Presses. Dustbooks annual 20th ed. 1985 $27.95 pap. $18.95. Serves a growing area of publishing.

International Literary Market Place. Bowker annual 1985 $75.00. Similar pattern to *Literary Market Place,* below, but covering more than 160 countries, and more than 10,000 book trade organizations, publishers, import-export services, and related·units.

Kingman, Lee. *Newbery and Caldecott Medal Books, 1966–1975.* Horn Bk. 1975 $22.00. Accounts of and excerpts from each of the annual prize winners for children's literature and illustration, with each acceptance speech. Earlier volumes include: *Newbery Medal Books, 1922–1955*, ed. by Bertha Mahony Miller and Elinor Whitney Field (1955) $22.00; *Caldecott Medal Books, 1938–1957*, ed. by Bertha Mahony Miller and Elinor Whitney Field (1957) $22.00; *Newbery and Caldecott Medal Books, 1956–1965*, ed. by Lee Kingman (1965) $22.00.

Knowledge Industry Publications. *U.S. Book Publishing Yearbook and Directory.* Facts on File annual 1982 $65.00. Chronology, operating expense ratios, financial reports, statistical tables, associations.

Literary Agents of North America Marketplace, 1984–1985. Aid-Research Associates 1984 pap. $16.95. A new source.

Literary and Library Prizes. Ed. by Olga S. Weber, Bowker 10th ed. 1980 $26.95. More than 650 literary awards, with history, description, rules of each, and winners up to November 1979.

Literary Market Place (LMP): The Directory of American Book Publishing. Bowker annual 1986 $59.95. Names, addresses, departments, personnel, and types of products or services, of the active U.S. and Canadian publishers. Also includes book-related and national associations, production services, review media, reference sources, and suppliers. Approximately 1,000 pages: includes a yellow-page section of Names and Numbers with quick contact information for 25,000 key people in book publishing.

Mayer, Debby. *Literary Agents: A Writers' Guide.* Pushcart Pr. 1983 pap. $5.95. Where authors can get help in finding publishers.

Peters, Jean, ed. *The Bookman's Glossary.* Bowker 6th ed. 1983 $24.95. Extensive revision. More than 1,800 terms plus 150 biographical notes. Publishing, bookselling, graphic arts, bibliography; includes current technology.

Plotnik, Arthur. *The Elements of Editing: A Modern Guide for Editors and Journalists.* Macmillan 1982 $9.50 pap. $3.95. A distinguished editor provides practical advice on copyright, permissions, relations among author, publisher, and printer.

Publishers Directory. Gale 5th ed. 1984 $200.00. Notes on more than 4,500 private, special, avant-garde, organizational, governmental, and institutional presses.

Smith, Peggy. *Proofreading Manual and Reference Guide.* Editorial Experts 1981 $38.00. Comprehensive reference and self-study text. Examples, workbook.

Sutherland, Zena, and others. *Children and Books.* Scott, Foresman 6th ed. 1981 $25.95. Children's books and their audience. A comprehensive, standard reference.

Ulrich's International Periodicals Directory. Bowker annual 2 vols. 1985 $139.95. Subject-arranged, detailed data about more than 70,000 publications, worldwide, including buying and bibliographic information.

UNESCO Statistical Yearbook. Unipub annual 1983 $111.50. Massive collection of worldwide tabulations, by nation and region, on education, book output, libraries, newspapers and periodicals, museums, film, broadcasting, and cultural expenditures.

BOOKMAKING, PRINTING, TYPOGRAPHY: HISTORY AND BIOGRAPHY

The history of the book goes back 5,000 years or so; there seems to be no end to the fascination that the subject arouses—hence the length of this list. Letterforms alone stir compulsive interest. Printing as an art and as a practical necessity, the book as an art form and as a practical object—the two aspects of the study make it rich and endlessly delightful. Moreover, the field of books and printing has always been blessed with strong and colorful personalities, and their stories are among the most readable parts of the literature. It should be noted, too, that books in these categories are among those that especially appeal to collectors.

Barker, Nicolas. *Stanley Morison.* Harvard Univ. Pr. 1972 $35.00. Morison, who died in 1967, was without question the greatest influence in the mid-twentieth century on type and typography. He was also a man of widely versatile interests. A massive biography, called "definitive."

Blades, William. *The Life and Typography of William Caxton, England's First Printer, 1861–1863.* Burt Franklin 2 vols. o.p. Long considered "the standard life."

Blumenthal, Joseph. *The Art of the Printed Book, 1455–1955.* Godine 1974 $50.00 pap. $28.50. Succinct, careful survey of the finest book printing, with 126 facsimiles.

——. *The Printed Book in America.* Godine 1977 $45.00. Fifty full-page reproductions in black and white, with well-defined historical text.

——. *Typographic Years: A Printer's Journey through a Half Century, 1925–1975.* Beil 1982 $26.50. The founder and operator of one of the finest of fine printer-publishers, the Spiral Press, recounts his experiences as printer, typographer, designer, historian, and teacher.

Chappell, Warren. *A Short History of the Printed Word.* Godine 1980 pap. $9.95. A famous artist, designer, and teacher produced this handsomely illustrated, concise history.

Clair, Colin. *A History of European Printing.* Academic Pr. 1977 $69.50. The origins of printing in all countries and its spread from the early beginnings constitute Clair's broad field of interest.

——, ed. *Early Printing in. . . .* Schram 1971–73 pap. *Australia, Burma, Caribbean, Ceylon, Greenland, Iceland, India, Indonesia, Madagascar & Seychelles, Malta, New Zealand* ea. $9.75; *South Africa* $18.00

Cobden-Sanderson, Thomas J. *Journals, 1879–1900: Together with The Ideal Book or the Book Beautiful—A Tract on Calligraphy, Painting and Illustration and on the Book Beautiful as a Whole.* Burt Franklin 2 vols. repr. of 1901–26 ed. $47.00. The ideas and work of the printer and binder of the Doves Press, collaborator with Sir Emery Walker.

Cohen, Arthur A. *Herbert Bayer: The Complete Work.* MIT 1984 $65.00. The famous émigré from the Bauhaus, a towering influence on graphic and industry design. Many illustrations.

Comparato, Frank F. *Books for the Millions.* Labyrinthos 1971 $12.50. The inventions that made possible the modern industry of printing and binding books.

Eisenstein, Elizabeth. *The Printing Press as an Agent of Change.* Cambridge Univ. Pr. 2 vols. in 1 repr. 1980 pap. $22.95. This scholar points out that all agree that printing led to a change in every aspect of life, but the process by which this came about, and what the cause-and-effect connections were, need much deeper examination.

——. *The Printing Revolution in Early Modern Europe.* Cambridge Univ. Pr. 1984 $34.50 pap. $9.95. A one-volume, heavily illustrated abridgment of *The Printing Press as an Agent of Change.* For college courses and the general reader.

Fairbank, Alfred. *A Book of Scripts.* Faber 1977 pap. $6.50. Showing of the great scripts, classic and modern, with commentary by the distinguished British calligrapher. Much used by teachers.

————. *The Story of Handwriting.* Watson-Guptill repr. of 1970 ed. 1976 pap. $5.95. Script and the origins of letterforms and type.

Glick, William J. *William Edwin Rudge.* Typophiles 1984 $20.00. Short, but carefully researched account of the company and its founder that did some of the finest book printing in the first third of the twentieth century and produced many of the best designers and printers.

Goines, David Lance. *A Constructed Roman Alphabet: A Geometric Analysis of the Greek and Roman Capitals and of the Arabic Numerals.* Godine 1982 $50.00. A leading calligrapher demonstrates how the majuscule letters are and have been made. A prize-winning work of book art.

Goudy, Frederic W. *Typologia: Studies in Type Design and Type Making—With Comment on the Invention of Typography, the First Types, Legibility and Fine Printing.* Univ. of California Pr. 1978 $27.50 pap. $3.95. The most prolific U.S. type designer was an expert in all these areas.

Grabhorn, Jane. *The Compleat Jane Grabhorn.* Grabhorn 1968 o.p. Writings and many reproduced or tipped-in actual specimens of the work of a great printer who died in 1973. Foreword by her husband, Robert Grabhorn, who, along with his brother Edwin and Jane, was a partner in the historic Grabhorn Press.

Grannis, Chandler B., ed. *Heritage of the Graphic Arts.* Bowker 1972 o.p. A selection of 22 of the lectures arranged in New York City by Dr. Robert L. Leslie on leaders in the graphic arts and bookmaking.

Hart, James D. *Fine Printing: The San Francisco Tradition.* Lib. of Congress 1985. Accounts of the Grabhorns and others, produced by Andrew Hoyem, a major inheritor of the tradition, who conducts the Arion Press.

Hunter, Dard. *Papermaking: The History and Technique of an Ancient Craft.* Dover 1978 pap. $8.95; Gannon 1978 lib. bdg. $17.50. The author studied papermaking throughout the world and founded the Paper Museum at MIT.

Kapr, Albert. *The Art of Lettering: The History, Anatomy and Aesthetics of the Roman Letter Forms.* Saur 1983 $90.00. Detailed history of letterforms from the earliest times to the era of modern typography. Heavily illustrated.

Lehmann-Haupt, Hellmut. *Gutenberg and the Master of the Playing Cards.* Yale Univ. Pr. 1967 o.p. A most interesting speculation, with illustrative evidence, about a decorative printing experiment that Gutenberg may have pursued.

————. *One Hundred Books about Bookmaking.* Greenwood repr. of 1949 ed. 1976 $15.00. Reprint of a small classic.

————, ed. *Bookbinding in America.* 1941. Bowker rev. ed. 1967 o.p. Contains three essays: "Early American Bookbinding" by Hannah Dustin French; "The Rise of American Edition Binding" by Joseph W. Rogers; and "On the Rebinding of Old Books" by Hellmut Lehmann-Haupt.

————. *The Göttingen Model Book.* Univ. of Missouri Pr. 1972 $50.00. The eminent historian of the book edits, with translation and commentary, a fifteenth-century manuscript book giving patterns and models of decorations for use by illuminators. All reproduced in full color.

Lewis, John. *The Twentieth-Century Book: Its Illustration and Design.* Reinhold 1984 $34.50 pap. $21.95. More than 400 illustrations. Highlights from the arts and crafts movement of the 1890s to the Swiss influences of the twentieth century.

————. *Typography: Design and Practice.* Taplinger 1978 $17.50 pap. $11.95. A broadscale view.

Lewis, Roy Harley. *Fine Bookbinding in the 20th Century.* Arco 1984 $29.95. Backgrounds, development of new attitudes, styles, and techniques. Attention to

Philip Smith, Ivor Robinson, and other leading contemporary binding artists of Europe and the United States.

Mardersteig, Giovanni. *The Officina Bodoni: An Account of the Work of a Hand Press, 1923–1977.* Ed. and trans. by Hans Schmoller, Chiswick Bk. Shop 1980 $95.00. Extensive account of the premier handpress printer of the twentieth century.

McLean, Ruari. *Modern Book Design.* Oxford 1959 $3.40. The range is from William Morris and his work in the nineteenth century to design in the late 1950s.

———. *Reynolds Stone.* Faber 1984 pap. $5.95. In wood, stone, or on paper, Stone was one of the greatest modern calligrapher-letterers and engravers.

———. *Victorian Publishers' Bookbindings on Paper.* Univ. of California Pr. $45.00. One of the author's careful studies of Victorian book arts. Heavily illustrated; many in color.

McMurtrie, Douglas C. *The Book: The Story of Printing and Bookmaking.* Oxford 2d ed. 1943 $60.00. The romantic story of printing and bookmaking from primitive human records to modern methods.

Meynell, Sir Francis, and Herbert Simon, eds. *The Fleuron Anthology.* Godine 1980 $45.00. Twenty-three colorful and scholarly articles reproduced from the famous journal, 1923–30, devoted to the modern typographic revival and the history of printing.

Miura, Kerstin Tini. *My World of Bibliophile Binding.* Univ. of California Pr. 1984 $125.00

Moran, James. *Printing Presses: History and Development from the 15th Century to Modern Times.* Univ. of California Pr. 1973 $46.00 pap. $7.95. This was the late English authority's field of expertise.

Morison, Stanley. *John Fell, 1745–1831: Bookseller, Printer, Publisher, Typefounder, Journalist.* Garland repr. of 1940 ed. 1978 $48.00. Characteristically thorough account by Morison of a versatile bookman.

———. *John Fell: The University Press and the Fell Types.* Garland repr. 1980 lib. bdg. $91.00. One of Oxford's great eighteenth-century printers and the typefaces he introduced.

———. *Politics and Script: Aspects of Authority and Freedom in the Development of Graeco-Latin Script from the Sixth Century B.C. to the Twentieth Century A.D.* Ed. by Nicolas Barker, Univ. Pr. of Virginia 1972 $35.00. Morison's classical scholarship came into play here, along with his political concerns.

———. *Selected Essays in the History of Letter Forms in Manuscript and Print.* Ed. by David McKitterick, Cambridge Univ. Pr. 2 vols. 1981 $275.00. This subject was Morison's primary fascination. Heavily illustrated.

———. *A Tally of Types: With Additions by Several Hands.* 1953. Ed. by Brooke Crutchley, rev. by M. K. Handover, Oak Knoll 1973 $55.00. A historical, critical, and functional account of the types cut by the Monotype Corporation under Morison's direction of its typographic revival program in the early 1920s and 1930s.

Morison, Stanley, and Kenneth Day. *The Typographic Book, 1450–1935: A Study of Fine Typography through Five Centuries Exhibited in Upwards of Three Hundred and Fifty Title and Text Pages Drawn from Presses Working in the European Tradition.* Ed. by Roger W. Shugg, Univ. of Chicago Pr. 1964 o.p. A massive work.

Morris, William. *The Ideal Book: Essays and Lectures on the Arts of the Book.* Ed. by William S. Petersen, Univ. of California Pr. 1982 $45.00. The most important of the essays and lectures, some not reprinted since the 1890s, on the book arts by the proprietor of the Kelmscott Press.

Moxon, Joseph. *Mechanick Exercises on the Whole Art of Printing.* 1683. Ed. by Herbert Davis and Harry Carter, Oxford 2d ed. 1962 o.p. A modern edition of the first—and very thorough—technical book on printing, with scholarly introduction and notes, and extensive illustrations and specimens.

Needham, Paul. *Twelve Centuries of Book-Bindings: 400–1600.* Oxford 1979 $75.00; Pierpont Morgan pap. $39.95. An outstanding exhibition provided the occasion for this detailed, heavily illustrated work.

Ogg, Oscar. *The 26 Letters.* 1948. Crowell 1971 $13.41; Van Nostrand rev. ed. 1983 pap. $9.95. Lavishly and delightfully illustrated by the author with line drawings and letterforms; relates the origins of calligraphy and lettering, development of the Roman alphabet, and the progress of printing.

Pederson, Johannes. *The Arabic Book.* Trans. by Geoffrey French, ed. by Robert Hillenbrand, Princeton Univ. Pr. 1983 $22.50 pap. $10.00. The production of books in medieval Islam.

Rogers, Bruce. *A Hodge-Podge of the Letters, Papers and Addresses Written during the Last Sixty Years.* Ayer repr. of 1953 ed. 1973 $18.00. Statements, formal and informal, by the graphic artist who led the modern movement for excellence in book design.

Rollins, Carl P. *Theodore Low De Vinne.* Typophiles 2 vols. 1968 o.p. Biographical essay by Rollins and an annotated bibliography and several major articles by the highly influential turn-of-the-century printer, typographer, and teacher.

Schreiber, Fred. *The Estiennes: An Annotated Catalogue of 500 Highlights of Their Various Presses.* Intro. by Nicolas Barker, Schreiber 1982 $65.00. Major aspects of printing and publishing by the Estienne family in Paris and other places in tumultuous times, 1502–1664.

Steinberg, S. H. *Five Hundred Years of Printing.* Penguin rev. ed. 1974 pap. $7.00. One-volume, concise, handy reference to the persons, places, machines, and events from the winepress to electronics.

Taylor, John B. *The Art Nouveau Book in Britain.* Taplinger 1980 $24.95. The William Morris era and after.

Thomas, Isaiah. *Diary of 1805–1828.* Johnson Repr. repr. of 1909 ed. 2 vols. ea. $35.00. Source material on the pioneer U.S. bookman.

———. *The History of Printing in America.* 1840. Burt Franklin repr. 2 vols. $55.50; Gordon 2 vols. $200.00; Johnson Repr. repr. of 1874 ed. pap. $35.00; ed. by Marcus A. McCorison, Univ. Pr. of Virginia and Crown (Weathervane) repr. 1975 pap. $5.95. By the versatile U.S. revolutionary, printer, publisher, scholar, bibliographer. Still considered an authoritative work.

Thompson, Susan Otis. *American Book Design and William Morris.* Bowker 1977 $39.95. Turn-of-the-century design and typography. The impact of the arts and crafts movement on publishing up to the 1930s.

Updike, Daniel Berkeley. *Printing Types: Their History, Forms and Use.* Dover 2 vols. repr. of 1922 ed. pap. ea. $9.95. The classic, still unmatched, Harvard work on the development of type for print. More than 300 illustrations of typefaces.

Walker, Gay, ed. *The Works of Carl P. Rollins.* Yale Univ. Lib. 1982 $9.00. Based on the collection left to Yale by Rollins, who was a major force for classical excellence in typography and printing design in the first half of the twentieth century.

Warde, Beatrice. *The Crystal Goblet: Sixteen Essays on Typography.* Ed. by Henry Jacob, World Publishing 1956 o.p. Writings by the promotion director of the Monotype Corporation, authority on typography and book design, who preached: "Printing should be invisible and should above all serve the text."

Winckler, Paul A. *The Reader in the History of Books and Printing.* Greenwood 1978

$28.50. A lengthy study. The author has also prepared a guide to sources on printing history for Gale.

Winship, George Parker. *Gutenberg to Plantin: An Outline of the Early History of Printing*. Burt Franklin repr. of 1926 ed. 1968 $20.50. This overview by a distinguished scholar relates to the period 1450–1600 in Europe.

Winterich, John T. *Early American Books and Printing*. Dover repr. of 1935 ed. 1981 pap. $4.95. Few writers about books, printing, and the book trade will ever match "Wint's" capacity to recount history with brevity and wit.

Wroth, Lawrence C. *The Colonial Printer*. 1931. Univ. Pr. of Virginia 1964 o.p. The beginnings of printing and publishing in the United States, including accounts of presses, typefounding, ink, paper, binding, employment and economic conditions, content and physical nature of products.

BOOKMAKING, PRINTING, TYPOGRAPHY: PROCEDURES AND PRACTICE

These titles are merely representative of classic works and outstanding current ones that are now in print or should be in print. The literature of instructional material for the student and practitioner in the printing industries is too vast, and in scores of instances, too specialized, for this list, but the titles may be found readily in specialized collections, good academic and public libraries, the *Subject Guide to Books in Print*, book trade and graphic arts periodicals, and other sources.

Bennett, Paul A., ed. *Books and Printing: A Treasury for Typophiles*. Peter Smith o.p. A collection of distinguished discussions on the art and craft of bookmaking. An invaluable anthology of key writings.

Dair, Carl. *Design with Type*. Univ. of Toronto Pr. rev. ed. 1982 pap. $12.95. One of the finest typographic designers in North America, this Canadian presented his working principles in a concise, comprehensive book.

Diehl, Edith. *Bookbinding: Its Background and Technique*. Dover repr. of 1940 ed. pap. $12.00; Hacker repr. of 1946 ed. 1979 lib. bdg. $60.00. The standard, comprehensive reference and art manual for many years.

Goudy, Frederic W. *The Alphabet and Elements of Lettering*. 1918. Dover 2 vols. in 1 repr. pap. $4.00; Peter Smith $11.50. By the famous typographer and type designer.

Johnson, Arthur W. *The Thames & Hudson Manual of Bookbinding*. Norton 1981 pap. $9.95; Thames & Hudson 1981 pap. $9.95. Detailed information and instructions, with clearly drawn illustrations throughout, for hand binding.

Johnson, Pauline. *Creative Bookbinding*. Univ. of Washington Pr. 1973 pap. $17.50. Contemporary fine binding explores new paths in "the arts of the book."

Johnston, Edward. *Writing and Illuminating and Lettering*. Taplinger 1977 pap. $10.95. By the father of the modern movement in writing and lettering, whose discoveries and type designs influenced Stanley Morison. A classic work.

Lawson, Alexander S. *Printing Types: An Introduction*. Beacon 1974 pap. $6.95. Derived from the author's course at the Rochester Institute of Technology, this is an excellent guide to type recognition and the elements of letters.

Lee, Marshall. *Bookmaking: The Illustrated Guide to Design/Production/Editing*. Bowker 2d ed. 1980 $39.95. Greatly expanded version of a standard manual on all aspects of the making of books under modern conditions, including a strong section that has been added on editing.

Morison, Stanley. *First Principles of Typography*. Cambridge Univ. Pr. 1951 o.p. The basics of classic typography.

Nesbitt, Alexander. *Decorative Alphabets and Initials*. Dover repr. of 1959 ed. pap. $6.00; Peter Smith $14.75. Sources for designers by a prominent practitioner and teacher.

————. *The History and Technique of Lettering (Lettering: The History and Technique of Lettering and Design)*. Dover repr. of 1950 ed. pap. $5.50; Peter Smith $14.50

————. *Two Hundred Decorative Title Pages*. Dover repr. of 1964 ed. pap. $6.00; Peter Smith $12.00. Sources and ideas for the designer.

Ogg, Oscar, ed. *Three Classics of Italian Calligraphy: Arrighi, Tagliente, Palatino*. Peter Smith repr. of 1953 ed. $9.00. Reprint of the writing specimen books of three sixteenth-century Italian masters who have influenced writing and type design ever since.

Rice, Stanley. *Book Design: Systematic Aspects*. Bowker 1978 $19.95. Manual on the essential, permanent features in a book.

————. *Book Design: Text Format Models*. Bowker 1978 $19.95. Alternate specifications, with visual samples, for all special items in a book: front matter, back matter, captions, etc. Companion volume to *Book Design: Systematic Aspects*.

Roberts, Matt T., and Don Etherington. *Bookbinding and the Conservation of Books: A Dictionary of Descriptive Terminology*. Lib. of Congress 1982 $27.00. Comprehensive, meeting specific needs of binders and conservators.

Rogers, Bruce. *Paragraphs on Printing*. Dover repr. 1980 pap. $6.95. Commentary on quality in the handling of type and presswork by the most respected U.S. book designer of the twentieth century.

Romano, Frank J. *The TypEncyclopedia: A User's Guide to Better Typography*. Bowker 1984 pap. $24.95. Key terms and definitions needed in copy-specifying and judging the quality of typesetting.

Sanders, Norman, and William Bevington. *Graphic Designer's Production Handbook*. Hastings 1982 pap. $9.95. Instructions given under 191 topical headings about design for printing. Details of making layouts and mechanicals, specifying production, handling current photo and printing techniques. Precise illustrations by William Bevington.

Society of Scribes and Illuminators (London). *Modern Scribes and Lettering Artists*. Taplinger 1980 $20.00. Presents a wide variety of contemporary scribal styles, mostly British and European. Omits several outstanding U.S. calligraphers.

Standard, Paul. *Calligraphy's Flowering, Decay and Restoration*. Taplinger 1977 $3.50. A contemporary master calligrapher, historian, and teacher produced, largely in his own hand, this study of the years before the revival of calligraphy in the United States. Standard was a dedicated promoter of the revival.

————, trans. *Arrighi's Running Hand*. Pentelic 1979 $7.95; Taplinger 1979 pap. $3.95. A presentation of the writing of the Renaissance master who was the chief inspirer of modern calligraphy.

Thames & Hudson Manual of Typography. Thames & Hudson 1980 $18.95. Comprehensive guide to every aspect of the craft in the light of contemporary and traditional standards.

Tschichold, Jan. *Asymmetric Typography*. Van Nostrand 1968 o.p. As a very young man, this distinguished German (later Swiss) typographer fervently advocated "modern" typography in the 1920s. This key statement, translated much later into English, remains a classic.

Tufte, Edward R. *The Visual Display of Quantitative Information*. Graphics Pr. $34.00. Fresh, dramatic, highly acclaimed approach to statistical graphics as honest, effective communication.

Watts, L., and J. Nisbett. *Legibility in Children's Books: A Review of Research*. Humanities Pr. 1974 pap. $13.75. What production factors help or hinder reading.

Williamson, Hugh. *Methods of Book Design: The Practice of an Industrial Craft*. Yale Univ. Pr. 1983 $40.00 pap. $12.95. Handsome, extensively detailed, and updated for current technology. Practical for publishers, editors, designers, producers.

Wilson, Adrian. *The Design of Books*. Gibbs M. Smith 1974 pap. $10.95. History and artistic development embodied in an inspiring, thoroughly illustrated how-to book.

Zapf, Hermann. *Manuale Typographicum*. MIT 1970 pap. $7.95. One hundred pages of quotations on types and printing, presented in typographic designs by Zapf.

———. *Typographic Variations*. Myriade 1977 pap. $9.95. Originally published in German and first issued in the United States in 1963, this book includes 78 text and title-page designs by Zapf.

Book Illustration

Only the merest sampling of books about book illustration is possible here. A rich mine of other related books may be found in the literature of the graphic arts, including printmaking and the history of the book, and in the biographies of illustrators and of artists whose work includes book illustration—artists from Dürer to Frederick Remington to Picasso, and from Howard Pyle to Leonard Baskin and Barry Moser.

de Maré, Eric. *The Victorian Woodblock Illustrators*. Beil 1982 $55.00; State Mutual Bk. 1981 $100.00. The development of illustration by engraving the end-grain of boxwood, from Thomas Bewick to William Morris. The craft and its role as a social force. Approximately 200 drawings.

Garrett, Albert. *British Wood Engraving of the 20th Century: A Personal View*. Scolar Pr. 1980 pap. $13.00. A fine selection of work by top artist-illustrators. Biographical outlines of more than 100 artists with more than 300 prints.

Hindman, Sarah, ed. *The Early Illustrated Book: Essays in Honor of Lessing J. Rosenwald*. Lib. of Congress 1982 $50.00. A handsome work, based on some of the lavish Rosenwald gifts to the library. Special attention to the major Dutch and Belgian presses.

Hunnisett, Basil. *Steel-Engraved Book Illustration in England*. Godine 1980 $40.00. A detailed survey of the illustrators, firms, styles, and methods of a previously little-researched period in the eighteenth and nineteenth centuries.

Illustrators of Children's Books, 1957–1966. Ed. by Lee Kingman and others, Horn Bk. 1968 $28.00

Johnson, Fridolf, ed. *Treasury of American Pen-and-Ink Illustration, 1881 to 1938*. Dover 1982 pap. $6.00. Portrayal of an intensely creative period in U.S. book and periodical art; introductory essay, 236 drawings by 103 artists.

Klemin, Diana. *The Art of Art for Children's Books*. Murton 1982 pap. $16.95. Relation of art to text, demonstrated, with comment, in reproduced pages of 60-odd books.

———. *The Illustrated Book: Its Art and Craft*. Murton 1983 pap. $19.95. Examples and explanations of works and techniques of 74 book illustrators.

Linton, William J. *American Victorian Wood Engraving*. Athenaeum of Philadephia,

Amer. Life Foundation, and Study Institute repr. of 1882 ed. 1976 $25.00. Extensive new bibliography by Nancy Carlson Shrock.

Mahony, Bertha, and Elinor Whitney. *Contemporary Illustrators of Children's Books.* Gale repr. of 1930 ed. 1978 $65.00. By the editors of the *Horn Book.*

McLean, Ruari. *Victorian Book Design and Colour Printing.* Univ. of California Pr. 2d ed. 1972 o.p. The flowering of book illustration in Britain, 1830–80.

Meyer, Susan E. *A Treasury of the Great Children's Book Illustrators.* Abrams 1983 $45.00. Examples and account of the works of 13 major illustrators from pre-1840 to about 1920.

Pippin, Brigid, and Lucy Mickle Thwaite. *Book Illustration of the 20th Century.* Arco 1984 $39.95. Short encyclopedia-style accounts of illustrators and portrayals of them and their work.

Ray, Gordon N. *The Art of the French Illustrated Book, 1700–1914.* Cornell Univ. Pr. 1982 o.p. Careful scholarship, full documentation, heavily illustrated. A major reference work on an exciting field.

———. *The Illustrator and the Book in England from 1790–1914.* Oxford 1976 $75.00. Catalog, heavily annotated, with sectional and general essays. A landmark exhibition.

Reed, Walt, and Roger Reed. *The Illustrator in America, 1880–1980.* Madison Square Pr. 1984 $48.50. Hundreds of brief biographies with samples of the artists' works.

Twyman, Michael. *Lithography, 1800–1850: The Techniques of Drawing on Stone in England and France and Their Application to Works of Typography.* Oxford 1970 $26.00. Twyman is a leading English historian of printing.

Wakeman, Geoffrey. *Victorian Book Illustration.* Gale 1973 $50.00. How the development of new printing processes continuously changed book illustration throughout the nineteenth century.

COPYRIGHT

Named here are a few useful books on a complicated subject—a list mainly for general purposes, but applicable especially to the many copyright issues related to books. The new U.S. Copyright Act, effective January 1, 1978, has been followed by many regulatory changes and some court actions, and has required the revision or replacement of many books on copyright. Thorny issues continue to include the application of international copyright agreements and questions arising from contemporary technology, notably electronic data storage and delivery systems and quick, cheap copying. The literature of copyright will continue to change accordingly.

Johnston, Donald F. *Copyright Handbook.* Bowker 2d ed. 1982 $29.95. Based on the new copyright law, with continuing interpretations and regulations.

Poets & Writers, Inc., and Carolina R. Harron. *A Writers' Guide to Copyright.* Poets & Writers 1979 pap. $4.95. A concise review of essentials.

Strong, William S. *The Copyright Book: A Practical Guide.* MIT 1981 $12.50. Authoritative work, also based on new law and regulations; of scholarly interest.

U.S. Copyright Office. *Library Reproduction of Copyrighted Works (17 U.S.C. 108): Report of the Register of Copyrights.* Copyright Office, Lib. of Congress 1982. Law and application.

Wittenberg, Philip. *Protection of Literary Property*. Writer 1978 $12.95. A work by a long-respected authority, published after the passage of the new copyright law.

CENSORSHIP AND THE FREEDOM TO READ

The last word is never said about censorship, nor is the necessity of the freedom to read ever sufficiently emphasized. The books named here cover the subject in fairly comprehensive, though often detailed, terms. More specialized studies may be found in the *Subject Guide to Books in Print*.

From the middle 1960s to the middle 1980s, different majorities on the U.S. Supreme Court have issued sharply differing—often confusing—rules concerning "community standards," "redeeming social value," privacy, civil rights, and the secrecy of information held by units of government. Certain government personnel face lifetime restrictions on speech and publication. Military censorship may be on the rise. "Whistle blowers" are often persecuted. Publishers face the continual threat and expense of litigation for alleged libel and other reasons. Self-censorship becomes increasingly tempting for publishers, editors, and authors to adopt as an option. A constitutional convention may result in new threats to the Bill of Rights. If untrammeled historical research and a robust press are to be maintained, the classic rule applies: "Eternal vigilance is the price of liberty."

Adams, Michael. *Censorship: The Irish Experience*. Biblo & Tannen repr. of 1968 ed. $15.00; Univ. of Alabama Pr. 1968 $18.25. Until Irish censorship was greatly mitigated in the middle 1960s, it sadly inhibited Irish literary publishing.

American Library Association, Office for Intellectual Freedom. *Censorship Litigation and the Schools*. Amer. Lib. Association text ed. 1983 pap. $17.50. Deals with the increasing attacks against school library operations and textbooks.

———. *Intellectual Freedom Manual*. Amer. Lib. Association 2d ed. 1983 $15.00. Guidance for defense of reading and libraries. Includes background history, documents, policies, and procedures.

Berninghausen, David K. *The Flight from Reason: Essays on Intellectual Freedom in the Academy, the Press and the Library*. Amer. Lib. Association 1975 $9.00. Statements by a leading association figure in this field.

de Grazia, Edward. *Censorship Landmarks*. Bowker 1969 o.p. Monumental compilation, with history and interpretation, by an attorney deeply involved in many such cases.

Downs, Robert, and Ralph E. McCoy. *The First Freedom Today: Critical Issues Related to Censorship and to Intellectual Freedom*. Amer. Lib. Association 1984 lib. bdg. $40.00. Specific kinds of attacks on free expression emerging in the 1980s.

Gregorian, Vartan. *Censorship: Five Hundred Years of Conflict*. Oxford 1984 $29.95. Lavishly illustrated catalog of a spectacular exhibit at the New York Public Library, by its dynamic director. Includes essays and references.

Haight, Anne Lyon. *Banned Books: 387 B.C. to 1978 A.D.* Bowker 4th ed. 1978 $18.50. Updated and enlarged by Chandler B. Grannis, with opening essay on censorship in the United States by Charles Rembar. Chronology of censored books and authors.

Jenkinson, Edward B. *Censors in the Classroom*. Southern Illinois Univ. Pr. 1979

$19.95. Effects of censorship activities on schools and libraries: why it happens, court rulings, the case for free access, free inquiry, and an open society.

Levy, Leonard W. *Treason against God: A History of the Offense of Blasphemy.* Schocken 1981 $24.95. Book banning and burning has been only one aspect of this story.

Lewis, Felice Flannery. *Literature, Obscenity and the Law.* Southern Illinois Univ. Pr. 1978 $19.95 pap. $9.95. Thorough, brightly written account of all aspects of the issue.

Milton, John. *Areopagitica.* AMS Pr. repr. of 1918 ed. $11.50; Harlan Davidson text ed. 1951 pap. $3.75; Saifer repr. of 1644 ed. 1972 $10.00. Milton's famous statement against licensing of books.

Oboler, Eli M., ed. *Censorship and Education.* Wilson 1982 pap. $7.00. Strong, representative, differing points of view. Discusses the impact of censorship on schools and libraries and major legal decisions.

———. *To Free the Mind: Libraries, Technology and Intellectual Freedom.* Libraries Unlimited 1983 $15.00. Essays on interrelated issues by the late university librarian, a leader in the defense of freedom of inquiry, writing, and reading.

Perrin, Noel. *Dr. Bowdler's Legacy: History of Expurgated Books in England and America.* Univ. Pr. of New England 1969. Not "banned" books, but "bowdlerized" ones. Amusing, factual.

Reisner, Robert George. *Show Me the Good Parts: The Reader's Guide to Sex in Literature.* Citadel Pr. 1964 $2.45. Examples of what may be censored.

Rembar, Charles. *The End of Obscenity.* Random 1968 o.p. Accounts of the trials of *Lady Chatterley's Lover, Tropic of Cancer,* and *Fanny Hill,* by the attorney for their defense.

BIBLIOPHILIA

"The love of books" is too broad a term to define precisely, and the titles listed here can represent only a few facets of the subject. Books on book collecting, for example, form a great portion of bibliophilic books, and they are covered in Chapter 2. Others will be found in the preceding sections of this chapter. Here, some well-known titles about the joys of knowing and using books are named, along with others that are intended to help lead the reader to some of the best and most enjoyable literature.

Altick, Richard D. *The Scholar Adventurers.* Macmillan (Free Pr.) 1966 pap. $9.95. Great episodes in literary detection: the exposure of the Wise forgeries, the uncovering of Boswell's papers at Malahide Castle, and the use of codes and ciphers in literature are among the stories told.

Barker, Nicolas, and John Collins. *A Sequel to An Enquiry: The Forgeries of Forman and Wise Reexamined.* Scolar Pr. 1984 $70.00. New research and evaluation on the subject of the famous exposé by John Carter and Graham Pollard.

de Bury, Richard (Bishop of Durham). *Love of Books: Philobiblon of Richard de Bury.* 1599. Trans. by E. C. Thomas, ed. by I. Gollancz, Cooper Square Pr. repr. of 1926 ed. $17.50. First translated in 1834. The oldest book about books.

Downs, Robert B. *Books and History.* Univ. of Illinois Lib. of Information Science 1974 $5.00. Role of books in affecting historical development.

———. *Books That Changed America.* Macmillan 1970 $7.95; New Amer. Lib. 1971 pap. $3.95. Selection and comment.

————. *Books That Changed the World*. Amer. Lib. Association 2d ed. 1978 $20.00; New Amer. Lib. 1971 pap. $3.95. Durable reference work.

Hanff, Helene. *Eighty-four Charing Cross Road*. Avon 1978 pap. $4.95; Viking 1975 $11.95. A novel told in the form of transatlantic correspondence between the staff of a London bookstore and a breezy New York City customer. It became a Broadway play.

Jackson, Holbrook. *The Anatomy of Bibliomania*. AMS Pr. repr. of 1950 ed. $30.00. This twentieth-century man of letters cites, with voluminous quotations, the pleasures of books under 23 headings.

————. *A Bookman's Holiday*. Folcroft repr. 1973 lib. bdg. $25.00. One of this literary historian's many books about books, authors, and bibliophilia.

Lanes, Selma. *Down the Rabbit Hole: Adventures and Misadventures in the Realm of Children's Literature*. Atheneum 1976 pap. $4.95. Assessments and observations.

Lang, Andrew. *Books and Bookmen*. AMS Pr. repr. of 1886 ed. $10.00; Arden Lib. repr. of 1892 ed. 1977 lib. bdg. $15.00. A standard work by a literary classicist and teacher.

McCullough, David W. *People, Books and Book People*. Crown 1981 $12.95. Essays and interviews by a contemporary book trade observer and literary critic.

Morley, Christopher. *The Haunted Bookshop*. Avon repr. of 1919 ed. 1983 pap. $4.95.

————. *Parnassus on Wheels*. Avon repr. of 1917 ed. 1983 $4.95. Both *The Haunted Bookshop* and *Parnassus on Wheels* are famous novels about bookselling—a detective tale and a clever romance—that have become part of the lore of booklovers.

Orcutt, William D. *In Quest of the Perfect Book*. Associated Faculty Pr. repr. of 1926 ed. 1969 $27.50; Ayer repr. of 1926 ed. $26.00. A booklover's classic.

Pearson, Edmund L. *Books in Black or Red*. Ayer repr. of 1923 ed. 1975 $21.50. Pearson was an entertaining essayist and literary historian.

Powell, Lawrence Clark. *Bookman's Progress*. Ed. by William Targ, Holmes Bk. repr. 1968 $10.00. Writings selected by a publisher-bibliographer, of essays by a famous librarian-bibliophile.

————. *Books in My Baggage: Adventures in Reading and Collecting*. Greenwood repr. of 1960 ed. 1973 $45.00. Librarian, book collector, and lecturer, Powell was a popular interpreter of the pleasures of books.

————. *A Passion for Books*. Greenwood repr. of 1958 ed. 1973 $15.00

Rosenbach, A. S. W. *Book Hunter's Holiday: Adventures with Books and Manuscripts*. Ayer repr. of 1936 ed. 1968 $21.50

Sabine, Gordon, and Patricia Sabine. *Books That Made a Difference: What People Told Us*. Shoe String 1983 pap. $13.50. A Center for the Book project. Two professional journalists interviewed people all over the country who told about books that "made the greatest difference in their lives."

Starrett, Vincent. *Bookman's Holiday: The Private Satisfactions of an Incurable Collector*. Ayer repr. of 1942 ed. $18.00

Thwaite, Mary F. *From Primer to Pleasure in Reading*. Horn Bk. repr. of 1963 ed. 1972 $14.00. Children's books printed in England from the 1400s to 1914, including authors, illustrators, publishers, representative books, and notes on other countries.

Waldhorn, Arthur, Olga S. Weber, and Arthur Zeiger, eds. *Good Reading: A Guide for Serious Readers*. Bowker 22d ed. 1985 $29.95. Notes on 2,500 outstanding books, with five broad areas, many subgroups, and special lists.

CHAPTER 2

Bibliography

Jean Peters

> What then is the business of the bibliographer? Primarily and essentially, I should say, the enumeration of books. His is the lowly task of finding out what books exist, and thereby helping to secure their preservation, and furnishing the specialist with information as to the extent of the subject-matter with which he has to deal.
> —A. W. POLLARD, *The Library: New Series* (1903)

Bibliography, by early definition, was "the writing or copying of books," the word coming from the Greek, *bibliographia*, book writing. This meaning was used until the middle of the eighteenth century, at which time the transition was made from the writing *of* books to the writing *about* books.

In the years since, bibliography has come to be recognized as an umbrella for two distinct sets of activities: (1) enumerative (or systematic) bibliography, the listing of books with some recognized relationship to one another; and (2) analytical (or critical) bibliography, the examination of books as material objects, with the purpose of discovering the details of their production process and analyzing the effects of this process on the physical characteristics of any given copy of a book. This chapter is largely concerned with enumerative bibliography; it deals with analytical bibliography only as it applies to the descriptive author bibliographies used by book collectors.

Enumerative bibliography is the most widely practiced form of bibliography. Its principal purpose is the mastery over written and published records known as bibliographic control—the effort to bring order out of chaos in the world of books. In the twentieth century the production of books has become so voluminous that every day, throughout the world, a flood of books and other bibliographic items is issued. It is the business of the bibliographer to identify this mass of material, classify, describe, and arrange it in a useful way for reference and study. It should be remembered that without bibliography, as Sir Frank C. Francis observed in the fifteenth edition of the *Encyclopaedia Britannica*, "the records of civilization would be an unchartered chaos of miscellaneous contributions to knowledge, unorganized and inapplicable to human needs."

GENERAL READINGS

Overviews and Anthologies

The Bibliographical Society of America, 1904–79: A Retrospective Collection. Univ. Pr. of Virginia 1980 $20.00. A collection of 39 articles taken from the society's *Papers* to commemorate its seventy-fifth anniversary in 1979. The selections represent, in the society's words, "the highest degree of excellence—articles of critical importance that have moved forward the art of bibliography."

Bowers, Fredson T. *Essays in Bibliography, Text and Editing.* Univ. Pr. of Virginia 1975 $30.00. Published for the Bibliographical Society of the University of Virginia.

Schneider, Georg. *Theory and History of Bibliography.* 1934. Trans. by Ralph R. Shaw, Gordon 1977 $69.95

Stokes, Roy. *The Function of Bibliography.* 1971. Lexington Bks. 2d ed. 1983 $22.00

Tanselle, G. Thomas. *Selected Studies in Bibliography.* Univ. Pr. of Virginia 1979 $15.00. Published for the Bibliographical Society of the University of Virginia. A collection of 11 articles, selected by the author and reprinted from the annual *Studies in Bibliography.* They are the most significant of the articles by G. Thomas Tanselle that appeared in *Studies in Bibliography.* The council of the Bibliographical Society of the University of Virginia points out in the foreword to the collection that "the *SB* articles as a group have had a major influence on the theory and practice of bibliography and textual criticism."

Enumerative (or Systematic) Bibliography

Besterman, Theodore. *The Beginnings of Systematic Bibliography.* 1935. Burt Franklin 2d ed. rev. 1966 $20.50

Krummel, D. W. *Bibliographies: Their Aims and Methods.* Mansell 1984 $30.00. A practical book for compilers of enumerative bibliographies and for those interested in bibliographic theory and practice. It examines the features that characterize the most respected bibliographies and suggests what makes other lists flawed. It concludes with a bibliography of major writings on the compiling of bibliographies (1883–1983) and a list of bibliographies that have received awards for graphic excellence.

Malcles, Louise N. *Bibliography (La Bibliographie).* 1956. Trans. by Theodore C. Hines, Scarecrow Pr. repr. of 1961 ed. 1973 o.p.

Van Hoesen, Henry B., and Frank K. Walter. *Bibliography, Practical, Enumerative, Historical: An Introductory Manual.* 1928. Burt Franklin 1971 $29.95

Analytical Bibliography

The books listed below complement one another and are the basic guides.

Bowers, Fredson T. *Principles of Bibliographical Description.* 1949. Russell Pr. 1962 o.p. A detailed treatment of analytical bibliography as applied to the description of books.

Gaskell, Philip. *A New Introduction to Bibliography.* Oxford 1972 $19.95. Updates and extends the period of coverage in McKerrow, listed below.

McKerrow, Ronald B. *An Introduction to Bibliography for Literary Students.* Oxford 1928 $24.95. Covers all aspects of the making of the printed book up to about 1800, and provides the background of knowledge requisite to bibliographic description.

BIBLIOGRAPHIES OF BIBLIOGRAPHIES

Other useful sources of bibliographies are: Eugene P. Sheehy, *Guide to Reference Books;* A. J. Walford, *Walford's Guide to Reference Material;* and Bohdan S. Wynar, *American Reference Books Annual;* all listed in this chapter under "Tools for Book Selection, Reference."

Beaudiquez, Marcelle. *Bibliographical Services throughout the World, 1970–74.* Unipub 1977 $22.50. The 1950–59 volume, ed. by Robert L. Collison, is also available from Unipub for $7.50. The volumes covering 1960–64 and 1965–69, both compiled by Paul Avicenne, are out of print.

Besterman, Theodore. *A World Bibliography of Bibliographies and of Bibliographical Catalogues, Calendars, Abstracts, Digests, Indexes, and the Like.* Rowman 5 vols. 4th ed. 1963 $275.00. Records approximately 117,000 volumes of bibliography under 16,000 headings.

The Bibliographic Index: A Cumulative Bibliography of Bibliographies. Wilson vol. 1 (1937–42) $85.00 vol. 2 (1943–46) $85.00 vol. 3 (1947–50) $85.00 vol. 4 (1951–55) $85.00 vol. 5 (1956–59) $170.00 vol. 6 (1960–62) $170.00 vol. 7 (1963–65) $170.00 vol. 8 (1966–68) $170.00 individual vols. for each year, 1969–79, ea. $100.00, 1980–84 service basis. Published twice a year with annual cumulations.

Toomey, Alice F. *A World Bibliography of Bibliographies, 1964–1974: A List of Works Represented by Library of Congress Printed Catalog Cards; A Decennial Supplement to . . . Besterman.* Rowman 2 vols. 1977 $95.00

TYPES OF ENUMERATIVE BIBLIOGRAPHIES

Although there is considerable overlap among the various types of enumerative bibliographies, they can be categorized as follows.

General bibliographies (also called *universal*) attempt to be all-inclusive and list books without limitations as to place of publication, time, subject, or author.

National bibliographies list books published *in* or *about* a country or region.

Trade bibliographies list books that are in print or for sale, and when, where, and by whom they were published. They usually also include the price of each item listed.

Author bibliographies list the complete works of an author, or works both by and about an author. They can run the gamut from the most simple, which provide only minimum identifying information (title and publication date)—these are called *checklists*—to those that provide descriptions extensive enough to approach the characteristics of a full-dressed descriptive bibliography.

Subject bibliographies list books about a specific subject. They may be comprehensive, or selective, or merely a reading list appended to an article or book. Unlike the types of bibliographies described above, the items listed are connected by *content*.

Bibliographies by *form* or *genre* include lists based either on the physical form in which the items were published, such as newspapers or periodicals (bibliographies of bibliographies fall into this category), or on genre, such as poetry or science fiction.

GENERAL BIBLIOGRAPHIES

There is not, nor will there ever be, a truly universal bibliography, complete and unlimited by language, period, or subject. The material is too vast. Attempts have been made to achieve this ideal, and some of the results are of great value. Recently, it seems reasonable to cite the printed catalogs of the great libraries of the world, comprehensive bibliographies of works from many countries and in many languages, as approaching nearest to the ideal universal bibliography. These catalogs have now reached such immense proportions that one of those listed below, *National Union Catalog* (Library of Congress), has ceased appearing in printed form, and since January 1983, has been available only on computer-generated microfiche.

UNITED STATES

A Catalog of Books Represented by Library of Congress Printed Cards, Aug. 1898–July 1942. Rowman 167 vols. $1,650.00; *Supplement, Aug. 1942–Dec. 1947* 42 vols. o.p.

Library of Congress Author Catalog, 1948–52. Rowman 24 vols. o.p.

Library of Congress Catalog—Books: Subjects, 1950–54 (Library of Congress Subject Catalog). Rowman 20 vols. 1955 o.p.

Library of Congress Catalog—Books: Subjects, 1955–59. Rowman 22 vols. 1960 $350.00

Library of Congress Catalog—Books: Subjects, 1960–64. J. W. Edwards 25 vols. 1965 o.p.

Library of Congress Catalog—Books: Subjects 1965–69. J. W. Edwards 42 vols. 1971 $600.00

Library of Congress Catalog—Books: Subjects, 1970–74. Rowman 100 vols. 1977 $1,740.00

National Union Catalog: A Cumulative Author List, 1953–57. Rowman 28 vols. $395.00. Vol. 27, *Music and Phonorecords,* and Vol. 28, *Motion Pictures and Film Strips,* are each $40.00.

National Union Catalog: A Cumulative Author List, 1958–67. Rowman 125 vols. $2,750.00

National Union Catalog: A Cumulative Author List, 1968–72. J. W. Edwards 128 vols. $1,950.00

National Union Catalog: A Cumulative Author List, 1973–77. Rowman 150 vols. $1,687.00. Cumulation includes *Films and Other Materials for Projection* and *Music, Books on Music, and Sound Recordings.*

National Union Catalog. Lib. of Congress (Cataloging Distribution Service) annual cumulations 1978 16 vols. $1,100.00, 1979 16 vols. $1,150.00, 1980 16 vols. $1,275.00, 1981 15 vols. $1,375.00, 1982 21 vols. $1,450.00. The *National Union Catalog* ceased publication as a book catalog at the end of 1982. Since January 1983, it has been published in computer-output microfiche and is available from the Cataloging Distribution Service, Lib. of Congress.

National Union Catalog: Books. Prepared under the editorial coordination of the Catalog Management and Publication Division, Lib. of Congress. Issued monthly on 48x microfiche, with separate cumulative name, title, subject, and series indexes. 1983 December index plus 12 monthly registers $100.00, 1984 December index plus 12 monthly registers $110.00, 1985 subscription $350.00. Contains bibliographic or catalog entries prepared by the Library of Congress, or by one of the libraries that contribute reports to the *National Union Catalog,* for books, pamphlets, and manuscripts, such as typescripts of theses, map atlases, monographic microform publications, and monographic government publications, both foreign and domestic. Entries encompass publications from all countries and in virtually every language.

National Union Catalog: U.S. Books. Prepared under the editorial coordination of the Catalog Management and Publication Division, Lib. of Congress. Issued monthly on 48x microfiche, with separate name, title, subject, and series indexes. 1983 December index plus 12 monthly registers $150.00, 1984 December index plus 12 monthly registers $145.00, 1985 subscription $245.00. Consists of records for monographs published in the United States in any language. This is a subset of the *National Union Catalog: Books.*

National Union Catalog: Cartographic Materials. Prepared under the editorial coordination of the Catalog Management and Publication Division, Lib. of Congress. Issued quarterly on 48x microfiche, with five separate indexes (name, title, subject, series, geographical classification code). 1983 registers $33.00, 1984 registers $6.50, 1985 subscription $130.00. Includes catalog records of single sheet maps, map sets, atlases, and maps treated as serials cataloged by the Library of Congress and records for atlases that have been cataloged by 1,500 contributing libraries. In 1983, the entire retrospective Library of Congress maps database was added to this publication.

National Union Catalog: Audiovisual Materials. Prepared under the editorial coordination of the Catalog Management and Publication Division, Lib. of Congress. Issued quarterly in 48x microfiche, with separate cumulative name, title, subject, and series indexes. 1983 register $7.00, 1984 register $12.00, 1985 subscription $65.00. Includes bibliographic records for motion pictures, filmstrips, transparency and slide sets, videorecordings, and kits currently cataloged by the Library of Congress.

The National Union Catalog Pre-1956 Imprints. National Union Catalog Pre-1956 Imprints (Vienna, Virginia) 754 vols. 1968–81, price available on request from the distributor. A cumulative author list representing Library of Congress printed cards and titles reported by other U.S. libraries. Also available on microfiche. A comprehensive retrospective catalog containing some 12 million entries for books, pamphlets, maps, atlases, music, and periodicals and indicating locations in some 1,100 libraries. A monumental work that supersedes the basic Library of Congress *Catalog of Books . . .* and its *Supplement* (1942–47), the *Library of Congress Author Catalog, 1948–52,* the *National Union Catalog . . . 1952–55 Imprints,* and the *National Union Catalog . . . 1953–57.* It also incorporates entries from the Union Catalog card file at the Library of Congress.

National Union Catalog, 1972: A Cumulative Author List Representing Library of Congress Printed Cards and Titles Reported by Other American Libraries. Lib. of Congress (Card Division) 9 monthly issues, 3 quarterly cumulations, and annual cumulation $375.00. This price also covers the *Catalog on Motion Pictures and Film Strips* (3 quarterly issues and annual cumulation $20.00) and *Catalog on Music and Phonorecords* (semiannual issue and annual cumulation $25.00)—both published by the Library of Congress.

GREAT BRITAIN

British Museum General Catalogue of Printed Books. Trustees of the British Museum 263 vols. 1960–66 annual and ten-year supplements. Previous editions issued as *Catalogue of Printed Books, 1881–1900*, Edwards Brothers 41 vols. 1946 o.p. Supplement, 10 vols. 1900–05 o.p.

EARLY AND RARE BOOKS

British Museum, Department of Printed Books. *Catalogue of Books Printed in the XVth Century Now in the British Museum.* British Lib. 1908–62.

The Eighteenth Century Short Title Catalogue: The British Library Collections. Ed. by R. C. Alston and M. J. Crump, British Lib. 1983 113 fiches £400.00. The machine-readable catalog is accessible in the United States through the Research Libraries Information Network (RLIN). The publication of this microfiche catalog of the British Library holdings of eighteenth-century imprints printed in Britain and in the English language anywhere in the world completes the first phase of the Eighteenth Century Short Title Catalog. Phase Two, the expansion of the database with records of the holdings of other libraries, is in progress. In the United States, the recording of North American copies of British eighteenth-century imprints is under way at Louisiana State University in Baton Rouge, and the recording of American eighteenth-century imprints is in progress at the American Antiquarian Society in Worcester, Massachusetts.

Goff, Frederick Richmond. *Incunabula in American Libraries: A Third Census of Fifteenth Century Books Recorded in North American Collections.* 1964. Kraus repr. 1973 $90.00; Bibliographical Society of Amer. supplement 1972 $10.00. Originally published by the Bibliographical Society of America. The Kraus reprint includes substantial annotations by the author in the margins to update the entries. The first census was compiled by the Bibliographical Society in 1919 and the second was compiled by Margaret Bingham Stillwell in 1940.

Incunable Short-Title Catalogue. Ed. by Lotte Hellinga, British Lib. in progress. Records compiled to date—some 18,000 at the end of 1984—are accessible in machine-readable form through the British Library Automated Information Service (BLAISE). When complete, this will be the only bibliography to record all surviving editions of books and other items printed from movable type in Europe from the beginning of printing in the mid-fifteenth century to 1500, and to list all known copies of each edition. Restricting its description of each edition to only what is required for identification, it will not supersede already existing bibliographies of incunables, but is intended to offer far broader coverage of the period than has ever been provided before.

The Nineteenth Century Short Title Catalogue. Chadwyck-Healey series 1 (1801–15) 5 vols. 1985 $1,495.00 series 2 (1816–70) in progress. A union catalog of all nineteenth-century imprints in English, wherever published, held by the Bodleian Library; the British Library; the University Library, Cambridge; Trinity College Library, Dublin; the National Library of Scotland; and the University Library, Newcastle.

Stillwell, Margaret Bingham. *The Beginning of the World of Books, 1450 to 1470: A*

Chronological Survey of the Texts Chosen for Printing during the First Twenty Years of the Printing Art. Bibliographical Society of Amer. 1972 $10.00
———. *Incunabula and Americana, 1450–1800: A Key to Bibliographical Study.* 1930. Cooper Square Pr. 1968 $29.50

NATIONAL BIBLIOGRAPHIES

UNITED STATES

Evans, Charles. *The American Bibliography: A Chronological Dictionary of All Books, Pamphlets and Periodical Publications Printed in the United States of America from the Genesis of Printing in 1639 down to and including the Year 1800; with Bibliographical and Biographical Notes.* 1903–34. Peter Smith repr. 1942 vols. 1– 12 set $180.00 vol. 13 $30.00 vol. 14 $30.00. Vol. 14 is a cumulated author-title index to the whole work. This is the most important general list of early American publications. For each book the author's name, along with birth and death dates, full title, date and place of publication, publisher or printer, number of pages, size, and, where possible, the name of a library owning a copy are supplied. In each volume, there is an index by author, subject, and publisher or printer. The first volume of this work was published in 1903; the twelfth, covering the years 1798–99, was published in 1934, just one year before the bibliographer's death.

Kelly, James. *The American Catalogue of Books (Original and Reprints). Published in the United States 1861 [to Jan. 1871].* Peter Smith 2 vols. 1938 ea. $18.00. A continuation of Roorbach's *Bibliotheca Americana.*

Leypoldt, Frederick. *American Catalogue . . . 1876–1910.* Peter Smith 13 vols. 1941 ea. $24.00–$30.00. A monumental bibliographic work, recording books in print and for sale, arranged by author, title, and subject.

The New Sabin: Books Described by Joseph Sabin and His Successors, Now Described Again on the Basis of Examination of Originals, and Fully Indexed by Title, Subject, Joint Authors, and Institutions and Agencies. Ed. by Lawrence S. Thompson, Whitston 10 vols. 1985 ea. $25.00–$30.00 cumulative index vols. 1–5 $30.00 vols. 6–10 in progress

Roorbach, Orville Augustus. *Bibliotheca Americana: A Catalogue of American Publications, Including Reprints and Original Works, from 1820 [to Jan. 1861].* 1852–61. Peter Smith 1939 vol. 1 o.p. vols. 2–4 (3 vols. in 1) $30.00. This is the direct ancestor of *The United States Catalog* and *The Cumulative Book Index*, see under "Trade Bibliographies, United States."

Sabin, Joseph, Wilberforce Eames, and R. W. G. Vail. *A Dictionary of Books Relating to America, from Its Discovery to the Present Time.* 1868–1936. Scarecrow Pr. 29 vols. in 2 miniprint vols. 1966 $199.00. Sabin's *Dictionary* is one of the great bibliographic reference works of the world in that it gives the bibliographic facts (including collations, locations, and notes on contents) of more than 100,000 books relating to U.S. history and social life. The *Dictionary* was begun in the middle of the nineteenth century by Joseph Sabin, distinguished American antiquarian. After approximately 15 years of research, Sabin published the first part of Volume 1 in 1868. He continued the work until his death in 1881, by which time he had gone as far as Volume 14, Part 82. After his death, the great task was continued by one of America's greatest bibliographers, Wilberforce Eames, who carried the work from Volume 14, Part 83, through Volume 20, Part 116, p. 196 (to the entry "Smith, Henry Hollingsworth"). The continuation by

Vail completed the set. The Scarecrow edition in miniprint is said to be readable without aids, but a free bar magnifier is included with each set. It is "the most handy Sabin for bookmen to use" (*Antiquarian Bookman*).

Shaw, Ralph R., and Richard H. Shoemaker. *American Bibliography: A Preliminary Checklist*. 1801–19. Scarecrow Pr. 22 vols. 1958–64 $290.00. A preliminary checklist gathered from secondary sources, designed to partially fill the gap in U.S. national bibliography between 1800, when Evans stops, and 1820, when Roorbach begins. Each volume covers one year.

Shipton, Clifford K., and James E. Mooney, eds. *National Index of American Imprints through 1800: The Short-Title Evans*. Univ. Pr. of Virginia 1969 $50.00. Provides an index to the Readex Microprint edition of Evans and also incorporates into the single alphabetical listing 10,035 additional items that have been identified since the publication of Evans's *The American Bibliography*.

Shoemaker, Richard H. *Checklist of American Imprints, 1820–1833*. Scarecrow Pr. 14 vols. plus *Title Index 1820–29* and *Author Index, Corrections and Sources, 1820–29* 1964–to date ea. $22.50–$32.50. Designed as a continuation of Shaw's *American Bibliography* to give more complete listings than those in Roorbach.

GREAT BRITAIN

British National Bibliography. British Lib. (Bibliographic Services Division) annual £76.00. An annual reference catalog of the new books published in Great Britain. Based on new books and new editions deposited with the Agent for the Copyright Libraries, with full bibliographic descriptions of every book. Dewey Decimal Classification (with modifications); author, title, and subject index. First issued for 1950.

Lowndes, William Thomas. *The Bibliographer's Manual of English Literature: Containing an Account of Rare, Curious, and Useful Books, Published in or Relating to Great Britain and Ireland, from the Invention of Printing; with Bibliographical and Critical Notices, Collations of the Rarer Articles, and the Prices at Which They Have Been Sold*. 1834. Ed. by Henry G. Bohn, Gale 8 vols. repr. of 1864 ed. corr. & enl. ed. 1967 $210.00

Pollard, A. W., and G. R. Redgrave. *A Short-Title Catalogue of Books Printed in England, Scotland and Ireland, and of English Books Printed Abroad, 1475–1640*. Ed. by N. A. Jackson, F. S. Ferguson, and K. F. Pantzer, Oxford 2d ed. rev. & enl. vol. 2 (I–Z) 1976 $165.00 vol. 1 in preparation.

Wing, Donald Godard, and Timothy J. Crist. *A Short-Title Catalogue of Books Printed in England, Scotland, Ireland, Wales and British America and of English Books Printed in Other Countries, 1641–1700*. MLA 2d ed. 1972 $325.00. A continuation of Pollard and Redgrave's *Short-Title Catalogue*.

TRADE BIBLIOGRAPHIES

Trade bibliographies are the basic reference tools for librarians, bibliographers, and booksellers seeking information as to which books are in print and when, where, by whom, and at what price they were published and made available for sale. The following list includes both current and retrospective sources.

UNITED STATES

The American Book Publishing Record Cumulative: An American National Bibliography. Bowker 15 vols. (1876–1949) 1980 $1,995.00, 15 vols. (1950–77) 1979 $1,995.00

Books in Print. Bowker 6 vols. 1985–86 $199.95. An annual publication listing all the in-print books of some 17,000 U.S. publishers by title and by author—more than 692,000 titles in all. Information provided includes author, title, edition, Library of Congress number, series information, language if other than English, whether illustrated or not, grade range, year of publication, type of binding, price, International Standard Book Number, publisher's order number, imprint, and publisher.

Books in Print Supplement. Bowker 2 vols. 1985–86 $110.00. An annual publication issued six months after the publication of *Books in Print* to update the information that appears there. Includes titles that have had price or other major changes, titles that have gone out of print, and titles that have been published or announced since the publication of the last edition of *Books in Print.* Also contains listings of new titles by subject.

The Cumulative Book Index. Wilson service basis. The *CBI* began publication in 1898. Since 1928, the last single-volume cumulation, it has been an author, title, and subject index to current books in the English language published worldwide. Monthly supplements are cumulated quarterly and then annually in bound volumes. Permanent volumes now in print are 1938–42, 1943–48, 1953–56, 1957–58, 1959–60, 1961–62, 1963–64, 1965–66, 1967–68, and annual volumes for each year from 1969 to 1984. Continually brought up-to-date.

The Cumulative Paperback Index, 1939–59: A Comprehensive Bibliographic Guide to 14,000 Mass-Market Paperback Books Issued under 69 Imprints. Ed. by Robert Reginald and M. R. Burgess, Gale 1973 $55.00

El-Hi Textbooks and Serials in Print. Bowker spring annual 1985 $60.00. Contains more than 40,000 entries, including textbooks, reference works, teaching aids, audiovisual materials, and periodicals, arranged within 21 broad subject categories.

Guide to Reprints: An International Bibliography of Scholarly Reprints. Guide to Reprints annual 1985 $85.00. A guide to books, journals, and other materials that are available in reprint form.

Paperbound Books in Print. Bowker spring and fall semiannual 3 vols. 1985 $85.95

Publishers' Trade List Annual. Bowker September annual 5 vols. 1985 $124.95. A collection of the booklists and catalogs of some 1,800 U.S. publishers bound together alphabetically.

Subject Guide to Books in Print. Bowker October annual 4 vols. 1985–86 $142.95. A subject guide to the nonfiction titles listed in *Books in Print;* titles arranged under some 63,000 headings with numerous cross-references.

The United States Catalog: Books in Print, January 1929. Wilson o.p. Continued by *The Cumulative Book Index.*

GREAT BRITAIN

British Books in Print. Whitaker (dist. by Bowker) annual 4 vols. 1985 $199.95. All British books in print at the end of April of each year. This is the continuation of *The Reference Catalogue of Current Literature* first published in 1874 and subsequently at four- or five-year intervals; provides access to close to 400,000 titles.

British Paperback Books in Print. Whitaker semiannual £25.00. A complete record of all paperbacks in print in the United Kingdom.

Whitaker's Cumulative Book List. Whitaker annual £18.00. A complete record of British publishing each year, with details as to title, subtitle, author, size, number of pages, price, month of publication, publisher, and classification.

CANADA

Canadian Books in Print: Author and Title Index. Univ. of Toronto Pr. 1985 $65.00

Canadian Books in Print: Subject Index. Univ. of Toronto Pr. 1985 $50.00

KEYS TO ANONYMOUS BOOKS

The books listed below are either reprints of earlier books or are now out of print. From 1950 on, authorship of anonymous and pseudonymous works in English and U.S. literature can usually be found in the *British National Bibliography* and in the *National Union Catalog.*

Cushing, William. *Anonyms: A Dictionary of Revealed Authorship.* 1889. Adler's 1968 $87.00

Halkett, Samuel, and John Laing. *Dictionary of Anonymous and Pseudonymous English Literature.* 1882–88 1926–34. Haskell 7 vols. $399.00. Vol. 8, *Third Supplement, 1900–1949*, by Dennis E. Rhodes and Anna E. C. Simoni, published by Barnes & Noble in 1956, is now out of print. Vol. 1 of the revised edition, covering 1475–1640 with addenda and corrigenda, ed. by John Horden, was published by Longman in 1980 at $150.00.

Initials and Pseudonyms: A Dictionary of Literary Disguises. 1885. Adler's 2 vols. 1969 $107.50; Gale 1982 $85.00

Stonehill, Charles A. *Andrew Block and H. Winthrop Stonehill: Anonyma and Pseudonyma.* 1927. Longwood 4 vols. in 2 1977 $55.00

Taylor, Archer, and Frederic J. Mosher. *The Bibliographical History of Anonyma and Pseudonyma.* Univ. of Chicago Pr. 1951 o.p.

TOOLS FOR BOOK SELECTION

[SEE ALSO "Trade Bibliographies" in this chapter
and appropriate sections in Chapter 1.]

Haines, Helen E. *Living with Books: The Art of Book Selection.* Columbia 2d ed. 1950 $30.00. The standard compendium.

General Book Selection Tools

Many book lists are compiled annually by libraries, wholesalers, and various organizations. The American Library Association catalogs are the highest type of evaluative bibliography. Entries are arranged according to the Dewey Decimal Classification. Each entry gives the author, birth and death dates, title, publisher, date of publication (except for fiction in the 1926 catalog), price, number of pages, and a description and evaluation of the contents.

A.L.A. Catalog, 1926: Annotated Basic List of 10,000 Books. Ed. by Isabella M. Cooper, Amer. Lib. Association 1926 o.p.

A.L.A. Catalog, 1926–1931: Annotated List of Approximately 3,000 Titles. Ed. by Marion Horton, Amer. Lib. Association 1933 o.p.

A.L.A. Catalog, 1932–1936: Annotated List of Approximately 4,000 Titles. Ed. by Marion Horton, Amer. Lib. Association 1938 o.p.

A.L.A. Catalog, 1937–1941: Annotated List of 4,000 Titles. Ed. by Marion Horton, Amer. Lib. Association 1943 o.p.

A.L.A. Catalog, 1942–1949: Annotated List of Approximately 4,500 Titles. Ed. by Florence Boochever, Amer. Lib. Association 1952 o.p.

Basic Book List. Amer. Booksellers Association 1984 free to members, extra copies to members $10.00, nonmembers $15.00. Titles arranged by subject and publisher. The subject classification is in accordance with the 26 standard categories of paperbacks determined by the Joint Associations Book Projects Committee.

Book Review Digest. 1905–to date. Wilson annual service basis. Approximately 6,000 books a year are listed by author with price, publisher, and descriptive notes. Published monthly (except February and July) with permanent bound annual cumulations. Every fifth year the annual volume contains a cumulated subject and title index of the previous five years. Reprints of annual volumes, from 1905 through 1969, are available at prices ranging from $50.00 to $90.00; annuals for 1970–84 are sold on a service basis.

Books for College Libraries: A Core Collection of 40,000 Titles. Amer. Lib. Association 6 vols. 2d ed. 1975 pap. $80.00. Preparation of this new and revised editon of Melvin J. Voight's and Joseph H. Treyz's *Books for College Libraries* (1967) was a project of the Association of College and Research Libraries. The titles selected are considered the minimum essential for the four-year undergraduate college. Subject specialists evaluated the titles in the earlier edition as well as titles published between 1964 and 1972. Titles are arranged by Library of Congress classification and are entered in the main catalog only once. Volume 6 contains author, title, and subject indexes. Each entry is a virtually complete MARC record.

The Fiction Catalog. Wilson 10th ed. 1980 $70.00 (plus 4 annual supplements $70.00). Lists 5,000 works of fiction that have been found most useful by experienced and outstanding librarians in U.S. and Canadian libraries. The four annual supplements cover approximately 1,600 additional titles.

Opening Day Collection. 1967. Choice 3d ed. 1974 $7.50. A listing of approximately 1,800 titles considered important for the collection of a new undergraduate library on its opening day.

Public Library Catalog (Standard Catalog for Public Libraries). Wilson 8th ed. 1984 $140.00 (plus 4 annual supplements). A classified and annotated list of some 8,000 nonfiction titles recommended for small and medium-sized libraries. Part 1 is a classified catalog arranged by Dewey Decimal Classification, with subject headings based on the *Sears List of Subject Headings.* Part 2 is an author, title, and subject index to Part 1, with approximately 13,000 analytical entries for parts of books. Part 3 is a directory of publishers and distributors.

Reference

Barton, Mary Neill, comp. *Reference Books: A Brief Guide.* Enoch Pratt 8th ed. 1978 $5.00

Cheney, Frances Neal. *Fundamental Reference Sources.* Amer. Lib. Association 2d ed. 1980 $15.00

Gates, Jean Key. *Guide to the Use of Books and Libraries*. McGraw-Hill 5th ed. 1983 $19.95 pap. $13.50

Kister, Kenneth F. *Encyclopedia Buying Guide: A Consumer Guide to General Encyclopedias in Print*. Bowker 3d ed. 1981 $29.95 pap. $19.95

————. *Kister's Atlas Buying Guide: General English-Language World Atlases Available in North America*. Oryx 1984 $37.50

Reference Sources for Small and Medium-Sized Libraries. Ed. by Jovian P. Lang and Deborah E. Masters, Amer. Lib. Association 4th ed. 1984 pap. $20.00

Sheehy, Eugene P. *Guide to Reference Books*. Amer. Lib. Association 9th ed. 1976 $40.00 supplements 1980 $15.00 1982 $15.00. One of the superior works, this guide is based on the edition by Constance M. Winchell and its three supplements, which it entirely supersedes.

Taylor, Margaret. *Basic Reference Sources: A Self-Study Manual*. Scarecrow Pr. 2d ed. 1981 pap. $13.50

Walford, A. J. *Walford's Guide to Reference Material*. Lib. Association 3 vols. 4th ed. vol. 1 (1980) $67.50 vol. 2 (1982) $67.50 vol. 3 (1985) $80.00. A guide to reference books published by the British Library Association. Although British items are given prominence, much U.S., Russian, French, German, and other material is included.

Wynar, Bohdan S. *American Reference Books Annual*. Libraries Unlimited vols. 1–11 (1970–80) o.p. vol. 12 (1981) $50.00 vol. 13 (1982) $55.00 vol. 14 (1983) $55.00 vol. 15 (1984) $65.00. Cumulative index to authors and titles (1980–84) $45.00.

Children's Books

The field of children's books has a literature of its own that goes beyond the scope of this chapter. Listed below are some of the basic book selection tools.

Books for Secondary School Libraries. Comp. by the Ad Hoc Library Committee of the National Association of Independent Schools, Bowker 6th ed. 1981 $34.95. "Designed to prepare secondary students for the subjects awaiting them at the college level. Helpful lists of library tools and reference materials are included. Fully indexed by author, title, and subject, with a special directory of publishers. Material arranged by Dewey Decimal Classification with Library of Congress Subject headings" (Publisher's catalog).

Children's Catalog. Wilson 14th ed. 1981 (plus 4 annual supplements 1982–85) $54.00. A catalog of children's books found useful in public and elementary school libraries. This edition covers nearly 6,000 books arranged in three parts. Part 1 is a classified catalog giving full cataloging information for each book; Part 2 is an author, title, and subject index with analytical entries; Part 3 is a directory of publishers and distributors.

The Elementary School Library Collection: A Guide to Books and Other Media. Ed. by Lois Winkel, Brodart 14th ed. 1984 $79.95

Gillespie, John T. *More Juniorplots: A Guide for Teachers and Librarians*. Bowker 1977 $15.95

Gillespie, John T., and Christine B. Gilbert. *Best Books for Children: Preschool through the Middle Grades*. Bowker 3d ed. 1985 $34.50

Gillespie, John T., and Diana L. Lembo. *Juniorplots: A Book Talk Manual for Teachers and Librarians*. Bowker 1967 $15.95. "Plot summaries of 80 books for young people 9 to 16, arranged according to 8 basic behavioral themes that a librarian or educator might want to use in giving a book talk. Thematic analysis, suggested discussion material, and a list of other related titles are given for each book described" (Publisher's catalog).

Junior High School Library Catalog. Wilson 5th ed. 1985 (plus 4 annual pap. supplements) in preparation. An annotated list of approximately 4,000 in-print fiction and nonfiction titles essential to the junior high school library collection (grades 7–9).

Larrick, Nancy. *A Parent's Guide to Children's Reading.* Westminster 5th ed. 1983 $12.95

Lima, Carolyn W. *A to Zoo: Subject Access to Children's Picture Books.* Bowker 2d ed. 1985 $39.95

Senior High School Library Catalog (Standard Catalog for High School Libraries). Wilson 12th ed. 1982 (plus 5 annual supplements) 1983–86 $70.00. This edition offers a select list of more than 5,000 in-print fiction and nonfiction titles for secondary school students (grades 9–12).

Subject Guide to Children's Books in Print. Bowker December annual 1985–86 $62.95. A subject listing of 45,000 juvenile titles under more than 7,100 subject headings. Provides complete ordering information: author, title, publisher, date of publication, price, and, when available, grade level, binding, and edition.

LISTS OF "BEST" BOOKS

The making of lists of "best books" is a form of book selection that is ever popular, both with the makers and with the readers. One of the earliest lists is Sir John Lubbock's famous Hundred Best Books in *The Pleasures of Life* (o.p.), published first in 1887.

Dickinson, Asa Don. *The World's Best Books: Homer to Hemingway.* Wilson 1953 $10.00

Downs, Robert B. *Books That Changed the World.* Amer. Lib. Association 2d ed. 1978 $2.00; New Amer. Lib. (Mentor) pap. $3.95

———. *Famous American Books.* McGraw-Hill 1971 $16.95

———. *Famous Books: Great Writings in the History of Civilization.* Littlefield 1975 pap. $4.95

Fadiman, Clifton. *The Lifetime Reading Plan.* Crowell rev. ed. 1978 $13.41. A guide to his famous "100 books."

Waldhorn, Arthur, and others, eds. *Good Reading.* Bowker 22d ed. 1985 $29.95. An annotated guide to more than 2,500 of the world's best books.

TOOLS FOR PERIODICAL SELECTION

Ayer Directory of Publications. Ayer annual $99.00. Indexes newspapers and magazines published in the United States and its territories; also includes Canada, Bermuda, Panama, and the Philippines. Arranged geographically with classified lists.

Irregular Serials and Annuals: An International Directory. Bowker 11th ed. 1986 $139.95. This bibliography brings together current data on more than 37,000 serials, annuals, continuations, proceedings of national and international conferences, and other publications issued irregularly or less frequently than twice a year. Arrangement is by subject, with title and subject indexes. Each entry gives title, subtitle or annotation, date of first issue, frequency (if scheduled), editor, name and address of publisher, price in the currency of the country of publication, and International Standard Serial Number.

Katz, William, and Linda Sternberg Katz. *Magazines for Libraries*. Bowker 5th ed. 1986 $95.00

New Serial Titles, 1950–70 Cumulative. Bowker 4 vols. 1973 o.p. A microfilm edition is available for $100.00; xerographic reprints cost $250.00 each. This is a compilation of the new serial titles commencing publication after December 31, 1949. It includes approximately 260,000 titles, alphabetically arranged. Information includes issuing body, place of publication, date of first issue, and date of last issue if publication has ceased. Dewey Decimal Classification number, country code, and International Standard Serial Number are included. There is a separate list of 20,000 cessations and changes since 1950.

Spahn, Theodore J., Janet M. Spahn, and Robert H. Muller. *From Radical Left to Extreme Right: A Bibliography of Current Periodicals of Protest, Controversy, Advocacy or Dissent, with Dispassionate Content-Summaries to Guide Librarians and Other Educators*. Scarecrow Pr. 1976 $30.00

The Standard Periodical Directory. Oxbridge 8th ed. 1983 $160.00. A guide to more than 60,000 U.S. and Canadian periodicals. Alphabetical subject arrangement with author index and subject guide. Gives name and address of publisher, editorial content and scope, year founded, subscription rate, etc.

Ulrich's International Periodicals Directory. Bowker 24th ed. 1985 $139.95. Provides in-depth information for some 69,000 periodicals from all over the world, arranged by subject. Special sections list periodicals that have been launched or ceased publication since 1983, and indexing and abstracting services are also included. Updated by *Ulrich's Quarterly: A Supplement to Ulrich's International Periodicals Directory and Irregular Serials and Annuals*, annual subscription $60.00.

Working Press of the Nation. National Research Bureau annual 5 vols. 1984 ea. $110.00 set $241.00. Vol. 1, *Newspaper Directory*; Vol. 2, *Magazine Directory*; Vol. 3, *TV and Radio Directory*; Vol. 4, *Feature Writer and Photographer Directory*; Vol. 5, *Internal Publications Directory*.

BOOK TRADE AND LIBRARY TERMINOLOGY

Included here are glossaries dealing with the language of the book trade. For glossaries dealing specifically with the terminology of book collecting and the rare book trade, see under "Book Collecting: Glossaries of Terminology" in this chapter.

Glaister, Geoffrey A. *Glaister's Glossary of the Book*. Univ. of California Pr. 1979 $75.00

Orne, Jerrold. *The Language of the Foreign Book Trade: Abbreviations, Terms and Phrases*. 1949. Amer. Lib. Association 3d ed. 1976 $20.00

Peters, Jean, ed. *The Bookman's Glossary*. Bowker 6th ed. 1983 $24.95

Roberts, Matt T., and Don Etherington. *Bookbinding and the Conservation of Books: A Dictionary of Descriptive Terminology*. Lib. of Congress 1982 $27.00

Young, Heartsill. *ALA Glossary of Library and Information Science Terms*. Amer. Lib. Association 1983 $50.00

DIRECTORIES AND YEARBOOKS
Book Trade

American Book Trade Directory. Bowker annual 31st ed. 1985 $119.95. Includes lists
   of booksellers, book clubs, rental library chains, wholesalers, etc., in the United
   States and Canada.

Book Buyer's Handbook. Amer. Booksellers Association free to members. A periodically updated guide to publishers' discounts, terms, policies, and trade features,
   issued in a ring-binder format with correction sheets supplied from time to
   time.

The Book Publishing Annual: Highlights, Analyses and Trends. Bowker 3d ed. 1985
   $60.00. Prepared by the editors of *Publishers Weekly* in collaboration with the
   Book Division of R. R. Bowker.

*Cassell and the Publishers Association Directory of Publishing in Great Britain, the
   Commonwealth, Ireland and South Africa.* International Publications 10th ed.
   1982 pap. $32.50. Covers book publishing and its ancillary services.

International Literary Market Place. Bowker annual 1985 pap. $75.00. A directory to
   approximately 10,000 active publishers throughout the world.

Kim, Ung Chon. *Policies of Publishers: A Handbook for Order Librarians.* Scarecrow
   Pr. 1982 pap. $15.00

*Literary Market Place, with Names and Numbers: The Directory of American Book Pub-
   lishing.* Bowker annual 1986 pap. $59.95

*Publishers Directory, 1984–85: A Guide to More Than 9,000 New and Established, Com-
   mercial and Nonprofit, Private and Alternative, Corporate and Association, Government and Institution Publishing Programs and Their Distributors.* Ed. by Linda S.
   Hubbard and Monica M. O'Donnell, Gale 2 vols. 5th ed. 1984 $200.00. Includes
   information on approximately 9,350 publishers in the United States and Canada, excluding only vanity presses and publishers listed in Bowker's *Literary
   Market Place.*

*Publishers, Distributors, and Wholesalers of the United States: A Directory of 57,000
   Publishers, Distributors, Associations, Wholesalers and Software Producers and
   Manufacturers Listing Editorial and Ordering Addresses, and an ISBN Publisher
   Prefix Index.* Bowker annual 7th ed. 1985 $59.95

Publishers' International Directory. Ed. by Barbara Verrel and others, Saur 2 vols.
   10th ed. 1984 $145.00. "The directory gives names and addresses of publishers
   around the world—arranged geographically. . . . Includes an index listing publishers by subject interests; a guide to publishers' and booksellers' associations
   and lists of national and international book trade associations around the
   globe" (Publisher's catalog).

Taubert, Sigfred, ed. *The Book Trade of the World.* Bowker 4 vols. 1972–84 ea. $70.00.
   A country-by-country survey of publishing and bookselling around the world, describing in detail the structure of each country's book trade, providing such information as history, statistics, and industry organizations and publications.

*Who Distributes What and Where: An International Directory of Publishers, Imprints,
   Agents, and Distributors.* Bowker 3d ed. 1983 $65.00. Provides full contact infor-
   mation on 6,500 publishers and their imprints, representatives, and distributors
   in 140 countries.

Library

American Library Directory. Bowker annual 38th ed. 1985 $119.95 updating service (6
   bimonthly bulletins) $65.00. Includes public libraries, county and regional ex-

tension systems, college and university libraries, junior college libraries, major research libraries overseas, and so on. Arranged geographically by state and city with information as to key personnel, volumes, budget, special departments, branches, salaries, etc.

Bowker Annual of Library and Book Trade Information. Ed. by Filomena Simora, Bowker annual 31st ed. 1986 $79.95. Sources of listings, charts, associations, and articles of interest to the library and book world.

Directory of Special Libraries and Information Centers. Gale 9th ed. 1985 $320.00 supplement (4 issues per year) $275.00

Subject Collections: A Guide to Special Book Collections and Subject Emphases as Reported by University, College, Public, and Special Libraries and Museums in the United States and Canada. Ed. by Lee Ash and William G. Miller, Bowker 2 vols. 6th ed. 1985 $165.00. "A companion to the 'American Library Directory,' this volume indexes the book resources of college, special and public libraries under subjects based upon Library of Congress subject headings, plus innumerable author, place and name collections. Within the subject categories, entries are arranged alphabetically in geographic order. Typical entries include name and location of library holding the collection, name of curator, whether indexed, book budget, etc." (Publisher's catalog).

Subject Collections in European Libraries. Ed. by Richard C. Lewanski, Bowker 2d ed. 1978 $57.00. Provides such information as name and location of collection, its size and type of material, name of curator, interlibrary loan and photoreproduction facilities, copyright privileges, number of volumes held, and a bibliographic citation of printed catalogs, guides, and other descriptive and historical monographs on the library.

World Guide to Libraries. Ed. by Helga Lengenfelder, Saur 6th ed. 1983 $190.00. Lists special, university, and public libraries from countries in Europe, Africa, America, Asia, and Oceania. For each library, the guide provides name and address, subject specialties, year of establishment, and number of books. The subject index, subdivided by country, pinpoints all the libraries of any country with particular subject collections.

Rare Book Trade

AB Bookman's Yearbook. Ed. by Jacob L. Chernofsky, AB Bookman's Weekly March annual 2 pts. pap. $15.00. Free with *AB* subscription. The *Yearbook* includes such book-trade features as a "Directory of Specialist and Antiquarian Booksellers."

Bookdealers in North America: A Directory of Dealers in Secondhand and Antiquarian Books in Canada and the United States of America, 1983–85. Seven Hills Bks. 9th ed. 1983 $25.00

The Collector's Guide to Antiquarian Bookstores. Comp. by Modoc Pr., intro. by Leona Rostenberg and Madeleine B. Stern, Macmillan 1984 $20.75

Dealers in Books: A Directory of Dealers in Secondhand and Antiquarian Books in the British Isles, 1984–86. Seven Hills Bks. 1984 $21.00

Directory of Specialized American Bookdealers, 1984–1985. Moretus Pr. 1984 $36.50. Prepared by the staff of *American Book Collector.*

European Bookdealers: A Directory of Dealers in Secondhand and Antiquarian Books on the Continent of Europe, 1982–84. Seven Hills Bks. 1982 $21.00

The International Directory of Book Collectors. Comp. by Roger Sheppard and Judith Sheppard, Trigon Pr. 4th ed. 1985 $35.00

Rare Books 1983–84: Trends, Collections, Sources. Ed. by Alice D. Schreyer, Bowker

1984 $49.95. A combination directory and year-in-review that covers the antiquarian and rare book world. The directory section contains full contact and descriptive listings for rare book libraries, antiquarian book dealers, and appraisers.

Robinson, Ruth E., and Daryush Farudi. *Buy Books Where—Sell Books Where: A Directory of Out of Print Booksellers and Their Author-Subject Specialties.* Robinson Bks. 1984 pap. $21.50

BOOK COLLECTING

The books included here relate to the individual collector, the institutional collector, and the book dealer. They are a representative selection only from the vast literature of book collecting. Directories for the rare and antiquarian book trade are not listed below, but are included in this chapter under "Directories and Yearbooks: Rare Book Trade."

Glossaries of Terminology

Included here are glossaries of terms used specifically in book collecting and the rare book trade. Glossaries that include the terminology of book collecting as one aspect of the language of the book trade can be found in this chapter under "Book Trade and Library Terminology."

Carter, John. *ABC for Book Collectors.* With corrs. and adds. by Nicolas Barker, Grenada 6th ed. 1980 $15.00

Malkin, Sol M. *ABC of the Book Trade.* AB Bookman's Weekly pap. $3.00

General Introductions and Manuals

Berkeley, Edmund, Jr., and others. *Autographs and Manuscripts: A Collector's Manual.* Scribner 1978 $24.95. A collection of articles sponsored by the Manuscript Society, offering the collector of autographs a comprehensive manual covering the history and fundamentals of autograph collecting.

Book Collecting: A Modern Guide. Ed. by Jean Peters, Bowker 1977 $23.95. A collection of 12 original essays by a group of prominent book professionals on the techniques of book collecting, offering advice on practical ways of building, organizing, and caring for a personal or special collection of books and manuscripts. Concludes with an excellent bibliographic essay on "The Literature of Book Collecting," by G. Thomas Tanselle.

Carter, John, ed. *New Paths in Book Collecting: Essays by Various Hands.* 1934. Ayer facsimile ed. 1967 $16.00. A collection of essays by a group of English collectors and dealers, offering excellent examples of imaginative approaches to book collecting. Areas covered include detective fiction, "yellow backs," serial fiction, and musical first editions.

———. *Taste and Technique in Book Collecting.* Private Libraries Association 1970 £8.00. A gracefully written and intelligent work on the nature of book collecting; one of the great classics in the field.

Collectible Books: Some New Paths. Ed. by Jean Peters, Bowker 1979 $19.95. A collection of essays by a group of librarians, scholars, and book collectors on nontraditional areas of collecting. Among the collecting areas covered are nonfirsts, anthologies, mass-market paperbacks, American trade bindings, photography as book illustration, publishers' imprints, and American fiction since 1960.

Wilson, Robert A. *Modern Book Collecting*. Knopf 1980 $12.95. A guide for the beginning collector of modern first editions. Included is a key to identifying first editions of nearly 200 American and British publishers and a list of bibliographies of collected modern authors.

Zempel, Edward N., and Linda A. Verkler. *First Editions: A Guide to Identification*. Spoon River Pr. 1984 $20.00. Statements of selected North American, British Commonwealth, and Irish publishers on their methods of designating first editions.

Bibliographies and Checklists

Whether one collects an author, a subject, or a printing or publishing imprint, bibliographies are essential in helping to identify and describe the material to be collected. In the nineteenth century, it was still possible to prepare comprehensive bibliographies that attempted to list *all* rare and collectible books. Today, works such as this have been superseded by hundreds of specialized bibliographies, so that it is necessary now to consult such works as Theodore Besterman's *A World Bibliography of Bibliographies*, the Wilson Company's *Bibliographic Index*, and others grouped together under "Bibliographies of Bibliographies" to learn what individual bibliographies are available on a particular collecting interest.

In the field of literature, where author collecting is probably the most predominant form, the collecting rules are set down in descriptive author bibliographies. These may be collective, providing descriptions of the works of a number of authors, such as the monumental *Bibliography of American Literature* compiled by Jacob Blanck; or they may be of individual authors, of which excellent examples are B. C. Bloomfield's *Philip Larkin: A Bibliography* and B. J. Kirkpatrick's *A Bibliography of Virginia Woolf*. A full range of descriptive author bibliographies in English and American literature can be located in the works listed below.

Howard-Hill, T. H. *Bibliography of British Literary Bibliographies*. Oxford (Clarendon Pr.) 1969 o.p. Supplemented by the last half of his *Shakespearian Bibliography and Textual Criticism: A Bibliography* (Oxford 1971 $39.95).

The New Cambridge Bibliography of English Literature. Cambridge Univ. Pr. 4 vols. ea. $135.00–$145.00. Vol. 1–3, ed. by George Watson; Vol. 4, ed. by I. R. Willison.

Tanselle, G. Thomas. *Guide to the Study of United States Imprints*. Harvard Univ. Pr. 1971 $75.00

Rare Book Prices

American Book Prices Current Annual. 1895–to date. Amer. Book Prices Current vol. 91 1985 $90.95. Earlier volumes are all out of print. This distinguished series, issued continuously for more than 75 years, covers all principal book auction sales in the United States and London—and, with the newest volumes, covers also some major Continental sales. It was issued originally by Dodd, later by Dutton, then by Bowker, and from 1953 through 1965 by Edward Lazare, a leading rare book expert, as editor and Ramona J. Lazare as publisher. It was subsequently issued by Columbia University Press for five years before it was acquired by its present owner.

American Book Prices Current Index. Amer. Book Prices Current 1916–1983 12 vols.
o.p.

Author Price Guides. Quill & Brush 1984–to date. ea. $1.00–$7.00. Separate guides issued for each author, printed on three-ring binder paper. A series of bibliographic checklists of the first editions of collectible authors, with estimated retail price ranges noted.

Book Auction Records (English) Annual. 1902–to date. International Publications vol.
73 (1977) $82.50 vol. 74 (1978) $82.50 vol. 75 (1979) $125.00 vol. 76 (1980)
$162.50 vol. 77 (1981) $130.00 vol. 78 (1982) $130.00 vol. 79 (1983) $130.00 vol.
80 (1984) $135.00. A priced and annotated annual record of book auctions
throughout the world.

Bradley, Van Allen. *The Book Collector's Handbook of Values 1982/83.* Putnam 1982
$29.95. The Chicago book critic, journalist, and one-time bookseller lists (by au-
thor) some 15,000 old and contemporary editions desired by collectors, along
with approximate prices. Bradley's popular column about rare books, "Gold in
Your Attic," led to a book by that title and a sequel, *New Gold in Your Attic.*

Heard, J. Norman, and Jimmie H. Hoover. *Bookman's Guide to Americana.* Scarecrow Pr. 8th ed. 1981 $17.50. An alphabetical cumulation from antiquarian
booksellers' catalogs in Americana, offering a cross-section of market prices.

Howes, Wright. *U.S.Iana.* Bowker 2d ed. 1962 $49.95. A selective bibliography of
Americana identifying significant and collectible works. Titles are keyed to rela-
tive grades of value, importance, and scarcity.

McGrath, Daniel, ed. *The Bookman's Price Index.* 1964–to date. Gale ea. $145.00.
Each volume contains entries selected from the catalogs of leading antiquarian
and specialist book dealers of the United States and Great Britain.

CHAPTER 3

Reference Books: Literature

Barbara Turman Wilkie

> Literature is a transmission of power. Text books and treatises, dictionaries and encyclopedias, manuals and books of instruction—they are communications; but literature is a power line, and the motor, mark you, is the reader.
> —CHARLES P. CURTIS, *A Commonplace Book*

Given the enormous amount of material published annually in the field of literature, it would be impossible to keep abreast of major trends and developments without reference books. Reference tools may be an end in themselves, but usually they are just another step leading to a more specific work. The reference books listed in this chapter are among the more important and useful tools currently used in literary research. Citations indicate the latest edition at the time of publication. The more general literary sources are listed first, followed by the more specialized titles in U.S. and British literature. Within each section, books are organized by type of material, e.g., bibliography, dictionary, and so on.

As with other nonfiction, reference works duplicate information among themselves; yet each has its individual strengths and deficiencies. One will know these best through use and comparison; stated purposes in prefaces are not always fulfilled, and copyright dates are no proof of up-to-date material. Although many reference works are beyond the budget of individuals, public and academic libraries should have some titles from each section below. For more specialized reference books on specific subjects, see the individual chapters of this volume.

BIBLIOGRAPHY

The Bibliographic Index: A Cumulative Bibliography of Bibliographies. Wilson vol. 1 (1937–42) $85.00 vol. 2 (1943–46) $85.00 vol. 3 (1947–50) $85.00 vol. 4 (1951–55) $85.00 vol. 5 (1956–59) $170.00 vol. 6 (1960–62) $170.00 vol. 7 (1963–65) $170.00 vol. 8 (1966–68) $170.00 individual vols. for each year, 1969–79, ea. $100.00, 1980–84 service basis. A subject list of English and foreign-language bibliographies, which contain 40 or more bibliographic citations. Includes bibliographies published separately or as parts of books and pamphlets. In addition, the editors search 1,900 periodicals for material. Published in April and August, with a bound cumulation each December.

Modern Language Association International Bibliography of Books and Articles on the Modern Languages and Literatures. 1921–to date. New York Univ. Pr. $15.00. Most comprehensive annual listing of books and articles on modern languages and literature in the United States and Great Britain. Includes sections on U.S. and English literature, as well as Medieval, neo-Latin, and Celtic literatures and folklore, divided first by century, then by authors writing in that century.

Pownall, David E., ed. *Articles on Twentieth Century Literature: An Annotated Bibliography, 1954–1970.* Kraus 8 vols. lib. bdg. $480.00. Based on the annotated bibliographies appearing in the journal *Twentieth Century Literature.* Includes scholarly and critical articles.

Schwartz, Narda Lacey, ed. *Articles on Women Writers, 1960–1975: A Bibliography.* ABC-Clio text ed. 1977 $26.50. Lists English-language articles published between 1960 and 1975 on approximately 600 women.

Women and Literature: An Annotated Bibliography of Women Writers. Women & Lit. Collective 1976 o.p. Focuses on fiction and other prose by women writers.

DICTIONARIES AND ENCYCLOPEDIAS

Barnet, Sylvan. *A Dictionary of Literary, Dramatic, and Cinematic Terms.* Little, Brown 2d ed. 1971 pap. $6.95. Fewer terms are discussed than in Holman, but Barnet offers some of the fullest and most allusive definitions; bibliographies.

Beckson, Karl, and Arthur Ganz. *A Reader's Guide to Literary Terms: A Dictionary.* Farrar 1975 pap. $6.95. Gives definitions and meanings of literary terms.

Bédé, Jean-Albert, and William Edgerton, eds. *Columbia Dictionary of Modern European Literature.* Columbia Univ. Pr. 2d ed. 1980 $60.00. Includes 1,853 writers selected on the basis of their relevance to twentieth-century literature, as well as survey articles on various national literatures.

Benet, William R., ed. *The Reader's Encyclopedia.* Crowell 2d ed. 1965 $21.63. Brief descriptions of writers, literary allusions and expressions, literary schools, plots and characters, criticism, etc.

Buchanan-Brown, John. *Cassell's Encyclopaedia of World Literature.* Morrow 3 vols. o.p. Volume 1 includes histories and general articles; Volumes 2 and 3 include biographies of literary figures.

Carrier, Warren, and Kenneth Oliver, eds. *Guide to World Literature.* National Council of Teachers of Eng. 1980 pap. $11.00. Discusses almost 200 literary classics from 26 countries.

Cuddon, J. A. *Dictionary of Literary Terms.* Doubleday 1977 $17.95; Penguin 1982 pap. $8.95. Contains more than 2,000 literary terms.

Fowler, Roger, ed. *A Dictionary of Modern Critical Terms.* Routledge & Kegan 1973 pap. $7.95

Freeman, William, ed. *Dictionary of Fictional Characters.* Writer rev. ed. 1973 $13.95. Indexes more than 20,000 fictional characters from literature, plays, and operas written in English during the last six centuries. Includes more than 2,000 works by approximately 500 U.S. and British authors.

Holman, C. Hugh. *A Handbook to Literature.* Bobbs 4th ed. 1980 $18.76 pap. $13.24. Contains more than 1,560 entries, including literary terms and movements, British and U.S. literary history, winners of major literary prizes, structuralism, semiotics, and phenomenology.

Klein, Leonard S., and Paula R. Sonntag, eds. *Encyclopedia of World Literature in the 20th Century.* Ungar 1985 $40.00. A reliable reference work that upholds the standards established by the first edition. Articles on living authors and bibliographies have been updated. Especially strong in covering European authors. Complements the *Columbia Dictionary of Modern European Literature.*

The Penguin Companion to World Literature. McGraw-Hill 1969–71 o.p.

Scott, A. F., ed. *Current Literary Terms.* St. Martin's repr. 1980 lib. bdg. $16.95. Alphabetical arrangement of literary and critical terms used in poetry and drama.

Shaw, Harry. *Dictionary of Literary Terms.* McGraw-Hill 1972 $29.95. Includes approximately 2,000 terms. Some terms originate from mass media.

Shipley, Joseph T., ed. *Dictionary of World Literary Terms.* Writer $15.95

Thorlby, Anthony, ed. *The Penguin Companion to European Literature.* McGraw-Hill 1969 o.p. Important European authors, with editions and translations of their works, summaries, and critical commentaries; guide to entries by language and country. Also available as Volume 2 of *The Penguin Companion to World Literature.*

DIGESTS

Bradbury, Malcolm, and others, eds. *Penguin Companion to USA and Latin American Literature.* McGraw-Hill 1971 o.p. Colonial days to the 1970s. Bibliographies and summaries.

Haydn, Hiram, and Edmund Fuller, eds. *Thesaurus of Book Digests: Digests of the World's Permanent Writings from the Ancient Classics to Current Literature.* Crown 1949 o.p. Arrangement is by title with indexes to authors and characters.

Keller, Helen R. *The Reader's Digest of Books.* Macmillan enl. ed. 1936 o.p. Good for summaries of older, lesser-known works.

Magill, Frank N., ed. *Masterplots. British Fiction Ser.* Salem Pr. 12 vols. 1976 $400.00 rev. ed. 1985 lib. bdg. $120.00

––––––. *Survey of Contemporary Literature.* Salem Pr. 12 vols. 1977 $350.00. Contains 2,300 essays on works by more than 1,300 international authors.

Magill, Frank N., and others, eds. *Magill's Literary Annual.* 1977–to date. Salem Pr. ea. $50.00. Includes 200 outstanding new books written in the United States during the previous year.

Weiss, Irving, and Anne D. Weiss. *Thesaurus of Book Digests: 1950–1980.* Crown 1980 $14.95. This supplements *Thesaurus of Book Digests* (1949) with summaries of approximately 1,700 fiction and nonfiction books published since 1949.

INDEXES

Chicorel Index Series. 1970–84. Amer. Lib. various prices. Contents: Vols. 1–3, *Chicorel Theater Index to Plays in Anthologies, Periodicals, Discs and Tapes;* Vol. 3A, *Chicorel Bibliography to the Performing Arts;* Vol. 4, *Chicorel Index to Poetry on Discs, Tapes and Cassettes;* Vols. 5A–C, *Chicorel Index to Poetry in Collections (Poetry-in-Print);* Vols. 6A–C, *Chicorel Index to Poetry;* Vols. 7–7A, *Chicorel Index to the Spoken Arts on Discs, Tapes and Cassettes;* Vol. 8, *Chicorel Theater Index to Plays in Anthologies, Periodicals, Discs, and Tapes;* Vol. 9, *Chicorel Theater Index to Plays for Young People;* Vol. 10, *Chicorel Bibliography to Books on Music and Musicians;* Vols. 11–11A, *Chicorel Index to Abstracting and Indexing Services: Periodicals in Humanities and the Social Sciences;* Vols. 12–12A, *Chicorel Index to Short Stories in Anthologies and Collections;* Vols. 13–13C, *Chicorel Index to the Crafts;* Vol. 14, *Chicorel Index to Reading Disabilities;* Vol. 14A, *Chicorel Index to*

Reading and Learning Disabilities; Vols. 15–15A, *Chicorel Index to Biographies;* Vols. 16–16A, *Chicorel Index to Environment and Ecology;* Vols. 17–17A, *Chicorel Index to Urban Planning and Environmental Design;* Vols. 18–18A, *Chicorel Index to Learning Disorders: Books;* Vol. 19, *Chicorel Abstracts to Reading and Learning Disabilities;* Vols. 20–20A, *Chicorel Index to Poetry and Poets;* Vol. 21, *Chicorel Theater Index to Drama Literature;* Vols. 22–22A, *Chicorel Index to Film Literature;* Vols. 23–23B, *Chicorel Index to Literary Criticism;* Vol. 24, *Chicorel Index to Parapsychology and Occult Books;* Vol. 26, *Chicorel Index to Video Tapes and Cassettes;* Vol. 27, *Chicorel Index to Mental Health Book Reviews.*

HANDBOOKS

Abrams, M. H. *A Glossary of Literary Terms.* Holt 4th ed. text ed. 1981 pap. $11.95. Ranked among the outstanding literary handbooks.

Atkinson, Frank. *Dictionary of Literary Pseudonyms: A Selection of Popular Modern Writers in English.* Shoe String 1982 $19.50. Identifies the pen names of more than 4,000 British and North American authors of the twentieth century.

Brewer, E. Cobham. *Brewer's Dictionary of Phrase and Fable: Centenary Edition.* Ed. by Ivor H. Evans, intro. by John Buchanan-Brown, Harper rev. ed. 1981 $25.91. References colloquial and proverbial phrases, mythological and biographical figures, etc.

Magill, Frank N., ed. *Cyclopedia of Literary Characters.* Harper 1964 $22.50; Salem Pr. 2 vols. 1963 $75.00. Contains 16,000 characters from 1,300 works of all periods and literatures. Includes index of authors and characters.

The Writer's Handbook. Ed. by Sylvia K. Burack, Writer 1985 $22.95 1984 $21.95 1983 $19.95. In four parts, describes various phases of professional writing.

DIRECTORY

Writers' and Artists' Year Book. 1906–to date. Macmillan. Useful to writers wishing to submit manuscripts to English, Commonwealth, or U.S. journals. Contains descriptions of materials accepted, rate of payment, etc.

LITERARY AWARDS

Clapp, Jane. *International Dictionary of Literary Awards.* Scarecrow Pr. 1963 o.p. "A selected list of major literary honors granted internationally and in countries other than the United States, Canada, and the United Kingdom" (Preface).

Hohenberg, John. *The Pulitzer Prizes: A History of the Awards in Books, Drama, Music, Journalism Based on the Private Files over Six Decades.* Columbia Univ. Pr. 1974 $26.00

Roginski, Jim. *Newbery and Caldecott Medalists and Honor Book Winners: Bibliographies and Resource Material through 1977.* Libraries Unlimited 1982 $47.50. Collectors of children's literature will find this tool of great value.

Stuart, Sandra Lee. *Who Won What When.* Lyle Stuart 1977 $12.00 1980 $12.00 pap. $8.95. Lists winners of U.S. and major foreign prizes since 1900.

Walter, Claire, ed. *Winners: The Blue Ribbon Encyclopedia of Awards.* Facts on File rev. ed. 1982 $39.95. Covers major U.S. honors in various fields.

Wasserman, Paul, ed. *Awards, Honors and Prizes: United States and Canada.* Gale 2 vols. 5th ed. 1982 ea. $125.00–$140.00. Includes more than 5,250 awards and prizes in different areas including literature.

Weber, Olga S., ed. *Literary and Library Prizes.* Bowker 10th ed. 1980 $26.95. Gives information on the history, condition, and rules of international, U.S., Canadian, and British prizes. Hundreds of winning authors and their works are listed.

World Dictionary of Awards and Prizes. Gale 1979 $60.00. Includes 2,000 international and national awards from 62 countries.

BIOGRAPHIES

Biography Index. Wilson 13 vols. 1946–82 ea. $125.00. Issued quarterly with annual and permanent three-year cumulations. "Covers biographical material appearing in approximately 1,900 periodicals indexed in other Wilson indexes; current books of individual and collective biography in the English language; obituaries, including those of national interest published in the *New York Times;* and incidental biographical material in otherwise nonbiographical books. Bibliographies and portraits and other illustrations are noted when they appear in connection with indexed material. Biography Index consists of a main or 'name' alphabet and an index by professions and occupations" (Publisher's catalog).

Havlice, Patricia P. *Index to Literary Biography.* Scarecrow Pr. 2 vols. 1975 $52.50 supplement 2 vols. 1983 $67.50. Contains biographical information on 68,000 authors appearing in collective biographies and dictionaries of literature.

Kunitz, Stanley J., and Vineta Colby, eds. *European Authors, 1000–1900.* Wilson 1967 $40.00. Contains 967 biographies of authors from 31 countries born after 1000 A.D. and dead by 1925.

Kunitz, Stanley J., and Howard Haycraft, eds. *Twentieth-Century Authors.* Wilson 1942 $52.00 supplement 1955 $38.00. A revision of Kunitz's *Living Authors* (o.p.) and *Authors Today and Yesterday* (o.p.), with additional material. Contains 1,850 biographies. The supplement brings the original biographies and bibliographies up to 1955, adding some 700 biographies.

La Beau, Dennis, ed. *Author Biographies Master Index. Gale Biographical Index Ser.* 2 vols. 1978 $140.00. Indexes approximately 413,000 entries in more than 140 biographical dictionaries and directories of writers.

Magill, Frank N., ed. *Cyclopedia of World Authors.* Harper 1958 lib. bdg. $19.79; Salem Pr. 3 vols. $100.00. Fine collection of 753 biographies and appraisals by authorities; signed articles.

Metzger, Linda, ed. *Contemporary Authors New Revision Series.* Gale 1985 vols. 14–15 ea. $85.00. This is the latest effort to keep the biographical data in this series current. Libraries must keep the existing and ongoing volumes along with the *NRS* volumes.

Seymour-Smith, Martin. *Who's Who in Twentieth-Century Literature.* Holt 1976 o.p. Includes approximately 700 dramatists, poets, novelists, and essayists of the twentieth century. Biased toward British and U.S. authors.

Vinson, James, and Daniel Kirkpatrick, eds. *Contemporary Dramatists.* Pref. by Ruby Cohn, *Contemporary Writers Ser.* St. Martin's 3d ed. 1982 $55.00. Approximately 300 brief biographies of contemporary dramatists writing in English.

——. *Contemporary Novelists.* Pref. by Jerome Klinkowitz and Walter Allen, *Contemporary Writers Ser.* St. Martin's 3d ed. 1982 $65.00. Contains information on 564 novelists, both living and dead, since the 1950s.

————. *Contemporary Poets.* Pref. by Marjorie Perloff and C. Day Lewis, *Contemporary Writers Ser.* St. Martin's 3d ed. 1980 lib. bdg. $65.00. Bio-bibliographic information provided for approximately 800 poets, both living and dead, since 1950.
————. *Great Writers of the English Language.* St. Martin's 3 vols. 1979 ea. $50.00–$55.00
Vrana, Stan. *Interviews and Conversations with 20th-Century Authors Writing in English: An Index.* Scarecrow Pr. 1982 $16.00
Wakeman, John, ed. *World Authors: 1950–1970.* Wilson 1975 $75.00
————. *World Authors: 1970–1975.* Wilson 1979 $52.00. A companion to *World Authors: 1950–1970*, it does not update biographies found in the earlier volume.
The Writers Directory: 1976–1978. St. Martin's 1976 $35.00. Who's who information on writers, poets, dramatists, and others who have written and published at least one full-length book in English.

U.S. AND ENGLISH LITERATURE: BIBLIOGRAPHY

Allibone, Samuel Austin. *A Critical Dictionary of English Literature and British and American Authors, Living and Deceased: From the Earliest Accounts to the Latter Half of the Nineteenth Century, Containing over 46,000 Articles (Authors) with 40 Indexes of Subjects.* Gordon repr. of 1872 ed. 3 vols. $300.00. A valuable standard work.
Annual Bibliography of English Language and Literature. 1921–to date. Modern Humanities Research Association $16.87. Includes a section on U.S. literature, but is heavily weighted toward English scholarship.
Redmond, J., and others, eds. *Year's Work in English Studies.* Humanities Pr. vols. 57–61 1977–82 text ed. $36.50–$44.25

U.S. LITERATURE: BIBLIOGRAPHY

American Literary Scholarship: An Annual. 1965–to date. Ed. by James L. Woodress, Duke Univ. Pr. 1963 (1965) $15.00; 1964 (1966) $15.00; 1965 (1967) $15.00; 1966 (1968) $15.00; 1967 (1969) $20.00; 1973 (1975) $25.00; 1974 (1976) $25.00; 1975 (1977) $25.00; 1977 (1979) $25.00; 1980 (1982) $37.75; 1981 (1983) $37.75; ed by J. Albert Robbins, 1968 (1970) $20.00; 1969 (1971) $20.00; 1970 (1972) $20.00; 1971 (1973) $20.00; 1972 (1974) $20.00; 1976 (1978) $25.00; 1978 (1980) $25.00; ed. by Warren G. French, 1983 (1985) $37.75
Articles on American Literature, 1968–1975. Comp. by Lewis Leary and John Auchard, Duke Univ. Pr. 1979 $48.75. A supplement to Leary's earlier works, which covered the periods 1900–50 and 1950–67. An important reference tool.
Blanck, Jacob. *Bibliography of American Literature.* Yale Univ. Pr. 7 vols. vol. 1 (1955) $65.00 vol. 2 (1957) $65.00 vol. 3 (1959) $65.00 vol. 4 (1963) $65.00 vol. 5 (1969) $65.00 vol. 6 (1973) $55.00 vol. 7 (1983) $75.00. A selective bibliography that includes approximately 300 U.S. literary figures. Volume 8 is still in progress.
Gohdes, Clarence, and Stanford E. Marovitz, eds. *Bibliographical Guide to the Study of the Literature of the U.S.A.* Duke Univ. Pr. 5th ed. rev. 1984 lib. bdg. $29.75. More than 400 new items have been added to the latest revision.
Nilon, Charles H. *Bibliography of Bibliographies in American Literature.* Bowker 1970 o.p. Lists bibliographies published separately, as well as those published in journals and as parts of books.

ENGLISH LITERATURE: BIBLIOGRAPHY

Annals of English Literature, 1475–1950: The Principal Publications of Each Year Together with an Alphabetical Index of Authors and Their Works. Rev. by R. W. Chapman, Oxford 1961 o.p.

Cambridge Bibliography of English Literature. Ed. by F. W. Bateson, Cambridge Univ. Pr. 5 vols. 1940–57 ea. $90.00–$135.00. Volume 5 is the supplement.

Concise Cambridge Bibliography of English Literature, 600–1950. Ed. by George Watson, Cambridge Univ. Pr. 2d ed. 1965 $49.50 pap. $15.95. A greatly abridged version of the *CBEL* that offers the general reader a select list of the best editions by and secondary works about the major English writers.

Howard-Hill, Trevor H. *Bibliography of British Literary Bibliographies.* Oxford (Clarendon) 1969 o.p.

New Cambridge Bibliography of English Literature. Ed. by George Watson and others, Cambridge Univ. Pr. 5 vols. 1969–76 $475.00. This work is based on the *CBEL* published in 1940 and 1957 (the supplement), now out of print. Expanded and brought up-to-date, it retains the systematic arrangement of the earlier work. Owners of the *CBEL* are urged to keep their volumes, however, as certain materials have been omitted in the *NCBEL*: the literatures of Canada, Australia, India, and New Zealand, and such nonliterary sections as those on science, law, economics, and political and social backgrounds. The scope, as stated by the editor, is nothing less than to "represent the whole of English studies, so far as concern the life of the British Isles, both in primary and secondary materials, 'works by' and 'works about.' " Nevertheless this work is the definitive retrospective coverage of the entire spectrum of English literature. Volume 5 is an index compiled by J. D. Pickles.

The Shorter New Cambridge Bibliography of English Literature. Ed. by George Watson, Cambridge Univ. Pr. 1981 $79.95. Intended for smaller libraries, for which the cost of the *NCBEL* is prohibitive.

U.S. LITERATURE: DICTIONARIES AND HANDBOOKS

Burke, W. J., and Will D. Howe, eds. *American Authors and Books: 1640 to the Present Day.* Rev. by Irving Weiss and Anne Weiss, Crown 1972 o.p. An "encyclopedia of U.S. books, authors, personalities, periodicals, awards, organizations, and other pertinent information covering all aspects of the literary world." Information is through 1971.

Duyckinck, Evert A., and George L. Duyckinck. *Cyclopedia of American Literature.* Gale 2 vols. repr. of 1875 ed. 1965 $110.00. This older work, cited in bibliographies, is arranged chronologically. Includes survey articles on "The New England Preachers," "Ballad Literature of the Indian," "French and Revolutionary Wars," etc.

Ehrlich, Eugene, and Gorton Carruth. *The Oxford Illustrated Literary Guide to the United States.* Oxford 1982 $35.00. Locates places associated with 1,527 U.S. authors in 1,586 cities and towns in the United States, covering U.S. literature from the beginning to the present.

Hart, James D. *The Oxford Companion to American Literature.* Oxford 5th ed. rev. 1983 $49.95. Standard reference tool.

Herzberg, Max J., and others. *The Reader's Encyclopedia of American Literature.* Intro. by Van Wyck Brooks, Crowell 1962 o.p. A quick reference companion volume to Benet's *The Reader's Encyclopedia*. Contains 6,500 articles dealing with authors, titles, and topics; 8 special charts.

ENGLISH LITERATURE: DICTIONARIES AND HANDBOOKS

Barnhart, Clarence L., and William D. Halsey, eds. *New Century Handbook of English Literature*. Prentice-Hall rev. ed. 1956 $32.95. Some 14,000 entries for authors, titles, plots, etc.

Concise Oxford Dictionary of English Literature. Ed. by Dorothy Eagle, Oxford 2d ed. rev. 1970 $35.00 pap. $9.95. This edition "contains much new and revised material, especially with reference to the literature of the twentieth century. . . . The articles on general literary topics have been revised to take account of developments and research during the last thirty years" (Preface).

Drabble, Margaret, ed. *The Oxford Companion to English Literature*. Oxford 5th ed. 1985 $35.00. Authors, characters, plots, mythological references, general topics, etc. ". . . this attractively produced work, rich in conventional intelligence, offers real delight . . . Britannia may no longer rule the waves, but she rules serenely over this pigheaded and fussy but still admirable volume" (*N.Y. Times*).

Eagle, Dorothy, and Hilary Carnell, eds. *The Oxford Illustrated Literary Guide to Great Britain and Ireland*. Oxford 1981 $35.00

Fisher, Lois. *A Literary Gazetteer of England*. McGraw-Hill 1980 $59.95

U.S. LITERARY HISTORY

Cambridge History of American Literature. Ed. by W. P. Trent and others, Macmillan 3 vols. in 1 1943 $26.95. This work is modeled on the *Cambridge History of English Literature*.

Spiller, Robert E., and others. *Literary History of the United States: Bibliography*. Macmillan 2 vols. 1974 o.p. Volume 1, the literary history, contains articles by distinguished contributors, divided according to historical periods; Volume 2 is the bibliographic supplement.

ENGLISH LITERARY HISTORY

Cambridge History of English Literature. Ed. by A. W. Ward and A. R. Waller, Cambridge Univ. Pr. 15 vols. ea. $65.00. Every chapter of this monumental work is written by a specialist. The unique feature is the discussion according to type: "Political Literature"; "Ballad Literature"; "Literature of Science"; "The Literature of Travel"; "Memoir Writers"; "The Essay"; etc. Of special value are "Book Production and Distribution" by H. G. Aldis, "The Foundation of Libraries," "Children's Books" by Harvey Darton, and "The Introduction of Printing into England and the Early Work of the Press." Originally published in 14 volumes between 1907 and 1917 (o.p.). The present edition omits the bibliographies, which are now revised and published separately as the four-volume *Cambridge Bibliography of English Literature* (see under "English Literature: Bibliography" in this chapter). In the original edition each volume was indexed separately, but now Vol. 15 is the general index to the entire work.

Garnett, Richard, and Edmund Gosse. *English Literature: An Illustrated Record*. Macmillan 4 vols. in 2 repr. of 1903 ed. 1935 o.p. Provides literary history and biographical and critical sketches of authors.

The Oxford History of English Literature Series. Ed. by Bonamy Dobrée and Norman Davis. Each volume or half-volume will be an independent book, but the whole series will form a continuous history. All the contributors will be acknowledged authorities on their periods, and each volume will incorporate in text and bibliography the results of the latest research. A standard reference history. Volumes now in print are:

Bennett, H. S. *Chaucer and the Fifteenth Century.* 1947 $42.50

Bush, Douglas. *English Literature in the Earlier Seventeenth Century: 1600–1660.* 2d ed. 1962 $42.50 1975 pap. $7.95

Butt, John. *The Mid-Eighteenth Century.* 1979 $47.50

Chambers, Edmund K. *English Literature at the Close of the Middle Ages.* 1945 $42.00

Dobrée, Bonamy. *English Literature in the Early Eighteenth Century, 1700–1740.* 1959 $42.00

Jack, Ian. *English Literature, 1815–1832.* 1963 $45.00

Lewis, C. S. *English Literature in the Sixteenth Century (Excluding Drama).* 1954 $39.50 1975 pap. $6.95

Renwick, William L. *English Literature, 1789–1815.* 1963 $29.95

Stewart, J. I. M. *Eight Modern Writers.* 1963 $39.50 1975 pap. $5.95

Sutherland, James R. *English Literature of the Late Seventeenth Century.* 1969 $39.50

Wilson, Frank Percy. *The English Drama, 1485–1585.* 1969 $35.00

Rogal, Samuel J. *A Chronological Outline of British Literature.* Greenwood 1980 lib. bdg. $35.00

U.S. LITERARY BIOGRAPHIES

Faust, Langdon L., ed. *American Women Writers: A Critical Reference Guide from Colonial Times to the Present.* Ungar 2 vols. abr. ed. 1983 pap. ea. $14.95. A more affordable alternative to the four-volume edition by Mainiero and Faust cited below, but it contains only 400 entries of the original 1,000.

Kunitz, Stanley J., and Howard Haycraft, eds. *American Authors, 1600–1900.* Wilson 8th ed. 1977 $33.00

Mainiero, Lina, and Langdon L. Faust, eds. *American Women Writers: A Critical Reference Guide.* Ungar 4 vols. 1979–82 ea. $60.00. Contains bio-bibliographic essays on U.S. women writers of all periods.

Rush, Theressa G., and others. *Black American Writers Past and Present: A Biographical and Bibliographical Dictionary.* Scarecrow Pr. 2 vols. 1975 $39.50. Contains bio-bibliographic information on 2,000 black writers.

Unger, Leonard, ed. *American Writers.* Scribner 8 vols. 1979 $460.00. Includes the supplement edited by A. Walton Litz.

ENGLISH LITERARY BIOGRAPHIES

Kunitz, Stanley J., and Howard Haycraft, eds. *British Authors before Eighteen Hundred.* Wilson 1952 $24.00. Biographies of 650 writers from the beginnings of English literature to Cowper and Burns.

——. *British Authors of the Nineteenth Century.* Wilson 1936 $27.00. Complete in one volume with 1,000 biographies and 350 portraits.

Scott, Kilvert Ian, ed. *British Writers.* Scribner 8 vols. 1979–84 lib. bdg. ea. $50.00–
$65.00. Includes bibliographies and index.

LITERARY CRITICISM

Adelman, Irving, and Rita Dworkin. *The Contemporary Novel: A Checklist of Critical
Literature on the British and American Novel since 1945.* Scarecrow Pr. 1972
$22.50. Surveys the critical literature on novels, citing scholarly rather than
popular reviews.
Bell, Inglis F., and Donald Baird. *The English Novel, 1578–1956: A Checklist of Twenti-
eth-Century Criticisms. Novel Explication Ser.* Shoe String repr. of 1959 ed. 1974
$12.00
Borklund, Elmer. *Contemporary Literary Critics.* St. Martin's 1978 $30.00. A guide to
the works of 115 modern U.S. and British critics.
Cassis, A. F. *The Twentieth-Century English Novel.* Garland 1977 lib. bdg. $50.00
Contemporary Literary Criticism. Ed. by Sharon R. Gunton and Jean Stine, Gale 30
vols. 1973–85 vols. 1–22 ea. $80.00 vols. 23–24 ea. $78.00 vols. 25–30 ea. $82.00
Curley, Dorothy N., ed. *Modern American Literature. Lib. of Literary Criticism Ser.* Un-
gar 3 vols. 4th ed. enl. text ed. 1969 $165.00
Dunn, Richard, ed. *The English Novel: Twentieth-Century Criticism, Defoe through
Hardy.* Ohio Univ. Pr. (Swallow) 1976 $20.00
Eichelberger, Clayton L. *A Guide to Critical Reviews of U.S. Fiction, 1870–1910.*
Scarecrow Pr. 2 vols. 1971–74 ea. $16.50–$17.50
Gerstenberger, Donna, and George Hendrick. *The American Novel, 1789 to 1959.*
Ohio Univ. Pr. (Swallow) 2 vols. 1961 $12.50
Kearney, E. I., and L. S. Fitzgerald. *The Continental Novel: A Checklist of Criticism in
English, 1900–1966.* Scarecrow Pr. 1968 o.p.
Magill, Frank N. *Magill's Bibliography of Literary Criticism: Selected Sources for the
Study of More Than 2,500 Outstanding Works of Western Literature.* Salem Pr. 4
vols. 1979 o.p.
Palmer, Helen, and Anne J. Dyson. *English Novel Explication: Criticisms to 1972.
Novel Explication Ser.* Shoe String 1973 o.p. Continues Bell and Baird, *The En-
glish Novel,* listing criticism from 1958 to 1972.
Schlueter, Paul, and June Schlueter. *English Novel Twentieth-Century Criticism:
Twentieth-Century Authors.* Ohio Univ. Pr. (Swallow) 1982 lib. bdg. $35.00
Tucker, Martin, ed. *The Critical Temper: A Survey of Modern Criticism on English and
American Literature from the Beginnings to the Twentieth Century. Lib. of Literary
Criticism Ser.* Ungar 3 vols. 1969 $165.00 1979 supplement $55.00
Walker, Warren S., ed. *Twentieth-Century Short Story Explication: Supplement Two to
the Third Edition.* Shoe String (Archon) 1984 $35.00

DRAMA: BIBLIOGRAPHY

Arata, Esther S., and Nicholas J. Rotoli. *Black American Playwrights, 1800 to the Pres-
ent: A Bibliography.* Scarecrow Pr. 1976 $16.50
Drury, Francis Keese Wynkoop. *Drury's Guide to Best Plays.* Ed. by James M. Salem,
Scarecrow Pr. 1978 o.p.
Hatch, James V., and Abdullah Omanii. *The Black Playwrights, 1823–1977: An Anno-
tated Bibliography of Plays, 1823–1977.* Bowker 1977 $24.95

King, Kimball. *Twenty Modern British Dramatists, 1956–1976: An Annotated Bibliography.* Garland 1977 lib. bdg. $39.00

Palmer, Helen H. *European Drama Criticism, 1900–1975. Drama Explication Ser.* Shoe String 2d ed. 1977 $35.00

Palmer, Helen H., and Anne Jane Dyson. *American Drama Criticism.* Supplement by Floyd E. Eddelman, Shoe String (Archon) 1984 $29.50

DRAMA: INDEXES

Connor, John M., and Billie M. Connor. *Ottemiller's Index to Plays in Collections: An Author and Title Index to Plays Appearing in Collections Published between 1900 and Early 1975.* Scarecrow Pr. 6th ed. rev. & enl. 1976 $23.00. The first edition (1943) covered 1900–1942. The current edition indexes 3,049 different plays by 1,644 different authors; 1,047 collections are analyzed. Limited to books published in England and the United States. Only complete texts are indexed. Foreign plays translated into English are entered under English titles with references from translated titles.

Index to Full-Length Plays, 1895–1925. Comp. by Ruth G. Thomson, Faxon 1956 lib. bdg. $11.00

Index to Full-Length Plays, 1926–1944. Comp. by Ruth G. Thomson, Faxon 1946 o.p.

Index to Full-Length Plays, 1944–1964. Comp. by Norma O. Ireland, Faxon 1965 o.p. Of this volume, *Library Journal* reports: "Continuation of important earlier work by Ruth Thomson, . . . the most important feature of this volume is its subject approach to plays found in collections, Broadway plays, and many pamphlet plays. Many new subject headings have been added with cross-references. Single-alphabet index of authors, subjects, and titles; the main entry is by play title and for each is given the author, number of characters, number of acts, and whether it is an adaptation."

Index to One-Act Plays, 1900–1924. Comp. by Hannah Logasa and Winifred Ver Nooy, Faxon 1924 o.p. Supplement, 1924–31 (1932) $11.00; Second Supplement, 1932–40 (1941) o.p.; Third Supplement, 1941–48 (1950) o.p.; Fourth Supplement, 1948–57 (1958) $12.00; Fifth Supplement, 1958–64 (1966) $11.00. The index covers 5,000 one-act plays; the 1932 supplement covers 7,000. Indexed by title, author, and subject; states the number of characters in each play. The second supplement includes more than 500 collections, many separate plays from pamphlets and periodicals. The fourth and fifth volumes provide information on characters, setting, background, suitability for school production, etc. The last three supplements are by Hannah Logasa.

Keller, Dean H. *Index to Plays in Periodicals.* Scarecrow Pr. rev. & enl. ed. 1979 $42.50

Patterson, Charlotte A. *Plays in Periodicals: An Index to English Language Scripts in Twentieth-Century Journals.* G. K. Hall 1972 lib. bdg. $22.50. More than 4,000 plays printed in 97 English-language journals published from 1900 through 1968.

Play Index. Wilson 6 vols. 1953–83 ed. by Dorothy H. West and Dorothy M. Peake, vol. 1, 1949–52 (1953) $12.00; ed. by Estelle A. Fidell and Dorothy M. Peake, vol. 2, 1953–60 (1963) $17.00; ed. by Estelle A. Fidell, vol. 3, 1961–67 (1968) $20.00; vol. 4, 1968–72 (1973) $25.00; vol. 5, 1973–77 (1978) $33.00; vol. 6, 1978–82 (1983) $40.00. Indexed by author, title, and subject, with cast analysis and publisher.

DRAMA: ENCYCLOPEDIAS AND HANDBOOKS

Anderson, Michael. *Crowell's Handbook of Contemporary Drama.* Crowell 1971
$10.00. A guide to drama developments in Europe and the United States since
World War II.

Matlaw, Myron. *Modern World Drama: An Encyclopedia.* Dutton 1972 o.p.

McGraw-Hill Encyclopedia of World Drama. Ed. by Stanley Hochman, pref. by Daniel
Gerould, McGraw-Hill 5 vols. 2d ed. 1983 $295.00. Concerned with dramatists
and the literature of the theater.

POETRY: BIBLIOGRAPHIES AND INDEXES

Chapman, Dorothy H. *Index to Black Poetry.* G. K. Hall 1976 lib. bdg. $26.00. "Black
poetry is here defined in the broadest manner. . . . References are included for the
work not only of black poets but also of those poets who have in some way dealt
with the black experience or written within the black tradition, regardless of their
racial origins" (Foreword). One hundred twenty-five collections are indexed.

Comprehensive Index to English-Language Little Magazines, 1890–1970: Series One.
Ed. by Marion Sader, Kraus 1976 8 vols. lib. bdg. $695.00

Granger, Edith. *Granger's Index to Poetry, 1970–1977.* Ed. by William James Smith,
Columbia Univ. Pr. 1978 o.p. Covers seven years rather than the usual five. One
hundred twenty new anthologies are included. More than 25,000 poems are indexed. Contains title, first line, and author indexes. Recommended anthologies
for priority acquisitions is a new feature of this volume.

Granger's Index to Poetry. 1904. Columbia Univ. Pr. 7th ed. 1982 $130.00. Useful in-
dex to standard and popular collections of poetry.

Granger's Index to Poetry: Indexing Anthologies Published from 1970 through 1981. Ed.
by William James Smith and William F. Bernhardt, Columbia Univ. Pr. 1982
$124.00. Supplements the 6th edition, covering 248 anthologies published be-
tween 1970 and 1981. One hundred twenty-eight titles are new and were not incorporated from *Granger's Index to Poetry, 1970–1977.*

Index of American Periodical Verse. 1971–to date. Scarecrow Pr. 1973–84 ea. $25.00–
$37.50. An important tool to locate poetry printed in journals. One hundred and
seventy U.S. periodicals are indexed.

Poetry Index Annual. Granger 1982–84 ea. $54.99. Index to poems from 46 antholo-
gies that were copyrighted or available in 1982. Includes author, title, and subject index. Serves as a supplement to *Granger's Index to Poetry.*

Reardon, Joan, and Kristine A. Thorsen. *Poetry by American Women, 1900–1975: A
Bibliography.* Scarecrow Pr. 1979 $30.00. Includes 9,500 volumes of poetry writ-
ten by more than 5,500 women.

Sears, Minnie E., and Phyllis Crawford, eds. *Song Index: An Index to More Than
12,000 Songs.* 1926. Shoe String (Archon) 2 vols. in 1 1966 $47.50. Contains po-
ems set to music. Many of the titles are not included in Granger. Includes more
than 7,000 songs.

POETRY: DICTIONARIES AND ENCYCLOPEDIAS

Deutsch, Babette. *Poetry Handbook: A Dictionary of Terms.* Barnes & Noble 4th ed.
1982 pap. $5.05

Murphy, R., ed. *Contemporary Poets.* St. Martin's 1971 $30.00. Bio-bibliographies of 1,000 contemporary poets writing in English.

Preminger, Alex, ed. *The Princeton Encyclopedia of Poetry and Poetics.* Princeton Univ. Pr. rev. ed. 1974 $70.00 pap. $16.50. An authoritative and scholarly encyclopedia with all articles written by authorities on the subject. International in scope.

Spender, Stephen, and Donald Hall. *Concise Encyclopedia of English and American Poets and Poetry.* Hawthorne Bks. 1963 o.p.

Vinson, James, and Daniel Kirkpatrick, eds. *Contemporary Poets. Contemporary Writers Ser.* St. Martin's 3d ed. 1980 lib. bdg. $65.00. Revised, expanded, and updated edition. A number of poets have been added and dropped.

POETRY: CRITICISM

Cline, Gloria S., and Jeffrey A. Baker. *An Index to Criticisms of British and American Poetry.* Scarecrow Pr. 1973 $15.00. Indexes critical literature published on British and American poetry from 1960 through 1970.

Kuntz, Joseph. *Poetry Explication: A Checklist of Interpretation since 1925 of British and American Poems Past and Present.* Ohio Univ. Pr. (Swallow) rev. ed. 1962 $16.00

FICTION: BIBLIOGRAPHIES

Coan, Otis W., and Richard G. Lillard. *America in Fiction: An Annotated List of Novels That Interpret Aspects of Life in the United States, Canada, and Mexico.* Pacific Bks. 6th ed. o.p.

Dickinson, A. T., Jr. *American Historical Fiction.* Scarecrow Pr. 3d ed. 1971 $12.50

Dyson, A. E., ed. *The English Novel: Select Bibliographical Guides.* Oxford 1974 $23.95 pap. o.p.

McGarry, Daniel D., and Sarah H. White. *World Historical Fiction Guide: Annotated Chronological, Geographical and Topical List of Selected Historical Novels (Historical Fiction Guide).* 1963. Scarecrow Pr. 2d ed. 1973 $20.50. Contains 6,455 works arranged by geography and chronology to 1900. Author-title index. All works are in English, although some are translations into English.

FICTION: INDEXES

Bogart, Gary L. *Short Story Index, Supplement, 1974–78: An Index to Stories in Collections and Periodicals.* Wilson 1979 $27.00

———. *Short Story Index, 1979: An Index to Stories in Collections and Periodicals.* Wilson 1980 pap. $25.00

Cook, Dorothy E., and Isabel S. Monro, eds. *Short Story Index: Basic Volume, 1900–1949.* Wilson 1953 $27.00. Supplement 1955–58, ed. by Estelle A. Fidell and Esther V. Flory, 1960 $15.00; Supplement 1959–63, ed. by Estelle A. Fidell, 1965 $19.00; Supplement 1964–68, ed. by Estelle A. Fidell, 1969 $24.00; Supplement 1969–73, ed. by Estelle A. Fidell 1974 $35.00; Supplement 1974–78, ed. by Gary L. Bogart 1979 $60.00

Gerhardstein, Virginia B. *Dickinson's American Historical Fiction*. Scarecrow Pr. 4th ed. 1981 $17.50
Hicken, Marilyn E. *Cumulative Fiction Index, 1975–79*. State Mutual Bk. 1980 $60.00
Magill, Frank N., ed. *Critical Survey of Long Fiction*. Eng. Language Ser. Salem Pr. 8 vols. 1983 $350.00
————. *Critical Survey of Short Fiction*. Salem Pr. 1981 o.p.
Short Story Index: Collections Indexed, 1900–1978. Wilson 1979 $25.00
Smith, Raymond Ferguson, and A. J. Gordon. *Cumulated Fiction Index, 1970–74*. State Mutual Bk. 1978 $60.00
Yaakov, Juliette, and Gary L. Bogart, eds. *Fiction Catalog*. Wilson 10th ed. 1980 $70.00

ESSAYS: INDEXES

Essay and General Literature Index. Wilson 9 vols. 1900–79 ea. $160.00. Alphabetical by author, subject, and (in the case of documents) title. Kept up-to-date by semi-annual supplements, with annual cumulations. Since 1960 the cumulative period for permanent volumes has been five years.
Essay and General Literature Index: Works Indexed, 1900–1969. Wilson 1972 $25.00. Cites all 9,917 titles that are analyzed in the first seven permanent cumulations.

SPEECHES: INDEXES

Manning, Beverley. *Index to American Women Speakers, 1828–1978*. Scarecrow Pr. 1980 lib. bdg. $32.50
Sutton, Roberta B., and Charity Mitchell. *Speech Index: An Index to Collections of World Famous Orations and Speeches for Various Occasions; Supplement 1966 to 1970*. Scarecrow Pr. 4th ed. 1972 $10.00. The supplement indexes 58 books published between 1966 and 1970.

SCOTTISH LITERATURE

Royle, Trevor. *Companion to Scottish Literature*. Gale 1983 $68.00. Devoted to Scotland's writers, culture, and history.

IRISH LITERATURE

Hyde, Douglas. *A Literary History of Ireland from Earliest Times to the Present Day*. Longwood Pr. repr. of 1910 ed. 1979 lib. bdg. $65.00. A standard history.
Mikhail, E. H. *An Annotated Bibliography of Modern Anglo Irish Drama*. Whitston 1981 $20.00

AUSTRALIAN AND NEW ZEALAND LITERATURE

Burns, James. *New Zealand Novels and Novelists, 1861–1979: A Bibliography*. Heinemann text ed. 1981 $20.00; International Specialized Bk. 1983 lib. bdg. $10.95

Lock, Fred, and Alan Lawson. *Australian Literature: A Reference Guide. Australian Bibliographies Ser.* Oxford 2d ed. text ed. 1980 pap. $12.95

McNaughton, Howard. *New Zealand Drama. Twayne's World Authors Ser.* G. K. Hall 1981 lib. bdg. $16.95

CANADIAN LITERATURE

Fee, Margery, and Ruth Cawker. *Canadian Fiction: An Annotated Bibliography.* Peter Martin 1976 pap. $8.95

Klinck, Carl F., ed. *Literary History of Canada: Canadian Literature in English.* Univ. of Toronto Pr. 3 vols. 1976 ea. $37.50 pap. ea. $12.50

Lecker, Robert, and others, eds. *Annotated Bibliography of Canada's Major Authors, Vol. I: Margaret Atwood, Margaret Laurence, Hugh Maclennan, Mordecai Richler, Gabrielle Roy.* G. K. Hall 5 vols. 1980–84 lib. bdg. ea. $25.00–$45.00

Story, Norah, ed. *The Oxford Companion to Canadian History and Literature.* Oxford 1967 o.p. The *Companion* has 450 literary and 1,500 historical entries.

Toye, William, ed. *The Oxford Companion to Canadian Literature.* Oxford 1983 $49.95. Covers developments from 1967 to 1972.

————. *Supplement to the Oxford Companion to Canadian History and Literature.* Oxford 1973 $21.00

CLASSICAL AND MYTHOLOGICAL DICTIONARIES

Cavendish, Richard, and Trevor Ling, eds. *Mythology: An Illustrated Encyclopedia.* Rizzoli 1980 $37.50

Cotterell, Arthur. *A Dictionary of World Mythology.* Putnam 1980 $12.95; Putnam (Perigee) 1982 pap. $8.95

Feder, Lillian. *Crowell's Handbook of Classical Literature.* Crowell 1964 o.p.

Gayley, Charles M. *The Classic Myths in English Literature and Art.* Longwood Pr. repr. of 1911 ed. 1977 lib. bdg. $45.00

Grant, Michael. *Greek and Latin Authors, 800 B.C.–A.D. 1000.* Wilson 1980 $35.00

Grimal, Pierre, ed. *Larousse World Mythology.* Bookthrift 1981 o.p.

Hamilton, Edith. *Mythology.* New Amer. Lib. 1971 pap. $2.95

Harnsberger, Caroline T. *Gods and Heroes: A Quick Guide to the Occupations, Associations and Experiences of the Greek and Roman Gods and Heroes.* Whitston 1977 $20.00

Harsh, Philip W. *A Handbook of Classical Drama.* Stanford Univ. Pr. 1944 $35.00 pap. $10.95

Harvey, Paul, ed. *Oxford Companion to Classical Literature.* Oxford 2d ed. 1937 $35.00 pap. $9.95

Kravitz, David. *Who's Who in Greek and Roman Mythology.* Crown (C. N. Potter) 1977 pap. $3.95

MacCulloch, John A., ed. *Mythology of All Races.* Cooper Square Pr. 13 vols. repr. of 1932 ed. $304.00

Oxford Classical Dictionary. Ed. by N. G. Hammond and H. H. Scullard, Oxford 2d ed. 1970 $45.00. "A compendium of modern scholarship designed to meet the needs of the general reader and of the specialist in all fields of ancient Greek and Roman civilization" (Publisher's catalog).

Shapiro, Max S., and Rhoda A. Hendricks, eds. *Mythologies of the World: A Concise Encyclopedia*. Doubleday 1979 $10.95

Sykes, Egerton. *Everyman's Dictionary of Nonclassical Mythology*. Dutton 3d ed. 1961 o.p.

Tripp, Edward. *Crowell's Handbook of Classical Mythology*. Crowell 1970 $17.50

CHAPTER 4

Broad Studies and General Anthologies: Literature

Robert Balay

Anthology. n. A collection of flowers.
—SAMUEL JOHNSON, *A Dictionary of the English Language*

A well chosen anthology is a complete dispensary of medicine for the more common mental disorders, and may be used as much for prevention as cure.
—ROBERT GRAVES, *On English Poetry*

This chapter lists histories, critical studies, reference works, and anthologies that are aimed at the general reader rather than the specialist in the field of literature. Many anthologies, critical studies, and reference books may be found in other chapters, particularly those on comparative literature in Volume 2, but the works listed here contain more than one form of expression (poetry, prose, and drama, for example) or treat the literature of more than one nation. Only prose, prose fiction, poetry, and criticism are treated in this chapter; works on drama may be found in Chapter 1 of Volume 2.

REFERENCE AND BACKGROUND

Background Reading

Altick, Richard D. *The Art of Literary Research*. Ed. by John J. Fenstermaker, Norton 3d ed. 1982 $16.95. An excellent and sensible guide to literary research; discusses attributes and limitations of various tools of research.
——. *Scholar Adventurers*. Macmillan (Free Pr.) text ed. 1966 pap. $9.95. Literary research as adventure: finding manuscripts (Boswell at Malahide Castle, Edward Taylor at Yale), unmasking forgeries (Thomas Wise), etc. Gripping.
Barzun, Jacques, and Henry Graff. *The Modern Researcher*. Harcourt 3d ed. 1977 pap. $13.95. The nature of research and its embodiment in scholarly writing: revision, use of quotation, style, citation form, verification, evidence, and the like.
Bateson, Frederick W. *The Scholar-Critic: An Introduction to Literary Research*. Routledge & Kegan 1972 $12.50. Densely written advice to the prospective literary scholar: use of reference works, evidence, accuracy, style, interpretation, and like matters.

Grierson, H. J. C. *The Background of English Literature: Classical and Romantic and Other Collected Essays and Addresses. Essay Index Repr. Ser.* Core Collection 1978 $23.75; Darby repr. of 1962 ed. 1983 lib. bdg. $45.00; Greenwood repr. of 1970 ed. 1978 lib. bdg. $24.75. Essays and addresses. Consistently intelligent and interesting.

Hadas, Moses. *Ancilla to Classical Reading.* Columbia Univ. Pr. 1954 pap. $12.00

Highet, Gilbert. *Classical Tradition.* Oxford 1949 $29.95

Thomson, James A. *The Classical Background of English Literature.* Somerset 1950 $39.00

van Leunen, Mary-Claire. *A Handbook for Scholars.* Knopf 1978 pap. $5.95. Hints for those preparing manuscripts for submission. Much commonsensible advice.

Guides

Altick, Richard D., and Andrew Wright. *A Selective Bibliography for the Study of English and American Literature.* Macmillan 6th ed. 1978 o.p. A classified list of bibliographies and other works of use to students of literature, with frequent lists of books the student should know. Includes a glossary of literary terms.

Bateson, Frederick W., and Harrison T. Meserole. *A Guide to English and American Literature.* Longman 3d ed. text ed. 1976 pap. $13.95; Gordian 3d ed. 1977 $15.00. Includes illuminating introductions—e.g., "A Common Culture," introducing the section on the eighteenth century.

Esdaile, Arundell J. *Sources of English Literature: A Guide for Students.* Burt Franklin repr. of 1928 ed. 1970 $17.00

Patterson, Margaret C., ed. *Literary Research Guide.* Gale 1976 $38.00; MLA 2d ed. rev. 1983 $28.00 pap. $12.50. Thoughtfully compiled, very useful to students.

Biographical Sources

Berkland, Elmer. *Contemporary Literary Critics.* St. Martin's 1977 $30.00. Life, writings, and assessment of the critical viewpoint of 115 British and U.S. critics.

Concise Encyclopedia of English and American Poets and Poetry. Ed. by Stephen Spender and Donald Hall, Hutchinson 2d ed. 1970 o.p. Too good to miss. Brief, pithy accounts of poets and of issues in poetry (e.g., "New Criticism"). Occasional long articles (e.g. "Foreign Influences on English Poetry").

Scott-Kilvert, Ian, ed. *British Writers.* Scribner 8 vols. 1979–84 ea. $50.00–$65.00. *American Writers*, ed. by Leonard Unger and listed below, and *British Writers* resemble one another in format and share their publisher, but are alike in little else. *British Writers* limits its scope to major authors, giving for each a discursive essay by a specialist, including life, critical survey of important works, estimate of stature in literary history, bibliography. *American Writers* treats a larger number of writers, including some distinctly minor figures, but provides uneven treatment, sometimes omitting critical estimates or bibliographies.

Unger, Leonard, ed. *American Writers: A Collection of Literary Biographies.* Scribner 8 vols. 1979 lib. bdg. $460.00. See annotation above for *British Writers*, ed. by Ian Scott-Kilvert.

Vinson, James, and Daniel Kirkpatrick, eds. *Contemporary Novelists.* Pref. by Jerome Klinkowitz and Walter Allen, *Contemporary Writers Ser.* St. Martin's 3d ed. 1982 $65.00

———. *Contemporary Poets.* Pref. by Marjorie Perloff and C. Day Lewis, *Contemporary Writers Ser.* St. Martin's 3d ed. 1980 lib. bdg. $65.00. Both of the works edited by Vinson and Kirkpatrick include brief biographies, lists of publications, critical estimate, and in many cases, comment by the writer on his or her work.

Encyclopedias

Annals of English Literature, 1475–1950: The Principal Publications of Each Year Together with an Alphabetical Index of Authors and Their Works. Comp. by J. C. Ghosh and E. G. Withycombe, rev. ed. by R. W. Chapman and others, Oxford 2d ed. 1961 o.p. Chronological tables of each year's publication. Useful and reliable.

Balmires, Harry, ed. *Guide to Twentieth Century Literature in English.* Methuen 1983 $32.00 pap. $15.95. The United Kingdom, the Commonwealth, and British possessions. The United States is omitted.

Bédé, Jean-Albert, and William Edgerton, eds. *Columbia Dictionary of Modern European Literature.* Columbia Univ. Pr. 2d ed. 1980 $60.00. Literature of the continent. Articles on the literature of various nations, as well as individual writers.

Brewer, E. Cobham. *Brewer's Dictionary of Phrase and Fable.* Ed. by Ivor H. Evans, Harper 1981 $25.95. Allusions, names from mythology and fiction, phrases in popular usage, eponymous tags, linguistic oddities, etc. "Will be wanted . . . both for its reference value and for the pleasure of its company" (*ARBA*).

Browning, D. S. *Everyman's Dictionary of Literary Biography. Everyman's Reference Lib.* Biblio Dist. 3d ed. 1969 $13.50

Curtius, E. R. *European Literature and the Latin Middle Ages.* Trans. by Willard R. Trask, *Bollingen Ser.* Princeton Univ. Pr. 1953 pap. $12.50. Useful compendium of information on a wide range of topics—ancient rhetoric, classicism, mannerism, etc.

Hornstein, Lillian H., and others, eds. *The Reader's Companion to World Literature.* New Amer. Lib. rev. ed. 1973 pap. $4.95

Oxford Companion series. An unequaled series of encyclopedic guides to the literature of various Western nations and languages. Each companion contains entries for individual writers, synopses of important works, factual oddities of interest to students of literature, literary forms, movements, etc.

   Carpenter, Humphrey, and Mari Prichard. *The Oxford Companion to American Literature.* 1984 $35.00

   Drabble, Margaret, ed. *The Oxford Companion to English Literature.* 5th ed. 1985 $29.95

   Garland, Henry, and Mary Garland, eds. *The Oxford Companion to German Literature.* 1976 $39.95

   Hart, James D. *The Oxford Companion to American Literature.* 5th ed. rev. 1983 $49.95

   Harvey, Paul, ed. *The Oxford Companion to Classical Literature.* 2d ed. 1937 $35.00 pap. $9.95

   Harvey, Paul, and Janet E. Heseltine, eds. *The Oxford Companion to French Literature.* 1959 $49.50

   Toye, William, ed. *The Oxford Companion to Canadian Literature.* 1983 $49.95

   Ward, Philip. *The Oxford Companion to Spanish Literature.* 1978 $39.95

Preminger, Alex, ed. *The Princeton Encyclopedia of Poetry and Poetics.* Princeton Univ. Pr. rev. ed. 1974 $70.00 pap. $16.50. Contains long articles on the poetry of various national or linguistic groups, but also offers informative entries on themes, genres, topics, forms—e.g., "Epigram."

Stapleton, Michael, ed. *The Cambridge Guide to English Literature.* Fwd. by Norman

Cousins, Cambridge Univ. Pr. 1983 $29.95. Treats literature of the English-speaking world. For the most part, entries are for writers and titles of works.

Ward, A. C. *Longman Companion to Twentieth Century Literature*. Longman 3d ed. text ed. 1981 $30.00. Topics and authors in twentieth-century literature. Opinionated but useful.

Dictionaries, Mostly of Literary Terms

Deutsch, Babette. *Poetry Handbook: Dictionary of Terms*. Barnes & Noble 4th ed. repr. of 1974 ed. 1982 pap. $5.72; Crowell 4th ed. repr. of 1974 ed. 1982 pap. $5.72; Harper 4th ed. 1974 $10.95

Fowler, Roger, ed. *A Dictionary of Modern Critical Terms*. Routledge & Kegan 1973 pap. $7.95

Holman, C. Hugh. *A Handbook to Literature*. Bobbs 4th ed. 1980 $18.76 pap. $13.24. "This is one of the standard sources for literary reference. . . . The handbook remains a remarkable work" (*Choice*).

Pech, John, and Martin Coyle. *Literary Terms and Criticism: A Student's Guide*. Macmillan 1984 pap. $3.95

Shipley, Joseph T. *Dictionary of World Literary Terms: Forms, Technique, Criticism*. Writer rev. ed. 1970 $15.95

Smith, Eric. *A Dictionary of Classical Reference in English Poetry*. Barnes & Noble 1984 $39.50

Special Topics

MYSTERY WRITERS

Reilly, John M., ed. *Twentieth-Century Crime and Mystery Writers*. Twentieth-Century Writers Ser. St. Martin's 1980 $65.00

Tymn, Marshall B. *The Year's Scholarship in Science Fiction, Fantasy and Horror Literature. Annotated Bibliography of Scholarly Bks.* Kent State Univ. Pr. 1981 $34.95 pap. $24.95 1983 pap. $7.50 1984 pap. $7.50 1985 pap. $7.50

SCIENCE FICTION WRITERS

Smith, Curtis S. *Twentieth-Century Science Fiction Writers*. Macmillan 1981 $65.00

AFRO-AMERICAN WRITERS

Fairbanks, Carol, and Eugene A. Engeldinger. *Black American Fiction: A Bibliography*. Scarecrow Pr. 1978 $19.50

Rush, Theressa G., and others. *Black American Writers Past and Present: A Biographical and Bibliographical Dictionary*. Scarecrow Pr. 2 vols. 1975 $39.50

WOMEN WRITERS

Duke, Maurice, and others, eds. *American Women Writers: Bibliographical Essays*. Greenwood 1983 lib. bdg. $39.95. Long essays on individual American women writers. Some odd omissions—e.g., Willa Cather.

Mainiero, Lina, and Langdon L. Faust, eds. *American Women Writers: A Critical Reference Guide*. Ungar 4 vols. 1979–82 ea. $60.00

GENERAL AND COMPREHENSIVE
ANTHOLOGIES OF LITERATURE

Listed here are anthologies that contain both poetry and prose. Anthologies of fiction, poetry, and criticism appear later in this chapter.

Some publishers' series constitute anthologies on a grand scale. The *Harvard Classics*, that "five-foot shelf" of the best books, was intended to bring culture and enlightenment from the centers of Eastern culture to the rest of the country. Now out of print, it is readily available from second-hand book dealers, often at bargain prices. The *Great Books of the Western World* set, published in 1952 by the Encyclopaedia Britannica Educational Corporation in 54 volumes, is still available at $869.00 for the set. The Great Books program did not stop with publishing, but sponsored classes and other educational programs based on the texts of the works reprinted in the *Great Books* set; study guides and the classified index to the set (called the *Syntopicon*) are still in print. Both *Everyman's Library*, published since 1906 by Dent in England and Dutton in the United States, and the *Modern Library*, published since 1915, first by Boni and Liveright but since 1925 by Random House, sought to publish inexpensive editions of standard works for consumption by the general reading public. *Everyman* began by issuing only titles out of copyright, but in later years began to reprint a few contemporary titles. The *Modern Library* has always emphasized works of the twentieth century, but both series rely on reprints in standard format of accepted works in many fields. Viking issues *Viking Portable Library* editions, sometimes selecting from the works of a single writer, sometimes issuing collections (e.g., *The Portable Irish Reader*). At their best, the portables make unique contributions to the study of a writer—*The Portable Faulkner*, for example, edited by Malcolm Cowley, which is still the best place to begin reading Faulkner, contains an illuminating introduction and explanatory passages by Cowley, as well as some material that Faulkner wrote for the *Portable* that is not available elsewhere. Oxford University Press issues several ongoing series—the *Oxford English Texts*, the *Oxford Standard Authors*, and the *Oxford English Novels*, among others. Norton publishes *Norton Critical Editions*, carefully edited texts of poets or novelists with selections of critical papers. Most recently, the *Library of America* has begun to issue authoritative editions of the works of established U.S. authors in pleasing and durable format. This venture, which constitutes an act of national piety, is appropriately supported by funds from the Ford Foundation and the National Endowment for the Humanities. The books are distributed by Viking.

General Anthologies

This section contains anthologies of writings from more than one country or written in various genres—poetry, fiction, essays, criticism.

Blanchard, Harold Hooper, ed. *Prose and Poetry of the Continental Renaissance in Translation*. Longman 2d ed. 1955 o.p. One of the best source books for the Renaissance, reprinting generous excerpts from many of the period's formative thinkers.

Brooks, Cleanth, and Robert Penn Warren. *An Approach to Literature.* Prentice-Hall 5th ed. 1975 $26.95. A fine general anthology, one of the best introductions to literature, widely used as a text. Includes glossary of literary terms.

Curtis, Charles P., Jr., and Ferris Greenslet. *The Practical Cogitator: The Thinker's Anthology.* Houghton Mifflin 1983 pap. $8.95. Its unfortunate title notwithstanding, this book contains some useful material. The editor includes "nothing that is not worth re-reading."

Ellmann, Richard, and Charles Feidelson, Jr. *The Modern Tradition: Backgrounds of Modern Literature.* Oxford 1965 $29.95. Attempts to assemble the texts from "101 poets, novelists, scientists, artists and speculative thinkers whose writings constitute the main documents of 'the modern tradition.'" A provocative collection, constituting the intellectual baggage of the modern literary scholar.

Fadiman, Clifton. *Reading I've Liked.* Simon & Schuster 1958 pap. $3.50. Good for its chatty introductions.

Giamatti, A. Bartlett. *Western Literature.* Harcourt 3 vols. 1971 ea. $12.95

Gottesman, Ronald, and others, eds. *The Norton Anthology of American Literature: Shorter Edition.* Norton text ed. 1980 $19.95 pap. $16.95. Very comprehensive, in keeping with other anthologies from this publisher.

Haydn, Hiram C., and John C. Nelson, eds. *Renaissance Treasury.* Greenwood repr. of 1953 ed. 1969 lib. bdg. $24.75. Italy, Spain, France, middle Europe.

Hibbard, Addison, and Horst Frenz, eds. *Writers of the Western World.* Houghton Mifflin 2d ed. text ed. 1967 $30.95. Includes illustrations, chronological tables, and indexes of authors, titles, and first lines.

Mack, Maynard, ed. *Norton Anthology of World Masterpieces.* Norton 2 vols. 5th ed. text ed. 1985 ea. $20.95 pap. ea. $18.95. From the Bible to Solzhenitsyn.

Quiller-Couch, Arthur, ed. *The Oxford Book of English Prose.* Oxford 1925 o.p. A standard anthology of examples of prose in English.

Ross, James B., and Mary M. McLaughlin, eds. *Portable Medieval Reader. Viking Portable Lib.* Penguin 1977 pap. $6.95

———. *Portable Renaissance Reader. Viking Portable Lib.* Penguin 1977 pap. $6.95. Brief excerpts from records left by an amazing variety of Renaissance writers, some well known (Luther, Rabelais, Leonardo), others obscure. Many curious and delightful passages—e.g., "The Judgment of a Witch" from the *Fugger Newsletter.*

Ross, Ralph, John Berryman, and Allen Tate, eds. *The Arts of Reading.* Apollo o.p. Distinguished by the commentary of its eminent editors.

Scholes, Robert, ed. *Some Modern Writers: Essays and Fiction by Conrad, Dinesen, Lawrence, Orwell, Faulkner and Ellison.* Oxford 1971 pap. $8.95. "The selections . . . have been made so as to afford the opportunity to consider the different ways these six writers approach similar situations and problems . . ." (Introduction).

Thomas, David, ed. *Everyman Anthology.* Biblio Dist. 1966 $7.95

Thompson, Karl F. *Classics of Western Thought.* Harcourt 4 vols. 1964 vols. 1–3 ea. $12.95 vol. 4 $11.95

Trilling, Lionel. *Experience of Literature.* Holt text ed. 2nd ed. 1970 pap. $16.95

———. *Prefaces to the Experience of Literature.* Harcourt 1981 $12.95 pap. $8.95. Contains "1,316 pages of drama, fiction and poetry, beginning with Sophocles and ending with Allen Ginsberg. . . . Occasionally . . . there comes along a text so remarkably good and interesting that it can no longer be merely studied; it demands to be read" (Robie Macauley, *N.Y. Times*). Although the anthology itself is out of print, the introductory essays have been reprinted.

Woods, Ralph L., ed. *The Golden Treasury of the Familiar.* Macmillan 1980 $29.95. Includes indexes by title, author, and "familiar lines."

Anthologies of National Literatures

ENGLAND

Abrams, M. H. *The Norton Anthology of English Literature.* Norton 2 vols. 4th ed. 1979 ea. $19.95 pap. ea. $18.95. One of the best of the blockbuster anthologies. Includes explanatory notes, bibliographies, biographical and critical commentaries, and generous excerpts from writers of each period.

Baugh, Albert C., and G. W. McClelland. *English Literature: A Period Anthology.* Appleton 2 vols. 1954 o.p. Still a standard anthology.

Kermode, Frank, and John Hollander. *The Oxford Anthology of English Literature.* Oxford 2 vols. 1973 ea. $24.95 pap. ea. $22.50. A splendid collection. "This 4600-page work features a general introduction to each of the six periods; brief biographical and critical essays on major authors; glossaries of literary and historical terms; modernized texts . . . explanatory notes; lists of suggested further readings; indexes; and 192 pages of illustrations" (*LJ*).

IRELAND

Green, David Herbert, ed. *Anthology of Irish Literature.* New York Univ. Pr. 2 vols. 1971 pap. $20.00. Twelve centuries of Irish writing, from early lyrics through modern Irish literature in English.

O'Connor, Frank, ed. *A Book of Ireland.* Irish Bk. Ctr. repr. of 1959 ed. 1971 pap. $5.95

UNITED STATES

Benet, William Rose, and Norman Holmes Pearson, eds. *The Oxford Anthology of American Literature.* Oxford 2 vols. 1938 o.p. Now dated, but still a valuable collection.

Bradley, Sculley, and others, eds. *The American Tradition in Literature.* Random 2 vols. 5th ed. text ed. 1981 pap. ea. $15.00

Foerster, Norman. *American Prose and Poetry.* Century Bookbindery 2 vols. repr. of 1934 ed. 1977 $20.00. Sections on the "Colonial Mind," the "Romantic Movement," the "Realist Movement." Critical notes.

Gottesman, Ronald, ed. *The Norton Anthology of American Literature.* Norton 2 vols. text ed. 1979 ea. $19.95 pap. ea. $16.95. A very comprehensive anthology.

Haslan, Gerald W., ed. *Forgotten Pages of American Literature.* Houghton Mifflin 1970 o.p. Useful because it reprints writers ignored by the standard anthologies: American Indians, Asian-Americans, Latino-Americans, Afro-Americans.

McMichael, George, ed. *Anthology of American Literature.* Macmillan 2 vols. 2d ed. 1980 write publisher for information. Some 4,000 pages, closely typeset. Generous selections from major works—*The Pathfinder, The Scarlet Letter, Huckleberry Finn, The Hairy Ape,* three long Melville stories—all complete.

Miller, Perry, ed. *Major Writers of America.* Harcourt text ed. 1962 vol. 1 $21.95. Thirty writers, Bradford to Faulkner. Generous selections, with discursive critical introductions.

Rahv, Philip. *Literature in America: An Anthology of Literary Criticism.* Peter Smith

$15.00. Essays, 1935 to 1956, arranged chronologically with emphasis on "national characteristics and relations to the national experience."

LATIN AMERICA

Rodríguez Monegal, Emir, ed. *The Borzoi Anthology of Latin American Literature.* Knopf 2 vols. 1977–84 pap. ea. $10.95. English translations of Latin American writers.

Specialized Subjects

Lewis, Arthur O. *Of Men and Machines.* Dutton 1963 o.p. A fascinating collection of writings on the relationship of men and machines: the problem, machine as friend, machine as thing of beauty, machine as enemy, futures.

MacDonald, Dwight, and Veronica Geng, eds. *Parodies: An Anthology from Chaucer to Beerbohm and After.* Quality Pap. Ser. Da Capo repr. of 1960 ed. 1985 pap. $12.95. A malicious gathering of parodies from many languages and cultures, with emphasis on the English language. Contains an interesting discussion of the distinctions among satire, burlesque, parody. For those who lived through the Eisenhower years, the Gettysburg Address as Eisenhower might have delivered it is not to be missed.

Moffat, Mary J. *In the Midst of Winter: Selections from the Literature of Mourning.* Random (Vintage) 1982 pap. $5.95

Seaver, Richard, and others. *Writers in Revolt: An Anthology.* Fell 1963 o.p. Rebels from the Marquis de Sade to writers of the present, such as Henry Miller, Iris Murdoch, Genet, Ionesco, Beckett.

Swados, Harvey, ed. *American Writer and the Great Depression.* Bobbs 1966 o.p. "Part of the 'American Heritage Series,' this brilliantly edited anthology offers selections from novels, poems and other writings, with photographs, from the Depression years" (*LJ*).

Wells, Carolyn. *A Parody Anthology.* Dover repr. of 1904 ed. 1967 pap. $2.50; Gale repr. of 1904 ed. 1968 $30.00; Gordon $59.95

White, E. B., and Katherine S. White, eds. *A Subtreasury of American Humor.* Telegraph Bks. repr. of 1941 ed. lib. bdg. $49.50

AFRO-AMERICAN WRITERS

Barksdale, Richard, and Kenneth Kinnamon. *Black Writers of America: A Comprehensive Anthology.* Macmillan text ed. 1972 o.p. One of the largest and most intelligently chosen of the Afro-American collections. Includes literature from the oral tradition: blues, prison songs, work songs, bad man songs, etc.

Chapman, Abraham, ed. *Black Voices: An Anthology of Afro American Literature.* New Amer. Lib. 1968 pap. $4.95

———. *New Black Voices.* New Amer. Lib. pap. $4.95. Fiction, autobiography, poetry, criticism.

Davis, Arthur P. *From the Dark Tower: Afro American Writers, 1900–1960.* Howard Univ. Pr. 1974 $12.95 1981 pap. $7.95

Davis, Charles T., and Daniel Walden, eds. *On Being Black: Writings by Afro-Americans from Frederick Douglass to the Present.* Fawcett 1970 o.p. An excellent anthology.

Emanuel, James A., and Theodore L. Gross, eds. *Dark Sympathy: Negro Literature in America.* Macmillan (Free Pr.) 1968 pap. $17.95. Four sections: "Early Literature"; "The Negro Awakening"; "Major Authors"; "Contemporary Literature." A comprehensive anthology, with biographical and critical introductions. Includes bibliography and index.

Turner, Darwin T. *Black American Literature: Essays, Poetry, Fiction, Drama.* Merrill text ed. 1970 pap. $15.95

JEWISH WRITERS

Alter, Robert, ed. *Modern Hebrew Literature. Lib. of Jewish Studies.* Behrman text ed. 1975 pap. $9.95. Prose fiction only, chiefly twentieth century.

Chapman, Abraham, ed. *Jewish American Literature: An Anthology.* New Amer. Lib. 1974 pap. $2.25

Gross, Theodore L. *Literature of American Jews.* Macmillan (Free Pr.) 1973 $14.95. Fiction, poetry, criticism, chiefly post-World War II. Includes Lazarus, Harold Roth, Bellow, Mailer, Schwartz, Ginzburg, etc.

POETRY

Histories of Poetry

For whatever reason, this is not the age for survey histories of literature. Most of the Olympian surveys belong to the years before World War I, or even to the nineteenth century. Studies of individual writers or single poems abound, but present-day scholars seem uncomfortable with the detachment that a survey history requires. For English poetry, the standard history is still Courthope's, which began to be published in 1895. The only recent rival is the Routledge history, which promises to be far less expansive. The reader who wants a history of poetry in English will have to find it in histories of English literature (themselves somewhat in eclipse) or will have to assemble it from biographies of poets or critical studies of discrete periods in poetic history.

Bateson, Frederick W. *English Poetry: A Critical Introduction.* Greenwood repr. of 1966 ed. 1978 lib. bdg. $24.75. Historical and literary context of poetry, Chaucer to W. H. Auden, with critical analyses of poems.

———. *English Poetry and the English Language: An Experiment in Literary History.* Russell Pr. repr. of 1934 ed. 1961 o.p. Concentrates on the period 1660–1800.

Bush, Douglas. *English Poetry: The Main Currents from Chaucer to the Present.* Oxford 1963 o.p.

———. *Science and English Poetry: A Historical Sketch, 1590–1950.* Greenwood repr. of 1950 ed. 1980 lib. bdg. $27.50

Courthope, William J. *History of English Poetry.* Russell Pr. 6 vols. in 3 repr. of 1895–1910 ed. 1962 $100.00. The standard history, treating English poetry from the middle English through the romantic periods.

Fairchild, Hoxie N. *Religious Trends in English Poetry.* Columbia Univ. Pr. 6 vols ea. $40.00

Gelpi, Albert. *The Tenth Muse: The Psyche of the American Poet.* Harvard Univ. Pr. text ed. 1975 $18.50

Grierson, H. J. C., and J. C. Smith. *A Critical History of English Poetry.* Arden Lib. repr. of 1950 ed. 1979 lib. bdg. $30.00; Humanities Pr. repr. of 1963 ed. text ed. 1983 $23.00. A distinguished history of 1,200 years of English poetry, Anglo-Saxon times to 1939.

Pearce, Roy H. *The Continuity of American Poetry.* Princeton Univ. Pr. 1961 pap. $11.50

Pearsall, Derek. *Old English and Middle English Poetry*. Routledge & Kegan 1985 pap. $10.95

Perkins, David. *History of Modern Poetry: From the Eighteen Nineties to the High Modernist Mode*. Harvard Univ. Pr. 1976 $27.50 pap. $10.00

Saintsbury, George E. *History of English Prosody from the 12th Century to the Present Day*. Russell Pr. 3 vols. 2d ed. repr. of 1923 ed. 1961 $40.00

Untermeyer, Louis. *Lives of the Poets: The Story of One Thousand Years of English and American Poetry*. Simon & Schuster 1972 pap. $6.95. Busily selling the many on the few, Untermeyer writes, for general consumption, of the lives, work, and background of 133 English and U.S. poets.

Waggoner, Hyatt H. *American Poets: From the Puritans to the Present*. Louisiana State Univ. Pr. text ed. 1984 $30.00 pap. $14.95. A study by a critic "who finds Emerson all-persuasive as an influence." "A princely view of our poetic experience and history" (*N.Y. Times*).

Wagner, Jean. *Black Poets of the United States: From Paul Laurence Dunbar to Langston Hughes*. Trans. by Kenneth Douglas, fwd. by Robert Bone, Univ. of Illinois Pr. repr. of 1963 ed. 1973 $25.00 pap. $12.50. A "full-length study of the major Black poets of the United States from early slavery times to Langston Hughes, now available in English. First published in France in 1963 . . ." (Publisher's note).

Critical Studies of Poetry

Auden, W. H. *Dyer's Hand and Other Essays*. Random (Vintage) 1968 pap. $4.95. Collected prose pieces, some written when he held the chair of poetry at Oxford, by one of the most distinguished twentieth-century poets.

Bloom, Harold. *The Anxiety of Influence: A Theory of Poetry*. Oxford 1973 $14.95 pap. $7.95

Brooks, Cleanth. *The Well Wrought Urn: Studies in the Structure of Poetry*. Harcourt 1956 pap. $5.95. Provocative essays on ten poems, Donne to Yeats, by one of the best known of the New Critics.

Ciardi, John, and Miller Williams. *How Does a Poem Mean*. Houghton Mifflin 2d ed. 1975 $18.95

Culler, Jonathan. *Structuralist Poetics: Structuralism, Linguistics and the Study of Literature*. Cornell Univ. Pr. 1976 pap. $8.95

De Selincourt, Ernest. *Oxford Lectures on Poetry*. Essay Index Repr. Ser. Ayer repr. of 1934 ed. $17.00; Folcroft repr. of 1934 ed. $30.00. Chaucer, Spenser, Blake, Wordsworth, Keats, Bridges.

Eastman, Max. *Enjoyment of Poetry*. Scribner 1951 $20.00

Eliot, T. S. *Selected Essays*. Harcourt 1950 $19.95. Among the twentieth century's most influential criticism.

Empson, William. *Seven Types of Ambiguity*. New Directions 1947 pap. $6.95

Frye, Northrop. *Fables of Identity: Studies in Poetic Mythology*. Harcourt 1963 pap. $5.95

Graves, Robert. *On English Poetry: Being an Irregular Approach to the Psychology of This Art, from Evidence Mainly Subjective*. Arden Lib. repr. of 1922 ed. 1980 lib. bdg. $20.00; Folcroft repr. of 1922 ed. 1975 lib. bdg. $17.50; Haskell repr. of 1922 ed. 1972 lib. bdg. $39.95; Somerset repr. of 1922 ed. $20.00. Brief, almost epigrammatic essays on English poetic style, diction, direction.

Gross, Harvey. *Sound and Form in Modern Poetry: A Study of Prosody from Thomas Hardy to Robert Lowell*. Univ. of Michigan Pr. 1964 $8.50 1968 pap. $9.95

Highet, Gilbert. *Powers of Poetry.* Oxford 1960 $22.50

Jarrell, Randall. *Poetry and the Age.* Ecco Pr. repr. of 1953 ed. 1980 pap. $6.95; Farrar 1972 pap. $2.85; Octagon 1972 lib. bdg. $20.50. Poetry of the present day; witty and readable.

Johnson, Samuel. *Lives of the English Poets.* Ed. by George B. Hill, Adler's 3 vols. repr. of 1905 ed. 1968 $159.00; Octagon 3 vols. 1967 lib. bdg. $126.50. Not simply biography, but a magisterial summing up of the history and state of English poetry by one of the greatest of critics. Some sections (e.g., the lives of Chatterton and Pope) are deeply moving. ". . . a work of memory, judgment and love, not a work of research" (John Wain, *Samuel Johnson*).

Krieger, Murray. *The New Apologists for Poetry.* Greenwood repr. of 1956 ed. 1977 lib. bdg. $24.75

Leavis, Frank R. *New Bearings in English Poetry: A Study of the Contemporary Situation.* AMS Pr. repr. of 1938 ed. $26.50

Lewis, C. Day. *Enjoying Poetry.* Folcroft 1947 $8.50

———. *The Lyric Impulse.* Harvard Univ. Pr. 1965 o.p. Musical elements in English verse.

MacLeish, Archibald. *Poetry and Experience.* Houghton Mifflin 1961 $6.95. Based on MacLeish's lectures as Boylston Professor at Harvard. Emphasis on Emily Dickinson, Yeats, Rimbaud, Keats.

———. *Poetry and Journalism.* Folcroft 1973 lib. bdg. $10.00

———. *Poetry and Opinion. Studies in Poetry* Haskell 1974 lib. bdg. $39.95

Reeves, James. *Understanding Poetry.* Heinemann text ed. 1965 $10.00. "An excellent antidote to the semantic orientation of the text [with the same title] by Brooks and Warren" (*LJ*).

Spender, Stephen. *The Making of a Poem.* Greenwood repr. of 1955 ed. 1973 lib. bdg. $45.00. On the creative process, by one of the century's most eminent practitioners.

Tuve, Rosemond. *Elizabethan and Metaphysical Imagery.* Univ. of Chicago Pr. (Phoenix Bks.) 1961 pap. $9.00

Vivante, Leone. *English Poetry and Its Contribution to the Knowledge of a Creative Principle.* Folcroft repr. of 1950 ed. 1975 lib. bdg. $25.00; Richard West repr. of 1950 ed. 1980 lib. bdg. $25.00

Anthologies of Poetry in English

In the days when students received a classical education, the term "anthology" was understood to refer to the *Greek Anthology,* a collection of 4,500 fugitive pieces by more than 300 writers, originally collected and circulated in manuscript, but with the advent of printing transcribed and published in book form. The pieces in the *Greek Anthology* have proved valuable for historians and archaeologists as well as students of the Greek language and literature, providing insights into the life of the ancient world. The collection is available in five volumes of the *Loeb Classical Library.* The earliest English anthology was the "Exeter Book," a manuscript collection made about 975 A.D. and kept at Exeter Cathedral. The first published anthology of poems in English was the so-called "Tottel's Miscellany," a collection of 271 poems by such poets as Wyatt, Surrey, Heywood, and Thomas, first issued in 1557. Compiled by Richard Tottel, the "Miscellany" (whose published title was *Songs and Sonnets*), went through eight editions before the end of the century.

In 1765, Bishop Thomas Percy published his *Reliques of Ancient Poetry,* an effort to collect early examples of ballads, sonnets, historical songs, and metrical romances, most of them drawn from a manuscript collection known as the "Percy Folio." Francis T. Palgrave's *Golden Treasury*, a collection of English lyric poetry through Tennyson, is perhaps the most famous anthology of poetry in the English-speaking world, going through many editions in the nineteenth and twentieth centuries, and still in print. The *Oxford Book of English Verse*, originally edited by Sir Arthur Quiller-Couch, had wide circulation, although it contained some corrupt texts. The *English and Scottish Popular Ballads*, edited by an American, Francis James Child, began to appear in 1882. It was thoroughly scholarly, presenting textual notes, background material, and variant readings.

Allen, Gay W. *American Poetry*. Harper text ed. 1965 $27.50. Includes bibliographies, commentary, and notes.

Auden, W. H., and Norman Holmes Pearson, eds. *Poets of the English Language. Viking Portable Lib*. Penguin vol. 2 (1977) pap. $6.95 vol. 4 (1977) pap. $7.95. Vols. 1, 3, and 5 are out of print. One of the best collections of poetry in English.

Baring-Gould, William S. *The Lure of the Limerick: An Uninhibited History, with Over Five Hundred Examples, British and American*. Crown 1967 $8.95 pap. $4.95. This collection bears witness to the fatal hold this limited form has over otherwise sensible readers. In spite of that, everyone has a favorite.

Benet, William Rose, ed. *Fifty Poets: An American Auto Anthology. Granger Poetry Lib*. repr. of 1933 ed. 1976 $19.75

Brooks, Cleanth, and Robert Penn Warren. *Understanding Poetry*. Holt 4th ed. 1976 pap. $18.95. After some decades in the field, this is still one of the most widely used texts in introductory courses. Comes with a teaching apparatus of introductory comments and study questions, and may be purchased with a teacher's manual. In spite of reservations by critics (some of whom have edited competing texts), this is one of the best introductory collections.

Bruchac, Joseph, ed. *Breaking Silence: An Anthology of Contemporary Asian American Poets*. Greenfield 1984 pap. $9.95. Poetry by Americans of Asian extraction (Chinese, Japanese, Filipinos, etc.) in English.

Carruth, Hayden, ed. *Voice That Is Great Within Us. Bantam Classic Ed. Ser*. 1970 pap. $4.95

Coffin, Charles Malone. *The Major Poets, English and American*. Rev. by Gerrit H. Roelofs, Harcourt 2d ed. rev. 1969 pap. $20.95. Chaucer to Lowell.

Cook, Roy J., ed. *One Hundred and One Famous Poems: With a Prose Supplement. Granger Poetry Lib*. repr. of 1929 ed. 1982 $17.50. Selection based on popularity.

Danziger, Marlies, and Wendell Stacy Johnson. *A Poetry Anthology*. Random 1967 $14.00. Indexes to poetic genres and first lines.

de la Mare, Walter. *Come Hither: A Collection of Rhymes and Poems for the Young of All Ages*. Knopf 1957 $25.00. Compiled by a poet who was himself one of the best children's poets.

Eastman, Arthur M., ed. *Norton Anthology of Poetry: Shorter Edition*. Norton 1970 pap. $5.25

Eastman, Arthur M., and others, eds. *Norton Anthology of Poetry*. Norton rev. ed. text ed. 1975 $19.95 pap. $16.95

Ellmann, Richard, and Robert O'Clair, eds. *Norton Anthology of Modern Poetry*. Norton 1973 $28.95 pap. $21.95. "The poets are presented chronologically, with American poets merged with those from Great Britain, Ireland and the Commonwealth. . . . A chronological table makes it possible to consider each poet . . . within the historical, intellectual and literary context" (Publisher's note).

Gardner, Helen, ed. *A Book of Religious Verse*. Oxford 1972 $17.95. ". . . an admirable selection of poems ranging from 'The Dream of the Rood' to poems by W. H. Auden, Louis Macneice, David Gascoyne and R. S. Thomas. . . ." (*Choice*).

Grigson, Geoffrey, ed. *The Faber Book of Nonsense Verse*. Faber 1979 $12.95 1982 pap. $7.95

Halpern, Daniel, ed. *The American Poetry Anthology*. Avon 1983 pap. $9.95. Contemporary poets.

Hodnett, Edward, ed. *Poems to Read Aloud*. Norton rev. ed. 1967 $12.95. Contains 295 English and American poems chosen for "readability, literary excellence and variety."

Hollander, Joan, and Harold Bloom, eds. *Wind and the Rain*. Granger Index Repr. Ser. Ayer repr. of 1961 ed. 1972 $18.00. Begins with a section with the book's title, followed by sections based on the seasons. "A miracle of freshness and originality. All the poems are chosen with flawless taste, and each is surprising, illuminating, in its aptness" (Saul Maloff, *Nation*).

Hughes, Langston, and Arna Bontemps, eds. *Poetry of the Negro, 1746–1970*. Doubleday 1970 $15.95. Contains 163 poets. Includes a section of white poets writing on blacks.

Lowry, Howard F., and Willard Thorp, eds. *Oxford Anthology of English Poetry*. Granger Poetry Lib. 2 vols. text ed. repr. of 1935 ed. 1979 $79.50. From medieval lyrics to Housman and Bridges.

Nims, John Frederick. *The Harper Anthology of Poetry*. Harper text ed. 1981 $13.50 pap. $14.95

Oxford Books of Verse Series. The Oxford Books are notable for their clarity of printing, quality of bookmaking, and distinction of editorship—e.g., Yeats as the editor for the modern verse volume.

  Auden, W. H. *The Oxford Book of Light Verse*. 1938 pap. $8.95

  Chambers, E. K. *The Oxford Book of Sixteenth-Century Verse*. 1932 $45.00

  Gardner, Helen. *The New Oxford Book of English Verse, 1250–1950*. 1972 $29.95. "The original 'Oxford Book of English Verse' came out in 1900, was revised by its editor, Sir Arthur Quiller-Couch, in 1939 . . . and has kept going to this day. . . . Dame Helen has remade the book for a new public" (Frank Kermode, *Atlantic*).

  Grierson, H. J. C., and Geoffrey Bullough, eds. *The Oxford Book of Seventeenth Century Verse*. 1934 $45.00

  Grigson, Geoffrey, ed. *The Oxford Book of Satirical Verse*. 1980 $29.95 pap. $10.95

  Harmon, William. *The Oxford Book of American Light Verse*. 1979 $25.00

  Hayward, John. *The Oxford Book of Nineteenth Century English Verse*. 1964 $45.00

  Kinsley, James, ed. *The Oxford Book of Ballads*. Oxford repr. of 1969 ed. 1982 pap. $12.95

  Larkin, Philip. *The Oxford Book of Twentieth-Century Verse*. 1973 $29.95

  Lonsdale, Roger, ed. *The New Oxford Book of Eighteenth Century Verse*. Oxford 1985 $25.00

  Matthiessen, F. O., ed. *Oxford Book of American Verse*. Oxford 1950 $29.95

  Opie, Peter, and Iona Opie, eds. *The Oxford Book of Children's Verse*. Oxford 1973 $25.00

  ———. *The Oxford Book of Narrative Verse*. 1983 $19.95

  Stallworthy, Jon. *The Oxford Book of War Poetry*. Oxford 1984 $19.95

  Woods, Fredrick, ed. *The Oxford Book of English Traditional Verse*. Oxford 1983 $19.95

  Yeats, William B., ed. *Oxford Book of Modern Verse, 1892–1935*. Oxford 1936 $22.50

Palgrave, Francis T., ed. *Golden Treasury of the Best Songs and Lyrical Poems in the English Language*. Oxford Stand. Authors Ser. 5th ed. 1964 $32.50. Continuously in print since 1861. Poems are in rough chronological order, without notes or critical apparatus. Selections are notable for sobriety and leaden morality; emphasis on Tennyson (a personal friend of Palgrave) and Gray. "Palgrave's sins of omission are famous, shameless and ludicrous. . . . The absence of any line by Donne, the failure to include Marvell's *To His Coy Mistress*, the inability to suggest Pope's quality . . . these are merely the opening shots which should ridicule the wretched boat's mean sail" (Brigid Brophy and Charles Osborne, *Fifty Works of English [and American] Literature We Could Do Without*).

Smith, Dave, ed. *The Morrow Anthology of Younger American Poets*. Intro. by Anthony Hecht, Morrow 1985 $17.95 pap. $10.00

Stanford, Ann, ed. *The Women Poets in English: An Anthology*. McGraw-Hill 1972 o.p.

Strand, Mark, ed. *Contemporary American Poets: American Poetry since 1940*. New Amer. Lib. (Meridian) 1969 pap. $6.95

Thwaite, Anthony, ed. *Six Centuries of Verse*. Methuen 1985 pap. $9.95. Copious commentary, among which poems are scattered. Includes illustrations.

Australian, Canadian, Irish, Scottish, and Welsh Anthologies

Bradley, Anthony, ed. *Contemporary Irish Poetry: An Anthology*. Univ. of California Pr. 1980 $19.95. Contains introduction, notes, and indexes of poets, titles, and first lines.

Cooke, John, ed. *The Dublin Book of Irish Verse, 1728–1909. Granger Index Repr. Ser.* Ayer repr. of 1909 ed. $38.50; Folcroft repr. of 1909 ed. lib. bdg. $20.00. Satisfactory for poets before 1900, but that not insignificant poet W. B. Yeats is represented by only four poems.

Eyre-Todd, George, ed. *Scottish Poetry of the Eighteenth Century*. Greenwood repr. of 1896 ed. $23.50

——. *Scottish Poetry of the Sixteenth Century*. Darby repr. of 1895 ed. 1983 $45.00

Hall, Rodney, ed. *Collins Book of Australian Poetry*. Collins 1981 $13.50. A comprehensive collection.

Kennelly, Brendan, ed. *The Penguin Book of Irish Verse*. Penguin 1982 pap. $4.95

Lindsay, Maurice, ed. *Modern Scottish Poetry: An Anthology of the Scottish Renaissance, 1925–1975*. Humanities Pr. text ed. 1976 pap. $9.00

MacDonagh, Donagh, and Lennox Robinson, eds. *Oxford Book of Irish Verse Seventeenth to Twentieth Century*. Oxford 1958 $29.95

MacQueen, John, and Tom Scott, eds. *Oxford Book of Scottish Verse*. Oxford 1966 $35.00. "[This] volume, which includes authors from the 13th century up to those born before 1930, is carefully chosen and edited and presents the most representative selection to date. It must be considered the best one-volume anthology of Scottish verse available" (*LJ*).

Montague, John, ed. *The Book of Irish Verse: An Anthology of Irish Poetry from the Sixth Century to the Present*. Macmillan 1983 $14.95 pap. $7.95; Peter Smith 1984 $15.25

Murdoch, Walter. *A Book of Australasian Verse*. Arden Lib. repr. of 1924 ed. 1979 lib. bdg. $30.00; Century Bookbindery repr. of 1924 ed. 1977 $20.00

Murphy, Gerard, ed. *Early Irish Lyrics: Eighth to Twelfth Century*. Oxford 1956 $29.00

Parry, Thomas, ed. *Oxford Book of Welsh Verse*. Oxford 1962 $15.50

Shapcott, Thomas, ed. *Contemporary American and Australian Poetry*. Univ. of Queensland Pr. text ed. 1976 $19.95 pap. $12.95. The juxtaposition of American and Australian poetry is based on the similarities of the two countries as developing societies and cultures.

Anthologies of World Poetry

Burnshaw, Stanley, ed. *The Poem Itself.* Horizon Pr. 1980 pap. $7.95. "45 modern poets in a new presentation: more than 150 original French, German, Italian, Portuguese and Spanish poems, with literal renderings and explanatory discussions." Translations are in prose.

Conniff, Richard, ed. *The Devil's Book of Verse.* Dodd 1983 $15.95. Poetry written with the pen dipped in acid. See especially Phyllis McGinley, "Home Is the Sailor." A useful antidote to *The Golden Treasury.*

Creekmore, Hubert, ed. *Lyrics of the Middle Ages.* Greenwood repr. of 1959 ed. lib. bdg. $19.75

Drachler, Jacob, and Virginia R. Terris, eds. *The Many Worlds of Poetry.* Knopf 1969 o.p. Poems, some in translation, on a variety of topics: "Blood Ties," "The Question of Progress," "The War Dead," etc. Includes study questions.

Lowell, Robert. *Imitations.* Farrar rev. & enl. ed. 1961 pap. $3.95. From various languages, all the translations by Lowell.

Nims, John Frederick, ed. *Sappho to Valéry: Poems in Translation.* Princeton Univ. Pr. 1980 $22.50 pap. $11.95. Original and translation on facing pages.

Pound, Ezra, and Marcella Spann, eds. *Confucius to Cummings: An Anthology of Poetry.* New Directions 1964 $10.00 pap. $6.95. Emphasis on Greek, Latin, Chinese, Troubadour, Renaissance, and Elizabethan poets.

Tomlinson, Charles, ed. *The Oxford Book of Verse in English Translation.* Oxford 1980 pap. $12.95. Organized chronologically by translator.

Van Doren, Mark. *An Anthology of World Poetry.* Harcourt rev. ed. 1936 $45.00. All the world of poetry in 1,200 pages. ". . . there is no poet in history who might not have found a place in [this book] had he ever fallen into the hands of a becoming translator" (Preface).

FICTION

Studies of Fiction

Allen, Walter. *The Short Story in English.* Oxford 1981 $25.00

Auchincloss, Louis. *Pioneers and Caretakers: A Study of Nine American Women Novelists.* Univ. of Minnesota Pr. 1965 $13.95. Jewett, Wharton, Glasgow, Cather, Roberts, Porter, Stafford, McCullers, McCarthy.

Axthelm, Peter M. *The Modern Confessional Novel. College Ser.* Yale Univ. Pr. 1967 $16.50. Dostoevsky, Gide, Sartre, Camus, Golding, Bellow. Includes a comprehensive bibliography.

Baker, Ernest A. *A History of the English Novel.* Barnes & Noble 11 vols. repr. of 1924–67 ed. 1966–79 ea. $19.50 set $214.50. The standard work on the English novel.

Booth, Wayne C. *The Rhetoric of Fiction.* Univ. of Chicago Pr. (Phoenix Bks.) 2d ed. 1983 pap. $30.00

Chase, Richard. *The American Novel and Its Tradition.* Gordian repr. of 1957 ed. 1978 $12.50; Johns Hopkins Univ. Pr. repr. of 1957 ed. 1980 pap. $6.95

Daiches, David. *The Novel and the Modern World.* Univ. of Chicago Pr. rev. ed. repr. of 1939 ed. text ed. 1984 pap. $9.00. "[The chapters] are all intended to illustrate . . . the main problems that have faced the writer of fiction in the present century" (Preface).

Fiedler, Leslie. *Love and Death in the American Novel.* Stein & Day 1975 pap. $12.95.

A famous, penetrating, and at times baffling analysis of American fiction, 1789 to 1959. Fiedler contends that Americans have developed a literature embarrassed by adult sexuality and obsessed with death.

Forster, E. M. *Aspects of the Novel.* Harcourt 1956 pap. $3.95. A very influential study, first published in 1927. "We discover under his casual and wittily acute guidance, many things about the literary magic which transmutes the dull stuff of He-said and She-said into characters, stories, and intimations of truth" (Jacques Barzun, *Harper's*).

Friedman, Norman. *Form and Meaning in Fiction.* Univ. of Georgia Pr. 1975 $28.00

James, Henry. *The Art of the Novel: Critical Prefaces.* Fwd. by R. W. Lewis, intro. by Richard P. Blackmur, Northwestern Univ. Pr. repr. of 1907 ed. 1984 pap. $9.95

Kennedy, Margaret. *The Outlaws on Parnassus.* Fwd. by Malcolm Cowley, Arden Lib. repr. of 1958 ed. 1979 lib. bdg. $20.00; Ayer repr. of 1960 ed. $18.00. ". . . one of the most urbane, perceptive and readable books about the art of fiction that I have ever read. . . . [Novels] can be written with a variety of technical devices, which she brilliantly describes, and they provide guided tours to their authors' visions of life" (Orville Prescott, *N.Y. Times*).

Kermode, Frank. *Sense of an Ending: Studies in the Theory of Fiction.* Oxford 1967 pap. $8.95. Six lectures delivered at Bryn Mawr in 1965. Formidable; for the advanced student.

Kettle, Arnold. *An Introduction to the English Novel.* Humanities Pr. 2 vols. repr. of 1963 ed. 1974 pap. ea. $11.00

Leavis, Q. D. *Fiction and the Reading Public.* Folcroft 1932 lib. bdg. $40.00

Lubbock, Percy. *The Craft of Fiction.* 1921. Fwd. by Mark Schorer, Viking 1957 o.p. An influential work for many decades. ". . . a Poetics of the novel" (Rene Wellek and Austin Warren, *Theory of Literature*).

Lukács, Georg. *The Historical Novel.* Trans. by Hannah Mitchell and Stanley Mitchell, Humanities Pr. repr. of 1962 ed. text ed. 1978 $15.50; Univ. of Nebraska Pr. repr. of 1937 ed. 1983 pap. $8.95. A Marxist approach.

———. *Theory of the Novel.* Trans. by Anna Bostock, MIT 1971 pap. $6.95

Moore, Harry T., ed. *Contemporary American Novelists.* Southern Illinois Univ. Pr. 1974 pap. $7.95

Price, Martin. *Forms of Life: Character and Moral Imagination in the Novel.* Yale Univ. Pr. text ed. 1983 $28.50

Quinn, Arthur Hobson. *American Fiction: An Historical and Critical Survey.* Irvington repr. of 1947 ed. 1982 $32.50

Rosenberg, Edgar. *From Shylock to Svengali: Jewish Stereotypes in English Fiction.* Stanford Univ. Pr. 1960 $27.50

Rubin, Louis D., Jr. *Curious Death of the Novel: Essays in American Literature.* Louisiana State Univ. Pr. 1967 $25.00. Poe to Flannery O'Connor. The novel is not dead.

Shapiro, Charles. *Twelve Original Essays on Great American Novels.* Wayne State Univ. Pr. 1959 pap. $5.95. On American novels from Cooper's *Deerslayer* and Hawthorne's *Scarlet Letter* to Hemingway's *The Sun Also Rises* and Faulkner's *Light in August.* Includes essays written for this volume by Malcolm Cowley, Granville Hicks, Alfred Kazin, and others.

Snell, George. *The Shapers of American Fiction, 1798–1947.* Cooper Square Pr. repr. of 1947 ed. 1961 $23.50

Snow, C. P. *The Realists.* Scribner 1978 $3.25. Stendhal, Balzac, Dickens, Dostoevsky, Tolstoy, Galdos, Henry James, Proust.

Stevenson, Lionel. *The English Novel: A Panorama.* Greenwood repr. of 1968 ed. 1978 lib. bdg. $42.50. A survey history by a highly regarded specialist on the novel.

Stevick, Philip. *The Theory of the Novel.* Macmillan (Free Pr.) 1967 $13.95

Sundquist, Eric J., ed. *American Realism: New Essays.* Johns Hopkins Univ. Pr. 1982 $27.50 pap. $8.95. Collected essays on novels of the period of American realism, Hawthorne to Dreiser.

Van Ghent, Dorothy. *The English Novel: Form and Function.* Harper 1961 pap. $6.50

General Collections of Fiction

Abrahams, William, ed. *Prize Stories: The O. Henry Awards.* Doubleday (Anchor) 1984 pap. $8.95. An annual selection of stories from U.S. and Canadian periodicals that have won the O. Henry Prize. The awards have been given annually since 1918.

————. *Prize Stories of the Seventies: From the O. Henry Awards.* Washington Square Pr. 1981 pap. $4.95

Angus, Douglas, ed. *The Best Short Stories of the Modern Age.* Fawcett rev. ed. 1974 pap. $2.75. The editor's courage is to be admired.

Best American Short Stories. 1916–to date. Houghton Mifflin annual 1984 $14.95 pap. $8.95. Edited by Edward J. O'Brien (1915–41), then Martha Foley (1942–77). Selections taken from U.S. and Canadian periodicals.

Brooks, Cleanth, and Robert Penn Warren, eds. *Understanding Fiction.* Prentice-Hall 3d ed. 1979 pap. $15.95. An introductory text, in use for many years, with explanatory notes and study questions. Based on the principles of the New Criticism.

Cahill, Susan, ed. *Women and Fiction 2: Short Stories by and about Women.* New Amer. Lib. 1978 pap. $3.95

Cassill, R. V., ed. *The Norton Anthology of Short Fiction.* Norton 2d ed. 1981 $13.95. An excellent collection.

Cowley, Malcolm, and Howard E. Hugo, eds. *The Lesson of the Masters: An Anthology of the Novel from Cervantes to Hemingway.* Scribner 1971 o.p. Excerpts from novels, with introductory matter and concluding statements (afterwords) by the editors. A fine anthology.

Cuddon, J. A., ed. *The Penguin Book of Ghost Stories.* Penguin Fiction Ser. 1985 pap. $6.95

————. *The Penguin Book of Horror Stories.* Penguin Fiction Ser. 1985 pap. $6.95

Davis, Robert G. *Ten Modern Masters.* Harcourt 3d ed. text ed. 1972 pap. $14.95. Three stories each by Borges, Chekhov, Faulkner, Joyce, Lawrence, Malamud, Mann, O'Connor, and Welty, and two longer stories by Conrad. Also includes nine stories by other writers and selections on writing by the ten featured writers.

Forkner, Ben, ed. *Modern Irish Short Stories.* Pref. by Anthony Burgess, Viking 1980 $15.95

Forkner, Ben, and Patrick Samway, eds. *Stories of the Modern South.* Penguin 1981 pap. $5.95; Peter Smith 1984 $13.75

Goodman, Robert B., ed. *Seventy-Five Short Masterpieces: Stories from the World's Literature.* Bantam 1961 pap. $3.50. Many unexpected choices: "Charles" by Shirley Jackson (not "The Lottery"); "The Oval Portrait" by Poe (instead of any number of stories more frequently chosen); "The Upturned Face" by Ambrose Bierce (not "An Occurrence at Owl Creek Bridge").

Gordon, Caroline, and Allen Tate, eds. *House of Fiction.* Scribner 2d ed. text ed. 1960
pap. $9.95. A well-known collection.
Hall, James B., and Elizabeth Hall. *The Realm of Fiction: 74 Short Stories.* McGraw-
Hill 3d ed. text ed. 1977 pap. $18.95
Henderson, Bill, ed. *The Pushcart Prize: Best of the Small Presses.* 1976–to date. Avon
annual 1985 pap. $9.95. An annual selection from reviews, little magazines,
small presses. "Some of the freshest, most innovative writing today" (*Booklist*).
Hills, L. Rust, ed. *Great Esquire Fiction: The Finest Stories from the First Fifty Years.*
Pref. by Phillip Moffitt, Penguin rev. ed. 1984 pap. $7.95. Stories selected from
Esquire, 1933–83.
Howe, Irving, ed. *Classics of Modern Fiction: Ten Short Novels.* Harcourt 3d ed. text
ed. 1980 pap. $16.95. Includes Dostoevsky, Tolstoy, James, Forster, Conrad,
Mann, Kafka, Flannery O'Connor, Bellow, Solzhenitsyn.
Marcus, Steven, ed. *World of Modern Fiction.* Simon & Schuster 2 vols. 1966 $17.50
Murphy, George E., Jr., ed. *The Editor's Choice: New American Stories.* Bantam 1985
pap. $6.95. Intended as an annual publication.
Pritchett, V. S., ed. *The Oxford Book of Short Stories.* Oxford 1981 $22.50
Raffel, Burton. *The Signet Classic Book of American Short Stories.* New Amer. Lib.
(Signet Class.) 1985 pap. $3.95
Schorer, Mark, ed. *Story: A Critical Anthology.* Prentice-Hall 2d ed. text ed. 1967 pap.
$15.95. Includes explanatory comments preceding and following most selec-
tions.
Six Great Modern Short Novels. Dell 1967 pap. $3.95. *The Bear, The Dead, Billy Budd,
The Overcoat, Noon Wine, The Pilgrim Hawk.*
Stern, Richard. *Honey and Wax: Pleasures and Powers of Narrative.* Univ. of Chicago
Pr. (Phoenix Bks.) 1969 pap. $3.95
Thorburn, David, ed. *Initiation: Stories and Short Novels on Three Themes.* Harcourt
2d ed. text ed. 1976 pap. $11.95. The themes: initiation, love, outsiders.
Tuska, John, ed. *The American West in Fiction.* New Amer. Lib. 1982 pap. $3.95
Washington, Mary Helen, ed. *Black-Eyed Susans: Classic Stories by and about Black
Women.* Doubleday (Anchor) 1975 pap. $4.50

GENERAL WORKS OF CRITICISM

Atkins, J. W. H. *Literary Criticism in Antiquity.* Arden Lib. 2 vols. repr. of 1952 ed.
1978 $65.00
Auden, W. H. *The Enchafed Flood: Three Critical Essays on the Romantic Spirit.* Univ.
Pr. of Virginia 1974 $8.95 pap. $3.95
——. *Forewords and Afterwords.* Random 1973 $19.95 pap. $3.95
Auerbach, Erich. *Mimesis: The Representation of Reality in Western Literature.* Prince-
ton Univ. Pr. 1953 $35.00 pap. $8.95. Homer to Virginia Woolf. Penetrating in-
sights expressed with clarity and simplicity.
——. *Scenes from the Drama of European Literature: Six Essays.* Peter Smith $18.50
Brophy, Brigid, and Charles Osborne. *Fifty Works of English and American Literature
We Could Do Without.* Stein & Day 1968 pap. $1.95. Brief, malicious, completely
unfair, and thoroughly delightful attacks on numerous classic works of English
and American literature.
Burke, Kenneth. *The Philosophy of Literary Form.* Univ. of California Pr. repr. of 1941
ed. 1974 pap. $10.95
Coveney, Peter. *The Image of Childhood: The Individual and Society—A Study of the
Theme in English Literature.* Intro. by Frank R. Leavis, Gannon 1957 $15.00.

Originally entitled *Poor Monkey: The Child in Literature from Rousseau's 'Emile' to the Freudian Novelists*. "This original and interesting book" starts from "a brilliant initial perception—the recognition that the whole of the romantic movement can be freshly charted in terms of the treatment of the child in literature. And although he has kept scrupulously to his apparently limited and limiting theme, what Mr. Coveney has achieved is a new and illuminating study of the main tradition of English literature since Wordsworth" (Philip Toynbee, *Observer*).

Emerson, Everett H., ed. *Major Writers of Early American Literature: Introductions to Nine Major Writers*. Univ. of Wisconsin Pr. 1972 $25.00 pap. $9.95. "An outstanding collection of original critical essays by a distinguished specialist. . . . Both a chronological survey of nearly 200 years of American literature and an exciting reappraisal of the major figures of that period . . ." (*Choice*).

Foerster, Norman. *American Criticism: A Study in Literary Theory from Poe to the Present*. Russell Pr. repr. of 1928 ed. 1962 $15.00. American literary theory, primarily as expressed and exemplified by Poe, Emerson, Lowell, and Whitman.

Frye, Northrop. *Anatomy of Criticism*. Princeton Univ. Pr. 1957 $36.00 pap. $7.95

Gardner, Helen. *The Business of Criticism*. Century Bookbindery repr. 1982 lib. bdg. $30.00

Gordon, Ian A. *The Movement of English Prose*. Midway Repr. Ser. Longman text ed. 1980 pap. $10.95. A study of changes in English prose style from Anglo-Saxon times onward. Exercises at the end of the text.

Hartman, Geoffrey. *The Fate of Reading: And Other Essays*. Univ. of Chicago Pr. repr. of 1975 ed. text ed. 1984 pap. $9.00

Howard, Leon. *Literature and the American Tradition*. Gordian repr. of 1960 ed. 1972 $15.00. The formation of American literary individuality.

Jones, Edmund D., ed. *English Critical Essays: Sixteenth, Seventeenth and Eighteenth Centuries*. Arden Lib. repr. 1983 lib. bdg. $20.00; Darby repr. of 1947 ed. 1983 lib. bdg. $25.00; Oxford repr. of 1916 ed. 1971 $16.95 pap. $3.95

———. *English Critical Essays: Nineteenth Century*. Darby repr. of 1947 ed. 1983 lib. bdg. $25.00; *Oxford Pap. Ser.* repr. of 1916 ed. 1971 pap. $3.95

Jones, Howard Mumford. *The Theory of American Literature*. Cornell Univ. Pr. rev. ed. 1967 o.p. "Brief, trenchant, authoritative, [his] pioneer study of American literary histography . . . well deserves a new lease on life" (*TLS*).

Kaplan, Charles, ed. *Criticism: The Major Statements*. St. Martin's text ed. 1975 $15.95. Plato, Aristotle, Longinus, Horace, Sidney, Dryden, Pope, Edward Young, Samuel Johnson, Wordsworth, Coleridge, Lamb, Keats, Shelley, Poe, Arnold, Pater, Henry James, Tolstoy, Eliot. A section of discussion questions at the end.

Kostelanetz, Richard, ed. *On Contemporary Literature: An Anthology of Critical Essays on the Major Movements and Writings of Contemporary Literature*. Essay Index Reprint Ser. Ayer repr. of 1964 ed. $40.00. Essays on such topics as U.S. fiction, U.S. theater, British poetry, Canadian writing, and on individual writers, mostly U.S., British, or French. Contributors include Kazin, Fiedler, Rexroth, Kermode, Jarrell, Eric Bentley, etc.

Krieger, Murray. *Theory of Criticism: A Tradition and Its System*. Johns Hopkins Univ. Pr. 1976 pap. $6.95

Kwiat, Joseph J., and Mary C. Turpie. *Studies in American Culture: Dominant Ideas and Images*. Johnson Repr. repr. of 1960 ed. 1971 $22.00

Langer, Suzanne K. *Philosophy in a New Key: A Study in the Symbolism of Reason, Rite and Art*. Harvard Univ. Pr. 3d ed. 1957 $18.50 pap. $6.95

Leavis, Frank R. *The Common Pursuit*. New York Univ. Pr. 1964 $12.50; Merrimack 1984 pap. $8.95

Levin, Harry. *Refractions: Essays in Comparative Literature*. Oxford 1966 $13.95 pap. $5.95

Lewis, R. W. B. *The American Adam*. Univ. of Chicago Pr. 1955 pap. $6.95

Orwell, George. *Collection of Essays*. Harcourt repr. of 1954 ed. 1970 pap. $4.95. Personal reminiscences and literary essays, the latter including the influential "Charles Dickens" and "Politics and the English Language."

Poirier, Richard. *A World Elsewhere: The Place of Style in American Literature*. Oxford 1966 pap. $4.95. Discusses "the creation of those works that allow their characters 'unhampered freedom of consciousness.'"

Praz, Mario. *The Romantic Agony*. Trans. by Angus Davidson, *Oxford Pap. Ser.* 2d ed. text ed. 1951 pap. $12.95. A well-known and provocative study of romanticism.

Richards, I. A. *Principles of Literary Criticism*. Harcourt 1961 pap. $5.95

Rowse, A. L. *The English Spirit: Essays in History and Literature*. Arden Lib. repr. of 1944 ed. $30.00; Folcroft repr. of 1964 ed. 1977 $20.00. On George Herbert, Swift, Walpole, Wordsworth, Carlyle, Macaulay, by an English historian famous for his ventures into literary studies.

Smith, Henry Nash. *Virgin Land: The American West as Symbol and Myth*. Harvard Univ. Pr. 1970 pap. $6.95

Spiller, Robert E. *The Cycle of American Literature: An Essay in Historical Criticism*. 1955. Macmillan (Free Pr.) 1967 pap. $13.95

Symons, Arthur. *The Symbolist Movement in Literature*. AMS Pr. repr. of 1899 ed. 1980 $17.50

Tate, Allen. *Essays of Four Decades*. Apollo 1970 o.p.; Swallow 1969 o.p. Forty-two essays and six prefaces.

Trilling, Lionel. *The Liberal Imagination: Essays on Literature and Society*. Harcourt 1979 $10.00

Wellek, Rene. *A History of Modern Criticism: 1750 to 1950*. Cambridge Univ. Pr. 4 vols. 1983 pap. ea. $14.95–$18.95. When complete, will stand as the standard history of modern criticism.

Wellek, Rene, and Austin Warren. *Theory of Literature*. Harcourt rev. ed. 1956 pap. $5.95. An influential study.

Wilson, Edmund. *Axel's Castle: A Study in the Imaginative Literature of 1870–1930*. Norton 1984 pap. $6.95. Originally published in 1931. A study in the use of symbolism by a group of writers of the period (Yeats, Valéry, Eliot, Proust, Joyce, Stein, Rimbaud) who shared certain literary tendencies.

Wimsatt, William K., and Cleanth Brooks. *Literary Criticism: A Short History*. Univ. of Chicago Pr. repr. of 1957 ed. 1978 pap. ea. $11.00. A well-known attempt to summarize the key issues in literary theory.

WRITERS ON WRITING

Bennett, Patrick. *Talking with Texas Writers: Twelve Interviews*. Texas A & M Univ. Pr. 1980 $17.50 pap. $9.95. Larry McMurtry, Tom Lea, William Goyen, others.

Booth, Wayne C. *The Rhetoric of Fiction*. Univ. of Chicago Pr. (Phoenix Bks.) 2d ed. 1983 pap. $30.00. "My goal is not to set everyone straight about my favorite novelists, but rather to free both readers and novelists from the constraints of abstract rules about what novelists must do, by reminding them in a systematic way of what good novelists have done in fact" (Preface).

Bruccoli, Matthew J., and others, eds. *Conversations with Writers*. Gale 1977 $46.00
———. *Conversations with Writers II*. Bruccoli 1978 $46.00. First series: Dickey, Gardner, Warren, others; second series: Farrell, Loos, Welty, others. Questions by the interviewers are highly informed and elicit illuminating responses.

Hersey, John. *Writer's Craft*. Random 1973 $13.95. Selections from writers on all aspects of the craft of writing by the likes of James, Forster, Robbe-Grillet, Burroughs, Lubbock, Flaubert. "I envy [Hersey's students] their time to study the book in relative leisure. . . . I envy them their chance to read slowly and carefully . . . Leo Tolstoy's 'What Is Art?,' Elizabeth Bowen's 'Notes on Writing a Novel,' Gertrude Stein's 'Poetry and Grammar,' and Edgar Allan Poe's 'The Philosophy of Composition' " (Christopher Lehmann-Haupt, *N.Y. Times*).

James, Henry. *Literary Reviews of American, English and French Literature*. New College & Univ. Pr. 1957 pap. $9.95

Jones, John Griffin, ed. *Mississippi Writers Talking*. Univ. Pr. of Mississippi 2 vols. 1982–83 ea. $15.00 pap. ea. $8.95. Welty, Foots, Percy, Willie Morris, others.

Ruas, Charles. *Conversations with American Writers*. Knopf 1985 $17.45. Recorded conversations over three decades with a variety of writers—Vidal, Toni Morrison, Mailer, others.

Solzhenitsyn, Alexander. *The Nobel Lecture on Literature*. Trans. by F. D. Reeve, Harper bilingual ed. 1972 $5.95. ". . . an extraordinarily moving testament to the power of art and literature as a uniting force in the modern world" (M. S. Cosgrave).

Todd, Janet, ed. *Women Writers Talking*. Holmes & Meier 1983 $27.50 pap. $12.50. Margaret Drabble, Alison Lurie, Erica Jong, others.

Writers at Work: The Paris Review Interviews. Penguin series 1–3 1977 pap. ea. $7.95 series 4–5 1977–81 pap. ea. $8.95; Viking series 6 1984 $22.50. The first series was edited by Malcolm Cowley; series 2–5 were edited by George Plimpton. Interviews with writers of many stripes—Dorothy Parker, Frank O'Connor, Capote, Huxley, Porter, James Jones, Waugh, others.

CHAPTER 5

British Poetry: Early to Romantic

Norman Fruman

> [The Poet] is the rock of defence for human nature; an upholder and pre-
> server, carrying everywhere with him relationship and love. In spite of dif-
> ference of soil and climate, of language and manners, of laws and customs:
> in spite of things silently gone out of mind, and things violently destroyed;
> the Poet binds together by passion and knowledge the vast empire of hu-
> man society, as it is spread over the whole earth, and over all time.
> —WILLIAM WORDSWORTH, Preface to *Lyrical Ballads* (1800)

This chapter covers the finest flowering of English literature— the period
from *Beowulf* (c.750 A.D.) to the death of Keats (1821). That "period" in fact
encompasses at least five literary periods: Old English, which (as a written
literature) began in the seventh century; Middle English (twelfth to fifteenth centuries), dominated by Chaucer; the Renaissance—Elizabethan
and Jacobean—with its wealth of gifted poets, above all Spenser, SHAKE-
SPEARE (see Vol. 2), Donne and Milton; the Restoration and the eighteenth
century, when the brilliant satirical achievements of Dryden and Pope led,
through such transitional poets as Gray and Cowper, to the period of the
great romantics—Blake, Wordsworth, Coleridge, Byron, Shelley, and Keats,
a perhaps unprecedented upwelling of poetic genius in so short a time.

The term *period*, of course, is purely conventional. Pope did not think of
himself as a "neoclassic" poet, and Shelley would have been surprised to be
called a "romantic." Nevertheless it seems in retrospect that certain epochs
have in common a tone and character that justifies particular nomencla-
tures. The cool rationalism of much eighteenth-century verse contrasts
sharply with the emotional turbulence of early nineteenth-century poetry.
As a whole, seventeenth-century poetry is apt to be ironic, analytic, somewhat melancholy; by contrast, the Elizabethans were far more confident,
passionate, brimming with joy and a zest for life. Although each "period"
may differ sharply from another, there is a sense of continuing tradition
that echoes down the generations covered in this chapter. Greek and Roman literature and thought, Christian belief (rooted in the Bible), and Renaissance Italian literature are perhaps the dominant influences. Thus Chaucer recalls and reveres "olde bokes" written in Latin, while he imitates and
improves on literary models provided by DANTE (see Vol. 2) and BOCCACCIO
(see Vol. 2). Centuries later, Keats would also be influenced by, and improve

on, Boccaccio. As Spenser acknowledges the influence of VIRGIL (see Vol. 2) and Chaucer, so his own Christian humanism anticipates that of Milton's poetry. Shelley will adopt Spenser's complex stanza in his elegy on the death of Keats (*Adonais*); Wordsworth, in trying times, longs for Milton's "cheerful godliness," and uses Milton's sonnet form, itself derived from Petrarch. The influence of Greek sculpture on Keats was profound, and Byron's great satires draw on Italian stanza forms. Nor is the force of literary tradition transmitted in an exclusively chronological fashion; Old English poetry was scarcely known before the early nineteenth century, and the popular ballad had virtually no written existence before the middle of the eighteenth century. Each kind of poetry therefore entered the stream of English literary tradition centuries after its composition, and this very tardiness enhanced and brightened the distinctly original character of ancient themes and techniques. Imitation and originality, tradition and experiment, then, combine and fuse in the unparalleled poetic richness of these centuries.

Although this great body of poetry is to some degree timeless and universal, poetry is also a social act, rooted in particular human lives and in a particular social context. Poetry can, therefore, speak with particular force to readers who know something of the special circumstances in which the poems were written. In the following pages the reader will find an abundance of titles of enduring value. As Dryden said of the characters in Chaucer's *Canterbury Tales*, "Here is God's plenty."

SELECTED BIBLIOGRAPHY

Old English Poetry

Greenfield, Stanley B. *A Critical History of Old English Literature*. New York Univ. Pr. 1965 $25.00 pap. $12.50

Matthews, William, ed. *Old and Middle English Literature. Goldentree Bibliographies in Language and Lit. Ser.* Harlan Davidson 1968 pap. $5.95. A classic bibliography of English literature until 1525.

Pearsall, Derek. *Old English and Middle English Poetry*. Routledge & Kegan 1985 pap. $10.95. Perhaps the best survey of the poetry.

Stevens, Martin, and Jerome Mandel, eds. *Old English Literature: Twenty-two Analytical Essays*. 1968. Univ. of Nebraska Pr. 1976 $25.50

Wrenn, Charles L. *A Study of Old English Literature*. Norton 1967 pap. $3.95. From Caedmon to the Norman Conquest. Probably the best survey of the field.

The Middle English Period

Blake, Norman L. *The English Language in Medieval Literature*. Methuen 1979 pap. $9.95; Rowman 1977 $17.50

Burrow, John A. *Medieval Writers and Their Work: Middle English Literature, 1100–1500*. Oxford text ed. 1982 pap. $6.95. An outstanding brief introduction.

Chambers, Edmund K. *English Literature at the Close of the Middle Ages. Oxford History of English Lit. Ser.* 1945 $42.00. Contains Medieval Drama, The Carol and the Fifteenth-Century Lyric, Popular Narrative Poetry and the Ballad, Malory.

Kane, George. *Middle English Literature: A Critical Study of the Romances, the Religious Lyrics, "Piers Plowman."* Folcroft repr. of 1951 ed. 1977 lib. bdg. $30.00; Greenwood repr. of 1970 ed. 1980 lib. bdg. $27.50

Ker, William P. *English Literature: Medieval.* Folcroft repr. of 1912 ed. 1977 lib. bdg. $30.00. Still valuable.

Lewis, Clive S. *The Allegory of Love: A Study of Medieval Tradition.* Oxford 1936 $22.00 pap $8.95. A classic on the tradition of courtly romance that affected Spenser and other English poets.

Maresca, Thomas E. *Three English Epics: Studies of "Troilus and Criseyde," "The Faerie Queene," and "Paradise Lost."* Univ. of Nebraska Pr. 1979 $17.95

Plummer, John F. *Vox Feminae: Studies in Medieval Women's Songs.* Medieval Institute 1981 pap. $10.95

Schlauch, Margaret. *English Medieval Literature and Its Social Foundations.* Cooper Square Pr. repr. of 1956 ed. 1971 lib. bdg. $25.00; Gordon 1977 lib. bdg. $59.95. An important work by a Marxist scholar.

Sisam, Kenneth. *Fourteenth-Century Prose and Verse.* Oxford 1921 $15.95

Speirs, John. *Mediaeval English Poetry: The Non-Chaucerian Tradition.* Hillary House 1958 o.p. A badly needed book, enthusiastically written; for laymen and scholars.

Tuve, Rosemond. *Allegorical Imagery: Some Medieval Books and Their Posterity.* Princeton Univ. Pr. 1966 $47.00 pap. $13.50

Waddell, Helen. *Poetry in the Dark Ages.* Folcroft repr. of 1948 ed. 1974 lib. bdg. $10.00; *Studies in Poetry* Haskell repr. of 1948 ed. pap. $22.95

Wilson, R. M. *Early Middle English Literature.* Folcroft repr. of 1939 ed. lib. bdg. $20.00. Comprehensive and trustworthy.

Zesmer, David M. *Guide to English Literature from Beowulf through Chaucer and Medieval Drama.* Greenwood repr. of 1961 ed. 1982 lib. bdg. $42.50. A basic introduction and survey, with annotated bibliography. Dated but useful.

The Renaissance: The Sixteenth Century

Bush, Douglas. *Mythology and the Renaissance Tradition in English Poetry.* Harvard Univ. Pr. rev. ed. 1969 $32.50; *Norton Lib.* rev. ed. 1963 pap. $3.45. Masterful studies of a crucial subject.

———. *Prefaces to Renaissance Literature.* Harvard Univ. Pr. 1965 $7.95. Five important essays on backgrounds of Renaissance poetry.

Hutton, James. *Essays on Renaissance Poetry.* Ed. by Rita Guerlac, fwd. by D. P. Walker, Cornell Univ. Pr. 1980 $37.50

Lewis, Clive S. *English Literature in the Sixteenth Century (Excluding Drama).* Oxford History of Eng. Lit. Ser. 1954 $39.50

Smith, Hallett D. *Elizabethan Poetry: A Study in Conventions, Meaning, and Expression.* Harvard Univ. Pr. 1952 $20.00. Probably the best general survey.

Tuve, Rosemond. *Elizabethan and Metaphysical Imagery.* Univ. of Chicago Pr. (Phoenix Bks.) 1961 pap. $9.00

Wilson, Frank P. *Elizabethan and Jacobean.* Oxford 1945 $12.95. Provocative essays on the literature of this period and its cultural background.

The Renaissance: The Early Seventeenth Century

Beer, Patricia. *An Introduction to the Metaphysical Poets.* Humanities Pr. repr. of 1972 ed. text ed. 1981 $9.50; Rowman 1972 $7.50

Bennett, Joan. *Five Metaphysical Poets: Donne, Herbert, Vaughan, Crashaw, Marvell.* Cambridge Univ. Pr. 1964 $32.50 pap. $9.95

Bradbury, Malcolm, and David Palmer, eds. *Metaphysical Poetry.* Crane Russak 1970 $9.00; Holmes & Meier text ed. 1970 $19.50; Indiana Univ. Pr. 1971 pap. $2.95

Bush, Douglas. *English Literature in the Earlier Seventeenth Century, 1600–1660.* Oxford History of Eng. Lit. Ser. 2d ed. 1962 $42.50 pap. $7.95. A masterful analysis.

Cruttwell, Patrick. *The Shakespearian Moment and Its Place in the Poetry of the Seventeenth Century.* Columbia Univ. Pr. 1954 $29.00

Keast, William R., ed. *Seventeenth-Century English Poetry.* Oxford rev. ed. 1971 pap. $13.95. Twenty-nine essays discussing seventeenth-century poetry generally, and the major poets of the era, exclusive of Milton.

Martz, Louis. *The Poetry of Meditation: A Study of English Religious Literature of the Seventeenth Century.* Yale Univ. Pr. 1962 pap. $7.95

Mazzaro, Jerome. *Transformations in the Renaissance English Lyric.* Cornell Univ. Pr. 1970 $20.00

Miner, Earl. *The Cavalier Mode from Jonson to Cotton.* Princeton Univ. Pr. 1971 $25.00

White, Helen C. *The Metaphysical Poets: A Study in Religious Experience.* AMS Pr. repr. of 1936 ed. $39.50

Willey, Basil. *The Seventeenth-Century Background: Studies in the Thought of the Age in Relation to Poetry and Religion.* Columbia Univ. Pr. 1942 $27.50

Williamson, George. *Six Metaphysical Poets: A Reader's Guide.* Farrar 1967 o.p.

The Restoration and the Eighteenth Century

Clifford, James L., ed. *Eighteenth-Century English Literature: Modern Essays in Criticism.* Oxford 1959 pap. $6.95

Davie, Donald. *Purity of Diction in English Verse.* Schocken 1967 $5.00. Superb discussions of eighteenth-century poetry.

Dobree, Bonamy. *English Literature in the Early Eighteenth Century, 1700–1740.* Oxford History of Eng. Lit. Ser. 1959 $42.00

Mahoney, John L. *The Enlightenment and English Literature: Prose and Poetry of the Eighteenth Century with Selected Modern Critical Essays.* Heath text ed. 1980 $26.95. Good selection of poetry and critical articles.

McKillop, Alan D. *English Literature from Dryden to Burns.* Irvington repr. of 1948 ed. $59.50; Somerset repr. of 1948 ed. $69.00. A model of condensation and critical judgment.

Rogers, Pat. *The Augustan Vision.* Methuen 1978 $10.95. One of the best modern studies.

Sherburn, George, and Donald F. Bond. *Literary History of England: The Restoration and Eighteenth Century, 1660–1789.* Irvington 2d ed. text ed. 1967 pap. $19.95

Spacks, Patricia Meyer. *The Poetry of Vision: Five Eighteenth-Century Poets.* Harvard Univ. Pr. 1967 o.p. Brilliant study of Thomson, Collins, Smart, and Cowper.

Sutherland, James R. *Preface to Eighteenth-Century Poetry.* Oxford Pap. Ser. 1948 pap. $5.75. An invaluable introduction.

Willey, Basil. *Eighteenth-Century Background: Studies on the Idea of Nature in the Thought of the Period.* Columbia Univ. Pr. 1941 $20.00

Romantic Poetry

Abrams, Meyer H. *The English Romantic Poets: Modern Essays in Criticism.* Oxford
2d ed. 1975 pap. $9.95
————. *The Mirror and the Lamp: Romantic Theory and the Critical Tradition.* Oxford
1953 $27.50 1971 pap. $9.95. A modern classic.
Bloom, Harold. *The Visionary Company: A Reading of English Romantic Poetry.* Cornell Univ. Pr. rev. ed. 1971 pap. $14.95. Interprets Blake, Wordsworth, Cole-
ridge, Byron, Shelley, and Keats.
Bowra, C. Maurice. *The Romantic Imagination.* Oxford 1961 pap. $9.95. A study of
major English romantic poets.
Bush, Douglas. *Mythology and the Romantic Tradition in English Poetry.* Harvard
Univ. Pr. rev. ed. 1969 $32.50
Elton, Oliver. *A Survey of English Literature, 1780–1830.* Folcroft 2 vols. repr. of 1912
ed. 1977 lib. bdg. $97.50; Richard West 2 vols. repr. of 1912 ed. 1980 lib. bdg.
$100.00. Magnificently informed and insightful survey.
Gleckner, Robert, and Gerald Enscoe, eds. *Romanticism: Points of View.* Wayne
State Univ. Pr. repr. of 1962 ed. 2d ed. text ed. 1975 pap. $5.95
Herford, Charles H. *The Age of Wordsworth. Select Bibliographies Repr. Ser.* Ayer repr.
of 1897 ed. $22.00; Folcroft 1973 lib. bdg. $12.95. Dated but still valuable, espe-
cially for minor figures.
Houtchens, Carolyn Washburn, and Lawrence Huston Houtchens, eds. *The English
Romantic Poets and Essayists: A Review of Research and Criticism.* New York
Univ. Pr. rev. ed. 1966 $30.00. Includes Blake and some of the lesser romantics.
Jack, Ian. *English Literature, 1815–1832. Oxford History of Eng. Lit. Ser.* 1963 $45.00
Jordan, Frank, ed. *The English Romantic Poets: A Review of Research and Criticism.
Reviews of Research.* MLA 4th ed. rev. 1985 $37.50 pap. $20.00
Renwick, W. L. *English Literature, 1789–1815. Oxford History of Eng. Lit. Ser.* 1963
$29.95
Woodring, Carl. *Politics in English Romantic Poetry.* Harvard Univ. Pr. 1970 $25.00.
The best book on the subject.

General Books on Early British Poetry

Bateson, Frederick W. *English Poetry: A Critical Introduction.* Greenwood repr. of
1966 ed. 1978 lib. bdg. $24.75
Baugh, A. C., and others, eds. *A Literary History of England.* Prentice-Hall 2d ed. 1967
$55.95
Courthope, William J. *A History of English Poetry.* Russell 6 vols. in 3 repr. of 1895–
1910 ed. 1962 $100.00. Old-fashioned, but thorough.
Fairchild, Hoxie N. *Religious Trends in English Poetry.* Columbia Univ. Pr. 6 vols.
1942–68. ea. $42.00
Ford, Boris, ed. *The New Pelican Guide to English Literature: A Guide for Readers.* Penguin 1984 pap. $5.95. Uneven but sometimes brilliant essays by scholars influ-
enced by F. R. Leavis.
Grierson, Herbert J., and J. C. Smith. *A Critical History of English Poetry.* Arden Lib.
repr. of 1950 ed. 1979 lib. bdg. $30.00; Humanities Pr. repr. of 1963 ed. text ed.
1983 $25.50 pap. $16.50
Johnson, Samuel. *The Lives of the English Poets.* Ed. by George B. Hill, Adler's 3 vols.
repr. of 1905 ed. 1968 $159.00; ed. by George B. Hill, Octagon 3 vols. 1967 lib.
bdg. $126.50. The first and still the best study of the whole period. Johnson's of-

ten sharp and unorthodox opinions of some 50 poets—well known and less so—including Milton, Dryden, Addison, Congreve, Gay, Swift, Pope, Collins, Young, and Gray. Taken in small doses, these are entertaining and enlightening, particularly for the informed reader.

Miles, Josephine. *Eras and Modes in English Poetry.* Greenwood repr. of 1964 ed. 1976 lib. bdg. $24.75. An acute study of the language in major poets.

Preminger, Alex, ed. *The Princeton Encyclopedia of Poetry and Poetics.* Princeton Univ. Pr. rev. ed. 1974 $72.50 pap. $17.50. Indispensable. A treasure trove of information.

Saintsbury, George E. *A History of English Prosody from the 12th Century to the Present Day.* Russell 3 vols. 2d ed. repr. of 1923 ed. 1961 $40.00. Dated, but still valuable.

Tillyard, Eustace M. *The English Epic and Its Background.* Greenwood repr. of 1966 ed. 1976 lib. bdg. $42.50. A discussion of English epics from the fourteenth to the nineteenth century, with emphasis on Greek, Latin, and Italian sources.

ANTHOLOGIES OF POETRY

Old English Poetry

Crossley-Holland, Kevin. *The Anglo-Saxon World. World's Class. Ser.* Oxford 1984 pap. $6.95

Kennedy, Charles W., ed. *An Anthology of Old English Poetry.* Oxford 1960 pap. $8.95

———. *Early English Christian Poetry.* Gordon 1977 lib. bdg. $59.95; Oxford 1963 pap. $5.95

Malone, Kemp. *Ten Old English Poems Put into Modern Alliterative Verse.* Octagon repr. 1980 lib. bdg. $13.00

Pope, John C., ed. *Seven Old English Poems.* Bobbs 1966 pap. $5.55; Norton repr. of 1966 ed. text ed. 1981 pap. $8.95

Raffel, Burton. *Poems from the Old English.* Univ. of Nebraska Pr. 2d ed. rev. 1964 pap. $3.95

Sweet, Henry. *Anglo-Saxon Reader in Prose and Verse.* Ed. by Dorothy Whitelock, Oxford 15th ed. 1967 pap. $11.50. A classic text.

The Middle English Period

Brown, Carleton, ed. *English Lyrics of the Thirteenth Century.* Oxford 1932 $26.00

———. *Religious Lyrics of the Fifteenth Century.* Oxford 1939 $32.50

———. *Religious Lyrics of the Fourteenth Century.* Oxford 2d ed. 1952 $13.00

Chambers, Edmund K., and F. Sidgwick. *Early English Lyrics, Amorous, Divine, Moral and Trivial.* AMS Pr. repr. of 1921 ed. $34.50; Ayer repr. of 1926 ed. $24.50; October House 1967 $6.95 pap. $2.95

Davies, Reginald T., ed. *Medieval English Lyrics. Granger Index Repr. Ser.* Ayer repr. of 1964 ed. 1972 $21.00; Faber 1966 pap. $8.95. Contains 187 of the most interesting and best shorter poems, each with translation.

French, Walter H., and Charles B. Hale, eds. *Middle English Metrical Romances.* Russell 2 vols. in 1 repr. of 1930 ed. 1964 $32.50

Gibbs, A. C., ed. *Middle English Romances. York Medieval Texts* Northwestern Univ. Pr. 1966 $11.95. Extracts from nine romances in a brief, attractive volume, with critical notes and glossary. The *York Medieval Texts* are designed to make important Middle English writings accessible to the reader or beginning student.

Loomis, Roger S. *Mirror of Chaucer's World.* Princeton Univ. Pr. 1965 pap. $12.95. A beautiful collection of relevant pictures.

The Renaissance: The Sixteenth Century

Auden, W. H. *An Elizabethan Song Book.* Ed. by Noah Greenberg, Faber 1968 pap. $8.95

Ault, Norman, ed. *Elizabethan Lyrics from the Original Texts.* Somerset repr. of 1949 ed. 3d ed. $69.00

Bullett, Gerald, ed. *Silver Poets of the Sixteenth Century.* Biblio Dist. repr. of 1947 ed. 1978 $12.95 pap. $4.50; Folcroft repr. of 1947 ed. 1978 lib. bdg. $15.00. Sir Thomas Wyatt; Henry Howard, Earl of Surrey; Sir Philip Sidney; Sir Walter Raleigh; Sir John Davies. Good biographical information in the introduction.

Cain, T. G., ed. *Jacobean and Caroline Poetry: An Anthology.* Methuen 1981 pap. $10.95. A generous, up-to-date selection.

Chambers, Edmund K., ed. *Oxford Book of Sixteenth-Century Verse.* Oxford 1932 $45.00

MacDonald, Hugh, ed. *Englands Helicon.* Harvard Univ. Pr. 1949 pap. $7.95

Sylvester, Richard S., ed. *Anchor Anthology of Sixteenth-Century Verse.* Doubleday (Anchor) 1974 pap. $6.95; Peter Smith $17.25

The Renaissance: The Early Seventeenth Century

Brinkley, Roberta F., ed. *English Poetry of the Seventeenth Century.* Norton rev. ed. 1936 pap. $8.95

Clayton, Thomas. *The Cavalier Poets.* Oxford Stand. Authors Ser. text ed. 1978 pap. $6.95. Highly recommended.

Gardner, Helen. *The Metaphysical Poets.* Oxford 2d ed. 1967 $14.95; *Penguin Poets Ser.* 1960 pap. $4.95. More than 200 poems by some 40 poets, among them Donne, Herbert, Crashaw, Vaughan; provides explanatory and biographical notes.

Grierson, Herbert J., and Geoffrey Bullough, eds. *Oxford Book of Seventeenth-Century Verse.* Oxford 1934 $45.00

Howarth, R. G., ed. *Minor Poets of the Seventeenth Century.* Biblio Dist. 1953 $12.95

Lewalski, Barbara K., and A. J. Sabol, eds. *Major Poets of the Earlier Seventeenth Century.* Bobbs 1973 o.p. Copious selections from Donne, Herbert, Vaughan, Crashaw, Jonson, Herrick, and Marvell.

Sylvester, R. S., ed. *The Anchor Anthology of Seventeenth Century Verse.* Peter Smith 2 vols. $17.25. Volume 1 is a full collection of metaphysical verse, a revised and enlarged edition of Martz's *The Meditative Poem.* Volume 2 is a full collection of Jonsonian and Cavalier verse.

The Restoration and the Eighteenth Century

Bredvold, L. I., and others, eds. *Eighteenth-Century Poetry and Prose.* Wiley 3d ed. text ed. 1973 $25.95

Lonsdale, Roger, ed. *The New Oxford Book of Eighteenth-Century Verse.* Oxford 1985 $25.00. A huge, original selection.

Mahoney, John L., ed. *The Enlightenment and English Literature: Prose and Poetry of the Eighteenth Century with Selected Modern Critical Essays.* Heath text ed. 1980 $26.95

Pinto, Vivian de Sola. *Poetry of the Restoration, 1653–1700.* Heinemann text ed. 1966 pap. $5.00

Tillotson, Geoffrey, and others. *Eighteenth-Century English Literature.* Harcourt text ed. 1969 $28.95

Romantic Poetry

Bernbaum, Ernest, ed. *Anthology of Romanticism.* Wiley 3d ed. enl. 1948 $15.50. A pioneering text that remains one of the very best.

Mahoney, John L., ed. *The English Romantics: Major Poetry and Critical Theory.* Heath text ed. 1978 $21.95

Noyes, Russell, ed. *English Romantic Poetry and Prose.* Oxford 1956 $29.95

Perkins, David, ed. *English Romantic Writers.* Harcourt text ed. 1967 $28.95. An anthology of both poetry and prose, concentrating on 20 major authors. Includes biographical information and a bibliography for each.

Reeves, James, ed. *Five Late Romantic Poets.* Heinemann text ed. 1974 pap. $5.00

Popular Ballads

[SEE page 127 in this volume.]

BEOWULF. c.750 A.D.

The oldest English epic, one of the oldest in any Teutonic language, written in strongly accentual alliterative verse, celebrates in two parts the feats of the hero Beowulf in Denmark and Sweden. It contains both pagan and Christian elements and is evidently older than the one extant manuscript, in the British Museum, written by two scribes about the year 1000. This copy was owned by a sixteenth-century British collector, Sir Robert Bruce Cotton, whose descendants turned his library over to the government in 1700. Much of the collection was destroyed in a fire in 1731. An Icelandic scholar, Grimur Jonsson Thorkelin, in London looking for historical data, copied *Beowulf* without realizing its literary significance. His transcripts, in the Great Royal Museum of Denmark, survived the British bombardment of Copenhagen in 1807 and are part of an ambitious plan to preserve valuable Anglo-Saxon manuscripts.

EDITIONS OF BEOWULF

Beowulf and the Fight at Finnsburg. Ed. by F. Klaeber, Heath 3d ed. 1936 pap. $20.95. With bibliography, notes, and glossary. Considered the best edition.

Beowulf and Judith, Done in a Normalized Orthography. Ed. by Francis P. Magoun, Jr., Harvard Univ. Pr. rev. ed. 1966 pap. $3.50

Beowulf. Ed. by D. H. Crawford, Cooper Square Pr. repr. of 1926 ed. $17.50; trans. by Burton Raffel, New Amer. Lib. pap. $1.95; trans. by E. Talbot Donaldson, ed. by Joseph F. Tuso, Norton text ed. 1975 pap. $4.95; ed. by Charles Keeping and Kevin Crossley-Holland, Oxford $11.95; trans. by Michael Alexander, *Penguin Class. Ser.* 1973 pap. $2.25; ed. by Whitney F. Bolton, St. Martin's text ed. 1982 $16.95

BOOKS ABOUT BEOWULF

Chambers, Raymond W., ed. *Beowulf: An Introduction*. Cambridge Univ. Pr. 1959
$65.00. The authoritative, indispensable critical work.

Fry, Donald K. *Beowulf and the Fight at Finnsburg: A Bibliography*. Univ. Pr. of Virginia 1969 $15.00

Nicholson, Lewis E., ed. *An Anthology of Beowulf Criticism*. Essay Index Repr. Ser.
Ayer repr. of 1963 ed. $17.75; Univ. of Notre Dame Pr. 1963 pap. $9.95. Major articles from British and American scholarly journals.

Tolkien, J. R. *Beowulf: The Monster and the Critics*. Folcroft repr. of 1936 ed. lib. bdg.
$15.00

Tripp, Raymond P., Jr. *More about the Fight with the Dragon: Beowulf 2208B–3182,
Commentary, Edition, and Translation*. Univ. Pr. of Amer. 1983 lib. bdg. $33.75
text ed. pap. $19.50

Williams, David. *Cain and Beowulf: A Study in Secular Allegory*. Univ. of Toronto Pr.
1981 $25.00

BLAKE, WILLIAM. 1757-1827

Blake, an engraver by training, is unique in English literature as a man who was a great pictorial artist as well as a great poet. He printed and published all his own works. Every page was hand-lettered, and had to be cut in reverse, mirror fashion, in copper, before being printed. It was then ornamented and illustrated and painted over in water colors by the poet-engraver and his wife. Every copy was in a sense a first edition because every copy differs from every other copy. Blake's illustrations of the Book of Job, reproduced in *Blake's Job* and for Blair's *Grave* (published as *Blake's Grave*), are his masterpieces. He also illustrated DANTE (see Vol. 2), Thomas Gray, *The Canterbury Pilgrims*, and *Paradise Lost*.

Blake was a visionary whose social criticism was much ahead of his day. He worked as an illustrator and engraver against financial odds and in poor health—for clients whom his independence often displeased—assisted by his acquiescent and childless wife and encouraged by a few believing friends. He was quite isolated from other poets of his time and was usually considered slightly mad when noticed at all in the literary world. But the short poems of the *Innocence* (1789) and *Experience* (1794) volumes—such as *The Tyger*—have come to be recognized as among the finest and most enduring of the English language. The long and difficult "Prophetic Books" develop an elaborate religious mythology, which Blake said he derived from his "visions." He was a Christian with a difference, despising the hypocrisy he found in religious institutions and preaching a sort of natural Christianity in which human beings were free to develop—and to love each other—without artificial restraints. His genius has been fully appreciated only in the twentieth century, and an enormous body of commentary has developed around all his works. Even his most complex "prophetic" poems are now held to be fully intelligible, and the simplest of his lyrics may contain the essence of a profound philosophy. Critical disputes abound and sharply divergent interpretations are commonplace.

BOOKS BY BLAKE

The Complete Poetry and Prose of William Blake. Ed. by David V. Erdman, commentary by Harold Bloom, Univ. of California Pr. rev. ed. 1981 $38.50. One of the three standard editions. Punctuation sparse and Bloom's readings, highly influential, are often eccentric. See entries for Keynes and Bentley editions below.

Selected Prose and Poetry. Ed. by Northrop Frye, *Modern College Lib. Ser.* Random text ed. 1966 pap. $4.95. Judicious selection, introduction, and notes by a preeminent Blake scholar.

William Blake's Poetry and Designs. Ed. by John E. Grant and Mary L. Johnson, *Norton Critical Eds.* 1979 pap. $12.95. An especially useful volume. Valuable criticism and good bibliography.

Complete Writings of William Blake, with Variant Readings. Ed. by Geoffrey Keynes, *Oxford Stand. Authors Ser.* 1966 $39.95 pap. $9.95. Long the standard edition, it remains the easiest to use.

William Blake's Writings. Ed. by Gerald E. Bentley, Jr. *Oxford Eng. Texts Ser.* 2 vols. 1979 $185.00. Not quite as easy to use as the Keynes edition above, but more reliable than the Erdman edition below.

Portable Blake. Ed. by Alfred Kazin, *Viking Portable Lib.* Penguin 1977 pap. $7.95; Viking 1956 $14.95. Good introduction.

Poems and Prophecies. Ed. by Max Plowman, Biblio Dist. (Everyman's) repr. of 1927 ed. 1978 $9.95 pap. $3.50

Blake's America, a Prophecy, and Europe, a Prophecy. Fine Arts Ser. Dover 1984 pap. $5.95

William Blake's Illustrations of the Book of Job. Ed. by S. Foster Damon, Univ. Pr. of New England 1966 $17.50 1982 pap. $8.95

Tiriel. 1789. Ed. by Gerald E. Bentley, Jr. Oxford 1967 o.p. A reproduction of the drawings and a commentary on the poem.

The Book of Thel: A Facsimile and a Critical Text. 1789. Ed. by Nancy Bogen, fwd. by David V. Erdman, NYPL 1971 $20.00. A reproduction in full color of the copy in the Berg Collection of the New York Public Library. The textual annotations are based on all the extant original copies. A new interpretation is given in the foreword.

The Marriage of Heaven and Hell, Combined with Songs of Innocence and of Experience. 1790. Oxford 2 vols. 1975 $34.00

Songs of Innocence and of Experience. 1794. Dover repr. of 1954 ed. 1971 pap. $3.00; ed. by Ruthven Todd, Folcroft repr. of 1794 ed. lib. bdg. $16.50; intro. by Geoffrey Keynes, Oxford 1977 $19.95 pap. $9.95

The Book of Urizen. 1794. Univ. of Miami Pr. 1966 pap. $6.95

BOOKS ABOUT BLAKE

Bentley, Gerald E., Jr., ed. *William Blake: The Critical Heritage. Critical Heritage Ser.* Routledge & Kegan 1975 $29.00. Especially valuable in demonstrating the extraordinary shifts in the critical attitudes toward Blake.

Blackstone, Bernard. *English Blake.* Shoe String (Archon) repr. of 1949 ed. 1966 $27.00

Bloom, Harold. *Blake's Apocalypse.* Cornell Univ. Pr. 1970 o.p.

Bronowski, Jacob. *William Blake: A Man without a Mask.* Gordon 1976 lib. bdg. $59.95; Haskell repr. of 1947 ed. 1969 lib. bdg. $49.95

Damon, S. Foster. *A Blake Dictionary: The Ideas and Symbols of William Blake.* Shambhala 1979 pap. $15.00; Univ. Pr. of New England text ed. 1965 $40.00. An extremely useful guide to the meanings of Blake's language and symbols, but must be supplemented by opposing views.

———. *William Blake: His Philosophy and Symbols.* Peter Smith $20.25. One of the pioneering books in the modern study of Blake and still indispensable.

Erdman, David V. *Blake: Prophet against Empire.* Princeton Univ. Pr. rev. ed. 1969 $47.00 pap. $15.95. Demonstrates Blake's unexpectedly deep involvement in the political controversies of his day.

———. *Concordance to the Writings of William Blake.* Concordance Ser. Cornell Univ. Pr. 2 vols. 1968 $95.00

Fisher, Peter. *The Valley of Vision: Blake as Prophet and Revolutionary.* Ed. by Northrop Frye, Univ. of Toronto Pr. 1961 o.p. A basic guide to Blake's thought.

Frye, Northrop. *Fearful Symmetry: A Study of William Blake.* Princeton Univ. Pr. 1947 pap. $9.95. Perhaps the most influential study of Blake ever written.

Gilchrist, Alexander. *The Life of William Blake.* Ed. by Ruthven Todd, Biblio Dist. (Everyman's) repr. of 1945 ed. 1982 text ed. pap. $8.95; Rowman repr. of 1880 ed. 1973 $20.00. The first life; flawed, but still a necessary source.

Gleckner, Robert. *The Piper and the Bard: A Study of William Blake.* Wayne State Univ. Pr. 1959 $9.95

Murry, John M. *William Blake.* Folcroft repr. of 1933 ed. lib. bdg. $17.50; Haskell repr. of 1933 ed. 1971 lib. bdg. $49.95

Percival, Milton O. *William Blake's Circle of Destiny.* Octagon 1964 lib. bdg. $27.50. A controversial guide to Blake's thought.

Schorer, Mark. *William Blake: The Politics of Vision.* Peter Smith $11.50. An interpretation of the moral and intellectual structure of Blake's "visionary" art.

Swinburne, Algernon C. *William Blake: A Critical Essay.* Ayer repr. of 1868 ed. $25.50; Folcroft 1973 lib. bdg. $39.50; ed. by Hugh J. Luke, Univ. of Nebraska Pr. (Bison) 1970 pap. $4.75

Wilkie, Brian, and Mary Lynn Johnson. *Blake's Four Zoas: The Design of a Dream.* Harvard Univ. Pr. 1978 $17.50

Wilson, Mona. *The Life of William Blake.* Cooper Square Pr. repr. of 1927 ed. 1969 $24.00; ed. by Geoffrey Keynes, Oxford 3d ed. 1971 $23.95. Not altogether reliable, but highly readable.

BURNS, ROBERT. 1759–1796

Robert Burns, the greatest of Scotland's poets, and for generations one of the most popular of all poets, has been shockingly neglected in recent years, possibly because of the direct appeal of his work. Songs like "Auld Lang Syne" and "A Red, Red Rose" are loved everywhere, and poems like *Tam O'Shanter* and *To a Mouse* are universal favorites. His love lyrics are irresistible, his celebrations of the joy of drinking and hearty companionship are inimitable. He was also a master satirist, as his devastating attack on religious hypocrisy, *Holy Willie's Prayer*, demonstrates. Burns was the son of a poor farmer, but was far better educated than the early legends allowed. His first book, *Poems, Chiefly in the Scottish Dialect*, printed at Kilmarnock in 1786, raised him from obscurity to great though short-lived fame. Burns struggled for the rest of his life against poverty, occasional hard drinking, a highly volatile temperament, and a passionate nature. Many legends followed upon his early death, many of them quite false, and they have clouded his reputation ever since. Almost all his great poems are in the Scots dialect, but are easily accessible.

BOOKS BY BURNS

Poems and Songs of Robert Burns. Ed. by James Kinsley, *Oxford Eng. Texts Ser.* 3 vols. 1968 $149.00. Supersedes all previous editions. Includes all extant poems and songs, with their eighteenth-century musical settings. The third volume contains invaluable notes on the texts in the previous volumes.

Poems and Songs. Beekman 1978 $9.95; ed. by James Kinsley, *Oxford Stand. Authors Ser.* 1969 $35.00 pap. $12.95

Songs of Robert Burns. Ed. by James C. Dick, AMS Pr. repr. of 1903 ed. $37.50. Contains words and music of all 361 songs with James Dick's notes; includes bibliography and indexes of first lines and tunes.

The Letters of Robert Burns. Ed. by J. De Lancey Ferguson and G. Ross Roy, Oxford 2 vols. 2d ed. 1985 ea. $65.00

The Merry Muses of Caledonia. c.1800. Ed. by James Barke and Sidney G. Smith, State Mutual Bk. 1983 $35.00

The Jolly Beggars. Ed. by John C. Weston, Univ. of Massachusetts Pr. 1967 $6.00

Poems, Chiefly in the Scottish Dialect. AMS Pr. repr. of 1786 ed. $12.50

BOOKS ABOUT BURNS

Crawford, Thomas. *Burns: A Study of the Poems and Songs.* Stanford Univ. Pr. 1960 $30.00 pap. $8.95. One of the best critical studies and particularly good on Burns's sources.

Daiches, David. *Robert Burns and His World.* Thames & Hudson 1978 $8.95. A delightful, frank, and erudite study, more critical than biographical.

Ferguson, J. De Lancey. *Pride and Passion: Robert Burns, 1759–1796.* Russell repr. of 1939 ed. 1964 $15.00

Lindsay, Maurice. *The Burns Encyclopedia.* St. Martin's 1980 $17.95

Lockhart, John G. *Life of Robert Burns.* Ed. by William S. Douglas, AMS Pr. repr. of 1892 ed. $20.00; Biblio Dist. (Everyman's) 1976 $12.95. The best of the older biographies.

Low, Donald A., ed. *Robert Burns: The Critical Heritage. Critical Heritage Ser.* Routledge & Kegan 1974 $38.00 1984 pap. $15.00

Reid, J. B. *A Complete Word and Phrase Concordance to the Poems and Songs of Robert Burns.* Burt Franklin repr. of 1889 ed. 1969 $30.50; Richard West repr. of 1889 ed. 1977 lib. bdg. $65.00; Russell repr. of 1889 ed. 1967 $25.00. Includes a glossary of Scots words, with notes, index, and appendix of readings.

Snyder, Franklin B. *The Life of Robert Burns.* Shoe String (Archon) repr. of 1932 ed. 1968 $32.00. Probably the most reliable biography.

BYRON, GEORGE GORDON NOËL, 6th Baron Byron. 1788–1824

Byron's life was so spectacularly glamorous and notorious that it is almost impossible to disentangle fact from legend. At his death, fighting for the liberation of Greece, he was among the most famous people in Europe. Handsome, club-footed, a lord of the realm, irresistible to women, precocious physically and intellectually, he was also a dazzlingly gifted poet whose genius embraced satire both in the eighteenth-century tradition of Pope and in swashbuckling narratives of picturesque adventure.

Both gifts were displayed early. *English Bards and Scotch Reviewers* (o.p.), a devastating attack on certain critics, was published when he was just age 21. *Childe Harold's Pilgrimage*, published at age 24, made him famous overnight. This long narrative poem of exotic travels also featured the first appearance of the "Byronic hero," a powerful, mysterious figure, haunted by some nameless and unspeakable crime. Byron dashed off a long series of immensely popular romantic tales that are little read today.

As a result of a scandalous divorce and rampant rumor of dark crimes, Byron was hounded out of England and spent the rest of his life in Europe, mainly in Italy. Here his art deepened and he turned increasingly to social and political satire. His masterpiece, *Don Juan* (1819–24), unfinished in 16 long cantos, is founded on the old Spanish saga made supremely famous by Mozart's *Don Giovanni*. Often neglected in the nineteenth century, *Don Juan* has come to be ranked among the comic and satirical masterpieces of English poetry.

BOOKS BY BYRON

Works. Ed. by E. H. Coleridge and R. E. Prothero, Octagon 13 vols. 1967 lib. bdg. $518.00. Although the texts of both the poetry and the prose have been superseded by the editions of McGann and Marchand (cited below), this edition is very rich in notes and supporting materials much worth consulting.

The Complete Poetical Works of Byron. Ed. by Jerome J. McGann, *Oxford Eng. Texts Ser.* vols. 2–3 1980–81 ea. $105.00 pap. ea. $64.00. When complete will supersede all previous editions.

Byron's Poetry. Ed. by Frank D. McConnell, *Norton Critical Eds.* text ed. 1978 $12.95 pap. $9.95. Judicious selection, important critical articles, and excellent bibliography to 1978.

Byron's Letters and Journals. Ed. by Leslie A. Marchand, Harvard Univ. Pr. 12 vols. 1973–85 ea. $15.00–$18.50. The only unexpurgated edition of Byron's incomparably vivid correspondence. A fine one-volume selection, published in 1984, is available from Harvard University Press.

Byron: A Self-Portrait. Ed. by Peter Quennell, Humanities Pr. 2 vols. 1967 $30.00

Byron's Hebrew Melodies. Ed. by Thomas L. Ashton, Univ. of Texas Pr. 1971 $16.95

Childe Harold's Pilgrimage (1812–1818). Ed. by Samuel C. Chew, Odyssey Pr. 1936 o.p. Superb notes.

Don Juan. 1819–24. Amereon $24.95; ed. by Leslie A. Marchand, Houghton Mifflin 1958 pap. $6.50; ed. by W. W. Pratt, *Yale Eng. Poets Ser.* text ed. 1982 $31.00 pap. $9.95

BOOKS ABOUT BYRON

Asimov, Isaac. *Asimov's Annotated Don Juan.* Doubleday 1972 $29.95

Boyd, Elizabeth F. *Byron's Don Juan: A Critical Study.* Humanities Pr. repr. of 1945 ed. 1975 $13.00

Dubois, Charles. *Byron and the Need of Fatality.* Haskell repr. of 1932 ed. 1970 lib. bdg. $49.95. An old but still influential study by an eminent French scholar.

Faulkner, Claude W. *Byron's Political Verse Satire.* Folcroft repr. of 1947 ed. lib. bdg. $8.50

Fuess, Claude M. *Lord Byron as a Satirist in Verse.* Haskell 1974 lib. bdg. $39.95

Gleckner, Robert F. *Byron and the Ruins of Paradise.* Greenwood repr. of 1967 ed. 1980 lib. bdg. $37.50

Guiccoli, Countess. *My Recollections of Lord Byron.* Gordon $59.95

Hagelman, Charles W., Jr., and Robert J. Barnes, eds. *Concordance to Byron's "Don Juan."* Concordance Ser. Cornell Univ. Pr. 1967 $57.50

Hogg, James. *New Light on Byron. Salzburg Studies in Eng. Lit., Romantic Reassessment* Humanities Pr. text ed. 1978 pap. $25.50

Hunt, Leigh. *Lord Byron and Some of His Contemporaries.* AMS Pr. repr. of 1828 ed. $25.00

James, D. G. *Byron and Shelley.* Folcroft repr. of 1951 ed. lib. bdg. $9.50

Lovell, Ernest J., Jr., ed. *His Very Self and Voice: Collected Conversations of Lord Byron.* Octagon repr. of 1954 ed. 1980 lib. bdg. $56.00

———. *Lady Blessington's Conversations of Lord Byron.* Princeton Univ. Pr. 1969 $26.00

Manning, Peter J. *Byron and His Fictions.* Wayne State Univ. Pr. 1978 $17.50

Marchand, Leslie A. *Byron: A Portrait.* Univ. of Chicago Pr. 1979 pap. $7.95. A one-volume condensation of the standard biography.

———. *Byron's Poetry: A Critical Introduction.* Harvard Univ. Pr. 1965 $14.00. A masterful distillation of learning and critical acumen.

Marshall, William H. *The Structure of Byron's Major Poems.* Univ. of Pennsylvania Pr. 1974 pap. $7.95

Martin, Philip W. *Byron: A Poet before His Public.* Cambridge Univ. Pr. 1982 $42.50 pap. $13.95. Provocative, dissenting estimate of Byron's poetry.

Maurois, André. *Byron.* Arden Lib. repr. of 1930 ed. 1979 lib. bdg. $22.50; Ungar $20.00

McGann, Jerome J. *Don Juan in Context.* Univ. of Chicago Pr. 1976 lib. bdg. $16.00

———. *Fiery Dust: Byron's Poetic Development.* Univ. of Chicago Pr. 1980 $22.00. A brilliant work by a preeminent Byron scholar.

Nicolson, Harold G. *The Poetry of Byron.* Folcroft repr. of 1943 ed. lib. bdg. $9.50; Richard West repr. of 1943 ed. 1980 lib. bdg. $10.00

Quennell, Peter. *Byron: The Years of Fame.* Haskell 1974 lib. bdg. $39.95; Merrimack 1978 $16.95; Shoe String (Archon) rev. ed. 1967 $18.50. Highly readable, as is *Byron in Italy* (below).

———. *Byron in Italy.* Ayer repr. of 1941 ed. $16.25

Raphael, Frederic. *Byron.* Thames & Hudson 1982 $18.95

Robson, W. W. *Byron as Poet.* Folcroft repr. of 1957 ed. lib. bdg. $12.50

Rutherford, Andrew. *Byron: A Critical Study.* Stanford Univ. Pr. 1961 $20.00 pap. $7.95

Thomas, Gordon K. *Lord Byron's Iberian Pilgrimage.* Brigham Young Univ Pr. 1983 pap. $7.95

Trelawney, Edward J. *Recollections of the Last Days of Shelley and Byron. Select Bibliographies Reprint Ser.* Ayer repr. of 1906 ed. $17.00; Richard West repr. of 1906 ed. 1973 $10.95

Young, Ione D., ed. *A Concordance to the Poetry of Byron.* I. Young 4 vols. repr. of 1975 ed. $32.00

CAMPION, THOMAS. 1567–1620

A practicing physician throughout his life, Campion wrote poetry, songs, masques, and a treatise on music and poetry. In his introduction to Campion's collected works, Walter R. Davis says, "Campion's pursuit of the movements of sound is recorded in that strange but subtle treatise, *Observations in the Art of English Poesie* [1602], and its fruits are preserved in his songbooks. He is a poet—perhaps *the* poet—of the auditory rather than the visual imagination. . . . He offers us experiences that strike the ear."

BOOKS BY CAMPION

Works of Thomas Campion. Ed. by Walter R. Davis, *Norton Lib.* 1970 pap. $2.95; ed. by Percival Vivian, *Oxford Eng. Texts Ser.* 1909 $34.95
The Selected Songs of Thomas Campion. Intro. by John Hollander, Godine 1972 $15.00 1974 pap. $7.50
Songs and Masques: With Observations in the Art of English Poesy. Ed. by A. H. Bullen, Folcroft repr. of 1889 ed. 1973 lib. bdg. $30.00

BOOKS ABOUT CAMPION

Kastendieck, Miles M. *England's Musical Poet: Thomas Campion.* 1938. Russell 1963 o.p.
Lowbury, Edward, and others. *Thomas Campion: Poet, Composer, Physician.* Barnes & Noble 1970 o.p.

CHATTERTON, THOMAS. 1752–1770

Chatterton has long been regarded as the archetypal poet of romantic legend. He was born very poor, and his poetic genius flowered earlier than that of any other English poet. He perpetrated a hoax in pretending that he had discovered an ancient manuscript of poems by Thomas Rowley, a fifteenth-century poet-priest. They were his own work, and as his deception was about to be discovered he committed suicide, a few months before his eighteenth birthday. Chatterton is an important figure in the development of romanticism, but his poems are valuable in their own right. One of Coleridge's early poems is a *Monody on the Death of Chatterton.*

BOOKS BY CHATTERTON

The Complete Works of Thomas Chatterton. Ed. by Donald S. Taylor and B. B. Hoover, *Oxford Eng. Texts Ser.* 2 vols. $89.00. The standard edition.
The Rowley Poems. Ed. by S. E. Hare, Somerset repr. of 1911 ed. $21.00. Good introduction.

BOOK ABOUT CHATTERTON

Meyerstein, Edward H. *A Life of Thomas Chatterton.* Richard West repr. of 1930 ed. $24.50; Russell repr. of 1930 ed. 1972 $25.00. The standard life.

CHAUCER, GEOFFREY. 1340?–1400

Chaucer has been called the "Prince of Story-tellers" because of his great narrative skill, his acute penetration, his mixture of humor and somber realism, and his remarkable accuracy in describing the real world. The technical perfection and extraordinary grace of Chaucer's verse are a discovery of recent centuries. His work has often been divided into three major periods: French, Italian, and English. In the first he was influenced by the major French poets of the time; the second results from his trip to Italy, and especially the influence of Boccaccio; the final English period includes his greatest works, especially *The Canterbury Tales* (1387–1400) and *Troilus and Criseyde* (c.1385). The sources and dates of many Chaucer works remain disputed, nor are all questions of authorship settled.

The Canterbury Tales is one of the world's chief collections of stories. Many of the tales are borrowed from BOCCACCIO's (see Vol. 2) *Decameron;* few, if any, are Chaucer's own invention. (Originality was not, at this time, regarded as a literary virtue.) The 24 stories are supposed to be told by pilgrims journeying on horseback from the Tabard Inn, Southwark, to the shrine of the martyred St. Thomas of Becket in Canterbury Cathedral. Chaucer never completed his vast scheme, which might have summarized the whole of medieval society. What he did achieve fully justifies Dryden's immortal statement: "Here is God's plenty."

His poems are usually printed today with a glossary, as a key to his Middle English, but it will be found that his language does not vary from our own nearly so much in vocabulary as in spelling.

Of the *Canterbury Tales*, any list of the best and most popular would include *The Pardoner's Tale, The Wife of Bath's Prologue and Tale, The Merchant's Tale, The Clerk's Tale* (of Patient Griselda), and *The Nun's Priest's Tale* (of Chanticleer and the Fox). *Troilus and Cressida*, a separate narrative of well-ordered plot, shows the influence of Italian literature. *The House of Fame* (o.p.), borrowed from Ovid's *Metamorphoses*, and *The Legend of Good Women* (o.p.)—among whom he numbers Cleopatra, Medea, and Ariadne—are his other important works. Chaucer is the greatest poet of his age and one of the three or four major figures in the history of English poetry. Modern English derives from the Middle English London dialect in which he wrote—basically a fusion of Norman and Saxon speech.

Chaucer created and used two metrical forms: the seven-line stanza, which was later called "rime royal" because James I of Scotland used it in *The King's Quair*, and the rhyming or "heroic" couplet. Chaucer's later and best work was done in such couplets, the form of *The Knight's Tale, The Nun's Priest's Tale*, and *The Legend of Good Women*.

Son of a London wine merchant, Chaucer served as a page to Elizabeth, Countess of Ulster; as a soldier in Edward's army in France; as a diplomat; and as a government official in various capacities. He is buried in Westminster Abbey, which eventually established a "Poet's Corner" for the interment of such great literary figures.

BOOKS BY CHAUCER

Works of Geoffrey Chaucer. Ed. by F. N. Robinson, *New Cambridge Eds.* Houghton Mifflin 2d ed. text ed. 1957 $29.95. Best one-volume edition.

Complete Works. Ed. by Walter W. Skeat, Oxford 7 vols. 2d ed. 1894–1900 $195.00. Still the basic text.

The Complete Poetry and Prose of Geoffrey Chaucer. Ed. by John H. Fisher, Holt text ed. 1977 $39.00

Geoffrey Chaucer: A Selection of His Works. Ed. by Kenneth Kee, *College Class. in Eng. Ser.* Odyssey Pr. 1966 pap. $5.95

Chaucer's Poetry: An Anthology for the Modern Reader. Ed. by E. Talbot Donaldson, Ronald Pr. 1958 o.p. Admirably organized.

The Canterbury Tales. Ed. by A. Kent Hieatt and Constance Hieatt, Bantam 1981 pap. $2.95; Biblio Dist. 1976 $12.95 pap. $3.95; ed. by John Halverson, *Lib. of Lit.* Bobbs text ed. 1971 pap. $12.19; ed. by Donald R. Howard and James M. Dean, New Amer. Lib. (Signet Class.) 1969 pap. $2.95; ed. by Walter W. Skeat, *World's Class. Ser.* Oxford $15.59; trans. by Nevill Coghill, *Penguin Class. Ser.* 1951 pap. $2.95; ed. by Diane Stewart, Raintree 1981 $15.15 1983 pap. $9.27; trans. by R. M. Lumiansky, Washington Square Pr. pap. $3.95

Canterbury Tales of Geoffrey Chaucer. Ed. by Daniel Cook, Doubleday (Anchor) abr. ed. pap. $2.95

The Canterbury Tales (Selected): An Interlinear Translation. Ed. by Vincent F. Hopper, Barron text ed. 1970 pap. $6.95

Clerk's Prologue and Tale. Ed. by James Winny, Cambridge Univ. Pr. text ed. 1966 $5.95

Franklin's Prologue and Tale. Ed. by A. C. Spearing, Cambridge Univ. Pr. text ed. $5.95

The Friar's Summoner and Pardoner's Tales. Ed. by N. R. Havely, Holmes & Meier $16.50 pap. $9.00

The General Prologue to the Canterbury Tales. Ed. by James Winny, Cambridge Univ. Pr. text ed. 1965 $5.95; ed. by Phyllis Hodgson, Longwood Pr. 1969 pap. $8.95

Merchant's Prologue and Tale. Ed. by M. Hussey, Cambridge Univ. Pr. text ed. 1966 $5.95

Nun's Priest's Prologue and Tale. Ed. by M. Hussey, Cambridge Univ. Pr. text ed. 1966 $5.95

The Knight's Tale or Palamon and Arcite by Geoffrey Chaucer Done into Modern English by the Rev. Professor Walter W. Skeat. Ed. by Walter W. Skeat, Richard West repr. of 1904 ed. lib. bdg. $25.00

Pardoner's Prologue and Tale. Ed. by A. C. Spearing, Cambridge Univ. Pr. text ed. 1966 $5.95

The Portable Chaucer. Ed. by Theodore Morrison, *Viking Portable Lib*. Penguin rev. ed. 1977 pap. $7.95

The Prioress' Prologue and Tale. Ed. by James Winny, Cambridge Univ. Pr. text ed. 1974 pap. $5.95

The Reeve's Prologue and Tale. Ed. by A. C. Spearing, Cambridge Univ. Pr. 1979 $5.95

Troilus and Cressida in Modern English Verse. Trans. by George F. Krapp, Random (Vintage) 1957 pap. $3.95

Troilus and Criseyde. Biblio Dist. 1974 $9.95 pap. $6.95; ed. by Barry A. Windeatt, Longman text ed. 1983 pap. $90.00

Wife of Bath's Prologue and Tale. Ed. by James Winny, Cambridge Univ. Pr. text ed. 1966 $5.95

BOOKS ABOUT CHAUCER

Baugh, Albert C., ed. *Chaucer. Goldentree Bibliographies in Language and Lit. Ser.* Harlan Davidson text ed. 1977 pap. $13.95

———. *Chaucer's Major Poetry*. Prentice-Hall 1963 $28.95

Bennett, Henry S. *Chaucer and the Fifteenth Century. Oxford History of Eng. Lit. Ser.* 1947 $42.50

Bowden, Muriel. *A Reader's Guide to Geoffrey Chaucer*. Farrar 1964 pap. $2.25; Octagon 1971 lib. bdg. $18.50

Brewer, Derek, ed. *Chaucer: The Critical Heritage. Critical Heritage Ser.* Routledge & Kegan 2 vols. 1978 $50.00

Coghill, Nevill. *The Poet Chaucer.* Oxford 2d ed. 1967 pap. $3.50

Donaldson, E. Talbot. *Speaking of Chaucer.* Labyrinth Pr. repr. of 1970 ed. 1983 pap. $7.95; *Norton Lib.* repr. of 1970 ed. 1972 pap. $3.95. Fine guide.

French, Robert D. *A Chaucer Handbook.* AMS Pr. repr. of 1947 ed. 2d ed. $35.00

Hinckley, Henry B. *Notes on Chaucer: A Commentary on the Prologue and Six of the Canterbury Tales.* Haskell repr. of 1907 ed. 1972 lib. bdg. $49.95

Huppe, Bernard F. *A Reading of the Canterbury Tales.* State Univ. of New York repr. of 1964 ed. $29.50 pap. $7.95

Hussey, S. S. *Chaucer: An Introduction.* Methuen 2d ed. 1981 $22.00 pap. $10.50

Kean, P. M. *Chaucer and the Making of English Poetry.* Routledge & Kegan 2d ed. 1982 pap. $12.95

Ker, William P. *Essays on Medieval Literature.* Folcroft repr. of 1905 ed. lib. bdg. $32.00

Kerhof, J. *Studies in the Language of Geoffrey Chaucer.* Folcroft repr. of 1966 ed. lib. bdg. $30.00

Kiser, Lisa J. *Telling Classical Tales: Chaucer and the "Legend of Good Women."* Cornell Univ. Pr. 1983 $19.50. A brilliant study.

Kittredge, George L. *Chaucer and His Poetry.* Intro. by B. J. Whiting, Harvard Univ. Pr. 1970 $10.00 pap. $2.95

Lowes, John L. *Art of Geoffrey Chaucer. Select Bibliographies Repr. Ser.* Ayer repr. of 1930 ed. $12.00; Folcroft repr. of 1930 ed. lib. bdg. $8.50. A superb book, still fresh.

Lumiansky, R. M. *Of Sondry Folke: The Dramatic Principle in the "Canterbury Tales."* Univ. of Texas Pr. 1980 pap. $8.95

Malone, Kemp. *Chapters on Chaucer.* Greenwood repr. of 1951 ed. 1979 lib. bdg. $27.50

Owen, Charles A., ed. *Discussions of the Canterbury Tales.* Greenwood repr. of 1961 ed. 1978 lib. bdg. $19.75

Robertson, D. W. *Preface to Chaucer: Studies in Medieval Perspectives.* Princeton Univ. Pr. 1962 pap. $19.50. Lively and digestible.

Root, Robert K. *The Poetry of Chaucer: A Guide to Its Study and Appreciation.* Gordon $59.95; Peter Smith rev. ed. $11.25; Somerset repr. of 1957 ed. $20.00

Rowland, Beryl, ed. *Companion to Chaucer Studies.* Oxford rev. ed. text ed. 1979 pap. $12.95. An extremely useful introduction especially for those with limited library facilities. A whole range of Chaucer scholarship written by major authorities. Excellent bibliographies at the end of each chapter.

Traversi, Derek. *The Canterbury Tales: A Reading.* Univ. of Delaware Pr. 1983 $25.00

Wagenknecht, Edward, ed. *Chaucer: Modern Essays in Criticism.* Oxford 1959 pap. $9.95

COLERIDGE, SAMUEL TAYLOR. 1772–1834

Coleridge wrote almost all his great poems in just 14 months, soon after he and Wordsworth became neighbors. *The Ancient Mariner, Kubla Khan,* the first part of *Christabel*—the so-called "Mystery Poems"—were part of this miraculous year (1789), as were the best of the "Conversations Poems," such as *Frost at Midnight.* Four years later, he wrote his heartbreaking *Ode to Dejection* (1802), a kind of farewell to poetry. Opium addiction, a desperately unhappy private life, and severe personality disorders combined to destroy his confidence and his capacity to work effectively.

In middle age he became a permanent guest-patient of a young doctor and his wife, with whom he spent the rest of his life. Although the great poetic gift never returned, Coleridge made a spectacular recovery as a critic, aesthetician, and philosopher. His lectures on SHAKESPEARE (see Vol. 2) and *Biographia Literaria* (1817) are among the masterworks of world criticism. Today he is regarded as one of the supreme figures in English literature and his influence extends everywhere.

Coleridge's reputation has been embroiled in constant controversy because of the repeated disclosures of unacknowledged borrowings in his major prose works, mainly from German philosophers and critics. But the major poetry remains untouched by such charges. The first comprehensive edition of Coleridge's writings, now in progress, has considerably extended the range of his intellectual activities, and his reputation is higher than ever. Coleridge is an extremely complex figure, who has aroused sharply divergent responses, but it is universally agreed that his greatest poetry is inimitable, an unforgettable amalgam of mystery, beauty, and intellectual depth.

BOOKS BY COLERIDGE

The Collected Works. Ed. by Kathleen Coburn and others, Princeton Univ. Pr. 14 vols. 1970–84 consult publisher for prices of individual volumes. When complete, this edition will comprise some 30 volumes. It will be the definitive edition for generations to come. The editing is authoritative, but represents a single perspective about Coleridge.

Complete Poetical Works. Ed. by E. H. Coleridge, *Oxford Eng. Texts Ser.* 2 vols. 1912 $89.00. Long the standard edition, this will almost certainly be superseded by the forthcoming volumes in the *Collected Works* (cited above).

Coleridge: Selected Poems. Ed. by R. C. Bald, *Crofts Class. Ser.* Harlan Davidson text ed. 1956 $3.25

Poems. Ed. by John Beer, Biblio Dist. 1974 $9.95 pap. $4.50

Poems of Samuel Taylor Coleridge. Ed. by E. H. Coleridge, *Oxford Stand. Authors Ser.* 1912 $29.95 pap. $8.95

Selected Poetry and Prose. Ed. by Donald Stauffer, *Modern Lib. College Ed. Ser.* Random text ed. 1951 pap. $6.00

The Portable Coleridge. Ed. by Ivor A. Richards, *Viking Portable Lib.*, Penguin 1977 pap. $7.95

Collected Letters of Samuel Taylor Coleridge. Ed. by Earl L. Griggs, Oxford 6 vols. 1956–71 $98.00.

Notebooks. Ed. by Kathleen Coburn, Princeton Univ. Pr. 3 vols. 1957–73 ea. $100.00–$110.00. When complete this magnificent edition will comprise five double volumes; a volume of text and another of notes. Among the most amazing notebooks ever written.

Biographia Literaria. Ed. by George Watson, Biblio Dist. (Everyman's) 1978 pap. $5.95. Lightly annotated, omits two chapters added by Coleridge that were not part of his original plan, and text more readable than many editions.

Biographia Literaria. Ed. by John Shawcross, Oxford 2 vols. 1907 $54.00. Highly influential introduction, with notes not easy to consult.

Biographia Literaria. Ed. by James Engell and W. J. Bate, Princeton Univ. Pr. 1984 pap. $19.95. Now regarded as the standard edition, highly tendentious with partisan notes and introduction, includes annotation of German sources.

Coleridge on Shakespeare: The Texts of the Lectures of 1811–12. Ed. by R. A. Foakes, Univ. Pr. of Virginia 1971 o.p. Based on previously unpublished transcripts of J. P. Collier's notes, now in the Folger Shakespeare Library. The most reliable text.

Shakespearean Criticism. Ed. by T. M. Rayser, Biblio Dist. 2 vols. repr. of 1960 ed. 1974–80 ea. $8.95

Inquiring Spirit: A New Presentation of Coleridge from His Published and Unpublished Writings. Ed. by Kathleen Coburn, Hyperion repr. of 1951 ed. 1980 $35.00

Table Talk of Samuel Taylor Coleridge. Richard West repr. of 1884 ed. $30.00

BOOKS ABOUT COLERIDGE

Beer, John, ed. *Coleridge's Variety: Bicentenary Studies.* Univ. of Pittsburgh Pr. 1974 $22.95

Byatt, A. S. *Wordsworth and Coleridge in Their Time.* Crane Russak 1973 $19.50

Chambers, Edmund K. *Samuel Taylor Coleridge: A Biographical Study.* Greenwood repr. of 1967 ed. 1978 lib. bdg. $27.50. There is no satisfactory biography of Coleridge. This one is dull, but thoroughly reliable as to facts. Some Coleridgeans have objected severely to Chambers's obvious disapproval of his subject.

Coburn, Kathleen, ed. *Coleridge: A Collection of Critical Essays.* Prentice-Hall 1967 $12.95

Crawford, Walter B., and others. *Samuel Taylor Coleridge: An Annotated Bibliography of Criticism and Scholarship, 1900–1939.* G. K. Hall 1983 vol. 2 lib. bdg. $59.50

Doughty, Oswald. *Perturbed Spirit: The Life and Personality of Samuel Taylor Coleridge.* Fairleigh Dickinson Univ. Pr. 1981 $40.00

Everest, Kevin. *Coleridge's Secret Ministry: The Context of the Conversation Poems 1795–1798.* Barnes & Noble text ed. 1979 $27.50

Fruman, Norman. *Coleridge: The Damaged Archangel.* Braziller 1971 $12.50. One of the most controversial books ever written about Coleridge. A comprehensive study of Coleridge's mind, character, and creative style. Several chapters deal with the literary and emotional sources of Coleridge's poetry.

Holmes, Richard. *Coleridge.* Oxford 1982 $13.95 pap. $3.95

Jackson, J. R., ed. *Coleridge: The Critical Heritage.* Routledge & Kegan 1970 $40.00

Lefebure, Molly. *Samuel Taylor Coleridge: A Bondage of Opium.* Stein & Day 1974 $15.00 1975 pap. $7.95. Attributes Coleridge's many personal and creative problems to his opium addiction. Well written but unreliable.

Logan, Eugenia. *A Concordance to the Poetry of Samuel Taylor Coleridge.* Telegraph Bks. repr. of 1940 ed. 1983 lib. bdg. $65.00

Lowes, John L. *The Road to Xanadu: A Study in the Ways of the Imagination.* Darby repr. of 1977 ed. 1985 lib. bdg. $65.00; Houghton Mifflin pap. $2.85; Princeton Univ. Pr. 1986 $50.00 pap. $14.95. A great scholarly work that reads like a detective story. Traces the sources of *The Ancient Mariner* and *Kubla Khan* in an attempt to unravel the mysteries of the imagination.

Margoliouth, H. M. *Wordsworth and Coleridge, 1795–1834.* Shoe String (Archon) repr. of 1953 ed. 1966 $15.00

Milton, Mary Lee. *The Poetry of Samuel Taylor Coleridge: An Annotated Bibliography of Criticism, 1935 to 1970.* Garland 1981 lib. bdg. $39.00

Nethercot, Arthur H. *The Road to Tryermaine: A Study of the History, Background and Purposes of Coleridge's "Christabel."* Greenwood repr. of 1962 ed. 1978 lib. bdg. $22.50

Potter, Stephen. *Coleridge and S. T. C.: A Study of Coleridge's Dual Nature.* Russell
    repr. of 1935 ed. 1965 $8.50
Prickett, Stephen. *Coleridge and Wordsworth.* Cambridge Univ. Pr. 1980 pap. $11.95
Schneider, Elisabeth. *Coleridge, Opium and Kubla Khan.* Octagon 1966 lib. bdg.
    $27.50. A brilliant scholarly and critical study that has undermined belief in the
    famous "dream" origin of *Kubla Khan.*
Woodring, Carl R. *Politics in the Poetry of Coleridge.* o.p. The best book on the sub-
    ject.

COLLINS, WILLIAM. 1721–1759

Collins published only a handful of poems before insanity clouded the remainder of his brief life. Neglected in his own time, Collins is one of the few
eighteenth-century poets whose reputation has continued to grow. His odes
and lyrics, often difficult to grasp by the casual reader, have come to be regarded by some eminent critics as masterworks and touchstones of political
taste. The young Coleridge wrote that Collins's *Ode on the Poetical Character*
(o.p.) had moved him as much as anything in Shakespeare.

BOOKS BY COLLINS

Works of William Collins. Ed. by Richard Wendorf and Charles Ryskamp, *Oxford
    Eng. Texts Ser.* 1979 $52.00
Poems of Gray, Collins, Goldsmith. Ed. by Roger Lonsdale. *Annotated Eng. Poets Ser.*
    Longman text ed. 1976 pap. $18.00. Superbly annotated. By far the best edition.

BOOKS ABOUT COLLINS

Garrod, H. W. *Collins.* Octagon repr. of 1928 ed. 1973 lib. bdg. $16.50. An acutely per-
    ceptive, brief study.
Sigworth, Oliver F. *William Collins. Twayne's Eng. Authors Ser.* G. K. Hall $14.95;
    Twayne's Eng. Authors Ser. Irvington text ed. 1965 $15.95
Wendorf, Richard. *William Collins and 18th-Century Poetry.* Univ. of Minnesota Pr.
    1981 $25.00
Williams, W. T., and G. H. Vallins. *Gray, Collins, and Their Circle.* Richard West repr.
    of 1937 ed. $17.00

COWPER, WILLIAM. 1731–1800

Wordsworth and Coleridge regarded Cowper as the greatest of living poets, the master of the most natural blank verse written in the late eighteenth century. For generations Cowper's profound influence on the English
romantic revolution was taken for granted. His easy, intimate, and completely unaffected personal correspondence marked a new departure in the
art of letter writing, and recent reexaminations of his poetic and epistolary
art suggest that a revival of interest is well under way. Cowper suffered
from intermittent attacks of insanity and melancholia throughout his life.
His powerful poem *The Castaway* (1796) carries a terrifying sense of despair
and isolation. He was deeply religious and convinced that he was destined
to eternal damnation. Devoted friends like the Unwins sheltered him
against the constant threat of overwhelming dread. After their deaths he
sank into a frightful apathy. His *Olney Hymns* (1779, o.p.) have long been

popular devotional works. It is ironic that his most beloved poem should be the comic narrative of John Gilpin.

BOOKS BY COWPER

The Poems of William Cowper. Ed. by John D. Baird and Charles Ryskamp, *Oxford Eng. Texts Ser.* text ed. 1980 vol. 1 $79.00. As with the edition of prose by King and Ryskamp (cited below), when complete this will be standard for generations to come.

Verse and Letters. Ed. by Brian Spiller, *Reynard Lib.* Harvard Univ. Pr. 1968 $20.00

The Letters and Prose Writings of William Cowper. Ed. by James King and Charles Ryskamp, Oxford 4 vols. 1979–84 ea. $69.00–$84.00. Nearing completion, this great edition will supersede all others.

BOOKS ABOUT COWPER

Cecil, David. *The Stricken Deer or the Life of Cowper.* Richard West repr. of 1929 ed. $20.00. A beautifully written, sympathetic life.

Fausset, Hugh I. *William Cowper.* Russell repr. of 1928 ed. 1968 $9.00

Hutchings, Bill. *The Poetry of William Cowper.* Longwood Pr. 1983 $25.25. An excellent introduction.

Neve, J. *Concordance to the Poetical Works of William Cowper.* Burt Franklin repr. of 1887 ed. 1967 $21.00; Greenwood repr. of 1887 ed. 1969 lib. bdg. $19.25; *Studies in Poetry* Haskell repr. of 1887 ed. 1969 lib. bdg. $49.95

Newey, Vincent. *Cowper's Poetry: A Critical Study and Reassessment. Eng. Texts and Studies* Barnes & Noble text ed. 1982 $29.50. Especially good on *The Task.* This and Hutchings's volume (cited above) are the most comprehensive modern studies.

Nicholson, Norman. *William Cowper.* Folcroft 1973 lib. bdg. $10.00; Richard West repr. of 1951 ed. text ed. 1980 $25.00

Quinlan, Maurice J. *William Cowper: A Critical Life.* Greenwood repr. of 1953 ed. lib. bdg. $18.75

Ryskamp, Charles. *William Cowper of the Inner Temple.* Cambridge Univ. Pr. 1959 o.p. Concentrates on the poet's early life. A fine biography by one of the leading Cowper scholars.

CRABBE, GEORGE. 1754–1832

Crabbe was a parson as well as a poet. He was as ordinary a parson as he was an extraordinary poet—the extraordinariness lying in his power to put mussels, eels, colds, weeds, teapots, and so on, and also whole villages of sympathetically observed characters into couplets that are undeniably poetry. Benjamin Britten's highly popular opera *Peter Grimes* is based on a section of Crabbe's *The Borough* (1810, o.p.). His deeply pessimistic view of human nature, his rejection of rural life as spiritually ennobling, have made him seem a cynic to some, sober realist to others.

BOOKS BY CRABBE

The Poetical Works of George Crabbe. 1914. Ed. by A. J. Caryle and R. M. Caryle, Scholarly repr. of 1932 ed. 1971 $79.00

Selected Poems. Ed. by C. Day Lewis, Penguin 1973 o.p.

Tales, 1812, and Other Selected Poems. Ed. by Howard W. Mills, Cambridge Univ. Pr. 1967 pap. $16.95

BOOKS ABOUT CRABBE

Bareham, Terence, and S. Gatrell. *Bibliography of George Crabbe.* Shoe String (Archon) 1978 $22.50

———. *George Crabbe. Critical Studies Ser.* Barnes & Noble 1977 $25.00

Burne, Neville B. *The Restless Ocean.* State Mutual Bk. 1979 $20.00

Chamberlain, Robert L. *George Crabbe. English Authors Ser.* Irvington 1965 lib. bdg. $8.95 text ed. pap. $4.95

Crabbe, George, Jr. *The Life of George Crabbe.* Arden Lib. repr. 1980 lib. bdg. $25.00. Written by his son. An enduring, minor classic.

Edgecombe, Rodney S. *Theme, Embodiment and Structure in the Poetry of George Crabbe.* Humanities Pr. text ed. 1983 pap. $25.50

Evans, John H. *The Poems of George Crabbe: A Literary and Historical Study.* Ayer $20.25. Still much worth consulting.

Haddakin, Lilian. *The Poetry of Crabbe.* Humanities Pr. text ed. 1955 $4.50. Excellent.

Nelson, Beth. *George Crabbe and the Progress of Eighteenth-Century Narrative Verse.* Bucknell Univ. Pr. 1976 $18.00

Pollard, Arthur. *Crabbe: The Critical Heritage. Critical Heritage Ser.* Routledge & Kegan 1972 $38.50 1985 pap. $15.00

Sigworth, Oliver. *Nature's Sternest Painter: Five Essays on the Poetry of George Crabbe.* Univ. of Arizona Pr. $6.50. One of the best modern studies. The title derives from Byron's tribute to Crabbe.

CRASHAW, RICHARD. 1613–1649

Crashaw differs from other English Metaphysical poets chiefly by virtue of his intense attachment to Roman Catholicism and to the spirit of the Counter-Reformation. The son of a Puritan clergyman, he took Anglican orders in 1638; but during the Civil Wars he was converted to the Church of Rome, and (in 1646) went to Italy, where he was made a canon shortly before his death there. His poetry is strongly influenced by Spanish and Italian models, notably the work of Giambattista Marino, whose poetry is marked by extravagantly sensuous conceits. Crashaw obsessively employs the imagery of wounds, kisses, nests, breasts, milk, and blood; his poetry is not to every critic's taste. After many years of neglect, and even contemptuous dismissal, Crashaw's poetry has experienced an extraordinary revival and is now much admired for its originality and dazzling imagery.

BOOKS BY CRASHAW

The Complete Poetry of Richard Crashaw. Ed. by George W. Williams, New York Univ. Pr. 1972 $25.00; ed. by George W. Williams, *Norton Lib.* repr. of 1970 ed. 1974 pap. $5.95

Poems, English, Latin and Greek, of Richard Crashaw. Ed. by Leonard C. Martin, *Oxford Eng. Texts Ser.* 2d ed. 1957 $59.00

BOOKS ABOUT CRASHAW

Bennett, Joan. *Five Metaphysical Poets: Donne, Herbert, Vaughan, Crashaw, Marvell.* Cambridge Univ. Pr. 1964 $32.50 pap. $9.95. One of the best introductions to a remarkable group of poets.

Cooper, Robert M. *A Concordance to the English Poetry of Richard Crashaw.* Whitston 1980 $35.00

Parish, Paul A. *Richard Crashaw. Twayne's Eng. Authors Ser.* G. K. Hall 1980 lib. bdg. $15.95. A useful brief life and survey of contemporary views. Excellent bibliography to 1980.

Rickey, Mary E. *Rhyme and Meaning in Crashaw's Poetry.* Haskell repr. of 1957 ed. 1972 lib. bdg. $39.95

Willey, Basil. *Richard Crashaw.* Folcroft repr. of 1949 ed. lib. bdg. $12.50

Williams, George W. *Image and Symbol in the Sacred Poetry of Richard Crashaw.* Univ. of South Carolina Pr. 2d ed. 1967 $17.95

DONNE, JOHN. 1573–1631

The dean of St. Paul's, the foremost preacher of his day, Donne has had an influence on English literature that is singularly wide and deep. In his own time he was far more famous as a preacher than as a poet, and for generations after his death his poetry was regarded as eccentric and rhythmically ungainly. Yet it is no exaggeration to say that he was the greatest single influence on English poetry between the two world wars. The great revival of Donne in the twentieth century is reflected in the poetry of many poets, notably T. S. Eliot.

Donne was educated at Oxford and Cambridge. His early career was ruined by his secret marriage to the niece of his employer, the Lord Keeper Sir Thomas Egerton. His early poetry—sensual love lyrics and satires on society—was cynical and realistic. After 1601, when he began his satirical *Progresse of the Soule* (o.p.), it became more serious in tone. The greatest of the Metaphysical poets, he was an exquisite shaper of ideas in compact form and characteristically made use of conceits and inversions to produce verse of great subtlety and power. He became dean of St. Paul's in 1619, and his prose *Sermons* and satires are his most important contribution to literature after some of the lyrics and elegies. His earnest and vigorous mind, expressed in flashing wit and startling beauty, his daring phrases—coupled with a certain roughness of form—have made him attractive to modern readers. Izaak Walton, his intimate and adoring friend, wrote the famous contemporary biography in his *Lives,* first published in 1640.

BOOKS BY DONNE

The Complete English Poems: John Donne. Ed. by A. J. Smith, *Penguin Poets Ser.* 1977 pap. $7.95

Poems. Ed. by Herbert J. Grierson, *Oxford Eng. Texts Ser.* 2 vols. 1912 $89.00. The standard edition for over 50 years, but contains many disputed readings. The Gardner and Milgate editions (cited below) are regarded as more reliable.

Selected Poems. Ed. by Matthias A. Shaaber, *Crofts Class. Ser.* Harlan Davidson text ed. 1958 pap. $3.50

John Donne's Poetry: An Annotated Text with Critical Essays. Ed. by Arthur L. Clements, *Norton Critical Eds.* 1966 pap. $6.95

The Divine Poems. Ed. by Helen Gardner, *Oxford Eng. Texts Ser.* 2d ed. 1979 $45.00 pap. $11.95. Supersedes all previous editions.

The Love Poems of John Donne. Ed. by Charles Fawkes, St. Martin's 1982 $8.95

Poetry and Prose. Ed. by Frank J. Warnke, *Modern Lib. College Ed. Ser.* Random 1967
    pap. $5.00
The Elegies, and the Songs and Sonnets. Ed. by Helen Gardner, *Oxford Eng. Texts Ser.*
    1965 $54.00
Satires, Epigrams and Verse Letters. Ed. by Wesley Milgate, *Oxford Eng. Texts Ser.*
    1967 $54.00. Supersedes all previous editions.
The Songs and Sonnets of John Donne. Ed. by Theodore Redpath, Methuen 1967 pap.
    $8.95. The copious annotations make this one of the most useful of editions.
The Sermons of John Donne. Ed. by Evelyn M. Simpson, Univ. of California Pr. 10
    vols. o.p. The publication of the 160 extant sermons is completed, and this may be
    considered the standard edition. Volume 1 contains essays on the bibliography of
    the printed sermons; a study of manuscripts, textual problems, and literary
    value; and an introduction on background and context. The sermons are pre-
    sented in exact transcriptions with introductions on their contents and circum-
    stances of delivery, and with textual notes. Volume 10 contains "appendixes on
    Donne's sources (a study of high scholarship), notes on the printed folios of 1640,
    1649, and 1661, an index of Biblical texts, addenda and corrigenda, and a general
    index."
*John Donne's Sermons on the Psalms and Gospels: With a Selection of Prayers and
    Meditations.* Ed. by Evelyn M. Simpson, Univ. of California Pr. 1963 pap. $6.95.
    Contains 10 sermons and a few prayers and meditations with explanatory foot-
    notes; a good introduction to Donne's prose.
The Anniversaries. 1611. Ed. by Frank Manley, Johns Hopkins Univ. Pr. 1963 o.p. An
    especially fine commentary.
The Epithalamions, Anniversaries, and Epicedes. Ed. by Wesley Milgate, Oxford 1978
    $49.00
Paradoxes and Problems. Ed. by Helen Peters, Oxford 1980 $47.50

BOOKS ABOUT DONNE

Bald, R. C. *John Donne: A Life.* Ed. by Wesley Milgate, Oxford 1970 $29.95
Brooks, Cleanth. *The Well-Wrought Urn: Studies in the Structure of Poetry.* Harcourt
    1956 pap. $5.95. Contains Brooks's classic analysis of *The Canonization.*
Carey, John. *John Donne: Life, Mind and Art.* Oxford 1981 $25.00. An especially bril-
    liant book by a remarkably gifted critic and scholar.
Clements, Arthur L. *John Donne's Poetry. Norton Critical Eds.* 1966 pap. $6.95. Good
    selection and valuable collection of critical essays.
Combs, H. C., and Z. R. Sullens. *Concordance to the English Poems of John Donne.
    Studies in Poetry* Haskell repr. of 1940 ed. 1970 lib. bdg. consult publisher for in-
    formation
Eliot, T. S. *Selected Essays.* Harcourt 1950 $19.95. Indispensable discussions of
    Donne.
Grierson, Herbert J. *Criticism and Creation.* Core Collection 1978 $17.50; Folcroft
    repr. of 1949 ed. lib. bdg. $17.50. An outstanding book by one of the greatest of
    Donne authorities.
Lewalski, Barbara K. *Donne's Anniversaries and the Poetry of Praise: The Creation of a
    Symbolic Mode.* Princeton Univ. Pr. 1973 $42.00. One of the most influential stud-
    ies of the past generation.
Martz, Louis L. *John Donne in Meditation: The Anniversaries. Eng. Lit. Ser.* Haskell
    repr. of 1947 ed. 1970 lib. bdg. $22.95
Parker, Derek. *John Donne and His World.* Scribner 1977 $4.95

Partridge, A. C. *John Donne: Language and Style*. Basil Blackwell 1978 $24.95; Westview Pr. 1979 lib. bdg. $30.00

Roberts, John R. *John Donne: An Annotated Bibliography of Modern Criticism, 1968–1978*. Univ. of Missouri Pr. 1982 $32.00

——, ed. *Essential Articles for the Study of John Donne's Poetry*. Essential Articles Ser. Shoe String (Archon) 1975 $25.00

Roston, Murray. *The Soul of Wit: A Study of John Donne*. Oxford text ed. 1974 $36.00

Rugoff, Milton A. *Donne's Imagery: A Study in Creative Sources*. Russell repr. of 1939 ed. 1962 $16.00

Sanders, Wilbur. *John Donne's Poetry*. Cambridge Univ. Pr. 1971 $34.50 pap. $11.95

Smith, A. J., ed. *John Donne: The Critical Heritage*. Critical Heritage Ser. Routledge & Kegan 1975 $40.00 pap. $15.00. A superb survey of Donne criticism from the beginnings to the present.

Spencer, Theodore, ed. *A Garland for John Donne, 1631–1931*. Peter Smith $11.25. Valuable essays by T. S. Eliot and others.

Stein, Arnold S. *John Donne's Lyrics*. Octagon repr. of 1962 ed. 1980 lib. bdg. $20.00

Unger, Leonard. *Donne's Poetry and Modern Criticism*. Russell repr. of 1950 ed. 1962 $8.00

Williamson, George. *The Donne Tradition: A Study in English Poetry from Donne to the Death of Cowley*. Octagon repr. of 1930 ed. 1973 lib. bdg. $20.00

Winny, James. *A Preface to Donne*. Longman text ed. 1983 pap. $8.95

Zunder, William. *The Poetry of John Donne: Literature and Culture in the Elizabethan and Jacobean Period*. Barnes & Noble text ed. 1982 $27.50

DRYDEN, JOHN. 1631–1700

As one of the first English writers to make a living by his pen alone, Dryden had to cater to popular public taste. His long career was astonishingly varied, and he turned his exceptional gifts to almost all the major literary forms. He dominated the entire Restoration period as a poet, playwright, and all-around man of letters. He was the third poet laureate of England, but was dismissed when he refused to take the oath of allegiance to William and Mary (Protestants) after the Revolution of 1688. In his old age he was the acknowledged literary dictator of England, and his influence on eighteenth-century poetry was immense, especially on Alexander Pope. His development of the couplet form, his brilliant satires, all became models for other poets to imitate but rarely equal. His many plays were popular in his own time, but it is his *MacFlecknoe* (1682), a devastating assault on his literary rival Thomas Shadwell, and *Absalom and Achitophel* (1681, 1682), a masterful satire on the political scene, that are especially admired today.

Dryden defended the Church of England in his *Religio Laici* (1682), and when he became a Roman Catholic wrote *The Hind and the Panther* (1687), a religious allegory in which the Roman Catholic Church is hounded by various wild beasts. Dryden was also a master of lyrical forms, and of translation. His *Essay of Dramatic Poesy* (1668) is a classic critical statement. Dryden's last work, the *Fables* of 1699, is regarded by some as his greatest achievement.

Books by Dryden

Works. Univ. of California Pr. 19 vols. 1973–79 ea. $50.00–$55.00. In progress since 1956, this will be the standard edition for generations.

Selected Works. Ed. by William Frost, *Rinehart Ed.* Holt text ed. 1971 $13.95

Complete Poetical Works. Ed. by George R. Noyes, Houghton Mifflin $12.50. Excellent notes.

Poems of John Dryden. Ed. by James Kinsley, *Oxford Eng. Texts Ser.* 4 vols. 1958 $154.00. Superior texts. Skimpier notes than Noyes (cited above).

Poems and Fables of John Dryden. Ed. by James Kinsley, *Oxford Stand. Authors Ser.* 1962 $32.50

Of Dramatic Poesy and Other Critical Essays. Biblio Dist. 2 vols. repr. of 1962 ed. 1968–71 ea. $9.95

The Best of Dryden. Ed. by Louis I. Bredvold, Somerset repr. of 1933 ed. $26.00

Selected Criticism. Ed. by James Kinsley and G. A. Parfitt, Oxford text ed. 1970 pap. $8.95

Selected Poetry and Prose. Modern Lib. College Ed. Ser. Random text ed. 1969 pap. $4.00

An Essay of Dramatic Poesy and Other Critical Writings. Ed. by John L. Mahoney, Irvington 1982 pap. $7.95

Books about Dryden

Bredvold, Louis I. *The Intellectual Milieu of John Dryden: Studies in Some Aspects of Seventeenth-Century Thought.* Univ. of Michigan Pr. 1956 o.p. One of the most influential books ever written about Dryden. Possibly superseded by Philip Harth.

Eliot, T. S. *Homage to John Dryden.* Arden Lib. 1974 $15.00; Gordon 1973 lib. bdg. $59.95; Haskell 1970 pap. $16.95

Hall, James M. *John Dryden: A Reference Guide.* G. K. Hall 1984 lib. bdg. $50.00

Harth, Philip. *Contexts of Dryden's Thought.* Univ. of Chicago Pr. 1968 o.p.

Kinsley, James, and Helen Kinsley. *Dryden: The Critical Heritage.* Routledge & Kegan 1971 $38.00

Miner, Earl. *Dryden's Poetry.* Indiana Univ. Pr. 1967 $15.00. Indispensable.

Montgomery, Guy, ed. *Concordance to the Poetical Works of John Dryden.* Russell repr. of 1957 ed. 1967 $30.00

Nicoll, Allardyce. *Dryden and His Poetry.* Folcroft repr. of 1923 ed. lib. bdg. $12.50

Saintsbury, George E. *Dryden.* Ed. by John Morley, *Eng. Men of Letters* AMS Pr. repr. of 1888 ed. lib. bdg. $7.80; Arden Lib. repr. of 1881 ed. 1977 lib. bdg. $15.00; Folcroft 1973 lib. bdg. $10.00; Gale repr. of 1881 ed. 1968 $43.00. Dated as to facts but the book is still worth consulting for its critical perceptions.

Scott, Walter. *The Life of John Dryden.* Ed. by Bernard Kreissman, Univ. of Nebraska Pr. (Bison) 1963 pap. $5.95. Despite the primacy of Ward's biography, this should not be overlooked.

Smith, David N. *John Dryden.* Folcroft repr. of 1950 ed. lib. bdg. $10.00

Swedenburg, H. T., Jr. *Essential Articles for the Study of John Dryden.* Shoe String (Archon) 1966 $25.00

Van Doren, Mark. *The Poetry of John Dryden.* Haskell repr. of 1920 ed. 1969 lib. bdg. $49.95. Perceptive, original, and still one of the best guides to Dryden.

Ward, Charles E. *The Life of John Dryden.* Univ. of North Carolina Pr. 1961 $19.50. The definitive life of Dryden since its publication, and also an important study of seventeenth-century England.

Zamonski, John A. *An Annotated Bibliography of John Dryden: Text and Studies, 1949–1973.* Garland 1974 lib. bdg. $25.00

GRAY, THOMAS. 1716–1761

Gray was an extremely shy, almost reclusive person. His nature was scholarly and he sought perfection in everything he did. He did not write much poetry, but what he did finish is of such high quality that he is sometimes considered the most important figure in English poetry between Pope and Blake. His *Elegy Written in a Country Churchyard* (1751) has long been one of the supremely popular poems in the English language, rivaling any poem ever written for quotable lines. Gray's language is extremely formal, often archaic. Much influenced by the Greek and Roman poets, and by Dryden, Gray later turned to Norse mythology for thematic material. *The Progress of Poesy* (1757) and *The Bard* (1757) contributed to the revival of the ode form, especially among the romantics. His letters have long been admired as among the best in the English language. Wordsworth regarded his *Ode to Adversity* as a masterpiece.

BOOKS BY GRAY

Poems of Gray, Collins, Goldsmith. Ed. by Roger Lonsdale, *Annotated Eng. Poets Ser.* Longman text ed. 1976 pap. $18.00. By far the best edition. Copious, superb notes.
Correspondence. Ed. by Paget Toynbee and Leonard Whibley, Oxford 3 vols. 1935 $109.00; Somerset 3 vols. repr. of 1935 ed. $75.00
Gray: Poetry and Prose. Ed. by J. Crofts, AMS Pr. repr. of 1926 ed. $18.50

BOOKS ABOUT GRAY

Brooks, Cleanth. *The Well-Wrought Urn: Studies in the Structure of Poetry.* Harcourt 1956 pap. $5.95. The essay on the *Elegy* has been immensely influential.
Cecil, David. *The Poetry of Thomas Gray: A Lecture.* Folcroft repr. of 1945 ed. lib. bdg. $5.00. A fine introduction.
———. *Two Quiet Lives: Dorothy Osborne and Thomas Gray.* Arden Lib. repr. of 1949 ed. 1981 lib. bdg. $30.00
Cook, Albert S. *A Concordance to English Poems of Thomas Gray.* Folcroft repr. of 1908 ed. lib. bdg. $30.00; Peter Smith $16.50
Ketton-Cremer, R. W. *Thomas Gray: A Biography.* Cambridge Univ. Pr. 1955 o.p. The standard life.
McKenzie, Alan T. *Thomas Gray: A Reference Guide.* G. K. Hall 1982 lib. bdg. $36.50
Sells, A. L. *Thomas Gray: His Life and Works.* Allen & Unwin text ed. 1980 $29.50

HERBERT, GEORGE. 1593–1633

One of the most important of the Metaphysical poets, George Herbert led a life that, though brief, was singularly pure, pious, and intensely devoted to his office as an Anglican priest. The 129 sacred poems in the collection known as *The Temple* (1633) are a spiritual autobiography of extraordinary intensity. Herbert was fond of traditional poetic forms, but he infused them with a meditative pathos that results in original effects. He was fond of simple diction and the rhythms of speech, at the same time that he freely used arcane symbols and arranged the poems in strange shapes on the page.

BOOKS BY HERBERT

Works. Ed. by F. E. Hutchinson, *Oxford Eng. Texts Ser.* 1941 $52.00
The English Poems of George Herbert. Ed. by C. A. Patrides, Biblio Dist. repr. of 1974 ed. 1981 pap. $5.00; ed. by C. A. Patrides, Rowman 1974 $11.50 pap. $5.00
The Williams Manuscript of George Herbert's Poems. Ed. by Amy Charles, Scholars' Facsimiles 1977 $50.00
George Herbert and the Seventeenth Century Religious Poets. Ed. by Mario Di Cesare, *Norton Critical Eds.* text ed. 1978 pap. $8.95. Excellent selection of poems, valuable critical articles, and a useful selected bibliography.
The Temple: Sacred Poems and Private Ejaculations. Select Bibliographies Repr. Ser. Ayer 6th ed. repr. of 1882 ed. 1972 $18.00

BOOKS ABOUT HERBERT

Benet, Diana. *Secretary of Praise: The Poetic Vocation of George Herbert.* Univ. of Missouri Pr. text ed. 1984 $22.50 pap. consult publisher for information
Bennett, Joan. *Five Metaphysical Poets: Donne, Herbert, Vaughan, Crashaw, Marvell.* Cambridge Univ. Pr. 1964 $32.50 pap. $9.95
Block, Chana. *Spelling the Word: George Herbert and the Bible.* Univ. of California Pr. 1985 consult publisher for price
Charles, Amy. *A Life of George Herbert.* Cornell Univ. Pr. 1977 $25.00
Di Cesare, Mario, and Rigo Mignani, eds. *A Concordance to the Complete Writings of George Herbert.* Cornell Univ. Pr. 1977 $67.50
Empson, William. *Seven Types of Ambiguity.* New Directions 1947 pap. $6.95. Brilliant but eccentric. Enormously influential in the modern revival of Herbert.
Fish, Stanley E. *The Living Temple: George Herbert and Catechizing.* Univ. of California Pr. 1978 $24.50. A fine, original study by an outstanding critic and scholar.
Higgins, Dick. *George Herbert's Pattern Poems: In Their Tradition.* Printed Edns. 1977 pap. $5.95
Patrides, C. A., ed. *George Herbert: The Critical Heritage. Critical Heritage Ser.* Routledge & Kegan 1983 $37.95. An unrivaled survey of Herbert criticism from the beginnings to today.
Roberts, John R., ed. *Essential Articles for the Study of George Herbert.* Shoe String (Archon) 1979 $32.50
———. *George Herbert: An Annotated Bibliography of Modern Criticism, 1905–1974.* Univ. of Missouri Pr. text ed 1978 $23.00
Stein, Arnold. *George Herbert's Lyrics.* Johns Hopkins Univ. Pr. 1968 $20.00. A work of permanent value.
Tuve, Rosemond. *A Reading of George Herbert. Midway Repr. Ser.* Univ. of Chicago Pr. 1982 pap. $12.00. Like all Tuve's work, rewarding.
Westerweel, Bart. *Patterns and Patterning: A Study of Four Poems by George Herbert.* Humanities Pr. text ed. 1984 pap. $37.50

HERRICK, ROBERT. 1591–1674

Herrick is one of the Cavalier lyricists, and the most gifted of "The Tribe of Ben," the small band of poets much under the influence of Ben Jonson. Herrick has been called one of the very greatest of English songwriters, and certainly the conflict within him between the pagan and the priest infuses his best poetry with a peculiar power and complexity. Herrick published only one volume of verse, the astonishing collection of 1,200 poems known as the *Hesperides and Noble Numbers* (1648, o.p.). Many of the poems deal with wine, women, and song—the need to *carpe diem* (seize the day), for youth and joy are fleeting. Intensely musical, his verse is by no means trivial, reflecting as it does classical and Anglican ceremony, English folklore, and timeless myth. Herrick lived a long life in holy orders, but with the Puritan victory he was pushed out of favor. Herrick almost disappeared from English literature until well into the nineteenth century. Since then his fame has steadily grown, and some of his poems are among the most popular in the language.

BOOKS BY HERRICK

Works. Ed. by F. E. Hutchinson, *Oxford Eng. Texts. Ser.* 1941 $52.00
The Complete Poetry of Robert Herrick. Ed. by J. Max Patrick, *Norton Lib.* repr. 1968 pap. $2.95
Poetical Works. Ed. by Leonard C. Martin, *Oxford Eng. Texts Ser.* 1956 $55.00

BOOKS ABOUT HERRICK

Chute, Marchette. *Two Gentle Men: The Lives of George Herbert and Robert Herrick.* Dutton 1959 $6.95; Folcroft repr. of 1960 ed. lib. bdg. $50.00
Hageman, Elizabeth H. *Robert Herrick: A Reference Guide.* G. K. Hall 1983 lib. bdg. $35.50
Macaulay, Rose. *The Shadow Flies. Lit. Ser.* Scholarly repr. of 1932 ed. 1972 $59.00. An absorbing novel based on the life of Herrick.
MacLeod, Malcolm L. *A Concordance to the Poems of Robert Herrick.* Folcroft repr. of 1977 ed. lib. bdg. $35.00; Haskell repr. of 1936 ed. 1970 lib. bdg. $49.95
Moorman, Frederick. *Robert Herrick: A Biographical and Critical Study.* 1910. Russell 1962 o.p.
Musgrove, S. *The Universe of Robert Herrick.* Folcroft repr. of 1950 ed. lib. bdg. $7.50
Rollin, Roger B., and J. Max Patrick, eds. *Trust to Good Verses: Herrick Tercentenary Essays.* Univ. of Pittsburgh Pr. 1977 $19.95

JOHNSON, SAMUEL. 1709–1784

Johnson so dominates the eighteenth century as a critic, essayist, biographer, lexicographer, and literary dictator that it is easy to neglect his considerable achievement as a poet. *London* (1738) and *The Vanity of Human Wishes* (1749), as T. S. ELIOT has said, are among the unique achievements in English poetry. Boswell's *Life* is often regarded as the greatest biography in any language. (See also Chapter 17.)

BOOKS BY JOHNSON

Yale Edition of the Works of Samuel Johnson. Ed. by A. T. Hazen and others, Yale Univ. Pr. 15 vols. 1958–85 ea. $31.00–$52.00. Supersedes all previous editions.
The Poems of Samuel Johnson. Ed. by David N. Smith and Edward L. McAdam, rev. by J. D. Fleeman, *Oxford Eng. Texts Ser.* 2d ed. 1974 $37.95. Revised by E. L. McAdam, Jr., and George Milne for the Yale edition, with fewer notes.
Johnson: Selected Writings. Ed. by Patrick Cruttwell. Penguin 1982 pap. $5.95

BOOKS ABOUT JOHNSON

Bate, Walter J. *The Achievement of Samuel Johnson.* Univ. of Chicago Pr. (Phoenix Bks.) 1978 pap. $4.95

———. *Samuel Johnson.* Harcourt 1977 $19.95 1979 pap. $7.95

Boswell, James. *Life of Johnson.* Intro. by S. C. Roberts, Biblio Dist. (Everyman's) 2 vols. in 1 repr. of 1976 ed. 1978 $17.95; ed. by F. Brady, New Amer. Lib. 1968 pap. $3.95; ed. by George B. Hill and L. F. Powell, Oxford 6 vols. 1934 $195.00; ed. by R. W. Chapman and J. D. Fleeman, intro. by Pat Rogers, *World's Class. Ser.* Oxford 1982 pap. $12.95; ed. by R. W. Chapman and C. B. Tinker, Oxford $36.00; ed. by R. W. Chapman and J. D. Fleeman Oxford 1970 pap. $8.95; *Penguin Eng. Lib. Ser.* 1979 pap. $3.95; *Modern Lib. College Ed. Ser.* Random text ed. 1964 pap. $3.95

Boulton, James T., ed. *Johnson: The Critical Heritage.* Routledge & Kegan 1978 $38.00

Chapman, R. W., ed. *The Letters of Samuel Johnson with Mrs. Thrale's Genuine Letters to Him.* Oxford 3 vols. 1984 ea. $34.50

Naugle, Helen H., ed. *A Concordance to the Poems of Samuel Johnson. Concordance Ser.* Cornell Univ. Pr. 1973 $45.00

Wain, John. *Samuel Johnson.* McGraw-Hill 1976 pap. $4.95

JONSON, BEN. 1572–1637

One of the great figures of English literature, Jonson's reputation has suffered a severe and undeserved decline in the twentieth century. For generations after his death he was regarded as almost the equal of Shakespeare as a playwright, and a poet of towering achievement. One of the first great all-around men of letters, he was by turns actor and playwright, poet and critic, scholar and soldier. In his later years he was the acknowledged arbiter of literary taste in London. Jonson was a great comic dramatist and a critic of enduring influence. He was also the author of many lyrics, epigrams, verse-letters, satires, and odes in various meters, reflecting his interest in classical literature and his command of its various modes of poetry. His poems in turn influenced the taste and style of his contemporaries and successors, especially the group known as "The Tribe of Ben," which included Herrick, Thomas Carew, and others. The Cavalier poets (Lovelace, Suckling, and many lesser figures) looked chiefly to Jonson's verse for their model.

BOOKS BY JONSON

Complete Works. Ed. by C. H. Herford and others, Oxford 11 vols. 1925–52 ea. $47.00–$49.00. Jonson's poems appear in Volume 8 of this definitive edition; notes on the poems are in Volume 11.

Complete Poetry of Ben Jonson. Ed. by William B. Hunter, Jr., *Norton Lib.* repr. of 1968 ed. pap. $5.95. Easier to use than the Herford edition cited above.

Ben Jonson: The Complete Poems. Ed. by G. A. Parfitt, *Eng. Poets Ser.* Yale Univ. Pr. text ed. 1982 $42.00 pap. $10.95

Poems. Ed. by Ian Donaldson, Oxford 1975 $29.95 text ed. pap. $7.95

Ben Jonson and the Cavalier Poets. Ed. by Hugh McLean *Norton Critical Eds.* 1975 $12.50 pap. $6.95. A superb edition, with invaluable critical articles, and an extremely useful selected bibliography.

Ben Jonson's Plays and Masques. Ed. by Robert M. Adams, *Norton Critical Eds.* text ed. 1979 $22.95 pap. $5.95

A Book of Masques. Ed. by T. J. Spenser and others, Cambridge Univ. Pr. 1981 pap. $19.95

BOOKS ABOUT JONSON

Bamborough, J. B. *Ben Jonson. Eng. Lit. Ser.* Humanities Pr. text ed. 1970 pap. $5.25

Blissett, William. *A Celebration of Ben Jonson.* Univ. of Toronto Pr. 1974 pap. $7.50

Brock, D. Herward, and James M. Welsh. *Ben Jonson: A Quadricentennial Bibliography. Author Bibliography Ser.* Scarecrow Pr. 1974 $15.00

Di Cesare, Mario, and Ephim Fogel, eds. *A Concordance to the Poems of Ben Jonson.* Cornell Univ. Pr. 1978 $62.50

Fletcher, Angus. *The Transcendental Masque: An Essay on Milton's Comus.* Cornell Univ. Pr. 1972 $24.50. A brilliant book with many illuminating observations on Jonson's art.

Johnston, George B. *Ben Jonson: Poet.* Octagon repr. 1970 lib. bdg. $18.50

Parfitt, G. A. *Ben Jonson: Public Poet and Private Man.* Barnes & Noble text ed. 1976 $22.50

Summers, Claude J., and Ted Larry Pebworth. *Ben Jonson. Twayne's Eng. Authors Ser.* G. K. Hall 1979 $13.50

Swinburne, A. C. *A Study of Ben Jonson.* Ed. by Howard B. Norland, Univ. of Nebraska Pr. 1969 pap. $3.65

Trimpi, Wesley. *Ben Jonson's Poems: A Study of the Plain Style.* Stanford Univ. Pr. 1962 $25.00. One of the best books on Jonson ever written.

KEATS, JOHN. 1795–1821

The critic Douglas Bush has said that if one poet could be recalled to life to complete his career, the almost universal choice would be Keats, who died at 25 and is now regarded as one of the three or four supreme masters of the English language. Orphaned early, Keats trained for a medical career but gave it up to write poetry. His early work is badly flawed in both technique and critical judgment, but from his casually written but brilliant letters one can trace the development of a genius who, through fierce determination in the face of great odds, fashioned himself into an incomparable artist.

In his tragically brief career, cut short by tuberculosis, Keats constantly experimented, often with dazzling success, and always with steady progress over previous efforts. The unfinished *Hyperion* is the only English poem after *Paradise Lost* worthy to be called an epic, and breathtakingly superior to his early *Endymion* (1818), written just a few years before. *Isabella* is a fine narrative poem, but *The Eve of St. Agnes,* written soon after, is peerless. In *Lamia* Keats revived the couplet form, long thought to be dead, in a gorgeous, romantic story.

Above all it was in his development of the ode that Keats's supreme achievement lies. In just a few months he wrote the odes *On a Grecian Urn, To a Nightingale, To Melancholy,* and the marvelously serene *To Autumn.* Keats is the only romantic poet whose reputation has steadily grown through all changes in critical fashion. Once patronized as a poet of beautiful images but no intellectual content, Keats is now appreciated for his powerful mind, profound grasp of poetic principles, and ceaseless quest for new forms and techniques. For many readers, old and young, Keats is a heroic figure.

BOOKS BY KEATS

The Complete Poems. Ed. by Miriam Allott, *Annotated Eng. Poets Ser.* Longman 1972 o.p. Probably the most useful student edition.

The Complete Poems. Ed. by John Barnard, *Penguin Poets Ser.* 1977 pap. $6.95. Easy-to-use one-volume edition. Good notes.

Complete Poems and Selected Letters. Ed. by Clarence D. Thorpe, Odyssey Pr. 1935 $20.51. Copious notes, superb introduction.

John Keats: Complete Poems. Ed. by Jack Stillinger, Harvard Univ. Pr. text ed. 1982 $22.50 pap. $9.95. The most reliable text, with detailed textual but no critical notes.

Poetical Works of John Keats. Ed. by H. W. Garrod, *Oxford Eng. Texts Ser.* 2d ed. 1958 $52.00. Long the standard edition. Still worth consulting.

Letters of John Keats. Ed. by Robert Gittings, *Oxford Pap. Ser.* 1970 pap. $9.95. The best one-volume edition. Very good notes.

Letters of John Keats, 1814–1821. Ed. by Hyder E. Rollins, Harvard Univ. Pr. 2 vols. 1958 $55.00. The standard edition.

Selected Poems and Letters. Ed. by Douglas Bush, Houghton Mifflin 1959 pap. $5.50. The authoritative notes are masterpieces of compression and critical judgment.

The Keats Circle, 1816–1878. 1948. Ed. by Hyder E. Rollins, Harvard Univ. Pr. 2 vols. 1965 o.p. Invaluable materials dealing with Keats and his family and friends.

BOOKS ABOUT KEATS

Bate, Walter J., ed. *John Keats*. Harvard Univ. Pr. 1979 $30.00 pap. $12.50. A superb life, particularly strong on critical analysis of poems.

Becker, Michael G., and Robert Dilligan. *A Concordance to the Poems of John Keats*. *Garland Reference Lib. of the Humanities* 1979 lib. bdg. $176.00

Bridges, Robert. *John Keats*. Haskell repr. of 1895 ed. 1972 lib. bdg. $29.95. An acute early analysis, not to be neglected.

Bush, Douglas. *John Keats: His Life and Writings*. Macmillan 1966 o.p. The best brief life and critical study. Beautifully written.

Evert, Walter H. *Aesthetic and Myth in the Poetry of Keats*. Princeton Univ. Pr. 1965 $30.00 pap. $3.95. Original and illuminating.

Finney, Claude L. *Evolution of Keats's Poetry*. Russell 2 vols. in 1 repr. of 1936 ed. $50.00. A huge, immensely rewarding study.

Gittings, Robert. *John Keats*. Greenwood repr. of 1968 ed. 1978 lib. bdg. $24.75. A comprehensive, fact-laden, authoritative biography.

———. *The Mask of Keats*. Darby repr. of 1979 ed. lib. bdg. $25.00

Little, Judy. *Keats as a Narrative Poet: A Test of Invention*. Univ. of Nebraska Pr. 1975 $14.50

Lowell, Amy. *John Keats*. Shoe String (Archon) 2 vols. repr. of 1925 ed. 1969 $50.00

Murry, John M. *Keats*. Octagon repr. of 1955 ed. 1976 lib. bdg. $19.50

———. *Keats and Shakespeare: A Study of Keats' Poetic Life from 1816–1820*. Greenwood repr. of 1951 ed. 1978 lib. bdg. $27.50

Perkins, David. *The Quest for Permanence: Symbolism of Wordsworth, Shelley, and Keats*. Harvard Univ. Pr. 1959 $18.50

Ricks, Christopher. *Keats and Embarrassment*. Oxford 1984 pap. $9.50

Ridley, M. R. *Keats' Craftsmanship: A Study in Poetic Development*. Univ. of Nebraska

Pr. (Bison) 1963 pap. $3.95. A masterpiece. Keats's manuscript revisions bring the reader close to the creative process.

Sharp, Ronald A. *Keats, Skepticism, and the Religion of Beauty.* Univ. of Georgia Pr. 1979 $17.00

Sperry, Stuart M., Jr. *Keats the Poet.* Princeton Univ. Pr. 1973 $37.50

Van Ghent, Dorothy. *Keats: The Myth of the Hero.* Ed. by Jeffrey C. Robinson, Princeton Univ. Pr. 1983 $25.00

Vendler, Helen. *The Odes of John Keats.* Harvard Univ. Pr. (Belknap Pr.) 1983 $18.50 1985 pap. $7.95. An acclaimed work by one of the most respected of contemporary critics.

Ward, Eileen. *John Keats: The Making of a Poet.* Octagon repr. of 1963 ed. lib. bdg. $40.00. Not so detailed a biographical account as that of Bate (above), but better on Keats's artistic psychology.

LANDOR, WALTER SAVAGE. 1775–1864

Landor's long life was filled with endless quarrels, lawsuits, and controversy. His temper was violent, his convictions absolute. But his writings in poetry are astonishingly serene, disciplined, and elevated. His youthful *Gebir* (1798) is the best of his long narrative poems, but it is with the short lyric that he is an enduring master. His prose *Imaginary Conversations* (1824–53) remains widely read.

BOOKS BY LANDOR

Poetical Works. Ed. by Stephen Wheeler, Oxford 3 vols. 1937 o.p.

The Complete Works of Walter Savage Landor. Ed. by T. E. Welby and Stephen Wheeler, AMS Pr. 16 vols. repr. of 1936 ed. $200.00

Poetry and Prose. Ed. by E. K. Chambers, AMS Pr. repr. of 1946 ed. $14.50. Excellent selection; important critical articles by major critics.

Selected Imaginary Conversations of Literary Men and Statesmen. Ed. by Charles L. Proudfit, Univ. of Nebraska Pr. 1969 $21.50

Imaginary Conversations. AMS Pr. 10 vols. repr. of 1893 ed. 1983 $445.00 ea. $44.50; Richard West 1985 lib. bdg. $25.00

BOOKS ABOUT LANDOR

Bradley, William. *Early Poems of Walter Savage Landor.* Folcroft repr. of 1914 ed. lib. bdg. $15.00

Davie, Donald. *Purity of Diction in English Verse.* Schocken 1967 o.p. An interesting dissent.

Elwin, Malcolm. *Savage Landor.* Arden Lib. repr. of 1941 ed. 1983 lib. bdg. $40.00. Good biography.

Pinsky, Robert. *Landor's Poetry.* Univ. of Chicago Pr. 1968 o.p. The most important modern study.

Super, Robert H. *Walter Savage Landor.* Greenwood repr. of 1954 ed. 1977 lib. bdg. $37.25. The standard life.

LANGLAND, WILLIAM. c.1332–c.1400

Little is known of the life of this early English poet, who was a contemporary of Chaucer. Langland represents the close of the period of Old English alliterative verse. His *Vision of Piers Plowman* (c.1360–c.1400), an allegorical and satirical poem, survives in many manuscripts, representing three separate versions known as the A, B, and C texts. The A text is about 2,400 lines long; the B is almost 4,000 and the C is a revision of B. The poem contains vivid pictures of contemporary life and is in two parts: The first, a dream vision, examines the proper use of material possessions in the quest for knowledge, and the second, in allegorical form, deals with the individual's pursuit of self-knowledge and perfection. It is not certain that Langland is the author of all three versions. *Piers Plowman* is one of the supreme medieval masterpieces: intense, exalted, biting, but also rambling. Some 47 manuscripts exist, testifying to the great popularity of the poem in the fourteenth and fifteenth centuries.

BOOKS BY LANGLAND

The Vision of Piers Plowman. Ed. by J. F. Goodridge, *Penguin Class. Ser.* 1959 pap. $3.95. The best translation in prose of the B text. Good introduction and notes.
Piers Plowman. Biblio Dist. 1978 $14.95 pap. $6.95; ed. by Walter W. Skeat, Cooper Square Pr. repr. of 1900 ed. $18.50; ed. by Jack A. Bennett, Oxford 1972 pap. $12.95; ed. by Derek Pearsall, Univ. of California Pr. 1979 $48.50

BOOKS ABOUT LANGLAND

Blanch, Robert J., ed. *Style and Symbolism in Piers Plowman: A Modern Critical Anthology.* Univ. of Tennessee Pr. 1969 text. ed. pap. $8.95
Bloomfield, Morton W. *Piers Plowman as a Fourteenth Century Apocalypse.* Rutgers Univ. Pr. 1962 $16.00
Chadwick, Dorothy. *Social Life in the Days of Piers Plowman.* Russell repr. of 1922 ed. 1969 $7.00
Chambers, R. W. *Man's Unconquerable Mind.* Haskell repr. of 1939 ed. 1969 lib. bdg. $49.95; Saifer $15.00. Superb general introduction to the poem.
Coghill, Nevill. *The Pardon of Piers Plowman.* Arden Lib. repr. of 1946 ed. 1978 lib. bdg. $10.00; Folcroft repr. of 1945 ed. lib. bdg. $8.50
Colaianne, A. J. *Piers Plowman: An Annotated Bibliography of Editions and Criticism, 1550–1977. Reference Lib. of the Humanities* Garland 1978 lib. bdg. $28.00
Donaldson, E. Talbot. *Piers Plowman: The C-Text and Its Poet.* Yale Univ. Pr. 1959 o.p. Ranges well beyond its title and one of the very best studies of Langland.
Dunning, Thomas P. *Piers Plowman: An Interpretation of the A Text.* Folcroft repr. of 1937 ed. lib. bdg. $25.00; Greenwood repr. of 1937 ed. 1971 lib. bdg. $18.75; ed. by T. P. Dolan, Oxford 2d ed 1980 $39.95
Fowler, David C. *Piers the Plowman: Literary Relations of the A and B Texts. Publications in Language and Lit.* Univ. of Washington Pr. 1961 $15.00
Lawlor, John. *Piers Plowman: An Essay in Criticism.* Barnes & Noble 1962 o.p.

MARVELL, ANDREW. 1621–1678

This enchanting poet was at once a Puritan and sympathetic to the Cavaliers. A partisan of Charles I, he became tutor to Cromwell's ward, a friend of Milton, and assistant Latin Secretary in the Cromwell government; he was later a member of the Restoration Parliament, surviving very well in the shifting political climate of his age. Close to the Metaphysical poets in method and diction, Marvell is usually secular in approach; he is fascinated by the charm and also the rude power of nature, with which his poetry is centrally concerned. His best-known poem, *To His Coy Mistress*, rings witty changes on the theme of *carpe diem* (seize the day).

Marvell's reputation has never stood higher than it does today. His verse combines wit, satire, intellectual depth, playfulness, complexity, and deep seriousness in a way perfectly suited to modern taste.

BOOKS BY MARVELL

The Complete Poems. Ed. by Elizabeth S. Donno, *Poets Ser.* Penguin 1977 pap. $5.95
Complete Poetry. Ed. by George D. Lord, Biblio Dist. 1984 pap. $5.95
The Poems of Andrew Marvell. Ed. by Hugh MacDonald, Routledge & Kegan 1969 pap. $5.95
Poems and Letters. Ed. by H. M. Margoliouth, *Oxford Eng. Texts Ser.* 2 vols. 3d ed. 1971 $81.00; Somerset repr. of 1952 ed. 2d ed. $45.00. Contains the complete poems and letters.

BOOKS ABOUT MARVELL

Bennett, Joan. *Five Metaphysical Poets: Donne, Herbert, Vaughan, Crashaw, Marvell.* Cambridge Univ. Pr. 1964 $32.50 pap. $9.95
Brett, R. I., and G. F. Grant, eds. *Andrew Marvell: Essays on the Tercentenary of His Death.* Oxford 1979 $19.95
Collins, Dan S. *Andrew Marvell: A Reference Guide.* G. K. Hall 1981 lib. bdg. $33.50
Craze, Michael. *The Life and Lyrics of Andrew Marvell.* Barnes & Noble text ed. 1979 $28.50
Donno, Elizabeth S., ed. *Andrew Marvell: The Critical Heritage. Critical Heritage Ser.* Routledge & Kegan 1978 $29.95. An indispensable survey of criticism from the beginnings to the present day.
Eliot, T. S. *Selected Essays.* Harcourt 1950 $19.95. Contains an indispensable essay on Marvell.
Guffey, George R., ed. *A Concordance to the English Poems of Andrew Marvell.* Univ. of North Carolina Pr. text ed. 1974 $35.00
Kelliher, Hilton. *Andrew Marvell: Poet and Politician, 1621–1678.* Longwood Pr. 1978 pap. $6.75; State Mutual Bk. 1978 $26.00
Legouis, Pierre. *Andre Marvell: Poète, Puritain, Patriote, 1621–1678.* Russell repr. of 1929 ed. 1965 $16.50. Available now in the original French version. A shorter version in English was published in 1964.
Wallerstein, Ruth C. *Studies in Seventeenth-Century Poetic.* Univ. of Wisconsin Pr. 1950 pap. $7.50

MILTON, JOHN. 1608–1674

Milton's tremendous poetic gift showed itself early: in the two companion pieces written in 1633, *L'Allegro* (the mirthful man) and *Il Penseroso* (the contemplative man); in *Comus, A Masque,* which was acted in 1634; and *Lycidas,* 1637, a pastoral elegy mourning the death of the poet's college friend Edward King, who was drowned in crossing the Irish Channel.

Milton's prose belongs to his middle life, when he turned away from poetry for a time, to help bring about "the establishment of real liberty" (as he wrote in 1654); from 1640 to 1660 he actively supported the Puritan cause, serving Cromwell as Latin Secretary from 1649 to 1655. His greatest prose work, the *Areopagitica* (1644) or *Speech for the Liberty of Unlicensed Printing,* took its name from the hill of Ares, on the site of the Acropolis in Athens, where a judicial court met.

Paradise Lost, one of the world's supreme epics, was published in 1667, in 10 books; the second edition (1674) contains 12 books, of which books 1, 2, 4, and 9 are the most admired. Its mighty theme is the fall of man from the Garden of Eden, and its purpose is "to justify the ways of God to man." Milton had been destined for the church, but while in Cambridge gave up his intention of taking orders. Theology continued throughout his life to occupy his thoughts, particularly in the great epic poem of the Fall of Man, *Paradise Lost. Paradise Regained* (1671) is its sequel.

For the last 22 years of his life Milton was blind. His three daughters, children of his first wife, Mary Powell, read aloud to him in Greek, Latin, and Hebrew, and the youngest took down all of *Paradise Lost* in dictation. Mary Powell died in 1652; Milton married Katherine Woodcock in 1656, and, after her death in 1658, married Elizabeth Minshull in 1663. These later marriages seemed to have alienated his children from him. Something of Milton's unhappy experience in marriage certainly echoes in his last great poem, *Samson Agonistes* (Samson the Athlete or Wrestler) (1671). This is written in the style of a Greek tragedy, the story founded on the biblical account of Samson's blindness and his deception at the hands of Delilah.

Milton's sonnets are few in number but are unsurpassed; *On His Blindness* is perhaps the most famous. He was a great Latin scholar, who wrote poetry in Latin that has been widely admired by classicists. Milton is one of the two or three greatest poets ever to write in English, and the peculiar power of his blank verse has earned him the title "the organ voice of England."

BOOKS BY MILTON

Works. Ed. by Frank Allen Patterson and others, Columbia Univ. Pr. 2 vols. in 4 pts. 1940 ea. $25.00. The first complete and definitive edition contains all the poetry considered to be genuine and all the variant readings of other editors, together with translations of such works as were not originally written in English.

John Milton: Complete Poems and Major Prose. Ed. by Merritt Y. Hughes, Odyssey Pr. 1957 $26.56. In many respects the best one-volume edition. Fine commentary and copious notes.

Poetical Works. Ed. by Helen Darbishire, *Oxford Eng. Texts Ser.* 2 vols. 1952–55 ea. $42.00. This may be a final text from a scholar's point of view.

Complete Poetical Works. Ed. by Douglas Bush, Houghton Mifflin text ed. 1965 $22.50

The Poems of John Milton. Ed. by John Carey and Alastair Fowler, *Norton Critical Eds.* 1972 o.p. A worthy rival to the Hughes edition listed above.

John Milton: Complete Shorter Poems. Ed. by John Carey, Longman text ed. 1971 pap. $14.50

The English Poems. Ed. by Walter W. Skeat, *World's Class. Ser.* Oxford $7.95

The Complete Prose Works. Ed. by Don M. Wolfe and others, Yale Univ. Pr. 8 vols. 1953–82 ea. $65.00–$90.00

The Portable Milton. Ed. by Douglas Bush, *Viking Portable Lib.* Penguin 1976 pap. $7.95; *Viking Portable Lib.* 1955 $14.95. Includes *Paradise Lost, Paradise Regained, Samson Agonistes,* complete; early poems and sonnets; selections from prose works, including *Areopagitica* complete. Concentrated authoritative notes.

Odes, Pastorals, Masques. Ed. by John Broadbent, Cambridge Univ. Pr. text ed. 1975 pap. $9.95

On the Morning of Christ's Nativity: Milton's Hymn with Illustrations by William Blake. Ed. by Geoffrey Keynes, Folcroft repr. of 1923 ed. lib. bdg. $12.50

Areopagitica. Ed. by George H. Sabine, *Crofts Class. Ser.* Harlan Davidson text ed. 1951 pap. $3.75

Of Education. 1644. Ed. by George H. Sabine, *Crofts Class. Ser.* Harlan Davidson text ed. 1951 pap. $3.75

Paradise Lost. 1667. Ed. by L. J. Potter and others, Cambridge Univ. Pr. bks. 1–2 1972 pap. $7.95 bks. 3–4 1976 pap. $7.50 bks. 5–6 1975 pap. $7.95 bks. 7–8 1973 pap. $7.95; New Amer. Lib. pap. $3.50; ed. by Merritt Y. Hughes, Odyssey Pr. 1962 pap. $5.99; ed. by F. T. Prince and others, Oxford bks. 1–2 1962 $6.95 bks. 9–10 1969 pap. $6.95

Paradise Lost. Ed. by Scott Elledge, *Norton Critical Eds.* 1975 $19.95 pap. $8.95. Excellent text, good section on backgrounds and sources, major critical essays, and useful biography.

Paradise Regained, the Minor Poems and Samson Agonistes. Ed. by Merritt Y. Hughes, Odyssey Pr. 1937 $12.50

Paradise Lost and Paradise Regained. Ed. by Christopher Ricks, New Amer. Lib. (Signet Class.) 1968 pap. $3.95

Paradise Lost and Selected Poetry and Prose. Ed. by Northrop Frye, *Rinehart Ed.* Holt text ed. 1951 pap. $13.95

Samson Agonistes. 1671. Ed. by F. T. Prince, Oxford 1957 pap. $6.95. Superb notes.

BOOKS ABOUT MILTON

Barker, Arthur E., ed. *Milton: Modern Essays in Criticism.* Oxford 1965 pap. $6.95

Broadbent, John. *Introduction to Paradise Lost.* Cambridge Univ. Pr. 1971 $32.50 pap. $10.95

Bush, Douglas. *John Milton: A Sketch of His Life and Writings.* Macmillan 1964 o.p. Concentrated, authoritative, and elegantly written.

——. *Paradise Lost in Our Times.* Peter Smith $10.25

Daiches, David. *Milton: Paradise Lost. Studies in Eng. Lit.* E. Arnold text ed. 1983 pap. $6.95; *Norton Lib.* 1966 pap. $4.95

Darbishire, Helen, ed. *Early Lives of Milton.* Scholarly repr. of 1932 ed. 1971 $49.00

——. *Milton's Paradise Lost.* Folcroft repr. of 1951 ed. lib. bdg. $8.00

Elton, Oliver. *Milton Il Penseroso.* Folcroft repr. of 1891 ed. lib. bdg. $8.00

Empson, William. *Milton's God.* Cambridge Univ. Pr. 1981 pap. $16.95; Greenwood repr. of 1961 ed. 1978 lib. bdg. $27.50. A controversial discussion of the religion of *Paradise Lost* by the eminent British critic.

Fish, Stanley E. *Surprised by Sin: The Reader in Paradise Lost.* Univ. of California Pr. 1971 pap. $8.95. One of the most influential recent readings of the epic.

Frye, Northrop. *The Return of Eden: Five Essays on Milton's Epics.* Univ. of Toronto Pr. 1975 $15.00 pap. $5.00. Absorbing essays by one of the century's most respected critical theorists.

Gardner, Helen. *A Reading of Paradise Lost.* Oxford 1965 pap. $12.50

Hall, William C. *Milton and His Sonnets.* Folcroft 1973 lib. bdg. $8.50

Hanford, James H. *John Milton: Poet and Humanist.* Case Western Reserve 1966 o.p.

Hanford, James H., and William A. McQueen. *Milton. Goldentree Bibliographies in Language and Lit.* Harlan Davidson text ed. $24.50 pap. $13.95

Hanford, James H., and James G. Taaffe. *A Milton Handbook.* 1939. Appleton 5th ed. 1970 o.p. Invaluable.

Hill, Christopher. *Milton and the English Revolution.* Penguin 1979 pap. $6.95; Viking 1978 $20.00

Hughes, Merritt Y., ed. *A Variorum Commentary on the Poems of John Milton.* Columbia Univ. Pr. 2 vols. ea. $42.00

Hunter, G. K. *Paradise Lost.* Allen & Unwin 1982 pap. $8.95

Hunter, William B., Jr. *A Milton Encyclopedia.* Bucknell Univ. Pr. 8 vols. ea. $30.00 set. $220.00

Ingram, William, and Kathleen M. Swain, eds. *A Concordance to Milton's English Poetry.* Oxford 1972 $118.00

Kermode, Frank, ed. *The Living Milton: Essays by Various Hands.* Routledge & Kegan 1960 $12.95 pap. $6.50

LeComte, Edward. *Dictionary of Puns in Milton's English Poetry.* Columbia Univ. Pr. 1981 $28.50

Lewalski, Barbara K. *Milton's Brief Epic: The Genre, Meaning, and Art of "Paradise Regained."* Univ. Pr. of New England 1966 $30.00

Lewis, Clive S. *A Preface to Paradise Lost.* Oxford 1942 pap. $6.95. An interpretation of Milton's purpose in writing the epic.

Martz, L. L., ed. *Milton: A Collection of Critical Essays.* Prentice-Hall $8.95 (Spectrum Bks.) pap. $2.95. This focuses primarily on *Paradise Lost.* Contains 11 important articles by English and American authorities like T. S. Eliot, C. S. Lewis, and Douglas Bush.

Nicolson, Marjorie H. *John Milton: A Readers' Guide to His Poetry.* Farrar 1963 pap. $5.95; Octagon 1971 lib. bdg. $27.50

Osgood, Charles G. *The Classical Mythology of Milton's English Poems.* Gordian repr. of 1900 ed. 1964 $10.00; Haskell repr. of 1900 ed. 1969 lib. bdg. $49.95; Irvington repr. of 1900 ed. lib. bdg. $34.00

Parker, William R. *Milton: A Biography.* Oxford 2 vols. 1968 $85.00. Authoritative, scholarly biography.

Patrides, C. A., ed. *Milton's "Lycidas": The Tradition and the Poem.* Univ. of Missouri Pr. rev. ed. text ed. 1983 $30.00 pap. $13.50

Radzinowicz, Mary Ann. *Toward Samson Agonistes: The Growth of Milton's Mind.* Princeton Univ. Pr. 1978 $47.50

Raleigh, Walter A. *Milton.* Ayer repr. of 1900 ed. 1967 $17.00; Richard West 1973 $10.00

Ricks, Christopher. *Milton's Grand Style.* Oxford 1963 pap. $10.95

Thorpe, James. *John Milton: The Inner Life.* Huntington Lib. 1983 $17.50

Tillyard, Eustace M. *The Miltonic Setting Past and Present.* AMS Pr. repr. of 1949 ed. $24.50

Visiak, E. H. *Milton's Agonistes.* Haskell 1970 pap. $29.95

Waldock, A. J. *Paradise Lost and Its Critics.* Peter Smith $11.50

Warner, Rex. *John Milton.* Folcroft repr. of 1949 ed. lib. bdg. $10.00

Wilson, A. N. *The Life of John Milton.* Oxford 1983 $19.95 pap. $8.95

Woodhouse, A. S. *The Heavenly Muse: A Preface to Milton.* Ed. by Hugh R. MacCallum, Univ. of Toronto Pr. 1972 $35.00

THE PEARL-POET. c.1390

The Pearl is a poet's exquisite lament, depicting a mystical, allegorical vision seen at the grave of a baby girl, possibly his daughter Margaret (from the French *Marguerite,* meaning "pearl" or "daisy," both symbols of virginity). It is one of four anonymous alliterative poems all in the same handwriting and in the same difficult West Midland dialect, in an illustrated British Museum manuscript, not discovered until the late nineteenth century. The other three are *Cleanness, Patience,* and *Gawaine and the Green Knight.* The resemblances among the four poems have persuaded some scholars that they are all the work of a single poet, but the issue remains hotly disputed. *Gawain* is the gem of medieval English metrical romances, unrivaled for artistic unity, stylistic color, and energy. The manuscript features the famous motto: "Evil to him who evil thinks."

WORKS OF THE PEARL-POET

Pearl Poems: An Omnibus Edition. Ed. by William Vantuono, Garland 2 vols. 1983–84 lib. bdg. ea. $75.00–$80.00

The Poems of the Pearl Manuscript. Ed. by Malcolm Andrew and Ronald Waldron, Univ. of California Pr. 1979 $55.00 pap. $11.95

Syr Gawayne: A Collection of Ancient Romance Poems by Scottish and English Authors. Ed. by Frederick Madden, AMS Pr. repr. of 1839 ed. $35.00; Johnson repr. of 1839 ed. $45.00

Sir Gawain and the Green Knight. Intro. by B. Raffel, New Amer. Lib. (Mentor) 1970 pap. $2.25; ed. by J. R. R. Tolkien and E. V. Gordon, Oxford 1967 pap. $8.95; ed. by Theodore Silverstein, Univ. of Chicago Pr. 1984 lib. bdg. $30.00 text ed. pap. $15.00; ed. by J. A. Burrow, *Eng. Poets Ser.* Yale Univ. Pr. 1982 text ed. $16.00 pap. $4.95

BOOKS ABOUT THE PEARL-POET

Benson, Larry. *Art and Tradition in Sir Gawain and the Green Knight.* Rutgers Univ. Pr. 1965 o.p. Perhaps the best book on the subject.

Blanch, Robert J. *Sir Gawain and the Green Knight: A Reference Guide.* Whitston 1984 $22.50

Boroff, Marie. *Sir Gawain and the Green Knight.* Yale Univ. Pr. 1962 o.p.

Burrow, J. A. *A Reading of Sir Gawain and the Green Knight.* Routledge & Kegan repr. of 1965 ed. 1978 pap. $7.95. Analyzes the poem section by section, using many allusions to other literature, and many quotations.

Fox, Denton. *Twentieth Century Interpretations of Sir Gawain and the Green Knight.* Prentice-Hall 1968 o.p.

Howard, Donald R., and Christian K. Zacher, eds. *Critical Studies of Sir Gawain and the Green Knight.* Univ. of Notre Dame Pr. 1968 $4.95. A collection of critical essays written since 1960.

Spearing, A. C. *The Gawain-Poet.* Cambridge Univ. Pr. 1971 pap. $14.95. A discussion of *Pearl, Cleanness, Patience,* and *Sir Gawain,* beginning with a general study of the whole group, followed by an analysis of each one individually.

POPE, ALEXANDER. 1688–1744

Because he was born a Roman Catholic at a time of severe government repression, Pope did not attend public schools or a university. He was educated at home, studied hard, and began writing poetry very early. A childhood illness left him dwarfish and sickly for the rest of his life.

Extraordinarily precocious, Pope wrote his verse *Essay on Criticism* (1711) at the age of 21. This, together with *The Rape of the Lock* (1714) and *Windsor Forest* (1713, o.p.), made him famous. *The Rape of the Lock* is a dazzling work, widely regarded as the finest mock epic in English. It deals with the loss of a lock of hair by a lady of fashion to a daring suitor; Pope treats this trifling theme with all the pomp and ceremony of a Homeric epic and the result is brilliant, preposterous, and serious by turns.

Pope spent years of his life translating the *Iliad* and the *Odyssey* into elegant heroic couplets. Regarded as a grotesque misrepresentation of the spirit of Homer by some critics, they have come to be regarded as masterpieces in their own right. Immensely popular, these translations added greatly to Pope's fame and wealth.

Profoundly influenced by Dryden, particularly his *MacFlecknoe*, Pope devoted his later years to *The Dunciad* (1728–43), a scathing attack on his critics and on the world of commercial literature in general. Pope had a wide circle of friends, and enemies, and spent much of his life in controversy. He is by far the most important poet between Dryden and Blake. His *Moral Essays* (1731–35) and *Essay on Man* (1734) have been somewhat neglected in recent generations, but his reputation as a great master is secure.

BOOKS BY POPE

Twickenham Edition of the Poems of Alexander Pope. Yale Univ. Pr. 1967 $90.00. Now complete, this will be the standard edition for generations to come.

Poetical Works. Ed. by Herbert Davis, Oxford 1966 $29.95 pap. $9.95. Lacks notes. Complete but for the translations of Homer.

The Prose Works of Alexander Pope. Ed. by Norman Ault, Greenwood repr. of 1936 ed. 1977 vol. 1 lib. bdg. $26.25

The Best of Pope. Ed. by George Sherburn, Scholarly repr. of 1929 ed. $26.00

Selected Poetry and Prose. Ed. by William K. Wimsatt, Jr., *Rinehart Ed.* Holt 2d ed. text ed. 1972 pap. $14.95. Widely regarded as the best selection. Excellent introduction and valuable bibliographical notes.

Poetry and Prose of Alexander Pope. Ed. by Aubrey Williams, Houghton Mifflin 1969 pap. $6.50

The Rape of the Lock. 1714. Ed. by Geoffrey Tillotson, Methuen 3d ed. 1971 pap. $3.95; ed. by J. S. Cunningham, Oxford 1966 pap. $4.95

An Essay on Man. 1733–34. Ed. by Frank Brady, Bobbs 1965 pap. $3.56; ed. by Maynard Mack, Methuen 1982 $44.00

The Art of Sinking in Poetry: Martinus Scriblerus' Peri Bathous—A Critical Edition. Ed. by Edna L. Steeves, Russell repr. of 1952 ed. 1968 $10.00

BOOKS ABOUT POPE

Barnard, John. *Pope: The Critical Heritage. Critical Heritage Ser.* Routledge & Kegan 1973 $42.00 pap. $15.00

Bedford, Emmett G., and Robert J. Dilligan, eds. *Concordance to the Poems of Alexander Pope.* Gale 2 vols. 1974 $160.00

Brower, Reuben A. *Alexander Pope: The Poetry of Allusion.* Oxford 1959 o.p. Influential readings in the New Critical mode.

Brownell, Morris R. *Alexander Pope and the Arts of Georgian England.* Oxford text ed. 1978 $64.00

Dixon, Peter. *Writers and Their Background: Alexander Pope.* Ohio Univ. Pr. 1972 $15.00 pap. $7.00

Dobrée, Bonamy. *Alexander Pope.* Greenwood repr. of 1951 ed. lib. bdg. $18.75

Edmunds, E. *Pope and His Poetry. Eng. Biographies Ser.* Haskell 1974 lib. bdg. $39.95
Erskine-Hill, Howard, and Anne Smith, eds. *The Art of Alexander Pope.* Barnes & Noble text ed. 1979 $24.50
Gooneratne, Yasmine. *Alexander Pope. British Authors Ser.* Cambridge Univ. Pr. 1976 $29.95 pap. $9.95
Gordon, I. R. *A Preface to Pope.* Longman text ed. 1976 $8.95
Jackson, Wallace. *Vision and Re-Vision in Alexander Pope.* Wayne State Univ. Pr. 1983 $17.95
Kinsley, William. *Contexts Two: The Rape of the Lock.* Ed. by Maynard Mack, Shoe String (Archon) 1979 $22.50
Knight, Douglas. *Pope and the Heroic Tradition: A Critical Study of His Iliad.* Shoe String (Archon) repr. of 1951 ed. 1969 $14.50
Kowalk, Wolfgang. *Alexander Pope: An Annotated Bibliography of Twentieth Century Criticism, 1900–1979.* Peter Lang 1981 pap. $43.75
Mack, Maynard. *The Garden and the City: Retirement and Politics in the Later Poetry of Pope, 1731–1743.* Univ. of Toronto Pr. 1969 $25.00. A brilliant, far-ranging study of Pope's imagination.
Mackail, John W. *Pope.* Folcroft 1973 lib. bdg. $8.50
Nuttall, A. D. *Pope's Essay on Man.* Allen & Unwin text ed. 1984 $24.50
Parkin, Rebecca P. *The Poetic Workmanship of Alexander Pope.* Octagon 1968 lib. bdg. $18.50. A very readable analysis of Pope's work from the point of view of "irony," "humor," "metaphor," "the approach to correctable evil," "Pope's poetic world," and so on.
Quennell, Peter. *Alexander Pope: The Education of Genius, 1688–1728.* Stein & Day 1970 pap. $6.95
Rogers, Pat. *Introduction to Pope.* Methuen 1976 pap. $11.95
Root, Robert K. *The Poetical Career of Alexander Pope.* Peter Smith $12.00
Sherburn, George. *The Early Career of Alexander Pope.* Oxford 1934 $24.95; Russell repr. of 1934 ed. 1963 $11.00. Definitive, but carries the life only through 1726.
Sitwell, Edith. *Alexander Pope. Select Bibliographies Repr. Ser.* Ayer repr. of 1930 ed. 1972 $24.00
Spacks, Patricia. *An Argument of Images: The Poetry of Alexander Pope.* Harvard Univ. Pr. 1971 o.p.
Stephen, Leslie. *Alexander Pope.* Richard West repr. of 1880 ed. $12.50
Tillotson, Geoffrey. *On the Poetry of Pope.* Oxford 2d ed. 1950 $6.00. One of the best guides.
Warren, A. *Alexander Pope as Critic and Humanist.* Peter Smith $8.50
Williams, Aubrey L. *Pope's Dunciad: A Study of Its Meaning.* Shoe String (Archon) repr. of 1955 ed. 1968 $16.50. The most illuminating analysis of this masterpiece.

POPULAR BALLADS

The English ballads (anonymous narrative songs preserved by oral transmission) were probably composed over a period of some 500 years, from 1200 to 1700; but very few were printed before the eighteenth century, when Bishop Thomas Percy discovered a seventeenth-century manuscript containing a number of ballads and other poems. He published these under the title *Reliques of Ancient English Poetry* in 1765; this volume stimulated an interest in the subject on the part of other writers, notably Sir Walter Scott. Ballads are typically simple in form (normally combining tetrameter quatrains with a repeated refrain), spare, and dramatically tragic in content. The ballads crossed the Atlantic with Scottish and Irish immigrants to America, and thrived in various regions of the United States.

English and Scottish Popular Ballads. Ed. by Francis J. Child, Dover 5 vols. 1965 pap. ea. $7.50

English and Scottish Popular Ballads. Ed. by George L. Kittredge and C. H. Sargent, Gordon 2 vols. $250.00. Good headnotes.

English Folk Songs from the Southern Appalachians. Ed. by C. J. Sharp and Maud Kerpeles, Oxford 2 vols. 1932 o.p.

The Oxford Book of Ballads. 1911. Ed. by Arthur Quiller-Couch, rev. by James Kinsley, Oxford 1955 o.p. Only the older ballads. No introduction; some music.

The Traditional Tunes of the Child Ballads. Ed. by Bertrand H. Bronson, Princeton Univ. Pr. 4 vols. $210.00. Covers more than the tunes; a valuable supplement to the Child edition cited above.

The Viking Book of Folk Ballads of the English-Speaking World. Ed. by Albert B. Friedman, Penguin 1982 pap. $6.95; Viking 1956 $17.95

Books about the Popular Ballad

Entwistle, William J. *European Balladry.* Oxford repr. of 1939 ed. 1951 $22.00

Gummere, Francis B. *The Popular Ballad.* Gordon $69.95; Peter Smith $5.50

Hodgart, Matthew J. *The Ballads.* Norton Lib. 1966 pap. $4.95

Wells, Evelyn K. *The Ballad Tree: A Study of British and American Ballads.* Ronald Pr. 1950 o.p.

SCOTT, SIR WALTER. 1771–1832

[See Chapter 11 in this volume.]

SHELLEY, PERCY BYSSHE. 1792–1822

Shelley was by far the most radical of the English romantic poets, and for much of his adult life he called for the complete overthrow of the existing order of things, especially organized religion. Expelled from Oxford because he refused to retract his atheistic beliefs, he soon quarreled with his wealthy father and was banished from home. Shelley married impulsively and then abandoned his young wife to run off to Italy with the 16-year-old Mary Wollstonecraft Godwin (the daughter of the radical feminist and the anarchist philosopher, who was eventually to write *Frankenstein*). Shelley and Byron became close friends in Italy and the objects of endless, notorious rumor.

Shelley's personal character was revered by almost everyone who knew him. Extremely generous toward others, frugal with himself, he strove tirelessly for the betterment of humanity. *Prometheus Unbound* (1820), a lyrical drama in four acts, calls for the regeneration of society through love, and for the destruction of all repressive institutions. *The Cenci* (o.p.), a verse drama based on real events, is one of the few plays from the romantic period still produced. Shelley's lyrics are marvelously varied and rich in sound and rhythm. Wordsworth regarded him as the best artist among living poets. *Adonais* (1821, o.p.), written to honor the memory of John Keats, is one of the supreme elegies in English. *The Triumph of Life* has been hailed by T. S. ELIOT as the nearest approach in English to DANTE (see Vol. 2). The *Ode to the West Wind* and *To a Skylark* are anthologized everywhere. His early death by drowning ended his career just as it was coming into full flower.

BOOKS BY SHELLEY

The Complete Poetical Works of Percy Bysshe Shelley: 1814–1817. Ed. by Neville Rogers, *Oxford Eng. Texts Ser.* 2 vols. 1972–74 ea. $59.00

Shelley. Ed. by Kathleen Raine, *Penguin Poets Ser.* 1978 pap. $4.95

Selected Poetry and Prose. Ed. by Kenneth N. Cameron, *Rinehart Ed.* Holt text ed. 1951 pap. $9.50. Excellent selection and notes.

Shelley's Poetry and Prose. Ed. by Donald H. Reiman, *Norton Critical Eds.* text ed. 1977 pap. $12.95. Excellent selection, introduction, notes, and bibliography.

Shelley on Love: An Anthology. Ed. by Richard Holmes, Univ. of California Pr. 1981 $17.95. A particularly interesting anthology by one of Shelley's most original biographers.

Shelley's Literary and Philosophical Criticism. Ed. by John Shawcross, Folcroft 1973 lib. bdg. $30.00

Prometheus Unbound. 1820. Ed. by Vida D. Scudder, Century Bookbindery repr. of 1904 ed. 1980 lib. bdg. o.p.

The Triumph of Life. Ed. by Donald H. Reiman, Garland 1984 lib. bdg. $60.00

BOOKS ABOUT SHELLEY

Abbey, Lloyd. *Destroyer and Preserver: Shelley's Poetic Skepticism*. Univ. of Nebraska Pr. 1980 $15.50

Allott, Miriam, ed. *Essays on Shelley*. *Eng. Texts and Studies* Barnes & Noble 1982 $28.50

Barcus, James E., ed. *Shelley: The Critical Heritage*. *Critical Heritage Ser.* Routledge & Kegan 1975 $36.00

Bloom, Harold. *Shelley's Mythmaking*. Cornell Univ. Pr. repr. of 1959 ed. 1969 pap. $5.95. A key work in the recent reassessment of Shelley.

Cameron, Kenneth N. *Shelley: The Golden Years*. Harvard Univ. Pr. text ed. 1974 $32.50

———. *The Young Shelley: Genesis of a Radical*. Century Bookbindery repr. of 1951 ed. 1980 lib. bdg. $30.00; Octagon repr. of 1950 ed. 1973 lib. bdg. $31.50. Indispensable.

Cronin, Richard. *Shelley's Poetic Thoughts*. St. Martin's 1981 $25.00

Curran, Stuart. *Shelley's Annus Mirabilis: The Maturing of an Epic Vision*. Huntington Lib. 1975 $14.50. An especially lucid study.

———. *Shelley's Cenci: Scorpions Ringed with Fire*. Princeton Univ. Pr. 1970 $31.00

Ellis, Frederick S. *Lexical Concordance to the Poetical Works of Percy Bysshe Shelley*. Burt Franklin repr. of 1892 ed. 1968 $33.50; Johnson Repr. repr. of 1892 ed. $55.00

Fogle, Richard H. *The Imagery of Keats and Shelley: A Comparative Study*. Univ. of North Carolina Pr. repr. of 1949 ed. $22.50

Grabo, Carl A. *Prometheus Unbound: An Interpretation*. Gordian repr. of 1935 ed. 1968 $9.00

Holmes, Richard. *Shelley: The Pursuit*. Charles River Bks. $11.95. Provocative, controversial, and highly readable life.

King-Hele, Desmont. *Shelley: His Thought and Work*. Fairleigh Dickinson Univ. Pr. 1971 $27.50. Valuable because of its attention to Shelley's scientific interests.

Knerr, Anthony D. *Shelley's Adonais: A Critical Edition*. Columbia Univ. Pr. 1984 $25.00

Peacock, Thomas L. *Peacock's Memoirs of Shelley*. Folcroft 1977 lib. bdg. $30.00

Pulos, C. E. *Deep Truth: A Study of Shelley's Scepticism*. Univ. of Nebraska Pr. (Bison) 1962 pap. $2.25. A very influential study.

Raine, Kathleen, ed. *Shelley*. Penguin Poets Ser. 1978 pap. $4.95

Reiman, Donald H. *Percy Bysshe Shelley*. Twayne's Eng. Authors Ser. G. K. Hall lib. bdg. $13.50; St. Martin's 1975 pap. $4.95

Rieger, James. *Mutiny Within*. Braziller $6.50 pap. $2.50

Roe, Ivan. *Shelley: The Last Phase*. Cooper Square Pr. repr. of 1953 ed. 1973 lib. bdg. $25.00; Folcroft repr. of 1953 ed. lib. bdg. $7.45

Trelawney, Edward J. *Records of Shelley, Byron, and the Author*. Ayer 2 vols. in 1 repr. of 1878 ed. 1968 $33.00

Wasserman, Earl R. *Shelley: A Critical Reading*. Johns Hopkins Univ. Pr. text ed. 1971 pap. $10.95. Extreme critical readings, highly influential.

Weaver, Bennett. *Toward the Understanding of Shelley*. 1966. Octagon 1967 lib. bdg. $18.50

Webb, Timothy. *Shelley: A Voice Not Understood*. Humanities Pr. text ed. 1977 $31.75

White, Newman Ivey. *Shelley*. 1940. Octagon 2 vols. 1972 lib. bdg. $109.00

Wilson, Milton T. *Shelley's Later Poetry*. Greenwood repr. of 1959 ed. 1974 lib. bdg. $22.50. A sensible and useful guide through some difficult works.

SIDNEY, SIR PHILIP. 1554–1586

Sidney is perhaps the supreme example of the ideal Elizabethan gentleman, embodying those traits as soldier, scholar, and courtier that Elizabethans most admired. As the nephew of Robert Dudley, Earl of Leicester (the favorite of Queen Elizabeth), and the son of a lord deputy of Ireland, his social and court connections were impeccable. He traveled widely in France, Germany, and Italy, and served the queen as courtier and ambassador before his death in battle in the Low Countries, a death that added to his glamor. His writings in prose and poetry were not intended for publication but for private circulation among aristocratic friends. His pastoral prose romance *Arcadia* (1590) is sprinkled with poetry and was much admired in his day, as it is in ours. His *A Defence of Poesie* (1595) is one of the great critical treatises in English and brilliantly summarizes the Renaissance ideal in literature: to instruct as well as to delight. His sonnet sequence *Astrophil and Stella* (1591, o.p.) is one of the first and perhaps the finest of the great Elizabethan sonnet cycles. Its influence on subsequent love poetry has been enormous. What gives the sequence its special appeal is Sidney's ability to bring fresh vigor to poetical conventions and to dramatize the entire sequence of 108 sonnets.

BOOKS BY SIDNEY

The Poems of Sir Philip Sidney. Ed. by William A. Ringler, Jr. Oxford Eng. Texts Ser. 1962 $59.00. The definitive edition.

An Apology for Poetry. c.1580. Ed. by Forrest Robinson, Bobbs 1970 pap. $5.99

Arcadia. 1590. Kent State Univ. Pr. 1971 pap. $7.25; ed. by Maurice Evans, *Penguin Eng. Lib. Ser.* 1977 pap. $7.95
The Countesse of Pembroke's Arcadia. Ed. by Katherine Duncan Jones, Oxford 1985 pap. $6.95; Scholars' Facsimiles 2 vols. 1983 $80.00
A Defence of Poetry. Ed. by J. A. Van Dorsten, Oxford 1966 pap. $4.95; ed. by Lewis Soens, Univ. of Nebraska Pr. 1970 $10.95

BOOKS ABOUT SIDNEY

Kalstone, David. *Sidney's Poetry. Norton Lib.* repr. of 1965 ed. 1970 pap. $1.85. The best general study of Sidney's art.
Montgomery, Robert L. *Symmetry and Sense: The Poetry of Sir Philip Sidney.* Greenwood repr. of 1961 ed. lib. bdg. $18.75
Myrick, Kenneth. *Sir Philip Sidney as a Literary Craftsman.* Peter Smith $5.00; Univ. of Nebraska Pr. (Bison) 1966 pap. $5.95
Nichols. *The Poetry of Sir Philip Sidney.* State Mutual Bk. 1982 $39.00. Very good.
Osborn, James M. *Young Philip Sidney: 1572–1577.* Yale Univ. Pr. 1972 o.p. The best of the fairly recent books on Sidney.
Rose, Mark. *Heroic Love: Studies in Sidney and Spenser.* Harvard Univ. Pr. 1968 $8.95. A fine book.
Wallace, Malcolm W. *Life of Sir Philip Sidney.* Octagon repr. of 1967 ed. lib. bdg. $31.50. Scholarly.
Waller, Gary, and Michael Moore, eds. *Sir Philip Sidney and the Interpretation of Renaissance Culture.* Barnes & Noble 1984 $26.50
Wilson, Mona. *Sir Philip Sidney.* Folcroft repr. of 1950 ed. lib. bdg. $25.00. Not as reliable as Wallace title cited above, but more readable.

SKELTON, JOHN. c.1460–1529

As a royal tutor, parson, orator, poet-satirist, and courtier, Skelton has been called "the most considerable figure in poetry between Chaucer and Spenser, a lonely star shooting his fiery and erratic spears into the twilight dawn before the rise of the Elizabethans." *A Ballade of the Scottysshe Kynge* (1513) celebrates the victory of the English forces of Henry VIII under the Earl of Surrey over the army of James IV at the battle of Flodden. *Magnificence* is an allegory in which the generous prince Magnificence is first destroyed by his own ill-advised generosity, then restored by Goodhope, Perseverance, and related virtues.

He was awarded the degree of laureate by the universities of Oxford and Cambridge, and was chosen as tutor to the young Prince Henry, who became Henry VIII. When Erasmus visited England, he called Skelton "the one light and glory of British letters," mainly because of his translations of the classics and his Latin verses.

Skelton directed his satire against the clergy, particularly Cardinal Wolsey, the target of *Colin Clout* (1522). After a lifelong hatred of Henry's chancellor, Skelton was finally forced to the sanctuary of Westminster in 1523 for writing *Why Came Ye Not to Court.* While in confinement he purified and simplified his style. He died before Wolsey met his downfall.

BOOKS BY SKELTON

John Skelton: The Complete English Poems. Ed. by John Scattergood, *Yale Eng. Poets Ser.* text ed. 1983 $30.00 pap. $9.95. Supersedes all previous editions.
The Poems. Ed. by Richard Hughes, Folcroft repr. of 1924 ed. 1974 lib. bdg. $30.00
John Skelton: A Selection from His Poems. Ed. by Vivian De Sola, AMS Pr. repr. of 1950 ed. $22.00
A Ballade of the Scottysshe Kynge. Gale repr. of 1882 ed. 1969 $40.00.
Magnificence. AMS Pr. repr. of 1910 ed. $49.50; Johns Hopkins 1980 $18.50

BOOKS ABOUT SKELTON

Fish, Stanley E. *John Skelton's Poetry. Yale Studies in Eng. Ser.* Shoe String (Archon) repr. of 1961 ed. 1976 $21.50. A major reevaluation and explication of the Skelton canon.
Heiserman, Arthur Ray. *Skelton and Satire.* Univ. of Chicago Pr. 1961 o.p.
Nelson, William. *John Skelton, Laureate.* Russell repr. of 1939 ed. 1964 $8.50

SMART, CHRISTOPHER. 1722–1771

Smart spent his early years as a journalist and writer of occasional verse. Subject to religious mania and an overexcited mind, Smart suffered a breakdown and spent several years in mental asylums. During his confinement, deprived of paper and pen, it is said that he scratched with a key on the wainscot of his room his masterpiece, *A Song to David* (1763). In 1771, in debt and sunk in drunkenness, Smart was confined to King's Bench Prison, where he died.

In his greatest poetry, Smart wrote rationally, but ecstatically, shedding the narrow poetic shackles of his time and anticipating the poetry of Blake, especially in *Jubilate Agno* (Rejoice in the Lamb), also from Smart's "mad" period, in which the poet glorifies all the creatures of God; there is a charming section on his cat Jeoffry. Benjamin Britten has set *Rejoice in the Lamb* to music.

BOOKS BY SMART

The Poetical Works of Christopher Smart. Ed. by Karina Williamson, *Oxford Eng. Texts. Ser.* vol. 1 1980 $39.95. This edition will supersede all others.
Jubilate Agno. Ed. by W. H. Bond, Greenwood repr. of 1954 ed. lib. bdg. $18.75; Telegraph Bks. repr. of 1954 ed. lib. bdg. $30.00. Good notes.
For I Will Consider My Cat Jeoffry. Atheneum 1984 $10.95

BOOKS ABOUT SMART

Dearnley, Moira. *The Poetry of Christopher Smart.* Barnes & Noble 1969 o.p. Clear and comprehensive.
Rizzo, Betty, and Robert Mahoney. *Christopher Smart: An Annotated Bibliography.* Garland 1983 lib. bdg. $76.00
Sherbo, Arthur. *Christopher Smart: Scholar of the University.* Michigan State Univ. Pr. 1967 $8.50. The best biography.

SPENSER, EDMUND. 1552–1599

"The poet's poet"—as Charles Lamb was to call Spenser two centuries later—was born in London, where he attended school before going to Cambridge in 1569. About 1579 he came to know Sir Philip Sidney; his first significant work, *The Shepheardes Calendar*, published under a pseudonym in 1580 and consisting of 12 "ecologues" (one for each month of the year), was dedicated to Sidney. Spenser hoped for advancement at the court of Queen Elizabeth, but in August 1580 he took a minor position in Ireland, where he spent the rest of his life, save for two visits to England. In 1594, he married Elizabeth Boyle, in Cork; the sonnet sequence *Amoretti* (1595) bears on his courtship, and the great marriage hymn, *Epithalamion* (1595), celebrates the wedding.

The first three books of Spenser's allegorical epic-romance, *The Faerie Queene*, appeared in 1590; three more in 1596. A fragment, the *Cantos of Mutabilitie*, which may or may not have been intended to form part of the great poem, appeared in 1609, after Spenser's death. Spenser appended a letter to his friend Sir Walter Raleigh to the edition of 1590, explaining "the general intention and meaning" of *The Faerie Queene* (1589) and giving some account of his sources and allegorical method. Although Spenser planned to write 12 books in all, only 6, and the two *Cantos of Mutabilitie*, survive. The rest may possibly have been destroyed by Irish rebels when, in 1598, they sacked Spenser's Irish residence at Kilcolman, but it is equally possible that the poet never managed to bring his massively planned work to completion.

Spenser's *Amoretti* is a great sonnet sequence on love, and *Colin Clout's Come Home Again* (1595) is an allegorical attack on the taste of the court. His influence on the romantic poets, especially Keats, was immense. He is buried in Westminster Abbey, near Chaucer, to whom he owed more as an artist than to anyone else.

BOOKS BY SPENSER

The Works of Edmund Spenser: A Variorum Edition. Ed. by Edwin Greenlaw and others, Johns Hopkins Univ. Pr. 11 vols. 1932–45 $325.00. This exhaustive edition follows in the main the edition of 1596, all other important editions and variants being noted, and summarizes all the older scholarship.

The Poetical Works. Ed. by J. C. Smith and Ernest de Selincourt, *Oxford Pap. Ser.* 1961 pap. $11.95

Edmund Spenser's Poetry. Ed. by Hugh MacLean, *Norton Critical Eds.* 2d ed. text ed. 1982 pap. $9.95. Probably the most useful edition, with much valuable criticism and a helpful bibliography.

Minor Poems. Ed. by Ernest de Selincourt, *Oxford Eng. Texts Ser.* 1910 $22.00

Spenser: Selections, with Essays by Hazlitt, Coleridge and Leigh Hunt. Intro. by W. L. Renwick, AMS Pr. repr. of 1923 ed. 1977 $19.50

Spenser: Selected Poetry. Ed. by A. Kent Hieatt and Constance Hieatt, *Crofts Class. Ser.* Harlan Davidson text ed. 1970 pap. $1.95

Faerie Queene: The Mutability Cantos and Selections from the Minor Poems. Ed. by Robert L. Kellogg and Oliver L. Steele, Odyssey Pr. 1965 bks. 1–2 pap. $14.47

Shepheardes Calendar. 1580. Burt Franklin 1980 $32.00

The Faerie Queene. 1590. Biblio Dist. 1978 pap. $3.95; ed. by J. C. Smith, *Oxford Eng. Texts Ser.* 2 vols. 1909 $98.00; ed. by P. C. Bayley, Oxford 2 bks. 1965–66 pap. $8.95
The Faerie Queene. Ed. by A. C. Hamilton, Longman 1978 $60.00 pap. $21.00. Copiously annotated; very helpful.
The Faerie Queene. Ed. by Thomas Roche, *Eng. Poets Ser.* Yale Univ. Pr. 1981 pap. $14.95. One of the best editions, with very full notes.

BOOKS ABOUT SPENSER

Alpers, Paul J. *Edmund Spenser.* Penguin 1970 o.p.
Bennett, Josephine W. *Evolution of the Faerie Queene.* Burt Franklin repr. of 1942 ed. 1962 lib. bdg. $21.00; Somerset repr. of 1942 ed. $27.00
Berger, Harry, Jr. *Spenser: A Collection of Critical Essays.* Prentice-Hall 1968 o.p.
Fletcher, Angus. *The Prophetic Moment: An Essay on Spenser.* Univ. of Chicago Pr. 1971 $20.00. Brilliant.
Hamilton, Albert Charles. *The Structure of Allegory in the Faerie Queene.* Oxford 1961 o.p.
————, ed. *Essential Articles for the Study of Edmund Spenser.* Shoe String (Archon) 1972 $25.00
Hoffman, Nancy J. *Spenser's Pastorals: The Shepheardes Calendar and "Colin Clout."* Johns Hopkins Univ. Pr. text ed. 1978 $14.50
Jones, Harry V. *A Spenser Handbook.* Irvington 1930 $38.50 text ed. pap. $18.95
Judson, A. C. *Notes on the Life of Edmund Spenser.* Kraus repr. of 1949 ed. 1978 pap. $6.00. Definitive.
Lewis, Clive S. *Spenser's Images of Life.* Ed. by A. Fowler, Cambridge Univ. Pr. 1967 $29.95 pap. $8.95
Lotspeich, Henry C. *Classical Mythology in the Poetry of Edmund Spenser.* Princeton Studies in Eng. Gordian repr. of 1932 ed. 1965 $7.50; Octagon 1965 lib. bdg. $16.00. Lists of Spenser's classical allusions with a valuable introductory essay.
McLane, Paul. *Spenser's "Shepheardes Calendar": A Study in Elizabethan Allegory.* Univ. of Notre Dame Pr. 1969 $18.95 pap. $14.50
McNeir, Waldo F., and Foster Provost. *An Annotated Bibliography of Edmund Spenser.* AMS Pr. repr. of 1962 ed. lib. bdg. $32.50; Humanities Pr. rev. ed. text ed. 1975 $25.50
Nelson, William, ed. *Form and Convention in the Poetry of Edmund Spenser.* Essays of the Eng. Institute Ser. Columbia Univ. Pr. 1961 $21.50. These well-written critiques add much to the modern understanding of the poet.
Osgood, Charles G. *Concordance to the Poems of Edmund Spenser.* Peter Smith repr. of 1915 ed. $42.00
Renwick, W. L. *Edmund Spenser.* Folcroft 1952 lib. bdg. $10.00

THOMSON, JAMES. 1700–1748

Thomson, the son of a Scottish clergyman, was educated for the ministry, but went instead to London, where he joined Pope's literary circle. His boyhood in the country greatly influenced his mature poetry. *The Seasons* (1730), a series of nature poems, grew to more than 5,000 lines in its final version; it became the most popular poem of the eighteenth century and inspired Haydn's great musical setting. Thomson can justly be credited with undermining the supremacy of the couplet and with changing poetic taste. With Thomson, the center of poetic interest moved from the city to the country. Thomson was a deeply committed humanitarian poet, convinced that human nature was basically benevolent and that physical nature was a manifestation of the divine spirit. For this reason he is often regarded as a "preromantic." He is also the author of the supremely famous *Rule, Britannia* (1740).

BOOKS BY THOMSON

Complete Poetical Works. Ed. by J. L. Robertson, *Oxford Stand. Authors Ser.* 1908 o.p. No notes.
Poems, Essays, and Fragments. Arden Lib. repr. of 1905 ed. 1977 lib. bdg. $20.00
The Seasons. Darby repr. of 1939 ed. 1982 lib. bdg. $30.00; ed. by James Sambrook, *Oxford Eng. Texts Ser.* 1981 $110.00
Seasons and the Castle of Indolence. Ed. by James Sambrook, Oxford 1972 pap. $9.95

BOOKS ABOUT THOMSON

Campbell, H. H. *James Thomson. Twayne's Eng. Authors Ser.* G. K. Hall 1979 lib. bdg. $15.95
————, ed. *James Thomson: An Annotated Bibliography.* Garland 1976 lib. bdg. $31.00
Cohen, Ralph. *The Art of Discrimination: Thomson's "Seasons" and the Language of Criticism.* Univ. of California Pr. 1963 o.p. A masterful study.
Dobell, Bertram. *Laureate of Pessimism.* Associated Faculty Pr. repr. of 1910 ed. 1970 $14.50; Richard West repr. of 1910 ed. 1973 $8.50
Salt, Henry S. *Life of James Thomson B.V.* Associated Faculty Pr. repr. of 1889 ed. 1971 $27.50; Richard West repr. of 1889 ed. 1973 $14.25
Walker, Imogene B. *James Thomson (B.V.): A Critical Study.* Greenwood repr. of 1950 ed. lib. bdg. $18.75

VAUGHAN, HENRY. 1622–1695

Henry Vaughan was born in South Wales. He studied at Oxford with his twin brother, Thomas; Thomas became an alchemist and a dealer in magic, and studied the hermetic philosophy that is also reflected in Henry's poems. Henry left Oxford for London, and, after serving as a Royalist soldier during the Civil War, retired to Wales, where he served as a physician for the last 20 years of his life. His early work was secular, but he is best remembered for his religious verse in *Silex Scintillans* (1650; second part, 1655). The best of his work shines with a childlike innocence and clarity of vision. He wrote about nature as a reflection of God: "All things that be, praise him. . . . Stones are deep in admiration." Vaughan's views on nature and childhood may have influenced Wordsworth.

BOOKS BY VAUGHAN

The Complete Poems. Ed. by Alan Rudrum, *Eng. Poets Ser.* Yale Univ. Pr. repr. of 1976 ed. text ed. 1981 $42.00 pap. $10.95. The most recent comprehensive edition, incorporating the results of modern scholarship.
The Complete Poetry of Henry Vaughan. Ed. by French Fogle, *Norton Lib.* repr. of 1964 ed. 1969 pap. $8.95

Books about Vaughan

Blunden, Edmund C. *On the Poems of Henry Vaughan: Characteristics and Intimations.* Russell repr. of 1927 ed. 1979 $6.00

Calhoun, T. O. *Henry Vaughan: The Achievement of Scintillans.* Univ. of Delaware Pr. 1981 $25.00

Grant, Patrick. *The Transformation of Sin: Studies in Donne, Herbert, Vaughan and Traherne.* Univ. of Massachusetts Pr. 1974 $17.50

Marilla, E. L. *Comprehensive Bibliography of Henry Vaughan.* Univ. of Alabama Pr. 1948 pap. $1.45

———. *The Secular Poems of Henry Vaughan: Essays and Studies on English Language and Literature.* Ed. by S. B. Lijergren, Telegraph Bks. repr. of 1958 ed. 1983 lib. bdg. $50.00

Marilla, E. L., and James D. Simmonds, eds. *Henry Vaughan: A Bibliographical Supplement.* Univ. of Alabama Pr. 1963 pap. $1.25

Pettet, E. C. *Of Paradise and Light: A Study of Vaughan's Silex Scintillans.* Telegraph Bks. repr. of 1960 ed. 1983 lib. bdg. $40.00

Post, Jonathan F. *Henry Vaughan: The Unfolding Vision.* Princeton Univ. Pr. 1983 $25.00

Simmonds, James D. *Masques of God: Form and Theme in the Poetry of Henry Vaughan.* Univ. of Pittsburgh Pr. 1972 $19.95

Wells, H. W. *The Tercentenary of Henry Vaughan.* Folcroft 1973 lib. bdg. $10.00

WIAT, SIR THOMAS THE ELDER. 1503–1542

[See under WYATT (OR WIAT), SIR THOMAS THE ELDER in this chapter.]

WORDSWORTH, WILLIAM. 1770–1850

Born in the "Lake Country" of northern England, Wordsworth was orphaned early, had an undistinguished career at Cambridge, spent a year in revolutionary France, and returned to England a penniless radical. For five years he and his sister, Dorothy, lived very frugally in rural England, where they met Coleridge. *Lyrical Ballads,* published anonymously in 1798, led off with Coleridge's *Ancient Mariner* and ended with Wordsworth's *Tintern Abbey.* Between these two masterworks are at least a dozen other great poems. The volume is often said to mark the beginning of the English romantic revolution. A second, augmented edition in 1800 was prefaced by one of the great manifestos in world literature, an essay that called for natural language in poetry, subject matter dealing with ordinary men and women, and a return to emotions and imagination. The preface and poems were violently attacked and Wordsworth's ride to fame was long and slow.

Before he was 30, Wordsworth had begun the supreme work of his life, *The Prelude,* an immensely long autobiographical work on "The Growth of the Poet's Mind," a theme unprecedented in poetry. Although first finished in 1805, *The Prelude* was never published in Wordsworth's lifetime. Between 1797 and 1807, he produced a steady stream of magnificent works, but little of his work over the last four decades of his life matters greatly. *The Excursion,* a poem of epic length, has never been popular, despite superb passages.

After *Lyrical Ballads*, Wordsworth turned to his own life, his spiritual and poetical development, as his major theme. More than anyone else, he dealt with mysterious affinities between nature and humanity. Poems like the *Ode on the Intimations of Immortality* have a mystical power quite independent of any particular creed, and simple lyrics like *The Solitary Reaper* produce amazing powerful effects with the simplest materials. Wordsworth also revived the sonnet and is the greatest master of the form after Milton, whom he resembles in many ways. Wordsworth is one of the giants of English poetry and criticism, and his work ranges from the almost childishly simple to the philosophically profound.

BOOKS BY WORDSWORTH

Wordsworth: Poetical Works. Ed. by Ernest de Selincourt, *Oxford Stand. Authors Ser.* rev. ed. repr. of 1936 ed. 1950 $60.00 pap. $35.00. This great edition is now being revised.

Poetical Works. Ed. by Thomas Hutchinson and Ernest de Selincourt, *Oxford Stand. Authors Ser.* 1950 $35.00 pap. $11.50. Small print makes the notes difficult to read. Otherwise a superb one-volume edition.

William Wordsworth. Ed. by Stephen Gill, *Oxford Authors Ser.* 1984 $29.95 pap. $10.95. For the first time, Wordsworth's poems appear in their original versions, and not as later revised. Indispensable, but must be augmented by other editions.

The Letters of William Wordsworth: A New Selection. Ed. by Alan G. Hill, Oxford 1984 pap. $7.95

The Letters of William and Dorothy Wordsworth: The Later Years, 1835–1839. Ed. by Ernest de Selincourt, rev. by Chester L. Shaver, Mary Moorman, and Alan G. Hill, Oxford 6 vols. 2d ed. 1967–82 ea. $58.00–$85.00

The Love Letters of William and Mary Wordsworth. Ed. by Beth Darlington, Cornell Univ. Pr. 1981 $27.50. These recently discovered letters throw invaluable light on the poet's marriage and middle years.

(and Samuel Taylor Coleridge). *Lyrical Ballads, 1798.* Ed. by W. J. Owen, Greenwood repr. of 1957 ed. 1979 lib. bdg. $24.75; ed. by W. J. Owen, Oxford 2d ed. 1969 pap. $5.95

(and Samuel Taylor Coleridge). *Wordsworth and Coleridge: Lyrical Ballads, 1805.* Ed. by Derek Roper, International Ideas 2d ed. 1986 pap. $14.95

The Prelude: 1799, 1805, 1850. Ed. by Jonathan Wordsworth, *Norton Critical Eds.* 1980 $22.95; ed. by Ernest de Selincourt, corrected by Stephen Gill, *Oxford Stand. Authors Ser.* 1970 pap. $5.95. The only edition that contains the 1799, 1805, and 1850 versions of this much-revised poem. Good notes, superb supporting materials, valuable criticism, and useful bibliography.

Home at Grasmere: Part First, Book First, of "The Recluse." Ed. by Beth Darlington, Cornell Univ. Pr. 1977 $55.00. Like all the titles in the "Cornell Wordsworth" now in progress (see the citations below), this volume features a "reading text" and photographs of many manuscript pages. Extremely valuable for detailed study of textual variants and stages of development in the poem.

Benjamin the Waggoner. Ed. by Paul Betz, Cornell Univ. Pr. 1980 $44.50

The Borderers. Ed. by Robert Osborn, Cornell Univ. Pr. 1981 $99.50

Descriptive Sketches. Ed. by Eric Birdsall and Paul M. Zall, Cornell Univ. Pr. 1984 $48.50

An Evening Walk. Ed. by James Averill, Cornell Univ. Pr. 1980 $38.50

BOOKS ABOUT WORDSWORTH

Abrams, Meyer H., ed. *Wordsworth: A Collection of Critical Essays.* Prentice-Hall (Spectrum Bks.) 1972 $12.95

Bateson, Frederick W. *Wordsworth: A Re-Interpretation.* AMS Pr. repr. of 1954 ed. $27.50. Among the most controversial books about Wordsworth because of its claim that William and Dorothy felt more than family affection for each other. Sensational, but a very important study.

Beatty, Arthur. *William Wordsworth: His Doctrine and Art in Their Historical Relations.* AMS Pr. repr. of 1927 ed. 2d ed. $32.50

Bialostosky, Don H. *Making Tales: The Poetics of Wordsworth's Narrative Experiments.* Univ. of Chicago Pr. 1984 lib. bdg. $26.00 pap. $12.50

Burra, Peter. *Wordsworth.* Folcroft repr. of 1936 ed. 1974 lib. bdg. $17.50; Haskell repr. of 1935 ed. 1972 lib. bdg. $31.95

Clarke, Colin C. *Romantic Paradox: An Essay on the Poetry of Wordsworth.* Greenwood repr. of 1963 ed. 1979 lib. bdg. $22.50

Coleridge, Samuel Taylor. *Biographia Literaria.* Ed. by George Watson, Biblio Dist. (Everyman's) 1978 pap. $5.95; ed. by John Shawcross, Oxford 2 vols. 1907 $54.00; ed. by James Engell and W. Jackson Bate, Princeton Univ. Pr. 1984 pap. $19.95. Still regarded as the classic analysis of Wordsworth's art.

Darbishire, Helen. *The Poet Wordsworth.* Greenwood repr. of 1965 ed. 1980 lib. bdg. $27.50. A miracle of compression and judicious criticism.

Ferry, David. *The Limits of Mortality: An Essay on Wordsworth's Major Poems.* Greenwood repr. of 1959 ed. 1978 lib. bdg. $19.75

Garrod, H. W. *Wordsworth: Lectures and Essays.* AMS Pr. repr. of 1923 ed. $12.50; Arden Lib. repr. of 1923 ed. 1978 lib. bdg. $12.50

Grob, Alan. *The Philosophic Mind: A Study of Wordsworth's Poetry and Thought, 1797–1805.* Ohio State Univ. Pr. 1973 $10.00

Harper, George M. *William Wordsworth: His Life, Works and Influence.* Russell 2 vols. in 1 repr. of 1929 ed. rev. ed. 1960 $25.00. Although superseded in many ways by Mary Moorman's more recent biography (cited below), this remains unrivaled for intellectual background and critical penetration.

Hartman, Geoffrey H. *Wordsworth's Poetry, 1785–1814.* Yale Univ. Pr. rev. ed. 1964 pap. $11.95. Among the most influential studies of the century. Absorbing, but lacks balance.

Havens, Raymond D. *The Mind of a Poet: A Study of Wordsworth's Thought with Reference to The Prelude.* AMS Pr. repr. of 1941 ed. $57.50. A masterful analysis of *The Prelude.*

Jones, Henry J. *The Egotistical Sublime: A History of Wordsworth's Imagination.* Greenwood repr. of 1954 ed. 1979 lib. bdg. $24.75

Legouis, Emile. *Early Life of William Wordsworth, 1770–1799: A Study of The Prelude.* Folcroft 1973 lib. bdg. $9.45; trans. by T. W. Matthews, Scholarly repr. of 1921 ed. 1971 $49.00

Lindenberger, Herbert S. *On Wordsworth's Prelude.* Greenwood repr. of 1963 ed. 1976 lib. bdg. $60.50

Miles, Josephine. *Wordsworth and the Vocabulary of Emotion.* Octagon 1965 lib. bdg. $18.00

Moorman, Mary. *William Wordsworth.* Oxford 2 vols. 1957–65 o.p. The standard life, but needs to be augmented by other perspectives.

Parrish, Stephen M. *The Art of the Lyrical Ballads.* Harvard Univ. Pr. 1973 $16.50

Perkins, David. *Quest for Permanence: Symbolism of Wordsworth, Shelley, and Keats.* Harvard Univ. Pr. 1959 $18.50

Purkis, John. *A Preface to Wordsworth.* Longman text ed. 1970 pap. $6.95
Raleigh, Walter A. *Wordsworth.* Scholarly repr. of 1903 ed. 1970 $29.00
Read, Herbert E. *Wordsworth.* AMS Pr. repr. of 1949 ed. $25.00; Greenwood repr. of 1958 ed. 1983 lib. bdg. $27.50
Sheats, Paul D. *The Making of Wordsworth's Poetry, 1785–1798.* Harvard Univ. Pr. 1973 $18.50
Stam, David H. *Wordsworthian Criticism, 1964–1973: An Annotated Bibliography.* NYPL 1974 $15.00
Woodring, Carl R. *Wordsworth.* 1965. Harvard Univ. Pr. 1968 o.p.
Wordsworth, Jonathan. *William Wordsworth: The Borders of Vision.* Oxford 1982 $39.50 pap. $23.95. A valuable study of the poet's mystical states of mind.

WYATT (OR WIAT), SIR THOMAS THE ELDER. 1503–1542

Wyatt served King Henry VIII as a diplomat and as ambassador to Spain and to the Emperor Charles V. His poetry reflects the influence of French and Italian literature (notably the Italian sonneteer Petrarch), and also the troubled course of his career as a courtier. Wyatt introduced the Italian sonnet into English verse, for the most part translating and paraphrasing Petrarchian originals, and employing rhyme schemes derived from other Italian poets. The sonnet, of course, was to become one of the chief English poetic forms. Wyatt's poetry also includes epigrams, satires, and devotional works, as well as many lyrics that look to Chaucerian precedent in form and outlook.

He and Henry Howard, Earl of Surrey, who established the "English" sonnet form (three quatrains and a couplet, rhyming *abab, cdcd, efef, gg*), have justly been called the first reformers of English meter and style.

BOOKS BY WYATT

Sir Thomas Wyatt: The Complete Poems. Ed. by R. A. Rebholz, Yale Univ. Pr. text ed. 1981 $31.00 pap. $8.95. The best modern edition.
Collected Poems of Sir Thomas Wyatt. Ed. by Kenneth Muir, Harvard Univ. Pr. 1950 pap. $5.95
Poetry of Sir Thomas Wyatt: A Selection and Study by E. M. W. Tillyard. Somerset repr. of 1929 ed. $29.00

BOOKS ABOUT WYATT

Foxwell, Agnes K. *Study of Sir Thomas Wyatt's Poems.* Russell repr. of 1911 ed. 1964 $7.50
Hangen, Eva C. *Concordance to the Complete Poetical Works of Sir Thomas Wyatt. English Literary Reference Ser.* Johnson Repr. repr. of 1941 ed. 1969 $45.00
Jentoft, Clyde W. *Sir Thomas Wyatt and Henry Howard, Earl of Surrey: A Reference Guide.* G. K. Hall 1980 lib. bdg. $25.00
Muir, Kenneth, ed. *The Life and Letters of Sir Thomas Wyatt.* State Mutual Bk. 1963 $35.00. The standard biography.
Thomson, Patricia. *Sir Thomas Wyatt and His Background.* Stanford Univ. Pr. 1964 $25.00
———. *Wyatt: The Critical Heritage. Critical Heritage Ser.* Routledge & Kegan 1974 $29.95

CHAPTER 6

British Poetry: Middle Period

Hartley S. Spatt

Vague words! but ah, how hard to frame
In matter-moulded forms of speech.

—ALFRED TENNYSON, *In Memoriam*

People seldom think of themselves as belonging to a "middle period." Perhaps they see themselves at times on the threshold of new opportunities, or participating in some grand procession toward greatness; or, in darker moments, they may see themselves as the last of a formerly great line, inheritors of a tradition that is dying with them. In neither case, though, is there a sense of "middle." This truism is especially applicable to the Victorian poets, subject of this chapter. For them, as for most Victorians, the sense of self-confident progress was uppermost in their minds: "The best is yet to be" (Robert Browning, "Rabbi Ben Ezra"). Matthew Arnold, one of the few Victorians to feel himself trapped "between two worlds, one dead, the other powerless to be born" ("Stanzas from the Grand Chartreuse"), gave up the practice of poetry as a result. So the primary assumption a reader must bring to the works of the Victorian poets is a belief in their own self-assurance.

Artistically, though, the Victorians did face a severe test to their sense of self-worth. Their immediate predecessors, the romantic poets, were very great indeed; and several of them lived into Victorian times. Those who died young or neglected—KEATS, SHELLEY, BLAKE—the early Victorians could embrace as models for their own developing ideas on poetry; but COLERIDGE and WORDSWORTH were another story. It was Wordsworth, not Browning or Tennyson, whom Queen Victoria chose as her first poet laureate (in 1843); it was Wordsworth's *Prelude* that was in everyone's hands in late 1850, not Tennyson's masterpiece *In Memoriam*, Browning's "Christmas-Eve and Easter-Day," or Rossetti's *The Germ*. As late as 1866, when Robert Buchanan wanted to condemn the poetry of Swinburne, all he had to do was invoke "the sweetness" of the romantics (*Athenaeum*).

Thus the first generation of Victorian poets—Tennyson, Robert Browning, Elizabeth Barrett Browning, and Arnold—must be seen primarily as sharers in the romantic ferment that stirred the world of the nineteenth century: political reform, religious evangelism, technological invention, and literary upheaval. But that generation inevitably became middle-aged; by

140

1851, when the romantics were finally gone and Tennyson could assume the post of poet laureate, he was more than 40. And the economic woes of the Hungry Forties, followed by the European revolutions, a disastrously muddled war in the Crimea, and mutiny in India, seemed to reveal a system more noted for its inadequacies than its greatness. "Why should I strive," asked William Morris, "to set the crooked straight?" ("The Earthly Paradise")—yet the conviction of progressibility remained strong in him and his generation, because Morris and his contemporaries *did* strive for beauty in the arts, and justice in the lives, of English men and women.

Already by the 1860s, though, such doubts had begun to generate a sense of disillusionment in those who would be called the third generation of Victorians. "Day and night I deplore/My . . . foundering own generation," laments the greatest of them, Gerard Manley Hopkins ("The Loss of the Eurydice"). It was a generation that would adopt neither revolution nor reform as its rallying cry, merely sensation. Trading the sense of a world reborn for the despairing conviction of a world in shreds and tatters, these last "romantics" shattered the tradition of a century or more; and as fire burns away stubble and leaves a field fresh for new growth, the fin-de-siècle flame illuminated a way for modernism.

HISTORY AND CRITICISM

Attridge, Derek. *The Rhythms of English Poetry*. Longman 1983 $30.00 pap. $17.95

Ball, Patricia M. *The Heart's Events: The Victorian Poetry of Relationships*. Longwood Pr. 1976 $36.50

Benziger, James. *Images of Eternity: Studies in the Poetry of Religious Vision, from Wordsworth to T. S. Eliot*. Southern Illinois Univ. Pr. 1962 pap. $2.25

Buckley, Jerome H. *The Victorian Temper: A Study in Literary Culture*. Cambridge Univ. Pr. 1981 pap. $11.95. A clear, well-structured overview of the period.

Christ, Carol T. *Victorian and Modern Poetics*. Univ. of Chicago Pr. 1984 lib. bdg. $16.00. A new addition to the argument over just how Victorian turned into modern.

Colville, Derek. *Victorian Poetry and the Romantic Religion*. State Univ. of New York Pr. 1970 pap. $19.95

Fairchild, Hoxie N. *Religious Trends in English Poetry*. Columbia Univ. Pr. 6 vols. ea. $40.00

Faverty, Frederic E., ed. *Victorian Poets: A Guide to Research*. Harvard Univ. Pr. 2d ed. 1968 $27.50. The starting point for any serious study of Victorian poets.

Fletcher, Pauline. *Gardens and Grim Ravines: The Language of Landscape in Victorian Poetry*. Princeton Univ. Pr. 1983 $27.50

Gaunt, William. *The Pre-Raphaelite Dream (The Pre-Raphaelite Tragedy)*. Richard West repr. of 1943 ed. $30.00; Schocken 1966 pap. $3.95

Houghton, Walter E. *The Victorian Frame of Mind, 1830–1870*. Yale Univ. Pr. 1963 pap. $9.95. One of the formative works of Victorian studies, analyzing more than a dozen themes and attitudes visible in the public and private writings of the early Victorians.

Hunt, John D. *The Pre-Raphaelite Imagination, 1848–1900*. Landmark Ed. Univ. of Nebraska Pr. 1969 $19.95

Kaplan, Fred. *Miracles of Rare Device: The Poet's Sense of Self in Nineteenth-Century Poetry.* Wayne State Univ. Pr. 1972 $10.95
Langbaum, Robert. *The Poetry of Experience: The Dramatic Monologue in Modern Literary Tradition.* Norton Lib. 1963 pap. $4.95. The book that defined how the dramatic monologue works.
————, ed. *The Victorian Age: Essays in History and in Social and Literary History.* Academy Chicago repr. of 1967 ed. 1983 pap. $6.95
Levine, Richard A., ed. *The Victorian Experience: The Poets.* Ohio Univ. Pr. 1982 text ed. $21.95 1983 pap. $12.00
Lucas, F. L. *Ten Victorian Poets.* Shoe String (Archon) repr. of 1948 ed. 1966 $16.50
Meisel, Martin. *Realizations: Narrative, Pictorial, and Theatrical Arts of the Nineteenth Century.* Princeton Univ. Pr. 1984 $52.50
Mermin, Dorothy. *The Audience in the Poem: Five Victorian Poets.* Rutgers Univ. Pr. 1983 $20.00. A useful complement to Langbaum's earlier work.
Sambrook, James. *Pre-Raphaelitism: A Collection of Critical Essays.* Univ. of Chicago Pr. 1976 $17.50 pap. $4.95
Stevenson, Lionel. *The Pre-Raphaelite Poets.* Univ. of North Carolina Pr. 1972 $25.00; Norton Lib. 1974 pap. $3.95
Tennyson, G. B. *Victorian Devotional Poetry: The Tractarian Mode.* Harvard Univ. Pr. text ed. 1980 $18.50
Thesing, William B. *The London Muse: Victorian Poetic Responses to the City.* Univ. of Georgia Pr. 1982 $22.00
Warren, Alba H. *English Poetic Theory, 1825–1865.* Biblio Dist. 1967 $27.50

COLLECTIONS

Barnes, William. *A Selection from Poems of Rural Life in the Dorset Dialect.* Century Bookbindery repr. of 1909 ed. 1977 $20.00. An important collection of dialect poetry, which was influential in the late Victorian era.
Brett, R. L., ed. *Poems of Faith and Doubt: The Victorian Age.* Univ. of South Carolina Pr. text ed. 1970 pap. $4.95
Buckler, William E., ed. *The Major Victorian Poets.* Houghton Mifflin (Riv. Eds.) 1973 pap. $6.50. A good, usable text edition.
Caldwell, Thomas, ed. *The Golden Book of Modern English Poetry: 1870–1920.* Arden Lib. repr. of 1922 ed. 1978 lib. bdg. $25.00. A fascinating index of Georgian taste.
Carr, Arthur S. *Victorian Poetry: Clough to Kipling.* Irvington repr. of 1972 ed. 1982 $18.95
Garrett, Edmund H., ed. *Victorian Songs.* Intro. by E. Gosse, *Granger Index Repr. Ser.* Ayer repr. of 1895 ed. $18.00. A useful collection of a neglected genre.
Hayward, John, ed. *The Oxford Book of Nineteenth-Century English Verse.* Oxford 1964 $45.00
Hickock, Kathleen. *Representations of Women: Nineteenth-Century British Women's Poetry.* Greenwood 1984 $29.95. Not a true anthology, since the poetry is available in short quotations only; but this work makes available far more women's poetry than has been accessible before, and is therefore vital.
Houghton, Walter E., and G. Robert Stange. *Victorian Poetry and Poetics.* Houghton Mifflin 2d ed. 1968 $30.95. Perhaps the most comprehensive text.
Lang, Cecil Y., ed. *The Pre-Raphaelites and Their Circle.* Univ. of Chicago Pr. 2d ed. 1975 pap. $12.95. The best anthology of Pre-Raphaelite works.
Messenger, Nigel P., and J. Richard Watson, eds. *Victorian Poetry: "The City of Dreadful Night" and Other Poems.* Rowman & Littlefield Univ. Lib. 1974 pap. $6.00

Miles, Alfred H., and others. *The Poets and the Poetry of the Nineteenth Century.* AMS
    Pr. 12 vols. repr. of 1907 ed. ea. $42.50 set $510.00. The official collection of ro-
    mantic and Victorian poets, selected by the Victorians.
Richards, Bernard. *English Verse, 1830–1890.* Longman 1980 pap. $19.95
Stanford, Derek, ed. *Pre-Raphaelite Writing.* Biblio Dist. (Everyman's) 1984 pap.
    $5.95; *Rowman & Littlefield Univ. Lib.* 1973 $11.50
Stedman, Edmund C. *Victorian Anthology, 1837 to 1895: Selections Illustrating the
    Editor's Critical Review of British Poetry in the Reign of Victoria.* Arden Lib. repr.
    of 1895 ed. 1977 lib. bdg. $30.00; Folcroft 1973 lib. bdg. $32.00; Greenwood repr.
    of 1895 ed. lib. bdg. $37.50; Scholarly 2 vols. repr. of 1895 ed. 1969 $29.00
Symons, Arthur, ed. *An Anthology of Nineties' Verse.* Scholarly repr. of 1928 ed.
    $29.00
Trilling, Lionel, and Harold Bloom, eds. *Victorian Prose and Poetry.* Oxford 1973 pap.
    $15.95
Watson, J. Richard, ed. *Everyman's Book of Victorian Verse.* Biblio Dist. 1982 $19.50
Wiley, P. L., and Harold Orel, eds. *British Poetry, 1880–1920: Edwardian Voices.* Ir-
    vington 1969 $39.50 pap. $19.95
Wright, David, ed. *Seven Victorian Poets.* Heinemann 1964 pap. $5.00

ARNOLD, MATTHEW. 1822–1888

Arnold's career as a poet was brief, especially in relation to his long ten-
ure as the acknowledged champion of high culture in mid-Victorian England. His career as inspector of schools ran from 1851 to his death in 1888,
and essays on social, literary, and religious questions were flowing from his
pen even before he was voted the professorship of poetry at Oxford (1857),
and continued through *Discourses in America* (1885) nearly 30 years later.

His poetic output, however, is more meager. As a young man, Arnold attempted to create poems through which contemporary readers could touch
worlds of remoteness—the people and places of legend. But by 1855 he had
realized that his poetry could never achieve the popularity of Tennyson's,
nor the influence among the great that might have compensated for his
smaller audience. Declaring that "it is a pity that power should be wasted"
(preface to *Poems*, 1855), he turned to prose. Then, after the death of his
dear college friend and fellow poet, Arthur Hugh Clough, in 1861, Arnold
wrote a number of poems on the subject of doubt and willed conviction, including *Thyrsis*, often called his greatest poem. Arnold's works are characterized by brilliant romantic images, set within earnestly Victorian discourse.
(See also Chapter 16 in this volume.)

BOOKS BY ARNOLD

The Works of Matthew Arnold. AMS Pr. 15 vols. repr. of 1903–04 ed. $425.00; Schol-
    arly 15 vols. repr. of 1903–04 ed. 1970 $265.00
Poems. Biblio Dist. (Everyman's) 1965 $9.95
Poetical Works. Ed. By C. B. Tinker and Howard F. Lowry, *Oxford Stand. Authors Ser.*
    1950 $35.00. With the Longman edition out of print, this is the second-best.
The Poetical Works of Matthew Arnold. Arden Lib. repr. of 1893 ed. 1978 lib. bdg.
    $30.00

Poetry and Criticism of Matthew Arnold. Ed. by Arthur D. Culler, *Riv. Eds.* Houghton Mifflin 1961 pap. $6.50

The Portable Matthew Arnold. Ed. by Lionel Trilling, *Viking Portable Lib.* Penguin 1980 pap. $7.95

Essays and Poems of Arnold. Ed. by Frederick W. Roe, Richard West repr. of 1928 ed. 1980 $30.00

Matthew Arnold: An Introduction and a Selection. Ed. by Clifford Dyment, Richard West repr. of 1948 ed. 1977 $25.00

Letters of Matthew Arnold to Arthur Hugh Clough. Ed. by Howard F. Lowry, Russell repr. of 1932 ed. 1968 $8.00

Unpublished Letters of Matthew Arnold. Folcroft repr. of 1923 ed. 1977 lib. bdg. $17.00

BOOKS ABOUT ARNOLD

Buckler, William E. *On the Poetry of Matthew Arnold. Gotham Lib.* New York Univ. Pr. 1982 $32.50

Dawson, Carl, ed. *Matthew Arnold: The Poetry. Critical Heritage Ser.* Routledge & Kegan 1973 $38.50

Eells, John S., Jr. *The Touchstones of Matthew Arnold.* AMS Pr. repr. of 1955 ed. $22.50; New College & Univ. Pr. 1955 pap. $8.95

Fulweiler, Howard W. *Letters from the Darkening Plain: Language and the Grounds of Knowledge in the Poetry of Arnold and Hopkins.* Univ. of Missouri Pr. 1972 $14.00

Honan, Park. *Matthew Arnold: A Life.* Harvard Univ. Pr. text ed. 1983 pap. $9.95; McGraw-Hill 1981 $19.95. The definitive biography.

Jamison, William A. *Arnold and the Romantics.* Folcroft 1958 lib. bdg. $20.00

Johnson, W. Stacy. *The Voices of Matthew Arnold.* Greenwood repr. of 1961 ed. 1973 lib. bdg. $18.75

MacDonald, Isobel. *The Buried Self: A Background to the Poems of Matthew Arnold.* Folcroft repr. of 1949 ed. 1974 $15.00

Saintsbury, George E. *Matthew Arnold.* Russell repr. of 1899 ed. 1967 $7.50

Smart, Thomas B. *Bibliography of Matthew Arnold.* Burt Franklin repr. of 1892 ed. $18.50; Folcroft 1974 lib. bdg. $18.50; Porter 1979 $28.50

Stange, G. Robert. *Matthew Arnold: The Poet as Humanist.* Gordian repr. of 1967 ed. 1979 $12.50

Super, R. H. *The Time-Spirit of Matthew Arnold.* Univ. of Michigan Pr. 1970 $6.95

Tollers, Vincent L., ed. *Bibliography of Matthew Arnold, 1932–1970.* Pennsylvania State Univ. Pr. 1974 $24.95

BROWNING, ELIZABETH BARRETT. 1806–1861

The story of Elizabeth Barrett's elopement with Robert Browning has been told many times, most succinctly perhaps by Samuel C. Chew: "Browning's virile confidence triumphed over paternal despotism and ill-health" (*A Literary History of England*). When the lovers left England on September 12, 1846, Barrett was a famous poet and Browning known more as a difficult and obscure thinker; her *Poems*, first published in 1844, had already made her a voice for women of her generation. That reputation was reinforced with the publication of her second edition of *Poems* in 1850, containing "Sonnets from the Portuguese," and reached its peak with her publication in 1857 of *Aurora Leigh.*

Barrett Browning's enduring fame has rested on these last two works, one a celebration of woman as man's other half, the second a celebration of woman's potential to stand on her own. During the Edwardian and later periods, it was "Sonnets from the Portuguese" that embodied Barrett Browning; since the rise of feminism, it has been *Aurora Leigh*. Most recently, a third side of Barrett Browning has been revealed: the incisive critical and political commentator, seen in her letters. As an invalid and a resident in Italy, she was of necessity a detached observer of events; but she was a passionately interested one. The projected multivolume edition of *The Brownings' Correspondence* promises to be a landmark in this newest revival.

BOOKS BY ELIZABETH BARRETT BROWNING

The Complete Works of Elizabeth Barrett Browning. Ed. by Charlotte Porter and Helen A. Clarke, AMS Pr. 6 vols. repr. of 1900 ed. $240.00. The standard edition, extensively annotated.

Complete Poetical Works. Scholarly repr. of 1900 ed. 1972 $69.00

Poetical Works of Elizabeth Barrett Browning. Intro. by Ruth Adams, *Cambridge Eds. Ser.* Houghton Mifflin 1974 $22.95

The Earlier Poems of Elizabeth Barrett Browning, 1826–1833. Arden Lib. repr. of 1878 ed. 1978 lib. bdg. $30.00

Aurora Leigh. Academy Chicago 1979 lib. bdg. $14.95 pap. $5.95

Sonnets from the Portuguese. Intro. by J. Mersand, Avon 1966 pap. $.75; Harper 1932 $10.95; Peter Pauper $4.95

Sonnets from the Portuguese and Other Love Poems. Doubleday $9.95

The Letters of Elizabeth Barrett Browning. Ed. by Frederic G. Kenyon, Telegraph Bks. 2 vols. repr. of 1897 ed. 1981 lib. bdg. $75.00

(and Robert Browning). *The Brownings' Correspondence.* Ed. by Philip Kelley and Ronald Hudson, Wedgestone Pr. 4 vols. 1984–85 ea. $47.50. This massive project promises to print everything written by or to Elizabeth and Robert; when completed, it will be the definitive collection of Browningiana.

The Letters of Elizabeth Barrett Browning to Mary Russell Mitford, 1836–1854. Ed. by Mary R. Sullivan, Wedgestone Pr. 3 vols. 1983 $160.00

Twenty-Two Unpublished Letters of Elizabeth Barrett Browning and Robert Browning. Folcroft repr. of 1935 ed. 1973 lib. bdg. $17.50; Haskell repr. of 1935 ed. 1971 lib. bdg. $39.95

(and Robert Browning). *New Poems.* Arden Lib. repr. of 1915 ed. 1977 $25.00

BOOKS ABOUT ELIZABETH BARRETT BROWNING

Hewlett, Dorothy. *Elizabeth Barrett Browning.* Octagon repr. of 1952 ed. 1972 lib. bdg. $27.50

Hudson, Gladys W., ed. *Elizabeth Barrett Browning Concordance.* Gale 4 vols. 1973 $165.00

Kelley, Philip, and Ronald Hudson, eds. *The Brownings' Correspondence: A Checklist.* Wedgestone Pr. 1978 $95.00

Loth, David. *The Brownings: A Victorian Idyll.* Richard West repr. of 1932 ed. 1973 $25.00; Telegraph Bks. 1982 lib. bdg. $35.00

Lubbock, Percy. *Elizabeth Barrett Browning in Her Letters.* AMS Pr. repr. of 1906 ed. $21.45; Folcroft repr. of 1906 ed. lib. bdg. $25.00

Radley, Virginia L. *Elizabeth Barrett Browning. Twayne's Eng. Authors Ser.* G. K. Hall lib. bdg. $13.95

BROWNING, ROBERT. 1812–1889

Browning's reputation has suffered, both during his lifetime and since, from the charge of obscurity. "Sordello," published in 1840, only his third published work, remains an enigma even to those who read it with the benefit of a recent annotated edition. Marriage to Elizabeth Barrett in 1846 brought a new lightness and openness of voice to Browning's verse during the next 21 years, resulting in the great dramatic monologues of *Men and Women* in 1855 and the epic *The Ring and the Book* in 1867. It is not that these are the most beautiful poems of the Victorian age, but they are the most perceptive; they reveal more clearly the men and women who speak the monologues, and the poet who conceived them, than any comparable works of the century. During the last 20 years of his career, however, the clotted quality of his verse returned, aggravated by his efforts to transform such subjects as contested wills (in "Red-Cotton Night Cap Country") and the political career of George Bubb Doddington (in "Parleyings with Certain People of Importance in Their Day") into poetry.

These notorious difficulties with Browning's poetry have led successive editors into apparently impassable morasses. Between the demands of textual exegesis on the one side, and the long-time bias toward encyclopedic annotation of the Browning Society on the other, any editor foolhardy enough to tackle Browning's works deserves thanks for even partial success. The Ohio University Press edition, under the direction of Roma A. King, Jr., completed five volumes in 15 years; the new Oxford English Text edition, under Ian Jack and Margaret Smith, has just reached "Sordello" without succumbing. Perhaps by the year 2000 there will be more progress.

The other side of Browning, alluded to in Henry James's famous story "The Private Life," promises to be illuminated by the forthcoming volumes of *The Brownings' Correspondence*, edited by Philip Kelley and Ronald Hudson; Volume 3 of that series will contain the first of Robert Browning's letters, along with everything ever written to or by either of the Brownings. Further recent biographical material was incorporated into William Irvine's and Park Honan's *The Book, The Ring, and the Poet*, now unfortunately out of print.

BOOKS BY ROBERT BROWNING

The Complete Works of Robert Browning, with Variant Readings and Annotations. Ed. by Roma A. King, Jr., Ohio Univ. Pr. 5 vols. 1967–82 ea. $30.00–$40.00. An ambitious effort to record all the poetry, in all its states.

Works. Ed. by Frederic G. Kenyon, AMS Pr. repr. of 1912 centenary ed. $250.00

The Poetical Works of Robert Browning. Ed. by Ian Jack and Margaret Smith, *Oxford Eng. Texts Ser.* 2 vols. ea. $69.00–$74.00. Additional volumes are in preparation.

The Poetical Works of Robert Browning. Intro. by G. Robert Stange, *Cambridge Eds. Ser.* Houghton Mifflin 1974 $27.50

Poetical Works, 1833 to 1864. Ed. by Ian Jack, *Oxford Stand. Authors Ser.* 1970 $29.95 pap. $6.95

Poems, 1835–1889. Ed. by Humphrey Milford, *Oxford World's Class. Ser.* 1954 $12.95

Robert Browning: The Poems. Ed. by John Pettigrew, Yale Univ. Pr. 2 vols. text ed. 1981 ea. $52.00 pap. ea. $14.95

Poems of Robert Browning. Ed. by Donald Smalley, Houghton Mifflin (Riv. Eds.) 1956 pap. $6.50

Robert Browning: Poetry and Prose. Ed. by Simon Nowell Smith, *Reynard Lib.* Harvard Univ. Pr. 1967 pap. $7.95

Robert Browning's Poetry. Ed. by James M. Loucks, *Norton Critical Eds.* 1980 pap. $6.95

Selected Poetry of Browning. Ed. by George Ridenour, New Amer. Lib. (Signet Class.) pap. $2.95

Pauline. Folcroft repr. of 1931 ed. 1977 lib. bdg. $25.00

Sordello: A Marginally Annotated Edition. Ed. by Morse Peckham, Whitston 1977 $18.50

Dramatic Idylls. Foundation Class. repr. of 1879 ed. 1981 $59.25

Robert Browning: Men and Women and Other Poems. Ed. by J. W. Harper, Biblio Dist. (Everyman's) 1985 pap. $5.95; *Rowman & Littlefield Univ. Lib.* 1975 $9.50 pap. $5.00

The Pied Piper of Hamelin. Putnam 1971 $5.29; Scroll Pr. $9.95; Warner repr. of 1889 ed. $10.95

The Ring and the Book. Intro. by John Bryson, Biblio Dist. (Everyman's) repr. of 1911 ed. 1968 $8.95; intro. by W. Sypher, *Norton Lib.* 1967 pap. $8.95; ed. by Richard D. Altick, Yale Univ. Pr. text ed. 1981 $42.00 pap. $11.95

A Critical Edition of Robert Browning's "Bishop Blougram's Apology." Ed. by Frank C. Allen, Humanities Pr. 1976 $25.50

Dearest Isa: Robert Browning's Letters to Isabella Blagden. Ed. by Edward C. McAleer, Greenwood repr. of 1951 ed. lib. bdg. $18.75; Univ. of Texas Pr. repr. of 1951 ed. text ed. 1977 pap. $17.50

Intimate Glimpses from Browning's Letter File. Folcroft repr. of 1934 ed. 1976 lib. bdg. $20.00

Learned Lady: Letters from Robert Browning to Mrs. Thomas Fitzgerald, 1876–1889. Ed. by Edward C. McAleer, Harvard Univ. Pr. (Belknap Pr.) 1966 $15.00

The Letters of Robert Browning and Elizabeth Barrett Browning, 1845–1846. Arden Lib. 2 vols. 1899 $85.00; ed. by Elvan Kinter, Harvard Univ. Pr. 2 vols. 1969 $55.00

(and Elizabeth Barrett Browning). *The Brownings' Correspondence.* Ed. by Philip Kelley and Ronald Hudson, Wedgestone Pr. 4 vols. 1984–85 ea. $47.50. This massive project promises to print everything written by or to Elizabeth and Robert; when completed, it will be the definitive collection of Browningiana.

BOOKS ABOUT ROBERT BROWNING

Armstrong, Isobel, ed. *Writers and Their Background: Robert Browning. Writers and Their Background Ser.* Ohio Univ. Pr. 1975 $20.00 pap. $10.00

Berdoe, Edward. *The Browning Cyclopedia: A Guide to the Study of the Works of Robert Browning.* Longwood Pr. repr. of 1916 ed. 1980 lib. bdg. $55.00; Richard West repr. of 1912 ed. 1977 lib. bdg. $65.00

Broughton, Leslie N. *Robert Browning: A Bibliography, 1830–1950.* Burt Franklin repr. of 1953 ed. 1970 $29.50

Broughton, Leslie N., and Benjamin F. Stelter. *Concordance to the Poems of Robert Browning, 1924–1925.* Haskell 4 vols. repr. of 1924 ed. 1970 lib. bdg. $325.00

Buckler, William E. *Poetry and Truth in Robert Browning's "The Ring and the Book."* New York Univ. Pr. 1985 $42.50

Carleton, Frances B. *The Dramatic Monologue: Vox Humana. Salzburg Studies in Eng. Lit.* Humanities Pr. text ed. 1977 pap. $25.50

Davies, Hugh S. *Browning and the Modern Novel.* Folcroft repr. of 1962 ed. 1976 lib. bdg. $6.00

Erickson, Lee. *Robert Browning: His Poetry and His Audiences.* Cornell Univ. Pr. 1984 $25.00

Gest, John M. *The Old Yellow Book: Source of Robert Browning's "The Ring and the Book."* Haskell repr. of 1924 ed. lib. bdg. $58.95; Richard West repr. of 1924 ed. 1973 $29.75. The original material transformed by Browning.

Gridley, Roy E. *The Brownings and France: A Chronicle with Commentary.* Longwood Pr. 1982 $38.00. Especially helpful in illuminating Browning's French poems.

Hair, D. S. *Browning's Experiments with Genre.* Univ. of Toronto Pr. 1972 $20.00

Harrold, William E. *The Variance and the Unity: A Study of the Complementary Poems of Robert Browning.* Ohio Univ. Pr. 1973 $12.00

Hassett, Constance W. *The Elusive Self in the Poetry of Robert Browning.* Ohio Univ. Pr. 1982 $19.95

Honan, Park. *Browning's Characters: A Study in Poetic Technique.* Shoe String (Archon) repr. of 1961 ed. 1969 $20.00

Kelley, Philip, and Ronald Hudson, eds. *The Brownings' Correspondence: A Checklist.* Wedgestone Pr. 1978 $95.00

Korg, Jacob. *Browning and Italy.* Ohio Univ. Pr. 1983 $24.95

Lawson, E. Leroy. *Very Sure of God: Religious Language in the Poetry of Robert Browning.* Vanderbilt Univ. Pr. 1974 $8.95

Litzinger, Boyd, and K. L. Knickerbocker, eds. *The Browning Critics.* Univ. Pr. of Kentucky 1965 pap. $12.00

Maynard, John R. *Browning's Youth.* Harvard Univ. Pr. 1977 $27.50

Mayne, Ethel C. *Browning's Heroines.* Richard West 1973 $35.00

Pearsall, Robert B. *Robert Browning. Twayne's Eng. Authors Ser.* G. K. Hall 1974 lib. bdg. $13.95

Ryals, Clyde De L. *Becoming Browning: The Poems and Plays of Robert Browning, 1833–1846.* Ohio State Univ. Pr. 1983 $25.00. Ryals stresses Browning's development of an ironic stance; the study complements Tucker's (see below), which argues for openness in Browning's style.

———. *Browning's Later Poetry, 1881–1889.* Cornell Univ. Pr. 1975 $25.00. Almost makes one want to read Browning's late poetry.

Siegchrist, Mark. *Rough in Brutal Print: The Legal Sources of Browning's "Red-Cotton Night Cap Country."* Ohio State Univ. Pr. 1981 $15.00

Slinn, E. Warwick. *Browning and the Fictions of Identity.* Barnes & Noble 1982 $28.50

Southwell, Samuel B. *Quest for Eros: Browning and "Fifine."* Univ. Pr. of Kentucky 1980 $25.00. Fascinating life-into-art study, although "Fifine" does tend to become a roman-à-clef in the process.

Thomas, Donald. *Robert Browning: A Life within Life.* Viking 1983 $18.75

Tucker, Herbert F. *Browning's Beginnings: The Art of Disclosure.* Univ. of Minnesota Pr. 1980 $22.50

Ward, Maisie. *Robert Browning and His World: The Printer Face (1812–1861).* Telegraph Bks. repr. of 1967 ed. 1984 lib. bdg. $40.00

CLOUGH, ARTHUR HUGH. 1819–1861

The Victorians' insistence on facing doubts, and prevailing through them to achieve true conviction, made it inevitable that there would be failures: those who were faced down by their doubts. Some turned to Catholicism;

some turned to a secularized "muscular Christianity"; some, like Arthur Hugh Clough, found no place to stand. But in the course of his search, while his loss of faith could still be thought of as healthy skepticism, Clough wrote three fine poems that keep his name and mind alive after a century and a half: *The Bothie* (1848), *Amours de Voyage* (published posthumously), and *Dipsychus* (unfinished). During the same period, he was Matthew Arnold's closest friend and most earnest correspondent; most of Arnold's critical ideas were worked out in letters to Clough before they were published in essays or prefaces. Clough's works have all been well and recently edited, making study of his poems and letters a pleasure, not just a requirement.

BOOKS BY CLOUGH

Poems and Prose Remains of Arthur Hugh Clough with a Selection from His Letters and Memoirs. Scholarly 2 vols. repr. of 1869 ed. 1970 $69.00

The Poems of Arthur Hugh Clough. Ed. by F. L. Mulhauser, *Oxford Eng. Texts Ser.* 2d ed. 1974 $79.00. The definitive edition of the poems.

Selections from the Poems of Arthur Hugh Clough. Norwood repr. of 1894 ed. 1977 lib. bdg. $10.00

Amours de Voyage. Ed. by Patrick G. Scott, Univ. of Queensland Pr. 1974 $14.95 pap. $8.95

The Bothie: The Text of 1848. Ed. by Patrick G. Scott, Univ. of Queensland Pr. 1977 $10.95 pap. $6.25

BOOKS ABOUT CLOUGH

Greenberger, Evelyn B. *Arthur Hugh Clough: Growth of a Poet's Mind.* Harvard Univ. Pr. 1970 $17.50

Houghton, Walter E. *The Poetry of Clough.* Octagon repr. of 1963 ed. 1979 lib. bdg. $18.50

Scott, Patrick G. *The Early Editions of Arthur Hugh Clough. Reference Lib. of the Humanities* Garland 1977 lib. bdg. $25.00

Thorpe, Michael, ed. *Clough: The Critical Heritage.* Routledge & Kegan 1972 $34.00

HARDY, THOMAS. 1840–1928

Hardy won fame as a great Victorian novelist; then, in 1895, he abandoned the novel and began writing poetry. During the last 30 years of his life he won new acclaim as a fine modern poet. His great epic is *The Dynasts* (1903–08), a saga of the Napoleonic Wars, which attempts to recapitulate all of English and human history. Of the nearly 1,000 other poems, several have achieved the status of school classics: "The Blow," "The Convergence of the Twain," "The Darkling Thrush," and Hardy's own favorite, "A Tramp-Woman's Tragedy." Hardy's poetic vision, expressed with a sparseness and directness that owe more to Hardy's remembrance of childhood hymns than to the poems of his contemporaries, bridges the gap (half-perceived, half-created) between the last century and our own. (See also Chapter 11 in this volume.)

BOOKS BY HARDY

The Complete Poetical Works. Ed. by Samuel Hynes, Oxford 2 vols. 1982–84 ea. $39.50–$47.50. The new standard edition.

The Variorum Edition of the Complete Poems of Thomas Hardy. Ed. by James Gibson,
Macmillan 1980 $60.00
The Complete Poems. Ed. by James Gibson, Macmillan 1982 pap. $12.95. The student
text.
The Complete Poems of Thomas Hardy. Macmillan 1978 $29.95. Superseded by Gib-
son's variorum edition and the new Oxford, but still usable.
The Works of Thomas Hardy in Prose and Verse. Johnson Repr. $3,000.00. All the
works, novels and poetry.
The Thomas Hardy Omnibus. St. Martin's 1979 $15.00
The Collected Letters of Thomas Hardy. Ed. by Richard L. Purdy and Michael Mill-
gate, Oxford 4 vols. 1978–84 ea. $35.95–$49.50
The Life and Work of Thomas Hardy. Ed. by Michael Millgate, Univ. of Georgia Pr.
1985 $35.00. The reconstructed work of the manuscripts by Hardy originally
published under his wife's name, Florence Hardy (see below).

BOOKS ABOUT HARDY

Bailey, J. O. *Thomas Hardy and the Cosmic Mind: A New Reading of "The Dynasts."*
Greenwood repr. of 1956 ed. 1977 $20.00
Bowra, C. M. *The Lyrical Poetry of Thomas Hardy.* Folcroft repr. of 1946 ed. 1975
$7.50; Haskell 1975 $22.95
Clements, Patricia, and Juliet Grindle, eds. *The Poetry of Thomas Hardy.* Barnes &
Noble 1980 $27.50. Essays of a consistently high standard.
Das, Manas M. *Thomas Hardy—Poet of Tragic Vision: A Study of Hardy's Poetic Sensi-
bility.* Humanities Pr. 1983 $11.25
Davie, Donald. *Thomas Hardy and British Poetry.* Oxford 1972 $18.95. One of the best
works of criticism of modern poetry generally.
Dean, Susan. *Hardy's Poetic Vision in The Dynasts: The Diorama of a Dream.* Prince-
ton Univ. Pr. 1977 $31.50
Garrison, Chester A. *The Last Venture: Hardy's Epic-Drama The Dynasts.* Humanities
Pr. 1973 pap. $25.00
Hardy, Florence, comp. *The Early Life of Thomas Hardy.* Scholarly repr. of 1928 ed.
1971 $14.00
————. *The Life of Thomas Hardy, 1840–1928.* Shoe String (Archon) repr. of 1962 ed.
1970 $27.50. The ghost-written biography/autobiography.
Lewis, C. Day. *Lyrical Poetry of Thomas Hardy.* Folcroft repr. of 1953 ed. lib. bdg.
$9.50
Millgate, Michael. *Thomas Hardy: A Biography.* Random House 1982 $25.00. The
new standard biography.
Orel, Harold. *Thomas Hardy's Epic-Drama: A Study of The Dynasts.* Greenwood repr.
of 1963 ed. $15.00
Page, Norman, ed. *Thomas Hardy: The Writer and His Background.* St. Martin's 1980
$27.50. Sets Hardy in both his contexts.
Paulin, Thomas. *Thomas Hardy: The Poetry of Perception.* Rowman 1975 $18.50.
Probably the best single book on Hardy's poetry.
Pinion, F. B. *A Commentary on the Poems of Thomas Hardy.* Barnes & Noble 1976
$10.00. Mainly biographical and geographical notes.
Richardson, James. *Thomas Hardy: The Poetry of Necessity.* Univ. of Chicago Pr. 1977
$12.00. One of the few books on Thomas Hardy's poetry by a poet.
Taylor, Dennis. *Hardy's Poetry, 1860–1928.* Columbia Univ. Pr. 1981 $24.00
Wright, Walter F. *The Shaping of "The Dynasts": A Study in Thomas Hardy.* Univ. of
Nebraska Pr. 1968 $24.50

Zietlow, Paul. *Moments of Vision: The Poetry of Thomas Hardy.* Harvard Univ. Pr. 1974 $20.00

HOPKINS, GERARD MANLEY. 1844–1889

Hopkins and his near contemporary Oscar Wilde represent the two extremes of the late Victorian dichotomy. Starting in the aesthetic center shared by Ruskin and Pater, the heroes of the university, one moved toward flamboyance, decadence, and ruin; the other moved toward asceticism, self-denial, and what some might call an equivalent end.

Before Hopkins converted to Catholicism and became a Jesuit in 1868, he had been considered the star of Balliol College; but when he entered the novitiate he burned all his youthful poems. Seven years later, at the instigation of his superiors, he resumed the practice of poetry in the composition of his finest long work, "The Wreck of the Deutschland." But the Jesuit magazine to which he submitted it declined to print it, and declined again with a later poem; so none of his poems had more than manuscript existence until 1918, when his closest friend and fellow poet, Robert Bridges, collected them, wrote a short prefatory study of Hopkins's innovations, and published the *Poems.*

Hopkins's verse, with its fusion of romantic and Christian images and its sophisticated metrical patterning, can appear difficult at first reading. But because Hopkins was a brilliant theorist and analyst of his own work, and left so many letters explaining his otherwise obscure concepts, such as "inscape," "instress," and "sprung rhythm," his poetry has been well served by critics. With the *Poems,* a selection of the prose, and any one of the secondary works listed below, a reader will encounter few obstacles to Hopkins's grandeur.

BOOKS BY HOPKINS

Poems. Ed. by W. H. Gardner and Norman H. Mackenzie, Oxford 4th ed. 1967 $29.95 pap. $7.95. The definitive edition.
Poems and Prose of Hopkins. Ed. by W. H. Gardner, Penguin 1953 pap. $4.95. The student text, combining poems and needed letters.
Major Poems. Biblio Dist. (Everyman's) 1979 pap. $2.75
Gerard Manley Hopkins. Pocket Poets Ser. Dufour 1969 pap. $2.00
The Wreck of the Deutschland. Godine 1971 $6.00 pap. $2.95

BOOKS ABOUT HOPKINS

Bender, Todd K. *Gerard Manley Hopkins: The Classical Background and Critical Reception of His Work.* Johns Hopkins Univ. Pr. 1966 $14.50
Bump, Jerome. *Gerard Manley Hopkins.* Twayne's Eng. Authors Ser. G. K. Hall 1982 $13.50. Rises far above the usual Twayne level.
Cotter, James F. *Inscape: The Christology and Poetry of Gerard Manley Hopkins.* Univ. of Pittsburgh Pr. 1972 $24.95
Downes, David A. *The Great Sacrifice: Studies in Hopkins.* Univ. Pr. of Amer. 1983 $21.50 pap. $8.75
Dunne, Tom. *Gerard Manley Hopkins: A Comprehensive Bibliography.* Univ. Pr. of Virginia 1983 $35.00

Harris, Daniel A. *Inspirations Unbidden: The "Terrible Sonnets" of Gerard Manley Hopkins.* Univ. of California Pr. 1982 $23.00. An outstanding study.
Heuser, Alan. *The Shaping Vision of Gerard Manley Hopkins.* Shoe String (Archon) repr. of 1958 ed. 1968 $12.50
Kenyon Critics. *Gerard Manley Hopkins.* New Directions 1973 pap. $2.45. The special Hopkins number of the *Kenyon Review.*
MacKenzie, Norman H. *A Reader's Guide to Gerard Manley Hopkins.* Cornell Univ. Pr. 1981 $26.95 pap. $9.95
Robinson, John. *In Extremity.* Cambridge Univ. Pr. 1980 pap. $8.95
Schneider, Elisabeth. *The Dragon in the Gate: Studies in the Poetry of Gerard Manley Hopkins.* Univ. of California Pr. 1968 $37.50
Sprinker, Michael. *A Counterpoint of Dissonance: The Aesthetics and Poetry of Gerard Manley Hopkins.* Johns Hopkins Univ. Pr. 1980 $14.00. A post-structuralist account.
Storey, Graham. *A Preface to Hopkins.* Longman 1981 $12.95 pap. $6.95. The best general introduction.
Sulloway, Alison G. *Gerard Manley Hopkins and the Victorian Temper.* Columbia Univ. Pr. 1972 $25.00
Walhout, Donald. *Send My Roots Rain: A Study of Religious Experience in the Poetry of Gerard Manley Hopkins.* Ohio Univ. Pr. 1981 $16.95

HOUSMAN, A(LFRED) E(DWARD). 1859–1936

Housman's great poetic work *A Shropshire Lad* (1896) is one of a number of works written in the 1890s that reflect the late Victorians' sense that an era was drawing to a close; with Queen Victoria in her dotage, and the very millennium ending, a kind of late adolescent nostalgia for the disappearing pastoral world of the early 1800s was inevitable. Housman himself did not share the simplistic fantasies of love, rejection, and despair mirrored in his quatrains, concentrating instead on his career as a professor of Latin; he translated such kindred spirits as JUVENAL (see Vol. 2) and Manilius.

But after the Great War, with places like Shropshire a cherished memory even for those who (like Housman himself) had never really known its pastoral charms, thousands fell into the spell of Housman's poems. Responding to the clamor, Housman produced *Last Poems* in 1922; after his death, a third volume was cobbled together out of his old notebook jottings. Writers who came of age anytime during the first quarter of the twentieth century were perhaps more strongly marked by Housman's poetry than by the new modern masters.

BOOKS BY HOUSMAN

Collected Poems of A. E. Housman. Holt rev. ed. 1971 pap. $7.95. The standard edition.
Collected Poems. Buccaneer Bks. repr. of 1983 ed. lib. bdg. $16.95
A Shropshire Lad. Intro. by J. Mersand, Avon 1964 pap. $.60; Beaufort Bks. 1985 pap. $6.95; intro. by William S. Braithwaite, Branden pap. $2.50; Buccaneer Bks. repr. 1981 lib. bdg. $14.95; ed. by Carl J. Weber, Greenwood repr. of 1946 ed. 1980 lib. bdg. $22.50; Peter Pauper $4.95
The Making of "A Shropshire Lad": A Manuscript Variorum. Ed. by Tom B. Haber,

Univ. of Washington Pr. 1966 $20.00. Each poem is printed in draft and final form, plus critical apparatus.

Satires of Juvenal. Foundation Class. 2 vols. repr. of 1911 ed. 1985 $237.45

BOOKS ABOUT HOUSMAN

Carter, John, and John Sparrow, eds. *A. E. Housman: A Bibliography.* Univ. Pr. of Virginia 1982 $25.00

Haber, Tom B. *A. E. Housman. Twayne's Eng. Authors Ser.* G. K. Hall 1967 $12.50

Leggett, B. J. *The Poetic Art of A. E. Housman: Theory and Practice.* Univ. of Nebraska Pr. 1978 $14.50

Page, Norman. *A. E. Housman: A Critical Biography.* Schocken 1983 $29.95

Richards, Grant. *Housman, 1897–1936.* Octagon 1972 lib. bdg. $31.50

Ricks, Christopher, ed. *A. E. Housman: A Collection of Critical Essays. Twentieth-Century Views Ser.* Prentice-Hall 1968 pap. $1.95

Withers, Percy. *A Buried Life: Personal Recollections of A. E. Housman.* Gordon $59.95

KIPLING, RUDYARD. 1865–1936 (NOBEL PRIZE 1907)

Kipling is the only nineteenth-century English poet to win the Nobel Prize; he won not alone on the basis of his short stories, which more closely mirror the ambiguities of the declining Edwardian world than has commonly been recognized, but also on the basis of his tremendous ability as a popular poet. His reputation was first made with *Barrack Room Ballads* (1892), and in "Recessional" he captured a side of Queen Victoria's final jubilee no one else dared to address. Kipling's genius lies not in his patriotic fervor, nor in his music hall rhythms, but in the underlying spirit that, as J. I. M. Stewart said in his study of Kipling (o.p.), always manages to "pluck something affirmative from the abyss." (See also Chapter 11 in this volume.)

BOOKS BY KIPLING

Collected Works. AMS Pr. 28 vols. repr. of 1941 ed. $1,120.00. The Burwash Edition, authorized.

Rudyard Kipling's Verse. Doubleday 1940 $19.95. The definitive edition; includes the verses he liked to append to his stories.

A Choice of Kipling's Verse. Ed. by T. S. Eliot, Faber 1963 pap. $4.95

Kipling: A Selection of His Stories and Poems. Ed. by John Beercroft, Doubleday 2 vols. 1956 $19.95

BOOKS ABOUT KIPLING

Durand, R. A. *A Handbook to the Poetry of Rudyard Kipling.* Kraus repr. of 1914 ed. $24.00

Harrison, James. *Rudyard Kipling. Twayne's Eng. Authors Ser.* G. K. Hall 1982 $13.00

Orel, Harold, ed. *Kipling: Interviews and Recollections.* Barnes & Noble 2 vols. 1983 ea. $26.50. Must reading for any Kipling enthusiast.

Stewart, J. I. M. *Rudyard Kipling.* Dodd 1966 o.p.

Tompkins, J. M. *The Art of Rudyard Kipling.* Univ. of Nebraska Pr. (Bison) 1965 pap. $5.95

Wilson, Angus. *The Strange Ride of Rudyard Kipling.* Penguin 1979 pap. $6.95; Viking 1978 $17.50

MEREDITH, GEORGE. 1828–1909

George Meredith was known in his own time as one of the era's finest novelists, but he was also known and respected as the author of seven books of poetry, representing the distillation of his thought from his earliest years (his first book was *Poems* in 1851) to his last (*A Reading Life* was published in 1901). Even today, Meredith's poetry is capable of arousing controversy. Some readers strongly prefer the clearness and naturalistic spirit of his early works, like "Love in the Valley," while others stand firm in defense of such late works as "Ode to the Great Comic Spirit," written in a much denser style. But all readers agree that his sonnet sequence *Modern Love*, published in 1862, captures the mingled laughter and despair of human sexual relationships with a brilliance and realism seldom found in the poetry of any period. (See also Chapter 11 in this volume.)

BOOKS BY MEREDITH

Works of George Meredith. Ed. by Arundell Esdaile, Russell 29 vols. repr. of 1909–12 ed. 1963 $325.00

The Poems of George Meredith. Ed. by Phyllis B. Bartlett, Yale Univ. Pr. 1978 $137.00. The definitive edition of Meredith's poetry.

Selected Poems. Ed. by Graham Hough, Greenwood repr. of 1962 ed. 1980 lib. bdg. $22.50

The Notebooks of George Meredith. Ed. by Gillian Beer and Margaret Harris, Humanities Pr. 1984 pap. $25.00

BOOKS ABOUT MEREDITH

Bernstein, Carol L. *Precarious Enchantment: A Reading of Meredith's Poetry.* Catholic Univ. Pr. 1979 $17.50. A series of excellent, sensitive readings of the poems.

Olmsted, John C. *George Meredith: An Annotated Bibliography, 1925–1975.* Garland 1978 lib. bdg. $25.00

Sawin, Lewis. *A Concordance to the Poetry of George Meredith.* Garland 1981 lib. bdg. $165.00. Based on Bartlett's Yale Univ. Press edition, this should be definitive as well.

Wilt, Judith. *The Readable People of George Meredith.* Princeton Univ. Pr. 1975 $24.00

Woods, Alice. *George Meredith's Poems.* Porter 1982 lib. bdg. $34.50

———. *Some of George Meredith's Poems.* Folcroft 1973 lib. bdg. $10.00

MORRIS, WILLIAM. 1834–1896

Morris was the Victorian age's model of the Renaissance man. Arrested in 1885 for preaching socialism on a London street corner (he was chairman of the Hammersmith Socialist League and editor of its paper, *The Commonweal*, at the time), he was called before a magistrate and asked for identification. He modestly described himself upon publication (1868–70) as "Author of 'The Earthly Paradise,' pretty well known, I think, throughout Europe." He might have added that he was also: the head of Morris and Company, makers of fine furniture, carpets, wallpapers, stained glass, and other crafts; founder of the Society for the Protection of Ancient Buildings; and founder as well as chief designer for the Kelmscott Press, which set a standard for fine book design that has carried through to the present.

Morris's literary productions spanned the spectrum of styles and subjects. He began under the influence of Dante Gabriel Rossetti with a Pre-Raphaelite volume called *The Defence of Guenevere and Other Poems* (1858, o.p.); he then turned to narrative verse, first in the pastoral mode ("The Earthly Paradise") and then under the influence of the Scandinavian sagas ("Sigurd the Volsung"). After "Sigurd," his masterpiece, Morris turned for a time exclusively to social and political affairs, becoming known as a master of the public address; then during the last decade of his life, he fused these two concerns in a series of socialist romances, the most famous of which is *News from Nowhere*.

BOOKS BY MORRIS

Collected Works. Ed. by May Morris, Gordon 24 vols. repr. of 1910–15 ed. $600.00. The standard edition of Morris's works, with revealing biographical introductions.

A Choice of William Morris' Verse. Ed. by Geoffrey Grigson, Faber 1969 $7.50 pap. $3.95. A usable student text.

News from Nowhere and Selected Writings and Design. Ed. by Asa Briggs, Penguin 1984 $4.95. A new student edition, weighted toward the late work.

Stories in Prose, Stories in Verse, Shorter Poems, Lectures and Essays. Ed. by G. D. H. Cole, AMS Pr. repr. of 1934 ed. $31.50

News from Nowhere. Routledge & Kegan repr. 1970 pap. $6.95

The Letters of William Morris to His Family and Friends. Ed. by Philip Henderson, AMS Pr. repr. of 1950 ed. $28.25

Collected Letters. Ed. by Norman Kelvin, Princeton Univ. Pr. 1984 vol. 1 $55.00. The first volume in what will be the definitive letters.

BOOKS ABOUT MORRIS

Banham, Joanna, and Jennifer Harris, eds. *William Morris and the Middle Ages.* Manchester Univ. Pr. 1984 $32.50 pap. $10.50

Cole, G. D. H. *William Morris as a Socialist.* Folcroft 1960 $10.00

Faulkner, Peter. *Against the Age: An Introduction to William Morris.* Allen & Unwin text ed. 1980 $28.50. The best general introduction to the man and his milieu.

———. *William Morris: The Critical Heritage.* Routledge & Kegan 1973 $38.50 pap. $15.00

Kirchhoff, Frederick. *William Morris. Twayne's Eng. Authors Ser.* G. K. Hall 1979 lib. bdg. $15.95

Lindsay, Jack. *William Morris: His Life and Work.* Taplinger 1979 $14.95

Mackail, J. W. *The Life of William Morris.* Ayer 2 vols. repr. of 1899 ed. 1968 $30.00. One of the best Victorian official biographies.

Needham, Paul, ed. *William Morris and the Art of the Book: A Pierpont Morgan Library Volume.* Ed. by Joseph Dunlap and John Dreyfus, Oxford 1976 $59.95

Oberg, Charlotte. *A Pagan Prophet: William Morris.* Univ. Pr. of Virginia 1978 $13.95

Silver, Carole. *The Romance of William Morris.* Ohio Univ. Pr. 1982 $20.95 pap. $12.95. The best current critical study.

Stansky, Peter. *Redesigning the World: William Morris, the 1880's, and the Arts and Crafts.* Princeton Univ. Pr. 1984 $27.50

———. *William Morris.* Oxford 1983 $12.95 pap. $3.95

Thompson, E. P. *William Morris.* Pantheon repr. of 1955 ed. 1977 $17.95. A major biography, stressing Morris's political development and influence.

Thompson, Paul Van K. *The Work of William Morris.* Charles River Bks. $7.95

Watkinson, Ray. *William Morris as Designer.* Eastview Pr. repr. 1980 $22.50; Van Nostrand 1983 pap. $12.95

William Morris Society in the United States. *Studies in William Morris.* Wedgestone Pr. 5 vols. repr. ea. $6.00–$11.00

ROSSETTI, CHRISTINA. 1830–1894

Christina Rossetti was for decades treated primarily as "the sister of Dante Gabriel Rossetti." She rejected her brother's flamboyance, remained at home, and wrote a far greater volume of poetry than her brother. With the rise of feminism and the growing recognition of the aesthetic possibilities of religious poetry, Christina Rossetti's work has become the subject of an increasing volume of study.

Although "Goblin Market," published in 1862, remains her best-known poem, her sonnet sequence "Monna Innominata" has attracted growing attention as a work that can bear comparison with Elizabeth Barrett Browning's "Sonnets from the Portuguese" on the one side, and George Meredith's "Modern Love" on the other. A new edition of her complete poems is long overdue; a project under the editorship of Rebecca W. Crump, in conjunction with the Louisiana State University Press, promises to repair the fault.

BOOKS BY CHRISTINA ROSSETTI

Poetical Works: With Memoir and Notes by William Michael Rossetti. Ridgeway Bks. 1904 $85.00. To date, the standard work.

The Complete Poems of Christina Rossetti: A Variorum Edition. Ed. by Rebecca W. Crump, Louisiana State Univ. Pr. vol. 1 1979 $27.50; vol. 2 1985 text ed. $35.00 The definitive text.

A Choice of Christina Rossetti's Verse. Ed. by Elizabeth Jennings, Faber 1970 pap. $4.95

Selected Poems. Ed. by C. H. Sisson, Humanities Pr. text ed. 1984 pap. $8.50

Goblin Market. Beaufort Bks. 1985 pap. $6.95; Dover repr. of 1893 ed. 1983 pap. $2.50; Dutton 1970 $7.95; Godine 1984 $13.95 pap. $7.95

Maude: Prose and Verse. Ed. by Rebecca W. Crump, Shoe String (Archon) 1976 $15.00

Sing Song: A Nursery Rhyme Book. Dover repr. of 1872 ed. 1969 pap. $3.00

Family Letters of Christina Georgina Rossetti, with Some Supplementary Letters and Appendices. Ed. by William M. Rossetti, *Eng. Lit. Ser.* Haskell repr. of 1908 ed. 1969 lib. bdg. $39.95

BOOKS ABOUT CHRISTINA ROSSETTI

Battiscombe, Georgina. *Christina Rossetti.* State Mutual Bk. 1981 $39.00

Bell, Mackenzie. *Christina Rossetti: A Biographical and Critical Study.* AMS Pr. repr. of 1898 ed. $12.50; Haskell repr. of 1898 ed. 1971 lib. bdg. $56.95; Richard West repr. of 1898 ed. 1973 $14.95. For years the only work on Christina Rossetti.

Bellas, Ralph A. *Christina Rossetti.* Twayne's Eng. Authors Ser. G. K. Hall 1977 lib. bdg. $16.95

Crump, Rebecca W. *Christina Rossetti: A Reference Guide.* G. K. Hall 1976 lib. bdg. $22.00

Jimenez, Nilda, ed. *The Bible and the Poetry of Christina Rossetti: A Concordance.* Greenwood 1979 lib. bdg. $55.00

ROSSETTI, DANTE GABRIEL. 1828–1882

Around Rossetti swirled the currents of high Victorian revolt. From his formative influence on the Pre-Raphaelite Brotherhood (1847–54) and his publication of *The Germ* in 1850, to his later infamy as the butt of Robert W. Buchanan's moralistic attacks in *The Fleshly School of Poetry* of 1871, Dante Gabriel Rossetti attracted the scorn of many, and the wholehearted admiration of growing numbers. Rossetti's poetry ranged from the grand guignol of "A Last Confession," through the imagistic brilliance of "The Blessed Damozel" (1850) and his other poems for pictures, to his masterwork: the sonnet sequence "The House of Life," upon which Rossetti's contemporary poetic fame rests.

Rossetti was also known as a translator, producing the first modern translation of the early Italian poets and publishing the best Victorian translation of Dante's *Vita Nuova* in 1861. His paintings stand out among the general academic ruck of Victorian England and have been the subject of exhibitions in the last decade at the Delaware Art Museum, the Fogg Art Museum, and the Yale University Art Gallery. Finally, he was an important model for the generations that followed him, both in his willingness to indulge in sexual irregularities and even more importantly in his eagerness to *épater les bourgeoisie* (walking his pet wombat on the streets of London, for example), which became a religion for the decadents who grew up during the 1860s.

BOOKS BY DANTE GABRIEL ROSSETTI

Poems. Ed. by Oswald Doughty, Biblio Dist. (Everyman's) repr. of 1961 ed. 1977 $8.95

The Poetical Works of Dante Gabriel Rossetti. Folcroft repr. of 1903 ed. lib. bdg. $45.00

Works. Ed. by William M. Rossetti, Adler's repr. of 1911 ed. 1972 $60.00. In the absence of anything more definitive, the standard edition.

Jan Van Hunks. Ed. by John R. Wahl, Folcroft repr. of 1952 ed. lib. bdg. $15.00; NYPL 1952 $10.00

The Best Poems by Dante Gabriel Rossetti. Gloucester Art Pr. repr. of 1881 ed. $66.45

The Germ. AMS Pr. repr. 1973 $25.00; Folcroft $10.00. The place to go to read Rossetti in his purest, original form.

Dante and His Circle with the Italian Poets Preceding Him. Norwood 2 vols. repr. of 1900 ed. 1980 lib. bdg. $75.00; Richard West repr. of 1902 ed. 1973 $25.00

The Early Italian Poets. Folcroft repr. of 1905 ed. lib. bdg. $30.00; Foundation Class. 2 vols. repr. of 1911 ed. 1985 $237.50; intro. by John Wain, Univ. of California Pr. 1982 $16.95

Dante Gabriel Rossetti: His Family Letters. AMS Pr. 2 vols. repr. of 1895 ed. $42.50

The Letters of Dante Gabriel Rossetti to His Publishers, F. S. Ellis. Folcroft repr. of 1928 ed. 1977 lib. bdg. $25.00

Letters. Ed. by Oswald Doughty and John R. Wahl, Oxford 1965–67 vols. 1–2 o.p. vols. 3–4 ea. $75.00. In a life devoted to excess, one would expect letters more revelatory.

Pre-Raphaelite Diaries and Letters. Ed. by William M. Rossetti, AMS Pr. repr. of 1900

ed. $14.00. Essential source material for the Pre-Raphaelite Brotherhood, and
for much of the Rossetti family's activities.

BOOKS ABOUT DANTE GABRIEL ROSSETTI

Angeli, Helen R. *Dante Gabriel Rossetti*. Ayer repr. of 1949 ed. $22.00
Beerbohm, M. *Rossetti and His Circle*. Gordon $59.95. An early study of the Pre-
Raphaelites by the rapier-penned satirist.
Boos, Florence. *The Poetry of Dante Gabriel Rossetti: A Critical Reading and Source
Study*. Mouton 1976 $40.00
Buchanan, Robert W. *The Fleshly School of Poetry and Other Phenomena of the Day*.
AMS Pr. 1871 $14.00. Any serious student of Rossetti, Swinburne, and their con-
temporaries should know on just what the attacks on Rossetti were based.
Dobbs, Brian, and Judy Dobbs. *Dante Gabriel Rossetti: An Alien Victorian*. Humani-
ties Pr. 1977 $21.25
Doughty, Oswald. *A Victorian Romantic: Dante Gabriel Rossetti*. Telegraph Bks. repr.
of 1949 ed. 1981 lib. bdg. $40.00. The standard biography, although much has
come to light in the past 25 years.
Fennell, Francis L. *Dante Gabriel Rossetti: An Annotated Bibliography*. Ed. by Duane
Devries, Garland 1981 lib. bdg. $40.00
Fraser, Robert S., ed. *Essays on the Rossettis*. Princeton Lib. 1972 $10.00
Howard, Ronnalie R. *The Dark Glass: Vision and Technique in the Poetry of Dante Ga-
briel Rossetti*. Ohio Univ. Pr. 1972 $12.00
Rees, Joan. *The Poetry of Dante Gabriel Rossetti: Modes of Self-Expression*. Cambridge
Univ. Pr. 1981 $42.50. One of the better recent studies.
Riede, David G. *Dante Gabriel Rossetti and the Limits of Victorian Vision*. Cornell
Univ. Pr. 1983 $25.00. One of the best books on Rossetti, or on Victorian poetry
generally.
Rossetti, William M. *Bibliography of the Works of Dante Gabriel Rossetti*. AMS Pr.
repr. of 1905 ed. $9.50; Folcroft repr. of 1905 ed. lib. bdg. $16.50
————. *Dante Gabriel Rossetti as Designer and Writer*. AMS Pr. repr. of 1889 ed.
$18.00; Richard West repr. of 1889 ed. 1979 lib. bdg. $40.00
Scott, William B. *Autobiographical Notes and Notes on His Artistic and Poetic Circle
of Friends, 1830–1882*. Ed. by W. Minto, AMS Pr. 2 vols. repr. of 1892 ed. 1970
$32.50. Fascinating memoirs by Rossetti's friend and fellow artist.
Sonstroem, David. *Rossetti and the Fair Lady*. Wesleyan Univ. Pr. 1970 $17.50
Vogel, Joseph F. *Dante Gabriel Rossetti's Versecraft*. Univ. Pr. of Florida 1971 pap.
$4.00

SWINBURNE, ALGERNON CHARLES. 1837–1909

Swinburne was just old enough to get caught up in the Pre-Raphaelite
maelstrom. In 1857, when Rossetti, William Morris, and their friends
painted the ceiling of the new Oxford Union, Swinburne fell away from his
politically minded friends at Balliol College and into the set of aesthetic
young graduates. Within a year he had left Oxford, one step ahead of expul-
sion. In less than ten years he was the most notorious poet of Europe, accepted by Walter Savage Landor but savaged by John Morley; these early
poems are still his best known: "Atalanta in Calydon" (1865), *Poems and Ballads* (1866), and "A Song of Italy" (1867).

Stung by the critical attacks on *Poems and Ballads*, Swinburne turned for
a time to prose, writing the manifesto "Art for Art's Sake" in his *Notes on Po-*

ems and Reviews (o.p.), as well as still-readable essays on BLAKE, BYRON, and SHAKESPEARE (see Vol. 2). He also composed two novels, *Lesbia Brandon* (c.1864) and *Love's Cross-currents* (1877, o.p.), which are available in a combined volume.

But his reputation rests on his poems: the several above, *Songs before Sunrise* (1871, o.p.), *Tristram of Lyonesse* (1882, o.p.), and the many others that flowed, with increasing regularity but diminishing vitality, from the retreat at Putney where he was taken in 1879 to recover from the effects of his alcoholic and other debauches—and where he stayed for 30 years under the care of Theodore Watts. David G. Riede has written eloquently of these late poems, attributing to them a mythopoeic power equal to the rhythmic and melodic power of the early works; but to most readers, although the late poems may be masterful, they reveal little of that erotic energy that led Tennyson to call Swinburne's verses "poisonous honey."

BOOKS BY SWINBURNE

Poems of Algernon Charles Swinburne. AMS Pr. 6 vols. repr. of 1905 ed. $265.00. Originally prepared by Swinburne himself.
Poems and Ballads and Atalanta in Calydon. Bobbs 1970 $10.25; ed. by Morse Peckham, Irvington text ed. 1970 pap. $8.95
Selected Poems: Swinburne. Ed. by L. M. Findlay, Humanities Pr. text ed. 1982 $14.75
Ballads of the English Border. Folcroft 1973 lib. bdg. $29.50; Gordon $59.95
New Writings by Swinburne: A Medley of Poems, Critical Essays, Hoaxes and Burlesques. Ed. by Cecil Y. Lang, Syracuse Univ. Pr. 1964 $14.95
Swinburne Replies. Ed. by Clyde K. Hyder, Syracuse Univ. Pr. 1966 $14.00
The Novels of Algernon Charles Swinburne: Love's Cross-currents, Lesbia Brandon. Greenwood repr. of 1962 ed. 1978 $28.50
A Year's Letters. Ed. by Francis J. Sypher, New York Univ. Pr. 1974 pap. $12.50
The Swinburne Letters. Ed. by Cecil Y. Lang, Yale Univ. Pr. 1959–62 6 vols. ea. $42.00. The model for all later collections.

BOOKS ABOUT SWINBURNE

Beetz, Kirk H. *Algernon Charles Swinburne: A Bibliography of Secondary Works, 1861–1980. Author Bibliographies Ser.* Scarecrow Pr. 1982 $16.50
Chew, Samuel C. *Swinburne.* Richard West repr. of 1929 ed. $30.00; Shoe String (Archon) repr. of 1929 ed. $22.00. As Philip Henderson's 1974 biography is out of print, this is probably the most accessible general account of Swinburne, though silent about sexual matters.
Connolly, Thomas E. *Swinburne's Theory of Poetry.* State Univ. of New York Pr. 1965 $22.50
Hyder, Clyde K., ed. *Swinburne: The Critical Heritage.* Routledge & Kegan 1970 $24.00 1984 pap. $15.00. Useful for its tracing of Swinburne's violent reception.
McGann, Jerome J. *Swinburne: An Experiment in Criticism.* Univ. of Chicago Pr. 1972 $20.00
McSweeney, Kerry. *Tennyson and Swinburne as Romantic Naturalists.* Univ. of Toronto Pr. 1981 $27.50
Raymond, Meredith B. *Swinburne's Poetics: Theory and Practice.* Mouton 1971 pap. $26.00

Riede, David G. *Swinburne: A Study in Romantic Mythmaking.* Univ. Pr. of Virginia 1978 $14.95
Thomas, Donald. *Swinburne: The Poet of His World.* Oxford 1979 $19.95

TENNYSON, ALFRED, 1ST BARON. 1809–1892

If there were a contest for the title "greatest Victorian poet," Tennyson would in death as in life obtain the prize. He had the finest ear of any English poet, admitting to know the metrical value of every word in the English language except "scissors." In addition, his ability to evoke a closely rendered scene was unsurpassed. Therefore, those who sought to attack Tennyson called him "the stupidest of the English poets"; but he remains the only one ennobled for his poetry.

Tennyson trumpeted the creed of the benevolent tyrant in poems as wide apart as "Ulysses," "The Princess," and "Idylls of the King"; it was this embrace of an authoritarian universe that, as much as his versecraft, earned him the respect of Prince Albert and the nomination as poet laureate in 1850. With that one stroke Tennyson became the poet of the establishment, and for 40 years the Parnassian idol whom younger poets would vainly seek to topple.

Tennyson's letters show almost nothing of the vividness and brilliance of his poetry, but Cecil Y. Lang and Edgar F. Shannon have begun publishing them for their sidelights. More importantly for an understanding of Tennyson's poetry, the century-long ban on publishing the contents of Tennyson's notebooks, held by Trinity College in Cambridge, was lifted a few years ago; a new edition of *In Memoriam*, incorporating these variants, has been brought out by Susan Shatto and Marion Shaw, and with luck the rest of the manuscripts will be made available in the near future. At the same time, the best annotated edition—that by Christopher Ricks—has been allowed to go out of print (*Poems*, Annotated English Poets Ser., Norton, 1972).

BOOKS BY TENNYSON

Works of Alfred Lord Tennyson: Annotated. Ed. by Hallam Tennyson, AMS Pr. 9 vols. repr. of 1907–08 ed. $202.50; Greenwood 9 vols. repr. of 1907–08 ed. lib. bdg. $148.50. The official text, incorporating all author's revisions.
Poems and Plays. Ed. by T. Herbert Warren and Frederick Page, Oxford repr. of 1953 ed. 1971 pap. $9.50
Poetical Works of Tennyson. Intro. by G. Robert Stange, *Cambridge Eds. Ser.* Houghton Mifflin 1974 $25.00
Poems of Tennyson. Ed. by Jerome H. Buckley, Houghton Mifflin (Riv. Eds.) 1958 pap. $6.50
Selected Poems. Ed. by Michael Millgate, *New Oxford Eng. Ser.* text ed. 1973 pap. $6.95
Tennyson's Poetry. Ed. by Robert W. Hill, Jr., *Norton Critical Eds.* 1972 pap. $13.95
A Choice of Tennyson's Verse. Ed. by David Cecil, Faber 1971 pap. $2.95
Unpublished Early Poems. Ed. by Charles Tennyson, Arden Lib. repr. of 1932 ed. 1980 lib. bdg. $20.00; Folcroft repr. of 1932 ed. lib. bdg. $12.50
Poems of 1842. Ed. by Christopher Ricks, International Ideas repr. of 1968 ed. 1981 $14.95

The Lover's Tale. Porter 1977 $12.50

In Memoriam. Ed. by Robert H. Ross, *Norton Critical Eds.* 1974 $8.95 pap. $3.95; ed. by Susan Shatto and Marion Shaw, Oxford Univ. Pr. 1982 $65.00. The Ross edition has a readable text with insightful essays attached. The Shatto and Shaw edition is essential for any serious study.

Alfred Tennyson: "In Memoriam," "Maud," and Other Poems. Ed. by John D. Jump, *Rowman & Littlefield Univ. Lib.* 1974 pap. $4.00

Idylls of the King. Ed. by J. M. Gray, *Eng. Poets Ser.* Yale Univ. Pr. 1983 $26.00 pap. $7.95. The best working edition of the *Idylls.*

Idylls of the King and a Selection of Poems. Fwd. by G. Baker, New Amer. Lib. (Signet Class.) pap. $2.50

The Letters of Alfred Lord Tennyson, 1821–1850. Ed. by Cecil Y. Lang and Edgar F. Shannon, Harvard Univ. Pr. 1981 $30.00. An excellent edition of material that illuminates very little about Tennyson.

BOOKS ABOUT TENNYSON

Baker, Arthur E. *A Concordance to the Poetical and Dramatic Works of Alfred, Lord Tennyson.* Barnes & Noble repr. of 1914 ed. 1966 o.p.

Baum, Paul F. *Tennyson Sixty Years After.* Octagon repr. of 1948 ed. 1976 lib. bdg. $26.00

Buckler, William E. *Man and His Myths: Tennyson's "Idylls of the King" in Critical Context.* New York Univ. Pr. 1984 $42.50

Buckley, Jerome H. *Tennyson: The Growth of a Poet.* Harvard Univ. Pr. 1974 pap. $7.95; Houghton Mifflin 1965 pap. $5.50. The ideal critical introduction to Tennyson's poetry and life.

Colley, Ann C. *Tennyson and Madness.* Univ. of Georgia Pr. 1983 $20.00. Must be read with care, but thought-provoking.

Culler, Arthur D. *The Poetry of Tennyson.* Yale Univ. Pr. 1977 $24.50. An excellent overview of the poetry.

Gray, J. M. *Thro' the Vision of the Night: A Study of Source, Evolution and Structure in Tennyson's "Idylls of the King."* McGill Queens Univ. Pr. 1980 $25.00. Lacks a complete sense of recent critical work.

Hagen, June S. *Tennyson and His Publishers.* Pennsylvania State Univ. Pr. 1979 $24.95

Hair, Donald S. *The Domestic and Heroic in Tennyson's Poetry.* Univ. of Toronto Pr. 1981 $27.50

Hellstrom, Ward. *On the Poems of Tennyson.* Univ. Pr. of Florida 1972 $8.25

Jones, Richard. *The Growth of the Idylls of the King.* Gordon $59.95

Joseph, Gerhard. *Tennysonian Love: The Strange Diagonal.* Univ. of Minnesota Pr. 1969 $10.00

Killham, John, ed. *Critical Essays on the Poetry of Tennyson.* Darby repr. of 1960 ed. 1981 lib. bdg. $30.00; Routledge & Kegan 1960 pap. $10.00. Mostly superseded now, but several of these essays were critical in the Tennyson revival.

Kissane, James D. *Alfred Tennyson. Twayne's Eng. Authors Ser.* G. K. Hall lib. bdg. $13.50

Kozicki, Henry. *Tennyson and Clio: History in the Major Poems.* Johns Hopkins Univ. Pr. 1979 $17.50

Layard, George S. *Tennyson and His Pre-Raphaelite Illustrators.* Folcroft repr. of 1894 ed. 1978 $12.50; Norwood repr. of 1894 ed. $12.50

Martin, Robert B. *Tennyson: The Unquiet Heart.* Faber 1983 pap. $12.95; Oxford 1980

$35.00. The fullest recent biography, which is marred only by its overemphasis on the strain of madness in the Tennyson family.

Paden, W. D. *Tennyson in Egypt: A Study of the Imagery in His Earlier Work.* Folcroft 1973 lib. bdg. $20.00; Octagon repr. of 1942 ed. 1971 lib. bdg. $18.00

Palmer, David J., ed. *Writers and Their Background: Alfred Tennyson. Writers and Their Background Ser.* Ohio Univ. Pr. 1973 $18.00 pap. $9.00

Pattison, Robert. *Tennyson and Tradition.* Harvard Univ. Pr. 1980 $14.00. A study of the idyll tradition and its relation to the domestic and heroic poems.

Pinion, F. B. *A Tennyson Companion: Life and Works.* St. Martin's 1984 $27.50

Pitt, Valerie. *Tennyson Laureate.* Telegraph Bks. repr. of 1962 ed. 1981 lib. bdg. $30.00; Univ. of Toronto Pr. 1962 $15.00 pap. $4.50

Rader, Ralph W. *Tennyson's Maud: The Biographical Genesis. Lib. Repr. Ser.* Univ. of California Pr. 1978 $31.00. Although Martin's recent biography disputes Rader's conclusions, this remains a stimulating essay in the life-into-art tradition.

Rosenberg, John D. *The Fall of Camelot: A Study of Tennyson's Idylls of the King.* Harvard Univ. Pr. (Belknap Pr.) 1973 $8.95

Shannon, Edgar F. *Tennyson and the Reviewers: A Study of His Literary Reputation and of the Influence of the Critics upon His Poetry, 1827–1951.* Shoe String (Archon) repr. of 1952 ed. 1967 $18.50

Shaw, W. David. *Tennyson's Style.* Cornell Univ. Pr. 1976 $24.95

Staines, David. *Tennyson's Camelot: The Idylls of the King and Its Medieval Sources.* Humanities Pr. 1982 $20.00

Tennyson, Charles. *Alfred Tennyson.* Shoe String (Archon) repr. of 1949 ed. 1968 $29.50. The fuller, nearly definitive biography by the poet's grandson.

Tennyson, Hallam, ed. *Studies in Tennyson.* Fwd. by John Benjamin, Barnes & Noble 1981 $28.50

Tennyson, Hallam T. *Alfred Lord Tennyson: A Memoir by His Son.* AMS Pr. 4 vols. repr. of 1899 ed. $34.50; Folcroft repr. of 1906 ed. 1974 lib. bdg. $65.00; Greenwood 2 vols. repr. of 1899 ed. lib. bdg. $47.50; Richard West 2 vols. in 1 repr. of 1897 ed. $75.00; Scholarly 2 vols. repr. of 1899 ed. $32.00. The "authorized," collaborative biography, containing all the material Tennyson, his wife, and his son wanted to see preserved.

THOMPSON, FRANCIS. 1859–1907

In the eighteenth century, Thomas Chatterton provided a warning case of what happened when genius was neglected; in the nineteenth century that model was provided by Francis Thompson. A dropout from a small Catholic school, Thompson drifted to London in the 1880s; there, selling matches on the street and living off the charity of the street's denizens, he somehow produced "The Hound of Heaven." When the poem appeared in 1891, Wilfred Meynell assumed protectorship over Thompson, by then nearly dead from consumption and opium addiction. Thompson managed to produce several subsequent volumes of poetry and prose, but never regained the seemingly miraculous voice that had earned him, and Meynell, their place in Victorian myth.

Books by Thompson

Works. Ed. by Wilfred Meynell, AMS Pr. 3 vols. repr. of 1913 ed. $87.50
Poems of Francis Thompson. Ed. by Terence L. Connolly, Greenwood repr. of 1941 ed. 1979 $37.50

The Hound of Heaven. Dimension Bk. 1983 $3.95; Morehouse repr. of 1890 ed. pap.
$1.00
The Hound of Heaven and Other Poems. 1936. Branden pap. $2.50

BOOKS ABOUT THOMPSON

Meynell, Everard. *The Life of Francis Thompson.* Richard West repr. of 1913 ed. 1973
$19.50; Scholarly repr. of 1913 ed. $18.00. The standard life.
Thomson, Paul Van K. *Francis Thompson: A Critical Biography.* Gordian repr. of
1961 ed. 1973 $10.00

WILDE, OSCAR. 1854–1900

It is sometimes said that Oscar Wilde's life was his greatest poem. Certainly the life of the man who is known more for parading down Pall Mall with an oversized flower than for his literary works may encourage that view. But if Wilde wrote little that transcends his age, he certainly wrote a series of works that embody that age more fully than any other works written in the Yellow Nineties: *The Picture of Dorian Gray* (1891), *The Critic as Artist,* "The Importance of Being Earnest"(1895)—and, lamentably, "The Ballad of Reading Gaol" (1898), written during Wilde's imprisonment for homosexual practices. The lurid light surrounding his downfall should not, however, blind readers to the very real merits of his earlier poetry, especially "Ravenna" (1878) and "Panthea."

BOOKS BY WILDE

Works. Ed. by Robert Ross, AMS Pr. 15 vols. repr. of 1909–22 ed. ea. $27.50 set
$412.50. The original collected edition.
The Portable Oscar Wilde. Ed. by Stanley Weintraub and Richard Aldington, Penguin
1981 pap. $7.95
The Ballad of Reading Gaol. Lawrence Hill 1981 pap. $4.50
De Profundis and Other Writings. Penguin Eng. Lib. Ser. 1976 pap. $3.95
Selected Letters of Oscar Wilde. Ed. by Rupert Hart-Davis, Oxford 1979 $9.95

BOOKS ABOUT WILDE

Ackroyd, Peter. *The Last Testament of Oscar Wilde.* Harper 1983 $12.45 1985 pap.
$3.00
Beckson, Karl. *Oscar Wilde: The Critical Heritage.* Routledge & Kegan 1984 $30.00
Bentley, Joyce. *The Importance of Being Constance: A Biography of Oscar Wilde's
Wife.* Beaufort Bks. 1984 $12.95
Cohen, Philip K. *The Moral Vision of Oscar Wilde.* Fairleigh Dickinson Univ. Pr. 1978
$25.00
Ericksen, Donald H. *Oscar Wilde.* Twayne's Eng. Authors Ser. G. K. Hall 1977 $12.50
Kronenberger, Louis. *Oscar Wilde.* Little, Brown 1976 $8.95
Mikhail, E. H. *Oscar Wilde: An Annotated Bibliography of Criticism.* Rowman 1978
$25.00
————. *Oscar Wilde: Interviews and Recollections.* Barnes & Noble 2 vols. 1979 ea.
$26.50
Shewan, Rodney. *Oscar Wilde: Art and Egotism.* Barnes & Noble 1977 $25.00. The
best single book on Wilde.

CHAPTER 7

Modern British and Irish Poetry

George Bornstein

> Those were years in which we were struggling to revive old communications and to create new ones.
>
> —T. S. ELIOT, *The Sacred Wood* (1928)

"The language is now in the keeping of the Irish (Yeats and Joyce); apart from Yeats, since the death of Hardy, poetry is being written by Americans," declared the iconoclastic EZRA POUND in the late 1920s. "All the developments in English verse since 1910 are due almost wholly to Americans." Pound's exaggeration contains an important kernel of truth. Until almost the end of the nineteenth century, the most important poetry in the English language was written in Great Britain. But the situation changed in the twentieth century, due largely to the immense contribution of American poetry and the independence of countries such as Ireland from Britain. As a result, their poets can no longer easily be labeled "British" (indeed, the best contemporary Irish poet, Seamus Heaney, has objected to his inclusion in the *Penguin Book of Contemporary British Poetry* [o.p.]). Now British poetry ranks as only one strand, albeit an important one, of poetry being written in English. A glance at the three major poets covered in this chapter—W. B. Yeats, T. S. Eliot, and W. H. Auden—illustrates the point. Yeats considered himself an Irish poet and served in the senate of his country after its independence. Eliot was born and raised in the United States and only became a British subject in 1927, well after the composition of "Prufrock," *The Waste Land*, and other important works. Only Auden was born in England, and he chose to become a U.S. citizen in 1946 after several years of residency.

Modern British poetry bears a close relation to political and social events. World War I looms ominously over the century. Its extensive slaughter, horrifying new weaponry, and political ineptitude destroyed the complacency, optimism, and sense of fixity of much prewar culture. The savage war poetry of Wilfred Owen and others replaced the sentimental patriotism of Rupert Brooke. Postwar poetry combined social pessimism with technical experimentation, as exemplified in the early and influential poetry and criticism of T. S. Eliot, whose title *The Waste Land* caught much of the intellectuals' response to their era. With the economic problems of the 1930s, the generation of W. H. Auden, Stephen Spender, Louis MacNeice, and C. Day Lewis turned temporarily leftward, toward a more socially engaged poetry. This in turn yielded to World War II, from which England emerged victorious but diminished. Many of the best poets who came to prominence during the 1950s, like Philip Larkin, formed a loose group called the Movement and produced a polished, restrained, ironic verse eschewing the large claims of the high modernist mode. Contemporary British verse seems more open to various influences and to be awaiting a decisive direction of its own. During the twentieth century, of course, many poets took independent paths, such as the neoromantic Dylan Thomas who produced his great poetry of vibrant rhetoric from the 1930s through the early 1950s. And Irish poetry, like Irish politics (Ireland remained neutral in World War II), took a separate course. After the great achievement of Yeats, the generation of Patrick Kavanagh and Austin Clarke dealt more with Irish themes and the shadow of Yeats than with the modernist main current. A different group of poets succeeded them, and of the newest generation Seamus Heaney seems to many the strongest voice.

Although 30 years ago critics tended to think of modern poetry as antiromantic, more recent voices have argued plausibly that it is more properly postromantic, whether overtly continuing or opposing romantic tradition. Certainly, the romantics began a poetry of mind (Wordsworth called the mind of man "my haunt, and the main region of my song"), which poets have followed ever since. Recent critics have argued that the structure, imagery, and subjects of modern verse owe much to romantic forebears. Yeats avowed the connection frankly, calling himself and his coworkers "the last romantics," and even the antiromantic polemics of Eliot betray a continuing connection. But modernism has not merely repeated romanticism. It drew also on traditions as disparate as the folk, the French, the classical, and even the oriental. Its restless technical explorations and troubled modes of consciousness have resulted in a distinctive poetry of high quality. The story of the interaction between what Eliot called "tradition" and the individual talent is far from over.

ANTHOLOGIES

Bradley, Anthony, ed. *Contemporary Irish Poetry: An Anthology*. Univ. of California Pr. 1980 $19.95. Begins with poets who started their careers after World War I; useful introduction and biographical sketches.

Cameron, Moven, ed. *Voices of Our Kind: An Anthology of Contemporary Scottish Verse*. State Mutual Bk. 1975 $15.00

Ellmann, Richard, and Robert O'Clair, eds. *The Norton Anthology of Modern Poetry*. Norton 1973 $28.95 pap. $21.95. Excellent, capacious gathering (1,456 pages) with helpful, brief bibliographies.

Harmon, Maurice, ed. *Irish Poetry after Yeats: Seven Poets*. Little, Brown 1981 $15.45 pap. $8.95. Ample representations of the poets and useful introduction.

Heath-Stubbs, John F., and David H. Wright, eds. *The Faber Book of Twentieth Century Verse: An Anthology of Verse in Britain*. Faber 3d ed. 1975 $12.95 pap. $7.95; Somerset repr. of 1900 ed. $39.00

Jones, Gwyn, ed. *The Oxford Book of Welsh Verse in English*. Oxford 1977 $22.50

Larkin, Philip, ed. *The Oxford Book of Twentieth Century English Verse*. Oxford 1973 $29.95. An important collection.

Lindsay, Maurice, ed. *Modern Scottish Poetry: An Anthology of the Scottish Renaissance 1925–1975*. Humanities Pr. text ed. 1976 pap. $9.00

MacQueen, John, and Tom Scott, eds. *Oxford Book of Scottish Verse*. Oxford 1966 $35.00

Montague, John, ed. *The Book of Irish Verse: An Anthology of Irish Poetry from the Sixth Century to the Present*. Macmillan 1983 $14.95 pap. $7.95; Peter Smith 1984 $16.75

Sanders, G. D., and others, eds. *Chief Modern Poets of Britain and America*. Macmillan 2 vols. 5th ed. text ed. 1970 pap. $13.95

Thwaite, Anthony, and John Mole, eds. *Poetry, 1945–1980*. Longman text ed. 1983 pap. $7.95. Good short gathering of mostly British and Irish poets; contains notes and biographical sketches.

Untermeyer, Louis. *Modern British Poetry*. Harcourt new & enl. ed. 1969 o.p. Contains critical introductions to each poet.

Yeats, William Butler, ed. *Oxford Book of Modern Verse, 1892–1935*. Oxford 1936 $22.50. Historically important gathering of British, Irish, and American verse with a brilliant if biased introduction by a great poet.

HISTORY AND CRITICISM

Alvarez, A. *Stewards of Excellence: Studies in Modern English and American Poets*. Gordian repr. of 1958 ed. text ed. 1971 $12.00. Readable comments on Yeats, Auden, William Empson, and D. H. Lawrence, together with various American poets.

Bedient, Calvin. *Eight Contemporary Poets: Charles Tomlinson, Donald Davie, R. S. Thomas, Philip Larkin, Ted Hughes, Thomas Kinsella, Stevie Smith, W. S. Graham*. Oxford 1974 pap. $3.95. Perceptive essays and a bibliography.

Bornstein, George. *Transformations of Romanticism in Yeats, Eliot and Stevens*. Univ. of Chicago Pr. 1976 lib. bdg. $25.00. Modern poetry as an "act of mind" for poets both continuing and opposing romantic tradition.

Brooks, Cleanth. *Modern Poetry and the Tradition*. 1939. Univ. of North Carolina Pr. 1970 pap. $6.95. Historically important and still worth reading; heavily influenced by the views of T. S. Eliot.

Daiches, David. *The Present Age in British Literature*. Indiana Univ. Pr. 1958 o.p. Survey of trends since 1914; includes bibliography.

Davie, Donald. *Thomas Hardy and British Poetry*. Oxford 1972 $18.95. Important argument for the "native strain" in modern British verse.

Fallis, Richard. *Irish Renaissance*. Syracuse Univ. Pr. 1977 $22.00 pap. $9.95. The best general history of its subject.

Feder, Lillian. *Ancient Myth in Modern Poetry*. Princeton Univ. Pr. 1972 $36.00 pap. $9.95. Emphasis on Yeats, Pound, Eliot, and Auden.

Gross, Harvey. *Sound and Form in Modern Poetry: A Study of Prosody from Thomas Hardy to Robert Lowell*. Univ. of Michigan Pr. 1968 pap. $9.95

Harrison, John R. *The Reactionaries—Yeats, Wyndham, Lewis, Pound, Eliot, Lawrence: A Study of the Anti-Democratic Intelligentsia*. Schocken 1967 o.p. Explores the political stance of the great modernists.

Hollander, John, ed. *Modern Poetry: Essays in Criticism*. Oxford 1968 pap. $10.95. A good collection of essays by both poets and critics.

Kenner, Hugh. *A Colder Eye: The Modern Irish Writers*. Knopf 1983 $16.95; Penguin

1984 pap. $8.95. Lively, controversial study; emphasizes Yeats, Kavanagh, and Clarke among poets.

————. *The Pound Era*. Univ. of California Pr. 1971 $37.50 pap. $10.95. Broad, often brilliant re-creation of the literary milieu.

Kermode, Frank. *The Romantic Image*. Chilmark Pr. 1963 o.p. Important study of the postromantic in modern poetry, with emphasis on Yeats, Eliot, and T. E. Hulme.

Langbaum, Robert. *The Poetry of Experience: The Dramatic Monologue in Modern Literary Tradition*. Norton Lib. 1963 pap. $4.95; Univ. of Chicago Pr. 1985 pap. $9.95. An influential study aligning modern poetry with that of the nineteenth century.

Leavis, Frank R. *New Bearings in English Poetry: A Study of the Contemporary Situation*. AMS Pr. repr. of 1938 ed. $26.50. First published in 1932, this was an influential interpretation, with particular emphasis on T. S. Eliot and Ezra Pound.

Loftus, Richard J. *Nationalism in Modern Anglo-Irish Poetry*. Univ. of Wisconsin Pr. 1964 o.p. The standard book in its field.

Miller, J. Hillis. *Poets of Reality: Six Twentieth-Century Writers*. Atheneum repr. of 1965 ed. text ed. 1969 pap. $4.25. The six writers include Yeats, Eliot, Thomas, Stevens, and Williams, with an introductory chapter on Conrad.

Perkins, David. *History of Modern Poetry: From the Eighteen Nineties to the High Modernist Mode*. Harvard Univ. Pr. 1976 $27.50 pap. $10.00. The most encyclopedic history of the period; surveys a very large number of poets.

Pinsky, Robert. *The Situation of Poetry: Contemporary Poetry and Its Traditions*. Princeton Essays in Lit. Ser. text ed. 1977 $20.00 pap. $7.95

Press, John. *Map of Modern English Verse*. Oxford 1969 pap. $7.95. Useful survey.

Rosenthal, M. L. *Modern Poets: A Critical Introduction*. Oxford 1960 $11.95 1965 pap. $8.95. Good survey of poetry from Yeats to World War II, with a final chapter on postwar poetry.

————. *The New Poets: American and British Poetry since World War II*. Oxford 1967 o.p. Good survey of the first 20 years of postwar poetry in America, Britain, and Ireland.

Scully, James, ed. *Modern Poetics*. McGraw-Hill 1965 pap. $3.95. Essays on poetry by 15 modern poets from Yeats to Robert Lowell.

Spears, Monroe K. *Dionysus and the City: Modernism in Twentieth-Century Poetry*. Oxford 1970 o.p. Considers the major changes around World War I and again after World War II.

Spender, Stephen. *The Struggle of the Modern*. Univ. of California Pr. 1963 o.p. Fascinating study by an important poet, with emphasis on the poetic imagination.

Stead, Christian K. *The New Poetic: Yeats to Eliot*. AMS Pr. repr. of 1964 ed. $24.50. Covers a variety of figures besides the two mentioned in the title; particularly good on Eliot.

Wilson, Edmund. *Axel's Castle: A Study in the Imaginative Literature of 1870–1930*. Norton repr. of 1931 ed. 1984 pap. $6.95; Scribner 1931 $6.95 text ed. pap. $5.95. A classic older study, still worth reading.

AMIS, KINGSLEY. 1922–

[SEE Chapter 12 in this volume.]

AUDEN, W(YSTAN) H(UGH). 1907–1973

The most important British poet of the generation after T. S. Eliot, W. H. Auden was born in York, England. The son of a doctor and a nurse, he passed through a series of private schools on his way to Oxford University, where he intended to study science but then changed to English literature. Although he graduated with only a mediocre degree, the force of his personality and brilliance of his intellect established him as an important figure even during his student days. After graduation, he quickly gained recognition as the foremost poet in a brilliant circle that also included C. Day Lewis, Stephen Spender, and Louis MacNeice. Active in leftist politics during the 1930s, Auden visited both Spain and China. He had a lifelong passion for travel, and in 1938 immigrated to the United States, where he became a naturalized citizen in 1946. In America he divided his time principally between Greenwich Village and California. A series of academic opportunities culminated in a term as professor of poetry at Oxford from 1956 to 1961. In later life, he also maintained a residence in Kirchstetten, Austria. His many honors included the Pulitzer Prize, the Bollingen Prize, and the National Book Award.

Auden's lifelong prolific output in both verse and prose was matched by a number of stylistic and thematic changes. As a teenager he composed copious verses in the Wordsworth tradition, but tore them up at Oxford because they were "based on Wordsworth. No good nowadays." Auden soon found a new mentor in T. S. Eliot, whose urbanity, intellectual compression, and modernistic technique attracted him. During the 1930s, Auden's work entered its most political phase, with an amalgam of MARX (see Vol. 3) and FREUD (see Vols. 3 and 5) driving his verse intellectually and a new-found affinity for BYRON affecting it literarily. By the end of the decade Auden moved toward a more religious phase, and the later poetry took on a decidedly Christian cast. Simultaneously, Auden came to doubt the social efficacy of verse, writing in his great elegy for Yeats that "poetry makes nothing happen." Auden produced work in a bewildering variety of forms, including long poems, short poems, verse drama, light and occasional verse, songs, opera libretti, and verse epistles, along with numerous editions and translations. His habit of continually revising his verse makes study of his career and even establishment of his basic canon particularly difficult. Auden also deserves high status as critic. Three important collections are *The Enchafed Flood* (1950), his study of romanticism; *The Dyer's Hand* (1962), which includes many pieces written while he held the chair of poetry at Oxford; and *Forewords and Afterwords*, an excellent selection.

BOOKS BY AUDEN

Selected Poems of W. H. Auden. Ed. by Edward Mendelson, Random (Vintage) 1979 pap. $5.95

The Orators: An English Study. Scholarly repr. of 1932 ed. o.p.

Look, Stranger! AMS Pr. repr of 1936 ed. o.p.

The Double Man. Greenwood repr. of 1941 ed. 1979 lib. bdg. $27.50. Also known as *New Year Letter.*

Nones. Random 1951 $6.95

Homage to Clio. Random 1960 o.p.

The Enchafed Flood. Univ. Pr. of Virginia repr. of 1967 ed. 1979 $9.95 pap. $4.95. A study of romanticism.

The Dyer's Hand and Other Essays. Random (Vintage) 1968 pap. $4.95

Epistle of a Godson and Other Poems. Random 1972 $10.95. The last volume published in Auden's lifetime.

Forewords and Afterwords. Random (Vintage) 1973 $19.95 pap. $2.95

The English Auden: Poems, Essays and Dramatic Writings. Random 1978 o.p.

BOOKS ABOUT AUDEN

Beach, Joseph W. *Making of the Auden Canon.* Russell repr. of 1957 ed. 1971 $15.00. Controversial, somewhat critical study of Auden's revisions.

Bloomfield, B. C., and Edward Mendelson. *W. H. Auden: A Bibliography, 1924–1969.* Univ. Pr. of Virginia 2d ed. 1973 $25.00

Callan, Edward. *Auden: A Carnival of Intellect.* Oxford 1983 $25.00

Carpenter, Humphrey. *W. H. Auden: A Biography.* Houghton Mifflin 1981 $10.95. Very readable.

Fuller, John. *A Reader's Guide to Auden.* Farrar 1970 o.p. Poem-by-poem commentary.

Haffenden, John, ed. *W. H. Auden: The Critical Heritage.* Critical Heritage Ser. Routledge & Kegan 1983 $39.95. Historical anthology of criticism about Auden.

Hynes, Samuel. *The Auden Generation: Literature and Politics in England in the 1930's.* Princeton Univ. Pr. repr. of 1977 ed. 1982 $35.00 pap. $9.95; Viking 1977 $12.50. Especially good on the literary and political context of the 1930s.

Johnson, Richard. *Man's Place: An Essay on Auden.* Cornell Univ. Pr. 1973 $19.50

Mendelson, Edward. *Early Auden.* Harvard Univ. Pr. 1983 pap. $9.95; Viking 1981 $20.00. The fullest study of this phase of Auden's career.

Replogle, Justin. *Auden's Poetry.* Washington Pap. Ser. Univ. of Washington Pr. repr. of 1969 ed. 1971 $15.00 pap. $2.95

Spears, Monroe K. *The Poetry of Auden: The Disenchanted Island.* Oxford 1963 o.p.

———. ed. *Auden: A Collection of Critical Essays.* Prentice-Hall 1964 o.p.

Wright, George T. *W. H. Auden.* Twayne's U.S. Authors Ser. G. K. Hall rev. ed. 1981 lib. bdg. $13.50

BETJEMAN, JOHN. 1906–1984

A leading modern champion of the values of an older England, John Betjeman was born in Highgate, London, to a well-off merchant family. The loneliness and suffering of his upbringing, first by nursemaids and then at a series of schools culminating in Marlborough, often surface in his poetry. He went to Magdalene College, Oxford, where he belonged to the same smart social set as Evelyn Waugh. Betjeman worked in a variety of media and achieved wide public attention as host for a television series on the history of British architecture, one of his prime enthusiasms (he was particularly fond of Victorian Gothic).

Deliberately free from the difficulties of much modern verse, Betjeman's poetry harks back to a more accessible British tradition that includes Tennyson and Hardy. With quiet wit he resisted the debasements of modern mass culture in favor of an older England—simpler, more rural, and more religious than the current one. Both Auden and Larkin especially admired his work, and Auden even edited a selection of it. His harsher critics have found him unintellectual and sentimental. His poetry has achieved a huge circulation in England, with the *Collected Poems* reputedly selling more than 100,000 copies.

Books by Betjeman

Collected Poems. Intro. by Lord Birkenhead, Merrimack 1985 pap. $9.95
John Betjeman. Pocket Poets Ser. Dufour 1958 pap. $2.00
An American's Guide to English Parish Churches. Astor-Honor 1959 $15.00
Victorian and Edwardian London. David & Charles 1969 pap. $10.50
A Nip in the Air. Norton 1976 pap. $2.50. Poetry.

Books about Betjeman

Delaney, Frank. *Betjeman Country.* David & Charles 1984 $18.95
Stapleton, Margaret L. *Sir John Betjeman: A Bibliography of Writings by and about
   Him. Author Bibliographies Ser.* Scarecrow Pr. 1974 $16.50

BROOKE, RUPERT. 1887–1915

The best known of the poets who took a patriotic, somewhat idealized,
view of World War I, Brooke was born in Rugby, where his father was head-
master of a house at the elite Rugby School. Blond, athletic, and intelligent,
Brooke embodied the English stereotype of the golden youth; even Yeats
called him "the handsomest man in England." Graduating from Rugby
School to King's College, Cambridge, Brooke joined the Apostles, a venera-
ble intellectual club, which counted Tennyson among its earlier members.
His verse moved from fashionably decadent to nearly Georgian, often with
a quiet pastoralism that now seems conventional. Brooke joined the Royal
Navy Volunteer Reserve in August 1914, served in Belgium, and was sent to
Gallipoli with the Hood Battalion but died en route in the Aegean. He is
best remembered for his war poetry, which idealizes both combat and patriotic feelings in a way that other war poets would react against sharply. Modern taste rates him lower than more disillusioned and more innovative writers like Wilfred Owen.

Books by Brooke

The Complete Poems of Rupert Brooke. AMS Pr. repr. of 1942 ed. 2d ed. $17.50
The Poetical Works of Rupert Brooke. 1946. Faber 1970 $13.95 pap. o.p. The standard
   edition.
The Collected Poems of Rupert Brooke. 1915. Dodd 1980 pap. $4.95

Books about Brooke

Hassall, Christopher. *Rupert Brooke: A Biography.* Faber 1972 pap. $5.95
Lehmann, John. *The Strange Destiny of Rupert Brooke.* Holt 1981 $12.95
Pearsall, R. B. *Rupert Brooke: The Man and Poet.* Humanities Pr. text ed. 1975 pap.
   $14.25
Rogers, Timothy. *Rupert Brooke: A Reappraisal and Selection.* Routledge & Kegan
   1971 o.p.

BUNTING, BASIL. 1900–

Ever the maverick, Basil Bunting is one of the most English as well as the
most Americanized of modern British poets. Born in Northumbria in northern England and educated largely at Quaker boarding schools, he declared
himself a conscientious objector in World War I and served a term in

prison. After a year and a half at the London School of Economics, he traveled extensively—particularly to Paris and then Italy—and supported himself through journalism, often doing music reviews. During World War II, he worked for the British merchant navy and was then sent to Persia by the government, eventually becoming Persian correspondent for the *London Times*. Work for an English provincial newspaper followed, and in the mid-sixties he returned to poetry and achieved his first public success with the autobiographical poem *Briggflatts*.

The unlikely duo of Wordsworth and Pound exerted major influences on Bunting's work. From WORDSWORTH came the preoccupation with rural life in his native Northumbria, which constitutes his best subject. From Pound came the verse techniques of American modernism with which Bunting presents his material. Yeats described him as "one of Ezra's more savage disciples," and Pound helped him get his first volume of verse published. Almost ignored in England until the late 1960s, Bunting has become an influential conduit of modernist techniques into native English poetry. His own formal innovations consist principally in his detailed adaptations of musical structures and forms for verbal art.

BOOK BY BUNTING

Collected Poems. Moyer Bell Ltd. 1985 $19.95 pap. $12.95; Oxford 2d ed. 1980 pap.
$9.95

BOOKS ABOUT BUNTING

Guedalla, Roger. *Basil Bunting: A Bibliography of Works and Criticism.* Folcroft 1976
lib. bdg. $20.00
Terrell, Carroll F., ed. *Basil Bunting: Man and Poet. Man and Poet Ser.* National Poetry Foundation 1981 $22.50 pap. $12.95. Comprehensive collection of essays, with annotated bibliography.

CLARKE, AUSTIN. 1896–1974

One of the leading Irish poets of the generation after Yeats, Clarke also wrote verse drama, novels, and criticism. From his parents he imbibed the Irish nationalism of his father and the stern religious conscience of his mother. As a boy he attended the same Belvedere College as JAMES JOYCE, with much the same reaction. He completed his B.A. at University College, Dublin, the same year as the Easter Rising (1916); on the execution of his teacher and friend Thomas MacDonagh, he was appointed to MacDonagh's teaching post for a three-year term. A nervous breakdown, an abortive marriage (it lasted ten days), and the nonrenewal of his teaching job led to Clarke's departure in 1922 for England, where he spent most of the next 15 years and began a successful marriage. Chosen as a charter member of the Irish Academy of Letters in 1932, Clarke returned to Dublin permanently in 1937 and devoted himself largely to verse drama in the 1940s and early 1950s. A lifelong Catholic, he took a leading role in the battle against censorship, which had already banned some of his books from his native country. His final years saw a renewed outpouring of poetry, much of it on social issues.

Clarke's early poetry turned often to Celtic themes and adaptations. Unlike Yeats and others, he knew enough Gaelic to read his sources in the original, and he tried to reproduce some of their complex patterns of assonance in his own verse. He then turned to the Celtic Romanesque period (fifth through twelfth centuries) for his middle verse as well as his three prose romances and some of his verse plays. For the last 20 years of his career he focused more on contemporary social issues. Throughout his poetry Clarke displayed both technical skill (particularly in his complex assonance) and a thematic preoccupation with the struggle between conscience and repression. When asked by ROBERT FROST to describe his poetry, he remarked, "I load myself with chains and then try to get out of them."

BOOKS BY CLARKE

The Collected Poems of Austin Clarke. AMS Pr. repr. of 1936 ed. $24.50
Poetry in Modern Ireland. Arden Lib. repr. of 1951 ed. 1978 lib. bdg. $15.00; Folcroft 1973 lib. bdg. $12.00; Irish Bk. Ctr. 2d ed. pap. $1.25
Twice around the Black Church. 1962 o.p. An autobiographical volume.
Poems. Oxford 1964 pap. $1.75. The standard edition.
Echo at Coole and Other Poems. Dufour 1968 $12.95
Celtic Twilight and the Nineties. Intro. by R. McHugh, Dufour 1970 $12.95
The Selected Poetry of Austin Clarke. Ed. by Thomas Kinsella, Wake Forest Univ. Pr. 1976 $13.50
The Third Kiss. Humanities Pr. text ed. 1976 $20.00. Drama.
Liberty Lane: A Ballad Play of Dublin in Two Acts with a Prologue by Austin Clarke. Humanities Pr. text ed. 1978 $22.75
The Frenzy of Sweeney. Humanities Pr. text ed. 1980 $26.50
The Singing Men at Cashel. Humanities Pr. text ed. 1980 pap. $16.25

BOOKS ABOUT CLARKE

Alpern, Susan. *Austin Clarke: His Life and Works.* Humanities Pr. 1974 text ed. $15.50
Jordan, John. *Austin Clarke.* Bucknell Univ. Pr. 1970 o.p. The first full-length study.
Montague, John, and Liam Miller, eds. *A Tribute to Austin Clarke on His Seventieth Birthday.* Dufour 1966 o.p.
Tapping, G. Craig. *Austin Clarke: A Study of His Writings.* Barnes & Noble 1981 lib. bdg. $29.00; Univ. Pr. 1981 pap. $11.50. Excellent study with useful bibliography.

COLUM, PADRAIC. 1881–1972

Born in a Longford workhouse where his father was first teacher and then master, Padraic Colum grew into an important figure in the Irish literary renaissance before immigrating to the United States. Invited by the Fay brothers to join the National Theatre Society, Colum soon came into contact with Yeats, Synge, Lady Gregory, and other major figures of the day. In 1912 he married the teacher and writer Mary Maguire, with whom he undertook several joint projects. The Colums immigrated to the United States in 1914. They eventually settled in New York, with intervening periods in Europe and in Connecticut. Colum kept up a varied production of verse, plays, fiction, criticism, and children's literature, together with active lecturing. His most extended teaching appointment was at Columbia Unviersity, where he and his wife offered a joint course in comparative literature.

Colum felt that his Catholic and peasant roots gave him a closer tie to the Irish folk than did the Protestant, Anglo-Irish background of many writers of the Irish renaissance. His poetry usually deals with common people and rural landscapes in a forthright manner. Colum was resolutely Irish, and his work for the most part avoids didacticism or sentimental nationalism in favor of straightforward presentation. As his best critic, Zack Bowen, remarked, Colum puts his trust in the "world of visible experience."

BOOKS BY COLUM

The Children of Odin: The Book of Northern Myths. Darby repr. of 1920 ed. $35.00; Havertown Bks. 1920 $40.00; Macmillan 1984 $10.95 pap. $5.95. Norse myth for children.

Collected Poems. Devin 1953 $12.00

Images of Departure: Poetry. Dufour o.p.

The Poet's Circuits: Collected Poems of Ireland. Humanities Pr. repr. of 1960 ed. text ed. 1981 pap. $12.75

Irish Elegies. 1966. Humanities Pr. 4th ed. text ed. 1976 $12.25

Golden Fleece. Macmillan 1967 $12.95. Greek myth for children.

Golden Fleece and the Heroes Who Lived before Achilles. Macmillan 1983 $12.95 pap. $5.95

(and Mary Colum). *Our Friend James Joyce.* 1958. Peter Smith $11.25

Selected Short Stories. Ed. by Sanford Sternlicht, Syracuse Univ. Pr. 1985 $19.95

BOOKS ABOUT COLUM

Bowen, Zack. *Padraic Colum: A Biographical-Critical Introduction.* Pref. by H. T. Moore, *Crosscurrents Modern Critiques Ser.* Southern Illinois Univ. Pr. 1970 $6.95

Colum, Mary. *Life and the Dream: Autobiography.* 1947 o.p. By the author's wife.

DE LA MARE, WALTER. 1873–1956

Born in a Kent village, Walter de la Mare grew up with late Victorian tastes, which he never wholly left behind. After his school days at St. Paul's Cathedral Choir School in London, he joined the London office of the Anglo-American Oil Company (a branch of Standard Oil) as a bookkeeper in 1890. He continued with that firm until 1908, when a Civil List pension enabled him to retire from business and concentrate entirely on writing. Devoted to children's literature and to prose tales as well as to poetry, de la Mare began his career with a volume of children's verse, followed it with a novel, and only in 1906 produced his first book of poetry for adults. *Listeners and Other Poems* (o.p.) established his reputation. Along with adult verse, he continued his interest in prose and in children's literature throughout his career; *Memoirs of a Midget* (1921) is his finest novel.

De la Mare's early success was an early casualty of the modernist movement and of the academic criticism (chiefly by the Leavis group in England and the New Critics in the United States) that supported it. They saw him as a typical promulgator of a nineteenth-century dream world detached from modern life. Yet, at his best, de la Mare was more than that, with his pervasive sense of a lost visionary world of childhood or of a symbolic one behind nature coexisting with the frustrations of an unsuccessful quest to recover it. He was also a skilled craftsman, and could count both W. H. Auden and T. S. Eliot among the admirers of his technical ability. In some ways, his mixture of formal technique with somewhat conventional appearance recalls the poetry of the Georgians, who respected him and included his verse in their anthologies.

BOOKS BY DE LA MARE

A Choice of de la Mare's Verse. Ed. by W. H. Auden, Faber 1963 o.p.
Complete Poems. Faber 1969 $26.00
Collected Poems. Faber 1979 $19.50 pap. $9.95
Selected Poems. Ed. by R. N. Green-Armitage, Faber 1973 pap. $5.95
Best Stories of Walter de la Mare. Faber 1983 pap. $7.95. A selection made by the author himself.
Peacock Pie: A Book of Rhymes. 1913. Faber 1958 $7.95 1980 pap. $3.50. Children's verse.
Songs of Childhood. Dover pap. $3.50; Garland repr. of 1902 ed. 1976 $42.00; Peter Smith $13.50. His first book of verse.
Memoirs of a Midget. 1921. AMS Pr. repr. of 1941 ed. $28.00. The finest of de la Mare's five novels.
Pleasures and Speculations. Essay Index Repr. Ser. Ayer repr. of 1940 ed. $19.50. A collection of essays.
Private View: Essays on Literature. Hyperion Pr. repr. of 1953 ed. $24.20. Another collection of essays.

BOOKS ABOUT DE LA MARE

Atkins, John A. *Walter de la Mare: An Exploration.* Folcroft 1973 lib. bdg. $8.50; Haskell 1975 lib. bdg. $46.95; Norwood repr. of 1947 ed. 1976 lib. bdg. $15.00
Brain, Russell. *Tea with Walter de la Mare.* Faber 1957 o.p. Informal memoir with valuable record of conversations in de la Mare's later years.
Brett, W. R., ed. *A Tribute to Walter de la Mare on His Seventy-fifth Birthday.* Faber 1948 o.p. Good collection of articles.
Clark, Leonard, and Edmund Blunden. *A Tribute to Walter de la Mare.* Small Pr. Dist. 1974 $6.00
Duffin, H. C. *Walter de la Mare: A Study of His Poetry. Studies in Poetry* Ayer repr. of 1949 ed. $21.00; Folcroft 1973 lib. bdg. $15.00; Haskell repr. of 1949 ed. 1970 lib. bdg. $48.95
Hopkins, Kenneth, ed. *Walter de la Mare: A Selection from His Writings.* Norwood repr. of 1956 ed. 1977 lib. bdg. $25.00
McCrosson, Doris Ross. *Walter de la Mare. Twayne's Eng. Authors Ser.* 1966 o.p.

DURRELL, LAWRENCE. 1912–

[SEE Chapter 12 in this volume.]

ELIOT, T(HOMAS) S(TEARNS). 1888–1965 (NOBEL PRIZE 1948)

Important as both poet and critic, Eliot became perhaps the most influential man of letters during the half-century after World War I. Born in St. Louis, he traced his descent from Andrew Eliot—who emigrated to Massachusetts from East Coker, Somerset, in the mid-seventeenth century—through a distinguished line of New England forebears. He was educated first at Smith

Academy in St. Louis and then at Harvard University both as undergraduate and graduate student from 1906 to 1914, with time abroad pursuing graduate studies in philosophy at the Sorbonne, Marburg, and finally Oxford. With the outbreak of war, he settled in England and in 1915 married Vivien Haigh-Wood. Having left his early, derivative verse far behind, he began under the encouragement of Ezra Pound to publish avant-garde poetry (including "The Love Song of J. Alfred Prufrock") exploiting fresh rhythms, abrupt juxtapositions, contemporary subject matter, and witty allusion.

After marrying Vivien he worked first as a schoolteacher and then in the foreign department of Lloyds Bank for eight years. During this time he published his influential early criticism, much of it written as occasional pieces for literary periodicals. He developed such doctrines as the "dissociation of sensibility" and the "objective correlative" and elaborated his views on wit and on the relation of tradition to the individual talent. Conceived partly to defend the kind of poetry he was writing, his critical theories shaped the taste of a generation, particularly through their impact on such critics as F. R. Leavis and I. A. Richards in England and the New Critics in America. This early period of creativity resulted in another collection of verse (which included "Gerontion") and culminated in *The Waste Land*, a masterpiece published in 1922 and produced partly during a period of psychological breakdown.

After becoming a director of the Faber publishing house in 1922 and joining the Church of England in 1927, Eliot's career underwent a change, with his published poetry such as *Ash Wednesday* (1930, o.p.) becoming overtly Christian. He edited his influential literary magazine *The Criterion* from 1922 to 1939 and turned his hand to social as well as literary criticism, with an increasingly conservative orientation. The religious poetry culminated in his great sequence *Four Quartets*, published individually from 1936 onward and collectively in 1943, after which his poetic career came to an end. He continued as playwright and critic, however, and achieved particular success with the verse dramas *Murder in the Cathedral* (1935) and *The Cocktail Party* (1950). Having separated from his first wife in the 1930s, he married his secretary Valerie Fletcher in 1957.

In contrast to his period of greatest influence, when his literary views were accepted as gospel, recent critics have seen Eliot as a more divided figure, often covertly attracted to the very elements (romanticism, personality, "heresy") that he overtly condemned. His early attacks on romantic poets, for example, often reveal him as a romantic against the grain, and his work shows the strong impress of his personality. The same divisions carry over into his verse, where violence struggles against restraint, emotion against order, and imagination against ironic detachment. This newer Eliot is at once more human and more attractive to contemporary taste.

BOOKS BY ELIOT

Collected Poems, 1909–1962. Harcourt 1963 $12.95

The Complete Poems and Plays, 1909–1950. Harcourt 1952 $18.95. Includes the first three of Eliot's five plays; the other two are listed separately, below.

Selected Poems. Harcourt 1967 pap. $2.95. The best short selection.

Elizabethan Essays. Gordon 1973 lib. bdg. $69.95; Haskell repr. of 1934 ed. 1969 lib.
bdg. $39.95

Selected Essays. Harcourt 1950 $19.95. The most capacious collection of his prose.

Selected Prose of T. S. Eliot. Ed. by Frank Kermode, Farrar 1975 $10.95 pap. $4.95;
Harcourt 1975 $10.95. The best one-volume selection, with notes by a leading
scholar.

Christianity and Culture. Harcourt 1960 pap. $5.95. Social criticism.

*The Use of Poetry and the Use of Criticism: Studies in the Relation of Criticism to Po-
etry in England.* 1933. Barnes & Noble repr. of 1964 ed. 2d ed. 1975 pap. $6.75;
Faber repr. 1985 pap. $3.95. Originally given as the Charles Eliot Norton Lec-
tures at Harvard University, 1932–33.

Old Possum's Book of Practical Cats. Harcourt 1939 o.p. Comic verse, the basis for
the musical *Cats.*

Four Quartets. 1943. Ed. by Bernard Bergonzi, Aurora text ed. 1970 pap. $2.50; Har-
court 1968 pap. $1.95. Eliot's last great sequence.

Sacred Wood. Methuen 7th ed. 1960 pap. $10.95. Famous early collection of prose.

The Confidential Clerk. Harcourt 1954 $9.95 1964 pap. $6.95. Drama.

On Poetry and Poets. Farrar 1957 pap. $7.95; Octagon repr. of 1957 ed. 1975 lib. bdg.
$21.50

The Elder Statesman. Farrar 1959 $4.95. Drama.

Poems Written in Early Youth. Farrar 1967 pap. $4.95. Juvenilia not included in the
collected editions.

*The Waste Land: A Facsimile and Transcript of the Original Drafts, including the Anno-
tations of Ezra Pound.* 1922. Ed. by Valerie Eliot, annotated by Ezra Pound, Harcourt 1971 $25.00 1974 pap. $9.95. Facsimile and drafts of *The Waste Land* manuscripts, with corrections and annotations by Eliot and Ezra Pound.

To Criticize the Critic. Octagon repr. 1980 lib. bdg. $19.50

BOOKS ABOUT ELIOT

Ackroyd, Peter. *T. S. Eliot: A Life.* Simon & Schuster 1984 $24.95. The best biogra-
phy to date.

Bergonzi, Bernard. *T. S. Eliot.* Macmillan (Collier Bks.) 1972 o.p. Excellent introduction to the work and life; one of the first "revisionist" interpretations.

Bornstein, George. *Transformations of Romanticism in Yeats, Eliot and Stevens.* Univ.
of Chicago Pr. 1976 lib. bdg. $25.00. Covers both criticism and poetry.

Bush, Ronald. *T. S. Eliot: A Study in Character and Style.* Oxford 1984 $25.00. Major,
controversial reassessment.

Gallup, Donald. *T. S. Eliot: A Bibliography.* Faber 1969 $14.95. Revised version.

Gardner, Helen. *The Composition of Four Quartets.* Oxford 1978 $35.00. Best work on
the subject.

Gordon, Lyndall. *Eliot's Early Years.* Oxford 1977 $16.95 pap. $4.95. Careful examination perhaps overstressing the religious orientation.

Kenner, Hugh. *The Invisible Poet: T. S. Eliot.* Harcourt 1959 o.p. A major study.

Litz, A. Walton, ed. *Eliot in His Time.* Princeton Univ. Pr. 1973 $20.00. Important col-
lection by major critics.

Margolis, John D. *T. S. Eliot's Intellectual Development, 1922–1939.* Univ. of Chicago
Pr. 1972 $16.00

Matthiessen, F. O. *Achievement of T. S. Eliot: An Essay on the Nature of Poetry.* Oxford 3d ed. 1959 pap. $3.95. Revised edition with chapter on the later works by
C. L. Barber. One of the early books, still one of the best.

Newton-De Molina, David, ed. *The Literary Criticism of T. S. Eliot: New Essays.* Humanities Pr. 1977 o.p. Good recent collection on the prose.

Smith, Carol H. *T. S. Eliot's Dramatic Theory and Practice: From Sweeney Agonistes to the Elder Statesman.* Gordian repr. of 1963 ed. 1977 $12.50. Perhaps the most helpful book on the plays.

Smith, Grover Cleveland. *T. S. Eliot's Poetry and Plays: A Study in Sources and Meaning.* Univ. of Chicago Pr. 1956 o.p.

Southam, B. C. *A Guide to the Selected Poems of T. S. Eliot.* Harcourt 1970 pap. $5.95. Provides helpful notes and glosses allusions.

Spender, Stephen. *T. S. Eliot.* Penguin 1975 o.p. Good survey by a distinguished poet and critic.

Tate, Allen, ed. *T. S. Eliot: The Man and His Work.* Delacorte 1967 o.p. Critical evaluations, biographical reminiscences, and commemorative poems by 26 distinguished writers.

Williamson, George. *Reader's Guide to T. S. Eliot with an Epilogue Entitled T. S. Eliot, 1888–1965.* Farrar rev. ed. 1953 pap. $3.95; Octagon repr. of 1974 ed. lib. bdg. $20.00. Poem-by-poem analysis helpful for the beginning reader.

FULLER, ROY. 1912–

Like the American WALLACE STEVENS, Roy Fuller has pursued simultaneous careers as writer and business attorney. Born of a middle-class family in Lancashire (his father managed a factory), he qualified as a solicitor in 1933 and spent most of his career with the Woolwich Equitable Building Society, of which he became a director in 1959. He married in 1936 and during the war served as a radar mechanic with the Royal Navy. From 1968 to 1973 he acted as professor of poetry at Oxford University, and since 1972 as a governor of the BBC. Besides poetry, Fuller has written numerous novels, including several for children, and some literary criticism. His only child is the poet and critic John Fuller.

Fuller first came to notice as a war poet during World War II. He has named Auden as a major influence on his verse, which in its regular form and restrained tone ultimately harks back to the English tradition of THOMAS HARDY. Always conscious of the relation between poetry and society, Fuller has sought a steady accessibility rather than recondite arcana. He often writes of domestic or natural subjects and resists what he sees as the debasement of traditional English culture. Fuller's inclusion in Robert Conquest's 1961 anthology *New Poetry* has resulted in his being viewed as part of the loose grouping of postwar poets known as the Movement.

BOOKS BY FULLER

Buff: Poems. Dufour 1965 pap. $8.50

Collected Poems, 1936–1961. Dufour 1962 $13.95

New Poems. Dufour 1968 $10.00

Owls and Artificers: Oxford Lectures on Poetry. Open Court 1971 $14.95

Professors and Gods. St. Martin's 1974 $20.00

From the Joke Shop. Dufour 1975 $10.95

Souvenirs. State Mutual Bk. 1980 $25.00

The Individual and His Times: A Selection of the Poetry of Roy Fuller. Ed. by V. J. Lee, Longwood Pr. 1982 pap. $8.95

BOOK ABOUT FULLER

Austin, Allan E. *Roy Fuller*. *Twayne's Eng. Authors Ser.* G. K. Hall 1979 lib. bdg.
    $15.95

GRAVES, ROBERT. 1895–1985

Born in Wimbledon near London to an Irish father and German mother,
Robert Graves has led one of the most varied and productive careers in
twentieth-century literature. Although devoted primarily to his poetry,
Graves has produced a vast array of other works, including historical novels
like *I, Claudius*, plays, criticism, translations, and his great autobiography
Goodbye to All That. He was educated at Charterhouse School, and after serving in France during World War I, he completed his formal education at St.
John's College, Oxford. His tangled private life has included, besides his two
marriages, a liaison with the poet LAURA RIDING from 1926 to 1939. During
his time with Riding, he settled in Majorca, where he spent most of his life.
Both accomplished and quirky, Graves's early poetic criticism was more influential than his later attacks on the great modernists. From 1961 to 1966
he was professor of poetry at Oxford.

Graves's early, Georgian poetry soon yielded to a more psychological orientation. Treated after the war by the psychiatrist W. H. R. Rivers, Graves developed a theory of poetry as the writer's expression of internal psychological
conflicts, which informed much of his work during the 1920s. Under Riding's
tutelage he turned outward in the 1930s toward a more objective stance in
which the poet discovers a reality beyond himself. From the 1940s onward,
his work was dominated by the theories he explicated in *The White Goddess*,
which he subtitled *A Historical Grammar of Poetic Myth*. For Graves, the ancient Greeks and Hebrews perverted an originally matriarchal society,
whose underlying mythology of a White Goddess with three aspects—
mother, beloved, and crone—true poets must seek to recover. Scholars do not
agree with all of Graves's conclusions, but the book does illuminate the most
obscure area of a poetry otherwise clear, craftsmanlike, and accessible.

BOOKS BY GRAVES

New Collected Poems. 1975. Doubleday 1977 $10.00 Contains biographical introduc-
    tion by James McKinley.
Over the Brazier. Folcroft repr of 1916 ed. lib. bdg. $22.00. Reprint of Graves's first
    volume.
*On English Poetry: Being an Irregular Approach to the Psychology of This Art, from Evi-
    dence Mainly Subjective*. Arden Lib. repr. of 1922 ed. 1980 lib. bdg. $20.00; Fol-
    croft repr of 1922 ed. 1975 lib. bdg. $17.50; *Eng. Lit Ser.* Haskell repr. of 1922 ed.
    1972 lib. bdg. $39.95; Somerset repr. of 1922 ed. $20.00
Whipperginny. Folcroft repr. of 1923 ed. lib. bdg. $25.00
Goodbye to All That. Doubleday (Anchor) 1929 o.p. Famous autobiography.
I, Claudius. 1934. Modern Lib. $8.95; Random (Vintage) 1977 pap. $4.95. Historical
    fiction.
Wife to Mr. Milton. Academy Chicago repr. of 1944 ed. 1979 pap. $5.95; Octagon
    repr. of 1944 ed. 1979 lib. bdg. $26.00; *Penguin Fiction Ser.* 1984 pap. $6.95. His-
    torical fiction.

Poems, 1938–1945. Farrar 1946 $4.95

The White Goddess: A Historical Grammar of Poetic Myth. 1947. Farrar rev. & enl. ed. 1966 pap. $8.25; Octagon 1972 lib. bdg. $26.00; Peter Smith 1983 $13.25

Claudius the God. Modern Lib. $8.95; Random (Vintage) 1977 pap. $4.95. Historical fiction.

(and Laura Riding). *A Survey of Modernist Poetry.* Doubleday 1928 o.p.

BOOKS ABOUT GRAVES

Canary, Robert H. *Robert Graves. Twayne's Eng. Authors Ser.* G. K. Hall 1980 lib. bdg. $12.50. Good general account.

Day, Douglas. *Swifter Than Reason: The Poetry and Criticism of Robert Graves.* Univ. of North Carolina Pr. 1963 o.p. The first major study.

Higginson, Fred H. *A Bibliography of the Works of Robert Graves.* Shoe String (Archon) 1966 $25.00. Supplements of this 1966 work appear in scholarly journals.

Hoffman, Daniel. *Barbarous Knowledge: Myth in the Poetry of Yeats, Graves, and Muir.* Oxford 1967 $10.95 1970 pap. $4.95. Perhaps the best single piece of criticism on Graves.

Keane, Patrick J. *A Wild Civility: Interactions in the Poetry and Thought of Robert Graves.* Univ. of Missouri Pr. 1980 pap. $6.95

Kirkham, Michael. *The Poetry of Robert Graves.* Oxford 1969 o.p. Important book.

Snipes, Katherine. *Robert Graves. Lit. and Life Ser.* Ungar 1979 $15.50

Stade, George. *Robert Graves. Columbia Essays on Modern Writers* 1967 pap. $2.50. Helpful pamphlet for the general reader.

Vickery, John B. *Robert Graves and the White Goddess.* Univ. of Nebraska Pr. 1972 $9.50. Emphasizes Graves's mythopoeic thought.

GUNN, THOM(SON). 1929–

Both literally and figuratively, Thom Gunn may have traveled the farthest of any of the original Movement poets of the 1950s in Britain. Born in Gravesend, he moved often as a child because his journalist father frequently worked for different newspapers. After two years in the British army and some months in Paris, he enrolled in Trinity College, Cambridge, from which he graduated in 1953. He then went to the United States for graduate study at Stanford University and an assistant professorship from 1958 to 1966 at the University of California, Berkeley. Important influences during that period were the older poets Yvor Winters and J. V. Cunningham and his contemporaries Gary Snyder and Ted Hughes (who was at Cambridge with Gunn). Since then he has lived in San Francisco and supported himself as a free-lance writer.

Gunn's literal journeys mirror psychological ones reflected in his poetry. Influenced by French existentialist thought, he first came to public attention as a skilled craftsman of anguished lyrics in traditional forms. Moving to California, he experimented with the drug LSD and a looser artistic structure, which he used to present often violent subjects (such as motorcycle gangs). Correspondingly, Gunn's erotic verse changed from the early heterosexual lyrics to a frank portrayal of homosexual love. Although he claims to be an atheist, Gunn often conveys a passionate, nearly mystical, identification with the world of nature. The title poem of his important volume *Moly* shows his understandable fascination with the theme of metamorphosis.

BOOKS BY GUNN

Selected Poems. Faber 1962 pap. $3.95
Selected Poems, 1950–1975. Farrar 1979 $12.95 pap. $5.95
(and Ander Gunn). *Positives: Verses by Thom Gunn.* Faber 1966 pap. $4.95; Univ. of
    Chicago Pr. 1967 $10.00. Contains verse by Gunn and photographs by his
    brother, Ander Gunn.
The Sense of Movement. Faber 1968 pap. $3.95
Moly and My Sad Captains. Farrar 1973 $7.50 pap. $4.95
To the Air. Ed. by Jan Schreiber, Godine 1974 $5.00
Jack Straw's Castle and Other Poems. Farrar 1976 $8.95 pap. $3.45
Talbot Road. Ill. by Bill Schuessler, Helikon 1981 pap. $7.00 signed ltd. ed. $20.00
The Menace. Man-Root 1982 $20.00
The Occasions of Poetry: Essays in Criticism and Autobiography. Ed. by Wilmer Clive,
    Farrar 1982 $15.00
The Passages of Joy. Farrar 1982 $10.00 pap. $6.95

BOOK ABOUT GUNN

Bold, Alan. *Thom Gunn and Ted Hughes.* Barnes & Noble 1976 text ed. $11.00

HEANEY, SEAMUS (JUSTIN). 1939–

Often viewed as the leading poet of his generation, Seamus Heaney was
born in Castledawson, County Derry, in Northern Ireland. Educated entirely in Irish schools, he graduated from Queen's University, Belfast, with a
first-class honors degree in English. He has held a variety of teaching jobs,
including a post at Queen's University from 1966 to 1972. In 1972 he left the
turbulence of Belfast for a four-year stay in a cottage at Glanmore, County
Wicklow, where he produced the *Glanmore Sonnets* and other works. He
and his family now live in Dublin, and he spends part of each year teaching
at Harvard University in the United States. A gifted critic as well as poet,
Heaney has also written a book of literary essays.

Heaney's first book, *Death of a Naturalist,* established his reputation,
which has grown with each successive volume. He often writes of rural life
in his native Ulster in an unsentimental and moving way. A poem like "Dig-
ging" establishes analogies between rural hardship and the poet's own labor. When he turns to the past, he favors the Viking rather than the Celtic
heroes of most Irish poets. Under the fascination of P. V. Glob's book *The
Bog People,* he produced a powerful group of poems about the preservation
of ancient and savage tribal culture in Irish peat bogs, again finding analogies to the poet's own condition. Political themes connected to the troubles
in Northern Ireland also appear in his work. Recently, Heaney published a
superb version of the story of one Irish hero who fascinates him, the medieval king Sweeney, in *Sweeney Astray.*

BOOKS BY HEANEY

Poems, 1965–1975. Farrar 1980 text ed. $12.95 pap. $7.25. Combined printing of his
    first four volumes.
Preoccupations: Selected Prose, 1968–1978. Farrar 1980 $15.00 pap. $7.95
Death of a Naturalist. 1966. Faber 1969 pap. $4.95

Door into the Dark. Faber 1972 pap. $4.95
Field Work. Farrar 1979 $8.95 pap. $5.25
Sweeney Astray. Farrar 1984 $13.95 1985 pap. $7.95. Translation of the medieval Irish work.

BOOKS ABOUT HEANEY

Buttel, Robert. *Seamus Heaney. Irish Writers Ser.* Bucknell Univ. Pr. 1975 $4.50
Morrison, Blake. *Seamus Heaney. Contemporary Writers Ser.* Methuen 1982 pap. $4.25

HUGHES, TED (EDWARD JAMES). 1930–

Hughes attended a grammar school in his native Yorkshire before spending two years as a ground mechanic in the Royal Air Force. He went on to Pembroke College, Cambridge, where he studied first literature and then anthropology in amassing some of the primitive lore that underlies his work. There he also met the American poet SYLVIA PLATH, whom he married in 1956. Their troubled marriage produced two children and ended with Plath's suicide in 1963. Hughes remarried in 1970. He has worked as a rose gardener and night watchman as well as reader for the Rank Organisation, and in 1965 became coeditor of the magazine *Modern Poetry in Translation.* Besides his adult poetry, he has done children's verse, translations, and several plays. Hughes's long list of honors and prizes culminated in his appointment as poet laureate in December 1984.

Violent in both subject matter and technique, Hughes stands as a major force against the more restrained and traditional verse of the Movement poets. His first book, *The Hawk in the Rain,* created a sensation on publication in 1957. Hughes finds a favorite subject in animals, particularly horses and birds of prey, and has developed a character called Crow in several volumes. His poetry aims to shock and disturb. Often it favors atavistic and instinctual forces beyond human involvement; the animal poems often stem from the point of view of the animal rather than of a human observer and have something in common with the work of the American poet ROBINSON JEFFERS. Hughes's predilection for raw energy, rarer in English than in American poetry, displays itself technically in daring diction, compression, and jarring rhythms.

BOOKS BY HUGHES

Selected Poems, 1957–1967. Harper 1974 $14.37
New Selected Poems. Harper 1982 $14.90 pap. $6.68. The best one-volume edition.
The Hawk in the Rain. 1957. Faber 1968 pap. $4.95
Wodwo. Harper 1967 o.p.
Lupercal. Faber 1970 pap. $4.95
Crow: From the Life and Songs of the Crow. Harper 1971 $8.95 pap. $5.29
The Tiger's Bones and Other Plays for Children. Viking 1974 $9.95
Season Songs. Viking 1975 $11.95
Gaudete. Harper 1977 $12.45
Cave Birds: An Alchemical Cave Drama. Viking 1979 $14.95
Remains of Elmet. Harper 1979 $16.95. For children.
Moortown. Harper 1980 $12.45 1983 pap. $5.72

Under the North Star. Viking 1981 $16.95
River. Harper 1984 pap. $12.45

BOOKS ABOUT HUGHES

Bold, Alan. *Thom Gunn and Ted Hughes.* Barnes & Noble 1976 text ed. $11.00
Roberts, Neil, and Terry Gifford. *Ted Hughes: A Critical Study.* Faber 1981 $25.00
Sagar, Keith, ed. *The Achievement of Ted Hughes.* Univ. of Georgia Pr. 1983 $25.00
Sagar, Keith, and Stephen Tabor. *Ted Hughes: A Bibliography, 1945–1980.* Wilson 1982 $47.00
West, Thomas. *Ted Hughes.* Methuen 1985 pap. $4.95

JENNINGS, ELIZABETH. 1926–

The only woman included in the *New Lines* anthology, which announced the Movement, Elizabeth Jennings was born in Boston, England. Educated at Oxford High School and St. Anne's College, Oxford, she worked in the Oxford City Library from 1950 to 1958 and then as a reader for the publishers Chatto & Windus. Since 1961 she has been a free-lance writer. She lives in Oxford but often visits Italy, where many of her poems are set. After a difficult middle period, which included stays in a mental hospital, Jennings has been writing even more strongly religious verse recently. She has said that "my Roman Catholic religion and my poems are the most important things in my life."

Jennings writes a restrained, craftsmanlike, sometimes lapidary, poetry of lucid diction and traditional meters. Other writers and artists, religious personalities like St. John of the Cross or St. Theresa, and nature figure among her favorite subjects. The Italian setting and profound religious conviction distinguish her work from that of the other Movement writers, as does the more personal and confessional stance of two of her collections during the 1960s. She has done numerous translations, including an interesting version of Michelangelo's sonnets.

BOOKS BY JENNINGS

Selected Poems. 1979. Carcanet pap. $8.00
The Secret Brother and Other Poems for Children. Dufour 1967 o.p.
The Animals' Arrival. Dufour 1969 $10.95
Consequently I Rejoice. Humanities Pr. 1980 $11.00 pap. $6.25
Moments of Grace. Humanities Pr. 1980 pap. $11.00
Celebrations and Elegies. Humanities Pr. text ed. 1982 pap. $11.00
In Praise of Our Lady. David & Charles 1982 $12.95

BOOK ABOUT JENNINGS

Schmidt, Michael, and Grevel Lindop, eds. *British Poetry since 1960.* Carcanet 1972 o.p. Contains a study of Jennings by Margaret Byers.

JONES, DAVID (MICHAEL). 1895–1974

David Jones did not publish his first book of poetry until his forties. Although he was born in Kent, his Welsh father instilled in him a love for the culture of Wales that pervades his work. At first Jones intended to be an artist, and he left grammar school for Camberwell School of Art. With the outbreak of war he enlisted in the Royal Welsh Fusiliers (Robert Graves served as an officer in the same regiment) and served in Flanders and France. After the war, he completed his education and began a successful artistic career, during which he became perhaps best known as an engraver and watercolorist. Immersed in legend, myth, and romance, he held that man was fundamentally religious. His own religious beliefs led him to convert to Roman Catholicism in 1921.

Although Yeats saluted his first book, Jones stood apart from the literary mainstream of his day, despite obvious debts to the methods of POUND, Eliot, and Joyce. His first volume, *In Parenthesis*, combines both poetry and prose in chronicling the wartime career of its major figure, John Ball. His even more ambitious second book, *The Anathemata: Fragments of an Attempted Writing*, uses the structure of the Tridentine Mass to chronicle the history of Britain from early geological times through preindustrial London. Some of its techniques of presentation and counterparting of myths and factual materials resemble Pound's *Cantos*. Auden judged it the best modern long poem in English. The later works *The Tribune's Visitation* (o.p.) and *The Sleeping Lord* deal with the Roman Empire in the time of Jesus. Readers will appreciate Jones's inclusion of his own notes to his difficult, allusive verse.

BOOKS BY JONES

In Parenthesis. 1937. Faber 1975 pap. $8.95. His first book of poetry, mingled with prose.

The Anathemata: Fragments of an Attempted Writing. 1952. Faber 1972 $9.95. His major poem.

Epoch and Artist. Faber 1973 pap. $6.95

The Sleeping Lord and Other Fragments. Faber 1974 $11.95

The Dying Gaul and Other Writings. Ed. by Harman Grisewood, Faber 1978 $23.50

Roman Quarry and Other Sequences. Sheep Meadow 1982 $27.50 pap. $14.95

Introducing David Jones: A Selection of His Writings. Ed. by John Matthias, Faber 1980 o.p.

Dai Greatcoat: A Self-Portrait of David Jones in His Letters. Ed. by René Hague, Faber 1980 $27.95

BOOKS ABOUT JONES

Hague, René. *A Commentary on "The Anathemata" of David Jones*. Univ. of Toronto Pr. 1978 $20.00. Line-by-line guide.

Rees, Samuel. *David Jones*. Twayne's Eng. Authors Ser. G. K. Hall 1978 $13.00

———. *David Jones: An Annotated Bibliography and Guide to Research*. Reference Lib. of the Humanities Garland 1977 lib. bdg. $22.00

KAVANAGH, PATRICK. 1905–1967

"My life has in many ways been a tragedy and a failure," wrote Patrick Kavanagh toward his death. Yet posterity has increasingly viewed him as one of the major Irish poets after Yeats. Born in Innishkeen, County Monaghan, Kavanagh ended his formal education after grammar school. He lived on a farm in his native parish until moving to Dublin in 1939, which he later described as one of the great mistakes of his life. There he supported himself primarily through journalism until awarded a sinecure of £400 a year for extramural lectures at University College, Dublin. After an illness in the mid-1950s, he grew resigned to obscurity and mellowed in his long literary war with both Irish repression and the Irish literary establishment. Besides his journalism, he also wrote novels of an autobiographical cast. He married for the first time during the last years of his life.

Sprung from Catholic peasant stock, Kavanagh saw himself as voicing his own heritage against more anglicized (and more famous) writers. His first volume, *Ploughman and Other Poems* (o.p.), established the rural themes that mark much of his verse. His best-known poem, *The Great Hunger*, follows a potato farmer named Patrick Maguire through the famine of the 1840s and presents a blistering attack on the sexual and spiritual deprivation of rural Irish peasantry. Kavanagh later criticized the poem as lacking humor, and his later work shows a more temperate acceptance of the ironic comedy of life, as in "Canal Bank Walk." He never lost his acerbity.

BOOKS BY KAVANAGH

Collected Poems of Kavanagh. Norton Lib. 1973 pap. $5.95
Complete Poems. Kavanagh 1972 $25.00
The Great Hunger. Biblio Dist. repr. of 1942 ed. 1971 $10.00. Reprint of his best-known poem.
Lapped Furrows: Correspondence, 1933–1967. Kavanagh 1969 $25.00
November Haggard: Uncollected Prose and Verse. Kavanagh 1971 $25.00
The Green Fool. Irish Bk. Ctr. 1975 pap. $4.95. Heavily autobiographical novel.
By Night Unstarred: An Autobiographical Novel. Kavanagh 1978 $25.00
Tarry Flynn. Irish Bk. Ctr. 1978 pap. $4.95. Heavily autobiographical novel, later made into a play.

BOOKS ABOUT KAVANAGH

Kavanagh, Peter. *Garden of the Golden Apples: A Bibliography of Patrick Kavanagh.* Kavanagh 1972 pap. $5.00
———. *Sacred Keeper: A Biography of Patrick Kavanagh.* Humanities Pr. text ed. 1980 $21.00. By the poet's brother.
Nemo, John. *Patrick Kavanagh. Twayne's Eng. Authors Ser.* G. K. Hall 1979 lib. bdg. $15.95. Probably the best general study; contains a useful bibliography.
Warner, Alan. *Clay Is the Word: Patrick Kavanagh, 1905–1967.* Humanities Pr. text ed. 1974 $11.00 pap. $4.50. The first full-length study, and still the liveliest.

LARKIN, PHILIP. 1922–1985

Born in Coventry where his father served as city treasurer for 22 years, Larkin was educated at King Henry VIII School in his native city and at St. John's College, Oxford. Perhaps his most important friend at Oxford was Kingsley Amis, who dedicated the novel *Lucky Jim* (1954) to him; Larkin reciprocated by dedicating *XX Poems* (o.p.) to Amis. A librarian by profession, Larkin held various posts in British libraries after graduation from college, and since 1955 had been the librarian of Brynmor Jones Library, University of Hull. Besides his verse, Larkin wrote two novels in the 1940s, *Jill* (1940) and *A Girl in Winter* (1947). An enthusiastic jazz buff, he did feature stories on that subject for the newspaper *The Daily Telegraph* from 1961 to 1971, and reviews of jazz recordings. Larkin was a private man who discouraged publication of details of his life.

Influenced at first by Yeats, Larkin soon became perhaps the finest of the Movement poets who eschewed both rhetorical excess and cosmic themes in the service of a restrained, conversational idiom presenting more ordinary subjects. Never a prolific poet, Larkin earned his high public esteem through the quality rather than quantity of his verse. Poems like "Church Going" or "The Whitsun Weddings" combine extraordinary skill with an ironic integrity to succeed in making major statements in spite of themselves. Like Auden, Larkin can also excel in wryly comic verse, as in his toad poems. In the introduction to his volume *The North Ship* (1946) he declared Hardy his favorite poet.

BOOKS BY LARKIN

Jill. 1940. Overlook Pr. 1984 pap. $7.95
The North Ship. Faber 1974 pap. $4.95
A Girl in Winter. 1947. Overlook Pr. 1976 $8.95
The Whitsun Weddings. Faber 1964 pap. $4.95
(ed.). *The Oxford Book of Twentieth Century English Verse.* Oxford 1973 $29.95
High Windows. Farrar 1974 pap. $6.95
Required Writing: Miscellaneous Pieces, 1955–1982. Farrar 1984 $17.95 pap. $9.95

BOOKS ABOUT LARKIN

Bloomfield, B. C. *Philip Larkin: A Bibliography.* Faber 1980 $54.95
Brownjohn, Alan. *Philip Larkin.* British Bk. Ctr. 1976 pap. o.p.
Kuby, Lolette. *An Uncommon Poet for the Common Man: A Study of the Poetry of Philip Larkin.* Mouton text ed. 1974 pap. $21.00
Martin, Bruce K. *Philip Larkin. Twayne's Eng. Authors Ser.* G. K. Hall 1978 $15.95
Motion, Andrew. *Philip Larkin. Contemporary Writers Ser.* Methuen 1982 pap. $4.25
Thwaite, Anthony. *Larkin at Sixty.* Faber 1982 $15.95
Timms, David. *Philip Larkin.* Barnes & Noble 1973 o.p. The first book published on Larkin; particularly good on the biographical and British contexts of the poems.

LAWRENCE, D(AVID) H(ERBERT). 1885–1930

[SEE Chapter 12 in this volume.]

LEWIS, C(ECIL) DAY. 1904–1972

The grandfather of C. Day Lewis changed the family name of Day to Day-Lewis. In a fit of inverse snobbery, the poet dropped the hyphen, to the confusion of librarians and bibliographers ever since. His own father was a priest in the Church of Ireland, and the poet was born in Ballintubber, Northern Ireland, but was educated in English boarding schools and at Oxford. There he met the young W. H. Auden and eventually became part of the circle that Auden once facetiously dubbed "Daylewisaudenmacneicespender." After a stint as a schoolteacher, he married and supported himself partly through writing a series of highly successful detective novels under the pseudonym Nicholas

Blake. Active in leftist political affairs during the 1930s, he left the Communist party, and political activity generally, in 1938.

His later honors include a year as Charles Eliot Norton professor of poetry at Harvard and as Clark lecturer at Cambridge, and a term as professor of poetry at Oxford from 1951 to 1956. He served as director of the publishing house of Chatto & Windus from 1954 until his death in 1972 and was named poet laureate in 1968.

C. Day Lewis began as a nearly Georgian poet but changed direction radically at Oxford under the influence of Auden. His verse for the next decade and a half showed greater intellectual tightness, contemporary diction, and social relevance. In his influential literary manifesto *A Hope for Poetry*, he named GERARD MANLEY HOPKINS, Wilfred Owen, and T. S. Eliot as literary ancestors. Moving to the Devon village of Musbury in 1938, Lewis entered a new phase of more private poetry marked by a strong interest in nature. An avid student of Virgil, he translated the *Georgics*, the *Aeneid*, and *Eclogues*. In his autobiography Lewis confessed that he found it difficult "to decide between contrary opinions, or to form any coherent idea of my own identity." Perhaps because he wrote well in a variety of styles but lacked a distinctive speaking voice, the public reputation of his poetry has declined in recent years.

BOOKS BY LEWIS

A Hope for Poetry. 1934. Porter 1978 $14.50. Prose manifesto, first published in 1934.
Poems, 1925–1972. Ed. by Ian Parsons, Hogarth Pr. 1977 o.p.

BOOKS ABOUT LEWIS

Dyment, Clifford. *C. Day Lewis*. British Bk. Ctr. o.p.
Riddel, Joseph N. *C. Day Lewis*. *Twayne's Eng. Authors Ser.* G. K. Hall 1971 lib. bdg.
    $10.95

MACBETH, GEORGE (MANN). 1932–

Born in the Scots mining village of Shotts but educated at King Edward VII School in Sheffield, Yorkshire, George MacBeth graduated with first-class honors from New College, Oxford. In the late 1950s, he belonged to The Group, an informal association of young writers, mostly poets, which in 1965 became the more structured Writers' Workshop. For 21 years, beginning in 1955, MacBeth produced programs on poetry and the arts for the BBC. Both the oral presentations of The Group and the BBC broadcasts whetted MacBeth's interest in the oral aspect of his own work. He has published numerous volumes of poetry, along with plays and (beginning in 1975) novels.

A prolific poet, MacBeth has worked in an almost chameleonlike variety of forms and styles. This eclecticism has made it difficult to establish a distinctive voice, yet his different styles have influenced numerous contemporaries in England. He has also tried to keep his poems accessible to the general public, and has achieved a reasonably wide popularity. Sometimes didactic, MacBeth often treats his subjects—death and life, war and love, tradition and the present day—with a linguistic playfulness that delights in the resources of language itself. His rephrasing of Keats's "Ode on a Grecian Urn" and pseudotranslations of Chinese poetry are memorably comic.

Books by MacBeth

Collected Poems, 1958–1970. Atheneum 1972 $7.50
Shrapnel and the Poet's Year. Atheneum 1974 $7.50. Two volumes in one.
Buying a Heart. Atheneum 1978 pap. $4.95
The Survivor. Harcourt 1978 $7.95. Fiction.
Poems of Love and Death. Atheneum 1980 $9.95 pap. $5.95
The Katana. Simon & Schuster 1982 $13.95
Poems from Oby. Atheneum 1983 $12.95 pap. $5.95
Anna's Book. Holt 1984 $16.95
The Long Darkness. Atheneum 1984 $13.95 pap. $7.95

MACDIARMID, HUGH (pseud. of Christopher Murray Grieve). 1892–1978

The leading Scottish poet of the twentieth century, Hugh MacDiarmid was the son of a postman in the Scottish border country. Educated at a local school and then at Edinburgh University, he served in World War I and then worked as a journalist and lecturer. His active political life involved membership in the Communist party, which expelled but later readmitted him, and in the Scottish Nationalist party, which he helped to found. These elements combined in his poetry, which often uses Scottish dialect and confronts political themes. His Scottish poetry reached perhaps its highest point in his major sequence *A Drunk Man Looks at the Thistle* (published in 1926, revised 1956) and his English poetry in the *Second Hymn to Lenin,* published in 1935. Tempestuous, irascible, surprising, and brilliant, MacDiarmid sought struggle rather than calm and suffered through periods of poverty and neglect as well as of public recognition. Throughout his long life he strove to create a Scottish culture in opposition to the dominant English one; in *Who's Who* he listed "Anglophobia" as his preferred recreation.

Books by MacDiarmid

Complete Poems of Hugh MacDiarmid. Ed. by Michael Grieve and William Aitken, Flatiron 2 vols. 1983 $65.00
More Collected Poems. Ohio Univ. Pr. (Swallow) 1970 $8.95
A Drunk Man Looks at the Thistle. 1926. Ed. by John C. Weston, Univ. of Massachusetts Pr. 1971 $9.50 pap. $5.50
The Hugh MacDiarmid Anthology: Poems in Scots and English. Ed. by Michael Grieve and Alexander Scott, Routledge & Kegan 1972 $18.95
Lucky Poet: A Self Study in Literature and Political Ideas Being the Autobiography of Hugh MacDiarmid. Univ. of California Pr. 1972 $26.50

Books about MacDiarmid

Buthlay, Kenneth. *Hugh MacDiarmid. Scottish Writers Ser.* Columbia Univ. Pr. 1983 pap. $6.50. The best general book.
Scott, P. H., and A. C. Davis, eds. *The Age of MacDiarmid: Essays on Hugh MacDiarmid and His Influence on Contemporary Scotland.* Barnes & Noble 1981 $25.00

MACNEICE, LOUIS. 1907–1963

Born in Belfast and raised in Carrickfergus, MacNeice never lost his sense of Irish roots, even after his education in English schools and Oxford University made him ill at ease with his Puritan upbringing. His father was a minister who later became a bishop in the Anglo-Irish Church of Ireland. At Oxford, MacNeice became friends with Stephen Spender and, later, W. H. Auden, with whom he collaborated on *Letters from Iceland*. After graduating with a double first, MacNeice accepted a lectureship in the classics at Birmingham University and, after the traumatic elopement of his first wife, at Bedford College of the University of London. He joined the BBC as scriptwriter and producer in 1941 and remained with it for the remainder of his career. He also did an admired translation of Aeschylus's *Agamemnon* and the well-known book *The Poetry of W. B. Yeats*.

MacNeice defended his own poetry and that of Auden, Spender, and Lewis in his book *Modern Poetry*. There he called for an "impure poetry" that would react against the giants of the previous generation by embracing the partisanship that he missed in Yeats and involvement with life that he found lacking in Eliot, both of whom had otherwise influenced him. While engaged with personal and political issues of the 1930s, MacNeice maintained a more skeptical stance than many of his contemporaries. His best verse—like "Valediction" or "Bagpipe Music"—brings wit and strong rhythms to bear on contemporary life and often harks back to scenes of his youth. After joining the BBC, he also wrote more than 150 scripts, of which a dozen radio dramas have been published.

BOOKS BY MACNEICE

Selected Poems. Faber 1964 pap. $5.95
(and E. R. Dodds, eds.). *Collected Poems.* Faber $22.00 pap. $11.50
Modern Poetry. Haskell repr. of 1938 ed. 1969 lib. bdg. $39.95; Richard West repr. of 1938 ed. $5.00
The Poetry of W. B. Yeats. Greenwood repr. of 1941 ed. 1979 lib. bdg. $24.75; intro. by Richard Ellmann, Oxford repr. of 1941 ed. 1969 pap. $3.95
Christopher Columbus: A Radio Play. AMS Pr. repr of 1944 ed. $20.00

BOOKS ABOUT MACNEICE

Brown, Terence. *Louis MacNeice: Sceptical Vision.* Barnes & Noble 1975 o.p.
Brown, Terence, and Alec Reid, eds. *Time Was Away: The World of Louis MacNeice.* Humanities Pr. text ed. 1974 $12.00. Mixture of critical essays and personal recollections.
Coulton, Barbara. *Louis MacNeice in the BBC.* Faber 1980 $27.95
Marsack, Robyn. *The Cave of Making: The Poetry of Louis MacNeice.* Oxford 1982 $17.95. Important recent study.
McKinnon, William T. *Apollo's Blended Dream: A Study of the Poetry of Louis MacNeice.* Oxford 1971 $12.75
Smith, Elton E. *Louis MacNeice. Twayne's Eng. Authors Ser.* o.p. Contains useful bibliography.

MASEFIELD, JOHN. 1878–1967

Once one of the most popular English poets of the century, Masefield has fallen into recent and undeserved neglect since his death. He was born in a Victorian house with rural vistas, which he later recalled as "living in Paradise." In childhood he had a series of intense, visionary experiences inspired by both nature and literature, which gave him a habitual sense of participation in a greater life. These had weakened by 1891, when he entered training for the merchant naval service. An officer on the White Star Line's *Adriatic*, he jumped ship in New York in 1895 and roamed across America, returning to England two years later when a recovery of his intense childhood visions convinced him he could succeed as a writer.

Masefield excelled more at narrative than at symbolism. His first book, *Salt Water Poems and Ballads*, displayed the allegiance to outcasts and wanderers that marks his subject matter. The musicality of that volume derives partly from the strong early influence of W. B. Yeats. Increasingly, Masefield experimented with colloquial diction, particularly from the lower classes; his *The Everlasting Mercy* (1911, o.p.) recounted the conversion of a rural scoundrel in language that astonished many readers. Immensely productive, he produced more than 20 volumes of fiction, 17 plays, and other prose work besides his major volumes of poetry; unfortunately, much of his work is now out of print. Masefield still appeals particularly to the common reader. He was appointed poet laureate in 1930.

BOOKS BY MASEFIELD

Poems. Macmillan 1953 o.p.
Salt Water Poems and Ballads. 1902. Macmillan 1953 o.p.
Tarpaulin Muster. Short Story Index Repr. Ser. Ayer repr. of 1907 ed. $14.00. Fiction.
Some Memories of W. B. Yeats. Biblio Dist. repr. of 1940 ed. 1971 $11.00; Folcroft 1977 lib. bdg. $10.00
Grace before Plowing: Fragments of an Autobiography. Macmillan 1966 o.p.
Letters of John Masefield to Florence Lamont. Ed. by Corliss Lamont and Lansing Lamont, Columbia Univ. Pr. 1979 o.p.

BOOKS ABOUT MASEFIELD

Drew, Fraser. *John Masefield's England: A Study of the National Themes in His Work.* Fairleigh Dickinson Univ. Pr. 1973 $24.50
Handley-Taylor, G. *John Masefield; or The Queen's Poet Laureate: A Bibliography.* Saifer $15.00
Lamont, Corliss. *Remembering John Masefield.* Fairleigh Dickinson Univ. Pr. 1971 $14.50. Contains valuable letters.
Smith, Constance Babington. *John Masefield: A Life.* Oxford 1978 o.p.
Sternlicht, Sanford. *John Masefield. Twayne's Eng. Authors Ser.* G. K. Hall 1978 lib. bdg. $13.50. Good, recent study.
Strong, L. A. G. *John Masefield.* British Bk. Ctr. o.p. Brief overview.

MUIR, EDWIN. 1887–1959

One of the foremost men of modern Scottish letters, Edwin Muir was born to a farming family in the remote Orkney Islands. Forced to move with his family to the industrial city of Glasgow when he was 13, Muir held a series of minor and often grubby jobs before supporting himself mainly through journalism and occasional teaching. In 1919 he married Willa Anderson, and in his *An Autobiography* (1940) would describe their marriage as "the most fortunate event in my life." Willa Muir not only encouraged her husband to write but collaborated with him on numerous translations and other works. Her own, moving autobiography, *Belonging*, is both an engrossing account and a minor masterpiece in its own right. In later life Muir worked for the British Council, was warden of an adult educational college in Scotland, and served as visiting Charles Eliot Norton professor at Harvard.

Muir's poetry stands somewhat aloof from more flamboyant varieties of modernism, yet won the respect of both Eliot and Yeats. Often cast in seemingly traditional rhymes and meters, his verse depended on a vision, which Kathleen Raine described as "the perennial philosophy." Muir looked beneath surfaces of the world for archetypes of a primal and now-lost unity of the soul with the world. Sometimes he used the Scottish landscape and sometimes earlier mythology to convey his vision, as in *One Foot in Eden* (1956). Muir's criticism and translations are still worth reading as well.

BOOKS BY MUIR

Collected Poems. Faber 1984 pap. $9.95; Oxford 2d ed. 1965 $19.95. The standard edition.

Selected Poems. Faber 1965 pap. $4.95

Transition: Essays on Contemporary Literature. Essay Index Repr. Ser. Ayer repr. of 1926 ed. $18.00; Folcroft 1976 lib. bdg. $25.00

John Knox: Portrait of a Calvinist. Associated Faculty Pr. repr. of 1929 ed. 1971 $26.00; *Select Bibliographies Repr. Ser.* Ayer repr. of 1929 ed. $21.00; Folcroft repr. of 1930 ed. 1978 lib. bdg. $30.00

Scottish Journey. Norwood repr. of 1935 ed. 1979 lib. bdg. $30.00; State Mutual Bk. 1981 $30.00

An Autobiography. Norwood repr. of 1954 ed. 1979 lib. bdg. $30.00. Revised version of *The Story and the Fable: An Autobiography.*

Estate of Poetry. Fwd. by A. MacLeish, Harvard Univ. Pr. 1962 $8.95. Critical essays originally delivered as the Charles Eliot Norton lectures at Harvard.

Scott and Scotland: The Predicament of the Scottish Writer. Folcroft repr. of 1936 ed. lib. bdg. $20.00

Selected Letters. Ed. by Peter H. Butter, Hogarth Pr. 1974 o.p.

BOOKS ABOUT MUIR

Butter, Peter H. *Edwin Muir: Man and Poet.* Greenwood repr. of 1966 ed. 1977 lib. bdg. $24.75. The authorized biography, also contains previously unpublished material.

Hoffman, Daniel. *Barbarous Knowledge: Myth in the Poetry of Yeats, Graves, and Muir.* Oxford 1967 $10.95 1970 pap. $4.95

Huberman, Elizabeth L. *Poetry of Edwin Muir: The Field of Good and Ill.* Oxford 1971 $11.95. Close study of the poems.

Knight, Roger. *Edwin Muir: An Introduction to His Work.* Longman text ed. 1980 $23.00

Mellown, Elgin W. *Bibliography of the Writings of Edwin Muir: Bibliography and Supplement Bound Together.* Univ. of Alabama Pr. 1970 $10.75
———. *Edwin Muir. Twayne's Eng. Authors Ser.* G. K. Hall 1979 lib. bdg. $15.95
Muir, Willa. *Belonging: A Memoir.* Hogarth Pr. 1968 o.p.

OWEN, WILFRED. 1893–1918

Born in the village of Oswestry in Shropshire, Owen began to compose poems at age 10 or 11 and continued steadily thereafter. He continued to hone his technique during a checkered academic career, which included Shrewsbury Technical School, a brief stint at University College, Reading, matriculation and then withdrawal from the University of London, a short effort at studying for priestly orders, and language teaching at the Berlitz school in Bordeaux. Returning to England in 1915 to enlist in the army, he was commissioned in the Manchester Regiment and went to the front in January 1917. Sent back to England to recuperate from the rigors of a winter campaign, he met Siegfried Sassoon at the Craiglockhart War Hospital in Edinburgh. During the year from August 1917 to September 1918 he produced much of his best work. Sent back to the front in 1918, he was awarded the Military Cross for gallantry in action and was killed by machine-gun fire on November 4 while in action at the Sambre Canal.

Although he produced other work, Owen's reputation depends on his war poetry. "My subject is War, and the pity of War," he wrote. Yet as his sometime mentor Siegfried Sassoon observed, "He pitied others; he did not pity himself." Owen's realistic depiction of the carnage of war, and his savage indignation at it, inform his best work. His themes gain power through his skillful technique, particularly the play of sound. He pioneered the technique of pararhyme, the use of rhyming words with similar consonants but differing vowels (as in "flashes/fleshes"). "Strange Meeting" is one of his finest poems.

BOOKS BY OWEN

The Complete Poems and Fragments. Ed. by Jon Stallworthy, Norton 2 vols. 1984 $65.00
Collected Poems. Ed. by C. Day Lewis, New Directions rev. ed. 1964 pap. $5.95
Collected Letters. Ed. by Harold Owen and John Bell, Oxford 1967 $45.00

BOOKS ABOUT OWEN

Owen, Harold. *Journey from Obscurity: Memoirs of the Owen Family—Wilfred Owen, 1893–1918.* Oxford 3 vols. $12.00. By the poet's brother.
Stallworthy, Jon. *Wilfred Owen: A Biography.* Oxford 1975 $27.50 1978 pap. $4.95. The standard biography.
Welland, D. S. R. *Wilfred Owen.* Fernhill 2d ed. 1978 o.p.
White, Gertrude M. *Wilfred Owen. Twayne's Eng. Authors Ser.* o.p.

SITWELL, (DAME) EDITH. 1887–1964

The first child of baronet Sir George Sitwell and Lady Ida Sitwell, Edith Sitwell became famous both as poet and bohemian. Reacting against what she called the "dim bucolics" of the Georgians, she and her brothers Osbert

and Sacheverell constituted a kind of aristocratic bohemian vanguard after
World War I. Diaghilev's Russian Ballet joined T. S. Eliot and, improbably,
ALEXANDER POPE among the early influences on her work. A skilled publicist
as well as poet, Sitwell exploited her upper-class nonconformity in numerous public controversies. Her collaboration with William Walton to produce musical settings of the *Facade* poems (1923) created an uproar when
the work was performed. Sitwell also put her talents to work for young writers in whom she believed, chief among them Dylan Thomas, whose reputation she helped launch. Despite later public honors—Elizabeth II created
her a Dame Grand Cross of the British Empire, and Oxford and Cambridge
bestowed honorary degrees—she remained proudly eccentric throughout
her celebrated career.

Sitwell's early poetry displayed a pyrotechnic surface of dazzling images
and leaps. She saw Eliot's "Prufrock" as heralding "a new era in poetry,"
which would lead to seeing the world with new eyes. Breakthroughs in perception often became the themes as well as goals of her poetry. Interested
particularly in French symbolist theories of sound, she developed an intricate tonal play of verbal patterns in her verse. Her work displayed an increasingly religious orientation, and during World War II she engaged public themes like politics more overtly in works like *Three Poems for an Atomic
Age*. Besides her own verse, she wrote several books of prose and edited numerous anthologies of poetry.

BOOKS BY SITWELL

Collected Poems. Vanguard 1954 $17.50
Poetry and Criticism. Folcroft repr. of 1925 ed. 1977 lib. bdg. $15.00
Bath. Greenwood repr. of 1932 ed. lib. bdg. $24.75; Hyperion Pr. repr. of 1932 ed.
    1981 $28.00
Aspects of Modern Poetry. Essay Index Repr. Ser. Ayer repr. of 1934 ed. $17.00
I Live under a Black Sun: A Novel. Greenwood repr. of 1938 ed. lib. bdg. $17.00
The Shadow of Cain. Folcroft repr. of 1947 ed. 1977 lib. bdg. $17.50
A Poet's Notebook. Greenwood repr. of 1950 ed. lib. bdg. $20.50
Music and Ceremonies. Vanguard 1963 $6.95
Taken Care Of: The Autobiography of Edith Sitwell. Atheneum 1965 o.p.
Edith Sitwell: Selected Letters, 1919–1964. Vanguard 1970 $12.50
English Eccentrics. Vanguard $12.50

BOOKS ABOUT SITWELL

Brophy, James D. *Edith Sitwell: The Symbolist Order*. Pref. by H. T. Moore, *Crosscur-
    rents Modern Critiques Ser.* Southern Illinois Univ. Pr. 1968 $7.95
Fifoot, Richard. *Bibliography of Edith, Osbert and Sacheverell Sitwell*. Shoe String (Ar-
    chon) 2d ed. 1971 $27.50
Glendinning, Victoria. *Edith Sitwell: A Unicorn among Lions*. Knopf 1981 $17.95
Lehmann, John. *A Nest of Tigers: Edith, Osbert, and Sacheverell Sitwell in Their Times*.
    Little, Brown 1969 o.p.
Villa, José García, ed. *A Celebration for Edith Sitwell*. 1948. Bks. for Libraries 1972
    o.p.

SMITH, STEVIE. 1902–1971

Florence Margaret Smith adopted her nickname, Stevie, as a nom de plume after a friend's joking comparison of her small stature to that of the jockey Steve Donoghue. She was born in Hull but after her parents' separation moved with her mother, aunt, and sister to a house in the London suburb of Palmers Green. There she lived for the rest of her outwardly uneventful life. After graduation from school, she worked as a private secretary with the London magazine publishing firm George Newnes until 1953, when partly due to ill health she retired to devote her full time to writing and to BBC broadcasts. Besides her verse, her other works include three novels published between 1936 and 1949.

Although she had a minor success with *Novel on Yellow Paper* and subsequent verse in the late 1930s, Smith came to wider public attention after the publication of her *Selected Poems* in England in 1962 and the United States in 1964. Praised by ROBERT LOWELL and others, her poetry does not fit easily into any school or influence. Rather, her mixture of nursery or children's rhythms with a mature irony leads to a voice at once individualized yet accessible. Smith's poems often deal with death, loneliness, absent parents, and what she described as a backsliding rejection of orthodox Christianity. After 1938 she illustrated her own books with line drawings that some critics find distracting but others judge as often ironic commentaries on the text. "Not Waving but Drowning," perhaps her best-known poem, illustrates her disconcerting blend of wit and seriousness at its best.

BOOKS BY SMITH

Collected Poems. Ed. by James MacGibbon, New Directions repr. of 1975 ed. 1983 pap. $12.95; Oxford 1976 $22.50
Selected Poems. New Directions 1964 pap. $4.95
Novel on Yellow Paper. 1936. Pinnacle Bks. 1982 pap. $3.50. Fiction.
The Holiday. 1949. Pinnacle Bks. 1982 pap. $2.75. Fiction.
Me Again: Uncollected Writings of Stevie Smith. Ed. by Jack Barbera and William McBrien, Farrar 1982 $15.95; Random (Vintage) repr. of 1981 ed. 1983 pap. $6.95
Over the Frontier. Pinnacle Bks. 1982 pap. $3.50. Fiction.
Stevie Smith: A Selection. Ed. by Hermione Lee, Faber 1983 $18.95 pap. $6.95

BOOKS ABOUT SMITH

Bedient, Calvin. *Eight Contemporary Poets.* Oxford 1974 pap. $3.95
Dick, Kay. *Ivy and Stevie.* Schocken 1983 pap. $5.95

SPENDER, STEPHEN. 1909–

The youngest of the group that included Auden, Lewis, and MacNeice, Stephen Spender was born in London and educated at Oxford. He produced his most memorable verse in the 1930s, when his leftist orientation led him briefly to join the Communist party. Coeditor of *Horizon* magazine before World War II, he served in the National Fire Service during the war. He worked as an editor of *Encounter* magazine from 1953 to 1967, resigning after the revelation that the magazine had relied on funding from the American CIA. Since the war, Spender has produced more prose than poetry, including the fine autobiography *World within World* (1951, o.p.) and the valuable literary analysis *The Struggle of the Modern* (1963). After his first visit to the United States in 1947 to see his old friend Auden, Spender began to spend half the year in England and the other half abroad, often in the United States on visiting appointments at universities. In 1970 he was appointed professor of English literature at the University of London.

Spender's poetry lacks both the wit and quietly authoritative tone of Auden's. Instead, he takes a more questioning, self-divided stance, in which his modern diction and subjects often serve a romantic preoccupation with the self. Spender's prose shows him the most proromantic of his circle. Even in the socially engaged verse of the 1930s, Spender often dramatized individual yearnings or projected them onto only apparently objective social circumstances. He has found his true themes in relationships, whether of individuals or of groups. A gifted critic, his recent work has included studies of T. S. Eliot, the 1930s poets, and the sculptor Henry Moore.

BOOKS BY SPENDER

Selected Poems. Faber 1965 pap. $4.95; Random 1964 pap. $8.95
Letters to Christopher: Stephen Spender's Letters to Christopher Isherwood, 1929–1939, with "The Line of the Branch"—Two Thirties Journals. Ed. by Lee Bartlett, Black Sparrow 1980 $14.00 pap. $7.50
The Destructive Element: A Study of Modern Writers and Beliefs. Folcroft repr. of 1935 ed. lib. bdg. $25.00; Saifer 1970 $10.00
Forward from Liberalism. Arden Lib. repr. of 1937 ed. 1977 lib. bdg. $27.50; Darby repr. of 1937 ed. 1981 lib. bdg. $30.00; Norwood repr. of 1937 ed. 1979 lib. bdg. $25.00; Richard West repr. of 1937 ed. 1979 lib. bdg. $25.00
Learning Laughter. Greenwood repr. of 1953 ed. lib. bdg. $16.00. On Israel.
Engaged in Writing: Two Novels. Saifer $10.00
The Thirties and After: Poetry, Politics, People, 1930s–1970s. Random (Vintage) 1979 pap. $10.00

BOOKS ABOUT SPENDER

Kulkarni, H. B. *Stephen Spender: An Annotated Bibliography.* Pref. by Stephen Spender, Garland 1976 lib. bdg. $34.00
Weatherhead, A. K. *Stephen Spender and the Thirties.* Bucknell Univ. Pr. 1975 $22.50

THOMAS, DYLAN. 1914–1953

The most important Welsh poet of the twentieth century, Thomas was born in Swansea, about which he remembered unkindly "the smug darkness of a provincial town." He attended Swansea Grammar School, but received his real education in the extensive library of his father, a disappointed schoolteacher with higher ambitions. Refusing university study in favor of immediately becoming a professional writer, Thomas worked first in Swansea and then in London at a variety of literary jobs, which included journalism and, eventually, filmscripts and radio plays. In 1936 he began the satisfying but stormy marriage to the bohemian writer and dancer Caitlin MacNamara that would endure for the rest of his career. His life fell into a pattern of oscillation between work and dissipation in London and recovery and relaxation in a rural retreat, usually in Wales. Thomas worked in a documentary film unit during the war. Besides his poetry, he wrote plays and fiction. In the early 1950s, he gave three celebrated poetry-reading tours of the United States, during which his outrageous behavior vied with his superb reading ability for public attention. Aggravated by chronic alcoholism, his health collapsed during the last tour, and he died in a New York City hospital.

In his poetry, Thomas embraced an exuberant romanticism in the encounter between self and world and a joyous riot in the lushness of language. His work falls into three periods—an early "womb-tomb" phase during which he produced a notebook, which he later mined for further poems, a middle one troubled by marriage and war, and a final acceptance of the human condition. The exuberant rhetoric of his work belies an equally strong devotion to craftsmanship and artistry, what he once called "my craft or sullen art." His great "Fern Hill," for example, builds its imagery of the rejoicing innocence of childhood on a strict and demanding syllabic count. A recollection of boyhood holidays on the farm of his aunt and uncle, that poem places its emotion within an Edenic framework typical of Thomas's work. The impressive sonnet sequences "Altarwise by Owl-Light" (1936) combines the internal quest of romanticism with a more elaborate religious outlook in tracing the birth and spiritual autobiography of a poet. Almost at the end of his career he produced the moving elegy "Do Not Go Gentle into That Good Night" (1952), written during the final illness of his father. Despite his periods of doubt and dissipation, Thomas celebrated the fullness of life. As he wrote in a note to his *Collected Poems,* "These poems, with all their crudities, doubts, and confusion, are written for the love of Man and in praise of God, and I'd be a damn fool if they weren't."

BOOKS BY THOMAS

Collected Poems, 1934–1953. 1952. New Directions 1971 pap. $5.95

Collected Stories. New Directions 1984 $16.95

Poems of Dylan Thomas. Ed. by David Jones, New Directions 1971 $14.00

Selected Letters. Commentary by Constantine FitzGibbon, New Directions 1967 $10.00

Letters to Vernon Watkins. Ed. by Vernon Watkins, Greenwood repr. of 1957 ed. 1982 lib. bdg. $25.00

The Notebooks, 1930–1934. Ed. by Ralph Maud, New Directions $10.00

Portrait of the Artist as a Young Dog. 1940. New Directions 1956 pap. $5.25

A Child's Christmas in Wales. 1954. Godine 1980 $10.95 1984 pap. $5.95; New Directions 1969 $12.00

Under Milk Wood: A Play for Voices. 1954. New Directions 1959 pap. $3.95

Adventures in the Skin Trade and Other Stories. New Directions 1955 pap. $4.95

The Doctor and the Devils and Other Scripts. New Directions 1970 pap. $6.25

BOOKS ABOUT THOMAS

Cox, Charles B., ed. *Dylan Thomas: A Collection of Critical Essays.* Prentice-Hall (Spectrum Bks.) 1966 $12.95

Ferris, Paul. *Dylan Thomas.* Penguin repr. of 1977 ed. 1979 pap. $4.95

FitzGibbon, Constantine. *The Life of Dylan Thomas.* Little, Brown 1965 o.p. The earliest good biography.

Kershner, R. B., Jr. *Dylan Thomas: The Poet and His Critics.* Amer. Lib. Association 1976 lib. bdg. $20.00. Contains useful bibliography.

Kidder, Rushworth M. *Dylan Thomas: The Country of the Spirit.* Princeton Univ. Pr. 1973 $23.00

Korg, Jacob. *Dylan Thomas. Twayne's Eng. Authors Ser.* G. K. Hall 1964 lib. bdg. $13.50

Maud, Ralph. *Dylan Thomas in Print: A Bibliographical History.* Univ. of Pittsburgh Pr. 1970 $14.95

————. *Entrances to Dylan Thomas' Poetry. Critical Essays in Modern Lit. Ser.* Univ. of Pittsburgh Pr. 1963 pap. $5.95. Good introduction.

Olsen, Elder. *The Poetry of Dylan Thomas.* Univ. of Chicago Pr. 1954 o.p.

Read, Bill. *The Days of Dylan Thomas.* McGraw-Hill 1965 o.p. Useful, sometimes overly schematic.

Tindall, William Y. *A Reader's Guide to Dylan Thomas.* Octagon 1973 lib. bdg. $22.50. Poem-by-poem analysis.

TOMLINSON, CHARLES. 1927–

Distinguished both as poet and painter, Tomlinson was born in Stoke-on-Trent and received his B.A. from Queen's College, Cambridge, in 1948. After a few years of elementary school teaching and a period as private secretary in northern Italy, he returned to study at London University, from which he received an M.A. in 1955. Since then he has taught in the English department at the University of Bristol and visited the United States to teach at the University of New Mexico and at Colgate.

One of the English poets most open to transatlantic influences, Tomlinson has profited from an array of modern American poets, including MARIANNE MOORE, WALLACE STEVENS, WILLIAM CARLOS WILLIAMS, EZRA POUND, and the objectivist group. Having begun as a painter, he often emphasizes visual elements in his verse. "My theme is relationship," he has said, "a phenomenological poetry, with roots in Wordsworth and in Ruskin, is what I take myself to be writing." Many of Tomlinson's best poems, like "At Barstow" and "Two Views of Two Ghost Towns," concern the American West. He has also done critical essays and some fine translations of Spanish writers, including the poetry of ANTONIO MACHADO Y RUIZ (see Vol. 2).

BOOKS BY TOMLINSON

Seeing Is Believing. Astor-Honor 1958 $7.95
American Scenes and Other Poems. Oxford 1966 $3.75
The Matachines. San Marcos 1968 pap. $5.00
The Shaft. Oxford text ed. 1978 pap. $6.95
The Flood. Oxford 1981 pap. $11.95
Some Americans: A Personal Record. Univ. of California Pr. 1981 $13.95
Poetry and Metamorphosis. Cambridge Univ. Pr. 1983 $19.95
Translations. Contemporary Poetry Ser. Oxford 1983 $15.95

BOOK ABOUT TOMLINSON

Bedient, Calvin. *Eight Contemporary Poets.* Oxford 1974 pap. $3.95. Good chapter on Tomlinson.

WATKINS, VERNON (PHILLIPS). 1906–1967

One of the leading Welsh poets of the twentieth century, Vernon Watkins came from the town of Maesteg in South Wales. After a series of preparatory schools he enrolled in Magdalene College, Cambridge, and then withdrew because he felt the intellectual atmosphere threatened his poetry. He returned to Wales, where his father—a branch manager at Lloyd's Bank— got him a job as cashier. During a mental collapse he experienced a religious vision that provided the ground of much of his later verse. Refusing promotion because it would distract him from poetry, Watkins continued as cashier until retirement from the bank. During World War II he served first in the home guard and then as a policeman in the Royal Air Force. In the 1960s, he taught poetry both at the University of Washington and at Swansea University in his native Wales.

Watkins did not publish his first book until his thirty-fifth year. His verse avoids topical subjects (except for tributes to Yeats and Dylan Thomas) in favor of religious or mystical ones, often set in the Welsh countryside. Watkins's particular vision fuses Christian and neo-Platonic traditions in a way that has led critics like Kathleen Raine to value him highly. Influenced early by Blake and later by Yeats, he belongs in the ranks of romantic moderns. The most important contemporary poet to Watkins was his great friend Dylan Thomas, whom he first met in 1935 and who first persuaded Watkins to let his work be published. Watkins also did verse translations, especially of Heine.

BOOKS BY WATKINS

Selected Poems. New Directions 1967 pap. $2.25
Selected Verse Translations. Intro. by Michael Hamburger, Small Pr. Dist. 1977 $8.00
Dylan Thomas: Letters to Vernon Watkins. Ed. by Vernon Watkins, Greenwood repr. of 1957 ed. 1982 lib. bdg. $25.00
Fidelities. 1967. New Directions 1969 $5.00. Poetry.
Unity of the Stream. Lit. Ser. Black Swan 1983 $17.50

BOOKS ABOUT WATKINS

Norris, Leslie. *Vernon Watkins, 1906–1967.* Faber 1970 o.p.
Polk, Dora. *Vernon Watkins and the Spring of Vision.* Humanities Pr. text ed. 1977 $14.50

YEATS, WILLIAM BUTLER. 1865–1939 (NOBEL PRIZE 1923)

In his 1940 memorial lecture in Dublin, T. S. Eliot pronounced Yeats "one of those few whose history is the history of their own time, who are a part of the consciousness of an age which cannot be understood without them." Modern readers have increasingly agreed, and now view Yeats even more than Eliot as the greatest modern poet in our language. Son of the painter

John Butler Yeats, the poet divided his early years among Dublin, London, and the port of Sligo in western Ireland. Sligo furnished many of the familiar places in his poetry, among them the mountain Ben Bulben and the lake isle of Innisfree. Important influences on his early adulthood included his father, the writer and artist William Morris, the Nationalist leader John O'Leary, and the occultist Madame Blavatsky. In 1889 he met the beautiful Nationalist Maud Gonne; his long and frustrated love for her would inspire some of his best work. Often and mistakenly viewed as merely a dreamy Celtic twilight, Yeats's work in the 1890s involved a complex attempt to unite his poetic, Nationalist, and occult interests in line with his desire to "hammer [his] thoughts into unity."

By the turn of the century, Yeats was immersed in the work with the Irish dramatic movement that would culminate in the founding of the Abbey Theatre in 1904 as a national theater for Ireland. Partly as a result of his theatrical experience, his poetry after 1900 began a complex "movement downwards upon life" fully evident in the *Responsibilities* volume of 1914 (o.p.). After that he published the extraordinary series of great volumes, all written after age 50, that continued until the end of his career. Widely read in various literary and philosophic traditions, Yeats owed his greatest debt to romantic poetry and once described himself, along with his coworkers John Synge and Lady Gregory, as a "last romantic." Yet he remained resolutely Irish as well and presented in his verse a persona bearing a subtle, idealized relationship to his everyday self. Political events like the Easter Rising and the Irish civil war found their way into his poetry, as did personal ones like marriage to Georgie Hyde-Lees in 1917, the birth of his children, and his sometime home in the Norman tower at Ballylee. So, too, did his increasing status as a public man, which included both the Nobel Prize and a term as senator of the Irish Free State (1922–28).

Yeats's disparate activities led to a lifelong quest for what he called "unity of being," which he pursued by what he called "antinomies," or opposites. These included action and contemplation, life and art, fair and foul, and other famous pairs from his poetry. The most original poet of his age, he was also in ways the most traditional, and certainly the most substantial. His varied literary output included not only poems and plays but an array of prose forms like essays, philosophy, fiction, reviews, speeches, and editions of folk and literary material. He also frequently revised his own poems, which exist in various published texts helpfully charted in the *Variorum* edition.

BOOKS BY YEATS

The Variorum Edition of the Poems of W. B. Yeats. Ed. by P. Allt, Macmillan 1957 $24.95. Helpful correlation of the various published revisions (often substantial) to Yeats's poems, together with his own notes and prefaces. The first two printings contain errors corrected in the third (1966) and later versions.

Collected Poems. Macmillan 1956 o.p. Long the standard collection, the description of this on the title page as "Definitive Edition, With the Author's Final Revisions" is misleading.

The Poems of W. B. Yeats. Ed. by Richard J. Finneran, Macmillan 1983 $19.95. Contains more than 100 poems not in the *Collected Poems*, together with extensive textual and explanatory notes.

The Early Poetry. Ed. by George Bornstein, Cornell Univ. Pr. 1986 in prep.

The Variorum Edition of the Plays of W. B. Yeats. Ed. by Russell K. Alspach, Macmillan 1966 o.p. Helpful correlation of the various published revisions, together with Yeats's own notes and prefaces.

The Collected Plays of W. B. Yeats. Macmillan new ed. 1953 $17.95

Uncollected Prose. Ed. by John P. Frayne and Colton Johnson, Columbia Univ. Pr. 2 vols. 1970–76 ea. $42.50. These two volumes contain material not in the other collections.

The Secret Rose: Stories by W. B. Yeats—A Variorum Edition. Ed. by Phillip L. Marcus, Warwick Gould, and Michael J. Sidnell, Cornell Univ. Pr. 1981 $34.95

The Letters of W. B. Yeats. Ed. by Allan Wade, Octagon repr. of 1955 ed. 1980 lib. bdg. $65.00

Letters to the New Island. Ed. by Horace Reynolds, Harvard Univ. Pr. 1970 $10.00

Autobiography. Macmillan (Collier Bks.) 1965 pap. $5.95

Essays and Introductions. Macmillan o.p. Includes much of Yeats's important literary criticism.

Explorations. Macmillan (Collier Bks.) 1973 pap. $2.95. Various prose works, including important section on the Irish dramatic movement.

A Vision. Macmillan 1961 pap. $8.95. A reissue with the author's final revisions.

Mythologies. Macmillan (Collier Bks.) 1969 pap. $8.95

Memoirs: Autobiography—First Draft and Journal. Ed. by Denis Donoghue, Macmillan 1973 o.p.

The Senate Speeches. Ed. by Donald R. Pearce, Indiana Univ. Pr. 1960 o.p.

John Sherman & Dhoya. Ed. by Richard J. Finneran, Wayne State Univ. Pr. 1969 o.p. A novella and a short story.

BOOKS ABOUT YEATS

Bloom, Harold. *Yeats.* Oxford 1970 $16.95 1972 pap. $8.95. Controversial reading of Yeats in terms of his relation to romantic tradition.

Bornstein, George. *Yeats and Shelley.* Univ. of Chicago Pr. 1970 $15.00. Yeats's relation to the poet whom he said "shaped my life."

Bradford, Curtis B. *Yeats at Work.* Ecco Pr. repr. of 1965 ed. 1978 pap. $5.95. Good study of Yeats's habits of composition, using many manuscript drafts.

Diggory, Terrence. *Yeats and American Poetry: The Traditional of the Self.* Princeton Univ. Pr. 1983 $29.50

Donoghue, Denis. *William Butler Yeats.* Viking 1971 o.p. Short introduction, perhaps stressing Nietzsche too much.

Ellmann, Richard. *Eminent Domain: Yeats among Wilde, Joyce, Pound, Eliot, and Auden.* Oxford 1967 o.p.

———. *The Identity of Yeats.* Oxford 1954 2nd ed. 1964 $22.50 pap. $5.95

———. *Yeats: The Man and the Masks.* Dutton 1948; Norton rev. ed. 1978 pap. $6.95. Still the best single introductory volume to Yeats's life and art.

Engelberg, Edward. *Vast Design: Patterns in W. B. Yeats's Aesthetic.* Univ. of Toronto Pr. 1964 $15.00 pap $4.50. The best study of Yeats's aesthetics and philosophy of art.

Finneran, Richard J., ed. *Yeats: An Annual of Critical and Textual Studies, 1983.* Cornell Univ. Pr. 3 vols. 1983–85 ea. $27.50–$39.95. Important annual collections of much of the best current work on Yeats.

Harris, Daniel A. *Yeats: Coole Park and Ballylee.* Johns Hopkins Univ. Pr. 1974 $22.50. Emphasis on Yeats's poetry dealing with Lady Gregory's Coole Park and his own tower at Ballylee.

Henn, Thomas R. *The Lonely Tower: Studies in the Poetry of W. B. Yeats.* Methuen 2d ed. 1979 $55.00

Hone, J. M. *William Butler Yeats: The Poet in Contemporary Ireland.* Folcroft repr. of 1916 ed. 1973 lib. bdg. $10.00; Gordon lib. bdg. $59.95; *Eng. Lit. Ser.* Haskell 1972 lib. bdg. $39.95. An early biography, still useful.

Jeffares, A. Norman. *A New Commentary on the Poems of W. B. Yeats.* Humanities Pr. text ed. 1983 $46.25; Stanford Univ. Pr. 1984 $39.50. Glosses many allusions, especially helpful for its reprinting of parallel passages from Yeats's prose.

——. *W. B. Yeats: Man and Poet.* Routledge & Kegan 1949 $22.50

Jochum, K. P. *W. B. Yeats: A Classified Bibliography of Criticism.* Univ. of Illinois Pr. 1978 $49.95

Marcus, Phillip L. *Yeats and the Beginnings of the Irish Renaissance.* Cornell Univ. Pr. 1970 o.p. Good on Yeats's relation to personalities and events of the 1890s.

Parkinson, Thomas. *W. B. Yeats: Self Critic—A Study of His Early Verse and the Later Poetry.* Univ. of California Pr. 1971 pap. $8.50. Covers the development of Yeats's entire poetic career.

Parrish, Stephen M., and James A. Painter, eds. *The Concordance to the Poems of W. B. Yeats.* Cornell Univ. Pr. 1963 $85.00

Stallworthy, Jon. *Between the Lines: Yeats's Poetry in the Making.* Oxford 1963 $29.95. Like Bradford (cited above), good study of Yeats's habits of composition; uses manuscripts of several major poems.

Torchiana, Donald. *W. B. Yeats and Georgian Ireland.* Northwestern Univ. Pr. o.p.

Unterecker, John. *Reader's Guide to William Butler Yeats.* Octagon repr. of 1959 ed. 1971 lib. bdg. $22.50. Poem-by-poem analysis with helpful introduction on Yeats's life and thought.

——, ed. *Yeats: A Collection of Critical Essays.* Prentice-Hall (Spectrum Bks.) 1963 $8.95 pap. $2.45

Whitaker, Thomas R. *Swan and Shadow: Yeats's Dialogue with History.* Univ. of North Carolina Pr. 1964 $26.00

CHAPTER 8

American Poetry: Early Period

James M. Cox

> If I read a book and it makes my whole body so cold no fire can ever warm me, I know that it is poetry. If I feel physically as if the top of my head were taken off, I know that is poetry. These are the only ways I know it. Is there any other way?
>
> EMILY DICKINSON, *The Life and Letters of Emily Dickinson*

The task facing the American poet from the beginning has been to make a national poetry without benefit of a native language. Even before the Declaration of Independence, the Puritan poets Anne Bradstreet and Edward Taylor felt the pressure of the wild, savage country and showed a marked tendency to reach through their English form and language toward the rude, homely experience of a new land. Although such groping roughened their meter and almost breached sentence structure, they both occasionally achieved a power that still seems immediate and striking.

Beside them, Philip Freneau, Joel Barlow, and Phillis Wheatley, although much more literary, seem less original. Unlike Barlow, who lost himself in a grandiose attempt to cast his American epic vision—*The Columbiad*—in heroic couplets, Freneau mastered eighteenth-century satiric and elegiac forms, and, in such a poem as "The Indian Burying Ground," he beautifully enclosed an American subject in traditional English form. But it is William Cullen Bryant who emerges as the first sure-handed poet in America. Writing after COLERIDGE and WORDSWORTH, Bryant achieved a form that invaded postromantic vision with preromantic diction. His blank verse, in such a poem as "Thanatopsis," echoes the stateliness and sententiousness of James Thompson and Edward Young at the same time that it clearly reflects Wordsworth's abiding trust in nature.

Bryant's successful work sets the stage for the genteel American poetry that followed. Henry Wadsworth Longfellow, John Greenleaf Whittier, James Russell Lowell, and Oliver Wendell Holmes combined to write a poetry disclosing that there were American poets who could hold their own on the terms that English poetry had established for them. Every one of these poets cultivated the English tradition in a new country. That is why there is always an element of competitive imitation in their work. They were trying to be new yet were always a bit old-fashioned. The old eighteenth-century didacticism thus stands alongside their nineteenth-century awareness of issues and attitudes. For a relatively young nation that had retained the language of its parent, these poets provided models of excellence—a proof that Americans would at once accommodate themselves to English forms and at the same time establish American letters as a cultural reality. It is small wonder that they came to be known as the Schoolroom Poets, for their success both here and in England was a promise that this nation could, with education and effort, emulate the literature of its language. Longfellow, perhaps more than any of the others, embodied the possibilities of such a poetic identity. Marvelously proficient in European languages, he was at once remarkably popular and extraordinarily urbane.

Accomplished though these poets were, their conventionality outweighed their originality. Although they were able to set American subjects to English meters, they were unable to discover new forms for their new subjects. That was the true task—the burden and the glory—of the American poetic imagination. Fortunately for American literature, there were poets who took the risk. First, there was Edgar Allan Poe. Scorning the didactic element in poetry, Poe sought to separate beauty from morality. At his best, he achieved an intensification of sound sufficient to threaten the common sense of the poetic line and release a buried, even a morbid, sense that, clinging to his redoubled rhyme, would be spellbound in the sonic pitch of the poem. Defining poetry as "the rhythmic creation of beauty," Poe not only sought the dream buried beneath the poetic vision—Coleridge had done that—but he abandoned the moral rationale that gave the buried dream symbolic meaning. The dream, or nightmare, was thus released to sound itself as the very rationale of verse.

If Poe threatened sense with sound, Ralph Waldo Emerson threatened sound with sense. Insisting that poetry was "a meter making argument," Emerson sought a meter that would be equal to the rude strokes of nature he feared were being lost to the civilizing process of gentility. He realized that blank verse, which was both the natural and the royal line of English poetry, would have to be naturalized and democratized if it was ever to be true to the America he meant to find in the West. For the most part, he eschewed blank verse altogether, seeking four-, three-, and even two-foot lines to sound the primordial sense of nature he tried so hard to hear. More than any other American writer, he called American literature into being. Like the true prophet he was, he did not so much predict the future as he made the future happen. It is no wonder that EZRA POUND, looking back on him, would say that he broke the back of blank verse.

The poet that Emerson prophesied was Walt Whitman. Whereas Poe had threatened poetic sense with sound and Emerson had threatened poetic sound with sense, Walt Whitman threatened poetic form itself. Releasing himself from the uniformly measured line, Whitman all but broke down the distinction between poetry and prose. He wanted a freedom of verse equal to the freedom of his vision; he wanted the poet to be equal to the reader and was able to imagine the two figures as identical. He thus envisioned himself dying into his words and being reborn as the reader's voice. Realizing that, in the English pronominal system, the pronoun *you* retains its form whether singular or plural, Whitman made that linguistic fact the heart of his poetic program. Thus, in any one of his poems the *you* always refers to the simple separate reader as well as to the mass of readers Whitman dreamed of as an audience. His poetry is at once incredibly public and wonderfully intimate, just as his vision is at once extraordinarily general and remarkably concrete. In going forward into his free democratic vision, Whitman actually went back behind both English and classical meters to a Biblical past. His poetry is more like the Psalms than anything else, which is as it should be, since Whitman imagined himself a god incarnating the word that would in turn embody his readers.

After Whitman, there was Emily Dickinson who, instead of expanding broadly and horizontally over the landscape as Whitman had done, contracted and concentrated into riddling quatrains. Drawing heavily on Protestant hymns, she so slanted her rhymes, buckled sentence patterns, and transported herself into metaphor that each of her poems became overcharged with meaning and spirit. If Whitman had played God in order to incarnate himself into all readers, Emily Dickinson played the devil and democratically voted herself into heaven, thus claiming a divine election that would have startled and staggered her Calvinistic ancestors.

There were other poets of course. There were the vernacular poets John Hay, BRET HARTE, James Whitcomb Riley, and PAUL LAURENCE DUNBAR, but their dialect poems tended to be performances—poems whose fate was to be memorized and recited rather than remembered. And there were southern poets like Henry Timrod and Sidney Lanier but in one way or another they followed the genteel poets. Then, too, there were the strong minor poets Jones Very and Frederick Goddard Tuckerman, who found themselves in mastering a single form—the sonnet. Although unknown to many readers of American poetry, both these poets are unforgettable the moment their work is read.

Yet it was Poe, Emerson, Whitman, and Dickinson who truly sounded an American poetry. After them an American poetry was not only possible, it was inevitable. Moreover, poetry in English would never be quite the same.

HISTORY AND CRITICISM

[SEE ALSO the reading lists on poetry in Chapter 3 in this volume.]

Allen, Gay W. *American Prosody.* Octagon repr. 1966 lib. bdg. $27.50

Arms, George. *The Fields Were Green: A New View of Bryant, Whittier, Holmes, Lowell and Longfellow, with a Selection of Their Poems.* Stanford Univ. Pr. 1953 $20.00

Burke, W. J. *American Authors and Books.* Crown 1972 o.p. The biographies of American poets and the titles of their best-known books, without critical evaluation, are included. Short articles on "Little Magazines" and the "Beat Generation" and a list of Pulitzer Prizes are valuable.

Eberwein, Jane D. *Early American Poetry: Bradstreet, Taylor, Dwight, Freneau and Bryant.* Univ. of Wisconsin Pr. 1978 pap. $13.50

Fussell, Edwin. *Lucifer in Harness: American Meter, Metaphor and Diction.* Princeton Univ. Pr. 1973 $21.00

Gelpi, Albert. *The Tenth Muse: The Psyche of the American Poet.* Harvard Univ. Pr. text ed. 1975 $18.50

Pearce, Roy H. *The Continuity of American Poetry.* Princeton Univ. Pr. 1961 pap. $11.50. Covers poetry from the seventeenth century to the present.

Scheick, William J., and Joella Doggett. *Guide to Seventeenth-Century American Poetry: A Reference Guide.* G. K. Hall 1977 lib. bdg. $19.00

Shapiro, Karl. *American Poetry.* Harper 1960 o.p. Bibliography and biographical notes on 54 poets from Anne Bradstreet to Allen Ginsberg, arranged chronologically. List of selected critical readings.

Untermeyer, Louis. *Lives of the Poets.* Simon & Schuster 1972 o.p. Many Americans are included among the 133 poets in this far-reaching history.

Waggoner, Hyatt H. *American Poets: From the Puritans to the Present.* Louisiana State Univ. Pr. text ed 1984 $30.00 pap. $14.95

Wallace, Ronald. *God Be with the Clown: Humor in American Poetry.* Univ. of Missouri Pr. text ed. 1984 $23.00

Wegelin, O. *Bibliography of American Poetry, 1650–1820.* Peter Smith 2 vols. in 1 $16.25

Williams, Stanley T. *Beginning of American Poetry.* Cooper Square Pr. repr. of 1951 ed. $20.00

COLLECTIONS

General and Comprehensive

[SEE ALSO Chapter 4 in this volume.]

Allen, Gay W. *American Poetry.* Harper text ed. 1965 $29.95. An "impressive volume" of nearly 700 poems from colonial times to the present day, including the much neglected poets Jones Very and Frederick Tuckerman. "All has been sown with a full and generous hand, so the variety and the striking originality of the period's poetry . . . are brilliantly displayed" (*New Yorker*).

Ehrenpreis, Irvin, ed. *American Poetry.* Darby repr. of 1965 ed. 1983 lib. bdg. $40.00

Ellmann, Richard, ed. *The New Oxford Book of American Verse.* Oxford 1976 $29.95

Gelpi, Albert. *The Poet in America, 1650 to Present.* Heath text ed. 1973 o.p.

Halpern, Daniel, ed. *The American Poetry Anthology.* Avon 1983 pap. $9.95

Harmon, William. *Oxford Book of American Light Verse.* Oxford 1979 $25.00

Matthiessen, F. O., ed. *Oxford Book of American Verse.* Oxford 1950 $29.95. Fifty-one poets are arranged in this excellent anthology. The earlier *Oxford Book of American Verse* was compiled by Bliss Carman in 1927.

Untermeyer, Louis. *An Anthology of the New England Poets from Colonial Times to the Present Day.* Random 1948 o.p. Thirty-three poets from Anne Bradstreet to Robert Lowell, with valuable biographical and critical comments—liberal representation of Longfellow.

Van Nostrand, Albert D., and Charles H. Watts, III, eds. *The Conscious Voice: An Anthology of American Poetry from the Seventeenth Century to the Present. Granger Index Repr. Ser.* Ayer repr. of 1959 ed. $26.50

Whicher, George F. *Poetry of the New England Renaissance, 1790–1890.* Holt 1950 o.p.

Whicher, Stephen, and Lars Ahnebrink, eds. *Twelve American Poets.* Oxford 1961 o.p. A discriminating selection of poems by Longfellow, Poe, Whitman, Dickinson,

Robinson, Frost, Stevens, Williams, Pound, Jeffers, Cummings, and Lowell, with substantial commentary.

Williams, Oscar, ed. *The Mentor Book of Major American Poets*. New Amer. Lib. pap. $4.95

———. *The New Pocket Anthology of American Verse*. Washington Square Pr. 1961 o.p. abr. ed. 1972 o.p.

American Indian and Black Poetry

Barksdale, Richard, and Kenneth Kinnamon. *Black Writers of America: A Comprehensive Anthology*. Macmillan text ed. 1972. An excellent anthology of black writing in America, containing a generous selection of poetry.

Bontemps, Arna, ed. *American Negro Poetry*. Hill & Wang 1963 o.p. Selections from more than 55 poets, including Leroi Jones, Richard Wright, and Langston Hughes. Biographical notes.

Cronyn, George W. *The Path on the Rainbow: An Anthology of Songs and Chants from the Indians of North America*. Arden Lib. repr. of 1918 ed. 1977 o.p.; Century Bookbindery repr. of 1918 ed. 1977 o.p.

Hughes, Langston, and Arna Bontemps, eds. *Poetry of the Negro, 1746–1970*. Doubleday 1970 $15.95. The works of 147 black poets from prerevolutionary to modern times.

Johnson, James W., ed. *The Book of American Negro Poetry*. Harcourt rev. ed. repr. of 1922 ed. 1969 pap. $7.95. Forty writers with biographical and critical sketches.

Turner, Frederick W., III, ed. *The Portable North American Indian Reader. Viking Portable Lib*. 1974 $14.95; Penguin 1977 pap. $7.95. Contains an impressive and discriminating selection of Indian poetry.

BARLOW, JOEL. 1754–1812

Barlow was a member of "The Connecticut Wits," a group of nine ambitious young writers determined to celebrate as well as satirize the young American democracy. The two other most famous members of the group—Timothy Dwight and John Trumbull—pursued their satiric muse until they became conservative Federalists in the face of Jeffersonian republicanism. But Barlow, who had been born and reared on a Connecticut farm before going first to Dartmouth College and then to Yale University, went first to Europe for 17 years, where, despite becoming wealthy, he became a passionate supporter of the French Revolution and saw to the publication of THOMAS PAINE's *The Age of Reason* (see Vol. 3). While running for election as a deputy to the French National Assembly, he wrote his best-known poem, the mock epic "The Hasty Pudding," which brought him celebrity in his native land. When he returned to the United States in 1805, he turned away from his ponderous epic *The Columbiad* (1807), in which he celebrated the future of the United States in the context of deploring the European past. As a reward for and acknowledgment of his support of Jeffersonianism, JAMES MADISON (see Vol. 3) appointed him minister to France. Following Napoleon to Poland in an effort to persuade the emperor to favor U.S. commerce, Barlow missed Napoleon, who was making his way back to Europe with his defeated army. When Barlow began his own return, he caught pneumonia and died. He was buried in a village near Cracow.

BOOK BY BARLOW

Works. Intro. by William K. Bottorf and Arthur L. Ford, Scholars' Facsimiles 2 vols. 1970 $130.00

BOOKS ABOUT BARLOW

Ford, Arthur L. *Joel Barlow. Twayne's U.S. Authors Ser.* Irvington 1971 lib. bdg. $11.95 text ed. pap. $4.95
Howard, Leon. *The Connecticut Wits.* AMS Pr. repr. of 1943 ed. $40.00
Woodress, James L. *Yankee's Odyssey: Life of Joel Barlow.* Greenwood repr. of 1958 ed. 1969 o.p.

BRADSTREET, ANNE. c.1612–1672

Anne Bradstreet, daughter of an early governor of the Massachusetts colony (Thomas Dudley) and wife of another (Simon Bradstreet), came to the United States from England just ten years after the Pilgrims, in 1630. A Puritan matron who eventually had eight children, she loved books from childhood. She and Edward Taylor were the only two American poets of consequence in the seventeenth century, and her poetry only found its way into print through the agency of her brother-in-law, who carried it to England without her knowledge. There it was first published in 1650 as *The Tenth Muse, Lately Sprung Up in America.*

Much of her early work was competent, but conventional: "The Four Seasons," "The Four Monarchies," "Dialogue between Old and New," and the like. Her religious poems of spiritual struggle often read like something from an old hymnbook. It is in her love poems to her husband, particularly those expressing her longing for him when he had to travel away, and in her poems about family affairs that she shines. Anne Bradstreet felt the oddness of being a writing woman when others might think she should be sewing. Her gentle, accepting spirit was warm and feminine but endowed with strength and self-assertiveness that broke through the Puritan mold. Admirably she was never ashamed to be human. The poet JOHN BERRYMAN had discovered her by 1956, when he published his long poem *Homage to Mistress Bradstreet* with illustrations by Ben Shahn.

Library Journal called the Harvard *Works* "a brilliant and probably definitive edition of . . . America's first genuine poet. It supersedes all previous editions in thoroughness and scholarship."

BOOKS BY BRADSTREET

The Complete Works of Anne Bradstreet. Ed. by Joseph R. McElrath, Jr., and Allan P. Robb, G. K. Hall 1981 lib. bdg. $36.50
The Works of Anne Bradstreet. Ed. by Jeannie Hensley, fwd. by Adrienne Rich; *John Harvard Lib. Ser.* Harvard Univ. Pr. (Belknap Pr.) 1981 pap. $7.95
Works in Prose and Verse. 1867. Ed. by J. H. Ellis, Peter Smith $16.25

BOOKS ABOUT BRADSTREET

Crowell, Pattie, and Ann Stanford, eds. *Critical Essays on Anne Bradstreet. Critical Essays on Amer. Lit. Ser.* G. K. Hall 1983 lib. bdg. $44.50

Martin, Wendy. *An American Triptych: Anne Bradstreet, Emily Dickinson and Adrienne Rich.* Univ. of North Carolina Pr. 1984 $24.00 pap. $7.95

Piercy, Josephine K. *Anne Bradstreet. Twayne's U.S. Authors Ser.* New College & Univ. Pr. 1964 pap. $5.95

White, Elizabeth W. *Anne Bradstreet: The Tenth Muse.* Oxford 1971 o.p. Concerned with her personal life in England and America, her literary background, and her development as an artist.

BRYANT, WILLIAM CULLEN. 1794–1878

Bryant's simple nature poetry is unmistakably American. His most famous poem in his day was "Thanatopsis," the title being a compound of two Greek words meaning "a meditation on death." Written when he was 17 or 18, it was first published in the *North American Review* in 1817. Always solemn and stately, his verse seemed cold to Lowell, who spoke of Bryant's "iceolation." Bryant was editor in chief of the New York *Evening Post* from 1829 until his death. When he was nearly eighty, he translated Homer's *Iliad* and *Odyssey* into English blank verse.

BOOKS BY BRYANT

Poetical Works of William Cullen Bryant. Ed. by Parke Godwin, *Life and Works of William Cullen Bryant Ser.* Russell 2 vols. repr. of 1883 ed. 1967 o.p.

The Prose Writings of William Cullen Bryant. Ed. by Parke Godwin, *Life and Works of William Cullen Bryant Ser.* Russell 2 vols. in 1 repr. of 1884 ed. 1964 o.p.

BOOKS ABOUT BRYANT

Bigelow, John. *William Cullen Bryant. Amer. Journalists Ser.* Ayer repr. of 1890 ed. 1970 $23.53; intro. by John Hollander, *Amer. Men and Women of Letters Ser.* Chelsea House repr. of 1890 ed. 1980 pap. $5.95; *Lib. of Lives and Letters Ser.* Gale repr. of 1890 ed. 1970 $34.00

Bradley, William A. *William Cullen Bryant.* Arden Lib. 1978 lib. bdg. $20.00; Folcroft repr. 1972 lib. bdg. $15.00

Brown, Charles. *William Cullen Bryant.* Scribner 1971 $12.50. "Thoroughly researched and straightforward in manner and style" (*Choice*).

Godwin, Parke. *A Biography of William Cullen Bryant. Life and Works of William Cullen Bryant Ser.* Russell 2 vols. repr. of 1883 ed. 1967 o.p.

McLean, Albert F., Jr. *William Cullen Bryant. Twayne's U.S. Authors Ser.* G. K. Hall 1964 lib. bdg. $12.50; *Twayne's U.S. Authors Ser.* New College & Univ. Pr. 1964 pap. $5.95

Peckham, Harry H. *Gotham Yankee: A Biography of William Cullen Bryant.* Russell repr. of 1950 ed. 1971 $12.50

DICKINSON, EMILY. 1830–1886

Emily Dickinson is considered a very great American poet. "Wholly underivative, her poetry was unique; her influence, negligible at first, is now incalculable" (Louis Untermeyer). Her verses are all short, but her output was large—a total of 1,775 poems in Johnson's definitive edition. Except for a few poems in magazines, all her work was published after her death, augmented in 1945 by the 650 poems in *Bolts of Melody*. These had remained locked in a camphor wood box since 1896, when Mabel Loomis Todd abruptly ended her painstaking editorial work after the publication of *Poems, Third Series*. Todd, wife of the professor of astronomy at Amherst College, edited the first edition of poems in 1890 with Colonel Thomas Wentworth Higginson, a close friend of the Dickinson family, from the manuscripts she had received for the purpose from William Austin and Lavinia, the poet's brother and sister, shortly after Dickinson's death. Millicent Todd Bingham carried on the work after her mother died.

In 1956 Bingham gave to Amherst College one of the largest collections of American literary material ever received by an educational institution—some 900 manuscript poems, as well as letters and notes of Dickinson, correspondence of other members of the Dickinson family, Bingham's material relating to the work on the poet, first editions of the original volumes, and other Dickinson material.

Readers and critics were quick to appreciate the fine and unusual quality of the first three series of *Poems* when they were first published (1890, 1891, 1896), but public taste changed and the poet's audience grew very slowly for the next 40 years. In 1924, Martha Dickinson Bianchi's *Life and Letters of Emily Dickinson* was published. It was reissued as a centennial edition in 1930. In the same year, the first *Collected Poems* and the first British *Selected Poems*, with a penetrating foreword by CONRAD AIKEN, appeared. The literary excitement revived at that time and, by further publications during 1930, the centenary year, has never abated. Now we at last have the definitive variorum edition of the *Poems* and the *Letters*. "The six volumes, considered as a unit, contain every word, including prose fragments, that Emily Dickinson is known to have written" (*N.Y. Times*).

Dickinson's mysterious seclusion and the confused controversial problems of her life and family have been the subject of speculation by many of the admirers of her poetry. Nature, love, and death were her great themes. Her poems are as varied, as baffling as was she, and illustrate her love of words, "her insurgent imagination, her unconventional use of rhyme, her audacious experimentation with form and assonance" (Josephine Pollitt). Most of her poems are short, lyrical, with the intellectual precision (in Dickinson's case, rhymed and metered) of the modern MARIANNE MOORE. Her birthplace in Amherst, Massachusetts, was named a national historic landmark in 1964.

BOOKS BY DICKINSON

The Complete Poems of Emily Dickinson. Ed. by Thomas H. Johnson, Little, Brown 1960 $24.50 pap. $10.45

Final Harvest: Emily Dickinson's Poems. Ed. by Thomas H. Johnson, Little, Brown 1962 $14.95 pap. $6.70

Poems by Emily Dickinson. Ed. by Martha Dickinson Bianchi and Alfred L. Hampson, Little, Brown rev. ed. 1957 $16.45

Poems of Emily Dickinson. Ed. by Thomas H. Johnson, Harvard Univ. Pr. (Belknap Pr.) 3 vols. 1955 $55.00

Poems of Emily Dickinson. Ed. by Robert Kipness, *Poets Ser.* Crowell 1964 $11.49

The Manuscript Books of Emily Dickinson: A Facsimile Edition. Ed. by Ralph W. Franklin, Harvard Univ. Pr. (Belknap Pr.) 2 vols. 1981 $100.00

Bolts of Melody: New Poems of Emily Dickinson. Ed. by Millicent Todd Bingham and Mabel Loomis Todd, Harper 1945 $8.95

Selected Poems of Emily Dickinson. Ed. by James Reeves, *Poetry Bookshelf* Barnes & Noble 1966 o.p.

Selected Poems and Letters of Emily Dickinson. Doubleday (Anchor) pap. $5.95

Poems for Youth. Ill. by Doris Hauman, Little, Brown 1934 $10.45

Choice of Emily Dickinson's Verse. Ed. by Ted Hughes, Faber 1968 pap. $5.95

Selected Poems and Letters. Doubleday (Anchor) pap. $5.95

The Letters of Emily Dickinson. Ed. by Thomas H. Johnson and Theodora Ward, Harvard Univ. Pr. 3 vols. 1958 o.p.

Emily Dickinson Face to Face: The Unpublished Letters, with Reminiscences and Notes by Her Niece. Ed. by Martha Dickinson Bianchi, 1932. Shoe String 1970 o.p.

The Life and Letters of Emily Dickinson. Ed. by Martha Dickinson Bianchi, Biblo & Tannen repr. of 1924 ed. 1970 $15.00

Emily Dickinson: Selected Letters. Ed. by Thomas H. Johnson, Harvard Univ. Pr. (Belknap Pr.) repr. of 1958 ed. 1971 $25.00

Letter to the World. Ed. by Rumer Godden, ill. by Prudence Seward, Macmillan 1969 o.p.

Books about Dickinson

Anderson, Charles R. *Emily Dickinson's Poetry: Stairway of Surprise.* Greenwood repr. of 1963 ed. 1982 lib. bdg. $35.00. "The first sustained book-length study of Emily Dickinson's poetry that seems wholly adequate" is penetrating and discriminating. Anderson selected 25 poems as "great ones" for line-by-line analysis.

Bingham, Millicent Todd. *Ancestors' Brocades: The Literary Discovery of Emily Dickinson—The Editing and Publication of Her Letters and Poems.* Dover 1945 o.p.; Peter Smith o.p. The major source of information about the emergence of Dickinson as a poet. Documented with poems, letters, reviews, and personal recollections.

———. *Emily Dickinson's Home: The Early Years, as Revealed in Family Correspondence and Reminiscences.* 1955. Dover 1967 o.p. This study aids in dispelling the many myths about Dickinson.

Blake, Caesar R., ed. *Recognition of Emily Dickinson: Selected Criticism since 1890.* Ed. by Carlton F. Wells, Univ. of Michigan Pr. 1964 o.p. A selection of critical essays by American and British writers spanning the past 70 years. "The editors . . . serve as guides not only to the evolution of her reputation but to a better understanding of her poetry" (*LJ*). Among those included are Thomas Wentworth Higginson, Conrad Aiken, Sir Herbert Read, and Thomas Johnson.

Cameron, Sharon. *Lyric Time: Dickinson and the Limits of Genre.* Johns Hopkins Univ. Pr. text ed. 1979 $24.00 1981 pap. $7.95

Capps, Jack L. *Emily Dickinson's Reading, 1836–1886.* Harvard Univ. Pr. 1966 $16.50. A close examination of the reading matter (books, periodicals, newspapers, and early school texts) available to Emily Dickinson "to further the understanding of [the poet] and her poetry" (Jack L. Capps). "Well documented, with interesting appendixes" (*LJ*).

Chase, Richard V. *Emily Dickinson*. Greenwood repr. of 1951 ed. 1971 lib. bdg. $24.75

Cody, John. *After Great Pain: The Inner Life of Emily Dickinson*. Harvard Univ. Pr. (Belknap Pr.) 1971 $25.00

Ferlazzo, Paul J., ed. *Critical Essays on Emily Dickinson. Critical Essays on Amer. Lit. Ser.* G. K. Hall 1984 lib. bdg. $32.50

———. *Emily Dickinson. Twayne's U.S. Authors Ser.* G. K. Hall 1976 lib. bdg. $12.95 1984 pap. $5.95

Franklin, R. W. *Editing of Emily Dickinson: A Reconsideration*. Univ. of Wisconsin Pr. 1967 $17.00. A technical study of the nineteenth- and twentieth-century editions of Emily Dickinson's poems, describing certain inaccuracies. The author discusses the problems involved in editing Dickinson manuscripts.

Gelpi, Albert J. *Emily Dickinson: The Mind of the Poet. Norton Lib.* repr. of 1966 ed. 1971 o.p. "Mr. Gelpi performs well in considering the poet in the overall context of American literature. . . . His chapter entitled 'The Flower, the Bee, and the Spider: The Aesthetics of Consciousness' is a brilliant statement in itself of what constitutes poetry" (*LJ*).

Higgins, David. *Portrait of Emily Dickinson: The Poet and Her Prose*. Rutgers Univ. Pr. 1967 pap. $10.00. "A solid work of scholarship, carefully documented, that is based in large part on the letters of Emily Dickinson and those of her family and friends" (*LJ*).

Johnson, Thomas H. *Emily Dickinson: An Interpretive Biography*. Atheneum 1967 text ed. pap. $4.95. Johnson, editor of the three-volume variorum edition of the poems, has expanded his preface for this "reliable, scholarly—and fascinating" biography.

Juhasz, Suzanne, ed. *Feminist Critics Read Emily Dickinson*. Indiana Univ. Pr. 1983 $17.50

Keller, Karl. *The Only Kangaroo among the Beauty: Emily Dickinson and America*. Johns Hopkins Univ. Pr. 1980 text ed. $24.50 pap. $7.95

Leyda, Jay. *The Years and Hours of Emily Dickinson*. Shoe String (Archon) 2 vols. repr. of 1960 ed. 1970 o.p. This documentary biography, a compilation of relevant materials without editorial comment, is an "extraordinary, interesting and original approach" to the poet.

Mossberg, Barbara A. *Emily Dickinson: When a Writer Is a Daughter*. Indiana Univ. Pr. 1983 $22.50

Pollak, Vivian R. *Dickinson: The Anxiety of Gender*. Cornell Univ. Pr. 1984 $19.50

Porter, David. *Dickinson: The Modern Idiom*. Harvard Univ. Pr. text ed. 1981 $20.00

Rosenbaum, Stanford P., ed. *Concordance to the Poems of Emily Dickinson. Concordance Ser.* Cornell Univ. Pr. 1964 $85.00

Sewall, Richard B., ed. *Emily Dickinson: A Collection of Critical Essays*. Prentice-Hall (Spectrum Bks.) 1963 $12.95

———. *The Life of Emily Dickinson*. Farrar 2 vols. 1974 ea. $14.95

———. *The Lyman Letters: New Light on Emily Dickinson and Her Family*. Univ. of Massachusetts Pr. 1966 o.p.

Sherwood, William R. *Circumference and Circumstance: Stages in the Mind and Art of Emily Dickinson*. Columbia Univ. Pr. 1968 o.p.

Shurr, William H. *The Marriage of Emily Dickinson: A Study of the Fascicles*. Univ. Pr. of Kentucky 1983 $22.00

Ward, Theodore Van. *The Capsule of the Mind: Chapters in the Life of Emily Dickinson*. Harvard Univ. Pr. 1961 o.p. Six essays, of which the first three deal with the poet's emotional life and the last three discuss her friendships. "Of the many attempts to write a life," this one by the editor associated with T. H. Johnson "has the richest sources and the best authority."

Weisbuch, Robert. *Emily Dickinson's Poetry.* Univ. of Chicago Pr. 1981 pap. $6.00

Whicher, George F. *This Was a Poet: A Critical Biography of Emily Dickinson.* Shoe String (Archon) 1980 $22.50 pap. $9.50

Wolosky, Shira. *Emily Dickinson: A Voice of War.* Yale Univ. Pr. 1984 $16.50

EMERSON, RALPH WALDO. 1803–1882

Emerson regarded himself as "more of a poet than anything else." He wrote his verse for himself without regard for an audience, and his poetry has a more spontaneous quality than most of his prose. W. C. Brownell in *American Prose Masters* speaks of the poems as "a kind of intimate reverberation" of the essays. "They are largely Emerson's communion with himself, as the Essays are his communication with the world." His poems are nearly always short, lyrical, and meditative. He was a rebel in poetry as well as prose. Robert E. Spiller in *The Cycle of American Literature* writes " 'Poetry was all written before time was,' [Emerson] tells us in his essays on 'The Poet,' 'and whenever we are so finely organized that we can penetrate into that region where the air is music, we hear those primal warblings and attempt to write them down.' The poet has his special function in the order of nature; he is 'the sayer, the namer, and represents beauty.' '. . . The experience of each new age requires a new confession, and the world seems always waiting for its poet.' In stating so clearly his case for an organic view of art [says Spiller] Emerson was describing not only his own method but the instinctive approach of most really great American writers." (See also Chapter 16 in this volume.)

BOOKS BY EMERSON

Complete Works. Ed. by Edward W. Emerson, AMS Pr. 12 vols. repr. of 1904 ed. ea. $29.00 set $348.00

The Works of Ralph Waldo Emerson. Richard West 5 vols. $85.00

The Selected Writings of Ralph Waldo Emerson. Ed. by Brooks Atkinson, Modern Lib. 1940 $9.95

Selections from Ralph Waldo Emerson. Ed. by Stephen Whicher, Houghton Mifflin (Riv. Eds.) 1960 pap. $5.95

Selected Prose and Poetry. Ed. by Reginald Cook, *Rinehart Ed.* Holt 2d ed. 1969 text ed. pap. $12.95

The Portable Emerson. Ed. by Malcolm Cowley, Penguin 1981 pap. $6.95

BOOKS ABOUT EMERSON

Allen, Gay W. *Waldo Emerson: A Biography.* Viking 1981 $25.00

Bishop, Jonathan. *Emerson on the Soul.* AMS Pr. repr. of 1964 ed. $29.50

Burkholder, Robert E., ed. *Critical Essays on Ralph Waldo Emerson.* Ed. by Joel Myerson, *Critical Essays in Amer. Lit. Ser.* G. K. Hall 1983 lib. bdg. $62.50

Hopkins, Vivian C. *Spires of Form: A Study of Emerson's Aesthetic Theory.* AMS Pr. repr. of 1951 ed. $33.50

Levin, David, ed. *Emerson: Prophecy, Metamorphosis, and Influence. Essays of the Eng. Institute Ser.* Columbia Univ. Pr. 1975 $18.50

Loving, Jerome. *Emerson, Whitman, and the American Muse*. Univ. of North Carolina Pr. 1982 $22.00

McAleer, John. *Ralph Waldo Emerson: Days of Encounter*. Little, Brown 1984 $27.00

Paul, Sherman. *Emerson's Angle of Vision: Man and Nature in American Experience*. AMS Pr. repr. of 1952 ed. $33.50

Waggoner, Hyatt H. *Emerson as Poet*. Princeton Univ. Pr. 1974 $23.00

Yanella, Donald. *Ralph Waldo Emerson*. Twayne's U.S. Authors Ser. G. K. Hall 1982 lib. bdg. $11.50

Yoder, R. A. *Emerson and the Orphic Poet in America*. Univ. of California Pr. 1978 $26.50

FIELD, EUGENE. 1850–1895

Eugene Field was born in Missouri and there served his apprenticeship as a journalist. In 1882, he joined the staff of the Denver *Tribune* as a columnist, and in 1883 he began the column "Sharps and Flats" for the Chicago *Daily News*. His poems are simple dialect sketches (sometimes the dialect is an imaginary one), fairy tales, fables, and pictures of home life. He is now best known as a children's poet. "Wynken, Blynken and Nod" and "Little Boy Blue" were set to music by Reginald DeKoven and Ethelbert Nevin. Many of his publications are collections of his newspaper contributions. *The Love Affairs of a Bibliomaniac* (1896) reflected his devotion to McClurg's rare book department, which he named "The Saints and Sinners Corner."

BOOKS BY FIELD

With Trumpet and Drum. Granger Index Repr. Ser. Ayer repr. of 1892 ed. $12.00

Love Songs of Childhood. Granger Index Repr. Ser. Ayer repr. of 1894 ed. $12.00

A Little Book of Western Verse. Folcroft repr. of 1896 ed. 1978 lib. bdg. $17.50

Poems of Childhood. Airmont Class. Ser. 1969 pap. $1.50

The Gingham Dog and the Calico Cat. Ill. by Helen Page, New Century repr. of 1945 ed. o.p.

Wynken, Blynken and Nod. Dutton 1982 $9.95; Hastings 1980 $6.95

BOOKS ABOUT FIELD

Dennis, Charles H. *Eugene Field's Creative Years*. Richard West repr. of 1924 ed. $25.00; Scholarly repr. of 1924 ed. $19.00

Thompson, Slason. *Life of Eugene Field: The Poet of Childhood*. Richard West repr. of 1927 ed. $40.00

FRENEAU, PHILIP. 1752–1832

Son of wealthy parents in Manhattan, Freneau received a good enough education from tutors to enter the sophomore class at the College of New Jersey (now Princeton University), where he roomed with JAMES MADISON (see Vol. 3). After graduation, he taught school and unsuccessfully attempted a career as a writer before accepting a position as secretary on a plantation in the West Indies, where he remained from 1776 until 1778. Returning home, he enlisted as a seaman on a blockade runner, serving for two years before he was captured and imprisoned on the British ship *Scorpion*. Regaining health after the brutal treatment he received in prison, he moved to Philadelphia, where, as editor of the *Freeman's Journal*, he directed the whole force of his imaginative and poetic talents in support of the American Revolution. THOMAS JEFFERSON (see Vol. 3) offered him a position as translator in the Department of State. When Jefferson resigned as secretary of state in 1793, Freneau, who had edited *The National Gazette* in his spare time and devoted his writing talents to the support of the French Revolution, left Philadelphia and returned to sea as a ship's captain. He spent his final years on a New Jersey farm, which he was finally forced to sell. He died in a blizzard, hopelessly impoverished and unknown.

Although much of his verse, because of its political nature, is extremely occasional and topical, Freneau nonetheless demonstrated a strong attachment to American themes. His "The Indian Burying Ground" (1786) exemplifies an enviable lyric grasp of the elegiac possibilities inherent in the experience of the new nation.

BOOKS BY FRENEAU

The Last Poems of Philip Freneau. Ed. by Lewis Leary, Greenwood repr. of 1945 ed. lib. bdg. $18.75
Poems Written between the Years 1768 and 1794. Gordon $59.95; ed. by Lewis Leary, Scholarly repr. of 1795 ed. 1976 lib. bdg. $70.00

BOOKS ABOUT FRENEAU

Axelrad, Jacob. *Philip Freneau: Champion of Democracy.* Univ. of Texas Pr. 1966 $20.00
Leary, Lewis. *That Rascal Freneau.* Octagon 1964 lib. bdg. $29.00

HOLMES, OLIVER WENDELL. 1809–1894

Many of Holmes's best poems appeared first in his "Breakfast Table" series. "The Deacon's Masterpiece, or The Wonderful One-Hoss Shay," "The Chambered Nautilus," and "The Living Temple" may all be found in *The Autocrat of the Breakfast Table* (1858). So many events are commemorated in his verses—nearly half are of this nature—that a social history of the times may be read in his complete poems. His work has preserved the distinctive idiom of New England speech. (See Chapter 16 in this volume for a biocritical comment and bibliography on Holmes.)

BOOKS BY HOLMES

The Complete Works of Oliver Wendell Holmes. Scholarly 13 vols. repr. of 1892 ed. 1972 $490.00
The Political Works of Oliver Wendell Holmes. Ed. by Eleanor M. Tilton, *Cambridge Eds. Ser.* Houghton Mifflin 1975 $12.50
Oliver Wendell Holmes: Representative Selections. AMS Pr. repr. of 1939 ed. $34.75

BOOKS ABOUT HOLMES

Morse, John T. *Life and Letters of Oliver Wendell Holmes.* Richard West 2 vols. repr. of 1897 ed. $65.00
Small, Miriam R. *Oliver Wendell Holmes. Twayne's U.S. Authors Ser.* New College & Univ. Pr. 1962 pap. $5.95

Tilton, Eleanor M. *Amiable Autocrat: A Biography of Doctor Oliver Wendell Holmes.* Octagon repr. of 1947 ed. 1976 lib. bdg. $27.50

LANIER, SIDNEY. 1842–1881

Lanier is the foremost poet of the nineteenth-century South. He volunteered for the Confederate army, served, and was taken prisoner. In 1879, he was made lecturer on English at Johns Hopkins University. He died at an early age and left a slender volume of verse. Lanier's great poem "The Marshes of Glynn," "a symphony without musical score," won him the title of "the poet of the marshes." "He had a profound knowledge of the analogies between poetry and music and applied musical theory to his own verse. He left behind him no really finished work; he is a poet of magnificent fragments. He was too excited, too impetuous to finish anything." Lanier wrote works of criticism on English literature. His first publication was a novel, *Tiger Lilies* (1867). In his 1879 lectures at Johns Hopkins, published as *The Science of English Verse* (1880), he maintained that the artistic laws governing music and poetry were the same.

BOOKS BY LANIER

The Centennial Edition of the Works of Sidney Lanier. Ed. by Charles R. Anderson, Johns Hopkins Univ. Pr. 10 vols. 1945 o.p.
Selected Poems. Pref. by Stuart Young, AMS Pr. repr. of 1947 ed. $21.50
Poems and Letters. Ed. by Charles R. Anderson, Johns Hopkins Univ. Pr. 1970 o.p.
Collected Writings. Gordon $600.00
The Science of English Verse. Folcroft 1973 lib. bdg. $25.00; Norwood repr. of 1894 ed. 1980 lib. bdg. $37.50

BOOKS ABOUT LANIER

Graham, Philip, and Joseph Jones. *A Concordance to the Poems of Sidney Lanier: Including the Poem Outlines and Certain Uncollected Items. Eng. Literary Reference Ser.* Johnson Repr. repr. of 1939 ed. 1969 $45.00
Mims, Edwin. *Sidney Lanier.* Gordon $59.95
Starke, Aubrey H. *Sidney Lanier: A Biographical and Critical Study.* Russell repr. of 1933 ed. 1964 o.p.

LONGFELLOW, HENRY WADSWORTH. 1807–1882

"Modern criticism represents Longfellow as an adolescent balladist and romancer," John Reeve wrote. "Yet his popularity in his lifetime was as great as that of TENNYSON. Longfellow is the classic case of a poet who would have been better had he found it more difficult to express himself in verse. Unfortunately his mechanical facility spoils almost all his work, and it is difficult to find more than a few poems that are readable today." However, his experimentation with classical meters influenced many of the poets who followed him. His three most popular narrative poems are thoroughly rooted in American soil: "Evangeline," "the flower of American idylls"; "Hiawatha," "the first genuinely native epic in American poetry"; and "The Courtship of Miles Standish," a Puritan romance of Longfellow's own ancestors, John Alden and Priscilla. "Paul Revere," the best known of the "Tales of a Wayside Inn," is also intensely national.

Longfellow's home in the heart of the business district of Portland, Maine, has long been maintained as a shrine. In 1955 his birthplace near the waterfront was torn down. The poet traveled abroad, then lived in Maine, where he taught at Bowdoin College, until an appointment to Harvard brought him (eventually) to the beautiful Craigie House, still standing as Longfellow's landmark in Cambridge, Massachusetts. Here he enjoyed the fame and affluence of his later life in a manner somewhat more luxurious than was approved by the literary men and women of Concord. (Emerson commented on this wryly.) He outlived two beloved wives. The early letters, says Louis Untermeyer in *SR*, "fail to move us because, although a courteous correspondent, he hated to write them." He was "not an impassioned, provocative or even interesting letter writer." His translation of Dante (see Vol. 2), much admired in its day, is now out of print.

BOOKS BY LONGFELLOW

Works. AMS Pr. 14 vols. repr. of 1891 ed. ea. $30.00 set $420.00
Poetical Works. Oxford Stand. Authors Ser. 1904 $35.00
The Poetical Works of Longfellow. Ed. by George Monteiro, *Cambridge Eds. Ser.* Houghton Mifflin rev. ed. 1975 $25.00
Poems. Biblio Dist. (Everyman's) repr. of 1909 ed. 1978 $8.95 pap. $3.95
Selected Poems. Peter Pauper 1968 $4.95
The Writings of Henry Wadsworth Longfellow: The Riverside Edition. Richard West 11 vols. repr. of 1886 ed. $300.00
The Letters of Henry Wadsworth Longfellow. Ed. by Andrew Hilen, Harvard Univ. Pr. 1983 text ed. $80.00. Longfellow's letters—805 of them—many in print for the first time, give an account of the poet's life from age 7 to 36 with little reference to his ambitions as a poet. "Meticulously edited" (*SR*).
Evangeline. 1847. Avon pap. $.60
Kavanagh: A Tale. 1849. Ed. by Jean Downey, *Masterworks of Lit. Ser.* New College & Univ. Pr. 1965 $7.95 pap. $4.95
The Song of Hiawatha. 1855. *Childrens Ill. Class.* Biblio Dist. repr. of 1960 ed. 1975 pap. $9.00

BOOKS ABOUT LONGFELLOW

Arvin, Newton. *Longfellow: His Life and Work.* Greenwood repr. of 1963 ed. 1977 lib. bdg. $65.00. "A good study but a poor biography" (*LJ*).
Gorman, Herbert S. *A Victorian American: Henry Wadsworth Longfellow.* Richard West repr. of 1926 ed. 1979 lib. bdg. $35.00
Johnson, Carl L. *Professor Longfellow of Harvard.* Univ. of Oregon Pr. 1943 pap. $1.00
Longfellow, Samuel, ed. *Life of Henry Wadsworth Longfellow, with Extracts from His Journals and Correspondence.* Darby 3 vols. repr. of 1891 ed. lib. bdg. $150.00; Greenwood 3 vols. repr. of 1891 ed. 1969 lib. bdg. $62.75; Scholarly 3 vols. repr. of 1891 ed. 1968 $40.00
Norton, Charles E. *Henry Wadsworth Longfellow.* Folcroft repr. of 1906 ed. $12.50
Thompson, Lawrance. *Young Longfellow, 1807–1843.* Octagon 1969 lib. bdg. $27.50
Wagenknecht, Edward. *Henry Wadsworth Longfellow.* Ungar 1985 $15.50
Williams, Cecil B. *Henry Wadsworth Longfellow. Twayne's U.S. Authors Ser.* G. K.

Hall 1964 lib. bdg. $12.50; *Twayne's U.S. Authors Ser.* New College & Univ. Pr. 1964 pap. $5.95

LOWELL, JAMES RUSSELL. 1819–1891

"The Vision of Sir Launfal" was once regarded as a "high mark of American poetry." Today Lowell's reputation as a poet and essayist has diminished considerably, but his versatility as a lifelong leader of the Cambridge group of nineteenth-century literary New Englanders has never been denied. "He was at various times, and sometimes concurrently, a poet, a radical political writer, a conservative political writer, a satirist, an editor, a critic, a diplomat, and a teacher; and in all of these efforts he won the praise of his contemporaries." Lowell was particularly successful in his public poetry. His "Concord Ode," "Centennial Ode," and "Commemoration Ode" are poems of occasion that have shown enduring quality. *A Fable for Critics* (1848), a long literary comment in verse, helped establish his national reputation. It is interesting to remember that Lowell and Longfellow are two American authors who have been given monuments in Westminster Abbey.

BOOKS BY LOWELL

Complete Writings. Ed. by Charles E. Norton, AMS Pr. 16 vols. repr. of 1904 ed. ea. $24.50 set $392.00
The Complete Poetical Works of Lowell. Ed. by Horace E. Scudder, Houghton Mifflin 1952 o.p.
Letters of James R. Lowell. Ed. by Charles E. Norton, AMS Pr. 2 vols. repr. of 1894 ed. $35.00
Bigelow Papers. Scholarly repr. of 1885 ed. 1970 $7.00
James Russell Lowell: Representative Selections. Intro. by Harry H. Clark and Norman Foerster, Arden Lib. repr. of 1947 ed. 1977 lib. bdg. $40.00

BOOKS ABOUT LOWELL

Beatty, Richmond C. *James Russell Lowell.* Shoe String (Archon) repr. of 1942 ed. 1969 $25.00
Greenslet, Ferris. *James Russell Lowell: His Life and Work.* Richard West repr. of 1905 ed. 1973 $9.50
Scudder, Horace E. *James Russell Lowell: A Biography.* AMS Pr. 2 vols. repr. of 1901 ed. $27.50; Arden Lib. 2 vols. repr. of 1901 ed. 1983 lib. bdg. $65.00; Richard West 2 vols. repr. of 1901 ed. 1973 $50.00; Scholarly 2 vols. repr. of 1901 ed. 1969 $18.00
Wagenknecht, Edward C. *James Russell Lowell: Portrait of a Many Sided Man.* Portraits of Amer. Writers Ser. Oxford 1971 $17.95

MOODY, WILLIAM VAUGHN. 1869–1910

Born in Spencer, Indiana, Moody attended Harvard University before joining the faculty of the University of Chicago. His early poetry, modeled largely on the Elizabethan poets and Milton, concentrated primarily on personal themes. But probably under the influence of Hamlin Garland, Moody became passionately interested in political and social issues. His *Gloucester*

Moors displays fine lyric power informing a profound social vision. After writing other poems protesting U.S. imperialism, Moody turned to verse drama. His poetry represents a transition from nineteenth-century verse to the twentieth-century work of ROBINSON and FROST.

BOOKS BY MOODY

Poems and Plays. AMS Pr. 2 vols. repr. of 1912 ed. $57.50
Selected Poems of William Vaughn Moody. Ed. by Robert M. Lovett, AMS Pr. repr. of 1931 ed. $30.00

BOOKS ABOUT MOODY

Brown, Maurice F. *Estranging Dawn: The Life and Works of William Vaughn Moody.* Southern Illinois Univ. Pr. 1973 $12.50
Halpern, Martin. *William Vaughn Moody. Twayne's U.S. Authors Ser.* New College & Univ. Pr. 1964 pap. $3.95
Henry, David D. *William Vaughn Moody.* Arden Lib. repr. of 1934 ed. 1978 lib. bdg. $25.00; Folcroft repr. lib. bdg. $25.00

POE, EDGAR ALLAN. 1809–1849

Poe's life is the battleground of modern biographers, but his poetry is the meeting ground of poets. "No other American poet has been so unanimously accepted by all the poets of the world," said John Macy. The quantity of Poe's verse is small, but because he wrote so little, people who read him read all of him. He is known more thoroughly than most poets. His poems are melancholy, mysterious, but, above all, melodious. Sound is to him more than sense. Death is his favorite subject. Edmund C. Stedman said, "He was not a single-poem poet, but the poet of a single mood." EDMUND WILSON said that there was in Poe "a dash of the actor who delights in elaborating a part." He was a "precocious and imaginative youth whose first poems appeared when he was 18. Some of his work achieved popularity during his short life, and after death . . . his reputation for romantic decadence increased, especially in France. . . . He played no small part in the formation of the mind and character of the French poet Baudelaire, another and more gifted decadent. . . . Poe's poetry as a whole is a mixture of the tawdry and the inspired, and was ruined both by the increasing toll taken on him by his dissipation and by his obsession with the idea of poetry as a kind of magical incantation" (James Reeves). Two biographies of Poe, important in their day, are now out of print: *Israfel* by Hervey Allen and *The Life of Poe* by Thomas Holley Chivers. (For Poe's prose works, see Chapter 13 in this volume.)

BOOKS BY POE

Complete Works of Edgar Allan Poe. Ed. by James A. Harrison, AMS Pr. 17 vols. repr. of 1902 ed. ea. $17.50 set $295.00
Works of Edgar Allan Poe. Ed. by Edmund C. Stedman and George E. Woodberry, *Select Bibliographies Repr. Ser.* Ayer 10 vols. repr. of 1895 ed. $250.00
Collected Works of Edgar Allan Poe. Harvard Univ. Pr. (Belknap Pr.) 3 vols. vol. 1 (1969) $32.50 vols. 2 and 3 (1978) $55.00

Poems of Edgar Allan Poe. Ed. by Dwight MacDonald, ill. by Ellen Raskin, *Apollo Eds.* Crowell repr. of 1965 ed. 1971 pap. o.p.
The Selected Poetry and Prose. Ed. by Thomas O. Mabbott, *Modern Lib. College Ed. Ser.* Random 1951 pap. $4.50
Selected Prose and Poetry. Rinehart Ed. Holt rev. ed. 1969 text ed. pap. $13.95
Great Short Works of Edgar Allan Poe. Ed. by J. R. Thompson, Harper 1970 pap. $3.80
Complete Tales and Poems of Edgar Allan Poe. Intro. by Hervey Allen, Modern Lib. 1938 $9.95
Great Tales and Poems of Edgar Allan Poe. Washington Square Pr. 1982 pap. $2.95
Selected Writings of Edgar Allan Poe. Ed. by E. H. Davidson, Houghton Mifflin (Riv. Eds.) 1956 pap. $6.50
The Portable Poe. Ed. by Phillip V. Stern, *Viking Portable Lib.* Penguin 1977 pap. $7.95
Letters of Edgar Allan Poe. Ed. by John Ostrom, Gordian 2 vols. repr. of 1948 ed. 1966 $30.00

BOOKS ABOUT POE

Baudelaire, Charles P. *Baudelaire on Poe: Critical Papers.* Trans. by Francis Hyslop, *Bald Eagle Ser.* Pennsylvania State Univ. Pr. 1952 $19.75
Booth, Bradford, and C. E. Jones. *Concordance to the Poetical Works of Edgar Allan Poe.* Peter Smith $18.00
Buranelli, Vincent. *Edgar Allan Poe. Twayne's U.S. Authors Ser.* G. K. Hall 2d ed. 1977 lib. bdg. $11.50
Campbell, Killis. *Mind of Poe, and Other Studies.* Russell repr. of 1933 ed. 1962 o.p. The title essay of this important book is an invaluable summary.
Carlson, Eric W., ed. *Recognition of Edgar Allan Poe: Selected Criticism since 1829.* Univ. of Michigan Pr. 1970 o.p.
Davidson, Edward H. *Poe: A Critical Study.* Harvard Univ. Pr. (Belknap Pr.) 1957 $20.00. Sound and readable inquiry into the mind and writings.
Fruit, John P. *Mind and Art of Poe's Poetry.* AMS Pr. repr. of 1899 ed. $17.50; Arden Lib. repr. of 1899 ed. 1980 lib. bdg. $20.00; Folcroft repr. of 1899 ed. lib. bdg. $15.00. An interesting early study.
Krutch, Joseph W. *Edgar Allan Poe: A Study in Genius.* Russell repr. of 1926 ed. 1965 o.p. In *The Shores of Light*, Edmund Wilson called this "the ablest and most important of recent American books on Poe."
Levin, Harry. *The Power of Blackness: Hawthorne, Poe, Melville.* Ohio Univ. Pr. repr. of 1958 1980 pap. $6.95
Quinn, Arthur H. *Edgar Allan Poe.* Cooper Square Pr. 1970 o.p.
Quinn, Patrick F. *French Face of Edgar Poe.* Southern Illinois Univ. Pr. 1971 pap. $2.45
Regan, Robert, ed. *Poe: A Collection of Critical Essays.* Prentice-Hall (Spectrum Bks.) 1967 $12.95. "Here was an author, curiously able to see the reality of terror and the demonic, yet often paradoxically decking it out in obvious stage trappings. An interesting collection, for much-maligned Poe can neither be swallowed whole nor completely rejected" (*LJ*).
Reilly, John E. *The Image of Poe in American Poetry.* Enoch Pratt 1976 pap. $2.50
Thompson, G. R. *Poe's Fiction: Romantic Irony in the Gothic Tales.* Univ. of Wisconsin Pr. 1973 o.p.
Wagenknecht, Edward C. *Edgar Allan Poe: The Man behind the Legend.* Oxford 1963 o.p. "This volume tersely and impartially debunks and defends Poe.... An indispensable addition to the shelves of all libraries" (*LJ*).

Walsh, John. *Poe the Detective: The Curious Circumstances behind the Mystery of Marie Roget*. Intro. by Thomas O. Mabbott, Rutgers Univ. Pr. 1967 o.p.
Woodberry, George E. *Life of Edgar Allan Poe, Personal and Literary*. Biblo & Tannen 2 vols. repr. of 1909 ed. o.p.

RILEY, JAMES WHITCOMB. 1849–1916

Poet, lecturer, and journalist, Riley gained popularity with his series of poems in the Hoosier dialect written under the pseudonym "Benjamin F. Johnson of Boone." These originally appeared in the Indianapolis *Journal*, where he worked from 1877 to 1885; in 1883 they were published as *The Old Swimmin'-Hole* and *'Leven More Poems*. Riley went on numerous lecture tours, entertaining as an actor and humorist. Although best known for his dialect poetry—"comforting, familiar platitudes, restated in verse" (Richard Crowder)—he also wrote humorous sketches and other poems.

BOOKS BY RILEY

The Complete Works of James Whitcomb Riley. AMS Pr. 6 vols. repr. of 1913 ed. $270.00; Century Bookbindery 10 vols. repr. of 1916 ed. 1983 lib. bdg. $400.00
Songs of Summer. Folcroft repr. of 1883 ed. lib. bdg. $20.00
Joyful Poems for Children. Bobbs 1960 o.p.
A Child-World. Granger Index Repr. Ser. Ayer repr. of 1896 ed. $17.00
Riley Child-Rhymes. Granger Index Repr. Ser. Ayer repr. of 1898 ed. $15.00
Book of Joyous Children. Granger Index Repr. Ser. Ayer repr. of 1902 ed. $18.00
Love Letters of a Bachelor Poet. 1922. Gordon $59.95
The Eternal Poetry of Romantic Love. Gloucester Art Pr. 1983 $51.85

BOOKS ABOUT RILEY

Carman, Bliss. *James Whitcomb Riley: An Essay*. Folcroft repr. of 1925 ed. 1977 lib. bdg. $15.00
Dickey, Marcus. *The Youth of James Whitcomb Riley*. Richard West repr. of 1919 ed. 1973 $35.00
Manlove, Donald C. *The Best of James Whitcomb Riley*. Indiana Univ. Pr. $15.00 pap. $7.95
Revell, Peter. *James Whitcomb Riley. Twayne's U.S. Authors Ser.* G. K. Hall o.p.

TAYLOR, EDWARD. c.1642–1729

A Congregational minister engaged in the task of establishing a spiritual code in a new country, Taylor wrote in the metaphysical tradition of HERBERT, DONNE, and CRASHAW. Born in England, he was a graduate of Harvard College (1671). He went to Westfield, Massachusetts, and stayed there the rest of his life, acting as clergyman and physician. At his own request, he remained virtually unpublished in his lifetime, until 1939, when *The Poetical Works of Edward Taylor* was edited by Thomas H. Johnson.

His *Poems* "will stand at the fore of American belles lettres. . . . Stanford's careful 'Introduction' discusses in turn Taylor's life, deeply experienced Calvinist faith, the extant manuscripts, the publication record, and the establishment of the present text" (*LJ*).

BOOKS BY TAYLOR

The Poetical Works of Edward Taylor. 1939. Ed. by Thomas H. Johnson, Princeton
   Univ. Pr. 1944 pap. $8.95
The Poems of Edward Taylor. Ed. by Donald E. Stanford, Yale Univ. Pr. 1977 o.p.

BOOKS ABOUT TAYLOR

Gefvert, Constance J., ed. *Edward Taylor: An Annotated Bibliography, 1668–1970.*
   Kent State Univ. Pr. 1971 $10.00
Grabo, Norman S. *Edward Taylor. Twayne's U.S. Authors Ser.* New College & Univ.
   Pr. 1961 pap. $5.95
Stanford, Donald E. *Edward Taylor. Pamphlets on Amer. Writers Ser.* Univ. of Minne-
   sota Pr. 1965 pap. $1.25

TIMROD, HENRY. 1828–1867

Timrod was born in Charleston, South Carolina, and attended the University of Georgia (then Franklin College), where he developed an intense interest in the classical writers—an interest displayed in *Poems* published in
1860, the one volume of poetry published in his lifetime. Prevented by tuberculosis from serving in the Civil War, Timrod became a war correspondent
and rose to the position of editor of the Columbia *South Carolinian,* supporting the Confederate cause with his pen. But Sherman's capture and burning
of Columbia (February 17, 1865) marked the end of any chance Timrod had
for a secure life. He died in poverty and despair little more than two years
after Appomattox.

From the time that Paul Hamilton Hayne, Timrod's friend since their
Charleston school days, collected and published *The Poems of Henry Timrod*
in 1873, Timrod has been recognized as the laureate of the Confederacy. His
classical purity of form coupled with his intellectual and moral austerity
prevent his poetry from becoming mired in the sentimentality characteristic of so much southern poetry.

BOOKS BY TIMROD

The Poems of Henry Timrod: With a Sketch of the Poet's Life. Ed. by Paul Hamilton
   Hayne, *Romantic Tradition in Amer. Lit. Ser.* Ayer repr. of 1873 ed. 1972 $21.00
Essays of Henry Timrod. Ed. by Edd W. Parks, Univ. of Georgia Pr. 1942 $16.00

BOOKS ABOUT TIMROD

Parks, Edd W. *Henry Timrod. Twayne's U.S. Authors Ser.* New College & Univ. Pr.
   1964 pap. $5.95
Thompson, H. T. *Henry Timrod: Laureate of the Confederacy.* AMS Pr. repr. of 1928
   ed. $16.50; Gordon $59.95

TUCKERMAN, FREDERICK GODDARD. 1821–1873

Tuckerman was little known during his lifetime. After graduating from
Harvard University, he settled in Greenfield, Massachusetts, where he carefully observed nature, making notes on eclipses and local fauna. In 1860 he
published *Poems,* a slender volume of sonnets. Although Tuckerman received a letter of praise from Tennyson, to whom he had sent a copy, his vol-

ume of poems remained practically unknown. It was not until 1931, when Witter Bynner republished the best of *Poems* together with three unpublished sonnet sequences, that Tuckerman became recognized as a minor master of the sonnet form.

BOOKS BY TUCKERMAN

Complete Poems. 1860. Ed. by N. Scott Momaday, critical fwd. by Yvor Winters, Oxford 1965 o.p.
The Sonnets of Frederick Goddard Tuckerman. Ed. by Witter Bynner, Knopf 1931 o.p.

BOOK ABOUT TUCKERMAN

Golden, Samuel A. *Frederick Goddard Tuckerman. Twayne's U.S. Authors Ser.* Irvington 1966 lib. bdg. $7.95 text ed. pap. $3.25; *Twayne's U.S. Authors Ser.* New College & Univ. Pr. 1966 pap. $5.95

VERY, JONES. 1813–1880

The son of a sea captain, Very was born in Salem, Massachusetts, where he attended public schools. With the help of a tutor, he gained enough education to take a teaching position at a private school in Salem before entering Harvard University. Graduating in 1836, he continued his studies in the Harvard School of Divinity. Although he received no degree, he was licensed as a Unitarian preacher in 1843.

Returning to Salem, he led a retired life, devoting more and more of his time to the study of religion and literature. He was sufficiently subject to moments of religious ecstasy that his sanity was questioned, and he was briefly committed to the McLean Asylum in Somerville, Massachusetts.

Very was a peripheral follower of Concord transcendentalism and was much admired by Emerson, who saw in Very's commitment to mysticism and literature both nobility and magnanimity of character. Beyond his admiration of Very's character, Emerson was an enthusiastic supporter of his poetry, recognizing in Very's sonnets the intense love of nature, the mystical humility, and the submissive will that gave to Very's sonnets mystical intensity coupled with stillness of control.

BOOKS BY VERY

Essays and Poems. Ed. by Ralph Waldo Emerson. *Romantic Tradition in Amer. Lit. Ser.* Ayer repr. of 1839 ed. 1972 $19.00
Poems and Essays: With a Biographical Sketch by James Freeman Clarke. Romantic Tradition in Amer. Lit. Ser. Ayer repr. of 1886 ed. 1972 $42.00

BOOKS ABOUT VERY

Barlett, William I. *Jones Very: Emerson's Brave Saint.* Greenwood repr. of 1942 ed. 1968 lib. bdg. $18.55
Gittleman, Edwin. *Jones Very: The Effective Years, 1833–1840.* Columbia Univ. Pr. 1967 $32.00

WHEATLEY, PHILLIS. c.1753–1784

Phillis Wheatley's chief distinctions as a colonial American poet are that she not only showed mastery of the heroic couplet but also that she was a slave. Brought to Boston in 1761 from Africa, when she was about seven years old, she became the property of John and Susannah Wheatley. She was fortunate in her master and mistress, who both appreciated her intelligence and saw to it that she learned to read and write. She was later taken to London, where she met distinguished persons (among them the Countess of Huntington and the Lord Mayor of London), who recognized and assisted her poetic endeavors. Returning to the United States on hearing of her mistress's fatal illness, she was finally freed in 1778 after Mr. Wheatley died. She married John Peters, a freedman. Her final years were spent in great poverty. She died in 1784 and was buried in an unmarked grave.

In her own lifetime, her most famous poem was "On the Death of the Rev. Mr. George Whitefield, 1770," a poem that at once celebrated the achievement of the famous preacher and exemplified the poet's mastery of the heroic couplet. Although her poetry is relatively conventional in form, its themes of freedom (she wrote a poem "To His Excellency George Washington") and its recognition of labor and art (she also wrote a poem "To S. M., a Young African Painter, on Seeing His Works") possess a resonance transcending eighteenth-century poetic forms. Her sturdy devotion to the life of poetry looks forward to the achievements of PAUL LAURENCE DUNBAR, LANGSTON HUGHES, and COUNTEE CULLEN.

BOOKS BY WHEATLEY

Life and Works of Phillis Wheatley. Black Heritage Lib. Collection Ser. Ayer repr. of 1916 ed. $13.95

Phillis Wheatley: Poems and Letters. Ed. by Charles F. Heartman, *Black Heritage Lib. Collection Ser.* Ayer repr. of 1915 ed. $8.75

Poems of Phillis Wheatley. Ed. by Julian D. Mason, Jr., Univ. of North Carolina Pr. 1966 $15.00

BOOKS ABOUT WHEATLEY

Jensen, Marilyn. *Phillis Wheatley: Negro Slave of John Wheatley.* Lion Bks. 1985 $12.95 pap. $9.95

Robinson, William H. *Phillis Wheatley.* Broadside 1975 $5.95 pap. $3.25

WHITMAN, WALT. 1819–1892

The publication of the first two volumes of *The Collected Writings of Walt Whitman* in 1961 was a publishing event of the year. A citizens' and writers' group formed during 1961 and 1962 called on public officials to preserve the Brooklyn building where Walt Whitman helped to set type and print the first edition of *Leaves of Grass* in 1855. Among those on the committee were CARL SANDBURG, ROBERT FROST, MARIANNE MOORE, ARCHIBALD MACLEISH, Arthur Miller, Aaron Copland, and MALCOLM COWLEY.

Whitman's stature as a poet is constantly advancing. He used a verse form that was at first a stumbling block to many readers. The gains made by his literary descendants, the writers of *vers libre,* are gains in which he has shared. The nearest parallel to the verse form of *Leaves of Grass* is found in the poetry of the English Bible, where the structure is based on a symmetry of clauses called parallelism. While Whitman's is not a conventional poetic form, it is far from lawless. Its cadence and rhythm are carefully wrought. Occasionally he used rhyme, as in "O Captain, My Captain."

"Yet, in spite of Whitman's perplexing mannerisms, the poems justify their boundless contradictions. They shake themselves free from rant and bombastic audacities and rise into the clear air of major poetry. Such poetry is not large but self-assured; it knows, as Whitman asserted, the amplitude of time and laughs at dissolution. It contains continents; it unfolds the new heaven and new earth of the Western world" (Louis Untermeyer).

BOOKS BY WHITMAN

Poems and Prose: Complete Writings. Scholarly 12 vols. repr. of 1902 ed. $395.00

Complete Poetry and Selected Prose. Ed. by J. E. Miller, Jr., Houghton Mifflin (Riv. Eds.) 1959 pap. $5.95

Poetry and Prose. Ed. by Justin Kaplan, Literary Class. (Lib. of Amer.) 1982 $27.50

A Choice of Whitman's Verse. Ed. by Donald Hall, Faber 1968 pap. $5.95

The Portable Whitman. Ed. by Mark Van Doren, Viking 1974 pap. $14.95

Specimen Days. Ed. by Alfred Kazin, ill. by Matthew Brady, Godine 1971 o.p.

Collected Writings of Walt Whitman. Ed. by Gay W. Allen and Sculley Bradley, New York Univ. Pr. 22 vols. Consult publisher's catalog for individual titles and prices.

Calamus: A Series of Letters Written during the Years 1868–1880 by Walt Whitman to a Young Friend. Folcroft repr. of 1898 ed. lib. bdg. $30.00

Leaves of Grass. 1855. Ed. by Emory Holloway, Doubleday 1954 o.p. The standard one-volume edition based on the 1902 text. Contains Whitman's prefaces of 1855, 1872, 1876, and 1888, and the variorum readings by O. L. Triggs. Rejected poems are included.

Leaves of Grass. Intro. by K. A. Preuschen, Adler's repr. of 1855 ed. pap. $22.50; *Bantam Class. Ser.* 1983 pap. $2.95; Buccaneer Bks. 1983 lib. bdg. $19.95; Eakins repr. of 1855 ed. $35.00; Modern Lib. 1944 $6.95; New Amer. Lib. (Signet Class.) 1971 pap. $2.95; ed. by Sculley Bradley and Harold W. Blodgett, *Norton Critical Eds.* text ed. pap. $13.95; ed. by Malcolm Cowley, *Penguin Poets Ser.* repr. of 1959 ed. 1961 pap. $2.95; Peter Pauper 1968 $4.95

Leaves of Grass: Comprehensive Reader's Edition. Ed. by Harold W. Blodgett and Sculley Bradley, New York Univ. Pr. 1965 $45.00

Leaves of Grass: A Textual Variorum of the Printed Poems, 1855–1892. Ed. by Sculley Bradley, Harold W. Blodgett, and William White, *Collected Writings of Walt Whitman Ser.* New York Univ. Pr. 3 vols. 1980 $175.00

Walt Whitman's Blue Book: The 1860–61 Leaves of Grass Containing His Manuscript Additions and Revisions. NYPL 2 vols. 1968 $60.00

Leaves of Grass and Selected Prose. Ed. by Lawrence Buell, *Modern Lib. College Ed. Ser.* Random 1981 text ed. pap. $4.95

Leaves of Grass, and Selected Prose. Ed. by Sculley Bradley, *Rinehart Ed.* Holt 1949 text ed. pap. $13.95

BOOKS ABOUT WHITMAN

Allen, Gay W. *The New Walt Whitman Handbook.* New York Univ. Pr. 1975 $25.00

————. *The Solitary Singer: A Critical Biography of Walt Whitman.* Univ. of Chicago
Pr. repr. of 1955 ed. 1985 pap. $15.95

Arvin, Newton. *Whitman.* Russell repr. of 1938 ed. 1969 $13.00

Asselineau, Roger. *Evolution of Walt Whitman: The Creation of a Book.* Harvard
Univ. Pr. (Belknap Pr.) 1962 o.p.

Beaver, Joseph C. *Walt Whitman: Poet of Science.* Octagon 1972 lib. bdg. $16.00

Bucke, Richard M. *Walt Whitman.* Intro. by H. Jaffe, Gordon $59.95; Johnson Repr.
repr. of 1883 ed. 1970 $23.00

Carpenter, Edward. *Days with Walt Whitman: With Some Notes on His Life and Work.*
AMS Pr. repr. of 1906 ed. $21.50

Chase, Richard. *Walt Whitman. Pamphlets on Amer. Writers Ser.* Univ. of Minnesota
Pr. 1961 pap. $1.25

Faner, Robert D. *Walt Whitman and Opera.* Southern Illinois Univ. Pr. 1972 repr. of
1951 ed. lib. bdg. $7.00 pap. $2.55

Hindus, Milton, ed. *Walt Whitman: The Critical Heritage.* Routledge & Kegan 1971
$29.95

Kaplan, Justin D. *Walt Whitman: A Life.* Bantam 1982 o.p.; Simon & Schuster 1980
o.p.

Loving, Jerome. *Emerson, Whitman, and the American Muse.* Univ. of North Carolina
Pr. 1982 $22.00

Miller, Edwin Haviland. *Walt Whitman's Poetry: A Psychological Journey.* New York
Univ. Pr. 1968 $25.00

Miller, James E., Jr. *American Quest for Supreme Fiction: Whitman's Legacy in the Personal Epic.* Univ. of Chicago Pr. 1979 lib. bdg. 25.00; Univ. of Chicago (Phoenix
Bks.) 1981 $9.95

————. *Walt Whitman. Twayne's U.S. Authors Ser.* G. K. Hall lib. bdg. $11.50

Pearce, Roy H., ed. *Whitman: A Collection of Critical Essays.* Prentice-Hall (Spectrum
Bks.) 1962 $12.95

Stovall, Floyd. *The Foreground of "Leaves of Grass."* Univ. Pr. of Virginia 1974 o.p.

Traubel, Horace. *With Walt Whitman in Camden, September 15, 1889–July 6, 1890.*
Ed. by Gertrude Traubel and William White, Rowman 3 vols. repr. of 1905 ed.
1961 $37.50; Southern Illinois Univ. Pr. 1982 $35.00

Waskow, Howard J. *Whitman: Explorations in Form.* Univ. of Chicago Pr. 1966
$17.50

Woodress, James. *Critical Essays on Walt Whitman. Critical Essays on Amer. Lit. Ser.*
G. K. Hall 1983 lib. bdg. $36.50

Zweig, Paul. *Walt Whitman: The Making of the Poet.* Basic Bks. 1984 $18.95

WHITTIER, JOHN GREENLEAF. 1807–1892

Whittier, the Quaker poet, was the "man of peace and the poet militant."
He himself said that he "set a higher value on his name as appended to the
Anti-Slavery Declaration in 1833 than on the title page of any book." His
"Voices of Freedom," sung in the cause of abolition, was second only to *Un-
cle Tom's Cabin* in influencing the public against slavery.

Whittier's "Snow-Bound, a Winter Idyll" contains fine descriptions of
New England and was immensely popular in its day. The portraits are fire-
light sketches of the members of his home circle drawn from memory after
most of his family were dead. His uncollected criticism, *On Writers and Writings,* is edited by Edwin H. Cady and H. H. Clark.

Whittier's Unknown Romance (with Elizabeth Lloyd) by Marie V. Denervand (o.p.) contained a few of the Lloyd-Whittier letters that are now part of the Pickard-Whittier papers at Harvard University and were edited by T. Franklin Currier as *Elizabeth Lloyd and the Whittiers: A Budget of Letters* (1937, o.p.). *John Greenleaf Whittier: Friend of Man* by John Albert Pollard is a long, scholarly, meticulously documented biography of Whittier as abolitionist, poet, philosopher, and political leader—with chapters of criticism of his work.

BOOKS BY WHITTIER

The Poetical Works of Whittier. Ed. by Hyatt H. Waggoner, *Cambridge Eds. Ser.* Houghton Mifflin rev. ed. 1975 $15.00

Writings. Ed. by H. E. Scudder, AMS Pr. 7 vols. repr. of 1894 ed. $280.00

The Letters of John Greenleaf Whittier. Ed. by John B. Pickard, Harvard Univ. Pr. (Belknap Pr.) 3 vols. 1975 text ed. $100.00

Legends of New England. Intro. by John B. Pickard, Scholars' Facsimiles repr. of 1831 ed. 1972 $35.00

National Lyrics. Ill. by George G. White, H. Fenn, and Charles A. Barry, *Black Heritage Lib. Collection Ser.* Ayer repr. of 1865 ed. $14.25

Anti-Slavery Poems: Songs of Labor and Reform. Anti-Slavery Crusade in Amer. Ser. Ayer repr. of 1888 ed. 1969 $18.00

BOOKS ABOUT WHITTIER

Kribbs, Jayne K. *Critical Essays on John Greenleaf Whittier. Critical Essays on Amer. Lit. Ser.* G. K. Hall 1980 lib. bdg. $23.50

Leary, Lewis. *John Greenleaf Whittier. Twayne's U.S. Authors Ser.* G. K. Hall lib. bdg. $11.50; *Twayne's U.S. Authors Ser.* New College & Univ. Pr. 1961 pap. $5.95

Underwood, F. *John Greenleaf Whittier.* Gordon $59.95; Richard West 1973 $25.00

Wagenknecht, Edward C. *John Greenleaf Whittier: A Portrait in Paradox.* Oxford 1967 o.p. A "compact, meaty introduction to the mind, personality and writings" (*N.Y. Times*) of the popular and successful poet in his time.

Warren, Robert Penn. *John Greenleaf Whittier's Poetry: An Appraisal and a Selection.* Univ. of Minnesota Pr. 1971 $10.00 pap. $2.95. Thirty-six selections.

CHAPTER 9

Modern American Poetry

Charles Molesworth

> I venture to say that the idea of losing oneself up to the point of self-destruction, of surrendering oneself to experience without regard to self-interest or conventional morality, of escaping wholly from the societal bonds, is an "element" somewhere in the mind of every modern person who dares to think of what Arnold in his unaffected Victorian way called "the fullness of spiritual perfection."
>
> LIONEL TRILLING, *Beyond Culture*

When modern American poetry was born, with the work of Eliot, Pound, Williams, and others in the first two decades of the twentieth century, the dominant traditional literary forces were the aestheticism of late romanticism and the moralism of late Victorianism. In a sense these two forces were antagonistic. The first argued for something like "art for art's sake"; the latter insisted that the poet provide his audience with models and prescriptions for ethical probity and social decorum. Much of the struggle of modern poetry, its great riches and its inherent tensions, can be traced to these two antagonistic forces. For the aestheticism that had flowered since the death of KEATS, the modern poet substituted a desire to confront the surfaces of modern reality in all their abrasive particularity. For the moralism that had flourished since the careers of MATTHEW ARNOLD and THOMAS CARLYLE, the modern poet developed a keen interest in the "higher" morality of aesthetic discipline, simultaneously using irony and skepticism to question all the points of "official" ethical reality. Added to these two points of challenge was an interest in experimentalism at the level of technique; this interest was fostered by a knowledge of the major innovators in European poetry, especially RIMBAUD (see Vol. 2) and MALLARMÉ (see Vol. 2). But it was also spurred by a belief that new forms of expression were absolutely necessary for the new sensibility. Rimbaud's injunction that "you must be as modern as possible" becomes Pound's insistence that the poet "make it new!" Because of this spirit of experimentalism in technique and the challenge to the dominant literary values, modern poetry came to be regarded as unnecessarily obscure and difficult.

Such charges of obscurity were answered at length by many critics, most of them affiliated with academic institutions. But what I. A. Richards said of Eliot's *The Waste Land*—that "it ended poetry for little old ladies"—remained largely true. The academicism of modern poetry, or, to put it another way, its removal from the consciousness of the average reader, was perhaps the key development in twentieth-century verse. Although some figures, such as Carl Sandburg and Vachel Lindsay, set their efforts in opposition to this development, most major poets of the time were deeply engaged with what we can call, using the shorthand of terminology, the modernist struggle. Modernism was, of course, a movement that affected literature, painting, music, architecture, and all other fields of cultural activity. Although modernism accepts and even encourages much of what we think of as the advances in twentieth-century thought and living, it is also opposed to much of modern life as well. Indeed, modernism is often characterized by a profound double-mindedness about modernity and even about modern culture. This double-mindedness enters into modern poetry in a variety of ways, often providing it with the themes of cultural nostalgia and spiritual loss as well as the credos of secular progress and heroic irony.

The poets of the generation that came to fruition around World War I are generally known as the modern masters. This group, which includes not only Eliot and Pound but also Williams, Moore, H. D., and Stevens, left a large and impressive body of work that has been the focus of an ever-increasing amount of academic commentary, as well as an audience of devoted and delighted readers. In the late 1950s and early 1960s, this legacy was increasingly protected by the critical tenets of New Criticism, which held that the poetic text itself was autonomously meaningful and required no outside or collateral system of meaning to give it validation or veracity. The heyday of New Criticism was marked by the flourishing of such talents as Allen Tate, John Crowe Ransom, and Robert Penn Warren, all of whom were known as poet-critics. These poet-critics were masters of the short lyric and the literary values of irony, ambiguity, and paradox, and they established a dominance, especially in academic circles, that was considerably widespread. But eventually a new generation of poets came to challenge these second-generation modernists.

This new challenge took many forms; indeed, it was a whole set of challenges. Confessional poets, the New York school, the Black Mountain school, the Deep Image poets, and the Beats were the most well known of those who were dissatisfied with the assumptions and values of the New Criticism. Although there is great diversity in these groups, it can be argued that they are at least united in their mistrust of the formalism that animated New Criticism. In virtually every instance, formalism was challenged by the need to establish some extraliterary source for the poem's truth. Formalism held that the way a poem was structured constituted its most important truth, a truth that went well beyond any dogma or idea. But such formalist claims were answered by an appeal to other truths, for example, the truth of the poet's individual life history (confessionalism), or the collective unconscious (the Deep Image school), or the larger and irresistible forces of social pressure and individual freedom (the Beats). The antiformalism of the late 1960s and the 1970s left a whole new set of terms and concerns: "naked poetry," "projective verse," "the poetry of process," and so forth. Nevertheless, formalism ran deep in the traditions of twentieth-century lyric poetry (it might even be argued that it constituted the main tradition of that poetry), and other developments seemed more to reinvigorate formalism than to issue any real challenge to the assumptions of modernism. However, in the late 1970s and early 1980s talk of the new aesthetics of postmodernism was increasing.

Postmodernism has no clear definition. Yet, among many poets, chiefly John Ashbery, James Merrill, Adrienne Rich, and Gary Snyder, there is a sense that the older forms of modernist belief and practice are increasingly irrelevant. In place of the heroic irony of modernism is an emphasis on empathy and identification that cannot be contained within the tight borders of the short, formally structured lyric so highly praised by New Criticism. Postmodernism may be regarded as an attempt to open the lyric to the forces of personality and even ideology. At the same time, other poets are returning to a use of discursive and even openly ethical concerns in their poetry; here the names of Hass, Pinsky, and C. K. Williams are important. Clearly, postmodernism is not simply a reaction against the institutionalized values of the modern masters, but it will take time for readers and critics—as well as poets—to sort out the forces currently at work in American poetry.

Regardless of the forms that postmodernism might uncover in the pressures of its development, modern American poetry has already had a century of rich experimentalism as well as a series of constant struggles to verify the values of traditional literature. It has offered a greatly enriched language and wisdom, although it has often had to purchase such achievements at the cost of full comprehension. Modern American poetry must remain an open poetry, which means that it will be as open to knowing as it can, and its truths and values will finally be as rigorous and as pleasurable as its readers choose to make them.

HISTORY AND CRITICISM

A number of anthologies that contain biographical material and commentary are listed later under "Collections." Collections of interviews are included in this section.

Allen, Don Cameron, ed. *The Moment of Poetry*. Greenwood repr. of 1962 ed. 1980 lib. bdg. $22.50. Five poet-professors (May Sarton, Richard Eberhart, Richard Wilbur, Randall Jarrell, and John Holmes) speak about their craft.

Allen, Donald M., and Warren Taliman, eds. *The Poetics of the New American Poetry*. Irvington 1973 $27.00. A collection of statements by 25 major poets.

Altieri, Charles. *Enlarging the Temple: New Directions in American Poetry during the 1960's*. Bucknell Univ. Pr. 1979 $22.50 pap. $9.95. This important study provides the crucial theoretical background for contemporary poetry.

———. *Self and Sensibility in Contemporary American Poetry*. Cambridge Studies in Amer. Lit. and Culture 1984 $24.95. A study that focuses on Creeley, Rich, and Ashbery, but deals with other figures as well.

Bellamy, Joe David. *American Poetry Observed: Poets on Their Work*. Univ. of Illinois

HUF
F

Pr. 1984 $19.95. Interesting interviews that reflect both the diversity and the underlying assumptions behind the work of many contemporary poets.

Blackmur, Richard. *Language as Gesture.* Columbia Univ. Pr. repr. of 1952 ed. 1981 $10.00. Important collection of essays on modernist poets.

Bontemps, Arna, ed. *The Harlem Renaissance Remembered: Essays Edited with a Commentary by Arna Bontemps.* Dodd 1984 pap. $9.95

Boyers, Robert, ed. *Contemporary Poetry in America: Essays and Interviews.* Schocken 1974 o.p. A useful collection with important essays on such poets as James Wright, Sylvia Plath, Adrienne Rich, and others.

Breslin, James. *From Modern to Contemporary: American Poetry, 1945–1965.* Univ. of Chicago Pr. 1984 $20.00. This study relies on close readings of works from such poets as Lowell, O'Hara, Levertov, and Ginsberg, but also offers a historical framework.

Brooks, Cleanth. *Modern Poetry and the Tradition.* Univ. of North Carolina Pr. 1970 pap. $6.95

Charters, Samuel. *Some Poems and Some Poets: Studies in American Underground Poetry since 1945.* Oyez 1971 $5.95 pap. $2.95. Group of essays on Jack Spicer, Robert Duncan, Allen Ginsberg, Lawrence Ferlinghetti, Charles Olson, Robert Creeley, and Gary Snyder.

Cook, Bruce. *The Beat Generation: The Tumultuous '50's Movement and Its Impact on Today.* Greenwood repr. of 1971 ed. 1983 lib. bdg. $35.00

Cowan, Louise. *The Fugitive Group: A Literary History.* Louisiana State Univ. Pr. 1959 pap. $7.95. An examination of the poets who published in *The Fugitive* in Nashville in the early 1920s: John Crowe Ransom, Allen Tate, and Robert Penn Warren.

Cowley, Malcolm. *Exile's Return: A Literary Odyssey of the 1920's.* Penguin 1976 pap. $5.95; Peter Smith 1983 $10.75

Day, A. Grove. *The Sky Clears: Poetry of the American Indians.* Univ. of Nebraska Pr. (Bison) 1964 pap. $3.95. A discussion for the general reader of the best translations of American Indian poetry.

Dickey, James. *Babel to Byzantium: Poets and Poetry Now.* Ecco Pr. 1981 pap. $7.95; Octagon repr. of 1968 ed. 1973 lib. bdg. $24.00. Highly partisan criticism and appreciation, mostly on Dickey's contemporaries.

Eberhart, Richard. *Of Poetry and Poets.* Univ. of Illinois Pr. 1979 $19.95.

Fass, Ekbert, ed. *Towards a New American Poetics, Essays and Interviews: Olson, Duncan, Snyder, Creeley, Bly, Ginsberg.* Black Sparrow 1979 $14.00 pap. $7.50. Important source material for the Black Mountain and Beat poets.

Feder, Lillian. *Ancient Myth in Modern Poetry.* Princeton Univ. Pr. 1972 $36.00 pap. $9.95

Friebert, Stuart, and David Young. *A Field Guide to Contemporary Poetry and Poetics.* Longman text ed. 1980 pap. $11.95. An uneven collection that has some interesting essays.

Fussell, Edwin. *Lucifer in Harness: American Meter, Metaphor and Diction.* Princeton Univ. Pr. 1973 $21.00. A clearly written book about the forms and apparent formlessness of American poetics in the twentieth century.

Gayle, Addison, Jr. *The Black Aesthetic.* Doubleday 1972 pap. $3.50

Gibson, Donald B. *Modern Black Poets: A Collection of Critical Essays.* Prentice-Hall (Spectrum Bks.) 1973 $12.95

Heller, Michael. *Conviction's Net of Branches.* Southern Illinois Univ. Pr. 1985 $13.50 pap. $8.95. Essays on the objectivists, especially Oppen and Rakoski.

Howard, Richard. *Alone with America: Essays on the Art of Poetry in the United States since 1950.* Atheneum enl. ed. 1980 $25.00 pap. $12.95. This collection provides guidance and approach to a whole generation of poets, including A. R. Ammons, James Wright, James Dickey, James Logan, Mark Strand, Anne Sexton, and 35 others.

Jackson, Richard. *Acts of Mind: Conversations with Contemporary Poets.* Univ. of Alabama Pr. text ed. 1983 $19.95. Another collection of interviews; this one includes several "younger" poets.

Johnson, Joyce. *Minor Characters.* Houghton Mifflin 1983 $13.95. A memoir by a woman who knew many of the Beat poets during the 1950s.

Kalstone, David. *Five Temperaments: Elizabeth Bishop, Robert Lowell, James Merrill, Adrienne Rich, John Ashbery.* Norton 1985 pap. $4.95; Oxford 1977 $22.50. Criticism that is almost exclusively positive, but includes some useful information on the poets.

Kherdian, David. *Six Poets of the San Francisco Renaissance: Portraits and Checklists.* Giligia $17.50

Lieberman, Lawrence. *Unassigned Frequencies: American Poetry in Review, 1964–1977.* Univ. of Illinois Pr. 1977 $17.50. Useful information about single volumes of poetry by a wide range of contemporary poets.

Mazzaro, Jerome. *Postmodern American Poetry.* Univ. of Illinois Pr. 1980 $15.00

Middlebrook, Diane Wood, and Marilyn Yalom, eds. *Coming to Light: American Women Poets in the Twentieth Century.* Univ. of Michigan Pr. 1985 $25.00 pap. $12.95. Sixteen essays on such poets as H. D., Bishop, Plath, and Rich.

Molesworth, Charles. *The Fierce Embrace: A Study of Contemporary American Poetry.* Univ. of Missouri Pr. text ed. 1979 $19.50 pap. $9.00. Treats several poets in depth and such topics as the little poetry magazines and the poet's sense of belonging to a specific generation.

Nelson, Cary. *Our Last First Poets: Vision and History in Contemporary American Poetry.* Univ. of Illinois Pr. 1981 $15.95 1984 pap. $7.95. A searching book that asks serious questions about the poets' views.

Oberg, Arthur. *Modern American Lyric: Lowell, Berryman, Creeley and Plath.* Rutgers Univ. Pr. 1978 o.p. Sensitive readings that are especially alert to tones and emotional struggles in the poems.

Ostroff, Anthony, ed. *The Contemporary Poet as Artist and Critic: Eight Symposia.* Little, Brown 1964 o.p. A close-up look at how poets read other poets, and how they respond to criticism; the essays show the New Criticism in practice.

Pearce, Roy Harvey. *The Continuity of American Poetry.* Princeton Univ. Pr. 1961 pap. $11.50. A valuable study of the history of American poetry from the seventeenth century to the age of Eliot.

Perkins, David. *A History of Modern Poetry: From the Eighteen Nineties to the High Modernist Mode.* Harvard Univ. Pr. 1976 $27.50 pap. $10.00. This is a thorough, cautious study.

Pinsky, Robert. *The Situation of Poetry: Contemporary Poetry and Its Traditions.* Princeton Essays in Lit. Ser. text ed. 1977 $19.00 pap. $7.95. An excellent critique of assumptions that animate, and deaden, much of contemporary poetry.

Pritchard, William. *Lives of the Modern Poets.* Oxford 1980 $27.50 1981 pap. $8.95. Critical-biographical studies of such major modernist masters as Frost, Eliot, and Pound.

Quinn, Sister Bernetta. *Metamorphic Tradition in Modern Poetry: Essays on the Work of Ezra Pound and Other Poets.* Gordian repr. of 1955 ed. 1966 $12.50

Rosenthal, M. L. *The Modern Poets: A Critical Introduction.* Oxford 1965 pap. $8.95. An early study.

Simpson, Eileen. *Poets in Their Youth: A Memoir*. Random 1982 $25.50. A revealing look at Berryman, Lowell, and others by a woman who was married to Berryman.

Sutton, Walter. *American Free Verse: The Modern Revolution in Poetry*. New Directions 1973 pap. $3.95

Turner, Alberta, ed. *Fifty Contemporary Poets: The Creative Process*. Longman text ed. 1977 pap. $13.95

Unger, Leonard, ed. *Seven Modern American Poets: An Introduction*. Lib. on Amer. Writers Univ. of Minnesota Pr. 1967 $16.95. This volume comprises seven numbers from the excellent University of Minnesota Pamphlets on American Writers (Frost, Stevens, Williams, Pound, Ransom, Eliot, and Tate). Unger "has written a fine introduction on modern American poetry" (*LJ*).

Vendler, Helen. *Part of Nature, Part of Us: Modern American Poets*. Harvard Pap. Ser. 1981 $7.95. Miscellaneous reviews and essays on a wide range of poets, with little theoretical or contextual argument.

Wagner, Jean. *Black Poets of the United States: From Paul Laurence Dunbar to Langston Hughes*. Trans. by Kenneth Douglas, Univ. of Illinois Pr. 1973 $25.00 pap. $12.50

Weatherhead, A. Kingsley. *The Edge of the Image: Marianne Moore, William Carlos Williams, and Some Other Poets*. Univ. of Washington Pr. 1967 $20.00

Whittemore, Reed. *Little Magazines. Pamphlets on Amer. Writers Ser.* Univ. of Minnesota Pr. 1963 pap. $1.25. This is a historical survey of the little poetry magazines of the twentieth century. A good general outline.

Wildman, Eugene, ed. *Anthology of Concretism*. Ohio Univ. Pr. (Swallow) 2d enl. ed. 1969 $10.00 pap. $4.95. An international movement once in vogue in the United States, concretism presents poetry in graphic design.

Williamson, Alan. *Introspection and Contemporary Poetry*. Harvard Univ. Pr. text ed. 1984 $17.50. Sensitive readings of Plath, as well as of several "younger" poets, such as Louise Glück.

COLLECTIONS

Adoff, Arnold, ed. *The Poetry of Black America: Anthology of the Twentieth Century*. Harper 1973 $22.89. An excellent anthology—comprehensive selections from W. B. DuBois and James Weldon Johnson through Richard Wright, Sun Ra, Imamu Amiri Baraka (LeRoi Jones) to Nikki Giovanni and Victor Hernandez Cruz.

Allen, Donald M. *The New American Poetry, 1945–1960*. Grove 1960 o.p.; Peter Smith o.p. An important collection of 215 poems by 44 poets, arranged to illuminate some of their differences and similarities. Included are biographies, bibliographies, and statements on poetics by the poets themselves. This anthology had an impact that is hard to overestimate. Reissued in an enlarged edition entitled *The Post Modern Poets*.

Berg, Stephen, and Robert Mezey, eds. *Naked Poetry: Recent American Poetry in Open Forms*. Bobbs 1969 pap. $11.49. An anthology of the work of 19 major poets with brief biographical sketches and photographs of the poets. Includes Levertov, Creeley, Rexroth, Roethke, Patchen, Berryman, and Snyder.

Brooks, Gwendolyn. *A Broadside Treasury, 1965–1970*. Broadside $6.00 pap. $4.00. Poems by 50 black poets from the Broadside Press series. Includes work by Gwendolyn Brooks, LeRoi Jones, Nikki Giovanni, Lance Jeffers, Don L. Lee, and Sonia Sanchez, among others.

Carruth, Hayden. *The Voice That Is Great within Us: American Poetry of the Twentieth Century. Bantam Class. Ed. Ser.* 1970 pap. $4.95

Hall, Donald, ed. *Contemporary American Poetry. Poets Ser.* Penguin rev. ed. 1963 pap. $4.95

Heyen, William. *The Generation of 2000: Contemporary American Poets.* Ontario Review Pr. 1984 $24.95 pap. $14.95. A recent collection that makes several younger poets' work available, with short prose statements by each poet.

Padgett, Ron, and David Shapiro. *Anthology of New York Poets.* Random 1970 o.p. Important for the student of the New York school of poets; sizable selections from the work of James Schuyler, Clark Coolidge, Kenward Elmslie, and Ted Berrigan, among others.

Pearson, Norman Holmes. *Decade: A Collection of Poems from the First Ten Years of the Wesleyan Poetry Program.* Wesleyan Univ. Pr. 1969 pap. $6.95. This book gathers the work of 33 poets published by Wesleyan up to 1968, including John Ashbery, Robert Bly, James Dickey, and James Wright.

Poulin, A., Jr. *Contemporary American Poetry.* Houghton Mifflin 3d text ed. 1980 pap. $16.50. One of the anthologies most often used in college courses.

Sanders, Gerald De Witt, and others, eds. *Chief Modern Poets of Britain and America.* Macmillan 2 vols. in 1 text ed. 5th ed. 1970 $23.95; Macmillan 2 vols. 1970 pap. $13.95

Strand, Mark, ed. *Contemporary American Poets: American Poetry since 1940.* New Amer. Lib. 1969 pap. $6.95 1971 pap. $4.50. Selections from 92 poets published since the 1940s.

Untermeyer, Louis, ed. *Modern American Poetry.* Harcourt new & enl. text ed. 1962 o.p. A critical anthology enlarged to include 772 poems by 76 poets ranging from Whitman to Anne Sexton.

AIKEN, CONRAD. 1889–1973

Born in Georgia, Conrad Aiken graduated from Harvard University and for several years lived alternately in England and the United States. Although he knew all the major modernist poets, for many years he himself was comparatively unknown. He won the Pulitzer Prize (1930), the Bollingen Prize (1956), and a gold medal (1958) from the National Institute of Arts and Letters, among many other awards. He was also consultant in poetry at the Library of Congress (1950–52). Allen Tate once described him as the "perfection of a vanishing American type: the complete man of letters." His autobiographical work *Ushant: An Essay* is of considerable historical interest for the student of modernism.

BOOKS BY AIKEN

Collected Poems, 1916–1970. Oxford 2d ed. 1970 $35.00

Selected Poems. Schocken 1982 pap. $9.95. Representative of his most important work since 1917.

Ushant: An Essay. 1952. Oxford 1971 $27.50

BOOKS ABOUT AIKEN

Hoffman, Frederick J. *Conrad Aiken. Twayne's U.S. Authors Ser.* New College & Univ. Pr. 1962 pap. $3.45

Martin, Jay. *Conrad Aiken: A Life of His Art.* Princeton Univ. Pr. 1962 $30.00. "In me," commented Aiken in a letter to Malcolm Cowley, "you behold an almost unique phenomenon, a poet who has acquired a Reputation . . . without ever having been caught in the act."

AMMONS, A. R. 1926–

Considered by Daniel Hoffman to be an "American Romantic in the Tradition of EMERSON and WHITMAN," Ammons easily communicates to men and women of science as well as those of letters. After attending Wake Forest College, he studied at the University of California, Berkeley, and later became an executive in the biological glass industry. Since 1964 he has taught at Cornell University and his *Collected Poems, 1951–1971* won a National Book Award (1973).

Ammons's use of images of nature to impart his perception of human ambiguity is similar to Robert Frost's. He is one of the most prolifically inventive poets of recent times, and he has an astonishing range of moods, from philosophical to playful. He has remained a singular poet, though at the same time an absorber of influence from such diverse sources as Emerson, Marianne Moore, and William Carlos Williams.

BOOKS BY AMMONS

Collected Poems, 1951–1971. Norton 1972 $17.50
Selected Poems, 1951–1977. Norton 1977 pap. $5.95
Corson's Inlet. Norton 1965 $5.95
Northfield Poems. Norton 1966 $5.95
Briefings. Norton 1971 $6.00
Sphere: The Form of a Motion. Norton 1974 o.p. An important long poem that extends the tradition of Williams's *Paterson* and Merrill's *Changing Light.*
Diversifications: Poems. Norton 1975 $6.95
The Snow Poems. Norton 1977 $12.50
A Coast of Trees. Norton 1981 $12.95 pap. $4.95
Worldly Hopes: Poems. Norton 1982 $12.95 pap. $5.95
Lake Effect Country: Poems. Norton 1983 $15.50 pap. $5.95

ASHBERY, JOHN. 1927–

A contemporary and fellow classmate of Kenneth Koch at Harvard University, John Ashbery has been one of the most experimental of the New York school of poets. Noted for his mixture of diction and elegant wit, he was influenced by early AUDEN, Laura Riding, and Wallace Stevens.

Born in Rochester, New York, Ashbery grew up near Lake Ontario. After graduation from Harvard University, he studied at Columbia University, where he obtained his M.A. In 1955, he was awarded a Fulbright Scholarship to study in France, where he wrote art criticism for the Paris edition of the *N.Y. Herald Tribune*. Like others in the New York school, Ashbery was closely associated with art and artists and wrote for *Art News*. His first book, which contained a preface by Auden, won the *Yale Series of Younger Poets* prize.

Ashbery's plays *The Heroes* and *The Compromise or Queen of the Caribou* have both been produced—the former by the Living Theatre and the latter at the Poet's Theatre in Cambridge, Massachusetts. It is now virtually impossible to overstate Ashbery's influence and the fervor of his partisans. Since the death of Lowell, he has been the most discussed (and praised) of all American poets. Although his poetry is imbued with anxiety and uncertainty (or perhaps because of this), Ashbery has become the dominant poet of both the avant-garde and academic criticism—a position not held by one poet since T. S. Eliot in the 1930s and 1940s.

BOOKS BY ASHBERY

Some Trees. Corinth Bks. repr. of 1956 ed. 1970 $6.50; *Amer. Poetry Ser.* Ecco Pr. 1978 pap. $4.95

The Tennis Court Oath. Wesleyan Univ. Pr. 1962 pap. $6.95

Rivers and Mountains: Poems. 1966. *Amer. Poetry Ser.* Ecco Pr. 1977 pap. $4.95

Double Dream of Spring. 1970. *Amer. Poetry Ser.* Ecco Pr. 1976 $7.95 pap. $4.95

Three Poems. 1972. *Penguin Poets Ser.* 1977 pap. $4.95. Written in prose of great flexibility, this is an important book, central to Ashbery's canon.

Self-Portrait in a Convex Mirror. *Penguin Poets Ser.* 1976 pap. $4.95; Viking 1975 $9.95. This volume won three national awards and secured the poet's reputation.

Houseboat Days. *Penguin Poets Ser.* 1977 pap. $3.95

As We Know. *Penguin Poets Ser.* 1979 pap. $7.95; Viking 1979 $12.50

Shadow Train: Fifty Lyrics. *Penguin Poets Ser.* 1981 pap. $4.95; Viking 1981 $12.50. A book of 16-line sonnets.

A Wave. Viking 1984 $14.95

BOOKS ABOUT ASHBERY

Lehman, David, ed. *Beyond Amazement: New Essays on John Ashbery.* Cornell Univ. Pr. 1980 $32.50 pap. $8.95

Shapiro, David. *John Ashbery: An Introduction to the Poetry. Intro. to 20th-Century Amer. Poetry Ser.* Columbia Univ. Pr. 1979 $19.00

BARAKA, IMAMU AMIRI (LEROI JONES). 1934–

Baraka is so powerful, accomplished, and versatile in so many literary fields that he made himself a name in literature before he became a militant against the oppression of black Americans. His early poems were often personal, uncommitted, and diffuse; he showed in these a strong lyric talent.

Baraka was sentenced to prison in connection with the Newark, New Jersey, riots of 1967. Before serving his term of imprisonment, however, he and other black militants were instrumental in helping maintain order in Newark at the time of Martin Luther King, Jr.'s, assassination in 1968. Since then, he has become more active in the black nationalist movement, more recently espousing revolutionary Marxist-Leninist principles. The major black American poet of the postwar era, Baraka has refused in the last two decades to separate his revolutionary commitment and his literary art. This alone makes him unique among his peers.

BOOKS BY BARAKA

Black Magic Poetry: Collected Poetry, 1961–67. Bobbs 1970 o.p. Includes the following volumes: *Sabotage; Target Study; Black Art.*

Preface to a Twenty Volume Suicide Note. Corinth Bks. 1961 pap. $2.50
The Baptism (and *The Toilet*). Grove 1967 pap. $3.95
Raise Race Rays Raze: Essays since 1965. Univ. Place 1971 $10.00
Home: Social Essays. 1964. Morrow 1972 pap. $3.45
The System of Dante's Hell, The Dead Lecturer, and Tales. Grove 1976 pap. $4.95
Selected Poetry of Amiri Baraka-LeRoi Jones. Morrow 1979 pap. $5.95
Daggers and Javelins: Essays, 1974–1979. Morrow 1984 pap. $10.00
The Autobiography of LeRoi Jones-Amiri Baraka. Freundlich 1984 $16.95

BOOKS ABOUT BARAKA

Benston, Kimberly. *Baraka: The Renegade and the Mask.* Yale Univ. Pr. College Ser. 1976 $26.50

Hudson, Theodore. *From LeRoi Jones to Amiri Baraka: The Literary Works.* Duke Univ. Pr. 1973 $18.75 pap. $9.75

Sollars, Werner. *Amiri Baraka-LeRoi Jones: The Quest for a Populist Modernism.* Columbia Univ. Pr. 1978 o.p. An important critical study.

BENET, STEPHEN VINCENT. 1898–1943

John Brown's Body (1928), which won the Pulitzer Prize for poetry in 1929 and brought Benét instant popularity, is a history of the Civil War in rhyme and blank verse—a history told from the point of view of ordinary people, a rank-and-file history, of the North and of the South equally. This narrative of "the rich man's war and the poor man's fight" is a remarkable epic of the United States. Benét has not received high praise from academic critics.

BOOK BY BENÉT

Selected Poetry and Prose. 1942. Holt 1959 o.p. Contains the complete text of *John Brown's Body* and an early novel, *Spanish Bayonet*, with poems and stories from all his books, including four stories and two poems not published in other books.

BOOKS ABOUT BENÉT

Benet, William R. *Stephen Vincent Benét.* Folcroft repr. of 1943 ed. 1977 lib. bdg. $10.00; Porter 1979 $28.50

Fenton, Charles A. *Stephen Vincent Benét: The Life and Times of an American Man of Letters, 1898–1943.* Greenwood repr. of 1958 ed. 1978 lib. bdg. $37.50

BERRYMAN, JOHN. 1914–1972

John Berryman's poetry has a depth and obscurity that in turn discourage readers and entice critics. His major work, *The Dream Songs*, forms a poetic notebook, capturing the ephemera of mood and attitude of this most mercurial of poets. Born John Smith in McAlester, Oklahoma, and educated at Columbia University and Clare College, Cambridge, he later taught at several universities. He received the Shelley Memorial Award (1948), the Harriet Monroe Award (1957), the Loines Award for poetry of the National Institute of Arts and Letters (1964), and the fellowship of the Academy of American Poets (1966). In 1964 he won the Pulitzer Prize in poetry for *77 Dream Songs* (1964). His short story "The Imaginary Jew" received the Kenyon-Doubleday Award and was listed in *Best American Short Stories, 1946*. He also wrote *Stephen Crane* (1950) and is the author of a novel, *Recovery* (1973). In 1972, Berryman committed suicide. Often listed along with Sylvia Plath and Anne Sexton as a major confessional poet, he was as much concerned with literary artifice as he was with personal revelation.

BOOKS BY BERRYMAN

Short Poems. Farrar 1967 $4.95. A collection of 64 poems, including "The Dispossessed" (1948) and "Formal Elegy," written in 1963 on the occasion of John F. Kennedy's death.

Berryman's Sonnets. Farrar 1967 $5.50 pap. $4.95

Homage to Mistress Bradstreet and Other Poems. 1956. Farrar 1968 pap. $3.50

The Dream Songs. Farrar 1969 $17.50 pap. $8.95

Love and Fame. Farrar 1970 $12.95. Berryman annotated the second edition, explaining the deletion of some poems and voicing thoughts on the poems in general.

The Freedom of the Poet. Farrar 1976 $12.50 pap. $6.95. Berryman's essays.

BOOKS ABOUT BERRYMAN

Haffenden, John. *John Berryman: A Critical Commentary*. New York Univ. Pr. (Gotham Lib.) 1980 $26.00

———. *The Life of John Berryman*. Routledge & Kegan 1982 $29.95; Routledge & Kegan (Ark) 1984 pap. $7.95. An exhaustive—and exhausting—biography.

Kelley, Richard. *John Berryman: A Checklist*. Intro. by Michael Berryhill, fwd. by William Meredith, *Author Bibliographies Ser*. Scarecrow Pr. 1972 $13.00. Bibliographic reference tool.

Martz, William J. *John Berryman*. *Pamphlets on Amer. Writers Ser*. Univ. of Minnesota Pr. 1969 pap. $1.25. An introduction to Berryman's poetry.

BISHOP, ELIZABETH. 1911–1979

In his *N.Y. Times* column, the late Harvey Breit applauded the awarding of the Pulitzer Prize for 1956 to "the peripatetic Massachusetts-born poet, Elizabeth Bishop, Vassar '34, traveler through Europe and Africa, ex-resident of Key West and Mexico, and present dweller in Brazil. We applauded because she . . . once said she was opposed 'to making poetry monstrous or boring and proceeding to talk the very life out of it.' " About *Questions of Travel* (1965), Philip Booth said, "No poet now writing achieves more naturally right notes or greater flexibility in formally structured poems. . . . Bishop's skill is lyrically demonstrated by the 47 quatrains of 'The Burglar of Babylon,' and by the marvelous ease of 'Sestina.'. . . Bishop is not only our most valuable export to Brazil, she is one of the true poets of this, or any, hemisphere" (*Christian Science Monitor*). The *Complete Poems* (1969) won the National Book Award (1970). She also wrote the nonfiction *Brazil* (1967, o.p.) and with Emanuel Brasil edited *An Anthology of Twentieth Century Brazilian Poetry* (1972) (translated by Paul Blackburn and others). Her influence on other poets was not obvious during her life, but many have tried to emulate her distinctive talent, and her reputation continues to grow.

BOOKS BY BISHOP

Complete Poems. Farrar 1969 pap. $7.95. Includes: "North and South," "A Cold Spring," "Questions of Travel," "Elsewhere," "Translations from the Portuguese," and new and uncollected works.

The Complete Poems, 1927–1979. Farrar 1983 pap. $9.95. Includes the same books of poems as *Complete Poems* plus "Geography III."

The Collected Prose. Ed. by Robert Giroux, Farrar 1984 $17.50 pap. $8.95. Contains essays and stories of startling precision and ironic dryness.

BOOKS ABOUT BISHOP

Schwartz, Lloyd, and Sylvia P. Estees. *Elizabeth Bishop and Her Art. Under Discussion Ser.* Univ. of Michigan Pr. 1982 $18.50 pap. $8.95

Stevenson, Anne. *Elizabeth Bishop. Twayne's U.S. Authors Ser.* New College & Univ. Pr. 1966 pap. $3.45

BLY, ROBERT. 1926–

Robert Bly lives on a farm in his native state of Minnesota; in Madison, Wisconsin, he edited *The Seventies* magazine, which he founded as *The Fifties* and in the next decade called *The Sixties*. In 1966, with David Ray, he organized American Writers against the Vietnam War. "A pungent critic, an undaunted moralist, a hackled dissenter, he is the sworn enemy of worldliness in the conduct of life and in the conduct of poetry" (*Atlantic*). *The Light around the Body*, which won the National Book Award in 1968, "is strongly critical of the war in Vietnam, of the callousness of American foreign policy in other areas and of the general tenor of American life" (*N.Y. Times*).

Bly is also a translator of Scandinavian literature, his most recent translation being *Twenty Poems of Tomas Transtromer*. Through the Sixties Press and currently the Seventies Press, he has introduced little-known European and South American poets to American readers. His magazines have been the center of a poetic movement involving the poets Donald Hall, Louis Simpson, and James Wright.

BOOKS BY BLY

Silence in the Snowy Fields. Wesleyan Poetry Program 1962 $15.00 pap. $6.95

The Light around the Body. Harcourt 1967 $8.95

The Morning Glory: Prose Poems. 1969. Harper 1975 $8.95. Twelve prose poems with drawings by Tomi de Paola.

Sleepers Joining Hands (Shadow Mothers). 1970. Harcourt 1973 $8.95 pap. $4.50

The Sea and the Honeycomb. Beacon 1971 o.p. A book of tiny poems by Quasimodo, D. H. Lawrence, Machado, and Issa, with originals of foreign-language poems at the back of the volume.

Old Man Rubbing His Eyes. 1973. Unicorn Pr. 4th ed. 1975 $15.50 pap. $5.00. Twenty new poems with 20 drawings by Franz Richter.

This Body Is Made of Camphor and Gopherwood. Harcourt 1977 $7.95 pap. $3.95

This Tree Will Be Here for a Thousand Years. Harcourt 1979 $8.95 pap. $4.95

Talking All Morning. Poets on Poetry Ser. Univ. of Michigan Pr. 1980 pap. $7.95. A collection of essays and interviews.

The Man in the Black Coat Turns: Poems. 1981. Penguin 1983 pap. $6.95

Loving a Woman in Two Worlds: Love Poems. Doubleday 1985 $10.95

Books about Bly

Nelson, Howard. *Robert Bly: An Introduction to the Poetry.* Ed. by John Unterecker, *Intro. to 20th-Century Amer. Poetry Ser.* Columbia Univ. Pr. 1984 $20.00
Peseroff, Joyce, ed. *Robert Bly: When Sleepers Awake. Under Discussion Ser.* Univ. of Michigan Pr. 1984 $20.00 pap. $11.95. A collection of essays by various critics.

BOGAN, LOUISE. 1897–1970

The cowinner with Leonie Adams of the Bollingen Prize in poetry (1954), Louise Bogan also won the Academy of American Poets Fellowship (1959) and the Brandeis Prize for poetry (1961). Her *Achievement in American Poetry, 1900–1950* (1950, o.p.) is a spirited book of criticism. Bogan was for many years the poetry critic for the *New Yorker* magazine.

Books by Bogan

Blue Estuaries: Poems. 1923–1968. *Amer. Poetry Ser.* Ecco Pr. 1977 pap. $7.95; Octagon repr. 1974 lib. bdg. $16.00
Poet's Alphabet. McGraw-Hill 1970 o.p.

Book about Bogan

Frank, Elizabeth. *Louise Bogan: A Portrait.* Knopf 1984 $24.95

BROOKS, GWENDOLYN. 1917–

Gwendolyn Brooks was born in Topeka, Kansas, and published her first poem at age 13 in a children's magazine. After the publication of her first book of poetry, *A Street in Bronzeville* (1945, o.p.), she was chosen as one of the ten Women of the Year by *Mademoiselle* magazine. In 1946 she received an award for creative writing from the American Academy of Arts and Letters and a Guggenheim Fellowship. Early in 1968, Governor Otto Kerner of Illinois appointed her to succeed the late Carl Sandburg as state poet laureate. Her second book of poems, *Annie Allen* (1949), won the 1950 Pulitzer Prize.

Books by Brooks

Selected Poems. Harper 1963 $11.49. This volume includes some poems previously unpublished in book form.
Annie Allen. Greenwood repr. of 1949 ed. 1972 lib. bdg. $15.00
Bronzeville Boys and Girls. Harper 1956 $9.89
In the Mecca. Harper 1968 $11.49
Aloneness. Broadside 1971 $3.00 pap. $2.00. Handwritten with drawings.
Family Pictures. Broadside 1971 $5.00 pap. $1.00
World of Gwendolyn Brooks. Harper 1971 $15.00
Report from Part One: An Autobiography. Broadside new ed. 1972 $5.95
Beckonings. Broadside 1975 pap. $2.00

BUKOWSKI, CHARLES. 1920–

At age 35, after years of writing prose fiction, Charles Bukowski began writing poetry. He is the most famed of a breed called "street poets"—those destined to have poetry published by small presses, whose writings are not only derived from street life, but whose own life in some sense is also of the street. On and off, Bukowski has worked as a dishwasher and a mailman, in a dog biscuit factory and a slaughterhouse, and has hung posters in a New York subway. His writing is typified by a rough, large, prophetic style.

Born in Germany, Bukowski came to the United States when he was two years old. A resident of Los Angeles, he writes a weekly column there called "Notes of a Dirty Old Man" for *Open City*. He received the Discovery Award of the National Endowment for the Arts in 1973.

BOOKS BY BUKOWSKI

Days Run Away Like Wild Horses over the Hills. 1970. Black Sparrow 1983 $14.00 pap. $6.00
South of No North. 1973. Black Sparrow 1983 $14.00 pap. $7.00
Burning in Water, Drowning in Flame. 1974. Black Sparrow 1983 $14.00 pap. $7.50
Love Is a Dog from Hell: Poems, 1974–1977. Black Sparrow 1982 $14.00 pap. $7.50
Mockingbird Wish Me Luck. Black Sparrow 1982 $14.00 pap. $5.00
Hot Water Music. Black Sparrow 1983 $14.00 pap. $8.50
War All the Time: Poems, 1981–1984. Black Sparrow 1984 $14.00 pap. $8.50

BOOKS ABOUT BUKOWSKI

Blazek, Douglas, ed. *A Charles Bukowski Sampler.* Quixote 3d ed. 1979 pap. $3.00
Fox, Hugh. *Charles Bukowski: A Critical and Biographical Study.* Abyss 1968 pap. $3.75

CARRUTH, HAYDEN. 1921–

Hayden Carruth was born in Waterbury, Connecticut, and received degrees from the Universities of North Carolina and Chicago. He is presently a resident of Vermont and a professor at Syracuse University.

Carruth has been editor of *Poetry Magazine*, an associate editor of the University of Chicago Press, and the project administrator for International Publications. As a free-lance editor, he has published many reviews in *Poetry*, *The Nation*, *Hudson Review*, and *The New Republic*. He also edited *The Voice That Is Great within Us*, a popular anthology.

Carruth has been awarded numerous grants and poetry prizes, among them the Bess Hokin Prize (1954), the Levinson Prize (1958), the Harriet Monroe Poetry Prize with Yvor Winters (1960–61), the Eunice Tietjens Memorial Prize (1964), and the Morton Dauwen Zabel Prize (1968). His work is indebted both to Frost and Williams and combines the imagist precision of Pound with the emotional directness of a native strain in American poetry.

BOOKS BY CARRUTH

Working Papers: Selected Essays and Reviews. Ed. by Judith Weissman, Univ. of Georgia Pr. 1983 $21.95
For You. New Directions 1970 $5.95 pap. $1.95
From Snow and Rock, from Chaos. New Directions 1973 pap. $2.25
The Bloomingdale Papers. Contemporary Poetry Ser. Univ. of Georgia Pr. 1974 pap. $5.95
Dark World. Kayak 1974 $2.00
Brothers, I Loved You All. Sheep Meadow 1978 $8.95 pap. $3.95

CORSO, GREGORY. 1930–

In 1957 Allen Ginsberg wrote of Corso, "He's probably the greatest poet in America, and he's starving in Europe." According to Derek Parker, Corso is a "more introverted poet than Ginsberg. . . . [He] combines in his work an unlikely mixture of street language and slang with lofty poetic rhetoric." Rexroth describes Corso as "a genuine naif. A real wildman with all the charm of a hoodlum . . . a wholesome Antonin Artaud, or a 'sincere' Tristan Tzara." Corso's themes are death and beauty, always in American terms.

Virtually an orphan, Corso was born on Bleecker Street in New York's Greenwich Village, spending his childhood and youth in and out of foster homes. During his numerous prison terms he was introduced to literature by a fellow convict. On his release, he met Ginsberg, who immediately recognized his talent and helped him.

BOOKS BY CORSO

Gasoline: The Vestal Ladies on Brattle. Intro. by Allen Ginsberg, *Pocket Poets Ser.* City Lights 1958 new ed. pap. $2.95
The Happy Birthday of Death. New Directions 1960 pap. $4.95
Long Live Man. New Directions 1962 pap. $3.75
Elegiac Feelings American. New Directions 1970 pap. $3.95

CRANE, (HAROLD) HART. 1899–1932

Hart Crane's tortured, rootless life with its moments of mystic vision and inspired writing is clearly revealed in his letters. He shared with WHITMAN the feeling of the expanse of America and had a passion for the sea. He wrote *Voyages* while living in Brooklyn, overlooking the East River. Crane committed suicide by drowning. Crane's stature as a modernist remains great, despite his relatively small output.

BOOKS BY CRANE

The Complete Poems and Selected Letters and Prose of Hart Crane. Ed. by Brom Weber, *Anchor Literary Lib.* Doubleday 1966 pap. $5.95; *Black and Gold Ser.* Liveright 1946 $19.95
Letters of Hart Crane and His Family, 1923–1932. Ed. by Thomas S. W. Lewis, Columbia Univ. Pr. 1974 $50.00
Robber Rocks: Letters and Memories of Hart Crane, 1923–1932. Ed. by Susan J. Brown, Wesleyan Univ. Pr. 1969 $16.00. A well-edited scholarly edition that gives a glimpse into the day-to-day life of Crane.

BOOKS ABOUT CRANE

Landry, Elaine, and Hilton Landry. *A Concordance to the Poems of Hart Crane.* Rev. by Robert De Mott, *Concordance Ser.* Scarecrow Pr. 1973 $18.00
Lane, Gary. *Concordance to the Poems of Hart Crane. Reference Ser.* Haskell 1972 lib. bdg. $59.95.
Leibowitz, Herbert A. *Hart Crane: An Introduction to the Poetry. Intro. to 20th-Century Poetry Ser.* Columbia Univ. Pr. 1968 $27.50 pap. $11.00

Lewis, Richard W. *The Poetry of Hart Crane: A Critical Study.* Greenwood repr. of 1967 ed. 1978 lib. bdg. $32.25

Lohf, Kenneth A., comp. *The Literary Manuscripts of Hart Crane. Calendars of Amer. Literary Mss.* Ohio State Univ. Pr. 1967 $6.50

Paul, Sherman. *Hart's Bridge.* Univ. of Illinois Pr. 1972 $22.50

Quinn, Vincent. *Hart Crane. Twayne's U.S. Authors Ser.* New College & Univ. Pr. 1963 pap. $3.45

Schwartz, Joseph. *Hart Crane: A Reference Guide.* G. K. Hall 1983 $37.50. Contains a chronology.

Spears, Monroe K. *Hart Crane. Pamphlets on Amer. Writers Ser.* Univ. of Minnesota Pr. 1965 pap. $1.25

Unterecker, John. *Voyager: A Life of Hart Crane.* Farrar 1969 $15.00. This complete and readable biography includes letters and interviews with Crane's contemporaries.

CREELEY, ROBERT. 1926–

Robert Creeley, who has a large readership, belongs to the Black Mountain group of poets, who came to know each other while teaching or studying at Black Mountain College. He is a former editor of the *Black Mountain Review.*

Creeley was born in Massachusetts, attended Harvard University, and has lived abroad in France, Spain, and Guatemala. During World War II, he served in the American Field Service in India and Burma. In 1960 he won the Levinson Prize. Creeley has written a novel, *The Island* (1963), concerning the shifting marital moods of an American husband and wife in Mallorca, where Creeley himself once ran Divers Press, and a collection of short stories, *The Gold Diggers.* He also has taught English at the University of New Mexico in Albuquerque and at the State University of New York at Buffalo. Creeley's work has allegiances to the indigenous American tradition that reaches back to EMILY DICKINSON and THOREAU. His *Collected Poems* is an important testament to a career of integrity molded out of self-doubt and self-knowledge. Few other poets have so trusted their voice, in the physical and psychological sense, to provide them with their only theme and their only defense.

BOOKS BY CREELEY

Collected Poems. Univ. of California Pr. 1983 $28.50

For Love: Poems, 1950–1960. Scribner 1962 pap. $12.50

Charm: Early and Uncollected Poems. Writing Ser. Four Seasons Foundation 1969 pap. $2.50. Contains 75 poems and a preface by Creeley.

A Quick Graph: Collected Notes and Essays. Four Seasons Foundation 1970 $10.00

Hello: A Journal, Feb. 29–May 3, 1976. New Directions 1978 $7.50 pap. $2.95; Small Pr. Dist. 1976 pap. $5.00. An unusual and experimental book.

Later. New Directions 1979 pap. $4.95

Mirrors. New Directions 1983 pap. $6.95

BOOK ABOUT CREELEY

Novik, Mary. *Robert Creeley: An Inventory.* Kent State Univ. Pr. 1973 $12.00

CULLEN, COUNTEE. 1903–1946

Born in New York City, Countee Cullen was separated from his mother in early childhood. He was raised in part by the Reverend Frederick Cullen, a Methodist minister. In high school, Cullen was already praised for his poetry. The poem "Life's Rendezvous" was published in a high school literary magazine and won first prize in a citywide contest. Educated at New York and Harvard universities, Cullen worked as an assistant editor on the Urban League's *Opportunity: A Journal of Negro Life*, writing a monthly literary column. His many awards for poetry included the first Harmon Prize for distinguished achievement in literature by a black writer, and a Guggenheim Fellowship. He taught junior high school in New York City until his death.

BOOKS BY CULLEN

On These I Stand: An Anthology of the Best Poems of Countee Cullen Selected by Himself and Including Six New Poems Never Before Published. Harper 1947 $10.95
Color. Amer. Negro: His History and Lit. Ser. Ayer repr. of 1925 ed. 1970 $14.00. Written while Cullen was concerned primarily with Afro-American themes, this collection includes love poems and poems eliciting sympathy for the outcast.

BOOK ABOUT CULLEN

Shucard, Alan R. *Countee Cullen. Twayne's U.S. Authors Ser.* G. K. Hall 1984 lib. bdg. $15.95

CUMMINGS, E(DWARD) E(STLIN). 1894–1962

A Harvard University graduate, E. E. Cummings, who styled himself e. e. cummings, lived in Greenwich Village and spent his summers on a farm in New Hampshire. Many honors came to him, including the 1958 Bollingen Prize.

In describing his *I—Six Nonlectures*, the *Atlantic* wrote: "Full of originality, high spirits, and aphoristic dicta, they express a credo of intense individualism." Cummings delivered these unconventional lectures while at Harvard in 1952. He also wrote the delightful commentaries for the 50 photographs in *Adventures in Value* (o.p.) by his wife, Marion Morehouse, a fine and sensitive photographer. For a generation or so, Cummings was the very model of the "modern poet"—a difficult, experimenting bohemian. His work now seems more play than theater.

BOOKS BY CUMMINGS

Complete Poems, 1913–1962. Harcourt 1972 $19.95 1980 pap. $11.95. Includes the contents of 12 individual volumes as well as unpublished works.
Poems, 1923–1954. Harcourt 1954 $15.95. Some 600 poems from all collections.
I—Six Nonlectures. Harvard Univ. Pr. 1953 pap. $3.95

BOOK ABOUT CUMMINGS

Firmage, George J. *E. E. Cummings: A Bibliography.* Greenwood repr. of 1960 ed. 1974 lib. bdg. $15.00

DICKEY, JAMES. 1923–

James Dickey is an eccentric personality and one of the most audible voices in poetry the United States produced in the 1960s. Born in Atlanta, Georgia, Dickey was a pilot in World War II and the Korean War. He spent six years in advertising and gave it up in 1961. He was educated at Vanderbilt University and has taught at Rice Institute and the University of Florida. He has been poet-in-residence at Reed and San Fernando State colleges, writer-in-residence at the University of Wisconsin, and consultant in poetry in English to the Library of Congress (1966–68).

Dickey is the author of four collections of critical essays: *The Suspect in Poetry* (1964, o.p.); *Babel to Byzantium: Poets and Poetry Now*, which discusses some 80 contemporary British and American poets; *The Self as Agent* (1970, o.p.); and *Sorties: Journals and New Essays* (1972). Dickey's first novel, *Deliverance* (1969), was a major motion picture, featuring an appearance by Dickey himself as a backwoods sheriff. Dickey composed a poem for the inauguration of President Jimmy Carter.

BOOKS BY DICKEY

Poems 1957–1967. Wesleyan Univ. Pr. 1978 pap. $9.95
The Central Motion: Poems, 1968–1983. Wesleyan Univ. Pr. 1983 $18.50 pap. $8.95
Drowning with Others. Wesleyan Poetry Program 1962 $15.00
Helmets. Wesleyan Poetry Program 1964 $15.00
Buckdancer's Choice. Wesleyan Poetry Program 1965 pap. $6.95
Self-Interviews. 1970. Ed. by Barbara Reiss and James Reiss, Louisiana State Univ. Pr. 1984 pap. $6.95. The poet's criticism of his own work and his opinions on the work of others.
The Zodiac. Doubleday 1976 $6.00. A long poem built on an original Dutch poem.
The Strength of Fields. Doubleday 1979 $8.95. The title poem, written for President Carter's inauguration, shows Dickey's populist spirit in its purest form.
Falling: May Day Sermon and Other Poems. Wesleyan Univ. Pr. 1982 $15.00 pap. $6.95
Puella. Doubleday 1982 $10.95. A book whose title poem celebrates women.
Sorties. Louisiana State Univ. Pr. 1984 pap. $7.95. More of Dickey's opinions about other writers.

BOOKS ABOUT DICKEY

Ashley, Franklin. *James Dickey: A Checklist*. Bruccoli $15.00. A bibliographic work.
Bowers, Neal. *James Dickey: The Poet as Pitchman*. Univ. of Missouri Pr. 1985 $7.95
Weigl, Bruce, and T. R. Hammer, eds. *The Imagination as Glory: Essays on the Poetry of James Dickey*. Univ. of Illinois Pr. 1984 $17.50

DOOLITTLE, HILDA. 1886–1961

[SEE H. D. in this chapter.]

DORN, EDWARD. 1929–

One of the "younger" Black Mountain poets, Edward Dorn was a student of Robert Creeley and Charles Olson. His work is not so much influenced by the Black Mountain school as it is integral to it. A deep sense of the necessities of speech patterns transmitted by projective verse and geography, myth, and prehistoric times puts Dorn particularly close to the work and thought of Olson. In fact, Olson compiled his *Bibliography for Ed Dorn* to reflect this interest in the latter three subjects. Like Olson, Dorn finds his greatest challenge and accomplishment in the long poem. His *Gunslinger* series of books—a continuing epic of the American West ostensibly in a satiric-comic mode but actually a deep expression of the poet's concern with the idea of hero and "free ego"—is already a landmark.

BOOKS BY DORN

The Collected Poems, 1956–1974. Writing Ser. Four Seasons Foundation 1975 $15.00
    pap. $10.00
Geography. Telegraph Bks. 1964 $7.50
Hands Up. Ed. by LeRoi Jones, Corinth Bks. 1964 pap. $1.50
The North Atlantic Tribune. Telegraph Bks. 1967 $7.50
Gunslinger: Books One and Two. 1968–69. Telegraph Bks. 1970 $15.00.
Interviews. Ed. by Donald Allen, *Writing Ser.* Four Seasons Foundation 1980 pap.
    $5.00. Very distinctive views about contemporary poetry.

DUGAN, ALAN. 1923–

The *Saturday Review* said of *Poems*, the first volume by the native New Yorker Alan Dugan: "His poetry is a special way of looking at things. . . . Through personal experience of war he shapes universal messages, while he takes history, religion, and mythology and gives them an intimate meaning." This book won the National Book Award and the Pulitzer Prize in 1962, and in the same year the poet won a fellowship in literature at the American Academy in Rome. The *N.Y. Times* found that in *Poems 2* (1963, o.p.) Dugan reveals "a sharp eye for the sights and sounds of New York." In *Poems 3*, Dugan "writes with an anger at society that moves from artless outcry to black resignation in the face of the world's evils, and back again" (*SR*).

BOOKS BY DUGAN

New and Collected Poems, 1961–1983. Amer. Poetry Ser. Ecco Pr. 1983 $17.50. Poems
    from three earlier books: *Poems, Poems 2,* and *Poems 3.*
Poems. Fwd. by Dudley Fitts, *Yale Ser. of Younger Poets* AMS Pr. repr. of 1961 ed.
    $11.00

DUNBAR, PAUL LAURENCE. 1872–1906

The first important black poet in the United States was born in Ohio of parents who had been slaves. He did newspaper work, served on the staff of the Library of Congress, and died of tuberculosis at age 34. His collected poems include four earlier volumes of his poetry, one of them the *Lyrics of Lowly Life* (1896), with the original preface by WILLIAM DEAN HOWELLS.

BOOKS BY DUNBAR

Collected Works. Gordon $600.00

Life and Works: Containing His Complete Poetical Works, His Best Short Stories, Numerous Anecdotes and a Complete Biography. Kraus repr. of 1911 ed. o.p.
Complete Poems. Dodd 1980 pap. $4.95. Includes "Lyrics of Lowly Life," "Lyrics of the Hearthside," "Lyrics of Sunshine," and "Shadow."

BOOK ABOUT DUNBAR

Lawson, V. *Paul Laurence Dunbar Critically Examined.* Gordon Pr. 1941 $59.95

DUNCAN, ROBERT (EDWARD). 1919–

A leading poet of the San Francisco renaissance, Robert Duncan is a member of the international avant-garde. Born in Oakland, California, he has been an editor, a teacher at Black Mountain College, and assistant director of the Poetry Center at San Francisco State College. Highly regarded by fellow nonacademic poets, Duncan's poetry is at once learned and spontaneous. Its form seems at once innate and wrought, complex, and wonderfully musical.

He received the Harriet Monroe Memorial Prize (1960); a Guggenheim Memorial Award (1963); the Levinson Poetry Prize (1964); a National Endowment for the Arts grant (1967); and the Eunice Tietjens Memorial Prize (1967). After a self-imposed silence of many years, Duncan published a challenging volume in 1984, *The Ground Work*, a book he designed himself. He continues to be one of the chief spokesmen for the poem as "wisdom literature" and not just personable expression or artifact.

BOOKS BY DUNCAN

The Opening of the Field. 1960. New Directions rev. ed. 1973 pap. $4.95
Roots and Branches. 1964. New Directions 1969 pap. $4.95
The Years as Catches: First Poems. 1966. Oyez 1977 $3.00. Duncan's first poems (1939–46) with a retrospective introduction by the poet.
Bending the Bow. New Directions 1968 $6.50 pap. $4.95
The Ground Work: Before the War. New Directions 1984 $19.50 pap. $10.50

BOOKS ABOUT DUNCAN

Bertholf, Robert, and Ian W. Reid, eds. *Robert Duncan: Scales of the Marvelous.* New Directions Insights 1979 pap. $4.00
Ironwood 22: Robert Duncan—A Special Issue. Includes part of Duncan's book on H. D. (Hilda Doolittle), plus important Duncan letters and essays by several critics.

EBERHART, RICHARD. 1904–

Born in Minnesota and educated at Dartmouth College and Cambridge (on a Rhodes Scholarship) and Harvard universities, Richard Eberhart has served as consultant in poetry at the Library of Congress (1959–66), and has won the Bollingen Prize (1962) and the Pulitzer Prize (1966). Dame Edith Sitwell remarked of his poems that they have "strong intellectual sinews, are poems of ideas, but have a warmth of humanity as strong as their intellect." He is a member of the National Institute of Arts and Letters.

BOOKS BY EBERHART

Collected Poems, 1930–1976. Oxford 1976 $22.50
Selected Poems, 1930–1965. New Directions 1966 pap. $3.95

BOOKS ABOUT EBERHART

Mills, Ralph J., Jr. *Richard Eberhart. Pamphlets on Amer. Writers Ser.* Univ. of Minnesota Pr. 1966 pap. $1.25
Van Dore, Wade. *Richard Eberhart: Poet of Life in Death.* Amer. Studies Pr. 1982 pap. $1.50

ELIOT, T(HOMAS) S(TEARNS). 1888–1965

[SEE Chapter 7 in this volume.]

FROST, ROBERT. 1874–1963

Frost was, in a sense, our national poet laureate. Not only was he made Vermont's official poet laureate, but he received a special congressional medal during the Eisenhower administration and was invited to read a poem at the inauguration of President John Kennedy in January 1961. Such official recognition was ironic in view of the fact that his first books of poetry had to be published in England. (But this says as much about the moribund state of poetry in the United States at the turn of the century as it does about any experimentalism on Frost's part.) Such ironies involved with the line between innovation and official recognition are very much part of Frost's career. Frost's poetry is written in traditional language and form, but its content is often at odds with its surface features. Despite the easily recognizable subjects of pastoral quietism and New England dutifulness, Frost's poetry is often entangled with the issues of nihilism and despair. Frost did win recognition, however, including the Pulitzer Prize in 1924, 1931, 1937, and 1943 and honorary degrees from 17 colleges.

Although he was descended from New Englanders, Frost was born and raised in San Francisco; he returned to New England at the time of his father's death in 1884. He studied at Dartmouth College and Harvard University, but gave up college for teaching. In 1912 he went to England, where he lived for three years. After his return to the United States, he taught at various colleges and helped found the Bread Loaf School in Middlebury, Vermont. Both President Kennedy and Archibald MacLeish spoke on October 26, 1963, at a special Amherst College convocation held in conjunction with the dedication of the $3.5 million library built in honor of the poet.

Frost will no doubt be read first as a traditional poet, but the discriminating will also continue to turn to him as a spokesman for a special brand of modernist irony. His prose writings about the art and craft of poetry, although limited in volume, have had a considerable influence, and they contain many clues to his elaborate cunning and quick imagination, as well as his use of colloquial rhythms and conscious artifice. He was an artist who took great pains to hide his pain and still continue to speak truthfully about what he had seen.

BOOKS BY FROST

The Poetry of Robert Frost. Ed. by Edward C. Lathem, Holt 1969 $17.50 1979 pap. $9.95. An indispensable book.
Selected Poems. Ed. by Robert Graves, *Rinehart Ed*. Holt text ed. 1963 pap. $12.95
The Selected Letters of Robert Frost. Comp. by Lawrance Thompson, Holt 1964 $10.00
Robert Frost and Sidney Cox: Forty Years of a Friendship. Ed. by William Evans, Univ. Pr. of New England 1981 $25.00. Includes 50 previously unpublished letters.

BOOKS ABOUT FROST

Brower, Reuben A. *The Poetry of Robert Frost: Constellations of Intention*. Oxford 1963 o.p. This thorough appraisal by a professor of English at Harvard University has hardly been surpassed in the last two decades.
Cook, Reginald L. *Robert Frost: A Living Voice. New Eng. Writers Ser*. Univ. of Massachusetts Pr. 1974 $17.50. Transcripts of several talks given by Frost in the last ten years of his life.
Cox, James M., ed. *Robert Frost: A Collection of Critical Essays*. Prentice-Hall 1962 $12.95
Francis, Robert. *Frost: Time to Talk, Conversations and Indiscretions Recorded by Robert Francis. New Eng. Writers Ser*. Univ. of Massachusetts Pr. 1972 $7.50. These conversations and reminiscences are drawn from the author's journals during the 1930s and 1950s.
Frost, Lesley. *New Hampshire's Child: Derry Journals of Lesley Frost*. State Univ. of New York Pr. 1969 $44.50. A handsome facsimile edition of Frost's daughter's journals. The reader catches a fascinating glimpse of Frost's personality.
Gerber, Philip L. *Robert Frost. Twayne's U.S. Authors Ser*. G. K. Hall 1982 rev. ed. lib bdg. $12.50 1984 pap. $6.95; *Twayne's U.S. Authors Ser*. New College & Univ. Pr. 1966 pap. $3.45
Lentricchia, Frank. *Robert Frost: Modern Poetics and the Landscapes of the Self*. Duke Univ. Pr. 1975 $15.75
Poirier, Richard. *Robert Frost: The Work of Knowing*. Oxford 1977 $22.50 pap. $7.95. Frost viewed as a modernist master.
Pritchard, William H. *Frost: A Literary Life Reconsidered*. Oxford 1985 $15.95. Seeks to offset the negative view of Frost as a person that emerges from the Thompson biography.
Thompson, Lawrance, ed. *Robert Frost: The Early Years, 1874–1915*. Holt 1966 o.p. Thompson received the Melville Cane Award for this definitive early biography.
———. *Robert Frost: The Years of Triumph, 1915–1938*. Holt 1970 o.p. This second volume of the projected three-volume biography of Robert Frost evinces the same depth and perceptiveness as the award-winning *The Early Years*.
Winnick, R. H., and Lawrance Thompson, eds. *Robert Frost: The Later Years, 1938–1963*. Holt 1977 o.p. Though currently out of print, Thompson's three-volume biography is one of the most important studies of a major American poet to appear in the last two decades.

GINSBERG, ALLEN. 1926–

"I saw the best minds of my generation destroyed by madness. . . ." So begin the prophetic intonations of *Howl*, Ginsberg's strong indictment of his society. *Howl*, now acclaimed as *The Waste Land* of our time, which was first published in 1956 with an introduction by William Carlos Williams, created an immediate sensation. The first edition, printed in England for

Lawrence Ferlinghetti's City Lights Books, was seized by customs and impounded until cleared of obscenity charges by a San Francisco court. This publishing event, coupled with the appearance of JACK KEROUAC's novel *On the Road*, brought into focus a new movement in the literary world—Beat writing.

Ginsberg describes himself as "the son of Naomi Ginsberg, Russian émigré, and Louis Ginsberg, lyric poet and school teacher." In 1968 father and son gave a joint poetry reading at the Brooklyn Academy of Music. The younger Ginsberg was born in Paterson, New Jersey, and attended Columbia University. Since then he has traveled extensively.

His later poetry is concerned with subjects of contemporary interest, including drugs, sexual disorder, voluntary poverty, and rejection of society. Ginsberg is a serious poet with a serious message, and a phenomenon both critical and representative of American literary traditions.

BOOKS BY GINSBERG

Collected Poems, 1947–1980. Harper 1984 $21.63. Includes annotations and photographs, as well as the important prefaces and afterwords to the separate volumes.

Howl and Other Poems. Pocket Poets Ser. City Lights 1956 pap. $2.95

Kaddish and Other Poems, 1958–1960. Pocket Poets Ser. City Lights 1960 pap. $2.95. The title poem is perhaps the most important elegy by a postwar American poet.

The Empty Mirror: Early Poems. Corinth Bks. 1961 pap. $3.50

Reality Sandwiches: Poems 1953–1960. City Lights 1963 pap. $3.50

(and William Burroughs). *The Yage Letters*. City Lights 1963 pap. $3.00. Written in 1953 when Burroughs was in South America.

Planet News. Pocket Poets Ser. City Lights 1970 signed ed. $15.00 pap. $3.50. Forty poems on the United States, Indian religions, and cosmology.

Indian Journals: March 1962–May 1963. City Lights 1970 $6.50 pap. $3.00. With drawings and photographs by Ginsberg, this is a journal of a trip through northern India.

The Fall of America: Poems of These States, 1965–1971. Pocket Poets Ser. City Lights 1972 pap. $4.00. Continuation of *Planet News* with afterwords by Ginsberg. Winner of the National Book Award (1974).

Journals: Early Fifties–Early Sixties. Grove 1977 pap. $6.95

Mind Breaths: Poems, 1972–1977. City Lights 1978 pap. $3.50

BOOK ABOUT GINSBERG

Kramer, Jane. *Allen Ginsberg in America*. Random 1970 o.p. An interesting journalistic book about the poet.

GLÜCK, LOUISE. 1943–

Born in New York City and raised on Long Island, Glück studied at Sarah Lawrence College and Columbia University. She has won numerous awards, including grants from the Rockefeller Foundation, the National Endowment for the Arts, and the Guggenheim Foundation. She lives in Vermont and teaches at Goddard College. Although Glück's poetry originally resembled the work of confessional poets, it has become more entranced with myth and transcendental longings.

Books by Glück

The House on Marshland. Amer. Poetry Ser. Ecco Pr. 1976 pap .$4.95
Descending Figure. 1980. *Amer. Poetry Ser.* Ecco Pr. 1983 pap. $5.95
Firstborn. Amer. Poetry Ser. Ecco Pr. 1983 pap. $5.95

HALL, DONALD. 1928–

Donald Hall was born in New Haven, Connecticut, and attended Harvard and Oxford universities. The poem "Exile" from his first collection, *Exile and Marriages* (1955, o.p.), won the Newdigate Prize in England.

Hall has been poetry editor for the *Paris Review.* He has edited *Contemporary American Poetry* and (with Robert Pack) *New Poets of England and America.* He is also the editor of several anthologies, including *Modern Stylists: Writers on the Art of Writing;* and he is also the author of *Henry Moore: The Life and Work of a Great Sculptor.* He lives on a farm in New Hampshire that his family has occupied for generations.

Books by Hall

String Too Short to Be Saved: Recollections of Summers on a New England Farm. 1961. Godine (Nonpareil Bks.) 1979 pap. $7.95. About his childhood on his grandfather's farm; in prose.
Goatfoot Milktongue Twinbird. Poets on Poetry Ser. Univ. of Michigan Pr. 1976 pap. $7.95. Essays on many topics, especially the sources of poetry.
Kicking the Leaves. Harper 1978 pap. $4.95. Many of these poems deal with life on the family farm.
Remembering Poets: Reminiscences and Opinions. Harper 1979 o.p. Deals with Dylan Thomas, Pound, and Eliot.

HASS, ROBERT. 1941–

Robert Hass was born in San Francisco and studied at St. Mary's College and Stanford University. He has taught at the State University of New York in Buffalo and the University of California, Berkeley. Haas was recently awarded a MacArthur Foundation fellowship, and his book of prose, *Twentieth Century Pleasures,* was the winner in the criticism category of the National Book Critics Circle Award (1985). It contains some very interesting writing about contemporary poetry and other subjects. Hass's poetry combines great skill with intelligence and lyric grace. Few of his contemporaries can match his use of cultural allusion meshed with a sensitivity to shades of feeling and tenuous but deep moments of meditative insight. His first book was a selection in the *Yale Series of Younger Poets.*

Books by Hass

Field Guide. Yale Ser. of Younger Poets 1973 $12.00 pap. $5.95
Praise. Amer. Poetry Ser. Ecco Pr. 1979 $7.95 1980 pap. $4.95

H. D. (HILDA DOOLITTLE). 1886–1961

Born in Bethlehem, Pennsylvania, Hilda Doolittle was educated at Bryn Mawr College. In 1911, after a visit abroad, she helped to organize the imagists with Ezra Pound. She married Richard Aldington, the English poet and novelist, whom she later divorced. Written in poetic prose, her poignant and subtle *Tribute to Freud: With Unpublished Letters by Freud to the Author* (o.p.) is a record of her memories of her analytical experiences in 1933–34, a memoir of FREUD (see Vol. 3) in London in 1938–39, and a description of the impact of his unique personality. (A more recent edition published by David Godine in 1974 contains a fuller text of this intriguing work.) In *Palimpsest* (1926) she explored the difficulties a woman finds trying to cultivate both love and art in a world that is ugly, vulgar, and violent. Her novel *Bid Me to Live: A Madrigal* (1960, o.p.), about a woman's loneliness and self-discovery during World War I, is a poetic stream-of-consciousness study. She lived in London from 1911 through the bombings of two world wars and spent her later years in Zurich, Switzerland, coming to New York only for brief visits. She received the Brandeis University Creative Arts Award (1959) and the award of merit medal for poetry (1960) from the American Academy of Arts and Letters—the first time the latter was awarded to a woman. Her importance as a model for women writers has grown steadily, and her stature as a modernist innovator, as well as foremost Imagist poet, is assured.

BOOKS BY H. D. (HILDA DOOLITTLE)

Collected Poems, 1912–1944. Ed. by Louis Martz, New Directions 1983 $35.00
Selected Poems of H. D. Grove 1957 pap. $8.95. Forty-six poems, including excerpts from each of the three long poems in *Trilogy.*
Hermetic Definition. New Directions 1972 pap. $4.95
Trilogy: The Walls Do Not Fall; Tribute to the Angels; The Flowering of the Rod. New Directions 1973 pap. $5.95

BOOKS ABOUT H. D. (HILDA DOOLITTLE)

Friedman, Susan S. *Psyche Reborn: The Emergence of H. D.* Indiana Univ. Pr. 1981 $22.50
Quinn, Vincent. *H. D.* Irvington 1967 lib. bdg. $15.95; *Twayne's U.S. Authors Ser.* New College & Univ. Pr. 1967 pap. $3.45
Robinson, Janice. *H. D.: The Life and Work of an American Poet.* Houghton Mifflin 1982 $17.95

HOWARD, RICHARD. 1929–

Richard Howard was born in Cleveland and educated at Columbia University and the Sorbonne. Noted for his translations of French literature, including the works of ROBBE-GRILLET (see Vol. 2) and the memoirs of Charles de Gaulle, Howard is also the author of one of the more important books on contemporary American poetry, *Alone with America,* and a reviewer and critic for *Poetry* magazine. He was awarded a Guggenheim Fellowship for poetry in 1966–67.

Howard's most notable poetic achievement is his fine adaptation of BROWNING's dramatic monologues, first compiled in *Untitled Subjects.* Harold

Bloom writes of them: "Richard Howard's dramatic monologues with their intricate blendings of our emergent sensibility and the anguish and splendor of the great Victorians represent one of the handful of surprising and refreshing inventions in American poetry of the Sixties."

BOOKS BY HOWARD

Quantities. Wesleyan Poetry Program 1962 $15.00 pap. $4.95
The Damages. Wesleyan Poetry Program 1967 $15.00 pap. $6.95
Untitled Subjects. 1969. Atheneum 1983 pap. $6.95
Findings: A Book of Poems. Atheneum 1971 pap. $3.95
Two-Part Inventions. Atheneum 1974 pap. $4.95. Poems built out of dialogues between famous people, most of them writers.
Fellow Feelings. Atheneum 1976 pap. $4.95
Misgivings. Atheneum 1979 pap. $4.95. Includes a series of poems about the subjects of the great French photographer Nadar.
Alone with America. Atheneum 1980 $25.00 pap. $12.95

HUGHES, LANGSTON. 1902–1967

Langston Hughes was known as the chronicler of Harlem. As compared to black writers who came after him, "Hughes' approach to racial matters was more wry than angry, sly than militant" (*PW*). But he helped set the mood for the present firmness on the part of his people and deserves credit for improvements in their condition. Born in Missouri and educated in the Middle West, he was discovered, while working as a busboy in Washington, D.C., by Vachel Lindsay. He was in no sense a traditional poet, but took his poetic form and material from folk sources, a great deal of his work expressing in words the spirit of the musical blues. With Countee Cullen, he was outstanding in the Harlem literary renaissance of the 1920s.

BOOKS BY HUGHES

The Langston Hughes Reader. 1958. Braziller 1981 $15.00. Comprehensive edition of poems, songs, plays, and prose.
Selected Poems of Langston Hughes. 1959. Random 1974 pap. $4.95. Spanning his career from 1926 to 1958.

BOOKS ABOUT HUGHES

Berry, Faith. *Langston Hughes: Before and Beyond Harlem.* Lawrence Hill 1983 $19.95 pap. $12.95
Larson, Norita D. *Langston Hughes, Poet of Harlem. People to Remember Ser.* Creative Ed. 1981 lib. bdg. $8.95

HUGO, RICHARD. 1923–1982

Born in Seattle, Washington, Richard Hugo served in the army in World War II. Some of his experiences are recounted in his book of prose, *The Triggering Town: Lectures and Essays on Poetry and Writing.* His work was twice nominated for the National Book Award and he has received the Theodore Roethke Prize. He worked for the Boeing Company in Seattle for more than a decade before directing the Creative Writing Program at the University of

Montana. Shortly before his death, he was named the judge in the *Yale Series of Younger Poets*.

Hugo's poetry is plainspoken and almost shy of any literary overtones. "I had the need to relive over and over my early personal sense of defeat to some sort of poetic fulfillment," he claimed, and his poetry often deals with anguished loneliness and social failure. It has more affinity with the fiction of SHERWOOD ANDERSON and even BRET HARTE than with the verbal dexterity of high modernism.

BOOKS BY HUGO

Making Certain It Goes On: The Collected Poems of Richard Hugo. Norton 1984 $25.00
Selected Poems. Norton 1979 $5.95
The Lady in Kicking Horse Reservoir. Norton 1973 pap. $4.95
What Thou Lovest Well, Remains American: Poems. Norton 1975 $7.95
31 Letters and 13 Dreams: Poems. Norton 1977 $7.95 pap. $2.95
The Triggering Town: Lectures and Essays on Poetry and Writing. Norton 1979 $3.95
The Right Madness on Skye: Poems. Norton 1980 $12.95 pap. $5.95

IGNATOW, DAVID. 1914–

David Ignatow has been an instructor at the New School for Social Research (1964–65) and a lecturer at the Universities of Kentucky and Kansas and Vassar College. He was poet-in-residence at York College of the City University of New York in 1969, and has been a member of the faculty at Columbia University since 1969. He is the recipient of the National Institute of Arts and Letters Award (1964), a Guggenheim Fellowship (1965–66), a Shelley Memorial Prize (1966), and a Rockefeller grant (1968–69). In his *Notebooks* as much as in his poems, Ignatow is the recorder of the anxieties of middle-class life in an urbanized, industrialized world.

BOOKS BY IGNATOW

Poems, 1934–1969. Wesleyan Univ. Pr. 1970 pap. $10.95. The collected poems to date, including *Poems* (1948), *The Gentle Weight Lifter* (1955), *Say Pardon* (1961), *Figures of the Human* (1964), and *Rescue the Dead* (1968).
Notebooks. 1974. Ed. by Ralph J. Mills, Jr., Sheep Meadow 1981 $9.75 pap. $7.95
Rescue the Dead. Wesleyan Poetry Program 1968 $15.00
Whisper to the Earth. Atlantic Monthly Pr. 1981 $10.95 pap. $6.95

JARRELL, RANDALL. 1914–1965

In 1961, Randall Jarrell's *The Woman at the Washington Zoo* (1960) won the National Book Award. It was said that "each poem . . . has his usual expert technical skill in use of rhyme, of assonance, meter and imagery."

Poet, critic, novelist, and teacher, Jarrell was born in Nashville, Tennessee. He graduated from Vanderbilt University, where he received his M.A., and taught at the University of Texas, Sarah Lawrence College, and the Woman's College of the University of North Carolina. He won a Guggenheim Fellowship (1947) and was awarded a grant from the National Institute of Arts and Letters (1951). In 1956–58, Jarrell served as poetry consultant at the Library of Congress; later he became literary editor of *The Nation* and poetry editor for the *Partisan Review* and the *Yale Review*.

Jarrell's fictional comedy *Pictures from an Institution* (1954) is a brilliant comment on college faculty capers. *A Sad Heart at the Supermarket: Essays and Fables* (1962, o.p.) contains his ironic observations on the decline in taste, learning, and culture in the United States. He was also the author of a number of children's books. Fatally injured when hit by a car in Chapel Hill, North Carolina, in October 1965, Jarrell was one of the finest of the poet-critics who flourished during the era of new critical formalism.

BOOKS BY JARRELL

Complete Poems. Farrar 1969 $25.00 pap. $12.95
Selected Poems, Including The Woman at the Washington Zoo. Atheneum text ed. 1964
   pap. $5.95
Kipling, Auden & Co.: Essays and Reviews, 1935–1964. Farrar 1980 $17.95 pap. $9.95.
   This selection demonstrates Jarrell's critical acuity.

BOOKS ABOUT JARRELL

Ferguson, Suzanne. *Poetry of Randall Jarrell. Southern Literary Studies.* Louisiana
   State Univ. Pr. 1971 o.p. In this first major critical study of Jarrell, Ferguson sur-
   veys the poetry chronologically.
Jarrell, Mary, ed. *Randall Jarrell's Letters: An Autobiographical and Literary Selection.*
   Houghton Mifflin 1985 $29.95

JEFFERS, ROBINSON. 1887–1962

After years of traveling, Robinson Jeffers settled on a wild, sea-beaten cliff at Carmel, California, in what was virtually a literary hermitage, and there set down the tragic folktales of northern California in ironic epic. Jeffers was a poet concerned with cruelty and horror, whose dramatic narratives are filled with scenes of blood and lust, and whose verse shows vigorous beauty and great originality. He was a poet who is not easily contained within the regular framework of literary history.

BOOKS BY JEFFERS

Selected Poetry. Random 1938 $20.00. Some 125 poems arranged chronologically; se-
   lected by the poet and his wife.
The Beginning and the End and Other Poems. Random 1963 $10.95

BOOKS ABOUT JEFFERS

Brophy, Robert J. *Robinson Jeffers: Myth, Ritual and Symbolism in His Narrative Poems.* Shoe String repr. of 1973 ed. 1976 $23.00
Coffin, Arthur B. *Robinson Jeffers: Poet of Inhumanism.* Univ. of Wisconsin Pr. 1971
   $32.50. A scholarly work arguing that Jeffers was more influenced by Nietzsche
   and the cynical view of history than by Schopenhauer.
Vardamis, Alex A. *Critical Reputation of Robinson Jeffers: A Bibliographical Study.*
   Shoe String (Archon) 1972 $23.00. A brief discussion of the work and life of Jef-
   fers with a thorough bibliography.

JOHNSON, JAMES WELDON. 1871–1938

James Weldon Johnson was the first incumbent of the Spence Chair of Creative Literature at Fisk University. He was an educator, poet, author, and composer, whose books are classics of black literature. *God's Trombones* (1927) is considered his richest book of poems. *The Autobiography of an Ex-Colored Man* (1912) is a useful source book on the life of the black man in America. He edited *American Negro Poetry: An Anthology* and, with his brother J. Rosamond Johnson, *Lift Every Voice and Sing*.

BOOKS BY JOHNSON

God's Trombones: Seven Sermons in Verse. Penguin Poets Ser. 1976 pap. $3.95; Viking 1927 $13.95
Along This Way: The Autobiography of James Weldon Johnson. Civil Liberties in Amer. History Da Capo repr. of 1933 ed. 1973 lib. bdg. $49.50. Johnson's autobiography.

BOOK ABOUT JOHNSON

Levy, Eugene. *James Weldon Johnson: Black Leader, Black Voice*. Ed. by John H. Franklin. *Negro Amer. Biographies & Autobiographies Ser.* Univ. of Chicago Pr. 1973 $20.00 1976 pap. $5.95

JUSTICE, DONALD. 1925–

Donald Justice studied at the Universities of Miami, Iowa, and Stanford, and has taught at the Universities of Missouri, Syracuse, and California at Irvine, and the Writers Workshop of the University of Iowa, where he exercised great influence on a whole generation of poets, such as Mark Strand and Charles Wright. Justice currently teaches at the University of Florida. He has edited the *Collected Poems of Weldon Kees*. The Pulitzer Prize was awarded to his *Selected Poems* (1979) and he has won the Lamont Prize (1960) and the Harriet Monroe Memorial Prize, as well as grants from the Rockefeller and Guggenheim Foundations. Justice's poems are generally short and ironic. His reticence is never spoiled by cynicism, nor is his humor lightened by triviality. He sees life through the frame of a certain American survivalism, and his sensibility is singular and yet representative.

BOOKS BY JUSTICE

Selected Poems. Atheneum 1979 $10.95 pap. $7.95
The Summer Anniversaries. Wesleyan Poetry Program 1960 $15.00 pap. $6.95
Night Light. 1967. Wesleyan Univ. Pr. rev. ed. 1981 $15.00 pap. $6.95
Departures. Atheneum 1973 pap. $2.95

KINNELL, GALWAY. 1927–

A New Englander by birth, Galway Kinnell is a poet who eludes easy categorization. His poetry at its height speaks of city as well as country. Indeed, his "The Avenue Bearing the Initial of Christ into the New World" is a kind of literary landmark for New York City's lower East Side. At his best in long poems—his recent *The Book of Nightmares* is one 75-page poem—Kinnell is most famous for his masterpiece "The Bear," in which a hunter unites with the hunted and the poet unites with the prey and the predator. The large-ness of his vision is coupled with an intense ability to weave a detailed tap-estry out of American life and experience.

Kinnell has also written a novel, *Black Light* (1980), set in the Middle East. He has traveled extensively in Europe and the Middle East and has taught in Grenoble, France. Educated at Princeton University and the University of Rochester, Kinnell was the winner of a Fulbright Fellowship to study in Paris. His awards include a Guggenheim Fellowship (1961–62), a National Institute of Arts and Letters grant (1961), a Rockefeller grant (1967–68), the American Book Award (1983), and a Pulitzer Prize (1983). He has also translated poetry from the French.

BOOKS BY KINNELL

Selected Poems. Houghton Mifflin 1982 $12.50 pap. $6.95. This book won the Pulitzer Prize and the American Book Award.
The Book of Nightmares. Houghton Mifflin 1971 pap. $6.95. A book-length poem.
The Avenue Bearing the Initial of Christ into the New World: Poems, 1946–1964. Houghton Mifflin 1974 pap. $9.95
Walking Down the Stairs: Selections from Interviews. Ed. by Donald Hall, *Poets on Poetry Ser.* Univ. of Michigan Pr. 1978 pap. $7.95
Mortal Acts, Mortal Words: A Collection of Poems. Houghton Mifflin 1980 $10.95 pap. $5.95

KOCH, (JAY) KENNETH. 1925–

Born in Cincinnati, Ohio, Kenneth Koch began writing at age five and became serious about it at age 17. After serving in the army, he received his B.A. from Harvard University and, later, his Ph.D. from Columbia University, where he now teaches. He has taught creative writing to children and, using works of his own pupils as examples, has written several books on the subject, notably *Wishes, Lies and Dreams: Teaching Children to Write Poetry* (1970) and the most recent *Rose, Where Do You Get That Red?* (1973). Koch is the recipient of a Fulbright Fellowship (1950–51), a Guggenheim Fellowship (1961), and an Ingram-Merrill Foundation Fellowship (1969).

Koch is associated with the New York school of poets. Much of his early work was influenced largely by Jacques Prevert, among others, but his poetry has since taken on a simpler and more realistic style. Like other New York poets, Koch has been actively interested in theater, and many of his plays, including *Little Red Riding Hood*, *The Election*, and *Perides*, have been performed by off-Broadway groups.

BOOKS BY KOCH

Selected Poems 1950–82. Random 1985 $17.95 pap. $9.95
Days and Nights. Random 1982 $10.50

KUNITZ, STANLEY (JASSPON). 1905–

Kunitz served in World War II as a private and later taught at Bennington College in Vermont. He translated from the Russian and did much to popularize the work of the poets YEVTUSHENKO (see Vol. 2) and Voznesensky.

His *Selected Poems* won the Pulitzer Prize (1958), and he has been elected to the National Institute of Arts and Letters. Robert Lowell said of him, "He has been one of our masters for years."

BOOKS BY KUNITZ

Selected Poems, 1928–1978. Atlantic Monthly Pr. 1979 $12.50 pap. $6.95
Testing-Tree: Poem. Atlantic Monthly Pr. text ed. 1971 pap. $3.95. Thirty new poems
   including the four-page title poem.

LEVERTOV, DENISE. 1923–

Born in Essex, England, Denise Levertov became a U.S. citizen after her marriage to Mitchell Goodman, the writer who was indicted, with BENJAMIN SPOCK (see Vol. 5) and the Rev. William Sloane Coffin, for his antiwar activities. She came to New York to live in 1948.

Levertov acknowledges that her writing was influenced by William Carlos Williams, Charles Olson, and Robert Duncan. After her first book, *The Double Image* (o.p.), was published in England in 1946, she did not produce a volume until 1957, when City Lights brought out *Here and Now* (o.p.). In 1961 she was poetry editor for the *Nation*, and in 1965 she received the grant in literature from the National Institute of Arts and Letters. Her essays collected in *The Poet in the World* and *Light Up the Cave* are written with a penetrating intelligence. She is a poet of reverence and fierce moral drive.

BOOKS BY LEVERTOV

Collected Earlier Poems, 1940–1960. New Directions 1979 $9.50
Poems, 1960–1967. New Directions 1983 $14.50 pap. $6.25. Contains three previous
   volumes.
O Taste and See. New Directions 1964 pap. $3.95
Relearning the Alphabet. New Directions 1970 $6.00 pap. $3.95
To Stay Alive. New Directions 1971 $6.50 pap. $4.95
Footprints: Poems. New Directions 1972 pap. $4.95. A book of reflective poems writ-
   ten concurrently with *Relearning the Alphabet* and *To Stay Alive.*
The Poet in the World. New Directions 1973 $9.50 pap. $4.95. Contains essays and in-
   terviews.
The Freeing of the Dust. New Directions 1975 pap. $4.95
Life in the Forest. New Directions 1978 $8.00 pap. $4.95
Light Up the Cave. New Directions 1981 $15.95 pap. $6.95. Prose essays about poetry.

BOOKS ABOUT LEVERTOV

Atchity, John K. *Denise Levertov: An Interview.* New London Pr. 1980 $10.00 pap.
   $3.95
Wagner, Linda W. *Denise Levertov. Twayne's U.S. Authors Series.* New College and
   Univ. Pr. 1967 pap. $5.95

LINDSAY, (NICHOLAS) VACHEL. 1879–1931

The appeal of Vachel Lindsay's poetry is first and foremost one of sound. Many of the poems are meant to be chanted aloud, intoned, and sung. The poet was a phenomenon in his day, who became famous for the recitation of his poems. He preached a gospel of beauty expressed in almost primitive cadences; "The Congo" is a poem that became enormously popular. His early art studies under Robert Henri gave him the ability to illustrate his own poems, and he developed an elaborate theory of art that has gone largely ignored.

BOOKS BY LINDSAY

Collected Poems. 1923. Macmillan rev. ed. 1925 $19.95. Illustrated by Lindsay.
Selected Poems. Ed. by Mark Harris, Macmillan 1963 $12.95
Adventures, Rhymes and Designs: Early Writings. Intro. by Robert F. Sayre, Eakins 1968 $10.95 pap. $6.95
Letters of Vachel Lindsay. Ed. by Marc Chenetier, *Amer. Cultural Heritage Ser.* Burt Franklin 1979 $21.95. An important volume.
Johnny Appleseed and Other Poems. 1928. Buccaneer Bks. repr. 1981 lib. bdg. $11.95; Harmony Raine 1981 lib. bdg. $11.95. A selection made chiefly with children in mind.

BOOK ABOUT LINDSAY

Masters, Edgar Lee. *Vachel Lindsay: A Poet in America.* Biblo & Tannen repr. of 1935 ed. 1969 $10.00. A sensitively written and informative biography that is more personal than critical.

LOGAN, JOHN. 1923–

Born in Red Oak, Iowa, educated at Coe College, the University of Iowa, Iowa City, and Georgetown University, John Logan found inspiration for his early poetical works in his conversion to Catholicism. Influenced primarily by RAINER MARIA RILKE (see Vol. 2), his poetry has moved from a religious formalistic style to a freedom of line and voice.

Editor of *Choice,* a major magazine of poetry and photography, Logan has received the Indiana School Letters Fellowship (1965, 1969); the Miles Modern Poetry Award (1967); and a Rockefeller grant (1968). He presently resides in Buffalo, New York, where he teaches at the State University. He has read at the Poetry Center of the YMHA in New York City, where he has also taught poetry workshops from time to time.

BOOKS BY LOGAN

The Anonymous Lover. Liveright 1973 $5.95
The Bridge of Change: Poems, 1974–1980. Boa Eds. 1981 $12.00
Only the Dreamer Can Change the Dream. Boa Eds. 1982 pap. $7.95

LOWELL, AMY. 1874–1925

Although Amy Lowell did not look like a poet—she was of ample build and enjoyed smoking cigars in public—she did write verse that was revolutionary in its time. She was known as the leader of the Imagist school, and so thoroughly was she identified with this new precise and delicate style that Ezra Pound jokingly proposed to retitle it "Amygism." She came from a well-known and established Boston family that included JAMES RUSSELL LOWELL as one of her predecessors and was later to produce another well-known poet in the person of Robert Lowell. Louis Untermeyer said of Amy Lowell, in his introduction to *The Complete Poetical Works*, that "her final place in the history of American literature has not been determined, but the importance of her influence remains unquestioned. Underneath her preoccupation with the need for novelty . . . she was a dynamic force." She did much to introduce French literary figures to an American audience with her essays and wrote a large biography of KEATS. For many people she was the figure of the avant-garde poet, bohemian and yet comfortable, apparently experimental yet fully conscious of the need to create a traditional role for herself as a tastemaker and trendsetter. Her posthumous volume *What's O'Clock* was awarded the Pulitzer Prize for poetry in 1926.

BOOKS BY AMY LOWELL

The Complete Poetical Works of Amy Lowell. Intro. by Louis Untermeyer, *Cambridge Eds. Ser.* Houghton Mifflin 1955 $15.00
Selected Poems. Scholarly repr. of 1928 ed. 1971 $22.00

BOOK ABOUT AMY LOWELL

Benvenuto, Richard. *Amy Lowell (Tusas 483).* Twayne's U.S. Authors Ser. G. K. Hall 1985 lib. bdg. $16.95

LOWELL, ROBERT. 1917–1977

Born in Boston, Robert Lowell, great-grandnephew of JAMES RUSSELL LOWELL and distant cousin of Amy Lowell, was a brilliant (but rebellious) member of this distinguished family. He received his B.A. in 1940 from Kenyon College, where he had studied under John Crowe Ransom and had come to know Allen Tate. In 1940 he also converted to Catholicism. During World War II he tried twice to enlist, but by the time he was called his strong feelings against the bombing of civilians had made him a conscientious objector. He was married to Elizabeth Hardwick, editor of the *N.Y. Review of Books*. His subject matter includes New England and its traditions, colored in the early poems by an intellectualized religious symbolism and savage satire against the materialism of modern American life.

Lowell won the 1947 Pulitzer Prize for poetry for *Lord Weary's Castle*, in which religion was beginning to fade as a source of symbolism. In *Life Studies*, which won the National Book Award for poetry in 1960, his poetic focus is portraiture of his New England relatives, through whom he studies himself and his origins. It was with the approach of this volume that critics began to speak of him as a confessional poet. *For the Union Dead*, another collection, continued the exploration of his own and the United States' past and present. Among Lowell's other prizes were the Harriet Monroe Memorial Prize (1961) and the 1962 Bollingen Prize of $2,500, which he shared with Richmond Lattimore, for *Imitations*.

Lowell showed that a poet can concern himself actively with the quality of American life. Bitterly opposed to the Vietnam War, he caused a sensation in 1965 when he rejected a White House invitation to appear at a festival of the arts. In his letter to President Johnson he wrote: "Every serious artist knows that he cannot enjoy public celebration without making subtle public commitments." He demonstrated (notably with NORMAN MAILER at a vast gathering at the Pentagon in 1967), spoke repeatedly in favor of peace, and accompanied Senator Eugene McCarthy during his campaign for the 1968 presidential nomination. Lowell's thoughtful and visionary genius was clearly at once a response and challenge to his times, as well as a reflection of deep-seated historical anxieties. The poetry of Lowell's late period, especially the *Notebook* volumes, portrays the agonies of failed heroic values and the nearly debilitating effects of historical irony. This late poetry shows how all of Lowell's idealism was an inescapable struggle, with only tenuous victories. The self-consciousness and autobiographical shorthand of his final volume, *Day by Day*, give off an uncanny glow of sadness and weary acceptance, one that further typifies the sensibility of a person who was the leading poet of his generation.

BOOKS BY ROBERT LOWELL

Selected Poems. Farrar 1976 $17.50 pap. $10.50

Lord Weary's Castle and The Mills of the Kavanaughs. 1946. Harcourt 2 vols. in 1 1983 pap. $3.95

Imitations. Farrar 1961 pap. $3.95. English versions, not translations, of 66 poems ranging from a passage of Homer to Pasternak.

The Old Glory. 1965. Farrar rev. ed. 1968 o.p. Three plays: *Benito Cereno; My Kinsman Major Molineux;* and *Endecott and the Red Cross.*

Near the Ocean: Poems. Illus. by Sidney Nolan, Farrar 1967 $6.95 pap. $1.95

Life Studies and For the Union Dead. Farrar 1967 pap. $5.25

Prometheus Bound. 1967. Farrar 1969 $5.95. A free adaptation from Aeschylus.

Notebook. 1969. Farrar rev. ed. 1970 $7.50. The new expanded edition of the original *Notebook* includes changes in the original poems and 90 new poems.

The Dolphin. Farrar 1973 $6.95 pap. $2.95. Thirty-two-page poem sequence.

For Lizzie and Harriet. Farrar 1973 $6.95 pap. $2.95. Contains in complete form poems that were published earlier in *Notebook* (1967–68).

History. Farrar 1973 $7.95. Approximately 400 poems, 80 of which had not previously appeared in book form. The remainder appeared in *Notebook* (1967–68).

Day by Day. Farrar 1977 $8.95 pap. $4.95

BOOKS ABOUT ROBERT LOWELL

Axelrod, Steven Gould. *Robert Lowell: Life of Art.* Princeton Univ. Pr. text ed. 1978 $31.00 pap. $11.50

Bell, Vereen. *Robert Lowell: The Nihilist as Hero.* Harvard Univ. Pr. text ed. 1983 $17.50

Hamilton, Ian. *Robert Lowell: A Biography.* Random (Vintage) 1983 o.p. A massive work that sheds important light on Lowell's extremely troubled life.

Martin, Jay. *Robert Lowell.* Pamphlets on Amer. Writers Ser. Univ. of Minnesota Pr. 1970 pap. $1.25. A readable nonscholarly introduction to Lowell's poetry. With selected bibliography on plays, prose, and critical studies.

Meiners, Roger K. *Everything to Be Endured: An Essay on Robert Lowell and Modern Poetry.* Literary Frontiers Ser. Univ. of Missouri Pr. 1970 pap. $8.00

Rudman, Mark. *Robert Lowell: An Introduction to the Poetry.* Columbia Univ. Pr. 1983 $19.95

Williamson, Alan. *Pity the Monsters: The Political Vision of Robert Lowell.* Yale Univ.
  Pr. 1974 o.p. A clear and useful study.
Yenser, Stephen. *Circle to Circle: The Poetry of Robert Lowell.* Univ. of California Pr.
  1976 $34.50

MacLEISH, ARCHIBALD. 1892–1982

  MacLeish was librarian of Congress from 1939 to 1944. During World War
II, he was director of O.F.F. (the first U.S. ministry of information) and later
assistant secretary of state (1944–45). In November 1945, he went to London as chairman of the U.S. delegation to the first general conference of
UNESCO in Paris (1946) and resigned in 1947. Throughout his life Mac-
Leish played a public role as well as a private one and was fearless in battles against censorship, intimidation, and violations of civil liberties. In
1949, he became Boylston Professor at Harvard. *J.B.: A Play in Verse,* the
story of Job transferred to contemporary life, won the 1958 Pulitzer Prize
for drama. MacLeish had already won two previous Pulitzer Prizes in 1932
and 1953. In 1953 he was also awarded the Bollingen Prize in poetry and
the National Book Award.

BOOK BY MACLEISH

New and Collected Poems, 1917–1982. Houghton Mifflin 1985 $19.95 pap. $9.95

BOOKS ABOUT MACLEISH

Falk, Signi L. *Archibald MacLeish. Twayne's U.S. Authors Ser.* New College and Univ.
  Pr. 1965 pap. $5.95
Smith, Grover. *Archibald MacLeish. Pamphlets on Amer. Writers Ser.* Univ. of Minne-
  sota Pr. 1971 pap. $1.25

MASTERS, EDGAR LEE. 1869–1950

  The Kansas-born poet of "Spoon River," Edgar Lee Masters, wrote many
books but continues to be known for only one, so great was the extraordinary success of that performance. The character of the verses—short post-
mortem monologues in a cemetery in epitaph form—is borrowed from the
old *Greek Anthology.* Masters is often regarded as the last best-selling American poet.

BOOKS BY MASTERS

A Book of Verses. 1898. Gordon Pr. $59.95
Spoon River Anthology. 1915. Buccaneer Bks. repr. 1983 lib. bdg. $19.95; Macmillan
  (Collier) new ed. 1962 pap. $3.95; (and *With Additional Poems*) Macmillan text
  ed. 1963 pap. $12.95
Vachel Lindsay: A Poet in America. Biblo & Tannen repr. of 1935 ed. 1969 $10.00
Across Spoon River. 1936. Octagon repr. of 1936 ed. 1969 lib. bdg. $27.50. An autobi-
  ography.
Mark Twain: A Portrait. Biblo & Tannen 1938 $10.00

BOOKS ABOUT MASTERS

Masters, Hardin W. *Edgar Lee Masters: A Biographical Sketchbook about a Great American Author*. Fairleigh Dickinson 1978 $18.00

Wrenn, John H. and Margaret M. Wrenn. *Edgar Lee Masters. Twayne's U.S. Authors Ser.* G. K. Hall 1983 lib. bdg. $13.50

McCLURE, MICHAEL. 1932–

A native midwesterner, Michael McClure is associated with the San Francisco renaissance of the mid-1950s, and his work, in the tradition of BLAKE and Artaud, is prophetic in tone and usually quite experimental on the printed page. His plays *The Beard* and *The Tooth of Crime* are underground theater classics. He is part of the poet's-theater movement that is now being revived on the San Francisco scene.

BOOKS BY McCLURE

Ghost Tantras. Four Seasons Foundation 1969 pap. $2.25

September Blackberries. New Directions 1974 $7.50 pap. $3.25

Jaguar Skies. New Directions 1975 pap. $1.95

Gorf. New Directions 1976 pap. $1.95

Antechamber and Other Poems. New Directions 1978 pap. $2.95

Hymns to St. Geryon (and *Dark Brown*). Grey Fox 1980 pap. $5.95. Two volumes of poetry printed together.

Scratching the Beat Surface. North Point Pr. 1982 $17.50. An important memoir.

Fragments of Perseus. New Directions 1983 pap. $4.95

MERRILL, JAMES. 1925–

James Merrill was born in New York and attended Amherst College, where he later spent a year teaching English. An extensive traveler, he has lived in Italy and now divides his time between Stonington, Connecticut, and Greece. In *First Poems* (1951, o.p.), "Merrill's images derive from both Symbolist and metaphysical sources—substances such as glass, crystal, and flint are linked with apparatuses of one kind or another (compasses, barometers, spectrums, and hourglasses)—and he speaks of the 'machinery of light' and the 'machinery of decay' " (Louise Bogan, *New Yorker*). *Nights and Days* won Merrill a 1967 National Book Award for "his scrupulous and uncompromising cultivation of the poetic art, evidenced in his refusal to settle for an easy and profitable stance."

Merrill's play *The Immortal Husband* has been performed off-Broadway. He has also written two novels, *The Seraglio* (1957, o.p.), about an aging businessman, and *The (Diblos) Notebook*, which was a runner-up for the 1966 National Book Award in fiction. His epic poem *The Changing Light at Sandover* is the most impressive long poem written since the era of the modernist masters. It secures Merrill's place as one of the preeminent poets of his generation and certainly one of the most ambitiously inventive writers of the postwar decades.

BOOKS BY MERRILL

From the First Nine: Poems, 1946–1976. Atheneum 1983 $20.00 pap. $10.95. Merrill's
    selection from the books of lyric poems.
Water Street. Atheneum 1962 pap. $4.95
Nights and Days. Atheneum 1966 pap. $5.95
Fire Screen. Atheneum 1969 pap. $6.95
Braving the Elements. Atheneum 1972 $5.95 pap. $3.95
Divine Comedies. Atheneum 1976 $11.95 pap. $6.95
The Changing Light at Sandover. Atheneum 1982 $25.00 pap. $12.95. Includes
    "Scripts for the Pageant" and "Mirabell: Books of Number" to form an epic-
    length poem.

BOOKS ABOUT MERRILL

Lehman, David, and Charles Berger, eds. *James Merrill: Essays in Criticism.* Cornell
    Univ. Pr. 1982 $25.00
Moffett, Judith. *James Merrill: An Introduction to the Poetry. Intro.* to 20th-Century
    Amer. Poetry Ser. Columbia Univ. Pr. 1984 $19.95

MERWIN, W(ILLIAM) S(TANLEY). 1927–

Born in New York City and educated at Princeton University, W. S. Merwin has lived in Boston, Spain, France, and England. In a short space of
time, he published four volumes of verse and three of translations from the
Spanish. His first book of poetry, *A Mask for Janus* (1952), was sponsored by
the *Yale Series of Younger Poets;* his second, *The Dancing Bears* (1954, o.p.),
won the Kenyon Review Fellowship; and his third, *Green with Beasts* (1960,
o.p.), won a British Poetry Book Society award.

In his early work, Merwin "wrote . . . with a verse technique as dazzling
as that of any poet of his generation" (Peter Davison, *Atlantic*). Merwin has
remained loyal to the modernist dicta to "make it new" and to use no super-
fluous verbiage. But his poetry is essentially based on deep sentiment and
its occasional use of surrealist devices produces a unique, unsteady mix of
genuine emotion and linguistic tensions.

BOOKS BY MERWIN

A Mask for Janus. Yale Ser. of Younger Poets AMS Pr. repr. of 1952 ed. $11.00
The Moving Target. Atheneum 1963 pap. $4.95
The Lice. Atheneum 1967 pap. $6.95
(trans.). *Products of the Perfected Civilization: Selected Writings of Chamfort.* 1969.
    North Point Pr. 1984 pap. $12.50
Carrier of Ladders. Atheneum 1970 pap. $7.95
The Miner's Pale Children: A Book of Prose. Atheneum 1970 pap. $6.95
Writings to an Unfinished Accompaniment. Atheneum 1973 pap. $5.95
The Compass Flower. Atheneum 1977 pap. $5.95
House and Travellers: A Book of Prose. Atheneum 1977 pap. $9.95. Prose poems.
Finding the Islands. North Point Pr. 1982 $11.00 pap. $6.00
Opening the Hand. Atheneum 1983 $13.95 pap. $6.95
Unframed Originals: Recollections. Atheneum 1983 $14.95 pap. $8.95. A book of prose
    memoirs, beautifully written and truly haunting in their nostalgic accuracy.

MILLAY, EDNA ST. VINCENT. 1892–1950

Edna St. Vincent Millay was born in Maine and graduated from Vassar College. She joined the Provincetown Players, acting many leading roles including those of her own plays. Her earliest poem, "Renascence," written when she was 19, first appeared in *The Lyric Year* (1912), an anthology of competitive poems. Its philosophy marked it as one of the most thoughtful poems in the collection. She was awarded the Pulitzer Prize for poetry (1923) for *The Ballad of the Harp Weaver*. As the Bohemian spokesman of early twentieth-century youth, she won further fame with her poetry of love and gaiety and longing and death, especially her sonnets.

BOOKS BY MILLAY

Collected Poems. Ed. by Norma Millay, Harper 1981 pap. $11.49. The collected works without dramatic pieces.
Collected Lyrics. 1943. Harper 1981 pap. $5.72. Millay's own selection.
Collected Sonnets. 1941. Harper 1941 $14.37. Some 175 selected sonnets.
The Letters of Edna St. Vincent Millay. Ed. by Allan Ross McDougall, Greenwood repr. of 1952 ed. 1973 lib. bdg. $24.25
Renascence and Other Poems. Granger Index Repr. Ser. Ayer repr. of 1917 ed. $10.75

BOOKS ABOUT MILLAY

Brittin, Norman A. *Edna St. Vincent Millay. Twayne's U.S. Authors Ser.* New College and Univ. Pr. 1967 pap. $5.95; G. K. Hall rev. ed. 1982 lib. bdg. $13.50
Gray, James. *Edna St. Vincent Millay. Pamphlets on Amer. Writers Ser.* Univ. of Minnesota Pr. 1967 pap. $1.25

MOORE, MARIANNE. 1887–1972

Born in St. Louis, the "first lady of American poetry" Marianne Moore was graduated from Bryn Mawr College in 1909. A few of her friends pirated her work in 1921 and published it under the title *Poems.* On her seventy-fifth birthday, November 15, 1962, she was honored by the National Institute of Arts and Letters and, in a special interview for the *N.Y. Times,* she spoke of her feelings concerning the treatment of poetry: "I'm very doubtful about scholasticizing poetry," she said, "I feel very strongly that poetry should not be an assignment but a joy." Five years later she said: "I wonder that I can bear myself to be in a world where they don't outlaw war." In 1967 Miss Moore received both the MacDowell Medal and a Gold Medal. Mayor John Lindsay of New York City hailed her as "truly the poet laureate of New York City." The famed Rosenbach Museum in Philadelphia has a collection devoted to her work and a detailed replica of a room in her Brooklyn home. Her precision and intricate metrics make her perhaps the leading modernist poet who can intoxicate us with beauty alone.

BOOKS BY MOORE

Complete Poems. Viking 1967 $16.95. Includes the *Collected Poems* (1951); *Like a Bulwark* (1956); *O to Be a Dragon* (1959); *Tell Me, Tell Me* (1966); and a selection of *The Fables of La Fontaine.*

Collected Poems. Macmillan 1951 $10.95. Contains *Selected Poems* (1935); *What Are Years* (1941, o.p.); *Nevertheless* (1944); and *Hitherto Uncollected.*

BOOKS ABOUT MOORE

Costello, Bonnie. *Marianne Moore: Imaginary Possessions.* Harvard Univ. Pr. text ed. 1981 $18.50
Engel, Bernard F. *Marianne Moore. Twayne's U.S. Authors Ser.* New College & Univ. Pr. 1964 pap. $3.45
Nitchie, George W. *Marianne Moore: An Introduction to the Poetry. Intro. to 20th Century Amer. Poetry Ser.* Columbia Univ. Pr. 1969 $24.00 pap. $11.00

NEMEROV, HOWARD. 1920–

Nemerov has become known for his wit and intelligence. *The Blue Swallows* (o.p.) received mixed reviews, but won him the first Roethke Memorial Prize. He also received the Oscar Blumenthal Prize (1958), the Harriet Monroe Memorial Prize (1959), the National Institute and American Academy Award in literature (1961), and the Pulitzer Prize (1978). A lively and uncompromising critic, he has selected for his *Poetry and Fiction: Essays* (o.p.) essays of the seventies, emphasizing twentieth-century literature and the contemporary stance of the critic. *Journal of the Fictive Life* is Nemerov's somewhat grim introspective search for the conditions that make a writer most creative.

BOOKS BY NEMEROV

The Collected Poems of Howard Nemerov. Univ. of Chicago Pr. 1977 $20.00; Univ. of Chicago Pr. (Phoenix Bks.) 1981 $12.50
New and Selected Poems. 1960. Univ. of Chicago Pr. (Phoenix Bks.) 1963 pap. $3.95. Part 1 includes 15 new poems not heretofore collected; Part 2, poems selected from *The Salt Garden* (1955) and *Mirrors and Windows* (1958); Part 3, selected from *The Image and the Law* (1947) and *Guide to the Ruins* (1950), represents his early work.
The Next Room of the Dream: Plays and Two Plays. Univ. of Chicago Pr. (Phoenix Bks.) 1962 pap. $2.45. Poems and two poetic dramas: *Endor* and *Cain.*
Journal of the Fictive Life. 1965. Univ. of Chicago Pr. 1981 pap. $5.95
Gnomes and Occasions. Univ. of Chicago Pr. 1973 pap. $1.95
The Western Approaches. Univ. of Chicago Pr. (Phoenix Bks.) 1975 pap. $3.95
Inside the Onion. Univ. of Chicago Pr. 1984 $9.95

BOOKS ABOUT NEMEROV

Labrie, Ross. *Howard Nemerov. Twayne's U.S. Authors Ser.* G. K. Hall 1980 lib. bdg. $13.50
Meinke, Peter. *Howard Nemerov. Pamphlets on Amer. Writers Ser.* Univ. of Minnesota Pr. 1968 pap. $1.25

O'HARA, FRANK. 1926–1966

Frank O'Hara was born in Baltimore, Maryland, and raised in Worcester, Massachusetts. After serving in the navy during World War II, he graduated from Harvard University, where he met Kenneth Koch and John Ashbery, and helped found the Poet's Theatre. He later studied at the University of

Michigan. In 1951 he moved to New York City, where he became involved with the burgeoning art scene. He was an art critic, worked for *Art News,* and later became associate curator for exhibitions of paintings and sculpture. In the early sixties he became the center of the group to be known as the New York school of poets.

O'Hara's poetry has dreamlike, irrational sequences of images; one of the dominant qualities of his work is its visual imagery, influenced to some degree by the leading painters of the decade, Pollack, Kline, and de Kooning. His work also reflected the pop art culture manifested in movies, advertising, and billboards. At times, however, an almost classic simplicity appears; "To the Harbormaster" is a good example, beginning simply, "I wanted to be sure to reach you,/though my ship was on the way/it got caught/in some moorings. . . ."

O'Hara died tragically when a dune buggy ran over him on Fire Island. In 1972, after his death, he was given the National Book Award for his *Collected Poems.*

BOOKS BY O'HARA

Collected Poems of O'Hara. 1971. Knopf $25.00
Selected Poems. Ed. by Donald M. Allen, Random (Vintage) 1974 pap. $4.95
Meditations in an Emergency. Grove (Everyman's) 1957 pap. $4.95
Second Avenue. Corinth Bks. 1960 pap. $1.25
Lunch Poems. City Lights 1964 pap. $3.95
Art Chronicles, 1954–1966. Braziller 1975 $15.00
Standing Still and Walking in New York. Ed. by Donald M. Allen, Grey Fox 1975 pap. $6.95

BOOK ABOUT O'HARA

Perloff, Marjorie. *Frank O'Hara: Poet among Painters.* Univ. of Texas Pr. text ed. 1979 pap. $7.95

OLSON, CHARLES. 1910–1970

The elder statesman of the Black Mountain school of poets, Charles Olson directly impinged on the work of fellow-teachers Robert Duncan and Robert Creeley as well as students including John Wieners, Jonathan Williams, Joel Oppenheimer, and Edward Dorn. His catalytic theory of poetry, expounded in the essay *Projective Verse* (o.p.), was reprinted in part in William Carlos Williams's *Autobiography* and in Donald M. Allen and Warren Taliman, eds., *The New Poetics of the New American Poetry, 1945–1960.* In his *Selected Writings,* Olson emphasizes "how to restore man to his 'dynamic.' There is too much concern, he feels, with end and not enough with instant. It is not things that are important, but what happens between them. . . . He thinks of poetry as transfers of energy and he reminds us that dance is kinesis, not mimesis" (*N.Y. Times*). *Human Universe and Other Essays* (o.p.) is a collection of interesting pieces on subjects ranging from HOMER (see Vol. 2) to YEATS. *Propioception* (o.p.) is one of Olson's seminal essays on verse and the poet's awareness.

Born in Worcester, Massachusetts, Olson attended Wesleyan, Harvard, and Yale universities. He taught at Harvard University and Clark and Black Mountain colleges. He received two Guggenheim Fellowships and a grant from the Wenner-Gren Foundation to study Mayan hieroglyphs in Yucatan. His involvement with primitive Indian cultures stimulated his interest in mysticism and the drug culture.

BOOKS BY OLSON

Selected Writings. Ed. by Robert Creeley, New Directions 1967 pap. $6.95. Poetry and criticism, including selections from *The Maximus Poems, Projective Verse*, and *Human Universe*.
Charles Olson and Robert Creeley: The Complete Correspondence. Ed. by George F. Butterick, Black Sparrow 6 vols. 1980–84 ea. $20.00 pap. ea. $7.50–$9.50
The Complete Maximus Poems. 1960. Ed. by George F. Butterick, Univ. of California Pr. 1983 $35.00
Call Me Ishmael: Herman Melville, Moby Dick, and America. City Lights 1966 pap. $3.50
Archaeologist of Morning. Grossman (Cape Goliard) 1970 o.p. All the poems authorized for publication except the *Maximus* sequence.

BOOKS ABOUT OLSON

Butterick, George F. *A Guide to the Maximus Poems of Charles Olson*. Univ. of California Pr. 1978 $50.00 pap. $14.95
Byrd, Don. *Charles Olson's Maximus*. Univ. of Illinois Pr. 1980 $15.00
Christensen, Paul. *Charles Olson: Call Him Ishmael*. Univ. of Texas Pr. text ed. 1979 $15.00
Paul, Sherman. *Olson's Push: Origin, Black Mountain, and Recent American Poetry*. Louisiana State Univ. Pr. 1978 $25.00
Von Hallberg, Robert. *Charles Olson: The Scholar's Art*. Harvard Univ. Pr. 1979 $17.50

OPPEN, GEORGE. 1908–1984

Born in New Rochelle, New York, George Oppen traveled widely and had an assortment of vocations. He served in the U.S. Army during World War II, worked as a tool and die maker and a cabinet maker, and owned and managed a shop in Mexico City, where he built and designed furniture. In 1969 he received the Pulitzer Prize. Of all the objectivists, he is perhaps the most lyrical and the most indigenously American in his cadences and severities.

BOOKS BY OPPEN

Collected Poems. New Directions 1976 pap. $7.95
Of Being Numerous. New Directions 1965 $5.25
This Is Which. New Directions 1965 $3.50
Primitive. Black Sparrow 1979 $10.00 pap. $3.00

PATCHEN, KENNETH. 1911–1972

"One of America's most unusual and powerful contemporary poets," said the *San Francisco Chronicle* of this versatile West Coast poet, writer, and painter. Born in Niles, Ohio, Patchen worked in all sorts of jobs before settling in California. In 1957 he pioneered in the "public birth of poetry—jazz" by reading his poems to the accompaniment of the Chamber Jazz Sextet in nightclubs and concert halls on the West Coast, breaking attendance records in San Francisco and Los Angeles. In 1954 he received the Shelley Memorial Award. Patchen died in 1972 after a prolonged illness, during which he continued to write prolifically.

BOOKS BY PATCHEN

Out of the World of Kenneth Patchen. New Directions 4 vols. 1970 pap. set $5.50
Collected Poems. New Directions 1969 pap. $11.50. Patchen's own choice. Shows a wide range of techniques and ideas.
Selected Poems. New Directions 1958 $5.95. Some 130 poems chosen from ten volumes published during the last 20 years.
The Journal of Albion Moonlight. New Directions 1961 pap. $6.95. Written in the 1940s.
But Even So. New Directions 1968 $4.50 pap. $1.25

BOOKS ABOUT PATCHEN

Morgan, Richard G., ed. *Kenneth Patchen: A Collection of Essays. AMS Studies in Modern Lit.* AMS Pr. 1977 lib. bdg. $29.50
Nelson, Raymond. *Kenneth Patchen and American Mysticism.* Univ. of North Carolina Pr. 1984 $18.95

PINSKY, ROBERT. 1940–

Robert Pinsky was born in Long Branch, New Jersey, and studied at Rutgers and Stanford universities. He has taught at the University of Chicago, Wellesley College, and the University of California, Berkeley. For several years the poetry editor of *The New Republic,* he has won the Oscar Blumenthal Prize (1978) and Woodrow Wilson and Fulbright grants. His book of criticism *The Situation of Poetry: Contemporary Poetry and Its Traditions* is referred to often. He has argued for, and written, a poetry of discursiveness—one that can treat abstract thought and social reality as well as subjectivity and deep emotion.

BOOKS BY PINSKY

Sadness and Happiness: Poems. Princeton Ser. of Contemporary Poets 1975 pap. $5.95
An Explanation of America. Princeton Ser. of Contemporary Poets 1979 $12.50 pap. $4.95. An impressive poem of great scope and inventive form.
History of My Heart. Amer. Poetry Ser. Ecco Pr. 1984 $12.50 pap. $5.72

PLATH, SYLVIA. 1932–1963

Plath's best poetry was produced, tragically, as she pondered—in her poems as well as her life—self-destruction, and she eventually committed suicide. She had an extraordinary impact on British as well as American poetry in the few years before her death. She is a confessional poet, influenced by the approach of Robert Lowell and Anne Sexton.

Born in Boston, a graduate of Smith College, Plath attended Newnham College, Cambridge University, on a Fulbright Fellowship and married the British poet TED HUGHES. Of her first collection, *The Colossus and Other Poems*, the *Times Literary Supplement* remarked, "Plath writes from phrase to phrase as well as with an eye on the larger architecture of the poem; each line, each sentence is put together with a good deal of care for the springy rhythm, the arresting image and—most of all, perhaps—the unusual word."

Plath's second book of poetry, *Ariel*, written in 1962 in a last fever of passionate creative activity, was published posthumously and describes frankly the emotional makeup of women. Robert Lowell found the poet of *Ariel* "feminine, rather than female, though, almost everything we customarily think of as feminine is turned on its head." A revealing study of the doomed personality that was Sylvia Plath is her one novel, *The Bell Jar*, about a neurotic college girl's first experience in New York and its destructive effect on her. It was first published under a pseudonym in 1963 and under her own name (in England) in 1966. In 1982, she was posthumously awarded the Pulitzer Prize for poetry.

BOOKS BY PLATH

The Collected Poems of Sylvia Plath. Harper 1981 $17.26 pap. $7.64

The Journals of Sylvia Plath. Ed. by Ted Hughes and Frances McCullough, Ballantine 1983 pap. $4.50; Doubleday 1982 $16.95

Johnny Panic and the Bible of Dreams: Short Stories, Prose, and Diary Excerpts. Harper 1979 $13.41 1980 pap. $6.68

The Colossus and Other Poems. 1962. Random (Vintage) 1968 pap. $2.95

Winter Trees. 1962. Harper 1972 $9.95. These poems, written in the last months of Plath's life in 1962, were collected posthumously.

Ariel. 1965. Harper 1968 $13.41 pap. $5.72

Crossing the Water. Harper 1971 $8.95 pap. $4.76. Poems written between *The Colossus* (1960) and *Ariel* (1965).

BOOKS ABOUT PLATH

Broe, Mary L. *Protean Poetic: The Poetry of Sylvia Plath*. Univ. of Missouri Pr. 1980 $20.00

Butscher, Edward. *Sylvia Plath: Method and Madness*. Washington Square Pr. 1977 pap. $3.50. A full-length biography.

Holbrook, David. *Sylvia Plath: Poetry and Existence*. Humanities text ed. 1976 $19.00. A "depth-psychology" study.

Lane, Gary, ed. *Sylvia Plath: New Views on the Poetry*. Johns Hopkins Univ. Pr. 1979 $24.50

Rosenblatt, Jon. *Sylvia Plath: The Poetry of Initiation*. Univ. of North Carolina Pr. 1982 pap. $6.95

Steiner, Nancy H. *A Closer Look at Ariel: A Memory of Sylvia Plath*. Harper 1973 o.p. A biographical description and character analysis of Plath. Critical introduction by George Stade gives a biographical survey.

Wagner, Linda. *Critical Essays on Sylvia Plath*. G. K. Hall 1984 $35.00

POUND, EZRA. 1885–1972

With T. S. ELIOT, Ezra Pound was one of the two main influences on British and U.S. poetry between the two world wars. The collection of the *Letters, 1907–1941* revealed the great erudition of this most controversial expatriate poet. Born in Idaho, Pound was graduated from the University of Pennsylvania and went abroad to live in 1908. His first book, *A Lume Spento*, a small collection of poems, was published in Venice in 1908. With the publication of *Personae* in London in 1909, he became the leader of the imagists abroad.

Pound's writings have been subject to many foreign influences. First he imitated the troubadours; then he came under the influence of the Chinese and Japanese poets. *The Cantos* (1925–60), his major work, to which he added for many years, is a mixture of modern colloquial language and classical quotation. *The Pisan Cantos*, written during his imprisonment in Italy, is more autobiographical.

Pound's prose, as well as his poetry, has been extremely influential. *The Spirit of Romance* is a revision of his studies of little-known romance writers. *ABC of Reading* is a characteristic exposition of a critical method. Critical writings are *Literary Essays of Ezra Pound*, *Instigations* (1920, o.p.), and *Guide to Kulchur*.

Pound was a linguist, whom Eliot called "the inventor of Chinese poetry for our time." His greatest translating achievements from Japanese, Chinese, Anglo-Saxon, Italian, Provençal, and French are collected in *The Translations of Ezra Pound*. Among his other writings are *Make It New: Essays; Jefferson and/or Mussolini* (o.p.), a discussion of American democracy and capitalism and fascism; and *The Classic Noh Theatre of Japan* (o.p.), with Ernest Fenollosa.

Living in Italy, Pound felt that some of the practices of Mussolini were in accord with the doctrines of social credit, in which he had become interested in the 1920s and 1930s, and he espoused some of the general applications of fascism. During World War II, he broadcast a series of programs addressed to the Allied troops on Italian radio. Indicted for treason and brought to the United States to stand trial in 1946, he was adjudged mentally incompetent to prepare a defense and was committed to St. Elizabeth's Hospital in Washington, D.C. After a concerted appeal to the federal government by American poets, led by Robert Frost, Pound was at last released in 1958 and returned to Italy. Critics have only recently begun to face squarely the connections between his fascism and his poetry.

BOOKS BY POUND

Personae: Collected Poems. 1909. New Directions $12.95. All the early work Pound cared to preserve.
Selected Poems. New Directions rev. ed. 1957 pap. $4.95
The Cantos: No. 1–117. New Directions 1970 $21.95
Letters of Ezra Pound. Studies in Pound Haskell 1974 lib. bdg. $59.95
The Letters of Ezra Pound to James Joyce, with Pound's Essays on Joyce. Ed. by Forrest Read, New Directions 1970 pap. $5.45

Selected Prose, 1909–1965. Ed. by William Cookson, New Directions 1975 pap. $9.95.
  Gathers Pound's previously uncollected prose pieces, including pieces on reli-
  gion, Confucius, America, economics, and history.
Literary Essays of Ezra Pound. 1953. Intro. by T. S. Eliot, New Directions 1968 pap.
  $7.95
The Translations of Ezra Pound. New Directions 1953 pap. $10.00
The Spirit of Romance. 1910. New Directions 1968 pap. $7.75
Gaudier-Brzeska: A Memoir. 1916. New Directions 1970 pap. $5.95. This remarkable
  French sculptor was killed in World War I at age 24.
ABC of Reading. 1934. New Directions 1960 pap. $5.00
Make It New: Essays. Scholarly repr. of 1935 ed. $39.00
Guide to Kulchur. 1938. New Directions 1968 pap. $6.95
Pavannes and Divagations. 1958. New Directions 1975 pap. $5.45. Collection of
  lighter pieces, both prose and poetry.
Drafts and Fragments, Cantos 110–117. New Directions 1969 o.p.
Selected Cantos. New Directions text ed. 1970 pap. $3.95. Pound's own selection from
  the monumental *Cantos.* Of use to the general poetry reader and beginning
  Pound student.

Books about Pound

Bernstein, Michael. *The Tale of the Tribe: Ezra Pound and the Modern Verse Epic.*
  Princeton Univ. Pr. 1980 $33.00 pap. $12.50. An important critical study.
Brooke-Rose, Christine. *A ZBC of Ezra Pound.* Univ. of California Pr. 1971 pap. $7.50.
  As the author notes, this work is primarily a book for newcomers to the work of
  Pound.
Davie, Donald. *Ezra Pound: The Poet as a Sculptor.* Univ. of Chicago Pr. (Phoenix
  Bks.) 1982 pap. $4.95; *Modern Masters Ser.* Viking new ed. 1976 $9.95
Emery, Clark. *Ideas into Action: A Study of Pound's Cantos.* Univ. of Miami Pr. 1958
  $8.95. A work that tries to demonstrate that Pound's *Cantos* has a method be-
  hind them.
Froula, Christine. *"To Write Paradise": Style and Error in Pound's Cantos.* Yale Univ.
  Pr. text ed. 1984 $18.50. A sophisticated study.
Gallup, Donald. *Ezra Pound: A Bibliography.* Univ. Pr. of Virginia 1983 $30.00
Hesse, Eva, ed. *New Approaches to Ezra Pound: A Coordinated Investigation of
  Pound's Poetry and Ideas.* Univ. of California Pr. 1969 $30.00. These writings on
  Pound are by Richard Ellmann, Forrest Read, Christine Brooke-Rose, Hugh Ken-
  ner, Leslie Fiedler, and others.
Kenner, Hugh. *The Pound Era.* Univ. of California Pr. 1971 $35.00 pap. $10.95. This
  detailed account of Pound and the age that seems to have surrounded him, its
  chief characters (Eliot, Joyce, Lewis) and the chief work, is one of the most fascinating accounts of any period in twentieth-century literature.
Lane, Gary. *A Concordance to Personae: Concordance to the Poems of Ezra Pound. Reference Ser.* Haskell 1972 lib. bdg. $59.95. A useful reference book, particularly
  for a poet of Pound's diversity and difficulty.
Leary, Lewis, ed. *Motive and Method in the Cantos of Ezra Pound. Essays of the Eng.
  Institute* Columbia Univ. Pr. 1954 pap. $8.50. A collection of essays by Guy Dav-
  enport, Hugh Kenner, and others.
O'Connor, William Van. *Ezra Pound. Pamphlets on Amer. Writers Ser.* Univ. of Minne-
  sota Pr. 1963 pap. $1.25
Schneidau, Herbert N. *Ezra Pound: The Image and the Real.* Louisiana State Univ.
  Pr. 1969 $17.50. This work is an examination of the poetic interaction and rela-

tionships between Pound and Joyce, Eliot, Ernest Fenollosa, Ford Madox Ford, T. E. Hulme, and others.

Stock, Noel. *Life of Ezra Pound: An Expanded Edition.* North Point Pr. 1982 pap. $15.00. This is a large and well-documented biography, replete with literary, historical, and period detail.

Sutton, Walter, ed. *Ezra Pound.* Prentice-Hall 1963 o.p. A collection of critical essays.

Torrey, E. Fuller. *The Roots of Treason: Ezra Pound and the Secret of St. Elizabeth.* Harcourt 1984 pap. $9.95. A revealing and critical study.

RAKOSI, CARL (CALLMAN RAWLEY). 1903–

Like the other objectivists Charles Reznikoff and George Oppen, Carl Rakosi is enjoying a well-deserved return to fashion. Born in Berlin of Hungarian parentage, he was educated at the Universities of Wisconsin and Pennsylvania, where he received a degree in social work, a profession for which he gave up writing poetry for a long period. His output is limited but valued for its integrity.

BOOKS BY RAKOSI

Collected Prose. National Poetry Foundation 1984 $18.95 pap. $12.95
Amulet. Black Sparrow 1967 pap. o.p.
Ere-Voice. Black Sparrow 1971 $3.50 pap. $1.45

RANSOM, JOHN CROWE. 1888–1974

A Rhodes scholar who went to Oxford University from Vanderbilt University, John Crowe Ransom taught at Vanderbilt from 1914 to 1937. Professor of poetry at Kenyon College, Ohio, from 1937 to 1958, Ransom founded *The Kenyon Review* in 1939. He was also one of the seven residents of Nashville, Tennessee, who founded and edited *The Fugitive* (1922–25) and according to Louis Untermeyer, "He more than any of the others was responsible for the new awakening of poetry in the South." He won the Academy of American Poets's $5,000 fellowship prize (1962) for his "distinguished poetic achievement." He also won the Bollingen Prize in poetry and the Loines Award for poetry. By writing a handful of lyrics remarkable for their irony and structural tensions, and critical essays that praised just these virtues in the name of New Criticism, Ransom had an influence far beyond many of his peers.

BOOKS BY RANSOM

Selected Poems. Amer. Poetry Ser. Ecco Pr. 3d rev. ed. 1978 pap. $4.95; R. West repr. of 1947 ed. 1977 lib. bdg. $20.00
Selected Letters of John Crowe Ransom. Ed. by Thomas Young, Louisiana State Univ. Pr. 1985 $32.50

BOOKS ABOUT RANSOM

Cowan, Louise S. *The Fugitive Group: A Literary History.* Louisiana State Univ. Pr. 1959 pap. $7.95
Stewart, John L. *The Burden of Time: The Fugitives and Agrarians—The Nashville Groups of the 1920's and 1930's and the Writings of John Crowe Ransom, Allen Tate, and Robert Penn Warren.* Princeton Univ. Pr. 1965 $44.00

———. *John Crowe Ransom. Pamphlets on Amer. Writers Ser.* Univ. of Minnesota Pr. 1962 pap. $1.25. Brief critical introduction to Ransom's poetry with an original approach.

REXROTH, KENNETH. 1905–1983

Kenneth Rexroth was born in South Bend, Indiana, and worked at a wide variety of jobs, being largely self-educated. In the late 1950s, he won a number of awards, including an Amy Lowell Travelling Fellowship, the Shelley Memorial Award, and a National Institute of Arts and Letters Literature Award. He translated widely, mainly from the Japanese, and wrote a lively account of his life, *An Autobiographical Novel* (o.p.). His work influenced many younger poets, such as Snyder, and continued in part the traditions of imagism and objectivism.

BOOKS BY REXROTH

The Collected Shorter Poems. New Directions 1967 pap. $7.95
The Collected Longer Poems. 1968. New Directions 1970 $8.25 pap. $5.25

REZNIKOFF, CHARLES. 1894–1976

Born in Brooklyn, New York, Reznikoff worked as a lawyer and legal editor, a profession reflected in his *Testimony: The United States, 1885–1890,* which portrays lives of various people in criminal law cases. He was associated with such objectivists as George Oppen and William Carlos Williams.

BOOK BY REZNIKOFF

Testimony: The United States, 1885–1890. 1965. Ed. by Seamus Cooney, Black Sparrow vol. 1 (1978) vol. 2 (1979) ea. $14.00 pap. ea. $6.00

RICH, ADRIENNE. 1929–

On her graduation from Radcliffe in 1951, Adrienne Rich found that her first book of poems, *A Change of World,* was chosen by W. H. AUDEN for the *Yale Series of Younger Poets.* Both Auden and Rich's father, who had encouraged her writing throughout her childhood, strongly influenced her early writing. Her poetry was traditional, largely in emulation of Auden. When *The Diamond Cutters* (1955, o.p.) came out, she was married, had three children, and was struggling with being a woman and a poet in the American environment of that time. Her poetry started to change remarkably in the 1960s, when she started writing directly as a woman rather than in the tradition of the men before her. She moved to New York City, where she became involved in antiwar activities. Her poems now manifest a merging between highly personal experience and social themes, in which, she says, "at last the woman in the poem and the woman writing the poem become the same person."

BOOKS BY RICH

A Change of World. Fwd. by W. H. Auden, *Yale Ser. of Younger Poets* AMS Pr. repr. of 1951 ed. $11.00. The author's first book, which won the *Yale Series of Younger Poets* prize.

Necessities of Life. 1966. A reissue of the author's first book.
Snapshots of a Daughter-in-Law. Norton rev. ed. 1967 pap. $4.95
Leaflets: Poems 1965–68. Norton 1969 pap. $4.95
The Will to Change: Poems 1968–70. Norton 1971 pap. $4.95
Diving into the Wreck: Poems 1971–72. Norton 1973 $10.95 pap. $5.95. New poems
  with an intense personal and feminist slant. Winner of the National Book Award
  (1974).
Of Woman Born: Motherhood as Experience and Institution. Norton 1976 $12.95. An
  important book in the new feminism.
The Dream of a Common Language: Poems, 1974–1977. Norton 1978 $12.95 pap.
  $4.95
On Lies, Secrets, and Silence: Selected Prose, 1966–1978. Norton 1979 $15.95 pap.
  $5.95. Some of these essays have become well known for their exploration of
  feminism and its relation to literature.
A Wild Patience Has Taken Me This Far: Poems, 1978–1981. Norton 1981 $12.95 pap.
  $4.95
The Fact of a Door Frame: Poems Selected and New, 1950–1984. Norton 1984 $18.95
  pap. $9.95

BOOK ABOUT RICH

Rich, Adrienne, and Barbara Gelphi, eds. *Adrienne Rich's Poetry. Norton Critical Eds.*
  1975 $7.95 pap. text ed. $6.95

RIDING, LAURA. (LAURA [RIDING] JACKSON). 1901–

Laura Riding is surely one of the most mysterious and neglected poets of
the twentieth century. Although she is unknown to most casual readers of
poetry, Kenneth Rexroth has said that "Laura Riding is the greatest lost
poet in American literature."

Riding was born in New York City and educated at Cornell University.
Her work appeared in the 1920s in numerous small literary magazines, in-
cluding *The Fugitive.* In 1925 she went to Europe, where she and ROBERT
GRAVES ran the Seizin Press in Majorca. In 1939 she returned to the United
States, renounced poetry, and since then has lived in Florida writing stud-
ies on the nature of language with her husband, Schuyler.

BOOKS BY RIDING

Selected Poems: In Five Sets. Norton Lib. 1973 $6.95. All the poems Riding wishes to
  have preserved are included in this volume.
Voltaire: A Biographical Fantasy. Norwood repr. of 1927 ed. 1978 lib. bdg. $10.00

ROBINSON, EDWIN ARLINGTON. 1869–1935

Amy Lowell spoke of Edwin Arlington Robinson's "difficult and beautiful
poetry" and considered him "one of the most intellectual poets in America."
He was a slow writer and waited long for recognition. His gift is for the delineation of character; his study of Shakespeare in the volume *The Man
against the Sky* (1916) won much praise in its time.

Robinson won the Pulitzer Prize in 1922, 1925, and 1928. The third Pulitzer was for one of his most intricate works, *Tristram* (1927, o.p.), a single
poem of more than 40,000 words. It was a best-seller and with the later

works established the poet in popular favor. Although his works are currently out of print, he is an important figure and is represented in many anthologies, such as Louis Untermeyer's *Modern American Poetry* and Gerald De Witt Sanders's *Chief Modern Poets.*

BOOKS BY ROBINSON

Collected Poems. Macmillan new ed. 1937 o.p. A number of shorter poems and long narrative poems, not previously included in a book.
Selected Poems of Edwin Arlington Robinson. 1963. Ed. by Morton D. Zabel, Macmillan 1965 o.p.; Macmillan (Collier Bks.) 1965 o.p.
Selected Early Poems and Letters. Ed. by Charles Davis, Holt 1960 o.p.

BOOKS ABOUT ROBINSON

Coxe, Louis. *Edwin Arlington Robinson. Pamphlets on Amer. Writers Ser.* Univ. of Minnesota Pr. 1962 pap. $1.25
Franchère, Hoyt C. *Edwin Arlington Robinson. Twayne's U.S. Authors Ser.* G. K. Hall 1968 lib. bdg. $12.50
Neff, Emery. *Edwin Arlington Robinson.* Russell repr. of 1948 ed. 1968 $10.00. A critical biographical work.
Smith, Chard Powers. *Where the Light Falls: A Portrait of Edwin Arlington Robinson.* Macmillan 1965 o.p.
Winters, Yvor. *Edwin Arlington Robinson.* New Directions 1971 pap. $3.45. A study of Robinson's technique by a major critic readable enough for the general reader.

ROETHKE, THEODORE. 1908–1963

The Waking brought Theodore Roethke the Pulitzer Prize in 1954. In 1959, his *Words for the Wind* won the National Book Award for poetry, the Bollingen Prize, the Millay Memorial Award, and the Borestone Mountain Poetry Award. He won the Poetry Society of America annual award and the Shelley Award in 1962.

Roethke spent his childhood in Saginaw, Michigan, was educated at the University of Michigan and at Harvard University, and was a professor of English at the University of Washington at the time of his death. A Theodore Roethke Memorial Foundation to aid American poets has since been established in his honor.

On the Poet and His Craft (1965) contains Roethke's analyses of some of his own work as well as essays on Dylan Thomas and Louise Bogan. Roethke argued that it was necessary to "stand up against" a great style, and by wrestling with his influences, especially YEATS, he became one of the most distinctive and important poets since World War II. His work centers on the themes of the self-generating energies of the embattled ego, as well as the ecstatic occasions of nature.

BOOKS BY ROETHKE

Collected Poems. Doubleday (Anchor) 1975 pap. $7.95; Univ. of Washington Pr. 1982 $19.95
Words for the Wind: The Collected Verse of Theodore Roethke. 1959. Univ. of Washington Pr. 1981 pap. $7.95

Selected Letters. Ed. by Ralph J. Mills, Jr., Univ. of Washington Pr. 1968 $20.00
The Far Field. 1964. Doubleday (Anchor) 1971 o.p.
On the Poet and His Craft: Selected Prose of Theodore Roethke. Ed. by Ralph J. Mills,
    Jr., Univ. of Washington Pr. 1965 pap. $7.95
Straw from the Fire: From the Notebooks of Theodore Roethke, 1943–1963. Ed. by
    David Wagoner, Univ. of Washington Pr. 1980 pap. $8.95. A selection from the
    notebooks, including poems and fragments, with reproductions of manuscript
    pages and illustrations.

BOOKS ABOUT ROETHKE

Blessing, Richard. *Theodore Roethke's Dynamic Vision.* Indiana Univ. Pr. 1974 $10.00
Bowers, Neal. *Theodore Roethke: The Journey from I to Otherwise.* Univ. of Missouri
    Pr. text ed. 1981 $20.00
LaBelle, Jenijoy. *The Echoing Wood of Theodore Roethke.* Princeton Essays in Lit. Ser.
    1976 $21.00
Mills, Ralph J., Jr. *Theodore Roethke.* Pamphlets on Amer. Writers Ser. Univ. of Minne-
    sota Pr. 1963 $1.25
Parini, Jay. *Theodore Roethke: American Romantic.* Univ. of Massachusetts Pr. 1979
    lib. bdg. $13.50
Sullivan, Rosemary. *Theodore Roethke: The Garden Master.* Univ. of Washington Pr.
    1975 $20.00
Williams, Harry. *The Edge Is What I Have: Theodore Roethke and After.* Bucknell
    Univ. Pr. 1976 $20.00

SANDBURG, CARL. 1878–1967

At Carl Sandburg's death, Mark Van Doren, Archibald MacLeish, and
President Lyndon Johnson delivered eulogies. In his tribute, President Johnson said that "Carl Sandburg was more than the voice of America, more
than the poet of its strength and genius. He was America. . . . He gave us
the truest and most enduring vision of our own greatness." The *N.Y. Times*
described him as "poet, newspaper man, historian, wandering minstrel, collector of folk songs, spinner of tales for children, [whose] place in American
letters is not easily categorized. But it is a niche that he has made uniquely
his own." Sandburg was the labor laureate of the United States.

Sandburg received the Pulitzer Prize for poetry in 1951 for his *Complete
Poems.* (One of his most famous—and briefest—poems, "Fog," was written
in the anteroom of a juvenile court as he was waiting to interview a judge.)
The last four volumes of his life of Lincoln had brought him the Pulitzer
Prize for history in 1940. Sixteen years in the writing, it was longer than the
Bible or all the known works of SHAKESPEARE (see Vol. 2).

Among his many awards were the gold medal for history and biography
(1952) from the American Academy of Arts and Letters; the Poetry Society
of America's gold medal (1953) for distinguished achievement; and the Boston Arts Festival Award (1955) in recognition of "continuous meritorious
contribution to the art of American poetry." In 1959, he traveled under the
auspices of the Department of State to the United States Trade Fair in Mos-
cow, and to Stockholm, Paris, and London. In 1960, he received a citation
from the Chamber of Commerce of the United States as a great living Ameri-

can for the "significant and lasting contribution which he has made to American literature."

BOOKS BY SANDBURG

Complete Poems. 1950. Harcourt rev. ed. 1970 $24.95. All the poems in his six previously published volumes, with 74 poems not previously collected.

Harvest Poems: 1910–1960. Intro. by Mark Van Doren, Harcourt 1960 pap. $2.95. Representative selection including 13 poems never before in book form.

Letters. Ed. by Herbert Mitgang, Harcourt 1968 o.p. More than 600 letters covering 64 years.

Always the Young Strangers. Harcourt 1953 $12.95. An autobiography.

Honey and Salt. 1963. Harcourt 1967 $11.95 pap. $2.95. New verse written between 1958 and 1962, published on the poet's eighty-fifth birthday.

BOOKS ABOUT SANDBURG

Allen, Gay W. *Carl Sandburg. Pamphlets on Amer. Writers Ser.* Univ. of Minnesota Pr. 1972 pap. $1.25. A good introduction to the poetry of Sandburg, with a selected bibliography. Useful to the beginning student.

Callahan, North. *Carl Sandburg, Lincoln of Our Literature: A Biography.* New York Univ. Pr. 1970 $20.00. Illustrated with photographs of Sandburg and his family. A well-written biography with emphasis on the life of the poet, not his works.

Crowder, Richard. *Carl Sandburg. Twayne's U.S. Authors Ser.* G. K. Hall 1963 lib. bdg. $11.50; New College & Univ. Pr. 1964 pap. $3.45

Durnell, Hazel. *The America of Carl Sandburg: Sandburg Centennial Facsimile of First Edition.* Univ. Pr. of Washington 1978 lib. bdg. $7.00 text ed. $5.00

Longo, Lucas. *Carl Sandburg: Poet and Historian.* Ed. by D. Steve Rahmas, *Outstanding Personalities Ser.* SamHar Pr. 1972 lib. bdg. $3.25 pap. $1.95

SCHWARTZ, DELMORE. 1913–1966

Born in Brooklyn, New York, Delmore Schwartz was educated at Columbia University, the University of Wisconsin, and New York University. He taught at Harvard University (1940–47) and lectured at various other universities. He also was associated with *Partisan Review* (1943–55), served as literary consultant for *New Directions*, and was poetry editor of *The New Republic* (1955–57). His first volume, *In Dreams Begin Responsibilities*, received praise from many critics. He received the Bollingen Prize, the Shelley Memorial Prize, and two other poetry awards after the publication of *Summer Knowledge: New and Selected Poems, 1938–1958* in 1959. The youngest winner of the Bollingen Prize since its establishment, Schwartz had already received a Guggenheim Fellowship when only 26 years old.

Until a year before his death from a heart attack, he was teaching at Syracuse University. He is immortalized, after a fashion, as the main figure in SAUL BELLOW's novel *Humboldt's Gift*.

BOOKS BY SCHWARTZ

Selected Poems: Summer Knowledge (Summer Knowledge: Selected Poems). 1959. New Directions 1967 pap. $5.95

Letters. Ed. by Robert Phillips, Ontario Review Pr. 1984 $24.95

Selected Essays. Ed. by Donald A. Dike and David H. Zucker, Univ. of Chicago Pr. 1970 $15.00

In Dreams Begin Responsibilities. 1938. Ed. by James Atlas, New Directions 1978 pap. $6.25

SEXTON, ANNE. 1928–1977

Anne Sexton's painful personal experiences form the subject matter of most of her poetry, which is often called confessional because of its frank approach and compulsive energy. Her first collection, *To Bedlam and Part Way Back*, focuses on her mental illness and subsequent hospitalization. *Live or Die* also "palpates human suffering, personal, physical, psychic" (*LJ*).

Sexton was born in Newton, Massachusetts. She won the Robert Frost Fellowship in poetry (1959), became a scholar at the Radcliffe Institute (1961–63), received a fellowship from the American Academy of Arts and Letters (1963–64), and was awarded a Ford Foundation grant (1965). In 1965 she also won the first literary magazine travel grant from the Congress for Cultural Freedom and was elected a fellow of the Royal Society of Literature in London. In 1967 she received the Shelley Award for the excellence of her total work and the Pulitzer Prize for *Live or Die*.

BOOKS BY SEXTON

To Bedlam and Part Way Back. Houghton Mifflin 1960 pap. $3.95

All My Pretty Ones. Houghton Mifflin 1962 pap. $4.50

Live or Die. Houghton Mifflin 1966 $8.95 pap. $6.95

Love Poems. Houghton Mifflin 1969 pap. $4.95. Twenty-five poems.

Transformations. Houghton Mifflin 1972 pap. $6.95. Poem-stories derived from Grimm's fairy tales, with a preface by Kurt Vonnegut, Jr.

The Awful Rowing toward God. Houghton Mifflin 1975 $8.95 pap. $5.50

The Complete Poems, 1981. Houghton Mifflin 1982 $20.00 pap. $11.95

BOOKS ABOUT SEXTON

McClatchy, J. D., ed. *Anne Sexton: The Artist and Her Critics.* Indiana Univ. Pr. 1978 $12.95

Sexton, Linda, ed. *Anne Sexton: A Self-Portrait in Letters.* Houghton Mifflin 1979 pap. $6.95

SHAPIRO, KARL (JAY). 1913–

Karl Shapiro won the Pulitzer Prize in 1945 for *V-Letter and Other Poems* (o.p.). Born in Baltimore, he attended the University of Virginia and Johns Hopkins University. After service in the army, he was appointed consultant in poetry at the Library of Congress in 1946 and joined the faculty of Johns Hopkins. There he taught writing courses until his resignation in 1950 to become editor, for a period, of *Poetry*. He is now professor of English at the University of California. In *The Bourgeois Poet,* Shapiro "breaks with accepted metrical patterns to attempt a poetry of direct speech. . . . 'The Bourgeois Poet' definitely has about it the air of a new imaginative release. Irony and social criticism are still there, but autobiography, invective, heavy doses of sexuality . . . and an occasional prophetic note are now blended to-gether" (Ralph J. Mills, Jr., *Contemporary American Poetry*).

BOOK BY SHAPIRO

Collected Poems, 1940–1978. Random 1978 $17.95. The poet's choice of the contents
    of three previous books with 18 unpublished poems.

SIMIC, CHARLES. 1938–

   Charles Simic was born in Yugoslavia and educated at New York University. He was recently awarded a MacArthur Foundation fellowship. Among
his other awards have been a Guggenheim Foundation grant and a National
Endowment for the Arts award. "My poetry always had surrealistic tendencies, which were discouraged a great deal in the '50's," the poet said, but
such tendencies were applauded in the 1970s and his reputation consequently flourished. His poems are about obsessive fears and often depict a
world that resembles the animism of primitive thought. His work has affinities with that of Mark Strand and has in its turn produced several imitators.

BOOKS BY SIMIC

Dismantling the Silence. Ed. by Richard Howard, *Braziller Poetry Ser*. 1971 pap. $3.95
Return to a Place Lit by a Glass of Milk. Braziller 1974 $5.95 pap. $3.95
Charon's Cosmology. *Braziller Poetry Ser*. 1977 $6.95 pap. $3.95
Classic Ballroom Dances. Braziller 1980 $6.95 pap. $3.95
Austerities. *Braziller Poetry Ser*. 1982 $7.95 pap. $4.95

SIMPSON, LOUIS. 1923–

   Born in the British West Indies, Louis Simpson became a U.S. citizen after volunteering for service in the U.S. Army in 1943. He draws his material
from the daily events of his own life, and several of his best-known poems
are war poems that deal with the hardness and brutality of what he calls
"the other side of glory." His basically realistic verse has strains of imagism
and surrealism. With Robert Pack and Donald Hall, he edited *New Poets of
England and America* (1957, o.p.) and is well known for his *An Introduction
to Poetry*. His awards include a Hudson Review Fellowship (1957); the Millay Award (1960); Guggenheim Fellowships (1962, 1970); and the Pulitzer
Prize for poetry (1964) for *At the End of the Open Road*.

BOOKS BY SIMPSON

People Live Here: Selected Poems, 1949–1983. Boa Eds. 1983 $15.95 pap. $7.95
A Dream of Governors. *Wesleyan Poetry Program* 1959 $15.00 pap. $6.95
At the End of the Open Road. *Wesleyan Poetry Program* 1963 $15.00 1982 pap. $6.95
Searching for the Ox. Morrow 1976 $5.95 pap. $2.50
The Best Hour of the Night. Ticknor & Fields 1983 pap. $6.95

SMITH, DAVE. 1942–

   Born in Portsmouth, Virginia, Dave Smith attended the University of Virginia and Ohio University. He has edited *The Pure Clear Word: Essays on the*

Poetry of James Wright and has written essays on fellow poets for *The American Poetry Review*. He celebrates nature and the spirit of place in his poetry, which is often directly emotional as well as lushly descriptive. "To find the poem one must lose the poem, letting it go and drawing it back," he said, and his poems often trace a rhythm of discovery and loss.

BOOKS BY SMITH

The Fisherman's Whore. Ohio Univ. Pr. 1974 $7.50
Cumberland Station: Poems. Univ. of Illinois Pr. 1977 pap. $5.95
Goshawk, Antelope. Univ. of Illinois Pr. 1979 $10.00 pap. $5.95
Dream Flights. Univ. of Illinois Pr. 1981 $10.00 pap. $5.95
Homage to Edgar Allan Poe: Poems. Louisiana State Univ. Pr. 1981 pap. $5.95
Gray Soldiers: Poems. S. Wright 1983 $15.00

SNODGRASS, W(ILLIAM) D(EWITT). 1926–

In *Heart's Needle,* a collection of confessional poetry that won the 1960 Pulitzer Prize, Snodgrass "spoke in a distinctive voice. It was one that was jaunty and assertive on the surface . . . but somber and hurt beneath. His work had a colloquial ease but was traditional in form. It was one of the few books that successfully bridged the directness of contemporary free verse with the demands of the academy. His poetry was appealing in that the poet stood in front of the work."

BOOKS BY SNODGRASS

Heart's Needle. 1959. Knopf 1983 pap. $6.95
After Experience: Poems and Translations. Ultramarine 1968 $10.00
The Führer Bunker: A Cycle of Poems in Progress. Amer. Poets Continuum Ser. Boa Eds. 1977 $12.95 pap. $6.00

SNYDER, GARY. 1930–

Gary Snyder was born in San Francisco and received a B.A. in anthropology at Reed College. He attended Indiana University and pursued the study of oriental languages at the University of California at Berkeley. When he was 18 he shipped out of New York as a seaman. He later worked as a logger and forest lookout in Oregon, Washington, and California. Before moving to Japan to study in a Zen monastery under a Bollingen Foundation grant, Snyder worked on an American tanker in the Persian Gulf and South Pacific Islands, then spent four months in India (1961–62).

Snyder is one of the most famous Beat poets (others being Allen Ginsberg and Gregory Corso). He is the most controlled and concise of them. His adventurous life has given his verse a unique range of subject and feeling. Close to nature since childhood, he also is the most widely known poet of the ecology movement. Often his poems have a Zenlike stillness and sharpness of perception, which serves to define the connective web between man and the natural universe.

Snyder is deeply interested in the American Indian and the idea of tribe as an alternative to modern culture, or at least as an example for modern culture. Besides receiving the first Zen Institute of America Award in 1956,

Snyder was the recipient of an American Academy of Arts and Sciences poetry prize in 1966.

His essays, *Earth House Hold,* composed of journal notes and diary excerpts, have become a classic in the underground ecology movement.

BOOKS BY SNYDER

Myths and Texts. 1960. New Directions 1978 pap. $3.95
Riprap and Cold Mountain: Poems. Grey Fox 1965 pap. $3.95
Back Country. New Directions 1968 pap. $4.95
Regarding Wave. New Directions 1970 $6.00 pap. $5.25
Six Sections from Mountains and Rivers without End Plus One. Writing Ser. Four Seasons Foundation 1970 o.p. Contains the newest section of this continuing series, which is likely to be one of the major long poems of our time.
Turtle Island. New Directions 1974 pap. $4.95
The Real Work: Interviews and Talks, 1964–1978. Ed. by Scott McLean, New Directions 1980 $10.95 pap. $5.50
Axe Handles. North Point Pr. 1983 $12.50 pap. $7.50

BOOK ABOUT SNYDER

Molesworth, Charles. *Gary Snyder's Vision: Poetry and the Real Work. Literary Frontiers Ser.* Univ. of Missouri Pr. 1983 pap. $7.95

STAFFORD, WILLIAM (EDGAR). 1914–

Born in Kansas, William Stafford was educated in the Midwest and has taught at Lewis and Clark College in Oregon. He is a consciously "western" poet, a word-painter of western landscapes. He is often linked with Robert Bly and James Wright as a poet of deep imagery.

BOOKS BY STAFFORD

Travelling through the Dark. Harper 1962 o.p.
The Rescued Year. Harper 1966 pap. $4.95
Allegiances. Harper 1970 $7.95
Someday, Maybe. Harper 1973 $7.95

STEVENS, WALLACE. 1879–1955

After attending Harvard University and New York Law School, Wallace Stevens was admitted to the bar in 1904, was associated with the Hartford Accident and Indemnity Company after 1916, was made a vice-president in 1934, and was also vice-president of the Hartford Livestock Insurance Company. He believed that his character as a poet was enhanced by this daily contact with a regular job. He did not gain general recognition until Harriet Monroe included four of his poems in the war number of *Poetry* in 1914. In 1915, *Poetry* awarded him a prize for his *Three Travelers Watch a Sunrise,* a one-act play in free verse. He received the Bollingen Prize in poetry (1949) and the National Book Award for poetry (1950) for *The Auroras of Autumn* (o.p.). In 1955, he received the National Book Award for the second time for *The Collected Poems* and the Pulitzer Prize. *The Necessary Angel: Essays on Reality and the Imagination* stands as his poetic credo. Although it is easy to say his great theme is the shaping power of the imagination, it is considerably more difficult to say how various are his inventive explorations and restatements of this theme. His stature as one of the select modern masters grows more secure each year, and he is perhaps at once the most philosophical and the most sensuous poet in the American tradition.

Books by Stevens

The Collected Poems. Random 1982 pap. $8.95. Contains all but three of his previously published works and 25 later poems.

Opus Posthumous. Ed. by Samuel French Morse, Random 1982 pap. $6.95. Includes poems, plays, and prose works.

The Palm at the End of the Mind: Selected Poems and a Play. Ed. by Holly Stevens, Random 1972 pap. $4.95; Shoe String (Archon) repr. of 1971 ed. 1984 lib. bdg. $27.50

Letters of Wallace Stevens. Ed. by Holly Stevens, Knopf 1966 $25.00. This collection of more than 800 letters is selected by Stevens's daughter, who has, in addition, supplied extracts from his unpublished private journal and letters to him from his father. This is an extremely rich collection for what it shows about Stevens's unique sensibility. A forthcoming biography by Joan Richardson will for the first time use this material to show the autobiographical roots of his poetry.

The Necessary Angel: Essays on Reality and the Imagination. 1951. Random (Vintage) 1965 pap. $3.95

Books about Stevens

Baird, James. *The Dome and the Rock: Structure in the Poetry of Wallace Stevens.* Johns Hopkins Univ. Pr. 1968 $28.50

Benamou, Michel. *Wallace Stevens and the Symbolist Imagination. Princeton Essays in Lit. Ser.* 1972 $21.00. A study of Stevens's relationship to the symbolists of the French tradition.

Blessing, Richard A. *Wallace Stevens: Whole Harmonium.* Syracuse Univ. Pr. 1970 $15.95. A textual analysis of the poems, letters, and critical works of Stevens.

Bloom, Harold. *Wallace Stevens: The Poems of Our Climate.* Cornell Univ. Pr. 1980 pap. $9.95

Brazeau, Peter. *Parts of a World: Wallace Stevens Remembered.* Random 1983 $19.95. An oral biography by people who knew Stevens.

Burney, William. *Wallace Stevens. Twayne's U.S. Authors Ser.* New College & Univ. Pr. 1968 pap. $3.45

Doggett, Frank. *Stevens' Poetry of Thought.* Johns Hopkins Univ. Pr. 1966 pap. $5.95

Edelstein, J. M. *Wallace Stevens: A Descriptive Bibliography. Pittsburgh Ser. in Bibliography.* 1973 $45.00

Kessler, Edward. *Images of Wallace Stevens.* Gordian repr. of 1972 ed. 1983 $13.50. A discussion of the general patterns of Stevens's major imagery.

Morse, Samuel French. *Wallace Stevens Checklist and Bibliography of Stevens Criticism.* Ohio Univ. Pr. (Swallow) 1963 $8.95

Pearce, R. H., and J. Hillis Miller, eds. *Acts of the Mind: Essays on the Poetry of Wallace Stevens.* Johns Hopkins Univ. Pr. 1965 o.p.

Vendler, Helen H. *On Extended Wings: Wallace Stevens' Longer Poems.* Harvard Univ. Pr. 1969 $18.50 pap. $6.95

STRAND, MARK. 1934–

Although not associated with any one school of poetry, Mark Strand's work seems to possess qualities of the European and Latin American surrealists. As Strand is a translator of PAZ (see Vol. 2), BORGES (see Vol. 2), GUILLÉN (see Vol. 2), and QUASIMODO (see Vol. 2), this is not surprising. His poetry, often uttered matter-of-factly, seems singularly removed from the here and now, filled with the impossibilities of the restless world lying between dream and wakefulness.

This Canadian-born U.S. poet received his degree from Antioch College, attended Yale University, and studied in Florence on a Fulbright grant (1960–61) and later at the University of Iowa. He was a Fulbright lecturer (1965–66) and during 1966–67 he held an Ingram Merrill Fellowship and taught at Mount Holyoke College. His prizes include an award from the National Council on the Arts (1967–68) and a Rockefeller Fellowship (1968–69). He presently teaches in Utah.

BOOKS BY STRAND

Selected Poems. Atheneum 1980 $10.95 pap. $7.95
Reasons for Moving. Atheneum 1968 $4.95 pap. $3.95
Darker. Atheneum 1970 pap. $2.95
The Story of Our Lives. Atheneum 1973 pap. $3.95
The Late Hour. Atheneum 1978 pap. $3.95
The Monument. Ecco Pr. 1978 $7.95 1979 pap. $4.95. A book of prose.
The Planet of Lost Things. Crown (Potter) 1982 $9.95

SWENSON, MAY. 1919–

May Swenson was born in Utah and educated at Utah State University, Logan. A former editor at New Directions Publishing Corporation, she has been a poet-in-residence at Purdue University in Indiana and has taught poetry seminars at the University of North Carolina, Greensboro (1968–69). Twice a recipient of a Rockefeller Fellowship (1955–67), Swenson has also been awarded a Guggenheim Fellowship (1959); a National Institute of Arts and Letters Award (1969); a Ford Foundation grant (1964); a Lucy Martin Donnelly Fellowship from Bryn Mawr College (1968); and a Shelley Memorial Award (1968).

BOOK BY SWENSON

New and Selected Things Taking Place. Atlantic Monthly Pr. 1978 pap. $7.95

TATE, ALLEN. 1899–1979

Allen Tate—poet, essayist, novelist, biographer, critic, and professor emeritus of English at the University of Minnesota—was one of the founders, with the other southern poets, of *The Fugitive* in 1922. Elected to the National Institute of Arts and Letters in 1949, he won the Bollingen Prize in poetry (1956). He received the 1963 award of the Academy of American Poets. The autumn 1959 issue of the *Sewanee Review* was a collection of essays by 19 English and American writers in honor of Tate's sixtieth birthday. He was one of the chief voices in the New Criticism, and his career was marked by a struggle with modernist values, which he largely opposed. (See also Tate's main entry in Chapter 16 in this volume.)

BOOK BY TATE

Collected Poems, 1919–1976. Farrar 1977 $15.00 pap. $6.95

BOOKS ABOUT TATE

Bishop, Ferman. *Allen Tate. Twayne's U.S. Authors Ser.* New College & Univ. Pr. 1967 pap. $3.45
Hemphill, George. *Allen Tate. Pamphlets on Amer. Writers Ser.* Univ. of Minnesota Pr. 1964 pap. $1.25
Squires, Radcliffe, ed. *Allen Tate and His Works: Critical Evaluations.* Univ. of Minnesota Pr. 1972 $15.00. This book gathers together critical essays on Tate by numerous scholars, including John Crowe Ransom, Robert Lowell, Herbert Read, Richard Howard, Frank Kermode, and Cleanth Brooks.
Stewart, John L. *The Burden of Time: The Fugitives and Agrarians—The Nashville Groups of the 1920's and 1930's and the Writings of John Crowe Ransom, Allen Tate, and Robert Penn Warren.* Princeton Univ. Pr. 1965 $44.00

WAKOSKI, DIANE. 1937–

Diane Wakoski's work is confessional and surreal, but belongs to no specific school. She seems more related in language to the native American idiom of William Carlos Williams than to the French surrealists/imagists like Prevert or Reverdy. Wakoski has admitted a poetic kinship with Allen Ginsberg, yet her work is truly as unique as his. Contrasted with that of the other Beats, Wakoski's subject matter almost always is personal, not political or public, and like Ginsberg's work finds expression in long, rambling musical poems. Recently her work has become more didactic—a direction that she considers her main concern in poetry. She shows a great sense of whimsy and imagination even when writing of difficult subjects.

BOOKS BY WAKOSKI

Dancing on the Grave of a Son of a Bitch. 1973. Black Sparrow 1980 $14.00 pap. $5.00
Magellanic Clouds. 1973. Black Sparrow 1978 pap. $5.00
Virtuoso Literature for Two and Four Hands. 1975. Doubleday pap. $3.95
Waiting for the King of Spain. 1977. Black Sparrow 1980 $14.00 pap. $5.00
The Man Who Shook Hands. Black Sparrow 1978 $5.50
Cap of Darkness. Black Sparrow 1980 $14.00 pap. $5.00
The Collected Greed: Parts 1–13. Black Sparrow 1984 $14.00 signed ed. $25.00 pap. $10.00

WARREN, ROBERT PENN. 1905–

A Kentucky-born poet, editor, scholar, and novelist, Robert Penn Warren spent part of his boyhood in Tennessee. His education included a Rhodes Scholarship at Oxford University. With Cleanth Brooks, he was one of the managing editors of the *Southern Review*, forum of the New Criticism, and, after its demise in 1942, became associated with the *Kenyon Review* as advi-

sory editor. Extraordinarily active and versatile, he has taught fiction, poetry, and playwriting, and has produced work in all forms of literature. His
poetry is intellectual, rich in the powerful images of the imagination, and
has its roots in the pre-Civil War South. He has continued to write impressive poetry into his eightieth year and is a major man of letters. (See also
Chapter 14 in this volume.)

BOOKS BY WARREN

Selected Poems, 1923–1975. Random 1976 $17.95 pap. $9.95
Brother to Dragons: A Tale in Verse and Voices Random 1953 $10.95 1979 $12.95
Incarnations: Poems, 1966–68. Random 1968 pap. $10.95. Thirty-four new poems
    never before in book form, with photographs of the author.
Audubon: A Vision. Random 1969 $9.95. A beautifully produced series of poems sug-
    gested to the poet by episodes from the life and reading of John James Audubon.
Or Else: Poems, 1968–1973. Random 1974 $10.95
Now and Then: Poems 1976–1978. Random 1978 $11.95 pap. $5.95
Being Here: Poetry, 1977–1980. Random 1980 $10.95 pap. $4.95
Rumor Verified: Poems, 1979–1980. Random 1981 $9.95 pap. $5.95

BOOKS ABOUT WARREN

Bohner, Charles. *Robert Penn Warren. Twayne's U.S. Authors Ser.* G. K. Hall rev. ed.
    1981 lib. bdg. $13.95
Gray, Richard, ed. *Robert Penn Warren: A Collection of Critical Essays. Twentieth-
    Century Views Ser.* Prentice-Hall 1980 $11.95 pap. $3.95
Snipes, Katherine. *Robert Penn Warren. Lit. and Life Ser.* Ungar 1984 $13.95

WILBUR, RICHARD. 1921–

When Richard Wilbur's *Things of This World* won the 1957 Pulitzer Prize
and the National Book Award the same year, the *N.Y. Times* commented edi-
torially: "A seemingly effortless craftsman, Mr. Wilbur reveals a fine lyrical
gift, a searching wit and, in his translations, a sympathetic kinship to the
works of others."

Wilbur was born in New York City and educated at Amherst College and
Harvard University. He has been on the English faculty at Harvard and
Wellesley College, and he is a member of both the American Academy of
Arts and Sciences and the National Institute of Arts and Letters. With LIL-
LIAN HELLMAN (see Vol. 2) he wrote the libretto for the opera *Candide.* He
also is one of the premier translators of his generation. He has translated
MOLIÈRE's (see Vol. 2) *Tartuffe* and *Misanthrope* and many poems of Andrei
Voznesensky and others. He was corecipient of the Bollingen Translation
Prize in 1963.

BOOKS BY WILBUR

The Poems of Richard Wilbur. Harcourt 1963 pap. $3.95
Walking to Sleep: New Poems and Translations. 1969. Harcourt 1971 pap. $4.95. New
    poems and translations. The translations include the works of Borges, Akhma-
    tova, Villion, D'Orleans, and Voznesensky.
Opposites: Poems and Drawings. 1973. Harcourt 1979 pap. $1.75
Responses: Prose Pieces, 1948–1976. Harcourt 1976 $13.95 pap. $3.95

The Mind-Reader. Harcourt 1977 pap. $3.95

The Whale and Other Uncollected Translations. New Amer. Trans. Ser. Boa Eds. 1982
$10.00 pap. $5.00

BOOK ABOUT WILBUR

Salinger, Wendy, ed. *Richard Wilbur's Creation. Under Discussion Ser.* Univ. of Michigan Pr. 1983 $16.00 pap. $8.95

WILLIAMS, C. K. 1936–

C. K. Williams was born in Newark, New Jersey, and now teaches at George Mason University in Virginia. He has translated SOPHOCLES (see Vol. 2), but his own work is as contemporary as that of any other poet. His subjects are abjection and shame, but these are always seen as the threshold to illumination and love. His verse is distinctive in using a long line, but one that never grows slack or prosy. Morris Dickstein has called him "one of the unique voices in contemporary poetry."

BOOK BY C. K. WILLIAMS

Tar. Random (Vintage) 1983 $10.00 pap. $5.95. Contains a long poem, "One of the Muses," that differs in subject matter from the usual urban landscape of the poet's earlier volumes.

WILLIAMS, WILLIAM CARLOS. 1883–1963

Poet, artist, and practicing physician of Rutherford, New Jersey, William Carlos Williams wrote poetry that was experimental in form, ranging from imagism to objectivism with great originality of idiom and human vitality. Credited with changing and directing American poetry toward a new metric and language, he also wrote a large number of short stories and novels. *Paterson* (1946–58), about the New Jersey city of that name, was his epic and places him with the Ezra Pound of the *Cantos* as one of the great shapers of the long poem in this century.

National recognition did not come early, but eventually he received many honors, including a vice-presidency of the National Institute of Arts and Letters (1952); the Bollingen Prize (1953); the $5,000 fellowship of the Academy of American Poets; the Loines Award for poetry of the National Institute of Arts and Letters (1948); and the Brandeis Award (1957). Book II of *Paterson* received the first National Book Award for poetry in 1949. Williams was named consultant in poetry in English to the Library of Congress for 1952–53.

Williams's continuously inventive style anchored not only objectivism, the school to which he most properly belongs, but a long line of subsequent poets as various as Robert Lowell, Frank O'Hara, and Allen Ginsberg. With Stevens, he forms one of the most important sources of a specifically American tradition of modernism.

BOOKS BY WILLIAM CARLOS WILLIAMS

Collected Earlier Poems: Before 1940. New Directions 1951 $22.50

Collected Later Poems: 1949–1950. New Directions rev. ed. 1962 $14.00. Poetry written in the 1940s. In addition to "The Wedge" and "The Clouds," a large number of poems not previously published, notably the sequences entitled "The Pink Church" and "Two Pendants: For the Ears."

Selected Poems. Intro. by Randall Jarrell, New Directions rev. & enl. ed. 1969 pap. $4.95

Selected Letters. Ed. by John C. Thirwell, Astor-Honor 1957 $12.95

In the American Grain. New Directions 1956 pap. $4.95

Kora in Hell: Improvisations. 1957. *Pocket Poets Ser.* City Lights o.p.

I Wanted to Write a Poem. 1958. Ed. by Edith Heal, New Directions 1978 pap. $3.95. Williams tells how various poems came into being.

Paterson: Books I–V. New Directions 1963 pap. $5.25

Autobiography. New Directions 1967 pap. $6.95

Pictures from Brueghel: Collected Poems, 1950–1962. New Directions 1967 pap. $5.95. New poems and the complete texts of "The Desert Music" (1954) and "Journey to Love" (1955).

Books about William Carlos Williams

Breslin, James E. *William Carlos Williams: An American Artist.* Oxford 1970 o.p. A critical study that discusses not only his poetry but also his experiments with the historical essay, short story, novel, and epic.

Brinnin, John Malcolm. *William Carlos Williams. Pamphlets on Amer. Writers Ser.* Univ. of Minnesota Pr. 1963 pap. $1.25

Coles, Robert. *William Carlos Williams: The Knack of Survival in America.* Rutgers Univ. Pr. 1975 $17.50 pap. $7.95

Conarroe, Joel. *William Carlos Williams' Paterson: Language and Landscape.* Univ. of Pennsylvania Pr. 1974 pap. $8.95

Dijkstra, Bram. *Hieroglyphics of a New Speech: Cubism, Stieglitz and the Early Poetry of William Carlos Williams.* Princeton Univ. Pr. 1969 $24.00

Guimond, James. *The Art of William Carlos Williams: A Discovery and Possession of America.* Univ. of Illinois Pr. 1968 pap. $7.50

Ostrom, Alan. *The Poetic World of William Carlos Williams. Crosscurrents—Modern Critiques Ser.* Southern Illinois Univ. Pr. 1966 $6.95

Sankey, Benjamin. *A Companion to William Carlos Williams' Paterson.* Univ. of California Pr. 1971 $42.00. A book-length study of Williams's epic using manuscript material to elucidate the poems.

Sherman, Paul. *The Music of Survival: A Biography of a Poem by William Carlos Williams.* Univ. of Illinois Pr. 1968 $12.50. A study and explication of "The Desert Music" from *Desert Music and Other Poems* by Williams.

Wallace, Emily M. *A Bibliography of William Carlos Williams.* Wesleyan Univ. Pr. 1968 $28.50

Weaver, Mike. *William Carlos Williams: The American Background.* Cambridge Univ. Pr. 1977 $39.50 pap. $10.95. The author stresses the American viewpoint and attitudes that shaped Williams's work.

WRIGHT, CHARLES. 1935–

Charles Wright was born in a small town in Tennessee and took his degrees from Davidson College and the University of Iowa. He has won the American Book Award (1982) for *Country Music*, which contains poems from his first four books. He has also won the Edgar Allan Poe Award from the Academy of American Poets. His poetry is dense with an imagistic texture derived from Pound and the great Italian modernist MONTALE (see Vol. 2). Themes of redemption, memory, and the haunting spirits of place combine to make Wright one of the most lyric of poets.

BOOKS BY CHARLES WRIGHT

Southern Cross: Poems. Random 1981 $10.50 pap. $5.95
Country Music: Selected Early Poems. Wesleyan Univ. Pr. 1982 $17.00 pap. $8.95.
    Brings together the work from the first several books.
The Other Side of the River. Random (Vintage) 1984 $11.95 pap. $5.95

WRIGHT, JAMES. 1927–1980

James Wright's work is typified by a humanitarian tenderness, compassion, and a keen sense of man's alienation. He has written of his own work: "I have written about the things I am deeply concerned with—crickets outside my window, cold and hungry old men . . . a feeling of desolation in the fall, some cities I have known." His work presents an unusual vision of middle America: the decayed and yet beautiful landscapes of train yards, bars, and whore districts in Minneapolis. Stylistically, Wright moved from a traditional rhymed and metered verse, drawing on the techniques of the now classic modernists—Robinson, Masters, Frost, and even THOMAS HARDY—to experimentalism in form and language. His later poems exhibited an almost oriental delicacy, yet retain the peculiar vision of the native American idiom.

Born in Martin's Ferry, Ohio, Wright attended Kenyon College and the University of Washington. Recipient of a Fulbright Scholarship to study in Vienna, he was awarded a National Institute of Arts and Letters grant, a Guggenheim grant, the Oscar Blumenthal Award, and a Pulitzer Prize for his *Collected Poems* in 1972.

BOOKS BY JAMES WRIGHT

Collected Poems. Wesleyan Univ. Pr. 1971 $16.00 pap. $7.95
Collected Prose. Ed. by Anne Wright, *Poets on Poetry Ser.* Univ. of Michigan Pr. 1982 pap. $8.95
Saint Judas. Wesleyan Poetry Program 1959 pap. $6.95 1982 pap. $6.95. Poems collected from the following volumes: *The Green Wall, St. Judas, The Branch Will Not Break,* and *Shall We Gather at the River?*
The Branch Will Not Break. Wesleyan Poetry Program 1963 pap. $6.95
Shall We Gather at the River? Wesleyan Poetry Program 1968 $15.00 pap. $6.95
To a Blossoming Pear Tree. Farrar 1978 $7.95 pap. $4.95
This Journey. Random (Vintage) 1982 pap. $5.95

ZUKOFSKY, LOUIS. 1904–1978

Louis Zukofsky first achieved a reputation in the literary world during the 1920s, when Ezra Pound published his work in *Exile.* Later he became editor of *Poetry,* in which, in 1931, he actively promoted the as yet relatively unknown William Carlos Williams and Kenneth Rexroth, among others. Zukofsky was born in New York City and received both his A.B. and M.A. degrees from Columbia University and taught for two years at the Brooklyn Polytechnic Institute. Zukofsky's poetry is notoriously difficult, although it continues to generate its defenders and a small but gallant group of explainers.

BOOKS BY ZUKOFSKY

All: The Collected Short Poems, 1923–1958. Norton 1965 o.p.
All: The Collected Short Poems, 1956–1964. Norton 1966 $4.50 1971 pap. $4.95
A Test of Poetry. 1948. Norton 1981 $12.95 pap. $6.95
Autobiography. Grossman 1970 o.p. In prose and poetry, with music scores by Celia Zukofsky.
A. 1972. Univ. of California Pr. 1978 $17.95 pap. $9.95. The epic-length poem.
Prepositions: The Collected Critical Essays of Louis Zukofsky. Univ. of California Pr. 1981 $19.95 pap. $5.95

BOOK ABOUT ZUKOFSKY

Ahearn, Barry. *Zukofsky's "A." An Introduction.* Univ. of California Pr. 1983 $19.95 pap. $6.95

CHAPTER 10

British Fiction: Early Period

Morris Golden

> ...as histories of this kind ... may properly be called models of HUMAN
> LIFE, so, by observing minutely the several incidents which tend to the ca-
> tastrophe or completion of the whole, and the minute causes whence those
> incidents are produced, we shall best be instructed in this most useful of all
> arts, which I call the ART OF LIFE.
>
> —Henry Fielding, *Amelia*

Whatever the English novel is—whether essentially an exciting story, a conflict between individuals, a realistic portrayal of the outer details of life or
of psychological complexities, a social analysis, an allegory of human fate,
or, as E. M. Forster most generally defined it, a narrative prose fiction at
least fifty thousand words long—critics agree that it came to its first maturity in the eighteenth century in the masterpieces of Samuel Richardson,
Henry Fielding, and their contemporaries. Its name comes from the French
nouvelle, or short story, and from the Italian *novella*, a story of a kind popular in the Renaissance, both stemming from the Latin *novella*—"new things;
news"—and its characteristics derive from a great variety of sources across
the centuries. The major literary contributions of the Middle Ages include
the saints' lives, fables, sermons with illustrative examples, and romances,
which proliferated in the fourteenth and fifteenth centuries and culminated
artistically in Thomas Malory's *Morte d'Arthur*.

With the widespread use of the printing press in the late fifteenth century
came the mass production of books. This resulted in a wider and better educated audience for narrative prose. In the sixteenth century, the great humanist Thomas More wrote his *Utopia* in Latin, but the popular English
translation made his combination of satiric condemnation of the real with a
fanciful elaboration of the ideal available as an important influence. Toward the end of the century the traditions of the realistic and the fanciful
appear separately in two of the most notable works of prose fiction, Thomas
Nashe's *Unfortunate Traveler* and Sir Philip Sidney's pastoral *Arcadia*.
Shorter prose narratives continued to appear not only in translation and
imitation of the *novella*, but also in the inserted narratives in Sidney's *Arcadia* and in the works of such popular authors as Thomas Deloney and Robert Greene.

The seventeenth century opened with the single most lasting and massive influence on the later English novel, the publication and immediate translation of CERVANTES's *Don Quixote* (see Vol. 2). It provided the model of a continued narrative arising from the fundamental human paradoxes in its two singular and yet representative main characters—Quixote, the obsessed idealist, and Sancho, the spontaneous pragmatist, who both faced a world in danger of disintegration. The book also provided a unifying point of view, concentrated in the rational, aristocratic, and humane narrator Cide Hamete Benengeli, who could plausibly test the oddities of the main characters and himself be tested by Cervantes and the reader. Later in the century came the influences of the Theophrastan character sketch; the religious allegory; French courtly romances; the social-psychological elaborations of Scudery; and English romances, wonder tales, and love intrigues.

These elements came together in the eighteenth century with the rise of the bourgeoisie, to whom the developing novel taught manners as well as morals. The great masters of the eighteenth century—Daniel Defoe, Richardson, Fielding, and Laurence Sterne—and their lesser contemporaries left a rich legacy to their successors. They capitalized on the problems of making prose fiction artistically respectable by satisfying the reader's wishes for social and ethical guidance, as well as escape, and fashioning some sort of order in a world where the old rules were apparently breaking down. In the process, they incorporated a diversity of new techniques, notably the journalistic description of real or imagined places (particularly by Jonathan Swift, Defoe, and Tobias Smollett); the essay (by Fielding and Oliver Goldsmith); the eastern tale, developed after the translation of the *Arabian Nights* into French in 1700; the rogue biography as in Defoe's *Moll Flanders* and Fielding's *Jonathan Wild;* the dramatic scene, especially by Richardson and Fielding; and the miscellany, as in Swift's *Tale of a Tub* and Sterne's *Tristram Shandy*.

In technique, the eighteenth-century novelists explored a variety of points of view, particularly in the nature of the first-person narrator. Their fictional spokespeople range from Defoe's apparently simple autobiographers through Richardson's, Smollett's, and Fanny Burney's letter writers to the complexities of Swift's, Goldsmith's, and Sterne's narrators. Structurally, Fielding achieves in *Tom Jones* the Aristotelian ideal of unity, showing that plot, theme, characters, and scenes can all be brought together coherently around one main action—Tom's movement from chaos to prudence and harmony. After this model, any subsequent looseness in a novel indicates either deliberate subversion, as in Sterne, or a lesser degree of artistic commitment.

As another technical legacy, the novelists provided their successors with various forms of realism, from the literal to the psychological, which are united by their presentation of the way people's minds work in recognizable situations. Characters who respond to the ordinary details of life are more convincing to the reader.

In the latter part of the eighteenth century a pervasive concern with psychology became, in lesser hands than Richardson's and Sterne's, sentimental and melodramatic. In the sentimental novels, domestic problems of love, trust, marriage, education, friendship, and sibling relationships are likely to be explored in a tearful bourgeois milieu. The corresponding tendency toward romance developed in the Gothic novel, which came to prominence with Horace Walpole's *Castle of Otranto* and rode a strange course through such oddities as Ann Radcliffe's *Mysteries of Udolpho.*

These last are chiefly notable for what they led to: JANE AUSTEN's presentation of domestic situations, the social explorations of the Victorians, Scott's historical romances, and the incorporation of the eerie into the larger concerns of EDGAR ALLAN POE, EMILY BRONTË, and NATHANIEL HAWTHORNE. But the final achievement of the eighteenth-century novel, its chief legacy, is its small group of actual masterpieces, most notably, *Moll Flanders, Joseph Andrews, The Vicar of Wakefield, Rasselas, Humphrey Clinker,* and certainly *Gulliver's Travels, Clarissa, Tom Jones,* and *Tristram Shandy.*

ANTHOLOGIES, HISTORY, AND CRITICISM

Adams, Percy G. *Travel Literature and the Evolution of the Novel.* Univ. of Kentucky Pr. 1983 $30.00

Ashley, Robert, and E. M. Moseley, eds. *Elizabethan Fiction.* Peter Smith 1953 o.p. A substantial collection.

Baker, Ernest A. *A History of the English Novel.* 1924–67. Barnes & Noble 11 vols. 1966–79 ea. $19.50 set $214.50

Baugh, Albert C., and others, eds. *A Literary History of England.* Prentice-Hall 4 vols. in 1. 2d student ed. 1967 $54.95

Beasley, Jerry C. *Novels of the 1740's.* Univ. of Georgia Pr. text ed. 1982 $20.00

Booth, Wayne C. *The Rhetoric of Fiction.* Univ. of Chicago Pr. (Phoenix Bks.) rev. ed. 1982 pap. $9.95; 2d ed. 1983 pap. $30.00. One of the most influential studies of the last scholarly generation dealing largely with the nature of the fictional narrator.

Clifford, James L., ed. *Eighteenth Century English Literature: Modern Essays in Criticism.* Oxford 1959 pap. $6.95. Reprints a number of valuable essays on the ideas and literature of the time.

———. *Man versus Society in Eighteenth Century Britain.* Cambridge Univ. Pr. 1968; Norton Lib. 1972 o.p. A number of original essays by distinguished scholars on such matters as the condition of the musician or painter of the time.

Collier, J. Payne, ed. *Illustrations of Early English Popular Literature.* Ayer 2 vols. repr. of 1863 ed. ea. $20.00 set $40.00

Davis, Walter R. *Idea and Act in Elizabethan Fiction.* Princeton Univ. Pr. 1969 $30.00

Day, Robert Adam. *Told in Letters: Epistolary Fiction before Richardson.* Univ. of Michigan Pr. 1966 o.p. A valuable analysis of plots and themes from which Richardson's work derived.

George, M. Dorothy. *London Life in the Eighteenth Century.* Peter Smith 1965 o.p. An authoritative historical description based on the materials available 40 years ago and not yet superseded.

Golden, Morris. *The Self Observed: Swift, Johnson, Wordsworth.* Johns Hopkins Univ. Pr. 1972 $17.50. Some pertinent materials on the prose fictions of Swift and Johnson.

Goldgar, Bertrand A. *Walpole and the Wits: The Relation of Politics to Literature,*

1722–1742. Univ. of Nebraska Pr. 1976 $17.95. Particularly valuable material on Fielding.

Harrison, G. B., ed. *The Elizabethan Journals: Being a Record of Those Things Most Talked of during the Years.* Peter Smith 2 vols. 1928–33 o.p. "These delightful gossip books comprise what is virtually a day-by-day account of the things, serious and frivolous, which most Englishmen were talking about during the last 12 years of Elizabeth's reign" (*LJ*).

Huizinga, Johan. *The Waning of the Middle Ages: A Study of the Forms of Life, Thought and Art in France and the Netherlands in the 14th and 15th Centuries.* St. Martin's 1924 $25.00. The authoritative, influential study of the late medieval background of the novel.

Jones, Richard F., and others, eds. *The Seventeenth Century: Studies in the History of English Thought and Literature from Bacon to Pope.* Stanford Univ. Pr. 1951 $22.50 pap. $4.95. Reprints a number of essays by noted scholars on the intellectual context of the works discussed.

Kettle, Arnold. *An Introduction to the English Novel.* Humanities Pr. 2 vols. text ed. 1974 pap. vol. 1 $12.00 vol. 2 $11.00. An excellent, readable discussion of early British authors and their works.

Kunitz, Stanley J., and Howard Haycraft, eds. *British Authors before 1800: A Biographical Dictionary.* Wilson 1952 $22.00. Complete in one volume with 650 biographies and 220 portraits.

Lewis, C. S. *English Literature in the Sixteenth Century (Excluding Drama).* Oxford History of Eng. Lit. Ser. 1954 $39.50 pap. $6.95. On the medieval literature of Scotland and the works of Sidney, Spenser, and Hooker.

Lovejoy, Arthur O. *Essays in the History of Ideas.* Greenwood repr. of 1948 ed. 1978 $29.50. Reprints a number of the author's studies in the history of ideas, some of them (like the "Parallel between Classicism and Deism") fundamental to understanding the early eighteenth century.

McKillop, Alan Dugald. *Early Masters of English Fiction.* Greenwood repr. of 1956 ed. 1980 $24.75. A penetrating account of the originality and vigor of the essential contributions to the novel form made by Defoe, Richardson, Fielding, Smollett, and Sterne.

Miller, Edwin Haviland. *The Professional Writer in Elizabethan England: A Study of Nondramatic Literature.* Harvard Univ. Pr. 1959 o.p. A scholarly examination that "documents and analyzes the many social, political, and aesthetic tensions which attended the development of a new English creature—the would-be professional writer" (*LJ*).

Miller, Nancy K. *The Heroine's Text: Readings in the French and English Novel, 1722–1782.* Columbia Univ. Pr. 1980 $24.00

Mish, Charles C. *English Prose Fiction, 1600–1700: A Chronological Check List.* Univ. Pr. of Virginia 2d ed. 1967 o.p.

———, ed. *Restoration Prose Fiction, 1666–1700: An Anthology of Representative Pieces.* Univ. of Nebraska Pr. 1970 $19.95

O'Dell, Sterg. *A Chronological List of Prose Fiction in English Printed in England and Other Countries, 1475–1640.* Folcroft 1954 $20.00

Paulson, Ronald. *Emblem and Expression: Meaning in English Art of the Eighteenth Century.* Harvard Univ. Pr. text ed. 1975 $25.00. Visual imagery and social context.

———. *The Fictions of Satire.* Johns Hopkins Univ. Pr. 1967 o.p. Valuable both for theoretical positions and for analysis of specific works in this period.

———. *Popular and Polite Art in the Age of Hogarth and Fielding.* Ward-Phillips Lec-

tures in Eng. Language and Lit. Ser. Univ. of Notre Dame Pr. text ed. 1979 $20.00. Social context, often significantly related to the fiction.

————. *Satire and the Novel in Eighteenth-Century England.* Yale Univ. Pr. 1967 o.p. Authoritative examination of the relation between the two forms.

Perry, Ruth. *Women, Letters, and the Novel.* AMS Studies in the 18th Century 1980 $29.50

Richetti, John J. *The Popular Fiction before Richardson: Narrative Patterns, 1700– 1739.* Oxford 1969 o.p. An authoritative study of the context of the novel's birth.

Rose, Mark. *Heroic Love: Studies in Sidney and Spenser.* Harvard Univ. Pr. 1968 $8.95. Useful for its discussion of *Arcadia.*

Röstvig, Maren-Sofie. *The Happy Man: Studies in the Metamorphoses of a Classical Ideal.* Universitetsforlaget 2 vols. vol. 1 1600–1700 (1962) vol. 2 1700–1760 (1971) 2d ed. ea. $17.00

Schilling, Bernard N., ed. *Essential Articles for the Study of English Augustan Backgrounds. Essential Articles Ser.* Shoe String 1961 $25.00. Reprints a large number of valuable essays on the literature and ideas of the seventeenth and eighteenth centuries.

Sullivan, Alvin, ed. *British Literary Magazines: The Augustan Age and the Age of Johnson, 1698–1788. Historical Guides to the World's Periodicals and Newspapers* Greenwood 1983 lib. bdg. $55.00. Profiles, often excellent, of the magazines that formed a context and sometimes a source of income for the fiction writers.

Todd, Janet M. *Women's Friendship in Literature: The Eighteenth-Century Novel in England and France.* Columbia Univ. Pr. 1980 $29.00

Tompkins, J. M. S. *The Popular Novel in England, 1770–1800.* Univ. of Nebraska Pr. 1961 pap. $5.95

Van Ghent, Dorothy. *The English Novel: Form and Function.* Harper 1961 pap. $6.50. Eighteen superb essays on the major classics from Richardson to Lawrence.

Watkins, W. B. C. *Perilous Balance: The Tragic Genius of Swift, Johnson, and Sterne.* Somerset repr. of 1939 ed. $29.00. Perceptive study of how the sensitivities of the writers affected what they saw and how they described it.

Watt, Ian. *The Rise of the Novel: Studies in Defoe, Richardson and Fielding.* Univ. of California Pr. 1957 $24.50. Still the best book in the field; brilliant, learned, and immensely stimulating.

BUNYAN, JOHN. 1628–1688

John Bunyan was a tinker who created the most intense prose allegories in English. He was imprisoned for most of 1660–72 for preaching Puritan doctrine in an England barely recovering from a religious civil war. In his first, autobiographical work, *Grace Abounding*, he found his main theme— spiritual conversion. He treated this subject most magnificently in his *Pilgrim's Progress.* He wrote this most famous allegory while imprisoned again in 1675 for six months. Christian, the ordinary man, makes the painful journey from the City of Destruction to the Heavenly Gates through dangers set up by others and by his own mind. Bunyan's theme is universal; he brought to it intense conviction, brilliant economy and vigor of statement, and the ability to evoke living characters in the guise of allegorical figures. Although *Mr. Badman, The Holy War,* and *Pilgrim's Progress, Part II* are not quite up to the masterpiece, they constitute an impressive expansion of Bunyan's range of prose fiction. *Pilgrim's Progress* was one of the few books that the American pioneer carried along with the Bible; with the return to favor of allegory and symbolism, a resurgence of interest in Bunyan is evident.

BOOKS BY BUNYAN

Works: With an Introduction to Each Treatise, Notes and a Sketch of His Life, Times and Contemporaries. Ed. by George Offor, AMS Pr. 3 vols. repr. of 1856 ed. $225.00

Complete Works. Ed. by Henry Stebbing, *Lib. of Lit., Drama, and Criticism* Johnson Repr. 4 vols. repr. of 1859 ed. 1970 $230.00

Grace Abounding to the Chief of Sinners. 1666. Baker Bks. 1978 pap. $3.50; (and *The Life and Death of Mr. Badman*), Biblio Dist. 1979 pap. $3.95; (and *The Pilgrim's Progress*), ed. by Roger Sharrock, *Oxford Stand. Authors Ser.* 1966 $36.00. *Grace Abounding* is Bunyan's spiritual autobiography.

The Pilgrim's Progress from This World to That Which Is to Come. 1678 1679 1684. Ed. by James B. Wharey, rev. by Roger Sharrock, 1929 *Oxford Eng. Texts Ser.* 2d ed. 1960 $55.00. The edition by James B. Wharey is a collation of the 11 editions published during Bunyan's lifetime and the first really authentic text, with bibliographical analysis. For the 1960 edition, the late Professor Wharey's 1929 edition has been thoroughly revised by Roger Sharrock. The most important change is a return to the text of Bunyan's first edition, supplemented by Bunyan's afterthoughts and additions taken from the earliest edition in which each appears. Sharrock has added a full commentary in two new sections and revised the introduction.

The Pilgrim's Progress. Biblio Dist. 1978 $9.95 pap. $2.50; ed. by Gladys N. Larson, Covenant 1978 pap. $6.95; Lightyear 1976 lib. bdg. $15.95; ed. by Gladys N. Larson, *Moody Class. Ser.* 1984 pap. $2.95; *World's Class.-Pap. Ser.* Oxford 1984 $3.95; Revell (Spire Bks.) 1965 pap. $2.95; Whitaker House 1981 pap. $2.95

The Holy War. 1682. Ed. by Roger Sharrock and James F. Forrest, *Oxford Eng. Texts Ser.* 1980 $75.00; Baker Bks. 1977 pap. $5.95; *Wycliff Class. Ser.* Moody 1978 pap. $8.95; Reiner 1975 $12.95

BOOKS ABOUT BUNYAN

Brown, John. *John Bunyan, 1628–1688: His Life, Times and Work.* Ed. by Frank M. Harrison, Shoe String repr. of 1928 ed. 1969 $28.50. The standard biography.

Froude, James A. *Bunyan.* Ed. by John Morley, *Eng. Men of Letters* AMS Pr. repr. of 1888 ed. $12.50

Harrison, Frank M. *A Bibliography of the Works of John Bunyan.* Folcroft 1932 lib. bdg. $12.50

Harrison, G. B. *John Bunyan: A Study in Personality.* Folcroft 1973 lib. bdg. o.p.

Newey, Vincent, ed. *Pilgrim's Progress: Critical and Historical Views.* *Eng. Texts and Studies* Barnes & Noble 1980 $30.00

Tindall, William York. *John Bunyan, Mechanick Preacher.* Russell repr. of 1934 ed. 1964 $13.00

BURNEY, FANNY (MME [FRANCES] D'ARBLAY). 1752–1840

Although lovers of JANE AUSTEN may think of Fanny Burney as merely an essential precursor, at least the first of her novels, *Evelina*, deserves its devotees. Consisting largely of the letters of the heroine, a young marriageable girl visiting London and registering freshly the responses to the metropolis and its people, it shows sharp observations, a precise sense of the shifting feelings of the girl and the men who are interested in her, and a delight in and fear of the grotesque middle class and the foreign relatives she meets. After Fanny Burney was revealed as the author of the widely admired novel, she left the intellectually exciting household of her father, Charles Burney, the leading musicologist of his time and a friend of SAMUEL JOHNSON, for the onerous boredom of being a lady-in-waiting to Queen Charlotte. She married late, wrote *Cecilia* (1782, o.p.), *Camilla* (1796), and *Wanderer* (1802, o.p.), and lived with apparent contentment to a very old age.

BOOKS BY BURNEY

Early Diary of Fanny Burney, 1768–1778. Arden Lib. 2 vols. $45.00; ed. by Annie R. Ellis, Ayer 2 vols. repr. of 1889 ed. $47.50; Richard West 2 vols. 1913 $39.50

Diary and Letters of Mme D'Arblay, 1778–1840. Ed. by Charlotte Barrett, pref. and notes by Austin Dobson, Richard West 4 vols. $200.00. The volumes are profusely illustrated, and a bibliography is included. Charlotte Barrett was Fanny Burney's niece.

The Diary of Fanny Burney. 1842–46. Ed. by Lewis Gibbs, Dutton (Everyman's) o.p. A vivacious picture of life at George III's court.

Journals and Letters of Fanny Burney. Ed. by Joyce Hemlow and others, Oxford 12 vols. 1972–84 ea. $49.00–$175.00

Evelina, or A Young Lady's Entrance in the World. 1778. Norton 1965 pap. $6.95; ed. by Edward A. Bloom, *World's Class. Ser.* Oxford 1982 pap. $6.95

Camilla. 1796. Ed. by Edward A. Bloom and Lillian D. Bloom, *World's Class.-Pap. Ser.* Oxford 1983 pap. $8.95

Memoirs of Dr. Burney, Arranged from His Own Manuscripts, from Family Papers, and from Personal Recollections. AMS Pr. 3 vols. repr. of 1832 ed. $115.00

BOOK ABOUT BURNEY

Hemlow, Joyce. *The History of Fanny Burney.* Oxford 1958 $39.95. Based largely on her journal-letters, notebooks, unpublished works, voluminous correspondence, and on other previously unpublished sections of Burney papers. A standard reference book.

DEFOE, DANIEL. 1661–1731

Although *Robinson Crusoe,* based on the actual experience of Alexander Selkirk, who was alone on an island for years, will no doubt continue to be Defoe's most popular book for young readers, his masterpiece is now thought to be *Moll Flanders,* the brilliantly persuasive recollections of a long lifetime in the underworld as written by an early eighteenth-century criminal. In it, the heroine moves from her birth in prison through early respectability to seduction, polygamy, theft, prostitution, incest, arrest, religious salvation, reform, transportation to America, and wealth. Since Defoe was a notable ironist (witness his *The Shortest Way with Dissenters* [1702, o.p.], which advocated killing dissenters from the established church for everyone's good), critics have recently differed over the seriousness of Moll's claims to religious conversion while in jail awaiting execution.

Defoe's unsurpassed realism of detail, fostered by a lifetime of journalism, political activity (including espionage), and business ventures that involved careful analyses of people and circumstances, and his compassionate sense of individual courage in the face of a harsh society have been his most important legacies to later novelists as well as his most vivid gifts to his readers. Among his many works—usually published anonymously so that there may never be a reliable list of them—*Roxana*, the unfinished story of a late seventeenth-century courtesan, has been highly praised by Virginia Woolf; *Captain Singleton* and *Colonel Jack* are lively and at times earthy narratives of adventure in exotic parts of the world; and *A Journal of the Plague Year* (the year 1665, when Defoe was a little boy) so well simulates an eyewitness account that ALBERT CAMUS (see Vol. 2) could use it as a source of his graphic power in *The Plague*.

The most ambitious attempt to list all of Defoe's writing is *A Checklist of the Writings of Daniel Defoe* by Robert Moore (Shoe String 1960 1971 o.p.).

BOOKS BY DEFOE

Novels and Miscellaneous Works. AMS Pr. 20 vols. repr. of 1841 ed. ea. $31.50 set $630.00. With biographical memoir, notes, and literary prefaces attributed to Walter Scott.

Romances and Narratives. Ed. by George A. Aitken, AMS Pr. 16 vols. repr. of 1895 ed. ea. $32.50 set $520.00. With an etched portrait and 48 rotogravure illustrations.

Novels and Selected Writings. Shakespeare Head Ed. Rowman 14 vols. repr. of 1923 ed. 1974 $250.00

Defoe's Review. Intro. and biblio. by Arthur Wellesley Secord, AMS Pr. 9 vols. bd. in 22 pts. repr. of 1938 ed. $605.00

The Best of Defoe's Review. Ed. by William Lytton Payne, *Essay Index Repr. Ser.* Ayer facsimile ed. 1951 $22.50. Payne also compiled *Index to Defoe's Review*, which is now out of print.

Letters. Ed. by George Harris Healey, Century Bookbindery repr. of 1955 ed. 1984 lib. bdg. $75.00

The Consolidator. 1705. *Foundations of the Novel Ser.* Garland lib. bdg. $55.00

Robinson Crusoe (The Life and Strange Surprizing Adventures of Robinson Crusoe, of York, Mariner). 1719 1720. Biblio Dist. 1977 $9.95 pap. $2.50; New Amer. Lib. (Signet Class.) pap. $1.95; ed. by Michael Shinagel, *Norton Critical Eds.* text ed. 1975 pap. $5.95; ed. by Angus Ross, Penguin 1966 pap. $2.25; Scribner 1983 $17.95 deluxe, numbered, boxed ed. $75.00

Captain Singleton (The Life, Adventures and Piracies of the Famous Captain Singleton). 1720. Biblio Dist. repr. of 1906 ed. 1969 $8.95

Moll Flanders (The Fortunes and Misfortunes of the Famous Moll Flanders). 1722. Biblio Dist. 1977 $9.95 pap. $2.95; New Amer. Lib. (Signet Class.) 1962 pap. $2.75; ed. by Edward Kelly, *Norton Critical Eds.* text ed. 1973 pap. $8.95; *Penguin Eng. Lib. Ser.* 1978 pap. $2.50; Random (Modern Lib.) 1950 pap. $3.95

A Journal of the Plague Year. 1722. AMS Pr. repr. of 1895 ed. $27.50; intro. by George A. Aitken, Biblio Dist. 1977 $9.95 pap. $2.95; New Amer. Lib. 1984 pap. $4.95; ed. by Anthony Burgess, *Penguin Eng. Lib. Ser.* 1966 pap. $2.95

Colonel Jack. 1722. Ed. by S. H. Monk, *Oxford Eng. Novels Ser.* 1965 pap. $4.95

Roxana, or the Fortunate Mistress. 1724. New Amer. Lib. (Signet Class.) 1979 pap.

$2.25; ed. by Jane Jack, *World's Class. Ser.* Oxford 1981 pap. $3.95; ed. by David Blewett, Penguin 1982 pap. $4.95

A General History of the Robberies and Murders of the Most Notorious Pyrates. 1724. Ed. by Manuel Schonhorn, Univ. of South Carolina Pr. 1972 o.p.

A Tour through the Whole Island of Great Britain. 1724–27. Biblio Dist. repr. of 1962 ed. 1974 $12.95; ed. by P. Rogers, Penguin 1978 pap. $4.95

The Complete English Tradesman (and *An Humble Proposal to the People of England for the Increase of Their Trade and Encouragement of Their Manufactures*). 1726. Burt Franklin 3 vols. in 1 text ed. 1970 $36.50; Kelley 2 vols. with supplement repr. of 1727 ed. $35.00

The Complete English Gentleman. Ed. by Karl K. Bülbring, Folcroft repr. of 1890 ed. lib. bdg. $35.00. Written between 1726 and 1731, but first published in 1890.

Conjugal Lewdness, or Matrimonial Whoredom. Scholars' Facsimiles repr. of 1727 ed. 1967 $45.00

BOOKS ABOUT DEFOE

Alkon, Paul. *Defoe and Fictional Time.* Univ. of Georgia Pr. 1979 $23.00. A much admired study of time in fiction.

Blewett, David. *Defoe's Art of Fiction: Robinson Crusoe, Moll Flanders, Colonel Jack, and Roxana.* Univ. of Toronto Pr. 1979 $22.50

Byrd, Max, ed. *Daniel Defoe: A Collection of Critical Essays.* Prentice-Hall 1975 $12.95

Novak, Maximillian E. *Defoe and the Nature of Man.* Oxford 1963 o.p. Examines the moral and philosophical bases of Defoe's fiction.

———. *Realism, Myth, and History in Defoe's Fiction.* Univ. of Nebraska Pr. 1983 $17.95

Richetti, John J. *Defoe's Narratives: Situations and Structures.* Oxford 1975 o.p.

Starr, G. A. *Defoe and Spiritual Autobiography.* 1965. Gordian 1971 $12.50

Sutherland, James R. *Daniel Defoe: A Critical Study.* Harvard Univ. Pr. 1971 o.p. An examination of Defoe as journalist, poet, and novelist, by the most distinguished Defoe scholar.

———. *Defoe.* Folcroft repr. of 1950 ed. 1978 lib. bdg. $30.00. The best and most readable biography.

FIELDING, HENRY. 1707–1754

A successful playwright in his twenties, Fielding turned to the study of law and then to journalism, fiction, and a judgeship after his *Historical Register*, a political satire on the Walpole government, contributed to the censorship of plays that put him out of business. As an impoverished member of the upper classes, he knew the country squires and the town nobility; as a successful young playwright, the London "jet set"; as a judge at the center of London, the city's thieves, swindlers, petty officials, shopkeepers, and vagabonds; and as a political journalist (editor-author of *The Champion*, 1739–41; *The True Patriot*, 1745–46; *The Jacobite's Journal*, 1747–48; *The Covent-Garden Journal*, 1752), he participated in argument and intrigue over everything from London elections to national policy, knowledgeably attacking and defending a range of politicians from ward heelers to the Prince of Wales.

When Fielding undertook writing prose fiction to ridicule the simple morality of Richardson's *Pamela*, he first wrote the hilarious burlesque *Shamela*. Shortly, however, he found himself considering all the forces working on man, and in *Joseph Andrews* (centering on his invented brother of Pamela) he played with the patterns of HOMER (see Vol. 2), the Bible, and CERVANTES (see Vol. 2) to create what he called "a comic epic poem in prose." His preface describing this new art form is one of the major documents in literary criticism of the novel. *Jonathan Wild*, a fictional rogue biography of a year later, plays heavily with ironic techniques that leave unsettled Fielding's great and recurring theme: the difficulty of uniting goodness (an outflowing love of others) with prudence in a world where corrupted institutions support divisive pride rather than harmony and self-fulfillment.

In his masterpiece, *Tom Jones*, Fielding not only faces this issue persuasively, but shows for the first time the possibility of bringing a whole world into an artistic unity, as his model Homer had done in verse. Not only does Fielding develop a coherent and centered sequence of events—something CONGREVE (see Vol. 2) had done casually on a small scale in *Incognita* 60 years before—but he relates the plot organically to character and theme, giving us all of eighteenth-century England (if not indeed, as he wished, all humanity) in a vision of the archetypal good man (Tom) on a journey toward understanding, with every act by every character both reflecting the special and typical psychology of that character and incurring the proper moral response.

If in *Tom Jones* Fielding affirms the existence of an order under the surface of chaos, in his last novel, *Amelia*, which realistically examines the misery of London, he can find nothing reliable except the prudent good heart, and that only if its possessor escapes into the country. Himself ill, saddened by the deaths of his intensely beloved first wife and daughter, depressed by a London magistrate's endless toil against corruption, he saw little hope for goodness in that novel or in his informal *Journal of a Voyage to Lisbon*. Shortly after traveling to that city for his health, he died at the age of 47 having proved to his contemporaries and successors that the novel was capable of the richest achievements of art.

Wesleyan University Press, in cooperation with Oxford University Press, has undertaken the Wesleyan Edition of Fielding's Works.

BOOKS BY FIELDING

The Complete Works of Henry Fielding. Ed. by William E. Henley, Barnes & Noble 16 vols. repr. of 1902–03 ed. 1967 o.p.

Miscellanies, Volume 1. Ed. by Henry Knight Miller, text intro. by Fredson Bowers, *Works of Henry Fielding* Wesleyan Univ. Pr. repr. of 1743 ed. 1973 $35.00

An Apology for the Life of Mrs. Shamela Andrews. 1741. Ed. by Brian Downes, Folcroft repr. of 1930 ed. lib. bdg. $10.00; Richard West repr. of 1926 ed. 1980 lib. bdg. $12.50; (and Samuel Richardson, *Pamela*), New Amer. Lib. (Signet Class.) pap. $3.50. His famous parody of Richardson's *Pamela*.

Joseph Andrews. 1742. Ed. by Martin C. Battestin, Houghton Mifflin (Riv. Eds.) 1961 pap. $5.50; intro. by Mary Ellen Chase, *Norton Lib.* 1958 pap. $5.95; ed. by R. F.

Brissenden, *Penguin Eng. Lib. Ser.* 1977 pap. $2.95; *Works of Henry Fielding* Wesleyan Univ. Pr. 1984 $45.00 pap. $12.50

Jonathan Wild (and *Journal of a Voyage to Lisbon*). 1743. Biblio Dist. 1973 $9.95 pap. $4.50; New Amer. Lib. (Signet Class.) pap. $3.50; ed. by David Nokes, *Penguin Eng. Lib. Ser.* 1982 pap. $3.95

The True Patriot; and The History of Our Own Times. 1745–46. Ed. by Miriam Austin Locke, *Eng. Lit. Ser.* Haskell repr. of 1964 ed. 1972 $66.95

The Jacobite's Journal and Related Writings. 1747–48. Ed. by William J. Coley, *Works of Henry Fielding* Wesleyan Univ. Pr. 1975 $35.00

Tom Jones: The History of a Foundling. 1749. Biblio Dist. 2 vols. repr. of 1909 ed. 1974 vol. 1 $9.95 vol. 2 $8.95; New Amer. Lib. (Signet Class.) pap. $3.50; ed. by Sheridan Baker, *Norton Critical Eds.* 1973 $17.50 pap. $9.95; ed. by Reg Mutter, *Penguin Eng. Lit. Ser.* 1966 pap. $3.95; *Modern Lib. College Ed. Ser.* Random 1950 pap. $4.50; ed. by Martin C. Battestin and Fredson Bowers, *Works of Henry Fielding* Wesleyan Univ. Pr. 2 vols. 1974 $50.00 pap. $9.95

Amelia. 1751. Wesleyan Univ. Pr. 1983 $45.00

The Journal of a Voyage to Lisbon (and *Jonathan Wild*). 1755. Biblio Dist. 1973 $9.95 pap. $4.50

BOOKS ABOUT FIELDING

Battestin, Martin C. *The Moral Basis of Fielding's Art: A Study of Joseph Andrews.* Wesleyan Univ. Pr. 1959 $17.50 pap. $9.95. A basic study of Fielding's ideas in the novel.

———, ed. *Twentieth-Century Interpretations of Tom Jones.* Prentice-Hall 1968 o.p.

Cross, Wilbur L. *The History of Henry Fielding.* Russell 3 vols. repr. of 1918 ed. 1963 $60.00. The basic biography that has not been superseded.

Godden, Gertrude M. *Henry Fielding: A Memoir.* Arden Lib. repr. of 1909 ed. 1980 $40.00. Still a valuable source of information on documents relating to Fielding.

Golden, Morris. *Fielding's Moral Psychology.* Univ. of Massachusetts Pr. 1966 $15.00. Fielding's novels as reflections and exemplifications of his conceptions of human nature.

Johnson, Maurice. *Fielding's Art of Fiction: 11 Essays on Shamela, Joseph Andrews, Tom Jones, and Amelia.* Univ. of Pennsylvania Pr. 1961 o.p. Thoughtful, stimulating approach to the art of the novel as well as to Fielding.

Miller, Henry Knight. *Essays on Fielding's Miscellanies: A Commentary on Volume One.* Princeton Univ. Pr. 1961 o.p. The best study of Fielding's thought, essential for understanding his novels.

———. *Henry Fielding's Tom Jones and the Romance Tradition.* Eng. Lit. Ser. Univ. of Victoria Pr. 1976 o.p. A first-rate interpretation from the romance perspective.

Murphy, Arthur. *The Lives of Henry Fielding and Samuel Johnson, together with Essays from Gray's Inn Journal, 1752–1792.* Scholars' Facsimiles 1968 $54.00. Reprinted from *Works* of Arthur Murphy (1786), *Works* of Fielding (1762), and *Works* of Samuel Johnson (1792), with an introduction by Matthew Grace. The Fielding "life" is a superb essay by his friend Murphy, which accompanied the first collected edition of his works.

Paulson, Ronald, and Thomas Lockwood, eds. *Henry Fielding: The Critical Heritage. Critical Heritage Ser.* Routledge & Kegan 1969 o.p. A useful collection of essays going back to the mid-eighteenth century.

Rogers, Pat. *Henry Fielding.* Scribner 1979 o.p. A relatively brief, knowledgeable account.

Wright, Andrew H. *Henry Fielding: Mask and Feast.* Univ. of California Pr. 1965 pap.

$2.50. A close study of *Joseph Andrews, Tom Jones,* and *Amelia,* in which "Wright brilliantly interprets Fielding's conception of art as a rehearsal of civilization" (*Choice*).

GOLDSMITH, OLIVER. 1728–1774

As SAMUEL JOHNSON said in his famous epitaph on his friend, Goldsmith ornamented whatever he touched with his pen. A professional writer who died in his prime, Goldsmith wrote the best comedy of his day, *She Stoops to Conquer;* one of its finest poems, "The Desert Village"; its most engaging essays, particularly in his newspaper column of Chinese Letters, which were reprinted as *The Citizen of the World;* histories of Rome, Greece, and England that remained in use in schools for a century; a *History of the Earth and Animated Nature* that at times, as Johnson predicted, is as amusing as a Persian tale; biographies and even book reviews that still give pleasure in their wit and sympathy; and *The Vicar of Wakefield,* which, despite major plot inconsistencies and the intrusion of poems, essays, tales, and lectures apparently foreign to its central concerns, remains one of the most engaging fictional works in English. One reason for its appeal is the character of the narrator, Dr. Primrose, who is at once a slightly absurd pedant, an impatient traditional father of teenagers, a Job-like figure heroically facing life's blows, and an alertly curious, helpful, loving person. Another reason is Goldsmith's own mixture of delight and amused condescension (analogous to, though not identical with, Sterne's in *Tristram Shandy* and Johnson's in *Rasselas,* both contemporaneous) as he looks at the vicar and his domestic group, fit representatives of a ludicrous but workable world.

BOOKS BY GOLDSMITH

Collected Works. Ed. by Arthur Friedman, Oxford 5 vols. 1966 o.p. The standard edition of his original writings.

Collected Letters. Ed. by Katharine C. Balderston, Richard West repr. of 1928 ed. 1980 lib. bdg. $20.00

The Vicar of Wakefield. 1766. Arden Lib. repr. 1982 lib. bdg. $30.00; Biblio Dist. 1976 $9.95 pap. $2.95; ed. by Arthur Friedman, *Oxford Eng. Novels Ser.* 1974 $19.95 1981 pap. $4.95; Penguin 1982 pap. $2.50; Richard West repr. of 1906 ed. 1980 lib. bdg. $25.00

BOOKS ABOUT GOLDSMITH

Ginger, John. *The Notable Man: The Life and Times of Oliver Goldsmith.* David & Charles 1978 o.p. Pleasantly written and usually accurate biography.

Harp, Richard L. *Thomas Percy's Life of Dr. Oliver Goldsmith: A Critical Edition. Salzburg Studies in Eng. Lit.* Humanities Pr. text ed. 1976 pap. $25.50

Quintana, Ricardo. *Oliver Goldsmith: A Georgian Study. Masters of World Lit. Ser.* Macmillan 1967 o.p. The best book-length critical study of Goldsmith.

Wardle, Ralph M. *Oliver Goldsmith.* Shoe String (Archon) 1969 o.p. Useful for the facts of Goldsmith's life.

MALORY, SIR THOMAS. fl. 1470

Sir Thomas Malory's works (consisting of the legends of Sir Lancelot, Sir Gareth, Sir Tristram, and the Holy Grail, as well as the stories of Arthur's coming to the throne, his wars with the Emperor Lucius, and his death) are the most influential expression of Arthurian material in English. The author's sources are principally French romances, but his own contributions are substantial and the result is a vigorous and resonant prose. *Le Morte d'Arthur*, finished between March 1469 and March 1470, was first printed in 1485 by William Caxton, the earliest English printer.

Malory is presumed to have been a knight from an old Warwickshire family, who inherited his father's estates about 1433 and spent 20 years of his later life in jail accused of various crimes. The discovery of a manuscript version of *Le Morte d'Arthur* in 1934 in the library of Winchester College supported the identification of Malory the author with Malory the traitor, burglar, and rapist and showed that many of the inconsistencies in the printed text were traceable to the printing house rather than to the author. The most reliable modern version, therefore, is one like Eugène Vinaver's that is based on the Winchester manuscript.

BOOKS BY MALORY

The Works of Sir Thomas Malory. Ed. by Eugène Vinaver, *Oxford Eng. Texts Ser.* 3 vols. 2d ed. 1967 $160.00

Works. Ed. by Eugène Vinaver, *Oxford Stand. Authors Ser.* 2d ed 1971 $24.95 pap. $11.95

Le Morte d'Arthur. Ed. by H. Oskar Sommer, AMS Pr. 3 vols. in 2. repr. of 1891 ed. $95.00; Biblio Dist. 2 vols. 1953–76 ea. $9.95 pap. ea. $3.95; ed. by D. S. Brewer, Northwestern Univ. Pr. 1968 pap. $6.95; ed. by Janet Cowen, *Penguin Eng. Lib. Ser.* 2 vols. 1970 pap. ea. $3.95; ed. by Edward Strachey, Scholarly repr. of 1899 ed. 1972 $49.00; ed. by R. M. Lumiansky, Scribner $50.00

King Arthur and His Knights. Ed. by Eugène Vinaver, Oxford 1975 pap. $7.95

The Winchester Malory: A Facsimile. Intro. by N. R. Ker, *Early Eng. Text Society Ser.* Oxford 1976 $149.00

BOOKS ABOUT MALORY

Dillon, Bert, ed. *A Malory Handbook*. G. K. Hall 1978 lib. bdg. $20.00

Hicks, Edward. *Sir Thomas Malory: His Turbulent Career—A Biography*. Octagon repr. of 1928 ed. 1970 $16.50

Ihle, Sandra N. *Malory's Grail Quest: Invention and Adaptation in Medieval Prose Romance* Univ. of Wisconsin Pr. text ed. 1983 $22.50

Lambert, Mark. *Malory: Style and Vision in Le Morte d'Arthur*. Yale Studies in Eng. Ser. 1975 o.p.

Life, Page W. *Sir Thomas Malory and the Morte d'Arthur: A Survey of Scholarship and Annotated Bibliography*. Univ. Pr. of Virginia 1980 $14.95

Lumiansky, R. M., ed. *Malory's Originality: A Critical Study of Le Morte d'Arthur*. Richard West repr. 1980 lib. bdg. $30.00

Vinaver, Eugène. *Malory*. Folcroft 1977 lib. bdg. $27.50. Malory's foremost modern editor.

MORE, SIR THOMAS, ST. 1478–1535

More is probably best known for his *Utopia*, which was written in Latin (then the language of literary and intellectual Europe) and printed in Louvain in 1516, where the author was serving as envoy. It was translated into English in 1551. As the first part of this small masterpiece indicates, More was weighing an offer to be an adviser to Henry VIII. He was well aware of the compromises, bitterness, and frustration that such an office involved as the feudal world was replaced by nations led by greedy, warring princes unconcerned for the multitudes of uprooted and oppressed (a world well described in Huizanga's *Waning of the Middle Ages*). In the second part, More develops his famous utopia—a Greek word punning on the meanings "a good place" and "no place"—a religious communistic society where the common ownership of goods, obligatory work for everyone, and the regular life of all before the eyes of all ensure that one's baser nature will remain under control. Inspired by PLATO's *Republic* (see Vol. 4), More's *Utopia* became in turn the urbane legacy of the humanistic movement (in which More's friends were most notably Erasmus, Colet, and Grocyn) to succeeding ages. More's decision to accept Henry's employment led to an agonizing test of political loyalty and personal integrity, to martyrdom, and to eventual sainthood.

BOOKS BY MORE

The Complete Works of St. Thomas More. Complete Works of St. Thomas More Ser. Yale Univ. Pr. 16 vols. projected 1963–85 ea. $30.00–$155.00. It is generally accepted that More's *Richard III* initiated modern historical writing. The Yale University Press edition offers this work, complete with parallel English (1557) and Latin (1565) texts, major variant readings, a collation of all extant manuscript versions, and (for the first time in full) the important early draft of the Latin text, Manuscript Arundel 43 in the College of Arms. The first scholarly treatment of More's *Utopia* incorporates the advances made in Renaissance studies in the twentieth century and places the work within the context of its times. The definitive Latin text is based on the March 1518 edition, the last to be corrected by More himself. There is a complete list of variant readings from the editions of 1516, 1517, and November 1518, with a parallel English text, a revision of the G. C. Richards translation.

Correspondence. Ed. by Elizabeth Frances Rogers, *Select Bibliographies Repr. Ser.* Ayer facsimile repr. of 1947 ed. $30.00

Thomas More's Prayer Book: A Facsimile Reproduction of the Annotated Pages. Trans. by Louis L. Martz and Richard S. Sylvester, *Elizabethan Club Ser.* Yale Univ. Pr. 1969 $25.00. A facsimile reproduction of the annotated pages, with the English translation. Published for the Elizabethan Club, it is intended as a companion volume to *The Complete Works of St. Thomas More* (see earlier).

Utopia. 1516. Biblio Dist. 1978 $8.95 pap. $2.95; trans. by Robert M. Adams, *Norton Critical Eds.* 1975 $12.95 pap. $4.95; trans. by Paul Turner, *Penguin Class. Ser.* 1965 pap. $2.50; trans. by Peter Marshall, Washington Square Pr. pap. $2.95; ed. by Edward Louis Surtz, *Selected Works of St. Thomas More Ser.* Yale Univ. Pr. 1964 $20.00 pap. $5.95; ed. by Edward Louis Surtz and J. H. Hexter, *Complete Works of St. Thomas More Ser.* Yale Univ. Pr. 1965 $55.00

The Supplycacyon of Soulys: Agaynst the Supplycacyon of Beggars. Eng. Experience
Ser. Johnson Repr. repr. of 1529 ed. 1971 $14.00
The Apology. 1533. Ed. by J. B. Trapp, *Complete Works of St. Thomas More Ser.* Yale
Univ. Pr. text ed. 1979 $55.00
A Dialogue of Comfort against Tribulation. 1534. *Complete Works of St. Thomas More
Ser.* Yale Univ. Pr. 1976 $75.00

BOOKS ABOUT MORE

Bolt, Robert. *A Man for All Seasons.* Random 1962 $8.95; Random (Vintage) 1966
pap. $2.95. The thoughtful and immensely successful play and movie.
Chambers, Raymond W. *Thomas More.* Univ. of Michigan Pr. 1958 pap. $6.95
Guy, J. A. *The Public Career of Sir Thomas More.* Yale Univ. Pr. 1980 $32.00
Harpsfield, Nicholas. *The Life and Death of St. Thomas More.* Ed. from mss. by E. V.
Hitchcock, Somerset repr. 1932 $25.00
The Life and Illustrious Martyrdom of Saint Thomas More. 1588 1689. Trans. by Philip
E. Hallett, 1928, ed. and annot. by E. E. Reynolds, Fordham Univ. Pr. 1967 o.p.
The 1588 edition was part 3 of *Tres Thomae* (St. Thomas, Thomas à Becket, and
More). The 1689 edition, published in Frankfurt, was entitled *Vita Thomae Mori.*
The life is based on William Roper's (d. 1578) notes, incorporating the memoirs
of members of More's household. Roper was the son-in-law of Sir Thomas More.
Logan, George M. *The Meaning of More's Utopia.* Princeton Univ. Pr. 1983 $27.50
Marius, Richard. *Thomas More: A Biography.* Knopf 1984 $22.95
Roper, William. *The Mirror of Vertue, or The Life of Thomas More.* 1625. In Richard S.
Sylvester and Davis P. Harding, eds., *Two Early Tudor Lives.* Yale Univ. Pr. 1962
$7.95
Surtz, Edward Louis. *The Praise of Pleasure: Philosophy, Education, and Communism
in More's Utopia.* Harvard Univ. Pr. 1957 o.p. An intense and scholarly study
that endeavors to reconcile *Utopia*'s communist and Epicurean principles with
More's Catholicism. "The clearest elucidation so far given of the meaning of
More's enigmatic book" (*TLS*).
Sylvester, Richard S., and Germaine Marc'hadour, eds. *Essential Articles for the
Study of Thomas More. Essential Articles Ser.* Shoe String 1977 $25.00

SOME OF THE MORE FAMOUS UTOPIAS

For complete bibliographic data on the utopias by Bellamy, Butler, Huxley, and
Swift, see the main listings for these authors in this volume.

Bacon, Francis. *The New Atlantis* (and *Great Instauration*). Ed. by J. Weinberger,
Crofts Class. Ser. Harlan Davidson text ed. 1980 $10.95 pap. $3.95.
Bellamy, Edward. *Looking Backward.*
Butler, Samuel. *Erewhon.*
———. *Erewhon and Erewhon Revisited.*
Harrington, James. *James Harrington's Oceana.* Ed. by S. B. Liljegren, Hyperion Pr.
repr. of 1924 ed. 1979 $30.25
Huxley, Aldous. *Brave New World.*
———. *Brave New World Revisited.*
Plato. *The Republic.* Basic Bks. text ed. 1968 pap. $8.95; Biblio Dist. 1980 $12.95 pap.
$5.95; trans. by James Adams (Gr.), Cambridge Univ. Pr. 2 vols. text ed. vol. 1
$62.50 vol. 2 $69.50; trans. by Benjamin Jowett, Doubleday pap. $6.95; trans. by
A. D. Lindsay, Dutton 1957 pap. 1965; trans. and intro. by G. M. Grube, Hackett
1973 $12.50 pap. text ed. $4.95; trans. by Raymond Larson, *Crofts Class. Ser.* Har-

lan Davidson text ed. 1979 $14.95 pap. $6.95; *Loeb Class. Lib.* Harvard Univ. Pr.
2 vols. ea. $12.50; trans. by Benjamin Jowett, Modern Lib. 1982 $7.95; trans. by
Francis M. Cornford, Oxford 1955 pap. $4.95; trans. by H. D. Lee, *Penguin Class.
Ser.* 1955 $3.50; trans. by Benjamin Jowett, Random (Vintage) 1955 pap. $3.95

Skinner, B. F. *Walden II.* Irvington repr. of 1948 ed. 1980 o.p.

Swift, Jonathan. *Gulliver's Travels.*

BOOKS ABOUT UTOPIAS

Hertzler, Joyce O. *The History of Utopian Thought.* Cooper Square Pr. repr. of 1923
ed. 1965 $28.50. Analyzes the origin and strength of social ideas and ideals con-
ceived by exceptional minds.

Mannheim, Karl. *Ideology and Utopia: An Introduction to the Sociology of Knowledge.*
Harcourt 1955 pap. $4.95. Charles A. Beard said that this is "one of the three or
four books which must be read by everyone who wants to discuss public affairs
intelligently."

Manuel, Frank E., ed. *Utopias and Utopian Thought.* Beacon pap. o.p.; Houghton Mifflin 1966 o.p. This volume of scholarly essays, all but three reprinted from the
magazine *Daedalus,* includes opinions on utopias and utopian thinking by Crane
Brinton, Paul Tillich, Lewis Mumford, Northrop Frye, and others.

Mumford, Lewis. *The Story of Utopias.* 1924. Peter Smith $10.25

Parrington, Vernon L., Jr. *American Dreams: A Study of American Utopias.* Russell
repr. of 1947 ed. 1967 $15.00

RICHARDSON, SAMUEL. 1689–1761

A printer and bookseller who wrote love letters for servant girls as an apprentice, studied nights to improve himself, and married the boss's daughter, Samuel Richardson undertook at age 50 to write a book of sample cour-
tesy notes, marriage proposals, job applications, and business letters for
young people. While imagining situations for this book, he recalled an old
scandal and developed it into *Pamela, or Virtue Rewarded,* a novel about a
servant girl whose firmness, vitality, literacy, and superior intelligence turn
her master's lust into a decorous love that leads to their marriage. All of *Pamela*'s virtues of fresh characterization, immediacy (what Richardson called
"writing to the moment" of the character's consciousness), and the involvement of the reader in the character's intense and fluctuating fantasies, together with a much more focused seriousness, a more varied and differenti-
ated cast of letter writers, and a more fundamental examination of moral
and social issues, make his second novel, *Clarissa,* a masterpiece. Although
anyone who reads this huge novel for its plot may hang himself (as Richardson's friend SAMUEL JOHNSON said), readers have been fascinated by the complex conflict between Clarissa Harlowe and Robert Lovelace, two of the
most fully realized characters, psychologically and socially, in all literature.
Like such great successors as ROUSSEAU (see Vol. 3), an acknowledged follower of Richardson, DOSTOEVSKY (see Vol. 2), and D. H. LAWRENCE, Richardson understands and shows us, in DIDEROT's (see Vol. 2) appreciative image,
the black recesses of the cave of the mind.

Although Richardson's last novel, *Sir Charles Grandison,* like *Pamela, Part
II,* mainly undertakes comic delineation of manners, it also examines the se-

rious issue of love between a Protestant and a Catholic and it experiments technically with flashbacks, with stenographic reports, and most assertively with a pure hero, a male Clarissa of irresistible social class, charm, and power. At its best, Richardson's work fuses the epistolary technique, the use of dramatic scenes, the traditions of religious biography, and the elements of current romantic fiction to achieve precise analysis, an air of total verisimilitude, and a vision of a world of primal psychological forces in conflict.

BOOKS BY RICHARDSON

The Novels. AMS Pr. 19 vols. repr. of 1901–02 ed. 1970 ea. $35.00 set $665.00. Complete and unabridged, with a life of the author and introductions by William Lyon Phelps.

The Correspondence of Samuel Richardson. Ed. by Anna Laetitia Barbauld, AMS Pr. 6 vols. repr. of 1804 ed. ea. $35.00 set $210.00

Selected Letters of Samuel Richardson. Ed. by John Carroll, Oxford 1964 o.p.

Letters of Doctor George Cheyne to Samuel Richardson. Ed. by Charles F. Mullett, Folcroft repr. of 1943 ed. lib. bdg. o.p.

Pamela, or Virtue Rewarded. 1740. Biblio Dist. 2 vols. repr. of 1914 ed. 1974 ea. $9.95 1978 pap. ea. $4.95; ed. by T. C. Duncan-Eaves and B. D. Kimpel, Houghton Mifflin (Riv. Eds.) 1971 pap. $6.50; Norton 1958 pap. $3.95; ed. by Peter Sabor, *Penguin Eng. Lib. Ser.* 1981 pap. $4.95

Clarissa Harlowe, or The History of a Young Lady. 1747–48. Biblio Dist. 4 vols. repr. of 1932 ed. 1976–78 ea. $12.95; ed. and abr. by George Sherburn, Houghton Mifflin (Riv. Eds.) 1962 $6.50

The History of Sir Charles Grandison. 1753–54. Ed. by Jocelyn Harris, Oxford 3 vols. 1972 o.p.

BOOKS ABOUT RICHARDSON

Carroll, John, ed. *Samuel Richardson: A Collection of Critical Essays. Twentieth Century Views Ser.* Prentice-Hall 1969 $12.95. Reprints some major approaches to the novels.

Castle, Terry. *Clarissa's Ciphers: Meaning and Disruption in Richardson's Clarissa.* Cornell Univ. Pr. 1982 $19.50. A lively, feminist, close reading of the novel.

Cowler, Rosemary, ed. *Twentieth Century Interpretations of Pamela.* Prentice-Hall 1969 o.p. Reprints valuable essays on the novel.

Doody, Margaret A. *A Natural Passion: A Study of the Novels of Samuel Richardson.* Oxford 1974 o.p. The best general study since McKillop's.

Duncan-Eaves, T. C., and B. D. Kimpel. *Samuel Richardson: A Biography.* Oxford 1971 o.p. The only extensive and authoritative modern biography of the novelist.

Flynn, Carol Houlihan. *Samuel Richardson: A Man of Letters.* Princeton Univ. Pr. 1982 $27.50. The role of letters in Richardson's life and novels.

Golden, Morris. *Richardson's Characters.* Univ. of Michigan Pr. 1963 o.p. An examination of sexual, psychological, and social qualities.

McKillop, Alan Dugald. *Samuel Richardson, Printer and Novelist.* Univ. of North Carolina Pr. 1936 o.p. Still a valuable biographical and critical study.

Sale, William M. *Samuel Richardson: A Bibliographical Record of His Literary Career with Some Historical Notes.* Yale Univ. Pr. 1936 o.p. Still standard.

———. *Samuel Richardson, Master Printer. Cornell Studies in Eng.* Greenwood repr. of 1950 ed. 1978 $24.75

SMOLLETT, TOBIAS GEORGE. 1721–1771

Smollett, the only major eighteenth-century English novelist who can seriously be called picaresque, came to the writing of novels with a strong sense of Scottish national pride (an alienating element in the London of the 1750s and 1760s), a Tory feeling for a lost order, horrifying experiences as a physician, and a fierce determination to make his way in the literary world. Prolific in a variety of forms, he was particularly successful as a popular historian, magazine editor, translator of CERVANTES (see Vol. 2), and author of novels about adventurous, unscrupulous, poor young men. His work is marked by vigorous journalistic descriptions of contemporary horrors like shipboard amputations or the filthy curative waters of Bath; by a flair for racy narrative often built on violence and sentiment and a comedy often relying on practical jokes and puns; and by a great gift for creating comic caricatures. His peppery *Travels through France and Italy* was something of a spur to Sterne's *Sentimental Journey*, where Smollett is referred to as Dr. Smelfungus who "set out with the spleen and jaundice, and every object he passed by was discolored or distorted—He wrote an account of them, but 'twas nothing but the account of his miserable feelings."

Smollett's most notable novels are *Roderick Random, Peregrine Pickle, Ferdinand Count Fathom* (1753, o.p.), *Sir Launcelot Greaves* (1762, o.p.), which set a precedent by first being serialized in his *British Magazine* (Jan. 1760–Dec. 1761), and especially *The Expedition of Humphry Clinker,* a relatively mellow work that follows the travels of Matthew Bramble, an excitable Welshman, from his home through chaotic England to idyllic Loch Lomond and back. Bramble himself finds what Smollett had irrecoverably lost, his health, as well as a son from his youth. Smollett died in 1771, the year of the novel's appearance, in Leghorn, Italy.

A complete scholarly edition of Smollett's works is currently in preparation by the University of Delaware Press.

BOOKS BY SMOLLETT

Letters. Ed. by Edward S. Noyes, *Select Bibliographies Repr. Ser.* Ayer facsimile ed. 1926 $23.50

The Adventures of Peregrine Pickle. 1731. Ed. by James L. Clifford, *Oxford Eng. Novels Ser.* 1964 pap. $7.95; *World's Class.-Pap. Ser.* Oxford 1983 $8.95

Roderick Random. 1748. Biblio Dist. repr. of 1927 ed. 1973 $9.95 pap. 1982 $5.95; ed. by Paul-Gabriel Bouce, *Oxford Eng. Novels Ser.* text ed. 1979 $45.00 1981 pap. $6.95

The Expedition of Humphry Clinker. 1771. Ed. by James Thorson, *Norton Critical Eds.* 1983 $24.95 pap. $7.95; ed. by Lewis M. Knapp, *World's Class.-Pap. Ser.* Oxford 1984 $7.95; ed. by Angus Ross, *Penguin Eng. Lib. Ser.* 1967 pap. $3.95

Travels through France and Italy. 1766. Ed. by Frank Feldstein, *World's Class. Ser.* Oxford facsimile ed. 1981 $59.00 pap. $7.95

BOOKS ABOUT SMOLLETT

Bouce, Paul-Gabriel. *The Novels of Tobias Smollett.* Longman text ed. 1976 $32.00

Kahrl, George. *Tobias Smollett: Traveler-Novelist.* Octagon 1968 lib. bdg. $16.50

Knapp, Lewis M. *Tobias George Smollett, Doctor of Men and Manners.* Russell repr. of

1949 ed. 1963 o.p. The most authoritative full-scale study of the man and the writer.

Martz, Louis L. *The Later Career of Tobias Smollett. Yale Studies in Eng. Ser.* Shoe String repr. of 1942 ed. 1967 $15.00. A study of Smollett's creative work after 1753.

Spector, Robert D. *Tobias Smollett. Eng. Authors Ser.* Irvington 1968 lib. bdg. $6.95. An excellent biographical and critical study.

STERNE, LAURENCE. 1713–1768

If Fielding showed that the novel (like the traditional epic or drama) could make the chaos of life coherent in art, Sterne only a few years later in *The Life and Opinions of Tristram Shandy, Gentleman,* of which the best edition is by Melvyn New and Joan New, laughed away the notion of order. In Sterne's world, people are sealed off in their own minds so that only in unpredictable moments of spontaneous feeling can they have the sense of another human being. Reviewers attacked the obscenity of Tristram's imagined autobiography as it was published (two volumes each in 1759, early 1761, late 1761, 1765, and one in 1767), particularly when the author revealed himself as a clergyman, but the presses teemed with imitations of this great literary hit of the 1760s.

Through the mind of the eccentric hero, Sterne subverted accepted ideas on conception, birth, childhood, education, and the contemplation of maturity and death, so that Tristram's concerns touched his contemporaries and are still important. Since *Tristram Shandy* is patently a great and lasting comic work that yet seems, as E. M. Forster said, "ruled by the Great God Muddle," much recent criticism has centered on the question of its unity or lack of it; and its manipulation of time and of mental processes has been considered particularly relevant to the problems of fiction in our day.

Sterne's *Sentimental Journey,* the best edition of which is by Gardner D. Stout, Jr., has been immensely admired by some critics for its superb tonal balance of irony and sentiment. His *Sermons of Mr. Yorick* catches the spirit of its time by dramatically preaching benevolence and sympathy as superior to doctrine. Whether as Tristram or as Yorick, Sterne is the most memorably personal voice in eighteenth-century fiction.

The University Presses of Florida, which is planning an edition of Sterne's works, has begun with *Tristram Shandy.*

BOOKS BY STERNE

The Complete Works and Life of Laurence Sterne. Ed. by Wilbur L. Cross, with a life by Percy Fitzgerald, AMS Pr. 12 vols. in 6 repr. of 1904 ed. ea. $52.50 set $315.00

Works. Ed. by George Saintsbury, AMS Pr. 6 vols. repr. of 1894 ed. ea. $10.00 set $60.00

Memoirs of Mr. Laurence Sterne: The Life and Opinions of Tristram Shandy; A Sentimental Journey; Selected Sermons and Letters. Ed. by Douglas Grant, *Reynard Lib.* Harvard Univ. Pr. 1970 $20.00 pap. $7.50

Tristram Shandy. 1759–67. Ed. by Melvyn New and Joan New, *Collected Works of Laurence Sterne* Univ. Pr. of Florida 2 vols. 1978 ea. $37.50; ed. by Howard Anderson, *Norton Critical Eds.* 1980 $24.95 pap. $5.95; ed. by James A. Work, Odyssey Pr. 1940 pap. $11.49; ed. by Ian C. Ross, *World's Class.-Pap. Ser.* Oxford 1983 $5.95

Laurence Sterne's Sermons of Mr. Yorick. 1760–69. Ed. by Lansing Hammond, *Yale Studies in Eng. Ser.* Shoe String repr. of 1948 ed. 1970 $17.50

A Sentimental Journey through France and Italy. 1768. Intro. by Gardner D. Stout, Jr., Univ. of California Pr. rev. ed. 1967 $39.00; ed. by Graham Petrie, *Penguin Eng. Lib. Ser.* 1967 pap. $3.95

The Journal to Eliza and Letters to Eliza (and *A Sentimental Journey through France and Italy*). 1775. Biblio Dist. 1975 $9.95 pap. $2.50

BOOKS ABOUT STERNE

Cash, Arthur H. *Laurence Sterne: The Early and Middle Years.* Methuen 1975 $60.00. Now the standard biography of Sterne up to the time of publication of the first two volumes of *Tristram Shandy.*

———. *Sterne's Comedy of Moral Sentiments.* Duquesne Univ. Pr. 1966 o.p. A valuable analysis of Sterne's ideas, particularly in his *Sentimental Journey.*

Cash, Arthur H., and John Stedmond, eds. *Winged Skull: Papers of the Laurence Sterne Bicentenary Conference.* Kent State Univ. Pr. 1971 $21.00

Cross, Wilbur L. *The Life and Times of Laurence Sterne.* Russell 3d ed. repr. of 1929 ed. 1967 o.p. The standard biography.

Curtis, Lewis P. *The Politics of Laurence Sterne.* Arden Lib. repr. of 1929 ed. 1978 lib. bdg. $22.50; Folcroft repr. of 1929 ed. lib. bdg. $15.00

De Porte, Michael V. *Nightmares and Hobbyhorses: Swift, Sterne, and Augustan Ideas of Madness.* Huntington Lib. 1974 $12.50

Fluchère, Henri. *Laurence Sterne: From Tristram to Yorick—An Interpretation of Tristram Shandy.* Trans. by Barbara Bray, Oxford 1965 o.p. An extensive study of the life and ideas of the author as they appear in the novels.

Freedman, William. *Laurence Sterne and the Origins of the Musical Novel.* Univ. of Georgia Pr. 1978 $19.50

Hammond, Lansing. *Laurence Sterne's Sermons of Mister Yorick.* Yale Studies in Eng. Ser. Shoe String repr. of 1948 ed. 1970 $17.50

Hartley, Lodwick. *Laurence Sterne: An Annotated Bibliography, 1965–1977.* G. K. Hall 1978 lib. bdg. $14.50

———. *Laurence Sterne in the Twentieth Century.* Univ. of North Carolina Pr. 1966 $17.50

Holtz, William V. *Image and Immortality: A Study of Tristram Shandy.* Univ. Pr. of New England 1970 $14.00. An admirable discussion of Sterne's use of the visual arts.

Howes, Alan B., ed. *Sterne: The Critical Heritage. Critical Heritage Ser.* Routledge & Kegan 1974 $40.00

Loveridge, Mark. *Laurence Sterne and the Argument about Design.* Barnes & Noble 1982 $27.50

Moglen, Helene. *The Philosophical Irony of Laurence Sterne.* Univ. Pr. of Florida 1975 $10.00

Myer, Valerie G., ed. *Laurence Sterne: Riddles and Mysteries. Critical Studies* Barnes & Noble 1984 $27.50

Traugott, John. *Tristram Shandy's World: Sterne's Philosophical Rhetoric.* Russell repr. of 1954 ed. o.p. Still the best study of Sterne's thought in the novels.

SWIFT, JONATHAN. 1667–1745

Apparently doomed to an obscure Anglican parsonage in Laracor, Ireland, even after he had written his anonymous masterpiece *A Tale of a Tub*, Swift turned a political mission to England from the Irish Protestant clergy into an avenue toward prominence as the chief propagandist for the Tory government. His exhilaration at achieving importance in his forties appears engagingly in his *Journal to Stella*, addressed to Esther Johnson, a young protégée for whom Swift felt more warmth than for anyone else in his long life. At the death of Queen Anne and the fall of the Tories in 1714, Swift became dean of St. Patrick's Cathedral, Dublin. In Ireland, which he considered exile from a life of power and intellectual activity in London, Swift found time to defend his oppressed countrymen, sometimes in contraband essays like his *Drapier Letters*, and sometimes in short mordant pieces like the famous *Modest Proposal;* and there he wrote perhaps the greatest work of his time, *Gulliver's Travels*.

Using his characteristic device of the persona (a developed and sometimes satirized narrator like the anonymous hack writer of *A Tale of a Tub* or Isaac Bickerstaff in *Predictions for the Ensuing Year*, who exposes an astrologer), Swift created the hero Gulliver, who in the first instance stands for the bluff, decent, average Englishman, then for man generally, and most powerfully for us, the readers. Gulliver is a full and powerful vision of man in a world where violent passions, intellectual pride, and external chaos can degrade him—to animalism, in Swift's most horrifying images—but where man has scope to act, guided by the classical-Christian tradition. *Gulliver's Travels* has been an immensely successful children's book (though Swift did not care much for children), so widely popular through the world for its imagination, wit, fun, freshness, vigor, and narrative skill that its hero is in many languages a common noun. Perhaps as a consequence, its meaning has been the subject of continuing dispute, and its author has been called everything from sentimental to mad.

For Swift's poetry, see *The Poems of Jonathan Swift*, edited by Harold Williams (o.p.), and *Poetical Works*, edited by Herbert Davis.

BOOKS BY SWIFT

The Prose Works. Ed. by Temple Scott, bio. intro. by W. E. H. Lecky, AMS Pr. 12 vols. repr. of 1888–1909 ed. $495.00

The Prose Works. Ed. by Herbert Davis, *Shakespeare Head Ed.* Barnes & Noble 14 vols. repr. of 1939 ed. 1964–68 $475.00. The index was compiled by William J. Kunz, Steven Hollander, and Susan Staves under the supervision of Irvin Ehrenpreis. Addenda, errata, and corrigenda were edited by Herbert Davis and Irvin Ehrenpreis.

Correspondence. Ed. by Harold Williams, Oxford 5 vols. 1965 o.p. "Meticulously annotated" collection of Swift's correspondence—the largest to date. Included are letters from Pope, Addison, Steele, and others. "Swift's letters follow the shifts of his fortune and reveal his clarity of mind, the strength of his style, and his command of language" (*LJ*).

The Portable Swift: Gulliver's Travels, Satires, Poems, Letters, Journals. Ed. by Carl Van Doren, *Viking Portable Lib.* Penguin 1977 pap. $7.95

Writings of Jonathan Swift. Ed. by Robert A. Greenberg and William B. Piper, *Norton Critical Eds.* text ed. 1973 pap. $10.95

Gulliver's Travels and Other Writings. Modern Lib. 1958 $6.95; ed. by Ricardo Quintana, Random 1979 $6.95. Includes *Gulliver's Travels; A Tale of a Tub; The Battle of the Books; A Discourse Concerning the Mechanical Operation of the Spirit; A Meditation upon a Broom-Stick;* selected prose from the *Journal to Stella;* the Partridge-Bickerstaff Papers and other writings; selected letters; and selected verse, 1709–33.

Gulliver's Travels and Other Writings. Ed. by Miriam K. Starkman, *Bantam Class. Ser.* 1981 pap. $2.25. Includes *The Battle of the Books, A Tale of a Tub,* and *A Modest Proposal.*

Satires and Personal Writings. Ed. by W. A. Eddy, *Oxford Stand. Authors Ser.* 1932 $32.50

A Discourse of the Contests and Dissentions between the Nobles and the Commons in Athens and Rome with the Consequences They Had upon Both Those States. 1701. Ed. by Frank H. Ellis, Oxford 1967 o.p. Swift's first satire and first published work—an allegory of English history.

A Tale of a Tub: Written for the Universal Improvement of Mankind. 1704. Ed. by Edward Hodnett, AMS Pr. repr. of 1930 ed. $15.00; ed. by Kathleen Williams, Biblio Dist. 1975 $10.95 pap. $3.50; ed. by Robert Folkenflik, *Mind of Man Ser.* J. Simon 1979 $30.00; ed. by A. C. Guthkelch and David N. Smith, Oxford 2d ed. 1958 $42.00

Gulliver's Travels. 1726. Biblio Dist. 1978 $9.95 1984 pap. $3.95; Dell pap. 2.95; ed. by Louis A. Landa, Houghton Mifflin rev. ed. 1960 $6.50; ed. by Robert A. Greenberg, *Norton Critical Eds.* 1970 text ed. pap. $5.95 1965 $5.50; ed. by Paul Turner, Oxford 1971 pap. $6.95; ed. by Peter Dixon and J. Chalker, *Penguin Eng. Lib. Ser.* 1967 pap. $2.25; Schocken 1984 $21.95; Scholars' Facsimiles repr. of 1726 ed. 1981 $70.00; ed. by Harry Shefter, *Enriched Class. Ed. Ser.* Washington Square Pr. pap. $3.95

Polite Conversations (A Complete Collection of Genteel and Ingenious Conversations according to the Most Polite Mode and Method Now Used in Court and in the Best Companies of England). Folcroft repr. of 1738 ed. 1975 lib. bdg. $15.00

BOOKS ABOUT SWIFT

Ehrenpreis, Irvin. *Swift: The Man, His Works, and the Age.* Harvard Univ. Pr. 3 vols. text ed. 1983 vols. 1 and 2 o.p. vol. 3 $35.00. The authoritative biography of Swift so far, also featuring learned and perceptive criticism.

Fabricant, Carole. *Swift's Landscape.* Johns Hopkins Univ. Pr. text ed. 1982 $25.00

Golden, Morris. *The Self Observed: Swift, Johnson, Wordsworth.* Johns Hopkins Univ. Pr. 1972 $17.50. On Swift's projection of certain views of himself into the vision of man in his writings.

Harth, Philip. *Swift and Anglican Rationalism: The Religious Background of A Tale of a Tub.* Univ. of Chicago Pr. 1961 o.p. A learned discussion of the book's theological milieu.

Jaffe, Nora C. *The Poet Swift.* Univ. Pr. of New England text ed. 1977 $15.00. A perceptive study of the poetry.

Johnson, Maurice. *The Sin of Wit: Jonathan Swift as a Poet.* Gordian 1966 o.p. The first, and still useful, critical study of Swift's poetry.

Landa, Louis A. *Swift and the Church of Ireland.* Oxford 1954 o.p. The authoritative study of Swift's career as a churchman.

Paulson, Ronald. *Theme and Structure in Swift's Tale of a Tub.* Yale Studies in Eng.

Ser. Shoe String repr. of 1960 ed. 1972 $18.50. Still the best book on Swift's early masterpiece.

Starkman, Miriam Kosh. *Swift's Satire on Learning in "A Tale of A Tub."* Octagon. 1968 lib. bdg. $18.50. A valuable study of the victims of Swift's satire and of seventeenth-century controversies.

Steele, Peter. *Jonathan Swift: Preacher and Jester.* Oxford 1978 $31.00

Vickers, Brian, ed. *The World of Jonathan Swift: Essays for the Tercentenary.* Harvard Univ. Pr. 1968 $17.50. Interpretive essays.

Williams, Kathleen. *Jonathan Swift and the Age of Compromise.* Univ. Pr. of Kansas 1959 o.p. Clear and persuasive discussion of the works, particularly *Gulliver's Travels*, in relation to Swift's intellectual milieu.

WALPOLE, HORACE (or Horatio), 4th Earl of Orford. 1717–1797

[SEE Chapter 17 in this volume.]

CHAPTER 11

British Fiction: Middle Period

Fred Kaplan

> If the scene were truly and powerfully rendered, the improbability more or less necessary to all tales and allowable in them, would become a part of a thing so true and vivid, that the reader must accept it whether he likes it or not.
> —CHARLES DICKENS, *Letters*

> The changing wisdom of successive generations discards ideas, questions facts, demolishes theories. But the artist appeals to that part of our being which is not dependent on wisdom; to that in us which is a gift and not an acquisition—and, therefore, more permanently enduring. He speaks to our capacity for delight and wonder, to the sense of mystery surrounding our lives; to our sense of pity, and beauty, and pain; to the latent feeling of fellowship with all creation.
> —JOSEPH CONRAD, *The Nigger of the Narcissus*

British fiction exploded into sustained greatness in the middle period, which begins in the first 20 years of the nineteenth century with the panoramic historical romances of Sir Walter Scott and the carefully crafted character explorations of Jane Austen. Scott's combinations of romantic medievalism and contemporary sentiment were widely popular; Austen's careful and restrained illuminations of the relationship between character, environment, and moral choice were hardly read. But the modern judgment is that she was the most impressive literary artist working in the novel between the final publications of the major eighteenth-century novelists and the first novel of Charles Dickens in 1836.

The years between passed with interesting but secondary figures like Ann Radcliffe and Mary Shelley, who popularized Gothic fiction, Maria Edgeworth, who created the regional novel, and Thomas Love Peacock, whose novels emphasized intellectual wit and literary humor. Such special subject areas anticipated in the mid-century the sea-adventure novels of Marryat, the historical novels of Bulwer-Lytton and Ainsworth, the political novels of Disraeli, the Christian-socialist novels of Kingsley, the labor novels of Gaskell, the utopian novels of Butler, the proletarian novels of Gissing, the novels of international adventure and moral testing of Conrad, the novels of colonial empire of Kipling, and so on. Each represents a popular type of fiction whose many practitioners contributed to a form of communication and entertainment that dominated the Victorian age.

Interestingly, the novelist most acclaimed during the high years of Victorian culture, Charles Dickens, has returned from comparative neglect to a position of the highest esteem, valued for the depth and precision of his psychological insight, the brilliance of his metaphoric style, and his capacity to sustain complex structures in which purposeful artifice, accurately realized satire, and poetic invention are integrated successfully. Dickens contained within himself all the strands that his contemporaries and followers, extraordinary in their own right, wove separately. Thackeray became the master of satire, George Eliot of psychological realism, Trollope of behavioral norms, Collins of detective sensationalism, Hardy of the landscape of pessimistic despair.

No period in the history of the English novel reflects so dramatically the movement from the past to the present, from pastoral containment to urban chaos, from aristocratic forbearance to democratic emotionalism, from belief in firm opinions and a settled faith to uncertainty and relativism. But, at the same time, no literature since the Renaissance in England has communicated quite the fullness and variety of life, the sense of sustained explorations of the relationship between people and themselves and people and society, as the fiction of the middle period.

HISTORY AND CRITICISM

Altick, Richard D. *The English Common Reader: A Social History of the Mass Reading Public, 1800–1900. Midway Repr. Ser.* Univ. of Chicago Pr. 1983 $13.00

Auerbach, Nina. *Communities of Women: An Idea in Fiction.* Harvard Univ. Pr. 1978 $15.00

Baker, Ernest Albert. *A History of the English Novel.* 1929–39. Barnes & Noble 11 vols. 1966–1977 ea. $19.50. Volume 11 is by Lionel Stevenson.

Beer, Patricia. *Reader, I Married Him: A Study of the Women Characters of Jane Austen, Charlotte Brontë, Elizabeth Gaskell and George Eliot.* Barnes & Noble repr. of 1974 ed. 1977 $22.50

Block, Andrew. *The English Novel, 1740–1850: A Catalogue including Prose Romances, Short Stories and Translations of Foreign Fiction.* Greenwood rev. ed. repr. of 1961 ed. 1982 lib. bdg. $38.50. A valuable reference source.

Buckley, J. H. *Season of Youth: The Bildungsroman from Dickens to Golding.* Harvard Univ. Pr. 1974 $22.50

Caserio, Robert L. *Plot, Story, and the Novel: From Dickens and Poe to the Modern Period.* Princeton Univ. Pr. 1979 $26.50

Cunningham, Valentine. *Everywhere Spoken Against: Dissent in the Victorian Novel.* Oxford 1975 $29.95

Deidre, David. *Fictions of Resolution in the Victorian Novels.* Columbia Univ. Pr. 1981 $29.50

Eigner, Edwin. *The Metaphysical Mind in England and America.* Univ. of California Pr. 1978 $27.00

Elwin, Malcolm. *Victorian Wallflowers: A Panoramic Survey of the Popular Victorian Literature. Essay Index Repr. Ser.* Core Collection 1978 $27.25

Fairchild, Hoxie N. *The Noble Savage: A Study in Romantic Naturalism.* Russell repr. of 1928 ed. 1961 $15.00

Fleishman, Avrom. *The English Historical Novel: Walter Scott to Virginia Woolf.* Johns Hopkins Univ. Pr. 1971 pap. $6.95

Ford, Boris, ed. *From Dickens to Hardy: A Survey of the Literature of the Age in Its Social and Intellectual Context.* Volume 6 in *A Guide to English Literature.* Penguin pap. 1983 $5.95

Ford, G. H., ed. *Victorian Fiction: A Second Guide to Research.* Modern Language Association 1978 $22.50 pap. $12.50

Garrett, Peter K. *The Victorian Multiplot Novel: Studies in Dialogical Form.* Yale Univ. Pr. 1980 $23.00

Gilbert, Sandra M., and Susan Gubar. *The Madwoman in the Attic: A Study of Women and the Literary Imagination in the Nineteenth Century.* Yale Univ. Pr. 1979 $45.00 pap. $16.95

Gregor, Ian. *Reading the Victorian Novel: Detail into Form.* Critical Studies Ser. Barnes & Noble text ed. 1980 $28.50

Houghton, Walter E., ed. *The Victorian Frame of Mind, 1830–1870.* Yale Univ. Pr. 1963 pap. $9.95

———. *The Wellesley Index to Victorian Periodicals, 1824–1900.* Univ. of Toronto Pr. 2 vols. 1966–78 ea. $150.00 set $375.00. "It is no exaggeration to say that such a work might eventually produce a revolution in nineteenth-century studies" (*Victorian Studies*).

James, Lewis. *Fiction for the Working Man, 1830–1850.* Penguin 1974 o.p.

King, Jeanette. *Tragedy in the Victorian Novel: Theory and Practice in the Novels of George Eliot, Thomas Hardy, and Henry James.* Cambridge Univ. Pr. 1980 pap. $10.95

Knoepflmacher, U. C. *Laughter and Despair: Readings in Ten Novels of the Victorian Era.* Univ. of California Pr. 1973 $29.50 pap. $4.95

Leavis, F. R. *The Great Tradition: George Eliot, Henry James, Joseph Conrad.* New York Univ. Pr. (Gotham Lib.) 1963 pap. $12.50. Important study of the novel.

Levine, George. *The Realistic Imagination: English Fiction from Frankenstein to Lady Chatterley.* Univ. of Chicago Pr. 1981 pap. $10.95

Lucas, John. *The Literature of Change: Studies in the Nineteenth-Century Provincial Novel.* Barnes & Noble 2d ed. 1980 $26.50 pap. $11.50

Miller, J. Hillis. *The Disappearance of God: Five Nineteenth Century Writers.* Harvard Univ. Pr. text ed. 1976 $20.00

———. *The Form of Victorian Fiction.* Bellflower 1980 $12.50

Ousby, Ian. *Bloodhounds of Heaven: The Detective in English Fiction from Godwin to Doyle.* Harvard Univ. Pr. 1976 $14.00

Qualls, Barry. *The Secular Pilgrims of Victorian Fiction: The Novel as Book of Life.* Cambridge Univ. Pr. 1982 $39.50 pap. $11.95

Sanders, Andrew. *The Victorian Historical Novel, 1840–1880.* St. Martin's 1979 $25.00

Showalter, Elaine. *A Literature of Their Own: British Women Novelists from Brontë to Lessing.* Princeton Univ. Pr. 1976 $36.00 pap. $9.95

Sutherland, John A. *Victorian Novelists and Publishers.* Univ. of Chicago Pr. (Phoenix Bks.) 1978 pap. $5.75

Tillotson, Kathleen. *Novels of the Eighteen-Forties.* Oxford 1983 pap. $10.95. Discusses these novels in the context of their relationship to each other, their time, and their first readers.

Van Ghent, Dorothy. *The English Novel: Form and Function.* Harper pap. $6.50

Varma, Devendra P. *The Gothic Flame: Being a History of the Gothic Novel in England—Its Origin, Efflorescence, Disintegration, and Residuary Influences.* Russell repr. of 1957 ed. 1966 $16.00. "Both historically and analytically thorough, besides being entertaining, [it] is wide embracing and scholarly; a vast amount of reading has gone into it" (*TLS*).

Webb, Igor. *From Custom to Capital: The English Novel of the Industrial Revolution.* Cornell Univ. Pr. 1981 $22.50

Wilt, Judith. *Ghosts of the Gothic: Austen, Eliot, and Lawrence.* Princeton Univ. Pr. 1980 $26.00

AUSTEN, JANE. 1775–1817

Jane Austen's novels were largely neglected during her own lifetime and in the decades of high Victorian commitment to seriousness and social issues. But the subtleties of her art and of her moral vision, particularly as embodied in her masterpiece *Emma*, have attracted high praise from modern readers. Her fiction reveals the strong influence of eighteenth-century classicism in its concentration on the nuances of character and in its purposefully nonrealistic depiction of a limited and controlled environment. Like HENRY FIELDING, although with a great deal more restraint, her subject was human nature. She pursued through the dramatization of the daily activities of a small group of typological inhabitants of a specialized community the moral and social significance of basic relationships. Her style is spare, direct, her narrative rapidly paced and made effective by the skillful use of dialogue. Ultimately the dominant tone of her fiction is irony, the dramatization and revelation of pretension, falsity, ambition, selfishness, and, worst of all, bad judgment. Underlying her fiction is a vision of the partial perfectibility of the moral sensibility, which can, despite pervasive obstacles, create a balance of interests and an almost pastoral resolution of tensions.

BOOKS BY AUSTEN

Oxford Illustrated Jane Austen. Ed. by R. W. Chapman, Oxford 6 vols. 1933–1954 ea. $16.95–$17.95

Complete Novels of Jane Austen. Modern Lib. $10.95; Penguin 1983 pap. $8.95

Letters, 1796–1817. Ed. by R. W. Chapman, *World's Class. Ser.* Oxford 2d ed. 1952 o.p.

Letters to Her Sister Cassandra and Others. Ed. by R. W. Chapman, Oxford 2d ed. repr. of 1952 ed. $39.00

The Watsons. 1805. Greenwood repr. of 1958 ed. 1973 lib. bdg. $24.75. *The Watsons* was an unfinished fragment, first published posthumously in 1871, along with two other fragments, *Lady Susan* (c.1805) and *Sanditon* (1817), in J. E. Austen-Leigh's *A Memoir of Jane Austen. Lady Susan* and *Sanditon* are both out of print in separate editions.

Sense and Sensibility. 1811. *Bantam Class. Ser.* 1983 pap. $2.50; Biblio Dist. 1978 $9.95 pap. $2.95; *World's Class. Ser.* Oxford 1980 pap. $2.95; ed. by Tony Tanner, *Penguin Eng. Lib. Ser.* 1969 pap. $2.95

Pride and Prejudice. 1813. *Bantam Class. Ser.* 1981 pap. $1.75; Biblio Dist. 1978 $8.95 pap. $1.95; ed. by N. L. Clay, *Heinemann Guide Novel Ser.* text ed. pap. $4.50; ed. by Mark Schorer, Houghton Mifflin (Riv. Eds.) 1956 pap. $5.50; New Amer. Lib. (Signet Class.) 1962 pap. $1.50; ed. by Donald Gray, *Norton Critical Eds.* text ed. 1966 pap. $6.95; ed. by James Kinsley and F. W. Bradbrook, *World's Class. Ser.*

Oxford 1980 pap. $2.95; ed. by Tony Tanner, *Penguin Eng. Lib. Ser.* 1971 pap. $1.95

Mansfield Park. 1814. *Bantam Class. Ser.* 1983 pap. $3.50; Biblio Dist. 1980 $9.95 pap. $3.75; New Amer. Lib. (Signet Class.) 1964 pap. $3.50; ed. by James Kinsley and John Lucas, *World's Class. Ser.* Oxford 1981 pap. $3.95; ed. by Tony Tanner, *Penguin Eng. Lib. Ser.* 1966 pap. $3.50

Emma. 1816. Ed. by David Lodge, *Casebook Ser.* Aurora text ed. 1970 pap. $2.50; *Bantam Class. Ser.* 1981 pap. $1.95; Biblio Dist. 1976 pap. $2.75; ed. by Lionel Trilling, Houghton Mifflin (Riv. Eds.) 1957 pap. $5.95; New Amer. Lib. (Signet Class.) 1964 pap. $1.95; ed. by Stephen Parrish, *Norton Critical Eds.* 1972 pap. $7.95; ed. by David Lodge and James Kinsley, *World's Class. Ser.* Oxford 1980 pap. $2.95; ed. by Ronald Blyth, *Penguin Eng. Lib. Ser.* 1966 pap. $2.50

Northanger Abbey. 1818. Biblio Dist. 1980 $9.95 pap. $2.50; ed. by N. L. Clay, *Heinemann Guide Novel Ser.* text ed. pap. $4.50; (and *Lady Susan, The Watsons, Sanditon*). *World's Class. Ser.* Oxford 1981 pap. $4.95; ed. by Anne Ehrenpreis, *Penguin Eng. Lib. Ser.* 1972 pap. $2.50

Persuasion. 1818. *Bantam Class. Ser.* 1984 pap. $2.95; Biblio Dist. 1976 pap. $2.50; ed. by N. L. Clay, *Heinemann Guide Novel Ser.* text ed. pap. $4.50; ed. by John Davie, *World's Class. Ser.* Oxford 1981 pap. $2.95; ed. by D. W. Harding, *Penguin Eng. Lib. Ser.* 1967 pap. $2.95

BOOKS ABOUT AUSTEN

Apperson, George. *Jane Austen Dictionary. Studies in Fiction Ser.* Haskell repr. of 1932 ed. 1969 $49.95. "A citation, in a single alphabet, of every person, place, book, and author mentioned in Miss Austen's works, plus the names of her family and friends, and the names of all her works, together with the writing and publishing history of each one" (Publisher's catalog).

Austen-Leigh, J. E. *Memoir of Jane Austen.* Ed. by R. W. Chapman, Folcroft repr. of 1882 ed. 1979 lib. bdg. $22.50

Brown, Julia Polwitt. *Jane Austen: Social Change and Literary Form.* Harvard Univ. Pr. 1979 $14.00

Butler, Marilyn. *Jane Austen and the War of Ideas.* Oxford 1975 $34.00

Chapman, R. W. *Jane Austen: Facts and Problems.* Oxford 1948 o.p. Biographical and critical problems with bibliography, chronology, iconography, etc.

Halperin, John. *The Life of Jane Austen.* Johns Hopkins Univ. Pr. 1984 $25.00

Hardwick, Michael. *A Guide to Jane Austen.* Scribner 1982 pap. $6.95

Lascelles, Mary. *Jane Austen and Her Art.* Arden Lib. repr. of 1939 ed. 1977 lib. bdg. $40.00; Folcroft repr. of 1939 ed. lib. bdg. $27.50; *Oxford Pap. Ser.* 1939 pap. $8.50. "Not only a masterly study of one of the finest artists in English literature but also an outstanding contribution to the criticism of the craft of fiction" (*TLS*).

Mansell, Darrel. *The Novels of Jane Austen: An Interpretation.* Humanities Pr. repr. of 1973 ed. text ed. 1978 $20.50

Moler, Kenneth L. *Jane Austen's Art of Allusion. Landmark Ed.* Univ. of Nebraska Pr. 1968 $18.95

Monaghan, David, ed. *Jane Austen in a Social Context.* Barnes & Noble 1981 $27.50

Mudrick, Marvin. *Jane Austen: Irony as Defense and Discovery.* Univ. of California Pr. 1968 o.p.

Paris, Bernard J. *Character and Conflict in Jane Austen's Novels: A Psychological Approach.* Wayne State Univ. Pr. 1979 $15.95

BARRIE, SIR J(AMES) M(ATTHEW). 1860–1937

Barrie achieved success with both plays and fiction. His novels of homely Scottish life, with their blended pathos and humor, made Scots dialect stories popular. The publication of *The Little Minister* (1891) established him as a successful novelist, and its dramatization started his career as a successful playwright.

In *The Little White Bird*, a collection of fanciful reveries over "dream children," was a half-elfin child called Peter Pan. From this character came Barrie's most popular success, in 1904—*Peter Pan*, a play for children. *Margaret Ogilvy* (1896) is the story-life of Barrie's mother, a bit of true fiction. His autobiography, *The Greenwood Hat* (1938), is out of print.

BOOKS BY BARRIE

Works. AMS Pr. 18 vols. repr. of 1929–41 ed. ea. $32.50 set $585.00
Selections from the Prose Works. Richard West repr. of 1929 ed. $20.00
The Letters of James Matthew Barrie. Ed. by Viola Meynell, AMS Pr. repr. of 1947 ed. 1976 $18.50
Auld Light Idylls (and *Better Dead*). 1886. *Short Story Index Repr. Ser.* Ayer repr. $18.00
The Little Minister. Buccaneer Bks. repr. of 1891 ed. 1981 $18.95
A Window in Thrums. 1889. Scholarly repr. of 1896 ed. $39.00
A Holiday in Bed and Other Sketches: With a Short Biographical Sketch of the Author. *Short Story Index Repr. Ser.* Ayer repr. of 1892 ed. $14.00
The Tillyloss Scandal. *Short Story Index Repr. Ser.* Ayer repr. of 1893 ed. $17.00
The Little White Bird, or Adventures in Kensington Gardens. Longwood Pr. repr. of 1902 ed. 1977 lib. bdg. $25.00
Peter Pan. 1904. Adapted by Josette Frank, *Looking Glass Lib.* Random 1983 pap. $6.95; ed. by S. Trina, Scribner 1980 $14.95
George Meredith. Arden Lib. repr. of 1909 ed. 1978 lib. bdg. $8.50

BOOKS ABOUT BARRIE

Cutler, Bradley D. *Sir James M. Barrie: A Bibliography with Full Collations of the American Unauthorized Editions.* Burt Franklin repr. of 1931 ed. 1967 $24.50
Dunbar, Janet. *J. M. Barrie: The Man behind the Image.* Houghton Mifflin 1970 o.p.
Mackail, Denis G. *Barrie: The Story of J. M. B. Select Bibliographies Repr. Ser.* Ayer repr. of 1941 ed. $34.00

THE BRONTË SISTERS

The Brontë sisters lived most of their lives at the parsonage in Haworth where their father, the Reverend Patrick Brontë, had been appointed perpetual curate. The mother had died soon after they moved there, leaving six small children, who were cared for by Elizabeth Branwell, their mother's oldest sister. The two older girls died of tuberculosis within the next five years. Left very much to their own devices, the three remaining sisters and their brother, Branwell, entertained themselves with creative writings recorded in tiny volumes. When Charlotte went away to school, Emily and Anne started an imaginative saga of their own called *Gondal* (o.p.). When Charlotte returned, she attempted to revive their earlier work and expand it into a realm named Angria, but without success. From that time on Charlotte and Branwell played and wrote about Angria, Emily and Anne about Gondal. These experiments in writing led to a joint volume of verse printed at their own expense in 1846, *Poems by Currer, Ellis and Acton Bell*, of which only two copies were sold.

BOOK BY THE BRONTË SISTERS

The Life and Works of the Sisters Brontë (The Life and Works of Charlotte Brontë and Her Sisters). AMS Pr. 7 vols. repr. of 1903 ed. ea. $45.00 set $315.00. The *Life* is Elizabeth Gaskell's biography of Charlotte, with annotations of Clement K. Shorter. The prefaces to the works are by Mrs. Humphrey Ward. The Haworth edition.

BOOKS ABOUT THE BRONTË SISTERS

Allott, Miriam, ed. *The Brontës: The Critical Heritage.* Routledge & Kegan 1974 o.p.
Bentley, Phyllis. *The Brontës.* Folcroft 1973 lib. bdg. $10.00
Dimnet, Ernest. *The Brontë Sisters.* Richard West repr. of 1927 ed. $20.00
Eagleton, Terry. *Myths of Power: A Marxist Study of the Brontës.* Barnes & Noble 1975 o.p.
Morrison, N. Brysson. *Haworth Harvest: The Story of the Brontës.* Vanguard 1969 $10.00
Pascal, Anne, ed. *Charlotte and Emily Brontë: An Annotated Bibliography. Reference Lib. of the Humanities* Garland 1979 lib. bdg. $50.00
Ratchford, Fannie E. *The Brontës' Web of Childhood.* Russell repr. of 1941 ed. 1964 $17.00
Shorter, Clement K. *The Brontës: Life and Letters. Eng. Biographies Ser.* Haskell 2 vols. repr. of 1908 ed. 1969 $199.95
———. *The Brontës and Their Circle.* Kraus repr. of 1917 ed. $32.00. Includes some early letters, as does Ernest Dimnet's *The Brontë Sisters.*
Winnifrith, Tony. *The Brontës and Their Background: Romance and Reality.* Humanities Pr. text ed. 1973 $13.00

BRONTË, ANNE ("Acton Bell," pseud.). 1820–1849

Anne Brontë's *Agnes Grey* is the story of a governess, and *The Tenant of Wildfell Hall*, a tale of the evils of drink and profligacy. Her acquaintance with sin and wickedness, as shown in her novels, was so astounding that Charlotte Brontë saw fit to explain in a preface that the source of her sister's knowledge of evil was her brother Branwell's dissolute ways. A habitué of drink and drugs, he finally became an addict. Her *Complete Poems*, edited by Clement K. Shorter, with a biographical introduction by C. W. Hatfield, is again available.

BOOKS BY ANNE BRONTË

The Poems of Anne Brontë: A New Text and Commentary. Ed. by Edward Chitham, Rowman 1979 $21.50
Agnes Grey. 1847. Biblio Dist. 1982 pap. $3.75
The Tenant of Wildfell Hall. 1848. Biblio Dist. 1982 pap. $4.75; ed. by G. D. Hargreaves, *Penguin Eng. Lib. Ser.* 1980 pap. $4.95

Books about Anne Brontë

Gérin, Winifred. *Anne Brontë: A Biography*. Rowman 1976 o.p.
Harrison, Ada, and Derek Stanford. *Anne Brontë: Her Life and Work*. Shoe String (Archon) repr. of 1959 ed. 1970 $18.00; Telegraph Bks. repr. of 1959 ed. 1981 lib. bdg. $30.00. An excellent study.

BRONTË, CHARLOTTE ("Currer Bell," pseud.). 1816–1855

A psychological novelist whose depictions of feminine heroines, particularly Jane Eyre, have risen to the level of cultural myth, Charlotte Brontë's books were based on her somber surroundings and the tragic events of her life. *The Professor* was a short early sketch that she enlarged in *Villette*. In *Jane Eyre* she introduced the first "ugly" heroine in fiction, and immediately achieved success. The heroine of *Shirley* is modeled on her sister Emily, and the story describes the misery that followed the introduction of machinery into Yorkshire. *Villette* is set in Brussels, where the author once taught school. The original ending, so painful to her readers that she changed it in later editions, enforced her bleak view of the position of the sensitive woman in a hostile society.

The first biography of Charlotte was the famous one by Mrs. (Elizabeth) Gaskell, which appeared two years after Charlotte's death. The discovery of Charlotte's "Lost Letters to Constantin Heger" (the original of *The Professor*), juvenilia, and other later letters and data has led to several new interpretations. Of these, Margaret Lane's *The Brontë Story* is an excellent sequel to Mrs. Gaskell's book. In the foreword, Lane says: "This book, in fact, is offered as a sort of footnote to Mrs. Gaskell, bringing the reader back to every point in her incomparable text, and at the same time putting him in possession of everything of importance that has come to light in the century since she wrote. Provided with this footnote as well as her 'Life,' he will, I hope, have in his hands the whole of the Brontë story."

Books by Charlotte Brontë

Jane Eyre. 1847. *Bantam Class. Ser.* 1981 pap. $1.95; New Amer. Lib. (Signet Class.) 1971 pap. $1.75; ed. by Richard J. Dunn, *Norton Critical Eds.* text ed. 1971 pap. $7.95; ed. by Margaret Smith, *World's Class. Ser.* Oxford 1980 pap. $2.95; ed. by Q. D. Leavis, *Penguin Eng. Lib. Ser.* pap. $2.25
Shirley. 1849. Biblio Dist. repr. of 1908 ed. 1975 $9.95; ed. by Margaret Smith and Herbert Rosengarten, *World's Class.-Pap. Ser.* Oxford 1981 $6.95; ed. by Andrew Hook and Judith Hook, *Penguin Eng. Lib. Ser.* 1974 pap. $3.95
Villette. 1853. Biblio Dist. 1974 $9.95 pap. $2.75 1983 text ed. pap. $3.95; ed. by Mark Lilly, *Penguin Eng. Lib. Ser.* 1980 pap. $5.95
The Professor (and *Emma*). 1857. Dutton (Everyman's) $9.95 pap. $3.74; *World's Class. Ser.* Oxford $2.50
The Secret and Lily Hart: Two Tales. Ed. by William Holtz, Univ. of Missouri Pr. 1979 pap. $5.95
The Spell: An Extravaganza. Arden Lib. repr. of 1931 ed. 1979 lib. bdg. $27.00; ed. by George MacLean, Folcroft repr. of 1931 ed. lib. bdg. $25.00

POETRY

Complete Poems. Ed. by Clement K. Shorter and C. W. Hatfield, *Lit. Ser.* Scholarly
  repr. of 1924 ed. 1972 $39.00
Legends of Angria. Ed. by Fannie E. Ratchford and William C. DeVane, Kennikat
  1973 o.p.

BOOKS ABOUT CHARLOTTE BRONTË

Gaskell, Mrs. Elizabeth Cleghorn. *The Life of Charlotte Brontë.* Ed. by Alan Shelston,
  Penguin Eng. Lib. Ser. 1975 pap. $5.95; Richard West repr. of 1947 ed. $20.00. "A
  great reckless biography . . . the very manner seems touched by the Brontëan
  fire" (*N.Y. Times*).
Gérin, Winifred. *Charlotte Brontë: The Evolution of Genius.* Oxford 1967 $26.95; Gal-
  axy Bks. pap. $8.95. An excellent definitive biography.
Lane, Margaret. *The Brontë Story: A Reconsideration of Mrs. Gaskell's Life of Charlotte
  Brontë.* Greenwood repr. of 1953 ed. 1971 lib. bdg. $17.75; Telegraph Bks. repr.
  of 1953 ed. 1981 lib. bdg. $25.00
Linder, Cynthia A. *Romantic Imagery in the Novels of Charlotte Brontë.* Barnes & No-
  ble text ed. 1978 $24.75
Martin, Robert B. *The Accents of Persuasion: Charlotte Brontë's Novels.* Arden Lib.
  repr. of 1966 ed. 1983 lib. bdg. $30.00; Richard West repr. of 1966 ed. 1984 lib.
  bdg. $40.00
Moglen, Helene. *Charlotte Brontë: The Self Conceived.* Univ. of Wisconsin Pr. text ed.
  1984 $27.50 pap. $9.95
Pinion, F. B. *A Brontë Companion: Literary Assessment, Background and Reference.*
  Barnes & Noble 1975 o.p.

BRONTË, EMILY JANE ("Ellis Bell," pseud.). 1818–1848

In her one novel, *Wuthering Heights,* Emily Brontë draws on the Gothic
horror tradition and the romantic obsession with Byronic intensity and
wildness of feeling. *Wuthering Heights* depicts a series of tumultuous and
passionate relationships that dramatize the power of love. Set in the wild
Yorkshire moors, the novel emphasizes the connection between landscape
and character, between the physical environment and the psychological con-
tours of those who inhabit it. It is noteworthy, among other reasons, for its
innovative handling of point of view and narrative structure, its resonant
but flexible style, and its dramatic psychological realism. Widely read in its
own day, *Wuthering Heights* is even more widely read and highly thought of
today.

Emily Brontë's *Complete Poems* has been edited by C. W. Hatfield from
the manuscripts. MATTHEW ARNOLD said of her that "for passion, vehemence,
and grief she had no equal since Byron."

BOOKS BY EMILY BRONTË

Complete Poems. Ed. by C. W. Hatfield, Columbia Univ. Pr. 1941 $23.00
Wuthering Heights. 1847. *Bantam Class. Ser.* 1981 pap. $1.95; ed. by N. L. Clay, *Heine-
  mann Guide Novel Ser.* text ed. pap. $4.50; ed. by V. S. Pritchett, Houghton Mif-
  flin (Riv. Eds.) 1956 pap. $5.50; Modern Lib. 1950 $8.95; New Amer. Lib. (Signet
  Class.) 1973 pap. $1.75; ed. by William M. Sale, Jr., *Norton Critical Eds.* rev. ed.
  1972 $4.95; ed. by Ian Jack, *World's Class. Ser.* Oxford 1981 pap. $2.95; ed. by

David Daiches, *Penguin Eng. Lib. Ser.* 1965 pap. $2.50; Random text ed. 1950 pap. $5.00

Gondal's Queen: A Novel in Verse. 1855. Ed. by Fannie E. Ratchford, Univ. of Texas Pr. 1977 o.p.

Gondal Poems. Ed. from the manuscript in the British Museum by H. Brown and J. Mott, Folcroft repr. of 1938 ed. o.p.

BOOKS ABOUT EMILY BRONTË

Benvenuto, Richard. *Emily Brontë. Twayne's Eng. Authors Ser.* G. K. Hall 1982 lib. bdg. $12.50

Crandall, N. *Emily Brontë: A Psychological Portrait.* Kraus repr. of 1957 ed. $28.00

Gérin, Winifred. *Emily Brontë.* Oxford 1972 $26.95 pap. $8.95

Homans, Margaret. *Women Writers and Poetic Identity: Dorothy Wordsworth, Emily Brontë, and Emily Dickinson.* Princeton Univ. Pr. 1980 $24.00

Visick, Mary. *The Genesis of Wuthering Heights.* Intro. by Edmund Blunden, Meckler 1980 $18.95; Telegraph Bks. repr. of 1967 ed. 1982 lib. bdg. $40.00. A study of the apotheosis of the Gondal people of the poems into the immortals of *Wuthering Heights.*

BULWER-LYTTON (Edward George Earle Lytton, after 1st Baron Lytton of Knebworth). 1803–1873

Immensely popular in his own lifetime, Bulwer-Lytton introduced the "silver spoon" novel with *Pelham* and initiated a series of historical romances with *Falkland*, the most notable of which are *The Last Days of Pompeii, Rienzi*, and *Harold, the Last of the Saxons* (1848, o.p.). Bulwer-Lytton's versatility was equaled only by his eccentricity. He wrote essays, travel volumes, drama, poetry, heroicized romance, fictionalized fact and factualized fiction, domestic fiction (*The Caxtons*), mystery tales, and, as a deeply committed adept of magic and the occult, novels of the supernatural, the most readable of which is *Zanoni: A Rosicrucian Tale* (1842). The standard life is *The Life, Letters, and Literary Remains*, edited by his son (o.p.). Robert L. Wolff's *Strange Stories: An Examination of Victorian Literature* (o.p.) contains a long section on Bulwer-Lytton's fascination with the occult.

BOOKS BY BULWER-LYTTON

Letters of the Late Edward Bulwer, Lord Lytton, to His Wife. AMS Pr. repr. of 1889 ed. $24.50. Includes extracts from his wife's manuscript "Autobiography" and other documents, published in vindication of her memory by Louisa Devey.

Falkland. 1827. Ed. by Herbert Van Thal, *First Novel Lib.* Dufour 1967 $7.95 pap. $4.95

Pelham, or The Adventures of a Gentleman. 1828. Ed. by Jerome J. McGann, Univ. of Nebraska Pr. 1972 $29.50

England and the English. Development of Industrial Society Biblio Dist. repr. of 1833 ed. 1971 $45.00

The Last Days of Pompeii. 1834. Buccaneer Bks. repr. 1983 lib. bdg. $17.95; Feder Bks. 1979 pap. $11.95

Rienzi: The Last of the Roman Tribunes. 1835. Scholarly repr. of 1885 ed. 1971 $49.00

Zanoni: A Rosicrucian Tale. Spiritual Fiction Publications Ser. Garber Comm. repr. of 1842 ed. 1982 $15.00

The Caxtons: A Family Picture. 1849. Scholarly repr. of 1898 ed. 1971 $49.00
A Strange Story. 1862. Shambhala 1973 o.p.
Vril: The Power of the Coming Race (The Coming Race). 1871. *Spiritual Fiction Publications Ser.* Garber Comm. 2d ed. repr. of 1972 ed. 1982 $10.00

BOOKS ABOUT BULWER-LYTTON

Christensen, Allan C. *Edward Bulwer-Lytton: The Fiction of New Regions.* Univ. of Georgia Pr. 1976 o.p.
Escott, T. H. *Edward Bulwer, First Baron Lytton of Knebworth: A Social, Personal, and Political Monograph.* Arden Lib. repr. of 1910 ed. 1977 lib. bdg. $30.00; Associated Faculty Pr. repr. of 1910 ed. 1970 $25.50
Sadleir, Michael. *Bulwer: A Panorama.* Folcroft repr. of 1931 ed. 1977 lib. bdg. $30.00

BUTLER, SAMUEL. 1835–1902

A versatile genius, Samuel Butler was an artist who exhibited in the Royal Academy, a musician who composed a cantata and an oratorio of distinction, a man of science who contributed several books to the study of evolution (not taken very seriously by scientists), a translator of HOMER (see Vol. 2), and the author of various books of travel and at least one enduring novel. *The Way of All Flesh* is a biographical novel depicting three generations of the same family. It satirizes the hypocrisy of the ecclesiastical and educational systems in a surprisingly modern tone. *Erewhon* (an anagram for "nowhere") and its sequel are utopias. *The Notebooks*, edited by Henry F. Jones, contains Butler's best work.

The Family Letters, edited by Arnold Silver, is a selection from the correspondence of Butler and his father, with several letters to and from his mother and sisters and one or two other relatives. Two-thirds of these letters have never before been printed. Those between Butler and his father show how close the early part of *The Way of All Flesh* was to the events in the son's life. The great bulk of his revealing *Correspondence with His Sister May* (1962, o.p.) remained mostly untouched in the British Museum for more than a quarter of a century.

BOOKS BY BUTLER

Works. Ed. by Henry F. Jones and A. T. Bartholomew, AMS Pr. 20 vols. repr. of 1923–26. ed. ea. $40.00 set $800.00
The Family Letters of Samuel Butler, 1841–1846. Ed. by Arnold Silver, Fernhill 1962 o.p.
The Notebooks of Samuel Butler. Ed. by Henry F. Jones, Richard West repr. of 1919 ed. $20.00
Further Extracts from the Notebooks. Ed. by A. T. Bartholomew, Greenwood repr. of 1934 ed. lib. bdg. $20.00
Prose Observations. Ed. by Hugh De Quehen, *Oxford Eng. Texts Ser.* text ed. 1979 $74.00
Erewhon. 1872. *Penguin Eng. Lib. Ser.* 1970 pap. $3.95
The Fair Haven: A Work in Defence of the Miraculous Element in Our Lord's Ministry upon Earth. Ed. by Robert L. Wolff, *Victorian Fiction Ser.* Garland repr. of 1873 ed. 1975 lib. bdg. $66.00

Evolution, Old and New, or The Theories of Buffon, Dr. Erasmus Darwin and Lamarck as Compared with Mr. Charles Darwin. 1879. Gordon $59.95

The Authoress of the Odyssey. 1897. Intro. by David Grene, Univ. of Chicago Pr. (Phoenix Bks.) 1967 o.p. Butler's discussion of why he believed *The Odyssey* to have been written two centuries after *The Iliad* by a Sicilian noblewoman.

(ed.). *Shakespeare's Sonnets Reconsidered.* AMS Pr. repr. of 1899 ed. $15.00

Erewhon Revisited (and *Erewhon*). 1901. Biblio. Dist. 1950 $10.95 repr. of 1932 ed. 1979 $10.95

The Way of All Flesh. 1903. Biblio Dist. repr. of 1933 ed. 1976 $11.95; ed. by Robert L. Wolff, *Victorian Fiction Ser.* Garland repr. of 1903 ed. 1975 lib. bdg. $66.00; ed. by James Cochrane, *Penguin Eng. Lib. Ser.* 1966 pap. $3.50

Essays on Life, Art and Science. 1904. Ed. by Richard A. Streatfeild, Associated Faculty Pr. repr. of 1908 ed. 1970 $26.00; Richard West repr. of 1908 ed. $11.50

The Humour of Homer and Other Essays. Ed. by Richard A. Streatfeild, Arden Lib. repr. of 1913 ed. 1982 $25.00; ed. by Richard A. Streatfeild, *Essay Index Repr. Ser.* Ayer repr. of 1914 ed. $18.00; ed. by Richard A. Streatfeild, Richard West repr. of 1913 ed. 1978 lib. bdg. $20.00

BOOKS ABOUT BUTLER

Cole, G. D. H. *Samuel Butler.* Folcroft 1973 lib. bdg. $10.00

Furbank, P. N. *Samuel Butler, 1835–1902.* Shoe String (Archon) 2d ed. 1971 $14.00

Greenacre, Phyllis. *The Quest for the Father: A Study of the Darwin-Butler Controversy, as a Contribution to the Understanding of the Creative Individual.* New York Psychoanalytic Institute Freud Anniversary Lecture Ser. International Univ. Pr. text ed. 1963 $16.50

Harkness, Stanley. *The Career of Samuel Butler, 1835–1902. Bibliography and Reference Ser.* Burt Franklin repr. of 1955 ed. 1968 $20.50

Jeffers, Thomas. *Samuel Butler Revalued.* Pennsylvania State Univ. Pr. 1981 $14.95

Jones, Henry Festing. *Samuel Butler: A Memoir.* Folcroft 2 vols. 1973 lib. bdg. $24.50; Octagon 2 vols. 1968 lib. bdg. $57.50

Muggeridge, Malcolm. *Earnest Atheist: A Study of Samuel Butler. Eng. Lit. Ser.* Haskell repr. of 1936 ed. 1971 lib. bdg. $49.95. The author, critic, and editor of *Punch* maintains that Butler was the epitome of a Victorian writer, rather than a rebel against his times.

CARROLL, LEWIS (pseud. of the Rev. Charles Lutwidge Dodgson). 1832–1898

Lewis Carroll was a minister of the Church of England and a professor of mathematics at Christ Church College, Oxford, where he was considered conscientious but often dull. In his diary of July 4, 1862, Carroll described "an expedition up the river to Godstowe with the three Lidells," the daughters of the dean of Christ Church College, "on which occasion I told them the fairy tale of 'Alice's Adventures under Ground,' which I undertook to write out for Alice." The original manuscript is on display in the British Museum and has been published in facsimile in the United States.

Carroll's particular talent for mathematical puzzles and paradox, for charming and significant nonsense verse, for verbal ingenuity, and for identification with the distortions and dilemmas of a child's view of the world have made *Alice's Adventures in Wonderland* and *Through the Looking Glass* perennial favorites with children. But in recent years Carroll has been taken quite seriously as a major literary artist for adults as well. His major works have come under the scrutiny of critics who have explained his permanent attractiveness in terms of existential and symbolic drama: The Alice books dramatize psychological realities in symbolic terms, being commentary on the nature of the human predicament rather than escape from it.

BOOKS BY CARROLL

The Complete Works of Lewis Carroll. Modern Lib. repr. of 1936 ed. $10.95; Random (Vintage) 1976 pap. $9.95

The Complete Illustrated Works. Ed. by Edward Guiliano, Outlet (Avenel) 1982 $7.98

The Letters of Lewis Carroll. Ed. by Morton Cohen and Roger L. Green, Oxford 2 vols. 1979 $75.00

The Humorous Verse of Lewis Carroll (The Collected Verse of Lewis Carroll). Dover repr. of 1933 ed. pap. $6.50; Peter Smith repr. $9.75

Lewis Carroll's Symbolic Logic. Ed. by W. W. Bartley, Crown (Potter) 1978 pap. $6.95

Alice's Adventures in Wonderland. 1865. Knopf 1983 $16.95

Alice's Adventures Under-Ground. 1886. Dover 1965 pap. $2.50; Peter Smith repr. $12.25; *Facsimile Class. Ser.* Smith Publications (Rutledge Pr.) 1981 $7.95. This is Carroll's own neat hand-lettered early version of *Alice's Adventures in Wonderland*, written out for the real Alice Liddell and sent to her in 1864, illustrated with charming drawings by Carroll himself. The first of these recent editions (all are from the same British Museum manuscript) was that of University Microfilms, which contains a brief introduction by Luther H. Evans about the genesis of the present publication venture. Very soon afterward, Dover brought out the paperback facsimile containing a fascinating introduction by Martin Gardner and material added from the Macmillan facsimile edition of 1886: a poem of "Christmas Greetings" by Carroll, and Carroll's "Easter Greeting"—a sentimental preface in prose—as well as the original Macmillan table of contents. McGraw-Hill in 1966 brought out the Dover version in hardback. All contain an engaging photograph of the original Alice. The Peter Smith edition differs from the later Tenniel-illustrated *Alice:* The Cheshire Cat, the Mad Tea Party, and the Duchess have not yet, for example, been conceived. The manuscript is inscribed: "A Christmas Gift to a Dear Child in Memory of a Summer Day." "The later Alice is a work of literature," said *Time*, "the earlier is a work of love."

Through the Looking Glass and What Alice Found There: The California Edition of the Pennyroyal Press Book. 1871. Univ. of California Pr. 1983 $19.95. A sequel to, and usually published with, *Alice in Wonderland.*

Alice in Wonderland (and *Through the Looking Glass*). Bantam Class. Ser. 1981 pap. $1.95; Macmillan (Collier Bks.) 1982 pap. $1.95; New Amer. Lib. (Signet Class.) 1973 pap. $1.75; ed. by Roger L. Green, *World's Class. Ser.* Oxford repr. of 1897 ed. 1982 pap. $4.95; Schocken 1979 lib. bdg. $9.95. The Oxford reprint has all the important variations of earlier editions.

Alice in Wonderland. Crown (Potter) 1973 pap. $3.95; ed. by Donald J. Gray, *Norton Critical Eds.* 1971 $10.00 pap. $5.95; *Class. Ser.* Peter Pauper repr. of 1940 ed. 1984 boxed set $25.00

The Annotated Alice: Alice's Adventures in Wonderland and Through the Looking Glass. Intro. by Martin Gardner, New Amer. Lib. (Meridian) pap. $5.95. Explains, for adults, many now-unfamiliar allusions.

The Hunting of the Snark: An Agony in Eight Fits. 1876. Ed. by James Tanis and John

Dooley, Kaufmann $18.95; *Facsimile Class. Ser.* Smith Publications (Rutledge Pr.) 1981 $7.95

The Annotated Snark: Full Text of Lewis Carroll's Great Nonsense Epic "The Hunting of the Snark" and the Original Illustrations by Henry Holiday. Ed. by Martin Gardner, Kaufmann 1981 $18.95. See *The Annotated Alice.* Includes bibliography and interesting appendix.

The Rectory Umbrella and Mischmasch. 1882. Dover repr. of 1932 ed. pap. $2.95. *The Rectory Umbrella* was never published separately.

The Nursery Alice. 1889. Dover pap. $4.95; Peter Smith repr. $8.25; *Facsimile Class. Ser.* Smith Publications (Mayflower Bks.) repr. of 1890 ed. 1979 $6.95

BOOKS ABOUT CARROLL

Clark, Anne. *Lewis Carroll: A Biography.* Schocken 1979 $12.95

Guiliano, Edward. *Lewis Carroll: An Annotated International Bibliography, 1960– 1977.* Univ. Pr. of Virginia 1980 $15.00

Hudson, Derek. *Lewis Carroll.* Arden Lib. repr. of 1954 ed. 1981 lib. bdg. $20.00; Folcroft repr. of 1954 ed. $30.00; Greenwood repr. of 1954 ed. 1972 lib. bdg. $22.25; Richard West repr. of 1954 ed. $20.00

Lennon, Florence Becker. *The Life of Lewis Carroll.* Richard West 1947 $25.00

Phillips, Robert, ed. *Aspects of Alice: Lewis Carroll's Dreamchild as Seen through the Critics' Looking Glasses.* Vanguard 1971 $17.50

Williams, Sidney, and Falconer Madan. *The Lewis Carroll Handbook.* Ed. by Denis Crutch, Shoe String (Archon) rev. ed. $37.50. A new version of *A Handbook of the Literature of the Rev. C. L. Dodgson,* revised, augmented, and brought up to 1960.

COLLINS, WILKIE. 1824–1889

Wilkie Collins created the crime novel of intricate plot and baffling mystery. *The Woman in White* was his first success, followed later by his masterpiece *The Moonstone.* Both novels demonstrate Collins's fascination with psychological portraiture and sensationalistic complication. Collins was a close friend of Charles Dickens and collaborated with him. His mastery of plot influenced Dickens, and he was influenced by Dickens's mastery of character. T. S. ELIOT remarked, "To anyone who knows the bare facts of Dickens' acquaintance with Collins, and who has studied the work of the two men, their relationship and their influence upon one another is an important subject of study."

BOOKS BY COLLINS

Works. AMS Pr. 30 vols. repr. of 1900 ed. ea. $40.00 set $1,200.00

Little Novels. Dover 1978 pap. $4.50

Tales of Terror and the Supernatural. Ed. by Herbert Van Thal, Dover 1972 pap. $4.00

Hide and Seek, or The Mystery of Mary Grice. 1854. Dover 1982 pap. $5.95; Peter Smith repr. 1983 $11.50

The Dead Secret. 1857. Dover 1979 pap. $5.00

The Queen of Hearts. Lit. of Mystery and Detection. Ayer repr. of 1859 ed. 1976 $35.50

The Woman in White. 1860. Biblio Dist. 1982 pap. $4.95; ed. by Harvey P. Sucksmith, *World's Class.-Pap. Ser.* Oxford 1981 pap. $3.95; ed. by Julian Symons, *Penguin Eng. Lib. Ser.* 1975 pap. $2.95 1982 pap. $3.95

The Moonstone. 1863. Biblio Dist. 1977 $8.95; *Penguin Eng. Lib. Ser.* 1966 pap. $3.95

Armadale. Dover 1977 pap. $7.95; Scholarly 2 vols. repr. of 1866 ed. 1972 $69.00

Poor Miss Finch: A Novel. Lit. Ser. Scholarly repr. of 1872 ed. 1972 $49.00
The Haunted Hotel. 1875. *Dover Mystery Ser.* 1982 pap. $3.00

BOOKS ABOUT COLLINS

Andrew, Ray Vernon. *Wilkie Collins: A Critical Survey of His Prose Fiction with a Bibliography.* Ed. by E. F. Bleiler, *Fiction of Popular Culture Ser.* Garland 1979 lib. bdg. $42.00

Beetz, Kirk H. *Wilkie Collins: An Annotated Bibliography 1889–1976. Author Bibliographies Ser.* Scarecrow Pr. 1978 $15.00

Lonoff, Susan. *Wilkie Collins and His Victorian Readers: A Study in the Rhetoric of Authorship. AMS Studies in the 19th Century* 1980 $32.50

Page, Norman, ed. *Wilkie Collins: The Critical Heritage. Critical Heritage Ser.* Routledge & Kegan 1974 $27.00

Robinson, Kenneth. *Wilkie Collins: A Biography.* Greenwood repr. of 1951 ed. 1973 lib. bdg. $19.75. The first full-length biography, and a good one.

CONRAD, JOSEPH. 1857–1924

Born a Pole (Josef Konrad Korzeniowski), Joseph Conrad, like VLADIMIR NABOKOV (see Vol. 2), learned the language of his literary career as an adult and produced an important body of distinguished fiction. A master of the novella as well as the novel, Conrad takes much of the setting for his fiction from his youth as a merchant sailor. Some of his basic fictional situations develop out of the Victorian tradition of the sea-adventure tale, the spy and detective novel, and the novel of voyages to unknown countries.

Beginning with *Almayer's Folly* in 1895, he produced a series of outstanding fictions, a number of which are considered major modern literary landmarks, particularly *The Heart of Darkness, Lord Jim, Nostromo, Victory, The Secret Agent,* and *Under Western Eyes.* Conrad's ability to transform metaphor, imagery, and fictional situation into symbols of the moral and psychological condition of modern man and his civilization establishes his fiction as a force in modernism rather than in Victorianism. If he is a bridge between two centuries, most of the bridge is in the twentieth century. Conrad's use of indirect narrative and his psychological perceptiveness create a sense of inwardness and existential self within his main characters; his symbols directly foreshadow modernism's evocation of alienated and dehumanized man in a corrupt society; and his frequent use of indirect narrative and complicated points of view developed by fictional narrators is in the mainstream of such experiments in modern fiction.

As Morton D. Zabel said, "Conrad is at basis a tragic novelist, as he is also essentially a moral and psychological realist whose profounder themes are concerned with problems of guilt and honor, with the tests of conscience and moral justice, and with the secret recriminatory and retributive processes of the human personality . . . . And while some of the richest writing comes in his descriptive and atmospheric art, his greatest powers appear when he makes the form and structure of his tales, as well as their stylistic detail and analysis, convey the processes of character, of conscience, and of moral justice."

BOOKS BY CONRAD

Collected Works. Johnson Repr. 1968 $3,900.00

The Collected Letters of Joseph Conrad. Ed. by Frederick R. Karl and Lawrence Davies, Cambridge Univ. Pr. Vol. 1 1983 $39.50

The Portable Conrad. Ed. by Morton D. Zabel and Frederick R. Karl, *Viking Portable Lib.* Penguin rev. ed. 1976 pap. $7.95. Includes *The Nigger of the Narcissus, The Heart of Darkness, Typhoon,* shorter stories, letters, and autobiographical writings.

The Great Short Works of Joseph Conrad: The Nigger of the Narcissus; Youth; The Heart of Darkness; Typhoon; The Lagoon; and Secret Sharer. Ed. by Jerry Allen, Harper pap. $3.50; Peter Smith repr. $12.75

Shorter Tales. Short Story Index Repr. Ser. Ayer repr. of 1924 ed. $22.00

Last Essays. Essay Index Repr. Ser. Ayer repr. of 1926 ed. $17.00

Conrad's Prefaces to His Works. Intro. by Edward Garnett, *Select Bibliographies Repr. Ser.* Ayer repr. of 1937 ed. $16.00; *Eng. Lit. Ser.* Haskell 1971 lib. bdg. $39.95

Joseph Conrad on Fiction. Ed. by Walter F. Wright, *Regents Critics Ser.* Univ. of Nebraska Pr. 1964 $18.95 pap. $4.95

Joseph Conrad's Letters to R. B. Cunninghame Graham. Ed. by C. T. Watts, Cambridge Univ. Pr. 1969 $42.50

Conrad to a Friend: 150 Selected Letters to Richard Curle. Ed. by Richard Curle, Russell repr. of 1928 ed. 1968 $9.00

(and others). *Conrad under Familial Eyes.* Ed. by Najden Zdzislaw, trans. by Halina Carroll-Najder, Cambridge Univ. Pr. 1984 $37.50

Three Great Tales. Random (Vintage) 1958 pap. $3.95

Almayer's Folly. 1895. Bentley repr. 1971 lib. bdg. $12.50; Penguin 1976 pap. $2.95

An Outcast of the Islands. 1896. Penguin 1976 pap. $3.50

The Nigger of the Narcissus. 1897. Ed. by Robert Kimbrough, *Norton Critical Eds.* 1979 pap. $4.95; (and *Typhoon and Other Stories*). Penguin 1963 pap. $2.75; (and *Typhoon, Falk, and Other Stories*), ed. by Norman Sherry, Biblio Dist. 1978 $12.95 pap. $3.50

Tales of Unrest. Penguin 1977 pap. $2.95

Lord Jim. 1900. *Bantam Class. Ser.* 1981 pap. $1.95; Biblio Dist. 1974 pap. $1.95; ed. by Morton D. Zabel, Houghton Mifflin (Riv. Eds.) 1958 pap. $5.25; New Amer. Lib. 1961 pap. $1.95; ed. by Thomas Moser, *Norton Critical Eds.* text ed. 1968 pap. $8.95; ed. by John Batchelor, *World's Class.-Pap. Ser.* Oxford 1983 pap. $3.95; *Penguin Modern Class. Ser.* 1971 pap. $1.95

Youth (and *The End of the Tether*). 1902. Penguin 1976 pap. $2.95

Typhoon (and *Youth*). 1902. Ed. by N. L. Clay, *Heinemann Guide Novel Ser.* text ed. pap. $2.95

The Heart of Darkness. 1902. Bentley repr. of 1926 ed. 1982 $12.50; ed. by Robert Kimbrough, *Norton Critical Eds.* 1972 pap. $4.95; *Penguin Eng. Lib. Ser.* 1984 pap. $1.95

Nostromo. 1904. Biblio Dist. 1979 $14.95 pap. $8.95; Modern Lib. 1950 $8.95

The Secret Agent. 1907. Bantam 1984 text ed. pap. $2.50; Doubleday 1953 pap. $4.95; New Amer. Lib. (Signet Class.) 1983 pap. $2.50

Under Western Eyes. 1911. Doubleday (Anchor) 1963 pap. $1.95; Penguin 1979 pap. $3.95

Chance. 1914. Merrimack 1984 pap. $7.95

Victory. 1915. Doubleday (Anchor) 1957 pap. $5.50

The Shadow Lane. 1917. Doubleday o.p.; Dutton (Everyman's) o.p.

Arrow of Gold: A Story between Two Notes. 1919. Dutton o.p.; *Norton Lib.* o.p.

The Rescue. 1920. Norton 1968 o.p.
The Rover. 1923. Academy Chicago 1975 pap. $3.95

BOOKS ABOUT CONRAD

Baines, Jocelyn. *Joseph Conrad: A Critical Biography.* Greenwood repr. of 1961 ed. 1975 lib. bdg. $45.00

Berthoud, Jacques. *Joseph Conrad: The Major Phase. British Authors Ser.* Cambridge Univ. Pr. 1978 $29.95 pap. $10.95

Bonney, William. *Thorns and Arabesques: Contexts for Conrad's Fiction.* Johns Hopkins Univ. Pr. text ed. 1980 $22.50

Dowden, Wilfred S. *Joseph Conrad: The Imaged Style.* Vanderbilt 1970 $11.95. Conrad's use of imagery in the major works as well as some of the shorter fiction.

Fleishman, Avrom. *Conrad's Politics: Community and Anarchy in the Fiction of Joseph Conrad.* Johns Hopkins Univ. Pr. 1967 $22.50

Ford, Ford Madox. *Joseph Conrad.* Octagon 1965 lib. bdg. $23.00. Ford was Conrad's friend and collaborator.

Gillon, Adam. *Eternal Solitary: A Study of Joseph Conrad.* Irvington text ed. 1960 $19.50

——. *Joseph Conrad. Twayne's Eng. Authors Ser.* G. K. Hall 1982 lib. bdg. $12.50 1984 pap. $6.95

Glassman, Peter J. *Language and Being: Joseph Conrad and the Literature of Personality.* Columbia Univ. Pr. 1976 $25.00

Graver, Lawrence. *Conrad's Short Fiction.* Univ. of California Pr. 1968 $28.50

Guérard, Albert J. *Conrad the Novelist.* Harvard Univ. Pr. 1958 $20.00. "The best critical book on Conrad yet written" (*N.Y. Times*).

Hay, Eloise Knapp. *The Political Novels of Joseph Conrad.* Univ. of Chicago Pr. 1981 $16.00

Jean-Aubry, Georges. *Sea-Dreamer: A Definitive Biography of Joseph Conrad.* Trans. by Helen Sebba, Shoe String (Archon) repr. of 1957 ed. 1967 $18.50

Johnson, Bruce. *Conrad's Models of Mind.* Univ. of Minnesota Pr. 1971 $12.50. "The author analyzes a number of Conrad's works, explaining Conrad's changing conceptions or models of mind, the psychological assumptions which lie behind the creation of fiction" (Publisher's catalog).

Karl, Frederick R. *Joseph Conrad: The Three Lives.* Farrar 1979 $25.00 pap. $14.95

Meyer, Bernard C. *Joseph Conrad: A Psychoanalytic Biography.* Princeton Univ. Pr. 1967 pap. $11.50. "Meyer's book should be the standard work in this phase of Conrad scholarship" (*LJ*).

Said, Edward. *Joseph Conrad and the Fiction of Autobiography.* Harvard Univ. Pr. 1966 $14.00. Based on the relationship between Conrad's letters and his shorter fiction.

Schwarz, Daniel R. *Conrad: Almayer's Folly to "Under Western Eyes."* Cornell Univ. Pr. 1980 $27.50

Sherry, Norman. *Conrad's Eastern World.* Cambridge Univ. Pr. 1966 $49.50 pap. $15.95

——. *Conrad's Western World.* Cambridge Univ. Pr. 1971 $49.50 pap. $17.95

——, ed. *Conrad: The Critical Heritage. Critical Heritage Ser.* Routledge & Kegan 1973 $34.00

Stallman, R. W., ed. *The Art of Joseph Conrad: A Critical Symposium.* Ohio Univ. Pr. text ed. 1982 $22.95 text ed. pap. $11.95

Teets, Bruce E., and Helmut E. Gerber, eds. *Joseph Conrad: An Annotated Bibliogra-*

phy of Writings about Him. Annotated Secondary Bibliography Ser. on Eng. Lit. in Transition, 1880–1921 Northern Illinois Univ. Pr. 1971 $30.00

Thorburn, David. *Conrad's Romanticism.* Yale Univ. Pr. 1974 $15.00

Watt, Ian. *Conrad in the Nineteenth Century.* Univ. of California Pr. 1980 $17.95 pap. $7.95

DICKENS, CHARLES. 1812–1870

With a reputation that now places him among the half dozen most significant and formidable literary artists in English literature, Charles Dickens dominates modern critical opinion of the Victorian novel to the same extent that he dominated his contemporaries. Dickens was richly educated in the trials of a bankrupt household, in the difficulties of earning his own way from a young age, and in the pressures of modern urban life. London becomes in his fiction the symbol of the condition of modern man; the pressures of economic survival become the illuminator of character and environment; and the experiences of childhood are transformed into a threatening landscape of exploitation.

Dickens's first success, *Sketches by Boz*, a series of vignettes on London life and character, was followed by the immensely popular *Pickwick Papers*, which like all of Dickens's novels was published in serial form. His reputation was firmly established by a succession of novels between 1837 and 1848, in which the dominant tone of ironic satire, outraged liberalism, comic extravagance, and imaginative fancy dramatized his concern with the themes of power, ambition, exploitation, self-destruction, and dehumanization. He drew on traditions of fairy tale and fantasy, developed immense skill with narrative and characterization, and revealed a brilliant flair for metaphor, psychological realism, and symbolic action. After *David Copperfield*, his "favorite" but flawed child, Dickens's novels became dark with a kind of visionary pessimism. His earlier liberalism and optimism were replaced in *Bleak House, Little Dorrit*, and *Our Mutual Friend* with an increasing sense of the corruption and imperfectibility of man and society in general, although he maintained his belief in the capability of special individuals to live productive and even happy lives. Dickens's fiction, in its richness and variety, its fascination with people and society, its embrace of man and acceptance of the withdrawal of God, its emphasis on urban life, economic pressures, and psychological realism both embodies and transcends Victorian culture.

A definitive edition of his letters in 12 volumes, Oxford's *Pilgrim Edition of the Letters of Charles Dickens*, five volumes of which have been published, is in progress. For the time being, the Nonesuch Press edition (o.p.) of his letters is the most complete. The complete novels and short fiction are available in Penguin paperbacks.

BOOKS BY DICKENS

New Oxford Illustrated Dickens. 21 vols. ea. $17.95–$24.50 set $695.00. The complete novels, short fiction, and assorted journalism.

Letters. Ed. by Madeline House, Graham Storey, Kathleen Tillotson, and K. J. Fielding, Oxford (Pilgrim Ed.) 1965–81 ea. $59.00–$115.00. Expected to be completed in approximately 12 volumes.

Uncollected Writings from Household Words, 1850–1859. Ed. by Harry Stone, Indiana Univ. Pr. 1969 o.p.

Letters to Wilkie Collins. Ed. by Georgina Hogarth, Kraus repr. of 1892 ed. $15.00

Charles Dickens as Editor: Being Letters Written by Him to William Henry Wills, His Sub-editor. Ed. by R. C. Lehmann, *Studies in Dickens* Haskell repr. of 1912 ed. 1972 lib. bdg. $59.95; Kraus repr. of 1912 ed. $20.00; Richard West repr. of 1912 ed. $35.00

The Unpublished Letters of Charles Dickens to Mark Lemon. Ed. by Walter Dexter, *Studies in Dickens* Haskell repr. of 1927 ed. 1971 lib. bdg. $69.00. Mark Lemon was the first editor of *Punch* and shared with Dickens an interest in the stage.

Mr. and Mrs. Charles Dickens: His Letters to Her. Ed. by Walter Dexter, fwd. by Dickens's daughter, Kate Perugin, *Studies in Dickens* Haskell repr. of 1935 ed. 1972 lib. bdg. $52.95

Speeches of Charles Dickens. Ed. by K. J. Fielding, Oxford 1960 o.p. A definitive edition.

The Public Readings of Charles Dickens. Ed. by Philip Collins, Oxford 1975 $69.00

Christmas Books. Ed. by Michael Slater, *Penguin Eng. Lib. Ser.* 2 vols. 1971 ea. $3.95

Christmas Stories. Biblio Dist. 1971 pap. $3.95

The Comic World of Dickens. Peter Smith repr. $10.25

Sketches by Boz: Illustrative of Every-Day Life and Every-Day People. 1836. Oxford 1957 $22.50

The Pickwick Papers (The Posthumous Papers of the Pickwick Club). 1836–37. Bantam 1983 pap. $4.95; Biblio Dist. 1977 $10.95; ed. by Robert L. Patten, *Penguin Eng. Lib. Ser.* 1973 pap. $4.95

Oliver Twist (The Adventures of Oliver Twist). 1837–39. Bantam Class. Ser. text ed. 1981 pap. $2.50; Biblio Dist. repr. of 1907 ed. 1978 $8.95; ed. by Kathleen Tillotson, *World's Class. Ser.* Oxford 1982 pap. $3.50; ed. by Angus Wilson, *Penguin Eng. Lib. Ser.* 1971 pap. $4.95

Nicholas Nickleby (The Life and Adventures of Nicholas Nickleby). 1838–39. Bantam Class. Ser. 1983 pap. $4.50; Biblio Dist. 1977 $10.95 pap. $3.95; ed. by Michael Slater, *Penguin Eng. Lib. Ser.* 1978 pap. $.95; Oxford 1982 pap. $5.95

The Old Curiosity Shop. 1840–41. Biblio Dist. repr. of 1907 ed. 1977 $10.95; ed. by Angus Easson, *Penguin Eng. Lib. Ser.* 1972 pap. $4.95

Master Humphrey's Clock. 1841. In the *New Oxford Illustrated Dickens.* 1958 $19.95

Barnaby Rudge: A Tale of the Riots of Eighty. 1841. Biblio Dist. 1966 $14.95; ed. by G. W. Spence, *Penguin Eng. Lib. Ser.* 1974 pap. $5.95

American Notes. 1842. Peter Smith repr. $10.25

A Christmas Carol. 1843. David & Charles 1982 $12.50; St. Martin's 1979 $9.95; Simon & Schuster 1983 $11.95

Martin Chuzzlewit (The Life and Adventures of Martin Chuzzlewit). 1843–48. Biblio Dist. repr. of 1907 ed. 1973 $10.95; ed. by P. N. Furbank, *Penguin Eng. Lib. Ser.* 1975 pap. $5.95

The Chimes. 1844. See collection of *Christmas Stories* (above) and *A Christmas Carol.*

The Cricket on the Hearth. 1845. See collection of *Christmas Stories* (above).

Dombey and Son (Dealings with the Firm of Dombey and Son, Wholesale, Retail, and for Exportation). 1846–48. New Amer. Lib. (Signet Class.) pap. $3.95; ed. by Alan Horsman, *World's Class.-Pap. Ser.* Oxford 1982 pap. $5.95; *Penguin Eng. Lib. Ser.* 1970 pap. $5.95

David Copperfield (The Personal History of David Copperfield). 1849–50. *Bantam Class.*

Ser. text ed. 1981 pap. $2.50; Biblio Dist. repr. of 1907 ed. 1975 $10.95; New
Amer. Lib. (Signet Class.) 1962 pap. $2.50; ed. by Nina Burgin, *World's Class.-
Pap. Ser.* Oxford 1983 pap. $4.95; *Penguin Eng. Lib. Ser.* 1966 pap. $3.95
Bleak House. 1852–53. *Bantam Class. Ser.* 1983 pap. $3.95; New Amer. Lib. (Signet
Class.) 1964 pap. $4.95; *Norton Critical Eds.* 1977 pap. $9.95; *Penguin Eng. Lib.
Ser.* 1971 pap. $4.95
A Child's History of England. 1853. Biblio Dist. repr. of 1907 ed. 1978 $9.95
Hard Times (Hard Times for These Times). 1854. *Bantam Class. Ser.* 1981 pap. $1.95;
Biblio Dist. 1974 $9.95 pap. $3.95; ed. by N. L. Clay, *Heinemann Guide Novel Ser.*
text ed. pap. $4.50; ed. by George H. Ford and Sylvère Monod, *Norton Critical
Eds.* text ed. 1966 pap. $5.95; ed. by David Craig, *Penguin Eng. Lib. Ser.* 1969
pap. $2.25; ed. by William W. Watt, *Rinehart Ed.* Holt text ed. 1958 pap. $8.95
Little Dorrit. 1855–57. New Amer. Lib. (Signet Class.) 1980 pap. $3.50; ed. by Harvey
P. Sucksmith, *World's Class.-Pap. Ser.* 1982 pap. $6.95; *Penguin Eng. Lib. Ser.*
1968 pap. $4.95
A Tale of Two Cities. 1859. *Bantam Class. Ser.* 1981 pap. $2.25; Biblio Dist. 1979
$10.95 pap. $2.50; New Amer. Lib. (Signet Class.) 1960 pap. $1.95; ed. by George
Woodcock, *Penguin Eng. Lib. Ser.* 1970 pap. $2.25
The Uncommercial Traveller (and *Reprinted Pieces*). 1860. In *New Oxford Illustrated
Dickens.* 1958 $22.50
Reprinted Pieces. 1860. Biblio Dist. repr. of 1921 ed. 1970 $8.95
Great Expectations. 1861. *Bantam Class. Ser.* 1981 pap. $2.50; Biblio Dist. 1979 pap.
$2.25; *Rinehart Eds.* Holt 2d ed. text ed. 1972 pap. $12.95; ed. by Angus Calder,
Penguin Eng. Lib. Ser. 1965 pap. $2.95 1982 pap. $2.50
Our Mutual Friend. 1864–66. Biblio Dist. repr. of 1929 ed. 1978 $12.95; ed. by Marga-
ret Tarner and John Milne, *Heinemann Guided Readers Ser.* text ed. 1978 pap.
$2.50; ed. by Stephen Gill, *Penguin Eng. Lib. Ser.* 1971 pap. $4.95
The Mystery of Edwin Drood. 1870. *Studies in Dickens* Haskell 1974 lib. bdg. $49.95;
Penguin Eng. Lib. Ser. 1974 pap. $3.95; ed. by Margaret Cardwell, *World's Class.
Ser.* Oxford 1982 pap. $3.50; New Amer. Lib. (Meridian) 1984 pap. $3.95
The Magic Fishbone. Children's Theatre Playscript Ser. Coach House 1961 pap. $2.00;
Vanguard 1953 $8.95

Books about Dickens

Butt, John, and Kathleen Tillotson. *Dickens at Work. Lib. Repr. Ser.* Methuen 1982
$37.00
Chesterton, G. K., and F. G. Kitton. *Charles Dickens.* Folcroft repr. 1973 lib. bdg.
$17.50
Churchill, R. C. *A Bibliography of Dickensian Criticism, 1836–1974. Reference Lib. of
the Humanities* Garland 1975 lib. bdg. $44.00
Cohen, Jane R. *Charles Dickens and His Original Illustrators.* Ohio State Univ. Pr.
1980 $32.50
Collins, Philip, ed. *Dickens: Interviews and Recollections.* Barnes & Noble 2 vols. 1981
ea. $28.50
———, ed. *Dickens: The Critical Heritage. Critical Heritage Ser.* Routledge & Kegan
1971 o.p. A collection of contemporary criticism, grouped for each work and arranged chronologically.
De Vries, Duane. *Dickens's Apprentice Years: The Making of a Novelist.* Barnes & Noble text ed. 1976 $19.50
Fielding, K. J. *Charles Dickens: A Critical Introduction.* Houghton Mifflin (Riv. Eds.)
1958 o.p. A study of his career as a novelist, arranged as a biography.

Ford, George H. *Dickens and His Readers*. Gordian repr. of 1955 ed. 1974 $15.00

Ford, George H., and Lauriat Lane, Jr., eds. *The Dickens Critics*. Cornell Univ. Pr. 1966 pap. $6.95

Forster, John. *The Life of Charles Dickens*. Dutton (Everyman's) o.p. Written by Dickens's most intimate friend, a professional biographer.

Gissing, George. *Critical Studies of the Works of Charles Dickens. Studies in Fiction* Haskell repr. of 1924 ed. 1969 lib. bdg. A critical handbook to which have been added nine papers that Gissing originally wrote as introductions to Dickens's novels.

Gold, Joseph, comp. *Stature of Dickens: A Centenary Bibliography*. Univ. of Toronto Pr. 1971 $25.00

Hardwick, Michael, and Mollie Hardwick. *The Charles Dickens Encyclopedia*. Scribner 1973 $20.00

Hayward, Arthur L. *Dickens Encyclopedia: An Alphabetical Dictionary of Reference to Every Character and Place Mentioned in the Works of Fiction, with Explanatory Notes on Obscure Allusions and Phrases*. Shoe String (Archon) repr. of 1924 ed. 1968 $18.50.

Horsman, E. A. *Dickens and the Structure of the Novel*. Folcroft 1959 lib. bdg. $8.50

House, Humphrey. *The Dickens World*. Oxford Pap. Ser. 2d ed. 1960 pap. $7.95; Richard West 1950 $12.50

Johnson, Edgar. *Charles Dickens: His Tragedy and Triumph*. Viking (Richard Seaver) 1977 $19.95. The best modern biography.

Kaplan, Fred. *Dickens and Mesmerism: The Hidden Springs of Fiction*. Princeton Univ. Pr. 1975 $26.50

Kent, William C. *London for Dickens Lovers. Studies in Dickens* Haskell repr. of 1935 ed. 1972 lib. bdg. $49.95. The London backgrounds of Dickens's life and work.

Kitton, Frederic G. *Dickens and His Illustrators: Cruikshank, Seymour, Buss, Phiz, Cattermole, Leech, Doyle, Stanfield, Maclise, Frank Stone, Tenniel, Landseer, Palmer, Topham, Marcus Stone, and Luke Fildes*. Ayer repr. of 1899 ed. $32.50. Contains 22 portraits and 70 facsimiles of original drawings.

Leavis, F. R., and Q. D. Leavis. *Dickens the Novelist*. Rutgers Univ. Pr. 1979 pap. $10.00

Ley, J. W. T. *The Dickens Circle. Studies in Dickens* Haskell repr. of 1919 ed. 1972 lib. bdg. $52.95. An intimate portrait of Dickens, his family, and his friends.

Lucas, John. *Melancholy Man: A Study of Dickens' Novels*. Barnes & Noble 2d ed. 1980 $26.50

Mackenzie, Norman, and Jeanne Mackenzie. *Dickens: A Life*. Oxford 1979 $25.00

Marcus, Steven. *Dickens: From Pickwick to Dombey*. Basic Bks. 1965 o.p.

Miller, J. Hillis. *Charles Dickens: The World of His Novels*. Harvard Univ. Pr. 1959 $18.50

Monod, Sylvère. *Dickens the Novelist*. Univ. of Oklahoma Pr. 1968 o.p. The author's own translation and revision of *Dickens Romancier*, originally published in 1953. *David Copperfield* receives heavy emphasis.

Newsom, Robert. *Dickens on the Romantic Side of Familiar Things: Bleak House and the Novel Tradition*. Columbia Univ. Pr. 1977 $21.00

Partlow, Robert, ed. *Dickens Studies Annual: Essays on Victorian Fiction*. AMS Pr. ea. $37.50 set $487.00. The first series, 1970–78, was edited by Robert Partlow; the second series, 1979–84, was edited by Michael Timko, Fred Kaplan, and Edward Guiliano.

Patten, Robert L. *Charles Dickens and His Publishers*. Oxford 1978 $63.00

Pierce, Gilbert A. *The Dickens Dictionary. Studies in Dickens*. Haskell repr. of 1878 ed. lib. bdg. $68.95
Pope, Norris. *Dickens and Charity*. Columbia Univ. Pr. 1978 $25.00
Pope-Hennessy, Dame Una. *Charles Dickens, 1812–1870*. Telegraph Bks. repr. of 1945 ed. 1983 lib. bdg. $30.00. Based on the 8,000 collected letters published by Nonesuch Press in 1938.
Sanders, Andrew. *Charles Dickens: Resurrectionist*. St. Martin's 1982 $25.00
Slater, Michael. *Dickens and Women*. Stanford Univ. Pr. 1983 $28.50
Stewart, Garrett. *Dickens and the Trials of Imagination*. Harvard Univ. Pr. text ed. 1974 $16.50
Stone, Harry. *Dickens and the Invisible World: Fairy Tales, Fantasy, and Novel Making*. Indiana Univ. Pr. 1979 $17.50
Wilson, Angus. *The World of Charles Dickens*. Academy Chicago 1984 pap. $8.95. Shows how Dickens's private and public life fed the creative imagination of the novelist. Some 200 black-and-white illustrations; 40 color plates.

DISRAELI, BENJAMIN (1st Earl of Beaconsfield). 1804–1881

A great master of the political novel, Disraeli may be said to have originated the genre. Anthony Trollope in his parliamentary novels is his closest rival. Disraeli's early books were all *romans à clef*, novels in which he introduced real personages easily recognizable beneath fictitious names. With *Coningsby, Sybil*, and *Tancred*, Disraeli produced his best work, all political novels and more or less a trilogy, as the same characters appear and reappear. In these novels, Disraeli dramatized ambition, romantic egoism, and the role of the outsider, particularly the Jew, and revealed a strong sense of the social and economic problems of mid-Victorian Britain. He then gave up writing temporarily, "gradually rose to be three times Chancellor of the Exchequer, and finally, Prime Minister from 1867–68 and again from 1874–80. During his second term of office, when he was knighted, he took a name from his first novel and became the first Earl of Beaconsfield. In his later years he resumed his writing and became an intimate friend of Queen Victoria," who referred to his death as "a national calamity."

The Life of Benjamin Disraeli, Earl of Beaconsfield, was written by William Flavell Monypenny (1866–1912), and completed by George Earl Buckle (1854–1935). Robert Blake's *Disraeli*, the standard modern biography, is out of print.

BOOKS BY DISRAELI

Works. Critical intro. by Edmund Gosse, biographical pref. by Robert Arnot; AMS Pr. 20 vols. repr. of 1904 ed. ea. $40.00 set $800.00
Benjamin Disraeli's Letters, 1815–1837. Ed. by J. A. W. Gunn, John Matthews, Donald Schuman, and M. G. Wiebe, Univ. of Toronto Pr. 2 vols. 1982 ea. $50.00
Vivian Grey. 1826. Dufour 1969 o.p.
The Voyage of Captain Popanilla. 1828. Bks. for Libraries o.p. McGrath o.p.
Coningsby. 1844. Ed. by Sheila M. Smith, *World's Class. Ser.* Oxford 1982 pap. $7.95; ed. by Thomas Braun, *Penguin Eng. Lib. Ser.* 1983 pap. $5.95
Sybil, or The Two Nations. 1845. *World's Class.-Pap. Ser.* Oxford 1981 pap. $7.95; ed. by Thomas Braun, *Penguin Eng. Lib. Ser.* 1980 pap. $5.95

Tancred, or The New Crusade. 1847. Greenwood repr. of 1877 ed. lib. bdg. $19.00
The Young Duke: A Moral Tale, though Gay. 1853. Folcroft repr. of 1853 ed. lib. bdg.
$20.00
Lothair. 1870. Greenwood repr. of 1906 ed. lib. bdg. $17.25; Scholarly repr. 1971
$14.00

Books about Disraeli

Blake, Robert. *Disraeli.* Oxford o.p.; St. Martin's o.p. "[Blake] has portrayed, with
delicacy and penetration, the most exciting and, in a curious way, the most modern of all Victorian statesmen. A great book" (Harold Macmillan). "Blake's biography is a triumph . . . in Mr. Blake [Disraeli] has found a biographer to do his
complex personality justice" (*LJ*).
————. *Disraeli's Grand Tour: Disraeli in the Holy Land, 1830–31.* Oxford Univ. Pr.
1982 $16.95
Brandes, George. *Lord Beaconsfield.* Peter Smith repr. $11.00
Braun, Thomas. *Disraeli the Novelist.* Allen & Unwin text ed. 1981 $15.00
Pearson, Hesketh. *Dizzy: The Nature and Life of Benjamin Disraeli, Earl of Beaconsfield.* Greenwood repr. of 1951 ed. 1975 lib. bdg. $19.75; Richard West repr. of
1951 ed. 1973 $30.00
Schwarz, Daniel R. *Disraeli's Fiction.* Barnes & Noble text ed. 1979 $26.50

DOYLE, SIR ARTHUR CONAN. 1859–1930

In Sherlock Holmes, Conan Doyle created one of the most famous charac-
ters in popular fiction. The well-known detective appears in four novels (*A
Study in Scarlet, The Sign of the Four, The Hound of the Baskervilles,* and *His
Last Bow*), and 56 short stories (contained in *The Adventures of Sherlock
Holmes, The Memoirs of Sherlock Holmes, The Return of Sherlock Holmes,* and
The Case-Book of Sherlock Holmes). Holmes fans might continue their re-
search in two volumes, both by Vincent Starrett: *The Private Life of Sherlock
Holmes* and *221B: Studies in Sherlock Holmes* (o.p.). Sir Arthur's son,
Adrian, and John Dickson Carr have written *The Exploits of Sherlock
Holmes.* Doyle also won great success with his historical novels. *The White
Company* (1891, o.p.), a tale of the War of the Roses, is his masterpiece. In
his last years, Sir Arthur wrote several books on spiritualism.

Books by Doyle

THE SHERLOCK HOLMES BOOKS

The Complete Sherlock Holmes. Doubleday 1952 $15.95
The Annotated Sherlock Holmes. Ed. by William S. Baring-Gould (pseud.), Crown
(Potter) 2 vols. 1967 $39.95. The 4 novels and 56 stories complete. Includes a bib-
liography.
Sherlock Holmes: Selected Stories. World's Class. Ser. Oxford 1980 pap. $3.95
Best Supernatural Tales of Arthur Conan Doyle. Ed. by E. F. Bleiler, Dover 1979 pap.
$4.95
Tales of Terror and Mystery. Penguin 1979 pap. $3.50
A Study in Scarlet. 1887. Penguin 1982 pap. $2.95
The Sign of the Four. 1890. Penguin 1982 pap. $2.95
The Adventures of Sherlock Holmes. 1891. Macmillan (Collier Bks.) 1962 pap. $3.95

The Memoirs of Sherlock Holmes. 1894. Penguin 1971 pap. $2.95
The Hound of the Baskervilles. 1902. *Longman Simplified Eng. Ser.* 1976 pap. $1.95
The Return of Sherlock Holmes. 1905. Penguin 1982 pap. $2.95
His Last Bow. 1917. Berkley Publishing 1982 pap. $2.25
The Case-Book of Sherlock Holmes. 1927. Berkley Publishing 1982 pap. $2.25

HISTORICAL NOVELS

The Refugees: A Tale of Two Continents. 1891. Transatlantic $8.95
The Valley of Fear. 1915. Berkley Publishing pap. $2.25; Buccaneer Bks. lib. bdg. $15.95

BOOKS ABOUT DOYLE

Doyle, Adrian Conan, and John Dickson Carr. *The Exploits of Sherlock Holmes. Short Story Index Repr. Ser.* Ayer repr. of 1954 ed. $21.00
Hall, Trevor. *Sherlock Holmes and His Creator.* St. Martin's 1979 $27.50
Hardwick, Michael, ed. *The Private Life of Dr. Watson: Being the Personal Reminiscences of John H. Watson.* Dutton 1983 $13.95
Higham, Charles. *The Adventures of Conan Doyle: The Life of the Creator of Sherlock Holmes.* Norton 1976 $12.95
Pearson, Hesketh. *Conan Doyle: His Life and Art.* Taplinger 1977 $9.95
Starrett, Vincent. *The Private Life of Sherlock Holmes.* AMS repr. of 1960 ed. $17.50; *Eng. Lit. Ser.* Haskell repr. of 1934 ed. 1970 lib. bdg. $39.95; Pinnacle Bks. 1975 pap. $1.95
Tracy, Jack, ed. *The Encyclopaedia Sherlockiana.* Doubleday 1977 $12.95

DU MAURIER, GEORGE. 1834–1896

Du Maurier was first famous as an artist, contributing incomparable satirical drawings of society to *Punch* and illustrating novels by authors such as Mrs. Gaskell, Thackeray, and Meredith. *Peter Ibbetson*, his own first novel, is a fanciful romance of dream life, a work of rare imagination and charm of style. *Trilby* created a literary sensation and brought the name of the character "Svengali"—an evil person who bends others to his will—into the English language. The story is set in the Latin Quarter in Paris and is thoroughly French in atmosphere. Du Maurier was born in Paris, studied art there, and illustrated his own novels. *Trilby* contained a portrait of Whistler in caricature, which Du Maurier was forced by law to change.

BOOKS BY DU MAURIER

Young George Du Maurier: A Selection of His Letters, 1860–67. Ed. by his granddaughter, Daphne Du Maurier, Darby repr. of 1951 ed. 1982 lib. bdg. $30.00; Greenwood repr. of 1951 ed. lib. bdg. $15.00. This book includes illustrations from contemporary drawings by Du Maurier.
Peter Ibbetson. 1892. Intro. by Madge Plunket, Arden Lib. repr. of 1891 ed. 1979 lib. bdg. $25.00; Scholarly repr. of 1932 ed. 1971 $19.00
Trilby. 1894. Biblio Dist. 1977 $9.95 pap. $3.95
The Martian: A Novel. Century Bookbindery 1980 lib. bdg. $25.00; Scholarly repr. of 1897 ed. 1971 $19.00

BOOK ABOUT DU MAURIER

Ormond, Leonée. *George Du Maurier.* Univ. of Pittsburgh Pr. 1969 o.p. A critical biography.

EDGEWORTH, MARIA. 1767–1849

Following FANNY BURNEY, Maria Edgeworth wrote in the tradition of the novel of manners. Her stated purpose was to diminish the frivolity of the times. *Castle Rackrent* and *The Absentee,* considered her best novels and both based on personal observation, portray the degeneration of Irish estates. As the sympathetic interpreter of Irish national characteristics, she contributed to the Celtic revival and was one of the first to introduce the lower classes into fiction.

BOOKS BY EDGEWORTH

Tales and Novels. AMS Pr. 10 vols. repr. of 1893 ed. set $210.00
The Life and Letters of Maria Edgeworth. Ed. by Augustus J. Hare, *Select Bibliographies Reprint Ser.* Ayer repr. of 1894 ed. $40.00
The Education of the Heart: The Correspondence of Rachel Mordecai Lazarus and Maria Edgeworth. Ed. by Edgar E. MacDonald, Univ. of North Carolina Pr. 1977 $25.00
Maria Edgeworth: Chosen Letters. AMS Pr. repr. of 1913 ed. $32.00
Maria Edgeworth in France and England: Selections from the Edgeworth Family Letters. Ed. by Christina Colvin, Oxford 1979 $54.00
Castle Rackrent. Ed. by Robert L. Wolff, *Ireland 19th-Century Fiction Ser.* Garland repr. of 1800 ed. 1979 lib. bdg. $46.00; *Norton Lib.* 1965 pap. $3.95; ed. by George Watson, *World's Class. Ser.* 1982 pap. $3.95
Castle Rackrent (and *The Absentee*). Biblio Dist. 1976 $8.95
The Absentee. 1812. Ed. by Robert L. Wolff, *Ireland 19th-Century Fiction Ser.* Garland 1979 lib. bdg. $46.00
Ormond. Ed. by Robert L. Wolff, *Ireland 19th-Century Fiction Ser.* Garland 2 vols. 1979 lib. bdg. $92.00
(and Richard Edgeworth). *Practical Education.* Ed. by Gina Luria, *Feminist Controversy in Eng.* Garland 2 vols. 1974 lib. bdg. $110.00

BOOKS ABOUT EDGEWORTH

Butler, Marilyn. *Maria Edgeworth: A Literary Biography.* Oxford 1972 $27.50
Hawthorne, Mark D. *Doubt and Dogma in Maria Edgeworth. Univ. of Florida Humanities Monographs* 1967 pap. $3.50
Hurst, Michael. *Maria Edgeworth and the Public Scene.* Telegraph Bks. repr. of 1969 ed. 1981 $35.00

ELIOT, GEORGE (pseud. of Mary Ann, or Marian, Evans, afterward Cross). 1819–1880

Born Mary Ann Evans, George Eliot asserted her intellect in her early translations and journalism, her imagination in a series of extraordinary novels, and her independence in her pseudonym and in her personal life. Her first four novels moved from social to psychological realism. English rural life became the carefully delineated background for serious dramatizations of human character tested by the interplay between environment and moral choice. Her concern for philosophic and moral issues was illumined by her wide learning and deep compassion for the human situation. Her versatility and learning propelled her into trying the historical novel (*Romola*), the political novel (*Felix Holt*), and a novel about Zionism (*Daniel Deronda*). Her style resembled that of other Victorian novelists, particularly Dickens, in the triumph of selective realism and psychological perceptiveness. Although HENRY JAMES thought *Silas Marner* "nearly a masterpiece," recent opinion holds that her supreme achievement is *Middlemarch*.

Gordon S. Haight's edition of her *Letters* was a major "contribution to literary history, to letter writing and to a deeper interpretation of the novelist that readers once read and loved." It contains 2,760 letters and extracts from journals, nearly two thousand of them written by Eliot herself. "The dominant qualities in the letters are intellectual and moral integrity, with unfaltering courage in saying and doing what she thought right" (*SR*).

BOOKS BY ELIOT

Writings of George Eliot. AMS Pr. 25 vols. repr. of 1908 ed. ea. $34.50 set $862.50. With the *Life* by J. W. Cross.

Essays. 1879. Ed. by Thomas Pinney, Columbia Univ. Pr. 1963 $20.00

The George Eliot Letters: 1836–80. Ed. by Gordon S. Haight, Yale Univ. Pr. 9 vols. 1952–79 ea. $50.00

Selections from George Eliot's Letters. Ed. by Gordon S. Haight. Yale Univ. Pr. 1985 $25.00

George Eliot's Life as Related in Her Letters and Journal. Ed. by J. W. Cross, Scholarly 3 vols. repr. of 1885 ed. 1969 $89.00

Scenes of Clerical Life. 1858. Biblio Dist. 1976 $8.95; ed. by David Lodge, *Penguin Eng. Lib. Ser.* 1973 pap. $4.95

Adam Bede. 1859. Biblio Dist. 1978 $9.95 pap. $2.50; ed. by John Paterson, Houghton Mifflin (Riv. Eds.) 1968 pap. $6.50; *Penguin Eng. Lib. Ser.* 1980 pap. $4.95

The Mill on the Floss. 1860. Biblio Dist. 1978 $9.95 pap. $2.95; ed. by Gordon S. Haight, *World's Class. Ser.* Oxford 1982 pap. $4.95

Silas Marner. 1861. *Bantam Class. Ser.* 1981 text ed. pap. $1.75; Biblio Dist. 1978 $9.95 pap. $2.95; ed. by N. L. Clay, *Heinemann Guide Novel Ser.* text ed. $3.95; *Penguin Eng. Lib. Ser.* 1968 pap. $2.50

Romola. 1863. *World's Class. Ser.* Oxford $15.95; ed. by Andrew Sanders, *Penguin Eng. Lib. Ser.* 1980 pap. $4.95

Felix Holt, the Radical. 1866. Biblio Dist. repr. of 1909 ed. 1967 $12.95 text ed. pap. $4.95; ed. by Peter Coveney, *Penguin Eng. Lib. Ser.* 1973 pap. $4.95

Middlemarch: A Study of Provincial Life. 1871. *Norton Critical Eds.* 1977 pap. $9.95; *Penguin Eng. Lib. Ser.* 1965 pap. $4.95

Daniel Deronda. 1876. New Amer. Lib. (Signet Class.) 1979 pap. $3.50; ed. by Barbara Hardy, *Penguin Eng. Lib. Ser.* 1967 pap. $4.95

BOOKS ABOUT ELIOT

Adam, Ian, ed. *The Particular Web: Essays on Middlemarch*. Univ. of Toronto Pr. 1975 $15.00

Auster, Henry. *Local Habitations: Regionalism in the Early Novels of George Eliot*. Harvard Univ. Pr. 1970 $15.00

Beer, Gillian. *Darwin's Plots: Evolutionary Narrative in Darwin, George Eliot, and Nineteenth-Century Fiction.* Routledge & Kegan 1983 $35.00
Bennett, Joan. *George Eliot: Her Mind and Her Art.* Cambridge Univ. Pr. 1948 $29.95 pap. $11.95
Bonaparte, Felicia. *The Triptych and the Cross: A Key to the Central Myths of George Eliot's Poetic Imagination.* New York Univ. Pr. 1979 $32.50 pap. $16.00
———. *Will and Destiny: Morality and Tragedy in George Eliot's Novels.* New York Univ. Pr. 1975 $32.00 pap. $16.00
Carroll, David, ed. *George Eliot: The Critical Heritage.* Barnes & Noble 1971 o.p.
Emery, Laura Comer. *George Eliot's Creative Conflict: The Other Side of Silence.* Univ. of California Pr. 1976 $26.00
Haight, Gordon S. *George Eliot: A Biography.* Oxford 1976 pap. $8.95. A judicious, carefully written, and definitive biography that was the first to draw fully on the author's edition of the letters.
Hardy, Barbara. *The Novels of George Eliot: A Study in Form.* Longwood 1959 $31.50. A solid and well-written analysis, which approaches form through the naturalism in all of the works.
———. *Particularities: Readings in George Eliot.* Ohio Univ. Pr. text ed. 1983 $20.95 pap. $10.95
Jones, R. T. *George Eliot. British Authors Ser.* Cambridge Univ. Pr. 1971 $22.50 pap. $7.95. Discusses the novels in chronological order.
Knoepflmacher, U. C. *George Eliot's Early Novels: The Limits of Realism.* Univ. of California Pr. 1968 o.p.
Mintz, Alan. *George Eliot and the Novel of Vocation.* Harvard Univ. Pr. 1978 $15.00
Paris, Bernard J. *Experiments in Life: George Eliot's Quest for Values.* Wayne State Univ. Pr. 1979 $15.95
Pinion, F. B. *A George Eliot Companion: Literary Achievement and Modern Significance. Companion Ser.* Barnes & Noble 1981 $28.50
Pratt, John C., and Victor A. Neufeldt. *George Eliot's "Middlemarch" Notebooks.* Univ. of California Pr. 1979 $47.50
Witemeyer, Hugh. *George Eliot and the Visual Arts.* Yale Univ. Pr. 1979 $27.50

GASKELL, MRS. ELIZABETH (CLEGHORN STEVENSON). 1810–1865

Mrs. Gaskell's novels were avidly read by her contemporaries as effective dramatizations of the social problems of their poor (*Mary Barton*) and of the life of the small rural community (*Cranford*). Her growing modern reputation particularly emphasizes her artistry and her influence as a woman writer. She is of special interest to feminists. Her emphasis as a regional novelist on realistic depictions of provincial life has earned her comparisons with George Eliot and Thomas Hardy. Mrs. Gaskell knew the Brontë family personally and is particularly remembered for her *Life of Charlotte Brontë* (1857).

BOOKS BY MRS. GASKELL

Works. Ed. by A. W. Ward, AMS Pr. 8 vols. repr. of 1906 ed. ea. $47.50 set $380.00
The Letters of Mrs. Gaskell. Ed. by J. A. V. Chapple and Arthur Pollard, Harvard Univ. Pr. 1966 $60.00. Letters dating from her marriage to her death, 1832–64. A collection of all her letters extant. "Their value lies less in revealing [her] daily cares and preoccupations . . . than in the light they throw on . . . Dickens,

Florence Nightingale, Harriet Beecher Stowe, Carlyle, Ruskin, Thackeray—and on the vulgar commercial vitality of her home city of Manchester in its first flush of industrial wealth" (*N.Y. Times*).

Cousin Phyllis and Other Tales. Ed. by Angus Easson, *World's Class. Ser.* Oxford 1981 pap. $7.95

Mary Barton. 1848. *Norton Lib.* 1958 pap. $5.95

Cranford (and *Other Tales*). 1851–53. Biblio Dist. 1973 pap. $2.50; ed. by Elizabeth Watson, *World's Class. Ser.* 1980 pap. $2.95

Ruth. Ed. by Robert L. Wolff, *Victorian Fiction Ser.* Garland repr. of 1853 ed. 1975 lib. bdg. $66.00

Lizzie Leight and Other Tales. 1854. *Short Story Index Repr. Ser.* Ayer repr. of 1865 ed. $16.00

North and South. 1855. Scholarly repr. of 1914 ed. 1971 $12.00

Life of Charlotte Brontë. Ed. by Alan Shelston, *Penguin Eng. Lib. Ser.* 1975 pap. $5.95; Richard West repr. of 1947 ed. $20.00

Sylvia's Lovers. 1863. Biblio Dist. repr. of 1911 ed. 1971 $9.95

The Grey Woman and Other Tales. Short Story Index Repr. Ser. Ayer repr. of 1865 ed. $16.00

Wives and Daughters. 1866. Biblio Dist. 1982 pap. $4.75; ed. by Frank G. Smith, *Penguin Eng. Lib. Ser.* 1969 pap. $4.95

BOOKS ABOUT MRS. GASKELL

Chapple, J. A. V., and J. G. Sharps. *Elizabeth Gaskell: A Portrait in Letters.* Manchester Univ. Pr. 1982 pap. $8.00

Easson, Angus. *Elizabeth Gaskell.* Routledge & Kegan 1979 $22.00

Ganz, Margaret. *Elizabeth Gaskell: The Artist in Conflict.* Irvington 1969 $27.50

Gérin, Winifred. *Elizabeth Gaskell: A Biography.* Oxford 1976 pap. $9.95

Haldane, Elizabeth. *Mrs. Gaskell and Her Friends. Select Bibliographies Repr. Ser.* Ayer repr. of 1931 ed. $18.00; Folcroft repr. 1973 lib. bdg. $12.50

Hopkins, A. B. *Elizabeth Gaskell: Her Life and Work.* Octagon repr. 1970 lib. bdg. $27.50

Pollard, Arthur. *Mrs. Gaskell: Novelist and Biographer.* Harvard Univ. Pr. 1965 $15.00

Sanders, Gerald DeWitt. *Elizabeth Gaskell.* Bibliography by Clark S. Northrup, Russell repr. of 1929 ed. 1971 $13.00; Scholarly repr. of 1929 ed. 1971 $12.00

GISSING, GEORGE (ROBERT). 1857–1903

Recent years have seen a strong revival of interest in Gissing, almost all of whose novels are now available in reprints. A bridge between late Victorianism and early modernism, Gissing's novels combine two essential themes of the period, the isolation and struggle of the artist and the economic bondage of the proletariat. *New Grub Street* and his own indirect autobiography, *The Private Papers of Henry Ryecroft*, reveal the close connection in Gissing between fiction and autobiography, and *Workers in the Dawn* and *Demos: A Story of English Socialism* dramatizes Gissing's conviction that economic and class divisions are central to human character and individual destiny.

BOOKS BY GISSING

Letters of George Gissing to Members of His Family. Ed. by Algernon Gissing and Ellen Gissing, *Eng. Lit. Ser.* Haskell repr. of 1927 ed. 1970 lib. bdg. $58.95

George Gissing and H. G. Wells: Their Friendship and Correspondence. Ed. by Royal A.
   Gettmann, Telegraph Bks. repr. of 1961 ed. 1983 lib. bdg. $40.00
The Letters of George Gissing to Eduard Bertz, 1887–1903. Ed. by Arthur C. Young,
   Greenwood repr. of 1961 ed. 1980 lib. bdg. $32.50
Autobiographical Notes: With Comments on Tennyson and Huxley. Gordon $59.95
*London and the Life of Literature in Late Victorian England: The Diary of George Gis-
   sing, Novelist.* Ed. by Pierre Coustillas, Bucknell Univ. Pr. 1978 $60.00
The House of Cobwebs and Other Stories. 1906. Telegraph Bks. repr. of 1914 ed. 1980
   lib. bdg. $25.00. Includes "The Work of George Gissing: An Introduction" by
   Thomas Seccombe.
A Victim of Circumstances and Other Stories. Short Story Index Repr. Ser. Ayer repr. of
   1927 ed. $17.00
Workers in the Dawn. AMS Pr. repr. of 1880 ed. $55.00
Thyrza: A Tale. 1887. AMS Pr. repr. of 1893 ed. $30.00; ed. by Jacob Korg, Fairleigh
   Dickinson Univ. Pr. $24.50
Life Morning. AMS Pr. repr. of 1888 ed. $30.00; Richard West 1947 $25.00
The Nether World. 1889. Methuen 1983 pap. $7.50
The Emancipated. AMS Pr. repr. of 1890 ed. $30.00; ed. by Pierre Coustillas, Fair-
   leigh Dickinson Univ. Pr. 1978 $22.50
New Grub Street. 1891. Ed. by Bernard Bergonzi, *Penguin Eng. Lib. Ser.* 1976 pap.
   $4.95
Demos: A Story of English Socialism. AMS Pr. repr. of 1892 ed. $15.00; Methuen 1983
   pap. $10.95
Born in Exile. AMS Pr. 3 vols. in 1 repr. of 1892 ed. $37.50; ed. by Pierre Coustillas,
   Society and Victorians Ser. Humanities Pr. text ed. 1978 $22.25
Denzil Quarier. AMS Pr. repr. of 1892 ed. $18.50; ed. by John Halperin, *Harvester
   Complete Critical Eds. Ser.* Humanities Pr. text ed. 1980 $19.50
The Odd Women. AMS Pr. repr. of 1893 ed. $30.00; Norton 1971 pap. $3.25; Richard
   West repr. lib. bdg. $30.00
In the Year of Jubilee. AMS Pr. repr. of 1894 ed. $21.50; Dover 1982 pap. $6.00
Eve's Ransom. AMS Pr. repr. of 1895 ed. $18.50; Dover 1980 pap. $3.00
Paying Guest. AMS Pr. repr. of 1895 ed. $16.00
Sleeping Fires. 1895. Univ. of Nebraska Pr. (Bison) 1983 pap. $4.95
The Unclassed. AMS Pr. repr. of 1896 ed. $15.00; Methuen 1983 pap. $10.95
The Whirlpool. AMS Pr. repr. of 1897 ed. $18.00; ed. by Patrick Parinder, Fairleigh
   Dickinson Univ. Pr. $24.50; Merrimack 1984 pap. $7.95
The Town Traveller. AMS Pr. repr. of 1898 ed. $18.00; Century Bookbindery repr. of
   1927 ed. lib. bdg. $25.00; ed. by Pierre Coustillas, Humanities Pr. text ed. 1981
   $21.00; Richard West repr. of 1898 ed. lib. bdg. $30.00; Telegraph Bks. repr. of
   1898 ed. 1981 lib. bdg. $20.00
Charles Dickens: A Critical Study (Critical Study of Charles Dickens). Scholarly repr. of
   1898 ed. 1972 $29.00
Human Odds and Ends. 1898. Ed. by Ian Fletcher and John Stokes, *Decadent Con-
   sciousness Ser.* Garland 1978 lib. bdg. $42.00
The Crown of Life. AMS Pr. repr. of 1899 ed. $24.50
By the Ionian Sea. 1901. Dufour 1956 o.p.
Our Friend the Charlatan. AMS Pr. repr. of 1901 ed. $18.50
The Private Papers of Henry Ryecroft. 1903. Arden Lib. repr. of 1914 ed. $35.00; Rich-
   ard West repr. of 1914 ed. 1978 lib. bdg. $30.00
Veranilda: A Romance. AMS Pr. repr. of 1904 ed. $15.00
Will Warburton: A Romance of Real Life. AMS Pr. repr. of 1905 ed. $10.00

BOOKS ABOUT GISSING

Collie, Michael. *George Gissing: A Biography.* Shoe String (Archon) 1977 $19.50

Coustillas, Pierre, ed. *Collected Articles on George Gissing.* Biblio Dist. 1968 $28.50

Coustillas, Pierre, and Colin Partridge, eds. *Gissing: The Critical Heritage.* Critical Heritage Ser. Routledge & Kegan 1972 $40.00. Contemporary and near-contemporary criticisms and comments.

Goode, John. *George Gissing: Ideology and Fiction.* Critical Studies Ser. Barnes & Noble text ed. 1979 $23.50

Halperin, John. *Gissing: A Life in Books.* Oxford 1982 $29.95

Korg, Jacob. *George Gissing: A Critical Biography.* Univ. of Washington Pr. 1963 $17.50 pap. $8.95

Michaux, Jean-Pierre, ed. *George Gissing: Critical Essays.* Critical Studies Ser. Barnes & Noble 1981 $26.50

Selig, Robert L. *George Gissing. Twayne's Eng. Authors Ser.* G. K. Hall 1983 lib. bdg. $16.95

Wolff, Joseph J. *George Gissing: An Annotated Bibliography of Writings about Him.* Annotated Secondary Bibliography Ser. of Eng. Lit. in Transition, 1880–1920 Northern Illinois Univ. Pr. 1974 $20.00

HARDY, THOMAS. 1840–1928

A master of somber irony with a tragic view of human nature and destiny, Hardy is the outstanding novelist of the late nineteenth century and a major influence on the modern novel. He dramatizes the conflict between natural instinct and social restriction and between Darwinism and spiritual aspiration.

The setting of nearly all his books is the area of the ancient kingdom of Wessex (used as a fictitious county name by Hardy), the part of England that includes Dorsetshire. His first novel, *The Poor Man and the Lady*, was never published. When George Meredith, then reader for Chapman and Hall, turned it down because it "had not enough plot," Hardy destroyed the manuscript. *The Return of the Native, Tess of the D'Urbervilles*, and *Jude the Obscure* are generally considered his greatest works. He delights in portraying the grim irony of life with reserved sympathy. In 1895, when he published his last novel, *Jude the Obscure*, the storm of criticism that the book aroused led him to give up fiction for poetry. He had always preferred his poetry to his novels and wanted to be remembered as a poet. Carl J. Weber, the American authority on Hardy who died in 1966, wrote the standard critical biography. He also edited *Dearest Emmie* (o.p.), a collection of some 74 letters (1885–1911) from Hardy to his first wife. The *Notebooks of Thomas Hardy*, edited by Evelyn Hardy, is now out of print. (See also Chapter 6 in this volume.)

BOOKS BY HARDY

The Thomas Hardy Omnibus. St. Martin's 1979 $15.00

The Penguin Thomas Hardy. 2 vols. 1984 $8.95

The Works of Thomas Hardy in Prose and Verse. Johnson Repr. $3,000.00

The Works of Thomas Hardy in Prose. AMS Pr. 18 vols. 1984 ea. $32.50 set $585.00

Thomas Hardy's Personal Writings: Prefaces, Literary Opinions, Reminiscences. Ed. by

Harold Orel, Humanities Pr. text ed. 1981 $10.00. "Illustrates [Hardy's] sensitiv-
ity and defensiveness . . . and makes the reader aware once again of the unity
and force of other Hardy attitudes" (*LJ*).

The Collected Letters of Thomas Hardy. Ed. by Richard L. Purdy and Michael Millgate, Oxford 4 vols. 1978–1984 ea. $35.95–$49.50

Life and Art: Essays, Notes and Letters. Ed. by E. Brennecke, *Essay Index Repr. Ser.*
Ayer repr. of 1925 ed. $15.00

Thomas Hardy Selected Stories. St. Martin's 1980 pap. $3.95

The Distracted Preacher and Other Tales. Intro. by Susan Hill, *Penguin Eng. Lib. Ser.*
1980 pap. $4.95

Desperate Remedies. 1871. *Hardy New Wessex Ed. Ser.* St. Martin's 1977 o.p.

Under the Greenwood Tree, or The Mellstock Quire. 1872. *Penguin Eng. Lib. Ser.* 1978
pap. $3.95; *Hardy New Wessex Ed. Ser.* St. Martin's 1977 pap. $3.95

A Pair of Blue Eyes. 1873. *Hardy New Wessex Ed. Ser.* St. Martin's 1979 pap. $3.95

Far from the Madding Crowd. 1874. *Bantam Class. Ser.* 1982 pap. $2.75; Biblio Dist.
1984 pap. $1.95; ed. by Ronald Blythe, *Penguin Eng. Lib. Ser.* 1978 pap. $2.95;
Hardy New Wessex Ed. Ser. St. Martin's 1978 pap. $2.95

The Hand of Ethelberta. 1876. *Hardy New Wessex Ed. Ser.* St. Martin's 1978 pap. $2.95

The Return of the Native. 1878. *Bantam Class. Ser.* 1981 pap. $1.95; ed. by John Milne,
Heinemann Guided Readers Ser. text ed. 1980 pap. $2.50; ed. by A. Walton Litz,
Houghton Mifflin (Riv. Eds.) 1967 pap. $5.50; New Amer. Lib. (Signet Class.)
1973 pap. $1.95; ed. by James Gindin, *Norton Critical Eds.* 1969 pap. $8.95;
Hardy New Wessex Ed. Ser. St. Martin's 1978 pap. $2.95

The Trumpet Major. 1880. *Hardy New Wessex Ed. Ser.* St. Martin's 1978 pap. $2.95

Two on a Tower. 1882. *Hardy New Wessex Ed. Ser.* St. Martin's 1977 o.p.

A Laodicean: Story of To-Day. 1881. *Hardy New Wessex Ed. Ser.* St. Martin's 1978 pap.
$3.95

Wessex Tales. 1883. *Hardy New Wessex Ed. Ser.* St. Martin's 1977 o.p.

The Mayor of Casterbridge. 1886. *Bantam Class. Ser.* 1981 pap. $1.95; ed. by R. B. Heil-
man, Houghton Mifflin (Riv. Eds.) 1962 pap. $5.50; ed. by James K. Robinson,
Norton Critical Eds. 1977 text ed. pap. $7.95; *Penguin Eng. Lib. Ser.* 1978 pap.
$2.95; *Hardy New Wessex Ed. Ser.* St. Martin's 1977 pap. $2.95

The Woodlanders. 1887. Ed. by Dale Kramer, Oxford 1981 $79.00; *Penguin Eng. Lib.
Ser.* 1981 pap. $4.95; *Hardy New Wessex Ed. Ser.* St. Martin's 1978 pap. $2.95

Tess of the D'Urbervilles: Pure Woman. 1891. *Bantam Class. Ser.* 1981 pap. $2.95; ed.
by William E. Buckler, Houghton Mifflin (Riv. Eds.) 1960 pap. $5.50; ed. by
Scott Elledge, *Norton Critical Eds.* 2d ed. text ed. 1978 pap. $5.95; ed. by Juliet
Grindle and Simon Gatrell, Oxford 1983 $98.00; ed. by A. Alvarez and David
Skilton, *Penguin Eng. Lib. Ser.* 1978 pap. $2.95

The Well-Beloved: Sketch of a Temperament. 1892. *Hardy New Wessex Ed. Ser.* St. Martin's 1978 pap. $2.95

Our Exploits at West Poley. 1893. Folcroft repr. 1952 lib. bdg. $16.50

Life's Little Ironies and *A Few Crusted Characters.* 1894. St. Martin's o.p.

Jude the Obscure. 1895. *Bantam Class. Ser.* 1981 $2.75; ed. by F. R. Southerington,
Lib. of Lit. Bobbs 1972 pap. $12.04; ed. by Irving Howe, Houghton Mifflin (Riv.
Eds.) 1965 pap. $5.50; ed. by Norman Page, *Norton Critical Eds.* 1978 pap. $7.95;
Penguin Eng. Lib. Ser. 1978 pap. $2.95; *Hardy New Wessex Ed. Ser.* St. Martin's
1977 pap. $2.95

A Changed Man; The Waiting Supper; and Other Tales. 1913. St. Martin's o.p.

BOOKS ABOUT HARDY

Bayley, John. *An Essay on Hardy.* Cambridge Univ. Pr. 1978 $29.95 1981 pap. $13.95

Beach, Thomas Warren. *The Technique of Thomas Hardy.* Russell repr. of 1922 ed. 1962 $14.00

Carpenter, Richard C. *Thomas Hardy. Twayne's Eng. Authors Ser.* G. K. Hall 1964 lib. bdg. $12.50. "An intelligent and perceptive analysis of Hardy's work that is cognizant of the traditional viewpoint . . . as well as the more recent attitude toward his work" (*Choice*).

Gerber, Helmut E., and W. Eugene Davis, eds. *Thomas Hardy: An Annotated Bibliography of Writings about Him. Annotated Secondary Bibliography Ser. on Eng. Lit. in Transition, 1880–1920* Northern Illinois Univ. Pr. 1973 $25.00

Gregor, Ian. *The Great Web: The Form of Hardy's Major Fiction.* Faber 1982 $7.95

Hardy, Florence Emily Dugdale, comp. *The Life of Thomas Hardy.* Shoe String (Archon) repr. of 1962 ed. 1970 $27.50. The second Mrs. Hardy, who died in 1937, compiled this life of her husband largely from contemporary notes, letters, diaries, and biographical memoranda, as well as from oral information from conversations extending over many years. The general understanding is that Hardy himself wrote a good deal of the material and that the biography is autobiographical.

Howe, Irving. *Thomas Hardy. Masters of World Lit. Ser.* Macmillan 1973 pap. $2.95

Meisel, Perry. *Thomas Hardy: The Return of the Repressed—A Study of the Major Fiction.* Yale Univ. Pr. 1972

Miller, J. Hillis. *Thomas Hardy: Distance and Desire.* Harvard Univ. Pr. 1970 $18.50

Millgate, Michael. *Thomas Hardy: A Biography.* Random 1982 $25.00

Page, Norman, ed. *Thomas Hardy: The Writer and His Background.* St. Martin's 1980 $27.50

Pinion, F. B. *Thomas Hardy: Art and Thought.* Rowman 1977 $19.50

Saxelby, F. Outwin. *A Thomas Hardy Dictionary: The Characters and Scenes of the Novels and Poems Alphabetically Arranged and Described.* Greenwood repr. of 1911 ed. 1980 lib. bdg. $27.50. The characters and scenes of the novels and poems alphabetically arranged and described.

Vigar, Penelope. *The Novels of Thomas Hardy: Illusion and Reality.* Humanities Pr. text ed. 1974 $18.00

Weber, Carl J. *Hardy in America: A Study of Thomas Hardy and His American Readers.* Russell repr. of 1946 ed. 1966 $10.00

——. *Hardy of Wessex.* 1940. Columbia Univ. Pr. 1965 o.p. An outstanding critical biography, notable for its scholarly accuracy and balanced appraisal, but now replaced by Millgate.

Williams, Merryn. *A Preface to Hardy.* Longman text ed. 1976 pap. $6.95

HUDSON, WILLIAM HENRY. 1841–1922

William Henry Hudson, born in South America of American parents, was both a naturalist and a novelist. He chose to serve two masters and reached distinction under both. *The Purple Land* (1885) is a story of Uruguay, "the land that England lost." *A Crystal Age* is a utopia, a picture of a paragon world. *Green Mansions* is an idyllic romance of South America, an allegory. His autobiography, *Far Away and Long Ago* (1918), has a matchless charm. Hudson is a stylist whose books are rich in beautiful lyric prose. He combined a gift for storytelling with a deep feeling for nature. *W. H. Hudson's Diary, 1874: Voyages from Buenos Aires to Southampton* (o.p.) contains descriptions of great force and beauty. *W. H. Hudson: A Portrait*, by Morley Roberts, the authorized life, is usually considered defamatory.

BOOKS BY HUDSON

Collected Works. AMS Pr. 24 vols. repr. of 1923 ed. ea. $35.00 set $840.00. The volumes of fiction in this set are listed separately in the bibliography below. Under the subheading Works on Natural History is a selection of titles that should be of interest. For other titles, mostly ornithological, consult the AMS Press catalog.

The Purple Land: Being the Narrative of One Richard Lamb's Adventures in the Banda Oriental in South America as Told by Himself. AMS Pr. repr. of 1922 ed. $35.00

Far Away and Long Ago. AMS Pr. repr. of 1923 ed. $35.00; Folcroft repr. of 1923 ed. 1973 lib. bdg. $20.00

Fan: The Story of a Young Girl's Life. 1892. AMS Pr. repr. of 1923 ed. $35.00

El Ombú and Other South American Stories. 1902. AMS Pr. repr. of 1923 ed. $35.00

Green Mansions: A Romance of the Tropical Forest. 1904. AMS Pr. repr. of 1923 ed. $35.00

A Crystal Age. 1906. AMS Pr. repr. of 1922 ed. $35.00; Folcroft repr. 1973 lib. bdg. $20.00

A Little Boy Lost: Together with the Poems. 1905. AMS Pr. repr. of 1923 ed. $35.00

WORKS ON NATURAL HISTORY

Idle Days in Patagonia. 1893. AMS Pr. repr. of 1923 ed. $35.00

Hampshire Days. 1903. AMS Pr. repr. of 1923 ed. $35.00; Folcroft repr. 1973 lib. bdg. $25.00

The Land's End: A Naturalist's Impression in West Cornwall. 1908. AMS Pr. repr. of 1923 ed. $35.00

A Shepherd's Life: Impressions of the South Wiltshire Downs. 1910. AMS Pr. repr. of 1923 ed. $35.00

Dead Man's Plack; An Old Thorn; and Miscellanea. 1920. AMS Pr. repr. of 1923 ed. $25.00; Folcroft repr. 1973 lib. bdg. $20.00. With an appreciation by Viscount Grey of Fallodon.

A Traveller in Little Things. 1921. AMS Pr. repr. of 1923 ed. $35.00; Folcroft repr. 1973 lib. bdg. $20.00. With a note by Edward Garnett.

A Hind in Richmond Park. 1922. AMS Pr. repr. of 1923 ed. $35.00. With a prefatory note by Morley Roberts.

BOOKS ABOUT HUDSON

Payne, John R. *W. H. Hudson: A Bibliography.* Univ. Pr. of Virginia 1977 $22.50

Roberts, Morley. *W. H. Hudson: A Portrait.* Richard West repr. of 1924 ed. $40.00

Tomalin, Ruth. *W. H. Hudson: A Biography.* Faber 1982 $29.95; Greenwood repr. of 1954 ed. lib. bdg. $15.00

Wilson, G. F. *A Bibliography of the Writings of W. H. Hudson. Eng. Lit. Ser.* Haskell repr. of 1922 ed. 1972 lib. bdg. $45.95

KINGSLEY, CHARLES. 1819–1875

Charles Kingsley, a clergyman of the Church of England, who late in his life held the chair of history at Cambridge University, wrote mostly didactic historical romances. He put the historical novel to new use, not to teach history but to illustrate some religious truth. *Westward Ho!*, his best known, is a tale of the Spanish main in the days of Queen Elizabeth I. *Hypatia, or New Foes with Old Faces* is the story of a pagan girl-philosopher who was torn to pieces by a Christian mob. The story is strongly anti-Roman Catholic, reflecting Kingsley's controversy with Cardinal Newman at the time of the Oxford movement. *Hereward the Wake, or The Watchful* is a tale of a Saxon outlaw. *The Water-Babies*, written for Kingsley's youngest child, "would be a tale for children were it not for the satire directed at the parents of the period," said Andrew Lang. *Alton Locke* and *Yeast* reflect Kingsley's leadership in "muscular Christianity" and his dramatization of social issues.

Kingsley used the pseudonym "Parson Lot" on papers he wrote for magazines. Of his poems, the most characteristic is the ballad-song "Sands of Dee."

BOOKS BY KINGSLEY

Life and Works of Charles Kingsley. Adler's 28 vols. repr. of 1880 ed. 1969 set $1,200.00

Charles Kingsley: His Letters and Memories of His Life. Ed. by his wife, AMS Pr. 2 vols. repr. of 1877 ed. $37.50; Richard West repr. of 1877 ed. $25.00

Alton Locke: Tailor and Poet. 1850. Folcroft repr. of 1900 ed. lib. bdg. $20.00; Scholarly repr. of 1928 ed. 1971 $35.00; ed. by Elizabeth A. Cripps, *World's Class.-Pap. Ser.* Oxford 1983 pap. $6.95

Yeast: A Problem. 1851. Biblio Dist. 1976 $8.95; Folcroft repr. of 1897 ed. lib. bdg. $25.00

Hypatia, or New Foes with Old Faces. 1853. Biblio Dist. repr. of 1906 ed. 1968 $8.95; Folcroft repr. of 1902 ed. lib. bdg. $20.00; ed. by Robert L. Wolff, *Victorian Fiction Ser.* Garland 1975 lib. bdg. $60.00

Westward Ho! 1855. Buccaneer Bks. repr. 1982 lib. bdg. $18.95

The Heroes of Greek Fairy Tales for My Children. 1856. Folcroft repr. lib. bdg. $15.00; Smith Publications (Mayflower Bks.) 1980 $8.95

Two Years Ago. 1857. Arden Lib. repr. of 1887 ed. 1983 lib. bdg. $30.00

The Water-Babies. 1863. *Facsimile Class. Ser.* Smith Publications (Mayflower Bks.) 1979 $7.95

Hereward the Wake, or The Watchful. 1866. AMS repr. of 1935 ed. $36.00

At Last: A Christmas in the West Indies. 1871. Folcroft repr. of 1900 ed. lib. bdg. $45.00

The Hermits. 1878. Folcroft repr. lib. bdg. $20.00

BOOKS ABOUT KINGSLEY

Colloms, Brenda. *Charles Kingsley: The Lion of Eversley.* Barnes & Noble 1975 o.p.

Stubbs, Charles W. *Charles Kingsley and the Christian Social Movement.* AMS Pr. repr. of 1899 ed. $17.50

Uffelman, Larry K. *Charles Kingsley.* Twayne's Eng. Authors Ser. G. K. Hall 1949 $14.50

KIPLING, RUDYARD. 1865–1936 (NOBEL PRIZE 1907)

Kipling, who as a novelist dramatized the ambivalence of the British colonial experience, was born of English parents in Bombay and as a child knew Hindustani better than English. He spent an unhappy period of exile from his parents (and the Indian heat) with a harsh aunt in England, followed by the public schooling that inspired his "Stalky" stories. He returned to India at 18 to work on the staff of the Lahore *Civil and Military Gazette* and rapidly became a prolific writer.

Short stories form the greater portion of Kipling's work and are of several distinct types. Some of his best are such stories of the supernatural, the eerie and unearthly, as "The Phantom Rickshaw," "The Brushwood Boy," and "They." His tales of gruesome horror include "The Mark of the Beast" and "The Return of Imray." "William the Conqueror" and "The Head of the District" are among his political tales of English rule in India. The "Soldiers Three" group deals with Kipling's three musketeers—an Irishman, a Cockney, and a Yorkshireman. The Anglo-Indian Tales, of social life in Simla, make up the larger part of his first four books.

Kipling wrote equally well for children (*Just So Stories, The Jungle Book, Mowgli,* and *Kim*) and adults. Some critics, like GEORGE ORWELL and LIONEL TRILLING, have dismissed him from serious consideration; others, such as T. S. ELIOT and Bonamy Dobrée, have affirmed his genius. EDMUND WILSON, in *The Wound and the Bow,* sees his great failing as an artist in the fact that, although he sometimes appeared to be torn between two cultures, he avoided significant dramatic conflict (which would have brought his work stature) by ending up, predictably, on the side of authority. His short stories—although their understanding of the Indian is often moving—became minor hymns to the glory of Queen Victoria's empire and the civil servants and soldiers who staffed her outposts. *Kim,* an Irish boy in India who becomes the companion of a Tibetan lama, at length joins the British Secret Service, without, says Wilson, any sense of the betrayal of his friend this actually meant. Nevertheless, Kipling has left us a vivid panorama of the India of his day.

The chronology of Kipling's books is important in that his earlier works are his best. *Something of Myself,* his autobiography, is out of print, as is a volume of letters, *From Sea to Sea* (1907).

BOOKS BY KIPLING

The Collected Works. AMS Pr. 28 vols. repr. of 1941 ed. set $1,120.00

Letters of Travel, 1892–1913. 1920. Amereon repr. lib. bdg. $15.70

O Beloved Kids: Rudyard Kipling's Letters to His Children. Harcourt 1984 $16.95

Maugham's Choice of Kipling's Best. Ed. by W. Somerset Maugham, Amereon repr. lib. bdg. $17.50

Kipling: Short Stories. Ed. by Andrew Rutherford, Penguin 2 vols. 1977 pap. ea. $3.95

Kipling: A Selection of His Stories and Poems. Ed. by John Beecroft, Doubleday 1956 $19.95

Book of Words. Essay Index Repr. Ser. Ayer repr. of 1928 ed. $17.00. Contains 31 speeches.

The Light That Failed. 1890. Airmont 1969 pap. $1.50; Amereon repr. lib. bdg. $13.25

The Courting of Dinah Shadd and Other Stories. Short Story Index Repr. Ser. Ayer repr. of 1890 ed. $12.50

American Notes. Foreign Travelers in Amer. Ayer repr. of 1891 ed. 1974 $13.00; *Select*

Bibliographies Repr. Ser. Ayer repr. of 1891 ed. 1972 $18.00; ed. by Arrell M. Gibson, *Western Frontier Ser.* Univ. of Oklahoma Pr. 1981 $13.95
The Jungle Book. 1894–95. Schocken 1984 $9.95
The Second Jungle Book. 1895. Doubleday 1923 o.p.
Mulvaney Stories. Short Story Index Repr. Ser. Ayer repr. of 1897 ed. $15.00
The Seven Seas. Longwood Pr. repr. of 1897 ed. 1978 lib. bdg. $20.00 1984 pap. $6.95
Captains Courageous. 1897. *Bantam Class. Ser.* 1982 pap. $1.50
The Day's Work. Short Story Index Repr. Ser. Ayer repr. of 1898 ed. $23.00
Soldier Stories. Short Story Index Repr. Ser. Ayer repr. of 1899 ed. $16.00
Kim. 1901. *Bantam Class. Ser.* 1984 pap. $2.25
Just So Stories. Durst repr. of 1902 ed. 1978 lib. bdg. $9.95; New Amer. Lib. (Signet Class.) 1974 pap. $1.75
Puck of Pook's Hill. 1906. Peter Smith repr. o.p.

BOOKS ABOUT KIPLING

Cornell, Luis L. *Kipling in India.* Telegraph Bks. repr. of 1966 ed. 1982 lib. bdg. $35.00
Dobrée, Bonamy. *Rudyard Kipling: Realist and Fabulist.* Oxford 1967 o.p. A study of Kipling's work by an eminent critic, who rallies to his defense as a writer "grotesquely misunderstood" and "misrepresented." The first part of the book deals with Kipling's philosophy, milieu, and prose writing; the second part with his poetry.
Green, Roger L., ed. *Kipling: The Critical Heritage. Critical Heritage Ser.* Routledge & Kegan 1971 $33.75. Contemporary and near-contemporary criticism, reviews, and comments.
Livingston, Flora. *Bibliography of the Works of Rudyard Kipling. Lib. of Lit., Drama, and Criticism* Johnson Repr. repr. of 1927 ed. 1970 $45.00; Burt Franklin repr. of 1927 ed. $43.00
McClure, John. *Kipling and Conrad: The Colonial Fiction.* Harvard Univ. Pr. text ed. 1981 $16.50
Moss, Robert F. *Rudyard Kipling and the Fiction of Adolescence.* St. Martin's 1982 $22.50.
Rao, K. Bhaskara. *Rudyard Kipling's India.* Univ. of Oklahoma Pr. 1967 $6.95. A critical view of Kipling's political and racial attitudes (as expressed in his work), which Rao, an Indian living in the United States, regards as having strengthened the reactionary forces of British imperialism.
Rutherford, Andrew, ed. *Kipling's Mind and Art: Selected Critical Essays.* Stanford Univ. Pr. 1964 $22.50 pap. $3.95. A collection of 11 essays by English and American scholars who agree "that Kipling has been too easily dismissed . . . . These essays do examine Kipling's weakness, but they also note his achievements" (*LJ*).
Tompkins, J. M. *The Art of Rudyard Kipling.* Univ. of Nebraska Pr. (Bison) 1965 pap. $5.95
Wilson, Angus. *The Strange Ride of Rudyard Kipling: His Life and Works.* Penguin 1979 pap. $5.95; Viking 1978 $17.50
Younge, W. Arthur, and John H. McGivering. *A Kipling Dictionary.* Gordon $75.00. "[Younge's outdated *Dictionary*] recorded some six hundred and thirty titles; Kipling's post-1911 literary output has enabled the present compiler [McGivering] to bring the number up to just under a thousand" (*LJ*).

MARRYAT, CAPTAIN FREDERICK. 1792–1848

A master of the sea tale, Marryat wrote novels that deal with life in the English Navy, in which he himself served. His stories were written for children but read by old and young alike. *Masterman Ready* at one time stood next to *Robinson Crusoe* in popularity with boy readers. *Peter Simple* (1834, o.p.) is the most autobiographical of the novels, *Mr. Midshipman Easy*, the most humorous. *Percival Keene* (1842, o.p.), the least estimable of his heroes, is a melodramatic story. *The Little Savage* (1848, o.p.) is a horror tale of remarkable power, strong in plot and character development. Marryat's novels are all didactic, but his moral lessons never intrude or offend. The details of his adventurous life, so far as they are known, are well described in Oliver Warner's *Captain Marryat: A Rediscovery. A Diary in America* (o.p.) appeared first in 1839. The recognition now given to Marryat as a source for social history is fully deserved, since his opinionated account of his journey gives us "an invaluable view of American life at the time when Jacksonian democracy was in full development in the new nation" (*LJ*).

BOOKS BY MARRYAT

The Novels of Captain Marryat. Ed. by Johnson R. Brimley, Arden Lib. 24 vols. repr. of 1895 ed. 1978 lib. bdg. $600.00
Mr. Midshipman Easy. 1836. Biblio Dist. 1970 pap. $1.95
The Phantom Ship. AMS Pr. repr. of 1839 ed. $44.50
Masterman Ready. 1841. Biblio Dist. repr. of 1907 ed. 1970 $8.95
Narratives of the Travels and Adventures of Monsieur Violet. 1843. Gregg 1970 o.p.
The Children of the New Forest. 1847. Puffin Class. Ser. Penguin 1984 pap. $2.25
The Mission, or Scenes in Africa. 1845. Intro by Tony Harrison, *Colonial Novel Ser.* Holmes & Meier repr. of 1845 ed. 1970 $25.00

BOOK ABOUT MARRYAT

Warner, Oliver. *Captain Marryat: A Rediscovery.* Hyperion repr. of 1953 ed. $21.50

MEREDITH, GEORGE. 1828–1909

An intellectual novelist, George Meredith was leisurely, epigrammatic, and involved at a time when the public admired the swift narrative flow of Dickens and Thackeray. His novels were designed to penetrate the hidden motivations of character. He boasted that he never wrote a word to please the public, and counted as the greatest compliment ever paid to him the statement that he had brought about a change in public taste. Meredith's reputation grew slowly. His first important novel, *The Ordeal of Richard Feverel*, a fine study of the emotional growth of a young man, is his most epigrammatic work and had little popular success. *The Egoist*, a comedy in narrative, regarded by most critics as his masterpiece, was the first to receive popular attention. *Diana of the Crossways*, his most nearly popular book, gave to fiction a new and particularly well drawn heroine, the woman of fine brain and strong body.

His *The Essay on Comedy, and the Uses of the Comic Spirit* (1897) has been described as the key to his novels. But Meredith, like Hardy, thought more of his poems than of his novels and preferred to be remembered as a poet. In notes for *The Selected Poetical Works of George Meredith* (1955, o.p.), G. M. Trevelyan says: "His poems are more especially concerned with his philosophy, and the novels with his application of it to ethical problems." Meredith's philosophy was one of optimism, but it was "the optimism of temperament and not of creed."

BOOKS BY MEREDITH

Works. Ed. by William M. Meredith, Russell 29 vols. repr. of 1909–12 ed. $325.00
Letters. Ed. by C. L. Cline, Oxford 3 vols. 1970 $98.00; ed. by his son, Richard West 2 vols. repr. $30.00.
Letters of George Meredith to Alice Meynell: With Annotations There to 1896–1907. Ed. by E. Meynell, Folcroft repr. of 1923 ed. lib. bdg. $15.00
The Poems of George Meredith. Ed. by Phyllis B. Bartlett, Yale Univ. Pr. 1978 $135.00
The Ordeal of Richard Feverel: A Story of a Father and Son. 1859. Dover 1983 pap. $7.95
Evan Harrington. 1860. Boydell & Brewer 1983 pap. $9.95
The Adventures of Harry Richmond. 1871. Ed. by L. T. Hergenhan, Univ. of Nebraska Pr. 1970 $28.50
The Egoist. 1879. Ed. by Robert M. Adams, *Norton Critical Eds.* text ed. 1979 $19.95 pap. $5.95; *World's Class. Ser.* Oxford $12.95; ed. by George Woodstock, *Penguin Eng. Lib. Ser.* 1979 pap. $4.95
The Tragic Comedians: A Study in a Well-Known Story. 1880. Ayer rev. ed. repr. of 1922 ed. 1975 $14.00
Diana of the Crossways. 1885. Scholarly repr. of 1931 ed. 1971 $49.00
The Essay on Comedy, and the Uses of the Comic Spirit. Norwood repr. of 1897 ed. 1980 lib. bdg. $32.50; Richard West repr. of 1918 ed. $30.00
Short Stories. 1898. Arden Lib. repr. of 1914 ed. 1982 lib. bdg. $25.00; *Short Story Index Repr. Ser.* Ayer repr. of 1898 ed. $18.00

BOOKS ABOUT MEREDITH

Beach, Joseph Warren. *The Comic Spirit in George Meredith: An Interpretation.* Russell repr. of 1911 ed. 1963 $7.00
Collie, Michael. *George Meredith: A Bibliography.* Univ. of Toronto Pr. 1976 $20.00
Kelvin, Norman. *A Troubled Eden: Nature and Society in the Works of George Meredith.* Stanford Univ. Pr. 1961 $20.00
Olmstead, John Charles. *George Meredith: An Annotated Bibliography, 1925–1975.* Garland 1978 $25.00
Stevenson, Lionel. *The Ordeal of George Meredith.* Russell repr. of 1953 ed. 1967 o.p.
Williams, Ioan, ed. *Meredith: The Critical Heritage. Critical Heritage Ser.* Routledge & Kegan 1971 $28.75. Contemporary criticisms of both novels and poetry, arranged chronologically.
Wilt, Judith. *The Readable People of George Meredith.* Princeton Univ. Pr. 1975 $24.00
Wright, Walter F. *Art and Substance in George Meredith: A Study in Narrative.* Greenwood repr. of 1953 ed. 1980 lib. bdg. $24.75

MOORE, GEORGE. 1852–1933

George Moore, "the master of the most subtle rhythm in modern prose" (Austin Clarke, *N.Y. Times*), was an exponent of the experimental novel of EMILE ZOLA (see Vol. 2), the naturalistic novel written with a polished and

careful artistry. Many regard *Sister Teresa* (1901) as his masterpiece, although *Esther Waters*, his objective story of a servant girl's seduction and
struggle, is more widely read.

As an autobiographer Moore was prolific. His *Confessions of a Young
Man, Memoirs of My Dead Life* (1906, o.p.), and the trilogy *Hail and Farewell!*
are books about himself and his friends. In the latter, says Austin Clarke,
"He had mocked at his fellow writers, invented ludicrous conversations for
them and succeeded in turning literary Dublin into delightful, irresistible
legend. He . . . made many enemies by his candor." *Conversations in Ebury
Street* (1924, o.p.) is a volume of actual talks between Moore and his friends
in his London home.

BOOKS BY MOORE

Letters of George Moore. Folcroft 1977 lib. bdg. $17.50
Letters to Lady Cunard, 1895–1933. Greenwood repr. of 1957 ed. 1979 lib. bdg. $22.50
George Moore in Transition: Letters to T. Fisher Unwin and Lena Milman, 1894–1910.
    Ed. by Helmut E. Gerber, Wayne State Univ. Pr. 1968 $13.95. "This book con-
    tains about 300 items from the correspondence of the Irish novelist to his 'pub-
    lisher' and to Lena Milman, who first introduced him to Russian literature"
    (*Choice*).
A Drama in Muslin. 1886. Humanities Pr. text ed. 1981 $23.75 pap. $7.00
Esther Waters. 1894. Biblio Dist. repr. of 1936 ed. 1977 $9.95 1983 pap. $5.95; *Black
    and Gold Ser.* Liveright 1942 $7.95; ed. by David Skilton, *World's Class.-Pap. Ser.*
    Oxford 1983 pap. $7.95
Evelyn Innes (and *Sister Teresa*). Ed. by Robert L. Wolff, *Victorian Fiction Ser.* Gar-
    land repr. of 1898 ed. 1975 lib. bdg. $66.00
The Untilled Field. Short Story Index Repr. Ser. Ayer repr. of 1903 ed. $15.00. A group
    of excellent short stories.
The Lake. 1905. Humanities Pr. text ed. 1981 $24.75 pap. $8.50
The Brook Kerith. 1916. Liveright new ed. 1969 o.p.
A Story-Teller's Holiday. 1918. *Black and Gold Ser.* Liveright 1929 $7.95
In Single Strictness. Short Story Index Repr. Ser. Ayer repr. of 1922 ed. $20.00
Confessions of a Young Man. 1886. *Lit. Ser.* Scholarly repr. of 1925 ed. 1972 $29.00
Hail and Farewell. 1911–14. Ed. by Richard Allen Cave, Humanities Pr. text ed. 1980
    $45.00
A Communication to My Friends. Folcroft repr. of 1933 ed. 1974 lib. bdg. $10.00; *Eng.
    Lit. Ser.* Haskell 1974 lib. bdg. $49.95. This essay was used as the preface to the
    uniform and later editions of *A Mummer's Wife.*

BOOKS ABOUT MOORE

Cave, Richard Allen. *A Study of the Novels of George Moore. Irish Literary Studies*
    Barnes & Noble text ed. 1978 $24.75
Freeman, John. *Portrait of George Moore in a Study of His Work.* Folcroft 1973 lib.
    bdg. $25.00; Scholarly repr. of 1922 ed. $35.00
Gilcher, Edwin. *Bibliography of George Moore.* Northern Illinois Univ. Pr. 1970
    $20.00
Mitchell, Susan L. *George Moore. Irish Culture and History Ser.* Associated Faculty Pr.
    repr. of 1916 ed. 1970 $18.50
Sechler, Robert P. *George Moore: A Disciple of Walter Pater.* Folcroft repr. of 1931 ed.
    lib. bdg. $12.50

Wolfe, Humbert. *George Moore. Select Bibliographies Repr. Ser.* Ayer repr. of 1931 ed. $19.00; Porter 1982 lib. bdg. $34.50

PEACOCK, THOMAS LOVE. 1785–1866

A poet, novelist, and critic, Thomas Love Peacock was a close friend of Shelley and other romantics. Essentially a classicist in temperament, he was self-taught and well read in Latin and Greek. Peacock satirized radicalism, medievalism, and transcendentalism, as well as individual romanticists like Wordsworth, Coleridge, Byron, and Shelley. *Crotchet Castle* (1831), appealing for its wit, humor, and clever irony, has remained the most popular of his novels. His two early novels, *Headlong Hall* and *Nightmare Abbey*, are both short and both satirical in " 'romantic' settings."

BOOKS BY PEACOCK

Works. Ed. by H. F. Brett-Smith and C. E. Jones, AMS Pr. 10 vols. repr. of 1924–34 ed. ea. $28.00 set $280.00
Peacock's Memoirs of Shelley. Folcroft repr. 1977 lib. bdg. $30.00
Songs from the Novels of Thomas Love Peacock. Folcroft repr. 1972 lib. bdg. $17.50
Headlong Hall (and *Nightmare Abbey*). 1816. Biblio Dist. 1965 $9.95 pap. $3.50
Nightmare Abbey (and *Crotchet Castle* and *The Misfortunes of Elphin*). 1818. Penguin 1982 pap. $3.95

BOOKS ABOUT PEACOCK

Able, Augustus H. *George Meredith and Thomas Love Peacock: A Study in Literary Influence.* Arden Lib. repr. of 1933 ed. 1978 lib. bdg. $15.00; Folcroft repr. of 1933 ed. lib. bdg. $15.00; Phaeton repr. of 1933 ed. 1970 $10.00; Porter 1977 $16.00
Butler, Marilyn. *Peacock Displayed: A Satirist in His Context.* Routledge & Kegan 1979 o.p.
Campbell, Olwen W. *Thomas Love Peacock. Select Bibliographies Repr. Ser.* Ayer repr. of 1953 ed. 1972 $14.00
Mills, Howard W. *Peacock: His Circle and His Age.* Cambridge Univ. Pr. 1969 $52.50
Van Doren, Carl. *The Life of Thomas Love Peacock.* Russell repr. of 1911 ed. 1966 $8.50

RADCLIFFE, ANN (WARD). 1764–1823

Ann Radcliffe originated the romantic mystery novel known as "Gothic." It is characterized by vivid descriptions and by seemingly supernatural elements that are later explained by natural causes. Her novels—the best-known is *The Mysteries of Udolpho*—influenced Scott in his development of narrative method, and Lord Byron in his conception of the Byronic hero. *Udolpho* was one of the literary inspirations of Keats's "Eve of St. Agnes."

BOOKS BY RADCLIFFE

Poetical Works. AMS Pr. 2 vols. repr. of 1834 ed. ea. $42.50 set $85.00
A Sicilian Romance. Gothic Novels Ser. Ayer repr. of 1821 ed. 1971 $42.00; Johnson Repr. 2 vols. repr. of 1790 ed. 1971 $47.00
The Romance of the Forest: Interspersed with Some Pieces of Poetry. Ayer 3 vols. repr. of 1791 ed. 1974 $86.00. First published anonymously.

The Mysteries of Udolpho. 1794. Ed. by Bonamy Dobrée, *World's Class. Ser.* Oxford rev. ed. 1980 pap. $5.95
The Castles of Athlin and Dunbayne: A Highland Story. 1796. *Gothic Novels Ser.* Ayer repr. of 1821 ed. 1972 $46.50; Johnson Repr. repr. of 1796 ed. $30.00
The Italian, or The Confessional of the Black Penitents: A Romance. 1797. Ed. by Frederick Garber, *World's Class. Ser.* Oxford 1981 pap. $6.95; intro. by D. P. Varma, Russell 4 vols. in 2 repr. of 1828 ed. 1968 $25.00
Gaston de Blondeville, or The Court of Henry III Keeping Festival in Ardenne. Gothic Novels Ser. Ayer repr. of 1826 ed. 1972 $48.50. A metrical tale with some poetical pieces, published posthumously, with a memoir of the author.

BOOKS ABOUT RADCLIFFE

McIntyre, C. F. *Ann Radcliffe in Relation to Her Time. Yale Studies in Eng. Ser.* Shoe String (Archon) repr. of 1920 ed. 1970 $12.50
Murray, Gene. *Ann Radcliffe. Twayne's Eng. Authors Ser.* o.p.

READE, CHARLES. 1814–1884

An energetic playwright and dramatizer of the novel for the stage, Reade wrote the didactic novel, the novel with a lesson. But he also wrote, probably influenced by Dickens, such interesting psychological romances as *Hard Cash* (1863, o.p.), in which sexual tension and sensationalism dominate. His one historical romance, his masterpiece *The Cloister and the Hearth*, is a picture of life in Germany and Italy at the close of the Middle Ages, the hero being the father of Erasmus. Such novels were compiled rather than written. Reade did endless historical research and investigation for the facts they contain.

BOOKS BY READE

Works. AMS Pr. 17 vols. repr. of 1896 ed. ea. $37.50 set $637.00
It Is Never Too Late to Mend: A Matter-of-Fact Romance. 1857. AMS Pr. 3 vols. in 2 repr. of 1857 ed. $104.00
The Cloister and the Hearth. 1861. Intro. by Algernon Charles Swinburne, Biblio Dist. 1955 o.p.

BOOKS ABOUT READE

Elwin, Malcolm. *Charles Reade: A Biography.* Russell repr. of 1931 ed. 1969 $10.50
Reade, Charles L. *Charles Reade: Dramatist, Novelist, Journalist.* Folcroft 2 vols. repr. of 1887 ed. 1977 lib. bdg. $85.00
Smith, Elton E. *Charles Reade. Twayne's Eng. Authors Ser.* o.p.

SCOTT, SIR WALTER. 1771–1832

Scott began his literary career by writing metrical tales. "The Lay of the Last Minstrel," "Marmion," and "The Lady of the Lake" made him the most popular poet of his day. Sixty-five hundred copies of "The Lay of the Last Minstrel" were sold in the first three years, a record such as poetry had never made before. His later romances in verse, "The Vision of Don Roderick," "Rokeby" (both o.p.), and "The Lord of the Isles," met with waning interest owing to the rivalry of LORD BYRON, whose more passionate poetic romances superseded Scott's in the public favor. Scott then abandoned poetry for prose. In 1814, he anonymously published a historical novel, *Waverley, or Sixty Years Since*, the first of the series known as the Waverley novels. He wrote 23 novels anonymously during the next 13 years. The first master of historical fiction, Scott wrote novels that are historical in background rather than in character: A fictitious person always holds the foreground. In their historical sequence, the Waverley novels range in setting from the year 1090, the time of the First Crusade, to 1700, the period covered in *St. Ronan's Well* (1824, o.p.), set in a Scottish watering place. Starting with the eleventh century, Scott wrote novels covering every period of European history except the thirteenth century.

BOOKS BY SCOTT

The Journal of Sir Walter Scott. 1890. Greenwood repr. of 1950 ed. 1978 lib. bdg. $52.25. From the original manuscript at Abbotsford.
Letters. Ed. by Herbert J. Grierson and others, AMS Pr. 12 vols. repr. of 1932–37 ed. ea. $30.00 set $360.00. "Established wherever possible after original manuscripts and including many letters hitherto entirely unpublished, or printed in an abridged or garbled form. The centenary edition" (Publisher's catalog).
Letters of Sir Walter Scott. Ed. by Herbert J. Grierson, AMS Pr. 12 vols. repr. of 1937 ed. ea. $30.00 set $360.00
Letters on Demonology and Witchcraft. Gordon $75.00; Richard West repr. of 1887 ed. $25.00

THE WAVERLEY NOVELS

Waverley, or Sixty Years Since. 1814. *Penguin Eng. Lib. Ser.* 1981 pap. $4.95; ed. by Claire Lamont, Oxford 1981 $59.00
Guy Mannering. 1815. Biblio Dist. 1954 o.p.
The Antiquary. 1816. Biblio Dist. 1969 $11.95 pap. $2.95
Old Mortality. 1817. Ed. by Angus Calder, Penguin 1975 pap. $4.95
The Heart of Midlothian. 1818. Biblio Dist. 1977 $9.95 pap. $4.50; ed. by John H. Raleigh, Houghton Mifflin, rev. ed. pap. $6.50; ed. by Claire Lamont, *World's Class. Ser.* Oxford 1982 pap. $10.95
Rob Roy. 1818. Biblio Dist. 1976 $9.95 pap. $4.50
The Bride of Lammermoor. 1819. Biblio Dist. 1973 $9.95 pap. $3.95
The Abbot. Biblio Dist. repr. of 1906 ed. 1969 $12.95
Ivanhoe. 1820. Biblio Dist. 1977 $12.95 pap. $3.95; Greenwood repr. of 1950 ed. 1978 $52.25; ed. by A. N. Wilson, *Penguin Eng. Lib. Ser.* 1984 pap. $4.95
Kenilworth. 1821. *Airmont Class. Ser.* 1968 pap. $2.95; Biblio Dist. 1955 $10.95
The Fortunes of Nigel. 1822. Ed. by Frederick M. Link, Univ. of Nebraska Pr. (Bison) 1965 pap. $5.95
Quentin Durward. 1823. Airmont pap. $2.50
Redgauntlet. 1824. Biblio Dist. repr. of 1906 ed. 1970 $10.95 1982 pap. $4.95
The Talisman. 1825. Biblio Dist. 1980 pap. $4.50; Penguin 1981 pap. $3.50
Woodstock. 1826. Biblio Dist. repr. of 1906 ed. 1969 $9.95
The Monastery. 1826. Biblio dist. repr. of 1906 ed. 1969 $9.95
The Fair Maid of Perth. 1828. Dutton (Everyman's) o.p.

OTHER PROSE

(ed.). *The Bannatyne Miscellany.* 1827–1855. AMS Pr. 3 vols. repr. of 1927 ed. $7,000.00. Scott edited Volume 1; David Laing edited Volumes 2 and 3. The

Bannatyne Club, of which Scott was the first president, was founded in 1823 for the purpose of publishing old Scottish documents chiefly concerned with the history and literature of that country. It was disbanded in 1861.

Life of Dryden. 1808. Ed. by Bernard Kreissman, Univ. of Nebraska Pr. (Bison) 1963 pap. $5.95

The Prefaces to the Waverley Novels. Ed. by Mark A. Weinstein, Univ. of Nebraska Pr. 1978 $19.95

POETRY

Complete Poetical Works. Cambridge Eds. Ser. Houghton Mifflin $8.95

Selected Poems. Ed. by Thomas Crawford, Oxford 1972 pap. $8.95

(ed.). *Minstrelsy of the Scottish Border.* 1802. Ed. by T. F. Henderson, Gale 4 vols. repr. of 1902 ed. 1968 $150.00

The Lady of the Lake and Other Poems. 1810. *Airmont Class. Ser.* pap. $1.95

The Lord of the Isles. 1815. Scholarly repr. of 1914 ed. 1971 $19.50

BOOKS ABOUT SCOTT

Ball, Margaret. *Sir Walter Scott as a Critic of Literature.* Associated Faculty Pr. repr. of 1907 ed. $22.00. A standard work now back in print.

Corson, J. C. *Bibliography of Sir Walter Scott. Bibliography and Reference Ser.* Burt Franklin repr. of 1943 ed. $30.50

Gell, William. *Reminiscences of Sir Walter Scott's Residence in Italy, 1832.* Richard West repr. of 1937 ed. 1973 $17.50

Grierson, Herbert. *Sir Walter Scott, Bart.* Folcroft repr. of 1938 ed. lib. bdg. $15.00. Of the older biographies, this and Dame Una Pope-Hennessy's *Sir Walter Scott* (o.p.) are standard. For the definitive modern biography, see Edgar Johnson's *Sir Walter Scott: The Great Unknown.*

Hillhouse, J. T. *The Waverley Novels and Their Critics.* Octagon 1968 lib. bdg. $24.00. Useful study.

Johnson, Edgar. *Sir Walter Scott: The Great Unknown.* Macmillan 2 vols. 1970 o.p. An exhaustive and definitive modern biography, awarded the American Heritage Biography Prize.

Lauber, John. *Sir Walter Scott. Twayne's Eng. Authors Ser.* 1966 o.p.

Lockhart, John Gibson. *The Life of Sir Walter Scott.* Biblio Dist. repr. of 1906 ed. 1969 $8.95. An abridgment of the *Memoirs* below.

———. *Memoirs of Sir Walter Scott.* AMS Pr. 10 vols. repr. of 1902 ed. set $345.00. The standard authorized biography by Scott's son-in-law, regarded as one of the great literary biographies.

Mayhead, Robin. *Walter Scott. British Authors Ser.* Cambridge Univ. Pr. 1973 $27.95 pap. $8.95

Rogers, May. *The Waverley Dictionary: An Alphabetical Arrangement of All the Characters in Sir Walter Scott's Waverley Novels with a Descriptive Analysis of Each Character, and Illustrative Selections from the Text.* Gale 2d ed. repr. of 1885 ed. 1967 $45.00

Welsh, Alexander. *The Hero of the Waverley Novels.* Atheneum 1968 o.p.

Wilson, A. N. *The Laird of Abbotsford: A View of Sir Walter Scott.* Oxford text ed. 1981 $24.95

SHELLEY, MARY WOLLSTONECRAFT (née Godwin). 1797–1851

Mary Shelley, the daughter of William Godwin, the English philosopher and writer, and Mary Wollstonecraft, author of the *Vindication of the Rights of Women* (1792), fell in love with the poet SHELLEY, went to the Continent with him in 1814, and married him after the death of his first wife in 1816. She is best known for her novel of horror, *Frankenstein*, which she wrote when Lord Byron proposed that he and each of his companions write a tale of the supernatural. It was an immediate sensation. After Shelley's death, she edited his writings and wrote biographies, articles, and fiction to educate her surviving son. Because of her association with BYRON, Trelawny, and Leigh Hunt, her *Letters* and *Journal* are excellent sources of literary material on the period. *My Best Mary* (o.p.) reveals in detail Shelley's life and loves as well as his wife's feelings and flirtations. Her seminal use of a combination of a creation myth and science in *Frankenstein* and her prominence as a struggling literary female have made her of special interest to modern readers.

BOOKS BY SHELLEY

Mary Shelley: Collected Tales and Stories, with Original Engravings. Ed. by Charles E. Robinson, Johns Hopkins Univ. Pr. 1976 o.p.
The Letters of Mary Wollstonecraft Shelley. Ed. by Betty Bennett, Johns Hopkins Univ. Pr. 2 vols. Vol. 1 *A Part of the Elect* (1980) $32.50 Vol. 2 *Treading in Unknown Paths* (1983) $30.00
The Letters of Mary Wollstonecraft Shelley. Ed. by Howard Harper, Folcroft repr. of 1918 ed. 1974 lib. bdg. $35.00
Frankenstein, or The Modern Prometheus. 1818. Macmillan (Collier Bks.) 1961 pap. $3.95; ed. by James Kinsley and M. K. Joseph, *World's Class. Ser.* Oxford 1980 pap. $2.95; Univ. of California Pr. 1984 $29.50; ed. by James Rieger, Univ. of Chicago Pr. repr. of 1974 ed. 1982 pap. $7.95
The Last Man. 1826. Ed. by Hugh J. Luke, Jr., Univ. of Nebraska Pr. 1965 pap. $4.95
Falkner: A Novel. AMS Pr. 3 vols. in 1 repr. of 1837 ed. $44.50
The Choice: A Poem on Shelley's Death. Folcroft repr. of 1876 ed. $17.50

BOOKS ABOUT SHELLEY

Dunn, Jane. *Moon in Eclipse: A Life of Mary Shelley.* St. Martin's 1978 $20.00
Lyles, W. H. *Mary Shelley: An Annotated Bibliography. Reference Lib. of the Humanities* Garland 1975 lib. bdg. $41.00

STEVENSON, ROBERT LOUIS. 1850–1894

Stevenson revived DEFOE's novel of romantic adventure, adding to it psychological analysis. *Kidnapped*, with its sequel *David Balfour*, and *The Master of Ballantrae* are stories of adventure and at the same time studies of character. Stevenson died before having finished *St. Ives* (completed by Sir ARTHUR QUILLER-COUCH) and *The Weir of Hermiston* (issued in its incomplete form), considered by many his masterpiece. "He produced not only the best boy's book in English (*Treasure Island*) and several masterpieces of Scottish characterization," but his short stories are vivid, memorable and show a complete mastery of "the macabre, the eerie, the weird" (*British Authors of the Nineteenth Century). Our Samoan Adventure* (o.p.) by his American wife, Fanny, tells the story of their last years together, throwing light on an obscure period and on personal relationships.

BOOKS BY STEVENSON

Works. Ed. by L. Osbourne and F. Van de G. Stevenson, AMS Pr. 26 vols. repr. of 1921–23 ed. ea. $40.00 set $1,040.00

Works. Richard West 10 vols. repr. $300.00

Selected Writings. Ed. by Saxe Commins, *Essay Index Repr. Ser.* Ayer repr. of 1947 ed. $42.50. Three novels, ten short stories, three books of travel, and a selection of verse.

Letters. Ed. by Sidney Colvin, Greenwood 4 vols. repr. of 1911 ed. lib. bdg. $68.25

Vailima Letters: Being Letters Addressed to Sidney Colvin, November 1890–October 1894. Greenwood 2 vols. repr. of 1895 ed. $18.75

Essays. Folcroft repr. of 1892 ed. 1978 lib. bdg. $15.00

From Scotland to Silverado. Ed. by James D. Hart, Harvard Univ. Pr. 1966 $20.00 pap. $7.95

The Cevennes Journal: Notes on a Journey through the French Highlands. State Mutual Bk. 1978 $30.00

PROSE

An Inland Voyage (and *Travels with a Donkey in the Cevennes* and *Silverado Squatters*). 1878. Biblio Dist. repr. of 1925 ed. 1978 $8.95

Treasure Island. 1883. *Bantam Class. Ser.* text ed. 1981 pap. $1.75; Scribner 1981 $17.95

Dr. Jekyll and Mr. Hyde. 1886. *Airmont Class. Ser.* 1964 pap. $1.25; *Bantam Class. Ser.* text ed. 1981 $1.95; ed. by Jenni Calder, *Penguin Eng. Lib. Ser.* 1981 pap. $2.95

The Black Arrow: A Tale of the Two Roses. Arden Lib. repr. of 1889 ed. lib. bdg. $20.00

Kidnapped: Being Memoirs of the Adventures of David Balfour in the Year 1751. 1889. Airmont 1974 pap. $1.50; *Bantam Class. Ser.* 1982 pap. $1.50; Biblio Dist. 1977 pap. $1.95; Scribner 1982 $18.95

The Master of Ballantrae: A Winner's Tale. 1889. Ed. by Emma Letly, *World's Class.-Pap. Ser.* Oxford 1983 pap. $5.95

Island Nights' Entertainment: The Beach of Falesa; The Bottle Imp; and The Isle of Voices. Scholarly repr. of 1893 ed. 1970 $18.00; *Pacific Class. Ser.* Univ. of Hawaii Pr. 1975 pap. $4.95

The Wrong Box. 1889. Amereon repr. lib. bdg. $12.35

(and Lloyd Osbourne). *The Wrecker.* 1892. Dover 1982 pap. $6.95

In the South Seas. 1896. *Pacific Class. Ser.* Univ. of Hawaii Pr. 1971 pap. $4.95

St. Ives. 1894. Biblio Dist. 1958 $8.95

The Amateur Emigrant. 1895. Merrimack 1984 pap. $7.95

The Body Snatcher. 1895. Ed. by Raymond Harris, *Jamestown Class. Ser.* 1982 pap. $2.00

POETRY

Poems. Ed. by George S. Hellman, Folcroft repr. of 1916 ed. 1979 $60.00; ed. by Helen Plotz, *Poets Ser.* Harper 1973 $10.53

Complete Poems. Gordon $69.95

New Poems and Variant Readings. Century Bookbindery repr. of 1918 ed. 1981 lib. bdg. $20.00; Richard West repr. of 1918 ed. 1979 lib. bdg. $20.00

A Child's Garden of Verses. 1885. *Airmont Class. Ser.* 1969 pap. $1.25; Oxford $11.95; Scribner $14.95

BOOKS ABOUT STEVENSON

Balfour, Sir Graham. *The Life of Robert Louis Stevenson.* Darby repr. of 1901 ed. 1983 lib. bdg. $30.00; Richard West repr. of 1901 ed. 1973 $40.00; Scholarly repr. of 1901 ed. 1968 2 vols. $49.00. Written by Stevenson's cousin, this biography reveals a great family pride and maintains loyal silences on many passages in Stevenson's career. The authorized *Life.*

Calder, Jenni, ed. *Robert Louis Stevenson: A Critical Celebration.* Barnes & Noble 1980 $20.00

——. *Robert Louis Stevenson: A Life Study.* Oxford 1980 $27.50

Daiches, David. *Stevenson and the Art of Fiction.* Darby repr. of 1951 ed. 1980 lib. bdg. $9.50; Folcroft repr. of 1951 ed. lib. bdg. $8.50

Eigner, E. M. *Robert Louis Stevenson and Romantic Tradition.* Princeton Univ. Pr. 1966 o.p.

Furnas, Joseph Chamberlain. *Voyage to Windward: The Life of Robert Louis Stevenson.* Richard West repr. 1980 lib. bdg. $30.00

Maixner, Paul, ed. *Robert Louis Stevenson: The Critical Heritage.* Critical Heritage Ser. Routledge & Kegan 1981 $48.00

Saposnik, Irving S. *Robert Louis Stevenson.* Twayne's Eng. Authors Ser. G. K. Hall 1974 lib. bdg. $12.50

Swearingen, Roger G. *The Prose Writings of Robert Louis Stevenson: A Guide.* Shoe String (Archon) 1980 $29.50

THACKERAY, WILLIAM MAKEPEACE. 1811–1863

Generally considered the most effective satirist and humorist of the mid-nineteenth century, Thackeray moved from humorous journalism to successful fiction with a facility that was partially the result of a genial fictional persona and a graceful, relaxed style. At his best, he held up a mirror to Victorian manners and morals, gently satirizing, with a tone of sophisticated acceptance, the inevitable failures of the individual and of society. He took up the popular fictional situation of the young person of talent who must make his way in the world and dramatized it with satiric directness in *The Luck of Barry Lyndon,* with the highest fictional skill and appreciation of complexities inherent within the satiric vision in his masterpiece *Vanity Fair,* and with a great subtlety of point of view and background in his one historical novel, *Henry Esmond. Vanity Fair,* a complex interweaving in a vast historical panorama of a large number of characters, derives its title from BUNYAN's *Pilgrim's Progress* and attempts to invert for satirical purposes the traditional Christian image of the City of God. *Vanity Fair,* the corrupt City of Man, remains Thackeray's most appreciated and widely read novel. Constantly attuned to the demands of incidental journalism and his sense of professionalism in his relationship with his public, Thackeray wrote entertaining sketches and children's stories and published his humorous lectures on eighteenth-century life and literature. His own fiction shows the influence of his dedication to such eighteenth-century models as HENRY FIELDING, particularly in his satire, which accepts human nature rather than condemns it and takes quite seriously the applicability of the true English gentleman as a model for moral behavior.

Thackeray requested that no authorized biography of him should ever be written. Members of his family did write about him, but of these accounts only the article by Sir Leslie Stephens, his son-in-law, in the *Dictionary of National Biography* is in print.

BOOKS BY THACKERAY

Centenary Biographical Edition of the Works of Thackeray. Intro. by Anne T. Richie, memoir by Leslie Stephens, AMS Pr. 26 vols. repr. of 1910–11 ed. ea. $47.25 set $1,128.50

The Letters and Private Papers of William Makepeace Thackeray. Ed. by Gordon N. Ray, Octagon 4 vols. repr. of 1945 ed. 1980 lib. bdg. $287.50

Stray Papers: Reviews, Verses, Sketches. Ed. by Lewis Melville (pseud. of Lewis Saul Benjamin), Kraus repr. of 1901 ed. $23.00

The Hitherto Unpublished Contributions of W. M. Thackeray to "Punch." AMS Pr. repr. of 1899 ed. $14.00; *Eng. Lit. Ser.* Haskell 1971 lib. bdg. $55.95. Includes a complete and authoritative bibliography, 1843–48, by M. H. Spielman, with numerous illustrations and explanatory notes.

Contributions to the Morning Chronicle. Ed. by Gordon N. Ray, Univ. of Illinois Pr. 1955 pap. $4.95

The Luck of Barry Lyndon. 1844. Buccaneer Bks. repr. 1982 lib. bdg. $22.95

Vanity Fair. 1847. Biblio Dist. 1979 $13.95 pap. $6.95; ed. by John Sutherland, *World's Class.-Pap. Ser.* Oxford 1983 pap. $5.95

The Book of Snobs. 1848. Ed. by John Sutherland, St. Martin's 1978 $25.00

Pendennis. 1850. Intro. by M. R. Ridley, Dutton (Everyman's) o.p.

The English Humorists (and *The Four Georges*). 1851. Biblio Dist. repr. of 1912 ed. 1968 $8.95

A Shabby Genteel Story. 1852. New York Univ. Pr. 1971 o.p. A sequel, *The Adventures of Philip*, which appeared in *Cornhill Magazine* in 1861, is out of print.

Henry Esmond (The History of Henry Esmond, Esquire). 1852. Biblio Dist. 1976 $9.95; ed. by John Sutherland and Michael Greenfield, *Penguin Eng. Lib. Ser.* 1977 pap. $4.95

The Newcomes. 1853 Dutton (Everyman's) o.p.

The Rose and the Ring, or The History of Prince Giglio and Prince Bulbo. 1854. Dutton o.p.; Pierpont Morgan 1947 o.p.

The Virginians. 1859. Dutton (Everyman's) o.p.

BOOKS ABOUT THACKERAY

Carey, John. *Thackeray: Prodigal Genius.* Faber 1980 pap. $7.95

Colby, Robert A. *Thackeray's Canvass of Humanity: An Author and His Public.* Ohio State Univ. Pr. 1979 $25.00

Collins, Philip, ed. *Thackeray: Interviews and Recollections.* St. Martin's 2 vols. 1983 ea. $20.00

Flamm, Dudley. *Thackeray's Critics: An Annotated Bibliography of British and American Criticism, 1836–1901.* Univ. of Carolina Pr. 1967 o.p. An interesting introduction describes Thackeray's critical fortunes in his own century. More than 700 entries.

Harden, Edgar. *The Emergence of Thackeray's Serial Fiction.* Univ. of Georgia Pr. 1979 $30.00

Loofbourow, John. *Thackeray and the Form of Fiction.* Gordian repr. of 1964 ed. 1976 $12.50
McMaster, Juliet. *Thackeray: The Major Novels.* Univ. of Toronto Pr. 1971 pap. $7.50
Rawlins, Jack. *Thackeray's Novels: A Fiction That Is True.* Univ. of California Pr. 1975 $29.50
Ray, Gordon N. *The Buried Life: A Study of the Relation between Thackeray's Fiction and His Personal History.* Thackeray Ser. Haskell 1974 lib. bdg. $39.95
———. *Thackeray.* Octagon 2 vols. 1972 lib. bdg. $69.00
Stevenson, Lionel. *The Showman of Vanity Fair: The Life of William Makepeace Thackeray.* Russell repr. of 1947 ed. 1968 $15.00
Sutherland, John. *Thackeray at Work.* Longwood 1979 $36.50
Taylor, Theodore. *Thackeray the Humorist and the Man of Letters.* Eng. Lit. Ser. Haskell repr. of 1864 ed. 1971 lib. bdg. $49.95. Writing shortly after the death of Thackeray, Taylor was able to obtain much information from source material and from Thackeray's friends, while memories of him were still sharp.
Tillotson, Geoffrey, and Donald Hawes, eds. *Thackeray: The Critical Heritage.* Critical Heritage Ser. Routledge & Kegan 1968 $45.00. First edition reviews from Thackeray's time.

TROLLOPE, ANTHONY. 1815–1882

In recent decades, Trollope's reputation has grown considerably, with particular emphasis on his effectiveness as a gentle satirist and as a shrewd observer of British manners and morals in provincial and urban settings, in politics, in the church, and in finance. Trollope's comic novels present the panorama of Victorian British pride and power while dramatizing traditional and conservative virtues in their conflict with changing values. His works number 100 or more volumes, including novels, tales, history, travel, and biography. Forty-odd novels are divided into three series: *The Chronicles of Barsetshire, or The Cathedral Stories; The Parliamentary Novels;* and *The Manor House Novels.* In each series, the same characters appear repeatedly, but each volume is complete in itself. The Barsetshire novels, the most popular of the group, are all set in the imaginary town of Barchester (based on Winchester, according to Trollope), and the characters are mainly clergy of various ranks and their families.

Trollope's autobiography, published posthumously in 1883, has been blamed for the eclipse of Trollope's fame right after his death. In it he confesses his custom of writing with his watch before him, requiring of himself 250 words every quarter hour. He began this at 5:30 every morning without fail and prided himself on living a full, varied life the rest of the day—he was employed until afternoon in the post office until 1867. But Trollope's mechanical work habits did not produce mechanical novels, and his modern reputation acknowledges his comic genius, his social insights, and his general seriousness.

BOOKS BY TROLLOPE

The Letters of Anthony Trollope. Ed. by N. John Hall, Stanford Univ. Pr. 2 vols. 1983 $87.50
Collected Short Stories. Ayer repr. $30.00

The Complete Short Stories. Texas Christian Univ. Pr. 5 vols. 1979–83 ea. $17.50
The Selected Works of Anthony Trollope. Ed. by N. John Hall, *Selected Works of An-
thony Trollope Ser*. Ayer 62 vols. repr. 1981 lib. bdg. $1,994.00. Includes all of the
following volumes:
The Macdermots of Ballycloran. 3 vols. repr. of 1847 ed. $105.00
La Vendée. repr. of 1850 ed. $105.00
The Three Clerks. 3 vols. repr. of 1858 ed. $105.00
The Bertrams. 3 vols. repr. of 1859 ed. $105.00
Castle Richmond. repr. of 1860 ed. $105.00
Tales of All Countries. 2 vols. repr. of 1861 ed. $39.00
Rachel Ray. repr. of 1863 ed. 1981 $65.00
Hunting Sketches. repr. of 1865 ed. $15.00
Miss Mackenzie. 2 vols. repr. of 1865 ed. $65.00
Travelling Sketches. repr. of 1866 ed. $15.00
Lotta Schmidt and Other Stories. repr. of 1867 ed. $45.00
Nina Balatka: The Story of a Maiden of Prague. 2 vols. repr. of 1867 ed. $50.00
Linda Tressel. repr. of 1868 ed. $45.00
An Editor's Tales. repr. of 1870 ed. $45.00
The Struggles of Brown, Jones, and Robinson. repr. of 1870 ed. $29.00
Sir Harry Hotspur of Humblethwaite. repr. of 1871 ed. $35.00
The Golden Lion of Granpere. repr. of 1872 ed. $39.00
Harry Heathcote of Gangoil. repr. of 1874 ed. $35.00
Lady Anna. repr. of 1874 ed. $70.00
The American Senator. 3 vols. repr. of 1877 ed. $105.00
How the Mastiff Went to Iceland. repr. of 1878 ed. $15.00
Cousin Henry. repr. of 1879 ed. $50.00
An Eye for an Eye. repr. of 1879 ed. $45.00
The Life of Cicero. 2 vols. repr. of 1880 ed. $90.00
The Fixed Period. 2 vols. repr. of 1882 ed. $45.00
Marian Fay. repr. of 1882 ed. $90.00
Lord Palmeston. repr. of 1882 ed. $25.00
Why Frau Frohman Raised Her Prices (and *Other Stories*). repr. of 1882 ed. $45.00
The Land-Leaguers. 3 vols. repr. of 1883 ed. $105.00
The Noble Jilt—Did He Steal It. 2 vols. repr. of 1923 ed. $30.00
An Old Man's Love. repr. of 1884 ed. $50.00

THE CHRONICLES OF BARSETSHIRE

The Warden. 1855. Biblio Dist. 1975 $9.95; *World's Class. Ser*. Oxford 1980 pap. $3.95;
ed. by Robin Gilmour, *Penguin Eng. Lib. Ser*. 1984 pap. $3.95
Barchester Towers. 1857. Biblio Dist. 1975 $9.95 pap. $3.95; ed. by Arthur Mizener,
Norton Critical Eds. 1984 pap.; ed. by James R. Kincaid, *World's Class.-Pap. Ser*.
Oxford 1980 pap. $4.95; ed. by Robin Gilmour, Penguin 1983 pap. $4.95
Dr. Thorne. 1858. Biblio Dist. repr. of 1908 ed. 1978 $10.95; ed. by David Skilton,
World's Class.-Pap. Ser. Oxford 1980 pap. $7.95
Framley Parsonage. 1861. Biblio Dist. 1978 pap. $3.25; ed. by P. D. Edwards, Oxford
1980 pap. $7.95
The Small House at Allington. 1864. Biblio Dist. repr. of 1909 ed. 1976 $9.95; ed. by
James R. Kincaid, *World's Class.-Pap. Ser*. Oxford 1980 pap. $7.95
The Last Chronicle of Barset. 1867. Biblio Dist. 2 vols. 1978 $14.95; ed. by Arthur
Mizener, Houghton Mifflin (Riv. Eds.) 1964 pap. $6.50; ed. by Stephen Gill,

World's Class.-Pap. Ser. Oxford 1980 pap. $9.95; *Penguin Eng. Lib. Ser.* 1981 pap. $4.95

THE PARLIAMENTARY NOVELS

Can You Forgive Her? 1864. Oxford 1973 $12.50; *World's Class.-Pap. Ser.* Oxford 1982 pap. $6.95; ed. by Stephen Wall, *Penguin Eng. Lib. Ser.* 1978 pap. $5.95

Phineas Finn. 1869. *World's Class.-Pap. Ser.* Oxford 1982 pap. $6.95; ed. by John Sutherland, *Penguin Eng. Lib. Ser.* 1978 pap. $5.95

The Eustage Diamonds. 1873. Lightyear 1976 $14.95; ed. by W. J. McCormack, *World's Class.-Pap. Ser.* Oxford 1983 pap. $6.95; ed. by Stephen Gill and John Sutherland, *Penguin Eng. Lib. Ser.* 1978 pap. $5.95

Phineas Redux. 1874. Ed. by John C. Whale, *World's Class.-Pap. Ser.* Oxford 1983 pap. $6.95

The Prime Minister. 1876. Ed. by Jennifer Uglow, *World's Class.-Pap. Ser.* Oxford 1983 pap. $6.95

The Duke's Children. 1880. Ed. by Hermione Lee, *World's Class.-Pap. Ser.* Oxford 1983 pap. $6.95

THE MANOR HOUSE NOVELS

Orley Farm. 1862. Dover 1981 pap. $8.95

The Belton Estate. 1866. Oxford o.p.

The Way We Live Now. 1875. Dover 1982 pap. $7.95; *World's Class.-Pap. Ser.* Oxford 1982 pap. $9.95

Is He Popenjoy? 1878. Oxford o.p.

OTHER NOVELS IN PRINT

The Kellys and the O'Kellys, or Landlords and Tenants. 1848. Ed. by W. J. McCormack, *World's Class.-Pap. Ser.* Oxford 1982 pap. $6.95

The Claverings. 1867. Dover 1977 pap. $6.00

He Knew He Was Right. 1869. Ed. by P. D. Edwards, Univ. of Queensland Pr. 1974 $15.00

The Vicar of Bullhampton. 1870. Dover 1979 pap. $7.50

Ralph the Heir. 1870. Dover 1978 pap. $7.95

Kept in the Dark. 1882 Dover 1978 pap. $2.95

AUTOBIOGRAPHY

The West Indies and the Spanish Main. 1859. Biblio Dist. 3d ed. repr. 1968 $19.50. "This hitherto unpublished work of nonfiction provides an intimate, knowledgeable and comprehensive picture of Victorian England" (Publisher's catalog).

South Africa. 1878. Humanities Pr. o.p.

An Autobiography. 1883. Ed. by P. D. Edwards, *World's Class.-Pap. Ser.* Oxford 1980 pap. $4.95; Univ. of California Pr. 1979 pap. $3.95

BOOKS ABOUT TROLLOPE

apRoberts, Ruth. *The Moral Trollope.* Ohio Univ. Pr. 1971 o.p. $12.95

Hall, N. John. *Trollope and His Illustrators.* St. Martin's 1983 $4.95

———, ed. *The Trollope Critics.* Barnes & Noble 1981 $18.50

Halperin, John, ed. *Trollope Centenary Essays.* St. Martin's 1982 $22.50

Kincaid, James R. *The Novels of Anthony Trollope.* Oxford 1977 $36.95

Lansbury, Coral. *The Reasonable Man: Trollope's Legal Fictions*. Princeton Univ. Pr. 1981 $20.00

Letwin, Shirley R. *The Gentlemen in Trollope: Individuality and Moral Conduct*. Harvard Univ. Pr. text ed. 1982 $20.00

Macmaster, Juliet. *Trollope's Palliser Novels: Theme and Pattern*. Oxford 1978 $25.00

Pope-Hennessy, James. *Anthony Trollope*. Little, Brown 1972 o.p. A critical biography that includes 25 illustrations from the original editions of the novels.

Sadleir, Michael. *Trollope: A Commentary*. Darby repr. 1980 lib. bdg. $25.00; Octagon repr. of 1947 ed. lib. bdg. $29.00; Richard West repr. of 1945 ed. $20.00

Smalley, Donald, ed. *Trollope: The Critical Heritage*. *Critical Heritage Ser*. Routledge & Kegan 1969 $40.00. A collection of contemporary criticisms.

Stebbins, Lucy, and Richard Stebbins. *The Trollopes: The Chronicle of a Writing Family*. AMS Pr. repr. of 1945 ed. $26.50. Based on family journals and other writings; includes Frances and her two sons, the historian Thomas Adolphus and the novelist Anthony.

Tracy, Robert. *Trollope's Later Novels*. Univ. of California Pr. 1978 o.p.

CHAPTER 12

Modern British Fiction

Alan Warren Friedman

> No English novelist is as great as Tolstoy—that is to say has given so com-
> plete a picture of man's life, both on its domestic and heroic side. No En-
> glish novelist has explored man's soul as deeply as Dostoevsky. And no nov-
> elist anywhere has analysed the modern consciousness as successfully as
> Marcel Proust. Before these triumphs we must pause. English poetry fears
> no one—excels in quality as well as quantity. But English fiction is less tri-
> umphant: it does not contain the best stuff yet written, and if we deny this
> we become guilty of provincialism.
>
> —E. M. FORSTER, *Aspects of the Novel*

To E. M. Forster, writing in 1927, a favorable comparison between English
novelists and writers like TOLSTOY (see Vol. 2), DOSTOEVSKY (see Vol. 2), or
PROUST (see Vol. 2) seemed like provincialism. Certainly the writers he mentions have few equals; but Forster's remarks indicate that he was only partially aware of the greatness of the writers who were his contemporaries.

Forster's modest appraisal of the accomplishments of his compatriots illustrates the difficulty of attempting, even in the most sensible and well-
informed manner, to judge the art of one's contemporaries accurately. In
discussing contemporary writers, one finds it almost impossible to avoid
praising mediocrity or ignoring greatness; the objects closest to us are the
ones most difficult to see. And this perhaps is why Forster, five years after
the publication of Joyce's *Ulysses*, assumed that no novelist could rival
Proust in analyzing the modern consciousness.

Forster's remarks came at the end of an unusually productive period in
British fiction. In the 25 or 30 years prior to the publication of his comments, outstanding novels were published by realists like Arnold Bennett
and John Galsworthy; by masters of psychological symbolism like JOSEPH
CONRAD and D. H. Lawrence; by social observers like Henry James and Ford
Madox Ford; and by experimental innovators like James Joyce and Virginia
Woolf. And Forster himself contributed to the large number of masterpieces
produced in this era: Though he lived until 1970, his last great work, *A Passage to India*, was completed in 1924.

The best British novelists of the next generation, of the 1930s and 1940s,
were Aldous Huxley, Graham Greene, George Orwell, Evelyn Waugh, and
Anthony Powell. All are noted for their skill in writing social commentary
and satire—and satire, of course, is a form of social commentary. Since they

worked in turbulent times, it is natural enough to find these novelists preoccupied with social questions; and the turbulence may explain a decline both in the productivity and variety of English fiction in this period.

After World War II enough similarities appeared among the new novelists to make generalizations about the state of fiction possible once again. At one point the phrase "Angry Young Men" was very much in vogue; and when the writers in question protested that they were not really very angry, their protest was taken as a sign that they were. What many of these newer novelists did seem to have in common—unlike some of their American and French counterparts—was a fictional style that ignored almost entirely the experimental writing of the early decades of the century.

Novelists like Angus Wilson, C. P. Snow, Kingsley Amis, John Braine, Alan Sillitoe, Iris Murdoch, and Doris Lessing have, for the most part, returned to the traditional naturalism of the Victorian or the Edwardian novel. Few of these writers use devices like symbolism or stream of consciousness, or try to develop new techniques of their own; their main interest is in storytelling.

Recent British writers who are most interested in experiment—Samuel Beckett, Lawrence Durrell, and Anthony Burgess—have all (for a variety of reasons) gone to live abroad, and the expatriate experience of alienation remains central to their writings. Some interesting novels have been produced in this period, many of them by religious writers like Graham Greene, Muriel Spark, and William Golding. Otherwise, the most compelling recent novels seem to be by current and former academics—Malcolm Bradbury, Angela Carter, John Fowles, David Lodge, Iris Murdoch—many of whom are both successful critics and self-conscious novelists aware of the full responsibilities of both their craft and their art. They seek, like Amis in *Lucky Jim*, to make the ivory tower representative of larger social spheres, to explore the universal in the university. On the whole, English fiction today does not seem as exciting as it once did. But of course this state of affairs is perhaps an illusion; we may, like Forster in 1927, be guilty of underestimating the quality of the newest writers.

HISTORY AND CRITICISM

Aldridge, John W. *Time to Murder and Create: The Contemporary Novel in Crisis. Essay Index Repr. Ser.* Ayer repr. of 1966 ed. $26.50

——, ed. *Critiques and Essays on Modern Fiction, 1920–1951: Representing the Achievement of Modern American and British Critics.* Scott, Foresman text ed. 1952 $22.75; Wiley 1952 $15.95

Allen, Walter. *The Novel To-Day.* Folcroft repr. of 1955 ed. lib. bdg. $12.50

Atkins, John. *Six Novelists Look at Society.* Riverrun 1980 $11.95 pap. $7.95

Auerbach, Erich. *Mimesis: The Representation of Reality in Western Literature.* Trans. by W. R. Trask, Princeton Univ. Pr. 1953 $35.00 pap. $8.95. Rich, complex, brilliant on the vast subject indicated by its title.

Baker, Ernest A. *A History of the English Novel.* Barnes & Noble 11 vols. $247.50

Bergonzi, Bernard. *Heroes' Twilight*. Humanities Pr. text ed. 1980 $25.50. Excellent analysis of the writings resulting from World War I.

Blamires, Harry, ed. *A Guide to Twentieth-Century Literature in English*. Methuen 1983 $32.00 pap. $15.95

Booth, Wayne C. *The Rhetoric of Fiction*. Univ. of Chicago Pr. 2d ed. 1983 pap. $12.95; Univ. of Chicago Pr. (Phoenix Bks.) 1983 2d ed. pap. $30.00

Bradbury, Malcolm, and David Palmer, eds. *The Contemporary English Novel*. Holmes & Meier text ed. 1980 $31.75 pap. $15.50

Brown, E. K. *Rhythm in the Novel*. Univ. of Nebraska Pr. (Bison) 1978 $11.95 pap. $3.25

Cross, W. L. *Four Contemporary Novelists*. AMS Pr. repr. of 1930 ed $12.50; *Essay Index Repr. Ser.* Ayer repr. of 1930 ed. $17.00. Conrad, Bennett, Galsworthy, Wells.

Daiches, David. *The Novel and the Modern World*. Univ. of Chicago Pr. repr. of 1939 ed. rev. ed. text ed. 1984 pap. $9.00. Galsworthy, Conrad, Mansfield, Joyce, Woolf, and Huxley.

Edel, Leon. *Bloomsbury: A House of Lions*. Avon 1980 pap. $2.75; Harper 1979 $14.37
———. *Modern Psychological Novel (The Psychological Novel, 1900–1950)*. 1955. Peter Smith $11.25. A brilliant analysis of the stream of consciousness technique in the works of Joyce, Proust, Virginia Woolf, Dorothy Richardson, and Faulkner.

Forster, E. M. *Aspects of the Novel*. Harcourt 1947 $9.95 1956 pap. $2.95; ed. by Oliver Stallybrass, Holmes & Meier text ed. 1978 $11.00. An important study of the aesthetics of fiction, in which Forster introduces his idea of "flat" and "round" characters.

Fraser, George S. *The Modern Writer and His World*. Greenwood repr. of 1965 ed. 1976 lib. bdg. $70.00

Friedman, Alan W. *Multivalence: The Moral Quality of Form in the Modern Novel*. Louisiana State Univ. Pr. 1978 $22.50. Relates narration and ethical concerns in Conrad, Ford, Cary, Waugh, and others.

Gindin, James. *Postwar British Fiction*. Greenwood repr. of 1962 ed. 1976 lib. bdg. $25.00

Hall, James. *The Tragic Comedians: Seven Modern British Novelists*. Greenwood 1978 lib. bdg. $22.50. A sharp, bright, and thoughtful critique of the modern British comic novel as exemplified in Forster, Huxley, Evelyn Waugh, Henry Green, Cary, Hartley, and Anthony Powell. Also points out "similarities and differences in content, style and technique, and comments on such other contemporary novelists as Amis, Braine, Wain, and Sillitoe."

Howe, Irving. *Politics and the Novel*. *Essay Index Repr. Ser.* Ayer repr. of 1957 ed. $18.00; Horizon Pr. 1977 pap. $5.95. "An intelligent, penetrating, lucid, graceful, persuasive and altogether splendid book."

Humphrey, Robert. *Stream of Consciousness in the Modern Novel*. Univ. of California Pr. 1962 pap. $2.95. A rewarding discussion of the methods and devices used by Joyce, Faulkner, Woolf, and Dorothy Richardson.

Iser, Wolfgang. *The Implied Reader: Patterns of Communication in Prose Fiction from Bunyan to Beckett*. Johns Hopkins Univ. Pr. text ed. 1978 pap. $8.95. Pioneering study of reader-response criticism.

Johnstone, Richard. *The Will to Believe: Novelists of the 1930s*. Oxford 1982 $29.50 1984 pap. $5.95

Karl, Frederick R. *A Reader's Guide to the Contemporary English Novel*. Farrar rev. ed. 1972 pap. $3.50; Octagon repr. of 1972 ed. lib. bdg. $25.00. This useful study attempts to define and evaluate the main movements in the English novel since Joyce. Karl devotes separate chapters to each of the following: Snow, Beckett,

Compton-Burnett, Greene, Durrell, Elizabeth Bowen, Waugh, Orwell, Henry Green, and Joyce Cary. The "Angries" and others are discussed in the last three chapters.

Karl, Frederick R., and Marvin Magalaner. *A Reader's Guide to Great Twentieth-Century English Novels.* Octagon 1972 $22.50. An examination of the works of Conrad, Forster, Woolf, Lawrence, Joyce, and Huxley.

Kazin, Alfred. *Contemporaries, from the Nineteenth Century to the Present.* Horizon Pr. rev. ed. 1981 pap. $9.95. Many of these essays, originally published as book reviews, cover modern British novelists. Written with clarity and originality, the views expressed are personal and incisive.

Kenner, Hugh. *A Colder Eye: The Modern Irish Writers.* Knopf 1983 $16.95; Penguin 1984 pap. $8.95

——. *Gnomon: Essays in Contemporary Literature.* Astor-Honor 1958 $8.95 pap. $5.95

Kermode, Frank. *The Art of Telling: Essays on Fiction.* Harvard Univ. Pr. 1983 $15.00 1985 pap. $6.95

——. *Sense of an Ending: Studies in the Theory of Fiction.* Oxford 1967 pap. $8.95

Kettle, Arnold. *Introduction to the English Novel.* Humanities Pr. 2 vols. repr. of 1963 ed. text ed. 1974 pap. ea. $11.00–$12.50. Studies of Butler, Hardy, Joyce, Forster, Huxley, Cary, and Greene.

Kostelanetz, Richard, ed. *On Contemporary Literature: An Anthology of Critical Essays on the Major Movements and Writings of Contemporary Literature.* Essay Index Repr. Ser. Ayer repr. of 1964 ed. $40.00. Contains sections on British writing and on Burgess, Lawrence Durrell, Golding, Lessing, Murdoch, and Spark.

Krieger, Murray. *Classic Vision: The Retreat from Extremity in Modern Literature.* Johns Hopkins Univ. Pr. 1971 $16.50

Kumar, Shiv K. *Bergson and the Stream of Consciousness Novel.* Greenwood repr. of 1963 ed. 1979 lib. bdg. $24.75. Uses Bergson's concepts to analyze the work of Richardson, Woolf, and Joyce.

Lodge, David. *The Language of Fiction: Essays in Criticism and Verbal Analysis of the English Novel.* Columbia Univ. Pr. 1967 $27.50; Routledge & Kegan repr. 1967 pap. $9.95

——. *Working with Structuralism: Essays and Reviews on Nineteenth and Twentieth Century Literature.* Routledge & Kegan 1981 pap. $8.95

Mansfield, Katherine. *Novels and Novelists.* Somerset repr. of 1930 ed. $49.00

Miller, J. Hillis. *Fiction and Repetition: Seven English Novels.* Harvard Univ. Pr. text ed. 1982 $15.00 1985 pap. $7.95

Newby, Peter. *The Novel, 1945–1950.* Folcroft repr. of 1951 ed. 1974 lib. bdg. $19.95 pap. $9.50

O'Connor, William V. *The New University Wits and the End of Modernism. Crosscurrents Modern Critiques Ser.* Southern Illinois Univ. Pr. 1963 $6.96. An early study of the writers who came after World War II, with a discussion of their literary antecedents.

O'Faolain, Sean. *The Vanishing Hero. Essay Index Repr. Ser.* Ayer repr. of 1957 ed. $16.00. On the novelists of the 1920s, including Bowen, Greene, Huxley, Joyce, Waugh, and Woolf.

Russell, John. *Style in Modern British Fiction: Studies in Joyce, Lawrence, Forster, Lewis and Green.* Johns Hopkins Univ. Pr. text ed. 1978 $18.50

Shapiro, Charles, ed. *Contemporary British Novelists.* Pref. by Harry T. Moore, *Crosscurrents Modern Critiques Ser.* Southern Illinois Univ. Pr. 1965 $10.95 1969 pap.

$5.95. Essays by various hands on the most important post–World War II English writers.

Spender, Stephen. *The Creative Element: A Study of Vision, Despair, and Orthodoxy among Some Modern Writers. Select Bibliographies Repr. Ser.* Ayer repr. of 1953 ed. $20.00

———. *Destructive Element: A Study of Modern Writers and Beliefs.* Folcroft repr. of 1935 ed. lib. bdg. $25.00; Saifer 1970 $10.00

Tindall, William Y. *Forces in Modern British Literature, 1885–1946. Essay Index Repr. Ser.* Ayer repr. of 1947 ed. $26.50. Literary criticism of all the major writers, as well as many minor figures, written with wit and understanding.

Vinson, James, ed. *Contemporary Novelists of the English Language.* Pref. by Walter Allen, St. Martin's 1972 $30.00 1982 $65.00. An excellent reference work with a short essay and bibliography describing the works of every important contemporary novelist, with an emphasis on English and American writers.

Webster, Harvey C. *After the Trauma: Representative British Novelists since 1920.* Univ. Pr. of Kentucky 1970 $18.00. Includes discussions on Rose Macaulay, Huxley, Compton-Burnett, Waugh, Greene, Hartley, Snow, and others.

West, Rebecca. *Ending in Earnest: A Literary Log. Essay Index Repr. Ser.* Ayer repr. of 1931 ed. 1967 $15.50

Williams, Raymond. *English Novel from Dickens to Lawrence.* Merrimack 1984 pap. $8.95; Oxford 1970 $7.95. Williams, a social historian, examines the links between the fiction of the late nineteenth and early twentieth centuries and the social change that occurred during that period.

COLLECTIONS

Davis, Robert G. *Ten Modern Masters.* Harcourt 3d ed. text ed. 1972 pap. $14.95. Several stories each by Anderson, Chekhov, Conrad, Faulkner, James, Joyce, Mann, Mansfield, O'Connor.

Garrity, Devin A., ed. *Forty-four Irish Short Stories: An Anthology of Irish Short Fiction from Yeats to Frank O'Connor.* Devin 1980 $12.95

Hayman, David, and Eric S. Rabkin. *Form in Fiction.* St. Martin's 1974 text ed. pap. $13.95

Hudson, Derek, ed. *Modern English Short Stories.* Somerset repr. of 1956 ed. $27.00. A comprehensive anthology with many minor writers as well as familiar names represented.

Miller, Karl. *Writing in England Today: The Last Fifteen Years.* Peter Smith $10.00. An anthology of recent British writing; includes poets and essayists as well as novelists.

Schorer, Mark, ed. *Story: A Critical Anthology.* Prentice-Hall 2d ed. text ed. 1967 pap. $18.95

AMIS, KINGSLEY. 1922–

Kingsley Amis, born "of Baptist stock originating in southeast London," received his degree in English language and literature from St. John's College, Oxford, in 1947. He has written poems, stories, and criticism for various periodicals. Until 1961, Amis lectured in English at University College, Swansea, and was a Fellow of Peterhouse (Cambridge) until 1963, when he decided to devote all of his time to writing. It was Maugham who first attacked that group of English writers called the "Angry Young Men," of whom Amis is one of the best known.

Lucky Jim, an entertaining satire on the fortunes of a frivolous young scholar at an English university, won the Somerset Maugham Award in 1955, and made Amis's reputation. He followed with *That Uncertain Feeling* (1956, o.p.), which the *Times Literary Supplement* praised: "His dialogue is brilliant, his timing of comic situations could hardly be bettered . . . yet by intention he is a serious comic writer, one who apparently means to say something about society." There was a great diversity of critical opinion about *Take a Girl Like You*, but the *New Yorker* considered it his best work since *Lucky Jim:* "Mr. Amis treats his subject . . . with wit, shrewdness, and humanity, and he shows an uncommon understanding of a kind of girl who exists by the million and who has not been taken seriously in literature for quite some time." In *The Anti-Death League* (1966, o.p.), at once a comedy and a spy thriller with serious undertones, "what Mr. Amis has done, with some of his best writing, is to expound his philosophies through a vivid, exciting story and a superior character analysis that challenges your imagination and absorbs your interest" (*Baltimore Sunday Sun*). With Robert Conquest, he has edited *Spectrum* (o.p.), science-fiction anthologies of short stories by masters who write with imagination and style. A longtime James Bond devotee—who had proved his interest with a study of the superhero, *The James Bond Dossier* (o.p.)—Amis was delegated to produce more Bond books in the manner of the late Ian Fleming, Bond's creator. "The critics," said the *N.Y. Times*, "were outraged, but the public seems to be delighted." Of *Colonel Sun* (1968, o.p.), his first Bond adventure—written under the pseudonym Robert Markham—Amis said: "It was fun—a kind of holiday."

BOOKS BY AMIS

Collected Poems, 1944–1979. Viking 1980 $10.00
Lucky Jim. 1954. Amereon 1976 repr. of 1954 ed. $15.95; Penguin 1976 pap. $3.95
Take a Girl Like You. David & Charles 1960 $19.95; Penguin 1976 pap. $1.95
New Maps of Hell. Ayer repr. of 1975 ed. $13.00
The Alteration. 1976. Viking 1977 $9.95
Jake's Thing. 1978. Penguin 1980 pap. $4.95; Viking 1979 $11.95
Harold's Years: Impressions of the Harold Wilson Era. Charles River Bks. $12.95
Stanley and the Women. Summit 1985 $16.95

BOOKS ABOUT AMIS

Gohn, Jack. *Kingsley Amis: A Checklist.* Kent State Univ. Pr. 1976 $14.00
Salwak, Dale. *Kingsley Amis: A Reference Guide.* G. K. Hall 1978 lib. bdg. $22.00

BENNETT, ARNOLD. 1867–1931

"In his time, Arnold Bennett was the shrewdest and most successful tradesman in English letters" (V. S. Pritchett, *New Yorker*). *The Old Wives' Tale* is the masterpiece of this novelist who wrote about the lives of shopkeepers and potters in the north of England—his own boyhood background, though he became immensely successful. "A merchant of words, frankly writing for money," he was able nonetheless to make the dullest characters interesting. In 1968, reviewing *Darling of the Day*, a successful musical adaptation of *Buried Alive* (1923), Walter Kerr wrote: "I'd forgotten some of the nicer twists of . . . 'Buried Alive' . . . and so was charmed all over again." Bennett's other important novels are *The Clayhanger Trilogy* (1910), *Hilda Lessways* (1911), *These Twain* (1916), and *Riceyman Steps* (1923). Bennett's voluminous *Journal* is of special value for the light it throws on the novelist at work.

BOOKS BY BENNETT

The Collected Works of Arnold Bennett. Ayer 90 vols. repr. of 1976 ed. $1,897.50
Journal of Arnold Bennett. Ayer 3 pts. repr. of 1932–33 ed. 1976 ea. $29.00–$33.00
Grand Babylon Hotel: A Fantasia on Modern Themes. 1904. Penguin 1976 pap. $4.95; Scholarly 1904 $27.00
The Old Wives' Tale. Ayer repr. of 1911 ed. 1976 $43.25
The Matador of the Five Towns and Other Stories. Collected Works of Arnold Bennett Ser. Ayer repr. of 1912 ed. 1976 $31.50; Scholarly repr. of 1905 ed. 1971 $25.00
Pretty Lady. Scholarly repr. of 1918 ed. 1971 $18.00
Author's Craft and Other Critical Writings of Arnold Bennett. Ed. by Samuel Hynes, *Regents Critics Ser.* Univ. of Nebraska Pr. (Bison) 1968 $21.50 pap. $5.25

BOOKS ABOUT BENNETT

Allen, Walter E. *Arnold Bennett.* AMS Pr. repr. of 1949 ed. $7.50
Bennett, Mrs. Arnold. *Arnold Bennett.* Richard West repr. of 1925 ed. 1973 $20.00
Broomfield, Olga R. *Arnold Bennett. Twayne's Eng. Authors Ser.* G. K. Hall 1984 lib. bdg. $19.95
Hall, James. *Arnold Bennett: Primitivism and Taste.* Univ. of Washington Pr. 1959 $15.00
Hepburn, J. *The Art of Arnold Bennett. Studies in Fiction Ser.* Haskell repr. of 1963 ed. 1972 lib. bdg. $43.95
Johnson, L. G. *Arnold Bennett of Five Towns.* Richard West repr. of 1924 ed. 1973 $20.00
Pound, Reginald. *Arnold Bennett: A Biography.* Associated Faculty Pr. repr. of 1952 ed. 1971 $17.00; Richard West repr. of 1952 ed. 1973 $16.50
Wright, Walter F. *Arnold Bennett: Romantic Realist.* Univ. of Nebraska Pr. 1971 $15.95

BOWEN, ELIZABETH. 1899–1973

Elizabeth Bowen, distinguished Anglo-Irish novelist, was born in Dublin, traveled extensively, lived in London, and inherited the family estate—Bowen's Court—in County Cork. Her account of the house, *Bowen's Court* (1942, o.p.), with a detailed fictionalized history of the family in Ireland through three centuries, has "sober charm" and "a warmth and insight that suggest extraordinary imaginative virtuosity." *Seven Winters* is a fragment of autobiography published in England in 1942. The "Afterthoughts" of the original edition are critical essays, "indispensable documents," in which she discusses and analyzes, among others, such literary figures as Woolf, Forster, Katherine Mansfield, Trollope, and Welty. Her stories, mostly about people of the British upper middle class, portray relationships that her analysis shows are never simple, except, perhaps, on the surface. Her concern with time and memory is a major theme. Beautifully and delicately written, her stories, with their oblique psychological revelations, are symbolic, subtle, and terrifying. *A Time in Rome* (1960, o.p.) is her brilliant evocation of that city and its layered past. In 1948, she was made a Commander of the British Empire.

BOOKS BY BOWEN

The Collected Stories of Elizabeth Bowen. Intro. by Angus Wilson, Knopf 1981 $20.00; intro. by Angus Wilson, Random 1982 pap. $8.95
Ann Lee's and Other Stories. Short Story Index Repr. Ser. Ayer repr. of 1926 ed. $16.00
The Hotel. 1927. Avon 1980 pap. $2.25; Greenwood repr. of 1928 ed. 1972 lib. bdg. $15.50
Joining Charles and Other Stories. Scholarly repr. of 1929 ed. 1971 $29.00
The House in Paris. 1936. Avon 1979 pap. $2.50
The Death of the Heart. 1938. Avon 1984 pap. $2.25; Knopf 1939 $15.95; Modern Lib. 1984 $8.95; Penguin 1985 pap. $5.95; Random 1984 pap. $8.95
Bowen's Court. 1942. Ecco Pr. 1979 pap. $6.95
The Heat of the Day. 1949. Avon 1979 pap. $1.95; Buccaneer Bks. repr. 1981 lib. bdg. $16.95; *Penguin Fiction Ser.* Penguin 1986 pap. $5.95
Collected Impressions. AMS Pr. repr. of 1950 ed. $28.50
The Little Girls. 1963. Penguin 1985 pap. $5.95
Good Tiger. Knopf 1965 $4.69
Seven Winters. Biblio Dist. repr. of 1942 ed. 1971 $10.00. Her only autobiographical work.
Why Do I Write. Richard West repr. of 1948 ed. 1980 lib. bdg. $10.00
Friends and Relations. Avon 1980 pap. $2.25

BOOKS ABOUT BOWEN

Blodgett, Harriet. *Patterns of Reality: Elizabeth Bowen's Novels.* Mouton text ed. 1975 pap. $29.00
Coles, Robert. *Irony in the Mind's Life: Essays on Novels by James Agee, Elizabeth Bowen, and George Eliot.* New Directions 1978 pap. $4.95; Univ. Pr. of Virginia 1974 $12.95
Glendinning, Victoria. *Elizabeth Bowen.* Avon 1979 pap. $3.50
Kenney, Edwin J. *Elizabeth Bowen. Irish Writers Ser.* Bucknell Univ. Pr. 1975 $4.50
Sellery, J'nan M., and William O. Harris. *Elizabeth Bowen: A Descriptive Bibliography.* Univ. of Texas Harry Ransom Humanities Research Center 1981 $25.00

BRADBURY, MALCOLM (STANLEY). 1932–

A professor of English literature and American studies who has published numerous critical studies (on Shakespeare, Waugh, Forster, Bellow, twentieth-century fiction, among others), Malcolm Bradbury is also a novelist whose protagonists are academics who make muddles of their personal and professional lives. He maintains, however, that his "settings are relatively incidental . . . and my main concern has been, within a more or less comic framework, to explore problems and dilemmas of liberalism and issues of moral responsibility." The targets of Bradbury's satires include intellectual pretension, cultural myopia, and official smugness. His protagonists are largely sympathetic, if comic, failures at mastering their own fates in a world of absurd rules and regulations. His best novels include *Eating People Is Wrong* (o.p.), *Stepping Westward* (o.p.), and *The History Man* (o.p.). This last, a novel of intellectual and political conflict at an English university in the late 1960s, was made into a successful television minidrama.

BOOKS BY BRADBURY

All Dressed Up and Nowhere to Go. Merrimack 1983 $14.95
Rates of Exchange. Knopf 1983 $13.95; Penguin 1985 pap. $6.95

BRAGG, MELVYN. 1939–

Though known in England primarily as a television producer and personality, Melvyn Bragg is also a social novelist of distinction. His earliest novels—*For Want of a Nail* (o.p.), *The Second Inheritance*, and *Without a City Wall*—portray young male protagonists who struggle gamely, and at least partially successfully, to overcome heredity, environment, and class. His novels of the rural Tallentine family, *The Hired Man* and *A Place in England* (o.p.), sympathetically portray the emotional and economic struggles of two generations as they seek to make a place for themselves in a changing world. In all these books, as in much of Hardy and Lawrence, the rural setting occupies a central and active place, with a vitality and significance to equal those of the characters themselves. Later novels of interest include *The Nerve* (o.p.) and *The Hunt* (o.p.). Bragg has won the Silver Pen Award and is a Fellow of the Royal Society of Literature.

BOOKS BY BRAGG

The Second Inheritance. David & Charles 1966 $16.95
Without a City Wall. 1968. David & Charles 1973 $9.95
The Hired Man. David & Charles 1969 $16.95
Autumn Manoeuvres. David & Charles 1978 $11.50
Kingdom Come. David & Charles 1980 $16.95
Land of the Lakes. Norton 1984 $24.95

BRAINE, JOHN. 1922–

John Braine, a Yorkshireman by birth and inclination, started to write *Room at the Top* (1957, o.p.) while hospitalized and recovering from tuberculosis. It is the story of a man obsessed by the need for success who believes he can become an "insider" by donning the proper mask, but who finds he must compromise everything he values. The film version of *Room at the Top* won the British Oscar and was widely acclaimed in the United States. *From the Hand of the Hunter* (o.p.) deals with the fight against failure by a tubercular. *Life at the Top* (1962) is concerned with the hero of *Room at the Top* after he marries the boss's daughter. In *The Jealous God* (1964, o.p.), "an author whose earlier concerns have been mainly fiscal and physical now turns his attention to the soul" and what is "perhaps his best novel since 'Room at the Top' " (Eric Moon, *LJ*). *Waiting for Sheila*, Braine's most interesting formal experiment, occurs in a single evening during which the protagonist recounts the failures of his past and present.

John Braine has said: "A novelist's task is to present human beings as they are—why they are is not his concern. . . . A writer must have roots, must belong to his own part of the country. He must write only about what he knows—but he mustn't write autobiography, which is one of the curses of the modern novel. And he must love people and things. All people, all things."

BOOKS BY BRAINE

Waiting for Sheila. 1976. Methuen 1977 $9.95
Life at the Top. Methuen 1980 pap. $3.95

BOOK ABOUT BRAINE

Salwak, Dale. *John Braine and John Wain: A Reference Guide*. G. K. Hall 1979 lib.
   bdg. $31.50

BURGESS, ANTHONY (JOHN ANTHONY BURGESS WILSON). 1917–

Anthony Burgess wrote his first novel in 1949 while he was a teacher of linguistics and composer of music; *A Vision of Battlements* (o.p.) resulted from his being "empty of music but itching to create." Later he became a British colonial officer in Southeast Asia, and in that capacity produced the trilogy *The Long Day Wanes*. He has since scored an impressive record— some 15 works of fiction published within a decade. "Although there are suggestions of what has come to be called 'black humor' in both 'A Vision of Battlements' and 'The Long Day Wanes,' it was only when he turned to the English scene, as he did in 1960 with 'The Doctor Is Sick' and 'The Right to an Answer,' that Burgess showed how wry and bitter he could be" (*SR*). These two successful satires on present-day England paved the way for two more on the England of the future: *The Wanting Seed* shows a society where people are governed by rigorous laws, and homosexuality is encouraged to control a mounting population; *A Clockwork Orange* paints the bleak picture of a nation overridden by teenage gangs. These two exhibit Burgess's fascination (like that of Joyce and Nabokov) with oddities of language.

Other works include *Honey for the Bears*, which implies that the U.S.S.R. and the United States are both overconformist societies. In *Tremor of Intent* "using the spy as missile-era folk-hero, he creates a gleaming novel of ideas—troubling ideas about the survival value of ideology, the disease of our appetites, our malevolent innocence as we perpetrate incredible atrocities and feel no guilt. Brazenly clever, Burgess is . . . guided by a foolproof intellectual homing device and possessed by a black sense of humor that barely hold his hostility in check. Outraged by blasphemies against life, he attacks unreason with satire so swift we hardly know we've been hit before we're pronounced morally dead" (*N.Y. Times*). *Enderby*, about an antisocial poet confined to the bathroom of a small apartment and then pitched into the world again, inaugurated a marvelous series on a most unusual character. Burgess has also written several books of literary criticism.

Books by Burgess

The Long Day Wanes: A Malayan Trilogy. 1956–59. *Norton Lib.* 1977 pap. $4.95. Contains *Time for a Tiger, The Enemy in the Blanket,* and *Beds in the East.*
The Doctor Is Sick. Norton repr. of 1960 ed. 1979 pap. $3.95
The Right to an Answer. 1960. Norton 1978 $3.95
The Wanting Seed. 1962. *Norton Lib.* repr. of 1963 ed. 1976 pap. $6.95
A Clockwork Orange. 1962. Norton 1963 pap. $3.95
Enderby. 1963. Norton 1968 $5.95
Inside Mr. Enderby. 1963. McGraw-Hill 1984 pap. $5.95
Tremor of Intent: An Eschatological Spy Novel. Norton 1966 $4.95; *Norton Lib.* 1977 pap. $5.95
Enderby Outside. 1968. McGraw-Hill 1984 pap. $5.95
The Eve of St. Venus. 1970. Norton 1979 pap. $1.95
Beard's Roman Women. McGraw-Hill 1976 $8.95
The Clockwork Testament, or Enderby's End. 1976. McGraw-Hill 1984 pap. $5.95
Honey for the Bears. Norton 1978 pap. $3.95
Nineteen Eighty-Five. Little, Brown 1978 $8.95
Man of Nazareth. McGraw-Hill 1979 $10.95
Earthly Powers. Avon 1981 pap. $3.95; Bobbs 1980 $16.95
Napoleon Symphony. Norton 1980 pap. $4.95
The End of the World News: An Entertainment. McGraw-Hill 1983 $15.95; Penguin 1984 pap. $5.95
This Man and Music. Avon 1985 pap. $3.95; McGraw-Hill 1983 $14.95
Enderby's Dark Lady: Or, No End to Enderby. McGraw-Hill 1984 $14.95

Books about Burgess

Aggeler, Geoffrey. *Anthony Burgess: The Artist as Novelist.* Univ. of Alabama Pr. 1979 $19.50
Boytinck, Paul. *Anthony Burgess: A Bibliography.* Richard West repr. of 1977 ed. 1978 lib. bdg. $22.50
Brewer, Jeutonne. *Anthony Burgess: A Bibliography. Author Bibliographies Ser.* Scarecrow Pr. 1980 lib. bdg. $16.50
Mathews, Richard. *The Clockwork Universe of Anthony Burgess.* Borgo Pr. 1978 lib. bdg. $12.95 pap. $4.95
Morris, Robert K. *Consolations of Ambiguity: An Essay on the Novels of Anthony Burgess. Literary Frontiers Ser.* Univ. of Missouri Pr. 1971 pap. $7.95

CARTER, ANGELA. 1940–

A powerful and disturbing writer, Angela Carter creates haunting fiction about travelers surviving their passage through a disintegrating universe. Often based on myth or fairy tale—borrowed or invented for the occasion— her work evokes the most powerful aspects of sexuality and selfhood, of life and death, of apocalypse. Carter's most successful novels include *The Magic Toyshop* (o.p.), which won the John Llewellyn Rhys Prize; *Several Perceptions* (o.p.), which won the Somerset Maugham Award; and *The Passion of New Eve* (o.p.), a story of the end of the world and its possible new beginning with failed mankind replaced by a self-generating womankind. She has translated many fairy tales and has written several collections of short stories, including *The Bloody Chamber*, which won the Cheltenham Festival of Literature Award and was the basis for the powerful movie, *A Company of Wolves*. She has worked as a journalist and teacher (including appointments at Brown and the University of Texas), and has published two nonfiction books of interest: *Nothing Sacred*, selected writings, and *The Sadeian Woman*.

BOOKS BY CARTER

Fireworks: Nine Stories in Various Disguises. 1974. Harper 1981 $10.53 1982 pap. $4.09
The War of Dreams. Avon 1977 pap. $1.95; Harcourt 1974 $6.95
The Bloody Chamber. 1979. Harper 1980 $9.57 1981 pap. $3.95
The Sadeian Woman: And the Ideology of Pornography. Harper 1980 pap. $3.50; Pantheon 1979 $7.95
(trans.). *Sleeping Beauty and Other Favorite Fairy Tales*. Schocken 1984 $12.95

CARY, JOYCE. 1888–1957

Poet, amateur painter, political scientist, and novelist, Cary was born in Ireland of an old Devonshire family. Despite many hardships in childhood, Cary always associated Ireland with "my dearest memories." His autobiographical novels, *Castle Corner* (o.p.) and *A House of Children* (o.p.), represent Cary's family life in County Clare up to the time of his own youth. He studied art for several years, but gave it up to enter Oxford. There, he first studied history but changed to law. Resolved to become a writer when he left Oxford, he was eager for adventure and went to the Balkan War of 1912–13.

Later, in Africa, Cary served with the Nigerian colonial service, and during World War I with the West African Frontier Force in campaigns in the Cameroons. Nearly killed when he was shot in the head, he returned to government service and was finally invalided out. Having had some success at writing and selling short stories, he settled in Oxford and devoted himself full time to his writing. But it was more than ten years before he published his first novel, and more than 20 before he attained financial security.

Aissa Saved (1932, o.p.) was the first of many books that established his reputation as a novelist of great vigor and imagination, a superb craftsman. Some of the early ones about Nigeria show his knowledge of Africa and his perception, compassion, and imaginative power. *Mr. Johnson* (1939, o.p.) is the most powerful of these. Among his later works is the marvelous *Horse's Mouth*, the portrait of a good artist who is also an outrageous one—perhaps his masterpiece, although the other books of that trilogy are also compelling. The Nimmo trilogy (1952–55, o.p.) treats British parliamentary politics through intensely clashing perspectives and values. Cary's genius in the trilogies and his other successful novels lies in a kind of ventriloquism, the ability to create and sustain extraordinary vital characters, each of whom tells his or her own story with remarkable intensity and sympathy.

BOOKS BY CARY

Herself Surprised. 1941. Amereon repr. of 1948 ed. 1976 lib. bdg. $16.95; Riverrun 1980 pap. $4.95. The first novel of the first trilogy; the second is *To Be a Pilgrim* (1942, o.p.).
The Horse's Mouth. 1944. Amereon $17.95; Harper 1965 pap. $3.80. The third novel of the first trilogy.
A Fearful Joy: A Novel. Greenwood repr. of 1949 ed. 1973 lib. bdg. $66.00
The Captive and the Free. 1959. Amereon $19.95

BOOKS ABOUT CARY

Fisher, Barbara. *Joyce Cary: The Writer and His Theme.* Humanities Pr. text ed. 1980 $29.00
O'Connor, William V. *Joyce Cary.* Columbia Univ. Pr. 1966 pap. $2.50. Good brief introduction.
Roby, Kinley E. *Joyce Cary.* Twayne's Eng. Authors Ser. G. K. Hall 1984 lib. bdg. $16.95
Soderskog, Ingvar. *Joyce Cary's "Hard Conceptual Labour": A Structural Analysis of "To Be a Pilgrim."* Humanities Pr. text ed. 1977 pap. $19.50
Wright, Andrew. *Joyce Cary: A Preface to His Novels.* Greenwood repr. of 1958 ed. 1972 lib. bdg. $18.75. Excellent early critical study.

COMPTON-BURNETT, DAME IVY. 1892–1969

All Compton-Burnett's many novels, which have been called "morality plays for the tough-minded," are satires of the "least attractive aspects of human nature as found among the nobility and landed gentry" of the late Victorian world. She writes with subtle brilliance—her melodramatic plots are developed almost exclusively in dialogue. *The Mighty and Their Fall*, centering on a late Victorian family of three generations living in a country house attended by four servants, "holds the reader fascinated by the analysis of character and suspense and—always—detection." "Here is a writer in whom intelligence is paramount; a moralist without a trace of sensationalism; a novelist difficult at first to read, who repays a hundredfold the effort she exacts." In 1956 she won the James Tait Black Memorial Award for Fiction for *Mother and Son*. In 1967 she was made a Dame Commander of the Order of the British Empire.

BOOKS BY COMPTON-BURNETT

Dolores. 1911. State Mutual Bk. 1981 $15.00
Pastors and Masters. 1925. David & Charles 1952 $12.95; Schocken 1984 pap. $5.95
Brothers and Sisters. 1930. David & Charles 1950 $14.95; Schocken pap. consult publisher for information.
More Women than Men. David & Charles 1933 $14.95; Schocken 1984 pap. $5.95
Daughters and Sons. David & Charles 1937 $14.95; Schocken 1984 pap. $5.95
A Family and a Fortune. David & Charles 1939 $14.95; *Penguin Modern Class. Ser.* 1983 pap. $4.95
Elders and Betters. David & Charles 1944 $14.95; Schocken 1984 pap. $5.95
Manservant and Maidservant. David & Charles 1947 $14.95; Oxford 1984 $5.95. Also published in the United States under the title *Bullivant and the Lambs.* AMS Pr. repr. of 1948 ed. $29.50

Two Worlds and Their Ways. David & Charles 1949 $14.95
The Present and the Past. David & Charles 1953 $12.95
Mother and Son. David & Charles 1955. $14.95
A Heritage and Its History. David & Charles 1959 $12.95
The Mighty and Their Fall. David & Charles 1961 $12.95
A God and His Gifts. David & Charles 1963 $12.95; *Penguin Modern Class. Ser.* 1983
    pap. $3.95

BOOKS ABOUT COMPTON-BURNETT

Liddell, Robert. *The Novels of I. Compton-Burnett.* Folcroft repr. of 1975 ed. lib. bdg.
    $20.00
Sprigge, Elizabeth. *The Life of Ivy Compton-Burnett.* Braziller 1973 $7.95
Spurling, Hilary. *Ivy: The Life of I. Compton-Burnett.* Knopf 1984 $22.95

DOUGLAS, NORMAN. 1868–1952

One of the "liveliest, wittiest, and most original authors of his generation," Douglas exerted a strong influence on modern writers of fantasy. He
had tried his "deft hand at music, diplomacy, linguistics and science (zool-
ogy, geology, and archeology) before he wrote, and sold in 1917 for a pid-
dling £75, the novel 'South Wind,' a perennially popular satiric classic that
made him famous.... Douglas first journeyed to Capri in 1888, on the
trail of a rare species of blue lizard, fell in love with the island and made it
his soul's operating base." There he died in penury in a borrowed villa.

The setting of *South Wind,* which fascinated many generations after 1917,
is an island, not unlike Capri, called Nepenthe, "inhabited by an extraordinary group of eccentrics who have, in various ways, succumbed to the local
atmosphere. By viewing most of the story through the eyes of an English
Bishop, Douglas emphasized his theme: the eternal contrast between Northern and Southern Europe" (*Cyclopedia of World Authors*). Many of Douglas's
nonfictional books have recently been reissued, including *Siren Land, Old
Calabria* (1915), *D. H. Lawrence and Maurice Magnus, Birds and Beasts of the
Greek Anthology, Good-Bye to Western Culture: Some Footnotes on East and
West* (1930), *London Street Games,* and *Looking Back.*

BOOKS BY DOUGLAS

South Wind. 1917. Dover repr. 1982 pap. $5.95; Penguin 1976 pap. $2.95; Scholarly
    repr. of 1931 ed. 1971 $39.00
In the Beginning. Scholarly repr. of 1927 ed. 1971 $39.00
Late Harvest. AMS Pr. repr. of 1946 ed. $16.00. Autobiographical.

BOOKS ABOUT DOUGLAS

Cunard, Nancy. *Grand Man: Memories of Norman Douglas.* Arden Lib. repr. of 1954
    ed. 1979 lib. bdg. $25.00; Telegraph Bks. repr. of 1954 ed. 1981 lib. bdg. $30.00
McDonald, Edward D. *A Bibliography of the Writings of Norman Douglas.* Folcroft
    repr. of 1927 ed. 1974 lib. bdg. $15.00
Stonehill, C. A. *Bibliography of the Writings of Norman Douglas.* Folcroft repr. of 1926
    ed. lib. bdg. $10.00
Tomlinson, H. *Norman Douglas. Eng. Biography Ser.* Folcroft repr. of 1931 ed. lib.
    bdg. $9.50; Haskell 1974 lib. bdg. $43.95

DRABBLE, MARGARET. 1939–

Margaret Drabble graduated from Cambridge, worked for a while as an actress, and then married Clive Swift (an actor). The plots of a number of her novels reflect situations in her own life. *A Summer Bird-Cage* (1963, o.p.) tells of two sisters: One, very bright, has recently graduated from Oxford, the other, very pretty, is about to marry. *The Garrick Year* (1964, o.p.) is based on her experiences in the theatrical world. The heroine of *The Needle's Eye* is a divorced woman with three children; her involvement with a lawyer leads to Jamesian subtleties as the moral and spiritual dilemmas of her characters are set forth.

Drabble herself has three children, and the central problem in a number of her books is one that has received a good deal of attention recently: the divided loyalties of a mother who seeks more than the simple joys of family life. Like those of a number of her contemporaries, Drabble's books are written in a traditional novelistic style, with an emphasis on the social and moral issues raised by the predicaments of her characters. She has edited some of JANE AUSTEN (whose writings have greatly influenced her own), as well as the most recent edition of the *Oxford Companion to English Literature*.

BOOKS BY DRABBLE

The Millstone. 1965. New Amer. Lib. (Plume) 1984 pap. $5.95
The Needle's Eye. Knopf 1972 $11.95
Realms of Gold. 1975. Bantam 1982 pap. $3.95
The Ice Age. 1978. New Amer. Lib. (Plume) 1985 $6.95
The Middle Ground. Knopf 1980 $10.95

DURRELL, LAWRENCE. 1912–

A prolific and protean writer since the early 1930s, Durrell has led a life as rich and varied as his writings. Born of Anglo-Irish parents in Himalayan India, Durrell attended school in England but has spent most of his life abroad. Along with numerous odd jobs, he has taught at the English Institute in Athens and at the Greek gymnasium on Cyprus; edited (along with HENRY MILLER) a witty and avant-garde magazine in Paris; founded and edited several poetry magazines; worked as press attaché in Egypt and Yugoslavia; and lectured for the British Council in Argentina. The popular success of *The Alexandria Quartet* has enabled him to live solely by writing ever since it was first published.

His first important work, *The Black Book* (1938, o.p.), was greeted by T. S. ELIOT as "the first piece of work by a new English writer to give me any hope for the future of prose fiction." In it, Durrell has said, "I first heard the sound of my own voice. . . . This is an experience no artist ever forgets." *A Chronicle of the English Death* (the book's original subtitle)—spiritual sterility embodied by smug, decadent, cold England—*The Black Book* heralds Durrell's emergence into Greece's warmth, color, and fecundity, the setting for much of his later work. Appropriately, *The Black Book* was unavailable until 1962 in the English-speaking world that it attacked.

Durrell's fiction includes two apprentice novels, *Pied Piper of Lovers* (o.p.) and *Panic Spring* (o.p.); a psychological mystery set on Crete, *The Dark Labyrinth; The Revolt of Aphrodite;* and *The Avignon Quintet. Aphrodite,* a not wholly successful satire of science fiction, Gothic, romantic, and business exposé novels, concerns a young inventor's misadventures with modern technology and love. He is constrained to create an exact "living" replica of a beautiful deceased Greek actress, but the machine—the perfect illusion— commits suicide rather than inhabit the world's harsh reality.

The subject of much controversy, *The Alexandria Quartet* is Durrell's major achievement. It is a self-reflexive novel of great structural complexity; a rich evocation of a cultural crossroads in a time of rapid change (a city "the most various and colorful I could remember"); a political and diplomatic thriller; an analysis of art and love from a myriad of angles; an education and a romance; a fairy tale that *ends* with "Once upon a time . . . ," and many other things—perhaps, above all, a work self-delighted with the rhythms and nuances of language.

Like *Aphrodite, The Avignon Quintet* shares the *Quartet*'s aesthetic and thematic concerns. One of its narrators tells us that a quincunx is a form bearing mystical meaning derived from the pattern of trees in "an ancient Greek temple grove"—one at each corner of a square and one at the center. The mysticism expresses ancient Gnostic beliefs and relates to the Knights Templar (about whom one of the characters is writing a history), who were destroyed in the early fourteenth century but supposedly left a vast treasure buried at the quincunx's center. All of the characters, who are less vividly conceived than their *Quartet* counterparts, seek some metaphysical treasure or another.

Durrell's other writings include three verse plays with ancient settings, a dozen books of poetry, including his *Collected Poems,* five island books (the best of which, *Bitter Lemons,* won the Duff Cooper Prize), and several collections of "Sketches from Diplomatic Life."

BOOKS BY DURRELL

Collected Poems. Viking 1980 $22.95

Prospero's Cell. 1945. Penguin 1978 pap. $3.95. About Corfu.

The Dark Labyrinth. 1947. Penguin 1978 pap. $3.95

Reflections on a Marine Venus: A Companion to the Landscape of Rhodes. 1953. Penguin 1978 pap. $3.95

Stiff Upper Lip. 1958. Dutton 1959 $3.50; Faber 1983 pap. $3.95

The Alexandria Quartet: Justine, Balthazar, Mountolive, Clea. 1957–60. Dutton 1961 pap. $19.50

Bitter Lemons. Dutton 1959 pap. $7.95. The narrative of his life in a small village on Cyprus as civil war erupts.

Sauve Qui Peut. 1966. Faber 1979 pap. $4.95

The Revolt of Aphrodite: Tunc. 1968. Penguin 1979 pap. $4.95

Spirit of Place: Letters and Essays on Travel. Ed. by Alan G. Thomas, Dutton 1971 $10.00. Eight reproductions of paintings by the author.

The Avignon Quintet: Monsieur, or the Prince of Darkness; Livia, or, Buried Alive; Con-

stance, or, Solitary Practices; Sebastian, or, Ruling Passions; Quinx, or, The Ripper's Tale. 1974–85. Penguin pap. ea. $5.95–$6.95; Viking ea. $12.95–$15.95
Sicilian Carousel. Penguin 1978 pap. $3.95; Viking 1977 $13.95
The Greek Islands. Penguin 1980 pap. $14.95; Viking 1978 $25.00
(and Alfred Perles). Art and Outrage: A Correspondence about Henry Miller. Porter 1982 pap. $16.50

Books about Durrell

Durrell, Gerald. My Family and Other Animals. Penguin 1977 pap. $3.95; Peter Smith 1983 $12.75. This delightful, sun-soaked account of the gifted and happily eccentric Durrell family's Mediterranean island sojourn is by Lawrence Durrell's brilliant naturalist brother. It provides amusing sidelights on Lawrence as he appeared to his family in younger days, as well as on Gerald's pets and other wildlife passions—and an assortment of human beings.
Fraser, G. S. Lawrence Durrell: A Critical Study. Dutton 1968 o.p.; Faber 1973 o.p.
Friedman, Alan W. Lawrence Durrell and the Alexandria Quartet: Art for Love's Sake. Univ. of Oklahoma Pr. 1970 $13.50
Pinchin, Jane L. Alexandria Still: Forster, Durrell and Carafy. Princeton Univ. Pr. 1976 $23.00
Weigel, John A. Lawrence Durrell. Dutton 1966 pap. $1.25; Twayne's Eng. Authors Ser. G. K. Hall 1965 lib. bdg. $12.95

FIRBANK, (ARTHUR ANNESLEY) RONALD. 1886–1926

Edmund Wilson called Firbank "one of the finest English writers of his period." Firbank lived the life of a leisured aesthete and died, still a young man, in Rome. His original and subtle novels have appealed to a small but appreciative audience, and in the 1950s and early 1960s he "posthumously acquired a band of devoted disciples." Firbank had a fine disdain for plot and a taste for eccentric characters. "All in all, a felicity, undisturbed by fugues and hints of nonfulfillment, reigns over his novels. There can be no doubt that Firbank has earned his niche of fame. . . . As literature goes, it is a small and creditable world, a true one, looking back at the reader with laughter and sorrow" (TLS). From Firbank descend elements in the work of Waugh, Compton-Burnett, Huxley, Angus Wilson, and Murdoch. The Complete Ronald Firbank, with a preface by Anthony Powell (1961), is, unfortunately, now out of print.

Books by Firbank

Five Novels. 1949. Intro. by O. Sitwell, New Directions 1981 pap. $8.95. Contains Valmouth, The Artificial Princess, The Flower beneath the Foot, The Prancing Nigger, and Cardinal Pirelli.
Valmouth. 1919. Biblio Dist. 1977 $10.00 pap. $6.75
The Prancing Nigger. 1924. Biblio Dist. 1977 pap. $6.75

Book about Firbank

Muir, Percival H. A Bibliography of the First Editions of Books by Arthur Annesley Ronald Firbank. Folcroft repr. of 1927 ed. lib. bdg. $10.00; Richard West repr. of 1927 ed. lib. bdg. $15.00

FORD, FORD MADOX (originally Ford Madox Hueffer). 1873–1939

Ford, who changed his German name legally in 1919, was a grandson of the painter Ford Madox Brown, who, together with his cousins the Rossettis, founded the Pre-Raphaelite Brotherhood. While helping JOSEPH CONRAD master English, Ford collaborated with him on *The Inheritors* (1901) and *The Nature of a Crime* (1924). Ford established the *English Review* in 1908. Among his distinguished contributors were Conrad, HARDY, Galsworthy, Masefield, and WILLIAM JAMES (see Vol. 4). In his *Transatlantic Review* (published in Paris, 1924) he "discovered" Joyce and Hemingway. His reminiscences, *Return to Yesterday*, are a valuable record of these editorial years; the volume was suppressed in England because it quotes King George V as threatening to abdicate the throne.

Ford's masterpiece is *The Good Soldier* (1915), a work that many critics number among the finest British novels of the century. This novel contains an outstanding example of what Ford and Conrad called *progression d'effet*, a technique for the chronological rearrangement of incidents in a story in order to provide the greatest emotional impact on the reader. Ford's *Parade's End* (1924–28), a tetralogy set primarily in England during World War I, is a major achievement on a grand scale. Even more than the war, Ford's concern in these novels is a study of the psychology and interrelationships of people going through violent change.

Ford's reputation was of slow growth, perhaps because of his association with so many of the great literary figures of his time. His *Portraits from Life* (1960, o.p.) contains memories and criticisms of HENRY JAMES, Conrad, Hardy, Wells, Lawrence, Galsworthy, and others. But as shown in some of the recent critical appraisals, Ford is now considered an innovator, a major twentieth-century novelist. He also wrote several volumes of literary criticism.

BOOKS BY FORD

Fifth Queen. Intro. by G. Greene, Vanguard 1963 $19.50. Contains *The Fifth Queen, Privy Seal, The Fifth Queen Crowned*—a trilogy based on the life of Catherine Howard.

Collected Poems. AMS Pr. repr. of 1914 ed. $21.00

The Good Soldier. Octagon repr. of 1951 ed. 1980 lib. bdg. $24.50; Random (Vintage) 1951 pap. $3.95. A "Tale of Passion" with an interpretation by Mark Schorer.

Thus to Revisit: Some Reminiscences. Octagon 1966 lib. bdg. $17.00

Parade's End. Knopf rev. ed. 1961 $18.95. The four novels of "The Tietjans Saga": *Some Do Not, No More Parades, A Man Could Stand Up, The Last Post.*

Return to Yesterday. Liveright repr. 1972 $12.95 pap. $7.95

The Rash Act. Century Bookbindery repr. of 1933 ed. 1982 lib. bdg. $35.00; Carcanet 1985 $14.95 pap. $8.50

It Was the Nightingale. Octagon 1972 lib. bdg. $29.00

No Enemy. Ecco Pr. repr. of 1929 ed. 1984 pap. $8.50

BOOKS ABOUT FORD

Cassell, Richard A. *Ford Madox Ford: A Study of His Novels.* Greenwood repr. of 1962 ed. 1977 lib. bdg. $24.75

Harvey, David D. *Ford Madox Ford, 1873–1939*. Gordian repr. of 1962 ed. text ed. 1972 $20.00
Leer, Norman. *Limited Hero in the Novels of Ford Madox Ford*. Michigan State Univ. Pr. 1966 $6.00
Lid, R. W. *Ford Madox Ford: The Essence of His Art*. Univ. of California Pr. 1964 $26.00
MacShane, Frank, ed. *Ford Madox Ford: The Critical Heritage*. Routledge & Kegan 1972 $29.95
Mizener, Arthur. *The Saddest Story: A Biography of Ford Madox Ford*. Carroll & Graf 1985 pap. $12.95
Moser, Thomas C. *The Life in the Fiction of Ford Madox Ford*. Princeton Univ. Pr. 1981 $35.00 pap. $15.00
Stang, Sondra J. *Ford Madox Ford*. Ungar 1977 $13.95

FORSTER, E(DWARD) M(ORGAN). 1879–1970

E. M. Forster is noted for "the easy grace and lucidity of his style; his humor, his good taste, the wise humanism of his outlook" (C. J. Rolo, *Atlantic*). His *Collected Tales* displays wit and irony in the use of fantasy, of which "The Celestial Omnibus" is a most delightful example. His most popular book, *A Passage to India*, won both the James Tait Black and the Femina-Vie Heureuse prizes. It is a brilliant, discerning study of the British-Indian dilemma well before the days of Indian independence. The play *A Passage to India* opened in London in 1960 and on Broadway in 1962. It was made into a movie in 1984.

Howards End, another very fine novel, deals with the problems of the changing English class structure. *Maurice*, about homosexual love, was suppressed during the author's lifetime and published posthumously in 1972. Forster's last three novels are serious and deal with important social problems. His earlier novels often have similar concerns but are less successful. The best of these is *A Room with a View*, which contrasts English gravity and Italian lightheartedness; the book is warm, witty, and sensitive.

His most important critical work is *Aspects of the Novel* (1927), long considered a classic on the art of fiction. *Two Cheers for Democracy* (1951) is divided into two parts, "The Second Darkness" (political reflections) and "What I Believe" (his faith in the arts and personal relationships). *Abinger Harvest* (1936) is "one of the most notable miscellanies of our time" (John Crowe Ransom, *Yale Review*)—a collection of articles, essays, reviews, and poems. In 1953 Forster received high recognition for his work from the queen—the Order of Companion of Honor. Until his death in 1970 he lived quietly in a small apartment in King's College, Cambridge, where he was an Honorary Fellow.

BOOKS BY FORSTER

Collected Tales of E. M. Forster. Knopf 1974 $14.95
The Abinger Edition of E. M. Forster. Ed. by Oliver Stallybrass, Harcourt 9 vols. 1978–83 ea. $17.75–$125.00
The Eternal Moment and Other Stories. Harcourt repr. of 1928 ed. 1970 pap. $3.95

The Life to Come and Other Stories. Avon 1976 pap. $2.95; intro. by Oliver Stally-
    brass, Norton 1973 $7.95
Where Angels Fear to Tread. 1905. Ed. by Oliver Stallybrass, Holmes & Meier text ed.
    1978 $29.50; Lightyear repr. 1981 lib. bdg. $14.95; Random 1958 pap. $2.95
The Longest Journey. 1907. Ed. by Elizabeth Heine, Holmes & Meier 1985 $69.50;
    Knopf 1922 $3.95; Random (Vintage) 1962 pap. $3.95
A Room with a View. 1908. Ed. by Oliver Stallybrass, Holmes & Meier text ed. 1978
    $24.50; Random (Vintage) 1961 pap. $3.95
Howards End. 1910. Buccaneer Bks. repr. 1981 lib. bdg. $17.95; ed. by Oliver Stally-
    brass, Holmes & Meier text ed. 1978 $29.50; Random (Vintage) 1954 pap. $3.95
A Passage to India. 1924. Buccaneer Bks repr. 1981 lib. bdg. $16.95; Harcourt 1985
    pap. $5.95; ed. by Oliver Stallybrass, Holmes & Meier text ed. 1978 $64.50;
    Lightyear repr. 1981 lib. bdg. $14.95
Maurice. Norton 1981 pap. $6.95

BOOKS ABOUT FORSTER

Brander, Laurence. *E. M. Forster: A Critical Study.* Beekman 1979 $16.95 pap. $9.95;
    Bucknell Univ. Pr. $10.00; Humanities Pr. text ed. 1968 $7.50
Colmer, John. *E. M. Forster: The Personal Voice.* Routledge & Kegan 1981 $21.00
    1983 pap. $8.95
Das, G. K. *E. M. Forster's India.* Rowman 1978 $16.50
Finkelstein, Bonnie B. *Forster's Women: Eternal Differences.* Columbia Univ. Pr. 1975
    $18.00
Gardner, Philip, ed. *E. M. Forster: The Critical Heritage.* Routledge & Kegan 1973
    $38.50 1984 pap. $15.00
Kelvin, Norman. *E. M. Forster.* Pref. by Harry T. Moore, *Crosscurrents Modern Cri-
    tiques Ser.* Southern Illinois Univ. Pr. 1967 $7.95. Forster viewed as novelist,
    critic, and historian.
Macaulay, Rose. *The Writings of E. M. Forster.* Folcroft repr. of 1938 ed. 1974 lib.
    bdg. $20.00
Martin, J. S. *E. M. Forster, the Endless Journey.* Cambridge Univ. Pr. 1976 $29.95
    pap. $9.95
Martin, Richard. *The Love That Failed: Ideal and Reality in the Writings of E. M. For-
    ster.* Mouton text ed. 1974 $24.00
McDowell, Frederick P. *E. M. Forster. Twayne's Eng. Authors Ser.* G. K. Hall rev. ed.
    1982 lib. bdg. $12.95
———, ed. *E. M. Forster: An Annotated Bibliography of Writings about Him.* Northern
    Illinois Univ. Pr. 1976 $30.00
Scott, P. J. *E. M. Forster: Our Permanent Contemporary.* Barnes & Noble text ed. 1983
    $28.50
Shusterman, David. *Quest for Certitude in E. M. Forster's Fiction.* Haskell repr. of
    1965 ed. 1972 lib. bdg. $49.95
Stone, Wilfred. *The Cave and the Mountain: A Study of E. M. Forster.* Stanford Univ.
    Pr. 1966 $30.00. Excellent discussion of Forster's career and analysis of his
    work.
Trilling, Lionel. *E. M. Forster.* New Directions rev. ed. 1964 pap. $5.95

FOWLES, JOHN. 1926–

John Fowles's first novel, *The Collector* (1963), is about a lower-class
young man who wins a lottery and thus is able to afford the expenses of act-

ing out a fantasy: He abducts a pretty, talented girl he has admired from afar. Fowles is good at maintaining suspense and in providing realistic details of the kidnapping; but his understandable distaste for the demented protagonist limits the psychological depth of his characterizations. In *The Magus*, as in *The Collector*, Fowles is concerned with the issues of enslavement, moral responsibility and perspective, and psychological aberration.

The French Lieutenant's Woman (1969), perhaps Fowles's best-known book because of the excellent movie made from it, takes place in Lyme Regis, the small seacoast village where he makes his home. The time setting and plot of the novel are old-fashioned: a story about a betrayed woman who lived one hundred years ago. But this is much more than the remake of a Victorian novel; Fowles's narrator often reminds the reader that he lives in the twentieth century—anachronisms, philosophical speculations, parodies, and literary allusions are all used to provide a very modern effect. The novel is that rare beast, a work that utilizes unconventional techniques and still manages to get onto the bestseller lists. *The Aristos* is an essay in which Fowles sets forth the ideas that concern him most; prominent among these is his elevation of an ideal of excellence, which, he says, should always be at the core of an artist's motivating instinct. Those who can achieve only mediocrity despise excellence: It intimidates them. The artist's struggle, therefore, is not only to achieve excellence in his own works but to resist damaging or envious criticism from his inferiors. Fowles, who has published a collection of poems written over the course of 20 years, has said that he considers poetry a relief after the rigors of writing fiction.

Books by Fowles

The Collector. Dell 1975 pap. $3.95; Little, Brown 1963 $15.45

The Aristos. 1964. Little, Brown rev. ed. 1970 $14.45; New Amer. Lib. (Plume) 1975 pap. $5.95

The Magus. 1966. Dell 1985 pap. $4.95; Little, Brown rev. ed. 1978 $12.95

The French Lieutenant's Woman. Little, Brown 1969 $14.95; New Amer. Lib. (Signet Class.) pap. 1981 $3.50

The Ebony Tower. Little, Brown 1974 $12.95; New Amer. Lib. (Signet Class.) 1975 pap. $3.95

Daniel Martin. Little, Brown 1977 $15.00; New Amer. Lib. (Signet Class.) 1978 pap. $4.50

Islands. Little, Brown 1979 $10.95

Shipwreck. Little, Brown 1983 pap. $9.70; Merrimack 1979 $8.95

The Tree. Ecco Pr. 1983 $13.50 pap. $7.95; Little, Brown 1980 $24.95

Mantissa. Little, Brown 1982 $13.95; New Amer. Lib. (Plume) 1983 pap. $6.95

Books about Fowles

Fawkner, H. W. *Timescapes of John Fowles*. Fairleigh Dickinson Univ. Pr. 1983 $19.50

Olshen, Barry N., and Toni A. Olshen. *John Fowles: A Reference Guide*. G. K. Hall 1980 lib. bdg. $17.00

Wolf, Peter. *John Fowles, Magus and Moralist*. Bucknell Univ. Pr. 2d ed. 1979 $18.00

Woodcock, Bruce. *Male Mythologies: John Fowles and Masculinity*. Barnes & Noble 1984 $23.95. Focuses on Fowles's use of gender roles.

GALSWORTHY, JOHN. 1867–1933 (NOBEL PRIZE 1932)

Galsworthy wrote novels and plays alternately throughout his life. His master work, *The Forsyte Saga*, begun in 1906 and finished in 1928 and consisting of six separate novels and two linking interludes, is the most famous example of the sequence novel in English literature. It is a study of the property sense, the possessive spirit, in different individuals and generations of English middle-class society. His later years brought him many honors, including the presidency of P.E.N. and honorary degrees from Oxford, Cambridge, and several other universities. After World War I he was offered a knighthood, which he refused. He did, however, accept the Order of Merit in 1929, and in 1932 he was awarded the Nobel Prize.

Though his posthumous reputation had waned, the centenary of his death in 1967 brought a re-creation of *The Forsyte Saga* on British and American television in serial form. Interest in him skyrocketed, and the Forsyte novels again became bestsellers. With new popularity came fresh critical analysis. Pamela Hansford Johnson called *The Forsyte Saga* "a work of profound social insight and patchy psychological insight" (*N.Y. Times*). His critical writings include *The Inn of Tranquility: Studies and Essays* and *Author and Critic*. (See also Volume 2, Chapter 4.)

BOOKS BY GALSWORTHY

Letters from John Galsworthy 1900–1932. Ed. by Edward Garnett, Scholarly 1971 $39.00

Jocelyn. Greenwood repr. of 1898 ed. 1971 lib. bdg. $18.75; Holt 1977 $6.95; Scholarly repr. of 1898 ed. $13.00

The Forsyte Saga. 1906–21. Buccaneer Bks. 1983 lib. bdg. $32.95; Scribner 1933 $25.00 pap. $12.95. Contains *The Man of Property, In Chancery,* and *To Let.*

Motley. Scholarly repr. of 1910 ed. $21.00

Dark Flower. 1913. Scholarly repr. of 1923 ed. 1971 $39.00

Five Tales. 1915. Scholarly repr. of 1918 ed. 1971 $39.00

Captures. Scholarly repr. of 1923 ed. 1971 $12.00

Fraternity. Scholarly repr. of 1923 ed. 1971 $59.00

Strife. Methuen 1974 $3.95

BOOKS ABOUT GALSWORTHY

Barker, Dudley. *Man of Principle: A Biography of John Galsworthy.* Stein & Day 1970 pap. $4.95

Bellamy, William. *The Novels of Wells, Bennett and Galsworthy, 1890–1910.* Routledge & Kegan 1971 $19.95

Croman, Natalie. *John Galsworthy: A Study in Continuity and Contrast.* Folcroft repr. of 1933 ed. lib. bdg. $15.00

Gindin, James. *The English Climate: An Excursion into a Biography of John Galsworthy.* Univ. of Michigan Pr. 1979 lib. bdg. $12.00

Marrot, Harold V. *Bibliography of the Works of John Galsworthy.* Burt Franklin repr. of 1928 ed. $20.50; Folcroft repr. of 1928 ed. lib. bdg. $32.50

——. *Life and Letters of John Galsworthy.* Kelley repr. of 1936 ed. $47.50

Smit, J. Henry. *Short Stories of John Galsworthy.* Haskell repr. 1969 lib. bdg. $49.95; Richard West $8.75

Stevens, Earl E., and Ray H. Stevens, eds. *John Galsworthy: An Annotated Bibliography of Writings about Him.* Northern Illinois Univ. Pr. 1980 $30.00

GOLDING, WILLIAM (GERALD). 1911– (NOBEL PRIZE 1983)

Born in Cornwall and brought up as a scientist, Golding changed to English literature after two years at Oxford. Interested in classical Greek and archaeology, he says his literary influences have been Euripides and the anonymous Anglo-Saxon author of *The Battle of Maldon*. E. M. Forster called *Lord of the Flies* "the outstanding novel of the year" (1954). In the United States it got off to a slow start, however, until the paperback edition of 1959 led to its popularity among college students. Golding himself describes its theme as "an attempt to trace the defects of human nature. The moral is that the shape of a society must depend on the ethical nature of the individual and not on any political system however logical or respectable" (Introduction). It became a runaway bestseller and was made into a film.

Other novels include *The Inheritors*, which tells the story of innocent Neanderthal man's defeat and supersession by Homo sapiens; *Free Fall*, an artist's autobiographical reminiscent search for the mechanism of transition from the relatively guiltless sins of his free childhood to those of his unfree adult life; *The Spire*, in which Golding recreates the story behind the building of a great English cathedral, which might have been Salisbury; and *The Pyramid*, a lighthearted comedy of manners. *The Hot Gates and Other Occasional Pieces* consists of 20 brief essays (two are autobiographical). Among the most interesting is "Fable" in which he tells how the war transformed him into a moralist and how he came to write *Lord of the Flies*.

In 1940, Golding joined the Royal Navy and spent five years in command of a rocket ship. In 1961–62 he was a visiting professor at Hollins College in Virginia and lectured at American colleges and universities. He won the Nobel Prize for Literature in 1983.

BOOKS BY GOLDING

Lord of the Flies. 1954. Amereon $13.95; Putnam 1962 $16.95
The Inheritors. 1955. Harcourt 1963 pap. $3.95; Washington Square Pr. 1981 pap. $3.95
Pincher Martin (The Two Deaths of Christopher Martin). Harcourt repr. of 1957 ed. 1968 pap. $3.95
Free Fall. 1959. Harcourt 1962 pap. $3.95
The Spire. 1964. Harcourt 1965 pap. $3.95
The Pyramid. 1967. Harcourt 1981 pap. $3.95
The Brass Butterfly. Faber 1969 pap. $4.95
The Scorpion God: Three Short Novels. 1971. Harcourt 1984 pap. $3.95. Includes *The Scorpion God, Clonk, Clonk,* and *Envoy Extraordinary*.
Darkness Visible. Bantam 1981 pap. $3.95; Farrar 1979 $14.95; Harcourt 1985 pap. $5.95
Rites of Passage. Farrar 1980 $14.95
A Moving Target. Farrar 1984 $14.95 pap. $7.95
The Paper Men. Farrar 1984 $15.95; Harcourt 1985 pap. $5.95

BOOKS ABOUT GOLDING

Baker, James R., and Arthur B. Siegler, Jr., eds. *Lord of the Flies: Text, Notes and Criticism.* Putnam text ed. 1964 pap. $4.95. Many valuable essays.

Biles, Jack I., and Robert O. Evans, eds. *William Golding: Some Critical Considerations.* Univ. Pr. of Kentucky 1978 $27.00

Dick, Bernard F. *William Golding. Twayne's Eng. Authors Ser.* G. K. Hall 1968 lib. bdg. $12.50

Johnston, Arnold. *Of Earth and Darkness: The Novels of William Golding.* Univ. of Missouri Pr. text ed. 1980 $15.00

Tiger, Virginia. *William Golding: The Dark Fields of Discovery.* M. Boyars 1978 pap. $7.95

GRAVES, ROBERT. 1895–1985

[SEE Chapter 7 in this volume.]

GREEN, HENRY (pseud. of Henry Vincent Yorke). 1905–1974

ELIZABETH BOWEN called Henry Green "one of the novelists most to be reckoned with today," and W. H. AUDEN, "the best English novelist alive." Green's "subtly designed" novels, with their one-word titles, are what he calls "an advanced attempt to break up the old-fashioned type of novel." He does not describe his characters, but "has made pioneer explorations of all the ways in which they can describe themselves." "Anything which has a voice is invited to use it," he explains, "but, the reader is left to supply the shapes and colors out of his own head." This oblique method and a fondness for symbols make his novels difficult for readers who expect straight plot and action, but fascinating to others. He has described his background in the autobiographical *Pack My Bag* (1952), his only book of nonfiction. Among his best-known novels are *Living* and *Back.*

BOOKS BY GREEN

Living. Scholarly repr. of 1929 ed. 1971 $39.00

Back. New Directions repr. of 1946 ed. 1981 pap. $5.95

Nothing. Kelley repr. of 1950 ed. $19.50

Blindness. Viking 1978 $11.95

Concluding. Kelley repr. of 1950 ed. $19.50; fwd. by Eudora Welty, Univ. of Chicago Pr. 1961 pap. $7.95 1978 pap. $6.95

Party Going. Kelley repr. of 1951 ed. $19.50

Doting. Kelley repr. of 1952 ed. $19.50

Nothing, Doting, Blindness. Penguin 1980 pap. $6.95

BOOKS ABOUT GREEN

Bassoff, Bruce. *Toward Loving: The Poetics of the Novel and the Practice of Henry Green.* Univ. of South Carolina Pr. 1975 lib. bdg. $14.95

Odom, Keith C. *Henry Green. Twayne's Eng. Authors Ser.* G. K. Hall 1978 lib. bdg. $15.95

Weatherhead, A. Kingsley. *A Reading of Henry Green.* Univ. of Washington Pr. 1961 $20.00

GREENE, (HENRY) GRAHAM. 1904–

A convert to Catholicism, Graham Greene is "primarily and passionately concerned with good and evil," with God in a fallen world of frail mortals. Greene's characters always fall short of the standards by which they are being judged, but their anguish earns them great sympathy.

He has spent periods on the staff of the London *Times* and the *Spectator*. In World War II he served at the Foreign Office, with special duties in West Africa. *The Man Within* (1939), his first published novel, was not a success here. He wrote several thrillers, which he calls "entertainments," but *The Power and the Glory* and *The Heart of the Matter* (1948), considered his two finest novels, convinced critics of his serious intent, subtle characterization, and accomplished craftsmanship.

Greene names as two great influences on his writing John Buchan, a master of the spy thriller, and the Catholic novelist François Mauriac. Greene's work follows this split character, from those sinister spy-chase tales to works of serious moral and religious reflection. A number of his novels and short stories have been made into successful films, and two of his plays, *The Living Room* (1954, o.p.) and *The Potting Shed* (1957, o.p.), were produced on Broadway. *Carving a Statue* (o.p.), which played off-Broadway in 1968, had its premiere in London in 1964. His 1967 film adaptation of *The Comedians*, a bestselling novel set in contemporary Haiti under the terror-ridden dictatorship of President François Duvalier, drew protest from the Haitian government upon its release here. In 1952 Greene received the Catholic Literary Award for *The End of the Affair*, a powerful study of love and religion. His nonfictional writings include *The Lost Childhood and Other Essays*, an excellent critical collection, mostly on contemporaries.

BOOKS BY GREENE

Twenty-one Stories. Penguin 1981 pap. $3.95. Three stories added and one withdrawn from *Nineteen Stories* (o.p.) form this collection.
The Portable Graham Greene. Ed. by Philip Stratford, Penguin 1977 pap. $7.95. A cross section, chosen with the collaboration of the author.
Collected Stories. Viking 1973 $16.95
Collected Essays. Penguin 1981 pap. $4.95; Viking 1969 $20.95
The Man Within. Penguin 1982 pap. $3.95; Viking 1981 $14.95
It's a Battlefield. 1934. Penguin 1977 pap. $3.95; Viking 1982 $17.95
The Bear Fell Free. Folcroft repr. of 1935 ed. lib. bdg. $17.50
Brighton Rock: An Entertainment. 1938. Penguin 1977 pap. $3.95; Viking 1938 $14.95
The Power and the Glory (The Labyrinthine Ways). 1946. Amereon $17.95; Viking 1981 $16.95
The Heart of the Matter. Amereon $16.95; Penguin 1978 pap. $3.95; Viking 1948 $14.95
The End of the Affair. Penguin 1977 pap. $4.95; Viking 1951 $16.95
The Quiet American. 1956. Amereon $15.95; Penguin 1977 pap. $3.95; Viking 1982 $16.95
Our Man in Havana: An Entertainment. 1958. Penguin 1979 pap. $3.95; Pocket Bks. 1974 pap. $1.25; Viking 1981 $14.95
A Burnt-Out Case. 1961. Penguin 1977 pap. $3.95

Journey without Maps. 1961. Penguin 1978 pap. $3.95; Viking 1983 $20.95

The Comedians. Penguin 1976 pap. $3.95; Viking 1966 $14.95

Travels with My Aunt. Penguin 1977 pap. $3.95; Viking 1970 $14.95

A Sort of Life. 1971. Simon & Schuster (Touchstone Bks.) 1978 pap. $3.95; Washington Square Pr. 1982 pap. $2.95

In Search of a Character: Two African Journals. 1961. Penguin 1981 pap. $3.95. After he had conceived the theme of *A Burnt-Out Case* he traveled in the Belgian Congo in February 1959 to gather "an authentic medical background." Although the journals were not kept for publication, they are interesting "as an indication of the kind of raw material a novelist accumulates." The brief notes and his footnotes, showing what Greene did and did not retain for his novel, are especially interesting.

The Human Factor. Avon 1978 pap. $3.95; Simon & Schuster 1978 $10.95; Viking 1983 $20.95

May We Borrow Your Husband: And Other Comedies of the Sexual Life. Penguin 1978 pap. $3.95

Another Mexico. 1981. Viking 1982 $16.95

The Confidential Agent. Penguin 1981 pap. $3.95; Viking 1982 $17.95

Dr. Fisher of Geneva or the Bomb Party. Avon 1981 pap. $2.50

A Gun for Sale. Penguin 1982 pap. $3.95

Orient Express. Viking 1982 $16.95

Ways of Escape. Simon & Schuster 1981 $13.95; Washington Square Pr. 1982 pap. $3.95

The Honorary Consuling. Pocket Bks. 1983 pap. o.p.

Monsignor Quixote. Simon & Schuster 1982 $12.95 deluxe $75.00 (o.p.)

Getting to Know the General: The Story of an Involvement. Simon & Schuster 1984 $14.95

BOOKS ABOUT GREENE

Atkins, John. *Graham Greene.* Arden Lib. repr. of 1957 ed. 1979 lib. bdg. $35.00; Humanities Pr. rev. ed. text ed. 1970 $16.50; Richard West repr. 1980 lib. bdg. $30.00; Riverrun 1982 $14.95. Readable, "accurate, scrupulous and just" (*Spectator*).

Kunkel, Francis L. *The Labryinthine Ways of Graham Greene: A Critical Study.* Appel repr. of 1960 ed. 2d ed. enl. $12.00

Miller, Robert H. *Graham Greene: A Descriptive Catalog.* Univ. Pr. of Kentucky 1979 $13.00

Stratford, Philip. *Faith and Fiction: Creative Process in Greene and Mauriac.* Univ. of Notre Dame Pr. 1964 pap. $9.95. This thorough examination of the works of Greene and Mauriac deals comprehensively with all their novels, emphasizing aspects that are mutually illuminating and illustrative of their main differences.

Vann, J. Don. *Graham Greene: A Checklist of Criticism.* Kent State Univ. Pr. 1970 $10.00

Wolfe, Peter. *Graham Greene the Entertainer.* Crosscurrents Modern Critiques Ser. Southern Illinois Univ. Pr. 1972 $11.95

HARTLEY, L(ESLIE) P(OLES). 1895–1972

Novelist, short-story writer, and literary critic, L. P. Hartley won the James Tait Black Memorial Prize in 1947 for *Eustace and Hilda.* Part of a trilogy that offers a penetrating and disturbing psychological study of what

Hartley called "sisteritis" in an upper-middle-class family, the three books were described by the London *Times* as "unique in modern writing . . . diverting and disturbing. Beneath a surface 'almost overcivilized' the reviewer found 'a hollow of horror.' " One of Hartley's special interests is Henry James, to whom he has been compared.

In *The Tragic Comedians*, James Hall devotes a chapter to Hartley, who is respected but not popular in England, read by few in America, but praised by discerning critics in both countries: "Along with Green and Powell, Hartley has changed the direction of the comic novel, raising even more seriously than they the question of whether it remains comic at all. . . . His freshness consists at first in simply changing the patterns of the naturalist novel from social insights to emotional ones; yet in doing so he departs from both the older solid way of conceiving character and the more recent fluid way of conceiving consciousness." David Cecil called *The Go-Between* "impressive," and wrote: "Hartley is for me the first of living novelists in certain important respects; beauty of style, lyrical quality of feeling and, above all, the power and originality of his imagination, which wonderfully mingles ironic comedy, whimsical fancy and a mysterious Hawthorne-like poetry." *The Novelist's Responsibility* is a collection of essays and letters.

BOOKS BY HARTLEY

Eustace and Hilda. Stein & Day 1985 $18.95
The Go-Between. Dufour repr. of 1953 ed. 1978 $16.95: Stein & Day 1980 pap. $7.95
Hireling. Dufour repr. of 1957 ed. 1973 $15.95

BOOK ABOUT HARTLEY

Schardt, Alois J., and others. *Feininger-Hartley.* Ayer repr. of 1944 ed. $14.00

HUGHES, RICHARD (ARTHUR WARREN). 1900–1976

Welsh by birth and descent, Richard Hughes had a varied university life at Oxford—on vacations he tramped, begged, acted as a pavement artist, and once led an expedition through Central Europe on some obscure mission that involved political intrigue. As an undergraduate he wrote *The Sisters' Tragedy*, which George Bernard Shaw called "the finest one-act play ever written." Drama was his first effort—which he then abandoned for fiction.

A High Wind in Jamaica, a modern classic, is an extraordinary tale about the casual cruelty in children—captured, in this case, by softhearted pirates. *In Hazard*, the vivid description of sailors battling a crippling storm, although "ostensibly a sea story, is in reality a terrifying allegory of the British Empire at this crisis of its existence." The story of a young Englishman's visit to his cousin's home near Munich in 1923, the year of Hitler's aborted beer-hall "putsch," *The Fox in the Attic* is a novel of extraordinary brilliance. It was the first volume of a projected series, *The Human Predicament*, which the author describes as a long historical novel of his own times, culminating in World War II. The second volume of the series, *The Wooden Shepherdess* (1972, o.p.), was less successful. Hughes worked as a civilian for the Admiralty during World War II and later collaborated on its official history. An unpredictable writer, he "preserves the devastating innocence of the child reflected through a highly sophisticated mature intellect." "Hughes is inspired as Tolstoy was by the compulsion to create. Everything that he touches comes to life in a gusty, laughing, tender, tragic interpretation of the weird contradictions that jostle each other so pitifully in the human heart" (SR). His nonfiction works include *Theology and the Cain Complex* and *Fiction as Truth: Selected Literary Writings by Richard Hughes.*

BOOKS BY HUGHES

The Sisters' Tragedy. 1924. Branden pap. $4.00
A High Wind in Jamaica or The Innocent Voyage. 1929. Amereon $13.95; Harper 1972
    pap. $2.84
In Hazard: A Novel. 1938. Peter Smith $11.75
The Fox in the Attic. Harper 1962 $10.00. The first volume of the series *The Human
    Predicament.*
In the Lap of Atlas: Stories of Morocco. Merrimack 1980 $13.95

HUXLEY, ALDOUS. 1894–1963

Aldous Huxley was a grandson of the great Darwinian apostle, Thomas Huxley. He was a graduate of Eton and of Oxford and had a reputation for the wit and the wide, curious learning that he packed into his books. Vincent Spalding thought him enormously cultured but not a great novelist because he was not a storyteller; indeed, he produced fewer novels than books of nonfiction. While he is always interesting and engages our intelligence, Huxley seldom touches our emotions. Differentiating his characters by their views and opinions, he wrote novels of ideas, abounding in passages of moralizing and of nonnarrative matter. Huxley was a very influential writer, at once the satirist and the fascinated chronicler of the hedonism of the 1920s. *Brave New World* (1932), his avid, but entertaining—and in some respects prophetic—vision of the mechanized near future, became the classic satire on technology carried to extremes.

In *Literature and Science,* his forty-fifth and last book, he "is more concerned with the use that Literature can make of Science, and the proper attitude of a man of letters towards Science, than with what a scientist might derive from Literature or how Science might recognize, assimilate, and employ the realities proper to Literature." He believed that it was necessary to connect the worlds of science and art.

After immigrating to California in 1937, he became involved with the techniques of mysticism, and the possibilities of reaching "reality" through the drug mescaline were explored in some of his writings.

Huxley received the Award of Merit Medal (1959) from the American Academy of Arts and Letters. In 1962 he was elected a Companion of Literature of the British Royal Society of Literature, one of the highest literary awards in Britain (restricted to ten).

BOOKS BY HUXLEY

World of Aldous Huxley. Ed. by C. J. Rollo, Peter Smith $11.25. An omnibus collection of fiction and nonfiction covering three decades.
Crome Yellow. Harper repr. of 1922 ed. 1974 pap. $1.75
Antic Hay. 1923. Harper 1983 pap. $6.68
Point Counter Point. 1928. Harper 1965 pap. $3.37
Brave New World. Buccaneer Bks. repr. 1982 lib. bdg. $16.95; Harper 1932 $12.45 pap. $5.72
Beyond the Mexique Bay. Academy Chicago 1985 pap. $5.95; Greenwood repr. of 1934 ed. 1975 lib. bdg. $22.50
Eyeless in Gaza. Amereon repr. lib. bdg. $23.95; Harper repr. of 1936 ed. 1974 pap. $2.25
After Many a Summer Dies the Swan. 1939. Amereon repr. lib. bdg. $18.95; Harper 1983 pap. $4.76
Brave New World Revisited. 1958. Harper 1965 pap. $2.84
Island: A Utopian Novel. 1962. Harper 1973 lib. bdg. $8.97. A sequel and alternative to *Brave New World.*

BOOKS ABOUT HUXLEY

Birnbaum, Milton. *Aldous Huxley's Quest for Values.* Lib. of the Social Sciences 1971 $17.50; Univ. of Tennessee Pr. 1971 $14.50
Cockshott, Gerald. *Music and Nature: A Study of Aldous Huxley.* Humanities Pr. text ed. 1980 pap. $39.50
Ferns, C. S. *Aldous Huxley: Novelist.* Longwood Pr. 1980 $36.50
Greenblatt, Stephen J. *Three Modern Satirists: Waugh, Orwell and Huxley.* Yale Univ. Pr. 1965 $10.50
Holmes, Charles M. *Aldous Huxley and the Way to Reality.* Greenwood repr. of 1970 ed. 1978 lib. bdg. $27.50
Huxley, Laura. *This Timeless Moment: A Personal View of Aldous Huxley.* Celestial Arts 1975 pap. $4.95. Mrs. Huxley's memoir of his last years.
Kuehn, Robert E., ed. *Aldous Huxley: A Collection of Critical Essays. Twentieth-Century Views Ser.* Prentice-Hall (Spectrum Bks.) 1974 $12.95
Thody, Philip. *Huxley: A Biographical Introduction.* Scribner 1973 $5.95
Watt, Donald, ed. *Aldous Huxley: The Critical Heritage.* Routledge & Kegan 1975 $30.00
Woodcock, George. *Dawn and the Darkest Hour: A Study of Aldous Huxley.* Faber 1972 $9.95

ISHERWOOD, CHRISTOPHER. 1904–1986

Isherwood met W. H. AUDEN at an English boarding school. They collaborated on three fantasy verse-plays. In 1938 the two went to China together, financed by their publishers. *Journey to a War* (1939, o.p.) is their diary, kept alternately. In 1939 they came to the United States, intending to become permanent residents. In 1946 Isherwood became a U.S. citizen and in 1949 he was elected a member of the National Institute of Arts and Letters.

His excellent brief novels, largely autobiographical, are written with precision. He is still best known for the brilliance of his Berlin stories, written before World War II. He spent about four years in Germany; the eccentrics of *The Berlin Stories* (1946) symbolize the decadence of pre-Nazi Berlin. John

Van Druten adapted his successful play, *I Am a Camera* (1951), from these stories. Its 1966 musical version, *Cabaret*, won the N.Y. Drama Critics Circle Award and a Tony.

"Hinduism and homosexuality have long been favorite themes of Christopher Isherwood. [*A Meeting by the River*] combines them in a short novel, composed entirely of letters and diaries, that is rather old-fashioned in form but distinctly up-to-date in its descriptions of post-British India and post-Genet California" (*N.Y. Times*). The book, says Stanley Kauffmann (*New Republic*), "is credible, moving, and ultimately ironic. [Its] considerable work is accomplished with beautifully spare means, seemingly easy but possible only to an artist who has always been good and who has lost no refinement." *A Single Man* (1964), on the theme of homosexual love, portrays a college professor distraught over the death of his male lover.

In California, he wrote movie scripts and, with Huxley, became interested in the ancient Indian philosophy of the Vedas. With Swami Prabhavanda, he translated from the Sanskrit, in prose and poetry, the Mahabharata Bhagavadgita, *The Song of God*, with an introduction by Aldous Huxley. He edited a number of books on Vedanta and Yoga. *Exhumations* (o.p.) contains poems, articles, essays, and stories.

BOOKS BY ISHERWOOD

The Berlin Stories. Bentley repr. of 1946 ed. 1979 lib. bdg. $15.00; New Directions repr. of 1954 ed. pap. $6.95
The Memorial: Portrait of a Family. Avon 1977 pap. $2.75; Greenwood repr. of 1946 ed. lib. bdg. $15.00; Irvington repr. of 1946 ed. lib. bdg. $13.00
All the Conspirators. 1928. New Directions 1979 pap. $6.95
A Meeting by the River. 1967. Avon 1978 pap. $1.95
Christopher and His Kind. Avon 1977 pap. $3.95; Farrar 1976 $10.00
Down There on a Visit. Avon 1978 pap. $2.75
Prater Violet. Avon 1978 pap. $2.75
A Single Man. Avon 1978 pap. $2.95
People One Ought to Know. Fwd. by Andre Mangeot, Doubleday 1982 $12.95
October. Twelvetrees Pr. 1983 pap. $15.00

BOOKS ABOUT ISHERWOOD

Finney, Brian. *Christopher Isherwood: A Critical Biography.* Oxford 1979 $22.50
Funk, Robert W. *Christopher Isherwood: A Reference Guide.* G. K. Hall 1979 lib. bdg. $27.50
Piazza, Paul. *Christopher Isherwood: Myth and Anti-Myth.* Columbia Univ. Pr. 1978 $21.00
Spender, Stephen. *Letters to Christopher: Stephen Spender's Letters to Christopher Isherwood, 1929–1939.* Ed. by Lee Bartlett. Black Sparrow 1980 $14.00 pap. $8.50
Summers, Claude J. *Christopher Isherwood.* Life and Lit. Ser. Ungar 1980 $13.95 1981 pap. $6.95

JOYCE, JAMES. 1881–1941

For many critics, James Joyce is the most important novelist of the twentieth century. He perfected the stream of consciousness monologue (which Edouard Dujardin and Dorothy Richardson had used before him); emerged as the most inventive of the experimental novelists; was a polyglot who could pun in a dozen languages; and antagonized his friends because of his egoism, yet could write about characters unlike himself with great compassion. Joyce's life was filled with contrasts: He abandoned his home to become an artist and spent his life in exile writing about the city he had abandoned. He was thought of as a great writer by people who had read little of his work, for his books were banned in English-speaking countries. Though *Ulysses* (1922) was suppressed for its supposed obscenity, few books stress the virtues of family life as strongly.

There is always more to Joyce's works than first meets the eye. The stories in *Dubliners* are, on the surface, naturalistic descriptions of city life; but Joyce's irony and symbolism show the true sterility of Dublin. One of the stories, "The Dead," seems to be about a festive occasion, the Morkans' annual dance; but the ghostly imagery reveals that the dance is a dance of the dead.

A Portrait of the Artist as a Young Man (1916) is similarly undercut by irony. The novel tells of Stephen Daedalus—a protagonist seemingly very much like the young Joyce, though ultimately quite different—and his struggle to become a writer. The novel vibrates between the alternatives of greatness and inexperience, triumph and failure, art and sham. And it is filled with subtleties and hidden beauty: intricate imagery; compact, powerful prose; and musical, flowing language.

In Joyce's early works the innovative techniques are always subtle, concealed beneath a plain, seemingly conventional story. In his later works this is no longer true. The reader is immediately aware of the experimental techniques; the prose may seem strange or unusual; and very often the story is difficult or impossible to discern.

Ulysses is such a work—a novel with many strata of meaning. On one level the book tells of the need Stephen Daedalus has for a father, of Leopold Bloom's yearning for a son, and of how the two meet during the one day on which the novel takes place: June 16, 1904. It was a day of great significance for Joyce because on it he met Nora Barnacle, who later became his wife. On another level, Stephen is Telemachus, Bloom is Odysseus, and their story is a modern "odyssey." But here, again, irony is important, for it is in the way that Bloom is not Odysseus, in his compassionate and extraordinary humanity, that his greatness and universality are revealed.

Every chapter of *Ulysses* has its own technique, style, central symbols, colors—all ingeniously used to enhance the action. In a chapter where the chief event is the birth of a child, the style delineates the birth and evolution of the English language. Joyce accomplishes this by parodying great English writers, moving forward chronologically from the earliest to the most recent. *Ulysses* is a very demanding book; but after the initial difficulties are surmounted it yields many rewards.

Ulysses was so inventive that it seemed to exhaust the possibilities for innovation in the English novel. Joyce, therefore, moved beyond English and wrote *Finnegans Wake* in a language of puns, allusions, and neologisms. The prose demands a slow reading pace, for the words themselves are as important as the ideas they represent. It cannot be read like most novels, in a few sittings; it must be savored slowly, bit by bit, over months and years. A reader must come to it with a great store of patience, intelligence, and humor and perhaps also with a good supply of critical commentaries.

Sixty years ago, Joyce's frankness seemed obscene to some, and he encountered difficulty in finding publishers for his works. Typesetters refused to work on his books; *Ulysses* was published in Paris because it was banned in England and the United States; and Americans who were eager to read it had to smuggle the book past customs inspectors until 1933, when, in a historic decision, Judge Woolsey declared that it was not obscene.

Today, enthusiasm for Joyce continues to be strong. In 1967 the exciting film versions of *Ulysses* and of passages from *Finnegans Wake* played to eager audiences, as did the play *Stephen D*—an adaptation of *A Portrait of the Artist* and *Stephen Hero* (1944)—and the revival of *The Coach with the Six Insides*, Jean Erdman's award-winning dramatic dance interpretation of *Finnegans Wake*. The year 1967 was also notable for the discovery of "Giacomo Joyce," a poetic love story Joyce wrote for a young woman, his pupil in Trieste, with whom he became infatuated. Joyce himself did not publish it, but he worked passages from it into *Ulysses* and *Finnegans Wake*.

Joyce spent most of his life away from his native Ireland—mostly in Trieste, Rome, and Paris. He and his family were visiting in Vichy when France fell in 1940; they took refuge in Zurich, where Joyce soon died, thus ending a lifetime of struggle against poverty, obtuse and fearful publishers, and his daughter's madness.

BOOKS BY JOYCE

The Portable James Joyce. 1947. Intro. by Harry Levin, *Viking Portable Lib.* Penguin 1976 pap. $7.95. Includes *A Portrait of the Artist as a Young Man, Collected Poems, Exiles, Dubliners,* selections from *Ulysses* and *Finnegans Wake.*

Letters of James Joyce. Viking 3 vols. 1957–66 ea. $20.00

Dubliners. Ed. by Michael Groden, Garland repr. of 1914 ed. 1977 lib. bdg. $89.00; Modern Lib. repr. of 1926 ed. $5.95; Penguin 1982 pap. $5.95; Viking 1982 $17.50

A Portrait of the Artist as a Young Man: A Facsimile of the Manuscript Fragments of Stephen Hero. 1916. Ed. by Michael Groden, Garland 3 vols. 1979 lib. bdg. $375.00. Autobiographical novel, with text and criticism.

Exiles: A Play. Ed. by Michael Groden, Garland repr. of 1951 ed. 1978 lib. bdg. $125.00; intro. by Padraic Colum, Penguin 1977 pap. $4.95. Includes hitherto unpublished notes by the author, discovered after his death.

Ulysses. 1922. Farrar 3 vols. 1976 $200.00; ed. by Hans W. Melchior and Claus Melchior, Garland 3 vols. 1984 lib. bdg. $200.00; Modern Lib. repr. of 1940 ed. $12.95; Random (Vintage) 1986 pap. $11.95; Univ. Pr. of Virginia 3 vols. $100.00. The Random House paperback is the long-awaited corrected text.

Finnegans Wake. 1939. Viking 1982 $30.00; Penguin 1959 pap. $7.95

A Shorter Finnegans Wake. Ed. by Anthony Burgess, Penguin 1968 pap. $3.95. This abridged version, "with its interspersed commentary and its long introduction, will probably do more than any other work has done to bring to the serious general reader one of the most admired—and most difficult—books of this century. . . . A devoted Joycean, Burgess has reduced the text to somewhat over a third of its original length" (*LJ*).

Stephen Hero. Intro. by Theodore Spencer, New Directions rev. ed. 1969 pap. $6.95. In 1955, New Directions published a new edition, with a preface by John J. Slocum and Herbert Cahoon, which incorporated newly discovered sections of the manuscript and Theodore Spencer's essay on this early version of *A Portrait of the Artist*. This new edition adds five subsequently discovered manuscript pages.

BOOKS ABOUT JOYCE

Adams, Robert M. *James Joyce: Common Sense and Beyond.* Octagon repr. of 1966 ed. 1980 lib. bdg. $20.00

Atherton, James S. *The Books at the Wake: A Study of Literary Allusions in James Joyce's "Finnegans Wake."* Appel rev. ed. $15.00; Southern Illinois Univ. Pr. repr. of 1959 ed. 1974 pap. $7.95

Baker, James R., and Thomas F. Staley. *James Joyce's Dubliners.* Wadsworth 1969 pap. $4.95

Beck, Warren. *Joyce's Dubliners: Substance, Vision and Art.* Duke Univ. Pr. 1969 pap. $9.75

Begnal, Michael H., and Grave Eckley. *Narrator and Character in "Finnegans Wake."* Bucknell Univ. Pr. 1975 $22.50

Benstock, Bernard. *Joyce-Again's Wake: An Analysis of Finnegans Wake.* Greenwood repr. of 1966 ed. 1975 lib. bdg. $24.75

Benstock, Shari, and Bernard Benstock. *Who's He When He's at Home: A James Joyce Directory.* Univ. of Illinois Pr. 1980 $19.95 pap. $8.95

Blamires, Harry. *The Bloomsday Book: A Guide through Joyce's Ulysses.* Methuen 1966 pap. $11.95. Excellent on religious allusions.

Bonheim, Helmut. *Joyce's Benefictions.* Univ. of California Pr. 1964 $18.75. A scholarly work in Joyce's style with emphasis on *Finnegans Wake*.

Bowen, Zack R. *Musical Allusions in the Works of James Joyce: Early Poetry through "Ulysses."* State Univ. of New York Pr. 1974 $44.50

Brandabur, Edward. *A Scrupulous Meanness: A Study of Joyce's Early Work.* Univ. of Illinois Pr. 1971 $12.50

Budgen, Frank. *James Joyce and the Making of Ulysses.* Peter Smith $7.50; intro. by Hugh Kenner, Indiana Univ. Pr. 1960 pap. $5.95

Burgess, Anthony. *Joysprick: An Introduction to the Language of James Joyce.* Harcourt 1975 pap. $7.95

———. *Re Joyce.* Norton Lib. repr. 1968 pap. $6.95; Peter Smith $7.50. Clever, intelligent introduction to Joyce by a fine novelist.

Deming, Robert H., ed. *A Bibliography of James Joyce Studies.* G. K. Hall 2d ed. rev. 1977 lib. bdg. $41.50

———. *James Joyce: The Critical Heritage.* Routledge & Kegan 2 vols. 1970 $65.00

Edel, Leon. *James Joyce: The Last Journey.* Haskell 1977 lib. bdg. $38.95

Ellmann, Richard. *James Joyce.* Oxford rev. ed. 1982 pap. $14.95. Not only an excellent biography of Joyce but one of the best literary biographies ever written.

———. *Ulysses on the Liffey.* Oxford 1972 pap. $7.95

French, Marilyn. *The Book as World: James Joyce's Ulysses.* Harvard Univ. Pr. 1976 $20.00

Gilbert, Stuart. *James Joyce's "Ulysses."* Random (Vintage) 1955 pap. $4.95. An early study, but still very useful; Joyce explained the Homeric parallels to Gilbert while he was writing this study.

Glasheen, Adaline. *A Third Census of Finnegans Wake*. Univ. of California Pr. 1977 $32.50. Supersedes two earlier versions by the same author.

Gluck, Barbara R. *Beckett and Joyce: Friendship and Fiction*. Bucknell Univ. Pr. 1979 $22.50

Gorman, Herbert S. *James Joyce*. Arden Lib. repr. of 1926 ed. 1978 lib. bdg. $30.00; Folcroft repr. of 1924 ed. lib. bdg. $30.00; Haskell 1974 lib. bdg. $49.95; Octagon 1972 lib. bdg. $26.00

Gottfried, Roy K. *The Art of Joyce's Syntax in "Ulysses."* Univ. of Georgia Pr. 1980 $16.50

Hart, Clive. *A Concordance to Finnegans Wake*. Appel rev. ed. 1963 $35.00

Hart, Clive, and David Hayman, eds. *James Joyce's "Ulysses": Critical Essays*. Univ. of California Pr. 1974 pap. $6.95

Hayman, David. *Ulysses: The Mechanics of Meaning*. Univ. of Wisconsin Pr. 2d ed. 1982 pap. $7.95

Hayman, David, and Elliott Anderson, eds. *In the Wake of the "Wake."* Univ. of Wisconsin Pr. 1978 $7.95

Henke, Suzette A. *Joyce's Moraculous Sindbook: A Study of "Ulysses."* Ohio State Univ. Pr. 1978 $15.00

Kenner, Hugh. *Joyce's Voices*. Univ. of California Pr. 1978 $17.00 pap. $2.95

Kiely, Robert. *Beyond Egotism: The Fiction of James Joyce, Virginia Woolf and D. H. Lawrence*. Harvard Univ. Pr. text ed. 1980 $15.00

Levin, Harry. *James Joyce: A Critical Introduction*. New Directions 1960 pap. $6.95. A good introduction.

Litz, A. Walton. *Art of James Joyce: Method and Design in Ulysses and Finnegans Wake*. Oxford 1964 pap. $4.95

———. *James Joyce*. Twayne's Eng. Authors Ser. G. K. Hall 1966 lib. bdg. $13.95. Critical analysis relating the works to each other and to the main body of contemporary literature. Annotated bibliography.

MacCabe, Colin. *James Joyce and the Revolution of the Word*. Barnes & Noble text ed. 1979 $26.50

Magalaner, Marvin. *Time of Apprenticeship: The Fiction of Young James Joyce*. Ayer repr. of 1959 ed. $15.00

Magalaner, Marvin, and Richard M. Kain. *Joyce: The Man, the Work, the Reputation*. Greenwood repr. of 1956 ed. 1979 lib. bdg. $32.50

McHugh, Roland. *Annotations to Finnegans Wake*. Johns Hopkins Univ. Pr. 1980 $35.00 pap. $12.95

———. *The Finnegans Wake Experience*. Univ. of California Pr. 1981 $16.50

———. *The Sigla of "Finnegans Wake."* Univ. of Texas Pr. text ed. 1976 $17.50

Norris, Margot C. *The Decentered Universe of Finnegans Wake: A Structuralist Analysis*. Johns Hopkins Univ. Pr. text ed. 1977 pap. $4.95

O'Hehir, Brendan, and John M. Dillon. *A Classical Lexicon for Finnegans Wake: A Glossary of the Greek and Latin in Major Works of Joyce*. Univ. of California Pr. 1977 $44.50

Raleigh, John H. *The Chronicle of Leopold and Molly Bloom: "Ulysses" as Narrative*. Univ. of California Press 1978 $28.50

Reynolds, Mary T. *Joyce and Dante: The Shaping Imagination*. Princeton Univ. Pr. 1981 $35.00

Schlauch, Margaret. *The Language of James Joyce*. Folcroft 1973 lib. bdg. $15.00

Seidel, Michael A. *Epic Geography: James Joyce's Ulysses*. Princeton Univ. Pr. 1976 $29.00

Senn, Fritz, ed. *New Light on Joyce from the Dublin Symposium.* Indiana Univ. Pr. 1972 $20.00

Shechner, Mark. *Joyce in Nighttown: A Psychoanalytic Inquiry into Ulysses.* Univ. of California Pr. 1974 $26.50

Staley, Thomas F., ed. *James Joyce Today: Essays on the Major Works.* Greenwood repr. of 1966 ed. 1979 lib. bdg. $24.75. Seven essays by noted scholars treating each of the major works.

———. *Ulysses: Fifty Years.* Indiana Univ. Pr. 1974 $8.50

Steinberg, Erwin R. *The Stream of Consciousness and Beyond in Ulysses.* Univ. of Pittsburgh Pr. 1972 $17.95

Sultan, Stanley. *Argument of Ulysses.* Ohio State Univ. Pr. 1965 $22.00

Svevo, Italo. *James Joyce.* City Lights 1967 pap. $1.25. Svevo, himself a novelist, was a friend of Joyce in Trieste.

Thornton, Weldon. *Allusions in Ulysses: An Annotated List.* Univ. of North Carolina Pr. 1982 pap. $12.95. Explains many of Joyce's most important allusions.

Tindall, William Y. *James Joyce: His Way of Interpreting the Modern World.* Greenwood repr. of 1950 ed. 1979 lib. bdg. $22.50. A witty and intelligent discussion of Joyce's work.

———. *A Reader's Guide to James Joyce.* Farrar 1959 pap. $6.95; Octagon 1971 lib. bdg. $22.50. Very useful guide and introduction.

Tucker, Lindsay. *Stephen and Bloom at Life's Feast: Alimentary Symbolism and the Creative Process in James Joyce's "Ulysses."* Ohio State Univ. Pr. 1984 $20.00

KOESTLER, ARTHUR. 1905–1983

Born in Budapest and educated in Vienna, Arthur Koestler wrote his first books in German. He lived briefly in Palestine, then worked as a journalist in Berlin in the 1930s. As a member of the Communist party, he visited Russia and then Spain during the Civil War. There he was captured by the Fascists and condemned to death, but he was freed through a prisoner exchange. He fled nazism and settled in Paris, only to have to flee again, this time to England. His political writings—including *Spanish Testament* (1937) and *The Scene of the Earth*—are also autobiographical.

His novels, such as *The Gladiators* (o.p.) and *Darkness at Noon*, offer acute psychological and philosophical awareness of the individual victimized by dehumanizing institutions. Other novels concern Jews in Palestine—*Thieves in the Night* (1946, o.p.) and *Promise of Fulfillment* (o.p.); the end of Europe—*The Age of Longing* (1951, o.p.); and international conferences—*The Call Girls* (1973, o.p.). He died in London in a suicide pact with his third wife.

BOOKS BY KOESTLER

Darkness at Noon. 1940. Bantam 1970 pap. $3.95; Macmillan 1941 $15.95

Arrow in the Blue. 1952. Macmillan 1970 $14.95; Stein & Day 1984 $19.95 pap. $12.95

The Invisible Writing. 1954. Stein & Day 1984 $19.95 pap. $12.95

The Roots of Coincidence. Random 1972 $7.95 1973 pap. $3.95

The Case of the Midwife Toad. Random 1973 pap. $3.50

The Thirteenth Tribe: The Khazar Empire and Its Heritage. Random 1976 $8.95

Janus: A Summing Up. Random 1979 pap. $4.95

The Ghost in the Machine. Random 1982 $15.00
The God That Failed. Ed. by Richard H. Crossman, *Essay Index Repr. Ser.* Ayer repr.
of 1949 ed. $19.95; ed. by Richard H. Crossman, Regnery-Gateway 1982 pap.
$5.95

BOOKS ABOUT KOESTLER

Calder, Jenni. *Chronicles of Conscience: A Study of George Orwell and Arthur Koestler.*
Critical Essays in Modern Lit. Ser. Univ. of Pittsburgh Pr. 1969 pap. $5.95
Levene, Mark. *Arthur Koestler. Lit. and Life Ser.* Ungar 1984 $13.95 pap. $6.95
Merrill, Reed B., and Thomas Frazier, eds. *Arthur Koestler: An International Bibliography.* Ardis 1979 $20.00
Sperber, Murray, ed. *Arthur Koestler: A Collection of Critical Essays.* Prentice-Hall
1977 $12.95

LAWRENCE, D(AVID) H(ERBERT). 1885–1930

One of Lawrence's finest novels, traditional in form and unlike his later
work, is *Sons and Lovers* (1913), an epic of family life in a colliery district and
"unabashed autobiography." Lawrence himself was the son of a miner and
was born in the coal region of Nottinghamshire. *The Rainbow* (1915), with its
forthright treatment of sexual passion, was condemned as obscene in 1915
and the entire edition destroyed. *Lady Chatterley's Lover* (1928), which Lawrence considered his greatest work, was written in three versions. It was privately printed in Florence, Italy, and banned both in England and the United
States until 1959, when Grove Press undertook publication of the third manuscript version and issued the first U.S. unexpurgated version. It was immediately banned by the U.S. Post Office, but in a now-famous opinion, Judge
Frederick van Pelt Bryan ruled the ban "unconstitutional" and confirmed it
as "illegal and void."

Always in search of warm climates for his tuberculosis, Lawrence spent
some time in New Mexico in 1924 on a ranch presented to him by Mabel
Dodge Luhan. Here "he found himself as much at harmony as he was ever
to be with any place." After Lawrence's death, the battle waged by his (often jealous) disciples turned to civil warfare. Abuse, libel, recriminations
fill many of the early books about him. He left behind him "an extraordinarily large body of work for so short a career, nearly all of it strongly
marked by his unmistakable literary and philosophical imprint."

BOOKS BY LAWRENCE

Complete Short Stories of D. H. Lawrence. Penguin 3 vols. 1976 pap. ea. $3.95–$4.95.
Includes the collections originally published as *A Modern Lover, The Lovely Lady,
Love among the Haystacks,* and others.
Complete Poems. Ed. by Vivian De Sola Pinto and F. Warren Roberts, Penguin 1977
pap. $12.95
The Complete Plays. Viking 1966 $12.95. Contains all eight of his finished plays and
two fragments.
Reflections on the Death of a Porcupine. 1925. Indiana Univ. Pr. 1963 pap. $4.95. In
this collection of essays, he put down, sometimes in a poetic and allegorical
vein, sometimes satirically, his views on life and love, on war and peace, and on
the writer's craft.

Four Short Novels. Penguin 1976 pap. $4.95. Includes *Love among the Haystacks, The Ladybird, The Fox,* and *The Captain's Doll.*

The Portable D. H. Lawrence. Ed. by Diana Trilling, Penguin 1977 pap. $7.95

Collected Letters. Ed. by Harry T. Moore, Viking 2 vols. 1962 $40.00. Contains 1,200 letters with a very useful "Who's Who in the Lawrence Letters" by the editor.

The Centaur Letters: Unpublished Letters by D. H. Lawrence. Fwd. by Edward D. McDonald, Univ. of Texas Pr. 1970 $15.00

The White Peacock. 1911. Ed. by Andrew Robertson, Cambridge Univ. Pr. 1983 $49.50; intro. by Melvyn Bragg, Viking 1985 $22.50

Sons and Lovers. 1913. Ed. by Gamini Salgado, Aurora repr. of 1968 ed. text ed. 1970 pap. $2.50; Buccaneer Bks. 1982 lib. bdg. $17.95; intro. by Alfred Kazin, Modern Lib. 1962 $6.95; intro. by Benjamin Demott, New Amer. Lib. (Signet Class.) 1985 pap. $3.95; Penguin 1983 pap. $3.95; ed. by Mark Schorer, Univ. of California 1978 $160.00; Viking 1968 ed. $10.00

The Prussian Officer, and Other Stories. 1914. *Short Story Index Repr. Ser.* Ayer repr. of 1914 ed. $21.00; ed. by John Worthen, Cambridge Univ. Pr. 1983 $49.50; intro. by Melvyn Bragg, Viking 1985 $18.95

The Rainbow. 1915. Modern Lib. $6.95; ed. by John Worthen, *Penguin Eng. Lib. Ser.* 1982 pap. $4.95

Women in Love. 1920. Buccaneer Bks. 1984 lib. bdg. $18.95; Modern Lib. 1937 $6.95; ed. by Charles Ross, *Penguin Eng. Lib. Ser.* 1982 pap. $4.95

The Lost Girl. 1920. Amereon $19.95; ed. by John Worthen, Cambridge Univ. Pr. 1981 $49.50 pap. $14.95; Penguin 1978 pap. $4.95; Viking 1982 $22.95

Aaron's Rod. 1922. Penguin 1976 pap. $3.95

Kangaroo. 1923. Penguin 1980 pap. $4.95

(and M. L. Skinner). *The Boy in the Bush.* 1924. Penguin 1981 pap. $4.95

St. Mawr and Other Stories. 1925. Ed. by Lindeth Vasey, Cambridge Univ. Pr. 1983 $49.50

Plumed Serpent. 1926. Intro. by W. Y. Tindall, Random 1955 pap. $5.95

Lady Chatterley's Lover. 1928. Ed. by Lawrence Durrell, intro. by Ronald Friedband, *Bantam Class. Ser.* 1983 pap. $2.75; Buccaneer Bks. 1981 lib. bdg. $18.95; intro. by Archibald MacLeish, Grove 1969 pap. $3.95; Modern Lib. 2d ed. 1982 $7.95; New Amer. Lib. (Signet Class.) 1972 pap. $2.75

BOOKS ABOUT LAWRENCE

Daiches, David. *D. H. Lawrence.* Folcroft 1977 lib. bdg. $9.50; Richard West repr. of 1963 ed. 1980 lib. bdg. $10.00

Draper, R. P., ed. *D. H. Lawrence: The Critical Heritage. Critical Heritage Ser.* Routledge & Kegan text ed. 1970 $35.00

Goodheart, Eugene. *The Utopian Vision of D. H. Lawrence.* Univ. of Chicago Pr. 1963 $12.00

Gregory, Horace. *D. H. Lawrence, Pilgrim of the Apocalypse: A Critical Study. Select Bibliographies Repr. Ser.* Ayer repr. of 1933 ed. $15.00; Grove (Evergreen Bks.) 1970 pap. $1.95

Hochman, Baruch. *Another Ego: The Changing View of Self and Society in the Work of D. H. Lawrence.* Univ. of South Carolina Pr. 1970 $17.95

Hough, Graham. *The Dark Sun: A Study of D. H. Lawrence.* Octagon 1972 lib. bdg. $21.00

Lawrence, Ada, and George S. Gelder. *Young Lorenzo: The Early Life of D. H. Lawrence.* Russell repr. of 1931 ed. 1966 $8.50. Ada Lawrence is his sister.

Leavis, F. R. *D. H. Lawrence: Novelist.* Univ. of Chicago Pr. (Phoenix Bks.) 1979 pap. $6.95. A study by one of Lawrence's leading advocates in England.

Luhan, Mabel G. *Lorenzo in Taos.* Scholarly repr. of 1932 ed. $29.00

Miko, Stephen J. *Toward Women in Love: The Emergence of a Lawrentian Aesthetic.* Yale Univ. Pr. 1972 $30.00

Moore, Harry T. *The Life and Works of D. H. Lawrence.* Darby repr. of 1951 ed. 1981 lib. bdg. $30.00; (with the title *D. H. Lawrence: His Life and Works*) Irvington 1964 $34.50

————. *The Priest of Love: A Life of D. H. Lawrence.* Farrar rev. ed. 1974 $15.00; Penguin 1981 pap. $6.95; Southern Illinois Univ. Pr. repr. of 1954 ed. rev. ed. 1977 pap. $12.95

Moynahan, Julian. *Deed of Life: The Novels and Tales of D. H. Lawrence.* Princeton Univ. Pr. 1963 $25.00 pap. $6.95. A chronological analysis of ten novels and a group of shorter pieces.

Nehls, Edward H., ed. *D. H. Lawrence: A Composite Biography.* Univ. of Wisconsin Pr. 3 vols. 1957–59 ea. $35.00

Ruderman, Judith. *D. H. Lawrence and the Devouring Mother: The Search for a Patriarchal Ideal of Leadership.* Duke Univ. Pr. 1984 lib. bdg. $35.75

Sagar, Keith. *The Art of D. H. Lawrence.* Cambridge Univ. Pr. 1976 $47.50 pap. $13.95. A comprehensive view of Lawrence's writings in many genres.

————. *D. H. Lawrence: A Calendar of His Works.* Univ. of Texas Pr. text ed. 1979 $22.50

Smith, Anne, ed. *Lawrence and Women.* Critical Studies Ser. Barnes & Noble 1978 $26.50 text ed. pap. $8.95

Spender, Stephen, ed. *D. H. Lawrence: Novelist, Poet, Prophet.* Harper 1973 $17.50. Essays by Diana Trilling, Denis Donoghue, A. Alvarez, and others; the editor is the well-known British poet and critic.

Spilka, Mark. *Love Ethic of D. H. Lawrence.* Fwd. by F. L. Ravagli, Indiana Univ. Pr. 1955 pap. $4.95; Peter Smith $15.75

————, ed. *D. H. Lawrence: A Collection of Critical Essays.* Prentice-Hall (Spectrum Bks.) 1963 $12.95 pap. $2.45

Stoll, John E. *Novels of D. H. Lawrence: A Search for Integration.* Univ. of Missouri Pr. 1971 $13.50

Vivas, Eliseo. *D. H. Lawrence: The Failure and the Triumph of Art.* Northwestern Univ. Pr. 1960 $7.68

Weiss, Daniel. *Oedipus in Nottingham: D. H. Lawrence.* Univ. of Washington Pr. 1962 $16.50

Worthen, John. *D. H. Lawrence and the Idea of the Novel.* Rowman 1979 $22.50

LESSING, DORIS (MAY). 1919–

Professor R. J. Thompson wrote in *Choice* in October 1967: "probably the biggest 'sleeper' now at work in England is Doris Lessing." Born in Persia, Lessing grew up on a farm in Rhodesia, before immigrating to England. Her two great themes are the problems between the races in Africa and those of the intelligent, liberated woman in a man's world. *African Stories* "contains a wide variety of beautifully-wrought stories by a sensitive and thoughtful but fiercely honest writer whose humanity soon becomes as patent as her love of the sun-washed land where she spent her formative years. These stories are to be savored" (*SR*). *The Grass Is Singing*, her first published novel, is about a girl married to a white farmer in South Africa, and her relationship with a black servant. In *Children of Violence* (1965–69), a five-novel series, she combines her two main themes in the story of Martha Quest, the Marxist, feminist daughter of English settlers in "Zambesia," before and during World War II. Critics have found the going here heavy. Eliot Fremont-Smith noted in the *N.Y. Times:* "As Martha moves in and out of racial South African politics, and into and away from a bad marriage, she becomes, and it would shock her to realize how much, increasingly tiresome; for all her powers of observation, insight and will, her mind is uninformed with humor—and hence, uninformed." The English *Sunday Times* has called her "not only the best *woman* novelist we have, but one of the most serious, intelligent, and honest writers of the whole post-war generation."

After a series of science-fiction novels, Lessing returned to the more realistic style of her earlier career. This work, however, she had published under a pseudonym so that she could, as she said, "be reviewed on merit, as a new writer, without the benefit of a 'name.' " While critically well received, the pseudonymous Jane Somers books did not sell well until Lessing's authorship was revealed.

BOOKS BY LESSING

African Stories. 1964. Simon & Schuster (Touchstone Bks.) 1981 pap. $10.95

The Grass Is Singing. 1950. New Amer. Lib. (Plume) 1976 pap. $7.95

Martha Quest: A Complete Novel from Doris Lessing's Masterwork, Children of Violence. 1952. New Amer. Lib. (Plume) 1970 pap. $5.95

A Proper Marriage: A Complete Novel from Doris Lessing's Masterwork, Children of Violence. 1954. New Amer. Lib. (Plume) 1970 pap. $5.95

The Habit of Loving. Crowell repr. of 1957 ed. 1974 $10.53; New Amer. Lib. (Plume) 1976 pap. $8.95

A Ripple from the Storm: A Complete Novel from Doris Lessing's Masterwork, Children of Violence. 1958. New Amer. Lib. (Plume) 1970 pap. $6.95

Landlocked: A Complete Novel from Doris Lessing's Masterwork, Children of Violence. New Amer. Lib. (Plume) 1970 pap. $3.95

The Golden Notebook. 1962. Bantam 1973 pap. $4.95; Simon & Schuster 1984 $24.95

A Man and Two Women and Other Stories. 1963. Simon & Schuster (Touchstone Bks.) 1984 pap. $8.95. Sixteen sketches and three longer stories.

The Four-Gated City. 1969. Bantam 1970 o.p.

Briefing for a Descent into Hell. Knopf 1971 $2.95; Random (Vintage) 1981 pap. $3.95

The Summer before the Dark. 1973. Random (Vintage) 1983 pap. $3.95

Stories. Knopf 1978 $15.00 Random (Vintage) 1980 pap. $7.95

Shikasta: Canopus in Argos Archives. Knopf 1979 $10.95

The Marriages between Zones Three, Four and Five. Knopf 1980 $13.95; Random (Vintage) 1981 pap. $5.95

The Sirian Experiments. Knopf 1981 $11.95; Random (Vintage) 1982 $5.95

The Memoirs of a Survivor. Bantam text ed. 1981 pap. $3.95; Knopf 1975 $10.00

Re: Colonized Planet 5-Shikasta. Random (Vintage) 1981 pap. $5.95

The Making of the Representative for Planet Eight. Knopf 1982 $11.95; Random (Vintage) 1983 pap. $4.95

Documents Relating to the Sentimental Agents in the Volyen Empire. Knopf 1983 $12.95 1984; Random (Vintage) pap. $4.95

The Diaries of Jane Somers (The Diary of a Good Neighbor and *If the Old Could . . .).*
   Random (Vintage) 1984 pap. $6.95.
The Good Terrorist. Knopf 1985 $16.95. The winner of the 1985 Booker Prize.

BOOKS ABOUT LESSING

Barr, Marleen, and Nicholas D. Smith. *Women and Utopia: Critical Interpretations.*
   Univ. Pr. of Amer. 1984 lib. bdg. $22.75 text ed. pap. $10.25
Burkom, Selma R. *Doris Lessing: A Checklist of Primary and Secondary Sources.*
   Whitston 1973 $7.50
Dembo, L. S., and Annis Pratt, eds. *Doris Lessing: Critical Essays.* Univ. of Wisconsin
   Pr. 1974 pap. $4.50
Holmquist, Ingrid. *From Society to Nature: A Study of Doris Lessing's "Children of Vio-
   lence."* Humanities Pr. 1980 pap. $21.50
Knapp, Mona. *Doris Lessing.* Life and Lit. Ser. Ungar 1984 $15.50 pap. $6.95
Rubenstein, Roberta. *The Novelistic Vision of Doris Lessing: Breaking the Forms of
   Consciousness.* Univ. of Illinois Pr. 1979 $20.95
Thorpe, Michael. *Doris Lessing's Africa.* Holmes & Meier text ed. 1979 $19.50 pap.
   $12.50

LEWIS, C(LIVE) S(TAPLES) (pseud. of Clive Hamilton). 1898–1963

C. S. Lewis, professor of medieval and Renaissance English at Cambridge,
1954–63, and Fellow at Oxford, was a writer of many varied and exceptional gifts. He wrote novels of fantasy, scholarly literary essays, and expositions of Christian doctrine. He became known in the United States for the
demoniacal *The Screwtape Letters*—letters of instruction and encouragement
from a shrewd old devil to an undergraduate imp on earth, a revelation of
hell's best official secret, and for *The Chronicles of Narnia*, a seven-volume
Christian allegory in the form of a children's adventure fantasy. *Out of the
Silent Planet, Perelandra,* and *That Hideous Strength* form a trilogy of strange
and exciting philosophical fantasies of life on other planets and, at last, in
the earthly setting of a college community. Other novels include *The Great
Divorce, Four Loves,* and *Studies in Words.* Among his scholarly works on literature, *The Allegory of Love: A Study of Medieval Tradition* (1936) has become a classic.

BOOKS BY C. S. LEWIS

Out of the Silent Planet. 1938. Macmillan 1943 $10.95
The Screwtape Letters. 1943. Amereon $12.95; Doubleday 1981 pap. $5.95; Fortress
   Pr. 1980 $9.95; Macmillan rev. ed. 1982 pap. $2.95; Revell 1978 $10.00 pap.
   $2.95; Whitaker House 1984 pap. $3.50
Perelandra. 1944. Macmillan 1968 414.95 pap. $3.95
The Great Divorce. 1946. Macmillan 1978 pap. $3.95
That Hideous Strength: A Modern Fairy Tale for Grown-Ups. 1946. Macmillan 1968
   $12.95
Till We Have Faces: A Myth Retold. 1957. Eerdmans 1964 pap. $2.95; Harcourt 1980
   pap. $5.95
Letters to Malcolm: Chiefly on Prayer. Harcourt repr. of 1963 ed. 1973 pap. $3.95. The
   person to whom these letters are addressed is probably fictitious.
Letters to an American Lady. Ed. by Clyde S. Kilby, Eerdmans 1967 pap. $2.95. Over

100 letters, Christian in theme, to an American (her identity is withheld) whom Lewis had never met.

Surprised by Joy: The Shape of My Early Life. Harcourt 1956 $12.95 1966 pap. $3.95

Four Loves. 1960. Harcourt 1971 pap. $2.95

Studies in Words. Cambridge Univ. Pr. 2d ed. 1960 pap. $13.95

BOOKS ABOUT C. S. LEWIS

Arnott, Anne. *The Secret Country of C. S. Lewis.* Eerdmans 1975 $4.95

Christopher, J. R., and Joan K. Ostling. *C. S. Lewis: An Annotated Checklist.* Kent State Univ. Pr. 1974 $20.00

Green, Roger L., and Walter Hooper. *C. S. Lewis: A Biography.* Harcourt repr. of 1974 ed. 1976 pap. $7.95

Walsh, Chad. *The Literary Legacy of C. S. Lewis.* Harcourt 1979 $10.95 pap. $4.95

LEWIS, (PERCY) WYNDHAM. 1884–1957

Distinguished and highly original, Wyndham Lewis is known for his "darting wit and sardonic insight." A modern master of satire, expert at deflating the pretensions of democracy, he was born off the coast of Maine in his English father's yacht and grew up in England. He was associated with Roger Fry and EZRA POUND on the vorticist magazine *Blast* (1914–15). Lewis served in France in World War I, and his dynamic paintings of war scenes soon gained him wide recognition for his art, now represented in the Tate Gallery and the Victoria and Albert Museum, London, and in the Museum of Modern Art, New York. After the publication of his naturalistic novel *Tarr* (1918) he became prominent as a writer. His major work of fiction is the tetralogy *The Human Age* (1955–56, o.p.). Lewis "was one of those high-powered, controversial and prophetic figures to whom no one can react with indifference. He was a fellow-traveller with fascism who wrote enthusiastically about Hitler. . . . A toughy, you see: a would-be shocker: a braggart. But his eye for the comic surface of things is marvelous" (Philip Toynbee, *Observer*). T. S. ELIOT called Wyndham Lewis "the most fascinating personality of our time" and he was described by Yeats as having that rare quality in writers, intellectual passion. Yet his reactionary views, especially his anti-Semitism, have more or less consigned him to oblivion today. His views are clearly expressed in such works as *Hitler, the Germans and the Jews* and *The Jews, Are They Human?*

BOOKS BY WYNDHAM LEWIS

Letters of Wyndham Lewis. Ed. by W. K. Rose, New Directions 1964 $10.00. Letters to Pound, Eliot, Joyce, Augustus John, and others.

Tarr. Dufour repr. of 1918 ed. 1970 pap. $5.95; Penguin 1983 pap. $5.95

The Wild Body. Haskell repr. of 1927 ed. 1975 lib. bdg. $37.95. Includes short stories: "A Soldier of Humour," "Beau Jejour," "Bestre," "The Cornac and His Wife," "The Death of the Ankou," "Franciscan Adventures," "Brotcotnaz," "Inferior Religions."

The Childermass. Dufour repr. of 1928 ed. 1970 pap. $6.95; Riverrun 1980 pap. $5.95; Scholarly repr. of 1928 ed. 1972 $49.00

The Apes of God. Black Sparrow repr. of 1930 ed. 1981 $20.00 pap. $12.50

The Snooty Baronet. Afterword by Bernard Lafourcade, Black Sparrow 1984 $20.00
    pap. $12.50; *Eng. Lit. Ser.* Haskell repr. of 1932 ed. 1971 lib. bdg. $49.95
Blasting and Bombardiering: An Autobiography, 1914–1926. 1937. Riverrun 1982 pap.
    $8.95; Univ. of California Pr. 2d ed. rev. 1967 $37.50
Self-Condemned: A Novel of Exile. Afterword by Smith Rowland, Black Sparrow repr.
    of 1954 ed. 1983 $20.00 deluxe ed. $30.00 pap. $12.50

BOOKS ABOUT WYNDHAM LEWIS

Jameson, Fredric. *Fables of Aggression: Wyndham Lewis, the Modernist as Fascist.*
    Univ. of California Pr. 1979 $22.50 pap. $5.95
Kenner, Hugh. *Wyndham Lewis: A Critical Guidebook.* New Directions 1954 pap.
    $4.25
Materer, Timothy. *Vortex: Pound, Eliot, and Lewis.* Cornell Univ. Pr. 1979 $22.50
———. *Wyndham Lewis: The Novelist.* Wayne State Univ. Pr. text ed. 1976 $12.50
Meyers, Jeffrey. *Wyndham Lewis: A Revaluation.* McGill Queens Univ. Pr. 1980
    $34.00
Morrow, Bradford, and Bernard Lafourcade. *A Bibliography of the Writings of Wynd-
    ham Lewis.* Black Sparrow 1978 $40.00
Pound, Omar, and Philip Grover. *Wyndham Lewis: A Descriptive Bibliography.* Shoe
    String (Archon) 1978 $20.00
Richards, I. A., and others. *Essays on Wyndham Lewis.* Norwood 1974 $30.00

LODGE, DAVID. 1935–

An academic and a student of the novel, David Lodge writes criticism and
fiction that self-consciously reflect each other. He is, for example, sympathetic toward narrative experimentation in both. Nonetheless, he writes in
what he calls "a tradition of realistic fiction [about] what the writer has
himself experienced and observed . . . lower-middle-class life in the inner
suburbs of South East London; a war-time childhood and a post-war 'austerity' adolescence; Catholicism; education and the social and physical mobil-
ity it brings; military service, marriage, travel, etc." His earliest novels, especially *The Picturegoers* (o.p.) and *Out of the Shelter* (o.p.), reflect his own
early years, while *Ginger, You're Barmy* (o.p.) is a seriocomic evocation of
army life. *The British Museum Is Falling Down,* his first experimentally interesting novel, is both a parodic pastiche of earlier literature (Joyce's *Ulysses,* for example) and a witty complaint against the Catholic prohibition
against contraception. In *How Far Can You Go?* he traces the lives of young
adults in the 1960s as they turn away from outmoded Catholicism only to
discover their lives devoid of all spiritual values. His finest novels to date
are hilarious academic satires—*Changing Places* and its sequel, *Small World*
(o.p.)—on the petty quarrels, rigid structures, intellectual pretentiousness,
erotic and professional jealousies, and jet-setting conferences of present-day
university life.

BOOKS BY LODGE

The British Museum Is Falling Down. 1965. David & Charles 1981 $16.95
Changing Places. Penguin 1979 pap. $4.95
How Far Can You Go? David & Charles 1980 $15.95

MANSFIELD, KATHERINE. 1888–1923
[SEE Chapter 15 in this volume.]

MASEFIELD, JOHN. 1878–1967
[SEE Chapter 7 in this volume.]

MAUGHAM, W(ILLIAM) SOMERSET. 1874–1965

In 1959, when Maugham was 85, the *N.Y. Times* reported that he had decided that it was time to stop writing except for himself. He had retired gracefully from playwriting in 1934. Of his formidable body of work, his novel *Of Human Bondage* has become a modern classic. It reflects his early experiences as a physician in St. Thomas' Hospital, London. *The Moon and Sixpence*, based on the life of the artist Paul Gauguin, is still read. Many of his stories were set in far outposts of the British Empire, where he himself had observed the effect of tropical lands on the uprooted European. Maugham said of himself: "I have never pretended to be anything but a storyteller. It has amused me to tell stories and I have told a great many." *The Summing Up*, a review of his writing career, which might well be used as a handbook of authorship, largely explains his competent craftsmanship and his thoroughgoing professionalism as a writer.

A multimillionaire, he sold 38 of his art treasures at auction in 1962 for more than $1,400,000, "which along with most of the rest of his estate he . . . earmarked for Britain's Incorporated Society of Authors, Playwrights and Composers to spare 'needy authors from doing hack work.' " His last years were marred by a public dispute with his daughter over the disposition of some of his paintings. Before his death he stipulated that no unpublished work of his should be printed posthumously.

BOOKS BY MAUGHAM

The Works of W. Somerset Maugham. Ayer 1977 47 vols. $940.00

Collected Short Stories. Penguin 4 vols. 1977–78 pap. ea. $4.95

The Making of a Saint: A Romance of Mediaeval Italy. 1898. Ayer repr. of 1966 ed. 1977 $24.50

Of Human Bondage. 1915. Ayer repr. of 1915 ed. 1977 $8.95; Buccaneer Bks. repr. 1981 lib. bdg. $18.95; Doubleday 1942 $16.95; Folcroft repr. of 1946 ed. lib. bdg. $15.00; Penguin 1978 pap. $4.95; Pocket Bks. $1.95; Random pap. $3.95; Washington Square Pr. 1973 pap. $.95

The Moon and Sixpence. Ayer repr. of 1919 ed. 1977 $20.00; Penguin 1977 pap. $3.95; Pocket Bks. pap. $1.50

Ashenden, or The British Agent. 1928. Amereon $13.95; Ayer repr. of 1941 ed. 1977 $20.00

Cakes and Ale. Ayer repr. of 1930 ed. 1977 $20.00; Penguin 1977 pap. $3.95

The Narrow Corner. Ayer repr. of 1932 ed. 1977 $20.00; Penguin 1977 pap. $4.95

The Razor's Edge. Ayer repr. of 1943 ed. 1977 $5.95; Penguin 1984 pap. $4.95

A Writer's Notebook. Ayer repr. of 1949 ed. 1977 $24.50; Penguin 1984 pap. $5.95

The Writer's Point of View. Folcroft repr. of 1951 ed. lib. bdg. $15.00; Porter 1979 $28.50

Points of View: Five Essays. Ayer repr. of 1959 ed. 1977 $20.00; Greenwood repr. of 1959 ed. 1969 lib. bdg. $24.75

BOOKS ABOUT MAUGHAM

Aldington, Richard. *W. Somerset Maugham: An Appreciation.* Folcroft 1977 lib. bdg. $10.00

Bason, Frederick T. *A Bibliography of the Writings of William Somerset Maugham.* Arden Lib. repr. of 1931 ed. 1979 lib. bdg. $18.00; Folcroft repr. of 1931 ed. lib. bdg. $15.00; Haskell 1974 lib. bdg. $49.95

Morgan, Ted. *Maugham: A Biography.* Simon & Schuster 1980 $17.95 1984 pap. $12.95

Sanders, Charles, ed. *W. Somerset Maugham: An Annotated Bibliography of Writings about Him.* Northern Illinois Univ. Pr. 1970 $17.50

MUNRO, H(ECTOR) H(UGH) ("Saki"). 1870–1916

Saki's short stories at their best are extraordinarily compact and cameolike, wicked and witty, with a careless cruelty and a powerful vein of supernatural fantasy. They deal, in general, with the same group of upper-class Britishers, whose frivolous lives are sometimes complicated by animals—the talking cat who reveals their treacheries in love, the pet ferret who is evil incarnate. The nom de plume Saki was borrowed from the cup-bearer in Omar Khayyam's *The Rubaiyat.* He used it for political sketches contributed to the *Westminster Gazette* as early as 1896, later collected as *Alice in Westminster.* The stories and novels were published between that time and the outbreak of World War I, when he enlisted as a private, scorning a commission. He died of his wounds in a shell-hole near Beaumont Hamel.

BOOKS BY MUNRO

The Complete Works of Saki. Doubleday 1976 $17.95

The Novels and Plays of Saki. Carroll & Graf 1984 pap. $8.95; Scholarly repr. of 1945 ed. 1971 $39.00

Best of Saki. Amereon $13.95; ed. by Graham Greene, Penguin 1977 pap. $5.95

The Short Stories of Saki (H. H. Munro). Ed. by Corbin Hoopes, Darby repr. lib. bdg. $30.00

MURDOCH, IRIS. 1919–

Wit, variety, and unpredictability characterize the work of this English philosopher-novelist. Murdoch was born in Dublin and educated in England, where she attended Somerville College, Oxford. After several government jobs, she returned to academic life, studying philosophy at Newnham College, Cambridge. Since 1948, she has been a Fellow and Tutor at St. Anne's College, Oxford. In 1959, she lectured at Yale University. Her husband, John Bayley, is a novelist, poet, and critic.

Elizabeth Bowen has said: "Everything that she has written has been remarkable—stamped by the unmistakable authority of mind and vision." Her first novel, *Under the Net,* already showed "a deft touch, a delight in strange, intricate and puzzling plots, a wild intelligence and a defiance of the pigeonhole" (*PW*). In the world of *A Severed Head,* she depicted a London society devoid of passion or conviction, a modern world in which are contrasted the artificial and the real in her characters' emotions. Her subtle irony, her wit, her sense of the comic combine in this astonishing novel. Murdoch also wrote *An Unofficial Rose* (1962, o.p.), *The Unicorn* (1963, o.p.), *The Red and the Green* (1965, o.p.), and *The Time of the Angels* (1966, o.p.). Of *The Nice and the Good*, which treats the multiple facets of love, Elizabeth Janeway said in the *N.Y. Times:* "Sparkling, daring, great fun, the book sweeps up black magic, science fiction, thriller, and half-a-dozen kinds of novel into the wittiest sort of concoction. It is hard to imagine anyone not enjoying it."

Murdoch has also written a book on Jean-Paul Sartre and several nonfiction works, including *The Sovereignty of Good* (1971), in which she sets forth her ideas on ethics, and *The Fire and the Sun: Why Plato Banished the Artists.*

BOOKS BY MURDOCH

Under the Net. 1954. Penguin 1977 pap. $4.95
The Sand Castle. 1957. Penguin 1978 pap. $4.95
A Severed Head. 1961. Penguin 1976 pap. $4.95
The Italian Girl. 1964. Penguin 1979 pap. $4.95
The Nice and the Good. 1967. Penguin 1978 pap. $4.95
Bruno's Dream. 1969. Penguin 1976 pap. $4.95
A Fairly Honorable Defeat. 1970. Penguin 1979 pap. $4.95
The Black Prince. Penguin 1983 pap. $4.95; Viking 1973 $12.95
The Sacred and Profane Love Machine. Penguin 1984 pap. $4.95; Viking 1974 $12.95
A Word Child. Penguin 1976 pap. $4.95; Viking 1975 $12.95
Henry and Cato. Penguin 1977 pap. $6.95; Viking 1977 $12.95
The Sea, the Sea. Penguin 1980 pap. $5.95; Viking 1978 $12.95
Nuns and Soldiers. Penguin 1982 pap. $6.95; Viking 1981 $14.95
The Philosopher's Pupil. Penguin 1984 pap. $6.95; Viking 1983 $17.75

BOOKS ABOUT MURDOCH

Gerstenberger, Donna. *Iris Mudoch. Irish Writers Ser.* Bucknell Univ. Pr. 1975 $4.50 pap. $1.95
Rabinovitz, Reuben. *Iris Murdoch.* Columbia Univ. Pr. 1968 pap. $2.50
Tominaga, Thomas T., and Wilma Schneidermeyer. *Iris Murdoch and Muriel Spark: A Bibliography. Author Bibliographies Ser.* Scarecrow Pr. 1976 $20.00

NAIPAUL, V(IDIADHAR) S(URAJPRASAD). 1932–

[See Volume 2, Chapter 19.]

O'BRIEN, FLANN (pseud. of Brian Nolan). 1911–1966

This gifted Irish writer had three identities: Brian Nolan, an Irish civil servant and administrator; Myles na gCopaleen, columnist for the *Irish Times*, poet and author of *An Beal Bocht* (*The Poor Mouth: A Bad Story about the Hard Life*), a satire in Gaelic on the Gaelic revival; and Flann O'Brien, playwright and avant-garde comic novelist praised by James Joyce, Graham Greene, DYLAN THOMAS, and WILLIAM SAROYAN (see Vol. 2). Although these writers, as well as a few intellectuals on both sides of the Atlantic, were quick to grasp O'Brien's genius, his masterpiece, *At Swim-Two-Birds* (1939), went almost unrecognized in its time. This novel, which plays havoc with the conventional novel form, is about a man writing a book about characters in turn writing about him. O'Brien starts off with three separate openings: "One beginning and one ending for a book was a thing I did not agree with." Anthony Burgess has called it "one of the five outrageous fictional experiments of all time that come completely and triumphantly off. What a fuss the French anti-novelists make about their tedious exercises in *chosisme;* how little fuss has been made about Flann O'Brien's humour, humanity, metaphysics, theology, bawdry, mythopoeia, word-play and six-part counterpoint." *The Third Policeman,* funny but grim, plunges into the world of the dead, though one is not immediately aware that the protagonist is no longer living. This book, says the *Nation,* "secures his place, already indicated by 'At Swim-Two-Birds,' as the most original comic artist, after Joyce, to come out of Ireland in this century."

BOOKS BY O'BRIEN

Stories and Plays. Penguin 1977 pap. $3.95; Viking 1976 $13.95
A Flann O'Brien Reader. Ed. by Stephen Jones, Viking 1978 $17.95
At Swim-Two-Birds. New Amer. Lib. (Plume) 1976 pap. $7.95
The Hard Life: A Novel. Penguin 1977 pap. $3.50
The Poor Mouth: A Bad Story about the Hard Life. Seaver Bks. 1981 pap. $4.95
The Third Policeman. New Amer. Lib. (Plume) 1976 pap. $5.95

O'CONNOR, FRANK (pseud. of Michael O'Donovan). 1903–1966

An Irish master of the short story, Frank O'Connor was born Michael O'Donovan in Cork. It is not surprising to learn in the first part of his autobiography, *An Only Child,* that he took his adored mother's name. O'Connor's absorbing interest was the literary treasury of Ireland. He labored tirelessly over masterful translations of ancient Gaelic works. O'Connor wrote the well-received *A Short History of Irish Literature: A Backward Look* and edited an anthology of prose and poetry, *A Book of Ireland* (1959, o.p.), which contains some of his own translations from the Gaelic. His *Shakespeare's Progress* (o.p.) is an "audacious appraisal of the Great Bard." In *The Lonely Voice: A Study of the Short Story* (1963, o.p.), he examines the work of those he considers the great short-story writers of the past. In his last years O'Connor lived mostly in the United States, and taught at Harvard and Northwestern universities.

BOOKS BY O'CONNOR

The Big Fellow. 1937. Templegate 1965 $6.95
Three Tales. Biblio Dist. repr. of 1942 ed. 1971 $12.50
A Picture Book. Biblio Dist. repr. of 1943 ed. 1971 $12.50
Collected Stories. 1952. Knopf 1981 $20.00; Random 1982 pap. $8.95
Mirror in the Roadway. Select Bibliographies Repr. Ser. Ayer repr. of 1956 ed. $22.00
An Only Child. G. K. Hall 1985 pap. $7.95; Irish Bk. Ctr. repr. of 1961 ed. 1970 pap. $3.95
My Oedipus Complex. Irish Bk. Ctr. 1963 pap. $4.95

My Father's Son. G. K. Hall 1985 pap. $7.95; Irish Bk. Ctr. repr. of 1968 ed. 1971 pap.
$3.95

BOOK ABOUT O'CONNOR

Matthews, James. *Frank O'Connor. Irish Writers Ser.* Bucknell Univ. Pr. 1975 $4.50
pap. $1.95

O'FAOLAIN, SEAN. 1900–

"There is an element in Irish fiction that someone has aptly described as
malicious affection. O'Faolain has it to the greatest degree. All the 11 stories
in [*I Remember! I Remember!* (o.p.)] bare the faults and failings of the characters without losing the reader's sympathy and understanding for those
same characters. There is a melancholy strain along with the quiet chuckle,
the nostalgic findings of a man who has lived and learned well. He is indeed
a past master of the short story" (*LJ*), as evidenced in *The Heat of the Sun*
(1966, o.p.). In his autobiography, *Vive Moi!*, which contains lovely passages
descriptive of the Irish countryside, he tells about his six years in the rebel
Irish Republican Army, about Irish Catholicism, and about the position of
the Irish writer who at one time or another usually finds himself in voluntary exile. The first literary work of "Ireland's leading prose writer" was in
Gaelic, though this was acquired and not his native tongue. He first attracted wide attention with *A Nest of Simple Folk* (1933, o.p.). After his I.R.A.
experiences, O'Faolain did graduate work at Harvard. He returned to Ireland, but still frequently lectures, teaches, and travels in the United States.

BOOKS BY O'FAOLAIN

King of the Beggars. Greenwood repr. of 1938 ed. 1975 lib. bdg. $18.00 Irish Bk. Ctr.
1980 pap. $6.95
Come Back to Erin. Greenwood repr. of 1940 ed. 1972 lib. bdg. $32.50
The Man Who Invented Sin. Devin repr. of 1948 ed. 1974 $12.95
And Again. Irish Bk. Ctr. 1982 pap. $4.95
Midsummer Night Madness. Irish Bk. Ctr. 1982 pap. $7.95
The Collected Stories of Sean O'Faolain. Little, Brown $29.45

ORWELL, GEORGE (pseud. of Eric Blair). 1903–1950

A Bengal-born novelist, critic, and political satirist, a product of Eton, an
anticommunist wounded while fighting for the Republicans in Spain, Orwell was an independent radical who courageously battled all forms of dictatorship. He first gained recognition in the United States with *Animal
Farm*, his satiric fable on Stalin's Russia. His bestselling *1984* depicts the
horrors of a well-established totalitarian regime; "Big Brother," the government spy, has become common American parlance for the official snooper.
Several posthumous volumes of essays have appeared, including *Shooting
an Elephant* (1950) and *Collection of Essays.*

BOOKS BY ORWELL

The Orwell Reader: Fiction, Essays, and Reportage. Intro. by R. H. Rovere, Harcourt
1961 pap. $6.95. Contains fiction, essays, and reportage.

Collected Essays, Journalism and Letters of George Orwell. Harcourt 1971 4 vols. ea.
    $15.95–$17.95 pap. ea. $6.95–$8.95
Burmese Days. Harcourt repr. of 1934 ed. 1974 pap. $4.95. Autobiographical.
Animal Farm. 1946. Buccaneer Bks. repr. 1982 lib. bdg. $16.95; Harcourt 1954 $8.95;
    New Amer. Lib. 1983 pap. $4.95
1984. 1949. Buccaneer Bks. 1982 lib. bdg. $17.95; Harcourt 1983 $12.95; New Amer.
    Lib. 1983 pap. $5.95
Orwell's 1984: Text, Sources, Criticism. Ed. by Irving Howe, Harcourt 1982 2d ed.
    pap. text ed. $11.95
Coming Up for Air. Harcourt repr. of 1950 ed. 1969 pap. $4.95
Keep the Aspidistra Flying. Harcourt repr. of 1956 ed. 1969 pap. $4.95
A Clergyman's Daughter. Harcourt repr. of 1960 ed. 1969 pap. $8.95

BOOKS ABOUT ORWELL

Bolton, W. F. *The Language of 1984: Orwell's English and Ours.* Univ. of Tennessee Pr.
    text ed. 1984 $19.95
Greenblatt, Stephen J. *Three Modern Satirists: Waugh, Orwell and Huxley.* Yale Univ.
    Pr. 1965 $10.50
Kubal, David L. *Outside the Whale: George Orwell's Art and Politics.* Univ. of Notre
    Dame Pr. 1973 pap. $6.95
Lee, Robert A. *Orwell's Fiction.* Irvington 1972 $29.50; Univ. of Notre Dame Pr. 1972
    pap. $5.95
Lewis, Peter. *George Orwell: The Road to 1984.* David & Charles 1980 pap. $10.50
Lief, Ruth A. *Homage to Oceania: The Prophetic Vision of George Orwell.* Ohio State
    Univ. Pr. 1969 $6.50
Meyers, Jeffrey. *A Reader's Guide to George Orwell.* Little, Brown 1977 pap. $4.95
———, ed. *George Orwell: The Critical Heritage.* Routledge & Kegan 1975 $35.00
Meyers, Jeffrey, and Valerie Meyers. *George Orwell: An Annotated Bibliography of
    Criticism. Reference Lib. of the Humanities* Garland 1977 lib. bdg. $25.00
Patai, Daphne. *The Orwell Mystique: A Study in Male Ideology.* Univ. of Massachusetts
    Pr. 1984 lib. bdg. $30.00 pap. $14.95. Feminist approach: Orwell as misogynist
    welded to patriarchal values.
Stansky, Peter, and William Abrahams. *The Unknown Orwell.* Academy Chicago 1981
    pap. $6.95
———. *Orwell: The Transformation.* Academy Chicago 1981 pap. $6.95; Knopf 1980
    $12.95
Williams, Raymond. *George Orwell.* Columbia Univ. Pr. repr. of 1971 ed. 1981 $22.50
    pap. $8.00
Woodcock, George. *The Crystal Spirit: A Study of George Orwell.* Schocken 1984 pap.
    $9.95

POWELL, ANTHONY (DYMOKE). 1905–

Evelyn Waugh once said: "Each succeeding volume of Mr. Powell's 'Music
of Time' series enhances its importance. The work is dry, cool, humorous,
elaborately and accurately constructed and quintessentially English. It is
more realistic than 'A La Recherche du Temps Perdu,' to which it is often
compared, and much funnier." It has been Powell's fate, according to some
critics, to be praised as like someone else, and in the 1930s it was Waugh.
He was of Waugh's world and the conflicts in his book develop out of the re-
bellions of the first quarter of the century. With *The Kindly Ones* he reached

the halfway mark in his chronicle, the end of the uneasy decades between two world wars. The third trilogy is devoted to World War II and the fourth to the following decades. The whole is a complex fictional history of the first two-thirds of the twentieth century. Powell thinks of his work as one long novel appearing a volume at a time, and not like, say, C. P. Snow's *Strangers and Brothers*, a series of connected novels. Born in London, Powell was educated at Eton and Oxford.

Books by Powell

A Dance to the Music of Time. Little, Brown 4 vols. 1963–76 ea. $24.45. Vol. 1, *A Question of Upbringing, A Buyer's Market*, and *The Acceptance World;* Vol. 2, *At Lady Molly's, Casanova's Chinese Restaurant*, and *The Kindly Ones;* Vol. 3, *The Valley of Bones, The Soldier's Art*, and *The Military Philosophers;* Vol. 4, *Books Do Furnish a Room, Temporary Kings*, and *Hearing Secret Harmonies.*
Infants of the Spring. David & Charles 1980 $14.95; Holt 1977 $10.95
O, How the Wheel Becomes It! Holt 1983 $13.95
To Keep the Ball Rolling. Penguin 1984 pap. $7.95

Book about Powell

Tucker, James. *The Novels of Anthony Powell*. Columbia Univ. Pr. 1976 $24.00

PRITCHETT, V(ICTOR) S(AWDEN). 1900–

V. S. Pritchett attended a number of schools, worked in the leather trade and later as a commercial traveler and shop assistant. After World War II, he was literary editor of the *New Statesman and Nation* and has frequently contributed to American periodicals and the *N.Y. Times Book Review*. He is a distinguished short-story writer who has often appeared in the *New Yorker*. Pritchett has also collaborated with the photographer Evelyn Hofer on three charming and excellent portraits of London, New York, and Dublin. Pritchett has been called "one of the best critics writing in English." He has also written well on many fellow writers.

Books by Pritchett

Collected Stories. Random (Vintage) 1983 pap. $8.95
Midnight Oil. Random 1973 pap. $3.95
The Turn of the Years. Random 1982 $17.50

PYM, BARBARA. 1913–1980

Often compared to the works of Jane Austen in both manner and subject, the novels of Barbara Pym are apparently guileless evocations of the foibles of aging and isolated characters. She has a sure, if understated, sense of her characters' psychology and of their unintentionally comic revelations about themselves and their futile lives. After the publication of *No Fond Return of Love*, all her books were out of print until she was cited, coincidentally by both David Cecil and Philip Larkin, as among the most underestimated novelists of the twentieth century. She subsequently completed two successful novels, *The Sweet Dove Died* and *Quartet in Autumn*, the latter a comic/pathetic study of two men and two women in their sixties who work in the same office but lead separate, lonely lives outside. Many of her earlier books have since been reprinted, including *Excellent Women* and *A Glass of Blessings*, both perceptive psychological studies of aging women taken advantage of by others. A posthumous novel, *A Few Green Leaves*, is a superb comedy of village life.

Books by Pym

Excellent Women. 1952. Dutton 1978 $13.95; Harper repr. of 1978 ed. 1980 pap. $3.80
A Glass of Blessings. 1958. Dutton 1980 $13.95; Harper 1981 pap. $3.80
No Fond Return of Love. 1961. Dutton 1982 $13.95; Harper 1984 pap. $3.37
Quartet in Autumn. Dutton 1978 $13.95; Harper repr. of 1978 ed. 1980 pap. $3.37
The Sweet Dove Died. 1978. Dutton 1979 $13.95; Harper repr. 1980 pap. $3.80
A Few Green Leaves. Dutton 1980 $13.95; Harper 1981 pap. $3.37
Jane and Prudence. Dutton 1981 $13.95; Harper 1982 pap. $3.37
Less Than Angels. Dutton 1981 $13.95; Harper repr. of 1980 ed. 1982 pap. $3.37
An Unsuitable Attachment. Dutton 1982 $13.95; Harper 1983 pp. $3.37
Some Tame Gazelle. Dutton 1983 $15.95; Harper repr. of 1950 ed. 1984 pap. $3.37
Very Private Eye: An Autobiography in Diaries and Letters. Ed. by Hazel Holt and Hilary Holt, Dutton 1984 $19.95; Random (Vintage) 1985 pap. $6.95

RHYS, JEAN. 1894–1979

Born in Dominica in the West Indies, Jean Rhys was educated at the Royal Academy of Dramatic Art in London, where she subsequently worked as, among other things, a chorus girl, a mannequin, and an artist's model. In the decade after World War I she lived among bohemians, mostly in Paris, before entering into the first of her three marriages. Her first book, a collection of stories called *The Left Bank,* was published with the encouragement of Ford Madox Ford, with whom she had an unhappy love affair and on whom she partly based the egotistical Heidler in *Quartet* (1929, o.p.). During the last decades of her life she lived mostly in obscurity in Devon, England, until *Wide Sargasso Sea* won her the Royal Society of Literature and W. H. Smith awards and led to the republication of her earlier books. She subsequently published two fine volumes of stories, *Tigers Are Better-Looking* (1974, o.p.) and *Sleep It Off, Lady.*

Her finest novel, *Wide Sargasso Sea* (1966) is both a lushly intense evocation of the Caribbean world of her childhood and a "prequel" to CHARLOTTE BRONTË's *Jane Eyre.* In alternating narration, both Rochester and Antoinette, his first wife who becomes "the mad woman in the attic," represent themselves as tragic victims of tropical decadence with its primitive ambience of menace and disaster. The pattern is similar in her own life and in all her novels: Rebellious, intelligent, insecure, neurotic women find no place in a world that allows them no proper outlet for their emotions or talents.

Books by Rhys

The Letters of Jean Rhys. Ed. by Francis Wyndham and Diana Melly, Viking 1984 $22.50
The Left Bank, and Other Stories. Pref. by F. M. Ford, *Short Story Index Repr. Ser.* Ayer repr. of 1927 ed. $15.00

After Leaving Mr. Mackenzie. 1930. Harper 1972 $8.95 1982 pap. $2.84; Random (Vintage) 1974 pap. $1.65
Voyage in the Dark. 1934. Norton 1982 pap. $3.95
Good Morning Midnight. 1939. Harper 1982 pap. $2.84; Random (Vintage) 1974 pap. $2.95
Wide Sargasso Sea. Norton repr. of 1966 ed. 1982 pap. $3.95
My Day. Small Pr. Dist. 1975 $7.50 pap. $3.00
Sleep It Off, Lady. Harper 1976 $7.95
(and Diana Athill). *Smile Please: An Unfinished Autobiography.* Creative Arts Bks. repr. of 1979 ed. 1983 pap. $6.95; Harper 1980 $10.95

BOOKS ABOUT RHYS

Mellow, Elgin W. *Jean Rhys: A Descriptive and Annotated Bibliography of Works and Criticism.* Reference Lib. of the Humanities Garland 1984 lib. bdg. $47.00
Plante, David. *Difficult Women.* Atheneum 1983 $9.95; Dutton 1984 pap. $6.95

RICHARDSON, DOROTHY (MILLER). 1873?–1957

The work of Dorothy Richardson is significant in the development of the modern English novel. Like PROUST (see Vol. 2), Joyce, and Woolf—though her talent was less than theirs—she was one of the first to write in the stream of consciousness manner, although she hated this term. Her autobiographical novel, in 12 book-length "chapters," had enjoyed few recent readers until the posthumous discovery and publication of a thirteenth section, *March Moonlight* (o.p.), in 1967, aroused new interest and brought fresh evaluations of her work. Though she displayed astonishing self-perceptions, most critics find her writing flawed by its egotistical tone and by her unpoetic, humorless style. The fact that she was treated like a son by her father perhaps explains the strong feminist orientation of her life (and of *Pilgrimage* [1915–38, o.p.]) and her general distrust of men. She gloried in loneliness and independence in a day when these were difficult for women, but tempered these virtues with love affairs both lesbian and heterosexual. She was briefly a mistress of H. G. Wells (who is portrayed as "Hypo" in *Pilgrimage*), an affair that ended in pregnancy and miscarriage, and eventually married an artist, Alan Odle. Her book, disdaining "plot," runs to 2,210 pages and some of it is heavy going, largely because it lacks selectivity and intensity. Richardson was "hopelessly vague" about her birth date, says Horace Gregory, but on her gravestone (which contains an error in her name) it is given as May 17, 1873.

BOOKS BY RICHARDSON

Backwater. Buccaneer Bks. repr. of 1916 ed. 1977 lib. bdg. $13.85
Honeycomb. Buccaneer Bks. repr. of 1919 ed. 1977 lib. bdg. $13.95

BOOKS ABOUT RICHARDSON

Fromm, Gloria G. *Dorothy Richardson: A Biography.* Univ. of Illinois Pr. 1977 $24.95
Rosenberg, John. *Dorothy Richardson: The Genius They Forgot.* Biblio Dist. 1979 pap. $10.95

Staley, Thomas F. *Dorothy Richardson. Twayne's Eng. Authors Ser.* G. K. Hall 1976 lib. bdg. $15.95

SACKVILLE-WEST, VICTORIA (MARY). 1892–1962

Born at Knole Castle, scene of Virginia Woolf's novel *Orlando*, Sackville-West was educated in that 365-room dwelling. In 1913 she married Harold Nicolson, journalist, diplomat, and biographer. *Poems of East and West*, her first book, was published in 1917. She remained unknown except by a small group of literary connoisseurs until 1927, when she received the Hawthornden Prize for a second volume of poetry. At this time she lived in London and was part of the Bloomsbury group, which included Lytton Strachey, Forster, JOHN MAYNARD KEYNES (see Vol. 3), and Woolf.

Sackville-West published many novels and volumes of poems, biography, and family history and several books on gardening, as well as book reviews and criticism. All of her writings reflect the same unhurried approach, deep reflection, and brilliantly polished style. Her influence on other writers, especially Woolf, was perhaps greater than her own individual achievement. *The Edwardians* (1930) and *All Passion Spent* (1931) are her best-known novels.

BOOKS BY SACKVILLE-WEST

The Heir. Short Story Index Repr. Ser. Ayer repr. of 1922 ed. $10.00
All Passion Spent. Doubleday 1984 pap. $8.95; Telegraph Bks. repr. of 1932 ed. lib. bdg. $35.00
The Edwardians. Amereon repr. lib. bdg. $16.95; Avon 1983 $3.95; Telegraph Bks. repr. of 1947 ed. lib. bdg. $35.00
The Easter Party. Greenwood repr. of 1953 ed. 1972 lib. bdg. $24.75

BOOKS ABOUT SACKVILLE-WEST

Nicolson, Nigel. *Portrait of a Marriage.* Atheneum 1973 $10.00 pap. $7.95. Nicolson is the son of Harold Nicolson and Victoria Sackville-West; his book is based on his parents' journals and letters. It is the story of a marriage tested by emotional upheavals and homosexual encounters; it not only survived but it seems to have been successful.
Trautmann, Joanne. *The Jessamy Brides: The Friendship of Virginia Woolf and V. Sackville-West.* Pennsylvania State Univ. Pr. text ed. 1973 pap. $.50

SAKI

[SEE MUNRO, H(ECTOR) H(UGH) in this chapter.]

SCOTT, PAUL. 1920–1978

Born in London, Paul Scott served in the British and Indian armies (1930–46) and is best known for his novels about India during the last years of the British rule. His major achievement, *The Raj Quartet* (1976), which was translated into a major television miniseries, and its fine sequel, *Staying On*, depict the breakdown of the old balance between ruler and ruled, colonizer and colonized, in terms of individual, family, and social trauma. What interests Scott is not only the historical moment but its metaphorical and metaphysical significance, which he represents in a highly serious and invocative prose. Earlier novels—including *The Alien Sky* (o.p.), *The Mark of the Warrior* (o.p.), and *The Birds of Paradise* (o.p.)—also use an Indian background to depict tragedy resulting from the clash of cultural perspectives and values. Also of interest is *The Chinese Love Pavilion* (o.p.), a novel set in the Malayan jungle.

BOOKS BY SCOTT

The Raj Quartet. Avon 4 vols. 1984 pap. $18.00; Morrow 4 vols. 1978 $29.95. Contains *The Jewel in the Crown, The Day of the Scorpion, The Towers of Silence,* and *A Division of the Spoils.*
Staying On. Avon 1979 pap. $3.50

SILLITOE, ALAN. 1928–

Alan Sillitoe grew up in the slums of the industrial city of Nottingham. He began to write while in the Royal Air Force, stationed in Malaya. After the war he went to Majorca, where he became a friend of Robert Graves, who encouraged him to write *Saturday Night and Sunday Morning*. The *N.Y. Herald Tribune* said: "Alan Sillitoe has given us one of the better pictures of English working-class life since Arnold Bennett dealt with the Five Towns or D. H. Lawrence with Nottingham colleries." His authors' fee for the manuscript rescued him and his wife from poverty and enabled him to afford the balanced diet to which he attributes his recovery from tuberculosis. *Saturday Night* won the Author's Club Prize for the best English novel of 1958 and was made into a superb movie in 1960. His second book, *The Loneliness of the Long-Distance Runner*, was awarded England's Hawthornden Prize for 1960 and was made into an excellent film in 1962.

William Posters is Sillitoe's play on the words of the British "Bill Posters Will Be Prosecuted" (U.S. version—"Post No Bills"), a sentence that has haunted him. *The Death of William Posters* (1965, o.p.) is about yet another young man who must escape from the philistinism of the social milieu to which he has been born. *Tree on Fire* (o.p.), a novel with autobiographical elements, was published in Britain in 1968. *Travels in Nihilon* (o.p.) is a satirical novel about a country controlled by nihilism. *Raw Material* (o.p.) is a fictionalized memoir of his childhood and an exploration of the making of a writer.

BOOKS BY SILLITOE

Saturday Night and Sunday Morning. Knopf 1959 $8.95; New Amer. Lib. (Signet Class.) 1973 pap. $3.50
The Loneliness of the Long-Distance Runner. Knopf 1960 $10.95; New Amer. Lib. 1971 pap. $2.25. Short stories.
Her Victory. Academy Chicago pap. $6.95; Watts 1982 $16.95
The Lost Flying Boat. Little, Brown 1984 $15.95

BOOK ABOUT SILLITOE

Vaverka, Ronald D. *Commitment as Art: A Marxist Critique of a Selection of Alan Sillitoe's Political Fiction.* Humanities Pr. text ed. 1978 pap. $16.00

SNOW, SIR C(HARLES) P(ERCY). 1905–1980

Trained as a physicist and at one time a Fellow in physics at Cambridge, C. P. Snow wrote a number of papers on the problems of molecular structure. He was knighted in 1957 for his important work in organizing scientific personnel for the Ministry of Labour during World War II and for his services as a civil service commissioner. In *Variety of Men* (1967, o.p.), "highly polished" biographical essays on nine men—including Einstein, Frost, and Stalin—who have influenced the destiny of the twentieth century, his "professional experience in the worlds of science, literature, and public affairs . . . enables him to examine these unusual men with a force of objectivity, insight, and political sophistication that is most impressive" (*New Yorker*). Snow, an influential literary critic, was concerned with the problems of education and lectured at colleges and universities in the United States. His sequence of novels, *Strangers and Brothers*, occupied him for more than 20 years. *Strangers and Brothers*, the first to be written in the series that bears its name, was published in England in 1940 and released in the United States in 1960. The cycle relates the life story of a young English lawyer named Lewis Eliot who is very much like Snow himself.

Snow, who made several long visits to the United States, drew on his wide experience for his Godkin Lectures at Harvard. These have been published as *Science and Government* (1961, o.p.). This book "tells the story of the bitter wartime clash between two eminent British scientist-advisers to the government. On the left, Sir Henry Tizard, the loser but Snow's man for a' that—the man who saw that Britain had a radar when it was needed. On the right, F. A. Lindemann (later Lord Cherwell), bosom pal of Winston Churchill, and the villain of this piece. The story has a moral and purpose. We need more scientists and scientific foresight in government." Snow's view that society is split into two antagonistic groups, humanists and scientists, is discussed in *The Two Cultures and the Scientific Revolution* (1959, o.p.). A violent transatlantic debate resulted when F. R. Lewis wrote a diatribe against Snow as a novelist and thinker for the *Spectator*. Lady Snow was the novelist Pamela Hansford Johnson.

BOOKS BY SNOW

Death under Sail. Garland repr. of 1932 ed. 1976 lib. bdg. $17.50; Scribner 1981 $10.95 1982 pap. $5.95

Strangers and Brothers. 1940. Scribner 1960 $20.00

The Light and the Dark. 1948. Scribner 1961 $20.00

The Time of Hope. 1949. Scribner 1961 $20.00

The Masters. 1951. Scribner 1960 $20.00 1982 pap. $6.95

The Homecoming. 1956. Scribner 1956 $17.50

The Affair. Scribner 1960 $20.00

In Their Wisdom. Scribner 1974 $2.95

The Realists. Scribner 1978 $12.95

A Coat of Varnish. Scribner 1981 $10.95 1983 pap. $7.95

The Physicists. Intro. by W. Cooper, Little, Brown 1981 $15.95

Strangers and Brothers: Omnibus Edition. Scribner 3 vols. 1979 $67.50. Vol. 1, *The Time of Hope, George Passant* (originally entitled *Strangers and Brothers*), *The*

Conscience of the Rich, and *The Dark and the Light;* Vol. 2, *The Masters, The New Men, The Homecoming,* and *The Affair;* Vol. 3, *Corridors of Power, The Sleep of Reason,* and *Last Things.*

BOOKS ABOUT SNOW

Boytinck, Paul. *C. P. Snow: A Reference Guide.* G. K. Hall 1980 lib. bdg. $28.50
Green, Martin B. *Science and the Shabby Curate of Poetry: Essays about the Two Cultures.* Greenwood repr. of 1964 ed. 1978 lib. bdg. $17.00
Karl, Frederick. *C. P. Snow: The Politics of Conscience. Crosscurrents Modern Critiques Ser.* Southern Illinois Univ. Pr. 1963 $6.95 1965 pap. $1.65

SPARK, MURIEL. 1918–

Muriel Spark has been called "our most chillingly comic writer since Evelyn Waugh" by the London *Spectator,* and the *New Yorker* praised her novel *Memento Mori* as "flawless." Her fiction is marked by its remarkable diversity, wit, and craftsmanship. "She happens to be, by some rare concatenation of grace and talent, an artist, a serious—and most accomplished—writer, a moralist engaged with the human predicament, wildly entertaining, and a joy to read" (*SR*). She became widely known in the United States when the *New Yorker* devoted almost an entire issue to *The Prime of Miss Jean Brodie* (1961, o.p.). Set in Edinburgh in the 1930s, this is the story of a schoolteacher, her unorthodox approach to life, and its effect on her select group of adolescent girls. Though their idol turns out to have feet of clay, she leaves an indelible mark on their lives. *The Girls of Slender Means* (1963), also warmly praised, is "an ironic comedy about the exuberance and transcience of youth and the tensions of being young and female and not married." Reviewing *The Mandelbaum Gate* (1965) for the *New Republic,* Honor Tracy wrote: "There is an abundance here of invention, humor, poetry, wit, perception, that all but takes the breath away. . . . The story, in fact, is pure adventure, with the suspense as artfully maintained as anywhere by Graham Greene, but this is only one ingredient. There are memorable descriptions of the Holy Land, fascinating insights into the jumble of intrigue and piety surrounding the Holy Places, and penetrating studies of Arabs. . . . In each of [Spark's] novels heretofore one of her qualities has tended to predominate over the others. Here for the first time they are all impressively marshaled side by side, resulting in her best work so far."

Muriel Spark was born and educated in Edinburgh and lived for some years in Central Africa. During World War II, she returned to England, where she worked in the Political Intelligence Department of the Foreign Office. She has been a magazine editor and writes poetry and literary criticism. Spark has lived in London's Camberwell section, the setting of *The Ballad of Peckham Rye,* but now makes her home in New York. Her novels reflect her conversion to Catholicism.

BOOKS BY SPARK

Memento Mori. 1959. Putnam (Perigee) 1982 pap. $5.95
The Girls of Slender Means. Knopf 1963 $4.95; Putnam (Perigee) 1982 pap. $5.95
The Abbess of Crewe. Penguin 1977 pap. $1.95; Putnam 1984 pap. $6.95

Not to Disturb. 1966. Penguin 1977 pap. $3.95
The Driver's Seat. 1970. Putnam 1984 pap. $6.95
Territorial Rights. Putnam 1979 $9.95 1984 pap. $6.95
The Ballad of Peckham Rye. Putnam (Perigee) 1982 pap. $5.95
Loitering with Intent. Putnam (Perigee) 1982 pap. $5.95
The Bachelors. Putnam 1984 pap. $6.95
The Comforters. Putnam 1984 pap. $6.95
The Only Problem. Putnam 1984 $14.95 1985 pap. $7.95

BOOKS ABOUT SPARK

Bold, Alan, ed. *Muriel Spark: An Odd Capacity for Vision. Critical Studies* Barnes &
    Noble 1984 $27.50. Collection of essays on important aspects of Spark's fiction.
Stanford, Derek. *Muriel Spark.* Saifer $17.50
Tominaga, Thomas T., and Wilma Schneidermeyer. *Iris Murdoch and Muriel Spark:*
    A Bibliography. Author Bibliographies Ser. Scarecrow Pr. 1976 $20.00

SWINNERTON, FRANK. 1884–1982

As the writer of more than 30 novels, Frank Swinnerton has shown himself dependable, compassionate, and wise, but he has never been a critical
success. In the publishing field from the age of 14, he first came to the eye of
the British reading public with the fine and delicate *Nocturne* (o.p.), admired by his friends Arnold Bennett and H. G. Wells. His main fictional interest has been the treatment of English urban life. *Quadrille* (o.p.), tightly
constructed and set in present-day London, is the fourth novel tracing the
fortunes of the Grace family. *Sanctuary* (o.p.), says the *New Yorker*, is "a simple and delightful tale of fearsome crisis set in London, in a very unusual
home for retired old ladies." It shows that "the octogenarian author has lost
none of his vigor of attack on his subject. His opening chapter could serve
as a model of how to depict a scene, indicate character and establish a
mood" (*N.Y. Times*). Swinnerton's close association with publishers and authors makes his essays and his autobiography, *Swinnerton* (1936, o.p.), a
mine of literary history. He has written biographical and critical works on
Arnold Bennett, GEORGE GISSING, and ROBERT LOUIS STEVENSON. For many
years Swinnerton contributed occasional letters called "A Word from London," on the British book trade, to the (U.S.) *Publishers Weekly*.

BOOKS BY SWINNERTON

Tokefield Papers, Old and New. Essay Index Repr. Ser. Ayer repr. of 1949 ed. $18.00
Background with Chorus. Richard West repr. of 1956 ed. 1980 lib. bdg. $30.00
Figures in the Foreground. 1917–40. *Essay Index Repr. Ser.* Ayer repr. of 1963 ed.
    $19.00
On the Shady Side. 1970. Ed. by W. H. Taylor, Garland 1982 lib. bdg. $18.00
Reflections from a Village. David & Charles 1979 $19.95

BOOKS ABOUT SWINNERTON

Bennett, Arnold. *Frank Swinnerton: Personal Sketches: Together with Notes and Com-
    ments on the Novels of Frank Swinnerton.* Folcroft 1977 lib. bdg. $10.00
McKay, Ruth C. *George Gissing and His Critic, Frank Swinnerton.* Arden Lib. repr. of
    1933 ed. 1980 lib. bdg. $20.00; Folcroft repr. of 1933 ed. 1974 lib. bdg. $20.00

THOMAS, D. M. 1935–

Born in Cornwall and educated at New College, Oxford, D. M. Thomas was originally published as a poet: *Two Voices* (o.p.) and *Logan Stone* (o.p.). His major novels to date include *The Flute-Player*, which depicts free and artistic spirits at odds with totalitarian authority, and the international bestseller, *The White Hotel*, a richly layered exploration of female sexuality, Freudian analysis, and mass hysteria against the backdrop of the Holocaust and the founding of Israel.

BOOKS BY THOMAS

The Flute-Player. 1979. Washington Square Pr. 1984 pap. $3.95
The White Hotel. Pocket Bks. 1982 pap. $3.95; Viking 1981 $13.95
Ararat. Pocket Bks. 1984 pap. $3.50; Viking 1983 $13.50
Selected Poems. Penguin 1983 pap. $7.95; Viking 1983 $15.75
Swallow. Viking 1984 $16.95; Washington Square Pr. 1985 pap. $4.50

TOLKIEN, J(OHN) R(ONALD) R(EUEL). 1892–1973

This English writer of fantasies "is an author whose imagination is kindled by his philology. Language has always been the chief love and concern of this Oxford scholar of the early forms of English." In his greatest book, the trilogy *The Lord of the Rings* (1954–56), Tolkien has invented a language with vocabulary, grammar, syntax, even poetry of its own. Though readers have imagined various possible allegorical interpretations, Tolkien has said: "It is not about anything but itself. (Certainly it has no allegorical intentions, general, particular or topical, moral, religious or political.)" In *The Adventures of Tom Bombadil*, Tolkien tells the story of the "master of wood, water, and hill," a jolly teller of tales and singer of songs, one of the multitude of characters in his romance, saga, epic, or fairy tales about his country of the "Hobbits."

Tolkien was also a formidable medieval scholar, as attested to by, among other works, *Beowulf: The Monster and the Critics* and his edition of *Anciene Wisse: English Text of the Anciene Riwle*.

BOOKS BY TOLKIEN

Tolkien. Ballantine 4 vols. 1984 pap. $11.80
Tree and Leaf. Houghton Mifflin 1965 $8.95
The Hobbit. 1938. Houghton Mifflin 1984 $19.95
The Fellowship of the Ring. Houghton Mifflin rev. ed. 1954 $14.95
The Two Towers. 1955. Houghton Mifflin 1967 $11.95
The Return of the King. 1956. Ballantine 1976 pap. $2.95; Houghton Mifflin rev. ed. 1967 $12.95
Farmer Giles of Ham: A Short Story. Houghton Mifflin 1978 $6.95 pap. $4.95
Smith of Wooton Major and Farmer Giles of Ham. Ballantine 1984 pap. $2.25
Unfinished Tales. Ed. by Christopher Tolkien, Houghton Mifflin 1980 $15.00 1982 pap. $8.95
Silmarillion. Ballantine 1985 pap. $3.95; Houghton Mifflin 1983 $7.95
The Book of Lost Tales. Houghton Mifflin 2 vols. 1984 ea. $14.95–$16.95

BOOKS ABOUT TOLKIEN

Carpenter, Humphrey. *Tolkien: A Biography.* Ballantine 1985 pap. $3.50; Houghton
    Mifflin 1977 $10.00
Grotta, Daniel. *The Biography of J. R. R. Tolkien: Architect of Middle-Earth.* Running
    Pr. rev. ed. 1978 lib. bdg. $12.90 pap. $4.95
Harvard Lampoon. *Bored of the Rings or Tolkien Revisited.* New Amer. Lib. 1971 pap.
    $2.50
Helms, Randel. *Tolkien's World.* Houghton Mifflin 1975 $7.95 pap. $3.95
Kocher, Paul H. *Master of Middle Earth: The Fiction of J. R. R. Tolkien.* Ballantine
    1982 $9.75
Noel, Ruth S. *The Languages of Tolkien's Middle-Earth.* Houghton Mifflin 1980 $9.95
    pap. $7.95
———. *The Mythology of Middle Earth.* Houghton Mifflin 1977 $7.95 1978 pap. $3.95
Tyler, J. E. *The New Tolkien Companion.* St. Martin's 1979 $14.95

WAUGH, EVELYN. 1903–1966

Evelyn Waugh came from a literary family. His elder brother, Alec, is a
novelist and traveler. Their father, Arthur Waugh, was the influential head
of the London publishing house Chapman and Hall. Waugh's deeply religious temperament (he later became an ardent Catholic) and literary abili-
ties were occasionally evident during his school days. He joined the Royal
Marines at the beginning of World War II and was among the first to volunteer for commando service. In 1944 he survived a plane crash in Yugoslavia
and, while hiding in a cave, corrected the proofs of *Brideshead Revisited*
(1945). Through very conservative eyes looking coldly on the mad scramble
of the upper class in the 1930s and the struggle between the young and old
generations, Waugh saw his disenchanted world clearly and expressed his
cynicism with savage fantasy and satire. His early novels, *Decline and Fall*,
Vile Bodies, and *A Handful of Dust*, are brilliantly funny; *Decline and Fall*
took the British public by storm and made his youthful reputation. In the later, "serious" novels he became petulant at the disintegration of the staid,
stable, indeed snobbish values of the England he imagined to be his; especially interesting in this regard are his novel *Scoop* and *Waugh in Abyssinia*,
journalistic writings of 1936. Evelyn Waugh's novels of the 1920s and 1930s,
together with *The Loved One* (an ironic tale of the extravagant and sentimental Forest Lawn Cemetery in California), attack real follies, which can be
seen as such from any political or social vantage point. The satire is sharp,
unencumbered, and to the point; the stories are furiously witty and inventive. On these he may be judged the outstanding satirist of his day. His
greatest works, however, are *Brideshead Revisited*, his novel of Catholic conversion, and the masterful trilogy of World War II, *Sword of Honour* (*Men at
Arms, Officers and Gentlemen, The End of the Battle*).

He also wrote impressive biographies of Rossetti, Ronald Knox, and Edmund Campion. *A Little Learning* (1964, o.p.), the first volume of his autobiography, is "an amusing and thoughtful chronicle of the early years of a
man who [had] such a profound influence on the literature and thought of

his own day. The prose, as is usual with Mr. Waugh, is elegant and at all times lucid" (*LJ*).

BOOKS BY WAUGH

Tactical Exercise. Short Story Index Repr. Ser. Ayer repr. of 1954 ed. $18.00. A collection of shorter satiric works, including "Work Suspended" and "Love among the Ruins."

Black Mischief. Little, Brown 1977 $13.95 pap. $5.70

Decline and Fall. 1929. Little, Brown 1977 $13.95 pap. $7.70

Vile Bodies. 1930. Little, Brown 1977 $13.95 pap. $5.70

A Handful of Dust. 1934. Little, Brown 1977 $13.95 pap. $5.70

Scoop. 1938. Little, Brown 1977 $13.95 pap. $7.70

Put out More Flags. Little, Brown 1977 $13.95 pap. $6.70

Brideshead Revisited: The Sacred and Profane Memories of Charles Ryder. G. K. Hall 1982 lib. bdg. $15.95; Little, Brown 1982 pap. $7.70

When the Going Was Good. Greenwood repr. of 1946 ed. 1976 lib. bdg. $22.00; Little, Brown 1984 $14.45

The Loved One. 1948. Little, Brown rev. ed. 1977 $13.95 pap. $6.70

Men at Arms. 1952. Little, Brown 1979 $14.45 pap. $6.70

Officers and Gentlemen. 1955. Little, Brown 1979 $13.95 pap. $7.70. Second novel of *Sword of Honour* trilogy.

The Ordeal of Gilbert Pinfold. 1957. Little, Brown 1979 $13.95 pap. $6.70

Tourist in Africa. Greenwood repr. of 1960 ed. 1977 lib. bdg. $22.50

The End of the Battle 1961. Little, Brown 1979 $13.95 pap. $6.70. Last novel of *Sword of Honour* trilogy.

Charles Ryder's School Days and Other Stories. Little, Brown 1982 $12.95 pap. $7.70

BOOKS ABOUT WAUGH

Davis, Robert M., and others. *Evelyn Waugh: A Checklist of Primary and Secondary Material.* Whitston 1972 $12.50

Greenblatt, Stephen J. *Three Modern Satirists: Waugh, Orwell and Huxley.* Yale Univ. Pr. 1965 $10.50

Lodge, David. *Evelyn Waugh.* Columbia Univ. Pr. 1971 pap. $2.50

Phillips, Gene D. *Evelyn Waugh's Officers, Gentlemen and Rogues: The Fact behind His Fiction.* Nelson-Hall 1975 $18.95

Pryce-Jones, David. *Evelyn Waugh and His World.* Little, Brown 1973 $12.95

Sykes, Christopher. *Evelyn Waugh: A Biography.* Little, Brown 1975 $12.50

WELLS, H(ERBERT) G(EORGE). 1866–1946

Wells wrote (in a very readable, sometimes journalistic style) scientific and fantastic romances, short stories, realistic novels, sociology, history, science, and biography—after 1895, averaging a book or more a year. His sociological works usually take the form of utopias or of prophecies. His *Science of Life* (1931, o.p.), written with Sir Julian Huxley, is an outline of biology as comprehensive as his *Outline of History* (1920). "He insisted on the importance of science during a long epoch when men of letters were heinously ignorant of it. His sense of the continuity and logical development of human destiny is very valuable, and enabled him to make shrewd guesses at future happenings which sometimes have been impressively right" (Richard Aldington). Wells and Jules Verne wrote the first popular science fiction—and both are still widely read in this vein.

It is the opinion of more than one critic that Wells never wrote anything better than his early science-fiction novels and such sociological fiction as *Love and Mr. Lewisham* (1900) and *Kipps* (1905). *Mr. Britling Sees It Through* (1916, o.p.) was one of the best novels written during World War I. Later novels, many of them devoted to causes he favored, might be less successful as fiction, but they were genuine attempts to reform the novel and will still be interesting to the student of English social history. His frank and brilliant *Experiment in Autobiography* (1934, o.p.) describes his rise from humble beginnings to world fame and throws interesting light on the literary, social, and political life of his period.

BOOKS BY WELLS

Seven Science Fiction Novels. Amereon $40.95; Peter Smith $16.50; Dover 1950 $15.00. Contains *The First Men in the Moon, The Food of the Gods, In the Days of the Comet, The Invisible Man, The Island of Dr. Moreau, The Time Machine,* and *The War of the Worlds.*

Three Prophetic Novels. Ed. by E. F. Bleiler, Dover pap. $5.95; Peter Smith $14.75. Contains *When the Sleeper Wakes, A Story of the Days to Come,* and *The Time Machine.*

Twenty-eight Science Fiction Stories. 1905. Dover $9.95; Peter Smith $13.25

Selected Short Stories. Penguin 1979 pap. $3.95

The Wheels of Chance and The Time Machine. 1896. Biblio Dist. repr. of 1935 ed. 1969 $8.95

Best Science Fiction Stories. 1965. Dover pap. $4.95; Peter Smith $14.25

The Time Machine. 1895. Amereon $9.95; Bentley repr. 1971 lib. bdg. $8.50; Berkeley pap. $1.95; Biblio Dist. (Everyman's) repr. of 1935 ed. 1975 pap. $2.50; New Amer. Lib. (Signet Class.) 1984 pap. $3.50

The Island of Dr. Moreau. 1896. Airmont Class. Ser. pap. $1.75

The Invisible Man. 1897. Amereon $12.95; Bantam 1983 pap. $1.95; Berkeley 1982 pap. $1.95; Buccaneer Bks. repr. 1982 lib. bdg. $16.95

Thirty Strange Stories. 1897. Short Story Index Repr. Ser. Ayer repr. of 1897 ed. $27.50

The War of the Worlds. 1898. Buccaneer Bks. repr. 1981 lib. bdg. $16.95; Oxford text ed. 1972 pap. $1.95; Putnam 1978 $6.95; Random 1960 $5.39; Scholastic repr. of 1968 ed. 1982 pap. $2.25

The First Men in the Moon. 1901. Airmont Class. Ser. pap. $1.25

The Food of the Gods. 1904. Airmont Class. Ser. pap. $.95.

In the Days of the Comet. 1906. Airmont Class. Ser. pap. $1.25; intro. by Brian Aldiss, Merrimack 1985 pap. $6.95

Tono-Bungay. 1908. Amereon $17.95

The History of Mister Polly. 1910. Ed. by Gordon N. Ray, Houghton Mifflin 1961 pap. $5.50

The Country of the Blind, and Other Stories. 1911. Short Story Index Repr. Ser. Ayer repr. of 1913 ed. $25.00

The King Who Was a King: An Unconventional Novel. Greenwood repr. of 1929 ed. 1972 lib. bdg. $18.75

The Fate of Man. Essay Index Repr. Ser. Ayer repr. of 1939 ed. $19.00

Modern Utopia. Intro. by M. R. Hillegas, Univ. of Nebraska Pr. (Bison) 1967 pap. $5.95

Mr. Britling Sees It Through. 1979. Buccaneer Bks. 1983 lib. bdg. $16.95; Merrimack 1985 pap. $6.95; Norwood repr. of 1917 ed. 1979 lib. bdg. $30.00
Little Wars. Da Capo 1977 pap. $4.95

Books about Wells

Costa, Richard H. *H. G. Wells. Twayne's Eng. Author Ser.* G. K. Hall rev. ed. 1985 lib. bdg. $13.95
Hammond, J. R. *Herbert George Wells: An Annotated Bibliography of His Works. Reference Lib. of the Humanities* Garland 1977 lib. bdg. $36.00
Haynes, R. D. *H. G. Wells, Discoverer of the Future: The Influence of Science on His Thought.* New York Univ. Pr. 1980 $30.00
Huntington, John. *The Logic of Fantasy: H. G. Wells and Science Fiction.* Columbia Univ. Pr. 1982 $26.00
Parrinder, Patrick, ed. *H. G. Wells: The Critical Heritage.* Routledge & Kegan 1972 $32.50 1985 pap. $15.00
Ray, Gordon N. *H. G. Wells and Rebecca West.* Yale Univ. Pr. 1974 $15.00
Reed, John R. *The Natural History of H. G. Wells.* Ohio Univ. Pr. 1982 lib. bdg. $25.95
Wells, Geoffrey H. *The Works of H. G. Wells, 1887–1925: A Bibliography, Dictionary, and Subject Index.* Burt Franklin repr. of 1926 ed. $15.00; Century Bookbindery 1983 $65.00
West, Anthony. *H. G. Wells: Aspects of a Life.* New Amer. Lib. 1985 pap. $10.95; Random 1984 $22.95

WEST, DAME REBECCA (pseud. of Cicily Isabel Fairfield). 1892–1983

Taking her name from one of Ibsen's strong-minded women, Rebecca West was a politically and socially active feminist all her long life. She had an intense ten-year affair with H. G. Wells, with whom she had a son. The work of a brilliant and versatile novelist, critic, essayist, and political commentator, West's greatest literary achievement is perhaps her travel diary, *Black Lamb and Grey Falcon: A Journey through Yugoslavia* (1942, o.p.). Five years in the writing, it is the story of an Easter trip that she and her husband made through Yugoslavia in 1937. A historical narrative with excellent reporting, it is essentially an analysis of Western culture. During World War II, she superintended British broadcast talks to Yugoslavia. Her remarkable reports of the treason trials of Lord Haw and John Amery appeared first in the *New Yorker* and are included with other stories about traitors in *The Meaning of Treason* (1947, o.p.), which was expanded to deal with traitors and defectors since World War II as *The New Meaning of Treason* (o.p.). *The Birds Fall Down* (1966, o.p.), which was a bestseller, is the story of a young Englishwoman caught in the grip of Russian terrorists. From a true story told to her half a century ago by the sister of Ford Madox Ford (who had heard it from her Russian husband), West "created a rich and instructive spy thriller, which contains an immense amount of brilliantly distributed information about the ideologies of the time, the rituals of the Russian Orthodox Church, the conflicts of customs, belief, and temperament between Russians and Western Europeans, the techniques of espionage and counter-espionage, and the life of exiles in Paris" (*New Yorker*).

Unlike that of her more famous contemporaries, her fiction is stylistically and structurally conventional, but it effectively details the evolution of daily life amid the backdrop of such historical disasters as the world wars. Her critical works include *Arnold Bennett Himself, Henry James, Strange Necessity: Essays and Reviews*, and *The Court and the Castle* (1957), a study of political and religious ideas in imaginative literature. In 1949 she was made a Dame Commander of the Order of the British Empire.

BOOKS BY WEST

The Young Rebecca: Writings of Rebecca West, 1911–1917. Ed. by Jane Marcus, Viking 1981 $25.00
The Thinking Reed. AMS Pr. repr. 1936 ed. $28.00; Penguin 1985 pap. $7.95
The Judge. Dial 1981 pap. $6.95
The Return of the Soldier. Dial 1982 pap. $6.95
Harriet Hume. Virago Modern Classic Ser. Dial 1982 pap. $7.95
This Real Night. Fiction Ser. Viking 1985. $16.95. Sequel to *The Fountain Overflows*. First of six announced posthumous works.
Rebecca West: A Celebration, a Selection of Her Writings Chosen by Her Publishers and Rebecca West. Intro. by Samuel Hynes. Viking 1977 $20.00

BOOKS ABOUT WEST

Ray, Gordon N. *H. G. Wells and Rebecca West*. Yale Univ. Pr. 1974 $15.00
Wolfe, Peter. *Rebecca West: Artist and Thinker. Crosscurrents Modern Critiques Ser.* Southern Illinois Univ. Pr. 1971. $6.95

WHITE, T(ERENCE) H(ANBURY). 1906–1964

T. H. White began his excursions into Malory's medieval England with *The Sword in the Stone*, a fantasy about the education of the young King Arthur—"a rare concoction of wisdom and humor, fact and fancy, legend and history, wit and sarcasm." It was his eighth book and made his fame in England and the United States. *The Witch in the Wood, The Ill-Made Knight, The Candle in the Wind*, and the posthumous *The Book of Merlyn* comprise his modernized Arthurian cycle. In the fall of 1960 *The Once and Future King* (1939–58) was successfully produced on Broadway by Lerner and Loewe in musical form under the title of *Camelot*, the late President Kennedy's favorite musical. White died aboard the U.S. liner *Exeter* in the harbor at Piraeus, Greece. During a 1963 U.S. lecture tour just before his death, he recorded his candid impressions in a journal. *America at Last* (o.p.) "is unique in its easy, graceful, often humorous style, and in the way it reveals as much of its writer as it does of America" (*LJ*).

White made an authoritative and amusing translation, *The Book of Beasts: Being a Translation from a Latin Bestiary of the Twelfth Century* (1954). This medieval work brought together what was known or believed about animals, their habits, and symbolism at that time. The "dimension of the near tragic in which Tim White passed his life . . . makes it impossible to see him merely as another English eccentric. He was a man of quite terrifying self-knowledge. . . . He made at least two attempts to marry, but they got him nowhere. He was, and knew it, a homosexual and a sado-masochist. He came to believe that the condition deprived him of the right to a full relationship with any human being. Almost deliberately, it seems, he settled for the life of an odd-man-out" (Walter Allen).

BOOKS BY WHITE

Letters to a Friend: The Correspondence between T. H. White and L. J. Potts. Ed. by Francois Gallix, Berkley Publishing 1984 pap. $6.95; ed. by Francois Gallix, Putnam 1982 $14.95

The Sword in the Stone. 1938. Ill. by T. H. White, Putnam 1939. $11.95

Mistress Masham's Repose. 1946. Berkley Publishing repr. of 1946 ed. 1984 pap. $2.95; G. K .Hall 1980 $9.95

The Goshawk. 1951. Penguin 1979 pap. $3.95

The Once and Future King. Berkley Publishing 1983 pap. $3.95; Putnam 1958. $16.95

Darkness at Pemberley. Dover 1978 pap. $4.00

A Joy Proposed. Intro. by Kurth Sprague, Univ. of Georgia Pr. 1983 $8.95

BOOK ABOUT WHITE

Crane, John K. *T. H. White. Twayne's Eng. Author Ser.* G. K. Hall 1974 lib. bdg. $13.50

WILSON, ANGUS (ANGUS FRANK JOHNSTONE-WILSON). 1913–

Angus Wilson was born in Sussex, the youngest of six sons, and spent several of his childhood years in South Africa. A series of odd jobs was followed by a position in the Department of Printed Books in the British Museum, where he "worked on replacing as many as possible of the three hundred thousand books destroyed here during the bombing, and subsequently as deputy superintendent of the Reading Room." Writing short stories on weekends, he was immediately successful with them. In 1955 he left the museum to become a full-time writer.

James Gindin has, with some exaggeration, declared that "Angus Wilson is the best contemporary English novelist. . . ." *Anglo Saxon Attitudes* (1956, o.p.) is a long, intricate, and witty novel that satirizes, none too gently, such sacred British institutions as the Church, the universities, and Her Majesty's Government. *The Middle Age of Mrs. Eliot* (1958, o.p.) won the James Tait Black Memorial Award for fiction in 1959. *The Old Men at the Zoo* tells "crisply, wittily, and intelligently a story of conflict and conscience in a microcosm, the London Zoo in the 1970s. The characters are zany, but believably human. The plot reveals the tensions of modern society." In *Late Call* a retired couple face problems of readjustment when they go to live with their widowed son. *No Laughing Matter* traces the fortunes of a British family throughout half a century beginning in 1912.

In addition to short stories and novels, he has written *Emile Zola: An Introductory Study of His Novels* (1952), *Tempo: The Impact of Television on the Arts* (1966, o.p.), *The Strange Ride of Rudyard Kipling*, and *The World of Charles Dickens* (1970).

BOOKS BY ANGUS WILSON

For Whom the Cloche Tolls: A Scrapbook of the Twenties. 1953. Academy Chicago 1983 pap. $5.95
The Old Men at the Zoo. 1961. Academy Chicago 1983 pap. $5.95
Late Call. 1965. Academy Chicago 1983 pap. $5.95
No Laughing Matter. 1967. Academy Chicago 1983 pap. $5.95
As If by Magic. 1973. Penguin 1978 pap. $3.95
Setting the World on Fire. Viking 1980 $12.95
The Wrong Set. Academy Chicago 1983 pap. $5.95

BOOK ABOUT ANGUS WILSON

Faulkner, Peter. *Angus Wilson: Mimic and Moralist.* Viking 1980 $16.95

WILSON, COLIN. 1932–

Colin Wilson made his reputation in England and the United States on the publication of his first book, *The Outsider.* Sometimes known as the *enfant terrible* of English letters, whose soberer practitioners still do not take him entirely seriously, he has been prolific in many literary fields without ever quite reaching first rank as a novelist. He has written a number of competent thrillers. The Jack-the-Ripper story was the basis of his first novel, *Ritual in the Dark. The Sex Diary of Gerald Sorme* (o.p.), which is not as sensational as its title, grew out of the author's research for *The Origins of the Sexual Impulse* (o.p.). *The Violent World of Hugh Greene* (o.p.) is a "good, solid, rather old-fashioned novel of a young man making his way" (*Harper*). In *Necessary Doubt* (o.p.) a German philosopher is plagued by suspicions that a former student is a killer. In *The Glass Cage* (1966, o.p.), a mystery in which the murderer leaves quotations from WILLIAM BLAKE near his victims is solved by a Blake expert. Wilson has narrative skill, and James Gindin writes that his "heroes are innocents, seeking to understand all the violence and irrationality they find around them. . . . Yet, for all their naivete, his heroes do reflect something about contemporary Britain: the interest in violence and perversion; . . . the search for order and stability; the feeling that organized society is shallow and hypocritical."

Son of a Leicester factory worker, Colin Wilson left school at the age of 16. After a six-month period in the Royal Air Force, he held a succession of factory, office, hospital, and dishwashing jobs in both London and Paris, worked on the *Paris Review,* and began to write plays, short stories, essays, and poetry. Wilson spent several years in the 1960s as a Writer in Residence at Hollins College, Virginia.

BOOKS BY COLIN WILSON

Ritual in the Dark. Academy Chicago 1982 pap. $5.95
The Outsider. 1956. Tarcher 1982 pap. $7.95
The Mind Parasites. 1967. Wingbow Pr. pap. $3.95
The Occult. Random 1973 pap. $7.95
Mysteries. Putnam 1980 pap. $9.95
Schoolgirl Murder Case. Academy Chicago 1982 pap. $4.95

Poltergeist: A Study in Destructive Haunting. Putnam 1982. $13.95; Putnam (Perigee) 1983 pap. $6.95

BOOK ABOUT COLIN WILSON

Weigel, John A. *Colin Wilson. Twayne's Eng. Authors Ser.* G. K. Hall 1975 lib. bdg. $13.50

WOOLF, VIRGINIA. 1882–1941

Virginia Woolf was a great experimenter. She scorned the traditional narrative form and turned to expressionism as a means of telling her story. *Mrs. Dalloway* and *To the Lighthouse,* her two generally acknowledged masterpieces, are stream of consciousness novels in which most of the action and conflict occur beneath a surface of social decorum. *Mrs. Dalloway,* set in London shortly after the end of World War I, takes place on a summer's day of no particular significance, except that intense emotion, insanity, and death intrude. *To the Lighthouse'*s long first and third sections, each of which concerns one day ten years apart, of the same family's summer holidays, are separated and connected by a lyrical short section during which the war occurs, several members of the family die, and decay and corruption run rampant. *Orlando* is the chronological life story of a person who begins as an Elizabethan gentleman and ends as a lady of the twentieth century; Woolf's friend, Victoria Sackville-West, served as the principal model for the multiple personalities. *Flush* is a dog's soliloquy that, by indirection, recounts the Browning love story and elopement and life in Florence. Her last short novel, *Between the Acts,* was left without her final revision, but it is, nonetheless, a major representation of a society on the verge of collapse.

Fearing a final mental breakdown from which she might not recover, Woolf drowned herself in 1941. Her husband published part of her farewell letter to deny that she had taken her life because she could not face the terrible times of war. Leonard Woolf also edited *A Writer's Diary,* which provides valuable insights into his wife's private thoughts and literary development. Equally informative are his own autobiographies, particularly *Beginning Again* and *Downhill All the Way,* and *The Letters of Virginia Woolf and Lytton Strachey* (o.p.). Virginia Woolf's *Granite and Rainbow* contains 27 essays on the art of fiction and biography. There are many sidelights on Woolf in the writings, letters, and biographies of other members of her Bloomsbury circle, such as Roger Fry, JOHN MAYNARD KEYNES (see Vol. 3), and Lytton Strachey.

Also casting much light on her life, thought, and creative processes are *The Common Reader* (1925), *The Second Common Reader* (1933), *A Room of One's Own* (1929), *Three Guineas* (1938), *The Captain's Death Bed and Other Essays, The Death of the Moth and Other Essays* (1942), and various collections of her autobiographical writings, diaries, and letters.

BOOKS BY WOOLF

The Letters of Virginia Woolf. Ed. by Nigel Nicolson and Joanne Trautman, Harcourt 6 vols. 1977–82 ea. $5.94–$14.95

The Diary of Virginia Woolf. Ed. by Anne Oliver Bell, Harcourt 5 vols. 1977–84 ea. $15.95–$19.95
Jacob's Room. 1923. Harcourt 1978 $4.95
The Voyage Out. Harcourt repr. of 1926 ed. 1968 pap. $4.95
Mrs. Dalloway. 1925. Harcourt 1949 $11.95
To the Lighthouse. 1927. Harcourt 1981 $17.95; Harcourt 1964 pap. $4.95
To the Lighthouse: The Original Holograph Draft. Ed. by Susan Dick, Univ. of Toronto Pr. 1982. $65.00
Orlando: A Biography. 1928. Harcourt (Harvest Bks.) 1973 pap. $4.95
The Waves. 1931. Harcourt 1978 pap. $4.95; Peter Smith 1983 $13.50
The Waves: The Two Holograph Drafts. Ed. by J. W. Graham, Univ. of Toronto Pr. 1976. $50.00
Flush: A Biography. 1933. Harcourt 1976 pap. $4.95
The Years. Harcourt repr. of 1937 ed. 1969 pap. $7.95
Between the Acts. Harcourt repr. of 1941 ed. 1970 pap. $4.95
A Haunted House and Other Short Stories. 1944. Fwd. by Leonard Woolf, Harcourt 1966 pap. $2.95. Includes 12 stories hitherto unpublished in book form.

BOOKS ABOUT WOOLF

Apter, T. E. *Virginia Woolf: A Study of Her Novels. Gotham Lib.* New York Univ. Pr. 1979 $27.00 pap. $13.50
Bell, Quentin. *Virginia Woolf: A Biography.* Harcourt 1972 $12.50; Harcourt repr. of 1972 ed. 1974 pap. $9.95. The standard biography; especially revealing of her early years. The biographer is her nephew.
Brewster, Dorothy. *Virginia Woolf. Gotham Lib.* New York Univ. Pr. 1962 pap. $10.00. A study of the woman, the critic, and the artist of genius.
———. *Virginia Woolf's London.* Greenwood repr. of 1960 ed. 1979 lib. bdg. $22.50
Clements, Patricia, ed. *Virginia Woolf: New Critical Essays.* Ed. by Isobel Grundy, Barnes & Noble text ed. 1983 $28.50. Focuses on patterns of connection in Woolf's works and her relationship to other twentieth-century novelists.
Daiches, David. *Virginia Woolf.* Greenwood repr. of 1963 ed. 1979 lib. bdg. $24.75
DiBattista, Maria. *Virginia Woolf's Major Novels: The Fables of Anon.* Yale Univ. Pr. 1980 $27.00
Fleishman, Avrom. *Virginia Woolf: A Critical Reading.* Johns Hopkins Univ. Pr. 1977 pap. $7.95
Freedman, Ralph, ed. *Virginia Woolf: Revaluation and Continuity, a Collection of Essays.* Intro. by Ralph Freedman, Univ. of California Pr. 1980 pap. $4.95. Essays by major Woolf scholars representing the most interesting current approaches to her work.
Ginsberg, Elaine. *Virginia Woolf: Centennial Papers.* Ed. by Laura Moss Gottlieb, Whitston 1984 $25.00
Kelley, Alice V. *The Novels of Virginia Woolf: Fact and Vision.* Univ. of Chicago Pr. (Phoenix Bks.) 1976 pap. $4.95
Kumar, Shiv. *Virginia Woolf and Intuition.* Folcroft 1978 lib. bdg. $9.50
Leaska, Mitchell A. *The Novels of Virginia Woolf: From Beginning to End.* Afterword by John Lehmann, John Jay Pr. 1977 lib. bdg. $12.00; Univ. Pubs. 1977 lib. bdg. $12.00
Lehmann, John. *Virginia Woolf and Her World.* Harcourt 1976 $12.95
Majumader, Robin, and Allen McLaurin, eds. *Virginia Woolf: The Critical Heritage.* Routledge & Kegan 1975 $38.00

Marcus, Jane, ed. *New Feminist Essays on Virginia Woolf.* Univ. of Nebraska Pr. 1981 $21.50

———. *Virginia Woolf: A Feminist Slant.* Univ. of Nebraska Pr. 1983 $24.95

Marder, Herbert. *Feminism and Art: A Study of Virginia Woolf.* Univ. of Chicago Pr. (Phoenix Bks.) 1972 pap. $2.95

Naremore, James. *The World without a Self: Virginia Woolf and the Novel.* Yale Univ. Pr. 1973 $27.00

Poole, Rogers. *The Unknown Virginia Woolf.* Cambridge Univ. Pr. 1978 $27.95; Humanities Pr. text ed. 1982 pap. $11.45

Rose, Phyllis. *Woman of Letters: A Life of Virginia Woolf.* Oxford 1978 $22.50 pap. $6.95

Schlack, Beverly Ann. *Continuing Presences: Virginia Woolf's Use of Literary Allusion.* Pennsylvania State Univ. Pr. 1979 $22.50

Spater, George. *A Marriage of True Minds: An Intimate Portrait of Leonard and Virginia Woolf.* Pref. by Quentin Bell, Harcourt 1977 $12.95 1979 pap. $5.95

Sprague, Claire, ed. *Virginia Woolf: A Collection of Critical Essays. Twentieth-Century Views Ser.* Prentice-Hall 1971 $12.95

Squier, Susan M. *Virginia Woolf and London: The Sexual Politics of the City.* Univ. of North Carolina Pr. 1985 $19.95

CHAPTER 13

American Fiction: Early Period

William J. Stuckey

Some one said: "The dead writers are remote from us because we *know* so much more than they did." Precisely, and they are that which we know.
—T. S. ELIOT, *Selected Essays*

The earliest American literature consisted chiefly of travel books, diaries, sermons, and political writings. Imaginative literature was late in developing. This was, in part, because the early Puritan settlers were suspicious of the merely literary, but also because this continent was a wilderness to be explored, cleared, settled, and governed—all of which meant emphasis on the practical and utilitarian. Urban centers with printing houses and sufficient population with wealth and enough leisure time to support the development of nonutilitarian literature were long in coming, and when they did, American printers found it much more profitable to pirate the works of English authors than to pay royalties to lesser-known native authors.

Our earliest writers of fiction were, of course, recently transplanted Britishers who imitated the writers that were popular back home; most of them are unread today and largely forgotten except by specialists working in the period. Although many of them, from the standpoint of literary merit, deserve neglect, there are some who can still be read with interest. Ann Eliza Bleeker, for instance, who wrote the earliest fictional account of Indians in America, *History of Maria Kittle*, anticipated more skillfully written accounts of Indian and white encounters; and Hugh Henry Brackenridge's *Modern Chivalry*, inspired in part by eighteenth-century English satirists and by *Don Quixote*, was, for its time, a telling satire on certain aspects of American life. Despite obvious unoriginality of style and form, these and other writers of the early years managed to break ground for the growth and development of later novelists, partly by demonstrating that—popular prejudice to the contrary—the realities of American life could be converted into interesting and significant fiction, and also by discovering subjects and ways of feeling that would in time seem genuinely American.

The most important of these early writers was Charles Brockden Brown, a native of Philadelphia, whose novel *Wieland*, published in 1798, appeared more than 20 years before Washington Irving's *Sketch Book*. Although Brown never achieved Irving's popularity, his four Gothic novels were solid achievements in the art of fiction and marked the beginning of the kind of psychological-moral fiction that would later be written by Poe, Hawthorne, James, and FAULKNER. Somewhat later, Irving domesticated the German fairy tale by grounding it in the realities of life along the Hudson River. Irving also helped make the profession of authorship respectable in a country that still tended to wonder whether storytelling was not a waste of time, if not actually sinful. He also convinced the English that America was able to produce a writer who could write English almost as well as an Englishman.

James Fenimore Cooper's novels lacked the grace of Irving's—indeed his Leatherstocking Tales strike modern readers as heavy-handed and tedious—but in his rambling, melodramatic books about Natty Bumpo and his Indian friends and enemies, Cooper created a myth about pioneer America that has been heavily exploited by popular and serious writers ever since and has put a number of more recent novelists in his debt, including ERNEST HEMINGWAY. In Poe's and Hawthorne's tales and sketches one sees the beginning of the American short story and the development of an aesthetic that has influenced succeeding generations of short story writers in Europe as well as in the United States. And in the romances of Hawthorne and the great symbolic work *Moby Dick* by Herman Melville, one catches the American romance-novel (to use Richard Chase's phrase) at its most exciting point of development.

The local color impulses discernible in some of the earliest fiction about life in the New World were carried on and developed in the nineteenth century by lesser writers, each with his or her own motive and particular bent. Harriet Beecher Stowe, Joel Chandler Harris, Bret Harte, even, to some extent, Mark Twain, belong to this artistically less exacting fictional tradition.

Historically, the most important movement in the later period of American fiction was the realistic movement, exemplified by W. D. Howells, who was not only a self-appointed apostle for the movement but one of its chief exemplars as well. Between 1872 and 1920, the year of his death, he published almost 100 novels and travel books. Critics differ, sometimes violently, in their responses to the fiction of Henry James—Vernon L. Parrington, Jr., for one, found James entirely too mental and lacking in social awareness—but hardly anyone denies James's importance in the history of American fiction, for not only did he create an impressively large body of fictional work but he was an astute critic and scholar of the art of fiction as well. It was James, with his knowledge of French and Italian and his long residence abroad, who brought the American novel artistically into the mainstream of international fiction. Every American fiction writer of any stature who came after James has profited to some extent from his discoveries.

As the following selective list of scholarly and critical works suggests, a great deal has been written on the subject of early American fiction, in large part because prose fiction has been the most popular of the literary forms in the United States and also because it has seemed most central to the nature of American experience, at least during the past 185 years. Among the histories that might be singled out for special mention are Alexander Cowie's *The Rise of the American Novel* (o.p.) and Arthur Hobson Quinn's *American Fiction: An Historical and Critical Survey*, both of considerable use to those who want an overview of this period. Darrel Abel's four-volume history *American Literature* also contains detailed estimates of the major and minor fiction writers of these early years. Among the many theoretical works, two radically different approaches are exemplified in the work of Vernon L. Parrington, Jr., and Richard Chase. Parrington's three-volume *Main Currents in American Thought* strains all American literature through the author's liberal political sieve. In the controversial study *The American Novel and Its Tradition*, Chase limits his perspective to what he calls the romance-novel and produces a perceptive, if somewhat restricted, history of the American novel from Brown to Faulkner. The recent feminist movement has resulted in the publication of a number of books that focus exclusively on American women writers. One of the most useful of those dealing with women fiction writers of the early period is Nina Baym, *Woman's Fiction: A Guide to Novels by and about Women in America, 1820–1870.*

Two basic but very different bibliographic works are Jacob Blanck's *Bibliography of American Literature* and Robert E. Spiller and others' *Literary History of the United States.* Blanck's *Bibliography* describes the various editions of works published by American authors, includes a brief selection of secondary works, and when completed will cover 300 authors from the beginning of the Federal period up to and including writers who died before the end of 1930. Seven volumes have been published so far by Yale University Press. The Spiller bibliography lists the titles of individual authors but is mainly concerned with secondary materials on those works.

Three excellent books dealing with the social and historical perspective of the literary period between the Civil War and World War II are *Harvests of Change: American Literature, 1865–1914* by Jay Martin; *Realism and Naturalism in Nineteenth-Century Literature* by Donald Pizer; and *The American 1890's: Life and Times of a Lost Generation* by Larzer Ziff.

Critical appraisals and bibliographic and biographical information are included in two series on American writers: *Twayne's U.S. Authors Series* and the University of Minnesota's *Pamphlets on American Writers*, individual titles of which are listed below in the appropriate bibliographies.

Useful tools for the scholarly reader are the carefully edited texts of important American authors (including Twain, Hawthorne, Melville, Irving) sponsored by the Modern Language Association (MLA), originally by its Center for Scholarly Editions (CSE) of American Authors. Less-expensive volumes of carefully edited classic works by American authors published by the American Authors Series are convenient as well as reliable modern editions. Titles that have so far appeared in both series are listed under appropriate subheadings of individual authors.

In general, only volumes applying to American Fiction: Early Period, or closely related subjects are listed here. For further references, see Chapters 3 and 4 in this volume.

HISTORY AND CRITICISM

[SEE ALSO Chapters 2, 3, and 4 in this volume.]

Abel, Darrel. *American Literature*. Barron text ed. 4 vols. 1963 pap. ea. $4.95–$6.95. An account of American literature that describes and interprets American writing in the context of the personal lives of its authors.

Bartlett, Irving H. *The American Mind in the Mid-Nineteenth Century*. Amer. History Ser. Harlan Davidson text ed. 2d ed. pap. $7.95

Baym, Nina. *Woman's Fiction: A Guide to Novels by and about Women in America, 1820–1870*. Cornell Univ. Pr. 1978 $12.00. A study of fiction usually dismissed as trivial and sentimental.

Bewley, Marius. *The Eccentric Design: Form in the Classic American Novel*. Columbia Univ. Pr. 1959 pap. $14.00. Able criticism of James, Hawthorne, Cooper, Melville, and Scott Fitzgerald.

Cady, Edwin H. *Light of Common Day: Realism in American Fiction*. Indiana Univ. Pr. 1971 o.p. A scholarly discussion of the problem of realism and naturalism in writers from Hawthorne to James. Interesting, readable.

Chase, Richard. *The American Novel and Its Tradition*. Johns Hopkins Univ. Pr. repr. of 1957 ed. 1980 pap. $6.95. A discussion of major American novels in light of Chase's carefully worked out thesis that our best novelists have written novel-romances that express the contradictions in American life rather than the unities.

Davis, David B. *Homicide in American Fiction, 1798–1860: A Study in Social Values*. Cornell Univ. Pr. 1968 pap. $5.95. Primarily a study of the early nineteenth century, but also touches on modern fiction. Bibliography and analytical index.

Dick, Everett. *Tales of the Frontier: From Lewis and Clark to the Last Roundup*. Univ. of Nebraska Pr. (Bison) 1963 $25.95 pap. $5.95

Eichelberger, Clayton L. *A Guide to Critical Reviews of U.S. Fiction, 1870–1910*. Scarecrow Pr. 1974 $16.50. An index to critical comment on major and minor fiction taken from 30 selected periodicals of the nineteenth century.

Foerster, Norman, and others, eds. *American Poetry and Prose*. Houghton Mifflin 2 pts. 5th ed. 1970 pap. ea. $21.95

Foster, Richard, ed. *Six American Novelists of the Nineteenth Century: An Introduction*. Lib. on Amer. Writers Univ. of Minnesota Pr. 1968 $17.50. Cooper, Hawthorne, Melville, Twain, Howells, and James. Reprinted from the University of Minnesota *Pamphlets on American Writers Series*.

Gaston, Edwin W., Jr. *The Early Novel of the Southwest, 1819–1918*. Univ. of New Mexico Pr. 1961 o.p. A valuable critical study of southwestern fiction of the period, with synopses of the 40 novels discussed and biographical sketches of the authors.

Henderson, Harry B., III. *Versions of the Past: The Historical Imagination*. Oxford 1974 o.p. Focuses on the major figures.

Holman, C. Hugh. *The American Novel through Henry James*. Goldentree Bibliographies in Language and Lit. Harlan Davidson text ed. 2d ed. 1979 $24.95 pap. $14.95. Texts, bibliographies, and criticism of 42 novelists.

Howard, Leon. *Literature and the American Tradition*. Gordian text ed. repr. of 1960 ed. 1972 $15.00. An examination of the formation of our literary individuality.

Jones, Howard Mumford. *History and the Contemporary: Essays in Nineteenth-Century Literature*. Univ. of Wisconsin Pr. 1964 o.p.

———. *O Strange New World: American Culture—The Formative Years*. Greenwood repr. of 1964 ed. 1982 lib. bdg. $45.00

Kolb, Harold H., Jr. *Illusion of Life: American Realism as a Literary Form*. Univ. Pr. of Virginia 1969 o.p. Clearly written, with a new definition of realism.

Kunitz, Stanley J., ed. *American Authors, 1600–1900*. Ed. by Howard Haycraft, Wilson 8th ed. 1971 1977 $33.00. Contains 1,320 biographies. The standard reference.

Lawrence, D. H. *Studies in Classic American Literature*. Penguin 1977 pap. $3.95. Discussions of Whitman, Melville, Benjamin Franklin, Cooper, Poe, Hawthorne, and Dana. Eccentric but perceptive.

Levin, Harry. *The Power of Blackness: Hawthorne, Poe, Melville*. Ohio Univ. Pr. repr. of 1958 ed. 1980 pap. $6.95. "A remarkable, provocative, astute study attempts to demonstrate that the introspection, tragic awareness, and sense of alienation inherent in the works . . . give a [true] picture of the American mind and milieu" (*Booklist*).

The Literary History of the American Revolution. 1897. Burt Franklin 1970 $21.50

Literary History of the United States. 1948. Macmillan 3 vols. 3d ed. 1953 o.p. This is the standard modern history of American literature and is particularly useful because Volume 3 with the 2d supplement (the 1st supplement [1959] was incorporated into the 3d edition) is a bibliography that not only lists such useful information as where the chief research centers are in the United States and describes special catalogs, directories, dictionaries, and digests of interest to the student of American literature, but also includes detailed bibliographic entries on all significant American writers from the beginning up to 1970. It includes articles in journals and magazines as well as books and lists reprints of authors' works that have now gone out of print.

Martin, Jay. *Harvests of Change: American Literature, 1865–1914*. Prentice-Hall 1967 o.p.

Matthiessen, F. O. *American Renaissance: Art and Expression in the Age of Emerson and Whitman*. Oxford repr. of 1941 ed. 1968 pap. $16.95. A major study.

Maxwell, D. E. S. *American Fiction: The Intellectual Background*. Columbia Univ. Pr. 1963 o.p. Chapters on Poe, Cooper, Melville, Hawthorne, and others.

Miller, Perry. *The Raven and the Whale: The War of Words and Wits in the Era of Poe and Melville*. Greenwood repr. of 1956 ed. 1973 lib. bdg. $42.50. A lively chronicle of the literary scene in New York in the 1840s and the 1850s and the conflict between American- and foreign-oriented writers.

Morison, Samuel Eliot. *The Intellectual Life of Colonial New England*. Cornell Univ. Pr. 1960 pap. $9.95; Greenwood repr. of 1956 ed. 1980 lib. bdg. $24.75

Mott, Frank L. *A History of American Magazines*. Harvard Univ. Pr. (Belknap Pr.) 5 vols. ea. $30.00. The standard history.

Parrington, Vernon L., Jr. *Main Currents in American Thought*. 1927. Harcourt 3 vols. 1955 pap. ea. $6.95

Pattee, Fred L. *The Development of the American Short Story*. Biblo & Tannen 1923 $16.00. A study of the form as used by writers from Irving through O. Henry.

———. *First Century of American Literature, 1770–1870*. Richard West 1935 $18.00

Pizer, Donald. *Realism and Naturalism in Nineteenth-Century Literature*. Pref. by Harry T. Moore, Southern Illinois Univ. Pr. 1966 o.p.

Quinn, Arthur Hobson. *American Fiction: An Historical and Critical Survey*. Appleton 1964 o.p. A useful, if necessarily general, account of American fiction from the beginning to Willa Cather, with the final chapter "Retrospect and Prospect" and a bibliography.

———, ed. *Literature of the American People*. Irvington 1951 $127.50

Ringe, Donald A. *American Gothic: Imagination and Reason in Nineteenth Century*

Fiction. Univ. Pr. of Kentucky 1982 $17.00. A useful survey of the important writers of the period.

Scheick, William J. *The Half Blood: A Cultural Symbol in Nineteenth-Century American Fiction*. Univ. Pr. of Kentucky 1979 $9.75. An interesting account of the creation of half-blood characters in popular and serious novels.

Snell, George. *Shapers of American Fiction, 1798–1947*. Cooper Square Pr. repr. of 1947 ed. $23.50

Tyler, Moses C. *A History of American Literature, 1607–1765*. Corner House 2 vols. repr. of 1878 ed. 1973 $30.00

Voss, Arthur. *The American Short Story: A Critical Survey*. Univ. of Oklahoma Pr. 1980 pap. $9.95. A good general introduction.

Wegelin, O. *Bibliography of Early American Fiction, 1774–1830*. Peter Smith $9.75. Covers books printed before 1831.

Wright, Lyle H. *American Fiction: A Contribution towards a Bibliography*. Huntington Lib. 3 vols. $30.00. These bibliographies list American editions of prose written for adults by Americans and printed between 1774 and 1900. Research Publications, Inc., is reprinting on microfilm all the volumes of prose fiction listed by Wright.

Ziff, Larzer. *The American 1890's: Life and Times of a Lost Generation*. Univ. of Nebraska Pr. 1979 o.p.

BELLAMY, EDWARD. 1850–1898

It is as the "humane and romantic Utopian, campaigning for equality and social justice, rather than as a novelist or profound thinker, that Bellamy is remembered and read today." While working as a newspaperman in Springfield, Massachusetts, he began to write novels and later short stories, but did not achieve much success until the publication of *Looking Backward*. The hero of this fantasy falls asleep in 1887 and awakens in the year 2000 to find himself in a humane scientific and socialistic utopia. After selling fewer than 10,000 copies in its first year, *Looking Backward* became enormously popular. Clubs were formed to promote Bellamy's social ideas and he became a leader of a brief Nationalist movement, crusading for "economic equality, human brotherhood, and the progressive nationalization of industry." Americans as diverse as VEBLEN (see Vol. 3) and DEWEY (see Vol. 3) have been influenced by Bellamy's suggestion that the products of industrial energy, intelligently organized, could be used as a device for obtaining a nobler future. His *Religion of Solidarity* and *Talks on Nationalism* are again available.

BOOKS BY BELLAMY

Dr. Heidenhoff's Process. Works of Edward Bellamy Ser. AMS Pr. repr. of 1880 ed. lib. bdg. $29.00

Miss Ludington's Sister. Irvington repr. of 1884 ed. lib. bdg. $19.50

Equality. AMS Pr. repr. of 1887 ed. 1970 $10.00; Irvington repr. of 1887 ed. lib. bdg. $14.50 pap. text ed. $7.95; Scholarly repr. of 1887 ed. $8.00

Looking Backward, 2000–1887. 1888. Ed. by John L. Thomas, *John Harvard Lib. Ser.* Harvard Univ. Pr. 1967 $17.50; ed. by Frederic R. White, Hendricks House 1979 pap. $4.45; ed. by Robert C. Elliott, Houghton Mifflin (Riv. Eds.) 1966 pap.

$5.50; fwd. by E. Fromm, New Amer. Lib. (Signet Class.) pap. $1.95; ed. by
Cecelia Tichi, *Penguin Amer. Lib. Ser.* 1982 pap. $3.95; intro. by R. J. Wilson,
Modern Lib. College Ed. Ser. Random 1982 text ed. pap. $3.95
The Blindman's World and Other Stories. Irvington repr. of 1898 ed. 1972 $20.75; Som-
erset 1898 o.p.

Books about Bellamy

Bowman, Sylvia E. *Edward Bellamy Abroad.* New College & Univ. Pr. 1962 $15.95
Morgan, Arthur E. *The Philosophy of Edward Bellamy.* Greenwood repr. of 1945 ed.
1979 lib. bdg. $18.75; Hyperion Pr. repr. of 1945 ed. 1979 $12.00

BIERCE, AMBROSE (GWINNETT). 1842–1914?

Bierce has been called "bitter," "wicked," and "mysterious," the latter because of his dramatic disappearance into Mexico in 1913 and his probable
death there the following year. He served with distinction through the Civil
War, then went to San Francisco, where he contributed to periodicals. He
was early known for the vitriolic wit of his journalistic sketches. His short
stories, grim horror tales recalling those of Poe, are his best work. *Can Such
Things Be?*, a collection of supernatural tales, appeared in 1893. His poetry
is epigrammatic, but conventional. His *Fantastic Fables* and *The Devil's Dictionary* display his cynical aversion to "labor unions, democracy and socialism." Typical of his *Dictionary* definitions are: "Happiness, n. An agreeable
sensation arising from contemplation of the misery of another." "Prejudice,
n. A vagrant opinion without visible means of support."

Books by Bierce

Collected Works of Ambrose Bierce, 1909–1912. Gordian 12 vols. $185.00; Gordon 12
vols. $5,000.00
Collected Writings of Ambrose Bierce. Intro. by Clifton Fadiman, *Biography Index
Repr. Ser.* Ayer repr. of 1946 ed. $41.00; Citadel Pr. 1983 pap. $9.95
The Complete Short Stories of Ambrose Bierce. Ed. by Ernest J. Hopkins, fwd. by
Cathy N. Davidson, Univ. of Nebraska Pr. (Bison) 1984 pap. $10.95
Ghost and Horror Stories of Ambrose Bierce. Ed. by E. F. Bleiler, Dover 1964 pap.
$3.95; Gannon lib. bdg. $10.50; Peter Smith $12.75
The Fiend's Delight. Irvington repr. of 1873 ed. lib. bdg. $29.50
Letters. Ed. by B. C. Pope, Gordian repr. of 1921 ed. 1967 $12.50
Fantastic Fables. 1890. Dover repr. of 1898 ed. 1970 pap. $2.50
Tales of Soldiers and Civilians. Short Story Index Repr. Ser. Ayer repr. of 1891 ed.
$21.00
Black Beetles in Amber. 1892. Gregg 1970 o.p.
Can Such Things Be? 1893. Citadel Pr. 1977 pap. $2.95
The Devil's Dictionary (The Cynic's Word Book). Dover repr. of 1911 ed. pap. $2.50;
Gannon lib. bdg. $9.50; Peter Smith $12.25

Books about Bierce

Gaer, Joseph, ed. *Ambrose Gwinnett Bierce: A Bibliography and Biographical Data.*
1935. Burt Franklin 1968 $18.50. A useful scholarly work.
Grenander, M. E. *Ambrose Bierce. Twayne's U.S. Authors Ser.* G. K. Hall o.p.

McWilliams, Carey. *Ambrose Bierce: A Biography.* Shoe String (Archon) repr. of 1929 ed. 1963 o.p.

Neale, Walter. *Life of Ambrose Bierce.* AMS Pr. repr. of 1929 ed. $16.00; Richard West repr. of 1929 ed. $15.75

BROWN, CHARLES BROCKDEN. 1771–1810

Charles Brockden Brown, the first full-time man of letters in the United States, happens also to be the nation's first important novelist. He is noted chiefly for having written four Gothic novels, which were not only comparatively well written but were forerunners of what later developed into one of our most significant traditions, the kind of psychological-moral fiction written by Hawthorne, Poe, Henry James, FAULKNER, and FLANNERY O'CONNOR.

Brown was also admired and imitated by English writers such as MARY SHELLEY, PERCY SHELLEY, and THOMAS LOVE PEACOCK. Brown had his faults, some of which were indigenous to the Gothic tradition that he inherited, but he also had a considerable talent for invention and novelistic construction and also for realistic observation and what he called "moral painting." Within four years, from 1798 to 1801, he published six novels: *Wieland* (1798), his best-known and most-studied book, was based on an actual murder case in New York, but Brown was less interested in the sensational aspects than in the moral and psychological implications of the case. *Ormond* (1799) deals with an attempted seduction but is ultimately about the struggle of conflicting values. *Arthur Mervyn* (1799), the longest of Brown's books, is flawed by its didacticism and humorless but is of interest because of its realistic account of the yellow fever plague that occurred in Philadelphia in 1773. *Edgar Huntly* (1799), though in part incredible, is otherwise skillfully constructed and of significant moral complexity. Before he abandoned novel writing for a career in journalism in 1804, Brown published two more novels, *Clara Howard* (o.p.) and *Jane Talbot*, both in 1801.

Although Brown's work has received nothing like the kind of popular or critical attention accorded other writers of no more talent and lesser historical importance, scholarly interest has quickened somewhat over the past 30 years. All his fiction is once more in print, and carefully edited volumes of his works are being published by Kent State University Press.

BOOKS BY BROWN

Novels of Charles Brockden Brown. Burt Franklin 6 vols. repr. of 1887 ed. 1968 $114.00

The Novels and Related Works of Charles Brockden Brown: Wieland and Memoirs of Carwin. Ed. by Sydney J. Krause and S. W. Reid, Kent State Univ. Pr. 1977 $35.00

Wieland, or The Transformation. Doubleday (Anchor) pap. $4.95; ed. by Fred L. Pattee, Harcourt repr. of 1798 ed. 1969 pap. $6.95

Arthur Mervyn, or Memoirs of the Year Seventeen Ninety Three. 1799. Ed. by Sydney J. Krause and S. W. Reid, *Novels and Related Works of Charles Brockden Brown Ser.* Kent State Univ. Pr. 1980 $35.00

Ormond, or The Secret Witness. Ed. by Ernest Marchand, *Lib. of Class. Ser.* Hafner text ed. repr. of 1799 ed. 1962 $6.50; ed. by Sydney J. Krause, S. W. Reid, and

Russell B. Nye, *Novels and Related Works of Charles Brockden Brown Ser.* Kent State Univ. Pr. 1983 $35.00

Edgar Huntly: Memories of a Sleep Walker. 1799. Ed. by Sydney J. Krause and S. W. Reid, *Novels and Related Works of Charles Brockden Brown Ser.* Kent State Univ. Pr. 1984 $35.00; ed. by David Stineback, *Masterworks of Lit. Ser.* New College & Univ. Pr. 1973 pap. $6.95

Jane Talbot. 1801. Century Bookbindery repr. of 1857 ed. 1980 lib. bdg. $40.00; Saifer $10.00

BOOKS ABOUT BROWN

Clark, David L. *Brockden Brown and the Rights of Women.* Folcroft repr. of 1912 ed. lib. bdg. $10.00. Concerned with Brown as a proponent of radical ideas about the rights of women.

Dunlap, William. *The Life of Charles Brockden Brown.* Scholarly repr. 2 vols. 1977 $75.00. The original subtitle to this work was "Together with Selections from the Rarest of His Printed Works, from His Original Letters and from His Manuscripts before Unpublished." The work was begun by Brown's friend Paul Allen and completed by Dunlap. Although there are inaccuracies, it is the chief source of information about Brown, including letters and fragments of his works otherwise not available.

Grabo, Norman S. *The Coincidental Art of Charles Brockden Brown.* Univ. of North Carolina Pr. 1981 $19.00

Parker, Patricia. *Charles Brockden Brown: A Reference Guide.* G. K. Hall o.p. A useful bibliography.

Ringe, Donald A. *Charles Brockden Brown. Twayne's U.S. Authors Ser.* G. K. Hall $14.50; *Twayne's U.S. Authors Ser.* New College & Univ. Pr. 1966 pap. $5.95. A useful study.

Rosenthal, Bernard, ed. *Critical Essays on Charles Brockden Brown.* G. K. Hall 1981 $25.00

Vilas, Martin S. *Charles Brockden Brown.* Folcroft repr. of 1904 ed. lib. bdg. $10.00. One of the first studies that attempts historical criticism of Brown's work.

Warfel, Harry R. *Charles Brockden Brown: American Gothic Novelist.* Octagon repr. of 1949 ed. 1974 o.p. Reliable, useful biography with criticism of the novels.

CABLE, GEORGE WASHINGTON. 1844–1925

Although born and raised in New Orleans and well known for his stories about Creole life, Cable was always an outsider. He was much attracted to certain aspects of Creole life and anxious to record it before it entirely disappeared. His sympathies, however, did not extend to what he considered certain moral weaknesses in Creole civilization, particularly in its treatment of blacks. As time went on, Cable began to speak out ever more openly on racial injustices in Louisiana and in the South generally. This brought a great deal of bitter criticism from fellow southerners and ultimately resulted in his removal to Massachusetts. His most explicit fictional treatment of racial injustice is probably *John March: Southerner*, which he set in northern Alabama rather than Louisiana to emphasize the sectional aspect of the racial problem. He also gave speeches, wrote letters to editors, and published articles on the problems of blacks in the South.

Cable's most successful literary work is *The Grandissimes*, which has been compared in power and scope to the fiction of William Faulkner. The novel is somewhat marred by obvious editorializing and some wooden characterization, but it contains powerful scenes and deals with racial injustice, a subject all but taboo in the fiction of the time. Guy A. Cardwell has argued convincingly that Cable significantly altered Mark Twain's racial views when the two men were on a lecture tour together (*Twins of Genius*, o.p.). The number of Cable's works in print increased tremendously with the reprinting of the 19-volume *Collected Works*, along with the reprinting of other single titles such as *Doctor Sevier* and *Madame Delphine*.

BOOKS BY CABLE

Collected Works. Somerset 19 vols. $695.00. Reprints of original publications from 1879 to 1918.

Silent South: Including the Freedman's Case in Equity, the Convict Lease System and to Which Has Been Added Eight Hitherto Uncollected Essays by Cable on Prison and Asylum Reform and an Essay on Cable by Arlin Turner. Intro. by Arlin Turner, *Criminology, Law Enforcement, and Social Problems Ser.* Smith, Patterson 1969 $10.00. A collection of essays on the plight of the black in the South after the Civil War.

Creoles and Cajuns: Stories of Old Louisiana. Ed. by Arlin Turner, Peter Smith 1959 $10.25

The Grandissimes. 1880. Hill & Wang 1957 o.p.; intro. by Newton Arvin, Peter Smith o.p.

Doctor Sevier. Irvington repr. of 1884 ed. lib. bdg. $16.50 text ed. pap. $9.95

Bonaventure. Irvington repr. of 1888 ed. 1972 $18.00. lib. bdg. $12.50

Strange True Stories of Louisiana. Short Story Index Repr. Ser. Ayer repr. of 1889 ed. $22.00

John March: Southerner. Black Heritage Lib. Collection Ser. Ayer repr. of 1894 ed. $26.50

Madame Delphine. AMS Pr. repr. of 1896 ed. $11.50; Scholarly repr. of 1896 ed. $9.00

Strong Hearts. Short Story Index Repr. Ser. Ayer repr. of 1899 ed. $17.00; Irvington repr. of 1899 ed. 1972 lib. bdg. $13.00

Bylow Hill. Ill. by F. C. Yohn, AMS Pr. repr. of 1902 ed. $15.00; Scholarly repr. of 1902 ed. $9.00

BOOKS ABOUT CABLE

Bikle, Lucy L. *George W. Cable: His Life and Letters.* Russell repr. of 1928 ed. 1967 $8.50. Written by Cable's daughter.

Butcher, Philip. *George W. Cable.* Twayne's U.S. Authors Ser. Irvington 1962 lib. bdg. $15.95 pap. $3.25

Ekstrom, Kjell. *George Washington Cable: A Study of His Early Life and Works.* Amer. Biography Ser. Haskell repr. of 1950 ed. 1969 lib. bdg. $49.95; *Essays and Studies in Amer. Language and Lit.* Kraus repr. of 1950 ed. pap. $15.00

Turner, Arlin. *George W. Cable: A Biography.* Louisiana State Univ. Pr. 1966 pap. $7.95; Peter Smith $10.25

——, ed. *Critical Essays on George Washington Cable.* G. K. Hall 1980 $26.00

CHOPIN, KATE. 1851–1904

The rediscovery of Kate Chopin's fiction has been one of the important literary events of recent years. Historians of American literature had long regarded her as a talented writer of tales about life among Louisiana Creoles, a mere local colorist, and not, therefore, deserving of inclusion in the ranks of major writers of American fiction. With the republication of her novel *The Awakening* (1899) in 1964 and, four years later, of her short story collection *Bayou Folk* (1894), her reputation has steadily grown. Today, *The Awakening* is widely admired both for its subtle artistry and its "stern realism," and a number of her short stories, such as "Desirée's Baby," are frequently singled out for inclusion in anthologies of short fiction and textbooks on American literature. Kate Chopin has now taken her place among the pioneers of the 1890s—STEPHEN CRANE, THEODORE DREISER, and FRANK NORRIS— as a fiction writer of considerable stature. With all her fiction once more in print and easily available, the reader is able to judge the range and quality of Kate Chopin's work.

BOOKS BY CHOPIN

Complete Works of Kate Chopin. Ed. by Per Seyersted, fwd. by Edmund Wilson, Louisiana State Univ. Pr. 2 vols. 1969 $60.00
Collected Works. Somerset 4 vols. repr. of 1890–99 ed. $95.00. Includes the early novel *At Fault* (1890) and two collections of short stories, *Bayou Folk* (1894) and *A Night in Acadie* (1897).
The Awakening and Other Stories. Intro. by Lewis Leary, *Rinehart Ed.* Harcourt text ed. 1970 pap. $10.95; Peter Smith $17.00; ed. by Nina Baym, *Modern Lib. College Ed. Ser.* Random 1981 pap. text ed. $3.95
At Fault. 1890. Somerset repr. $25.00
Bayou Folk. Gordon 1974 lib. bdg. $69.95; Irvington repr. of 1894 ed. 1972 $18.95
A Night in Acadie. Gordon $69.95; Irvington repr. of 1897 ed. 1972 lib. bdg. $23.00. Chopin's collected stories.
The Awakening. 1899. Avon 1972 pap. $2.95; Charles River Bks. $3.95; Gordon 1974 $69.95; ed. by Margaret Culley, *Norton Critical Eds.* 1977 $10.00 text ed. pap. $4.95

BOOKS ABOUT CHOPIN

Seyersted, Per. *Kate Chopin: A Critical Biography.* Louisiana State Univ. Pr. repr. of 1969 ed. pap. $5.95. A readable scholarly work with notes and a useful bibliography of primary and secondary works published in periodicals.
Springer, Marlene. *Edith Wharton and Kate Chopin: A Reference Guide.* G. K. Hall 1976 o.p. An excellent bibliography.

COOPER, JAMES FENIMORE. 1789–1851

Cooper is best known for his novels of the American Indian and backwoodsman and of the sea. *The Spy*, a story of the American Revolution, was the first American novel to win popularity in foreign countries. Cooper was obliged to publish it first at his own expense, as no American publisher would accept it. Its unexpected success turned him decisively to authorship. The Leatherstocking Tales are a series of five stories which

Cooper wrote backwards, as it were, beginning with the old age and death of his hero, and later returning to Leatherstocking's earlier life. Natty Bumpo, known variously as Leatherstocking, Deerslayer, Pathfinder, Hawkeye, and *la longue Carabine*, is the noble, fearless frontier scout. The Leatherstocking Tales, when measured against the more skillfully written and psychologically more subtle novels of later American writers, are crude and melodramatic, but historically they are of great importance. In these tales Cooper managed to create an authentic American myth about pioneer life, including themes and character types still to be found in writers like Ernest Hemingway.

Cooper originated the tale of ships and the sea. Although SMOLLET's *Roderick Random* and *Peregrine Pickle* are known as the first sea tales, they are really stories of sailors. Cooper served as a midshipman in the U.S. Navy for four years and had the knowledge of a professional seaman. *The Pilot* was inspired by *The Pirate* of Sir WALTER SCOTT. Cooper regarded Scott's novel as inaccurate in seamanship, and he wrote *The Pilot* as a challenge to Scott.

Among Cooper's publications were 33 substantial fictional works, 3 books of explicit social and political commentary, 5 travel works, a monumental history of the U.S. Navy (1839), a book of naval biographies, and an impressive quantity of miscellaneous writings, much of it anonymous and some of it still unknown to scholars. There is as yet no complete edition of his works. His grandson and namesake edited the miscellaneous selections from the family papers, *The Correspondence of James Fenimore Cooper*, which has been reprinted; many titles long out of print are once again available in single volumes. Ten-volume and 16-volume editions of his works have been reprinted, and carefully edited scholarly editions have also been published by the State University of New York Press.

BOOKS BY COOPER

Works of Fenimore Cooper. Greenwood 10 vols. repr. of 1891–93 ed. lib. bdg. $330.00; Richard West 16 vols. $250.00

The Correspondence of James Fenimore Cooper. Ed. by James F. Cooper, *Select Bibliographies Repr. Ser.* Ayer 2 vols. repr. of 1922 ed. $53.00; *Amer. Biography Ser.* Haskell 12 vols. repr. of 1922 ed. 1971 lib. bdg. $79.95; Telegraph Bks. 2 vols. repr. of 1922 ed. 1983 lib. bdg. $200.00

The Letters and Journals of James Fenimore Cooper. Ed. by James F. Beard, Harvard Univ. Pr. (Belknap Pr.) 6 vols. 1–2 o.p. vols. 3–4 (1964) set $50.00 vols. 5–6 (1968) set $50.00

Precaution: A Novel. AMS Pr. 2 vols. repr. of 1820 ed. $12.50; Scholarly repr. of 1820 ed. $13.50

The Spy. 1821. Lightyear 1976 lib. bdg. $19.95; *Masterworks of Lit. Ser.* New College & Univ. Pr. 1971 pap. $8.95

The Pioneers. 1823. Buccaneer Bks. repr. lib. bdg. 1984 $19.95; Lightyear 1976 lib. bdg. $15.95; New Amer. Lib. (Signet Class.) pap. $3.50; ed. by James F. Beard, *Writings of James Fenimore Cooper Ser.* State Univ. of New York Pr. 1980 pap. $14.94

The Last of the Mohicans. 1826. *Bantam Class. Ser.* 1981 pap. $2.50; Buccaneer Bks. repr. 1983 lib. bdg. $18.95; Dodd 1984 $12.95; New Amer. Lib. (Signet Class.)

pap. $2.50; ed. by James A. Sappenfield and E. N. Feltskog, intro. by James F. Beard, *Writings of James Fenimore Cooper Ser.* State Univ. of New York Pr. 1982 $44.50 pap. $14.95

Prairie. 1827. Lightyear 1976 lib. bdg. $19.95; New Amer. Lib. (Signet Class.) 1964 pap. $3.95; ed. by James P. Elliot, *Writings of James Fenimore Cooper Ser.* State Univ. of New York Pr. 1984 $44.50 pap. $14.95

Notions of the Americans Picked Up by a Travelling Bachelor. 1828. Ungar 2 vols. o.p.

The Red Rover. 1828. Lightyear 1976 lib. bdg. $16.95

The Wept of Wish-Ton-Wish. Scholarly 2 vols. in 1 repr. of 1829 ed. 1971 $17.00

The Bravo. 1831. Ed. by Donald A. Ringe, *Masterworks of Lit. Ser.* New College & Univ. Pr. 1963 $10.95 pap. $7.95

The Water-Witch, or The Skimmer of the Seas. AMS Pr. repr. of 1896 ed. $14.50; Scholarly repr. of 1896 ed. $14.00

The Pathfinder, or The Inland Sea. 1840. Intro. by Richard D. Rust, *Writings of James Fenimore Cooper Ser.* State Univ. of New York Pr. 1980 $44.50 pap. $14.95

The Deerslayer. 1841. *Bantam Class. Ser.* 5th ed. 1982 pap. $2.95; Buccaneer Bks. 1984 lib. bdg. $19.95; Dodd 1979 $8.95; Lightyear 1976 lib. bdg. $19.95; New Amer. Lib. (Signet Class.) pap. $2.95

Home as Found. 1838. Putnam 1961 o.p.

Afloat and Ashore: A Sea Tale. Lightyear repr. of 1844 ed. 1980 lib. bdg. $18.25

Satanstoe, or The Littlepage Manuscripts. 1845. Univ. of Nebraska Pr. (Bison) 1962 o.p.

The Chainbreaker, or The Littlepage Manuscripts. 1845. AMS Pr. 2 vols. o.p.; Scholarly o.p. A sequel to *Satanstoe.*

The Crater, or Vulcan's Peak: A Tale of the Pacific. 1847. AMS Pr. repr. of 1896 ed. $37.50; *John Harvard Lib.* Harvard Univ. Pr. (Belknap Pr.) 1962 text ed. $18.50

Sea Lions. 1849. Ed. by Warren S. Walker, Univ. of Nebraska Pr. 1965 o.p.

The Ways of the Hour. Irvington repr. of 1850 ed. lib. bdg. $16.00

BOOKS ABOUT COOPER

House, Kay S. *Cooper's Americans.* Ohio State Univ. Pr. 1966 $6.25. A study of two main types from more than 400 American characters in Cooper's fiction.

Peck, H. Daniel. *A World by Itself: The Pastoral Moment in Cooper's Fiction.* Yale Univ. Pr. 1977 $20.00. A sympathetic, scholarly book.

Philbrick, Thomas L. *James Fenimore Cooper and the Development of American Sea Fiction.* Harvard Univ. Pr. 1961 o.p. A specialized historical and critical work with Cooper as its main interest. Freneau, Smollett, and Poe are among others discussed.

Railton, Stephen. *Fenimore Cooper: A Study of His Life and Imagination.* Princeton Univ. Pr. 1978 $31.00. An important study.

Ringe, Donald A. *James Fenimore Cooper. Twayne's U.S. Authors Ser.* G. K. Hall $11.50; *Twayne's U.S. Authors Ser.* New College & Univ. Pr. 1962 pap. $5.95

Spiller, Robert E. *Fenimore Cooper: Critic of His Times.* Russell repr. of 1931 ed. 1963 $17.00

————. *James Fenimore Cooper. Pamphlets on Amer. Writers Ser.* Univ. of Minnesota Pr. 1965 o.p. Traces the evolution of Cooper from social observer to social critic, and his steadily growing maturity as a novelist. The main events of his life and brief summaries of his major works are included. A readable pamphlet in the useful American Writers Series. Bibliography.

GARLAND, (HANNIBAL) HAMLIN. 1860–1940

Garland was born and raised on pioneer farms in the upper Middle West, and his earliest and best fiction (most of it collected in *Main Travelled Roads*, 1891) deals with the unremitting hardship of frontier life—angry, realistic stories about the toil and abuses to which farmers of the time were subjected. As his fiction became more popular and romantic, its quality seriously declined, and Garland is remembered today chiefly for a handful of stories, such as "Under the Lion's Paw" and "Rose of Dutcher's Coolly." His only contribution to literary theory is *Crumbling Idols* (o.p.), in which he argued for an art that was truthful, humanitarian, and rooted in a specific locale. The first volume of his autobiography, *A Son of the Middle Border*, was followed by the much-admired second volume, *A Daughter of the Middle Border*, which was awarded a Pulitzer Prize. He published several other volumes of reminiscence, all of which are once more available with the reprinting of the 45-volume collection of his works.

BOOKS BY GARLAND

Collected Works. Somerset 45 vols. repr. of 1890–1939 ed. $1,200.00. For titles and prices of individual volumes, consult the publisher's catalog.

Hamlin Garland's Diaries. Ed. by Donald Pizer, Huntington Lib. 1968 $10.00

A Member of the Third House. Irvington repr. of 1892 ed. lib. bdg. $18.50

A Spoil of Office. Intro. by Eberhard Alsen, *Amer. Studies Ser.* Johnson Repr. repr. of 1892 ed. 1969 $26.00

Wayside Courtships. Short Story Index Repr. Ser. Ayer repr. of 1897 ed. $18.00

Boy Life on the Prairie. Univ. of Nebraska Pr. (Bison) repr. of 1899 ed. 1961 pap. $9.95

Prairie Folks. AMS Pr. rev. & enl. ed. repr. of 1899 ed. $16.00

Rose of Dutcher's Coolly. AMS Pr. repr. of 1899 ed. $12.50; Folcroft repr. of 1895 ed. 1984 lib. bdg. $30.00; ed. by Donald Pizer, Univ. of Nebraska Pr. (Bison) 1970 pap. $5.95

A Son of the Middle Border. Intro. by Donald Pizer, Univ. of Nebraska Pr. (Bison) repr. of 1917 ed. 1979 $29.95 pap. $6.95

A Daughter of the Middle Border. 1921. Peter Smith 1960 $11.00

Trail-Makers of the Middle Border. 1927. Somerset $34.00

Prairie Song and Western Story. Short Story Index Repr. Ser. Ayer repr. of 1928 ed. $20.00

Roadside Meetings. Folcroft repr. of 1930 ed. lib. bdg. $50.00

Companions of the Trail: A Literary Chronicle. 1931. Somerset $44.00

My Friendly Contemporaries: A Literary Log. 1932. Somerset $45.00

Afternoon Neighbors: Further Excerpts from a Literary Log. 1934. Somerset $49.00

BOOKS ABOUT GARLAND

Ahnebrink, Lars. *Beginnings of Naturalism in American Fiction, 1891–1903. Essays and Studies on Amer. Language and Lit.* Kraus repr. of 1950 ed. pap. $15.00; Russell repr. of 1950 ed. 1961 o.p.

Bryer, Jackson. *Hamlin Garland and the Critics: An Annotated Bibliography.* Ed. by Eugene Harding and Robert Rees, Whitston 1973 $12.50

Holloway, Jean. *Hamlin Garland: A Biography. Select Bibliographies Repr. Ser.* Ayer repr. of 1960 ed. o.p. Most useful for criticism, analyses, and summaries of Garland's books, and the bibliography of his publications.

Pizer, Donald. *Hamlin Garland's Early Work and Career.* Russell repr. of 1960 ed. 1969 $9.00. A useful book, particularly for Garland specialists, it deals with Garland's earliest work, some of which is of minor interest.

HARRIS, JOEL CHANDLER. 1848–1908

Harris was a newspaper man whose stories in black dialect appeared first in the columns of the Atlanta *Constitution,* with which he was associated for 24 years. The character of Uncle Remus became immensely popular. The stories, ten volumes of which have been published, helped to show the literary value of the folklore of the old plantation and of the black songs and ballads. Harris was the first writer to create out of diverse black oral-dialect stories in the South, in the nineteenth century, a local-color literature of lasting form. With the intensifying of the civil rights movement in recent years, however, dialect stories have become suspect as patronizing; Harris has not escaped partial eclipse. *On the Plantation* (1892, o.p.) is the autobiography of his early life.

BOOKS BY HARRIS

Complete Tales of Uncle Remus. Ed. by Richard Chase, Houghton Mifflin 1955 $35.00

Favorite Uncle Remus. Ed. and ill. by George Van Santvoord and Archibald C. Coolidge, Houghton Mifflin 1948 $15.95

Uncle Remus: His Songs and His Sayings. 1880. Norwood repr. of 1908 ed. lib. bdg. $45.00; ed. by Robert Hemenway, *Penguin Amer. Lib. Ser.* 1982 pap. $4.95

Nights with Uncle Remus: Myths and Legends of the Old Plantation. Century Bookbindery repr. of 1883 ed. 1982 lib. bdg. $35.00. "This collection is the second of Harris's Uncle Remus series, valuable because of the introduction in which he gives detail of his methods of collection, and a comparison of the stories included here with a volume of South African Negro stories" (Publisher's catalog).

Mingo and Other Sketches in Black and White. Short Story Index Repr. Ser. Ayer repr. of 1884 ed. $19.00; Irvington text ed. repr. of 1884 ed. lib. bdg. $16.50 pap. $6.50; Telegraph Bks. repr. of 1884 ed. 1981 lib. bdg. $35.00

Daddy Jake, the Runaway, and Short Stories Told after Dark by Uncle Remus. Short Story Index Repr. Ser. Ayer repr. of 1889 ed. $16.00

Balaam and His Master and Other Sketches and Stories. Short Story Index Repr. Ser. Ayer repr. of 1891 ed. $18.00; Telegraph Bks. repr. of 1891 ed. 1981 lib. bdg. $35.00

Stories of Georgia. Gale repr. of 1896 ed. 1975 $40.00

Tales of the Home Folks in Peace and War. Short Story Index Repr. Ser. Ayer repr. of 1898 ed. $24.50; Telegraph Bks. repr. of 1898 ed. 1981 lib. bdg. $35.00

Plantation Pageants. Short Story Index Repr. Ser. Ayer repr. of 1899 ed. $18.00; Telegraph Bks. repr. of 1899 ed. 1981 lib. bdg. $35.00

The Chronicles of Aunt Minervy Ann. Irvington repr. of 1899 ed. 1972 $21.00

On the Wings of Occasions: Being the Authorized Version of Certain Curious Episodes of the Late Civil War, Including the Hitherto Suppressed Narrative of the Kidnapping of President Lincoln. Short Story Index Repr. Ser. Ayer repr. of 1900 ed. $19.00; Irvington repr. of 1900 ed. lib. bdg. $17.50; Telegraph Bks. repr. of 1905 ed. 1981 lib. bdg. $30.00

Gabriel Tolliver: A Story of Reconstruction. Amer. in Fiction Ser. Irvington repr. of
    1902 ed. lib. bdg. $23.00
The Making of a Statesman and Other Stories. 1902. Bks. for Libraries o.p.
Told by Uncle Remus: New Stories of the Old Plantation. Ill. by J. M. Conde, A. B.
    Frost, and Frank Verbeck, Telegraph Bks. repr. of 1903 ed. 1981 lib. bdg. $35.00
Uncle Remus Returns. 1905. Telegraph Bks. repr. of 1918 ed. 1981 lib. bdg. $35.00

BOOKS ABOUT HARRIS

Bickley, R. Bruce, Jr. *Critical Essays on Joel Chandler Harris. Critical Essays on Amer.
    Lit. Ser.* G. K. Hall (Twayne) 1981 $26.00
———. *Joel Chandler Harris. Twayne's U.S. Authors Ser.* G. K. Hall 1978 lib. bdg.
    $13.50
Cousins, Paul M. *Joel Chandler Harris: A Biography. Southern Literary Studies* Louisi-
    ana State Univ. Pr. 1968 $22.50

HARTE, (FRANCIS) BRET(T). 1836?–1902

Bret Harte's birth year is variously given as 1836 and 1839, and his tomb-
stone bears the date 1837. He is remembered especially for his two short stories "The Luck of Roaring Camp" and "The Outcasts of Poker Flat," both
achievements in local color. The former is the story of an orphaned baby
adopted by the men in a gold-rush-era mining camp; it was dramatized by
Dion Boucicault in 1894. The latter is a tale of four undesirables expelled
from a mining camp and their losing battle against a blizzard. Although he
was born in the East and lived there and in Europe most of his life, Harte's
17 years of residence in California have associated him most closely with
that state, and the scenes of all his successful stories are laid in the West.
His contemporary sketches of life in San Francisco in the 1860s, written
with Mark Twain, were first collected in book form as *Sketches of the Sixties.*
When he went east again to settle in Boston in 1871, his talent seems to
have deserted him. Much of his later life was spent in England.

BOOKS BY HARTE

The Writings of Bret Harte. AMS Pr. 20 vols. repr. of 1903 ed. $650.00
Condensed Novels. Short Story Index Repr. Ser. Ayer repr. of 1871 ed. $14.50; *Short
    Story Index Repr. Ser.* Ayer repr. of 1882 ed. $22.00; *Amer. Humorists Ser.* Irving-
    ton repr. of 1902 ed. lib. bdg. $24.50
The Queen of the Pirate Isle. 1866. Warne o.p.
The Luck of Roaring Camp. 1868. Ed. by Walter Pauk and Raymond Harris, ill. by
    Robert J. Pailthorpe, *Jamestown Class. Ser.* 1976 text ed. pap. $2.00; New Amer.
    Lib. (Signet Class.) pap. $2.50
The Outcasts of Poker Flat, The Luck of Roaring Camp, and Other Sketches. Amereon
    repr. of 1869 ed. 1976 lib. bdg. $14.40
Mrs. Scagg's Husband and Other Sketches. 1873. Somerset o.p.
Tales of the Argonauts and Other Sketches. Short Story Index Repr. Ser. Ayer repr. of
    1875 ed. $16.00
Gabriel Conroy. Irvington repr. of 1876 ed. lib. bdg. $16.50
Drift from Two Shores. Short Story Index Repr. Ser. Ayer repr. of 1878 ed. $18.00
Flip, and Other Stories. Short Story Index Repr. Ser. Ayer repr. of 1882 ed. $16.00
On the Frontier. Short Story Index Repr. Ser. Ayer repr. of 1884 ed. $16.50

The Heritage of Deadlow Marsh and Other Tales. Short Story Index Repr. Ser. Ayer
    repr. of 1889 ed. $16.00
Colonel Starbottle's Client and Some Other People. Short Story Index Repr. Ser. Ayer
    repr. of 1892 ed. $18.00
Sally Dows and Other Stories. Short Story Index Repr. Ser. Ayer repr. of 1893 ed.
    $18.00
In a Hollow of the Hills. Irvington repr. of 1895 ed. lib. bdg. $14.00
Maruja and Other Tales. Short Story Index Repr. Ser. Ayer repr. of 1896 ed. $27.50
Thankful Blossom, and Other Eastern Tales and Sketches. Short Story Index Repr. Ser.
    Ayer repr. of 1896 ed. $25.00
Stories in Light and Shadow. Short Story Index Repr. Ser. Ayer repr. of 1898 ed. $17.00
Tales of Trail and Town. Short Story Index Repr. Ser. Ayer repr. of 1898 ed. $21.00
Mr. Jack Hamlin's Meditation. Short Story Index Repr. Ser. Ayer repr. of 1899 ed. 1973
    $22.00
From Sand Hill to Pine. Short Story Index Repr. Ser. Ayer repr. of 1900 ed. $20.00
Three Partners, and Other Tales. Short Story Index Repr. Ser. Ayer repr. of 1900 ed.
    $23.50
Under the Redwoods. Short Story Index Repr. Ser. Ayer repr. of 1901 ed. $19.00
Openings in the Old Trail. Short Story Index Repr. Ser. Ayer repr. of 1902 ed. $19.00
(and Mark Twain). *Sketches of the Sixties.* Ed. by John Howell, AMS Pr. repr. of 1927
    ed. 1950 $19.50; Scholarly Pr. repr. of 1926 ed. 1970 $21.00

BOOKS ABOUT HARTE

Boynton, Henry W. *Bret Harte. Select Bibliographies Repr. Ser.* Ayer repr. of 1903 ed.
    1972 $10.00
Duckett, Margaret. *Mark Twain and Bret Harte.* Univ. of Oklahoma Pr. 1964 o.p. An
    attempt to offset the damage done to Harte's reputation by the derogatory com-
    ments about Mark Twain. "A useful study of two men whose careers began in
    the same place and ended worlds apart" (*Choice*).
Gaer, Joseph. *Bret Harte: Bibliography and Biographical Data.* Burt Franklin repr. of
    1935 ed. 1967 $23.50
Merwin, Henry C. *The Life of Bret Harte: With Some Account of the California Pio-
    neers.* Gale repr. of 1911 ed. 1967 $45.00
Morrow, Patrick. *Bret Harte.* Ill. by Arny Skov, *Western Writers Ser.* Boise State Univ.
    1972 pap. $2.00; Bowling Green Univ. 1979 $10.95
Pemberton, Thomas E. *The Life of Bret Harte. Select Bibliographies Repr. Ser.* Ayer
    repr. of 1903 ed. $21.00
Stewart, George R., Jr. *Bibliography of the Writings of Bret Harte.* Folcroft repr. of
    1933 ed. lib. bdg. $20.00

HAWTHORNE, NATHANIEL. 1804–1864

Compared to a more prolific writer like Cooper, Hawthorne's fictional output seems relatively small (four novels or, as he preferred to call them, "romances," three collections of short fiction for mature readers, as well as several children's books), but in quality Hawthorne has no rival in the nineteenth century except Melville. His stories, such as "Young Goodman
Brown," "Rappaccini's Daughter," and "My Kinsman, Major Molineaux,"
were remarkable achievements, and Hawthorne has been credited with
making a major contribution to the developing art of the American short
story. His greatest novel doubtless is *The Scarlet Letter*, a symbolic work of

subtle moral and psychological complexity. *The House of the Seven Gables* deals mainly with the destructive effects of the past. *The Blithedale Romance* is a skeptical study of various projects of social reform, including "equal rights for women" and socialism. *The Marble Faun* is a modern retelling of the fall of man, dealing with the ambiguous effects of sin. Hawthorne was well acquainted with other New England writers, notably EMERSON and THOREAU, and was a friend and mentor of the younger Herman Melville, on whose great work *Moby Dick* Hawthorne exerted an important influence. At his death Hawthorne left three unfinished romances and voluminous private journals, which have since been edited and published. The definitive edition of Hawthorne's work began to appear in 1964, and by 1972 all eight novels had appeared, including his apprentice work *Fanshawe* (1829), his collection of essays about England, *Our Old Home* (1863), and his children's books, *A Wonder Book* (1851) and *Tanglewood Tales* (1853), as well as *True Stories from History and Biography* and his American, French, and Italian notebooks.

BOOKS BY HAWTHORNE

The Centenary Edition of the Works of Nathaniel Hawthorne. Ed. by William Charvat and others, Ohio State Univ. Pr. 14 vols. 1962–80 ea. $8.00–$36.00

The Complete Novels and Selected Tales of Nathaniel Hawthorne. Ed. by Norman H. Pearson, Modern Lib. $10.95

Novels. Ed. by Millicent Bell, Literary Class. (Lib. of Amer.) 1983 $27.50. Contains all of Hawthorne's completed novels, from *Fanshawe* to *The Marble Faun.* A convenient and well-edited collection.

Complete Short Stories of Nathaniel Hawthorne. Doubleday 1959 $12.95

The Dolliver Romance, Fanshawe, and Septimus Felton. Short Story Index Repr. Ser. Ayer repr. of 1883 ed. $22.00. With an appendix containing *The Ancestral Footstep.* Hawthorne's first novel reprinted with his unfinished romances.

Tales, Sketches, and Other Papers. Short Story Index Repr. Ser. Ayer repr. of 1883 ed. $26.00

Best Known Works. Short Story Index Repr. Ser. Ayer repr. of 1941 ed. $31.50

Great Short Works of Nathaniel Hawthorne. Ed. by Frederick C. Crews, Harper 1967 pap. $3.80

The Portable Hawthorne. Ed. by Malcolm Cowley, *Viking Portable Lib.* Penguin rev. ed. repr. 1977 pap. $6.95

Selected Tales and Sketches. Ed. by Hyatt H. Waggoner, AMS Pr. repr. of 1950 ed. $37.00; *Rinehart Ed.* Holt text ed. 3d ed. pap. $13.95

Scarlet Letter and Other Tales of the Puritans. Ed. by Harry Levin, Houghton Mifflin (Riv. Eds.) pap. $5.50

Celestial Railroad and Other Stories. New Amer. Lib. (Signet Class.) pap. $2.95. Nineteen short stories that explore "the daydreams which edge toward nightmare."

The English Notebooks of Nathaniel Hawthorne. Ed. by Randall Stewart, Russell repr. of 1941 ed. 1962 o.p.

The Heart of Hawthorne's Journals. 1929. Ed. by Newton Arvin, Barnes & Noble 1967 o.p.

Twice Told Tales. 1837. Intro. by F. R. Gemme, *Airmont Class. Ser.* pap. $1.50

The Scarlet Letter. 1850. Ed. by Robert D. Spector, *Bantam Class. Ser.* 1981 pap. $1.50; Biblio Dist. (Everyman's) 1971 pap. $2.50; ed. by Harry Levin, Houghton

Mifflin (Riv. Eds.) 1960 pap. $5.50; ed. by Sculley Bradley and others, *Norton Critical Eds.* 2d ed. 1977 pap. $5.95; ed. by William Charvat and others, *Centenary Ed. of the Works of Nathaniel Hawthorne* Ohio State Univ. Pr. 1963 $20.00; ed. by Thomas E. Connolly, *Penguin Amer. Lib. Ser.* 1983 pap. $2.25

The House of the Seven Gables. 1851. *Bantam Class. Ser.* 1981 pap. $1.50; Biblio Dist. (Everyman's) 1973 $8.95 pap. $4.95; Macmillan (Collier Bks.) 1962 pap. $2.95; New Amer. Lib. (Signet Class.) pap. $1.50; ed. by Seymour L. Gross, *Norton Critical Eds.* text ed. 1967 pap. $9.95; ed. by William Charvat and others, *Centenary Ed. of the Works of Nathaniel Hawthorne* Ohio State Univ. Pr. 1965 $15.00; ed. by Milton R. Stern, *Penguin Amer. Lib. Ser.* 1981 pap. $2.95

A Wonder Book for Boys and Girls. 1851. Ed. by William Charvat and others, *Centenary Ed. of the Works of Nathaniel Hawthorne* Ohio State Univ. Pr. 1972 $25.00

The Blithedale Romance. 1852. Intro. by Alfred Kazin, New Amer. Lib. (Signet Class.) 1981 pap. $1.95; intro. by Arlin Turner, *Norton Lib.* 1958 pap. $2.45; intro. by Annette Kolodny, *Penguin Amer. Lib. Ser.* 1983 pap. $3.95

Tanglewood Tales. 1853. *Airmont Class. Ser.* 1968 pap. $1.25

Mosses from an Old Manse. Short Story Index Repr. Ser. Ayer repr. of 1854 ed. $24.50; ed. by William Charvat and others, *Centenary Ed. of the Works of Nathaniel Hawthorne* Ohio State Univ. Pr. 1974 $30.00

The Marble Faun. 1860. New Amer. Lib. (Signet Class.) pap. $2.95; ed. by William Charvat and others, *Centenary Ed. of the Works of Nathaniel Hawthorne.* Ohio State Univ. Pr. 1974 $30.00

BOOKS ABOUT HAWTHORNE

Bell, Millicent. *Hawthorne's View of the Artist.* State Univ. of New York Pr. 1962 $36.50

Fogle, Richard H. *Hawthorne's Fiction: The Light and the Dark.* Univ. of Oklahoma Pr. rev. ed. repr. of 1964 ed. 1975 o.p.

Gerber, John C., ed. *Twentieth Century Interpretations of the Scarlet Letter. Twentieth-Century Interpretations Ser.* Prentice-Hall (Spectrum Bks.) 1968 $8.95

James, Henry. *Hawthorne.* Ed. by John Morley, *Eng. Men of Letters* AMS Pr. repr. of 1887 ed. $12.50; Folcroft repr. of 1879 ed. lib. bdg. $30.00; Gordon $59.95. A perceptive estimate of some of Hawthorne's limitations as a writer.

Mellow, James R. *Nathaniel Hawthorne in His Times.* Houghton Mifflin 1980 $19.95 1982 pap. $10.95. A popular but scholarly biography.

Newman, Lea B. *A Reader's Guide to the Short Stories of Nathaniel Hawthorne.* G. K. Hall 1979 lib. bdg. $36.50. A useful bibliography.

Stoehr, Taylor. *Hawthorne's Mad Scientists: Pseudoscience and Social Science in Nineteenth-Century Life and Letters.* Shoe String (Archon) 1978 $21.50. Deals with the pseudoscience lore in the last century.

Turner, Arlin. *Nathaniel Hawthorne: A Biography.* Oxford 1980 $29.95. An excellent, reliable biography.

Waggoner, Hyatt H. *Hawthorne: A Critical Study.* Harvard Univ. Pr. (Belknap Pr.) rev. ed. 1963 $17.50

———. *The Presence of Hawthorne.* Louisiana State Univ. Pr. text ed. 1979 $15.00

HENRY, O. (pseud. of William Sydney Porter). 1862–1910

O. Henry left 250 short stories, an output of six years, which filled 15 volumes. These may be divided into his stories of the Southwest, of Latin America, and of New York City. *Cabbages and Kings* (1904, o.p.), his first book, deals with his South American adventures. *The Four Million* (1906) contains stories of New York life, a theme continued in *The Trimmed Lamp* (1907, o.p.) and *Strictly Business* (1910, o.p.). The typical O. Henry story is the expanded anecdote, ending in a sudden, humorous surprise, a formula imitated by many writers who followed him. Dale Kramer's sympathetic biography, *The Heart of O. Henry* (1955, o.p.), recounts the previously untold story of the author's early love affair and marriage, his conviction for embezzlement, his imprisonment, and the eight remaining years in New York where his writing made him famous. It is said that the most plausible explanation for his pen name is that he found it in the *U.S. Dispensatory* while serving as prison drug clerk. It was the name of a celebrated French pharmacist, Etienne-Ossian Henry, abbreviated. The authorized life is *O. Henry Biography* by C. Alphonso Smith (1916, o.p.); the definitive biography is *Alias O. Henry* by Gerald Langford (1957, o.p.). His two best-known stories, "The Gift of the Magi" and "The Ransom of Red Chief," are the title stories of two recently published collections of his works.

BOOKS BY O. HENRY

Complete Works of O. Henry. Fwd. by Harry Hansen, Doubleday 1953 $15.95
Best Short Stories. Buccaneer Bks. repr. 1983 lib. bdg. $16.95
The Best Short Stories of O. Henry. Modern Lib. $6.95
The Pocket Book of O. Henry Short Stories. Ed. by Harry Hansen, Washington Square Pr. pap. $3.95
My Tussle with the Devil and Other Stories. 1918. Bks. for Libraries o.p.
The Four Million and Other Stories. Airmont Class. Ser. 1964 pap. $1.25
The Ransom of Red Chief. Ed. by Walter Pauk and Raymond Harris, ill. by Robert J. Pailthorpe, *Jamestown Class. Ser.* text ed. 1979 pap. $2.00
The Gift of the Magi. Ill. by Shelley Freshman, Bobbs repr. 1978 $7.95; ed. by Walter Pauk and Raymond Harris, ill. by Robert J. Pailthorpe, *Jamestown Class. Ser.* text ed. 1979 pap. $2.00

BOOKS ABOUT O. HENRY

Current-Garcia, Eugene. *O. Henry.* Twayne's U.S. Authors Ser. G. K. Hall 1972 lib. bdg. $11.50
Langford, Gerald. *Alias O. Henry: A Biography of William Sydney Porter.* Greenwood repr. of 1957 ed. 1983 lib. bdg. $35.00
Long, Eugene H. *O. Henry: The Man and His Work.* Russell repr. of 1949 ed. 1969 o.p.
Moyle, Seth. *My Friend O. Henry.* Folcroft repr. of 1914 ed. $6.50. This is primary material for any account of O. Henry's life.
Smith, C. Alphonso. *O. Henry Biography.* Richard West repr. of 1916 ed. $30.00

HOLMES, OLIVER WENDELL. 1809–1894

[SEE Chapter 8 in this volume.]

HOWELLS, WILLIAM DEAN. 1837–1920

An editor of the *Atlantic Monthly* and later *Harper's Magazine*, W. D. Howells exercised a considerable influence on American letters during the latter third of the nineteenth century. He encouraged and helped publish such writers as Twain, CRANE, and Henry James, and for many years carried on a battle with the defenders of sentimental fiction and argued for the superiority of the new realistic mode. Howells was also a prolific writer, having published more than 100 works of fiction, travel, memoir, poetry, and drama. Among his early works were *Their Wedding Journey, A Chance Acquaintance, The Lady of the Aroostook,* and *A Modern Instance,* all forerunners of the book for which he is best remembered, *The Rise of Silas Lapham,* a novel about the moral rise of a self-made man who gives up his riches rather than profit from dishonesty. *A Hazard of New Fortunes* reflects Howells's later concern with social issues. Howells's *Criticism and Fiction and Other Essays* (1891) contains in the long title essay his reflections from his monthly department in *Harper's Magazine* (1869–92). Other nonfiction titles include a facsimile edition of his campaign biography of the *Life of Abraham Lincoln,* annotated in Lincoln's handwriting (1960, o.p.); the *Life and Character of Rutherford B. Hayes* (o.p.), another campaign biography; *The Complete Plays of W. D. Howells;* two autobiographical works, once more in print, both dealing with Howells's early life, *A Boy's Town* (1890) and *Years of My Youth;* as well as three literary reminiscences, *My Literary Passions, Literary Friends and Acquaintances* (1900), and *My Mark Twain* (1910). The two-volume edition of *Life in Letters of W. D. Howells* is again available.

BOOKS BY HOWELLS

A Selected Edition of W. D. Howells. Indiana Univ. Pr. 12 vols. 1968–73 o.p.

A Doorstop Acquaintance and Other Sketches. Folcroft repr. of 1867 ed. lib. bdg. $12.50

Their Wedding Journey. 1872. Indiana Univ. Pr. 1968 $20.00

A Chance Acquaintance. Folcroft repr. 1973 lib. bdg. $25.00; intro. by J. Thomas and David J. Nordloh, Indiana Univ. Pr. 1971 $20.00; Irvington repr. of 1873 ed. lib. bdg. $9.00; ill. by William S. Sheppard, Scholarly repr. of 1874 ed. 1970 $10.00

A Foregone Conclusion. Irvington repr. of 1875 ed. lib. bdg. $11.00; Scholarly repr. of 1905 ed. 1972 $12.00

The Lady of the Aroostook. 1879. Greenwood repr. of 1907 ed. lib. bdg. $18.75

The Undiscovered Country. Folcroft repr. 1973 lib. bdg. $25.00; Scholarly repr. of 1880 ed. 1971 $19.00

Doctor Breen's Practice. Greenwood repr. of 1881 ed. lib. bdg. $18.75; Scholarly repr. of 1881 ed. 1970 $10.00

A Fearful Responsibility, and Other Stories. Scholarly repr. of 1881 ed. 1970 $9.00

A Modern Instance. 1882. Intro. by George N. Bennett, Indiana Univ. Pr. 1977 $20.00; intro. by Edwin H. Cady, *Penguin Amer. Lib. Ser.* 1984 pap. $5.95

The Rise of Silas Lapham. 1885. Ed. by George Arms, *Rinehart Ed.* Holt text ed. 1949 pap. $9.95; ed. by Edwin H. Cady, Houghton Mifflin (Riv. Eds.) 1957 pap. $5.50; Macmillan (Collier Bks.) 1962 pap. $1.25; ed. by Don L. Cook, *Norton Critical Eds.* 1982 $24.95 text ed. pap. $7.95; *Penguin Amer. Lib. Ser.* 1983 pap. $4.95

The Minister's Charge, or The Apprenticeship of Lemuel Barker. Folcroft repr. 1973 lib. bdg. $25.00; Indiana Univ. Pr. 1978 $20.00; Scholarly repr. of 1887 ed. $19.00

Annie Kilburn: A Novel. 1888. Scholarly repr. of 1891 ed. 1972 $14.00

A Hazard of New Fortunes. 1890. Folcroft 1973 lib. bdg. $25.00; afterword by Benjamin Demott, New Amer. Lib. 1983 pap. $3.95. A novel of New York City life, with implicit social criticism.

The Quality of Mercy. 1890. Folcroft repr. 1973 lib. bdg. $25.00; intro. by James P. El-
liott, Indiana Univ. Pr. 1979 $20.00; Scholarly repr. of 1892 ed. $19.00
The Shadow of a Dream (and *An Imperative Duty*). 1892. Ed. by Edwin H. Cady, *Masterworks of Lit. Ser.* New College & Univ. Pr. 1962 $8.95 pap. $5.95
A Traveler from Altruria. 1894. Hill & Wang 1957 o.p. A utopian novel, pointing up
what Howells found wrong with America.
The Landlord at Lion's Head Inn. 1897. AMS Pr. repr. of 1897 ed. $27.50; Arden Lib.
repr. of 1900 ed. lib. bdg. $30.00; Richard West repr. of 1900 ed. 1979 lib. bdg.
$35.00
Suburban Sketches. Ill. by Augustus Hoppin, *Short Story Index Repr. Ser.* Ayer repr. of
1898 ed. $18.00
A Pair of Patient Lovers. Arden Lib. repr. of 1901 ed. 1978 lib. bdg. $20.00; *Short Story
Index Repr. Ser.* Ayer repr. of 1901 ed. $20.00
Kentons: A Novel. 1902. Folcroft repr. 1973 lib. bdg. $25.00; Greenwood repr. of 1902
ed. lib. bdg. $18.75; intro by G. C. Carrington, Jr., Indiana Univ. Pr. 1972 $15.00;
Scholarly repr. of 1902 ed. 1971 $10.00
Questionable Shapes. Short Story Index Repr. Ser. Ayer repr. of 1903 ed. $17.00
Leatherwood God. AMS Pr. repr. of 1916 ed. $16.00; Folcroft repr. 1973 lib. bdg.
$25.00; ed. by Eugene Pattison, Indiana Univ. Pr. 1976 $22.50; ill. by Henry Ra-
leigh, Scholarly repr. of 1916 ed. 1970 $14.00

BOOKS ABOUT HOWELLS

Brenni, Vito J. *William Dean Howells: A Bibliography. Author Bibliographies Ser.*
Scarecrow Pr. 1973 o.p.
Brooks, Van Wyck. *Howells: His Life and World.* Dutton 1959 o.p. Howells's experi-
ences are analyzed for the sources of characters, situations, plots, and social phi-
losophy.
Cady, Edwin H. *Critical Essays on William Dean Howells, 1866–1920.* Ed. by Norma
W. Cady, *Critical Essays on Amer. Lit. Ser.* G. K. Hall 1983 lib. bdg. $36.50
Eble, Kenneth E., ed. *Howells: A Century of Criticism.* SMU Pr. 1962 $12.95
Firkins, Oscar W. *William Dean Howells: A Study.* Russell repr. of 1924 ed. 1963 o.p.
Gibson, William M. *William D. Howells. Pamphlets on Amer. Writers Ser.* Univ. of Min-
nesota Pr. 1967 pap. $1.25
Kirk, Rudolf. *William Dean Howells.* Ed. by Clara M. Kirk, *Twayne's U.S. Authors Ser.*
New College & Univ. Pr. 1962 pap. $5.95
McMurray, William. *Literary Realism of William Dean Howells. Crosscurrents Modern
Critiques Ser.* Southern Illinois Univ. Pr. 1967 $6.95. A chapter is devoted to each
of 12 of Howells's novels, discussed in the light of his literary realism and philo-
sophic pragmatism—the latter influenced by William James.

IRVING, WASHINGTON. 1783–1859

Irving is the earliest American man of letters whose works are still popu-
larly read. He was "the first native writer to receive critical and popular approval in this country and in Europe." His works are diverse: essays, biographies, histories, short stories, and sketches. His imaginative works are the
short stories. Irving may be said to have assisted in the development of the
short story. The short stories consist of three volumes: *The Sketch Book of
Geoffrey Crayon*, containing his best works, "Rip Van Winkle" and "The Legend of Sleepy Hollow"; *Bracebridge Hall, or The Humorists: A Medley;* and
Tales of a Traveller, containing stories of action and adventure.

For two years Irving was attaché of the U.S. legation in Spain, and he later served as U.S. minister to Spain. His interest in Spanish history inspired four works: *The Life and Voyages of Columbus* and its sequel, *The Voyages and Discoveries of the Companions of Columbus* (1831, o.p.), which includes both titles, *A Chronicle of the Conquest of Grenada* (1829), and *The Alhambra*.

During a brief stay in the United States, Irving, as a member of a government commission, made a long trip into the West. In 1832, after a three-month tour of the Southwest, he wrote *The Western Journals* (o.p.). *A Tour on the Prairies* was published in 1835. *Astoria* (1836 rev. ed. 1849) was written from records furnished by John Jacob Astor and was done on commission from the Astor family. The sequel to *Astoria* was *The Adventures of Captain Bonneville U.S.A. in the Rocky Mountains and the Far West* (1837).

As a biographer Irving won little distinction. He wrote lives of Goldsmith, Mahomet and his successors, and George Washington, for whom he had been named.

A three-day celebration in Madrid in November 1959 commemorated the centenary of Irving's death. The mayor of Granada unveiled a plaque to the American whose "Tales of the Alhambra" had frequently been reprinted in both Spanish and English editions and who had devoted "more than 1,000,000 words to Spain, her people and her culture."

Books by Irving

Complete Works of Washington Irving: Journals and Notebooks. Ed. by Lillian Schlissel and Walter A. Reichart, *Twayne's Critical Eds. Program* G. K. Hall 1981 $33.50

Washington Irving: Representative Selections. Ed. by Henry A. Pochmann, Scholarly 1971 $39.00

Selected Works of Washington Irving. Ed. by William Kelly, *Modern Lib. College Ed. Ser.* Random text ed. 1983 pap. $5.95

The Sketch Book of Geoffrey Crayon, Gentn. Intro. by Andrew B. Myers, Sleepy Hollow Pr. repr. of 1852 ed. 1981 $23.95

Legend of Sleepy Hollow and Other Selections from Washington Irving. 1819–20. Ed. by Austin M. Fox, Washington Square Pr. pap. $3.95

Rip Van Winkle and the Legend of Sleepy Hollow. Intro. by Haskell S. Springer, ill. by Felix O. Darley, Sleepy Hollow Pr. 1974 o.p.; ill. by George H. Boughton, *Facsimile Class. Ser.* Smith Publications (Mayflower Bks.) 1980 $6.95

Bracebridge Hall, or The Humorists. 1822. Scholarly repr. of 1902 ed. $11.00

Tales of a Traveller. 1824. *Short Story Index Repr. Ser.* Ayer repr. of 1825 ed. $17.00

The Alhambra. 1832. Gordon 2 vols. 1976 $250.00; intro. by Andrew B. Myers, ill. by Felix O. Darley, Sleepy Hollow Pr. repr. of 1851 ed. 1982 $23.95

A Tour on the Prairies. 1835. Ed. by John F. McDermott, Univ. of Oklahoma Pr. repr. of 1956 ed. 1971 o.p.

Journals. 1919. Haskell 3 vols. repr. of 1919 ed. 1970 lib. bdg. $99.95

Journal of Washington Irving, 1823–1824. Ed. by Stanley T. Williams, Shoe String (Archon) repr. of 1931 ed. 1968 o.p.

Notes and Journal of Travel in Europe, 1804–1805. 1921. Scholarly 3 vols. in 1 lib. bdg. $69.00

BOOKS ABOUT IRVING

Brooks, Van Wyck. *The World of Washington Irving*. Dutton 1950 o.p.

Hedges, William L. *Washington Irving: An American Study, 1802–1832*. Greenwood repr. of 1965 ed. 1980 lib. bdg. $37.50

Irving, Pierre Monroe. *The Life and Letters of Washington Irving*. Intro. by Charles D. Warner, Darby 3 vols. repr. of 1869 ed. 1983 lib. bdg. $250.00; Gale 4 vols. repr. of 1863 ed. 1967 $85.00. By Irving's nephew and literary assistant.

Leary, Lewis. *Washington Irving*. Pamphlets on Amer. Writers Ser. Univ. of Minnesota Pr. 1963 o.p.

Myers, Andrew B., ed. *A Century of Commentary on the Works of Washington Irving*. Sleepy Hollow Pr. 1976 $20.00. Reprints the most important critical pieces of the period 1860–1960.

———. *The Worlds of Washington Irving*. Sleepy Hollow Pr. 1974 pap. $5.50. A scholarly but popular account of Irving's life.

Williams, Stanley T. *Life of Washington Irving*. Octagon 2 vols. repr. of 1935 ed. 1971 lib. bdg. $69.00

JAMES, HENRY. 1843–1916

James is one of the most prominent of a number of American writers who chose to live in Europe because it offered, among other things, a much richer texture of manners and morals. In most of his best fiction James's subject is the contrast between the simplicity (sometimes the simple-mindedness) and naturalness (sometimes the vulgarity) of Americans and the sophistication and decadence of Europeans. From *Daisy Miller* to the later novels like *The Ambassadors* and *The Golden Bowl*, James's ultimate concern is with drawing out of this contrast moral distinctions that have seemed too refined for many readers, including H. G. WELLS, who found James tediously complicated. James's reputation has not only survived such criticism, it has continued to grow; today even his detractors acknowledge his importance and influence. He is commonly regarded as our most technically gifted writer. CAROLINE GORDON has referred to him as "the scholar of the novel," for in addition to writing more than 20 novels and numerous short works of fiction (as well as sketches, plays, and memoirs), James wrote copiously on the art of fiction, on the fiction of other writers, and, most interesting of all, on his own fiction. The prefaces he did for the famous New York Edition (recently reprinted) of his own work were later edited by R. P. Blackmur and published as *The Art of the Novel*. These prefaces, along with *The Notebooks of Henry James*, provide a fascinating and instructive study of the development of the device of the "central intelligence," which paved the way for the "stream of consciousness" technique developed in the twentieth century by JOYCE and others.

James's biocritical work *Hawthorne* (1879) is perceptive, particularly about Hawthorne's limitations, but it tells a good deal about James as well. His *Letters* are once again in print, as well as his *Letters to A. C. Benson*. Several volumes of James's short stories have also been reprinted, including three volumes that were first published after his death: *Travelling Companions*, *The Landscape Painter*, and *Master Eustace*, all edited by Albert Mordell. The other four collections are *Terminations*, *The Better Sort*, *Embarrassments*, and *The*

Soft Side. Altogether, these seven volumes reprint 49 stories, many of them not available in standard collections. James's early novel *Watch and Ward* is also in print again as are a late one, *The Sacred Fount,* and his last novel, *The Sense of the Past,* which was published the year after his death. The great New York Edition is also back in print. (See also Chapter 16 in this volume.)

BOOKS BY JAMES

Novels and Tales of Henry James. Kelley 26 vols. repr. of 1907 ed. lib. bdg. $494.00. For information on volumes containing numerous shorter pieces, the reader should consult the publisher's catalog.

Novels, 1871–1880. Ed. by William T. Stafford, Literary Class. (Lib. of Amer.) 1983 $27.50

Great Short Works of Henry James. Ed. by Dean Flower, Harper pap. $4.33

Tales of Henry James. Ed. by Maqbool Aziz, Oxford 2 vols. 1973–79 ea. $39.00– $55.00

Tales of Henry James. Ed. by Christof Weglin, *Norton Critical Eds.* text ed. 1984 pap. $6.95

Eight Uncollected Tales. Ed. by Edna Kenton, *Short Story Index Repr. Ser.* Ayer repr. of 1950 ed. $18.00

The Portable Henry James. Ed. by Morton D. Zabel, *Viking Portable Library* Penguin rev. ed. 1977 pap. $6.95. Five of the shorter tales, three "nouvelles," criticism, essays, notebooks, memoirs, letters. Annotated bibliography.

Selected Short Stories. Penguin 1963 pap. $2.50

Henry James: Stories of the Supernatural. Ed. by Leon Edel, Taplinger repr. of 1970 ed. 1980 pap. $9.95

Tales of Art & Life. Union College 1984 pap. $14.75 text ed. pap. $4.75

The Art of the Novel: Critical Prefaces. 1934. Northeastern Univ. Pr. text ed. 1984 $9.95

The Notebooks of Henry James. Ed. by F. O. Matthiessen and Kenneth B. Murdock, Peter Smith $17.75; Univ. of Chicago Pr. $10.95

Letters of Henry James. Ed. by Leon Edel, Harvard Univ. Pr. 3 vols. 1974–80 ea. $25.00

Letters to A. C. Benson. Gordon $69.95

Roderick Hudson. 1876. *Novels and Tales of Henry James.* Kelley repr. of 1907 ed. lib. bdg. $27.50; intro. by Tony Tanner, Oxford 1980 pap. $4.95; Penguin 1981 pap. $3.95; intro. by Leon Edel, Peter Smith $10.25

The American. 1877. *Novels and Tales of Henry James.* Kelley repr. of 1907 ed. lib. bdg. $27.50; ed. by James W. Tuttleton, *Norton Critical Eds.* 1978 $14.95 text ed. pap. $9.95; ed. by William Spengemann, *Penguin Amer. Lib. Ser.* 1981 pap. $3.95

Watch and Ward. Intro. by Leon Edel, Grove repr. of 1960 ed. 1979 pap. $3.95

The Europeans. 1878. Ed. by Tony Tanner, *Penguin Eng. Lib. Ser.* 1985 pap. $2.50; Queens House repr. of 1878 ed. 1976 lib. bdg. $17.95

The Europeans: A Facsimile of the Manuscript. Intro. by Leon Edel, Fertig 1979 $35.00

Daisy Miller and Other Stories. 1878. Ed. by Michael Swan, Penguin 1984 pap. $2.50

A Bundle of Letters. Folcroft repr. of 1897 ed. lib. bdg. $15.00; Richard West repr. of 1880 ed. 1980 lib. bdg. $10.00. Written in 1879 for the *Parisian.* Unauthorized edition published in 1880.

Confidence. 1880. Ed. by Herbert Ruhm, Greenwood repr. of 1962 ed. 1977 lib. bdg. $24.75

The Portrait of a Lady. 1881. Ed. by Robert D. Bramberg, *Norton Critical Eds.* text ed. 1975 pap. $9.95; *World's Class. Ser.* Oxford 1981 pap. $4.95; ed. by Geoffrey Moore, *Penguin Eng. Lib. Ser.* 1984 pap. $3.95

Washington Square. 1881. New Amer. Lib. (Signet Class.) pap. $2.25; ed. by Mark Le Fanu, *World's Class. Ser.* Oxford 1982 pap. $2.95; ed. by Brian Lee, *Penguin Eng. Lib. Ser.* 1984 pap. $2.50

The Bostonians. 1886. *Bantam Class. Ser.* 1984 pap. $2.95; ed. by Alfred Habegger, Bobbs 1976 pap. $12.04; intro. by Louis Auchincloss, New Amer. Lib. (Signet Class.) 1984 $3.50; ed. by Charles Anderson, Penguin 1984 pap. $2.95; intro. by Irving Howe, *Modern Lib. College Ed. Ser.* Random 1964 pap. $3.95

The Princess Casamassima. 1886. *Apollo Eds.* Crowell 1976 pap. $5.95; *Novels and Tales of Henry James* Kelley repr. of 1908 ed. lib. bdg. $22.50; Penguin 1977 pap. $4.95; intro. by C. P. Oliver, Peter Smith $10.50

Tragic Muse. 1889. *Novels and Tales of Henry James* Kelley 2 vols. repr. of 1908 ed. lib. bdg. ea. $22.50; *Penguin Modern Class. Ser.* 1978 pap. $5.94

The Lesson of the Master. 1892. Darby repr. of 1915 ed. 1983 lib. bdg. $35.00

Real Thing and Other Tales. Short Story Index Repr. Ser. Ayer repr. of 1893 ed. $18.00; Folcroft 1973 lib. bdg. $35.00

The Siege of London. 1893. Gordon $59.95

Terminations. Short Story Index Repr. Ser. Ayer repr. of 1895 ed. $14.50; Folcroft 1973 lib. bdg. $40.00. Includes the title story and "The Death of the Lion," "The Coxon Fund," "The Middle Years," and "The Altar of the Dead."

The Spoils of Poynton (The Old Thing). 1896. Ed. by Bernard Richards, *World's Class. Ser.* Oxford 1982 pap. $4.95; Penguin 1977 pap. $3.50

Embarrassments. Short Story Index Repr. Ser. Ayer repr. of 1896 ed. $17.00. Contains title story and "The Figure in the Carpet," "Glasses," "The Next Time," and "The Way It Came."

What Maisie Knew. 1897. *Novels and Tales of Henry James* Kelley repr. of 1908 ed. $27.50; ed. by Douglas Jefferson and Douglas Grant, *World's Class.-Pap. Ser.* Oxford repr. 1980 pap. $3.50; Penguin 1974 pap. $3.95

The Turn of the Screw. 1898. Ed. by Robert Kimbrough, *Norton Critical Eds.* 1966 pap. $4.95

The Awkward Age. 1899. *Novels and Tales of Henry James* Kelley repr. of 1908 ed. lib. bdg. $27.50

The Soft Side. Arden Lib. repr. of 1900 ed. 1983 lib. bdg. $45.00; *Short Story Index Repr. Ser.* Ayer repr. of 1900 ed. $16.00; Folcroft 1973 lib. bdg. $35.00. Contains 12 stories, including "Europe" and "The Real Right Thing."

The Sacred Fount. 1901. Grove 1979 pap. $4.95

The Wings of the Dove. 1902. *Novels and Tales of Henry James* Kelley 2 vols. repr. of 1909 ed. lib. bdg. ea. $22.50; New Amer. Lib. (Signet Class.) pap. $3.95; ed. by Donald J. Crowley and Richard A. Hocks, *Norton Critical Eds.* 1978 $17.50 pap. $7.95; ed. by Peter Brooks, *World's Class. Ser.* Oxford 1984 pap. $4.95; Penguin 1974 pap. $3.95

The Ambassadors. 1903. *Novels and Tales of Henry James* Kelley 2 vols. repr. of 1909 ed. lib. bdg. ea. $20.00; ed. by S. P. Rosenbaum, *Norton Critical Eds.* text ed. 1964 pap. $7.95

The Better Sort. Short Story Index Repr. Ser. Ayer repr. of 1903 ed. $21.00

The Golden Bowl. 1904. Intro. by W. W. Robson, Biblio Dist. (Everyman's) 1984 pap. $5.95; *Novels and Tales of Henry James* Kelley 2 vols. repr. of 1909 ed. lib. bdg. ea. $22.50; ed. by Virginia L. Smith, *World's Class.-Pap. Ser.* Oxford 1983 pap. $4.95; ed. by Gore Vidal, *Penguin Eng. Lib. Ser.* 1985 pap. $3.95

The American Scene. 1907. Ed. by Leon Edel, Indiana Univ. Pr. 1968 $15.00 pap. $8.95

Sense of the Past. 1917. Folcroft repr. 1973 lib. bdg. $45.00; *Novels and Tales of Henry James* Kelley repr. of 1917 ed. lib. bdg. $20.00

Travelling Companions. Short Story Index Repr. Ser. Ayer repr. of 1919 ed. $17.00. A collection of seven stories written between 1868 and 1874.

The Landscape Painter. Short Story Index Repr. Ser. Ayer repr. of 1919 ed. $16.00; Darby repr. of 1919 ed. 1983 lib. bdg. $50.00. Contains four early uncollected stories: the title story, "Poor Richard," "A Day of Days," and "A Most Extraordinary Case."

Master Eustace. Short Story Index Repr. Ser. Ayer repr. of 1920 ed. $19.00. Includes four others besides the title story: "Longstaff's Marriage," "Theodolinde," "A Light Man," and "Benvolio."

BOOKS ABOUT JAMES

Beach, Joseph W. *Method of Henry James.* Saifer rev. ed. 1954 $10.00. An old study of James's development as a fictional artist, slightly revised, but one of the best ever written on the subject.

Canby, Henry S. *Turn West, Turn East: Mark Twain and Henry James.* Biblo & Tannen 1951 $18.00. A comparative biography showing two sharply different strains in American culture.

Dupee, Frederick W. *Henry James. Amer. Men of Letters Ser.* Greenwood repr. of 1951 ed. 1973 lib. bdg. $24.75

———, ed. *The Question of Henry James.* Octagon repr. of 1945 ed. 1973 lib. bdg. o.p. A useful collection of essays dealing with the controversial aspect of James's art.

Edel, Leon, and Gordon Ray, eds. *Henry James and H. G. Wells: A Record of Their Friendship and Their Quarrel.* Greenwood repr. of 1958 ed. 1979 $24.75. An interesting and instructive account of the differences between these two, as men and artists.

Leavis, F. R. *The Great Tradition: George Eliot, Henry James, Joseph Conrad. Gotham Lib.* New York Univ. Pr. 1963 pap. $12.50

Matthiessen, F. O. *Henry James: The Major Phase.* Oxford 1944 o.p.

———. *The James Family: A Group Biography—Together with Selections from the Writings of Henry James Senior, William, Henry, and Alice James.* Random (Vintage) repr. of 1947 ed. 1980 pap. $7.95

Putt, Samuel G. *Henry James: A Reader's Guide.* Intro. by Arthur Mizener, Cornell Univ. Pr. 1967 o.p. A good, readable introductory work to James's 22 novels and 112 tales.

JEWETT, SARAH ORNE. 1849–1909

Sarah Orne Jewett was one of the best writers of local color, a genre noted for emphasis on quaintness of place and oddness of character, and marked by sentimentality of tone. She was born in the town of South Berwick, Maine, daughter of a doctor and descendant of distinguished New Englanders. South Berwick and environs is the locale for much of her fiction, and many of her characters were evidently drawn from observations of rural patients of her father, whom she frequently accompanied on his "rounds." Early influences were Harriet Beecher Stowe and W. D. Howells, a writer whom she resembled in manner and in cheerfulness of outlook. Sarah Orne Jewett was, in turn, an important influence on WILLA CATHER.

BOOKS BY JEWETT

Collected Works. Somerset 14 vols. repr. of 1877–1901 eds. $395.00

Stories and Tales. AMS Pr. 7 vols. repr. of 1910 ed. $185.00

Best Stories. Pref. by Willa Cather, Peter Smith 2 vols. in 1 $14.75

World of Dunnet Landing: A Sarah Orne Jewett Collection. Ed. by David Green, Peter Smith $11.00

Deephaven and Other Stories. Ed. by Richard Cary, *Masterworks of Lit. Ser.* College & Univ. Pr. 1966 o.p.

Sarah O. Jewett: Letters. Ed. by Richard Cary, Colby rev. & enl. ed. 1967 o.p.

Old Friends and New. Short Story Index Repr. Ser. Ayer repr. of 1879 ed. $15.50

Country By-Ways. Arden Lib. repr. of 1881 ed. 1978 lib. bdg. $25.00; *Short Story Index Repr. Ser.* Ayer repr. of 1881 ed. $15.00; Darby repr. of 1881 ed. 1980 lib. bdg. $30.00

A Country Doctor. Irvington repr. of 1884 ed. 1972 $29.50

A White Heron. 1886. Crowell 1963 o.p.

Native of Winby and Other Tales. Short Story Index Repr. Ser. Ayer repr. of 1893 ed. $17.00

Tales of New England. Short Story Index Repr. Ser. Ayer repr. of 1894 ed. $16.00

Life of Nancy. Short Story Index Repr. Ser. Ayer repr. of 1895 ed. $19.00

The Queen's Twin and Other Stories. Short Story Index Repr. Ser. Ayer repr. of 1899 ed. $19.00; Irvington repr. of 1899 ed. 1972 lib. bdg. $16.00

The Country of the Pointed Firs. Intro. by Willa Cather, Arden Lib. repr. of 1927 ed. 1978 lib. bdg. $35.00; Avon 1977 pap. $1.75; Doubleday 1954 pap. $5.50; intro. by Marjorie Pryse, Norton 1982 pap. $6.95; pref. by Willa Cather, Peter Smith $11.00

BOOKS ABOUT JEWETT

Cary, Richard. *Sarah Orne Jewett. Twayne's U.S. Authors Ser.* New College & Univ. Pr. 1962 pap. $5.95

Donovan, Josephine L. *Sarah Orne Jewett. Lit. and Life Ser.* Ungar 1980 $12.95. A good, brief introduction.

Matthiessen, F. O. *Sarah Orne Jewett.* Peter Smith repr. of 1929 ed. $10.25

Thorp, Margaret F. *Sarah Orne Jewett. Pamphlets on Amer. Writers Ser.* Univ. of Minnesota Pr. 1966 pap. $1.25. Brief but useful.

MELVILLE, HERMAN. 1819–1891

Melville was a descendant of prominent Dutch and English families long established in New York. He grew up without much formal schooling and went to sea at age 20 after the financial failure and death of his father. He sailed on various ships, including a whaling ship, to and from the South Seas, and these experiences were to form the basis of his best fiction. His first two books, *Typee* and *Omoo*—partly romance and partly autobiographical travel books set in the South Seas—were popular successes, particularly *Typee*, which included a stay among cannibals and a romance with a South Sea maiden.

Moby-Dick also began as an adventure story, based on Melville's experience aboard the whaling ship, but in the writing of it—inspired in part by conversations with his friend and neighbor Hawthorne and partly by his own irrepressible imagination—Melville turned it into something so strange

that when it appeared in print his readers and critics alike were dumb-
founded, even outraged. His literary reputation was destroyed, and he was
obliged to live the rest of his life taking whatever jobs he could find and bor-
rowing money from relatives. He continued to write, however, published
some marvelous short fiction pieces—*Benito Cereno* (1855) and *Bartleby, the
Scrivener* are the best—and some Civil War poetry rivaled only by Whitman's *Drum Taps*. His posthumously published work *Billy Budd* is a brilliant short novel that although unfinished at Melville's death is a moving account of a young sailor's imprisonment and death.

Melville's reputation, however, rests most solidly on his great epic romance *Moby-Dick*. It is a difficult as well as a brilliant book, and many critics have offered interpretations of its complicated ambiguous symbolism.
Darrel Abel briefly summed up *Moby-Dick* as "the story of an attempt to
search the unsearchable ways of God," although the book has historical, political, and moral implications as well.

BOOKS BY MELVILLE

Great Short Works. Intro. by Warner Berthoff, Harper pap. $3.80; Peter Smith $14.00
Apple-Tree Table and Other Sketches. Greenwood repr. of 1922 ed. $15.00. Ten prose
    pieces originally published in periodicals, 1850–56, collected and originally pub-
    lished by Princeton University Press.
Selected Tales and Poems. Rinehart Ed. Holt text ed. 1950 pap. $12.95
The Portable Melville. *Viking Portable Lib*. Ed. by Jay Leyda, Penguin 1976 o.p. Selec-
    tions of letters linked by biographical comments, *Typee* and *Billy Budd* in full,
    parts of four other novels, and other writings.
Poems of Herman Melville. Ed. by Douglas Robillard, *Masterworks of Lit. Ser*. New
    College & Univ. Pr. 1976 pap. $6.95
Selected Poems. Ed. by F. O. Matthiessen, Folcroft 1973 lib. bdg. $17.50
Redburn, White-Jacket, Moby-Dick. Ed. by G. Thomas Tanselle, Literary Class. 1982
    $27.50
Typee, Omoo, Mardi. Ed. by G. Thomas Tanselle, Literary Class. 1983 $25.00
Typee: A Peep at Polynesian Life. 1846. New Amer. Lib. (Signet Class.) pap. $3.50;
    Writings of Herman Melville Ser. Northwestern Univ. Pr. 1968 $26.95 pap. $7.95;
    ed. by George Woodcock, *Penguin Eng. Lib. Ser*. 1972 pap. $2.95
Omoo: A Narrative of Adventures in the South Seas. 1847. Ed. by Harrison Hayford
    and Walter Blair, *Complete Works of Herman Melville Ser*. Hendricks House 1969
    $14.00. Sequel to *Typee*.
Redburn: His First Voyage. 1849. *Writings of Herman Melville Ser*. Northwestern Univ.
    Pr. 1972 $26.95 pap. $7.95; ed. by Harold Beaver, *Penguin Eng. Lib. Ser*. 1977
    pap. $4.95
White-Jacket, or The World in a Man-of-War. 1850. *Writings of Herman Melville Ser*.
    Northwestern Univ. Pr. 1970 $29.95 pap. $8.95
Moby-Dick, or The White Whale. 1851. Ill. by Mead Shaeffer, Dodd 1979 $8.95
Pierre, or The Ambiguities. 1852. *Writings of Herman Melville Ser*. Northwestern Univ.
    Pr. 1972 $28.95 pap. $8.95
The Piazza Tales and Other Prose Pieces, 1839–1860. 1856. Ed. by Hershel Parker,
    Writings of Herman Melville Ser. Northwestern Univ. Pr. 1985 $35.95 pap. $11.95.
    Includes "The Piazza," "Bartleby," "Benito Cereno," "The Lightning Rod Man,"
    "The Encantadas," and "The Bell Tower."

The Confidence Man: His Masquerade. 1857. Ed. by Elizabeth S. Foster, *Complete Works of Herman Melville Ser.* Hendricks House 1979 $14.00; New Amer. Lib. (Signet Class.) pap. $3.50; ed. by Harrison Hayford, Northwestern Univ. Pr. 1984 $32.95; ed. by Hershel Parker, *Norton Critical Eds.* text ed. 1971 pap. $8.95

Clarel: A Poem and Pilgrimage in the Holy Land. 1876. Gordon 2 vols. $250.00

Billy Budd, Sailor: An Inside Narrative. 1924. Ed. by Harrison Hayford and Merton M. Sealts, Jr., Univ. of Chicago Pr. (Phoenix Bks.) 1962 pap. $5.95. The definitive reading text, with extensive notes and commentary, together with a "genetic text" enabling the reader to follow the genesis and growth of the story; scholarship of the highest order. Published posthumously.

Journal Up the Straits, Oct. 11, 1856–May 5, 1857. Ed. by Raymond Weaver, Cooper Square Pr. repr. of 1935 ed. 1971 lib. bdg. $20.00. This is not very accurately edited, but it is the only transcription of Melville's "Journal Up the Straits, Oct. 11, 1856–May 5, 1857."

BOOKS ABOUT MELVILLE

Berthoff, Warner. *Example of Melville.* Norton Lib. repr. of 1962 ed. 1972 pap. o.p. A survey of the writer as a literary craftsman, his use of land- and seascapes, and the vitality of his imagination.

Bowen, Merlin. *The Long Encounter: Self and Experience in the Writings of Herman Melville.* Univ. of Chicago Pr. 1960 o.p. A reexamination from the viewpoint of his life-long preoccupation with the riddle of self and its relation to the world of experience. Index.

Chase, Richard, ed. *Melville: A Collection of Critical Essays.* Prentice-Hall (Spectrum Bks.) 1962 $12.95

Fisher, Marvin. *Going Under: Melville's Short Fiction and the American 1850's.* Louisiana State Univ. Pr. 1977 $20.00. Deals with Melville's struggle to write and survive in the America of his time.

Franklin, H. Bruce. *The Wake of the Gods: Melville's Mythology.* Stanford Univ. Pr. 1963 pap. $15.95. A reinterpretation of the major works, demonstrating how mythology determines and defines large parts of their structure and meaning.

Herbert, T. Walter, Jr. *Moby Dick and Calvinism: A World Dismantled.* Rutgers Univ. Pr. 1977 $22.50. An important book on the relationship of Calvinism and its decline in *Moby-Dick.*

Hillway, Tyrus. *Herman Melville.* Twayne's U.S. Authors Ser. G. K. Hall rev. ed. 1979 lib. bdg. $11.50

——. *Moby Dick Centennial Essays.* Ed. by Luther S. Mansfield, SMU Pr. 1953 $9.95

Howard, Leon. *Herman Melville: A Biography.* Univ. of California Pr. repr. of 1951 ed. 1981 pap. $7.95; *Pamphlets on Amer. Writers Ser.* Univ. of Minnesota Pr. 1961 pap. $1.25

Karcher, Carolyn L. *Shadow Over the Promised Land: Slavery, Race, and Violence in Melville's America.* Louisiana State Univ. Pr. 1980 o.p.

Parker, Hershel, ed. *The Recognition of Herman Melville.* Univ. of Michigan Pr. 1967 o.p. A collection of critical essays from 1846 on, in chronological order.

Rosenberry, Edward H. *Melville and the Comic Spirit.* Octagon repr. of 1955 ed. 1970 lib. bdg. $16.50. A survey of Melville's life and work. For the general reader.

Sedgwick, William E. *Herman Melville: The Tragedy of Mind.* Russell repr. of 1944 ed. 1962 o.p. One of the best and winner of a National Book Award.

Seelye, John. *Melville: The Ironic Diagram.* Northwestern Univ. Pr. 1970 o.p. A persuasive argument that for Melville truth "is question and answer, and by aban-

doning the answer imposed on existence by his questers, he only the more emphasized the final question. . . . "
Weaver, Raymond M. *Herman Melville: Mariner and Mystic.* Intro. by Mark Van Doren, Cooper Square Pr. repr. of 1921 ed. o.p. Follows Melville through his cruises to the South Seas and back again to America for a background study of his works.

POE, EDGAR ALLAN. 1809–1849

Poe was one of the few American writers to achieve international fame. His poetry influenced the French symbolists and his literary criticism, in which he disparaged sentimentality and insisted on the need for objective criteria, anticipated the modern formalist movement. His theory of the short story, as well as his own achievements in that genre, contributed very substantially to the development of the modern short story, in Europe as well as in the United States. Poe himself seems to have regarded his talent for fiction writing as of less importance than his poetry and criticism; and although his public preferred his detective stories *(Murders in the Rue Morgue, Marie Roget, The Gold Bug)* and other of his analytic tales *(A Descent into the Maelstrom, The Black Cat,* and *The Premature Burial),* his own preference was for works of the imagination *(Ligeia, The Fall of the House of Usher, The Masque of the Red Death),* which are tales of horror beyond that of the plausible kind found in the analytic stories. His *Letters* is "a virtually complete one-volume collection of 333 letters written . . . from 1824, when he was a 15-year-old cadet, to the year of his death in 1849." Most of the best criticism of Poe's fiction also deals with his poetry and criticism. However, three useful works that deal extensively with his fiction are cited below.

BOOKS BY POE

The Complete Works of Edgar Allan Poe. Ed. by James A. Harrison, AMS Pr. 17 vols. repr. of 1902 ed. ea. $17.50 set $295.00; intro. by Nathan H. Dole, Darby 10 vols. repr. of 1908 ed. 1981 lib. bdg. $400.00
The Complete Works of Edgar Allan Poe. Intro. by Nathan H. Dole, Darby 10 vols. repr. of 1908 ed. 1981 lib. bdg. $400.00
Works of Edgar Allan Poe. Ed. by Edmund C. Stedman and George E. Woodberry, *Select Bibliographies Repr. Ser.* Ayer 10 vols. repr. of 1895 ed. $250.00
Complete Stories and Poems of Edgar Allan Poe. Doubleday $15.95
Poems. Volume 1 in *Collected Works of Edgar Allan Poe.* Ed. by Thomas O. Mabbott, Harvard Univ. Pr. (Belknap Pr.) 1969 $32.50
Great Short Works of Edgar Allan Poe. Ed. by J. R. Thompson, Harper 1970 pap. $3.80
The Portable Poe. Ed. by Phillip V. Stern, *Viking Portable Lib.* Penguin 1977 pap. $7.95
Selected Prose and Poetry. Rinehart Ed. Holt text ed. rev. ed. 1969 pap. $13.95
Great Tales and Poems of Edgar Allan Poe. Washington Square Pr. 1982 pap. $2.95
Selected Tales. Ed. by Julian Symons, *World's Class. Ser.* Oxford 1980 pap. $4.95
Tales of Mystery and Imagination. Intro. by Padraic Colum, Biblio Dist. (Everyman's) repr. of 1908 ed. 1975 $8.95 pap. $3.95; Buccaneer Bks. repr. 1981 lib. bdg. $17.95; Lightyear repr. 1981 lib. bdg. $14.95
Letters of Edgar Allan Poe. Ed. by John Ostrom, Gordian 2 vols. repr. of 1948 ed. $30.00

The Narrative of Arthur Gordon Pym. 1838. *Amer. Century Ser.* Hill & Wang 1984 pap.
    $6.25; ed. by Harold Beaver, *Penguin Eng. Lib. Ser.* 1976 pap. $3.50
The Fall of the House of Usher and Other Tales. 1839. New Amer. Lib. (Signet Class.)
    pap. $2.75
Tales of the Grotesque and Arabesque. 1840. Peter Smith $11.00

BOOKS ABOUT POE

Buranelli, Vincent. *Edgar Allan Poe. Twayne's U.S. Authors Ser.* G. K. Hall 1977
    $11.50
Howarth, William L., ed. *Twentieth-Century Interpretations of Poe's Tales. Twentieth-
    Century Interpretations Ser.* Prentice-Hall (Spectrum Bks.) 1971 $9.95. A useful
    collection of essays by various critics.
Thompson, J. R. *Poe's Fiction: Romantic Irony in the Gothic Tales.* Univ. of Wiscon-
    sin Pr. 1973 o.p. A perceptive analysis of the tales.

STOWE, HARRIET BEECHER. 1811–1896

Harriet Beecher was born in Litchfield, Connecticut, one of nine children
of the distinguished Congregational clergyman and stern Calvinist Lyman
Beecher. Of her six brothers, five became clergymen, the most sympathetic
perhaps being Henry Ward Beecher. In 1832 she went with her family to
Cincinnati. There she taught in her sister's school and began publishing
sketches and stories. In 1836, she married the Reverend Calvin E. Stowe,
one of her father's assistants at the Lane Theological Seminary and a strong
antislavery advocate. They lived in Cincinnati for 18 years and six of her
seven children were born there. The Stowes moved to Brunswick, Maine, in
1850, when her husband became a professor at Bowdoin College.

The description of the death of Uncle Tom was written first, in one sit-
ting, on scraps of grocer's brown paper after her own supply gave out. She
then wrote the earlier chapters. *Uncle Tom's Cabin* was first published in
The National Era (1851–52), which paid $300 for the serial rights, and later
in book form in two volumes by John P. Jewett of Boston. It was an immediate bestseller; 10,000 copies were sold in less than a week, 300,000 within a
year. It was translated into 37 languages. The first American to use a black
as the hero of a novel, in the South she was hated and her accuracy questioned. Her reply was *A Key to Uncle Tom's Cabin.*

Always an industrious writer, she produced almost a novel a year. *Dred: A
Tale of the Great Dismal Swamp,* another tale of the South, sold well. *The
Minister's Wooing, The Pearl of Orr's Island, Oldtown Folks, Betty's Bright
Idea,* and *Agnes of Sorrento* have been reprinted. Among her English friends
were GEORGE ELIOT, the Ruskins, and Lady Byron, whom she defended in a
controversial article, "The True Story of Lady Byron's Life," in the *Atlantic
Monthly* in 1869.

BOOKS BY STOWE

The Writings of Harriet Beecher Stowe. AMS Pr. 16 vols. repr. of 1896 ed. $635.00
Regional Sketches. Ed. by John R. Adams, *Masterworks of Lit. Ser.* New College &
    Univ. Pr. 1972 $8.95 pap. $5.95
Uncle Tom's Cabin, or Life among the Lowly. 1852. *Bantam Class. Ser.* text ed. 1981

pap. $2.75; Biblio Dist. (Everyman's) 1976 $8.95 pap. $2.25; ed. by Ann Douglas, *Penguin Amer. Lib. Ser.* 1981 pap. $3.95

A Key to Uncle Tom's Cabin. 1853. *Amer. Negro: His History and Lit. Ser.* Ayer repr. of 1854 ed. 1968 $18.00; Scholarly repr. of 1853 ed. $11.00; Telegraph Bks. repr. 1981 lib. bdg. $50.00

Uncle Sam's Emancipation, Earthly Care, A Heavenly Discipline, and Other Sketches. *Black Heritage Lib. Collection Ser.* Ayer repr. of 1853 ed. $12.50

Dred: A Tale of the Great Dismal Swamp. AMS Pr. 2 vols. repr. of 1856 ed. $27.50; Scholarly 2 vols. repr. of 1856 ed. 1969 $35.00

The Minister's Wooing. Americans in Fiction Ser. Irvington repr. of 1859 ed. lib. bdg. $16.50; Scholarly repr. of 1859 ed. $12.00

The Pearl of Orr's Island: A Story of the Coast of Maine. Century Bookbindery repr. of 1886 ed. 1982 lib. bdg. $30.00; Irvington repr. of 1862 ed. lib. bdg. $13.00 text ed. pap. $5.95; Scholarly repr. of 1862 ed. $14.00

Oldtown Folks. AMS Pr. repr. of 1869 ed. $15.00; Scholarly repr. of 1869 ed. 1969 $14.00

Sam Lawson's Oldtown Fireside Stories. 1872. *Americans in Fiction Ser.* Irvington text ed. pap. $5.95

Palmetto Leaves. 1873. Ed. by Mary B. Graff, Univ. Pr. of Florida 1968 o.p.

Betty's Bright Idea. Short Story Index Repr. Ser. Ayer repr. of 1875 ed. $14.00

Agnes of Sorrento. Scholarly repr. of 1890 ed. $16.00

BOOKS ABOUT STOWE

Adams, John R. *Harriet Beecher Stowe. Twayne's U.S. Authors Ser.* G. K. Hall 1963 $11.50 pap. $3.45

Ammons, Elizabeth, ed. *Critical Essays on Harriet Beecher Stowe.* G. K. Hall 1980 $26.00

Foster, Charles H. *Rungless Ladder: Harriet Beecher Stowe and New England Puritanism.* Cooper Square Pr. repr. of 1954 ed. 1970 lib. bdg. $18.50. A useful analysis of her novels and the decay of puritanism.

Furnas, J. C. *Goodbye to Uncle Tom.* 1956. Apollo 1964 o.p. Condemns *Uncle Tom's Cabin* for fostering racial stereotypes.

Stowe, Charles Edward, and Lyman Beecher Stowe. *Harriet Beecher Stowe.* Richard West repr. of 1911 ed. $35.00. The authors were Stowe's son and grandson.

Wilson, Robert F. *Crusader in Crinoline: The Life of Harriet Beecher Stowe.* Greenwood repr. of 1941 ed. 1972 lib. bdg. $42.50. Most complete.

TWAIN, MARK (pseud. of Samuel Langhorne Clemens). 1835–1910

Samuel L. Clemens, steamboat pilot, prospector, and newspaper reporter, adopted the pen name "Mark Twain" when he began his career as a literary humorist. The pen name—a river pilot's term meaning "two fathoms deep" or "safe water"—appears to have freed him to develop the lecture personality and the deadpan manner that later became an important technique in the creation of his best work.

During his lifetime Twain wrote a great deal, much of it turned out like his public lectures, to make money. Even his least significant writing, however, reflects flashes of wit and reveals his marvelous command of colloquial American English still unrivaled in the history of American literature. His best work is his "Mississippi writing"—*Life on the Mississippi* and, especially, *The Adventures of Huckleberry Finn,* in which he was able to integrate his talent for comic invention with his satirical cast of mind and his tendency toward moral outrage. ERNEST HEMINGWAY declared *Huckleberry Finn* the greatest American book and the source of all modern American fiction. *The Adventures of Tom Sawyer,* although inferior to the two other Mississippi books, is notable for the creation of its hero, one of Twain's most memorable characters. *A Connecticut Yankee in King Arthur's Court* and *The Tragedy of Pudd'nhead Wilson* also belong toward the top of the list of Twain's achievements, but considerably below his best writings, for in these latter works the satire, moral outrage, and comedy fail to come together.

William Dean Howells, a friend of Twain's, encouraged him to write for the *Atlantic Monthly* and later wrote an affectionate memoir, *My Mark Twain,* in which he called Twain "the Lincoln of our literature." In 1894 a publishing house that Twain had invested in went bankrupt and Twain lost a fortune. This was but one of the fortunes he was to lose through money-making schemes. His personal life was further blighted with the death of an infant son and two grown daughters, and the long illness and death of his wife. These extremes of success, failure, and sorrow may help account for the contrasting extremes in his writing of humor and bitterness. Toward the close of his life the bitterness predominated and his writing became a satirical diatribe against God and man, so much so that his surviving daughter, Clara Clemens Samoussoud (d. 1962), refused to allow it to be published until after her death—*Letters from Earth* (o.p.).

Twain was the first of a number of American writers whose works are being edited and published in scholarly editions under MLA-approved programs, including discarded chapters and scenes from earlier works as well as items left unfinished (and sometimes in multiple versions) at Twain's death and later found among his papers. Among those to appear are *Fables of Man, Correspondence with Henry Huttleston Rogers, Mark Twain's Hannibal, Huck and Tom,* and *What Is Man? and Other Philosophical Writings.* Also, very minor works long out of print were reissued by reprint presses, as, for instance, *King Leopold's Soliloquy, Following the Equator,* and *The American Claimant.* Twain's works have also been issued in reliably edited, economical volumes in the Library of America Classics Series, as for example, *Mark Twain's Mississippi Writings,* which contains *The Adventures of Tom Sawyer, Life on the Mississippi, The Adventures of Huckleberry Finn,* and *Pudd'nhead Wilson.*

BOOKS BY TWAIN

The Complete Short Stories. Ed. by Charles Neider, Bantam pap. $3.95; Doubleday 1957 $15.95

The Complete Humorous Sketches and Tales. Doubleday 1961 $15.95. More than 200 pieces arranged chronologically from 1863.

Great Short Works of Mark Twain. Ed. by Justin Kaplan, Harper 1967 pap. $3.80

Selected Shorter Writings of Mark Twain. Ed. by Walter Blair, Houghton Mifflin (Riv. Eds.) 1962 pap. $5.50

The Portable Mark Twain. Ed. by Bernard De Voto, *Viking Portable Lib.* Penguin 1977 pap. $7.95

Mark Twain's Satires and Burlesques. Ed. by Franklin R. Rogers, *Mark Twain Papers Ser.* Univ. of California Pr. 1967 o.p. MLA-approved text of some minor works.

Mark Twain's "Which Was the Dream?" and Other Symbolic Writings of the Later Years. Ed. by John S. Tuckey, *Mark Twain Papers Ser.* Univ. of California Pr. 1966 $44.50. MLA-approved text of forgotten fiction from Mark Twain's darkest period.

The Adventures of Thomas Jefferson Snodgrass. Folcroft repr. of 1928 ed. lib. bdg. $20.00. Ten humorous letters first published in 1861 in the New Orleans *Daily Crescent.*

Mark Twain's Hannibal, Huck and Tom. Ed. by Walter Blair, *Mark Twain Papers Ser.* Univ. of California Pr. 1969 $38.50. Discarded material from early novels about Huck Finn and Tom Sawyer.

Mark Twain's Fables of Man. Ed. by John S. Tuckey, *Mark Twain Papers Ser.* Univ. of California Pr. 1972 $27.50

A Pen Warmed Up in Hell: Mark Twain in Protest. Harper 1979 pap. $5.72

What Is Man? and Other Philosophical Writings. Ed. by Paul Baender, *Mark Twain Papers Ser.* Univ. of California Pr. 1973 $26.50. The title essay is Twain's pessimistic view of man first published in 1917.

Mississippi Writings. Ed. by Guy Cardwell, Literary Class. 1982 $27.50

The Devil's Race Track, Mark Twain's Great Dark Writings: The Best from Which Was the Dream? and Fables of Man. Ed. by John S. Tuckey, Univ. of California Pr. 1980 $15.95 pap. $6.95

Mark Twain to Mrs. Fairbanks. Ed. by Dixon Wecter, Huntington Lib. 1949 o.p. "Mother" Fairbanks was one of Twain's early literary mentors.

The Correspondence of Samuel L. Clemens and William D. Howells, 1869–1910. Ed. by Henry Nash Smith and William M. Gibson, Harvard Univ. Pr. 2 vols. 1960 o.p.

Selected Mark Twain–Howells Letters. Ed. by Frederick Anderson, Atheneum 1968 pap. $5.95. The *Correspondence* above with unimportant matter and canceled words deleted to reduce it to one volume. Contains two new letters; otherwise "substantially the same," with editorial aids virtually unchanged *(LJ).*

Mark Twain's Letters to His Publishers, 1867–1894. Ed. by Hamlin Hill, *Mark Twain Papers Ser.* Univ. of California Pr. 1967 $35.00. Includes 290 letters, most of them previously unpublished. The MLA-approved text.

Mark Twain's Letters to Mary. Ed by Lewis Leary, Columbia Univ. Pr. 1961 o.p. These 30-odd letters and notes, characterized by "cheerful affection and prankish good humor," were addressed during the last four years of Twain's life to the young daughter-in-law of Henry H. Rogers, the Standard Oil Company executive who had become Mark Twain's business adviser and close friend.

Letters from the Sandwich Islands. Haskell 1972 o.p. A collection of Twain's contributions to the Sacramento *Union,* originally edited by G. Ezra Dane.

Mark Twain's Letters to Will Bowen. Folcroft repr. of 1941 ed. lib. bdg. $15.00. Letters to Twain's "first, oldest and dearest friend," first published in a collection edited by Theodore Hornberger.

Mark Twain's Correspondence with Henry Huttleston Rogers, 1893–1909. Ed. by Lewis Leary, *Mark Twain Papers Ser.* Univ. of California Pr. 1969 $44.50

Mark Twain's Notebooks and Journals. Ed. by Frederick Anderson and others, *Mark Twain Papers Ser.* Univ. of California Pr. 3 vols. vol. 1 (1976) $42.50 vol. 2 (1976) $42.50 vol. 3 (1980) $48.50

Autobiography of Mark Twain. Ed. by Charles Neider, Harper 1959 $20.00 1975 pap. $3.37

Mark Twain's Autobiography. Intro. by Albert B. Paine, Century Bookbindery 2 vols. repr. of 1924 ed. 1983 lib. bdg. $65.00

Mark Twain's Travels with Mr. Brown. Ed. by Franklin Walker and G. Ezra Dane, Russell 1971 o.p. A collection of sketches that Twain wrote for the San Francisco *Alta California,* 1866–67.

The Celebrated Jumping Frog of Calaveras County. 1867. Dover 1971 pap. $2.50

Traveling with the Innocents Abroad: Mark Twain's Original Reports from Europe and the Holy Land. Ed. by Daniel Morley McKeithan, Univ. of Oklahoma Pr. 1958 o.p. A collection of the 58 lively letters sent to American newspapers, describing Twain's experiences on a pleasure excursion to Europe, the Holy Land, and Egypt. Revised by Twain, they became the basis of *The Innocents Abroad.*

The Innocents Abroad, or The New Pilgrim's Progress. 1869. Airmont Class. Ser. 1967 pap. $1.25; New Amer. Lib. (Signet Class.) pap. $3.95

Roughing It. 1872. New Amer. Lib. (Signet Class.) pap. $2.95; ed. by Hamlin Hill, *Penguin Amer. Lib. Ser.* 1981 pap. $3.95; intro. by Franklin R. Rogers, *Iowa-California Ed. of the Works of Mark Twain,* Univ. of California Pr. 1972 $26.00 pap. $8.95

(and Charles Dudley Warner). *Gilded Age.* 1873. Ed. by Bryant M. French, Bobbs 1972 o.p.; ed. by Charles Dudley Warner, New Amer. Lib. (Signet Class.) pap. o.p.

The Adventures of Tom Sawyer. 1876. Ed. by Robert D. Spector, *Bantam Class. Ser.* 1981 pap. $1.75; Dodd 1984 $11.95; New Amer. Lib. (Signet Class.) 1959 pap. $1.50; ed. by John C. Gerber and others, *Iowa-California Ed. of the Works of Mark Twain* Univ. of California Pr. 1980 $32.50; Univ. of California Pr. 1983 $12.95 pap. $2.95

Tom Sawyer and Huckleberry Finn. Biblio Dist. (Everyman's) repr. of 1943 ed. 1972 $9.95 pap. $2.25

The Prince and the Pauper. 1882. New Amer. Lib. (Signet Class.) 1964 pap. $1.95; ed. by Victor Fischer and Lin Salamo, *Iowa-California Ed. of the Works of Mark Twain* Univ. of California Pr. 1980 $28.50; Univ. of California Pr. 1984 pap. $3.95

Stolen White Elephant and Others. 1882. Folcroft repr. 1973 lib. bdg. $30.00. The title story is also in the Neider collection (see above).

Life on the Mississippi. 1883. *Bantam Class. Ser.* 1981 pap. $1.95; *Penguin Amer. Lib. Ser.* 1984 pap. $4.95

The Adventures of Huckleberry Finn. 1885. Ed. by Leo Marx, Bobbs 1967 pap. $8.40; Dell 1960 pap. $2.95; ed. by Lionel Trilling, *Rinehart Ed.* Holt text ed. 1948 pap. $11.95; ed. by Henry Nash Smith, Houghton Mifflin (Riv. Eds.) 1958 pap. $5.95; New Amer. Lib. (Signet Class.) 1971 pap. $1.50; ed. by Peter Coveney, *Penguin Eng. Lib. Ser.* 1966 pap. $2.50

A Connecticut Yankee in King Arthur's Court. 1889. Bantam 1981 pap. $1.95; New Amer. Lib. (Signet Class.) pap. $1.75; *Penguin Eng. Lib. Ser.* 1972 pap. $2.95; ed. by Bernard L. Stein, *Iowa-California Ed. of the Works of Mark Twain* Univ. of California Pr. 1980 $37.50; Univ. of California Pr. 1983 $13.95

The Tragedy of Pudd'nhead Wilson. 1894. *Bantam Class. Ser.* 1981 pap. $1.95; New Amer. Lib. (Signet Class.) pap. $1.75; ed. by Malcolm Bradbury, *Penguin Eng. Lib. Ser.* 1969 pap. $2.50

Tom Sawyer Abroad (and *Tom Sawyer, Detective*). 1894–96. Airmont Class. Ser. pap. $1.50; Univ. of California Pr. 1982 $12.95 pap. $3.95

Personal Recollections of Joan of Arc. 1896. Harper repr. of 1896 ed. $10.95

The American Claimant. AMS Pr. repr. of 1897 ed. $27.50
Following the Equator. AMS Pr. repr. of 1897 ed. $32.50
Diaries of Adam and Eve (Extracts from Adam's Diary). Arden Lib. repr. of 1904 ed.
  1981 lib. bdg. $25.00; Coronado Pr. 1971 $6.50
King Leopold's Soliloquy. 1905. Ed. by Stefan Heym, International Publishing 1970
  pap. $1.50. A satiric sketch.
Mark Twain's Mysterious Stranger Manuscripts. Ed. by William M. Gibson, *Mark
  Twain Papers Ser.* Univ. of California Pr. 1969 $38.50 pap. $8.95. Text is based on
  three holograph manuscripts at the University of California, Berkeley, of the volume published posthumously in 1916, reconstructed by Albert Bigelow Paine,
  who is now known to have taken liberties with the manuscripts.
Mysterious Stranger and Other Stories. 1916. New Amer. Lib. (Signet Class.) 1962 pap.
  $1.95
The War Prayer. 1923. Ill. by John Groth, Harper 1984 pap. $2.84. An antiwar parable
  that Twain stipulated could be published only after his death.
Simon Wheeler, Detective. Ed. by Franklin R. Rogers, NYPL 1965 $15.00. An uncom-
  pleted novel that *Library Journal* finds a good one, with an "illuminating" introduction. First published in 1963.

BOOKS ABOUT TWAIN

Brooks, Van Wyck. *The Ordeal of Mark Twain.* AMS Pr. repr. of 1933 ed. $18.00. The
  celebrated attack on Twain. Now discredited.
Budd, Louis J. *Critical Essays on Mark Twain, 1867–1910. Critical Essays on Amer.
  Lit. Ser.* G. K. Hall (Twayne) 1982 lib. bdg. $30.00 1983 lib. bdg. $31.00
———. *Mark Twain: Social Philosopher.* Kennikat 1962 o.p. Based predominantly on
  contemporary speeches, newspaper interviews, and unpublished letters and
  manuscripts.
Canby, Henry S. *Turn West, Turn East: Mark Twain and Henry James.* Biblo & Tan-
  nen 1951 $18.00. A comparative biography of contrasting contemporaries.
Covici, Pascal, Jr. *Mark Twain's Humor: The Image of a World.* SMU Pr. 1962 pap.
  $9.95. A useful essay on Mark Twain's use of such devices as parody, burlesque,
  hoax, and bluff.
Cox, James M. *Mark Twain: The Fate of Humor.* Princeton Univ. Pr. 1966 $30.00 pap.
  $11.50
De Voto, Bernard. *Mark Twain at Work.* AMS Pr. repr. of 1942 ed. $38.50
———. *Mark Twain's America.* 1932. Greenwood repr. of 1967 ed. 1978 $25.75. De Vo-
  to's defense of Twain.
Fatout, Paul. *Mark Twain in Virginia City.* Associated Faculty Pr. repr. of 1964 ed.
  1973 o.p.
Foner, Philip S. *Mark Twain: Social Critic.* International Publishing repr. 1972 pap.
  $2.25. His thinking on major social, political, and economic issues of his day,
  based largely on previously unpublished material.
Gibson, William M. *The Art of Mark Twain.* Oxford 1976 $22.50. A major work on the
  artistry of Mark Twain.
Kaplan, Justin. *Mr. Clemens and Mark Twain.* Simon & Schuster (Touchstone Bks.)
  1983 pap. $10.95
Krause, Sydney J. *Mark Twain as Critic.* Johns Hopkins Univ. Pr. 1967 $25.00
Pettit, Arthur G. *Mark Twain and the South.* Univ. Pr. of Kentucky 1974 $22.00. Solid
  and clearly written on an important subject.
Scott, Arthur L. *Mark Twain: Selected Criticism.* SMU Pr. rev. ed. 1967 pap. $5.95

Smith, Henry Nash. *Mark Twain: The Development of a Writer*. Atheneum text ed. 1967 pap. $3.95; Harvard Univ. Pr. (Belknap Pr.) 1962 $15.00
Wecter, Dixon. *Sam Clemens of Hannibal*. Houghton Mifflin 1952 o.p.

WALLACE, LEWIS (LEW). 1827–1905

General Wallace was a soldier in the Mexican War and the Civil War. He began his first novel, *The Fair God*, a tale of Cortez and the conquest of Mexico, at age 18. *Ben Hur: A Tale of the Christ*, an outstanding bestseller, has been called "the only American novel which can be compared with 'Uncle Tom's Cabin' as a true folk possession." Although sentimentalized in action and language, it is "vivid and memorable in its authentic detail." "My God! Did I set all this in motion?" the author is said to have remarked when he saw the sets for the Broadway version in 1900. The chariot race, famous on the stage, was also the high point of the movies of 1927 and 1959—the latter costing $15 million. *Ben Hur* was published while Wallace was governor of the Territory of New Mexico. It sold 500,000 copies within eight years. While Ambassador to Turkey, Wallace wrote his last novel, *The Prince of India* (1893, o.p.). *Lew Wallace: An Autobiography* is his own account of his life to 1864 and his wife's account thereafter.

Books by Wallace

The Fair God: A Tale about the Conquest of Mexico. 1873. Popular Lib. o.p.
Ben Hur. 1880. Buccaneer Bks. repr. 1981 lib. bdg. $19.95; ed. by Naunerle Farr and Nestor Redondo, Pendulum Pr. text ed. 1978 $5.00 pap. $1.95
Lew Wallace: An Autobiography. Irvington 2 vols. repr. of 1906 ed. $48.95

WISTER, OWEN. 1860–1938

A Philadelphian and grandson of the actress Fanny Kemble, Owen Wister was educated in private schools in the United States and abroad and graduated from Harvard University with highest honors in music. After suffering a nervous breakdown, he traveled to Wyoming to recover his health. He then made frequent trips back to the West. His only well-known novel, *The Virginian*, a bestseller for years, is a pioneer western. It was dedicated to his lifelong friend THEODORE ROOSEVELT (see Vol. 3), another outdoorsman and lover of the West. Two of Wister's reprinted books are *Lin McLean* and *Lady Baltimore*. A study that includes a consideration of Wister is Edward G. White, *The Eastern Establishment and the Western Experience: The West of Frederic Remington, Theodore Roosevelt and Owen Wister* (o.p.)

Books by Wister

The West of Owen Wister: Selected Short Stories. Intro. by Robert L. Hough, Univ. of Nebraska Pr. (Bison) 1972 $18.50 pap. $4.50
Lin McLean. Irvington repr. of 1898 ed. lib. bdg. $24.00

The Jimmyjohn Boss and Other Stories. Irvington repr. of 1900 ed. 1972 lib. bdg.
    $19.00
The Virginian: A Horseman of the Plains. 1902. Citadel Pr. 1984 pap. $8.95; intro. by
    Max Westbrook, New Amer. Lib. (Signet Class.) 1983 pap. $2.50; Washington
    Square Pr. 1983 pap. $3.95
Lady Baltimore. Buccaneer Bks. repr. of 1906 ed. 1977 lib. bdg. $16.95; *Americans in
    Fiction Ser.* Irvington repr. of 1905 ed. lib. bdg. $16.50

CHAPTER 14

Modern American Fiction

Maurice Beebe

All modern American literature comes from one book by Mark Twain called
Huckleberry Finn. If you read it you must stop where the Nigger Jim is
stolen from the boys. That is the real end. The rest is just cheating. But it's
the best book we've had. All American writing comes from that. There was
nothing before. There has been nothing as good since.
—ERNEST HEMINGWAY, *The Green Hills of Africa*

Of Hemingway's statement above, Huck Finn himself might have said,
"He told the truth, mainly. There was things which he stretched, but
mainly he told the truth." The characteristic hero of American fiction
since the late nineteenth century has been a young man both naively innocent and worldly wise. In one of the best critical studies of the twentieth-
century American novel—the appropriately titled *Radical Innocence*—Ihab
Hassan finds that the most characteristic feature of American fiction is
"its typical antihero. The central and controlling image of recent fiction is
that of the rebel-victim. He is an actor but also a sufferer." Henry Fleming of Stephen Crane's *The Red Badge of Courage,* Clyde Griffiths of Theodore Dreiser's *An American Tragedy,* Jay Gatz of F. Scott Fitzgerald's *The
Great Gatsby,* J. D. Salinger's Holden Caulfield of *The Catcher in the Rye,*
Alexander Portnoy of Philip Roth's *Portnoy's Complaint,* and Ken Kesey's
MacMurphy in *One Flew over the Cuckoo's Nest* are easy-to-find examples
that illustrate Hassan's thesis. They are more likely to become like the
cynical antiheroes that dominate the work of a group of irreverent writers
raised in the postwar years who by pretending to see through everything
would appear to owe as much to the *Mad* magazine of their adolescence
as to such more immediate teachers as Joseph Heller, Kurt Vonnegut, Jr.,
and Thomas Pynchon.

Whereas Hassan's "controlling image" of the rebel-saint provides a workable thesis with which to describe American fiction for almost a century,
it does not account for several distinct phases within that period. Hemingway went on to praise HENRY JAMES in addition to MARK TWAIN—and he
might just as well have acknowledged also the considerable debt that later novelists have owed to WILLIAM DEAN HOWELLS, whose earnest and realistic novels about the social climate in various parts of the United
States helped to establish a tradition of the novel of manners that flour-

ished for more than a half-century in works by such writers as Edith
Wharton, Ellen Glasgow, and John O'Hara before falling off drastically in
recent years. Henry James's contribution is more difficult to assess, for although that author is justifiably considered the father of modern fiction
because he was one of the first to insist and to demonstrate that fiction
can be as much an art as poetry or drama, he produced a body of work
so distinctly his own that it has proved basically inimitable. One "lesson
of the Master," however, is an emphasis on sensibility—a story as told by
a sensitive and "aware" but somehow detached and passive observer who
looks on a counterpart who is more vital and engaged than himself. It is
Nick Carraway in *The Great Gatsby*, Jake Barnes of Hemingway's *The Sun
Also Rises*, or Jack Burden of Robert Penn Warren's *All the King's Men*.
Henry James taught writers of many lands how to fuse a story of dramatic action through the sensibility of a reflecting "center of consciousness." The earliest phase of modern American fiction was characterized
by its impressionistic techniques and a strong focus on individual sensibilities.

Beginning with the 1930s and continuing through World War II, the emphasis in American fiction shifted away from the individual toward society in general. Works such as John Dos Passos's *U.S.A.*, John Steinbeck's
The Grapes of Wrath, and Hemingway's *For Whom the Bell Tolls* heralded
a new awareness that man does not stand alone. The young American
writers who survived the war and began their literary careers shortly afterward may have come away from their shared experience with resent-
ment at the discipline they had undergone and some doubts about the
cause for which they fought, but they returned also with a mutual conviction that men must work together if they are to improve the human condition. Writers such as James Jones and Norman Mailer have continued to
see themselves as participants in the history of their time. The second
phase of modern American fiction is marked by group consciousness and
social awareness.

These qualities are especially apparent in the regional and ethnic literatures that tended to dominate American fiction after World War II. Beginning with Ellen Glasgow and continuing through Thomas Wolfe and William Faulkner to Eudora Welty, Truman Capote, Carson McCullers, and
Flannery O'Conner, a disproportionate number of the best American writers
have been southerners. C. Hugh Holman has said that "boundaries of experience" separate the South from the rest of America: "The only group of
Americans who have known military defeat, military occupation, and seemingly unconquerable poverty, they have the sense of failure, the sense of
guilt, which comes from having been America's classic symbol of injustice. . . . " This has resulted in a serious and tragic literature.

Similar factors help to explain the rise of ethnic literatures. The 1960s in
particular saw the ascendancy of Jewish and black writers. Like the southern novelists, they wrote with an awareness of a long tradition of deprivation and suffering behind them, but whereas southern fiction is characterized by scenes of Gothic decay and a sense of tragedy, the Jewish and

black writers have reacted in different ways to their heritage. Black writers from Richard Wright to Ralph Ellison and James Baldwin have produced angry fiction imbued with a sense of injustice, outrage, and the need to fight back. The antiheroes who dominate their fiction are rebels, outcasts, and exiles. The typical antihero in recent Jewish fiction, on the other hand, is a long-suffering buffoon buffeted by circumstances and his own neuroses, fears, and guilts. There is little humor in black fiction of this century, but black humor is the characteristic mode of the American Jewish novel as produced by such writers as Saul Bellow, Bernard Malamud, Stanley Elkin, and Philip Roth. They share a sense of the absurd that enables them to laugh at themselves, but theirs is the kind of laughter that often hides their tears.

Two other general trends have been apparent in fiction of the past two decades—the one a movement toward actual life, the other toward increasing artifice. The much-publicized "nonfiction novel" in which sophisticated literary techniques are used to narrate actual events may well have reached its peak almost at its inception with Truman Capote's *In Cold Blood* in 1966. Investigative reporters willing to look in depth at the events they narrate and to see them from their own frankly personal points of view have become culture heroes in recent years. Norman Mailer is perhaps the most successful and conspicuous recruit to a movement that increasingly blurs the distinctions between fiction and nonfiction; and the whole history of modern American prose literature may someday be summarized in terms of the progression from Thomas Wolfe to Tom Wolfe, whose *The New Journalism* is both a historical account of the movement and an anthology of representative examples from writers as diverse as Gay Talese, Terry Southern, George Plimpton, and Joan Didion. However, even as the nonfiction novel was being submerged within the broader movement of the New Journalism, some serious younger novelists sought to expand the frontiers of fiction toward an increasing insistence that art is art. In the fiction of writers such as John Barth, Donald Barthelme, Robert Coover, and William Gass, there is a reflexive, self-conscious tendency, which makes them write labyrinthine, ingenious stories that seem to deal ultimately with their own composition.

From the reviewers' response to some recent books of the reflexive type, many readers have grown weary of mere artifice. John Gardner's controversial attack on many of his contemporaries in *On Moral Fiction* may have struck some writers and critics as a throwback to old philistine attitudes toward the uses of fiction, but we can now recognize that Gardner's book seemed to look forward to a fresh emphasis on traditional human values. If there is a significant new direction to be found in the fiction of the 1980s, it would seem to be in the work of writers like E. L. Doctorow, Toni Morrison, and William Kennedy, who have shown that they know their craft well enough to avoid calling attention to it. And in finding a balance between fact and fantasy some of these new writers of the 1980s could succeed not only in joining actuality with artifice, but also in coming close to a northern version of the "magic realism" that distinguishes the literature produced by their neighbors to the south and makes it seem so vital.

COLLECTIONS OF MODERN AMERICAN SHORT STORIES

Why do short stories entice the writer? Here is Bernard Malamud's answer: "Within a dozen or more pages, whole lives are implied and even understood. Though events are endless, lives aren't, yet there is a temptation in telling of lives to spin them endlessly. But the short story, though it reconceives lives, must limit itself to the sweeping realization of its meaning, which is to say it quickly runs its course because that's its nature, its fate. And that relates it more fittingly to our short lives." The indispensable reference tool for locating a specific story is *The Short Story Index*, which is described in Chapter 3 in this volume.

Angus, Douglas, and Sylvia Angus, eds. *Contemporary American Short Stories*. 1967. Fawcett 1978 pap. $2.95

Bellow, Saul, ed. *Great Jewish Short Stories*. 1963. Dell 1985 pap. $4.95

Clarke, John H., ed. *American Negro Short Stories*. Hill & Wang 1966 $10.95 pap. $6.95

Current-Garcia, Eugene, and Walton R. Patrick, eds. *American Short Stories*. Scott, Foresman text ed. 4th ed. 1982 pap. $14.50

Elkin, Stanley, and Shannon Ravenel, eds. *The Best American Short Stories, 1980*. Penguin 1981 pap. $6.95

Foley, Martha, ed. *Two Hundred Years of Great American Short Stories*. Houghton Mifflin 1975 $14.95

Gold, Herbert, and David L. Stevenson, eds. *Stories of Modern America*. St. Martin's 1969 pap. $12.95

Henry, Dewitt, ed. *The Ploughshares Reader: New Fiction for the 80's*. Pushcart Pr. 1985 $24.95

Hills, L. Rust, and P. C. Hills. *How We Live*. 1968. Macmillan (Collier Bks.) 2 vols. 1971 pap. ea. $3.45

Kostelanetz, Richard. *Breakthrough Fictioneers: An Anthology*. RK Edns. 1972 pap. $10.00. Imaginative selection of highly experimental fiction.

Martin, Russell, and Marc Barasch. *Writers of the Purple Sage: An Anthology of Recent Western Writing*. Penguin 1984 pap. $7.95; Viking 1984 $19.95

Messerli, Douglas. *The Contemporary American Fiction*. Sun & Moon Pr. 1983 $14.95

Murphy, George E., Jr. *The Editor's Choice: New American Stories*. Bantam 1985 pap. $6.95. First in a projected series of stories selected by editors of leading magazines and literary reviews.

Oates, Joyce Carol. *Scenes from American Life: Contemporary Short Fiction*. Random 1972 pap. $10.95

Skaggs, Calvin. *The American Short Story*. Dell 2 vols. ea. $4.95

Stegner, Wallace, and Mary Stegner. *Great American Short Stories*. Dell 1957 pap. $4.95

Stevick, Philip. *Anti-Story: An Anthology of Experimental Writing*. Macmillan (Free Pr.) 1971 pap. $12.95. Excellent selection of unusual stories by various contemporary writers, mostly American.

Sullivan, Nancy. *Treasury of American Short Stories*. Doubleday 1981 $16.95

Wolff, Tobias. *Matters of Life and Death: New American Stories.* Wampeter Pr. 1983 $14.95

HISTORICAL AND CRITICAL WORKS

[SEE ALSO Chapters 3 and 13 in this volume.]

Aldridge, John W. *After the Lost Generation: A Critical Study of the Writers of Two Wars.* Ayer repr. of 1951 ed. $20.00. "A pioneer study. . . . The first serious and challenging book about the new novelists" (Malcolm Cowley, *N.Y. Tribune*), this work remains of more than historical interest. Aldridge contrasts the writers of the lost generation, principally Hemingway, Fitzgerald, and Dos Passos, with the then new writers of the 1940s.

————. *The American Novel and the Way We Live Now.* Oxford 1983 $16.96. Three decades later Aldridge surveys the contemporary novel and finds even less to his liking.

Allen, Mary. *The Necessary Blankness: Women in Major American Fiction of the Sixties.* Univ. of Illinois Pr. 1976 $15.95

Auchincloss, Louis. *Pioneers and Caretakers: A Study of Nine American Women Novelists.* Univ. of Minnesota Pr. 1965 $13.95

Balakian, Nona, and Charles Simmons, eds. *The Creative Present: Notes on the Contemporary American Novel.* 1963. Gordian 1972 $12.50. Leading critics evaluate the work of 17 writers; "a valuable and absorbing book that gives a moderately conservative view of the fiction being produced in America today" (*N.Y. Times*).

Baumbach, Jonathan. *The Landscape of Nightmare: Studies in the Contemporary American Novel.* New York Univ. Pr. 1965 $22.50 pap. $11.50. Perceptive analyses and interpretations of individual novels by Bellow, Ellison, Malamud, Morris, O'Connor, Salinger, Styron, Edward Lewis Wallant, and Warren.

Blake, Nelson Manfred. *Novelists' America: Fiction as History, 1910–1940.* Syracuse Univ. Pr. 1970 pap. $5.95. The author, a professional historian, turns to fiction in the search for historical truth in this rewarding study of three decades of U.S. life as viewed by eight novelists: Lewis, Fitzgerald, Faulkner, Wolfe, Steinbeck, Dos Passos, Farrell, and Wright.

Bluefarb, Sam. *The Escape Motif in the American Novel: Mark Twain to Richard Wright.* Ohio State Univ. Pr. 1972 $8.00

Bradbury, Malcolm. *The Modern American Novel.* Oxford 1983 $22.00. Bradbury discusses representative novels to illustrate prevailing movements and themes from the time of the naturalists to the present.

Bryer, Jackson R., ed. *Sixteen Modern American Writers: A Survey of Research and Criticism.* Duke Univ. Pr. rev. & enl. ed. 1973 $25.00. Prominent academic authorities describe and evaluate biographical, critical, and bibliographic writings on major writers of this century, including Anderson, Cather, Dreiser, Faulkner, Hemingway, Steinbeck, and Wolfe.

Caramello, Charles. *Silverless Mirrors: Book, Self and Postmodern American Fiction.* Florida State Univ. Pr. 1983 $25.00 pap. $12.00. A provocative study that discusses Barth and Gass, as well as some lesser known contemporary experimental writers.

Coindreau, Maurice Edgar. *The Time of William Faulkner: A French View of Modern American Fiction.* Ed. and trans. by George McMillan Reeves, Univ. of South Carolina Pr. 1971 $17.95. Coindreau deserves a major share of the credit for making modern American fiction popular in France and elsewhere in Europe. He sees Faulkner as the dominant American writer of the modern period. This collection brings together 11 commentaries on that writer as well as translated prefaces to French editions of books by Caldwell, Capote, William Goyen, O'Connor, and William Maxwell.

Cooperman, Stanley R. *World War I and the American Novel*. Johns Hopkins Univ. Pr. 1967 pap. $6.95

Davis, Thadious M., and Trudier Harris, eds. *Afro-American Fiction Writers after 1955*. Volume 33 in *Dictionary of Literary Biography*. Gale 1984 $82.00. This volume in the generously illustrated *Dictionary of Literary Biography* series features authoritative biographical and critical introductions to 49 established and promising writers.

French, Warren. *The Social Novel at the End of an Era*. Pref. by Harry T. Moore, *Crosscurrents Modern Critiques Ser*. Southern Illinois Univ. Pr. 1966 $7.95. Excellent study of the way in which social and historical events affected the writing of five novels published around 1940—Steinbeck's *The Grapes of Wrath*, Hemingway's *For Whom the Bell Tolls*, Faulkner's *The Hamlet*, Dalton Trumbo's *Johnny Got His Gun*, and Pietro di Donato's *Christ in Concrete*.

Frohock, W. M. *The Novel of Violence in America*. 1950. Southern Methodist Univ. Pr. 5th ed. 1971 $8.95

Galloway, David D. *The Absurd Hero in American Fiction: Updike, Styron, Bellow, Salinger*. 1966. Univ. of Texas Pr. 2d ed. rev. 1981 $22.50 pap. $10.95. A perceptive critic "shows how four American novelists . . . have used the novel to portray the absurd man in four aspects: as saint, as tragic hero, as picaro, as seeker for love" (Publisher's note).

Gardner, John. *On Moral Fiction*. Basic Bks. 1978 pap. $6.95. This controversial polemic has helped to draw a line between the traditionalists and the formalists among contemporary writers.

Girgus, Sam B. *The New Covenant: Jewish Writers and the American Idea*. Univ. of North Carolina Pr. 1984 $19.95

Harper, Howard M., Jr. *Desperate Faith: A Study of Bellow, Salinger, Mailer, Baldwin, and Updike*. Univ. of North Carolina Pr. 1967 pap. $7.00

Hassan, Ihab. *Radical Innocence: Studies in the Contemporary Novel*. Princeton Univ. Pr. 1961 $37.50 pap. $9.95. An exhaustive probing, by a distinguished critic, of McCullers, Mailer, Salinger, and others.

Helterman, Jeffrey, and Richard Layman, eds. *American Novelists since World War II*. Volume 2 in *Dictionary of Literary Biography*. Gale 1978 $80.00. Standard reference work. See also Kibler below.

Hendin, Josephine. *Vulnerable People: A View of American Fiction since 1945*. Oxford 1978 pap. $7.95

Hilfer, Anthony. *The Ethics of Intensity in American Fiction*. Univ. of Texas Pr. 1981 $22.50. Traces the conflict between moral codes imposed from without and the individual's need for emotional self-expression as reflected in fiction by James, Dreiser, Stein, and others.

Hoffman, Frederick J. *The Twenties: American Writing in the Postwar Decade*. 1955. Macmillan (Free Pr.) 1965 pap. $9.95. One of the best surveys of a pivotal period in modern literary history, this sophisticated study balances social awareness with literary values.

Holman, C. Hugh. *The Roots of Southern Writing: Essays on the Literature of the American South*. Univ. of Georgia Pr. 1972 $20.00. "Running throughout the essays is a strain of resigned but optimistic humanism which sees that only through its profound experience of suffering, defeat, and poverty could the

South produce the most distinctively tragic regional literature this country has known" (*Journal of Modern Lit.*).

———. *Three Modes of Modern Southern Fiction: Ellen Glasgow, William Faulkner and Thomas Wolfe.* Univ. of Georgia Pr. 1967 $9.00

Karl, Frederick R. *American Fictions, 1940–1980: A Comprehensive History and Critical Evaluation.* Harper 1983 $32.50. This solid and lengthy survey deals with types and trends as well as the work of the most seriously committed writers of literary fiction during four decades.

Kazin, Alfred. *Bright Book of Life: American Novelists and Storytellers from Hemingway to Mailer.* Little, Brown 1973 $9.95; Univ. of Notre Dame Pr. 1980 pap. $6.95. "Less ambitious than *On Native Grounds*, but a more than worthy continuation of that classic of modern criticism, *Bright Book of Life* is Kazin's somewhat personal response to the post-Hemingway generation of American writers of fiction" (*Journal of Modern Lit.*).

———. *On Native Grounds: An Interpretation of Modern American Prose Literature.* 1942. Harcourt 1983 $9.95. Brilliant and penetrating literary history of the "relation between American prose and our developing society in the years between 1890 and the present" (*New Yorker*). Highly recommended.

Kibler, James E., Jr. *American Novelists since World War II: Second Series.* Volume 6 in *Dictionary of Literary Biography.* Gale 1980 $80.00. Supplements the volume edited by Helterman and Layman listed above.

Klein, Marcus. *After Alienation: American Novels in Mid-Century.* 1963. Ayer repr. $20.00. An important analysis of Bellow, Ellison, Baldwin, Morris, and Malamud.

Klinkowitz, Jerome. *The Life of Fiction.* Univ. of Illinois Pr. 1977 $12.50. Graphics by Roy R. Behrens contribute to the innovative nature of this introduction to the work of 12 experimental writers.

———. *Literary Disruptions: The Making of a Post-Contemporary American Fiction.* Univ. of Illinois Pr. 2d ed. 1980 $19.95 pap. $6.50

Lynn, Kenneth Schuyler. *The Dream of Success: A Study of the Modern American Imagination.* Greenwood repr. of 1955 ed. 1972 $22.50

Lyons, John O. *The College Novel in America.* Southern Illinois Univ. Pr. 1962 $7.95. A first major attempt to bring the literature of college life together, this covers more than 200 novels from the early nineteenth century to the present.

Madden, David E. *American Dreams, American Nightmares.* Pref. by Harry T. Moore, Southern Illinois Univ. Pr. 1970 $19.95 pap. $9.95. Specially commissioned essays on the theme of the American dream and the awakening therefrom in representative literary texts, including novels by Ellison, Faulkner, Fitzgerald, Mailer, Miller, and Wolfe.

———. *Proletarian Writers of the Thirties.* Crosscurrents Modern Critiques Ser. Southern Illinois Univ. Pr. 1968 $19.95 pap. $9.95

———. *Tough Guy Writers of the Thirties.* Crosscurrents Modern Critiques Ser. Southern Illinois Univ. Pr. 1968 $16.95 pap. $9.95

Magny, Claude-Edmonde. *The Age of the American Novel: The Film Aesthetic of Fiction between the Two World Wars.* Trans. by Eleanor Hochman, Ungar 1972 $13.50. "This is the first translation into English of a book, originally published in France in 1968, which probably more than any other single critical text helped to turn postwar French novelists towards the 'sort of raw and savage novel' which during the classic period of modern American fiction had been written by Dos Passos, Hemingway, Steinbeck, and Faulkner" (*Journal of Modern Lit.*).

Malin, Irving. *New American Gothic. Crosscurrents Modern Critiques Ser.* Southern Illinois Univ. Pr. 1962 $11.95. Examines a dominant form of literary fiction that is marked by intensity of character, fierce struggle between self and antiself, and an unresolved blur of identity banging against walls of complex and equally unresolved reality. Included are Capote, McCullers, Salinger, O'Connor, Hawkes, and Purdy.

Martine, James J., ed. *American Novelists, 1910–1945.* Volume 9 in *Dictionary of Literary Biography.* Gale 3 vols. 1981 $240.00. Generously illustrated volumes that cover the careers of 140 novelists who came to some prominence during the years between the two world wars. For succeeding installments of this invaluable reference work, see listings above for Helterman and Layman and for Kibler.

May, John R. *Toward a New Earth: Apocalypse in the American Novel.* Univ. of Notre Dame Pr. 1972 pap. $2.95. Traces the theme of judgment, catastrophe, and renewal in 12 novels from Hawthorne to Vonnegut, among them works by Faulkner, West, O'Connor, Ellison, Barth, and Pynchon.

Mellard, James M. *The Exploded Form: The Modernist Novel in America.* Univ. of Illinois Pr. 1980 $15.00

Milne, Gordon. *The American Political Novel.* Univ. of Oklahoma Pr. 1966 pap. $6.95

Nadeau, Robert L. *Readings from the New Book of Nature: Physics and Metaphysics in the Modern Novel.* Univ. of Massachusetts Pr. 1981 $17.50. How the New Physics has influenced some modern writers is shown in chapters on Barth, Updike, Pynchon, Vonnegut, and others.

Olderman, Raymond. *Beyond the Waste Land: The American Novel in the Nineteen-Sixties.* Yale Univ. Pr. 1972 $24.50. Still another demonstration that American novelists have moved toward a more affirmative vision of life than that held by their predecessors. A worthwhile critical study particularly rich in its considerations of Kesey, Heller, Barth, Pynchon, Hawkes, and Vonnegut.

Payne, Ladell. *Black Novelists and the Southern Literary Tradition.* Univ. of Georgia Pr. 1981 $11.00

Peden, William. *The American Short Story: Continuity and Change, 1940–1975.* 1964. Houghton Mifflin 2d ed. rev. & enl. 1975 $7.95. More than 100 writers of short fiction are discussed in this standard critical survey.

Pinsker, Sanford. *Between Two Worlds: The American Novel in the 1960s.* 1971. Whitston 1980 $7.50

———. *The Schlemiel as Metaphor: Studies in the Yiddish and American Jewish Novel.* Pref. by Harry T. Moore, *Crosscurrents Modern Critiques Ser.* Southern Illinois Univ. Pr. 1971 $6.95

Pizer, Donald. *Twentieth-Century American Literary Naturalism: An Interpretation.* Southern Illinois Univ. Pr. 1982 $16.95. A leading scholar offers readings of six novels that belong to the tradition of literary naturalism. Considered are Farrell, Dos Passos, Steinbeck, Mailer, Styron, and Bellow.

Pizer, Donald, and Earl N. Harbert, eds. *American Realists and Naturalists.* Volume 12 in *Dictionary of Literary Biography.* Gale 1982 $70.00

Rubin, Louis D., Jr. *The Curious Death of the Novel.* Louisiana State Univ. Pr. 1967 $25.00. The title essay of this collection covering various topics is "sharp, funny, rabbit-punching" (Eliot Fremont-Smith). Rubin finds this recent era a "fallow period" for American fiction.

———. *Writers of the Modern South: The Faraway Country.* Univ. of Washington Pr. 1966 pap. $5.95. Discusses Faulkner, Wolfe, Warren, Welty, Ransom, Tate, and Styron.

Rupp, Richard H. *Celebration in Postwar American Fiction, 1945–1957*. Univ. of Miami Pr. 1970 $11.95. A critical study of ten contemporary novelists that sees a swing away from the alienation and despair of earlier periods. The subjects are Agee, Baldwin, Bellow, Cheever, Ellison, Malamud, O'Connor, Salinger, Updike, and Welty.

Schulz, Max F. *Black Humor Fiction of the Sixties: A Pluralistic Definition of Man and His World*. Ohio Univ. Pr. 1973 $12.95

Sullivan, Walter. *Death by Melancholy: Essays on Modern Southern Fiction*. Louisiana State Univ. Pr. 1972 $12.50. Several general essays accompany studies of Faulkner, Porter, Warren, O'Connor, and others.

Sundquist, Eric J., ed. *American Realism: New Essays*. Johns Hopkins Univ. Pr. 1982 $27.50 pap. $8.95. This collection brings together critical discussions of James, Crane, Norris, Wharton, Dreiser, and other novelists.

Tanner, Tony. *City of Words: American Fiction, 1950–1970*. Harper 1971 $12.50. A young British critic provides a fresh-eyed look at contemporary American fiction. Especially perceptive are his discussions of Mailer, Purdy, Hawkes, Heller, Roth, Pynchon, Vonnegut, Barth, Barthelme, and Gass.

Tuttleton, James W. *The Novel of Manners in America*. 1972. Norton 1974 pap. $3.45. "This solid work of scholarly criticism covers the novel of manners in America from Cooper to Auchincloss . . . [seen] against the background of a changing sociological matrix, but [Tuttleton] does not forget that he is dealing with the novel as a form of art as well as a reflection of social history. The result is an unusually responsible and discerning study of a kind of novel which was doomed to become unfashionable precisely because it was to a large extent concerned with fashions" (*Journal of Modern Lit.*). Discusses at length James, Wharton, Lewis, Fitzgerald, O'Hara, Marquand, and Cozzens.

Vinson, James, and Daniel Kirkpatrick, eds. *Contemporary Novelists*. 1972. St. Martin's 3d ed. 1982 $65.00. Some 600 American and British novelists are represented in this ambitious and useful reference work. Most entries include a list of writings, a personal statement by the author, and a signed critical commentary by one of the more than 200 prominent contributors.

Walden, Daniel, ed. *Twentieth-Century American-Jewish Fiction Writers*. Volume 28 in *Dictionary of Literary Biography*. Gale 1984 $80.00. This addition to the *Dictionary of Literary Biography* series includes entries on 51 writers.

Wallace, Ronald. *The Last Laugh: Form and Affirmation in the Contemporary American Comic Novel*. Univ. of Missouri Pr. 1979 $17.00. Works by Barth, Hawkes, Kesey, and Coover, among others, are placed against the literary traditions to which they belong.

Walsh, Jeffrey. *American War Literature: 1914 to Vietnam*. St. Martin's 1982 $25.00

Werner, Craig H. *Paradoxical Resolutions: American Fiction since James Joyce*. Univ. of Illinois Pr. 1982 $18.95. Werner traces the pervasive influence of Joyce on American fiction since the time of Faulkner and Wright.

Witham, W. Tasker. *The Adolescent in the American Novel, 1920–1960*. Ungar 1975 $15.00

Woodress, James. *American Fiction, 1900–1950: A Guide to Information Sources*. Gale 1973 $55.00. This useful volume describes literary scholarship devoted to more than 40 of the prominent fiction writers of the early twentieth century as well as general studies of modern American fiction.

Young, Thomas Daniel. *The Past in the Present: A Thematic Study of Modern Southern Fiction*. Louisiana State Univ. Pr. 1981 $14.95. Seven books of fiction are analyzed in terms of their dominant themes. Discusses Faulkner, Tate, Warren, Welty, O'Connor, Percy, and Barth.

Zavarzdeh, Mas'ud. *The Mythopoeic Reality: The Postwar American Nonfiction Novel.* Univ. of Illinois Pr. 1980 $21.50 pap. $5.95. Works by Capote and Mailer are among the writings considered in this somewhat theoretical study of a new kind of American fiction.

Ziff, Larzer. *The American 1890's: Life and Times of a Lost Generation.* 1976. Univ. of Nebraska Pr. 1979 pap. $6.95. A discussion that includes, among others, Crane, Norris, and Dreiser.

AGEE, JAMES. 1909–1955

Tennessee-born and Harvard-educated, Agee crowded a lot of versatile literary activity into his short and troubled life. In addition to two novels, he wrote short stories, essays, poetry, and screenplays; and he worked professionally as a journalist and film critic. Appropriately, he is best remembered for a work that combines several genres and literary approaches. *Let Us Now Praise Famous Men*, a documentary report on sharecropper life accompanied by vividly realistic photographs by Walker Evans, has been called "a great Moby-Dick of a book" (*N.Y. Times Bk. Review*). It may be considered an important precursor of the so-called nonfiction novel that was to gain prominence during the 1960s.

Belonging to more conventional types of fiction are *The Morning Watch* (1954, o.p.), a novel in the tradition of portraits of artists-to-be, and *A Death in the Family*, a moving account of domestic life based on the loss of his father, for which Agee was posthumously awarded the Pulitzer Prize in 1958. The 1960 dramatization by Tad Mosel, *All the Way Home*, also won a Pulitzer Prize and the New York Drama Critics Circle Award and was cited by *Life* as the "Best American Play of the Season."

Agee's work for the screen was highlighted by his scripts for *The African Queen* and *The Night of the Hunter*. *Agee on Film* (1958–60) consists of a gathering of reviews and comments as well as five scripts. With *Collected Poems* (1968) out of print, Agee's poetry is available only in part as *Permit Me Voyage*.

Prior to Laurence Bergreen's well-received 1984 biography of Agee, the principal source of information about his life was *Letters of James Agee to Father Flye*, which consists of 70 letters written by Agee to his instructor at St. Andrew's School and a close and trusted friend throughout his life. They show Agee most often in a reflective, self-condemning mood. The final ones, written from the hospital where he was battling daily heart attacks, are touching, as are his sad reflections on the work he yet wanted to do.

BOOKS BY AGEE

Collected Short Prose. 1969. Ed. by Robert Fitzgerald, Berg repr. 1978 $14.95. Features a valuable memoir by Fitzgerald as well as a selection of Agee's short stories, satiric pieces, movie scripts, and miscellanea.

Letters of James Agee to Father Flye. 1962. Berg repr. 1978 $14.95

(and Walker Evans). *Let Us Now Praise Famous Men.* 1941. Ballantine 1974 pap. $1.95; Houghton Mifflin 1960 $19.95 1980 pap. $11.95. "The centerpiece of Agee's career ..." Robert E. Burkholder (*Dictionary of Literary Biography*) wrote. "Not quite a novel, but too poetic to be nonfiction ... a supreme attempt at recreating the squalor and beauty of the tenant farmers' lives through use of experimental techniques, such as a shifting point of view, several narrative levels and time schemes, and a structure which combines elements of the Mass, five-act drama, and the sonata."
A Death in the Family. 1959. Bantam 1971 pap. $3.95

BOOKS ABOUT AGEE

Barson, Alfred T. *A Way of Seeing: A Critical Study of James Agee.* Univ. of Massachusetts Pr. 1972 $13.50
Bergreen, Laurence. *James Agee.* Dutton 1984 $20.00; Penguin 1985 pap. $8.95
Doty, Mark A. *Tell Me Who I Am: James Agee's Search for Selfhood.* Louisiana State Univ. Pr. 1981 $15.95
Larsen, Erling. *James Agee.* Pamphlets on Amer. Writers Ser. Univ. of Minnesota Pr. 1971 pap. $1.25
Madden, David, ed. *Remembering James Agee.* Louisiana State Univ. Pr. 1974 $13.95
Ohlin, Peter. *Agee.* Intro. by D. McDowell, Astor-Honor 1965 $12.50 pap. $7.95

ANDERSON, SHERWOOD. 1876–1941

The important but often misunderstood role that Sherwood Anderson played in modern literary history has tended to obscure his distinctive merits as a writer. In different ways he served as a catalyst for Hemingway and Faulkner at the beginnings of their careers, and although both repaid him with satiric mockery in early novels, Faulkner was generous enough to acknowledge in 1956 that "he was the father of my generation of American writers and the tradition of American writing which our successors will carry on. He has never received his proper evaluation."

Born in Camden, Ohio, of Scottish-American parents, Anderson led a varied, restless life as laborer, soldier, businessman, and newspaper proprietor. A highlight of *Sherwood Anderson's Memoirs: A Critical Edition* (o.p.), edited by Ray L. White, is his account of the pivotal moment in 1912 when he spontaneously walked away from the Ohio paint factory that he managed to start a precarious new career as a writer. His father served as the model for Windy in *Windy McPherson's Son* (1916, o.p.), his first novel, and many of his later works of fiction are based on autobiographical experience. *Poor White*, which first appeared in 1920 and is now available in *The Portable Sherwood Anderson* as the only one of his full-length novels in print, is generally considered the best of his novels. Such others as *Many Marriages* (1923), *Dark Laughter* (1925), and *Kit Brandon*, which seemed daring and progressive in their frank depiction of sex and in their author's probing of the subconsciousness of his characters, now appear somewhat wooden and dated, and most critics agree that he was at his best as a writer of short fiction.

Largely because of *Winesburg, Ohio*, Anderson's place in literary history owes much to his association with the revolt-from-the-village tradition of writers like Sinclair Lewis and EDGAR LEE MASTERS. Too often overlooked are the books in which Anderson presented a much more sympathetic view of small-town life. They include *Mid American Chants*, which uses somewhat Whitmanesque free verse to celebrate the Midwest and the common man, and *The Buck Fever Papers*, which brings together rather whimsical and good-humored news stories he wrote under the Buck Fever pseudonym for two newspapers he owned in southwestern Virginia.

BOOKS BY ANDERSON

The Portable Sherwood Anderson. 1949. *Viking Portable Lib.* Penguin 1977 pap. $6.95
The Teller's Tales: Short Stories. Ed. by Frank Gado, *Signature Ser.* Union College 1983 pap. $14.75
The Writer at His Craft. Ed. by Jack Salzman, Appel 1978 $22.50
Sherwood Anderson: Selected Letters. Ed. by Charles E. Modlin, Univ. of Tennessee Pr. text ed. 1983 $24.95
Winesburg, Ohio. 1919. Intro. by Malcolm Cowley, Penguin 1976 pap. $2.95; ed. by John Ferres, *Viking Critical Lib.* Penguin 1977 pap. $7.95; intro. by Malcolm Cowley, Viking 2d ed. 1960 $15.00. A unified collection of stories about grotesque and unfulfilled people in a small town. Considered a modern classic that can stand comparison with James Joyce's *Dubliners*.
Alice and The Lost Novel. Arden Lib. repr. of 1929 ed. 1978 lib. bdg. $8.50; Folcroft repr. of 1929 ed. lib. bdg. $10.00; Porter 1979 $28.50. Two novelettes, the first an attempt to define the inner beauty of an ideal woman, the second an exploration of the creative process experienced by an artist.
Beyond Desire. 1933. Intro. by Walter B. Rideout, *Black and Gold Lib.* Liveright 1961 $6.95 1970 pap. $2.45. Anderson fuses four interrelated short novels in an attempt to interpret the New South.
Sherwood Anderson's Notebook. 1926. Appel 1970 $10.00

BOOKS ABOUT ANDERSON

Anderson, David D. *Critical Essays on Sherwood Anderson. Critical Essays on Amer. Lit. Ser.* G. K. Hall (Twayne) 1981 $26.00
———, ed. *Sherwood Anderson: Dimensions of His Literary Art.* Michigan State Univ. Pr. 1976 text ed. $9.50
Appel, Paul P., ed. *Homage to Sherwood Anderson.* Appel 1970 lib. bdg. $12.00
Burbank, Rex. *Sherwood Anderson. Twayne's U.S. Authors Ser.* G. K. Hall 1964 lib. bdg. $12.95
Campbell, Hilbert, and Charles E. Modlin, eds. *Sherwood Anderson: Centennial Studies.* Whitston 1976 $12.50
Rideout, Walter B., ed. *Sherwood Anderson: A Collection of Critical Essays. Twentieth-Century Views Ser.* Prentice-Hall (Spectrum Bks.) 1974 $12.95 pap. $2.45
Rogers, Douglas. *Sherwood Anderson: A Selective, Annotated Bibliography. Author Bibliographies Ser.* Scarecrow Pr. 1976 $15.00
Taylor, Welford D. *Sherwood Anderson. Lit. and Life Ser.* Ungar 1977 $12.95
Weber, Brom. *Sherwood Anderson. Pamphlets on Amer. Writers Ser.* Univ. of Minnesota Pr. 1964 pap. $1.25
———. *Sherwood Anderson: A Biographical and Critical Study.* Stanford Univ. Pr. 1966 $22.50. Still the best balanced account of Anderson's life and writing career.
White, Ray L., ed. *The Achievement of Sherwood Anderson: Essays in Criticism.* Univ. of North Carolina Pr. 1966 $21.00 pap. $6.95

AUCHINCLOSS, LOUIS. 1917–

A practicing lawyer who has found time to write more than 35 books, 27 of them works of fiction, Louis Auchincloss calls himself a Jacobite proud to be an author in the tradition of HENRY JAMES and Edith Wharton. He followed in his family's solid tradition by attending Groton, Yale, and the University of Virginia Law School before serving in the Pacific during World War II. His first novel, *The Indifferent Children* (1947, o.p.), was published under the pseudonym Andrew Lee, but its kindly reception encouraged him to publish from then on under his own name. *Sybil*, a novel about an unhappy socialite in search of a real identity beneath the roles that have been imposed upon her, established Auchincloss as a male writer with a special understanding of feminine psychology. He has maintained that reputation throughout his career, but several of his most recent books seem particularly remarkable as explorations of different kinds of women portrayed with something less than complete sympathy. Another theme frequently explored by Auchincloss is the moral, legal, and psychological crises faced by his lawyer characters in works like *The Embezzler, The Country Cousin*, and the related stories about a law firm told in *The Partners*. In what is generally thought to be his most successful novel, *The Rector of Justin*, Auchincloss offers a somewhat ambiguous portrait of a deeply committed headmaster and good man whom no one ever sees truly or clearly. When Auchincloss returned to the theme of the dedicated man in *The House of the Prophet*, Robert Kiely (*N.Y. Times*) suggested that the book has a fatal weakness in offering as central character a "genius" with "mundane" ideas. In addition to his fiction, Auchincloss has written biographical and critical portraits of Edith Wharton, HENRY ADAMS, Ellen Glasgow, and other writers. Available nonfiction includes *Reflections of a Jacobite* (1961), a book of essays about literature with a "clearly defined class feeling," *Pioneers and Caretakers: A Study of Nine American Women Novelists*, and *A Writer's Capital*.

BOOKS BY AUCHINCLOSS

Sybil. 1952. Greenwood repr. $20.50
The Romantic Egoists: Short Stories. 1954. Greenwood repr. $15.00
The Great World and Timothy Colt. 1956. Queens House $16.95
The Rector of Justin. Houghton Mifflin 1964 pap. $3.95
The Embezzler. Houghton Mifflin 1966 $5.95
The Partners. Houghton Mifflin 1974 $6.95
The Dark Lady. Houghton Mifflin 1977 $8.95
The Country Cousin. Houghton Mifflin 1978 $8.95
The House of the Prophet. Houghton Mifflin 1980 $10.95 pap. $3.95
Watchfires. Houghton Mifflin 1982 $13.95
Exit Lady Masham. Houghton Mifflin 1983 $13.95
Narcissa and Other Fables. Houghton Mifflin 1983 $13.95
The Book Class. Houghton Mifflin 1984 $14.95

BALDWIN, JAMES. 1924–

EDMUND WILSON (*The Bit between My Teeth*) described James Baldwin as "not only one of the best black writers that we have ever had in this country, [but] one of the best writers that we have. He has mastered a taut and incisive style . . . and in writing about what it means to be a Negro he is writing about what it means to be a man." Looking back on Baldwin's career several decades after Wilson made his comment, it seems increasingly clear that if the main theme of Baldwin's writings is what it means to be a Negro and a man, he has approached that theme from the perspective of an outsider. His novels, plays, short stories, and essays are concerned again and again with problems of racial, sexual, and personal identity; and what makes those works especially remarkable is the uncompromising honesty of their author.

Baldwin emerged to prominence at an opportune time, during the 1950s and 1960s, when for the first time there was a large receptive audience ready to listen to articulate spokespeople from black America. His first novel, *Go Tell It on the Mountain* (1953), describes the growing up of a young man in Harlem. Clearly fictional, yet autobiographical in its setting and dominant psychological themes, the work raised expectations that Baldwin would serve as a leading force in a postmodern literature marked by passion and commitment to activist causes.

That promise has been only partly fulfilled. Baldwin left the United States for Paris in 1948 and has spent many of his subsequent years living abroad, but another explanation may be found in his increasing concern with questions of personal rather than racial identity. His second and third novels, *Giovanni's Room* (1956, o.p.) and *Another Country* (1962, o.p.), are remembered largely for what was considered a daring and advanced depiction of homosexuals. And although *If Beale Street Could Talk* (1974) was one of the bestsellers of 1975, its story of a young black couple victimized by the American judicial system ends on such a note of uncertainty that the book seems ineffective as an activist statement. Baldwin's latest novel, *Just Above My Head*, is a more ambitious, complex work. Baldwin commented, "What I've really been feeling is that I've come full circle. From 'Go Tell It on the Mountain' to 'Just Above My Head' sums up something of my experience— it's difficult to articulate—that sets me free to go someplace else" (*Dictionary of Literary Biography*).

Baldwin has written several plays. *Blues for Mister Charlie* (1964), which received mixed reviews on Broadway, is a powerful study of racial conflict in a southern town, while *The Amen Corner* movingly describes the desperate struggle of a woman minister in Harlem to keep her church and hold her family together.

BOOKS BY BALDWIN

Go Tell It on the Mountain. Dell 1965 pap. $2.50; Doubleday (Dial) 1953 $13.95
Notes of a Native Son. 1955. Beacon 1984 pap. $6.95; Doubleday (Dial) $7.95
Nobody Knows My Name. Doubleday (Dial) 1961 $7.95
Going to Meet the Man. 1965. Dell pap. $1.50; Doubleday (Dial) $7.95
If Beale Street Could Talk. Doubleday (Dial) 1974 $6.95; New Amer. Lib. (Signet Class.) 1975 pap. $2.95
Just Above My Head. Dell 1980 pap. $3.50; Doubleday (Dial) 1979 $12.95

BOOKS ABOUT BALDWIN

Clark, Kenneth B. *King, Malcolm, Baldwin: Three Interviews.* Wesleyan Univ. Pr. repr. of 1964 ed. 1985 pap. $9.95

Macebuh, Stanley. *James Baldwin: A Critical Study.* Okpaku 1973 $8.95

O'Daniel, Therman B., ed. *James Baldwin: A Critical Evaluation.* Howard Univ. Pr. 1977 $12.00 1981 pap. $7.95

Pratt, Louis H. *James Baldwin. Twayne's U.S. Authors Ser.* G. K. Hall 1978 lib. bdg. $11.50

Standley, Fred L., and Nancy V. Standley. *James Baldwin: A Reference Guide.* G. K. Hall 1979 lib. bdg. $36.50

Sylvander, Carolyn W. *James Baldwin. Lit. and Life Ser.* Ungar 1981 $12.95 pap. $6.95

BARNES, DJUNA. 1892–1982

Although Djuna Barnes was a New Yorker who spent much of her long life in Greenwich Village, where she died a virtual recluse in 1982, she resided for extended periods in France and England. Her writings, too, are representative modernist works in that they seem to transcend all national boundaries to take place in a land peculiarly her own. Deeply influenced by the French symbolists of the late nineteenth century and by the surrealists of the 1930s, she served also as the liberated woman, whose unconventional way of life is reflected in the uncompromising individuality of her literary style. Her dreamlike and haunted writings have never found a wide popular audience, but they have strongly influenced such writers as West, Algren, Dahlberg, Lowry, Miller, and especially Nin, in whose works a semifictional character named Djuna sometimes appears.

Barnes published *The Book of Repulsive Women* anonymously in 1915. Not long afterward she moved to Paris and became associated with the colony of writers and artists who made that city the international center of culture during the 1920s and early 1930s. Her *Ladies Almanack* was privately printed there in 1928, the same year that Liveright in America published her first novel, *Ryder* (o.p.). The book on which her fame largely depends is *Nightwood* (1936), a surrealistic story set in Paris and the United States, which deals with the complex relationships among a group of strangely obsessed characters, most of them homosexuals and lesbians.

She wrote little after *Nightwood*. In fact, she professed to Malcolm Lowry in 1952 that she had been so frightened by the experience of writing that searing work that she could not write anything afterward. Fortunately, her literary talents revived with *The Antiphon*, a verse-drama originally published in 1958, which is now available in *Selected Works*. EDWIN MUIR described that ambitious experimental work as "one of the greatest things that have been written in our time."

BOOKS BY BARNES

Selected Works of Djuna Barnes. Farrar 1962 $12.95

Smoke and Other Early Stories. Ed. by Douglas Messerli, Sun & Moon Pr. 1982 $12.95 pap. $8.00

Ryder. 1928. St. Martin's 1979 $10.95 1981 pap. $5.95

Nightwood. Intro. by T. S. Eliot, New Directions 1946 pap. $5.25. In his introduction
to the novel, Eliot wrote that it is a book that would "appeal primarily to readers of poetry." He found in it "the great achievement of a style, the beauty of
phrasing, the brilliance of wit and characterization, and a quality of horror and
doom very nearly related to that of Elizabethan tragedy."

BOOKS ABOUT BARNES

Field, Andrew. *Djuna: The Life and Times of Djuna Barnes.* Putnam 1983 $16.95
Kannenstine, Louis. *The Art of Djuna Barnes: Duality and Damnation.* New York
Univ. Pr. 1977 $26.00 pap. $13.50

BARTH, JOHN. 1930–

John Barth published an essay in the August 1967 issue of *Atlantic
Monthly* called "The Literature of Exhaustion," which has become a classic
of recent criticism. While describing the kind of self-consciously reflective
fiction that helps to distinguish the final period of high modernism, Barth
identified his own antecedents and set down some cautionary principles
that help to explain his work and that of other members of his generation.
He is often considered an American leader of the metafictional writers. Robert Scholes called him "the best writer of fiction we have at present, and
one of the best we have ever had."

Born in Cambridge, Maryland, Barth attended the Juilliard School of Music, but went on to Johns Hopkins for an M.A., became addicted to the academic life while working in the classics library, and now holds a professorship in creative writing at Johns Hopkins. His first novel, *The Floating Opera,* is an existentialist tale that is cynical, readable, funny, relatively brief.
His fourth novel, *Giles Goat-Boy,* is also picaresque—a 700-page allegorical
fantasy set in the present.

Barth's most recent fiction is even more experimental than his two long
novels. The stories in *Lost in the Funhouse* are reflexive to an extreme, self-
consciously concerned as they are with technical problems of storytelling.
Yet for all their difficulty, Barth's humor and virtuosity make his stories immediately enjoyable. His interest in classical themes and subjects is utilized
in *Chimera* (1972), which consists of retellings of the legends of Schehera-
zade, Perseus, and Bellerophon interlocked in such a way that the artist-as-
storyteller begins to take on the stature of a mythical hero. Most reviewers
in the commercial press found the book confusing and annoying, but it is
filled with the kinds of labyrinthian riddles and indigenous tricks that make
Barth's writings especially attractive to college audiences. In fact, to judge
from the sometimes hostile reception of Barth's latest novels, *Letters* and
Sabbatical: A Romance, the academic appeal of his kind of writing has
started to turn off some reviewers. Of *Letters,* Barth's attempt to revive the
epistolary novel in the form of another long and complicated work, both
John Leonard in the *N.Y. Times* and Robert Towers in the *N.Y. Review of
Bks.* suggested that it seemed to have been written only for "graduate students and other masochists" (Leonard) or "that little band of academic
scholar-critics, now mostly middle-aged, who, having locked themselves

into a room with POUND's 'Cantos' and 'Finnegans Wake,' glare balefully through barred windows at the rest of the literary scene" (Towers). On the other hand, Philip Stevick, a professor-critic writing in the *Nation,* found *Letters* to be "an extraordinary exercise in intersecting perspectives, intersecting rhetorics, intersecting ways of organizing the world. . . . It is a book that confirms one's conviction that, for pure talent, the ability to do anything with words, nobody is better than Barth."

BOOKS BY BARTH

The Floating Opera. 1956. Bantam 1972 pap. $3.95
The End of the Road. 1958. Bantam 1969 pap. $3.95; Doubleday 1967 $4.95
The Sot-Weed Factor. 1960. Bantam 1969 pap. $4.95. "A piece of ingenious linguistic play, a joyous series of raids on half-forgotten resources of language. . . . The book is a joke-book, an endless series of gags. . . . But the biggest joke of all is that Barth seems finally to have written something closer to the 'Great American Novel' than any other book of the last decades" (Leslie Fiedler).
Giles Goat-Boy; or The Revised New Syllabus. Doubleday 1966 ltd. ed. $25.00; Fawcett 1978 pap. $2.95. "Its greatness is most readily apparent in its striking originality of structure and language, an originality that depends upon a superb command of literary and linguistic tradition" (Robert Scholes, *N.Y. Times*).
Chimera. Fawcett 1978 pap. $2.95; Random 1972 $12.95
Letters. Random 1972 $12.95
Sabbatical: A Romance. Penguin 1983 pap. $5.95; Putnam 1982 $14.95

BOOKS ABOUT BARTH

Harris, Charles B. *Passionate Virtuosity: The Fiction of John Barth.* Univ. of Illinois Pr. 1983 $16.95
John Barth: An Annotated Bibliography. Author Bibliographies Ser. Scarecrow Pr. 1977 $15.00
Morrell, David. *John Barth: An Introduction.* Pennsylvania State Univ. Pr. 1976 $22.50
Tharpe, Jac. *John Barth: The Comic Sublimity of Paradox. Crosscurrents Modern Critiques Ser.* Southern Illinois Univ. Pr. 1974 $6.95 1977 pap. $4.95
Waldmeir, Joseph J. *Critical Essays on John Barth. Critical Essays on Amer. Lit. Ser.* G. K. Hall 1980 lib. bdg. $26.00
Weixlmann, Joseph. *John Barth: An Annotated Bibliography. Reference Lib. of the Humanities* Garland 1976 lib. bdg. $29.00

BARTHELME, DONALD. 1931–

According to *Newsweek,* Barthelme is "perhaps the most influential young fiction writer today." Born in Philadelphia, he served in the army, worked as a museum director in Houston during the mid-1950s, and did editorial work before establishing himself as a writer. His only novel, *Snow White,* took up almost an entire issue of the *New Yorker.* Few works have received such distinction, and Barthelme is the youngest writer to be so honored.

Snow White is hardly the typical *New Yorker* story. More surreal than realistic, more cynical than sensitive, it updates the fairy tale in startling ways. Barthelme's Snow White shares an apartment with seven short businessmen who have grown prosperous manufacturing oriental baby foods such as Baby Dim Sum and Baby Dow Shew. The evil stepmother is named Jane Villiers de l'Isle Adam, the prince-hero turns out to be a real frog, and the story ends in a way that will surprise readers of the Brothers Grimm. Whereas much modern fiction is reflexive in the sense that it deals with its own composition, making us conscious of the artist behind the work, Barthelme takes us a step further by pulling the reader into his stories. Thus, for example, *Snow White* is interrupted with a questionnaire in which the author solicits advice from his readers as to how his story should proceed.

Sixty Stories, which comprises approximately half of the short fiction he wrote between 1961 and 1981, offers what he and his editors consider the best of his shorter works. Most of those works are at least as experimental as his own novel—so much so that it is perhaps convenient to see them as exercises in verbal and visual effects rather than as traditional short stories. He likes to pepper his sketches with erudite literary references. He makes use of real people as fictional characters—as in the startling reversal of non-fiction fiction shown in "Robert Kennedy Saved from Drowning." He likes to break down barriers of time, as in "The Indian Uprising," in which an old-fashioned cowboys and Indians formula is used to tell about guerrilla warfare in a modern urban ghetto. Because he has been strongly influenced by the visual arts, including film, it is not surprising that recently he has devoted himself to breaking down the usual distinctions between the verbal and visual genres of art. *The Dead Father* (1975) and other late works combine illustrations with text in an unusually effective new way, which is beginning to find its imitators.

BOOKS BY BARTHELME

Sixty Stories. Dutton (Obelisk) 1982 pap. $8.95; Putnam 1981 $15.95
Come Back, Dr. Caligari. 1964. Little, Brown 1971 pap. $6.70
Snow White. Atheneum 1967 pap. $5.95
The Dead Father. Farrar 1975 $7.95; Pocket Bks. repr. 1978 pap. $2.25
Amateurs. Farrar 1976 $7.95
Great Days. Farrar 1979 $7.95; Pocket Bks. 1980 pap. $2.50
Presents. Ltd. Ed. Ser. Pressworks 1981 $60.00
Overnight to Many Distant Cities. Putnam 1983 $13.95

BOOKS ABOUT BARTHELME

Gordon, Lois. *Donald Barthelme. Twayne's U.S. Authors Ser.* G. K. Hall 1981 lib. bdg. $14.50
Klinkowitz, Jerome, and others. *Donald Barthelme: A Comprehensive Bibliography and an Annotated Secondary Checklist*. Shoe String (Archon) 1977 $15.00
McCaffery, Larry. *The Metafictional Muse: The Work of Robert Coover, Donald Barthelme, and William Gass. Critical Essays in Modern Lit. Ser.* Univ. of Pittsburgh Pr. 1982 $24.95
Molesworth, Charles F. *Donald Barthelme's Fiction: The Ironist Saved from Drowning. Literary Frontier Ed.* Univ. of Missouri Pr. text ed. 1982 pap. $7.95

BELLOW, SAUL. 1915–   (NOBEL PRIZE 1976)

Even before Saul Bellow won the Nobel Prize, *Newsweek* in a cover story of September 1, 1975, called him "the most honored American novelist of his age." By then he had received several Guggenheim Fellowships, a Pulitzer Prize, and no less than three National Book Awards in addition to other recognitions. Perhaps a major reason for his high respectability may be found in the representative nature of his work. Bellow has always seemed to exist comfortably between extremes. Neither too liberal nor too conservative in his politics but very much aware of changing social conditions, on occasion very funny and often quite profound, sophisticated in his literary knowledge yet sometimes loose and sprawling in his literary forms, Bellow has epitomized American literary culture of his time. *Newsweek* noted, "Philip Roth put it nicely when he referred to Bellow as 'closing the gap, as it were, between Damon Runyon and Thomas Mann.' "

He was born Solomon Bellows in a small town in Quebec, of Russian Jewish parents. His family moved to Chicago when he was nine. A graduate of Northwestern University, he did graduate work in anthropology at the University of Wisconsin until he decided to devote himself to writing. He served in the merchant marine during World War II and worked on the fringes of the New York publishing scene before returning to the Middle West and settling into an academic career. Since 1962 he has been a member and chairperson of the University of Chicago's Committee on Social Thought, a flexible department with restricted enrollment for people with broad intellectual interests.

The Adventures of Augie March (1953) is generally considered the pivotal book in his career as a writer. It was preceded by *Dangling Man* (1944) and *The Victim* (1947), comparatively short novels, which were well received by some of the most influential critics of the time and praised for the way in which they seemed to reflect the existential mood of the postwar years. With *Augie March*, a long picaresque novel centered on the misadventures of a kind of "Chicago Tom Jones" (Albert J. Guerard), Bellow began to develop what IRVING HOWE has called "the first major new style in American prose fiction since those of Hemingway and Faulkner." It is a style that combines the rhythms and energy of urban street talk with the plain speech of the Middle West and the bookish consciousness of an intellectual. *Augie March* brought Bellow not only the first of his National Book Awards, but wide public acceptance as a writer to be enjoyed as well as respected. However, Bellow turned back to shorter, tighter forms with his next book, and the novelette of the same title in his *Seize the Day* (1956) volume is generally considered one of his two or three outstanding works. *Henderson the Rain King* (1959) marked a return to the picaresque with its zesty account of the African adventure of the only WASP hero in the Bellow gallery of main characters, a larger-than-life Yankee millionaire.

Herzog (1964), the most autobiographical of his novels, is generally considered the best of his longer novels. It is the story of Moses Herzog (a name borrowed, significantly, from JOYCE's *Ulysses*), a kind of Leopold Bloom in reverse whose life seems to be one long anxiety attack as he looks back on the most recent of his domestic crises and what led to it. Herzog's letters to all sorts of people are included in the loosely structured novel, and its encyclopedic quality makes it seem in some ways as representative in its depiction of mid-century Chicago as *Ulysses* was in its coverage of Dublin in 1904. Bellow's next full-length novel, which also won a National Book Award, was *Mister Sammler's Planet* (1970), the story of an elderly man whose experiences and attitudes also suggest the collective unconsciousness of the century in which we live. *Humboldt's Gift*, Bellow's Pulitzer Prize novel, is a story told by a writer not unlike Bellow who looks back on the tragic career of a poet friend with traits reminiscent of both JOHN BERRYMAN and DELMORE SCHWARTZ. *The Dean's December*, on the other hand, depressed some reviewers because of what they considered its reflection of Bellow's own world-weary attitudes at a low point in his personal life. Fortunately, that mood seems to have been a passing one. Of *Him with His Foot in His Mouth and Other Stories*, Robert M. Adams said, "Of all the American novelists who don't have a foot in their mouth, he remains one of the most rewarding; and the new collection of stories provides encouraging evidence that this state of things is not about to change" (*N.Y. Review of Bks.*).

BOOKS BY BELLOW

The Portable Saul Bellow. Intro. by Gabriel Josipovici, *Viking Portable Lib*. Penguin 1977 pap. $9.95; Viking 1974 $14.95
Dangling Man. 1944. Avon 1975 pap. $2.25; New Amer. Lib. (Plume) pap. $3.95
The Victim. 1947. Avon 1975 pap. $1.95; New Amer. Lib. (Plume) pap. $3.95; Vanguard $11.95
The Adventures of Augie March. Avon 1977 pap. $3.95; Viking 1953 $12.95
Seize the Day. Avon 1977 pap. $2.95; Penguin 1984 pap. $3.95; Viking 1956 $7.95. A novella, three short stories, and a one-act play.
Henderson the Rain King. Avon 1976 pap. $2.95; Penguin 1984 pap. $4.95; Viking 1959 $12.95
Herzog. Avon 1976 pap. $3.95; Penguin 1984 pap. $4.95; Viking 1964 $12.95; ed. by Irving Howe, Viking 1976 $14.95
Mosby's Memoirs and Other Stories. Penguin 1984 pap. $4.95; Viking 1968 $10.95
Mister Sammler's Planet. Penguin 1984 pap. $4.95; Viking 1970 $12.95
Humboldt's Gift. Avon 1976 pap. $3.95; Viking 1975 $12.95. "An exuberant comedy of success and failure, in which Bellow deals directly for the first time with the writer's life in America, including, implicitly, his own. It is his funniest book and his most openly affectionate, even in its satiric side glances" (*Newsweek*).
The Dean's December. Harper 1982 $14.37
Him with His Foot in His Mouth and Other Stories. Harper 1984 $15.34

BOOKS ABOUT BELLOW

Bradbury, Malcolm. *Saul Bellow. Contemporary Writers Ser*. Methuen 1982 pap. $4.25
Braham, Jeanne. *A Sort of Columbus: The American Voyages of Saul Bellow's Fiction*. Univ. of Georgia Pr. text ed. 1984 $15.00
Clayton, John J. *Saul Bellow: In Defense of Man*. Indiana Univ. Pr. 2d ed. 1979 $15.00
Dutton, Robert R. *Saul Bellow*. 1971. *Twayne's U.S. Authors Ser*. G. K. Hall rev. ed. 1982 lib. bdg. $12.50

Fuchs, Daniel. *Saul Bellow: Vision and Revision.* Duke text ed. 1984 $35.00. First scholarly study of Bellow's text.

Goldman, L. H. *Saul Bellow's Moral Experiences: A Critical Study of the Jewish Experience.* Irvington 1983 $26.50 pap. $16.95

Harris, Mark. *Saul Bellow: Drumlin Woodchuck.* Univ. of Georgia Pr. 1980 $15.00

Malin, Irving. *Saul Bellow's Fiction.* Pref. by Harry T. Moore, *Crosscurrents Modern Critiques Ser.* Southern Illinois Univ. Pr. 1969 $7.95

Nault, Marianne. *Saul Bellow: His Works and His Critics—An Annotated International Bibliography. Reference Lib. of the Humanities* Garland 1977 lib. bdg. $28.00. Annotated bibliography with international coverage.

Newman, Judie. *Saul Bellow and History.* St. Martin's 1984 $20.00

Opdahl, Keith. *Novels of Saul Bellow: An Introduction.* Pennsylvania State Univ. Pr. 1967 $17.50

Porter, M. Gilbert. *Whence the Power: The Artistry and Humanity of Saul Bellow.* Univ. of Missouri Pr. 1974 $13.00

Rodrigues, Eusebio L. *Quest for the Human: An Exploration of Saul Bellow's Fiction.* Bucknell Univ. Pr. 1981 $27.50

Scheer-Schaezler, Brigitte. *Saul Bellow. Lit. and Life Ser.* Ungar 1972 $12.95

Sokoloff, B. A. *Saul Bellow: A Comprehensive Bibliography.* Folcroft 1972 lib. bdg. $20.00

Trachtenberg, Stanley, ed. *Critical Essays on Saul Bellow. Critical Essays on Amer. Lit. Ser.* G. K. Hall 1979 $29.00

BERGER, THOMAS (LOUIS). 1924–

Thomas Berger has been gradually building a reputation as a comic and satiric novelist of exceptional gifts. Born in Cincinnati, he served in the army from 1943 to 1946, graduated from the University of Cincinnati in 1948, did graduate work at Columbia, and held several editorial and librarian positions while beginning his writing career. His Reinhart series (*Crazy in Berlin, Reinhart in Love, Vital Parts,* and *Reinhart's Women*), which the *Washington Post* called "a great and unique achievement," follows the central character, big and clumsy Carlo Reinhart, from youth to middle age.

Like other writers of black humor, Berger sometimes slips into presenting life as such a horror that any laughter it may evoke is strained and hollow. For example, *Killing Time* is the story of a murderer who thinks that he is doing his victims a favor by killing them; and *Regiment of Women* is an unpleasant fantasy set in a future time when women roam the world like fierce Amazons raping and abusing men in a not very convincing thesis-novel about what would happen if the Women's Liberation movement did indeed triumph. A much more successful blend of horror and comedy is *Little Big Man,* which won the Rosenthal Award of the National Institute of Arts and Letters in 1965. In this best-known of Berger's novels—a fame due in large part to a successful movie adaptation starring Dustin Hoffman—the author makes good use of the tall tale. It is a big, sprawling novel about life in the Old West during the nineteenth century. This mock-hero saga gave Berger ample range and scope for his gifts as a satirist. Few writers since the time of SWIFT and POPE have made better use of extravagant caricature and wild exaggeration to expose the foibles and evils of what man has done in the name of civilization.

Although Berger claims that he wrote each book in a different style, most of them have in common a strong element of satire and parody. Of his more recent novels, *Who Is Teddy Villanova?* takes off as a spoof of popular detective novels; *Arthur Rex* is an irreverent retelling of the Camelot legend, which *Kirkus Reviews* called "the first really astute reworking of the Arthurian story in decades"; and *Neighbors*, Berger's personal favorite among his books, is like Kafka's *The Trial* in showing how "at any moment banality might turn sinister." Berger said of *Neighbors*, "It is for me the absolutely pure fiction that I have lately aspired to, with no taint of journalism, sociology, and the other corruptions." Berger continued his exposé of suburban and small-town America with *The Feud*, a story set in the 1930s.

BOOKS BY BERGER

Crazy in Berlin. 1958. Delacorte 1982 $16.95; Dell (Delta Bks.) 1982 pap. $8.95
Reinhart in Love. 1962. Delacorte 1982 $16.95; Dell (Delta Bks.) 1982 pap. $7.95
Little Big Man. 1964. Delacorte 1979 $10.95; Dell pap. $4.95; Fawcett 1978 pap. $3.50
Killing Time. 1967. Dell (Delta Bks.) 1981 pap. $7.95
Vital Parts. 1970. Delacorte 1982 $16.95; Dell (Delta Bks.) 1982 pap. $8.95
Regiment of Women. 1973. Dell (Delta Bks.) 1982 pap. $7.95
Sneaky People. Dell (Delta Bks.) 1983 pap. $7.95; Simon & Schuster 1975 $8.95
Who Is Teddy Villanova? 1977. Delacorte 1980 $9.95; Dell (Delta Bks.) 1978 pap. $3.95
Arthur Rex. Delacorte 1978 $11.95; Dell (Delta Bks.) repr. of 1978 ed. 1979 pap. $5.95 1985 pap. $4.95
Neighbors. 1980. Dell (Delta Bks.) 1981 pap. $5.95
Reinhart's Women. Delacorte 1981 $13.95; Dell (Delta Bks.) 1982 pap. $7.95
The Feud. 1982. Delacorte 1983 $14.95; Dell (Delta Bks.) 1984 pap. $7.95
Nowhere. Delacorte 1985 $14.95

BURROUGHS, WILLIAM S. 1914–

From hipster to so-called Godfather of Punk, William Burroughs has lived a controversial life as a leading member of the Beat Generation and a daring writer of psychedelic literary experiments, but when he reached his seventieth birthday in 1984, it was almost as if he had been overtaken by respectability.

Burroughs was born in St. Louis as the grandson of the man who invented the adding machine and a descendant of the Robert E. Lee of Civil War fame. After attending Harvard and while living a bohemian life in association with such Beat writers as ALLEN GINSBERG and Jack Kerouac (Burroughs appears as a character named Old Bull Lee in *On the Road*), he became addicted to morphine and under the pseudonym William Lee published his first novel, *Junkie*, in 1953 as half of an Ace Double Books paperback. Described on the jacket as "Confessions of an Unredeemed Drug Addict," it escaped critical notice, but may be seen now as the forerunner of his later fiction with its introduction of many of the themes, settings, characters, and amoral postures that became prominent with *Naked Lunch* and its successors. Refused by the American publishers to whom Burroughs submitted the manuscript, *Naked Lunch* first appeared in Paris under the Olympia Press imprint in 1959, the same year that Burroughs was permanently cured of his addiction, and although the introduction to the regular Grove Press edition continues to claim that the work was composed from "a stack of crazed scribblings" that Burroughs found he had written under the influence of heroin, he admitted to Jennifer Crichton in *PW*, "That was an exaggeration, . . . an *allegory*." It now seems apparent that much of the psychedelic effect of Burroughs's fiction is an illusion that masks rather deliberate methods of composition, which include "cut-out" techniques, pastiche, and the deliberate trying-out of styles derived from popular fiction genres to create literary montages that owe as much to fantasy and science as to the surrealism of avant-garde literature.

Naked Lunch might have remained ignored if both Mary McCarthy and Norman Mailer had not called attention to the work at the International Writers Conference held in Edinburgh in 1962. The difficulties experienced by Grove Press as it fought censorship of its first U.S. edition of the work, an important episode of modern literary history fully recounted in a book by Michael Barry Goodman cited below, helped to call public attention to the work, and although Burroughs's raw subject matter and seeming lack of discipline have alienated some of the more academic and genteel literary critics, he has been assured a loyal audience of appreciative readers ever since. *Naked Lunch* was followed by three additional novels about the Nova crime syndicate—*The Soft Machine, The Ticket That Exploded,* and *Nova Express*—which make use of overlapping characters and motifs. With *The Wild Boys* of 1971, Burroughs began to develop a new style more accessible to the general reader, and although *Cities of the Red Night* received mixed reviews, it was praised by such Burroughs experts as Jennie Skerl and Robert Burkholder (*Dictionary of Literary Biography*) as perhaps the best of his more recent novels. Of *The Place of Dead Roads*, Jennifer Crichton said that it "gives no indication of being the work of an older writer. Set in the nineteenth-century West, the novel is true to Burroughs's various obsessions: guns, homosexuality, the writer as 'shootist' blasting into his readers' heads and the terror produced by those addicted to power and control."

Books by Burroughs

Three Novels. Grove 1981 pap. $5.95. *The Soft Machine,* bound with *Nova Express* and *The Wild Boys.*
Junkie. 1953. Penguin 1973 pap. $3.50. New edition with restored complete text published as "Junky."
Naked Lunch. 1959. Grove 1962 pap. $3.95
The Soft Machine. 1961. Grove 1966 pap. $2.45
The Ticket That Exploded. 1962. Grove 1967 pap. $2.95
(and Allen Ginsberg). *Yage Letters.* City Lights 1963 pap. $3.00
Nova Express. Grove 1964 pap. $2.45
Exterminator! 1973. Penguin 1979 pap. $4.95
Port of Saints. 1975. Blue Wind 1980 $24.95
Blade Runner: A Movie. Blue Wind 1979 pap. $6.95

Roosevelt after Inauguration. City Lights 1979 pap. $3.00
The Last Words of Dutch Schultz. Seaver Bks. repr. 1981 pap. $4.95
Cities of the Red Night. Holt 1981 $14.95 1982 pap. $7.25
Ah Pook Is Here. Riverrun 1982 pap. $8.95
(and Brion Gysin). *The Third Mind.* Grove 1982 pap. $8.95; Seaver Bks. 1982 pap.
    $8.95; Viking 1978 $12.95
The Place of Dead Roads. Holt 1983 $15.95
The Burroughs File. City Lights 1984 $19.95 pap. $8.95. Miscellaneous essays and
    sketches.

BOOKS ABOUT BURROUGHS

Burroughs, William S., Jr. *Kentucky Ham.* Overlook Pr. 1984 $15.95. Includes remi-
    niscences of his father by a promising writer who died young (1947–1981).
Goodman, Michael Barry. *William S. Burroughs: An Annotated Bibliography of His
    Works and Criticism. Reference Lib. of the Humanities* Garland 1975 lib. bdg.
    $23.00
Maynard, Joe, and Barry Miles, eds. *William S. Burroughs, 1953–1973: A Bibliogra-
    phy.* Fwd. by William S. Burroughs, intro. by Allen Ginsberg, Univ. Pr. of Vir-
    ginia 1978 $15.00
Mottram, Eric. *William Burroughs: Algebra of Need. Critical Appraisals Ser.* Humani-
    ties Pr. text ed. 1977 $13.50
Odier, Daniel. *The Job: Interviews with William Burroughs.* Grove 1974 pap. $4.95

CALDWELL, ERSKINE. 1903–

Although Erskine Caldwell was for years one of the most popular of American writers, he once complained, "I'm not read very much in the South because they are very touchy about what they regard as unkind criticism,
and I'm not thought much of in the North either." He may well have
thought of himself as a prophet without honor in his home country, for his
fame elsewhere was quite spectacular. His more than 50 books were translated into more than 40 languages and have sold more than 75 million copies. But he was hardly neglected in his home country either. His third
novel, *Tobacco Road,* was both a bestselling book and in a stage adaptation by John Kirkland one of the most successful American plays. That
work, a seriocomic portrayal of a rural southern family struggling to eke
out a living in an impoverished backwoods area, set the pattern for much
of the fiction that followed, and although sophisticated southern readers
may have resented the implication of his work that the South was popu-
lated mostly by ignorant red-necks like the Lesters, the rest of the country
found many of his books both amusing and shockingly realistic. His popularity and his preference for low-life subjects may help to explain why he
has been more or less steadily ignored by the critical establishment, but
now that the weakest of his many books have quietly gone out of print, it
seems clear that what remains is likely to last. *Tobacco Road, God's Little
Acre,* and the best of his short stories show a highly original talent that
managed to capture once and for all what much of America was like during the period of the Great Depression, which has sometimes seemed
chronic. Caldwell was ahead of his time in his frank treatment of sex and

in a mixture of the funny with the vulgar grotesque in a way that antici-pated the black humor of the 1960s.

Caldwell has never quite managed to live down the image of a man con-fused with his fictional characters, but after graduating from the University of Virginia, he lived the cosmopolitan life of a reporter and correspondent who worked in many sections of America and traveled widely abroad. He provided the text for several books of photographs by his then-wife Marga-ret Bourke-White, including *You Have Seen Their Faces* (1937), which ranks among the best documentary accounts of depression America.

BOOKS BY CALDWELL

Stories of Life: North and South. Dodd 1983 $14.95
The Black and White Stories of Erskine Caldwell. Ed. by Ray McIver, Peachtree 1984 $12.95
Tobacco Road. 1932. New Amer. Lib. (Signet Class.) 1970 pap. $2.95
God's Little Acre. 1933. New Amer. Lib. (Signet Class.) 1976 $6.95 pap. $2.95
Deep South: Memory and Observation. Intro. by Guy Owen, Univ. of Georgia Pr. repr. of 1968 ed. 1980 pap. $6.95

BOOKS ABOUT CALDWELL

Devlin, James E. *Erskine Caldwell. Twayne's U.S. Authors Ser.* G. K. Hall 1984 lib. bdg. $15.95
Korges, James. *Erskine Caldwell. Pamphlets on Amer. Writers Ser.* Univ. of Minnesota Pr. 1969 pap. $1.25
MacDonald, Scott. *Critical Essays on Erskine Caldwell. Critical Essays on Amer. Lit. Ser.* G. K. Hall 1981 lib. bdg. $26.00

CAPOTE, TRUMAN. 1924–1984

Truman Capote made his special province the exploration of the dividing line between dream and reality, fiction and truth. Even before his first novel, *Other Voices, Other Rooms* (1948), brought him international recog-nition, he had written memorable short stories, such as "A Tree of Night," "Master Misery," and "Miriam," which combine romantic pathos with nightmarish horror. The short novel *Breakfast at Tiffany's* (1958), which in-troduced the delightfully free-spirited Hollie Golightly, also marks the transition in Capote's career from his early preoccupation with southern locales and themes to a concern with the sometimes campy, sometimes so-phisticated, lives of people associated with the arts, the theater, and high society.

Long before his *In Cold Blood* (1966) helped to make "nonfiction novel" a catchphrase of modern criticism, Capote was experimenting with in-depth reportage in profiles of celebrities or vividly personal descriptions of inter-esting places from New Orleans to Soviet Russia. Although such high-level journalism helped develop some of the techniques he was to use in *In Cold Blood*, his previous choice of subjects and his own well-publicized life with "the beautiful people" could not prepare readers for the startling impact of his nonfiction novel. In order to write *In Cold Blood*, the story of a senseless murder of a Kansas family and the background of the two murderers, Capote spent considerable time in the Midwest researching the lives of the victims and becoming close friends with both the police officer credited with solving the crime and the two young men responsible for it. The result is a remarkable and dramatic work. Although *Book Week* was justified in calling it "talented, powerful, and enigmatic" and finding that "the enigma lies in Capote's curious neutrality, in the blank eyes that stare up from the book's pages," it is also true that Capote's seemingly objective detachment only masks a deep compassion for human suffering and weakness. Capote's subsequent campaign against capital punishment testifies to his personal involvement, and Richard Brooks's vivid movie adaptation of *In Cold Blood* was faithful to the novel in emphasizing America's social responsibility for crime as well as the stupidity of this particular killing.

Capote was frequently in the limelight, partly through his appearances on talk shows, partly because of the widely publicized episodes involving drugs and drinking, and when he died suddenly in August 1984 there was much speculation about the unknown whereabouts of a long Proustian novel to be called "Answered Prayers," on which he said he had been working for years. Unless that manuscript is found and published, only the parts of it that appeared in *Esquire* as well as the experimental stories in *Music for Chameleons* will testify to the nature of the new style he was struggling to develop. To the end, Capote was a literary artist who kept challenging himself to find new forms of expression, and it is as perhaps the finest stylist of twentieth-century American prose literature that he will be remembered.

BOOKS BY CAPOTE

The Selected Writings of Truman Capote. Modern Lib. 1963 $6.95; Random 1963 $13.95. A selection of 117 titles representing 20 years of his writing, including *Breakfast at Tiffany's, The Muses Are Heard,* and parts of *A Tree of Night* and *Local Color.*

The Grass Harp (and *A Tree of Night and Other Short Stories*). 1941–51. New Amer. Lib. (Signet Class.) 1956 pap. $2.75

Other Voices, Other Rooms. 1948. New Amer. Lib. (Signet Class.) pap. $2.25; Random 1968 $11.95

Breakfast at Tiffany's. New Amer. Lib. (Signet Class.) 1959 pap. $2.50; Random 1958 $10.95

In Cold Blood. New Amer. Lib. (Signet Class.) 1971 pap. $3.95; Random 1966 $18.95

A Christmas Memory. Random 1966 $14.95

Music for Chameleons. New Amer. Lib. (Plume) 1983 pap. $6.95; New Amer. Lib. (Signet Class.) 1981 pap. $3.50; Random 1980 $11.95

BOOKS ABOUT CAPOTE

Garson, Helen S. *Truman Capote. Lit. and Life Ser.* Ungar 1980 $12.95 pap. $6.95

Rudisill, Marie, and James C. Simmons. *Truman Capote.* Morrow 1983 $12.95 pap. $5.95

Stanton, Robert J. *Truman Capote: A Reference Guide.* G. K. Hall 1980 lib. bdg. $22.50

Windham, Donald. *Footnote to a Friendship: A Memoir of Truman Capote and Others.*
Sandy Campbell ltd. ed. 1983 $35.00

CATHER, WILLA. 1876–1947

Of American women novelists of her time none is more highly regarded than Willa Cather. Most of her books are written in a style of disarming simplicity, and she usually preferred to write about quite ordinary people, but her work has proved lasting because of her delicate craftsmanship, artistic honesty, and ability to create memorable characters. Her best novels have in fact seemed to grow richer with the passing years, as may be suggested by the amount of criticism and the number of differing interpretations they continue to receive. *The Professor's House* (1925), for example, contrasts the life of a burnt-out middle-aged historian with that of a creative young inventor named Tom Outland who died in the war but left a positive legacy of integrity by which other lives are to be measured. Hence this novel with its mythical overtones and its sense of balance seems to be interpreted variously by each of its readers.

The most popular of her novels and the most widely taught is *My Antonia* (1918), the vivid life story of a farm wife of the prairie country, admired not only for its warm depiction of a remarkably human character, but for the subtlety of a point of view that lends a sort of double perspective to her portrait. *Death Comes for the Archbishop* (1927), her choice as her best book, is a fictionalized account of the first bishop appointed to the New Mexico Territory after its annexation. By means of loosely structured episodes covering more than 40 years, she raised a historical narrative to the level of a legend and wrote what is generally considered her masterpiece. Her other novels from *Alexander's Bridge* (1912) and *O Pioneers!* (1913, o.p.) to *Sapphira and the Slave Girl* vary in quality, but none is a shoddy piece of work and the total corpus of writings she left behind is clearly that of a dedicated professional writer. In addition to her work as a novelist, she served as an editor of *McClure's* magazine, produced journalism of various kinds, and wrote a number of short stories for the popular magazines of her day. Of her shorter fiction, "The Sculptor's Funeral," "Neighbor Rosicky," and the frequently reprinted "Paul's Case" are generally considered the most worthy.

In telling the story of Thea Kronberg, a Swedish girl from Colorado who becomes a great Wagnerian soprano in *The Song of the Lark* (1915), Cather disguised her own development from her childhood in rural Nebraska to her triumphant years in New York. Readers may well be skeptical about the approach used by Phyllis C. Robinson in the most recent biography of Cather. Jason Epstein (*New Criterion*) objected to the unproven assumption in *Willa* that she was a homosexual. Whatever her sexual inclinations may have been—and she seems to have been, like Henry James, peculiarly asexual—she saw herself as an artist before anything else, and if her will contained an unqualified prohibition against the publication of any of her letters, that may have been only because she wanted to be judged ultimately by the literary work she carefully shaped and presented to the world between the covers of books.

BOOKS BY CATHER

Willa Cather's Collected Short Fiction, 1892–1912. Intro. by Mildred R. Bennett, Univ. of Nebraska Pr. rev. ed. 1970 $22.95

Early Stories of Willa Cather. Ed. by Mildred R. Bennett, Dodd 1983 pap. $7.95

Five Stories. Random (Vintage) 1956 pap. $4.95

Uncle Valentine and Other Stories: Willa Cather's Uncollected Short Fiction, 1915–1929. Ed. by Bernice Slote, Univ. of Nebraska Pr. 1973 $15.95

The Troll Garden: A Definitive Edition. Afterword by Katherine Anne Porter, New Amer. Lib. (Signet Class.) 1984 pap. $3.95; ed. by James L. Woodress, Univ. of Nebraska Pr. 1983 $15.95. Short stories.

The Kingdom of Art: Willa Cather's First Principles and Critical Statements, 1893–1896. Ed. by Bernice Slote, Univ. of Nebraska Pr. 1967 $27.95

The World and the Parish: Willa Cather's Articles and Reviews, 1893–1902. Ed. by William M. Curtin, Univ. of Nebraska Pr. 2 vols. 1970 $39.50

Alexander's Bridge. Intro. by Bernice Slote, Univ. of Nebraska Pr. (Bison) repr. of 1912 ed. 1977 pap. $5.50. Cather's first novel.

The Song of the Lark. 1915. Houghton Mifflin 1983 pap. $8.95

My Antonia. 1918. Houghton Mifflin 1926 $16.95 pap. $5.95

Youth and the Bright Medusa. 1920. Random (Vintage) 1975 pap. $3.95. Short stories.

One of Ours. Knopf 1922 $12.95; Random (Vintage) 1971 pap. $4.95

A Lost Lady. 1923. Knopf 1973 $12.95; Random (Vintage) 1972 $12.95 pap. $3.95

The Professor's House. 1925. Random (Vintage) 1973 pap. $4.95

My Mortal Enemy. 1926. Random (Vintage) 1961 pap. $3.95

Death Comes for the Archbishop. 1927. Modern Lib. 1984 $8.95; Random (Vintage) 1971 pap. $3.95 1984 pap. $8.95

Shadows on the Rock. 1931. Random (Vintage) 1971 pap. $5.95

Obscure Destinies. 1932. Random (Vintage) 1974 pap. $4.95. Short stories.

Lucy Gayheart. Random (Vintage) repr. of 1935 ed. 1976 pap. $3.95

Sapphira and the Slave Girl. Random (Vintage) repr. of 1940 ed. 1975 pap. $4.95

The Old Beauty and Others. Random (Vintage) repr. of 1948 ed. 1976 pap. $3.95. Short stories.

BOOKS ABOUT CATHER

Bennett, Mildred R. *The World of Willa Cather.* Univ. of Nebraska Pr. (Bison) 1961 $22.50 pap. $8.25

Brown, Edward K., and Leon Edel. *Willa Cather: A Critical Biography.* Avon 1980 pap. $2.95

Crane, Joan. *Willa Cather: A Bibliography.* Univ. of Nebraska Pr. 1982 $35.00. Thorough textual bibliography of writings by Cather.

Daiches, David. *Willa Cather: A Critical Introduction.* Greenwood repr. of 1951 ed. 1971 lib. bdg. $27.50

Gerber, Philip L. *Willa Cather.* Twayne's U.S. Authors Ser. G. K. Hall 1975 lib. bdg. $11.50

Lathrop, Joanna. *Willa Cather: A Checklist of Her Published Writing.* Univ. of Nebraska Pr. 1975 pap. $4.95

McFarland, Dorothy T. *Willa Cather.* Lit. and Life Ser. Ungar 1972 $12.95

Randall, John H., III. *The Landscape and the Looking Glass: Willa Cather's Search for Value.* Greenwood repr. of 1960 ed. 1973 lib. bdg. $24.75

Robinson, Phyllis C. *Willa: The Life of Willa Cather.* Doubleday 1983 $17.95

Sergeant, Elizabeth S. *Willa Cather: A Memoir.* Univ. of Nebraska Pr. (Bison) 1963
    pap. $4.95
Stouck, David. *Willa Cather's Imagination.* Univ. of Nebraska Pr. 1975 $18.95
Woodress, James L. *Willa Cather: Her Life and Art.* Holt 1984 pap. $8.95; *Landmark
    Ed.* Univ. of Nebraska Pr. repr. of 1975 ed. 1982 $21.95

CHEEVER, JOHN. 1912–1982

Although John Cheever's first full-length novel won a National Book
Award and his last one a Pulitzer Prize, the publication of *The Stories of
John Cheever* in 1978 seemed to cap his career and to establish his reputation as a writer who was at his best with shorter forms of fiction. It was
largely on the strength of the collected edition of his stories that he was
given the National Medal for Literature at the American Book Awards in
1982. Accepting the award, Cheever said that he had always been devoted
to one fundamental thing—the creation of "a page of good prose."

A few months after that presentation Cheever died of cancer. An obituary
notice in *PW* offers this summary: "Cheever began his writing career early,
moving to New York at age 17 to write fiction rather than attend college.
The *New Yorker* accepted his first short story in 1935, and he soon became a
regular contributor to that magazine. Altogether he published more than
one hundred short stories, in which he explored the personalities and social
life of upper-middle-class characters who lived in Manhattan's Upper East
Side and the Westchester County and Connecticut suburbs. The stories re-
volved around spacious homes and apartments, Ivy League schools, the better families, hired help, well-paying jobs, alcohol, adultery, and a simmer-
ing but resigned, almost disappointed approach to that life."

Cheever's first novel, *The Wapshot Chronicle* (1958, o.p.), and its sequel,
The Wapshot Scandal, evoke his family and youth in New England.
Whereas the Wapshot novels celebrate life with reservations, *Bullet Park*
(1969) descends to a much more sinister and apocalyptic vision as it centers on the attempted immolation of a child on a church altar. Regeneration is the theme of *Falconer*, a widely acclaimed novel that won a Pulitzer
Prize, written after Cheever had been hospitalized following a period of
heavy drinking. Cheever's last book, *Oh What a Paradise It Seems*, is a novelette that some critics found a fitting summation of his work. Paul Gray
in *Time* saw the book as a kind of "coda" that provides final variations of
themes seen in earlier stories, and John Updike, a writer with whom Cheever is frequently compared, classified the work as "an ecological romance,
a parable and a tall tale" that reestablished Cheever's links to an American transcendentalist tradition of qualified idealism: "Ever more boldly
the celebrant of the grand poetry of life, Cheever, once a taut and mordant
chronicler of urban and suburban disappointments, now speaks in the
cranky, granular, impulsive, confessional style of our native wise men and
exhorters since Emerson" (*New Yorker*).

Susan Cheever's memoir of her father, *Home before Dark*, based in large
part on 30 volumes of intimate journals kept by Cheever, became one of the

nonfiction bestsellers of 1984. It was praised by reviewers for what Elizabeth Hardwick (*N.Y. Review of Bks.*) called its "tone of elegiac candor."

BOOKS BY CHEEVER

The Stories of John Cheever. Ballantine 1980 pap. $3.50; Knopf 1978 $17.50; Random
    (Vintage) 1981 pap. $7.95
Some People, Places, and Things That Will Not Appear in My Next Novel. 1961. *Short
    Story Index Repr. Ser.* Ayer 1979 $15.00
The Wapshot Scandal. 1965. Ballantine 1983 pap. $2.95; Harper 1973 pap. $2.25. "As
    for Mr. Cheever, he is a very good writer indeed. His new novel is rich and
    tricky and full of surprises. More than anyone except perhaps Nabokov (and he
    does not suffer from Nabokov's sudden plunges into grotesquerie), he is able to
    use objects, the scenes and the attributes of contemporary life for the purposes
    of art. Ugliness, pain, loneliness and horror are not softened but understood and
    valued without sentiment, without moralizing and (it seems to me) with pro-
    found good sense that approaches wisdom" (Elizabeth Janeway, *N.Y. Times*).
Bullet Park. Ballantine 1978 pap. $2.25; Knopf 1969 $10.95
Falconer. Ballantine 1978 pap. $2.75; Knopf 1977 $9.95
Oh What a Paradise It Seems. Ballantine 1983 pap. $2.50; Knopf 1982 $10.00

BOOKS ABOUT CHEEVER

Bosha, Francis J. *John Cheever: A Reference Guide.* G. K. Hall 1981 $23.00
Cheever, Susan. *Home before Dark: A Biographical Memoir of John Cheever.* Houghton
    Mifflin 1984 $15.95
Collins, Robert G. *Critical Essays on John Cheever. Critical Essays on Amer. Lit. Ser.*
    G. K. Hall 1982 lib. bdg. $33.50
Hunt, George W. *John Cheever: The Hobgoblin Company of Love.* Eerdmans 1983
    $17.95
Waldeland, Lynne. *John Cheever. Twayne's U.S. Authors Ser.* G. K. Hall 1979 lib. bdg.
    $12.50

COOVER, ROBERT. 1932–

Robert Coover is a midwesterner who has earned a reputation as one of
the most innovative of contemporary writers of fiction. Coover likes to experiment with an abundance of differing styles, and his stories are marked
by clever ingenuity and sometimes dizzying displays of verbal pyrotechnics.
The Origin of the Brunists, his first novel, is a religious parable heavily
loaded with symbolism and mythical parallels. It deals with the rise following an Appalachian coal-mine disaster of a sect of worshipers made up of
both fundamentalists and theosophists whose leader, Giovanni Bruno, is
less a preacher than a silent enigma. The principal analogue is apparently
meant to be the founding of the Christian religion, but Coover's extensive
irony requires that he reverse many of the traditional features of the Christian legend. *The Universal Baseball Association*, Coover's most accessible
novel to date, is also dominated by religious symbolism. Over the years
J. Henry Waugh, a middle-aged bachelor and accountant, has developed an
elaborately structured game, which he plays with dice. His game is based
on the mathematical probabilities of baseball. Every evening Henry plays
his game and maintains his extensive record books. "There are box scores to

be audited," he explains to a friend, "trial balances of averages along the way, seasonal inventories, rewards and punishments to be meted out, life histories to be overseen." J. Henry Waugh is thus a surrogate for God, and the participants in his imaginary baseball league seem almost to come to life, raising as they do age-old questions about fate and free will, success and failure, games and religions.

Coover's *Pricksongs and Descants* is a collection of 20 short pieces and a theoretical "Prologo" in which the author states his belief that contemporary fiction should be based on familiar historical or mythical forms not in the way of modernist works like JOYCE's *Ulysses* or T. S. ELIOT's *The Waste Land*, which simply use myths as a means of providing an arbitrary, skeletal framework, which has no particular thematic importance, but in order to break through the mythical forms and thus expose them, leading the reader "to the real, away from . . . mystery to revelation." Most of the stories in this volume, which was well received by critics, are based on biblical episodes or classical fairy tales retold in startling new ways.

The Public Burning (o.p.), based on the controversial trial of the Rosenbergs, is a hard-to-classify work in which an essentially tragic story is told in a broadly comic manner. *A Political Fable* is "a kind of warm-up exercise for 'The Public Burning,'" though it did not appear until afterward: "Published in book form by Viking to coincide with the 1980 election year, 'A Political Fable' remains a dazzling, often hilarious spoof of America's circuslike political operations" (Larry McCaffery and Sinda J. Gregory, *Dictionary of Literary Biography Yearbook, 1981*).

Coover's publications in recent years have consisted mainly of shorter works, written at various stages of his career, published in limited editions to appeal to collectors.

BOOKS BY COOVER

The Origin of the Brunists. 1966. Viking 1978 $12.50
The Universal Baseball Association, J. Henry Waugh, Prop. 1968. New Amer. Lib. (Plume) pap. $6.95
Pricksongs and Descants. 1969. New Amer. Lib. (Plume) 1970 pap. $5.95
In Bed One Night and Other Brief Encounters. Burning Deck 1983 $15.00

BOOKS ABOUT COOVER

Andersen, Richard. *Robert Coover.* Twayne's U.S. Authors Ser. G. K. Hall 1981 $11.50
Gordon, Lois. *Robert Coover: The Universal Fictionmaking Process.* Crosscurrents Modern Critiques New Ser. Southern Illinois Univ. Pr. 1983 $15.95
McCaffery, Larry. *The Metafictional Muse: The Work of Robert Coover, Donald Barthelme, and William Gass.* Critical Essays in Modern Lit. Ser. Univ. of Pittsburgh Pr. 1982 $24.95

COZZENS, JAMES GOULD. 1903–1978

Cozzens had earned a solid reputation as a novelist before the appearance of *By Love Possessed* (1957, o.p.), but that bestseller and Book-of-the-Month Club selection seemed to establish him as a major American writer. In 1960 he was awarded the Howells Medal of the American Academy of Arts and

Letters for *By Love Possessed*. In the years since then, however, Cozzens has seemed to "plateau-out" as a novelist whose works deserve respect for their craftsmanship and moral vision, but whose critical stature has not grown appreciably. The fact that he was guilty of writing a bestselling novel with "love" in its title may have caused some reviewers of his later works to question his artistic integrity, but a more likely explanation for the decline of readership in recent years is that, because Cozzens chose to write most often on topical subjects set at specific places and times involving particular occupations, his novels now seem dated.

Whatever the reasons, 10 of his 14 main works of fiction have been allowed to go out of print. His first novel, *Confusion* (o.p.), is a romantic story written when Cozzens was a sophomore at Harvard. He left college without graduating, produced three more youthful adventure stories, and, with *S.S. San Pedro* in 1931, the story of how disaster at sea tests the seamanship and character of his protagonists, wrote what he later considered the first of his works deserving of serious attention. Even before he wrote his sea novel, Cozzens had been concerned with what was to be his main theme—how men are tested by their professions. Both *Cock Pit* (o.p.) and *The Son of Perdition* deal with the Cuban sugar industry, while Cozzens's later "occupational" novels include *The Last Adam* (1933, o.p.), which is devoted to medicine; *Men and Brethren* (o.p.), to the ministry; *The Just and the Unjust* (1942) and *By Love Possessed*, to the law; the Pulitzer-Prize winning *Guard of Honor*, to the army air force; and *Morning, Noon and Night* (1968), to the business world. It may be that youthful distrust of all aspects of the establishment during the past few decades provides still another explanation for Cozzens's decline, but his concern with social responsibility could well lead to renewed appreciation.

BOOKS BY COZZENS

Just Representations: A James Gould Cozzens Reader. Ed. by Matthew J. Bruccoli, Harcourt 1978 pap. $6.95

Selected Notebooks: 1960–1967. Ed. by Matthew J. Bruccoli, Bruccoli 1984 $12.00

A Time of War: Air Force Diaries and Pentagon Memos, 1943–45. Ed. by Matthew J. Bruccoli, Bruccoli 1984 $29.95

The Son of Perdition. AMS Pr. repr. of 1929 ed. $29.00

S.S. San Pedro. Harcourt repr. of 1931 ed. 1968 pap. $1.15

Guard of Honor. 1948. Harcourt 1964 pap. $8.95

A Flower in Her Hair. Bruccoli ltd. ed. 1974 $40.00

A Rope for Dr. Webster. Bruccoli ltd. ed. 1976 $35.00

BOOKS ABOUT COZZENS

Bracher, Frederick G. *The Novels of James Gould Cozzens*. Greenwood repr. of 1959 ed. 1972 lib. bdg. $22.50

Bruccoli, Matthew J. *James Gould Cozzens: A Descriptive Bibliography. Pittsburgh Ser. in Bibliography* Univ. of Pittsburgh Pr. 1981 $32.95

———. *James Gould Cozzens: A Life Apart*. Harcourt 1983 $15.95 1984 pap. $9.95. Standard biography by the scholar and bibliophile who has done most to keep Cozzens's reputation alive.

————, ed. *James Gould Cozzens: New Acquist of True Experience. Crosscurrents Modern Critiques Ser.* Southern Illinois Univ. Pr. 1979 $17.95. Critical appreciations and studies.

Hicks, Granville. *James Gould Cozzens. Pamphlets on Amer. Writers Ser.* Univ. of Minnesota Pr. 1966 pap. $1.25

CRANE, STEPHEN. 1871–1900

Dead of tuberculosis before he was 30, Crane managed to combine an outstanding literary career with a flamboyant and adventurous life. He was born in New Jersey as a member of a large and devout family, and attended Syracuse University before beginning his career as a journalist in New York City and becoming a widely traveled newspaper correspondent. He then joined a filibustering expedition to Cuba near the end of 1896 and survived the sinking of the ship that was to take him from Jacksonville to Havana. Crane's newspaper stories about the wreck of the *Commodore* became the basis for his best-known short story, "The Open Boat," which is a gripping and profound narrative that is thought to contain in gist the main ideas of the existential philosophy that became dominant in modern literature several decades after Crane had so brilliantly anticipated it. With Cora Taylor, he spent the remaining months of his life in residence at Bredfe Place in Sussex, where he was a close friend and neighbor of such kindred literary artists as HENRY JAMES, JOSEPH CONRAD, and FORD MADOX FORD. If Crane had lived a normal life span, he might well have become recognized as one of the giants of the modernist tradition.

As it is, Crane made significant contributions. His first book, *Maggie: A Girl of the Streets* (1893), sold so few copies that any copy is now one of the most highly valued of modern rare books. *The Red Badge of Courage* (1895), his most famous work, blends a realistic depiction of the Civil War with an impressionistic style and profound religious symbolism. It is a triumph of imaginative avocation as Crane describes with deep psychological insight the experiences of a young recruit, Henry Fleming, who must undergo several baptisms under fire before knowing both shame and triumph. Crane's novel undoubtedly influenced Conrad's *Lord Jim* as well as Hemingway's writings about the war.

Crane's subsequent literary work is uneven in quality, but "The Open Boat," "The Blue Hotel," and "The Bride Comes to Yellow Sky" are among the most frequently anthologized stories in American literature. Like *The Red Badge* and the best of his poems, Crane's three most famous short stories reflect an existential view of man as an isolated being in a meaningless universe, yet capable of defiant heroism.

BOOKS BY CRANE

The Works of Stephen Crane. Ed. by Fredson Bowers, Univ. Pr. of Virginia 10 vols. 1969–76 ea. $15.00–$27.50. Recognized as an approved text by the Center for Editions of American Authors created by the Modern Language Association under the sponsorship of the National Foundation on the Arts and Humanities.

Prose and Poetry. Ed. by J. C. Levenson, Literary Class. 1984 $27.50. Now the best available one-volume selection of Crane's writings.

Great Short Works of Stephen Crane: Red Badge of Courage, Monster, Maggie, Open Boat, Blue Hotel, Bride Comes to Yellow Sky and Other Works. Ed. by James B. Colvert, Harper rev. ed. pap. $3.80

Stories and Tales. Ed. by Robert W. Stallman, Random 1955 pap. $2.95

The Portable Stephen Crane. Ed. by Joseph Katz, *Viking Portable Lib.* Penguin 1977 pap. $7.95; *Viking Portable Lib.* 1969 $10.00

The Blue Hotel and Other Stories (Maggie and Other Stories). Washington Square Pr. 1982 pap. $4.95

Maggie and Other Stories. Airmont Class. Ser. pap. $1.95

Red Badge of Courage and Selected Prose and Poetry. 1950. Ed. by William M. Gibson, *Rinehart Ed.* Holt text ed. 3d ed. 1969 pap. $12.95

The Red Badge of Courage and Other Writings. Ed. by Richard Chase, Houghton Mifflin (Riv. Eds.) 1960 pap. $5.95

Maggie: A Girl of the Streets. Fawcett 1978 pap. $2.25; ed. by Thomas A. Gullason, *Norton Critical Eds.* 1980 $20.95 pap. $5.95; Scholars' Facsimiles repr. of 1893 ed. 1978 $30.00

The Red Badge of Courage: An Episode of the American Civil War. 1895. Ed. by Henry Binder, Avon 1983 pap. $6.95; intro. by Alfred Vedro, *Bantam Class. Ser.* 1981 pap. $1.50; intro. by Malcolm Bradbury, Biblio Dist. text ed. 1983 pap. $3.95; ed. by Richard Lettis, Harcourt text ed. 1960 pap. $7.95; ed. by Henry Binder, Norton 1982 $14.95; intro. by Pascal Covici, *Penguin Amer. Lib. Ser.* 1983 pap. $2.95; intro. by Robert W. Stallman, *Modern Lib. College Ed. Ser.* Random 1951 pap. $3.75; ed. by Harry Shefter, *Enriched Class. Ed. Ser.* Washington Square Pr. pap. $2.95

The Little Regiment: And Other Episodes of the American Civil War. Arden Lib. repr. of 1897 ed. 1983 lib. bdg. $40.00; *Short Story Index Repr. Ser.* Ayer repr. of 1896 ed. $12.50

The Open Boat: And Other Tales of Adventure. Scholarly repr. of 1898 ed. $39.00

Whilomville Stories. Irvington repr. of 1900 ed. 1972 lib. bdg. $18.00; Scholarly repr. of 1900 ed. $19.00

Wounds in the Rain: A Collection of Stories Relating to the Spanish American War of 1898. Short Story Index Repr. Ser. Ayer repr. of 1900 ed. 1972 $24.50; Darby repr. of 1905 ed. 1983 lib. bdg. $40.00

Men, Women and Boats. Short Story Index Repr. Ser. Ayer repr. of 1921 ed. $19.00

BOOKS ABOUT CRANE

Bassan, M., ed. *Stephen Crane: A Collection of Critical Essays.* Prentice-Hall (Spectrum Bks.) 1967 $12.95

Beer, Thomas. *Stephen Crane.* Octagon repr. of 1923 ed. 1972 lib. bdg. $20.50. A brilliant biography, which helped launch the revival of interest in Crane.

Bergon, Frank. *Stephen Crane's Artistry.* Columbia Univ. Pr. 1975 $21.00

Berryman, John. *Stephen Crane: A Critical Biography.* 1975. Farrar 1982 pap. $9.25. Good critical biography with strong psychological slant.

Cady, Edwin H. *Stephen Crane. Twayne's U.S. Authors Ser.* G. K. Hall 1980 lib. bdg. $22.50; *Twayne's U.S. Authors Ser.* New College & Univ. Pr. 1962 pap. $5.95

———. *Stephen Crane in England: A Portrait of the Artist.* Ohio State Univ. Pr. 1965 $4.50

Cazemajou, Jean. *Stephen Crane. Pamphlets on Amer. Writers Ser.* Univ. of Minnesota Pr. 1969 pap. $1.25

Colvert, James B. *Stephen Crane. Album Biographies Ser.* Harcourt 1984 $24.95 pap. $12.95
Crosland, Andrew T. *A Concordance to the Complete Poems of Stephen Crane.* Gale 1975 $85.00
Delbanco, Nicholas. *Group Portrait: Conrad, Crane, Ford, Wells, and James.* Morrow 1982 $11.50 1984 pap. $6.20
Hoffman, Daniel G. *Poetry of Stephen Crane.* Columbia Univ. Pr. 1957 $27.50 pap. $12.00
Katz, Joseph, ed. *Stephen Crane in Transition: Centenary Essays.* Northern Illinois Univ. Pr. 1972 $10.00
Sherwood, John C. *Stephen Crane: An Annotated Bibliography.* Garland 1983 $20.00
Stallman, Robert W. *Stephen Crane: A Biography.* Braziller 1968 $12.50 pap. $4.95. Most thoroughly researched life of Crane.
———. *Stephen Crane: A Critical Bibliography.* Iowa State Univ. Pr. 1972 $26.00
Weatherford, Richard M., ed. *Stephen Crane: The Critical Heritage. Critical Heritage Ser.* Routledge & Kegan 1973 $30.00 1984 pap. $15.00
Wolford, Chester L. *The Anger of Stephen Crane: Fiction and the Epic Tradition.* Univ. of Nebraska Pr. 1983 $15.95

DOCTOROW, E(DGAR) L(AURENCE). 1931–

That E. L. Doctorow is a professional writer in the best sense may be indicated by the fact that he has yet to write two books alike. A New Yorker by birth and schooling, he prepared himself for the writing trade by attending Kenyon College when its literary program under John Crowe Ransom was at full crest, going on for graduate work at Columbia University, and working as a script reader for Columbia Pictures before becoming an editor with New American Library and Dial Press. He has written a serious western novel, a science-fiction fantasy, a play, a collection of short stories, and three novels of quite different types, one of which includes a considerable amount of poetry.

The practice in mixing the real with the fictional that Doctorow gained by writing *The Book of Daniel* (1971) was put to effective and spectacular use in *Ragtime* (1975). He interweaves the stories of three families, one WASPish, one Jewish, and one black, not only with one another but with such historical figures as J. P. Morgan, Houdini, FREUD (see Vol. 3), Jung, Scott Joplin, and THOMAS EDISON (see Vol. 5). These real people are put to work helping to disrupt or resolve some of the problems of the fictional people, and by the time the novel is concluded most readers feel that Coalhouse Walker, for instance, must have actually existed since he was so dramatically involved with people we remember from the history books. This ingenious fusion of fact and fiction annoyed such readers as Paul Levy (*Books and Bookmen*), who found that the characters who bear the famous names in the novel "are not historical personages; they are merely pawns in Doctorow's particularly dotty and tasteless game of chess." But other reviewers and a multitude of plain readers seemed to agree with Eliot Fremont-Smith (*The Village Voice*), who called the book "a bag of riches, totally lucid and accessible, full of surprises, epiphanies, little time-bombs that alter one's view of things, and enormous fun to read."

Doctorow's two most recent books of fiction have not had the impact of *Ragtime*, but they show him continuing to experiment with form and style. *Loon Lake* (1980), set in the time of the Great Depression, takes a young drifter named Joe Korzeniowski (Joseph Conrad's original name in Poland) to the opulent residence in the Adirondacks of an industrial magnate and his wife, a famous aviatrix. Joe's tale of his picaresque wanderings among carnival people is juxtaposed against the questionable stability of Loon Lake, and the novel seems rather heavily loaded with symbols of rebirth and regeneration. Doctorow's frequent shifting point of view as well as his juggling of prose, poetry, and "computerese" makes *Loon Lake* sometimes seem rather like the joint effort of a very talented class in creative writing. It may be no accident that Doctorow next tried his hand at a series of carefully wrought and deceptively simple short fiction that seems very traditional by comparison. The novella and six stories in *Lives of the Poets* are almost Chekhovian in their quiet, muted tone, but the use of recurring images and other interweaving devices between the story in the novella about the poet writing the book and the scenes he has transcribed would suggest that much is operating beneath the surface. His latest novel, *World's Fair*, is autobiographical.

Books by Doctorow

Welcome to Hard Times. 1960. Random 1975 pap. $7.95
The Book of Daniel. Bantam repr. 1984 pap. $3.95; Modern Lib. $8.95; Random 1971 $14.95
Ragtime. Bantam 1981 pap. $4.50; Random 1975 $12.95
Loon Lake. Bantam 1981 pap. $3.50; Random 1980 $11.95
Lives of the Poets: Six Stories and a Novella. Random 1984 $14.95
World's Fair. Random 1985 $17.95

Book about Doctorow

Trenner, Richard, ed. *E. L. Doctorow: Essays and Conversations*. Ontario Review Pr. 1983 $17.95 pap. $9.95. Nine critical assessments in addition to several personal statements by Doctorow and three interviews.

DOS PASSOS, JOHN. 1896–1970

It is as a social chronicler that John Dos Passos is most admired, for in addition to a large quantity of writing depicting his personal response to the events of his times, his best-known works of fiction are in general "documentary" accounts that mix the lives of real people with those of his fictional characters. The *U.S.A.* trilogy remains his most impressive achievement. Distributed through that work are 68 Newsreel sections composed of newspaper headlines and lines from popular songs as well as other materials; 27 short biographies of such people as Eugene Debs, Henry Ford, Isadora Duncan, and the Wright brothers; and 51 Camera Eye sections in which Dos Passos attempts a kind of kaleidoscopic view of experiences recounted by a poetic speaker who is different from the impersonal narrator of the other sections. The lives of 12 main fictional characters representing various walks of life are traced in the three volumes, and although *U.S.A.* may not be the Great American Novel, it comes close to living up to its title. A second trilogy, comprised of *Adventures of a Young Man* (1939, o.p.), *Number One* (1943), and *The Grand Design* (1949) grouped under the title *District of Columbia* (1952), lacks the cohesiveness of *U.S.A.* but finds a loosely linked kind of unity through Dos Passos's use of members of the same family in the three volumes.

Aside from his two trilogies, Dos Passos wrote eight individual novels. *One Man's Initiation—1917* (o.p.) is a highly subjective record of his experiences in the French ambulance service in World War I, while *Three Soldiers* is one of the first novels to reveal the sordidness of military life. *Manhattan Transfer* anticipates some aspects of the later style, and its comparatively shorter length makes it more accessible for college courses in the modern American novel than *U.S.A.* Many critics found the fiction published after the two trilogies to be somewhat disappointing. *Chosen Country* (o.p.), *Most Likely to Succeed* (o.p.), and *The Great Days* (o.p.) are of some biographical interest, but they lack the innovative excitement of the earlier works, and as Dos Passos grew older, his view of the life about him became increasingly pessimistic. Members of the liberal literary establishment found it hard to accept Dos Passos's spirited attack on labor unions in *Midcentury* (1961, o.p.), and in his final novel, the posthumously published *Century's Ebb*, he found "a further subsidence of American life during the years from the death of Malcolm X to the launching of Apollo 10" (George J. Becker). In that last work of fiction, he uses profiles of WALT WHITMAN and GEORGE ORWELL as positive touchstones by which to measure the failure of bureaucratic modern society to achieve true democracy. But as ALFRED KAZIN once observed, Dos Passos was a writer who, like EMERSON and some other Americans before him, seemed to like Man much more than men.

During and following World War II, as a correspondent for *Life* he reported on the various theaters of war, U.S. occupation of Germany, the Nuremberg trials, Socialist England, and the industrial United States. Books collecting some of those observations include *Journey between Wars* (1938, o.p.), *Brazil on the Move* (1963, o.p.), *Orient Express, The Prospect before Us*, and *Tour of Duty* (1946, o.p.).

Mr. Wilson's War is a narrative history of the U.S. government and its foreign relations from 1900 to just after World War I, informally written in terms of the people who made the headlines. His admiration for THOMAS JEFFERSON (see Vol. 3) is reflected in the biographical study *The Head and the Heart of Thomas Jefferson* (1954, o.p.). *The Shackles of Power: Three Jeffersonian Decades* is "entertaining popular history" (*LJ*). His highly adventurous memoirs, *The Best Times* (1967, o.p.), cover the years 1896 to 1936 and his friendship with JOYCE, Hemingway, Fitzgerald, and others.

BOOKS BY DOS PASSOS

U.S.A.: The Forty-Second Parallel, 1919, The Big Money. 1937. Houghton Mifflin 1963 $20.00

Century's Ebb: The Thirteenth Chronicle. Harvard Common Pr. 1975 $9.95

The Fourteenth Chronicle: Letters and Diaries. Ed. by Townsend Luddington, Gambit 1973 $15.00

Three Soldiers. 1921. Houghton Mifflin 1964 pap. $12.95

Manhattan Transfer. 1925. Bentley repr. of 1953 ed. 1980 lib. bdg. $16.50; Houghton
    Mifflin 1963 pap. $7.95
42nd Parallel. 1930. New Amer. Lib. (Signet Class.) 1983 pap. $3.95
The Big Money. 1936. Intro. by Alfred Kazin, New Amer. Lib. (Signet Class.) 1969
    pap. $3.95
Number One. Queens House repr. of 1943 ed. 1977 $18.95
The Grand Design. Queens House repr. of 1949 ed. 1977 lib. bdg. $18.95

BOOKS ABOUT DOS PASSOS

Becker, George J. *John Dos Passos. Lit. and Life Ser.* Ungar 1974 $12.95
Carr, Virginia S. *Dos Passos: A Life.* Doubleday 1984 $24.95. The most thorough and
    authoritative biography of Dos Passos available.
Colley, Iain. *Dos Passos and the Fiction of Despair.* Rowman 1978 $26.00
Davis, Robert G. *John Dos Passos. Pamphlets on Amer. Writers Ser.* Univ. of Minne-
    sota Pr. 1962 pap. $1.25
Hook, Andrew, ed. *Dos Passos: A Collection of Critical Essays.* Prentice-Hall (Spec-
    trum Bks.) 1974 pap. $2.45
Potter, Jack. *A Bibliography of John Dos Passos.* Folcroft 1977 lib. bdg. $20.00; intro.
    by John Dos Passos, A. S. Barnes ltd. ed. 1950 $22.50
Rohrkemper, John C. *John Dos Passos: A Reference Guide.* G. K. Hall 1980 lib. bdg.
    $23.00
Rosen, Robert C. *John Dos Passos: Politics and the Writer.* Univ. of Nebraska Pr. 1981
    $15.95
Wagner, Linda W. *Dos Passos: Artist as American.* Univ. of Texas Pr. 1979 $16.95
Wrenn, John H. *John Dos Passos. Twayne's U.S. Authors Ser.* G. K. Hall 1961 lib. bdg.
    $12.50; *Twayne's U.S. Authors Ser.* New College & Univ. Pr. 1961 pap. $5.95

DREISER, THEODORE. 1871–1945

Hardly anyone these days questions the stature of Theodore Dreiser as a
major writer, but only because he has survived decades of begrudging and
patronizing criticism from readers and critics who have found his ideas un-
sophisticated and his style fumbling and "elephantine." For all his flaws—
perhaps no other major novelist since DOSTOEVSKY (see Vol. 2) has suffered
from as many imperfections as Dreiser—there is a raw narrative force in his
better works that makes them compelling reading. His first two novels—*Sister Carrie* and *Jennie Gerhardt*, stories of girls from the Midwest who learn
some of life's bitter lessons—are considered landmark contributions to
American literary naturalism, and the number of editions of *Sister Carrie* in
print testifies to the rank of that novel as a modern classic widely taught in
schools and universities. However, *An American Tragedy* is usually considered Dreiser's best book. Based on an actual murder case, it is the story of a
young man, Clyde Griffiths, who finds himself in such a tangled web of social and psychological forces beyond his control that his tragic fate seems to
carry with it a relentless inevitability that keeps the story both tough-
minded and compassionate.

As an indictment of American social and business values, *An American
Tragedy* develops themes all too apparent in Dreiser's trilogy of works—*The
Financier, The Titan,* and *The Stoic*—about an unscrupulous and successful

businessman named Frank Cowperwood whose fictional story provides a vivid but devastating record of the boom period in American industry.

Dreiser was born in Terre Haute, Indiana, as a member of a large family that included several sisters whose experiences provided models for his first novels and a brother who, as Paul Dresser, was to achieve fame as the composer of "On the Banks of the Wabash" and other popular songs. Dreiser worked as a newspaper reporter and magazine editor. Among his several works of autobiography, *A Traveler at Forty* (1913), *A Book about Myself* (1922), and *Dawn* are currently out of print, but available are *A Hoosier Holiday* and *Newspaper Days* (1931). *Notes on Life* consists of reflections selected and edited by Marguerite Tjader and John McAleer. *The American Diaries, 1902–1926* (o.p.) is one of three titles issued to date in an authoritative edition of Dreiser's works being published by the University of Pennsylvania Press. The others are *The Pennsylvania Edition of Sister Carrie* and the first publication of an unfinished work of mixed autobiography and fiction written early in Dreiser's career and published as *An Amateur Laborer*.

BOOKS BY DREISER

Theodore Dreiser: A Selection of Uncollected Prose. Ed. by Donald Pizer, Wayne State Univ. Pr. 1977 $15.95

Sister Carrie. 1900. Ed. by E. L. Doctorow, *Bantam Class. Ser.* 1982 pap. $2.25; ed. by Jack Salzman, Bobbs 1970 pap. $6.65; ed. by Kenneth S. Lynn, *Rinehart Ed.* Holt text ed. 1957 pap. $9.95; Lightyear repr. of 1907 ed. 1980 lib. bdg. $23.95; New Amer. Lib. (Signet Class.) 1962 pap. $2.25; ed. by Donald Pizer, *Norton Critical Eds.* text ed. 1970 pap. $8.95; *Penguin Amer. Lib. Ser.* 1981 pap. $3.95; ed. by James L. West, III, and others, Univ. of Pennsylvania Pr. 1981 $45.00 pap. $16.95

Jennie Gerhardt. 1911. Fwd. by Helen Yglesias, Schocken repr. of 1960 ed. 1982 pap. $8.95

The Financier. 1912. New Amer. Lib. (Signet Class.) 1967 pap. $3.95

The Titan. 1914. AMS Pr. repr. of 1946 ed. $27.50

The Genius. 1915. Lightyear repr. of 1917 ed. 1980 lib. bdg. $24.95

Free and Other Stories. Scholarly repr. of 1918 ed. 1971 $49.00

Twelve Men. Scholarly repr. of 1919 ed. 1971 $49.00

An American Tragedy. 1925. New Amer. Lib. (Signet Class.) 1973 pap. $3.95

The Stoic. 1947. Intro. by Richard Lingerman, New Amer. Lib. (Signet Class.) 1981 pap. $3.95

BOOKS ABOUT DREISER

Atkinson, Hugh C. *Theodore Dreiser: A Checklist.* Kent State Univ. Pr. 1971 $10.00

Dudley, Dorothy. *Forgotten Frontiers: Dreiser and the Land of the Free.* AMS Pr. repr. of 1932 ed. $20.00; Scholarly repr. of 1932 ed. 1972 $21.00

Frohock, W. M. *Theodore Dreiser. Pamphlets on Amer. Writers Ser.* Univ. of Minnesota Pr. 1972 pap. $1.25

Gerber, Philip L. *Theodore Dreiser. Twayne's U.S. Authors Ser.* G. K. Hall 1963 lib. bdg. $11.50

Hakutani, Yoshinobu. *Young Dreiser: A Critical Study.* Fairleigh Dickinson Univ. Pr. 1980 $22.50

Hussman, Lawrence E. *Dreiser and His Fiction: A Twentieth Century Quest.* Univ. of Pennsylvania Pr. 1983 $22.50

Lehan, Richard D. *Theodore Dreiser: His World and His Novels.* 1969. Southern Illinois Univ. Pr. 1974 pap. $3.25

Lundquist, James. *Theodore Dreiser. Lit. and Life Ser.* Ungar 1974 $12.95

Matthiessen, F. O. *Theodore Dreiser. Amer. Men of Letters Ser.* Greenwood repr. of 1951 ed. 1973 lib. bdg. $24.75; *Amer. Men of Letters Ser.* Richard West repr. of 1951 ed. 1979 lib. bdg. $22.50. Still the best critical biography.

Pizer, Donald. *Critical Essays on Theodore Dreiser. Critical Essays on Amer. Lit. Ser.* G. K. Hall (Twayne) 1981 lib. bdg. $26.00

——. *The Novels of Theodore Dreiser: A Critical Study.* Univ. of Minnesota Pr. 1976 $25.00

Shapiro, Charles. *Theodore Dreiser: Our Bitter Patriot. Crosscurrents Modern Critiques Ser.* Southern Illinois Univ. Pr. 1962 $6.95

Stephancher, Stephen. *Dreiser among the Critics: A Study of American Reactions to the Work of a Literary Naturalist, 1900–1949.* Folcroft 1973 $9.50

Swanberg, W. A. *Dreiser.* Scribner repr. 1965 $30.00. "This will unquestionably remain the definitive biography of [a] major novelist. . . . Mr. Swanberg's prodigious research has sent him to the most obscure sources, to thousands of letters, and to scores of men and women who knew Dreiser, and with this massive detail he has constructed a fascinating story" (*LJ*).

Warren, Robert Penn. *Homage to Theodore Dreiser: On the Centennial of His Birth.* Random 1971 $12.95

ELKIN, STANLEY. 1930–

Without a bestseller to his credit or a lot of critical attention, Stanley Elkin has steadily, quietly worked his way into the higher ranks of contemporary American novelists. He was born in New York, but grew up in Chicago and has spent most of his life since in the Midwest, receiving his Ph.D. in English from the University of Illinois with a dissertation on Faulkner, and teaching since 1960 at Washington University in St. Louis. John Ditsky (*Hollins Critic*) places Elkin's fiction in these terms: "If Elkin seems to be some sort of spiritual descendant of Nathanael West in the ways in which he attaches out-loud, falling-on-the-floor humor to reflections on the human state as a steady downward plunge to death, he is nevertheless very much his own man in the manner in which he explores and develops that tradition." His recent novel *George Mills* provides a kind of hindsight focus on what makes Elkin's fiction peculiarly his own. The George Mills of this title is not one man, but a whole series of men named George Mills, whose lives bridge centuries of time and repeat much the same fate as again and again they are destined to serve as "God's blue collar worker." As if to deliberately confound those critics who had objected to Elkin's neglect of plot in his earlier novels, these George Millses go astray like sparks from an anvil as their author displays his stylistic virtuosity, yet taken together the many George Millses become an Everyman with mythical dimensions whose all-encompassing humanity remains after the laughter and the cleverness are stilled.

Reviewers found Elkin's first novel, *Boswell: A Modern Comedy* (o.p.), the story of an uninhibited modern-day counterpart of the eighteenth-century biographer, hilarious and promising, while the stories in *Criers and Ki-bitzers, Kibitzers and Criers* established Elkin as a writer capable of writing short stories of textbook-anthology quality. The ironically entitled *A Bad Man* is about a Jewish department store magnate who deliberately arranges to have himself convicted of several misdeeds so that he can experience the real world of a prison and carry on his own war with the warden in what takes on the dimensions of a burlesque existential allegory. *The Dick Gibson Show* uses the host of a radio talk show as a way of showing fancifully what it means to live "at sound barrier," and both *Searchers and Seizures* and *The Living End* (o.p.) are triptychs of related stories verging on surrealism. *The Franchiser*, generally considered Elkin's best novel before *George Mills*, uses the story of a traveling salesman of franchises to show the flattening homogenization of American life. But as usual what happens in this Elkin novel is less important than the way in which the story is told. As Thomas LeClair put it in *Contemporary Literature*, "Sentence for sentence, nobody in America writes better than Stanley Elkin. For him the novel is primarily a place for language, energized and figurative language, to happen."

BOOKS BY ELKIN

Criers and Kibitzers, Kibitzers and Criers. 1966. New Amer. Lib. (Plume) 1973 pap. $3.95

A Bad Man. 1967. *Obelisk Ser.* Dutton 1984 pap. $10.95

The Dick Gibson Show. 1971. Dutton 1983 pap. $8.95

Searchers and Seizures. 1973. Godine (Nonpareil Bks.) 1978 pap. $6.95. Three novellas.

The Franchiser. Farrar 1976 $8.95; afterword by William H. Gass, Godine (Nonpareil Bks.) repr. of 1976 ed. 1980 pap. $6.95

The First George Mills. 1981. *Ltd. Ed. Ser.* Pressworks 1981 $45.00

George Mills. Obelisk Ser. Dutton 1983 pap. $8.95

The Magic Kingdom. Dutton 1985 $15.95

ELLISON, RALPH (WALDO). 1914–

Unless the second novel on which he has been reported to be working for several decades is finally published, Ralph Ellison will have the distinction of being one of the few writers who have established a firm literary reputation on the strength of but a single work of long fiction. Writer and teacher, Ralph Ellison was born in Oklahoma City, studied at Tuskegee Institute, and has lectured at New York, Columbia, and Fisk universities and at Bard College. He received the Prix de Rome from the Academy of Arts and Letters in 1955, and in 1964 he was elected a member of the National Institute of Arts and Letters. He has contributed short stories and essays to various publications.

Invisible Man, his first novel, won the National Book Award for 1952 and is considered an impressive work. "Ellison's sensibility is unique and his novel is original—not because he has created a new form (in that sense he has written a traditional novel), but rather because he holds a view we have not known before, or only half knew, because he has managed to penetrate to a heart of our society which we have hidden, or half hidden, from ourselves. It is a vision of the underground man who is also the invisible Negro, and its possessor has employed this subterranean view and viewer to so extraordinary an advantage that the impression of the novel is that of a pioneer work. This impression was corroborated by James Baldwin, who in *Notes of a Native Son* wrote, 'Mr. Ellison, by the way, is the first Negro novelist I have ever read to utilize in language, and brilliantly, some of the ambiguity and irony of Negro life' " (Harvey Breit, *The Creative Present*). In 1964 appeared Ellison's book of essays, *Shadow and Act*, which discusses the black in America and Ellison's Oklahoma boyhood, among other topics.

Book by Ellison

Invisible Man: Thirtieth Anniversary Edition. 1952. Modern Lib. 1963 $3.95; Random 1982 $15.95; Random (Vintage) 1972 pap. $3.95

Books about Ellison

Covo, Jacqueline. *The Blinking Eye: Ralph Waldo Ellison and His American, French, German and Italian Critics, 1952–1971—Bibliographic Essays and a Checklist.* Author Bibliographies Ser. Scarecrow Pr. 1974 $15.00
Hersey, John, ed. *Ralph Ellison: A Collection of Critical Essays.* Twentieth-Century Views Ser. Prentice-Hall (Spectrum) 1973 $12.95 pap. $1.95
O'Meally, Robert G. *The Craft of Ralph Ellison.* Harvard Univ. Pr. text ed. 1980 $15.00

FARRELL, JAMES T. 1904–1979

If there is an American author of this century who has suffered from overexposure, it is James T. Farrell. Resisting commercial pressures and testing the patience of critics, he was too fiercely independent to compromise his personal standards in order to reach a wide audience. Yet he managed to publish more than 50 books, including 28 novels and 16 collections of short stories. Almost all of his novels form a part of four series on which his reputation largely rests, but the fact that only *Studs Lonigan: A Trilogy* remains in print would suggest that his place in literature is still to be determined. His second major cycle is the out-of-print Danny O'Neill pentalogy (1936–53)—*A World I Never Made, No Star Is Lost, Father and Son, My Days of Anger,* and *The Face of Time.* The Bernard Carr trilogy (1946–52) consists of *Bernard Clare, The Road Between,* and *Yet Other Waters,* all out of print. All three series are semiautobiographical works with the first two set in Chicago, where Farrell grew up in the Irish slums of the South Side, and the third showing how the central figure achieves success as a writer in New York City from 1927 to 1936.

After 1958 Farrell was engaged primarily in writing a new series called *The Universe of Time,* which also has a central autobiographical character, Eddie Ryan, but which Farrell envisioned as "a relativistic panorama of our times" dealing with "man's creativity and his courageous acceptance of impermanence." Of some 30 projected volumes in the series, 10 were published in Farrell's lifetime. They are *Boarding House Blues, The Silence of History* (1963), *What Time Collects* (1964), *When Time Was Born* (1966), *New*

Year's Eve 1929, A Brand New Life (1968), *Judith* (1969), *Invisible Swords* (1970), *The Dunne Family,* and *The Death of Nora Ryan.* In his review of the second volume Robert Gorham Davis commented: "It is an effort to recapture the sounds and inner rhythms of an American experience now gone forever. Sooner or later Farrell will be given his place as a sort of William Dean Howells of Jackson Park in recognition of the scope and faithfulness with which he recorded the day-to-day, almost hour-to-hour, suffering, sentimentality, dignity, coarseness and despair of an important part of the Nation's population at a time of decisive change in its psyche" (*N.Y. Times*).

Only *Studs Lonigan,* however, has captured a wide audience to date. That series is read largely for its historical interest as a vivid period piece of "slice-of-life" realism. Farrell's objective method of presenting experience, his reluctance to point a moral, and his naturalistic philosophy have offended some readers and critics, but time may show that it is Farrell's freedom from moralism and transient commitments that make him capable of seeing individual experience in broad and universal terms.

BOOKS BY FARRELL

Studs Lonigan: A Trilogy. Avon 1976 pap. $3.95; Vanguard 1979 $17.50. *Young Lonigan* (1932), *The Young Manhood of Studs Lonigan* (1934), *Judgment Day* (1935). With a new introduction by the author.
Father and Son. Irish-Amer. Ser. Ayer repr. of 1940 ed. 1976 $38.50
Reflections at Fifty and Other Essays. Vanguard 1954 $10.00
French Girls Are Vicious and Other Stories. Vanguard 1955 $11.95
What Time Collects. 1964. Woodhill repr. 1974 pap. $1.50
When Time Was Born. The Smith 1966 $3.50
New Year's Eve 1929. The Smith 1967 $4.50
Eight Short Stories and Sketches. Arts End 1981 pap. $10.00
This Man and This Woman. State Mutual Bk. 1981 $18.95
Sam Holman. Prometheus Bks. 1983 $16.95

BOOKS ABOUT FARRELL

Branch, Edgar M. *James T. Farrell. Pamphlets on Amer. Writers Ser.* Univ. of Minnesota Pr. 1963 pap. $1.25
Wald, Alan M. *James T. Farrell: The Revolutionary Socialist Years.* New York Univ. Pr. 1978 $25.00 pap. $12.50

FAULKNER, WILLIAM. 1897–1962 (NOBEL PRIZE 1949, awarded in 1950)

William Faulkner was awarded the Nobel Prize in 1950 "for his powerful and artistically independent contribution to the new American novel," but it would appear now that he deserved to win that honor also for his contribution to world literature at its highest level. Only a few American writers of this century really qualify as international modernists, and there can be little doubt that Faulkner is one of them. When reporting his death, the *Boston Globe* quoted Faulkner's having once told an interviewer: "Since man is mortal, the only immortality for him is to leave something behind him that is immortal since it will always move. That is the artist's way of scribbling 'Kilroy was here' on the wall of the final and irrevocable oblivion through which he must some day pass." In those terms Faulkner left an ineradicable mark deeper than that of almost any other writer of his times.

Faulkner was a Mississippi writer of great power who was drawn to times of abnormality and decadence. His novels are intense in their character portrayal of disintegrating southern aristocrats, poor whites, and Negroes. A complex, stream-of-consciousness rhetoric often involves him in lengthy sentences, though of such anguished power that impetus and meaning are seldom lost. Most of the tales are set in a place not found on any map— Yoknapatawpha County, Mississippi—and are characterized by the use of many recurring characters from families of different social levels spanning more than a century.

After a brief stint as a flier in the Royal Canadian Air Force near the end of World War I, Faulkner returned to his home in Oxford, Mississippi. Unable at first to make a living from his writing, he worked as night superintendent at a power plant, carpenter, roof painter, and postmaster at the university until such time as his growing reputation enabled him to place stories in popular magazines such as the *Saturday Evening Post* and brought him opportunities to write lucrative screenplays for Hollywood. *The Sound and the Fury* (1929) is considered his first major work. Also told from multiple viewpoints is *As I Lay Dying* (1930), a grotesquely sad-comic story about a family of poor southern whites. Less experimental in technique than these two works and therefore a better introduction to the Yoknapatawpha saga is *Light in August* (1932), a novel of sure-handed craftsmanship, which successfully blends violence with pathos. With *Absalom, Absalom!* (1936), the difficult parts of his famous short novel "The Bear" (as published in *Go Down, Moses*, 1942), and the allegorical *A Fable* (1954), a non-Yoknapatawpha novel set in France during World War I, Faulkner returned to an innovative and difficult style that is not likely to appeal to average readers. Yet, interspersed with the writings of such works are collections of easily readable stories originally published in popular magazines, and there seems to be a growing sentiment among critics that *The Snopes Trilogy*, for the most part an example of Faulkner's "moderate" style, could well be his most important single work.

In addition to the Nobel Prize he received the Howells Medal of the American Academy of Arts and Letters in 1950, and in 1951 the National Book Award for his *Collected Stories*. For his novel *A Fable* he received the National Book Award for the second time and the Pulitzer Prize in 1955. *The Reivers* (1962) was awarded the Pulitzer Prize in 1963. In 1957 and 1958 he was the University of Virginia's first writer-in-residence, and in January 1959 accepted an appointment as consultant on contemporary literature to the Alderman Library of the university.

Considering that Faulkner was not without honors in his lifetime and the world recognition that has come to him since then, it is surprising to learn that when MALCOLM COWLEY edited *The Portable Faulkner* in 1946, he found that almost all of Faulkner's books were out of print. By arranging selections from the works with intelligence and ingenuity to form a continuous chronicle, Cowley deserves much of the credit for making readers aware of the way in which Faulkner was creating a fictive world on a scale grander than that of any novelist since Balzac. Since 1946 criticism has proliferated at such a voluminous rate that although the list of books about Faulkner is longer than that for any other writer in this chapter, it nonetheless represents only a selection of some of the more important books currently available. Many others have gone out of print.

BOOKS BY FAULKNER

The Portable Faulkner. 1946. Ed. by Malcolm Cowley, *Viking Portable Lib.* Penguin rev. ed. 1977 pap. $7.95

The Faulkner Reader. Modern Lib. 1959 $8.95

Collected Stories. 1950. Random 1956 $22.95; Random (Vintage) 1977 pap. $8.95

Uncollected Stories of William Faulkner. Ed. by Joseph Blotner, Random (Vintage) 1981 $17.95 pap. $7.95

Selected Short Stories of William Faulkner. Modern Lib. 1962 $5.95

Three Famous Short Novels: Spotted Horses, Old Man, and The Bear. Random (Vintage) pap. $3.95

New Orleans Sketches. 1958. Ed. by Carvel Collins, Random 1968 $13.95. Early writings.

The Faulkner-Cowley File: Memories and Letters, 1944–1962. 1955. Ed. with extensive commentary by Malcolm Cowley, Penguin 1978 pap. $3.95

Selected Letters. Ed. by Joseph Blotner, Random (Vintage) 1978 pap. $4.95

Soldiers' Pay. 1926. Liveright 1954 $9.95 pap. $6.95

Mosquitoes. 1927. Liveright 1955 $6.95

Flags in the Dust. Ed. by Douglas Day, Random 1973 $13.95; Random (Vintage) 1974 pap. $3.95. Early version of what was to become *Sartoris.*

Sartoris. 1929. Fwd. by Robert Cantwell, afterword by Lawrance Thompson, New Amer. Lib. (Signet Class.) 1983 pap. $3.50; Random 1966 $15.95

The Sound and the Fury. 1929. Random (Vintage) 1954 pap. $3.95; *Modern Lib. College Ed. Ser.* Random 1967 pap. $2.95

As I Lay Dying. 1930. Random 1964 $13.95; Random (Vintage) 1964 pap. $2.95

Sanctuary: The Original Text. 1931. Ed. by Noel Polk, Random 1981 $14.95

Light in August. Random (Vintage) repr. of 1932 ed. 1972 pap. $4.95

Pylon. 1935. Random 1965 $13.95

Absalom, Absalom! Modern Lib. College Ed. Ser. Random 1966 $17.95; Random (Vintage) repr. of 1936 ed. 1972 pap. $3.95

The Unvanquished. 1938. Ill. by Edward Shenton, Random (Vintage) 1965 pap. $4.95. Short stories set during the Civil War.

Wild Palms. 1939. Random (Vintage) 1964 pap. $8.95. Two separate narratives—*Wild Palms* and *Old Man*—printed in separate chapters.

The Hamlet. 1940. Random (Vintage) 1956 pap. $4.95

Go Down, Moses and Other Stories. Random 1942 $13.95; Random (Vintage) 1978 pap. $2.95

Intruder in the Dust. Random 1948 $13.95; *Modern Lib. College Ed. Ser.* Random 1967 pap. $4.95

Knight's Gambit. 1949. Ed. by Joseph Blotner, Random (Vintage) 1978 pap. $2.95

Requiem for a Nun. Random 1951 $13.95; Random (Vintage) 1975 pap. $3.95

A Fable. Random 1954 $15.95; Random (Vintage) repr. of 1954 ed. 1978 pap. $3.95

The Town. Random 1957 $13.95; Random (Vintage) 1961 pap. $4.95

The Mansion. Random 1959 pap. $4.95

The Reivers: A Reminiscence. Random 1962 $13.95; Random (Vintage) 1962 pap. $3.95

BOOKS ABOUT FAULKNER

Adams, Richard P. *Faulkner: Myth and Motion.* Princeton Univ. Pr. 1968 $27.50
Bassett, John E., ed. *William Faulkner: The Critical Heritage. Critical Heritage Ser.* Routledge & Kegan 1975 $36.00
Bezzerides, A. I. *William Faulkner: A Life on Paper.* Univ. Pr. of Mississippi text ed. 1980 $10.00 pap. $5.00
Bleikasten, André. *The Most Splendid Failure: Faulkner's The Sound and the Fury.* Indiana Univ. Pr. 1976 $12.50
———. *William Faulkner's The Sound and the Fury: Selected Criticism.* Garland 1982 lib. bdg. $33.00
Brodhead, Richard. *Faulkner: A Collection of Critical Essays. Twentieth-Century View Ser.* Prentice-Hall 1983 $12.95 pap. $5.95
Brooks, Cleanth. *William Faulkner: First Encounters.* Yale Univ. Pr. 1983 $19.50 1985 pap. $7.95. Serviceable summaries and critical introductions for the reader new to Faulkner.
———. *William Faulkner: The Yoknapatawpha Country.* Yale Univ. Pr. 1963 $40.00 pap. $10.95. The most extensive study devoted exclusively to the Yoknapatawpha saga.
———. *William Faulkner: Toward Yoknapatawpha and Beyond.* Yale Univ. Pr. 1978 $35.00 pap. $10.95. Complements the 1963 study.
Broughton, Panthea R. *William Faulkner: The Abstract and the Actual.* Louisiana State Univ. Pr. 1974 $20.00
Brown, Calvin S. *A Glossary of Faulkner's South.* Yale Univ. Pr. 1976 $25.50 pap. $6.95
Canfield, J. Douglas, ed. *Sanctuary: A Collection of Critical Essays.* Prentice-Hall 1982 $10.95 pap. $4.95
Carey, Glenn O. *Faulkner: The Unappeased Imagination: A Collection of Critical Essays.* Whitston 1980 $18.50
Cox, Leland H. *William Faulkner: Biographical and Reference Guide.* Gale 1982 $60.00
———. *William Faulkner: Critical Collection.* Gale 1982 $60.00
Creighton, Joanne V. *William Faulkner's Craft of Revision: The Snopes Trilogy—The Unvanquished and Go Down, Moses.* Wayne State Univ. Pr. text ed. 1977 $12.95
Cullen, John B., and Floyd C. Watkins. *Old Times in the Faulkner Country.* Louisiana State Univ. Pr. 1975 $12.95
Davis, Thadious M. *Faulkner's "Negro": Art and the Southern Context.* Louisiana State Univ. Pr. 1982 $25.00 pap. $10.95
Faulkner, John. *My Brother Bill.* 1963. Yoknapatawpha 1975 $13.95
Faulkner, Murray C. *The Faulkners of Mississippi: A Memoir.* Louisiana State Univ. Pr. 1967 $20.00. Reminiscences by a brother.
Ford, Margaret P., and Suzanne Kincaid. *Who's Who in Faulkner.* 1963. Louisiana State Univ. Pr. text ed. 1966 pap. $5.95
Hoffman, Frederick J. *William Faulkner.* 1962. *Twayne's U.S. Authors Ser.* G. K. Hall 1985 pap. $6.95; *Twayne's U.S. Authors Ser.* New College & Univ. Pr. 1966 pap. $5.95
Howe, Irving. *William Faulkner: A Critical Study.* 1952. Univ. of Chicago Pr. (Phoenix Bks.) 3d ed. 1975 pap. $7.00
Kartiganer, Donald M. *The Fragile Thread: The Meaning of Form in Faulkner's Novels.* Univ. of Massachusetts Pr. 1979 $15.00

Kawin, Bruce F. *Faulkner and Film. Ungar Film Lib.* 1977 $12.95 pap. $5.95

Kerr, Elizabeth M. *William Faulkner's Gothic Domain.* Associated Faculty Pr. 1979 $21.50

———. *William Faulkner's Yoknapatawpha: "A Kind of Keystone in the Universe."* Fordham Univ. Pr. 1983 $40.00

Kinney, Arthur F. *Critical Essays on William Faulkner: The Compson Family. Critical Essays on Amer. Lit. Ser.* G. K. Hall 1982 lib. bdg. $33.50

———. *Faulkner's Narrative Poetics: Style as Vision.* Univ. of Massachusetts Pr. 1978 $17.50

Kreiswirth, Martin. *William Faulkner: The Making of a Novelist.* Univ. of Georgia Pr. 1984 $15.00

Longley, John Lewis, Jr. *The Tragic Mask: A Study of Faulkner's Heroes.* 1963. Univ. of North Carolina Pr. 1967 pap. $6.95

Matthews, John T. *The Play of Faulkner's Language.* Cornell Univ. Pr. 1982 $24.95

Millgate, Michael. *The Achievement of William Faulkner.* 1965. Random (Vintage) 1971 pap. $1.95; Univ. of Nebraska Pr. (Bison) repr. of 1966 ed. 1978 $15.00

Minter, David. *William Faulkner: His Life and Work.* Johns Hopkins Univ. Pr. text ed. 1982 $25.00 pap. $7.95

Polk, Noel. *Faulkner's Requiem for a Nun: A Critical Study.* Indiana Univ. Pr. 1981 $17.50

Powers, Lyall H. *Faulkner's Yoknapatawpha Comedy.* Univ. of Michigan Pr. 1980 $19.95

Ricks, Beatrice, ed. *William Faulkner: A Bibliography of Secondary Works. Author Bibliographies Ser.* Scarecrow Pr. 1981 lib. bdg. $35.00. Most exhaustive listing of secondary material usefully arranged for quick reference.

Ruppersburg, Hugh M. *Voice and Eye in Faulkner's Fiction.* Univ. of Georgia Pr. 1983 $16.00

Schoenberg, Estella. *Old Tales and Talking: Quentin Compson in William Faulkner's "Absalom, Absalom!" and Related Works.* Univ. Pr. of Mississippi 1977 $2.00

Stonum, Gary L. *Faulkner's Career: An Internal Literary History.* Cornell Univ. Pr. 1979 $21.50. Excellent study of Faulkner's development as a literary artist.

Strandberg, Victor. *A Faulkner Overview: Six Perspectives. Literary Criticism Ser.* Associated Faculty Pr. 1981 $13.50

Sundquist, Eric J. *Faulkner: The House Divided.* Johns Hopkins Univ. Pr. 1983 $16.95

Taylor, Walter. *Faulkner's Search for a South.* Univ. of Illinois Pr. 1982 $18.50

Vickery, Olga W. *Novels of William Faulkner: A Critical Interpretation.* 1959. Louisiana State Univ. Pr. rev. ed. 1964 $20.00. This pioneer interpretation has not been surpassed.

Volpe, Edmond. *A Reader's Guide to William Faulkner.* Farrar 1964 pap. $8.95; Octagon repr. of 1964 ed. 1975 lib. bdg. $27.50

Wasson, Ben. *Count No'count: Flashbacks to Faulkner.* Intro. by Carvel Collins, *Center for the Study of Southern Culture Ser.* Univ. Pr. of Mississippi 1983 $14.95

Welshimer, Linda. *William Faulkner: Four Decades of Criticism.* Michigan State Univ. Pr. 1973 $10.00

Wolfe, George H., ed. *Faulkner: Fifty Years after "The Marble Faun."* Univ. of Alabama Pr. 1976 $12.95

FITZGERALD, F(RANCIS) SCOTT (KEY). 1896–1940

F. Scott Fitzgerald remains one of the best-known American authors of the twentieth century in spite of the fact that only occasionally did he write works of genuine distinction. The uneven quality of his output may be attributed in part to his desiring fame, wealth, and a good time at least as much as he wanted to be a literary artist. Fitzgerald was born in St. Paul, Minnesota, and spent much of his childhood in upstate New York, then attended private schools in St. Paul and New Jersey before enrolling at Princeton in 1913. He left in 1917 without taking a degree, and while serving as an army lieutenant at Camp Sheridan near Montgomery, Alabama, he met and fell in love with Zelda Sayre, a beautiful and popular southern belle who had many suitors. When their engagement was broken because it seemed unlikely that Scott could support Zelda in her accustomed style, he wrote in cynical despair *This Side of Paradise* (1920). The spectacular success of this first of the lost-generation novels enabled Scott and Zelda to marry not long after its publication. They then embarked on a glamorous and well-publicized way of life that saw them traveling back and forth between the best hotels and speakeasies of America and the most fashionable resorts of Europe. Somehow Fitzgerald managed to write his best novel, *The Great Gatsby* (1925), in spite of the many distractions around him, but the wild life-style of the Fitzgeralds took its inevitable toll. Zelda gradually lapsed into incurable mental illness. After 1930 she spent much of her life in mental sanitariums before finally dying in an asylum fire in 1948.

Fitzgerald's writings after *Gatsby* are of uneven quality. *Tender Is the Night* (1934), his most ambitious novel, is a moving psychological narrative but one so close to the Fitzgeralds' own experiences that it lacks sufficient detachment for full artistic control. To pay for Zelda's medical expenses and their daughter's education in private schools, not to mention his own indulgences, Fitzgerald turned out numerous stories and articles for popular magazines between the time of the crash in 1929 and his own fatal heart attack in 1940. Only occasionally did his talent rise to the potential suggested by *The Great Gatsby*. His short story "Babylon Revisited" (1930) may convey better than any other work of fiction the atmosphere of Paris before and after the Fall; and some critics feel that his posthumously published *The Last Tycoon* (1941) might have been equal to *Gatsby* if Fitzgerald had lived long enough to polish and resolve the story. That short novel was edited by Fitzgerald's friend from Princeton days, EDMUND WILSON, who later collected other late pieces, notebook entries, and letters to and from Fitzgerald in a volume appropriately called *The Crack-up* (1945, o.p.).

The tormented yet glamorous lives of Scott and Zelda Fitzgerald have intrigued readers of several generations—so much so in fact that they themselves have become semifictional characters whose lives have been dramatized in movies and television specials as well as depicted in fiction by other writers. And every few years it seems that a new biography promising fresh revelations is published to critical acclaim and wide public interest. The popular attractiveness of the Fitzgeralds has tended to obscure the fact that Scott was indeed a writer of considerable talent who occasionally flashed into genius. His best works have been mainstays in college classrooms for half a century and have thus evoked almost as much criticism and scholarship as has been devoted to any American writer of the modern period.

BOOKS BY FITZGERALD

Three Novels: The Great Gatsby, Tender Is the Night, The Last Tycoon. Scribner text ed. 1953 pap. $11.95

The Stories of F. Scott Fitzgerald. Scribner 1984 $25.00 pap. $6.95

Six Tales of the Jazz Age and Other Stories. Scribner repr. of 1960 ed. 1968 pap. $5.95. Nine stories taken from *Tales of the Jazz Age* and *All the Sad Young Men.*

Afternoon of an Author: A Selection of Uncollected Stories and Essays. Intro. by Arthur A. Mizener, *Hudson River Ed. Ser.* Scribner 1981 $20.00; Scribner 1957 pap. $2.95

The Letters of F. Scott Fitzgerald. 1963. *Hudson River Ed. Ser.* Scribner 1981 $30.00

This Side of Paradise. Scribner repr. of 1920 ed. $17.50 pap. $5.95

The Beautiful and the Damned. Scribner repr. of 1922 ed. $20.00 pap. $7.95

The Great Gatsby. 1925. Arion Pr. 1984 $400.00; *Hudson River Ed. Ser.* Scribner 1981 $15.00

Tender Is the Night. Scribner repr. of 1934 ed. 1982 pap. $3.95

Taps at Reveille. Scribner repr. of 1935 ed. $17.50. Short stories.

The Last Tycoon. Ed. by Edmund Wilson, Scribner repr. of 1941 ed. 1958 $17.50 1983 pap. $2.95

The Pat Hobby Stories. Intro. by Arnold Gingrich, Scribner 1962 $15.00. A belated but authentic first edition of the 17 stories that deal with an aging Hollywood scriptwriter, a pathetic, courageous, amoral figure. Written during the last two years of Fitzgerald's life, the stories ran consecutively in *Esquire* magazine.

The Basil and Josephine Stories. Ed. by John Kuehl and Jackson R. Bryer, Scribner 1973 $8.95. Brings together for the first time two series of stories with autobiographical significance written for the *Saturday Evening Post* in the late 1920s and early 1930s.

The Crack-up. Ed. by Edmund Wilson, New Directions 1945 pap. $5.95

BOOKS ABOUT FITZGERALD

Allen, Joan M. *Candles and Carnival Lights: The Catholic Sensibility of F. Scott Fitzgerald.* New York Univ. Pr. 1978 $25.00 pap. $12.50

Bruccoli, Matthew J. *The Last of the Novelists: F. Scott Fitzgerald and "The Last Tycoon."* Southern Illinois Univ. Pr. 1977 $9.95

——. *Scott and Ernest: The Authority of Failure and the Authority of Success.* Southern Illinois Univ. Pr. 1980 pap. $7.95. Comparative study of Fitzgerald and Hemingway.

——. *Some Sort of Epic Grandeur: The Life of F. Scott Fitzgerald.* Harcourt 1981 $25.00. "Bruccoli has earned the right to pull everything together in a single, authoritative record that deserves to be called 'definitive'" (*Journal of Modern Lit.*).

Bryer, Jackson R., ed. *F. Scott Fitzgerald: The Critical Reception. Amer. Critical Tradition Ser.* Burt Franklin 1978 lib. bdg. $22.50

——. *The Short Stories of F. Scott Fitzgerald: New Approaches in Criticism.* Univ. of Wisconsin Pr. text ed. 1982 pap. $7.95

Donaldson, Scott. *Critical Essays on F. Scott Fitzgerald's "The Great Gatsby." Critical Essays on Amer. Lit. Ser.* G. K. Hall 1984 lib. bdg. $25.00

Eble, Kenneth. *F. Scott Fitzgerald. Twayne's U.S. Authors Ser.* Bobbs text ed. 1977 pap. $4.95; *Twayne's U.S. Authors Ser.* G. K. Hall rev. ed. 1977 lib. bdg. $11.50 1984 pap. $5.95; *Twayne's U.S. Authors Ser.* New College & Univ. Pr. 1963 pap. $3.45

Fitzgerald, Zelda. *Save Me the Waltz.* Intro. by Harry T. Moore, New Amer. Lib. (Signet Class.) repr. of 1967 ed. 1974 pap. $1.25; pref. by Harry T. Moore, *Crosscurrents Modern Fiction Ser.* Southern Illinois Univ. Pr. 1967 $7.95 pap. $8.95. Zelda Fitzgerald's fictional vision of the life she and Scott Fitzgerald had together.

Gallo, Rose A. *F. Scott Fitzgerald. Lit. and Life Ser.* Ungar 1978 $12.95 1984 pap. $6.95

Levot, Andre. *F. Scott Fitzgerald.* 1983. Warner Bks. 1984 pap. $9.95

Lockridge, Ernest, ed. *Twentieth Century Interpretations of the Great Gatsby.* Prentice-Hall (Spectrum Bks.) 1968 $9.95 pap. $2.95

Long, Robert E. *The Achieving of the Great Gatsby: F. Scott Fitzgerald, 1920–1925.* Bucknell Univ. Pr. 1979 $19.50 1981 pap. $9.95

Mellow, James R. *Invented Lives: The Marriage of F. Scott and Zelda Fitzgerald.* Ill. by James R. Mellow, Houghton Mifflin 1984 $22.50

Milford, Nancy. *Zelda: A Biography.* Avon repr. of 1970 ed. 1971 pap. $2.50; Harper 1970 $16.30 1983 pap. $8.61. This bestseller is a freshly researched study of the Fitzgeralds with emphasis on Zelda.

Miller, James E., Jr. *F. Scott Fitzgerald: His Art and His Technique.* New York Univ. Pr. (Gotham Lib.) 1964 pap. $9.50

Mizener, Arthur A. *The Far Side of Paradise: A Biography of F. Scott Fitzgerald.* Avon 1984 pap. $1.50; Houghton Mifflin rev. & enl. ed. pap. $4.95. A biography that does full justice to the writer as a man representative of his times.

———, ed. *F. Scott Fitzgerald: A Collection of Critical Essays.* Prentice-Hall (Spectrum Bks.) 1963 $12.95 pap. $2.95

Stanley, Linda C. *The Foreign Critical Reputation of F. Scott Fitzgerald: An Analysis and Annotated Bibliography.* Greenwood 1980 lib. bdg. $37.50

Turnbull, Andrew. *Scott Fitzgerald.* 1962. Scribner 1982 pap. $7.95. Turnbull, who knew Fitzgerald, writes: "Along the way I interviewed everyone I could find who had known him, and their testimony is part of the fabric of this book." "Here, unmistakably, is first-rate biography which displaces every work before it, including the earnest and admirable pioneering effort of Arthur Mizener a decade ago. Mr. Turnbull renders vividly the many people in Fitzgerald's life; and, most important of all, he re-creates in human and poignant terms Fitzgerald's tragic relationship with his wife Zelda" (*Atlantic*).

Way, Brian. *F. Scott Fitzgerald and the Art of Social Fiction.* St. Martin's 1980 $25.00

West, James L., III. *The Making of "This Side of Paradise."* Univ. of Pennsylvania Pr. 1983 $16.50

GADDIS, WILLIAM. 1922–

In Recognition of William Gaddis is a collection of essays supporting the view that Gaddis is the HERMAN MELVILLE of the twentieth century. The comparison may prove justified not only because of artistic similarities, but also because both writers suffered from years of neglect before achieving fame. *The Recognitions* baffled and angered most of its initial reviewers, but it has slowly, steadily attracted a growing number of appreciative readers willing to work through its more than 900 demanding pages. Its length and encyclopedic complexity caused some critics mistakenly to hail it as the American *Ulysses*, but Gaddis disclaimed much knowledge of JOYCE. Its central figure, Wyatt, is a painter who finds his natural talent misdirected away from original creation toward the forging of old masterpieces. Scores of other characters appear, and almost all of them are also forgers, imposters, counterfeiters, and plagiarists, for *The Recognitions* is essentially a deeply religious work about the nature of reality and creativity.

As if to make amends for the neglect of *The Recognitions*, most reviewers greeted Gaddis's second novel, *JR*, with respectful attention. Although not a popular success, it won the National Book Award. Of *Carpenter's Gothic*, Gaddis's most recent novel, *PW* wrote that readers "familiar with his virtuosity . . . will find his gifts very much intact here; the narrative spins and swirls at high voltage and with unflagging energy. Of the many pleasures the novel affords, however, the principal one remains Gaddis's eerily uncanny ear for American speech in all its broken rhythms, violence, expressiveness, booming narrative power."

BOOKS BY GADDIS

The Recognitions. 1955. Avon 1974 pap. $4.95
JR. 1975. Penguin 1985 pap. $12.95
Carpenter's Gothic. Viking 1985 $16.95

BOOKS ABOUT GADDIS

Kuehl, John, and Steven Moore. *In Recognition of William Gaddis*. Syracuse Univ. Pr. 1984 $25.00
Moore, Steven. *A Reader's Guide to William Gaddis's "The Recognitions."* Univ. of Nebraska Pr. 1982 $25.00

GARDNER, JOHN (C.). 1933–1982

One of the most lively literary controversies of recent years was stirred up by the publication of John Gardner's *On Moral Fiction*. He attacked many of his leading contemporaries for their world-weary despair, smart-alecky cleverness, and excessive concern for ingenious literary techniques at the expense of those solid human values that Gardner insisted lay at the core of the art of fiction. Whether or not one agreed with its main thesis, *On Moral Fiction* (the title essay won a Pushcart Prize) clearly stated the artistic credo of its author, and when Gardner's literary career was brought to a premature end several years later, critics found it tempting to evaluate his total output in terms of his own standards. The authors of the first full-length critical studies of Gardner would seem to agree wholeheartedly with David Cowart's statement that "the remarkable thing about Gardner's fiction is its consistent clarity of purpose and moral vision" (*Dictionary of Literary Biography*). It is important to realize, however, that by "moral" Gardner did not mean didactic, and the eight main novels he left behind offer no easy affirmations. "What is there in this world but accident?" asks one of his principal characters, and those works contain many instances of gratuitous violence and senseless sudden endings not unlike Gardner's own death in a motorcycle accident four days before he was to be married.

Gardner was born in Batavia, New York, and attended both DePauw University and Washington University of St. Louis before attaining a Ph.D. in English from the State University of Iowa in 1958, which qualified him for a career as a teacher of creative writing and a scholar of medieval literature.

He taught and lectured at a number of schools and universities, but his main academic affiliations were at Southern Illinois University and, from 1978 until his death, the State University of New York at Binghamton. An extremely productive and versatile writer, he published scholarly work on the medieval period as well as several study guides, and his creative efforts included not only adult fiction, but children's books, poetry, libretti for operas, and radio plays.

Gardner published two philosophical novels—*The Resurrection* (1966, o.p.) and *The Wreckage of Agathon* (o.p.)—without attracting much notice before *Grendel* established him as a major new talent. Already considered a modern classic, that short novel retells the Old English epic of *Beowulf* from the point of view of the dragon rather than the hero. The success of *Grendel* enabled Gardner to revise and publish several longer novels on which he had been working during the decade of the 1960s. *The Sunlight Dialogues* is a lengthy novel that deals, on perhaps the most fundamental of its many levels, with the conflict between an earnest but bumbling police chief in upstate New York and a bearded, mysterious transient who calls himself The Sunlight Man and epitomizes the spirit of freedom and anarchy as emphatically as the police chief represents law and order. Some critics think that it is Gardner's best novel set in contemporary times. *Nickel Mountain*, which Gardner called in a subtitle *A Pastoral Novel*, is the story of a developing love affair between a middle-aged man and a young woman in a somber country setting. *October Light*, which won the National Book Critics Circle Award in 1976, has a novel within a novel. Gardner's next full-length novel, *Freddy's Book*, is also a kind of double novel in that it provides at least a half-frame for its central narrative, a fablelike tale called *King Gustav and the Devil* set in sixteenth-century Scandinavia. What proved to be Gardner's last novel, *Mickelson's Ghosts*, is a lengthy, somewhat tortured account of the several crises faced by a middle-aged philosophy professor at SUNY-Binghamton. The reviews were largely negative with the principal complaint being the seeming lack of distance between the novel's hero and its author.

Gardner is a collectible author whose first editions and small-press publications have appeal in the rare book market. One reason may be that he worked in several attractive and unusual genres.

Books by Gardner

Grendel. Ballantine 1975 pap. $2.25; Knopf 1971 $12.95
The Sunlight Dialogues. 1972. Ballantine 1982 pap. $4.95
Nickel Mountain. Ballantine 1982 pap. $3.50; Knopf 1973 $15.95
October Light. 1976. Ballantine 1981 pap. $3.50
Freddy's Book. Ballantine 1981 pap. $2.95; Knopf 1980 $10.00
The Art of Living and Other Stories. Knopf 1981 $12.95
Mickelson's Ghosts. Knopf 1982 $16.95
On Becoming a Novelist. Intro. by Raymond Carver, Harper 1983 $13.41 1984 pap. $5.72

BOOKS ABOUT GARDNER

Cowart, David. *Arches and Light: The Fiction of John Gardner.* Southern Illinois Univ. Pr. 1983 $19.95

Morace, Robert A. *John Gardner: An Annotated Secondary Bibliography. Reference Lib. of the Humanities* Garland 1984 lib. bdg. $45.00

————, ed. *John Gardner: Critical Perspectives.* Ed. by Kathryn Vanspanckeren, afterword by John Gardner, *Crosscurrents Modern Critiques New Ser.* Southern Illinois Univ. Pr. 1982 $18.95

Morris, Gregory L. *A World of Order and Light: The Fiction of John Gardner.* Univ. of Georgia Pr. 1984 $22.50

GASS, WILLIAM. 1924–

William Gass is known as one of our best stylists, an experimental writer willing to take chances as he explores new dimensions of fictional form. He was born in Fargo, North Dakota, and after attending Kenyon College at a time when that school was in its heyday as a literary center, he went on to graduate study in philosophy at Cornell University, receiving his Ph.D. in 1954. From then until 1969 he taught at Purdue, and he now holds a distinguished professorship at Washington University in St. Louis.

His writing talent was first recognized in 1958, when the editors of *Accent* invited him—an unprecedented honor—to fill an entire issue of that distinguished little magazine with some of his stories and essays, but nine more years passed before he published his first book. The novel *Omensetter's Luck* (1966) was well received by critics, who praised it for its exceptional style and its rich evocation of a particular time and place. *Newsweek* described it as "a dense, provoking, vastly rewarding and very beautiful first novel." The following year his collection of stories, *In the Heart of the Heart of the Country*, attracted additional readers. The title story of that volume and several others, in particular the brilliant "The Pedersen Kid," have evoked considerable critical interest, as has his short novel *Willie Master's Lonesome Wife* (1968, o.p.), a wildly bawdy and richly allusive interior monologue by a latter-day Molly Bloom, which appeared originally as a special supplement to *Tri-Quarterly.* In recent years Gass has devoted himself to the writing of an ambitious longer work, which remains unpublished. In addition, he has become a busy contributor of essay-reviews and other prose pieces to *N.Y. Review of Books* and some of the other better literary journals. Some of his reviews of individual writers and essays on the theory of fiction are collected in *Fiction and Figures of Life* (1970), *The World within the Word*, and *The Habitations of the Word.* Difficult to classify is *On Being Blue: A Philosophical Inquiry*, though one might say that it is as brilliant and witty an exposition of the many meanings of the word "blue" as one would expect to come from the typewriter of a very bright professor of philosophy who loves languages.

BOOKS BY GASS

Omensetter's Luck. New Amer. Lib. (Plume) 1966 pap. $5.95

In the Heart of the Heart of the Country. Godine (Nonpareil Bks.) 1981 pap. $7.95;
Harper 1968 $10.00

BOOK ABOUT GASS

McCaffery, Larry. *The Metafictional Muse: The Work of Robert Coover, Donald Barthelme, and William Gass.* Univ. of Pittsburgh Pr. 1982 $24.95

GLASGOW, ELLEN. 1874–1945

Born in Richmond, Virginia, of a mother who traced her ancestry to the
Cavalier settlers of Tidewater Virginia and a father who descended from the
Scotch-Irish of the Shenandoah Valley, Ellen Glasgow was a writer whose divided background helps explain her ability to combine romantic sensibility
with tough-minded realism. For the Virginia Edition of her works, published
by Scribner in 1938 and now out of print, she chose 12 of her 18 novels and divided them into two main groups. What she called novels of character and
comedies of manners consist of five works: *The Battle-Ground; The Deliverance; They Stooped to Folly; Virginia* (1913); and *Barren Ground* (1925). The remaining seven novels she grouped under the heading "social history in the
form of fiction." Covering almost 100 years of life in the Old Dominion, they
are perhaps better read in historical sequence than in the order in which they
were originally published: *The Miller of Old Church; The Romantic Comedians*
(1926); *The Voice of the People; The Romance of a Plain Man; Life and Gabri-
ella; The Sheltered Life;* and *Vein of Iron* (1935). The new prefaces that she
wrote for each volume of the Virginia Edition form a valuable record of her
literary growth and a treatise on novel writing that compares favorably with
the prefaces that Henry James wrote for the New York Edition of his works.
With the addition of an introduction to the one novel she published subsequently, the Pulitzer Prize-winning *In This Our Life* (1941), these prefaces
were brought together and published as *A Certain Measure* (1943). *The
Woman Within* (1954, o.p.), her own story of her inner life, parallels her fiction in its account of a courageous woman who refused to become a victim of
the outmoded codes of chivalry and male domination that characterized the
Old South of her heritage. Although only six of her novels are currently in
print, she remains a transitional figure of considerable importance in the literary history of America not only because she was a conscious craftsperson
with high standards for her art, but also because as the first southern woman
writer to break through from romantic conventions to ironic and realistic literature of the top drawer, she showed the way for many of the southern
women writers who have followed her.

BOOKS BY GLASGOW

The Descendant. 1897. Ed. by Elizabeth Hardwick, Ayer repr. of 1926 ed. 1977 lib.
bdg. $26.00; Russell Pr. repr. of 1900 ed. lib. bdg. $20.00. Glasgow's first novel,
originally published anonymously, is republished with an introduction by Elizabeth Hardwick.
The Voice of the People. Irvington repr. of 1900 ed. lib. bdg. $18.50; ed. by W. L. God-
shalk, *Masterworks of Lit. Ser.* New College & Univ. Pr. 1972 $10.95 pap. $7.95

Barren Ground. 1925. *Amer. Century Ser.* Hill & Wang 1957 pap. $9.95; Peter Smith
$10.75

The Romantic Comedians. Ed. by Elizabeth Hardwick, Ayer repr. of 1926 ed. 1977
lib. bdg. $30.00; Russell Pr. repr. of 1926 ed. lib. bdg. $20.00

Vein of Iron. Harcourt 1935 pap. $7.95

In This Our Life. Rivercity Pr. repr. 1981

BOOKS ABOUT GLASGOW

Godbold, E. Stanly. *Ellen Glasgow and the Woman Within.* Louisiana State Univ. Pr.
1972 $27.50

McDowell, Frederick P. *Ellen Glasgow and the Ironic Art of Fiction.* Univ. of Wisconsin Pr. 1960 pap. $6.95

Richards, Marion K. *Ellen Glasgow's Development as a Novelist. Studies in Amer. Lit.*
Mouton 1971 text ed. $26.00

Rouse, Blair. *Ellen Glasgow. Twayne's U.S. Authors Ser.* Irvington 1962 lib. bdg. $8.95
text ed. pap. $2.95; *Twayne's U.S. Authors Ser.* New College & Univ. Pr. 1962
pap. $5.95

Thiebaux, Marcelle. *Ellen Glasgow. Lit. and Life Ser.* Ungar 1982 $15.50

Wagner, Linda W. *Ellen Glasgow: Beyond Convention.* Univ. of Texas Pr. 1982 text
ed. $15.95

GORDON, CAROLINE. 1895–1981

Caroline Gordon's controlled craftsmanship as well as her conservative attitudes stamped her as a traditionalist among modern writers. Born in Kentucky as the daughter of a classics teacher and graduated from Bethany College in 1916, she married the poet Allen Tate in 1924 and became an associate of the Fugitives and Southern Agrarian groups that helped to make Nashville a vital mecca for southern intellectuals during the 1970s. Her first novel, *Penhally* (1931, o.p.), traces the decline brought about by pride and jealousy as well as the devastation of the Civil War. *None Shall Look Back* (1937, o.p.), which had the misfortune to appear shortly after *Gone with the Wind*, is a distinguished but neglected novel with a theme similar to her first. Against the story of the Allard family, which, like the house of Penhally, deteriorates through internal weaknesses as well as because of the Civil War, Gordon sets off the heroic figure of the Confederate General Nathan Bedford Forrest. *The Garden of Adonis* picks up the story of the Allards, this time during the depression of the 1930s, and shows how social conditions as well as their own incapacities have put the men of the family at the mercy of their spoiled and neurotic women.

Aleck Maury, Sportsman, like Gordon's most famous short story "Old Red," is remarkable for its vivid hunting scenes. Probably no other woman has written so knowledgeably and sympathetically about the outdoor man's love of the fields and streams of his native region and the almost sacramental view of nature that accompanies such allegiance. *Green Centuries* is a novel about a pioneer couple who settle near the Cumberland Gap during the American Revolution. *The Women on the Porch, The Strange Children*, and *The Malefactors* (1956, o.p.) are novels about modern intellectuals found wanting when tested by nature and their own raw emotions.

Books by Gordon

The Collected Stories of Caroline Gordon. Farrar 1981 $17.95 pap. $9.95
The Southern Mandarins: Letters of Caroline Gordon to Sally Wood, 1924–1937. Ed. by
    Sally Wood, fwd. by Andrew Lytle, Louisiana State Univ. Pr. text ed. 1984
    $25.00
Aleck Maury, Sportsman: A Novel. Lost Amer. Fiction Ser. Cooper Square Pr. repr. of
    1934 ed. 1972 $18.50; Southern Illinois Univ. Pr. repr. of 1934 ed. 1980 $12.95
    pap. $6.95
The Garden of Adonis. Cooper Square Pr. repr. of 1937 ed. 1972 $22.50
Green Centuries. Cooper Square Pr. repr. of 1941 ed. 1972 $23.50
The Women on the Porch. Cooper Square Pr. repr. of 1944 ed. 1972 $19.50
The Strange Children. Cooper Square Pr. repr. of 1951 ed. 1972 $19.50
Old Red and Other Stories. Cooper Square Pr. repr. of 1963 ed. 1972 $18.50

Books about Gordon

Fraistat, Rose A. *Caroline Gordon as Novelist and Woman of Letters. Southern Literary
    Studies* Louisiana State Univ. Pr. text ed. 1984 $20.00
Landess, Thomas H., ed. *The Short Fiction of Caroline Gordon: A Symposium.* Univ.
    of Dallas Pr. 1972 $4.95

HAWKES, JOHN. 1925–

Robert Coover is quoted on the jacket of *Virginie: Her Two Lives* with the
suggestion that those discovering John Hawkes for the first time "might as
well begin right here with this lush, erotic masterpiece." However, for readers not already acquainted with Hawkes's singular writings, probably the
best entry is through *Humors of Blood and Skin: A John Hawkes Reader.*
From his nine novels and other writings Hawkes selected representative passages, which he has linked together to form a sort of literary montage. William Gass in his introduction praises the book as "the joyful showing forth
and celebration of Hawkes's healing art" and says of the Hawkes style, "*It is
a prose that breathes what it sees.*"

If Hawkes is an American writer whose works seem to put him in the company of such international modernists as NABOKOV (see Vol. 2) and BECKETT
(see Vol. 2), it is partly because he has himself traveled widely yet taken as
part of his imaginative luggage a strange and interior country of his own. After an early childhood in Connecticut and New York City, Hawkes moved to
Juneau, Alaska, when he was ten years old and spent his formative years
there before attending schools in New England and graduating from Harvard College. He served as an ambulance driver in Germany during World
War II, and he has spent considerable time in the south of France when free
from his teaching duties at Brown University, where he has been professor
of English since 1967.

The Cannibal, his short first novel, struck its readers as suggestive of KAF-
KA's (see Vol. 2) stories, Djuna Barnes's *Nightwood*, and the work of the
French surrealists; and although a similar vein of plotless narratives set in
strange and macabre landscapes is characteristic of his books through *The
Lime Twig* (1951) and *Second Skin* (1964), he began to place more emphasis
on story with *The Blood Oranges* (1971). Hawkes moved even further in that

direction when he changed publishers from New Directions to Harper & Row in a frankly acknowledged effort to reach a wider audience. *The Passion Artist*, the story of a celibate forced to purge the repressed traumas of his youth through sex and violence in middle age, was described by John Barth as "severe, horrific, and yet somberly hilarious; Hawkes's best since 'Second Skin,'" though Josephine Hendin entitled her review in the *N.Y. Times Book Review* "A Detour to Nihilism" and Paul Gray in *Time* said that the book "does not so much explore sex as mime its mysteries." *Virginie: Her Two Lives* is a kind of feminine counterpart of *The Passion Artist*, which, like *The Blood Oranges*, contrasts two historical periods. The heroine is an 11-year-old girl who lives both in the eighteenth century and in Paris after World War II. She is purged of innocence while remaining strangely invulnerable in her double lives, saved in each story by the *deus ex machina* of a maternal figure who puts an abrupt end to the "phallocentric" proceedings that have entrapped her.

BOOKS BY HAWKES

Humors of Blood and Skin: A John Hawkes Reader. Intro. by William Gass, New Directions 1984 $22.50 pap. $12.95
Lunar Landscapes. New Directions repr. 1969 $4.95. Contains *Charivari, The Goose on the Grave, The Owl*, and short stories.
The Cannibal. Intro. by Albert J. Guerard, New Directions 1949 pap. $5.95
The Beetle Leg. 1951. New Directions repr. 1967 pap. $4.95
The Owl. 1953. Intro. by Robert Scholes, New Directions 1977 pap. $3.95
The Lime Twig. Intro. by Leslie A. Fiedler, New Directions 1960 pap. $5.95
Second Skin. New Directions 1964 pap. $4.95
The Blood Oranges. New Directions 1971 $9.95 1972 pap. $7.95
Death, Sleep and the Traveler. New Directions 1974 $6.95 pap. $5.95
Travesty. New Directions 1976 pap. $4.95
The Passion Artist. Harper 1979 $11.49 1981 pap. $3.95
Virginie: Her Two Lives. Carroll & Graf 1983 pap. $7.95; Harper 1982 $13.41; New Directions ltd. ed. 1982 $75.00

BOOKS ABOUT HAWKES

Berry, Eliot. *A Poetry of Force and Darkness: The Fiction of John Hawkes*. Borgo Pr. 1979 lib. bdg. $10.95 pap. $3.95
Busch, Frederick. *Hawkes: A Guide to His Fictions*. Syracuse Univ. Pr. 1973 $10.00
Hryciw, Carol A. *John Hawkes: An Annotated Bibliography*. Author Bibliographies Ser. Scarecrow Pr. 1977 $15.00
Kuehl, John. *John Hawkes and the Craft of Conflict*. Rutgers Univ. Pr. 1975 $20.00
O'Donnell, Patrick. *John Hawkes*. Twayne's U.S. Authors Ser. G. K. Hall 1982 lib. bdg. $14.50
Santore, Anthony C., ed. *A John Hawkes Symposium: Design and Debris*. Ed. by Michael N. Pocalyko, New Directions 1977 pap. $4.95
Scotto, Robert M. *Three Contemporary Novelists: An Annotated Bibliography of Works by and about John Hawkes, Joseph Heller and Thomas Pynchon*. Reference Lib. of the Humanities Garland 1977 lib. bdg. $23.00

HELLER, JOSEPH. 1932–

Even if *Catch-22* (1961), Heller's first and most successful novel, did not have any other merits to keep it alive, it could well be remembered for introducing a new phrase into the English language. As explained by Captain Yossarian, the Assyrian bombardier in Heller's antiwar novel, the catch goes like this: "Anyone who is crazy must be grounded; anyone who is willing to fly combat missions must be crazy; ergo, anyone who flies should be grounded. But [you have to] request grounding; no one crazy enough to fly missions would ask; and if one should there's a catch: anyone who wants to get out of combat duty isn't really crazy." Nelson Algren wrote of the book in the *Nation:* "Below its hilarity, so wild that it hurts, . . . this novel is not merely the best American novel to come out of World War II; it is the best American novel that has come out of anywhere in years." Some critics found the satiric method repetitive and ultimately tiresome. Seven years later, after 2 million copies had been sold in paperback with total copies approaching 3½ million, *Catch-22* was again reviewed in the *N.Y. Times.* Josh Greenberg wrote, "I found the antic humor of Catch-22 . . . robustly fresh [and] sidesplittingly funny. I know of no book written in the last 20 years that continues to make me laugh out loud so much."

Like Yossarian, the Brooklyn-born Heller was a B-25 bombardier during World War II. He graduated from New York University, received an M.A. from Columbia, and attended Oxford University on a Fulbright Scholarship. He began *Catch-22* in 1953 and finished it in 1961 by working after his hours at advertising jobs at *McCall's, Look, Time,* and Remington Rand. He capitalized on his experience in the worlds of business and publishing in his second novel, *Something Happened* (1974), in which the unheroic hero, Bob Slocum, expresses the author's ideas in a gloomy and wryly humorous story about the moral bankruptcy of middle-class American life in the postwar years. In *Good as Gold* the Heller surrogate is a writer and college professor named Bruce Gold, the first Jewish protagonist in a Heller novel, and if it was less than enthusiastically received by some critics that may have been partly because still another novel about identity crises seemed rather tired and flat a whole decade after the vogue of Jewish black humor had reached its crest with Philip Roth's *Portnoy's Complaint.* Heller continued his exploration of ethnic identity with *God Knows,* one of the bestsellers of 1984.

BOOKS BY HELLER

Catch-22. Dell (Delta Bks.) 1982 pap. $3.50; Simon & Schuster 1961 $13.95
Something Happened. Ballantine repr. of 1978 ed. 1979 pap. $2.95; Dell 1985 pap. $4.95; Knopf 1974 $12.50
Good as Gold. Dell repr. of 1979 ed. 1985 pap. $4.95; Pocket Bks. 1980 pap. $2.95; Simon & Schuster 1979 $12.95
God Knows. Knopf 1984 $16.45

BOOK ABOUT HELLER

Potts, Stephen W. *From Here to Absurdity: The Moral Battlefields of Joseph Heller.* Borgo Pr. 1982 lib. bdg. $10.95 pap. $3.95

HEMINGWAY, ERNEST. 1899–1961 (NOBEL PRIZE 1954)

The announcement in early 1985 that an annual Ernest Hemingway Award would be presented for the best novel published in English anywhere in the world seemed fitting recognition that Charles Poore was right when he said that Hemingway "may be the strongest influence in literature that this age will give to posterity." Now, a half-century after the 1930s, it seems apparent that Hemingway was one of the literary giants of the whole twentieth century. Only William Faulkner among American writers after HENRY JAMES can claim equal stature with Hemingway, but whereas Faulkner made Yoknapatawpha County of Mississippi seem universal and mythical in the broadest sense, Hemingway quite literally was an international writer, taking as his range of coverage much of the world from Upper Michigan to "the green hills of Africa." Some members of the academic and literary establishments have long taken a somewhat patronizing attitude toward Hemingway, questioning the sincerity of his macho image and finding his ideas either too conservative or too superficial, but he seems more firmly entrenched than ever as one of the modern masters. More than any other writer of this century he showed that it is possible to be both popular and good.

Hemingway was born in Oak Park, near Chicago, the son of a doctor who loved outdoor sports and instilled in his son what were long considered masculine values. After graduation from high school, Hemingway gave up college to serve a journalistic apprenticeship with the *Kansas City Star*. He went to Italy as an ambulance driver in World War I, joined the Italian infantry, and was severely wounded. As a correspondent he covered disturbances in the Near East, and about 1921 settled with other American expatriates in Paris. His first books were published there. *The Torrents of Spring* (1926), a satiric burlesque of Sherwood Anderson's style, really acknowledges his debt to Anderson, who with Gertrude Stein was his teacher in the natural rhythms of American speech. His first successful novel, *The Sun Also Rises* (1926), is made up almost entirely of the conversations of a group of the "lost generation" artists and writers in Paris. *Men without Women* (1927) deals with deadpan gangsters and matadors. He used the Italy of World War I as the background for the love story of an English nurse and an American soldier in *A Farewell to Arms* (1929).

In 1927 he returned to America and, in 1930, bought a home in Key West, the scene of *To Have and Have Not*, which he considered "not so good." In 1936 he went to Spain at the beginning of the bloody civil war. His play *The Fifth Column* and his greatest novel, *For Whom the Bell Tolls* (1940), were the matured results of his Spanish experiences. For his many and varied services in World War II he was decorated with a Bronze Star. He returned to Cuba in 1946. While on assignment for *Look* magazine, he and his wife had two narrow escapes early in 1954 when two planes on which they were traveling crashed in Africa. Seven years later, in declining health, partly as a result of injuries suffered in these crashes, he shot himself in his home in Ketchum, Idaho. With hindsight it is impossible to avoid the knowledge that Hemingway had always been preoccupied with the theme of self-destruction.

In addition to his steady production of fiction, Hemingway wrote such distinguished works of nonfiction as *Death in the Afternoon* (1932), a vigorous account of bullfighting in Spain; *The Green Hills of Africa* (1935), memorable not only for descriptions of big game hunting on an African safari but for campfire discussions on life and literature; and *A Moveable Feast* (1964), a series of vivid character sketches about people he knew in Paris during the 1920s. In his foreword, Hemingway admitted that much of *A Moveable Feast* might be considered semifictional, but his portraits of Scott and Zelda Fitzgerald, Gertrude Stein, FORD MADOX FORD, and others are generally considered psychologically accurate. Almost all of Hemingway's fugitive journalistic writings from his high school days through two world wars to his last years are collected in three volumes—*Ernest Hemingway's Apprenticeship* (o.p.); *Ernest Hemingway, Cub Reporter* (o.p.); and *By Line: Ernest Hemingway*. The best edition of Hemingway's poetry is one edited by Nicholas Gerogiannis and published as *The Complete Poems*.

BOOKS BY HEMINGWAY

The Enduring Hemingway: An Anthology of a Lifetime in Literature. Ed. by Charles Scribner, Jr., Kelley 1974 $19.95; Scribner 1974 $7.95. *A Farewell to Arms* and *The Old Man and the Sea* as well as a generous selection of other writings.

A Hemingway Reader. Scribner repr. 1953 $35.00. *The Torrents of Spring* and *The Sun Also Rises* complete with episodes from other novels plus 11 short stories.

Three Novels: The Sun Also Rises; A Farewell to Arms; The Old Man and the Sea. 1962. Scribner 1972 pap. $11.95

Short Stories of Ernest Hemingway. Scribner repr. of 1938 ed. $27.50 pap. $8.95

The Snows of Kilimanjaro and Other Stories. 1961. Scribner 1982 pap. $2.95

The Fifth Column and Four Stories of the Spanish Civil War. Scribner 1969 pap. $4.95

Islands in the Stream. Hudson River Ed. Ser. Scribner 1970 $25.00 pap. $7.95

The Nick Adams Stories. 1972 Scribner 1981 pap. $6.95. The stories are rearranged in chronological sequence including eight previously unpublished.

Ernest Hemingway: Selected Letters, 1917–1961. Ed. by Carlos Baker, Scribner 1981 $10.95 pap. $12.95

In Our Time. 1925. Hudson River Ed. Ser. Scribner repr. of 1930 ed. $15.00 pap. $4.50

The Torrents of Spring. 1926. Scribner 1972 $5.95

The Sun Also Rises. 1926. Scribner 1982 pap. $3.95 1983 $12.95

Men without Women. 1927. Scribner 1983 pap. $2.95. Short stories.

A Farewell to Arms. 1929. Scribner 1982 pap. $3.95 1983 $13.95

Winner Take Nothing. 1933. Scribner 1982 $3.50. Short stories.

To Have and Have Not. 1940. Scribner 1983 $14.95 pap. $8.95

For Whom the Bell Tolls. 1940. Scribner 1982 pap. $4.95 1983 $14.95

Across the River and into the Trees. Scribner repr. 1950 $20.00 pap. $6.95

The Old Man and the Sea. 1952. Scribner 1983 $9.95; fwd. by Charles Scribner, Jr., Scribner 1984 $12.95 pap. $2.95

BOOKS ABOUT HEMINGWAY

Baker, Carlos. *Ernest Hemingway: A Life Story*. Avon 1980 pap. $5.95; Scribner repr. 1969 $40.00. The definitive biography and one of the best of any modern writer.

————. *Hemingway: The Writer as Artist.* 1952. Princeton Univ. Pr. 4th ed. rev. ed. 1972 $38.50 pap. $9.95. Still the best scholarly critical study of the development of Hemingway's literary career.

Benson, Jackson J., ed. *The Short Stories of Ernest Hemingway: Critical Essays.* Duke Univ. Pr. 1975 $21.00

Brenner, Gerry. *Concealments in Hemingway's Work.* Ohio State Univ. Pr. 1983 $23.50

Burgess, Anthony. *Ernest Hemingway and His World.* Scribner 1978 $12.50. Pictorial biography.

Fenton, Charles A. *The Apprenticeship of Ernest Hemingway.* Octagon repr. of 1954 ed. 1975 lib. bdg. $24.00. Scholarly study of the Kansas City and Toronto years.

Flora, Joseph M. *Hemingway's Nick Adams.* Louisiana State Univ. Pr. 1982 $20.00

Fuentes, Norberto. *Hemingway in Cuba.* Intro. by Gabriel Garcia Marquez, Lyle Stuart 1984 $22.50

Gajdusek, Robert E. *Hemingway's Paris.* 1978. Scribner 1982 pap. $12.95

Gellens, Jay, ed. *Twentieth Century Interpretations of A Farewell to Arms. Twentieth Century Interpretations Ser.* Prentice-Hall (Spectrum Bks.) 1970 $9.95

Grebstein, Sheldon N. *Hemingway's Craft. Crosscurrents Modern Critiques Ser.* Southern Illinois Univ. Pr. 1973 $14.95

Hardy, Richard E., and John G. Cull. *Hemingway: A Psychological Portrait.* Irvington repr. of 1977 ed. text ed. 1984 $16.95 pap. $8.95

Hemingway, Mary Welsh. *How It Was.* Knopf 1976 $12.50. Memoir by his widow.

Hotchner, A. E. *Ernest Hemingway: A Personal Memoir.* 1966. Morrow 1983 $16.95 pap. $8.95

Kert, Bernice. *The Hemingway Women.* Norton 1983 $20.00. Popular biography of the women in Hemingway's life.

Laurence, Frank M. *Hemingway and the Movies.* Univ. Pr. of Mississippi 1980 $20.00

Lee, A. Robert. *Ernest Hemingway: New Critical Essays.* Barnes & Noble 1983 $28.50

Meyers, Jeffrey, ed. *Hemingway: The Critical Heritage. Critical Heritage Ser.* Routledge & Kegan 1982 $32.50

Nagel, James, ed. *Ernest Hemingway: The Writer in Context.* Univ. of Wisconsin Pr. 1984 pap. $27.50

Nelson, Raymond S. *Hemingway: Expressionist Artist.* Iowa State Univ. Pr. text ed. 1979 pap. $6.95

Noble, Donald R. *Ernest Hemingway: A Revaluation.* Whitston 1984 $22.50

Oldsey, Bernard. *Ernest Hemingway: The Papers of a Writer.* Garland 1981 lib. bdg. $22.00

————. *Hemingway's Hidden Craft: The Writing of "A Farewell to Arms."* Pennsylvania State Univ. Pr. 1979 $19.75

Raeburn, John. *Fame Became of Him: Hemingway as Public Writer.* Indiana Univ. Pr. 1984 $17.50

Reynolds, Michael S. *Critical Essays on Ernest Hemingway's "In Our Time." Critical Essays on Amer. Lit. Ser.* G. K. Hall 1983 lib. bdg. $33.50

————. *Hemingway's First War: The Making of A Farewell to Arms.* Princeton Univ. Pr. 1976 $31.00

Rovit, Earl H. *Ernest Hemingway. Twayne's U.S. Authors Ser.* G. K. Hall 1963 lib. bdg. $11.50; *Twayne's U.S. Authors Ser.* New College & Univ. Pr. 1963 pap. $3.45

Ryan, Frank L. *The Immediate Critical Reception of Ernest Hemingway.* Univ. Pr. of Amer. text ed. 1980 $16.00 pap. $7.50

Sarason, Bertram D. *Hemingway and the Sun Set.* Bruccoli 1972 $10.00. Collection of memoirs by originals of characters in *The Sun Also Rises* along with a long scholarly introduction on the background of the novel.

Shaw, Samuel. *Ernest Hemingway. Lit. and Life Ser.* Ungar 1982 $12.95 pap. $6.95

Stephens, Robert O., ed. *Ernest Hemingway: The Critical Reception. Amer. Critical Tradition Ser.* Burt Franklin 1976 lib. bdg. $23.50

Svoboda, Frederic J. *Hemingway and The Sun Also Rises: The Crafting of a Style.* Univ. Pr. of Kansas 1983 $19.95

Wagner, Linda W., ed. *Ernest Hemingway: Five Decades of Criticism.* Michigan State Univ. Pr. 1974 $10.00

Waldhorn, Arthur. *A Reader's Guide to Ernest Hemingway.* Farrar 1972 $5.95; Octagon repr. of 1972 ed. 1977 lib. bdg. $20.00

Whitlow, Roger. *Cassandra's Daughters: The Women in Hemingway.* Greenwood 1984 lib. bdg. $25.00

Williams, Wirt. *The Tragic Art of Ernest Hemingway.* Louisiana State Univ. Pr. text ed. 1981 $20.00

Young, Philip. *Ernest Hemingway: A Reconsideration.* 1952. Pennsylvania State Univ. Pr. 2d ed. 1966 $22.50. Early critical study with psychological interpretations that proved to be prophetic.

——. *Hemingway Manuscripts: An Inventory.* Ed. by Charles W. Mann, Pennsylvania State Univ. Pr. 1969 $15.00

IRVING, JOHN. 1942–

John Irving has been one of the most visible and successful members of a postwar generation of American writers whose main literary lineage can be traced back to the black humor of the 1960s and from there perhaps back to the *Mad* magazine of their adolescent years. Irving's novels are filled with grotesque and bizarre characters ranging from bespectacled bears in the Vienna Zoo to a transsexual tight end for the Philadephia Eagles, but although he is capable of finding humor in such subjects as castration, speech impediments, and crippled ballerinas, there is an underlying humane seriousness in Irving's fiction that may help explain why he has found an eager audience among young readers who like his blend of toughness and kindness. Those readers quickly raised *The World according to Garp* from cult status to bestsellerdom and made *The Hotel New Hampshire* the second bestselling book of 1981. Irving prepared himself for that rather spectacular breakthrough by writing three earlier novels, which found only respectful attention from a few reviewers and muted enthusiasm from a small but growing corps of readers.

Irving grew up in New Hampshire, attending Exeter Academy, going on to the Universities of Pittsburgh and New Hampshire, and then attending the Iowa Writers' Workshop, where Kurt Vonnegut, Jr., was one of his teachers. Crucial to his development was a period spent in Vienna in 1963–64, where he married and became interested enough in the modern history of that pivotal Austrian city to make it a presence in all of his novels.

Setting Free the Bears, a first novel written while Irving was in Iowa, introduces many of his later concerns and themes in its farcical and extravagant account of what happens when the animals in the Vienna Zoo are freed from their cages by the idealistic Siggy Javotnik. *The Water-Method Man* is

Fred "Bogus" Trumper, who can neither urinate nor have sexual intercourse without experiencing excruciating pain unless he can bring himself to face an operation even more acutely painful. Trumper finds some solace by translating for his dissertation an "Old Low Norse" epic, finding it so dull that he keeps improving upon the original until he becomes its real author. Thus Irving introduces a reflexive fiction-within-fiction device that becomes increasingly central in his fiction after *The 158-Pound Marriage*, a book about the consequences of wife-and-husband swapping by two couples who seem rather like up-to-date counterparts of the tangled quartet in Ford Madox Ford's modern classic *The Good Soldier*.

Irving puts a writer with at least superficial similarities to himself at the center of *The World according to Garp*—T. S. Garp is writing a book called *The World according to Bensenhaver*—but the main appeal of Irving's fourth book is the zestful way in which he deals with a rather astonishing variety of subplots and casts a wary eye on some of the more trendy interests of contemporary society. *The Hotel New Hampshire* is a long and intricately structured book about various members of the Berry family and the people they meet at the hotel they run in New Hampshire. The great popular success of the novel was partly neutralized by the reservations of most reviewers, who found the novel a disappointment after *Garp*.

BOOKS BY IRVING

Setting Free the Bears. Pocket Bks. repr. 1979 pap. $3.50 1982 pap. $3.95
The Water-Method Man. 1972. Pocket Bks. 1982 pap. $3.95
The 158-Pound Marriage. Pocket Bks. 1978 pap. $3.95; Random 1974 $7.95
The World according to Garp. Dutton 1978 $10.95; Pocket Bks. 1982 pap. $4.95
The Hotel New Hampshire. Dutton 1981 $9.50; Pocket Bks. 1982 pap. $3.95 1984 pap. $3.95
The Cider House Rules. Morrow 1985 $18.95

JACKSON, SHIRLEY. 1919–1965

Shirley Jackson's literary reputation rests firmly but not solely on a short story that is considered a modern American classic. From the time of its first appearance in the June 28, 1948, issue of the *New Yorker*, "The Lottery" has been much discussed and often anthologized. The story of an ancient scapegoat ritual reenacted in a community of modern times, it offers a rather cynical view of human nature. Along with the other stories collected in *The Lottery; or The Adventures of James Harris*, it provides evidence that Shirley Jackson was "a literary sorceress of uncanny prowess" (Orville Prescott, *N.Y. Times*). Most of her longer fiction combines an interest in abnormal mental states with a sense of the uncanny and the supernatural. After her first novel, *The Road through the Wall* (1948), a somewhat satiric account of suburban life in California, she wrote *Hangsaman* (o.p.) about a woman on the verge of mental collapse; *The Bird's Nest* (o.p.), a dramatic tale of suspense based on a real-life case study of a woman afflicted with multiple personalities; and *The Sundial* (o.p.), a story about religious zealots awaiting the end of the world. The best known of her full-length novels are

The Haunting of Hill House, which as *The Haunting* became a classic movie chiller starring Julie Harris, and *We Have Always Lived in the Castle,* a frightening psychological thriller.

The somber side of Jackson's stories and novels is balanced to some extent by the lighthearted nature of two volumes of personal memoirs. *Life among the Savages* (1953, o.p.) and *Raising Demons* (1957, o.p.) are humorous chronicles of life in an intellectual family of a small Vermont town based on Jackson's experiences as the wife of the critic Stanley Edgar Hyman and the mother of four children. She died suddenly of heart failure at age 47. Her husband edited the posthumous *Come Along with Me* (1968), which consists of three lectures on the craft of writing along with the novel she was working on at the time of her death.

BOOKS BY JACKSON

The Road through the Wall. 1948. Woodhill 2d ed. repr. 1973 pap. $1.25
The Lottery; or The Adventures of James Harris. 1949. Bentley repr. 1980 $14.00; Farrar pap. $7.95
The Haunting of Hill House. 1959. Penguin 1984 pap. $4.95; Warner Bks. 1982 pap. $2.75
We Have Always Lived in the Castle. 1962. Penguin pap. $4.95

BOOK ABOUT JACKSON

Friedman, Lenemaja. *Shirley Jackson. Twayne's U.S. Authors Ser.* G. K. Hall 1975 $12.50

JONES, JAMES. 1921–1977

With the posthumous publication of *Whistle* (o.p.), it became apparent that the main achievement of James Jones was the writing of a trilogy of novels about U.S. Army life of the World War II years that may well stand among the best war fiction of all time. The same main characters appear in *From Here to Eternity, The Thin Red Line* (1962), and *Whistle,* though their names are changed, and Jeffrey Helterman (*Dictionary of Literary Biography*) has said that Jones may well have "produced an immense, vital trilogy on men at war which should earn him the place he had always wanted—to be the Thomas Wolfe of his generation." The first novel of the trilogy, *From Here to Eternity,* which won the National Book Award, was a controversial bestseller that was made into one of the best movies of 1953. Jones's novel is a brutal, almost ugly, picture of the peacetime army in Hawaii until the attack on Pearl Harbor. *The Thin Red Line* describes the Guadalcanal campaign, while *Whistle,* which was edited by Willie Morris from a nearly completed manuscript, shows Mort Winch (the Milt Warden of *From Here to Eternity*) returning wounded to the United States with three of his men and discovering that neither the army nor their country has any significant place for them.

Jones's other fiction is considered less successful. *Some Came Running* (1957, o.p.), an autobiographical novel about a veteran who returns to Illinois to write a war novel, was condemned for its undisciplined length, verbal excesses, and naive philosophizing, while the deliberately short and much tighter *The Pistol* proved to be the first of several works in which an almost obsessive concern with heavy symbolism suggested to some readers that Jones had veered too far away from the raw naturalism of his first novel. *Go to the Widow-Maker*, about a civilian's effort to prove his masculinity and courage in skin diving and shark shooting, was generally poorly received. Jones, who had taken up the expatriate life of a writer in Paris, was on the scene at the time of the students' rebellion in 1968, and his *The Merry Month of May* is a novelized version of those events. *A Touch of Danger* (o.p.) is a straightforward thriller in the manner of the tough-guy novelists of the thirties, and his short fiction was collected in *The Ice-Cream Headache and Other Stories* (o.p.).

BOOKS BY JONES

From Here to Eternity. 1951. Avon 1979 pap. $2.75; Delacorte 1980 $14.95; Dell 1985 pap. $5.95
The Pistol. 1959. Dell 1979 pap. $2.25
The Thin Red Line. Avon 1975 pap. $2.25; Dell 1985 pap. $5.95; Scribner 1962 $20.00
Go to the Widow-Maker. 1967. Dell pap. $2.75
Whistle: Chapter One of a Work in Progress. Bruccoli 1974 $25.00; Dell 1985 pap. $5.95

BOOKS ABOUT JONES

Garrett, George. *James Jones.* Harcourt 1984 pap. $10.95
Giles, James R. *James Jones. Twayne's U.S. Authors Ser.* G. K. Hall 1981 lib. bdg. $11.50
Hopkins, John R., ed. *James Jones: A Checklist.* Intro. by James Jones, Bruccoli $18.00; Gale 1974 $35.00

KENNEDY, WILLIAM. 1928–

When *Ironweed* won both the Pulitzer Prize and the National Book Critics Circle Award in 1983, recognition came to a writer who had quietly produced a small body of significant work that Saul Bellow praised in these terms: "These Albany novels will be memorable, a distinguished group of books." The Albany Cycle, as it is now called, consists so far of three novels set in the upstate capital of New York during the 1920s and 1930s with emphasis falling on the seamy side of Albany with its crooked politicians, gangsters, gamblers, and depression-era tramps. Good as the first two novels in the cycle are, *Ironweed* is artistically a much more assured performance. A wanderer's-return sort of mellowness replaces the wisecracks and the cynical tone of *Legs* (1975) while reinforcing the human values of *Billy Phelan's Greatest Game* (1978). The progression of Kennedy's development as a writer is all the more apparent when one compares *Ironweed* with Kennedy's first novel, *The Ink Truck.* The success of the Albany Cycle encouraged Viking Press to reissue in 1984 the novel first published in 1969, and in a new author's note Kennedy conceded that the unidentified locale of this novel about a newspaper strike is indeed Albany. The *Washington Post Book World* was no doubt prescient when it called the book "a fine debut by a writer of obvious talent and much promise." Kennedy has provided his own background gloss to the cycle with *O Albany! An Urban Tapestry*. In addition to teaching at the State University of New York in Albany, Kennedy worked as a newspaperman and free-lance journalist until his recent success, and the awarding to him of a MacArthur "genius grant" enabled him to devote full time to such writing chores as the screenplay for Francis Ford Coppola's *Cotton Club* film and the continuation of the Albany Cycle. He is at work on a novel that will deal with the ancestors of some of the characters already introduced.

BOOKS BY KENNEDY

The Ink Truck. 1969. Viking 1984 $15.95
Legs. Penguin 1983 pap. $5.95; Putnam 1975 $8.95
Billy Phelan's Greatest Game. Penguin 1983 pap. $5.95; Viking 1978 $9.95
Ironweed. *Contemporary Amer. Fiction Ser.* Penguin 1984 pap. $5.95; Viking 1983 $14.95

KEROUAC, JACK. 1922–1969

Now that *On the Road* has been sanctified as a *Penguin Modern Classic* and honored by inclusion in the *Viking Critical Library*, it no longer seems quite feasible to see Jack Kerouac as merely the spokesman for the Beat Generation, a latter-day bohemian and social rebel. Kerouac coined the phrase "Beat Generation" in 1952, and several years later the *American College Dictionary* used his definition: "*Beat Generation*—members of the generation that came of age after World War II who espouse mystical detachment and relaxation of social and sexual tensions, supposedly as a result of disillusionment stemming from the cold war." But when Kerouac himself protested, "I'm king of the beats, but I'm not a beatnik," he may have wanted to disclaim responsibility for the unwashed hippies who took to the road even while he stayed at home during the late sixties and early seventies. Kerouac himself was a conservative in both politics and religion, and if he was a revolutionary at all, it was in the tradition of romantic American individualism of a Thoreauvian kind. Nonetheless, his three bestselling works—*On the Road*, *The Dharma Bums*, and *The Subterraneans*—attracted hundreds of thousands of readers and remain social documents of great historical significance as manifestos of new attitudes that profoundly affected young people throughout the Western world.

Born in Lowell, Massachusetts, of French-Canadian extraction (he was christened as Jean Louis Lebris De Kerouac), he interrupted his education at Columbia University by serving in the merchant marine during World War II and spent the postwar years roaming the United States and Mexico often in association with such other writers-to-become-famous as ALLEN GINSBERG, William Burroughs, and GARY SNYDER, as well as the almost legendary Neal Cassaday, whom he was to immortalize as the Dean Moriarty of *On the Road* and the Cody of *Visions of Cody*. Kerouac's first novel, *The Town and the City*, is a rather conventional story of family disintegration written under the influence of Thomas Wolfe, but he found his own characteristic voice in his next work. *On the Road* was the first of his books to reflect his method of "spontaneous prose." Written in 20 days on a single 120-foot roll of teletype paper, it makes use of free association in a way that Kerouac likened to improvised jazz. He saw that novel and most of his subsequent works as installments in one vast autobiographical testament, which he hoped to see eventually published in a uniform edition as *The Legend of Duluoz* with the names of the real-life models for his characters substituted for their varying fictional monikers. According to Ann Charters (*Dictionary of Literary Biography*), one can read the whole Kerouac saga in 12 stages corresponding to the chronological periods in his life.

Kerouac's first book of poetry, *Mexico City Blues* (1959), consists of 242 jazz poems on such subjects as Zen, drug addiction, and childhood, while other volumes of poetry available are *Heaven and Other Poems, Scattered Poems,* and *Scripture of Golden Eternity.* A collection of travel sketches is *Lonesome Traveler.*

BOOKS BY KEROUAC

The Town and the City. Harcourt repr. of 1950 ed. 1970 pap. $8.95
On the Road. 1957. Buccaneer Bks. 1976 lib. bdg. $17.95; New Amer. Lib. (Signet Class.) pap. $3.50; Penguin repr. of 1959 ed. 1976 pap. $4.95; ed. by Scott Donaldson, *Viking Critical Lib.* Penguin 1979 $12.95 pap. $6.95
The Subterraneans. Grove 1958 pap. $1.95; intro. by Gerald Nicosia, Grove 2d ed. 1981 pap. $3.50
The Dharma Bums. 1958. Buccaneer Bks. 1976 lib. bdg. $16.95; New Amer. Lib. (Signet Class.) pap. $2.50; Penguin 1971 pap. $5.95
Doctor Sax. 1959. Buccaneer Bks. 1976 lib. bdg. $16.95
The Book of Dreams. City Lights 1961 pap. $4.00
Visions of Gerard. McGraw-Hill Pap. repr. of 1963 ed. 1976 pap. $4.95
Satori in Paris. Grove 1966 pap. $2.25
Pic. Grove (Everyman's) 1971 pap. $4.95. Story about a black baseball player.
Visions of Cody. 1972. *McGraw-Hill Pap.* 1974 pap. $6.95
Maggie Cassidy. McGraw-Hill 1978 pap. $4.95
Tristessa. McGraw-Hill Pap. 1978 pap. $4.95
Big Sur. McGraw-Hill Pap. 1981 pap. $5.95

BOOKS ABOUT KEROUAC

Challis, Chris. *Quest for Kerouac.* Faber 1984 pap. $7.95. A Britisher retraces Kerouac's paths across the United States.
Charters, Ann. *Jack Kerouac.* Phoenix Bk. Shop 2d ed. rev. 1975 $10.00
Clark, Tom. *Jack Kerouac.* Harcourt 1984 $22.95 pap. $10.95
Gifford, Barry, and Lawrence Lee. *Jack's Book: An Oral Biography of Jack Kerouac.* Penguin 1979 pap. $5.95; St. Martin's 1978 $10.95
Hipkiss, Robert A. *Jack Kerouac, Prophet of the New Romanticism: A Critical Study of the Published Works of Kerouac and a Comparison of Them to Those of J. D. Salinger, James Purdy, John Knowles and Ken Kesey.* Univ. Pr. of Kansas 1976 $17.95
Hunt, Tim. *Kerouac's Crooked Road: The Development of a Fiction.* Shoe String (Archon) 1981 $19.50
Jarvis, Charles E. *Visions of Kerouac: The Life of Jack Kerouac.* Ithaca Pr. 1975 pap. $4.95

McNally, D. *Desolate Angel: Jack Kerouac, the Beat Generation and America.* McGraw-Hill 1980 pap. $6.95

Milewski, Robert J., and others. *Jack Kerouac: An Annotated Bibliography of Secondary Sources, 1944–1979. Author Bibliographies Ser.* Scarecrow Pr. 1981 $15.00

Nicosia, Gerald. *Memory Babe: A Critical Biography of Jack Kerouac.* Ed. by Fred Jordan, Grove 1983 $22.50 1984 pap. $9.95

KESEY, KEN. 1935–

Born in Colorado, graduated from the University of Oregon, and since then a sometimes vagabond resident of the West Coast, Kesey has published only two full-length novels, but they have helped to give him a cult following. *One Flew over the Cuckoo's Nest* (1962) owes much to Kesey's own experience as a ward attendant in a mental hospital. This exciting first novel is told from the point of view of a half-breed who thinks of himself as the Big Chief pictured on the writing tablets of everybody's school days looking out at the other inmates in a Disneylike world.

Sometimes a Great Notion is a long, complex novel that troubled many of the readers of Kesey's first novel, for although this story of a lumbering family dynasty in the Northwest exalts the romantic values of nature and emotion over the feeble representatives of the establishment represented in the story, it also seems to champion strong, arrogant individualism against anything that smacks of conformity or easy concessions to group approval. The Ken Kesey who wrote *Sometimes a Great Notion* would not have been likely to attend the festivities at Woodstock. Yet, after publishing that daring and misunderstood novel, Kesey publicly renounced "literature" for "life" and allowed himself to become a cult hero for the commune-and-candlestick generation. Married and the father of four children, he has served as a kind of guru for an Oregon commune during the period since his second novel was published. Although he has thrown out hints that he may have written fiction under a pseudonym, his only books of record in recent years are *Kesey's Garage Sale*, a hodgepodge of survival-kit materials, which seems to have been derived from his many contributions to the last supplement of *The Whole Earth Catalog*, and *Kesey*, a collection of miscellaneous writings by Kesey, edited by Michael Strelow along with biographical and critical material by MALCOLM COWLEY and John Clark Pratt.

BOOKS BY KESEY

One Flew over the Cuckoo's Nest. New Amer. Lib. (Signet Class.) 1975 pap. $2.95; Penguin repr. of 1962 ed. 1976 pap. $3.95; ed. by John Clark Pratt, *Viking Critical Lib.* Penguin 1977 pap. $8.95; Viking 1962 $12.95

Sometimes a Great Notion. 1964. Bantam 1976 pap. $3.95; Penguin 1977 pap. $7.50

BOOKS ABOUT KESEY

Leeds, Barry H. *Ken Kesey. Lit. and Life Ser.* Ungar 1981 $12.95 pap. $6.95

Porter, M. Gilbert. *The Art of Grit: Ken Kesey's Fiction. Literary Frontiers Ser.* Univ. of Missouri Pr. 1982 pap. $8.00

Tanner, Stephen L. *Ken Kesey. Twayne's U.S. Authors Ser.* G. K. Hall 1983 lib. bdg. $14.50

KOSINSKI, JERZY. 1933–

Jerzy Kosinski, whose *Steps* won the National Book Award for fiction in 1968, grew up in Poland but emigrated to the United States in 1957 and became a naturalized citizen in 1965. His first two novels are set in Europe—not merely geographically, but in the wider, universal sense that makes the settings of works by Europeans. *The Painted Bird* is the story of a young boy wandering through Eastern Europe during the years of World War II. Looking on scenes of devastation and violence, the mute young observer somehow conveys a sense of mingled horror and compassion for the human condition. *Steps* presents even more neutralized vignettes of abuse, rape, and mutilation, but it achieves a kind of poetic grandeur in its unstated assumption that it is better to see horror than to see nothing at all. A novel without conventional narration, point of view, or dialogue, it harks back to works like Djuna Barnes's *Nightwood* in its surrealistic view of human bestiality, but it offers hope nonetheless if only in its demonstration that destruction must precede creation.

In the works after *Steps* Kosinski has sometimes succeeded in combining experimental techniques with popular appeal. Kosinski's name stayed prominently before the public when he was made the target of a *Village Voice* exposé in 1982, which accused him of being a CIA agent and writing his books with unacknowledged collaboration from paid helpers. Those charges have been more or less satisfactorily refuted, but not without apparent damage to Kosinski's reputation. Even before the furor caused by the *Voice* piece and reactions to it elsewhere in the media, *Pinball* (1982), like the novel before it, *Passion Play* (o.p.), had received a largely negative response from critics. Presumably a fair assessment of Kosinski cannot be made until the critical climate has time to cool, but if the promise that seemed to be offered by *The Painted Bird* and *Steps* turns out to be largely unfulfilled, the genuine merit of those first two novels is not likely to be seriously challenged. Kosinski is an author with a distinctive voice of his own that nonetheless seems to echo some main currents of international modernism.

BOOKS BY KOSINSKI

The Painted Bird. 1965. Bantam 1972 pap. $3.95; Houghton Mifflin 2d ed. 1976 o.p.; Modern Lib. 2d ed. repr. 1982 $6.95
Steps. Bantam repr. 1969 pap. o.p.; Modern Lib. 1968 $7.95
Being There. 1971. Bantam 1980 pap. $3.50
The Devil Tree. Bantam repr. of 1973 ed. 1974 pap. o.p.; Harcourt 1973 o.p.; St. Martin's rev. ed. 1981 o.p.
Cockpit. Bantam 1976 pap. o.p.; Houghton Mifflin 1975 o.p.
Blind Date. Bantam repr. 1978 pap. o.p.; Houghton Mifflin 1977 o.p.
Pinball. 1982. Bantam 1983 pap. $4.50

BOOKS ABOUT KOSINSKI

Bruss, Paul. *Victims: Textual Strategies in Recent American Fiction*. Bucknell Univ. Pr. 1981 $25.00
Lavers, Norman. *Jerzy Kosinski. Twayne's U.S. Authors Ser.* G. K. Hall 1982 $12.50

LARDNER, RING. 1885–1933

In the literary history of America from Huck Finn to Nick Adams and Holden Caulfield, Ring Lardner occupies an important place. He was for many years a sports reporter in Chicago who wrote in a distinctive style that was known as Lardner's Ringlish. Young Hemingway, growing up in nearby Oak Park, greatly admired Lardner's work, and later fiction about sports by such writers as Mark Harris and Dan Jenkins might never have been written if the imaginary letters that Lardner composed for a brash and uneducated bush-league baseball player named Jack Keefe had not made *You Know Me, Al* an American classic of its kind. Lardner's most famous short story is "Haircut," a frequently anthologized tale in which an ignorant and naive barber tells a horror story as if it were funny. There is a repetitious quality about Lardner's later work as he fell increasingly under "the spell of the misspelled" and "the lure of the illiterate," but in the comic tradition of American fiction he has long been assured a permanent niche.

BOOKS BY LARDNER

The Ring Lardner Reader. Ed. by Maxwell Geismar, Scribner 1963 $26.00. Geismar's introduction enhances the value of this standard collection of Lardner's writings.
The Best Short Stories of Ring Lardner. 1938. Scribner repr. 1957 $22.50 pap. $7.95
Haircut and Other Stories. 1922. Random (Vintage) 1984 pap. $5.95
Ring Lardner's "You Know Me, Al": The Comic Strip Adventures of Jack Keefe. Amereon repr. of 1914 ed. lib. bdg. $10.60; Harcourt 1979 pap. $6.95; Random (Vintage) 1984 pap. $5.95; Scribner repr. of 1914 ed. 1960 pap. $17.50
The Story of a Wonder Man: Being the Autobiography of Ring Lardner. Ill. by Margaret Freeman, Greenwood repr. of 1927 ed. 1975 lib. bdg. $22.50
Some Champions: Previously Uncollected Autobiographical Sketches and Fiction. Ed. by Richard Layman, Scribner 1976 pap. $3.95

BOOKS ABOUT LARDNER

Bruccoli, Matthew J., and Richard Layman. *Ring W. Lardner: A Descriptive Bibliography.* Univ. of Pittsburgh Pr. 1976 $48.00
Evans, Elizabeth. *Ring Lardner. Lit. and Life Ser.* Ungar 1980 $12.95
Patrick, Walton R. *Ring Lardner. Twayne's U.S. Authors Ser.* New College & Univ. Pr. 1963 pap. $5.95
Yardley, Jonathan. *Ring: A Biography of Ring Lardner.* Atheneum 1984 pap. $13.95

LEWIS, SINCLAIR. 1885–1951 (NOBEL PRIZE 1930)

The first American to win the Nobel Prize for literature, Sinclair Lewis was a busy and popular writer whose novels chronicle the social history of his time and constitute what Maxwell Geismar called "a remarkable diary of the middle class mind in America." Before he was honored with the Nobel Prize, he published a group of novels that realistically depicted various levels of American life. *Main Street* (1920), his first important novel, is a pitying picture of provincialism in the small town of Gopher Prairie, Minnesota, which Lewis modeled on his hometown of Sauk Centre, while *Babbitt* (1922), a moving account of midlife crisis experienced by an average American businessman, actually succeeded in adding a new word to the American dictionary. Continuing a blend of social criticism with sympathy, Lewis wrote *Arrowsmith* (1925), in which the idealism of a devoted scientist and physician is contrasted with the materialistic forces that try to capitalize on his discoveries. *Elmer Gantry* (1927) is a portrait of a dissolute but successful evangelist, while *Dodsworth* (1929) deals with a retired industrialist whose material success and the burden of an ambitious wife have failed to provide emotional sustenance. Lewis succeeded in bringing to life the talk and actions common to the middle classes of America. Although some of the conditions he describes now seem peculiarly dated, his people remain convincingly real.

Lewis's sense of responsibility to society seemed to become all the stronger after his Nobel Prize, and some of the books he wrote afterward have topical subjects that now seem rather dated. *It Can't Happen Here* (1935) forecast an imaginary coming of fascism to the United States, *Gideon Planish* exposed corruption in organized philanthropy, *Kingsblood Royal* (1947, o.p.) was one of the first novels to deal with the evils of racial prejudice, and *Cass Timberlane*, which was originally subtitled *A Novel of Husbands and Wives*, gave a long, clear look at the institution of marriage in its story of a Minnesota judge and his young second wife.

If American novelists of this century can be divided into opposing camps of social historians and literary artists, Lewis clearly belongs to the former group. As a result he has seemed to fade further into the past as writer after writer has taken his place as an authoritative observer of the times. It is ironic that no sooner had Mark Schorer's admirable *Sinclair Lewis: An American Life* appeared than interest in its subject seemed to decline drastically.

BOOKS BY LEWIS

Free Air. 1912. Arden Lib. repr. of 1919 ed. 1980 lib. bdg. $35.00; Scholarly repr. of 1919 ed. 1971 $49.00

Main Street. 1920. Buccaneer Bks. repr. 1984 lib. bdg. $18.95; *Modern Class. Ser.* Harcourt 1950 $14.95; New Amer. Lib. (Signet Class.) 1974 pap. $3.95

Babbitt. 1922. *Modern Class. Ser.* Harcourt 1949 $14.95; New Amer. Lib. (Signet Class.) pap. $3.50

Arrowsmith. 1925. Buccaneer Bks. repr. 1982 lib. bdg. $17.95; New Amer. Lib. (Signet Class.) pap. $3.95

Elmer Gantry. 1927. New Amer. Lib. (Signet Class.) 1971 pap. $2.95

Man Who Knew Coolidge: Being the Soul of Lowell Schmaltz, Constructive and Nordic Citizen. Short Story Index Repr. Ser. Ayer repr. of 1928 ed. $20.00

Dodsworth. 1929. New Amer. Lib. (Signet Class.) 1971 pap. $3.50

Ann Vickers. AMS Pr. repr. of 1933 ed. $44.50

Work of Art. AMS Pr. repr. of 1934 ed. $37.50

It Can't Happen Here: A Novel. AMS Pr. repr. of 1935 ed. $38.00

Gideon Planish. 1943. Woodhill 1974 pap. $1.95

Cass Timberlane. 1945. Buccaneer Bks. repr. 1982 lib. bdg. $18.95; Woodhill 1974 pap. $1.95

The God-Seeker. 1949. Woodhill 1975 pap. $1.95
World So Wide. 1950. Woodhill 1974 pap. $1.75

BOOKS ABOUT LEWIS

Fleming, Robert E., and Esther Fleming. *Sinclair Lewis: A Reference Guide.* G. K.
    Hall 1980 lib. bdg. $21.00
Grebstein, Sheldon N. *Sinclair Lewis. Twayne's U.S. Authors Ser.* G. K. Hall lib. bdg.
    $12.50; *Twayne's U.S. Authors Ser.* New College & Univ. Pr. 1962 pap. $5.95
Light, Martin. *The Quixotic Vision of Sinclair Lewis.* Purdue Univ. Pr. 1975 $6.50
Lundquist, James. *Sinclair Lewis. Lit. and Life Ser.* Ungar 1973 $12.95
Schorer, Mark. *Sinclair Lewis: An American Life. Pamphlets on Amer. Writers Ser.*
    Univ. of Minnesota Pr. 1963 pap. $1.25

LONDON, JACK. 1876–1916

Jack London died in his prime, having accomplished an enormous volume of work. He owed his first great success to dog stories: *The Call of the
Wild* (1903) is a study of reversion to type, the domesticated dog returning
to the wild after performing heroic deeds in man's corrupted world, while
White Fang reverses that situation by showing the wild dog tamed by kindness. *The Sea Wolf* is the best known of London's other adventure stories,
the exciting tale of the maddest captain in American sea fiction between
HERMAN MELVILLE's Ahab and Herman Wouk's Queeg. The autobiographical
Martin Eden stands up as one of the better bildungsroman written at a time
when many such self-portraits were being produced, and *The Iron Heel*
(1907) remains a vivid novel of social prophecy in which London anticipates
the threat of fascism. Of London's many excellent short stories, the often anthologized "To Light a Fire" is now considered a genuine classic of literary
naturalism.

In *On Native Grounds*, ALFRED KAZIN writes: "The clue to Jack London's
work is certainly to be found in his own turbulent life. . . . The greatest
story he ever wrote was the story he lived . . . ." He had become an ardent
socialist when, in his oyster pirate days in San Francisco, he read the *Communist Manifesto.* The radical undertone of his work in part accounts for his
continuing popularity in Eastern Europe, but only his undoubted skill as a
writer and a craftsman of fiction can explain why his stock seems to have
risen throughout the world in recent years. Critical appreciations appear
with increasing regularity, and he continues to be read widely. Students of
American literature who want to read only the best and most representative
of his literary fiction will find that they cannot do better than to read
through the two volumes in the Library of America series edited by Donald
Pizer.

BOOKS BY LONDON

Novels and Social Writings. Ed. by Donald Pizer, Literary Class. (Lib. of Amer.) 1982
    $27.50
Novels and Stories: The Call of the Wild; White Fang; The Sea-Wolf; Short Stories. Ed.
    by Donald Pizer, Literary Class. (Lib. of Amer.) 1982 $27.50
Best Short Stories of Jack London. 1953. Fawcett 1978 pap. $2.25

Great Short Works of Jack London: Call of the Wild, White Fang and Six Stories. Ed. by
   Earle Labor, Harper pap. $2.84
The Call of the Wild, White Fang and Other Stories. Ed. by Andrew Sinclair, intro. by
   James Dickey, *Penguin Amer. Lib. Ser.* 1981 pap. $2.95
The Call of the Wild and White Fang. Bantam Class. Ser. 1981 pap. $1.75; Washington
   Square Pr. pap. $2.95
The Call of the Wild. 1903. Buccaneer Bks. repr. 1983 lib. bdg. $17.95
The Sea Wolf. 1904. *Bantam Class. Ser.* 1981 pap. $1.75
White Fang. 1906. Ed. by Naunerle Farr, ill. by Fred Carrillo, Pendulum Pr. text ed.
   abr. ed. 1977 $5.00 pap. $1.95; ed. by Andrew Sinclair, *Penguin Amer. Lib. Ser.*
   1984 pap. $4.95
Martin Eden. 1909. *Airmont Class. Ser.* 1969 pap. $2.50

BOOKS ABOUT LONDON

Beauchamp, Gorman. *Reader's Guide to Jack London.* Ed. by Roger C. Schlobin, Star-
   mont House 1984 $13.95 text ed. pap. $5.95
Hedrick, Joan D. *Solitary Comrade: Jack London and His Work.* Univ. of North Caro-
   lina Pr. 1982 $21.00
Johnston, Carolyn. *Jack London: American Radical.* Greenwood repr. 1984 $29.95
Labor, Earle. *Jack London. Twayne's U.S. Authors Ser.* G. K. Hall 1974 lib. bdg.
   $12.50
Martin, Stoddard. *California Writers: Jack London, John Steinbeck, the Tough Guys.*
   St. Martin's 1984 $22.50
Perry, John. *Jack London: An American Myth.* Nelson-Hall text ed. 1981 $23.95 pap.
   $11.95
Sinclair, Andrew. *Jack: A Biography of Jack London.* Harper 1977 $12.95; Washing-
   ton Square Pr. 1983 pap. $4.95
Sisson, James E., and Robert W. Martens. *Jack London First Editions.* Star Rover
   1978 $39.50
Stone, Irving. *Jack London: Sailor on Horseback.* 1947. Doubleday 1978 $12.95
Tavernier-Courbin, Jacqueline. *Critical Essays on Jack London. Critical Essays on
   Amer. Lit. Ser.* G. K. Hall 1983 lib. bdg. $31.50
Walcutt, Charles C. *Jack London. Pamphlets on Amer. Writers Ser.* Univ. of Minnesota
   Pr. 1966 pap. $1.25
Walker, Dale L., comp. *The Fiction of Jack London: A Chronological Bibliography.*
   Texas Western Pr. 1972 $10.00
Walker, Franklin. *Jack London and the Klondike: The Genesis of an American Writer.*
   Huntington Lib. repr. of 1966 ed. 1978 pap. $5.00
Watson, Charles N., Jr. *The Novels of Jack London: A Reappraisal.* Univ. of Wisconsin
   Pr. 1983 $19.95
Woodbridge, H. C. *Jack London: A Bibliography.* Kraus rev. & enl. ed. 1973 $40.00

MAILER, NORMAN. 1923–

   Norman Mailer has been very much in the public eye ever since his first
novel, *The Naked and the Dead*, was a bestseller of 1948 that seemed to
many readers the best novel likely to come out of World War II. Prior to
bursting on the literary scene, Mailer had combined a Brooklyn childhood,
a Harvard education, and a two-year stint in the army to form an unusual
background that gave him several divergent angles from which to view the
world around him, and in the years since, he has increasingly placed him-

self within the history that he has recorded. As a result, it has become more and more difficult to separate his fiction from his nonfiction, and although he has never succeeded in being a true member of the avant-garde, he has usually managed to be just a step or two behind the first troops to enter conquered territories.

After *The Barbary Shore* (1951) and *The Deer Park* (1955), two fairly short novels of contemporary life, the turning point in Mailer's career came with *Advertisements for Myself* in 1959. In that bulky work he reprinted practically everything he had written. He has gone on to write works of semipure fiction such as the traumatic *An American Dream* (1966, o.p.), the long-awaited historical novel *Ancient Evenings*, and the ersatz thriller *Tough Guys Don't Dance*, but he has seemed at his best in crossover books like *Why Are We in Vietnam?* and *The Executioner's Song*. The former is generally thought to be Mailer's best novel after *The Naked and the Dead*, but it is as social commentary that the book made its chief impact. Called by its author a true life novel, *The Executioner's Song* recounts vividly the last year in the life of the murderer Gary Gilmore before his execution. In subject and technique it is a book much like Truman Capote's *In Cold Blood*, and it is to Mailer's credit that his intense and panoramic work does not suffer by comparison with Capote's.

Beginning with *The Armies of the Night: History as a Novel, the Novel as History* (1968), a book published the same year he ran unsuccessfully for mayor of New York City, Mailer has turned his considerable talents to his own particular brand of the New Journalism. Mailer has not been content to investigate the events of his time from the point of view of a detached observer. Instead, he has placed himself squarely in the center of the history he has traced. Books like *Some Honorable Men, The Fight*, and *Of a Fire on the Moon* (1971) are examples of what Richard Poirier calls narrative-journals, in which Mailer described his own less than detached presence at national political conventions, the heavyweight fight between Muhammad Ali and George Foreman, and U.S. Space Program preparations at Cape Canaveral. With *The Prisoner of Sex* (1971), he almost singlehandedly manned the bulwarks against the first fierce onslaught of the New Feminists. Providing a counterpart to the earlier summation of *Advertisements for Myself* is *Pieces and Pontifications*, the first half of which consists of previously uncollected articles and reflections, while *Pontifications* brings together 20 interviews with Mailer in which he expresses views on practically everything.

BOOKS BY MAILER

The Short Fiction of Norman Mailer. Fertig repr. of 1967 ed. 1980 $25.00; Pinnacle Bks. 1981 pap. $3.50
A Transit to Narcissus: A Facsimile of the Original Typescript. Fertig 1978 $39.50. Previously unpublished apprentice work.
The Naked and the Dead. 1948. Holt 1976 $16.95; Holt (Owl Bks.) 1980 pap. $7.95; New Amer. Lib. (Signet Class.) 1971 pap. $3.50
The Barbary Shore. Fertig repr. of 1951 ed. 1980 $25.00
The Deer Park. Fertig repr. of 1955 ed. 1980 $25.00; Putnam (Perigee) 1981 pap. $5.95

Advertisements for Myself. 1959. Putnam (Perigee) 1981 pap. $6.95
Why Are We in Vietnam? A Novel. 1967. Holt (Owl Bks.) 1982 pap. $6.25
The Executioner's Song. Little, Brown 1979 $19.45; Warner Bks. 1984 pap. $4.95
Ancient Evenings. Little, Brown 1983 $19.45; Warner Bks. 1984 pap. $4.95
Tough Guys Don't Dance. Ballantine 1985 pap. $3.95; Random 1984 $16.95
Pieces and Pontifications. Little, Brown 1982 $20.00

BOOKS ABOUT MAILER

Adams, Laura. *Existential Battles: The Growth of Norman Mailer.* Ohio Univ. Pr. 1976 $16.95 pap. $7.95

Bailey, Jennifer. *Norman Mailer: Quick Change Artist.* Barnes & Noble text ed. 1980 $27.50

Begiebing, Robert J. *Acts of Regeneration: Allegory and Archetype in the Works of Norman Mailer.* Univ. of Missouri Pr. 1980 $20.00

Braudy, Leo, ed. *Norman Mailer: A Collection of Critical Essays.* Prentice-Hall (Spectrum Books) 1972 pap. $1.95

Bufithis, Philip H. *Norman Mailer. Lit. and Life Ser.* Ungar 1978 $12.95 pap. $6.95

Ehrlich, Robert. *Norman Mailer: The Radical as Hipster.* Scarecrow Pr. 1978 lib. bdg. $15.00

Gordon, Andrew M. *An American Dreamer: A Psychoanalytic Study of the Fiction of Norman Mailer.* Fairleigh Dickinson Univ. Pr. 1980 $22.50

Manso, Peter. *Mailer: His Life and Times.* 1984. Simon & Schuster 1985 $19.95

Merrill, Robert. *Norman Mailer. Twayne's U.S. Authors Ser.* G. K. Hall 1978 $13.50

Mills, Hilary. *Mailer: A Biography.* Empire Bks. 1982 $14.95. "The fast-paced reportage in this highly readable book is appropriate to its subject" (*Journal of Modern Lit.*).

Poirier, Richard. *Norman Mailer.* Ed. by Frank Kermode, *Modern Masters Ser.* Viking 1972 $9.95

Sokoloff, B. A. *Norman Mailer: A Comprehensive Bibliography.* 1972. Folcroft text ed. 1975 $24.50

MALAMUD, BERNARD. 1914–1986

With the exception of *The Natural,* almost all of Bernard Malamud's works of fiction deal with Jewish characters, "because," he said, "I know them. But more important I write about them because the Jews are absolutely the very *stuff* of drama." Born in Brooklyn of immigrant parents, he was graduated from City College of New York and received his M.A. in English from Columbia. Beginning in 1949 he taught for 12 years at Oregon State University while he wrote his first four books, including *A New Life* (1961), the sometimes black-humored account of a Jewish intellectual from New York who accepts a teaching appointment in the Northwest. Partly because his lack of a Ph.D. prevented him from teaching advanced literature courses at Oregon State in spite of his growing literary fame, he left Corvallis in 1961 to accept an appointment at Bennington College in Vermont, where he taught until retirement. He served as a visiting lecturer at Harvard from 1966 to 1968 and was elected a member of the National Institute of Arts and Letters in 1964.

Interest in his first novel, *The Natural,* was revived in 1983 when a movie starring Robert Redford brought dramatically to life the highly symbolic story of baseball player Roy Hobbs and his homemade bat Wonderboy. *The Assistant* (1957), much of which takes place in a grocery store owned by a poor Jew named Morris Bober, also makes use of mythical themes, as does *The Fixer* (1966), which Malamud based on the case of a worker in a Kiev brickyard who was arrested in 1911 for the ritual murder of a Christian boy. *The Fixer* had the unusual distinction of winning both the National Book Award for fiction and the Pulitzer Prize. It was Malamud's second National Book Award, for *The Magic Barrel* (1958), his first collection of short stories, was also granted that recognition.

In his later novels Malamud had been concerned with the relation of art to life and love. Whereas the tone of *Pictures of Fidelman*, a loosely constructed gathering of episodes in the life of an unsuccessful painter, is largely comic and satiric, *The Tenants* marks a return to the profound compassion found in works like *The Assistant* and *The Fixer*. *Dubin's Lives* is a novel about an aging biographer who lives in New England and finds himself challenged to live passionately when he starts to write a book about D. H. LAWRENCE. Dubin's affair with a young woman is marked by comic misadventure, much more characteristic of Malamud's novels than Lawrence's, but there is a tone of mellow compassion in the book that keeps it from seeming to be a satire on the male climacteric. Malamud's last novel, *God's Grace*, is a fantasy on the last-survivor theme. Alan Lelchuk (*N.Y. Times Bk. Review*) called it "a fable by turns charming and foolish, topical and far-fetched, provocative and innocent."

BOOKS BY MALAMUD

The Stories of Bernard Malamud. 1983. New Amer. Lib. (Plume) 1984 pap. $7.95

A Malamud Reader. Farrar 1967 pap. $9.95. Includes *The Assistant;* ten stories from *The Magic Barrel* and *Idiots First;* excerpts from *The Natural, A New Life*, and *The Fixer*.

The Natural. 1953. Avon 1980 pap. $3.50; Farrar 1961 $13.95 pap. $6.25; Pocket Bks. pap. $2.25

The Assistant. Avon 1980 pap. $3.95; Farrar 1957 $12.95 pap. $4.95

The Magic Barrel. Avon 1980 pap. $2.95; Farrar 1958 $14.95 pap. $6.25; Pocket Bks. repr. 1972 pap. $1.95

A New Life. Avon 1980 pap. $2.95; Farrar 1961 $15.00

Idiots First. Farrar 1963 $10.95; Pocket Bks. 1975 pap. $1.75

The Fixer. Farrar 1966 $17.50 pap. $7.95; Pocket Bks. 1982 pap. $3.95; Washington Square Pr. 1976 pap. $2.95

Pictures of Fidelman: An Exhibition. Farrar 1969 $9.95; Pocket Bks. 1975 pap. $1.75

The Tenants. Avon 1981 pap. $2.95; Farrar 1971 $10.00; Pocket Bks. pap. $1.95

Rembrandt's Hat. 1971. Farrar 1973 $11.95; Pocket Bks. 1974 pap. $1.50

Dubin's Lives. Avon 1979 pap. $2.50; Farrar 1979 $10.00

God's Grace. Avon 1983 pap. $3.95; Farrar 1982 $13.50

BOOKS ABOUT MALAMUD

Alter, Iska. *The Good Man's Dilemma: Social Criticism in the Fiction of Bernard Malamud. Studies in Modern Lit.* AMS Pr. 1981 $29.50

Astro, Richard, and Jackson J. Benson. *The Fiction of Bernard Malamud*. Oregon State Univ. Pr. 1977 $12.00

Avery, Evelyn. *Victims: The Fiction of Richard Wright and Bernard Malamud*. Kennikat 1979 $12.00
Field, Leslie A., and Joyce W. Field, eds. *Bernard Malamud and His Critics*. New York Univ. Pr. 1970 $20.00 pap. $10.00
Hershinow, Sheldon J. *Bernard Malamud. Lit. and Life Ser.* Ungar 1980 $12.95 1984 pap. $7.95
Kosofsky, Rita N. *Bernard Malamud: An Annotated Checklist*. Kent State Univ. Pr. 1969 $10.00
Richman, Sidney. *Bernard Malamud. Twayne's U.S. Authors Ser.* G. K. Hall 1966 lib. bdg. $12.50; *Twayne's U.S. Authors Ser.* New College & Univ. Pr. 1966 pap. $3.45

McCARTHY, MARY. 1912–

Before *Cannibals and Missionaries* was published in 1979, Mary McCarthy announced that it would be her last novel. Appropriately that last novel raises serious questions about the value of art in a world full of social injustice, for when one looks back on McCarthy's career as a writer of fiction no theme seems more dominant than the conflict between aesthetics and morals. After a promising first novel, *The Company She Keeps*, and a short *conte philosophique* called *The Oasis* (1949), she brought together some of the stories she had written for literary magazines. Her next book, *The Groves of Academe*, is an effective satire about the crisis of hypocrisy brought about in a typical American college in New England by the pressures of the Senator McCarthy era. *A Charmed Life* deals with an intellectual woman at odds with herself and seems to look back obliquely on McCarthy's failed marriage with Edmund Wilson. *The Group* (1963), which became a bestseller almost immediately, tells of eight Vassar girls, class of 1933, and the seven eventful years that followed their commencement. *Birds of America* (1971), the story of a sensitive young man and his harpsichordist mother in a world they never made, caused Helen Vendler to write that "Mary McCarthy, for all her cold eye and fine prose, is an essayist, not a novelist. But then, if we can have nonfiction novels, why not a new McCarthy genre, the fictional essay? It is not an unworthy form, taken for what it is" (*N.Y. Times*).

Nonetheless, some readers continue to feel that McCarthy's best writing is her nonfiction. The best of her literary criticism appears in *The Writing on the Wall and Other Literary Essays* and *Ideas and the Novel*. *On the Contrary* is a collection of articles on politics and the social scene, women, and literature and the arts. Her art-history-travel books, *Venice Observed* (1956) and *The Stones of Florence* (1959), are notable for their combining sharp observation with personal intensity.

BOOKS BY McCARTHY

The Company She Keeps. 1942. Avon 1981 pap. $3.50; Harcourt 1967 pap. $5.95
The Oasis. 1949. Avon 1981 pap. $2.25
Cast a Cold Eye. Harcourt 1950 $12.95
The Groves of Academe. Avon 1981 pap. $2.95; Harcourt 1952 $9.50; New Amer. Lib. (Plume) pap. $3.95
A Charmed Life. Avon 1981 pap. $2.95; Harcourt 1955 $15.95; New Amer. Lib. (Plume) pap. $3.95

The Group. Avon 1980 pap. $3.95; Harcourt 1963 $8.50; New Amer. Lib. (Signet
   Class.) 1972 pap. $1.95
Birds of America. Avon 1981 pap. $3.95; Harcourt 1971 $11.95; New Amer. Lib. (Sig-
   net Class.) 1972 pap. $1.50
Cannibals and Missionaries. Avon 1980 pap. $2.75; Harcourt 1979 $10.95
The Hounds of Summer and Other Stories. Avon 1981 pap. $3.50. Two previously un-
   collected stories in addition to some from *Cast a Cold Eye.*

BOOKS ABOUT MCCARTHY

McKenzie, Barbara. *Mary McCarthy. Twayne's U.S. Authors Ser.* G. K. Hall $12.95;
   Twayne's U.S. Authors Ser. New College & Univ. Pr. 1966 pap. $5.95
Stock, Irvin. *Mary McCarthy. Pamphlets on Amer. Writers Ser.* Univ. of Minnesota Pr.
   1968 pap. $1.25

McCULLERS, CARSON. 1917–1967

Born in Columbus, Georgia, where she finished high school at a very early
age, McCullers began to write seriously from age 16. She ventured to New
York in 1934 and studied at intervals at Columbia and New York universities, while beginning a literary career that saw her first short stories accepted by *Story*. *The Heart Is a Lonely Hunter* (1940), her first novel, is the
story of a deaf-mute to whom secrets are confided by a number of sharply
drawn characters. Richard Wright wrote of "the astonishing humanity that
enabled a white writer, for the first time in Southern fiction, to handle Negro characters with as much ease and justice as those of her own race." The
domestic tragedy of an army officer in a southern camp in peacetime is the
main subject of *Reflections in a Golden Eye* (1941, o.p.), but again it is a gallery of supporting characters that stands out as the trademark of her distinctive art. *The Member of the Wedding* (1946) is a psychological study of a 12-
year-old girl. Her second play, *The Square Root of Wonderful* (1958), was not
as well received, and when her novella *The Ballad of the Sad Cafe* (1951) was
adapted by Edward Albee (1963) and produced on Broadway, the *N.Y.
Times* felt that a prose poem that seemed strangely tender had been transformed into "a play flecked with weird, halting poetry." *Clock without
Hands* (1961, o.p.) is a perceptive and poignant study of the change in southern mores brought about by the 1954 Supreme Court decision declaring public school segregation unconstitutional. McCullers suffered a series of debilitating strokes that made her last years a constant agony and cut short pre-
maturely a career that seemed about to break through to the higher ranks
of international fame. French and British critics in particular found her
work close to Faulkner's in quality and tone.

BOOKS BY MCCULLERS

The Ballad of the Sad Cafe and Other Stories. Bantam 1967 pap. $2.95
The Heart Is a Lonely Hunter. Houghton Mifflin 1940 $13.95
The Member of the Wedding. Houghton Mifflin 1946 $15.95; New Directions 1963
   pap. $4.95

MILLER, HENRY. 1891–1980

The apparent heir of D. H. Lawrence in championing the natural in man and hailed by Norman Mailer as one of the most vital writers of the century, Henry Miller had some 30 years of underground fame before Grove Press in 1961 successfully fought off the censors and published *Tropic of Cancer*—the first volume in the trilogy for which he is best known—for the first time legally in the United States.

Born and raised in New York City, the young Miller worked at various menial jobs before going to Paris as a nearly penniless and unproven writer. Because of his choice of subjects and the frankness of his treatment, his early picaresque novels were published only in Paris, although several of them were read in the United States in smuggled copies. *The Cosmological Eye* (1939), a collection of stories, essays, and other prose pieces that defies conventional classification, was the first book that an American publisher dared to publish, and Laughlin's New Directions went on to bring out such similar volumes as *The Wisdom of the Heart, Sunday after the War* (o.p.), *The Air-Conditioned Nightmare* (1945–47), *Remember to Remember*, and *Stand Still Like the Hummingbird*.

The Rosy Crucifixion, the collective title for the novels *Sexus* (1949), *Plexus* (1953), and *Nexus* (1960), is his second major trilogy. These provide yet more fictional autobiography covering, in his usual ribald fashion, the years of his "crucifixion" in the United States before he went to France.

Miller's busy writing hand and the complicated publication history of his works make it difficult to establish a canon of his writings, but among books currently in print are three installments of *Book of Friends: A Tribute to Friends of Long Ago;* literary criticism such as *Henry Miller on Writing, Books in My Life, Time of the Assassins: A Study of Rimbaud*, and *The World of Lawrence: A Passionate Appreciation;* books about places such as Greece in *The Colossus of Maroussi, Big Sur and the Oranges of Hieronymus Bosch* (1957), *Quiet Days in Clichy*, and *Under the Roofs of Paris. Just Wild about Harry* is a play, and some of Miller's work as a watercolor artist is available in *The Paintings of Henry Miller*.

BOOKS BY MILLER

The Henry Miller Reader. Ed. by Lawrence Durrell, New Directions repr. of 1959 ed. 1969 pap. $8.95

The Henry Miller Trilogy: Tropic of Cancer; Tropic of Capricorn; and Black Spring. Grove 3 vols. 1963 $9.95

The Rosy Crucifixion: Sexus, Plexus, and Nexus. Grove 3 vols. 1980 $12.85

Collector's Quest: The Correspondence of Henry Miller and J. Rives Childs, 1947–1965. Ed. by Richard C. Wood, Univ. Pr. of Virginia 1968 $7.50

Henry Miller: Years of Trial and Triumph, 1962–1964—The Correspondence of Henry Miller and Elmer Gertz. Ed. by Elmer Gertz and Felice F. Lewis, Southern Illinois Univ. Pr. 1978 $19.95

From Your Capricorn Friend: Henry Miller and the Stroker, 1978–1980. Intro. by Irving Stettner, New Directions 1984 $14.00 pap. $6.25

Tropic of Cancer. 1931. Grove 1961 pap. $3.95; pref. by Anais Nin, Modern Lib. 1983 $7.95

Tropic of Capricorn. 1938. Grove 1962 pap. $3.95
Black Spring. 1939. Grove 1964 pap. $4.95
Sexus. Grove 1965 pap. $5.95
Plexus. Grove 1965 pap. $6.95
Nexus. Grove 1965 pap. $5.95

BOOKS ABOUT MILLER

Durrell, Lawrence. *Art and Outrage.* 1960. Porter 1982 pap. $16.50
——. *Henry Miller: Happy Rock.* Porter 1982 o.p.
Gordon, William A. *The Mind and Art of Henry Miller.* Pref. by R. H. Fogle, fwd. by
    Lawrence Durrell, Louisiana State Univ. Pr. 1967 pap. $6.95. First serious criti-
    cal study. "By far the most intelligent thing I have ever read on Miller" (Ken-
    neth Rexroth).
Mailer, Norman. *Black Messiah.* Vagabond Pr. 1981 $20.00 pap. $9.00
Martin, Jay. *Always Merry and Bright: The Life of Henry Miller.* Capra Pr. 1978 $15.00;
    Penguin 1980 pap. $10.95. Thorough and readable biography.
Perles, Alfred. *Henry Miller in Villa Seurat.* Porter 1982 $16.50
Schnellock, Emil. *Henry Miller: Just a Brooklyn Boy.* Porter 1982 pap. $16.50
Shifreen, Lawrence J. *Henry Miller: A Bibliography of Secondary Sources.* Scarecrow
    Pr. 1979 lib. bdg. $26.00
Wickes, George. *Henry Miller. Pamphlets on Amer. Writers Ser.* Univ. of Minnesota Pr.
    1966 pap. $1.25
——, ed. *Henry Miller and the Critics. Crosscurrents Modern Critiques Ser.* Southern
    Illinois Univ. Pr. 1963 $12.95
Widmer, Kingsley. *Henry Miller. Twayne's U.S. Authors Ser.* New College & Univ. Pr.
    1963 pap. $5.95

MORRIS, WRIGHT. 1910–

Early in his career Wright Morris was called by Mark Schorer "probably
the most original young novelist writing in the United States," and in 1968
Leon Howard wrote: "Wright Morris has been the most consistently original of American novelists for a quarter of a century." Since then the University of Nebraska Press has brought out new editions of his first 17 novels,
and although both critical and popular appreciation of his work continues
to grow slowly, there is a general consensus that he ranks high among contemporary American novelists. Born in Central City, Nebraska (the Lone
Tree of his fiction), Morris attended Pomona College in California and had
an academic career chiefly at San Francisco State University until his retirement in 1975. Nebraska and California have provided the main settings for
his work, but he has traveled widely here and abroad and some of his best
novels are picaresque stories of odysseys made by engaging characters and
the people they meet along the way. For instance, his first novel, *My Uncle
Dudley* (1942), is a fictionalized account of a trip with his father to California that motherless Morris made as a youth. When almost 30 years later he
wrote about another east-to-west journey in *Fire Sermon* (1971), in which an
old man and a boy encounter three young hippies, Granville Hicks called
the book "simon-pure, dyed-in-the-wool honest-to-God Wright Morris of the
very highest grade" (*N.Y. Times*). *The Field of Vision,* which deals with "innocents abroad in Mexico," won the National Book Award for fiction in 1957

and ranks behind only *Ceremony in Lone Tree* as his most successful novel. *Ceremony* involves four generations at a family reunion as Morris ingeniously reconciles the past, present, and future in a story that avoids too much nostalgia without descending into the disillusionment of the you-can't-go-home-again theme that appears quite often in his other fiction. Critics attempting to define the originality of Morris have emphasized his distinctive style—a Faulknerlike ability to draw characters that come alive as individuals, his cross-country Americanness, and a strong sense of place that may owe something to Morris's considerable gifts as a photographer.

His fine feeling for the conjunction of time and place is evident in his several books of photographs with text: *The Inhabitants, The Home Place* (1948), *God's Country and My People, Photographs and Words,* and *Picture America.* Other nonfiction includes a collection of essays on contemporary social and political problems—*A Bill of Rites, a Bill of Wrongs, a Bill of Goods* (1967, o.p.)—and two widely praised volumes of criticism—*The Territory Ahead: Critical Interpretations in American Literature* (1958) and *Earthly Delights, Unearthly Adornments: American Writers as Image Makers.* Two volumes of personal memoirs are *Will's Boy* and *Solo: An American Dreamer in Europe, 1933–1934.*

Books by Morris

My Uncle Dudley. Greenwood repr. of 1942 ed. lib. bdg. $18.75; Univ. of Nebraska Pr. (Bison) repr. of 1942 ed. 1975 pap. $4.50

The Man Who Was There. Univ. of Nebraska Pr. (Bison) repr. of 1945 ed. 1977 $18.50 pap. $4.95

The World in the Attic. Univ. of Nebraska Pr. (Bison) repr. of 1949 ed. 1971 $15.95 pap. $3.50

Man and Boy. AMS Pr. repr. of 1951 ed. $23.00; Univ. of Nebraska Pr. (Bison) repr. of 1951 ed. 1974 pap. $4.25

The Works of Love. Univ. of Nebraska Pr. (Bison) repr. of 1952 ed. 1972 pap. $6.95

The Deep Sleep. Univ. of Nebraska Pr. (Bison) repr. of 1953 ed. 1975 pap. $5.95

The Huge Season. Univ. of Nebraska Pr. (Bison) repr. of 1954 ed. 1975 pap. $5.50

The Field of Vision. Univ. of Nebraska Pr. (Bison) repr. of 1956 ed. 1974 $18.50 pap. $7.95

Love among the Cannibals. Univ. of Nebraska Pr. (Bison) repr. of 1957 ed. 1977 $18.95 pap. $8.95

Ceremony in Lone Tree. Univ. of Nebraska Pr. (Bison) repr. of 1960 ed. 1973 pap. $6.95

What a Way to Go. Univ. of Nebraska Pr. (Bison) repr. of 1962 ed. 1979 $22.50 pap. $5.95

Cause for Wonder. Univ. of Nebraska Pr. (Bison) repr. of 1963 ed. 1978 $18.95 pap. $3.95

One Day. Univ. of Nebraska Pr. (Bison) repr. of 1965 ed. 1976 $28.95 pap. $6.95

In Orbit. Univ. of Nebraska Pr. (Bison) repr. of 1967 ed. 1976 pap. $5.95

Fire Sermon. Univ. of Nebraska Pr. (Bison) repr. of 1971 ed. 1979 $12.50 pap. $3.50

A Life. Univ. of Nebraska Pr. (Bison) repr. of 1973 ed. 1980 $12.95 pap. $3.95

The Fork River Space Project. Harper 1977 $8.95; Univ. of Nebraska Pr. (Bison) repr. of 1977 ed. 1981 pap. $5.95

Plains Song. Harper 1980 $12.45; *Contemporary Amer. Fiction Ser.* Penguin 1981 pap.
$5.95

BOOKS ABOUT MORRIS

Crump, G. B. *The Novels of Wright Morris: A Critical Interpretation.* Univ. of Nebraska
Pr. (Bison) 1978 $18.95

Howard, Leon. *Wright Morris. Pamphlets on Amer. Writers Ser.* Univ. of Minnesota Pr.
1968 pap. $1.25

Knoll, Robert E., ed. *Conversations with Wright Morris: Critical Views and Responses.*
Univ. of Nebraska Pr. (Bison) 1977. $16.95 pap. $4.95

Madden, David. *Wright Morris. Twayne's U.S. Authors Ser.* New College & Univ. Pr.
1964 pap. $5.95

MORRISON, TONI. 1931–

Publication of her fourth novel, *Tar Baby*, seemed to solidify Toni Morrison's reputation as one of today's leading novelists. One naturally writes "black women novelists" and strikes the first two words, for there are few writers white or black, male or female who take precedence over her. But Jean Strouse, who wrote the *Newsweek* cover story about her, says, "Morrison hates it when people say she is not a 'black writer.' " "Of course I'm a black writer. That's like saying Dostoevski's not a Russian writer. They mean I'm not *just* a black writer, but categories like black writer, woman writer, and Latin American writer aren't marginal anymore. We have to acknowledge that the thing we call 'literature' is pluralistic now, just as society ought to be."

Toni Morrison's four novels show a steady progression not only in artistic skill but in the range and scope of her subjects and settings. The first three take place in black communities in dominantly white small northern cities, where Toni Morrison, as Chloe Anthony Wofford, grew up as a member of a stable family of six headed by a father who often worked three jobs simultaneously in order to support his family during the depression years. She graduated from Howard University and received a master's degree from Cornell with a thesis on the theme of suicide in modern literature. She has taught writing courses at Bard College and several universities near New York City, where she works as a senior editor of Random House.

Her first novel, *The Bluest Eye*, is a deliberately composed experimental work that begins haltingly with the Dick-and-Jane language of a grade school primer and slowly develops the motifs thus introduced in the poetically tragic story of a little black girl. Her second novel, *Sula*, is the story of two women whose deep early friendship is severely tested when one of them returns after a ten-year absence as "a classic type of evil force" to disrupt the community. *Song of Solomon* has as central characters a young man named Milkman and his nemesis, Guitar, whose fates are as inextricably linked as those of the young women in *Sula*. *Song of Solomon* is a thoughtful work rich in symbols and mythical in its implications, yet readable enough to have been chosen a main selection of the Book-of-the-Month Club and as winner of the National Book Critics Circle Award for 1977. In *Tar Baby* Morrison extends her range to an island in the Caribbean and for the first time allows white characters to play prominent roles along with the black. *Tar Baby* is essentially a novel of ideas, but the ideas again are conveyed along with a fast-moving narrative with credible characters.

BOOKS BY MORRISON

The Bluest Eye. 1970. Washington Square Pr. 1972 pap. $3.95
Sula. Knopf 1973 $10.95; New Amer. Lib. (Plume) 1982 pap. $5.95
Song of Solomon. Knopf 1977 $10.95; New Amer. Lib. (Signet Class.) 1978 pap. $3.95
Tar Baby. Knopf 1981 $11.95; New Amer. Lib. (Signet Class.) 1983 pap. $3.95

NIN, ANAIS. 1903–1977

Anais Nin was a neglected and almost legendary figure in the history of modern art and letters until selections from her monumental diary—drawn from an original 150 volumes comprising 15,000 pages of typescript—began to appear in 1966. She was born in 1903, the daughter of a well-known Spanish pianist and composer who separated from his wife and daughter when Nin was 11 years old. Brought to the United States, she attended public schools only briefly before embarking on a remarkable program of self-education that included starting her diary as an unmailed letter to her lost father. She returned to Paris during the early 1930s, supporting herself as an artist's model and Spanish dancer while continuing to write. By 1939 she had published in Paris *D. H. Lawrence: An Unprofessional Study,* a prose poem called *House of Incest,* and three novelettes gathered under the title *Winter of Artifice* (1939). She had become close friends with many leading figures of the Parisian artistic and social scene, including the then-struggling writer Henry Miller, the young surrealist poet Antonin Artaud, with whom she had an affair, and the psychiatrist OTTO RANK (see Vol. 5). She returned to the United States at the outbreak of World War II in 1939. Because she could not place her writings with commercial publishers, she bought her own printing press and in 1944 produced a small, hand-set edition of her stories, *Under a Glass Bell.* Praised by EDMUND WILSON in the *New Yorker,* it was republished four years later by Dutton, and from then on she was able to publish regularly, though she found only a small, discriminating audience until publication of her diary and the representative role she seemed to play in the feminist movement helped to arouse interest in her creative work.

Anais Nin's fiction is marked by a dreamlike sensibility. Probably the best entry into her fictive world is the omnibus volume *Cities of the Interior,* which brings together five short novels to create a sustained narrative. Even the erotica she wrote on commission for a wealthy gentleman during her Paris years—published after her death in *Delta of Venus* and *Little Birds*—has a special poetic and transcendent aura about it, which makes it qualify as high-porn literature of a rather special kind.

Books by Nin

Anais Nin Reader. Ed. by Philip K. Jason, intro. by Anna Balakian, Ohio Univ. Pr. (Swallow) 1973 pap. $7.95. Selections from both her fiction and her nonfiction— a good introduction to this not easily classified writer.

Cities of the Interior. Intro. by Sharon Spencer, Ohio Univ. Pr. (Swallow) 1974 $19.95 pap. $12.95. An omnibus volume containing *Ladders to Fire, Children of the Albatross, The Four-Chambered Heart, A Spy in the House of Love,* and *The Seduction of the Minotaur.*

A Woman Speaks: The Lectures, Seminars, and Interviews of Anais Nin. Ed. by Evelyn J. Hinz, Ohio Univ. Pr. (Swallow) 1975 $13.95 pap. $6.95

House of Incest. 1931. Ohio Univ. Pr. (Swallow) 1958 pap. $3.95

Winter of Artifice. 1939. Ohio Univ. Pr. (Swallow) 1961 pap. $5.95

Under a Glass Bell. 1944. Ohio Univ. Pr. (Swallow) 1948 pap. $4.25. Short stories.

Ladders to Fire. 1946. Ohio Univ. Pr. (Swallow) 1959 pap. $5.95

Children of the Albatross. 1947. Ohio Univ. Pr. (Swallow) 1959 pap. $4.95

The Four-Chambered Heart. 1950. Ohio Univ. Pr. (Swallow) 1966 pap. $5.95

A Spy in the House of Love. 1954. Ohio Univ. Pr. (Swallow) 1959 pap. $5.95

The Seduction of the Minotaur. Ohio Univ. Pr. (Swallow) 1961 pap. $5.95

Collages. Ohio Univ. Pr. (Swallow) 1964 $3.95

Delta of Venus. Bantam repr. 1978 pap. $3.95; Harcourt 1977 $10.00

Little Birds. 1979. Bantam 1980 pap. $3.95

Books about Nin

Deduck, Patricia A. *Realism, Reality, and the Fictional Theory of Alain Robbe-Grillet and Anais Nin.* Univ. Pr. of Amer. 1982 $21.75 pap. $8.75

Evans, Oliver. *Anais Nin.* Pref. by Harry T. Moore, *Crosscurrents Modern Critiques Ser.* Southern Illinois Univ. Pr. 1968 $7.95

Franklin, Benjamin, and Duane Schneider. *Anais Nin: An Introduction.* Ohio Univ. Pr. 1980 $20.00 pap. $12.00

Knapp, Bettina L. *Anais Nin. Lit. and Life Ser.* Ungar 1978 $12.95 pap. $6.95

Scholar, Nancy. *Anais Nin. Twayne's U.S. Authors Ser.* G. K. Hall 1984 lib. bdg. $13.95

Snyder, Robert. *Anais Nin Observed: From a Film Portrait of a Woman as Artist.* Ohio Univ. Pr. (Swallow) 1976 pap. $9.95

Spencer, Sharon. *Collage of Dreams: The Writings of Anais Nin.* Harcourt 1981 $5.95; Ohio Univ. Pr. (Swallow) 1977 $12.95

NORRIS, FRANK. 1870–1902

Considered one of the leading pioneers in American realism, Frank Norris is read and studied for his vivid and honest depiction of life at the beginning of a lusty and developing new century. Born in Chicago, he moved to San Francisco with his well-to-do family when he was 14 and went on to attend the University of California and Harvard University before becoming a war correspondent in South Africa and Cuba. His early apprentice work consisted mostly of rather unremarkable adventure stories, but with the long-gestating *McTeague: A Story of San Francisco* he struck a new note that made him seem to some readers an American ZOLA (see Vol. 2). That powerful study of avarice in a seedy section of the Bay Area may well be Norris's masterpiece.

The Octopus, the first of the projected *Epic of the Wheat* series, deals with the raising of wheat in California and the struggle of ranchers against the railroads, while *The Pit* is a novel about speculation on the Chicago wheat exchange, but Norris died suddenly after an operation for appendicitis and did not write "The Wolf," in which the wheat as a symbol of life-force was to feed a famine-stricken village in Europe. *Vandover and the Brute* (1914, o.p.), the manuscript of which was lost during the San Francisco earthquake and rediscovered for publication in 1914, is an early work admired as a representative work of American naturalism.

Like Stephen Crane, a writer with whom Norris is frequently compared, Norris died too young to fulfill his considerable promise, but he has more than held his own ground among turn-of-the-century writers whose works have lived. One reason may be that he took his craft as a writer seriously and saw himself more the artist than the reporter, as is shown by his *Responsibilities of the Novelist and Other Literary Essays* (1903) and *The Literary Criticism of Frank Norris,* edited by Donald Pizer.

BOOKS BY NORRIS

A Novelist in the Making: A Collection of Student Themes and the Novels Blix and Vandover and the Brute. Ed. by James D. Hart, *John Harvard Lib. Ser.* Harvard Univ. Pr. 1970 $35.00

Frank Norris of "The Wave": Stories and Sketches from the San Francisco Weekly, 1893 to 1897. Folcroft repr. of 1931 ed. 1974 lib. bdg. $30.00; Scholarly repr. of 1931 ed. 1972 $39.00

Moran of the Lady Letty: A Story of Adventure off the California Coast. AMS Pr. repr. of 1898 ed. $12.45; Irvington repr. of 1898 ed. 1979 lib. bdg. $11.00 text ed. pap. $6.75

Blix. AMS Pr. repr. of 1899 ed. $19.00

McTeague: A Story of San Francisco. 1899. Intro. by B. Evans, Fawcett 1977 pap. $2.25; ed. by Carvel Collins, *Rinehart Ed.* Holt text ed. 1950 pap. $8.95; Lightyear 1976 lib. bdg. $18.95; New Amer. Lib. (Signet Class.) pap. $2.75; ed. by Donald Pizer, *Norton Critical Eds.* 1977 $12.95 1978 text ed. pap. $8.95; ed. by Kevin Starr, *Penguin Amer. Lib. Ser.* 1982 pap. $3.95; intro. by Carvel Collins, Peter Smith $16.75

Man's Woman. AMS Pr. repr. of 1900 ed. 1970 $17.00

The Octopus: A Story of California. 1901. Lightyear 1976 lib. bdg. $18.50; New Amer. Lib. (Signet Class.) pap. $3.50

Deal in Wheat and Other Stories of the New and Old West. Ill. by Remington Leyendecker, Scholarly repr. of 1903 ed. 1971 $6.00

The Pit: A Story of Chicago. 1903. Lightyear 1976 lib. bdg. $18.25; Richard West repr. of 1903 ed. 1978 lib. bdg. $25.00

Vandover and the Brute. Univ. of Nebraska Pr. (Bison) repr. of 1914 ed. 1978 $24.50 pap. $6.50

BOOKS ABOUT NORRIS

Ahnebrink, Lars. *The Influence of Emile Zola on Frank Norris.* Arden Lib. repr. of 1947 ed. 1978 lib. bdg. $16.00; Folcroft repr. of 1947 ed. lib. bdg. $15.00

Dillingham, William B. *Frank Norris: Instinct and Art.* Univ. of Nebraska Pr. 1969 $15.50

French, Warren. *Frank Norris. Twayne's U.S. Authors Ser.* New College & Univ. Pr. 1962 pap. $5.95

Frohock, W. M. *Frank Norris. Pamphlets on Amer. Writers Ser.* Univ. of Minnesota Pr. 1968 pap. $1.25

Graham, Don. *Critical Essays on Frank Norris.* G. K. Hall (Twayne) 1980 lib. bdg. $26.00

———. *The Fiction of Frank Norris: The Aesthetic Context.* Univ. of Missouri Pr. 1978 text ed. $15.00

Marchand, Leslie. *Frank Norris: A Study.* 1942. Octagon 1954 $20.00

McElrath, Joseph P., ed. *Frank Norris: The Critical Reception. Amer. Critical Tradition Ser.* Burt Franklin 1979 lib. bdg. $21.50

Pizer, Donald. *The Novels of Frank Norris. Studies in Fiction Ser.* Haskell repr. of 1966 ed. 1972 lib. bdg. $49.95

OATES, JOYCE CAROL. 1938–

Joyce Carol Oates would seem to live the life of a person of letters more fully than anyone else at this time. By the time she was 47 years old she had published at least that many separate books, including 16 full-length novels and more than a dozen collections of short stories. She has also written numerous poems collected in several volumes, at least three plays, many critical essays, and articles and reviews on various subjects while fulfilling her obligations as a professor of English at the University of Windsor, where with her husband Raymond Smith she edited the *Ontario Review* until they moved to Princeton in 1978. She has earned a reputation as indubitably one of our most prolific writers and very likely one of our best.

Her fiction alone demonstrates considerable variety in that it ranges from direct naturalism to complex experiments in form. However, what chiefly makes her work peculiarly her own is a quality of psychological realism, an uncanny ability to bring to the surface of her narratives an underlying sense of foreboding within her characters or a threat of violence that seems to lurk just around the corner from the everyday domestic lives she depicts so realistically. Her first six novels, including *Them* (1969), which won the National Book Award, express these qualities in varying ways.

Since 1975 her novels have shown her experimenting with several genres, ranging from such Gothiclike romances as *Bellefleur, A Bloodsmoor Romance,* and *Mysteries of Winterthur* at one pole to the most Joycean of her books at the other. Of *Childworld,* which makes use of stream of consciousness, shifting chronology, and other sophisticated techniques reminiscent of *Ulysses,* Irene Chayes (*New Republic*) wrote: "This is a novel that at last is comparable to the best of her short stories and by an evolutionary leap has already moved beyond them, into the tradition of literature, going back at least as far as the Romantics, in which the philosophical problems of man's existence and his destiny are bound up with the problems of art." *The Assassins: A Book of Hours,* a rather heavy treatment of politics, seemed to most reviewers a less successful experiment, and *Son of the Morning,* which the author described as "a first person narration by a man addressing himself throughout to God . . . the whole novel is a prayer," was only respectfully received. *Unholy Loves* is an academic novel set at a university in upstate New York that caters to Ivy League rejects and, in the cutting and catty way of the novel's narrator, provides abundant material for a satiric view of college and sexual politics. Both *Cybele* and *Angel of Light* are renderings of ancient myths in contemporary terms, the former about orgiastic rites performed by a kind of modern-day eunuch and the second a story set in our nation's capital loosely based on the fall of the house of Atreus. *Solstice,* her most recent novel, examines a close friendship between two women and seems to show Oates returning to the rich psychological penetration that has marked her best work.

Louisiana State University Press has issued five collections of poetry: *Anonymous Sins and Other Poems; Love and Its Derangements* (o.p.); *Angel Fire* (o.p.); *The Fabulous Beasts;* and *Women Whose Lives Are Food, Men Whose Lives Are Money.* Her literary criticism is collected in *The Edge of Impossibility: Tragic Forms in Literature; New Heaven, New Earth: The Visionary Experience in Literature; Contraries;* and *The Profane Art: Essays and Reviews.*

BOOKS BY OATES

Where Are You Going, Where Have You Been? Stories of Young America. Fawcett 1976 pap. $1.75. A selection of stories from previous collections.
By the North Gate. Fawcett 1978 pap. $1.50; Vanguard 1963 $14.95. Stories.
With Shuddering Fall. Fawcett 1976 pap. $1.75; Vanguard 1964 $14.95
Upon the Sweeping Flood and Other Stories. Vanguard 1966 $14.95
A Garden of Earthly Delights. Fawcett repr. 1977 pap. $1.95; Vanguard 1967 $14.95
Expensive People. Fawcett 1982 pap. $2.95; Vanguard 1968 $14.95
Them. Fawcett 1978 pap. $3.50; Vanguard 1969 $14.95
Wheel of Love and Other Stories. Vanguard 1970 $14.95
Wonderland. 1971. Fawcett 1979 pap. $1.95; Vanguard $14.95
Marriages and Infidelities. Fawcett repr. 1978 pap. $2.50; Vanguard 1972 $14.95. Stories.
Do with Me What You Will. Fawcett 1978 pap. $2.95; Vanguard 1973 $14.95
The Goddess and Other Women. Fawcett repr. 1976 pap. $1.95; Vanguard 1974 $14.95. Stories.
The Assassins: A Book of Hours. Fawcett repr. 1976 pap. $3.50; Vanguard 1975 $14.95
The Seduction and Other Stories. 1975. Black Sparrow 1976 $14.00; Fawcett 1980 pap. $2.75
Childworld. Fawcett pap. $2.95; Vanguard 1976 $14.95
Crossing the Border: Stories. Fawcett 1978 pap. $2.50; Vanguard 1976 $14.95
Night-Side: Stories. Fawcett pap. $2.50; Vanguard 1977 $14.95
Son of the Morning. Fawcett repr. 1979 pap. $2.75; Vanguard 1978 $14.95
Cybele. Black Sparrow 1979 $14.00 pap. $6.00
Unholy Loves. Fawcett pap. $2.95; Vanguard 1979 $14.95
Bellefleur. Dutton 1980 $13.95
A Sentimental Education: Stories. Dutton (Obelisk) 1982 pap. $4.95
Angel of Light. 1981. Warner Bks. 1982 pap. $3.95
A Bloodsmoor Romance. Dutton 1982 $16.95; Warner Bks. 1983 pap. $3.95
Mysteries of Winterthur. Dutton 1984 $16.95

Last Days: Stories. Dutton 1984 $15.95
Solstice. Dutton 1985 $15.95

BOOKS ABOUT OATES

Bastian, Katherine. *Joyce Carol Oates's Short Stories between Tradition and Innovation.* Peter Lang 1982 pap. $21.05

Creighton, Joanne V. *Joyce Carol Oates.* Twayne's U.S. Authors Ser. G. K. Hall 1979 lib. bdg. $11.50

Friedman, Ellen G. *Joyce Carol Oates.* Lit. and Life Ser. Ungar 1980 $15.50 1984 pap. $7.95

Norman, T. *Isolation and Contract: A Study of Character Relationships in Joyce Carol Oates's Short Stories, 1963–1980.* Humanities Pr. text ed. 1984 pap. $21.00

Wagner, Linda W. *Critical Essays on Joyce Carol Oates.* Critical Essays on Amer. Lit. Ser. G. K. Hall 1979 lib. bdg. $26.00

O'CONNOR, FLANNERY. 1925–1965

Although Flannery O'Connor produced only a small canon of work during her short life, no other American writer of her generation has received more critical attention. Her creative work was largely compressed within the decade of the 1950s, and according to Frederick R. Karl (*American Fictions, 1940–1980*) hers was "the most singularly unique voice" of the period: "Her mixture of wit, irony, paradox, and traditional belief in the devil and God gave her prose a maturity that belied the age at which most of her fiction was written." The victim of an inherited lupus disease that eventually crippled her and cut short her life, she had a quiet, bookish life as a child before attending Georgia State College for Women and going on to the Writers Workshop at the State University of Iowa, where she earned a master of fine arts degree.

Her 1949 dissertation consisted of six short stories, one of which was developed into her first novel, *Wise Blood* (1952). That highly symbolic story of a fanatical itinerant preacher who sets out to found a "church of truth without Jesus Christ crucified" introduces some of the religious themes that pervade her later work. *The Violent Bear It Away* (1960), her second novel, is a story of murder involving a Tennessee backwoods preacher and a small boy. Here O'Connor again exhibits her interest in the strange forms religion can take and in aberrant human personality; here too she shows herself a writer concerned with the oppressive mores of the Deep South in the Faulkner tradition.

As powerful as her novels are, they are in some ways less impressive than her short fiction. Her best-known story is "A Good Man Is Hard to Find," a psychological horror story about the murder of a family on vacation by an escaped convict called The Misfit. Frequently used in college textbooks, this story of grace and redemption is considered a modern American classic. Other stories frequently anthologized are "The Artificial Nigger," "Good Country People," and "Everything That Rises Must Converge."

Most critics who write about Flannery O'Connor emphasize her religious themes or her relation to a school of southern writers who favored the grotesque, seeing her as in some ways an American Graham Greene or a younger William Faulkner. But thanks in part to a current of comedy that runs through her writings, she is also unique enough to defy easy labeling. As she explained in a letter to Andrew Lytle, "To my way of thinking, the only thing that keeps me from being a regional writer is being a Catholic and the only thing that keeps me from being a Catholic writer (in the narrow sense) is being a Southerner."

BOOKS BY O'CONNOR

The Complete Stories of Flannery O'Connor. Farrar 1971 $25.00 pap. $8.95

Three by Flannery O'Connor: Wise Blood; The Violent Bear It Away; A Good Man Is Hard to Find. New Amer. Lib. (Signet Class.) 1980 pap. $3.50

Wise Blood (and *The Violent Bear It Away* and *Everything That Rises Must Converge*). 1952. Farrar 1962 $10.95 pap. $6.25

A Good Man Is Hard to Find. Harcourt 1955 $7.95 1977 pap. $4.95

The Violent Bear It Away. Farrar 1960 pap. $5.95

Everything That Rises Must Converge. Farrar 1965 $10.00 pap. $5.95

Mystery and Manners: Occasional Prose. Ed. by Robert Fitzgerald and Sally Fitzgerald, Farrar 1960 $10.95 pap. $6.95

The Habit of Being: Letters. Ed. by Sally Fitzgerald, Farrar 1979 $15.00

BOOKS ABOUT O'CONNOR

Asals, Frederick. *Flannery O'Connor: The Imagination of Extremity.* Univ. of Georgia Pr. 1982 $20.00

Coles, Robert. *Flannery O'Connor's South.* Louisiana State Univ. Pr. 1980 $17.50

Eggenschwiler, David. *The Christian Humanism of Flannery O'Connor.* Wayne State Univ. Pr. 1972 $9.95

Farmer, David. *Flannery O'Connor: A Descriptive Bibliography.* Garland 1981 lib. bdg. $22.00

Feeley, Kathleen. *Flannery O'Connor: Voice of the Peacock.* Fordham Univ. Pr. 2d ed. 1982 pap. $9.00

Friedman, Melvin J., ed. *The Added Dimension: The Art and Mind of Flannery O'Connor.* 1966. Fordham Univ. Pr. 2d ed. 1977 pap. $9.00. A collection of original critical pieces by various hands.

Getz, Lorine M. *Nature and Grace in Flannery O'Connor's Fiction. Studies in Art and Religious Interpretation* Mellen 1982 $39.95

Golden, Robert, and Mary C. Sullivan. *Flannery O'Connor and Caroline Gordon: A Reference Guide.* G. K. Hall 1977 lib. bdg. $28.50

Grimshaw, James A., Jr. *The Flannery O'Connor Companion.* Greenwood 1981 lib. bdg. $27.50. A compendium of information.

Humphries, Jefferson. *The Otherness Within: Gnostic Readings in Marcel Proust, Flannery O'Connor, and François Villon.* Louisiana State Univ. Pr. 1983 $25.00

Kinney, Arthur F. *Flannery O'Connor's Library: Resources of Being.* Univ. of Georgia Pr. text ed. 1985 $25.00

McFarland, Dorothy T. *Flannery O'Connor. Lit. and Life Ser.* Ungar 1976 $12.95

McKenzie, Barbara. *Flannery O'Connor's Georgia.* Univ. of Georgia Pr. 1980 $24.95 pap. $12.50

Miller, Gilbert H. *Nightmares and Visions: Flannery O'Connor and the Catholic Grotesque.* Univ. of Georgia Pr. 1972 $12.00

Orvell, Miles. *Invisible Parade: The Fiction of Flannery O'Connor.* Temple Univ. Pr. 1972 $27.95

O'HARA, JOHN. 1905–1970

Working comfortably within the tradition of social realism, John O'Hara turned out more than 20 novels and 200 short stories. According to Charles Bassett (*Dictionary of Literary Biography*), O'Hara "claimed to be the hardest working author in the United States." The eldest of eight children of a physician in Pottsville, Pennsylvania, whose sudden death seemed to make college impossible for his children, O'Hara used journalism as his path to a writing career, working as a Hollywood press agent, serving as secretary to Heywood Broun, and writing regularly for the *N.Y. Herald Tribune* and the *New Yorker* before his first novel, *Appointment in Samarra*, brought him immediate fame. Although its successor, *Butterfield 8*, was less a critical success, it too found a wide audience. These first two novels, comparatively short and more tightly constructed than most of his later works, are still thought to be among his best productions, though in retrospect it now seems that his career reached its peak with two long novels published during the mid-1950s. *Ten North Frederick* was given the National Book Award in 1955. O'Hara may have liked *From the Terrace* best of all his novels because it deals with a favorite theme—the emotional poverty of a man who in the eyes of the world is a great success.

As often happens with the prolific and bestselling writers, particularly those who choose to write about upper-crust WASPs at a time when the literary establishment tends to be liberal and egalitarian, O'Hara has suffered from the false assumption that he was part of the world he wrote about, one of "them" instead of like "the rest of us." As a result, his critical reputation is unsettled.

BOOKS BY O'HARA

Selected Short Stories of John O'Hara. Ed. by Lionel Trilling, Modern Lib. 1956 $6.95
Two by O'Hara. Ed. by Matthew J. Bruccoli, Harcourt 1979 $10.95
Appointment in Samarra. 1934. Random repr. 1982 pap. $3.95
Butterfield 8. 1935. Random repr. of 1980 ed. 1982 pap. $3.95
Pal Joey. 1940. Random (Vintage) repr. of 1976 ed. 1983 pap. $3.95
Ten North Frederick. 1955. Carroll & Graf 1985 pap. $4.50; Random 1955 $14.95
From the Terrace. 1958. Carroll & Graf 1984 pap. $4.95
Sermons and Soda Water. 1960. Random 3 vols. $12.50. Trilogy of short novels—*The Girl on the Baggage Truck, Imagine Kissing Pete*, and *We're Friends Again*.
Waiting for Winter. Random 1966 $14.95
And Other Stories. Random 1968 $14.95
Lovey Childs: A Philadelphian's Story. Random 1969 $14.95
The Ewings. Random 1972 $14.95
The Time Element and Other Stories. Random 1972 $14.95
The Second Ewings. Bruccoli 1977 $35.00
An Artist Is His Own Fault: John O'Hara on Writers and Writing. Ed. by Matthew J. Bruccoli, Southern Illinois Univ. Pr. 1977 $8.95

BOOKS ABOUT O'HARA

Bruccoli, Matthew J. *John O'Hara: A Descriptive Bibliography*. Pittsburgh Ser. in Bibliography Univ. of Pittsburgh Pr. 1978 $40.00

———. *The O'Hara Concern: A Biography of John O'Hara.* Random 1975 $15.00
Grebstein, Sheldon N. *John O'Hara. Twayne's U.S. Authors Ser.* New College & Univ.
　Pr. 1966 pap. $5.95
Long, Robert E. *John O'Hara. Lit. and Life Ser.* Ungar 1983 $12.95
MacShane, Frank. *The Life of John O'Hara.* Dutton 1981 $15.95
Walcutt, Charles C. *John O'Hara. Pamphlets on Amer. Writers Ser.* Univ. of Minnesota
　Pr. 1969 pap. $1.25

PARKER, DOROTHY. 1893–1967

During her years of greatest fame Dorothy Parker was known primarily as
a writer of light verse, an essential member of the Algonquin Round Table,
and a caustic and witty critic of literature and society. She is remembered
now as an almost legendary figure of the 1920s and 1930s. Her reviews and
staff contributions to three of the most sophisticated magazines of this century, *Vanity Fair*, the *New Yorker*, and *Esquire*, were notable for their put-
downs; and many of the most famous bright remarks of the time were attributed to her—some of them justly so. For all her highbrow wit, however,
Dorothy Parker was very liberal in her political views, and the hard veneer
of brittle toughness that she showed to the world was often a shield for frustrated idealism and soft sensibilities. The best of her fiction is marked by a
balance of ironic detachment and sympathetic compassion, as in "Big
Blonde," which won the O. Henry Award for 1929 and is still her best-re-
membered and most frequently anthologized story.

The best of Dorothy Parker is readily and compactly accessible in *The Portable Dorothy Parker.* Her own selection of stories and verse for the original
edition of that compilation, published in 1944, remains intact in the revised
edition, but included also are more than 200 pages of later stories, reviews,
and articles, including the complete text of her *Constant Reader* (o.p.), a collection of her book reviews for the *New Yorker. You Might as Well Live: The
Life and Times of Dorothy Parker* (o.p.), by John Keats, is a readable and balanced biography.

BOOK BY PARKER

The Portable Dorothy Parker. 1944. *Viking Portable Lib.* Penguin rev. ed. 1976 pap.
　$7.95; ed. by Brendan Gill, *Viking Portable Lib.* 1973 $14.95. Includes a very read-
　able biography.

BOOK ABOUT PARKER

Kinney, Arthur F. *Dorothy Parker. Twayne's U.S. Authors Ser.* G. K. Hall 1978 $12.50

PERCY, WALKER. 1916–

Walker Percy, born in Alabama, raised in Mississippi, and a resident now
of Louisiana, is a member of a prominent southern family who lost his parents at an early age and grew up as the foster son of his father's cousin.
Percy graduated from the University of North Carolina and received his
M.D. from Columbia, but is a nonpracticing physician who has devoted
much of his life to his writing. ALFRED KAZIN wrote that "the lean, subtle
Percy style, the unmistakable breeding behind the style, puts Percy among

the 'dandys' now when there are so many real and would-be roughnecks" (*Harper's*). However, it is not so much the genteel style of Percy that has attracted a steadily growing critical audience as the profoundly humanistic views and conservative tone of a writer who has described himself as a southern "philosophical Catholic existentialist" (*Dictionary of Literary Biography*).

Percy's witty and provocative first novel, *The Moviegoer*, won the 1962 National Book Award, but Charles Poore considers *The Last Gentleman* (1966) "an even better book." *Love in the Ruins* marks a sharp change in method and subject from the first two novels. A doomsday story set "at the end of the Auto Age," it exposes many foibles and abuses in contemporary life through sharp satire and extravagant fantasy. Whereas *Love in the Ruins* (1971) is funny, Percy's next novel, *Lancelot*, is the rather bleak and pessimistic story of a deranged man who blows up his home when he finds proof of his wife's infidelities and tells his story in an asylum for the mentally disturbed. Its apocalyptic vision is expressed in a more positive and affirmative way in *The Second Coming*, which takes its title from the fact that it resurrects the character of Will Barret from *The Last Gentleman* and locates him, a quarter-century older, finding love and meaning in a cave.

In addition to his six novels, Percy is the author of two volumes of philosophical reflections culled from his personal journals—*The Message in the Bottle* and *Lost in the Cosmos: The Last Self-Help Book*.

BOOKS BY PERCY

The Moviegoer. Avon 1979 pap. $3.50; Farrar 1967 pap. $2.95; Knopf 1961 $11.95
The Last Gentleman. Farrar 1966 $17.95 pap. $8.95
Love in the Ruins: The Adventures of a Bad Catholic at a Time Near the End of the World. Avon 1978 pap. $3.95; Farrar 1971 $15.95
Lancelot. Farrar 1977 $8.95
The Second Coming. Farrar 1980 $12.95; Pocket Bks. 1982 pap. $3.95; Washington Square Pr. 1981 pap. $3.95

BOOKS ABOUT PERCY

Broughton, Panthea Reid, ed. *The Art of Walker Percy: Stratagems for Being. Southern Literary Studies* Louisiana State Univ. Pr. 1979 $27.50
Coles, Robert. *Walker Percy: An American Search.* 1978. Little, Brown 1979 $15.00
Luschei, Martin. *The Sovereign Wayfarer: Walker Percy's Diagnosis of the Malaise. Southern Literary Studies* Louisiana State Univ. Pr. 1972 $22.50
Poteat, Patricia Lewis. *Walker Percy and the Old Modern Age: Reflections on Language, Argument, and the Telling of Stories.* Louisiana State Univ. Pr. text ed. 1985 $20.00

PORTER, KATHERINE ANNE. 1894–1980

This distinguished writer is known for her subtle and delicate perception, her careful, disciplined technique, and her precision of word and phrase. She wrote slowly and with restraint but achieved an impression of ease and naturalness that is close to perfection. She was born in Texas, schooled in Louisiana convents, and working as a newspaper reporter and free-lance journalist traveled to such places as Paris, Majorca, Berlin, Vienna, and Mexico. Her *Collected Stories*, which won both the Pulitzer Prize and the National Book Award in 1966, was written over a long lifetime, but includes works that have been a standard part of high school and college literature courses for a half-century. Among the best are "Noon Wine," "The Jilting of Granny Weatherall," and "Flowering Judas." "Pale Horse, Pale Rider," long enough to be considered a novelette, is one of several stories about a character named Miranda who as a girl and young woman undergoes experiences not unlike those of Porter. Other Miranda stories are "Old Mortality" and a group of seven gathered under the title "The Old Order" that deal with her childhood.

Her one and only full-length novel, *Ship of Fools*, 20 years in the writing, "is the story of a voyage. . . . A novel of character rather than of action, it has as its main purpose a study of the German ethos shortly before Hitler's coming to power in Germany. . . . 'Ship of Fools' is also a human comedy and a moral allegory" (*New Yorker*). To some critics the book was a disappointment, but all recognized its importance and it appeared on the best-seller list for 28 weeks in 1962.

"In my view," wrote Robert Penn Warren in a tribute published in *Saturday Review* after Porter's death in 1980, "the final importance of Katherine Anne Porter is not merely that she has written a number of fictions which have enlarged and deepened the nature of the story, both short and long, in our time, but that she has created an *oeuvre*—a body of work including fiction, essays, letters, and journals—that bears the stamp of a personality, distinctive, delicately perceptive, keenly aware of the depth and darkness of human experience, delighted by the beauty of the world and the triumphs of human kindness and warmth, and thoroughly committed to a quest for meaning in the midst of the ironic complexities of man's lot." Much of the nonfictional part of that body of work was gathered into *The Collected Essays and Occasional Writings of Katherine Anne Porter* (o.p.).

BOOKS BY PORTER

The Collected Stories of Katherine Anne Porter. 1965. Harcourt 1979 pap. $7.95
The Old Order: Stories of the South from Flowering Judas, Pale Horse, Pale Rider and The Leaning Tower. Harcourt 1955 pap. $3.95
Ship of Fools. Little, Brown repr. of 1962 ed. 1984 pap. $7.70

BOOKS ABOUT PORTER

Demouy, Jane K. *Katherine Anne Porter's Women: The Eye of Her Fiction*. Univ. of Texas Pr. text ed. 1983 $22.50
Givner, Joan. *Katherine Anne Porter: A Life*. Simon & Schuster (Touchstone Books) 1984 $10.95. "A judicious and balanced portrait" by a biographer chosen by Porter (*Journal of Modern Lit.*).
Hendrick, George. *Katherine Anne Porter*. Twayne's U.S. Authors Ser. G. K. Hall 1965 lib. bdg. $11.50; *Twayne's U.S. Authors Ser.* New College & Univ. Pr. 1965 pap. $5.95
Mooney, Harry J., Jr. *The Fiction and Criticism of Katherine Anne Porter*. Critical Essays in Modern Lit. Ser. Univ. of Pittsburgh Pr. rev. ed. 1962 pap. $4.95

Schwartz, Edward. *Katherine Anne Porter: A Critical Biography.* Folcroft 1953 lib.
  bdg. $15.00
Warren, Robert Penn. *Katherine Anne Porter: A Collection of Critical Essays. Twentieth
  Century Views Ser.* Prentice-Hall (Spectrum Bks.) 1978 $12.95 pap. $3.95
West, Ray B., Jr. *Katherine Anne Porter. Pamphlets on Amer. Writers Ser.* Univ. of Min-
  nesota Pr. 1963 pap. $1.25

POWERS, J(AMES) F(ARL). 1917–

"Powers is among the greatest of living storytellers," said FRANK O'CON-
NOR—and his modest production has been chiefly in the medium of the
short story. He has contributed to the *New Yorker* and other magazines.
Early in his career he wrote with anger at the plight of the black as well as
his own humiliation during the depression at being forced to accept jobs as
salesclerk and insurance salesman. Later, although "neither a determined
and conscious apologist for the church of Rome, nor blindly revolting
against her" (*SR*), he found his subjects in the lives of priests and their par-
ishes, which he has treated with gentle irony.

The *New Yorker* called *Prince of Darkness*, his first collection, "varied and
fresh stories, written in delightfully firm and straightforward prose, in
which Mr. Powers proves that he has few rivals at creating characters with
more than superficial reality." The *N.Y. Times* said of *Presence of Grace*
(o.p.), "J. F. Powers is a largely endowed, careful and important short-story
writer, one of the best in America. Some of the nine stories in his new collection are distinguished by a high astringent hilarity, and some are filled with
terror and pity." His first novel, *Morte d'Urban*, won him the 1963 National
Book Award. Its "prose is clear, lean, and supple: it is the work of a master
who has achieved virtuosity. . . . The gaiety of his wit . . . is pertinent here
because *Morte d'Urban* could have been bitter, even savage, in its ridicule of
a certain kind of priest" (*Commonweal*).

BOOKS BY POWERS

Prince of Darkness and Other Stories. 1947. Random (Vintage) 1979 pap. $2.95
Morte d'Urban. 1962. Random (Vintage) 1979 pap. $2.95

BOOK ABOUT POWERS

Hagopian, John V. *J. F. Powers. Twayne's U.S. Authors Ser.* New College & Univ. Pr.
  1968 pap. $5.95

PURDY, JAMES. 1923–

"The American dream turned nightmare" is how Warren French and Donald Pease (*Dictionary of Literary Biography*) characterize the strange Gothic
world of James Purdy's fiction. The "special kind of literary imagination"
that David Daiches praised in his preface to *Malcolm*, the first novel, runs
like a current through the nine novels and several volumes of short stories
that have followed, but it is the earliest works that have made the greatest
impact. Reticent about his personal life, Purdy has revealed little about his
past, but it is known that he was born in Ohio and educated in Mexico be-

fore taking an M.A. in Romance languages at the University of Chicago and spending some time at the University of Madrid. He has lived quietly in Brooklyn Heights for the past several decades.

Color of Darkness, his first collection of stories, was printed privately, then brought out in England before being published in his own country. In her introduction to the American edition, Dame EDITH SITWELL wrote: "Purdy does more in a whisper than most novelists do by yelling at the tops of their voices.... There is never a sentence too much, never a word too much.... He is a superb writer, using all the fires of the heart and the crystallizing powers of the brain." *Malcolm* is the story of a confused boy abandoned by his father in a sort of existential allegory. *The Nephew* depicts a woman in rural Ohio who tries to write a memorial to her orphaned nephew, missing in action in Korea, only to discover after her researches into his life that he is as faceless and absent as ever. *Cabot Wright Begins* (o.p.) is about a convicted rapist whose story is pieced together by a group of predatory writers who are trying to commercialize it into a bestselling sex novel.

Jeremy's Version (o.p.) and *The House of the Solitary Maggot* (o.p.) were announced as the first parts of a projected trilogy to be called *Sleepers in a Moon-Crowned Valley*. They have little in common with each other except as depictions of dying rural communities, but their tone of somber mellowness may be constrasted with the grotesque and sometimes precious exoticism of other later works, such as *I am Elijah Thrush* (o.p.), *In a Shallow Grave*, *Narrow Rooms*, and *The Mourners Below*.

Purdy remains a writer with a distinctive voice that not everyone hears clearly, but he has found an audience of readers mainly among academic critics who are willing to respond to the challenge of novels and stories that often seem to cry out for analysis and interpretation.

BOOKS BY PURDY

Dream Palaces: Malcolm, The Nephew and 63 Dream Palace. Viking 1980 $19.95
63 Dream Palace and Other Stories. 1956. Penguin 1981 pap. $4.95
The Nephew. 1960. Intro. by Edward Albee, Penguin 1980 pap. $3.95
In a Shallow Grave. Intro. by Jerome Charyn, Arbor House 1976 $7.50 1984 pap. $5.95
Narrow Rooms. Arbor House 1977 $9.95
The Mourners Below. Contemporary Amer. Fiction Ser. Arbor House 1980 $9.95; Penguin 1982 pap. $4.95; Viking 1981 $13.95
Proud Flesh. Lord John ltd. ed. 1981 $40.00
Old Glory's Course. Viking 1984 $18.95

BOOK ABOUT PURDY

Schwarzchild, Bettina. *The Not-Right House: Essays on James Purdy. Literary Frontiers Ser.* Univ. of Missouri Pr. 1968 pap. $6.95

PYNCHON, THOMAS. 1937–

If there is a legitimate American heir to JAMES JOYCE, it would appear to be Thomas Pynchon, and it is probably no accident that some of the same academic minds that have devoted years to the explication of *Ulysses* and *Finnegans Wake* have also turned their attention to Pynchon's three novels. He has steadfastly avoided personal publicity, and little is known of him other than that he was born in Glen Cove, New York, and graduated from Cornell, where he took VLADIMIR NABOKOV's (see Vol. 2) famous course in modern literature. George Plimpton (*N.Y. Times*) has commented, "Pynchon's remarkable ability includes a vigorous and imaginative style, a robust humor, a tremendous reservoir of information (one suspects he could churn out a passable almanac in a fortnight's time) and, above all, a sense of how to use and balance these talents."

In 1963 Pynchon won the Faulkner First Novel Award with *V*. The main character, Benny Profane, is determined to learn the identity of a woman identified only as "V" in the diary of his late father. Mary McCarthy suggests that the book could rank as "one of the most encyclopedic founts of fact in the history of the novel," with its detailed descriptions of a nose operation, the intricacies of British espionage in the Middle East, the history of Malta, and similar abstruse subjects.

The Crying of Lot 49 is the story of how Mrs. Oedipa Maas discovers a world within her world, an antiworld, an adversary world—or invents one in her imagination. The novel makes use of information and communications theory a la NORBERT WIENER (see Vol. 5), among other subjects. Here again the symbolism, the commentary on the United States and on human isolation are intricate and masterly—though some reviewers found it overingenious and maddeningly dense.

It is, however, *Gravity's Rainbow*, winner of the National Book Award for fiction in 1974, that is considered Pynchon's greatest fictional achievement to date. In part a fictional elegy and meditation on death, it is an encyclopedic work set back and forth from the time of the Second World War that is loaded with references to a multitude of topics ranging from light bulbs to a schematic history of German thought. The novel was enthusiastically received by most reviewers, with W. T. Lhamon, Jr., proclaiming (*New Republic*) that "this novel is going to change the shape of fiction, if only because its genius will depress all competitors" and Edward Mendelson announcing (*Yale Review*) "that few books in this century have achieved the range and depth of this one. . . . This is certainly the most important novel to be published in English in the past thirty years." Judging from the abundance of criticism and interpretation that the novel has evoked during the decade since that proclamation, it could well be that Lhamon and Mendelson were prophetically correct.

BOOKS BY PYNCHON

V. 1963. Bantam 1968 pap. $4.95

The Crying of Lot 49. Bantam 1966 pap. $3.50

Gravity's Rainbow. Bantam 1974 pap. $3.50; Penguin 1973 pap. $7.95; Viking 1973
    $17.95

Slow Learner: Early Stories. Little, Brown 1984 $14.45

BOOKS ABOUT PYNCHON

Clerc, Charles. *Approaches to "Gravity's Rainbow."* Ohio State Univ. Pr. 1983 $25.00

Cooper, Peter L. *Signs and Symptoms: Thomas Pynchon and the Contemporary World.* Univ. of California Pr. 1983 $22.50

Cowart, David. *Thomas Pynchon: The Art of Allusion. Crosscurrents Modern Critiques New Ser.* Southern Illinois Univ. Pr. 1980 $15.95

Fowler, Douglas. *A Guide to Pynchon's Gravity's Rainbow.* Ardis 1980 $18.95

Hipkiss, Robert A. *The American Absurd: Pynchon, Vonnegut, and Barth.* Associated Faculty Pr. 1984 $15.00

Hite, Molly. *Ideas of Order in the Novels of Thomas Pynchon.* Ohio State Univ. Pr. 1983 $17.50

Mackey, Douglas A. *The Rainbow Quest of Thomas Pynchon.* Borgo Pr. 1980 lib. bdg. $13.95

McConnell, Frank D. *Four Postwar American Novelists: Bellow, Mailer, Barth, and Pynchon.* Univ. of Chicago Pr. 1978 pap. $5.50

Mendelson, Edward, ed. *Pynchon: A Collection of Critical Essays. Twentieth-Century Views Ser.* Prentice-Hall (Spectrum Bks.) 1978 $12.95 pap. $3.45

Pearce, Richard. *Critical Essays on Thomas Pynchon. Critical Essays on Amer. Lit. Ser.* G. K. Hall 1981 $26.00

Plater, William M. *The Grim Phoenix: Reconstructing Thomas Pynchon.* Indiana Univ. Pr. 1978 $17.50

Schaub, Thomas H. *Pynchon: The Voice of Ambiguity.* Univ. of Illinois Pr. 1981 $13.50

Stark, John O. *Pynchon's Fictions: Thomas Pynchon and the Literature of Information.* Ohio Univ. Pr. 1980 $18.95

Tanner, Tony. *Thomas Pynchon.* Methuen 1982 pap. $4.25

Walsh, Thomas P., and Cameron Northouse. *John Barth, Jerzy Kosinski and Thomas Pynchon.* G. K. Hall 1978 lib. bdg. $17.00

ROTH, PHILIP. 1933–

" 'Goodbye, Columbus' is a first book but it is not the book of a beginner. Unlike those of us who come howling into the world, blind and bare, Mr. Roth appears with nails, hair, and teeth, speaking coherently. At 26 he is skillful, witty, and energetic and performs like a virtuoso"—so wrote Saul Bellow when Philip Roth made a loud entry onto the literary scene with a novella and short stories that won the 1960 National Book Award. Roth, born and raised in Newark, New Jersey, attended the public schools of that city and went on to Bucknell University before receiving his M.A. from the University of Chicago and publishing stories about contemporary Jewish life in such prestigious literary magazines as *Paris Review*, the *New Yorker*, and *Commentary*. Of *Letting Go*, a novel about young university teachers in the 1950s, the *Atlantic* said that "the sharply observant qualities of his first book have been expanded and enriched; he has become more probing, tentative, complex"; and "When She Was Good," his story of a gentile girl of the Midwest who in striving for moral perfection destroys her family and ultimately herself, was described by Raymond Rosenthal in the *New Leader*: "With a simplicity and modesty that are in the end lethal, Roth has written the most violently satiric book about American life since EVELYN WAUGH's 'The Loved One.' "

The bestselling *Portnoy's Complaint* (1969) caused a greater stir than any other novel of its time. Told in the form of a confession by Alexander Portnoy to his psychiatrist Dr. Spielvogel, this outrageous novel centers around the character of Alexander's archetypal Jewish mother. Virtually the apotheosis of the American Jewish novel, *Portnoy's Complaint* seems almost to have killed off the form it represents, and even Roth himself has been hard put to match or surpass this blackest of comedies. *Our Gang* (1971, o.p.) is a clever political satire directed at President Nixon and his pre-Watergate associates, but those prominent targets of Roth's venomous scorn seem pale and feeble when compared with the formidable mother in *Portnoy's Complaint*. *The Breast* finds Roth rather pathetically groping for a subject equally spectacular.

Roth has continued to produce novels at the rate of about one every two years, but none has come close to matching the impact of *Portnoy's Complaint*. In fact, Roth has linked together several of his recent works by means of a central character named Nathan Zuckerman who seems to be Philip Roth looking back on his literary career and wondering where he goes from there. Zuckerman is introduced in *My Life as a Man* (1974, o.p.) and takes the central role in *The Ghost Writer, Zuckerman Unbound,* and *The Anatomy Lesson*. In addition to the Zuckerman saga, Roth has produced two independent novels: *The Professor of Desire* and *The Great American Novel*. In *Reading Myself and Others*, Roth tries to step outside himself in order to look objectively at his own fiction. This collection of perceptive criticism is particularly strong on FRANZ KAFKA (see Vol. 2) and several of Roth's Jewish contemporaries such as Mailer, Malamud, and Bellow.

BOOKS BY ROTH

A Philip Roth Reader. Intro. by Martin Green, Farrar 1980 $17.50 pap. $9.95
Goodbye Columbus and Five Short Stories. 1959. Modern Lib. 1966 $5.95
Letting Go. Intro. by James Atlas, Farrar 1962 pap. $9.95; Fawcett repr. 1985 pap. $4.95; Random 1962 $12.50
When She Was Good. Penguin 1985 pap. $5.95; Random 1967 $10.95
Portnoy's Complaint. Fawcett repr. 1985 pap. $3.95; Modern Lib. 1982 $6.95; Random 1969 $15.00
The Breast. 1972. Farrar rev. ed. 1982 pap. $5.95
The Great American Novel. Farrar 1973 pap. $7.95
The Professor of Desire. Farrar 1977 $8.95
The Ghost Writer. Farrar 1979 $8.95; Fawcett 1983 pap. $2.95
Zuckerman Unbound. Farrar 1981 $10.95; Fawcett repr. 1982 pap. $3.50
The Anatomy Lesson. Farrar 1983 $14.95
Zuckerman Bound: A Trilogy and Epilogue. Farrar 1985 $22.50 pap. $9.95. Brings together the three Zuckerman novels along with "a wild short novel, 'The Prague Orgy,' which is at once the bleakest and the funniest writing Roth has done" (Harold Bloom, *N.Y. Times*).

BOOKS ABOUT ROTH

Jones, Judith, and Nancy Guinevera. *Philip Roth. Lit. and Life Ser.* Ungar 1981 $12.95 pap. $6.95

Lee, Hermione. *Philip Roth. Contemporary Writers Ser.* Methuen 1982 pap. $4.25
Pinsker, Sanford. *The Comedy That "Hoits": An Essay on the Fiction of Philip Roth.
Literary Frontiers Ser.* Univ. of Missouri Pr. 1975 pap. $7.95
———. *Critical Essays on Philip Roth. Critical Essays on Amer. Lit. Ser.* G. K. Hall
1982 lib. bdg. $30.00
Rodgers, Bernard F., Jr. *Philip Roth: A Bibliography. Author Bibliographies Ser.* Scarecrow Pr. 1974 $15.00

SALINGER, J(EROME) D(AVID). 1919–

More than 20 years of seclusion and silence have taken their toll with
J. D. Salinger's literary reputation, but the impact made by *The Catcher in
the Rye* (1951) and the Glass family stories was deep enough to make a lasting
impression and to assure continued readership. Salinger was born in New
York City of Jewish and Scottish-Irish extraction. He attended Manhattan
public schools, a military academy in Pennsylvania, and three colleges, but
received no degrees. "A happy tourist's year in Europe," he wrote in 1955,
"when I was eighteen and nineteen. In the Army from '42 to '46, most of the
time with the Fourth Division. . . . I've been writing since I was fifteen or so.
My short stories have appeared in a number of magazines over the last ten
years, mostly—and most happily—in the *New Yorker*. I worked on 'The
Catcher in the Rye,' on and off, for ten years" (*Twentieth Century Authors*). "Remarkable and absorbing . . . profoundly moving . . . magic," Harrison
Smith called this story. *The Catcher* has been an extremely popular book
among young people ever since its appearance and has brought Salinger an
international reputation. *Franny and Zooey* (1961) is composed of two long
New Yorker stories, which appeared in 1955 and 1957, recording a significant
weekend in the lives of Franny Glass, a troubled 20-year-old college student,
and her brother Zooey, a television actor. *Raise High the Roof Beam, Carpenters* is another story of the Glass family. There are seven Glass children, "two
of whom are now dead and all of whom were child prodigies."

Salinger gradually withdrew from public life and the literary scene during the 1950s. He had discovered Zen during his days in Greenwich Village
after the war, and that oriental philosophy may have encouraged his deeper
immersion in meditation and writing. Unfortunately, however, Salinger's
withdrawal has not led to increased creativity—at least not visibly. As of
early 1985, his years of seclusion since 1963 had produced only silence, and
his critical reputation, which peaked in the early sixties, has suffered accordingly. Little has been written about Salinger in recent years. *The Catcher in
the Rye*, however, remains a standard text in high school and college classrooms, and a loyal following of readers continues to hope for a continuation
of the Glass family saga. They feel that when and if that work is completed,
it will be one of the masterworks of twentieth-century fiction.

BOOKS BY SALINGER

Nine Stories. Bantam 1971 pap. $2.95; Little, Brown 1953 $15.45
The Catcher in the Rye. Bantam 1977 pap. $2.75; Little, Brown 1951 $14.45
Franny and Zooey. Bantam repr. 1969 pap. $2.95; Little Brown 1961 $12.95

Raise High the Roof Beam, Carpenters and Seymour: An Introduction. Bantam 1971
  pap. $3.50; Little, Brown 1963 $11.95. Two novellas.

BOOKS ABOUT SALINGER

French, Warren. *J. D. Salinger. Twayne's U.S. Authors Ser.* Bobbs text ed. 1963 pap.
  $4.95; *Twayne's U.S. Authors Ser.* G. K. Hall 2d ed. rev. ed. 1976 lib. bdg. $11.50
  1985 pap. $6.95; *Twayne's U.S. Authors Ser.* New College & Univ. Pr. 1963 pap.
  $3.45
Gwynn, Frederick L., and Joseph Blotner. *The Fiction of J. D. Salinger. Critical Essays in Modern Lit. Ser.* Univ. of Pittsburgh Pr. 1958 pap. $4.50
Lundquist, James. *J. D. Salinger. Lit. and Life Ser.* Ungar 1978 $12.95 pap. $6.95
Rosen, Gerald. *Zen in the Art of J. D. Salinger.* Creative Arts Bks. 1977 pap. $3.50
Starosciak, Kenneth. *J. D. Salinger: A Thirty Year Bibliography, 1938–1968.* Ross
  1971 $6.95

SINCLAIR, UPTON (BEALL). 1878–1968

Sinclair, a lifelong vigorous socialist, first came into fame with "the most
powerful of muck-raking novels," *The Jungle,* in 1906. Refused by five publishers and finally published by Sinclair himself, it became an immediate
bestseller, led to a government investigation of the Chicago stockyards, and
was fruitful of much reform. In 1967, he was invited by President Johnson
to "witness the signing of the Wholesome Meat Act, which will gradually
plug loopholes left by the first Federal meat inspection law" (*N.Y. Times*), a
law Sinclair had helped to bring about. Newspapers, colleges, schools,
churches, and industries have each been the subject of a Sinclair attack, ex-
posing their evils. Sinclair is not really a novelist, but a fearless and indefati-
gable journalist-crusader. All his early books are propaganda for his social
reforms. When regular publishers boycotted his work, he published himself,
usually at a financial loss. His 80 or so books have been translated into 47
languages, and his sales abroad, especially in Russia, have been enormous.

Dragon's Teeth, a "Lanny Budd" novel, won the Pulitzer Prize in 1942.
With *World's End* (1940), his sixty-fifth novel and a Literary Guild selection,
Sinclair had started his series of bestselling volumes in the ambitious saga
of his "hyperthyroid" hero Lanny Budd—a fictional history of contemporary
world events. *Presidential Mission* (1947) brings Lanny up to the invasion of
North Africa and the Casablanca Conference with Roosevelt, Churchill, and
others, and the eleventh volume, *The Return of Lanny Budd,* concerns the
growth of the Russian menace from 1946 through 1949. More than a million
copies of the Lanny Budd novels have been sold, and they have been translated into more than 20 languages.

BOOKS BY SINCLAIR

Springtime and Harvest. 1901. Scholarly repr. $23.00
Prince Hagen: A Phantasy. Ed. by R. Reginald and Douglas Melville, Ayer repr. of
  1903 ed. 1978 lib. bdg. $20.00
Manassas: A Novel of the War. Scholarly repr. of 1904 ed. 1969 $39.00
The Jungle. 1906. Intro. by Morris Dickstein, *Bantam Class. Ser.* text ed. 1981 pap.
  $1.95; Buccaneer Bks. repr. 1981 lib. bdg. $17.95; New Amer. Lib. (Signet Class.)

1973 pap. $1.95; *Penguin Modern Class. Ser.* 1980 pap. $2.25; *Penguin Fiction Ser.* 1985 pap. $4.95

Sylvia: A Novel. Scholarly repr. of 1913 ed. 1971 $29.00

King Coal: A Novel. 1917. Intro. by George Brandes, *Labor Movement Ser.* AMS Pr. repr. of 1921 ed. 1980 $24.00

The Brass Check: A Study of American Journalism. Arden Lib. 1979 lib. bdg. $15.00; *Amer. Journalists Ser.* Ayer repr. of 1919 ed. 1970 $25.50; Johnson Repr. repr. of 1920 ed. $35.00

Oil! Bentley repr. of 1927 ed. 1981 lib. bdg. $16.50

Boston: A Documentary Novel of the Sacco-Vanzetti Case. Intro. by Howard Zinn, Bentley repr. of 1928 ed. 1978 $16.50; Scholarly 2 vols. repr. of 1928 ed. $59.00

Little Steel. Labor Movement in Fiction and Nonfiction Ser. AMS Pr. repr. of 1938 ed. $23.00

BOOKS ABOUT SINCLAIR

Blinderman, Abraham, ed. *Critics on Upton Sinclair. Readings in Literary Criticism* Univ. of Miami Pr. 1975 $5.95

Bloodworth, William, Jr. *Upton Sinclair. Twayne's U.S. Authors Ser.* G. K. Hall 1977 lib. bdg. $13.50

Dell, Floyd. *Upton Sinclair: A Study in Social Protest.* AMS Pr. repr. of 1927 ed. $24.50

Gottesman, Ronald, and Charles Silet. *The Literary Manuscripts of Upton Sinclair.* Ohio State Univ. Pr. 1973 $12.50

Yoder, Jon A. *Upton Sinclair. Lit. and Life Ser.* Ungar 1975 $12.95

STEIN, GERTRUDE. 1874–1946

A dominant and central figure in modern cultural history, Gertrude Stein "left behind her the memory of a personage—not a great writer but a bold experimenter and a great woman" (MALCOLM COWLEY). She was born in Pennsylvania, but spent most of her childhood and early youth in California. After graduating from Radcliffe, where she was strongly influenced by the philosopher WILLIAM JAMES (see Vol. 4), she studied medicine for four years at Johns Hopkins but took no degree. In 1903 she went to Paris with her brother Leo.

From 1907 until her death, Stein lived in France with her lesbian friend and secretary Alice B. Toklas. Their apartment in Paris became renowned as one of the most celebrated and long-lived cultural salons in our century. Toklas, who died in 1967, described in her autobiography, *What Is Remembered* (1963, o.p.), their long friendship and the procession of artists, writers, philosophers, and critics who were their friends. Stein returned to the United States only once, in 1934, to give a lecture tour and to see her opera "Four Saints in Three Acts," with music by Virgil Thomson.

She was a master of words and used them entirely for their tonal and associational qualities. Such sentences as "A rose is a rose is a rose" baffled many of her contemporaries but seem less strange, and often masterly, in the light of today's changed taste, which she helped to mold. Her most ambitious novel was *The Making of Americans* (1925, o.p.); Ernest Hemingway corrected the original proofs. Her plays, *In Circles* and *What Happened*, have had great success in the New York off-Broadway theater. *What Happened* won an Obie Award in 1964. With the chief exception of *The Autobiography of Alice B. Toklas,* her most widely read work, and *Three Lives,* which includes *Melanchtha,* a brilliant portrait of a black girl, most of Gertrude Stein's writings are too difficult and experimental for general readers, but she has had considerable influence on other writers from the time of Ernest Hemingway and other members of what she called "the lost generation" to the present post-modernist period. Today's avant-garde writers often discover that their most daring innovations of language and style were anticipated by Gertrude Stein.

BOOKS BY STEIN

The Yale Edition of the Unpublished Writings of Gertrude Stein. Yale Univ. Pr. 8 vols. 1951–58 ea. $27.50

Selected Writings of Gertrude Stein. Ed. by Carl Van Vechten, Random (Vintage) 1972 pap. $7.95

Fernhurst, Q.E.D., and Other Early Writings. 1971. Liveright 1983 pap. $6.95

Three Lives. 1909. Intro. by Ann Douglas, New Amer. Lib. (Signet Class.) 1985 pap. $3.95; Random (Vintage) 1958 pap. $3.95

Tender Buttons. Gordon 1972 lib. bdg. $59.95; *Amer. Lit. Ser.* Haskell repr. of 1914 ed. 1970 lib. bdg. $50.00. Prose poems.

Lucy Church Amiably. Ultramarine repr. of 1930 ed. 1972 $20.00

Ida: A Novel. Cooper Square Pr. repr. of 1941 ed. 1971 $22.50; Random (Vintage) 1972 pap. $2.95

The Autobiography of Alice B. Toklas. 1933. Modern Lib. 1980 $6.95; Peter Smith $12.75; Random (Vintage) pap. $3.95. Stein's autobiography composed as though written by her companion.

BOOKS ABOUT STEIN

Bridgman, Richard. *Gertrude Stein in Pieces.* Oxford 1970 $27.50. Good critical introduction.

Copeland, Carolyn F. *Language and Time and Gertrude Stein.* Univ. of Iowa Pr. 1976 text ed. $15.00 pap. $7.50

DeKoven, Marianne. *A Different Language: Gertrude Stein's Experimental Writing.* Univ. of Wisconsin Pr. 1983 $22.50

Dubnick, Randa K. *The Structure of Obscurity: Gertrude Stein, Language, and Cubism.* Univ. of Illinois Pr. 1984 $19.50

Gertrude Stein and Alice B. Toklas: A Reference Guide. G. K. Hall 1984 $35.00

Hoffman, Frederick J. *Gertrude Stein. Pamphlets on Amer. Writers Ser.* Univ. of Minnesota Pr. 1961 pap. $1.25

Hoffman, Michael J. *Gertrude Stein. Twayne's U.S. Authors Ser.* G. K. Hall 1976 lib. bdg. $12.50

Liston, Maureen. *Gertrude Stein: An Annotated Critical Bibliography.* Kent State Univ. Pr. 1979 $15.00

Mellow, James R. *Charmed Circle: Gertrude Stein and Company.* 1974. Avon repr. 1982 pap. $4.95

Rogers, W. G. *When This You See Remember Me: Gertrude Stein in Person.* Darby repr. of 1948 ed. 1983 lib. bdg. $45.00; Greenwood repr. of 1948 ed. 1971 lib. bdg. $18.75

Sprigge, Elizabeth. *Gertrude Stein: Her Life and Work.* Arden Lib. repr. of 1957 ed. 1981 lib. bdg. $35.00

Steiner, Wendy. *Exact Resemblance to Exact Remembrance: The Literary Portraiture of Gertrude Stein.* Yale Univ. Pr. 1978 $23.50

Stewart, Allegra. *Gertrude Stein and the Present.* Harvard Univ. Pr. 1967 $20.00. Traces Stein's theories of writing as applied to her work.

Sutherland, Donald. *Gertrude Stein: A Biography of Her Work.* Greenwood repr. of 1951 ed. 1972 lib. bdg. $45.00

Walker, Jayne L. *The Making of a Modernist: Gertrude Stein from "Three Lives" to "Tender Buttons."* Univ. of Massachusetts Pr. 1984 $17.50

Wilson, Robert A. *Gertrude Stein: A Bibliography.* Phoenix Bk. Shop 1974 $15.00

STEINBECK, JOHN. 1902–1968

What amounts to a kind of Steinbeck boom in recent years has gone a long way toward elevating him to major status among American writers of his generation. If not quite at the world-class artistic level of a Hemingway or a Faulkner, he is nonetheless read very widely throughout the world by readers of all ages who consider him one of the most "American" of writers.

Born in Salinas County, California, Steinbeck was of German-Irish parentage. As a young man he went to New York where he worked as a reporter and as a hod carrier. Returning to California, he devoted himself to writing, with little success; his first three books sold fewer than 3,000 copies. *Tortilla Flat* (1935), dealing with the happy-go-unlucky *paisanos*, California Mexicans whose ancestors settled in the country 200 years ago, established his reputation. *In Dubious Battle* (1936), a labor novel of a strike and strike-breaking, won the gold medal of the Commonwealth Club of California. *Of Mice and Men* (1937), a long short story of a homeless moron, written almost entirely in dialogue, was an experiment and was dramatized in the year of its publication, winning the New York Drama Critics Circle Award. It gave him fame.

Out of a series of articles he wrote about the transient labor camps in California came the inspiration for his greatest book, *The Grapes of Wrath* (1939), the odyssey of the Joad family, dispossessed of their farm in the Dust Bowl and seeking a new home, only to be driven on from camp to camp. The fiction is interrupted at intervals by nonfiction, explaining this new sociological problem of American nomadism. As the American novel "of the season, probably the year, possibly the decade," it won the Pulitzer Prize. It roused America and won a broad readership by the unusual simplicity and tenderness with which Steinbeck treated social questions. Long after the social conditions it describes have been corrected if not forgotten, *The Grapes of Wrath* remains alive as a vivid account of believable human characters seen in symbolic and universal terms that transcend geography and history.

His best and most ambitious novel since *The Grapes of Wrath* is *East of Eden* (1952), a saga of two American families in California from about 1860 through World War I. *Cannery Row* (1945), *The Wayward Bus* (1947), and *Sweet Thursday* (1955) are lighter works that find Steinbeck returning to the lighthearted tone of *Tortilla Flat* as he recounts picaresque adventures of modern-day picaros. *The Winter of Our Discontent* (1961) struck some reviewers as being appropriately titled because of its despairing treatment of man's fall from grace in a wasteland world where money is king.

Steinbeck also wrote important nonfiction, including *Russian Journal* (1948, o.p.) in collaboration with the photographer Robert Capa; *Once There Was a War;* and *America and Americans* (1966, o.p.), which features pictures by 55 leading photographers and a 70-page essay by Steinbeck. His interest in marine biology led to two books primarily about sea life, *Sea of Cortez* (1941) (with Edward F. Ricketts) and *The Log from the Sea of Cortez* (1951). *Travels with Charley* is his engaging account of his journey of rediscovery of America, which took him through approximately 40 states.

BOOKS BY STEINBECK

The Portable John Steinbeck. Ed. by Pascal Covici, Viking 1946 pap. $7.95. Includes *Of Mice and Men, The Red Pony,* short stories, and other selections.
The Short Novels of John Steinbeck: Tortilla Flat, Of Mice and Men, The Red Pony, The Moon Is Down, Cannery Row, The Pearl. Viking 1963 $16.95
John Steinbeck: A Life in Letters. Ed. by Elaine Steinbeck and Robert Wallsten, Viking 1975 $22.50
A Cup of Gold. 1929. Penguin 1976 pap. $3.95
The Pastures of Heaven. 1932. Penguin 1982 pap. $3.95
Tortilla Flat. Penguin 1977 pap. $3.50; Viking 1935 $13.95
In Dubious Battle. 1936. Penguin 1979 pap. $3.95
Of Mice and Men. 1937. Bantam 1970 pap. $2.50; Modern Lib. 1938 $5.95
The Red Pony. 1937. Viking 1959 $9.95
The Grapes of Wrath. 1939. Penguin 1976 pap. $3.95; ed. by Peter Lisca, *Viking Critical Lib.* Penguin 1977 pap. $7.95
The Moon Is Down. 1942. Bantam 1970 pap. $1.95; Penguin 1982 pap. $3.95
Cannery Row. Viking 1945 $13.95
The Wayward Bus. Penguin repr. of 1947 ed. 1979 pap. $3.95
The Pearl. Viking 1947 $9.95 (and *The Red Pony*) Penguin 1976 pap. $2.95
Burning Bright: A Play in Story Form. Penguin repr. of 1950 ed. 1979 pap. $3.95
Sweet Thursday. Penguin repr. of 1955 ed. 1979 pap. $3.95
Short Reign of Pippin IV: A Fabrication. Penguin 1977 pap. $3.95
The Winter of Our Discontent. 1961. Penguin 1983 pap. $3.95

BOOKS ABOUT STEINBECK

Benson, Jackson J. *The True Adventures of John Steinbeck, Writer: A Biography.* Viking 1984 $35.00. "Of this splendid biography we will say only that it seems to us to rate with the half-dozen-or-so very best critical biographies of twentieth-century writers" (*Journal of Modern Lit.*).
Davis, Robert M., ed. *Steinbeck: A Collection of Critical Essays.* Prentice-Hall (Spectrum Bks.) 1972 $12.95
Demott, Robert. *Steinbeck's Reading: A Catalogue of Books Owned and Borrowed.* Garland 1983 lib. bdg. $47.00 1984 lib. bdg. $20.00
Fensch, Thomas. *Steinbeck and Covici: The Story of a Friendship.* Eriksson 1979 $12.95 pap. $9.95
French, Warren G., ed. *Companion to the Grapes of Wrath.* Kelley repr. 1963 lib. bdg. $17.50

Hayashi, Tetsumaro. *A New Steinbeck Bibliography (1929–1971). Author Bibliographies Ser.* Scarecrow Pr. 1973 $15.00

———. *A New Steinbeck Bibliography (1971–1981). Author Bibliographies Ser.* Scarecrow Pr. 1983 $15.00

———. *Steinbeck's Literary Dimension: A Guide to Comparative Studies.* Scarecrow Pr. 1973 $15.00

———. *A Study Guide to Steinbeck: A Handbook to His Major Works.* Scarecrow Pr. 1974 $15.00

Jain, Junita. *John Steinbeck's Concept of Man: A Critical Study of His Novels.* Humanities Pr. 1980 $11.00

Levant, Howard. *The Novels of John Steinbeck: A Critical Study.* Univ. of Missouri Pr. 1975 $20.00 pap. $9.50

Lisca, Peter. *The Wide World of John Steinbeck.* Gordian 1981 $15.00

McCarthy, Paul. *John Steinbeck. Lit. and Life Ser.* Ungar 1980 $12.95 pap. $6.95

Millichap, Joseph R. *Steinbeck and Film. Ungar Film Lib.* 1983 $12.95 pap. $6.95

St. Pierre, Brian. *John Steinbeck: The California Years.* Chronicle Bks. 1984 pap. $7.95

Watt, F. *Steinbeck. Writers and Critics Ser.* Chips 1978 $22.50

STYRON, WILLIAM. 1925–

When William Styron's first novel appeared in 1951, it seemed to some critics that the young author was the likely heir to William Faulkner. The story of a family doomed to decline and tragedy like Faulkner's Compsons, *Lie Down in Darkness* (1951) is a highly charged book that carries a quality of poetic brooding that seems both southern in the Faulkner sense and very modern in the way of a Kafka or Camus.

Born in Newport News, Virginia, Styron served in the U.S. Marine Corps before completing his studies at Duke University, where he studied creative writing with Professor William Blackburn, mentor to other writers of promise and achievement, and wrote his first stories. Not long after *Lie Down in Darkness* was accepted for publication, he was recalled to active duty because of the Korean crisis. He used some of his experiences for *The Long March* (1953), a short novel about individuality and authority in the military that was well received critically. His next full-length novel, *Set This House on Fire* (1960), is a tragicomedy, a satire, a bildungsroman, a portrait of the artist, and a whopping big novel in the Thomas Wolfe tradition that seemed to elevate Styron to the rank of major novelist.

Styron's bestseller, *The Confessions of Nat Turner*, received almost universal praise by the literary establishment before winning the Pulitzer Prize in 1967. Styron based his novel on a contemporary 20-page pamphlet about the actual Turner uprising published by a lawyer named Thomas Gray and hit upon the fictional device of having Nat dictate his account of the affair to Gray so that the rebellion is seen both from within and outside. Clifton Fadiman thought that Styron had "somehow thought himself inside the skin of one of the most remarkable, appalling and tragic figures in the entire chronicle of the American Negro." However, that judgment was severely contradicted by the contributions to *William Styron's Nat Turner: Ten Black Writers Respond* (o.p.), in which such prominent black writers as John

Oliver Killens and John Williams accused Styron of helping to perpetuate "just about every myth with which the black man has been shackled since slavery" (*PW*).

Styron turned to another moral issue in *Sophie's Choice*, a novel about the Holocaust as viewed retrospectively by one of its victims and survivors. Sophie Zawistowska tells her story to a young southern writer named Stingo who appears to be a surrogate for Styron himself. Reviewers differed in their assessment: Edith Milton (*Yale Review*), for instance, finding it "an ambiguous, masterful, and enormously satisfying novel" and Benjamin Demott (*Atlantic*) calling it "an over-reaching blockbuster." Just as black writers objected to *Confessions of Nat Turner* as a white man's distorted view of their race, Alvin Rosenberg (*Midstream*) insisted that Styron had written not so much a valid account of the Holocaust as a "spoof of the same."

BOOKS BY STYRON

Lie Down in Darkness. 1951. New Amer. Lib. (Plume) repr. 1978 pap. $6.95; Random 1979 $14.95
The Long March. Bantam 1981 pap. $2.95; Random (Vintage) 1953 $10.95
Set This House on Fire. Bantam 1981 pap. $3.95; New Amer. Lib. (Signet Class.) pap. $1.95; Random 1960 $15.00
The Confessions of Nat Turner. Bantam text ed. 1981 pap. $3.95; New Amer. Lib. (Signet Class.) repr. 1968 pap. $2.25; Random 1967 $16.95
Sophie's Choice. Bantam 1982 pap. $4.50; Random 1980 $15.95
This Quiet Dust: And Other Writings. Random 1982 $17.50. A potpourri of reminiscences, essays, and reflections on themes of Styron's fiction.

BOOKS ABOUT STYRON

Casciato, Arthur D., and James L. West, III. *Critical Essays on William Styron*. G. K. Hall 1982 $34.00
Friedman, Melvin J. *William Styron*. Bowling Green 1974 $2.50
Morris, Robert K., and Irving Malin, eds. *The Achievement of William Styron*. Univ. of Georgia Pr. 1975 $17.50 1981 $27.50 pap. $13.00
Pearce, Richard. *William Styron. Pamphlets on Amer. Writers Ser.* Univ. of Minnesota Pr. 1971 pap. $1.25

UPDIKE, JOHN. 1932–

When *Couples* was published in 1968, Wilfred Sheed (*N.Y. Times*) looked back on John Updike's career to that time and commented, "Updike can be quite a virtuoso. But with each book, his position seems a little less flashy and more solid." The mixture of flashy versatility and solid achievement has been apparent in Updike's writing since that judgment was made, but that he is a deeply committed literary artist is shown not only by the abundance of his works in several genres during the past quarter-century, but by his willingness to experiment with new forms and themes. Updike has shifted directions with each decade as he has responded to the changing times while at the same time maintaining a basic if sometimes ambiguous personal integrity.

Rabbit Run introduces Harry "Rabbit" Angstrom as a 26-year-old salesman of dime-store gadgets trapped in an unhappy marriage in a dismal Pennsylvania town who looks back wistfully on his days as a high school basketball star. *Rabbit Redux* (1971) takes up the story ten years later, and Rabbit's relationship with representative figures of the 1960s enables Updike to provide social commentary in a story marked by mellow wisdom and compassion in spite of some shocking jolts. In *Rabbit Is Rich*, Harry is comfortably middle-aged and complacent. Much of the book seems to satirize the country-club set and the swinging sexual/social life of Rabbit and his friends, but Updike again moves the story onto a higher plain, which would seem to justify those critics who think that Updike's vision is unquestionably religious in its essential nature.

Updike's other novels range widely in subject and locale from his first, *The Poorhouse Fair* (1959), about a home for the aged that seems to be a microcosm for society as a whole, through *The Coup*, about a revolution in Africa, to *The Witches of Eastwick*, in which Updike tries to write from inside the sensibilities of three witch-bitches of contemporary New England. *The Centaur* is a subtle, complicated allegorical novel that won the 1964 National Book Award. *Couples* was conceived, Updike said in a *N.Y. Times* interview, "to show a group of couples as an organism, something like a volvox, making demands on and creating behavior in the people in it."

Updike also has written short stories, poems, critical essays, and reviews. He was a staff member of the *New Yorker* for several years after graduating *summa cum laude* from Harvard and spending a year at the Ruskin School of Fine Arts in Oxford. His short fiction is notable for the crisp, efficient way in which he treats a wide variety of subjects. And that few contemporary authors make a more extensive attempt than Updike to keep up with the best work done by their writing contemporaries throughout the world is amply demonstrated by the abundance and range of the many critical pieces gathered in three thick volumes: *Assorted Prose, Picked-Up Pieces,* and *Hugging the Shore.*

BOOKS BY UPDIKE

Too Far to Go. Fawcett 1979 pap. $2.50. A selection of stories.
Same Door. Fawcett 1972 pap. $.95; Knopf 1959 $11.95; Random (Vintage) repr. of 1959 ed. 1981 pap. $4.95
The Poorhouse Fair. Fawcett 1981 pap. $2.50; Knopf repr. of 1959 ed. 1977 $13.95
Rabbit Run. Fawcett 1978 pap. $2.95; Knopf 1960 $13.95. With revised text.
Pigeon Feathers and Other Stories. Knopf 1962 $12.95
The Centaur. Fawcett 1977 pap. $2.75; Knopf 1963 $12.95
Of the Farm. Fawcett 1981 pap. $2.50; Knopf 1965 $10.95
The Music School. Fawcett 1977 pap. $1.75; Knopf 1966 $12.59; Random (Vintage) repr. of 1966 ed. 1980 pap. $4.95
Couples. Fawcett repr. 1985 pap. $4.50; Knopf 1968 $12.50
Bech: A Book. Knopf 1970 $13.95; Random (Vintage) 1980 pap. $4.95
Rabbit Redux. Fawcett repr. 1977 pap. $2.95; Knopf 1971 $14.95
Museums and Women and Other Stories. Knopf 1972 $15.00; Random (Vintage) repr. of 1972 ed. 1981 pap. $4.95

A Month of Sundays. Fawcett repr. 1985 pap. $3.50; Knopf 1975 $9.95
Marry Me. Fawcett repr. 1977 pap. $2.95; Knopf 1976 $9.95
The Coup. Fawcett 1980 pap. $2.95; Knopf 1978 $10.95
Problems and Other Stories. Fawcett 1981 pap. $2.95; Knopf 1979 $12.95
Rabbit Is Rich. Fawcett 1983 pap. $2.95; Knopf ltd. ed. 1981 $40.00
Bech Is Back. Fawcett 1983 pap. $2.95; Knopf 1982 $13.95
The Witches of Eastwick. Fawcett 1985 pap. $3.95; Knopf ltd. ed. 1984 $15.95

BOOKS ABOUT UPDIKE

Burchard, Rachael C. *John Updike: Yea Sayings. Crosscurrents Modern Critiques Ser.*
   Southern Illinois Univ. Pr. 1971 $7.95
Detweiler, Robert. *John Updike. Twayne's U.S. Authors Ser.* Bobbs text ed. 1972 pap.
   $4.95; *Twayne's U.S. Authors Ser.* G. K. Hall rev. ed. 1984 lib. bdg. $13.95 pap.
   $5.95
Gearhart, Elizabeth A. *John Updike: A Comprehensive Bibliography with Selected An-
   notations.* Folcroft repr. of 1978 ed. 1980 lib. bdg. $25.00; Norwood 1978 lib.
   bdg. $22.50
Greiner, Donald J. *John Updike's Novels.* Ohio Univ. Pr. text ed. 1984 $23.95. Comple-
   ments *The Other John Updike* (below) as a serviceable critical assessment of Up-
   dike's literary career.
————. *The Other John Updike: Poems, Short Stories, Prose, Play.* Ohio Univ. Pr. text
   ed. 1981 $20.95 pap. $10.00
MacNaughton, William R. *Critical Essays on John Updike. Critical Essays on Amer.
   Lit. Ser.* G. K. Hall 1982 lib. bdg. $30.00
Markle, Joyce B. *Fighters and Lovers: Theme in the Novels of John Updike.* New York
   Univ. Pr. 1973 $20.00
Olivas, Michael A. *Annotated Bibliography of John Updike Criticism.* Garland 1974
   $22.00
Sokoloff, B. A. *John Updike: A Comprehensive Bibliography.* Folcroft ltd. ed. 1972 lib.
   bdg. $20.00
Tallent, Elizabeth. *Married Men and Magic Tricks: John Updike's Erotic Heroes.* Cre-
   ative Arts Bks. 1982 pap. $6.95
Uphaus, Suzanne H. *John Updike. Lit. and Life Ser.* Ungar 1980 $12.95 pap. $6.95
Vaughan, Philip H. *John Updike's Images of America.* Mojave Bks. text ed. 1981 pap.
   $6.50

VIDAL, GORE. 1925–

When Gore Vidal's nineteenth novel, *Lincoln,* was published in 1984, Harold Bloom used it as the occasion to look back respectfully at Vidal's career
as a writer. In Bloom's view, Vidal has been most "gifted at re-imagining
history" so that such books as *Julian* (1964) about the pagan ruler of Rome
in the fourth century, *Burr* about America during the revolutionary period,
and *1876* about this nation 100 years later are probably his best achievements in fiction before *Lincoln.* In *Lincoln,* Vidal "found his truest subject,
which is our national political history during precisely those years when
our political and military histories were as one, one thing and one thing
only: the unwavering will of Abraham Lincoln to keep the states united"
(*N.Y. Review of Bks.*).

Gore Vidal was born at West Point, the U.S. Military Academy, and spent much of his childhood in Washington, D.C., with his maternal grandfather, a scholarly and witty senator from Oklahoma. His first book, *Williwaw,* reflected his own experiences on an army freight-supply ship in the Aleutian Islands during World War II, while *The City and the Pillar* (1948, o.p.) drew attention as one of the first honest and serious depictions of homosexuality in fiction. *Washington, D.C.* is a novel about corruption in that city from about 1937 to 1954 as seen from the perspective of a senator, and *Myra Breckenridge* (o.p.) achieved a certain notoriety both as a novel and a film dealing with the life of a transvestite. It is as an essayist, however, that Vidal finds his other chief distinction as a writer. He says of himself, "I am at heart a propagandist, a tremendous hater, a tiresome nag, complacently positive that there is no human problem which could not be solved if people would simply do as I advise."

BOOKS BY VIDAL

Williwaw: A Novel. AMS Pr. repr. of 1946 ed. $23.50
A Thirsty Evil: Seven Short Stories. Ayer repr. of 1956 ed. 11.00; Gay Sunshine repr. of 1956 ed. 1981 $20.00 pap. $7.95
Julian. Random (Vintage) repr. of 1964 ed. 1977 pap. $5.95
Washington, D.C. 1967. Ballantine repr. 1985 pap. $3.95; Random 1976 $14.95
Burr: A Novel. Ballantine 1985 pap. $3.95; Random 1973 $14.95
Myron: A Novel. Random 1974 $6.95
Kalki. Random 1978 $14.95
Creation. Ballantine 1985 pap. $3.95; Random 1981 $15.95
Duluth. Ballantine 1984 pap. $3.95; Random 1983 $13.95
Lincoln: A Novel. Ballantine repr. 1985 pap. $4.95; Random 1984 $19.95

BOOKS ABOUT VIDAL

Kiernan, Robert F. *Gore Vidal. Lit. and Life Ser.* Ungar 1982 $12.95 pap. $6.95
Stanton, Robert J. *Gore Vidal: A Primary and Secondary Bibliography.* G. K. Hall 1980 lib. bdg. $28.50
————, ed. *Views from a Window: Conversations with Gore Vidal.* Lyle Stuart 1980 lib. bdg. $14.95
White, Ray L. *Gore Vidal. U.S. Authors Ser.* G. K. Hall 1968 lib. bdg. $12.50; *Twayne's U.S. Authors Ser.* New College & Univ. Pr. 1968 pap. $5.95

VONNEGUT, KURT, JR. 1922–

The appeal of Kurt Vonnegut, Jr., especially to bright younger readers of the past few decades may be attributed partly to the fact that he is one of the few writers who have successfully straddled the imaginary line between science-fiction fantasy and whatever we mean by real literature. He was born in Indianapolis and attended Cornell University, but his college education was interrupted by World War II. Captured during the Battle of the Bulge and imprisoned in Dresden, he received a Purple Heart for what he calls a "ludicrously negligible wound." After the war he returned to Cornell and then earned his M.A. at the University of Chicago. He worked as a police reporter and in public relations before placing many short stories in the popular magazines and beginning his career as a novelist.

His first novel, *Player Piano*, is a highly credible account of a future mechanistic society in which people count for little. *The Sirens of Titan* is the story of a playboy whisked off to Mars and outer space in order to learn some humbling lessons about Earth's modest function in the total scheme of things. *Mother Night* satirizes the Nazi mentality in its narrative about an American writer who broadcasts propaganda in Germany during the war but may or may not be an Allied agent. *Cat's Cradle* makes use of some of Vonnegut's experiences in General Electric laboratories in its story about the discovery of a special kind of ice that destroys the world. *God Bless You, Mr. Rosewater* satirizes a benevolent foundation set up to foster the salvation of the world through love, an endeavor with, of course, disastrous results.

Slaughterhouse-Five; or The Children's Crusade is the book that marked a turning point in Vonnegut's career. Based on his experiences in Dresden, it is the story of another Vonnegut surrogate named Billy Pilgrim who travels back and forth in time and becomes a kind of modern-day Everyman. The novel was something of a cult book during the Vietnam era. *Breakfast of Champions*, the story of a Pontiac dealer who goes crazy after reading a science-fiction novel by Kilgore Trout, received generally unfavorable reviews, but was a commercial success. *Slapstick*, dedicated to the memory of Laurel and Hardy, is the somewhat wacky memoir of a 100-year-old ex-president who thinks he can solve society's problems by giving everyone a new middle name. In addition to his fiction, Vonnegut has published nonfiction on social problems and other topics, some of which is collected in *Wampeters, Foma and Granfalloons* (1974).

BOOKS BY VONNEGUT

Player Piano. 1952. Dell (Delta Bks.) 1972 pap. $6.95
The Sirens of Titan. 1959. Delacorte 1971 $9.95; Dell (Delta Bks.) 1971 pap. $2.95
Mother Night. 1962. Dell (Delta Bks.) 1972 pap. $5.95
Cat's Cradle. 1963. Dell (Delta Bks.) 1974 pap. $6.95
God Bless You, Mr. Rosewater. 1965. Delacorte 1971 $8.95; Dell (Delta Bks.) 1974 pap. $8.95
Welcome to the Monkey House. 1968. Dell (Delta Bks.) 1970 pap. $2.75
Slaughterhouse-Five; or The Children's Crusade. 1969. Dell (Delta Bks.) 1974 pap. $3.95
Between Time and Timbuktu; or Prometheus Five: A Space Fantasy. 1969. Dell (Delta Bks.) 1974 pap. $9.95
Breakfast of Champions. Delacorte 1973 $7.95; Dell 1982 pap. $2.95
Slapstick; or Lonesome No More. Delacorte 1976 $7.95; Dell 1982 pap. $2.95
Palm Sunday: An Autobiographical Collage. 1982. Dell 1984 pap. $3.95

BOOKS ABOUT VONNEGUT

Hudgens, Betty L., ed. *Kurt Vonnegut, Jr.: A Checklist. Modern Authors Checklist Ser.* Gale 1972 $35.00

Klinkowitz, Jerome. *Kurt Vonnegut. Contemporary Writers Ser.* Methuen 1982 pap. $4.25
Lundquist, James. *Kurt Vonnegut. Lit. and Life Ser.* Ungar 1977 $12.95 pap. $6.95
Mayo, Clark. *Kurt Vonnegut: The Gospel from Outer Space; or Yes We Have No Nirvanas.* Borgo Pr. 1977 lib. bdg. $10.95 pap. $3.95
Reed, Peter J. *Kurt Vonnegut, Jr. Writers for the Seventies Ser.* Crowell 1976 pap. $2.95
Schatt, Stanley. *Kurt Vonnegut, Jr. Twayne's U.S. Authors Ser.* Bobbs text ed. 1976 pap. $4.95; *Twayne's U.S. Authors Ser.* G. K. Hall 1976 lib. bdg. $13.50

WARREN, ROBERT PENN. 1905–

Robert Penn Warren is an unusually versatile writer who has tried his hand at almost every kind of literature. In all these forms he has achieved recognition and distinction, but it is as a poet, critic, and novelist that he is most widely known.

Writing almost always about his native South, Warren has produced ten novels and a collection of short stories, *The Circus in the Attic and Other Stories* (1948, o.p.). By far the most successful of his novels is *All the King's Men*, the story of a southern politician and demagogue named Willie Stark, which Warren based on the rise and fall of Huey Long. Warren was considered one of the most influential of the New Critics whose influence on the teaching of literature in American schools and universities during the late 1940s and 1950s could scarcely be overestimated, and because *All the King's Men* seemed to be the very epitome of what a good work of literature should be in New Critical terms—a complicated but highly readable narrative filled with irony and ambiguity—the novel came to be used widely in courses on modern fiction. It won both the Pulitzer Prize and the Southern Authors Award in 1947.

Warren's other novels are disappointing by comparison. Following the success of *All the King's Men*, however, Warren seemed to turn to more loosely told stories about dramatic and romantic subjects, such as the miscegenation theme of *Band of Angels* (1955, o.p.) or the natural catastrophes that serve as the crisis background for *The Cave* and *Flood: A Romance of Our Time* (1964, o.p.). *Wilderness: A Tale of the Civil War* (1961, o.p.) is an allegory of a man's spiritual quest for truth about himself and the world. *Meet Me in the Green Glen* (1971, o.p.), the story of a tragic love affair, seemed to mark a return to the tighter structure and more complex artistry of Warren's earlier novels, but *A Place to Come To*, apparently his last novel, in which an elderly and renowned scholar who seems to owe much to Warren himself looks back on his family's past in an effort to find the meaning of his life, struck some reviewers as a confused and tired work. Sometime midway through his career as a novelist it is as if Warren stopped thinking of himself as a southern writer in the tradition of William Faulkner and turned instead to Thomas Wolfe for inspiration. Although in retrospect that switch must be regretted, no one can deny the immense influence of Robert Penn Warren on modern letters. (See also Chapter 9.)

BOOKS BY WARREN

Night Rider. 1939. Random (Vintage) 1979 pap. $2.95
All the King's Men. 1945. Buccaneer Bks. repr. 1981 lib. bdg. $14.95; Harcourt 1982
    $5.95; Random 1960 $13.95
World Enough and Time. 1950. Random (Vintage) 1979 pap. $2.95
The Cave. Random 1959 $12.95
A Place to Come To. Random 1977 $12.95

BOOKS ABOUT WARREN

Bohner, Charles. *Robert Penn Warren. Twayne's U.S. Authors Ser.* G. K. Hall rev. ed.
    1981 lib. bdg. $13.50; *Twayne's U.S. Authors Ser.* New College & Univ. Pr. 1964
    pap. $5.95
Casper, Leonard. *Robert Penn Warren: The Dark and Bloody Ground.* Greenwood repr.
    1960 lib. bdg. $22.50
Chambers, R., ed. *Twentieth Century Interpretations of All the King's Men.* Prentice-
    Hall (Spectrum Bks.) 1977 $9.95 pap. $3.45
Clark, William B. *Critical Essays on Robert Penn Warren. Critical Essays on Amer. Lit.
    Ser.* G. K. Hall (Twayne) 1981 $26.00
Giordano, Frank. *Homage to Robert Penn Warren.* Logbridge-Rhodes 1982 $14.00
    pap. $5.00
Gray, Richard, ed. *Robert Penn Warren: A Collection of Critical Essays. Twentieth-Cen-
    tury Views Ser.* Prentice-Hall (Spectrum Bks.) 1980 $11.95 pap. $3.95
Grimshaw, James A., Jr. *Robert Penn Warren: A Descriptive Bibliography, 1922–1979.*
    Fwd. by Robert Penn Warren, Univ. Pr. of Virginia 1982 $30.00
Guttenberg, Barnet. *Web of Being: The Novels of Robert Penn Warren.* Vanderbilt
    Univ. Pr. 1975 $11.95
Justus, James H. *The Achievement of Robert Penn Warren. Southern Literary Ser.* Loui-
    siana State Univ. Pr. text ed. 1981 pap. $12.95
Light, James F. *Merrill Studies in All the King's Men.* Merrill text ed. 1971 pap. $3.95
Nakadate, Neil, ed. *Robert Penn Warren: A Reference Guide.* G. K. Hall 1977 lib. bdg.
    $33.50
———. *Robert Penn Warren: Critical Perspectives.* Univ. Pr. of Kentucky 1981 $26.00
Snipes, Katherine. *Robert Penn Warren. Lit. and Life Ser.* Ungar 1984 $12.95
Walker, Marshall. *Robert Penn Warren: A Vision Earned.* Barnes & Noble text ed.
    1979 $25.00

WELTY, EUDORA. 1909–

One of the most admired American writers, Eudora Welty has steadily
gone on writing short stories and novels that are entirely original, sometimes melodramatic, occasionally fantastic, and often concerned with psychological aberration. She has a fine ear for dialogue and a sense of style
that elevates her fiction above the ordinary. Born in Jackson, Mississippi,
she attended the Mississippi State College for Women before going north to
the University of Wisconsin and Columbia University. She worked for a
while in advertising, then returned to Jackson to take a government publicity job. She has remained in Jackson since then, living quietly with her family and pursuing a literary career that has brought her several awards and
much critical attention. Some of her better-known short stories, frequently
anthologized and thus widely taught and studied in classrooms, are "Why I

Live at the P.O.," "Death of a Traveling Salesman," "Petrified Man," and "A Worn Path."

Although Welty's critical reputation remains largely dependent upon her excellent short stories, she has also written four full-length novels, which have been well received. *Delta Wedding* is a densely plotted novel with many characters told from multiple points of view. It explores with intelligence and subtlety problems of domestic relationships and the mixing of social classes. *The Ponder Heart,* a more simply told story, centers around the murder trial of a man unjustly accused of killing his young wife. With *Losing Battles,* Welty deals again with the complexities of a large family gathering. *The Optimist's Daughter* is the story of tangled relationships between a 71-year-old judge undergoing a critical eye operation in a New Orleans hospital, his daughter, a withdrawn widow summoned from Chicago, and the judge's second wife of coarse breeding younger than his daughter. Gradually, this subtle story of father-daughter and husband-wives begins to reverberate with further complications. Howard Moss called the book "a miracle of compression. . . . The best book Eudora Welty has ever written" (*N.Y. Times*).

One Writer's Beginnings, an engaging volume of reminiscences originally given as lectures at Harvard, had the unusual distinction for a serious work of literary nonfiction published by a university press of climbing high on the bestseller lists during 1984. Her other nonfiction includes *One Time, One Place: Mississippi in the Depression* (1972), *A Snapshot Album,* and *The Eye of the Story: Selected Essays and Reviews.*

BOOKS BY WELTY

The Collected Stories of Eudora Welty. Harcourt 1980 $22.95 1982 pap. $9.95
Selected Stories. 1954. Intro. by Katherine Anne Porter, Modern Lib. $6.95
Thirteen Stories. 1956. Ed. by Ruth M. Vande Kieft, Harcourt 1965 pap. $3.95
A Curtain of Green and Other Stories. 1941. Harcourt 1979 pap. $4.95
The Wide Net and Other Stories. Harcourt repr. of 1943 ed. 1974 pap. $4.95
The Robber Bridegroom. 1942. Atheneum 1963 pap. $3.95; Harcourt repr. of 1948 ed. 1978 pap. $3.95
Delta Wedding. 1946. Harcourt 1979 pap. $4.95
The Golden Apples. Harcourt 1949 $12.95 pap. $5.95
The Ponder Heart. Harcourt 1954 $6.95 1967 pap. $3.95
The Bride of Innisfallen and Other Stories. Harcourt repr. of 1955 ed. 1972 pap. $4.95
Losing Battles. Random 1970 $13.95; Random (Vintage) 1978 pap. $4.95
The Optimist's Daughter. Random 1972 $10.00; Random (Vintage) 1985 pap. $3.95

BOOKS ABOUT WELTY

Abadie, Ann J., and Louis D. Dollarhide. *Eudora Welty: A Form of Thanks.* Univ. Pr. of Mississippi 1979 $9.95 pap. $4.95
Bryant, Joseph A., Jr. *Eudora Welty.* Pamphlets on Amer. Writers Ser. Univ. of Minnesota Pr. 1968 pap. $1.25
Desmond, John F., ed. *A Still Moment: Essays on the Art of Eudora Welty.* Scarecrow Pr. 1978 $15.00
Devlin, Albert J. *Eudora Welty's Chronicle: A Story of Mississippi.* Univ. Pr. of Missis-

sippi 1983 $20.00. Considers the stories in historical order as a chronicle that
can stand comparison with Faulkner's Yoknapatawpha saga.
Kreyling, Michael. *Eudora Welty's Achievement of Order. Southern Literary Ser.* Louisi-
ana State Univ. Pr. 1980 $10.00
Prenshaw, Peggy W., ed. *Conversations with Eudora Welty.* Univ. Pr. of Mississippi
1984 $17.95 pap. $9.95
————. *Eudora Welty: Thirteen Essays.* Univ. Pr. of Mississippi 1983 pap. $7.95
Randisi, Jennifer L. *A Tissue of Lies: Eudora Welty and the Southern Romance.* Univ.
Pr. of Amer. 1982 $25.00 text ed. pap. $12.00
Swearingen, Bethany C. *Eudora Welty: A Critical Bibliography, 1936–58.* Univ. Pr. of
Mississippi 1984 $10.00
Vande Kieft, Ruth M. *Eudora Welty. Twayne's U.S. Authors Ser.* New College & Univ.
Pr. 1962 pap. $3.45

WEST, NATHANAEL (pseud. of Nathan Wallenstein Weinstein). 1904–1940

Nathanael West's modest legacy of completed works reached its peak of
recognition during the period when later Jewish American writers were discovering black humor. Among novels that chronicle the wasteland despair
and grotesque comedy of the time between wars, West's *Miss Lonelyhearts*
(1933) and *The Day of the Locust* (1939) stand out as remarkable examples.
The first is about a young man conducting a column of advice to the love-
lorn who finds it increasingly impossible not to share the problems of his
readers, and *The Day of the Locust* is a surrealistic story about a riot that
ends with the burning of Los Angeles. If FRANZ KAFKA (see Vol. 2) had lived
to come to the United States and become a screenwriter, he might have written a book like *The Day of the Locust*, which MALCOLM COWLEY called the
best novel ever written about Hollywood. West's two other short novels, *The
Dream Life of Balso Snell* (1931) and *A Cool Million* (1934), are experimental
works that offer variations on the theme of reality and illusion; they too
look toward a literature of the absurd and deserve their place in literary history as influences on a school of American writers that came into prominence during the 1960s.

West's own life had aspects of tragic absurdity. He was married to Eileen
McKenney, the original of the central figure in *My Sister Eileen*, while his
own sister became the wife of humorist S. J. PERELMAN. After writing *Miss
Lonelyhearts*, West and his wife went to Hollywood and remained there until they were both killed in a car accident in 1940.

BOOKS BY WEST

The Complete Works of Nathanael West. Intro. by Alan Ross, Octagon repr. of 1957 ed.
1979 lib. bdg. $29.00
Miss Lonelyhearts and The Day of the Locust. New Directions pap. $5.25
The Dream Life of Balso Snell and A Cool Million. Farrar 1963 pap. $5.95
The Day of the Locust. Buccaneer Bks. repr. 1981 lib. bdg. $15.95; intro. by Alfred
Kazin, New Amer. Lib. (Signet Class.) 1983 pap. $2.95

BOOKS ABOUT WEST

Comerchero, Victor. *Nathanael West: The Ironic Prophet.* Univ. of Washington Pr. repr. 1967 pap. $5.95

Hyman, Stanley E. *Nathanael West. Pamphlets on Amer. Writers Ser.* Univ. of Minnesota Pr. 1962 pap. $1.25

Malin, Irving. *Nathanael West's Novels. Crosscurrents Modern Critiques Ser.* Southern Illinois Univ. Pr. 1972 $6.95

Martin, Jay. *Nathanael West: The Art of His Life.* Carroll & Graf 1984 pap. $8.95; Farrar 1970 $10.00. The standard biography.

Vannatta, Dennis P. *Nathanael West: An Annotated Bibliography. Reference Lib. of the Humanities* Garland 1975 lib. bdg. $28.00

White, William. *Nathanael West: A Comprehensive Bibliography.* Kent State Univ. Pr. 1975 $12.00

Widmer, Kingsley. *Nathanael West. Twayne's U.S. Authors Ser.* G. K. Hall 1982 lib. bdg. $12.50

WHARTON, EDITH. 1862–1937

A good friend and disciple of Henry James and a woman who moved in wealthy and fashionable circles throughout her life, Edith Wharton was well qualified to work within the tradition of social realism. She wrote novels of manners, but her attitude was rather consistently critical of the society she wrote about, and it is finally her irony and her satiric touches that make her best fiction worth reading today.

Ethan Frome (1911), the single work for which Wharton is best known, is in many ways the least characteristic of her writings. It is a taut and harsh short novel, still widely read in schools, about a domestic tragedy set in a rural area of New England. While Wharton lived, however, her most widely read book was *The Age of Innocence*, a novel of manners reinforced by strong psychological insights, which won the Pulitzer Prize in 1920. Since her death, *The House of Mirth* (1905) has become the most widely read and frequently taught of her longer novels. Its heroine, Lily Bart, is perhaps the best portrait of "the American girl" after Daisy Miller, and if her story is widely used in today's classrooms in spite of its pessimistic tone, that may be partly because it provides a salutary lesson for feminist critics and teachers: "Wharton's intimate and sympathetic portrait of Lily Bart is perhaps the finest example anywhere in American fiction of the tragedy of a woman who has come to regard herself primarily as a decorative object" (Cynthia Griffin Wolff, *Dictionary of Literary Biography*). *The Custom of the Country* (1913) is thought to be Wharton's most biting satire, while the four novelettes gathered together in *Old New York* are the most likely candidates for rediscovery. *The Reef,* a novel set in France, and the short novel *Madame de Treymes* are considered to be the most Jamesian of her books, but not necessarily among her best productions. Edith Wharton was reticent about her personal life, but her *A Backward Glance* (1934, o.p.) contains charming reminiscences of James and other contemporaries.

Books by Wharton

The Edith Wharton Omnibus. Intro. by Gore Vidal, Scribner 1978 $4.95
Short Stories of Edith Wharton, 1910–1937. Scribner 1975 $30.00
Ghost Stories of Edith Wharton. Scribner repr. 1973 $22.50
Madame de Treymes and Others: Four Novelettes. Scribner 1973 lib. bdg. $20.00 pap.
     $5.95. Includes *The Touchstone* (1900), *Sanctuary* (1903), *Madame de Treymes*
     (1907), and *The Bunner Sisters* (1916).
Roman Fever and Other Stories. Scribner 1978 lib. bdg. $20.00 pap. $5.95
The Great Inclination. 1899. AMS Pr. repr. $17.00; Scholarly $6.00
The Touchstone. AMS Pr. repr. of 1900 ed. $17.00
Crucial Instances. AMS Pr. repr. of 1901 ed. $17.00; Scholarly repr. of 1901 ed. $6.00
Valley of Decision. Scholarly 2 vols. repr. of 1902 ed. $13.00
The House of Mirth. Bantam Class. Ser. 1984 pap. $2.25; Berkley Publishing repr.
     1984 pap. $3.50; New Amer. Lib. (Signet Class.) 1964 pap. $2.95; ed. by R. W. B.
     Lewis, New York Univ. Pr. (Gotham Lib.) 1977 $25.00 pap. $8.50; intro. by Cyn-
     thia G. Wolff, *Penguin Amer. Lib. Ser.* 1985 pap. $4.95; Scribner repr. of 1905 ed.
     1976 $20.00 pap. $6.95
Ethan Frome. Scribner repr. of 1911 ed. $17.50 pap. $4.95
The Reef. Intro. by Louis Auchincloss, Scribner repr. of 1912 ed. 1984 $20.00 pap.
     $8.95
The Custom of the Country. Scribner repr. of 1913 ed. 1976 $25.00 pap. $5.95
Summer: A Novel. Intro. by Cynthia G. Wolff, Harper 1980 pap. $2.84; Scholarly
     repr. of 1917 ed. 1970 $39.00
The Age of Innocence. Scribner repr. of 1920 ed. 1968 $20.00 pap. $7.95 1983 pap.
     $3.95
Old New York. 1924. Intro. by Marilyn French, Berkley Publishing repr. 1981 pap.
     $2.95. Four novelettes.

Books about Wharton

Ammons, Elizabeth. *Edith Wharton's Argument with America.* Univ. of Georgia Pr.
     1980 $17.00
Gimbel, Wendy. *Edith Wharton: Orphancy and Survival. Landmark Dissertations in
     Women's Studies* Praeger 1984 $29.95
Lawson, Richard H. *Edith Wharton. Lit. and Life Ser.* Ungar 1977 $12.95
Lewis, R. W. B. *Edith Wharton: A Biography.* Harper 1975 $17.50. A masterful biogra-
     phy.
Loney, Glenn, ed. *The House of Mirth: The Play of the Novel.* Fairleigh Dickinson
     Univ. Pr. 1981 $21.50
McDowell, Margaret B. *Edith Wharton. Twayne's U.S. Authors Ser.* G. K. Hall 1976
     lib. bdg. $11.50
Nevius, Blake. *Edith Wharton: A Study of Her Fiction.* 1953. *California Lib. Repr. Ser.*
     Univ. of California Pr. 1976 $30.00
Rae, Catherine M. *Edith Wharton's New York Quartet.* Fwd. by R. W. B. Lewis, Univ.
     Pr. of America 1984 lib. bdg. $16.50 text ed. pap. $8.00
Walton, Geoffrey. *Edith Wharton: A Critical Interpretation.* 1970. Fairleigh Dickinson
     Univ. Pr. 2d ed. rev. 1982 $22.50
Wershoven, Carol. *The Female Intruder in the Novels of Edith Wharton.* Fairleigh Dick-
     inson Univ. Pr. 1982 $27.50
Wolff, Cynthia G. *A Feast of Words: The Triumph of Edith Wharton.* Oxford 1977
     $25.00 pap. $6.95

WILDER, THORNTON. 1897–1975

One of the most honored and versatile of modern writers, Thornton Wilder combined a career as a successful novelist with work for the theater that made him one of this century's outstanding dramatists. It was an early short novel, however, that first brought him fame. *The Bridge of San Luis Rey*, a bestseller that won the Pulitzer Prize in 1927, is the story of a group of assorted people who happen to be on a bridge in Peru when it collapses. Ingeniously constructed and rich in its philosophical implications about fate and synchronicity, Wilder's book would seem to be the first well-known example of a formula that has become a cliché in popular literature. His attraction to classical themes is manifested in *The Woman of Andros* (1930, o.p.), a tragedy about young love in pre-Christian Greece, and *The Ides of March* (1948, o.p.), set in the time of Julius Caesar and told in letters and documents covering a long span of years. *Heaven's My Destination* (1934, o.p.) is a seriocomic and picaresque story about a young book salesman traveling through the Midwest during the early years of the Great Depression. *Theophilus North* (1973), Wilder's last novel, disappointed many reviewers, but it provided its author with opportunities to offer some wry observations on the life of the idle rich in Newport during the summer of 1926 and to ponder in the story of his alter ego what might have happened if Wilder had stayed home, so to speak, instead of becoming Thornton Wilder.

As a serious writer of fiction, Wilder's main claim rests on *The Eighth Day* (1967), an intellectual thriller, which the *N.Y. Times* called "the most substantial fiction of his career." It won the National Book Award for fiction in 1968. (See also Volume 2, Chapter 5.)

BOOKS BY WILDER

The Bridge of San Luis Rey. 1927. Avon 1976 pap. $2.95; Harper 1967 $12.45
The Eighth Day. Avon 1976 pap. $2.95; Harper 1967 $11.95
Theophilus North. Avon 1981 pap. $3.95; Harper 1973 $10.95

BOOKS ABOUT WILDER

Burbank, Rex J. *Thornton Wilder. Twayne's U.S. Authors Ser.* G. K. Hall 2d ed. 1978 lib. bdg. $12.50; *Twayne's U.S. Authors Ser.* New College & Univ. Pr. 1961 pap. $5.95
Goldstone, Malcolm L. *The Art of Thornton Wilder*. Univ. of Nebraska Pr. 1965 pap. $4.25
Goldstone, Richard H., and Gary Anderson, eds. *Thornton Wilder: A Bibliographical Checklist of Work by and about Thornton Wilder. Studies in Modern Lit.* AMS Pr. 1982 $29.50
Grebanier, Bernard. *Thornton Wilder. Pamphlets on Amer. Writers Ser.* Univ. of Minnesota Pr. 1964 pap. $1.25
Harrison, Gilbert A. *The Enthusiast: A Life of Thornton Wilder*. Ticknor & Fields 1983 $19.95. Entertaining but a solid life.
Stresau, Hermann. *Thornton Wilder*. Trans. by Frieda Schutze, *Lit. and Life Ser.* Ungar 1971 pap. $5.95
Wilder, Amos N. *Thornton Wilder and His Public*. Fortress Pr. 1980 $8.95

WOLFE, THOMAS. 1900–1938

When William Faulkner was asked to rate his contemporaries, he put Thomas Wolfe at the top of the list—not so much for what Wolfe accomplished, said Faulkner, but for the magnitude of what he tried to do. Wolfe was born in Asheville, North Carolina, received his M.A. from Harvard, taught at New York University, and traveled abroad when he could. His one long autobiographical novel begins with *Look Homeward, Angel,* perhaps the best American bildungsroman ever written, the account of a sensitive young man named Eugene Gant. Eugene's story is continued in *Of Time and the River,* in which a publisher's note announced that "this novel is the second in a series of six" and gave the six titles. Wolfe lived to complete but four. Hurt and troubled by widespread rumors that his undisciplined manuscripts had been shaped into publishable form by Scribner's famous editor Maxwell Perkins, Wolfe changed publishers, moving from Scribner to Harper, and for legal reasons found it necessary to change the name of his fictional surrogate. The George Webber of *The Web and the Rock* and *You Can't Go Home Again* is essentially Eugene Gant continuing his search for the meaning of life, and Wolfe traces the turbulent path of his hero. His European experiences have shown George the beginnings of Hitlerism, and he tells his editor that henceforth he will write fiction of social protest. Wolfe, of course, did not live to write the books so bravely announced.

In addition to the four installments of the one long autobiographical novel on which his reputation must chiefly rest, Wolfe wrote some short stories that are collected in *The Hills Beyond* and *From Death to Morning.* As a student in the famous 47 Workshop at Harvard and afterward on his own, Wolfe wrote several plays, including *Welcome to Our City.* Wolfe's own plays were not as successful in the theater as Ketti Frings's adaptation of *Look Homeward, Angel* as a comedy-drama in three acts; it won a Pulitzer Prize in 1958 as well as the New York Drama Critics Circle Award as the best play of the season.

BOOKS BY WOLFE

The Short Novels of Thomas Wolfe. Scribner repr. 1962 $25.00

The Autobiography of an American Novelist. Ed. by Leslie A. Field, Harvard Univ. Pr. text ed. 1983 $15.00 pap. $5.95. Combines *The Story of a Novel* (1936) and *Writing and Living* (1964).

Thomas Wolfe's Letters to His Mother, Julia Elizabeth Wolfe. Ed. by John S. Terry, AMS Pr. repr. of 1943 ed. $36.00

Beyond Love and Loyalty: The Letters of Thomas Wolfe and Elizabeth Nowell. Ed. by Richard S. Kennedy, Univ. of North Carolina Pr. 1983 $18.95. Correspondence between Wolfe and his agent/biographer, together with a previously unpublished story, "No More Rivers."

My Other Loneliness: Letters of Thomas Wolfe and Aline Bernstein. Ed. by Suzanne S. Stutman, Univ. of North Carolina Pr. 1983 $30.00 pap. $14.95. Correspondence with the woman who served as model for Esther Jack in Wolfe's fiction.

Look Homeward, Angel. 1929. Buccaneer Bks. repr. 1981 lib. bdg. $16.95; Scribner 1979 $17.50 1982 pap. $6.95

Of Time and the River. Scribner repr. of 1935 ed. 1971 $17.50 1979 $17.50

From Death to Morning. Scribner repr. of 1935 ed. pap. $8.95

The Web and the Rock. Harper repr. of 1939 ed. 1973 pap. $3.95

You Can't Go Home Again. Buccaneer Bks. repr. 1981 lib. bdg. $16.95; Harper repr. of 1940 ed. 1973 pap. $4.33

The Hills Beyond. Harper repr. of 1943 ed. $12.50; New Amer. Lib. (Signet Class.) 1982 pap. $8.95

A Western Journal. Univ. of Pittsburgh Pr. 1968 pap. $4.95

BOOKS ABOUT WOLFE

Berger, Brian F. *Thomas Wolfe: The Final Journey.* Willamette River 1984 $10.00

Evans, Elizabeth. *Thomas Wolfe.* Ungar 1984 $12.95

Gurko, Leo. *Thomas Wolfe: Beyond the Romantic Ego. Twentieth-Century Amer. Writers Ser.* Crowell 1975 $11.49. Biography for young readers.

Holman, C. Hugh. *The Loneliness at the Core: Studies in Thomas Wolfe.* Louisiana State Univ. Pr. 1975 $17.50

Johnson, Elmer D. *Thomas Wolfe: A Checklist.* Kent State Univ. Pr. 1970 $13.00

Kennedy, Richard S. *The Window of Memory: The Literary Career of Thomas Wolfe.* Univ. of North Carolina Pr. 1962 $19.95 pap. $7.95. A penetrating scholarly and critical study of the genesis and composition of Wolfe's fiction.

————, ed. *Thomas Wolfe: A Harvard Perspective.* Croissant 1983 $12.95

McElderry, Bruce R., Jr. *Thomas Wolfe. Twayne's U.S. Authors Ser.* G. K. Hall 1963 lib. bdg. $12.50; *Twayne's U.S. Authors Ser.* New College & Univ. Pr. 1964 pap. $5.95

Muller, H. J. *Thomas Wolfe.* Krause repr. of 1947 ed. $17.00

Nowell, Elizabeth. *Thomas Wolfe: A Biography.* Greenwood repr. of 1960 ed. 1973 lib. bdg. $29.75. Excellent life of the man by one who knew him well.

Phillipson, John S. *Thomas Wolfe: A Reference Guide.* G. K. Hall 1977 lib. bdg. $20.00

Raynolds, Robert. *Thomas Wolfe: Memoir of a Friendship.* Univ. of Texas Pr. 1965 $10.95

Reeves, Pascal, ed. *Thomas Wolfe: The Critical Reception.* Burt Franklin 1974 $19.95

Rubin, Louis D., Jr., ed. *Thomas Wolfe: A Collection of Critical Essays. Twentieth-Century Views Ser.* Prentice-Hall (Spectrum Bks.) 1973 pap. $1.95

Walser, Richard. *Thomas Wolfe Undergraduate.* Duke Univ. Pr. 1977 $11.75

WRIGHT, RICHARD. 1908–1960

Richard Wright was "generally accounted the most gifted living American Negro writer," until the rise of James Baldwin. "With Wright, the pain of being a Negro is basically economic—its sight is mainly in the pocket. With Baldwin, the pain suffuses the whole man. . . . If Baldwin's sights are higher than Wright's, it is in part because Wright helped to raise them" (*Time*). He was born on a plantation near Natchez, Mississippi. At 15, he started to work in Memphis, then in Chicago, then "bummed all over the country" supporting himself by various odd jobs. His early writing was in the smaller magazines—first poetry, then prose. He won *Story*'s $500 prize—for the best story written by a worker on the Writer's Project—with "Uncle Tom's Children" in 1938, his first important publication. He wrote *Native Son* in eight months, and it made his reputation. Based in part on the actual case of a young black murderer of a white woman, it was one of the first of the black protest novels, violent and shocking in its scenes of cruelty, hunger, rape, murder, flight, and prison.

Black Boy is the simple, vivid, and poignant story of Wright's early years in the South. It appeared at the beginning of a new postwar awareness of the evils of racial prejudice and did much to call attention to the plight of the U.S. black. *The Outsider* is a novel based on Wright's own experience as a member of the Communist party, an affiliation he terminated in 1944. He remained politically inactive thereafter and from 1946 until his death made his principal residence in Paris. His nonfiction writings on problems of his race include *Black Power: A Record of Reactions in a Land of Pathos* (1954) about a visit to the Gold Coast, *White Man, Listen,* and *Twelve Million Black Voices: A Folk History of the Negro in the United States.*

BOOKS BY WRIGHT

Richard Wright Reader. Ed. by Ellen Wright and Michel Fabre, Harper 1978 pap. $7.95

Uncle Tom's Children: Four Novellas. 1938. Harper 1965 pap. $3.37

Native Son. Harper 1940 $14.37

The Outsider. 1953. Harper 1965 $2.84

Savage Holiday. 1954. Chatham repr. $8.50. Psychological thriller.

The Long Dream. 1958. Chatham repr. $9.50. Novel about the South.

Black Boy: A Record of Childhood and Youth. 1945. Harper 1969 $16.30 pap. $3.37

American Hunger. Harper 1977 $13.41 pap. $4.75. Continuation of autobiography started with *Black Boy.*

BOOKS ABOUT WRIGHT

Avery, Evelyn. *Rebels and Victims: The Fiction of Richard Wright and Bernard Malamud.* Associated Faculty Pr. 1979 $11.50

Bakish, David. *Richard Wright. Lit. and Life Ser.* Ungar 1973 $12.95

Brignano, Russell C. *Richard Wright: An Introduction to the Man and His Works.* Univ. of Pittsburgh Pr. 1969 pap. $6.95

Fabre, Michel. *The Unfinished Quest of Richard Wright.* Morrow 1973 $15.00 1979 pap. $7.95

Felgar, Robert. *Richard Wright. Twayne's U.S. Authors Ser.* G. K. Hall 1980 $11.50

Fishburn, Katherine. *Richard Wright's Hero: The Faces of a Rebel-Victim.* Scarecrow Pr. 1977 $15.00

Gayle, Addison. *Richard Wright: Ordeal of a Native Son.* 1980. Peter Smith repr. 1983 $13.25

Hakutani, Yoshinobu, ed. *Critical Essays on Richard Wright.* G. K. Hall 1982 $26.00

Ray, David, and Robert M. Farnsworth, eds. *Richard Wright: Impressions and Perspectives.* Univ. of Michigan Pr. 1973 pap. $4.95

Reilly, John M., ed. *Richard Wright: The Critical Reception.* Burt Franklin 1978 $21.50 pap. $7.95

Walker, Margaret. *The Daemonic Genius of Richard Wright.* Howard Univ. Pr. 1984 $15.95

CHAPTER 15

Commonwealth Literature

Catherine Griffiths

> Commonwealth Literature . . . is a term of art . . . which has now become widespread in Britain, the United States and other countries as a convenient shorthand indication and because it represents, in a reasonably uncontentious though perhaps clumsy way, a fact of history and substance about the situation of the writers.
> —WILLIAM WALSH, *A Manifold Voice: Studies in Commonwealth Literature*

The view that Commonwealth literature represents in any sense a genre has been the subject of some debate. Can diverse countries separated by culture and geography create a common literary context? In a limited way they can. The literatures of English Canada, New Zealand, and Australia are bonded not only by their mother tongue but by some common thematic preoccupations. A cursory survey of Commonwealth literature reveals a pervasive, often unconscious, recognition of the inherent tension that has helped to shape the cultures of these vestiges of British colonialism. As a single literature, the writing of the Commonwealth tends to group around various dichotomous themes: the tension between the shift in status from colony to independent nation; the sometimes volatile mixing of native peoples and settlers; or the pull, especially in Canada and Australia, between regional or ethnic ties and appeals to nationalism. One of the more pressing dilemmas faced by the earlier Commonwealth writers was the decision whether to imitate the literary forms of an older, richer European culture or to forge new standards for the New World.

Within these sorts of classifications, general patterns begin to emerge among the writers here represented. The clash between native and colonial cultures has been examined by New Zealand's Patricia Grace, Canada's Charles G. D. Roberts and Margaret Laurence, and Australia's Thomas Keneally and "The Jindyworobak" poetry movement. Examples of regionalist writing may be seen in the prairie or northern narratives of Sinclair Ross and Robert W. Service, or in Les A. Murray's poems of New South Wales. Ethnocentric authors including Hugh MacLennan (whose books are now out of print), with his acute awareness of Canada's dual cultural origin, Canadian-Jewish writers Mordecai Richler and A. M. Klein as well as Australia's Joseph Furphy capture the spectrum of cultures that characterize these Commonwealth nations.

589

The lure of the European literary scene has drawn many Commonwealth expatriates away from the rawer intellectual climates of their native lands. Katherine Mansfield, Leonard Cohen, Mavis Gallant, Christina Stead, and Henry Handel Richardson all have been notable participants in this artistic migration. Yet for every expatriate writer there are numerous others with a strong nationalistic streak: Canadian poet E. J. Pratt, Australia's Judith Wright, and New Zealand's Ronald Hugh Morrieson and Frank Sargeson.

Of course, there are Commonwealth poets and novelists whose major themes transcend the boundaries of these central trends. They range from authors with feminist concerns such as Margaret Atwood, Alice Munro, Margaret Laurence, Barbara Hanrahan, and Miles Franklin to intensely individualistic novelists like Canada's Michael Ondaatje and New Zealand's Janet Frame.

AUSTRALIA

General Works and Anthologies

Buckley, Vincent. *Essays in Poetry. Essay Index Repr. Ser.* Ayer 1957 $18.00. A selection of essays with individual studies of K. Slessor, R. D. Fitzgerald, A. D. Hope, J. Wright, and J. McAuley. Some of the studies are cursory but the essays are clear, informative, and worthwhile.

Cantrell, Leon, ed. *Bards, Bohemians and Bookmen: Essays in Australian Literature.* Univ. of Queensland Pr. 1977 $24.95. Nineteen essays by well-known Australian scholars representing a cross-section of work recently done in Australian literary history and criticism. Several explore areas on nineteenth-century Australian literature.

————, ed. *The Eighteen Nineties Stories: Verses and Essays. Portable Australian Authors Ser.* Univ. of Queensland Pr. 1978 $30.00 pap. $12.95. A selection of creative writing, both fiction and verse, from Australian writers of the 1890s. Includes works by H. Lawson, V. Daley, B. O'Dowd, and C. Brennan.

Coombes, Archie J. *Some Australian Poets. Essay Index Repr. Ser.* Ayer repr. of 1938 ed. $12.00. A dated but informative work that would have added value if a more generous supply of quotations had been provided from the various poems under discussion.

Diesendorf, Margaret, and Amanuddin Syed, eds. *New Poetry from Australia.* Poetry Eastwest 1973 pap. $2.00. A small anthology that contains selections from the poetry of, most notably, Thomas Shapcott and Norman Talbot. Biographies of the poets are included.

Elkin, P. K., ed. *Australian Poems in Perspective: A Collection of Poems and Critical Commentaries.* Univ. of Queensland Pr. 1978 $22.00 pap. $12.95

Elliott, Brian. *The Jindyworobaks.* Univ. of Queensland Pr. 1980 $30.00 pap. $12.95. A thorough exploration, through a presentation of poetry and criticism, of the nationalist Jindyworobak poetry movement, which flourished during the 1930s. This group held that "the only true and sincere Australian culture is that of the Aboriginal race."

Green, Henry M., ed. *Modern Australian Poetry.* Granger repr. of 1952 ed. 1979 $22.75. An anthology that illustrates the shift in Australian poetry from "romantic nationalism" to "modernity and disillusion." Contains biographical notes.

Hamilton, K. G. *Studies in the Recent Australian Novel.* Univ. of Queensland Pr. 1979 $23.50. Eight essays on 16 novels published mainly since 1965 including discussions of P. White, T. Keneally, and Hal Porter. An informative introduction by Hamilton traces the history and development of Australian literature between the early 1930s and the late 1970s—"the golden age" of the Australian novel.

Healy, J. J. *Literature and the Aborigine in Australia, 1770–1975.* St. Martin's 1979 $26.00. A finely balanced work that explores the moral, aesthetic, sociological, and historical factors involved in the works of white Australians who attempt to come to grips with the aborigine.

Heseltine, Harry, ed. *The Penguin Book of Australian Short Stories.* Penguin 1984 pap. $5.95. Twenty-five tales arranged chronologically. Contains short stories by P. White, Hal Porter, and many others as well as a particularly good representation of Michael Wilding's *As Boys to Wanton Flies.*

Hope, A. D. *Australian Literature, 1950–1962.* International Specialized Bk. 1963 pap. $3.50

Jones, Joseph, and Johanna Jones. *Australian Fiction. Twayne's World Authors Ser.* G. K. Hall 1983 lib. bdg. $18.95

Kramer, Leonie, ed. *The Oxford History of Australian Literature.* Oxford 1981 $55.00. A comprehensive guide to the fiction, drama, and poetry of Australia. Bibliography and biography are included.

Macartney, Frederick. *Australian Literary Essays.* Richard West repr. of 1958 ed. 1973 $20.00. A rather eclectic collection of essays that includes discussions of individual authors and the chapter "Literature and the Aborigines."

McAuley, James, ed. *A Map of Australian Verse: The Twentieth Century.* Oxford 1975 pap. $19.95. An excellent source of critical, biographical, and historical information about Australia's major poets, together with samples of their poetry.

McDonald, Roger. *The First Paperback Poets Anthology.* Univ. of Queensland Pr. 1974 $12.95 pap. $7.95. Some of the best new poetry in Australia. The poems are from 22 books of verse published by the University of Queensland Press. Includes biographical notes.

Moore, T. Inglis. *Social Patterns in Australian Literature.* Univ. of California Pr. 1971 $34.50. Moore analyzes Australian literature as an "expression of significant patterns of thought, feeling and behaviour distinguishing the Australian society." The chapters "The Spell of the Bush" and "The Creed of Mateship" are particularly insightful.

Shapcott, Thomas, ed. *Consolidation: The Second Paperback Poets Anthology.* Univ. of Queensland Pr. text ed. 1983 $18.00 pap. $9.50. A collection that illustrates why the later 1970s was "a period of rich consolidation" for Australian poetry.

———. *Contemporary American and Australian Poetry.* Univ. of Queensland Pr. text ed. 1976 $19.95 pap. $12.95. A fascinating attempt to compare "in a way not previously attempted, two late twentieth-century English language cultures, both of which share striking historical similarities and divergences at certain points of origin and development."

Stevens, Bertram. *The Golden Treasury of Australian Verse.* Arden Lib. repr. of 1909 ed. 1979 lib. bdg. $30.00; Folcroft repr. of 1909 ed. lib. bdg. $20.00. This dated work includes poems by A. L. Gordon, V. Daley, and B. O'Dowd.

Walker, Shirley, ed. *Who Is She? Images of Women in Australian Fiction.* St. Martin's 1983 $29.95. An excellent collection of essays in feminist criticism in relation to Australian fiction. Authors explored include C. Stead, P. White, T. Keneally, M. Franklin, and B. Hanrahan.

Wallace-Crabbe, Christopher, ed. *The Golden Apples of the Sun: Twentieth-Century*

Australian Poetry. International Specialized Bk. 1980 $15.50. A thoughtful selection of Australian poems in which the principle for selection was the quality of the poem rather than the fame of the poet.

————. *Six Voices: Contemporary Australian Poets.* Greenwood repr. of 1977 ed. 1979 lib. bdg. $22.50. A small anthology containing the verse of representative Australian poets: K. Slessor, R. D. Fitzgerald, A. D. Hope, D. Stewart, J. Wright, and J. McAuley.

ASTLEY, THEA. 1925–

Born in Brisbane, Queensland, Thea Astley is a novelist of local attitudes and values. Her style has been termed "exotic" or "arch," but her prose is generally redeemed by her ironic wit. Astley's fiction is at its best when she is portraying the mundane life. *The Acolyte,* a highly parodic novel, is a character study of a "genius." Astley's *A Boat Load of Home Folk* also sustains an ironic vision, although Astley once wryly protested that the work was an attempt to "wring those trachyte reviewing hearts with my sympathy for the misfits [the characters]." One of her more compelling works, *An Item from the Late News,* is the story of Wafer, "The Bomb Age Baby." Haunted by the threat of nuclear holocaust, he seeks the perfect bomb shelter in Allbut, Australia. But the parochial values of Allbut clash with Wafer's bizarre morality—he is kind to aborigines and does not drink—driving the novel toward a disturbing and brutal climax.

BOOKS BY ASTLEY

A Boat Load of Home Folk. 1968. Penguin 1983 pap. $4.95
The Acolyte. Univ. of Queensland Pr. repr. of 1972 ed. 1980 pap. $7.25
An Item from the Late News. 1982. Penguin 1984 pap. $4.95; Univ. of Queensland Pr. 1983 $12.95

BEAVER, BRUCE. 1928–

A poet known for his complicated and circuitous syntax, Bruce Beaver is one of the more important figures in the Australian poetry scene of the 1970s. Born in Sydney, he worked at a variety of jobs, most of them semi-skilled, before he published *Under the Bridge* (o.p.) at his own expense. However, his reputation was made with a later volume of verse, *Letters to Live Poets* (o.p.). Beaver's poetry is distinguished by a confessional and unpretentious style. His verse explores the less glamorous situations in life; yet this vision of ordinariness is rarely bleak but rather tempered with imagination and wit.

BOOK BY BEAVER

As It Was. Univ. of Queensland Pr. 1979 $14.95 pap. $9.95

BRENNAN, CHRISTOPHER. 1870–1932

In terms of other Australian poetry, Christopher Brennan's verse is uncharacteristically elitist. He is an unorthodox and passionate man. His work is distinguished by its contorted syntax and intense commitment to the methods of the symbolists. Brennan's style is reminiscent of Rilke's or Yeats's although he never achieved the classic status of these poets, perhaps because his work "is trapped in the iconography and the diction of an age too early," as Frank Kermode described it. Yet, along with the stiff, formal quality of his work, there is an undercurrent of intense feeling in Brennan's verse that both deepens and vivifies it. *Poems: 1913*, which represents the work of the years 1894–1902, contains his most important poetry. From 1923 to 1925, Brennan's passion for Violet Singer and grief for her death elicited a few more poems, the sonnet "You, the Woman" being one of the better known among them.

BOOK BY BRENNAN

Poems: 1913. International Specialized Bk. $22.00 pap. $16.00

FRANKLIN, (STELLA MARIA) MILES. 1879–1954

Miles Franklin was born in New South Wales. Involved in "feminist journalism," she worked as a free-lance writer in Sydney and Melbourne before embarking, in 1905, for the United States, where she remained for nine years. In Chicago, Franklin engaged in social work and suffragette activity for the National Women's Trade Union League. In 1927, she took up permanent residence in Australia. *My Brilliant Career* was published in 1901. This fictional autobiography of Sybylla Melvyn is certainly Franklin's most memorable work. The adventures of the lively and egocentric Sybylla are continued in *The End of My Career* (which can also be found under the title *My Career Goes Bung*), a work written immediately after *My Brilliant Career*, but not published until 1946.

Under the pseudonym "Brent of Bin Bin," six other novels depicting Australian life appeared. In addition to novels, Franklin wrote criticism and biographies. Following her death, the Miles Franklin Award for fiction was instituted, to be given to a novelist whose work authentically represented Australian life.

BOOKS BY FRANKLIN

My Brilliant Career. 1901. St. Martin's 1980 $9.95; Washington Square Pr. 1981 pap. $3.95
The End of My Career. 1946. Washington Square Pr. 1984 pap. $3.95
On Dearborn Street. Univ. of Queensland Pr. 1982 $14.95

FURPHY, JOSEPH. 1843–1912

The son of Irish immigrants, Joseph Furphy was born in Victoria. Recognition of Furphy as a major Australian writer rests solely on *Such Is Life*, a novel to which he brought not only his knowledge of bush life, but also a rich experience of literature that he acquired without formal training. *Such Is Life* consists of a number of variations on given themes, for the most part expounded through the persona of "Tom Collins." A. G. Stephens in a letter to Furphy refers to it as a "classic" that "embalms accurate representations of our character and customs, life and scenery." Furphy himself described it thus: "I have just finished writing a full-sized novel, title, *Such Is Life*, scene, Riverina and Northern Vic; temper, democratic; bias, offensively Australian." Yet, when Furphy died in 1912, his magnum opus was "little appreciated by the Australian public, and it was left to later generations to discover the measure of his achievement."

BOOK BY FURPHY

Portable Joseph Furphy. Univ. of Queensland Pr. text ed. 1982 $30.00 pap. $12.95. Includes a revised version of *Such Is Life*.

HALL, RODNEY. 1935–

Although born in Warwickshire, England, Rodney Hall, writer, actor, and musician, developed an emotional attachment to Australia through the reminiscences of his Australian family. His verse has been called impressionistic and disturbing. The source of his poetry's vitality can be traced to Hall's interest in the idiom and rhythm of the "living speech" of contemporary Australia. Hall's moving and somber verse is relieved by his consistently compassionate approach to his subject.

BOOKS BY HALL

Focus on Andrew Sibley. Univ. of Queensland Pr. 1968 $12.95
Black Bagatelles. Univ. of Queensland Pr. 1978 $12.95 pap. $7.95
Selected Poems. Univ. of Queensland Pr. 1978 $14.95 pap. $9.95
The Most Beautiful World. Univ. of Queensland Pr. text ed. 1982 $13.50 pap. $7.50
Just Relations. Penguin 1984 pap. $6.95; Viking 1983 $16.75

HANRAHAN, BARBARA. 1939—

Born in Adelaide, Barbara Hanrahan studied art in Australia and then in London. Her first novel, *The Scent of Eucalyptus* (o.p.), is a rich, sharp, and authentic evocation of a child's world with its mingling of fact and fantasy. *The Albatross Muff* is "a strangely captivating . . . fairy tale," a book of "complexity and power . . . meaty, unpredictable . . . combining the marvelous with the mundane" (Publisher's note). In *Where the Queens All Strayed*, Hanrahan again reveals her preoccupation with the waiflike, precocious child. *The Peach Groves* and *The Kewpie Doll* explore, in tones both sinister and erotic, the joys and terrors of growing up. Hanrahan's most compelling novel, *The Frangipani Gardens*, is the story of a woman who "faces . . . [a] decision between the kind of artistic mediocrity which brings filial approval, or truth to herself and her skills" (Shirley Walker, *Who Is She?*). Hanrahan is also a well-known printmaker.

BOOKS BY HANRAHAN

The Albatross Muff. 1977. Charles River Bks. $2.95
Where the Queens All Strayed. 1978. Univ. of Queensland Pr. 1984 pap. $7.95
The Peach Groves. 1979. Univ. of Queensland Pr. text ed. 1980 $12.00 pap. $6.00
The Frangipani Gardens. 1980. Univ. of Queensland Pr. 1985 pap. $7.95
Dove: A Novel. Univ. of Queensland Pr. 1982 $14.95 pap. $7.95
The Kewpie Doll. Merrimack 1984 $14.95 pap. $6.95

HOPE, A(LEC) D(ERWENT). 1907–

Probably one of the better-known Australian poets, Hope was born in Cooma, New South Wales. A man of erudition and wit, he exhibits in his verse "an insistent literariness" alien to most Australian poetry (*Collins Book of Australian Poetry*). His work reveals an obsession with the capacity that humanity has to rise up above the mundane; his verse consistently returns to the realm of the heroic. In the introduction to Hope's *Collected Poems, 1930–1970* (o.p.), Leonie Kramer notes that "there is little evidence in his own poetry that he has found any direct inspiration from his actual environment. . . . Hope is not an observer of nature or men; he is a witness rather, and a purveyor of ideas about them. . . . In temper his work is romantic rather than classical." Hope was for many years professor of English at the Australian National University.

BOOK BY HOPE

The Pack of Autolycus. Australia Northern Univ. Pr. text ed. 1979 $7.50

JOLLEY, ELIZABETH. 1923–

Elizabeth Jolley's fascinating novel *Miss Peabody's Inheritance* contains two parallel stories that deal with love, loneliness, and the need to create. Of this novel Nancy Keesing remarked: "Her writing is splendid, her characters various, her humor delicious."

Born in England, Elizabeth Jolley came to Australia in 1959. Apart from *Miss Peabody's Inheritance,* she is the author of three novels: *The Newspaper of Claremont Street* (o.p.), *Palomino* (o.p.), and *Mr. Scobie's Riddle,* as well as three collections of short stories.

BOOKS BY JOLLEY

Miss Peabody's Inheritance. 1983. Penguin pap. $5.95; Viking 1984 $13.95
Mr. Scobie's Riddle. 1983. *Penguin Fiction Ser.* 1984 pap. $5.95

JONES, EVAN. 1931–

Born in Melbourne, Evan Jones is probably best known as a member of the circle of poets who taught at Melbourne University during the 1950s. Although he is far from a prolific poet, his work has been described as "strikingly individual poetry [which] bears little suggestion of any recognizable period or manner, despite its strongly traditional values. . . . There is a recurrent vein of asperity and wit which runs through it and which is sometimes turned obliquely on himself in epigrams or lyrics with tart, ironic flavour" (C. Wallace-Crabbe, *Meanjin Quarterly*).

BOOKS BY JONES

Left at the Post. Univ. of Queensland Pr. 1984 $10.95 pap. $5.95
Recognitions. Australia Northern Univ. Pr. text ed. $7.25

KENEALLY, THOMAS. 1935–

Thomas Keneally was born in Sydney and educated at St. Patrick's College. For a time he studied for the priesthood, but left six months before ordination. His work reflects his Roman Catholic upbringing. Focusing on such themes as sin and expiation, his novels reveal a rather morbid preoccupation with violence and death. In describing his work, *The Oxford History of Australian Literature* states: "His novels explore conflicts of principle, and find their resolution in the affirmation of the basic human decencies: compassion, generosity, integrity. . . . Keneally has combined the advantages of the popular forms of fiction . . . with seriousness of theme and thoroughness of imaginative design."

Keneally has written more than a dozen books since 1964, as well as some successful stage plays. His reputation was established in Australia with his third novel, *Bring Larks and Heroes* (o.p.), the tale of an Irish soldier's fluctuating fortunes within a penal settlement suggestive of colonial Sydney. *Three Cheers for the Paraclete*, which the author describes as "a sort of ecclesiastical *Lucky Jim*," explores the life of a young priest who teaches at a seminary. With this work, Keneally arrived at "a clear, creative awareness of the distinctive nature of his powers, of the special shape of the imaginative responses," as Robert Burns said. Keneally's best-known work, *The Chant of Jimmie Blacksmith*, is based on an actual revolt led by two aborigines at the turn of the century. Jimmie, a half-caste, attempts to integrate into white society through marriage to a white woman. When she betrays him, Jimmie's response results in a climactic scene of mutilation and death.

BOOKS BY KENEALLY

Three Cheers for the Paraclete. 1968. Penguin 1984 pap. $5.95
The Chant of Jimmie Blacksmith. 1972. Penguin 1983 pap. $4.95
Confederates. Berkley Publishing 1983 pap. $3.95; Harper 1980 $12.95
Schindler's List. G. K. Hall 1985 $18.95; Penguin 1983 pap. $5.95

LINDSAY, NORMAN. 1879–1969

Norman Lindsay, born at Creswick, Victoria, became probably the most popular Australian illustrator of all time. Yet Lindsay was as gifted in literature as he was in the visual arts. Around the age of 16 he left home for Melbourne, where he worked as a journalistic illustrator for the yellow press newspapers. When his cartoons of street urchins were criticized as being too unrealistic, he responded by publishing some stories of his Creswick childhood; these were later collected as *Saturdee*, a work that has been dubbed "the Australian *Tom Sawyer*." Together with *Redheap* (o.p.) and *Halfway to Anywhere* (o.p.), it became part of the bildungsroman trilogy that many consider Lindsay's most important fiction. Never far from farcical, his novels made him enemies "as he took great delight in using both recognizable character sketches and related names in descriptions of past events" (*The Australian Encyclopedia*). Because of this, *Redheap* was banned in Australia until 1959.

For one who was regarded chiefly as an illustrator, Lindsay was a prolific writer. In addition to 11 novels, he published a dozen books on art. Most of Lindsay's life was spent in Sydney, where his studio became a meeting place for many members of Australia's artistic community.

BOOK BY LINDSAY

Saturdee. 1933. AMS Pr. repr. of 1939 ed. $18.45

McAULEY, JAMES. 1917–1976

From the beginning of his poetic career, and as the editor-founder of *Quadrant*, James McAuley injected an influential conservative element into the Australian literary scene. During the 1940s he effectively weakened the nationalist "Jindyworobak" and avant-garde "Angry Penguin" movements with arguments for formal control in poetry. McAuley maintained that "subtlety, complexity and balance are all on the side of traditional verse. It provides the best combination of freedom and order" (*Quadrant*).

From 1951 until his death, McAuley was professor of English at the University of Tasmania in Hobart. His carefully patterned verse still enjoys a high reputation.

BOOKS BY McAULEY

After the Blizzard: Poems. Univ. of Missouri Pr. 1975 $6.95
The Exiles Book of Hours: A Sequence. Confluence Pr. 1982 pap. $4.00

MURRAY, LES A. 1938–

Born in Bunyah, New South Wales, Murray is recognized as one of the more significant poets who began publishing in the 1960s. Perhaps because of his facility with languages (Murray was a translator of western European languages at the Australian National University), his poems display a unique and adventurous approach to English.

James McAuley sees the impetus for Murray's work to be "the dairy-farming country at Bunyah . . . where he grew up. This is the core of reality for him," from which Murray's verse reaches out "into the city, into other countries, into history, politics and anthropology; but everything is tested against the local reality." A versatile poet who uses both irregular and formal verse, Murray embraces a variety of tones and topics in his work.

BOOK BY MURRAY

The Peasant Mandarin: Prose Pieces. Univ. of Queensland Pr. 1979 $19.95 pap. $12.00

PORTER, HAL. 1911–

It was in his childhood home in Bairnsdale that Hal Porter developed his love for the countryside about which he has frequently written. In his stories, novels, and plays, Porter often attacks "the complicated deceits of urban Australians," which are seen in opposition to a nostalgic vision of "the simplicities of country life or childhood" (*The Portable Hal Porter*). In 1962, Porter produced a volume of short stories that labeled him in the eyes of

Australian critics such as A. D. Hope as "the most distinctive and perhaps most distinguished writer of short stories." Although best known for his short fiction, Porter has also emerged as a masterly satiric poet. Four examples of his carefully controlled ironic poetry are included in *The Portable Hal Porter*.

BOOKS BY PORTER

The Paper Chase. Univ. of Queensland Pr. repr. of 1966 ed. 1980 pap. $9.95. Porter's second volume of autobiography has particular interest for the readers of *Handful of Pennies* (o.p.) since many of the characters and situations from the novel emerge in *The Paper Chase* divested of their fictional disguises.
The Portable Hal Porter. Ed. by Mary Lord, Univ. of Queensland Pr. 1980 $30.00 pap. $12.95

RICHARDSON, HENRY HANDEL (pseud. of Ethel Florence Lindesay Richardson). 1870–1946

Richardson wrote the trilogy that has been described as "the most outstanding example of the naturalistic novel in Australian literature" (*Modern Australian Prose*). Richardson was born in East Melbourne in 1870, and at age 13, she became a boarder at the Ladies College in Melbourne. This became the setting for her novel *The Getting of Wisdom*. A musical scholarship allowed for further training in Leipzig, where her mother had hopes of a career for her as a concert pianist. Although this ambition was never realized, the trip to Europe resulted in permanent residence abroad. In 1895, she married John G. Robertson, a Scottish student whom she met in Leipzig. In 1903, when her husband was granted a professorship at the University of London, Richardson was able to settle in that city and work on her writing for the next 30 years. Always inspired by actual events in the lives of herself and her family, her first novel, *Maurice Guest*, tells the story of a young piano student at Leipzig. Her trilogy, *The Fortunes of Richard Mahony*, began to take shape in 1917 when the first volume, *Australia Felix* (o.p.), was published. This book begins the saga of Richard Townshend Mahony, a character loosely based on Richardson's physician/storekeeper father. The account of the rise and fall of Mahony's fortunes continues in *The Way Home* (o.p.) and culminates with *Ultima Thule*.

After her husband's death in 1933, Richardson moved to a country home in Sussex where she died, leaving an unfinished autobiography. In recognition of her literary achievements, Richardson was awarded the Australian Gold Medal and the King George Jubilee Medal.

BOOKS BY RICHARDSON

Maurice Guest. 1908. *Virago Modern Class. Ser.* Doubleday 1983 pap. $9.95
The Getting of Wisdom. 1910. *Virago Modern Class. Ser.* Doubleday 1981 pap. $5.95
The Fortunes of Richard Mahony. 1917. Century Bookbindery repr. of 1941 ed. 1985 lib. bdg. $45.00
Ultima Thule. 1929. Century Bookbindery repr. of 1929 ed. 1984 lib. bdg. $20.00

BOOKS ABOUT RICHARDSON

Buckley, Vincent. *Henry Handel Richardson.* Folcroft 1973 lib. bdg. $7.50
Nichols, J. R. *Art and Irony: The Tragic Vision of Henry Handel Richardson (A Discussion on the Relationship of Theme and Technique in Fiction).* Univ. Pr. of Amer. 1982 lib. bdg. $25.00 text ed. pap. $12.25

SHAPCOTT, THOMAS W. 1935–

Born in Ipswich, Queensland, Thomas W. Shapcott is one of twin brothers. Rodney Hall notes "that being a twin has haunted [Shapcott's] poetry though he rarely writes about it directly. There is a recurrent fear of being incomplete, imperfect, together with a powerful urge to give, to be generous and to be loved." Probably his most notable book of verse is *Shabbytown Calendar*, in which his poetry seems starker and further removed from the romantic preoccupations of his earlier work. A prominent spokesman for poetry in the 1960s, he is also deeply interested in the antiestablishment verse of the more recent Australian poets.

BOOKS BY SHAPCOTT

Inwards to the Sun. Univ. of Queensland Pr. 1969 $9.95
Begin with Walking. Univ. of Queensland Pr. 1972 pap. $4.95
Shabbytown Calendar. 1975. Univ. of Queensland Pr. 1976 $9.95 pap. $4.95

SHUTE, NEVIL (pseud. of Nevil Shute Norway). 1899–1960

Born in London, Nevil Shute earned a degree in engineering at Oxford, and then established an aircraft construction company. In 1938, he sold his company interests to become a full-time writer. He emigrated with his family to Australia in 1950 to a farm in Langwarin, Victoria. Nevil Shute was a prolific writer who explored widely disparate themes and situations. *In the Wet* is a wry account of the Queen of England's decision to move from Britain to progressive Australia. In *On the Beach*, Australia became the last refuge for a world ravaged by nuclear war. Shute's hugely successful *A Town Like Alice* is the story of an Australian soldier and a woman who survive a Japanese death march during World War II. Internationally respected, Shute's work has also found an appreciative audience in the popular market.

BOOKS BY SHUTE

Marazan. David & Charles 1982 $14.95
So Disdained. David & Charles 1980 $14.95
An Old Captivity. Amereon $18.95; David & Charles 1982 $14.95
Pastoral. Amereon $15.95; Greenwood repr. of 1944 ed. lib. bdg. $18.75
The Pied Piper. 1944. Amereon $17.95; David & Charles 1982 $14.95
A Town Like Alice. 1948. Ballantine 1985 pap. $2.95; David & Charles 1976 $14.95
The Chequer Board. Amereon $19.95; Ballantine 1985 pap. $2.95; David & Charles 1980 $14.95
No Highway in the Sky. Amereon $18.95; David & Charles 1980 $14.95
Ruined City. David & Charles 1982 $13.95
The Far Country. Amereon $18.95; David & Charles 1980 $14.95

Requiem for a Wren. David & Charles 1982 $14.95
Round the Bend: A Novel. Amereon $18.95; David & Charles 1980 $14.95; Greenwood
    repr. of 1951 ed. lib. bdg. $17.00; Queens House repr. of 1951 ed. 1977 lib. bdg.
    $19.95
In the Wet. 1953. David & Charles 1982 $14.95
On the Beach. 1957. Amereon $14.95; Ballantine 1978 pap. $2.50; David & Charles
    1980 $14.95; Morrow 1957 $12.95
Trustee from the Toolroom. Amereon repr. of 1960 ed. 1976 lib. bdg. $17.95
The Rainbow and the Rose. Ballantine 1985 pap. $2.95; David & Charles 1980 $11.50
What Happened to the Corbetts. David & Charles 1982 $14.95
Stephen Morris. David & Charles 1980 $14.95

SLESSOR, KENNETH. 1901–1971

Kenneth Slessor's collected poems, *One Hundred Poems* (o.p.), is a book
filled with accomplished and brilliant verse. After its publication he wrote
no more poetry, with the exception of a few random verses, for the remaining 30 years of his life. Yet, even with this comparatively small body of
work, he is still known as the father of modern Australian poetry. Influenced by such poets as T. S. ELIOT, E. E. CUMMINGS, and Wilfred Owen, he
helped to free Australian poetry from parochialism. A. C. W. Mitchell sees
Slessor's work "as a poetic rendering of the grotesque, not in any concern
with a play of conventional imagery, although there are examples of this,
but in the incongruous combination of unlikely elements."

Born in New South Wales, Slessor attended grammar school in Sydney
and in 1920 became a reporter with the *Sydney Sun.* During his long and distinguished career as a journalist he held a variety of positions, including
that of book reviewer for the *Sydney Daily Telegraph.* Slessor's verse can be
found in a number of anthologies.

BOOKS ABOUT SLESSOR

Frewin, Leslie, ed. *Parnassus Near Picadilly.* Sportshelf $15.00
Harris, Max. *Kenneth Slessor.* Sportshelf pap. $5.00

STEAD, CHRISTINA. 1902–1983

Christina Stead, daughter of a well-known naturalist, was a native of Sydney. In 1928, Stead went to London, where she lived until 1935. After extensive travel, Stead settled in the United States in 1937. For a period, she
wrote screenplays in Hollywood. In 1941, *The Man Who Loved Children* was
published. This book, with its economic synthesis of reflection and dialogue, reveals a thoughtful and intimate look at human emotions. It is the
story of Samuel Clemens Pollit, a man whose sadistic imagination tragically transforms his wife's existence. The reissue of this novel in 1966 gave
Stead international recognition. Robert Lowell called it "a classic," adding
that "there are few novels in English that are as large and beautifully written." *For Love Alone* is an early and unabashedly feminist novel that features Teresa, a heroine whose life illustrates Stead's conviction that women
have inherited a tradition of social subjugation. *Miss Herbert: The Suburban
Wife* tells the story of Eleanor, "the incarnation of the ancient Venus," a

woman who is at once "a powerful sexual being" and a "good, plain person," a contradiction that is finally resolved in a surprising and touching conclusion. *Letty Fox* is an earlier novel that explores the life of a promiscuous young woman. Until 1965, editions of *Letty Fox* were banned in Australia.

BOOKS BY STEAD

A Christina Stead Reader. Random 1979 $12.95
The Man Who Loved Children. 1941. Avon 1966 pap. $2.50; intro. by Randall Jarrell, Holt 1980 pap. $7.95
For Love Alone. 1944. Harcourt 1979 pap. $5.95
Letty Fox: Her Luck. 1946. Harcourt 1979 pap. $5.95
Miss Herbert: The Suburban Wife. 1976. Harcourt 1981 pap. $5.95; Random 1976 $8.95

BOOK ABOUT STEAD

Lidoff, Joan. *Christina Stead. Lit. and Life Ser.* Ungar 1982 $15.50 pap. $6.95

STEWART, DOUGLAS. 1913–

Although born and educated in New Zealand, Stewart has lived in Australia since 1938. An important poet, he is also one of Australia's most influential authors and critics. As a generalization, Stewart's poetry focuses on the beauty of the Australian landscape and its animals. His nature lyrics display a thematic coherence in that he consistently acknowledges the unity of creation, and the relationships within the natural order. Douglas Stewart's most successful verse is characterized by a good-natured tone. About his own conception of poetry, Stewart writes: "As well as the more exalted virtues of poetry—melody and feeling in the lyric, structure and movement in the narrative—I like things that are alive, odd, humorous out of the way. . . . The thing I do not enjoy is dullness."

BOOK BY STEWART

Fishing around the Monaro. Australia Northern Univ. Pr. 1978 pap. $2.75

BOOK ABOUT STEWART

Keesing, Nancy. *Douglas Stewart.* Sportshelf pap. $5.00

STOW, RANDOLPH. 1935–

Randolph Stow was born in Geraldton, Western Australia, and educated at the University of Western Australia where, as an undergraduate, he wrote his first novels. In 1958, he received the Miles Franklin Award for his third novel, *To the Islands.* It is the surreal saga of Herriot, a disillusioned missionary whose loss of faith compels him to embark on a pilgrimage of self-discovery through the desert wilderness to the aboriginal islands of the dead. The desert landscape is also the setting of *Tourmaline,* a novel in which a water-diviner comes to a drought-ridden settlement, promising water but discovering gold. *The Merry-Go-Round in the Sea* relies much less on the allusive symbolism inherent in Stow's earlier work. A more conventional novel, it records a young boy's transition to adolescence in a nostalgic and affectionate fashion. *The Suburbs of Hell* focuses on a series of brutal, motiveless murders that take place in the small community of Tornwhich. In *Visitants,* Stow fictionalizes his experiences as an assistant to the government anthropologist of Papua, New Guinea.

BOOKS BY STOW

To the Islands. 1958. Taplinger rev. ed. 1982 $9.95
Tourmaline: A Novel. 1963. Taplinger 1983 $10.95
The Merry-Go-Round in the Sea. 1965. Taplinger repr. of 1966 ed. 1984 $14.95
Visitants: A Novel. 1979. Taplinger 1981 $9.95
The Suburbs of Hell. Taplinger 1984 $13.95

WHITE, PATRICK. 1912–   (NOBEL PRIZE 1973)

Born in Britain of Australian parents, Patrick White has spent time in both places. But his heart and his genius are Australian: "Whatever has come since, I feel that the influences and impressions of this strange, dead landscape of Australia predominate." Following schooling in England, which he heartily disliked (though he later returned to Cambridge), White left for Australia and worked in a sheep station, intermittently writing fiction—in the stream-of-consciousness mode—and drama. His first successful novel, *Happy Valley* (1939, o.p.), an ironic tale of life in an Australian mining town, won the Australian Literature Society's Gold Medal. His next novel was *The Living and the Dead* (1941), about a young man in England and Europe in the early years of this century. The "dead" represent those caught in the stultifying traditions bequeathed to them by a dead past. *The Aunt's Story* (1948) chronicles the "lives" of an odd, ugly woman "whose instincts are greater than her adaptability to life" and her journeyings from Australia to Europe and America.

Of *Voss,* which concerns a German explorer in nineteenth-century Australia, Walter Allen wrote in the *New Statesman:* "I am happy to join in the chorus of praise for Mr. White. It is very fine indeed, by far the most impressive new novel I have read this year. At the least, it is a work of brilliant virtuosity, and I suggest that it is much more than that: I suppose it would need an Australian to gauge its full significance, for as it seems to me, Mr. White is attempting to create an Australian myth." The *New Yorker* said of *Voss:* "His prose, which floats heavily off either into semi-poetic passages full of Bunyan-size images like 'the reeling earth,' or into needlessly cramped, studied dialogue, tends to set up an obstinate and exasperating barrier between his subject matter and the reader. Nonetheless, this is a heroic and sometimes brilliant novel." In *The Solid Mandala,* White "further explores the Australian dilemma, the human condition, of life down under. He is a writer of genius, the finest novelist in the world of the Commonwealth [and] this book is one of the finest novels of this decade or any other" (*LJ*). *Four Plays* (1966, o.p.) contains "The Ham Funeral," written in 1947 but not produced until 1961, "The Season of Sarsaparilla," "A Cherry Soul," and "Night on Bald Mountain."

BOOKS BY WHITE

The Living and the Dead. AMS Pr. repr. of 1941 ed. $28.50; Penguin 1983 pap. $5.95
The Aunt's Story. Avon 1975 pap. $1.95; *Penguin Fiction Ser.* 1986 pap. $6.95; Viking 1948 $12.95
The Tree of Man. Avon 1975 pap. $1.95; Penguin 1984 pap. $5.95; Viking 1955 $13.95
Voss. Avon 1975 pap. $1.95; Penguin 1984 pap. $5.95; Viking 1957 $13.95
Riders in the Chariot. Avon 1975 pap. $2.25; *Penguin Fiction Ser.* 1985 pap. $6.95; Viking 1961 $13.95
The Solid Mandala. Avon 1980 pap. $1.95; Penguin 1983 pap. $4.95; Viking 1966 $12.95
The Vivisector. Avon 1975 pap. $2.25; Penguin 1985 $6.95; Viking 1970 $13.95
The Burnt Ones. *Penguin Fiction Ser.* 1985 pap. $6.95
The Eye of the Storm. Viking 1974 $13.95
The Cockatoos. Penguin 1983 pap. $4.95; Viking 1975 $12.95
A Fringe of Leaves. Penguin 1984 pap. $4.95; Viking 1977 $13.95
The Twyborn Affair. Penguin 1981 pap. $5.95; Viking 1980 $14.95
Flaws in the Glass: A Self Portrait. Penguin 1983 pap. $5.95; Viking 1982 $14.95

BOOKS ABOUT WHITE

Bjorkstein, Ingmar. *Patrick White: A General Introduction.* Trans. by Stanley Gerson, Humanities Pr. text ed. 1976 $13.00 pap. $7.00
Colmer, John. *Patrick White.* Methuen 1984 pap. $4.75
Dutton, Geoffrey. *Patrick White.* Folcroft 1962 $8.50
Dyce, J. R. *Patrick White as Playwright.* St. Martin's 1980 $20.00; Univ. of Queensland Pr. 1974 $19.95
Kiernan, Brian. *Patrick White.* St. Martin's 1980 $20.00
McCulloch, A. M. *A Tragic Vision: The Novels of Patrick White.* Univ. of Queensland Pr. text ed. 1983 $32.50
Morley, Patricia. *The Mystery of Unity: Theme and Technique in the Novels of Patrick White.* McGill Queens Univ. Pr. 1972 $15.00
Walsh, William. *Patrick White's Fiction.* Rowman 1977 $10.00
Weigel, John A. *Patrick White. Twayne's World Authors Ser.* G. K. Hall 1983 lib. bdg. $16.95
Wolfe, Peter. *Laden Choirs: The Fiction of Patrick White.* Univ. Pr. of Kentucky 1983 $25.00

WRIGHT, JUDITH. 1915–

Poet, critic, and anthologist, Judith Wright was born and currently resides in New South Wales. Her pastoral upbringing is reflected in the themes of her poetry, which focus on the country people and the wildlife of Australia. An active worker for conservation organizations, Wright expresses her concern for the environment and her boundless energy in much of her nature poetry.

BOOKS BY WRIGHT

The Cry for the Dead. Oxford 1981 $32.50
Charles Harpur. Sportshelf pap. $5.00

CANADA

General Works and Anthologies

Atwood, Margaret. *Survival: A Thematic Guide to Canadian Literature*. Univ. of Toronto Pr. 1972 pap. $6.95. A witty, informative guide to the significant patterns in Canadian literature.

Baker, Ray P. *A History of English-Canadian Literature to the Confederation*. Richard West repr. of 1920 ed. 1973 $30.00

Ballstadt, Carl, ed. *The Search for English-Canadian Literature: An Anthology of Critical Articles from the Nineteenth and Early Twentieth Centuries*. Univ. of Toronto Pr. 1975 pap. $8.50. "The main purpose of this book is to reflect the major issues in the critical search for distinctive literature in Canada during the nineteenth and early twentieth centuries" (Introduction).

Bourinot, J. G., and Roy Camille. *Our Intellectual Strength and Weakness: English Canadian Literature, French Canadian Literature*. Lit. of Canada Ser. Univ. of Toronto Pr. 1973 pap. $7.50. A wide-ranging view of Canada's cultural situation.

Broadus, Edmund K. *A Book of Canadian Prose and Verse*. Ed. by Eleanor H. Broadus, Norwood repr. of 1923 ed. lib. bdg. $30.00; ed. by Eleanor H. Broadus. Scholars Pr. repr. of 1923 ed. $20.00. "A picture of Canadian life past and present." Poets Bliss Carman and the lesser-known Archibald Lampman are especially well represented.

Carman, Bliss, ed. *Canadian Poetry in English*. 1922. Greenwood repr. of 1954 ed. 1976 lib. bdg. $32.50. Marred by the inclusion of third-rate nationalistic verse, Carman's 1922 anthology is a comprehensive and critical collection of early Canadian poetry. Biographies of poets included.

Cude, Wilfred. *A Due Sense of Differences: An Evaluative Approach to Canadian Literature*. Univ. Pr. of Amer. lib. bdg. $22.75 text ed. pap. $12.00. "Cude relies on deep reading, which he often does well; sour attitudes toward the skeptical critics; and an honest, exuberant defense of some decent books" (*Choice*).

Duffy, Dennis. *Gardens, Covenants, Exiles: Loyalism in the Literature of Upper Canada/Ontario*. Univ. of Toronto Pr. 1982 $27.50 pap. $10.95. An analysis of the effects of the United Empire Loyalism on the literary culture of what is now Ontario.

Frye, Northrop. *The Bush Garden: Essays on the Canadian Imagination*. Univ. of Toronto Pr. 1971 pap. $8.95. "A retrospective collection of [Northrop Frye's] writings on Canadian culture, mainly literature, extending over a period of nearly thirty years" (Preface).

Garvin, John W., ed. *Canadian Poets*. Granger Poetry Lib. repr. of 1926 ed. 1976 $38.50; Richard West repr. of 1926 ed. $40.00. A dated work that provides a sampling of the verse of 52 early Canadian poets. Included are contemporary reviews of the poetry, which prove to be delightful examples of "purple prose."

Jones, D. G. *Butterfly on Rock: A Study of Themes and Images in Canadian Literature*. Univ. of Toronto Pr. 1970 pap. $7.50. Less a survey or a comprehensive study of any single author or work than an attempt "to define more clearly some of the features that recur in the . . . Mirror of [Canadian] imaginative life" (Introduction).

Jones, Joseph, and Johanna Jones. *Canadian Fiction*. Twayne's World Authors Ser. G. K. Hall 1981 lib. bdg. $16.95. A "beginner's guide" to Canadian literature: "to reveal to the reader a dimension of literature in English with which, more than likely, he is not yet very familiar" (Preface).

Klinck, Carl F., ed. *Literary History of Canada: Canadian Literature in English*. Univ. of Toronto Pr. 3 vols. 1976 pap. $40.00. "A comprehensive reference book on the [English] literary history of [Canada]" (Introduction).

Knister, Raymond, ed. *Canadian Short Stories. Short Story Index Repr. Ser*. Ayer repr. of 1928 ed. $18.00. The work of "the best Canadian writers" according to the editor in 1928. Includes work by Callaghan, Leacock, and D. C. Scott.

Lee, Dennis. *Savage Fields: An Essay in Literature and Cosmology*. Univ. of Toronto Pr. 1977 $14.95 pap. $7.95. A critical look at Ondaatje's *The Collected Works of Billy the Kid* and Cohen's *Beautiful Losers*. Lee "is ultimately interested less in literary criticism than what he terms cosmology or 'an image of planet order' " (Sam Solecki, *Canadian Forum*).

Mandel, Eli, ed. *Contexts of Canadian Criticism. Patterns of Literary Criticism Ser*. Univ. of Chicago Pr. 1971 $21.00; Univ. of Toronto Pr. 1971 pap. $10.95. An interesting examination of what Mandel terms the "three major contexts" of Canadian criticism: historical, interpretive, and "literary tradition."

Metcalf, John, ed. *Making It New. Contemporary Canadian Stories Ser*. Methuen 1983 pap. $13.95. Three stories each by Clark Blaise, Mavis Gallant, Hugh Hood, Norman Levine, John Metcalf, Alice Munro, and Leon Rooke.

Norris, Ken. *Canadian Poetry Now: Twenty Poets of the 80s*. Univ. of Toronto Pr. 1984 pap. $12.95. An anthology that represents the "next wave" in Canadian poetry: the poets of the 1980s "just now coming into their own."

Pacey, Desmond. *Creative Writing in Canada: A Short History of English-Canadian Literature*. Greenwood 2d ed. repr. of 1961 ed. 1976 lib. bdg. $22.50. An adequate selective survey of Canadian belles lettres. Chronological discussions of fiction and poetry.

Phelps, Arthur L. *Canadian Writers. Essay Index Repr. Ser*. Ayer repr. of 1951 ed. $13.00. Individual studies of, among others, E. J. Pratt, T. C. Haliburton, F. P. Grove, S. Leacock, Hugh MacLennan, and W. O. Mitchell.

Staines, David, ed. *Canadian Imagination: Dimensions of a Literary Culture*. Harvard Univ. Pr. $14.00

Stevenson, Lionel. *Appraisals of Canadian Literature*. Folcroft repr. of 1926 ed. lib. bdg. $20.00. A dated work that attempts to show that this literature warrants acceptance "as a separate entity in the intellectual geography of the world" (Introduction).

Stouck, David. *Major Canadian Authors: A Critical Introduction*. Univ. of Nebraska Pr. 1984 $22.95. Authors are situated in their historical context, which thereby provides a brief outline of the development of Canadian literature. From T. C. Haliburton to Alice Munro.

Toye, William, ed. *The Oxford Companion to Canadian Literature*. Oxford 1983 $49.95. An indispensable collection, arranged alphabetically, of articles on writers and genres.

Weaver, Robert, ed. *Canadian Short Stories*. Oxford pap. $10.95. Included are stories by Margaret Atwood, Mavis Gallant, Alice Munro, and Rudy Wiebe.

Wilson, Edmund. *O Canada: An American's Notes on Canadian Culture*. Farrar 1965 $4.95; Octagon repr. of 1966 ed. 1976 lib. bdg. $18.00. "Notes" featuring Wilson's impressions of Callaghan, Hugh MacLennan, and Mavis Gallant.

Woodcock, George. *The World of Canadian Writing: Critiques and Recollections*. Univ. of Washington Pr. 1980 $20.00. An eclectic collection of essays on such Canadian writers as Margaret Laurence, Margaret Atwood, Hugh Hood, Earle Birney, and A. M. Klein.

ATWOOD, MARGARET. 1939–

A critic, editor, and poet and prose writer of international reputation, Margaret Atwood has been one of the most significant voices in Canadian literature since the publication of her first full-length book of poems, *The Circle Game*. Atwood initially gained critical attention with her lean, unconventional verse. *The Journals of Susanna Moodie* is an innovative collection of poems that takes as its narrator the convention-bound colonialist of the title. *Procedures from Underground* (o.p.) relies on native Indian mythology for its particular vision. With *Power Politics* (o.p.), Atwood established herself as a feminist poet through her exploration of the destructive and alienating aspects of sexual relationships.

Toward the end of the 1960s, Atwood shifted from poetry to fiction. Her novels, with the exception of *Life before Man*, feature a female protagonist who, because of various circumstances, must radically reassess her own existence. The most compelling of these are *Lady Oracle*, in which the heroine decides to stage her death in order to escape into a new life, and *Surfacing*, the story of a woman who sets out to find her botanist father in the Quebec bush and instead discovers a new perspective on the union of nature and humanity. Atwood has also written two volumes of short fiction: *Dancing Girls* and *Murder in the Dark* (o.p.).

The daughter of an entomologist, Margaret Atwood was born in Ottawa and grew up in northern Ontario and Quebec. She received a B.A. from the University of Toronto and an A.M. from Harvard.

BOOKS BY ATWOOD

The Circle Game. 1966. Univ. of Toronto Pr. 1967 pap. $4.95
The Edible Woman. Warner Bks. 1983 pap. $3.50
The Journals of Susanna Moodie: Poems. Oxford 1970 pap. $5.95
Surfacing. 1972. Warner Bks. 1983 pap. $3.50
Survival: A Thematic Guide to Canadian Literature. Univ. of Toronto Pr. 1972 pap. $6.95
Lady Oracle. 1976. Avon 1977 pap. $3.95
Dancing Girls: And Other Stories. 1977. Bantam 1985 $8.95; Simon & Schuster 1982 $14.95
Life before Man. 1979. Simon & Schuster 1980 $11.95; Warner Bks. 1983 pap. $3.95
True Stories. Simon & Schuster 1982 $13.50 pap. $4.95
Bodily Harm. Bantam 1983 pap. $3.95; Ultramarine 1982 $15.00
Second Words: Selected Critical Prose. Beacon 1984 $18.95 pap. $9.95; Univ. of Toronto Pr. 1982 $17.95

BIRNEY, (ALFRED) EARLE. 1904–

Earle Birney was born in Calgary, Alberta, and raised in rural Alberta and British Columbia. To earn money for university, Birney held a variety of manual jobs before enrolling at the University of British Columbia in 1922. Clearly, both his studies and his experience in the labor force gave to his poetry a wide variety of themes and situations. After receiving his Ph.D.

in 1938, Birney accepted a position at the University of Toronto, where he worked until he joined the army in 1942. After serving as a personnel officer during the war, he obtained a professorship in medieval literature, a post from which he retired in 1965.

Earle Birney's poetry has received recognition both in Canada and abroad. His first book of verse, *David and Other Poems* (o.p.), which contains his most important long poem, *David*, won a Governor General's Award. Always concerned with the technical aspects of poetry, Birney was the first Canadian writer to opt for a more relaxed cadence to reflect a more colloquial style. One of numerous collections of Birney's poetry, *The Mammoth Corridors* is characteristic of his later work in which the humanistic themes of his earlier verse are abandoned "to envision a vast, indifferent cosmos in whose 'mammoth corridors' human energy is little more than a glorious absurdity" (*The Oxford Companion to Canadian Literature*).

BOOK BY BIRNEY

The Mammoth Corridors. Stone Pr. 1980 pap. $5.00

CALLAGHAN, MORLEY. 1903–

A master of the short story and author of several excellent novels, Morley Callaghan has long been a writer of international reputation. Callaghan was born and raised in Toronto, educated at St. Michael's College, University of Toronto, and Osgoode Hall law school. Working as a reporter for the *Toronto Daily Star,* he met ERNEST HEMINGWAY, who was also working with the newspaper. In 1929, the same year as his first volume of short stories, *Native Argosy,* was published, Callaghan traveled to Paris where he became reacquainted with Hemingway and met JAMES JOYCE and F. SCOTT FITZGERALD. *That Summer in Paris* contains Callaghan's memoirs of his experiences with these famous expatriates.

Morley Callaghan is renowned for the clarity and economy of his prose, a style that is most akin to Hemingway's. One of Callaghan's finest novels, *Such Is My Beloved* (1934, o.p.), is the tale of an idealistic young priest and his attempts to "reform" two prostitutes. *A Time for Judas* is Callaghan's most recent novel.

BOOKS BY CALLAGHAN

Native Argosy. Short Story Index Repr. Ser. Ayer repr. of 1929 ed. $18.00
That Summer in Paris: Memories of Tangled Friendships with Hemingway, Fitzgerald and Some Others. 1963. Penguin 1979 pap. $3.95
A Time for Judas. 1983. St. Martin's 1984 $12.95

CARMAN, BLISS. 1861–1929

A first cousin of Sir Charles G. D. Roberts and a distant relation of Ralph Waldo Emerson, Bliss was born in Fredericton, New Brunswick, and educated at the Universities of New Brunswick, Oxford, Edinburgh, and Harvard. Always a restless and emotionally unstable man, Carman attempted a fitful career as a journalist in New York before devoting himself fully to poetry. In 1921, he embarked on a poetry-reading tour across Canada. This proved so successful that by its completion Carman was hailed as Canada's unofficial poet laureate.

Enormously popular in his day, Carman produced more than 50 volumes of poetry, most of it heavily influenced by Wordsworth, Emerson, and the Pre-Raphaelites. His most important verse was produced in collaboration with his friend Richard Hovey: The resulting "Vagabondia" series eventually ran to four volumes—*Songs from Vagabondia, Last Songs from Vagabondia, Echoes from Vagabondia* (o.p.), and *More Songs from Vagabondia.*

Bliss Carman's best poetry reflects his sincere joy in nature and the affirmation of a divine presence, which its cyclical rhythms suggested. He is at his weakest when a growing interest in transcendentalism and a rather vague form of pantheism mired his poems in abstractions and repetitiveness.

Books by Carman

Letters of Bliss Carman. Ed. by H. Pearson Gundy, McGill Queens Univ. Pr. 1981 $25.00

(and Richard Hovey). *Songs from Vagabondia.* Gordon $59.95; Greenwood repr. of 1895 ed. lib. bdg. $24.75; Johnson Repr. repr. of 1907 ed. 1969 lib. bdg. $12.00

(and Richard Hovey). *Last Songs from Vagabondia.* Gordon $59.95

(and Richard Hovey). *More Songs from Vagabondia.* Gordon $59.95

Books about Carman

Cappon, J. *Bliss Carman and the Literary Currents and Influences of His Time.* Gordon $59.95

Shepard, Odell. *Bliss Carman.* Gordon $59.95

COHEN, LEONARD. 1934–

Leonard Cohen should properly be described as an artist rather than a poet or prose writer. Born and raised in the affluent Westmount district of Montreal, Cohen graduated from McGill in 1955 and for a short time attended graduate school at Columbia. With the decision to become a professional writer, he returned to Montreal. In 1963 he became an expatriate, and lived intermittently on the Greek island of Hydra, in California, New York, and occasionally Montreal.

Throughout the 1960s Cohen's verse, both as song and poetry, became extremely popular. His "Suzanne" was one of the most-recorded songs of the decade. Always a poet whose work reflected the attitudes of society's nonconformists, Cohen successively identified with the Beat Generation of the 1950s, the rhetoricians of protest of the mid-1960s, and the more meditative disillusionment of the 1970s.

Cohen's best-known work, *Beautiful Losers* (o.p.), is a psychedelic novel that is an abstraction of all searches for a lost innocence. *Death of a Lady's Man* is one of Cohen's recent collections of poetry. Here, his preoccupation with the duality of beauty and decadence is once again explored.

BOOKS BY COHEN

Songs of Leonard Cohen. Macmillan (Collier Bks.) 1969 pap. $3.95
Death of a Lady's Man. 1978. *Penguin Poets Ser.* 1979 pap. $4.95; Viking 1979 $15.00
Choosing to Work. Reston 1979 $22.95
Book of Mercy. Random 1984 $9.45

DAVIES, ROBERTSON. 1913–

Playwright, journalist, actor, and novelist, Robertson Davies is one of Canada's best-known authors. Born in Thamesville, he grew up in Kingston, Ontario, where he later attended Queen's University. A member of Balliol College's dramatic society, he received a B.Litt. from Oxford in 1938, whereupon he joined the prestigious Old Vic Theatre Company. Returning to Canada in 1940, he served as editor of the influential publication *Saturday Night* until 1942. From 1953 to 1971 he was a member of the board of the Stratford Festival. In 1963, Davies became the first master of Massey College, a graduate college at the University of Toronto.

In the 1970s Davies published the Deptford Trilogy—*Fifth Business, The Manticore,* and *World of Wonders*—a series of novels that relies heavily on Carl Jung's theory of archetypes. This trilogy may be contrasted with Davies's earlier novels, which are largely comedies of manners. The Salterton Trilogy—*Tempest Tost, Leaven of Malice,* and *A Mixture of Frailties* (o.p.)—is the most important in this genre of "satiric romance." Here, Davies explores the pettiness and pretensions of small-town university life in Salterton (Kingston). *The Rebel Angels* is set in Ploughwright (Massey) College. A bizarre and dramatic work, it examines the way an individual's primitive beliefs influence his or her intellectual ones.

BOOKS BY DAVIES

Tempest Tost. 1951. Penguin 1980 pap. $3.95
Leaven of Malice. 1954. Penguin 1980 pap. $4.95
Fifth Business. 1970. Penguin 1977 pap. $4.95
The Manticore. 1972. Penguin 1977 pap. $4.95
World of Wonders. 1975. Penguin 1977 pap. $4.95; Viking 1976 $12.95
One Half of Robertson Davies. Penguin 1978 pap. $5.95; Viking 1978 $12.95
The Rebel Angels. 1981. Penguin 1983 pap. $4.95; Viking 1982 $13.95
High Spirits. Penguin 1983 pap. $5.95; Viking 1983 $14.95
The Mirror of Nature. Univ. of Toronto Pr. 1983 pap. $6.50

FINDLEY, TIMOTHY. 1930–

A native of Toronto, novelist and playwright Timothy Findley initially embarked upon an acting career. In its first season (1953), Findley worked for the Canadian Stratford Festival and later, after study at London's Central School of Speech and Drama, he toured Britain, Europe, and the United States as a contract player. While performing in Thornton Wilder's *The Matchmaker,* Findley was encouraged by the playwright to write fiction. Influenced by film techniques, Findley's first novel, *The Last of the Crazy People,* is a penetrating look at a family of "emotional cripples" from a child's perspective. With his character Hooker, Findley captures "the irrational logic of a child's mind, while avoiding the pitfall of treating childhood sentimentally" (*Journal of Canadian Studies*). *The Butterfly Plague* (o.p.) followed in 1969. *The Wars*, Findley's most successful novel, has been translated into nine languages and in 1982, was made into a film. In *The Wars*, "the device of a story-within-a-story is used to illustrate how a personality transcends elemental forces even while being destroyed by them, and how the value of past experience is a function of the skill with which we recreate it imaginatively, transcending the chaos of time and history" (*Canadian Literature*). In 1981 *Famous Last Words* was published. This fictionalization of Ezra Pound's *Hugh Selwyn Mauberley*, already a "fictional fact," presents a brilliant study of fascism in the form of a daring literary experiment.

Books by Findley

The Last of the Crazy People. 1967. Dell 1985 pap. $4.50
The Wars. Dell 1983 pap. $3.95
Famous Last Words. 1981. Dell 1983 pap. $3.95

GALLANT, MAVIS (DE TRAFFORD YOUNG). 1922–

Born in Montreal, Mavis Gallant had a fairly cosmopolitan youth, attending 17 different schools in Canada and the United States. In 1950, after working for the Canadian National Film Board and the *Montreal Standard*, she ended her marriage to John Gallant and settled in Europe. It was at this point that her stories—from the first, deft, witty, and sophisticated—began to appear regularly in the *New Yorker*. Gallant's expatriate status often provided the thematic focus for her most compelling fiction. According to Martin Knelman, her work is "full of brilliant little observations about what transpires in the fine print of human relationships. The prose is cool, elegant, precise and totally stripped of sentimentality."

Books by Gallant

Other Paris: Stories. Short Story Index Repr. Ser. Ayer repr. of 1955 ed. $18.00
From the Fifteenth District: A Novella and Eight Short Stories. Random 1979 $8.95

HALIBURTON, THOMAS CHANDLER. 1796–1865

Although he died before Canada achieved Confederation in 1867, Thomas Chandler Halburton's depiction of prefederation Nova Scotia has given him a prominent place in Canadian literature. Born in Windsor, Nova Scotia, he was the son of Connecticut and Rhode Island Loyalists. In 1826 he was made a member of Nova Scotia's provincial assembly, a post he held until his appointment as a circuit judge in 1829. At this point a confirmed Burkean-Tory, Haliburton began writing satiric sketches for the *Nova Scotian*. Encouraged by their local popularity, he had them published as *The Clockmaker; or The Sayings and Doings of Samuel Slick of Slickville* (the first Canadian bestseller). *The Clockmaker* follows the adventures of Sam Slick, the unscrupulous Connecticut clock peddler. An uneasy embodiment of Yankee shrewdness and Tory-Loyalist principles, Sam Slick instantly became an international comic hero whose travels were eventually chronicled in seven volumes.

In 1841, Haliburton was appointed to the Supreme Court of Nova Scotia; in 1856 he retired to England, where he held a seat in the House of Commons. Two years later he was awarded an honorary degree for literary merit by Oxford University—the first colonial to be so honored.

Today, Haliburton is widely regarded as one of the fathers of American humor. His folksy subjects and colloquial dialogue influenced such later humorists as Mark Twain and Stephen Leacock.

BOOKS BY HALIBURTON

The Clockmaker. 1836. Irvington repr. of 1838 ed. 1979 lib. bdg. $34.75
The English in America. AMS Pr. 2 vols. repr. of 1851 ed. $60.00. Haliburton's attack on Canada's "responsible government," which he saw as a threat to British imperialism.
Sam Slick. Ed. by Ray P. Baker, Arden Lib. repr. of 1923 ed. 1981 lib. bdg. $45.00

BOOK ABOUT HALIBURTON

Chittick, Victor L. *Thomas Chandler Haliburton, "Sam Slick."* AMS Pr. repr. of 1924 ed. $20.00

HINE, DARYL. 1936–

Born in Vancouver, Daryl Hine studied philosophy and classics at McGill University and received an M.A. and Ph.D. in comparative literature from the University of Chicago. From 1968 to 1978 he edited the influential periodical *Poetry*. Hine's verse is marked by familiarity with the classics, its sophistication and complicated rhyme schemes. His poems are a unique blend of archaic forms and modern concerns. Hine is the author of ten books of poetry. *Five Poems, The Carnal and the Crane, Heroics, The Devil's Picturebook, Wooden Horse*, and *In and Out* are out of print.

BOOKS BY HINE

Minutes. Atheneum 1968 pap. $2.45
Resident Alien. Atheneum 1975 $6.95
Daylight Saving. Atheneum 1978 $6.95
Selected Poems. Atheneum 1981 $11.95 pap. $6.95

HOOD, HUGH. 1928–

While he is best known as a writer of short stories, Hugh Hood's fourth novel, *You Can't Get There from Here*, exhibits his usual skill at characterization and a concern with descriptive prose, dialogue, and ironic humor. Hood's humor features universal themes and a strong moral tone, the latter being a product of the author's Roman Catholic sensibility. *You Can't Get There from Here* is a satirical look at multinational corporations and philanthropists who descend on Third World countries. *The Fruit Man, the Meat Man and the Manager* (o.p.) is Hood's best collection of short fiction to date.

Hugh Hood was born in Toronto and received his B.A., M.A., and Ph.D. from the University of Toronto. Until 1961 Hood taught English at St.

Joseph's College, Hartford, Connecticut. He now teaches at the University of
Montreal.

BOOK BY HOOD

You Can't Get There from Here. 1972. Beaufort Bks. 1984 pap. $3.95

KLEIN, A(BRAHAM) M(OSES). 1909–1972

Ludwig Lewisohn wrote in the foreword to A. M. Klein's first book of poems, *Hath Not a Jew . . .* (o.p.), that Klein was "the first contributor of authentic Jewish poetry to the English language." Indeed, Klein's impact on
the Canadian literary scene, with his open exploration of Jewishness, paved
the way for later Jewish writers such as Irving Layton, Leonard Cohen, Mordecai Richler, Miriam Waddington, and Adele Wiseman.

Born in the Ukraine, Abraham Moses Klein left at the age of one with his
parents for Montreal, where he remained for the rest of his life. A brilliant
student of orthodox background, he resisted family pressure to become a
rabbi and enrolled at McGill University in 1926. In 1933 he graduated from
the law school at the University of Montreal and established a practice.
Deeply involved with the Jewish community, Klein early exhibited a commitment to the Zionist movement. From 1936 to 1937 he edited *The Canadian Zionist* and from 1939 to 1954 he held the editorship of *The Canadian
Jewish Chronicle.*

Most of Klein's work reveals his debt to James Joyce. His reliance upon
Joycean allusions, multilingual puns, and complex metaphors is especially
prevalent in *The Rocking Chair* (o.p.), considered by many to contain Klein's
finest verse. These poems are somewhat of a departure from his earlier
work, exemplified in *Poems*, which is more traditional in theme and technique. Klein also wrote some short stories and a highly successful novel,
The Second Scroll (o.p.).

BOOKS BY KLEIN

Poems. Modern Jewish Experiences Ser. Ayer repr. of 1944 ed. 1975 $13.00
Short Stories. Ed. by M. W. Steinberg, Univ. of Toronto Pr. 1983 $35.00 pap. $14.50
Beyond Sambation: Selected Essays and Editorials, 1928–1955. Univ. of Toronto Pr.
    1982 $35.00

KROETSCH, ROBERT. 1927–

Robert Kroetsch was born in Heisler, Alberta, and received his B.A. from
the University of Alberta. In 1954 he studied creative writing at McGill University under Hugh MacLennan. He obtained a Ph.D. in creative writing
from the University of Iowa in 1961. For 14 years Kroetsch taught English
at the State University of New York, in Binghamton. He is currently a professor of English at the University of Manitoba.

With the trilogy *The Words of My Roaring* (o.p.), *The Studhorse Man*, and
Gone Indian (o.p.), Kroetsch departed from realism to experiment with a
surreal or fabulous approach to literature. An updated version of Homer's
Odyssey, The Studhorse Man chronicles a loner's search for the perfect mare

to produce the ultimate breed of horses. *Badlands*, Kroetsch's fifth novel, is a postmodern *Huckleberry Finn* narrated in the form of notes written by a paleontologist rafting through the Alberta Badlands. *Alibi* is a mythic tale of the quest for the perfect spa, a novel that operates in a more realistic vein than Kroetsch's earlier fiction.

BOOKS BY KROETSCH

The Studhorse Man. 1969. Beaufort Bks. 1984 pap. $3.95
Badlands. 1975. Beaufort Bks. 1983 pap. $3.95
Field Notes: The Collected Poetry of Robert Kroetsch. Beaufort Bks. 1981 o.p.
Alibi: A Novel. Beaufort Bks. 1983 $14.95

LAURENCE, (JEAN) MARGARET (WEMYSS). 1926–

"Canada's most successful novelist" was born in Neepawa, Manitoba. Like so many of the waiflike girls of her fiction, Laurence was orphaned at an early age and brought up by relatives. In 1947, she graduated from United College in Winnipeg, Manitoba, and worked as a reporter. A year later she married engineer Jack Laurence. The couple lived in England, Somalia, and Ghana. Yet, it was Laurence's birthplace, fictionalized as "Manawaka," that became the setting for four interconnecting works beginning with *The Stone Angel* and concluding with *The Diviners*. Laurence's protagonists see life as a quest, sometimes joyful but inevitably alienating. *The Stone Angel* is the story of Hagar Shipley, an old woman who, like King Lear, must come to terms with her own sins. Both *A Jest of God* (1966, o.p.) and *The Fire-Dwellers* (1969, o.p.) focus on women who battle a life-denying, self-imposed isolation. Laurence's finest novel, *The Diviners*, reveals her preoccupation with the concept of heritage. The heroine, Morag, and her Métis lover, Jules, both discover that the past has bequeathed to them the strength to resist society's attempts to mold or reject the outsider. Margaret Laurence currently resides in Lakefield, Ontario.

BOOKS BY LAURENCE

A Tree for Poverty: Somali Poetry and Prose. Biblio Dist. 1954 $12.50
The Stone Angel. 1964. Bantam 1981 pap. $3.95
The Diviners. 1974. Bantam 1982 pap. $4.50
The Christmas Birthday Song. Knopf 1980 $6.99

LAYTON, IRVING. 1912–

Irving Layton was born in Romania in 1912; a year later he and his parents arrived in Montreal. Educated in the same city, he received his B.Sc. in agriculture from Macdonald College and an M.A. in political economy from McGill University. Throughout his career Layton has been writer-in-residence at several Canadian universities. Easily the most controversial Canadian poet, Layton was professor of English at Toronto's York University, a post from which he retired in 1978. His verse has been variously described as dazzling, vulgar, sexist, and hyperbolic, yet Layton has always redeemed himself by the integrity with which he approaches his craft. His poetry avoids sentimentality, often centering on decidedly unpoetic, mundane images. Layton is a self-proclaimed "public exhibitionist," and his frank, bawdy verse and antagonist persona have tended to alienate him from both intellectual circles and the general public.

BOOK BY LAYTON

The Selected Poems of Irving Layton. Intro. by Hugh Kenner, New Directions 1977 $8.50 pap. $2.25

LEACOCK, STEPHEN (BUTLER). 1869–1944

Born in Swanmore, England, Stephen Leacock was one of 11 children of an unsuccessful farmer and an ambitious mother, a woman to whom Leacock no doubt owed his energetic and status-conscious nature. In 1891, while teaching at the prestigious Upper Canada College in Toronto, Leacock obtained a modern language degree from the University of Toronto. In 1903, after receiving a Ph.D. in political economy from the University of Chicago, he joined the staff of McGill University, Montreal, as professor of politics and economics. Leacock's career as a humorist began when he had some comic pieces published as *Literary Lapses* in 1910. This successful book was followed by *Nonsense Novels* (1911, o.p.) and *Sunshine Sketches of a Little Town.* Leacock continued this frantic literary output for the remainder of his career, producing more than 30 books of humor as well as biographies and social commentaries. The Stephen Leacock Medal for Humour was established after his death to honor annually an outstanding Canadian humorist.

BOOKS BY LEACOCK

The Social Criticism of Stephen Leacock: The Unsolved Riddle of Social Justice and Other Essays. Intro. by Alan Bowker, *Social History of Canada Ser.* Univ. of Toronto Pr. 1973 pap. $5.95
Literary Lapses. 1910. *Short Story Index Repr. Ser.* Ayer repr. of 1911 ed. $16.00
Sunshine Sketches of a Little Town. Short Story Index Repr. Ser. Ayer repr. of 1912 ed. $21.95
Frenzied Fiction. Short Story Index Repr. Ser. Ayer repr. of 1917 ed. $16.00
Winsome Winnie, and Other New Nonsense Novels. Short Story Index Repr. Ser. Ayer repr. of 1920 ed. $13.00
Here Are My Lectures and Stories. Essay Index Repr. Ser. Ayer repr. of 1937 ed. $18.25
Humour and Humanity. Century Bookbindery repr. of 1938 ed. 1980 lib. bdg. $35.00
Model Memoirs: And Other Sketches from Simple to Serious. Essay Index Repr. Ser. Ayer repr. of 1938 ed. $19.00
Laugh with Leacock. Dodd text ed. 1981 pap. $5.95

BOOKS ABOUT LEACOCK

Lomer, Gerhard R. *Stephen Leacock: A Check-List and Index of His Writings.* Folcroft repr. of 1954 ed. lib. bdg. $20.00; Richard West repr. of 1954 ed. 1978 lib. bdg. $25.00
McArthur, Peter. *Stephen Leacock.* Folcroft repr. of 1923 ed. 1974 lib. bdg. $10.00

MACPHERSON, JAY. 1931–

Although her literary production has been small, Jay Macpherson has proved to be an excellent and influential poet. Born in England, she moved with her mother and brother to Newfoundland in 1940. She attended university in Ottawa and in Toronto, where she received a Ph.D. in English literature in 1964. In 1957, Oxford University Press published what subsequently became her best-known work, *The Boatman* (o.p.), winner of the Governor General's Award. *Poems Twice Told* reprints *The Boatman* and *Welcoming Disaster* (o.p.) in one volume. Heavily influenced by the eminent Canadian critic Northrop Frye, Macpherson is at the hub of the "mythopoeic school" that sprang from Frye's literary theory. She is currently a professor of English at Victoria College, University of Toronto.

BOOK BY MACPHERSON

Poems Twice Told: Containing The Boatman and Welcoming Disaster. Oxford 1981 $10.95

MOODIE, SUSANNA (STRICKLAND). 1803–1885

Susanna Moodie, born in Suffolk, England, was the youngest of five daughters, four of whom became writers of fiction and poetry. (Moodie's elder sister, Catharine Parr Traill, a lesser-known British colonial author, wrote *The Backwoods of Canada*.) Before immigrating to Canada, in 1832, Moodie penned numerous poems and stories, all heavily didactic and decidedly second-rate. However, once she had settled in Upper Canada (now Ontario) with her husband, John Dunbar Moodie, the harsh life of the settler provoked a more realistic literary response. Her autobiographical *Roughing It in the Bush*, published in 1852, is a series of sketches stitched into a larger narrative. It is a book expressing the hopes and defeat, the pride and the anger the early settlers felt toward their new home, the Canadian bush. A sequel, *Life in the Clearings versus the Bush* (o.p.), appeared in 1853. Throughout her life Susanna Moodie's literary output continued to be prolific. Yet it is the frank and colorful quality of *Roughing It* that has placed her in the forefront of early Canadian writers.

BOOK BY MOODIE

Roughing It in the Bush. Irvington repr. of 1852 ed. lib. bdg. $19.50

MUNRO, ALICE (LAIDLAW). 1931–

Alice Munro was born in Wingham, Ontario. An avid writer from an early age, Munro is a particularly gifted author of short stories. Her first collection, *Dance of the Happy Shades* (o.p.), won a Governor General's Award. *Lives of Girls and Women* and *Who Do You Think You Are?* (published in the United States as *The Beggar Maid*) are episodic novels in which the incidents are self-contained but feature a consistent protagonist. Her colloquial, realistic prose is characterized by an attention to detail and a preoccupation with women's relationships, usually ordinary women or girls living in rural Ontario towns. Other collections of Munro's short fiction are *Something I've Been Meaning to Tell You* and *The Moons of Jupiter.*

BOOKS BY MUNRO

Lives of Girls and Women. 1971. New Amer. Lib. (Plume) 1983 pap. $6.95
Something I've Been Meaning to Tell You. 1974. New Amer. Lib. (Signet) 1984 pap. $7.95
The Beggar Maid: Stories of Flo and Rose. Bantam 1982 pap. $2.95; Knopf 1979 $8.95; *Penguin Fiction Ser.* 1984 pap. $4.95
The Moons of Jupiter. 1982. Knopf 1983 $13.95; *Penguin Fiction Ser.* 1984 pap. $4.95

ONDAATJE, MICHAEL. 1943–

Although Michael Ondaatje has written four volumes of excellent poetry including *There's a Trick with a Knife I'm Learning to Do,* it is his fiction that has gained widespread attention.

A writer quite unconcerned with typical Canadian themes, Ondaatje focuses his craft on the bizarre, which he renders through surreal, innovative techniques. In *The Collected Works of Billy the Kid,* Ondaatje toys with various literary genres—drama, interviews, lyrics—to relate the life of Billy the Kid. *Coming through Slaughter* is the "biography" of jazz musician Charles "Buddy" Bolden, a book in which Ondaatje uses Bolden's life to illustrate the artistic dichotomy of creativity and destruction. *Running in the Family* is a fictionalized account of Ondaatje's Ceylonese ancestors.

Michael Ondaatje was born in Ceylon (now Sri Lanka) and moved to Canada in 1962. He earned a B.A. from the University of Toronto and an M.A. from Queen's University, Kingston. He has taught English at the University of Western Ontario and York University, Toronto.

BOOKS BY ONDAATJE

The Collected Works of Billy the Kid. 1970. Norton 1974 $9.95; Penguin 1984 pap. $5.95; Wingbow Pr. 1978 pap. $3.50
Coming through Slaughter. 1976. Norton 1977 $9.95; Penguin 1984 pap. $5.95
There's a Trick with a Knife I'm Learning to Do: Poems, 1962–1978. Norton 1979 $12.95 pap. $4.95
Running in the Family. Norton 1982 $12.95; Penguin 1984 pap. $5.95

PRATT, E(DWIN) J(OHN). 1883–1964

E. J. Pratt is considered to be the poet who initiated the Canadian modernist movement. Yet, unlike his literary contemporaries, Pratt was attracted to the convention of epic poetry: *Brébeuf and His Brethren* (1940) and *Towards the Last Spike,* both out of print, are impressive examples of this style, and are also ambitious attempts to forge a national mythology through verse.

Edwin John Pratt was born at Western Bay, Newfoundland. As he grew up in this desolate coastal town, Pratt's association with the sea impressed him with an image that would later reverberate throughout his poetry. Although trained as a Methodist minister, Pratt evidently experienced a crisis of faith following his studies in philosophy and psychology at the University of Toronto, where he received a Ph.D. in theology. In 1920, largely because of his promise as a poet, he was given an English professorship at Victoria College, University of Toronto, a post from which he retired in 1953.

Pratt's verse is aptly described by E. K. Brown as the "work of an experimenter who is continuing to clutch at a tradition although that tradition is actually stifling him." All 12 volumes of Pratt's poetry are out of print in this country, yet his colossal stature as a Canadian poet commands our consideration. Samples of his verse can be found in many Canadian poetry anthologies.

BOOK BY PRATT

(ed.). *Heroic Tales in Verse*. Granger repr. of 1941 ed. 1977 consult publisher for information

RICHLER, MORDECAI. 1931–

A consummate and caustic novelist, Mordecai Richler is one of the Montreal Jewish writers whose work has gained both critical attention and a strong public following. Born in Montreal at the onset of the Depression, Richler reflects in his best work, in a wry and engaging manner, his experiences in the Jewish ghettos around St. Urbain Street. Richler left Sir George Williams College without obtaining a degree, to travel to Europe and begin a writing career. After a sojourn in Canada, he became an expatriate writer in England, returning to Montreal only in 1972.

Richler has been described as "the loser's advocate," an author who can elicit sympathy for unsympathetic characters. One of the more famous of these creations is Duddy Kravitz, hero of *The Apprenticeship of Duddy Kravitz* (1959, o.p.). An amoral trickster, Duddy schemes his way out of the Jewish ghetto to become a landowner. A pivotal work, *Duddy Kravitz* paved the way for novels with similar themes. *Saint Urbain's Horseman* is a superb, ironic examination of Jake Hersch, who must come to terms with his dual (Canadian and Jewish) heritage. *Joshua Then and Now* has as its protagonist Joshua Shapiro, a man who must confront the mistakes of the past and present in order to evaluate what has become the prevalent theme in Richler's fiction: the question of moral responsibility.

BOOKS BY RICHLER

Saint Urbain's Horseman. 1971. Bantam 1972 pap. $3.95
Joshua Then and Now. Bantam 1981 pap. $4.95; Knopf 1980 $11.95
Home Sweet Home: My Canadian Album. Knopf 1984 $16.95; Penguin 1985 pap. $4.95

ROBERTS, CHARLES G. 1860–1943

Roberts is considered by many to be the dean of Canadian poetry. His English-Loyalist background and close contact with the untamed Canada of the Confederation combined to provide a rich source for his creative writing. A cousin of Bliss Carman, Roberts was born in Douglas, New Brunswick. While pursuing a degree, Roberts began writing poetry. This early productivity yielded three books of verse. The first of these, *Orion* (1880, o.p.), garnered the praise of Matthew Arnold.

A prolific writer, Roberts was an outspoken supporter of Canadian literature; however, this did not prevent the Confederation poet from spending a sizable portion of his life in New York and later London (from 1895 to 1925). Apart from his influential poetry, with its presentation of divinely ordered nature, Roberts produced a highly successful series of animal stories, tales that portrayed the violence involved in survival and avoided the moral tone often associated with such works (see *Earth's Enigmas*). Roberts wrote several adult romances that invariably feature the English/French tension in eighteenth-century Canada (see *By the Marshes of Minas*). Roberts was knighted in 1935.

Books by Roberts

Earth's Enigmas. Short Story Index Repr. Ser. Ayer repr. of 1895 ed. $18.00
By the Marshes of Minas. Short Story Index Repr. Ser. Ayer repr. of 1900 ed. $19.00

ROSS, SINCLAIR. 1908–

Born near Prince Albert, Saskatchewan, Sinclair Ross grew up on the prairies. Apart from his service in the Canadian army (1942–46), Ross worked at the Union Bank of Canada (which later became the Royal Bank of Canada) from his completion of high school to his retirement in 1968. He now resides in Vancouver.

Together with two collections of short stories, *The Lamp at Noon and Other Stories* (o.p.) and *The Race and Other Stories* (o.p.), Ross has written four novels: *As for Me and My House*, *The Well* (o.p.), *Whir of Gold* (o.p.), and *Sawbones Memorial* (o.p.). Ross's reputation rests on his first novel, *As for Me and My House*. Ross was inspired by the hardships of the depression, as are many western Canadian writers. *As for Me and My House* is a bleak yet richly textured look at the relationship between a disillusioned minister and his wife, whose diary serves as the vehicle for the tale. Little appreciated when it first appeared in print, *As for Me and My House* is now firmly established as a Canadian classic.

Book by Ross

As for Me and My House. 1941. Univ. of Nebraska Pr. (Bison) 1978 $14.95 pap. $3.25

SCOTT, DUNCAN CAMPBELL. 1862–1947

Born in Ottawa, Duncan Campbell Scott was the son of a Methodist minister. On joining the civil service, Scott became a clerk and later commissioner to the Indian tribes of the James Bay Region. It was in these positions that Scott gained a firsthand knowledge of Canada's native peoples, a knowledge reflected in much of his verse. Eventually, Scott was made deputy minister of Indian affairs, a post from which he retired in 1932. Good collections of Scott's poetry, now out of print, may be found in *Selected Poems of Duncan Campbell Scott* or *Duncan Campbell Scott: Selected Poetry*.

Scott is a fine example of a "Confederation Poet," one who was influenced by both nineteenth-century British and American thought but at the same time developed a commitment to the presentation of his native land and its people. Scott also published two collections of short stories: *In the Village of Viger* (o.p.) and *The Witching of Elspie*.

BOOK BY SCOTT

The Witching of Elspie: A Book of Stories. Short Story Index Repr. Ser. Ayer repr. of 1923 ed. $18.00

SERVICE, ROBERT W(ILLIAM). 1874–1958

Robert William Service was born in Preston, England, and raised in Scotland. He worked at the Commercial Bank of Scotland from 1889 until his departure for Canada in 1896. After traveling through western Canada, the United States, and Mexico, he resumed his banking career. In 1908, Service was transferred to a bank in Dawson, Yukon Territory, a setting that became the impetus for most of his verse.

Service is almost exclusively associated with the colorful, humorous ballads about life on the northern frontier, "The Cremation of Sam McGee" and "The Shooting of Dan McGrew" being easily the most familiar of these. Service left Canada in 1912 to act as a foreign correspondent. This enormously popular "Northern Poet" died in Monte Carlo.

BOOKS BY SERVICE

Collected Poems of Robert Service. Dodd 1944 $17.95
More Collected Verse. Dodd 1955 $19.95
Later Collected Verse. Dodd 1965 $17.95
The Best of Robert Service. Amereon $14.95; Dodd pap. $4.95
More Selected Verse of Robert Service. Amereon $14.95; Dodd pap. $4.95
Spell of the Yukon and Other Verses. Dodd $6.95
Best Tales of the Yukon. Running Pr. 1983 lib. bdg. $12.90 pap. $4.95
Yukon Poems. Filter 1967 $8.00 pap. $1.50

WADDINGTON, MIRIAM (DWORKIN). 1917–

Born in Winnipeg, Manitoba, into a Jewish family, Miriam Waddington received a B.A. in 1939 from the University of Toronto, and then studied social work in Toronto and Philadelphia. Married to Patrick Waddington, whom she later divorced, she became active in the Montreal poets' circle during the 1940s. From 1964 to 1983, Waddington held a teaching position at York University, Toronto. *Driving Home* is a lackluster collection of Waddington's verse that combines new and old pieces. A stronger work is *The Visitants*, in which a series of intense images serves to express Waddington's outrage over various forms of social injustice.

BOOKS BY WADDINGTON

Driving Home: Poems New and Selected. Oxford 1972 pap. $4.50; Small Pr. Dist. 1973 pap. $5.95
The Visitants. Oxford 1981 pap. $9.95

NEW ZEALAND

General Works and Anthologies

Adcock, Fleur, ed. *The Oxford Book of Contemporary New Zealand Poetry.* Oxford 1982 pap. $14.95. A comprehensive guide to the subject. Most of the poems collected here were first published in the 1970s or later.

Curnow, Wystan, ed. *Essays on New Zealand Literature.* Heinemann 1974 $15.00; International Specialized Bk. text ed. 1983 pap. $9.95. An introduction to the subject through nine specific studies by various critics. Good discussions of New Zealand literary history.

Hankin, Cherry, ed. *Critical Essays on the New Zealand Short Story.* International Specialized Bk. text ed. 1983 pap. $9.95. Especially written for this volume, these essays discuss 13 different writers, including Sargeson and Mansfield, using a variety of approaches, styles, and ideas.

Jones, Joseph, and Johanna Jones. *New Zealand Fiction. Twayne's World Authors Ser.* G. K. Hall 1983 lib. bdg. $20.95. A chronological guide to the main writers and tendencies to be found in New Zealand fiction.

Mulgan, Alan. *Literature and Authorship in New Zealand.* Folcroft lib. bdg. $17.50. A monograph of New Zealand literature that includes a historical survey as well as a discussion of the New Zealand novelist.

Stead, C. K. *In the Glass Case: Essays on New Zealand Literature.* Oxford 1981 $32.50. An excellent collection of essays and reviews on both fiction and poetry. Includes discussions of Mansfield, Sargeson, Frame, Brasch, Baxter, and Curnow.

Wilkes, G. A., and J. C. Reid. *Literatures of Australia and New Zealand.* Ed. by A. L. McLeod, Pennsylvania State Univ. Pr. 1971 $24.95. A historical survey of Australian literature and a discussion of New Zealand literature according to genre.

BAXTER, JAMES KEIR. 1926–1972

James K. Baxter's father was a farmer, a descendant of Scots settlers; his mother, who took a degree at Cambridge, was the daughter of J. Macmillan Brown, a scholar who played a significant role in New Zealand university life. Widely acclaimed as one of New Zealand's finest poets, Baxter from an early age exhibited a precocious facility with verse. Throughout his life, Baxter's unorthodox views received attention. As a young man he argued that "the poet or prose writer who ignores human suffering is betraying himself"; his verse is characterized by a technical conservatism and an adherence to formality as well as an easy familiarity with the classics. Baxter spent most of his life in New Zealand where, after an unsuccessful university career, various jobs, and a battle with alcoholism, he converted to Catholicism in 1958. In 1970 he established a commune at Jerusalem, a Maori settlement on the Wanganui River.

BOOK BY BAXTER

Collected Poems. Ed. by J. E. Weir, Oxford 1979 $65.00

BRASCH, CHARLES ORWELL. 1909–1973

Charles Brasch's father was a self-made lawyer; his mother, the daughter of a prosperous businessman. Both parents were of Jewish descent though they had not been practicing members of that faith for generations. At the age of 17 Brasch was sent by his ambitious father to St. John's College, Oxford, to read history. Ill-prepared for the rigors of the university, he took a rather disappointing third class in the final examinations. After Oxford, he traveled extensively in Europe and the Near East. In 1932 Brasch decided, against his father's wishes, to renounce a business career and take up poetry. As a literary figure Brasch had double significance for his homeland. In an attempt to consolidate the arts in New Zealand, he became the founder and editor of *Landfall*, an enormously influential quarterly that would offer a forum for New Zealand writers.

BOOKS BY BRASCH

Collected Poems. Ed. by Alan Roddick, Oxford 1984 $34.95
Indirections. Oxford 1980 $35.00

DAVIN, DANIEL MARCUS. 1913–

Irish-Catholic in background, Daniel Davin was born in Invercagill. Although the son of a poorly educated family whose first language was Gaelic, Davin distinguished himself at Sacred Heart College, Auckland, the University of Otago, and Oxford, where as a Rhodes scholar he read classics. During World War II, Davin served as an intelligence officer. In 1945 he joined Clarendon Press in Oxford; in 1978 he retired from the position of Academic Publisher to the University. His works (most of which are out of print) include the novels *Cliffs of Fall; For the Rest of Our Lives; Roads from Home; The Sullen Bell; No Remittance; Not Here, Not Now; Brides of Price;* his best collection of short fiction is *The Gorse Blooms Pale,* a group of stories that deal with life in London before and during the war. *Closing Times* is a book of critical essays that commemorate Davin's literary friends: Dylan Thomas, Joyce Cary, Louis MacNeice, and the little-known Julian Maclaren-Ross.

BOOK BY DAVIN

Closing Times. Oxford 1975 $17.50

FRAME, JANET. 1924–

Janet Frame has been praised as "the most talented writer to come out of New Zealand since Katherine Mansfield." Her first novel, *Owls Do Cry* (1957), a study of the disintegration of a poor New Zealand family, was considered "a superior performance." *Faces in the Water* (1961), a novel "presented as the memoir of a cured mental patient," was presumably based on her own experience. *Time* said of it: "Her writing is sensitive and her evocation of madness is unforgettable." *The Edge of the Alphabet* (o.p.) is a "strange book about three wasted days in a dim world." *Scented Gardens for the Blind* (1963), a bizarre, "perfervid, stream-of-consciousness novel with a limited audience, albeit haunting appeal," tells the bleak story of a family who alienate one another and "shut themselves in separate graves" (*LJ*). *A State of Siege*, with all the elements of a psychological thriller, provides a portrait of an aging teacher. Charles Rolo (*Atlantic*) has said that Frame is "endowed with a poet's imagination, and her prose has beauty, precision, a surging momentum and the quality of constant surprise." Her talent, particularly her poetic power with words, is considered brilliant, but far too often "she has used it only to express her own emotions—her melancholy, disillusion and despair."

Yellow Flowers in the Antipodean Room is the story of a young man who is mistakenly pronounced dead after an accident; when he is roused from deep coma, his world, which had accepted his "death," resented his "resurrection" and his life became a downhill slide. Frame's book of poems, *The Pocket Mirror*, is "a rich mixture of narrative and lyric modes [looking] backward to childhood and forward to death" (*LJ*).

BOOKS BY FRAME

Owls Do Cry. Braziller 1982 pap. $5.95
Faces in the Water. Braziller 1982 pap. $5.95
Scented Gardens for the Blind. Braziller 1980 pap. $5.95
A State of Siege. Braziller 1981 pap. $4.95
The Pocket Mirror: Poems. Braziller 1967 $4.95
Yellow Flowers in the Antipodean Room. Braziller 1969 $5.95
Living in the Maniototo. Braziller 1979 $8.95 pap. $4.95
To the Is-Land. Braziller 1982 $10.95

GRACE, PATRICIA. 1937–

Born in Wellington in 1937, Patricia Grace is of Maori descent. She has taught in country schools and is now teaching at Porirua. Both Grace's first collection of short fiction, *Waiariki*, and *The Dream Sleepers and Other Stories* explore what it means to be Maori in a predominantly white society. Her first novel, *Mutuwhenua: The Moon Sleeps*, tells the story of a young Maori girl and a *pakeha* (white) schoolteacher who plan to marry. With insight and compassion, Grace describes the bicultural tensions that inevitably develop from this relationship.

BOOKS BY GRACE

Waiariki. 1975. Three Continents 1976 pap. $7.00
Mutuwhenua: The Moon Sleeps. Three Continents 1978 pap. $7.00
The Dream Sleepers and Other Stories. Three Continents 1980 pap. $7.00

MANSFIELD, KATHERINE. 1888–1923

Katherine Mansfield was born in New Zealand and her native country colors her short stories. She died at the early age of 35. Mansfield was chiefly responsible for the renaissance of the short story in England that took place during and after her lifetime. The Femina-Vie Heureuse prize was awarded to "Bliss" in 1921. One of her best and best-known stories is "The Garden Party," based on the memories of her New Zealand childhood.

The wife of John Middleton Murry, editor of the *Nation* and *Athenaeum*, she wrote reviews of fiction that appeared over the signature "K. M." in her husband's paper and attracted wide attention. Her "Journal" and "Letters" are remarkable records of her constant search for truth in fiction, undistorted by artificiality or sophistication. Among her other books are *The Garden Party and Other Stories* (1922, o.p.), *Poems* (1924, o.p.), and *Bliss and Other Stories* (1920, o.p.).

BOOKS BY MANSFIELD

Short Stories. Knopf 1947 $22.95
The Short Stories of Katherine Mansfield. Ecco Pr. repr. of 1920 ed. 1983 pap. $9.95; intro. by John M. Murry, Knopf 1947 $22.95
The Scrapbook of Katherine Mansfield. Fertig repr. of 1939 ed. 1975 $29.50
Stories. Ed. by Elizabeth Bowen, Random (Vintage) 1956 pap. $4.95
The Urewera Notebook. Ed. by Ian Gordon, Oxford 1978 text ed. pap. $12.95

BOOKS ABOUT MANSFIELD

Alpers, Anthony. *Life of Katherine Mansfield.* Penguin 1982 pap. $7.95; Viking 1980 $16.95
Clarke, Isabel C. *Katherine Mansfield: A Biography.* Arden Lib. repr. of 1944 ed. 1978 lib. bdg. $15.00; Folcroft repr. of 1944 ed. lib. bdg. $10.00
————. *Six Portraits. Essay Index Repr. Ser.* Ayer repr. of 1935 ed. $20.00
Eustace, Cecil J. *Infinity of Questions. Essay Index Repr. Ser.* Ayer repr. of 1946 ed. $16.50; Richard West repr. of 1946 ed. $8.50; Saifer 1946 $10.00
Friis, Anne. *Katherine Mansfield: Life and Stories.* Folcroft repr. of 1946 ed. lib. bdg. $27.50
Gurr, Andrew, and Clare Hanson. *Katherine Mansfield.* St. Martin's 1981 $18.95
Hankin, C. A. *Katherine Mansfield and Her Confessional Stories.* St. Martin's 1983 $22.50
————, ed. *The Letters of John Middleton Murry to Katherine Mansfield.* Watts 1983 $28.95
Hormasji, Nariman. *Katherine Mansfield: An Appraisal.* Century Bookbindery repr. of 1967 ed. 1982 lib. bdg. $35.00
Mantz, Ruth E. *Bibliography of Katherine Mansfield.* Porter 1979 lib. bdg. $42.50
Mantz, Ruth E., and John M. Murry. *The Life of Katherine Mansfield.* Haskell 1974 lib. bdg. $55.95; Scholarly repr. of 1933 ed. $27.00
Meyers, Jeffrey. *Katherine Mansfield: A Biography.* New Directions 1980 pap. $10.50
Morris, G. N. *Mansfieldiana: A Brief Katherine Mansfield Bibliography.* Folcroft repr. of 1948 ed. lib. bdg. $12.50
Sewell, Arthur. *Katherine Mansfield: A Critical Essay.* Folcroft repr. of 1973 ed. lib. bdg. $15.00

MORRIESON, RONALD HUGH. 1922–1972

Ronald Hugh Morrieson was not a prolific writer. His first novel, *The Scarecrow*, was completed at the age of 41; three more followed before his early death at 50. Two short stories were also published after his death. Yet based on this limited output, over the last few years Morrieson's status as a novelist of merit has been established. Morrieson was born, lived, and died in the same house in Hawera, South Taranaki. From this bucolic locale, he explored themes quite alien to the provincial fiction predominant in New Zealand. *The Scarecrow*, a unique combination of comedy and violence, focuses on "The Scarecrow," an evil magician whose presence threatens a small community. This novel of the grotesque has been described by Peter Simpson as "a kind of extraordinary comic fugue . . . [with] horror answering laughter and ugly death answering ripe youth."

BOOK BY MORRIESON

The Scarecrow: Novel. 1963. International Specialized Bk. 1983 o.p.

SARGESON, FRANK. 1903–1982

Frank Sargeson won international recognition as a master of a definitively New Zealand prose. Born and raised in Hamilton, he trained as a lawyer. Fleeing from the puritan restraints of his family, he left for England in 1926 to embark on a stint of self-education at the British Museum. In 1928 he returned to New Zealand, where he waited five years before any of his laboriously written stories were published. With his shift from short stories to novels, Sargeson gradually abandoned the trademark "narrative dialect" of his short fiction to embrace the playful, "self-delighting" rhetoric of his later achievements. *Memoirs of a Peon* is a comic look in the picaresque tradition at the New Zealand lower classes.

BOOK BY SARGESON

Memoirs of a Peon. 1965. International Specialized Bk. 1983 pap. $4.95

CHAPTER 16

Essays and Criticism

Kathleen Bonann Marshall
and
Donald G. Marshall

> The essay has to create from within itself all the preconditions for the effectiveness and validity of its vision.
> —GEORGE LUKACS, *Soul and Form*

Dr. Samuel Johnson, the "great cham" of common sense in the late eighteenth century, regarded the essay as "a loose sally of the mind, an irregular, undigested piece, not a regular and ordinary performance." T. W. Adorno, in his *Essay as Form*, insists that "the essay remains what it always was, the critical form par excellence; specifically it constructs the immanent criticism of cultural artifacts, and it confronts that which such artifacts are within their concept; it is the critique of ideology." Clearly, there exists a tension either within the essay itself, or in one's conception of the essay form. And this contrast—between a loose, informal piece of prose and a serious, rigorous argument—has been present since the essay's inception. MICHEL DE MONTAIGNE (see Vol. 2), who invented the essay in the sixteenth century, named it on the grounds that it was a form in which he could "essay" or try out his ideas by reflecting upon various subjects in writing without claiming to be definitive. Francis Bacon, whose essays appeared only a few years after Montaigne's, was more interested in imposing his views than in trying them out. His essays reflect his intention in their rigor of style and tone.

From the beginning, the modern English essay divided into the formal and the informal styles: the formal after Bacon, who tells us nothing about himself; the informal after Montaigne, who tells us everything. From Bacon, the essay assumed the characteristics of a closely argued, logical, tightly organized, possibly philosophical piece of studied prose. Montaigne's style established the more tentative, relaxed, confidential, even musing, tone that would be more closely associated with a highly personal piece of writing. The intimate relationship between author and form is indicated by his observation, "Everyone recognizes me in my book, and everyone recognizes my book in me."

The personal essay could not flourish until two matters were settled: The arts, particularly literature, had to provide ample room for subjective and personal expression; and literature had to acknowledge the fact that prose was not merely "prosaic" but capable of artistic purpose. In the eighteenth century, the latter was achieved, especially with the rise of the periodicals. The tenor of the age, however, was objective and rational. Thus the periodical essays of Joseph Addison, Sir Richard Steele, Samuel Johnson, and others are eloquent compromises of the two possible natures of the form. But when romanticism in art dominated the spirit of literature, in the early nineteenth century, the informal essay blossomed in the works of Charles Lamb, William Hazlitt, Thomas De Quincey, and others. Many of their finest essays first appeared in a new sort of periodical, the "magazine," so named to indicate its inclination to be a storehouse of verbal odds and ends. *Blackwoods* and *The London Magazine* aimed at a wider and less "serious" audience than did the political and literary periodicals of the time, and encouraged writings of a light tone and on popular topics. Throughout the century, and to a significant extent in our own time, English and American essayists have found the magazine to be their most congenial host. Today the familiar form is widely employed, though often under the name of editorial, political column, humerous column, or book, play, or film review. Many distinguished people in other fields have contributed to these forms: the paleontologist Stephen Jay Gould, the food and travel writer M. F. K. Fisher, the research physician Lewis Thomas, the screenwriter Woody Allen.

The formal essay, on the other hand, has tended to concern itself rather thoroughly with literary criticism. In Montaigne's time, but on the English side of the Channel, Sir Philip Sidney wrote *The Apologie for Poetrie*, to defend the art against the attacks of Stephen Gosson. Sidney's essay is methodical, thorough, and objective and constitutes perhaps the earliest significant single piece of English literary criticism still vital today. Other purposes dominated the prose writings of the seventeenth century, but the thriving periodicals of the eighteenth century gave ample opportunity to the analytical minds of the Age of Reason, who found much to say about the nature, history, and principles of the arts. Literary criticism of the nineteenth century was often impressionistic rather than objective, and the familiar essay was a conducive form. At present, literary criticism has become one of the dominating concerns of writers, and the critical essay the dominant form of academic commentary on literature. During the past 20 years, critics in colleges and universities have brought into their essays a new field labeled "literary theory" or "critical theory." International and multidisciplinary in its range, literary theory has kept the critical essay open to its traditional movement from commentary on literary works to reflection on the widest social and moral themes.

GENERAL READING

Dobrée, Bonamy. *English Essayists*. Folcroft 1973 lib. bdg. $10.00
Farrington, Davis D. *The Essay*. Norwood repr. of 1924 ed. $20.00

Kostelanetz, Richard. *Essaying Essays: Alternative Forms of Exposition.* R. K. Eds. 1975 pap. $20.00

MacDonald, W. L. *Beginnings of the English Essay.* Folcroft repr. of 1914 ed. 1972 lib. bdg. $15.00

O'Leary, R. D. *The Essay.* Arden Lib. repr. of 1928 ed. $30.00; Richard West repr. of 1928 ed. 1973 $30.00

Robinson, Ian. *The Survival of English Essays in the Criticism of Language.* Cambridge Univ. Pr. 1973 pap. $34.00

Walker, Hugh. *The English Essay and Essayists.* 1900. AMS Pr. repr. of 1915 ed. $34.50; Arden Lib. repr. of 1928 ed. $13.75

Williams, Orlo. *The Essay.* Arden Lib. $10.00; Folcroft 1977 lib. bdg. $10.00

Wylie, Laura J. *The English Essay.* Folcroft 1973 lib. bdg. $10.00; Norwood repr. of 1916 ed. 1980 lib. bdg. $10.00

COLLECTIONS

Brewer, David J., ed. *The World's Best Essays from the Earliest Period to the Present Time.* Arden Lib. 10 vols. repr. of 1900 ed. 1982 lib. bdg. $500.00

Bronson, Walter C., ed. *English Essays. Essay Index Repr. Ser.* Ayer repr. of 1905 ed. $24.50

Cochrane, Robert, ed. *The English Essayists: A Comprehensive Selection from the Works of the Great Essayists from Lord Bacon to John Ruskin.* Arden Lib. repr. of 1881 ed. 1978 lib. bdg. $40.00

Cody, Sherwin, ed. *Selection from the Best English Essays, Illustrative of the History of English Prose Style. Essay Index Repr. Ser.* Ayer repr. of 1903 ed. $21.50

Collins, Vere Henry, ed. *Three Centuries of English Essays: From Francis Bacon to Max Beerbohm.* Arden Lib. repr. of 1931 ed. 1979 lib. bdg. $12.50; *Essay Index Repr. Ser.* Ayer repr. of 1931 ed. $11.00

Earl of Birkenhead, ed. *The Hundred Best English Essays.* Norwood repr. of 1929 ed. $15.00

Fiedler, Leslie, ed. *The Art of the Essay.* 1959. Crowell 2d ed. 1969 o.p. An illuminating, entertaining collection of 60 essays covering the whole field from Montaigne to the present.

Howard, Maureen, ed. *The Penguin Book of Contemporary Essays.* Viking 1984 $16.95

Makower, Stanley V., and Basil H. Blackwell, eds. *A Book of English Essays, 1600–1900. Essay Index Repr. Ser.* Ayer repr. of 1912 ed. $26.50; Norwood repr. of 1914 ed. 1979 lib. bdg. $15.00

Milford, Humphrey S., ed. *Selected Modern English Essays.* Greenwood repr. of 1932 ed. 1981 lib. bdg. $32.50

Moore, John R., ed. *Representative Essays: English and American. Essay Index Repr. Ser.* Ayer repr. of 1930 ed. $20.00

Newbolt, Henry, ed. *Essays and Essayists.* Norwood repr. of 1928 ed. 1979 lib. bdg. $10.00

Peacock, William, ed. *Selected English Essays.* Norwood repr. of 1935 ed. 1979 lib. bdg. $12.50; *World's Class. Ser.* Oxford $9.95

Priestley, John B., ed. *Essayists Past and Present. Essay Index Repr. Ser.* Ayer repr. of 1925 ed. $18.00

Pritchard, Francis H., ed. *The World's Best Essays.* Norwood repr. of 1929 ed. $45.00

Rhys, Ernest, ed. *A Century of English Essays.* Arden Lib. repr. 1979 lib. bdg. $10.00;

Richard West repr. of 1913 ed. 1978 lib. bdg. $15.00. A selection ranging from
Caxton to R. L. Stevenson and the writers of the early twentieth century.
Sampson, George, ed. *Nineteenth-Century Essays. Essay Index Repr. Ser.* Ayer repr. of
1912 ed. $16.00
Smithberger, Andrew T., ed. *Essays: British and American.* Greenwood repr. of 1953
ed. lib. bdg. $20.25
Williams, W. E., ed. *A Book of English Essays. Penguin Eng. Lib. Ser.* 1981 pap. $4.95
Winchester, Caleb T., ed. *A Book of English Essays. Essay Index Repr. Ser.* Ayer repr.
of 1914 ed. $24.50

CONTEMPORARY CRITICISM

Altieri, Charles. *Act and Quality: A Theory of Literary Meaning and Humanistic Understanding.* Univ. of Massachusetts Pr. 1981 $27.50 pap. $12.95. Draws on Wittgenstein and language analysis to link meaning to use and action; analyzes poetry
by William Carlos Williams.
Bakhtin, Mikhail. *The Dialogic Imagination: Four Essays.* Trans. by Caryl Emerson
and Michael Holquist, ed. by Michael Holquist, Univ. of Texas Pr. 1981 pap.
$12.95. Important essays on time, language, and the novel.
Barfield, Owen. *Poetic Diction: A Study in Meaning.* 1928. Arden repr. of 1975 ed.
1982 lib. bdg. $45.00; Wesleyan Univ. Pr. 3d ed. 1973 pap. $9.50
――――. *Saving the Appearances: A Study in Idolatry.* Harcourt 1965 pap. $4.95
Bleich, David. *Subjective Criticism.* Johns Hopkins Univ. Pr. text ed. 1978 $28.50 pap.
$9.95
Bleicher, Josef. *Contemporary Hermeneutics: Hermeneutics as Method, Philosophy and
Critique.* Routledge & Kegan 1980 $28.00 pap. $14.00. Discusses general issues
and history of reflections on how the reader understands texts.
Booth, Wayne. *Critical Understanding: The Powers and Limits of Pluralism.* Univ. of
Chicago Pr. 1979 $22.50 pap. $8.95
――――. *The Rhetoric of Fiction.* 1961. Univ. of Chicago Pr. 2d ed. 1983 pap. $30.00
Borkland, Elmer. *Contemporary Literary Critics.* Gale 2d ed. 1982 $64.00. Short es-
says and bibliographies of 124 British and American critics.
Brooks, Cleanth. *Modern Poetry and the Tradition.* 1939. Univ. of North Carolina Pr.
1970 pap. $6.95. Essays applying close attention to language and imagery in
Elizabethan and modern poems.
――――. *The Well-Wrought Urn: Studies in the Structure of Poetry.* 1947. Harcourt 1956
pap. $5.95. Presents and applies a method of "close reading" to a variety of En-
glish poems.
Bruns, Gerald L. *Inventions: Writing, Textuality, and Understanding in Literary His-
tory.* Yale Univ. Pr. 1982 $21.00. A brilliant collection of essays, wide ranging in
topic and texts discussed.
Butler, Christopher. *Interpretation, Deconstruction and Ideology: An Introduction to
Some Current Issues in Literary Theory.* Oxford 1984 $24.95 pap. $10.95
Culler, Jonathan. *On Deconstruction: Literary Theory in the 1970s.* Cornell Univ. Pr.
1982 $24.95 pap. $8.95. Good introduction to this important and difficult mod-
ern critical movement.
――――. *The Pursuit of Signs: Semiotics, Literature, Deconstruction.* Cornell Univ. Pr.
1981 $19.95 pap. $8.95
――――. *Structuralist Poetics: Structuralism, Linguistics, and the Study of Literature.*
Cornell Univ. Pr. 1976 pap. $8.95. Good introduction to structuralism.

Donoghue, Denis. *Ferocious Alphabets*. Columbia Univ. Pr. repr. of 1981 ed. 1984 pap. $9.00; Little, Brown 1981 $14.95. Critical study of contemporary criticism, especially deconstruction.

Eagleton, Terry. *Criticism and Ideology: A Study in Marxist Literary Theory*. Schocken 1978 pap. $6.50

———. *Literary Theory: An Introduction*. Univ. of Minnesota Pr. 1983 $29.50 pap. $9.95. Surveys contemporary criticism from a Marxist perspective.

———. *Marxism and Literary Criticism*. Univ. of California Pr. 1976 pap. $3.95

Empson, William. *Seven Types of Ambiguity*. 1930. New Directions 1947 pap. $6.95. Intense concentration on ambiguous language in poetry.

———. *Some Versions of Pastoral*. 1938. New Directions 1960 pap. $8.95. Broadens the concept of pastoral and extends it to nineteenth- and twentieth-century works.

———. *The Structure of Complex Words*. Rowman repr. of 1951 ed. 3d ed. 1979 $22.50. On key words in literary contexts, including "wit," "sense," "honest," in Pope, Shakespeare, and others.

Graff, Gerald. *Literature against Itself: Literary Ideas in Modern Society*. Univ. of Chicago Pr. 1979 $17.00 pap. $8.50. A controversial polemic on political grounds against the pretenses of modernist literature and critical theory.

Harari, Josue V., ed. *Textual Strategies: Perspectives in Post-Structuralist Criticism*. Cornell Univ. Pr. 1979 $35.00 pap. $10.95. Well-chosen introductory anthology with excellent bibliography.

Hirsch, E. D. *The Aims of Interpretation*. Univ. of Chicago Pr. (Phoenix Bks.) 1978 pap. $7.00. Essays, including reconsiderations of his earlier theories.

Howard, Roy J. *Three Faces of Hermeneutics: An Introduction to Current Theories of Understanding*. Univ. of California Pr. 1982 $21.00 pap. $5.95. Describes analytic, Marxist, and phenomenological hermeneutics.

Hoy, David Couzens. *The Critical Circle: Literature, History, and Philosophical Hermeneutics*. Univ. of California Pr. 1978 $25.00 1982 pap. $5.95. Excellent introduction to hermeneutics in relation to contemporary philosophy and criticism.

Kurzweil, Edith, and William Phillips, eds. *Literature and Psychoanalysis*. Columbia Univ. Pr. 1983 $34.00 pap. $13.00. Traces psychoanalytic criticism from Freud to the present.

Lawall, Sarah. *Critics of Consciousness: The Existential Structures of Literature*. Harvard Univ. Pr. 1968 $17.50. General introduction to critics who describe how an author's consciousness structures the world presented in the work.

Leavis, F. R. *The Great Tradition: George Eliot, Henry James, Joseph Conrad*. Gotham Lib. New York Univ. Pr. 1963 pap. $12.50

Lentricchia, Frank. *After the New Criticism*. Univ. of Chicago Pr. 1980 $21.00 pap. $13.00. Reflections on developments in literary theory since the 1960s, emphasizing the social and political context of key issues.

———. *Criticism and Social Change*. Univ. of Chicago Pr. 1984 lib. bdg. $15.00

Levin, Harry. *Grounds for Comparison. Studies in Comparative Lit.* Harvard Univ. Pr. 1972 $27.50. Collected essays.

———. *Refractions: Essays in Comparative Literature*. Oxford 1966 pap. $13.95 pap. $5.95

Natoli, Joseph P., ed. *Psychological Perspectives on Literature: Freudian Dissidents and Non-Freudian, A Casebook*. Shoe String (Archon) 1984 $29.50

Norris, Christopher. *Deconstruction: Theory and Practice*. Methuen 1982 $21.00 pap. $9.95. Good introduction to the background and ideas of deconstruction.

Richards, I. A. *Practical Criticism: A Study of Literary Judgment.* 1929. Harcourt 1956 pap. $7.95. Influential manifesto for "close reading" instead of impressionistic criticism.

———. *Principles of Literary Criticism.* 1925. Harcourt 1985 pap. $7.95. Influential in the founding of modern approaches to reading poetry.

Said, Edward. *Beginnings: Intention and Method.* Basic Bks. 1975 $18.95; Columbia Univ. Pr. repr. of 1975 ed. 1984 $30.00 pap. $12.00; Johns Hopkins Univ. Pr. 1978 pap. $5.95

———. *The World, the Text, and the Critic.* Harvard Univ. Pr. 1983 $20.00 pap. $7.95. Broad survey and critique of contemporary critical movements.

Scholes, Robert. *Structuralism in Literature: An Introduction.* Yale Univ. Pr. 1974 $24.00 pap. $7.95. Good introduction to an important contemporary critical approach.

Skura, Meredith. *The Literary Use of the Psychoanalytic Process.* Yale Univ. Pr. 1983 $26.50 pap. $9.95

Strelka, Joseph, ed. *Literary Criticism and Myth.* Pennsylvania State Univ. Pr. text ed. 1980 $24.50

Suleiman, Susan R., and Inge Crosman, eds. *The Reader in the Text: Essays on Audience and Interpretation.* Princeton Univ. Pr. 1980 $45.00 pap. $13.95. Stimulating collection of essays by leading critics with bibliography.

Tompkins, Jane P., ed. *Reader-Response Criticism: From Formalism to Structuralism.* Johns Hopkins Univ. Pr. 1980 $20.00 pap. $6.95. A collection of key essays with an excellent introduction and analysis by the editor and annotated bibliography.

Wellek, Rene. *The Attack on Literature and Other Essays.* Univ. of North Carolina Pr. 1982 $18.00 pap. $8.95

———. *Concepts of Criticism.* Ed. by Stephen G. Nichols, Jr., Yale Univ. Pr. 1963 pap. $13.95

———. *Discriminations: Further Concepts of Criticism.* Yale Univ. Pr. 1970 $37.50

Wimsatt, W. K. *Day of the Leopards: Essays in Defense of Poems.* Yale Univ. Pr. 1976 $24.50

———. *Hateful Contraries: Studies in Literature and Criticism.* Univ. Pr. of Kentucky 1965 $25.00 pap. $8.00

———. *The Verbal Icon: Studies in the Meaning of Poetry.* Univ. Pr. of Kentucky 1954 pap. $8.00. One of the great books in contemporary reflection on poetry and criticism.

Winters, Yvor. *In Defense of Reason: Three Classics of Contemporary Criticism.* Ohio State Univ. Pr. (Swallow) 1947 pap. $12.95. Includes "Primitivism and Decadence" and other essays and studies of poetry, mostly modern and American.

Wright, Elizabeth. *Psychoanalytic Criticism: Theory in Practice.* Methuen text ed. 1985 $19.95 pap. $8.95. Broad survey of psychoanalytic critical theory to the present.

FEMINIST CRITICISM

Over the past 15 years, the literary and critical essay has proved congenial to reflections on the broad social and political movement called "feminism." Feminist critics have discovered neglected women writers and commented on literary forms—letters, diaries, detective fiction, romances—that were especially attractive to women authors and readers. Contemporary women writers have frequently supplemented their imaginative representations of their society with wide-ranging essays. Only a small sampling of this important work is listed here.

Abel, Elizabeth, ed. *Writing and Sexual Difference.* Univ. of Chicago Pr. (Phoenix Bks.) 1983 pap. $8.95. Anthology of essays on issues of writing and gender.

Abel, Elizabeth, and Emily K. Abel, eds. *The Signs Reader: Women, Gender, and Scholarship.* Univ. of Chicago Pr. lib. bdg. 1983 $25.00 pap. $8.95. Essays from the prominent feminist journal *Signs.*

Bernikow, Louise. *Among Women.* Harper 1981 pap. $4.95. Wide-ranging essays on women in literature.

Bradbrook, Muriel C. *Women and Literature, 1779–1982.* Barnes & Noble text ed. 1983 $26.75. Essays on literature by and about women and on lives led by women in fiction and reality.

Christian, Barbara. *Black Feminist Criticism: Perspectives on Black Women Writers.* Pergamon 1985 $29.95 pap. $13.50

Donovan, Josephine, ed. *Feminist Literary Criticism: Explorations in Theory.* Univ. Pr. of Kentucky 1975 pap. $5.00. Six essays, one bibliographic.

Eisenstein, Hester. *Contemporary Feminist Thought.* G. K. Hall (Twayne) 1984 lib. bdg. 1983 $17.95 pap. $6.95. An intellectual history.

Ellmann, Mary. *Thinking about Women: Conceptions of Femininity.* Harcourt repr. of 1968 ed. 1970 $4.95

French, Marilyn. *Beyond Power: On Women, Men, and Morals.* Summit 1985 $19.95. Far-ranging historical discussion by the noted novelist.

Frye, Marilyn. *The Politics of Reality: Essays in Feminist Theory.* Crossing Pr. 1983 $18.95 pap. $8.95

Gilbert, Sandra M., and Susan Gubar. *The Madwoman in the Attic: The Woman Writer and the Nineteenth-Century Literary Imagination.* Yale Univ. Pr. 1979 $45.00 pap. $16.95. One of the most widely influential studies.

Hardwick, Elizabeth. *Seduction and Betrayal: Women and Literature.* Peter Smith 1983 $13.00; Random (Vintage) 1974 pap. $3.95

Heilbrun, Carolyn G. *Reinventing Womanhood.* Norton 1979 $14.95 pap. $5.95

———. *Toward a Recognition of Androgyny.* Norton repr. of 1973 ed. 1982 pap. $4.95

Kahn, Coppelia, and Gayle Green, eds. *Making a Difference: Feminist Literary Criticism.* Methuen 1985 $22.00 pap. $9.95. Ten wide-ranging essays introducing the field.

Marks, Elaine, and Isabelle de Courtivron, eds. *New French Feminisms: An Anthology.* Schocken 1981 pap. $8.95; Univ. of Massachusetts Pr. 1979 $15.00. Excellent selections, many first translated here.

Moi, Toril. *Sexual/Textual Politics.* Methuen 1985 $25.00 pap. $9.95. Comprehensive survey of feminist criticism.

Olsen, Tillie. *Silences.* Dell 1983 pap. $4.50. Peter Smith 1984 $15.75. Essays by the distinguished short-story writer.

Ostriker, Alicia. *Writing Like a Woman. Poets on Poetry Ser.* Univ. of Michigan Pr. 1983 pap. $8.95

Ruthven, K. K. *Feminist Literary Studies: An Introduction.* Cambridge Univ. Pr. 1985 $32.50 pap. $8.95

Showalter, Elaine, ed. *The New Feminist Criticism: Essays on Women, Literature, and Theory.* Pantheon 1985 $22.95 pap. $13.95

Smith, Barbara. *Toward a Black Feminist Criticism.* Crossing Pr. 1977 pap. $2.50

Walker, Alice. *In Search of Our Mothers' Gardens: Womanist Prose.* Harcourt 1983
    $14.95 1984 pap. $6.95. Essays by the black feminist and Pulitzer Prize winner.

ADDISON, JOSEPH. 1672–1719

Addison, son of the Dean of Litchfield, took high honors at Oxford and
joined the army. He first came to literary fame by writing a poem, "The
Campaign," to celebrate the Battle of Blenheim. When Steele, whom he had
known in school, started *The Tatler* in 1709, Addison became a regular contributor. But his contributions to a later venture, *The Spectator* (generally
considered the zenith of the periodical essay), were fundamental: Steele can
be credited with the editorial direction of the journal; but Addison's essays,
ranging from gently satiric to genuinely funny, secured the journal's success. In *The Spectator*, No. 10, Addison declared that the journal aimed "to
enliven morality with wit, and to temper wit with morality." His brilliant
character of Sir Roger de Coverley (followed from rake to reformation) distinguishes the most popular essays.

Books by Addison

Essays in Criticism and Literary Theory. Ed. by John Loftis, *Crofts Class. Ser.* Harlan
    Davidson text ed. 1975 pap. $3.95
The Miscellaneous Works of Joseph Addison. Ed. by A. C. Guthkelch, Scholarly 2 vols.
    repr. of 1914 ed. 1971 $79.00
The Coverley Papers from The Spectator. Scholarly repr. 1980 lib. bdg. $29.00
Critical Essays from The Spectator. Ed. by Donald F. Bond, Oxford 1970 pap. $5.95
Criticism of Milton's Paradise Lost, from The Spectator, 1711–1712. 1868. Ed. by Ed-
    ward Arber, Saifer 1983 $15.00
The Freeholder, or Political Essays. Scholarly repr. of 1716 ed. 1976 $19.00

ALLEN, WOODY. 1935–

Allen's favorite personality—the bemused neurotic, the perpetual worry-
wart, the born loser—dominates his plays, his movies, and his essays. A native New Yorker, Allen attended local schools and despised them, turning
early to essay writing as a way to cope with his personal (and apparently
self-imposed) isolation and to distinguish himself at school. Since his apprenticeship, writing gags for comedians like Sid Caesar and Garry Moore,
the image he projects—of a "nebbish from Brooklyn"—has developed into a
personal metaphor of life as a concentration camp from which no one escapes alive. Allen wants to be funny, but isn't afraid to be serious either—
even at the same time. *Annie Hall*, which won four Academy Awards, was a
subtle, dramatic development of the contemporary fears and insecurities of
American life. In her review of *Love and Death* (o.p.), Judith Crist wrote that
Allen goes "for the character rather than the cartoon, the situation rather
than the set-up, the underlying madness rather than the surface craziness."
In Allen's essays reprinted from the *New Yorker*, *Getting Even* and *Without
Feathers*, the situations and characters don't just speak to us, they are us.

BOOKS BY ALLEN

Getting Even. Random 1971 $10.95 pap. $2.95
Without Feathers. Random 1975 $8.95; Ballantine 1983 pap. $2.95
Side Effects. Random 1980 $8.95; Ballantine 1981 pap. $2.75
The Floating Light Bulb. Random 1982 $10.50

ARNOLD, MATTHEW. 1822–1888

Son of the famous headmaster at Rugby, Arnold established himself in an Oxford professorship (of poetry in 1857) and pursued relentlessly the theme of social integration. A poet and literary critic influenced initially by Goethe and Wordsworth, Arnold gradually became a trenchant social critic. In his essay "Culture and Anarchy" (1869) he inveighed against the barbarian aristocracy for its materialism, against the philistine middle class for its vulgarity, against the populace lower class for its ignorance. He sought wider respect for education and coined the phrase "disinterestedness" to suggest that culture should be disseminated equally among all social classes. His *Essays in Criticism* (1865) established a broader intellectual scope for the literary critic: Criticism was to be more comprehensive, with social and political considerations equal in importance to scholarship. In his efforts to integrate literature and life, and to bring higher cultural standards to all ranks of society, Arnold had an influence extending well beyond his own time. (See also Chapter 6 in this volume.)

BOOKS BY ARNOLD

Works. AMS Pr. 15 vols. repr. of 1904 ed. 1972 $425.00; Scholarly 15 vols. repr. 1903 ed. 1970 $395.00
The Complete Prose Works of Matthew Arnold. Univ. of Michigan Pr. 11 vols. 1960–76 ea. $19.95
On Translating Homer. 1862. AMS Pr. repr. of 1905 ed. 1978 $16.25
On the Study of Celtic Literature and Other Essays. 1867. Biblio Dist. 1976 $9.95
Literature and Dogma: An Essay Towards a Better Apprehension of the Bible. AMS Pr. repr. of 1883 ed. 1970 $15.00; Folcroft repr. of 1873 ed. lib. bdg. $20.00; ed. by James C. Livingston, Ungar 1970 $8.50 pap. $3.45
Letters of Matthew Arnold, 1848–1888. 1904. Ed. by George W. Russell, Scholarly 2 vols. repr. of 1969 $59.00
Essays in Criticism. Folcroft repr. of 1910 ed. 1974 lib. bdg. $25.00
(and Walter Pater). *Sweetness and Light: An Essay on Style.* Arden Lib. repr. of 1910 ed. 1979 lib. bdg. $12.50
Unpublished Letters of Matthew Arnold. Folcroft repr. of 1923 ed. 1977 lib. bdg. $17.00; Porter 1985 $42.50
Four Essays on Life and Letters. Ed. by E. K. Brown, *Crofts Class. Ser.* Harlan Davidson text ed. pap. 1947 pap. $1.25
Poetry and Criticism of Matthew Arnold. Ed. by A. Dwight Culler, Houghton Mifflin (Riverside ed.) 1961 pap. $6.95
The Portable Matthew Arnold. Ed. by Lionel Trilling, *Viking Portable Lib.* Penguin 1980 pap. $7.95
Selected Prose. Ed. by P. J. Keating, *Penguin Class. Ser.* 1983 pap. $6.95; ed. by P. J. Keating, Peter Smith $6.00

BOOKS ABOUT ARNOLD

McCarthy, Patrick J. *Matthew Arnold and the Three Classes.* Columbia Univ. Pr. 1964 $27.50. "Clear exposition of the many forces intellectual and political, which made their impact upon a complex mind" (*LJ*).

Trilling, Lionel. *Matthew Arnold.* Harcourt 1979 $12.95 pap. $6.95

BACON, FRANCIS. 1561–1626

Learned, widely experienced, ambitious, even reckless, Bacon rose from Grey's Inn to serve as Lord Chancellor in the reign of James I. His public life was distinguished by service to the king and interpretations of the laws of England. But his career ended abruptly with a bribery conviction and imprisonment in the Tower. His life in retirement produced works both of philosophy and literature. In his works of philosophy, including the *Novum Organum* (1620) and *The Advancement of Learning* (1605), Bacon intended to supersede the Aristotelian system. His essays, primarily on literary topics, numbered only 10 in the first edition of 1597; but the final version, of 1625, includes 58. The *Essays* was written over many years and documents the development of Bacon's attitudes and his especial style.

BOOKS BY BACON

Essays. AMS Pr. repr. of 1940 ed. 1983 $31.50; *Essay Index Repr. Ser.* Ayer 5th ed. rev. 1973 $29.50; Rowman 1972 $11.75 pap. $5.25

Essays: Religious Meditations, Places of Perswasion and Disswasion. Eng. Experience Ser. Walter J. Johnson repr. of 1597 ed. 1968 $9.50

New Organon and Other Essays. Ed. by Fulton H. Anderson, Bobbs 1960 pap. $9.63

Essays and Colours of Good and Evil. 1842. *Select Bibliographies Repr. Ser.* Ayer repr. of 1862 ed. 1972 $20.25

Francis Bacon: A Selection of His Works. Ed. by Sidney Warhaft, *College Class. in Eng. Ser.* Odyssey Pr. 1965 pap. $13.24

The Advancement of Learning. Ed. by William A. Armstrong, Athlone 1975 $29.50; Longwood Pr. pap. $14.95; ed. by G. W. Kitchin, Rowman 1973 $13.00 pap. $7.50

Great Instauration and New Atlantis. Ed. by J. Weinberger, *Crofts Class. Ser.* Harlan Davidson text ed. 1980 $10.95 pap. $3.95

BARZUN, JACQUES. 1907–

Barzun, born in France and educated in America, became professor of history at Columbia in 1945 and served as dean of faculties and provost until 1967. He has written with wisdom and tact on history, criticism, education, and musicology. He calls himself a "student of cultural history," but his learned interpretations of historical fact and critical theory, educational policy, and research techniques demonstrate a penetrating grasp of relevant issues. His *Teacher in America* was called "one of the few volumes on education by which no intelligent reader can be bored." He writes of his adopted country, America, with humor and perception in *God's Country and Mine.* He is frank and genial, but ready to challenge the establishment: In *The House of Intellect* he attacks the whole intellectual (or pseudo-intellectual) world for its betrayal of true intellect in such areas as public administration, communications, conversation and home life, education, business, and scholarship.

Books by Barzun

Race: A Study in Superstition. 1937. AMS Pr. repr. of 1965 ed. rev. ed. 1978 $28.50
Teacher in America. 1945. Liberty Fund 1981 $9.00 pap. $4.00
God's Country and Mine. Greenwood repr. of 1954 ed. Greenwood 1973 lib. bdg. $17.50
The Energies of Art: Studies of Authors Classic and Modern. Greenwood repr. of 1956 ed. 1975 lib. bdg. $65.00
Darwin, Marx, Wagner: Critique of a Heritage. 1958. Univ. of Chicago Pr. 2d ed. 1981 pap. $6.95
The House of Intellect. Greenwood repr. of 1959 ed. 1978 lib. bdg. $24.50
Of Human Freedom. Greenwood repr. of 1964 ed. 2d ed. rev. 1977 lib. bdg. $17.75
Berlioz and His Century: An Introduction to the Age of Romanticism. 1969. Univ. of Chicago Pr. 1982 pap. $8.95
On Writing, Editing and Publishing: Essays Explicative and Hortatory. Univ. of Chicago Pr. (Phoenix Bks.) 1971 pap. $1.50
Clio and the Doctors: History, Psycho-History, Quanto History. Univ. of Chicago Pr. 1974 pap. $3.45
The Use and Abuse of Art. Bollingen Ser. Princeton Univ. Pr. 1974 $19.00 pap. $6.95
Classic, Romantic and Modern. Univ. of Chicago Pr. 1975 pap. $5.50
Critical Questions: On Music and Letters, Culture and Biography. Ed. by Bea Friedland, Univ. of Chicago Pr. 1982 lib. bdg. $20.00 1984 pap. $8.95

BEERBOHM, SIR MAX. 1872–1956

When Beerbohm succeeded Bernard Shaw as drama critic of the *Saturday Review* in 1898, Shaw introduced his successor as "the incomparable Max." Beerbohm was decadent, witty, graceful, and urbane—fitting for a critic who carried on the high tradition of satire in English letters. His works of social and literary criticism, and of fiction, mask serious dissatisfaction with contemporary pretenses and poses behind a patina of highly polished prose. In *A Christmas Garland* (1912, o.p.) Beerbohm uses parody to expose the artifice of literary manner in his contemporaries (including BENNETT, CONRAD, WELLS, and Chesterton). His only novel, *Zuleika Dobson*, is a delightful burlesque of his own college days at Oxford. Like his essays and short stories, it is light, witty, and stimulating. Beerbohm was an accomplished caricaturist. Of his 46 portrait drawings in *Max's Nineties: Drawings 1892–1899* (1958, o.p.), most were taken from periodicals of that period.

Books by Beerbohm

Works and More. Scholarly repr. of 1896 ed. $25.00
Around Theaters. 1898–1903. Greenwood repr. of 1954 ed. 1969 lib. bdg. $24.50. Essays originally published in the *Saturday Review.*
More. Essay Index Repr. Ser. Ayer repr. of 1899 ed. 1921 $17.00
Last Theaters. 1904–10. Ed. by Rupert Hart-Davis, Taplinger 1970 $15.00
Zuleika Dobson. 1911. Dodd 1984 $19.95; Penguin 1983 pap. $4.95
Observations. Haskell repr. of 1925 ed. 1971 lib. bdg. $56.95

Mainly on the Air. 1946. *Essay Index Repr. Ser.* Ayer repr. of 1957 ed. 1972 $17.00.
   Broadcasts, essays.
Seven Men and Two Others. World's Class. Ser. Oxford 1980 pap. $4.95

BOOKS ABOUT BEERBOHM

Lynch, Bohun. *Max Beerbohm in Perspective.* Folcroft repr. of 1921 ed. lib. bdg.
   $14.75; Gale repr. of 1922 ed. 1977 $45.00; Haskell 1974 $53.95; Richard West
   repr. of 1921 ed. 1979 lib. bdg. $25.00
Riewald, J. G., ed. *The Surprise of Excellence: Modern Essays on Max Beerbohm.* Shoe
   String (Archon) 1974 $18.50

BELLOC, HILAIRE. 1870–1953

Belloc was born in France but was naturalized as a British subject in
1902. Though he began as a humorist—with children's verse—his works include satire, poetry, history, biography, fiction, and many volumes of essays. With his close friend and fellow Catholic, G. K. Chesterton, Belloc
founded the *New Witness,* a weekly newspaper opposing capitalism and free
thought and supporting a philosophy known as distributism. The pair were
so close in thought and association that GEORGE BERNARD SHAW (see Vol. 2)
nicknamed them "Chesterbelloc." Belloc lived quietly in the country in England until his tragic death in 1953 from burns caused when his dressing
gown caught fire from the hearth. In *Shandygaff* Christopher Morley said:
"In Belloc we find the perfect union of the French and English minds. Rabe-
laisian in fecundity, wit, and irrepressible sparkle, he is also of English
blood and sinew." (See also Volume 3, Chapter 9.)

BOOKS BY BELLOC

Avril. Essay Index Repr. Ser. Ayer repr. of 1904 ed. $19.00. Essays on the poetry of the
   French Renaissance.
On Nothing and Kindred Subjects. Essay Index Repr. Ser. Ayer repr. of 1908 ed. $19.00
On Anything. Essay Index Repr. Ser. Ayer repr. of 1910 ed. $18.00
On Everything. Essay Index Repr. Ser. Ayer repr. of 1910 ed. $19.00
On Something. Essay Index Repr. Ser. Ayer repr. of 1910 ed. 1968 $15.00
First and Last. Essay Index Repr. Ser. Ayer repr. of 1911 ed. $18.00
This and That, and the Other. Essay Index Repr. Ser. Ayer repr. of 1912 ed. 1968
   $21.50
At the Sign of the Lion, and Other Essays. Essay Index Repr. Ser. Ayer repr. of 1916 ed.
   $12.00
On. Essay Index Repr. Ser. Ayer repr. of 1923 ed. $17.00
Short Talks with the Dead and Other Essays. Essay Index Repr. Ser. Ayer repr. of 1926
   ed. $18.00
Conversation with an Angel, and Other Essays. Essay Index Repr. Ser. Ayer repr. of
   1929 ed. 1968 $20.00; Gordon 1976 lib. bdg. $59.95
Conversation with a Cat and Others. 1929. *Essay Index Repr. Ser.* Ayer repr. of 1931
   ed. $17.00
Essays of a Catholic. Essay Index Repr. Ser. Ayer repr. of 1931 ed. $18.00
Characters of the Reformation. Essay Index Repr. Ser. Ayer repr. of 1936 ed. $24.00
Great Heresies. Essay Index Repr. Ser. Ayer repr. of 1938 ed. $18.00

Silence of the Sea. Essay Index Repr. Ser. Ayer repr. of 1940 ed. $16.00
Places. Essay Index Repr. Ser. Ayer repr. of 1941 ed. $18.00

BOOKS ABOUT BELLOC

Braybrooke, Patrick. *Some Thoughts on Hilaire Belloc: Ten Studies.* Haskell repr. of
   1923 ed. 1969 $48.95
Wilhelmsen, Frederick. *Hilaire Belloc: No Alienated Man.* Richard West repr. of 1953
   ed. $20.00

BLACKMUR, R(ICHARD) P(ALMER). 1904–1965

R. P. Blackmur, a native of Massachusetts, was one of America's foremost
critics. Though lacking a college education, he was on the Princeton faculty
from 1940 until his death, and in 1961–62 was Pitt Professor of American History and Institutions at Cambridge University. He contributed criticism to literary journals and "little" magazines, chiefly on nineteenth- and twentieth-
century novelists and poets. As a leader in the New Criticism—an academic
movement that advocated close rhetorical analysis of texts—he rejected the
traditional historicism of literary criticism. In *A Burden for Critics* (1948,
o.p.) he called for "modern criticism to enlarge its scope, and to add to analysis, elucidation, and comparison the important function of judgment based
on rational standards." Blackmur's development of a New Critical theory depended in large part on Matthew Arnold's conviction that literary study was
and should be the pivotal feature of "culture."

BOOKS BY BLACKMUR

Dirty Hands, or The True-Born Censor. Folcroft repr. of 1930 ed. lib. bdg. $10.00
The Double Agent: Essays in Craft and Elucidation. 1935. Peter Smith 1962 $10.50
The Expense of Greatness. Peter Smith $10.50; Somerset repr. of 1940 ed. $39.00
Language as Gesture: Essays in Poetry. Greenwood repr. of 1952 ed. lib. bdg. $25.75;
   Columbia Univ. Pr. 1981 pap. $10.00
The Lion and the Honeycomb: Essays in Solicitude and Critique. Greenwood repr. of
   1955 ed. lib. bdg. $20.75
Anni Mirabiles, 1921–1925: Reason in the Madness of Letters. Folcroft repr. of 1956
   ed. 1974 lib. bdg. $8.50

BLOOM, HAROLD. 1930–

Bloom's central idea has been that poets must struggle against the existing body of poetry in order to make room for their own writing and personal style. In various works, he has elaborated the steps or stages in this
struggle, which can be interpreted as psychological moments in the poet's
career, but also as poetic images and devices, which Bloom believes are
found in a specific sequence in all great lyric poetry in English after MILTON.
Only poets who pass through all the stages and record that passage in their
lyric poetry achieve greatness or "strength" in Bloom's term. He has applied
his ideas in books on YEATS and WALLACE STEVENS and in essays on many
other poems and poets.

Books by Bloom

Yeats. Oxford (Galaxy Bks.) 1972 pap. $8.95
The Anxiety of Influence: A Theory of Poetry. Oxford (Galaxy Bks.) 1973 pap. $7.95
Ringers in the Tower: Studies in Romantic Tradition. Univ. of Chicago Pr. 1973 pap.
    $3.45
Kabbalah and Criticism. Continuum 1975 $8.95; Crossroads 1983 pap. $7.95. Draws
    on Gershom Scholem's studies of Jewish mystical writings to extend Bloom's
    theories of poetic creation.
A Map of Misreading. Oxford 1975 pap. $7.95. Elaborates Bloom's theory of poetic
    creation on imagistic, rhetorical, and psychological dimensions.
Figures of Capable Imagination. Continuum 1976 $11.95
Wallace Stevens: The Poems of Our Climate. Cornell Univ. Pr. 1977 $32.00 1980 pap.
    $9.95
The Flight to Lucifer: A Gnostic Fantasy. Farrar 1979 $9.95
Agon: Towards a Theory of Revisionism. Oxford 1982 $25.00 pap. $7.95
The Breaking of the Vessels. Univ. of Chicago Pr. 1982 $10.00 pap. $4.95

Book about Bloom

Fite, David. *Harold Bloom: The Rhetoric of Romantic Vision.* Univ. of Massachusetts
    Pr. lib. bdg. 1985 $25.00. Good survey of Bloom's entire work.

BROWNE, SIR THOMAS. 1605–1682

Browne, a learned and devoted physician, wrote some of the loveliest ba-
roque prose in the English language. His *Religio Medici* (1642–43), immensely popular among his contemporaries, appeared in nine English editions, five Latin editions, and Dutch, German, and French translations—all
before his death. In *Religio Medici* he managed to write with clarity and conviction about the interrelatedness of the laws of God and the laws of nature
(science): "those that never saw Him in the one have discovered Him in the
other." While his ideas have encouraged generations of physicians, his prose
style has influenced generations of writers. His delight in curious or learned
words has been widely imitated, in particular by Charles Lamb and in general by the nineteenth-century romantic writers.

Books by Browne

Selected Writings. Ed. by Geoffrey Keynes, Univ. of Chicago Pr. (Phoenix Bks.) 1970
    pap. $3.50
Prose. Ed. by Norman J. Endicott, *Norton Lib.* 1972 pap. $5.95. Includes *Religio Me-
    dici*, *Hydriotaphia*, letters, and short texts.
Hydriotaphia (Urne-Burial) and The Garden of Cyrus. 1658. Ed. by Frank L. Huntley,
    Crofts Class. Ser. Harlan Davidson text ed. 1966 pap. $3.25
Religio Medici, Hydriotaphia and The Garden of Cyrus. ed. by R. H. Robbins, Oxford
    1972 pap. $7.95

Book about Browne

Bennett, Joan. *Sir Thomas Browne: A Man of Achievement in Literature.* Cambridge
    Univ. Pr. 1962 o.p. An authoritative study of the man and his work, including
    skillful analysis of his arguments. Bibliography and index.

BURKE, KENNETH. 1897–

Omnivorously eclectic, Burke has found in the analysis of human symbolic activities a key to the largest cultural issues. For Burke, literature is the most prominent and sophisticated form of "symbolic action," one that provides "equipment for living" by allowing us to try out hypothetical strategies for dealing with the endless variety of human situations and experiences. Human society demands some principle of order, but the language and reason that create order can fall into rigid abstractions that can be destructive and violently imposed. Literature shows us an image of sacrifice, forgiveness, and flexibility that plays an important role in keeping society functioning flexibly. Burke's writing is extensive, complex, and wide ranging, but also unique and uniquely important among current critical approaches.

Books by Burke

Counter-Statement. Univ. of California Pr. repr. of 1931 ed. 1968 pap. $6.95

Permanence and Change: An Anatomy of Purpose. 1935. Intro. by Hugh Dalziel Duncan, Bobbs 2d ed. rev. 1965 o.p.

Attitudes toward History. 1937 Hermes 2d ed. rev. 1959 o.p.

The Philosophy of Literary Form: Studies in Symbolic Action. Univ. of California Pr. repr. of 1941 ed. rev. ed. 1974 pap. $10.95

A Grammar of Motives. Univ. of California Pr. repr. of 1945 ed. 1969 pap. $10.95

A Rhetoric of Motives. Univ. of California Pr. repr. of 1950 ed. 1969 pap. $8.95

The Rhetoric of Religion: Studies in Logology. 1961. Univ. of California Pr. 1970 pap. $5.95

Perspectives by Incongruity: Studies in Symbolic Action and Terms for Order. Ed. by Stanley Edgar Hyman and Barbara Karmiller, Indiana Univ. Pr. 1964 o.p. Selections from his criticism and creative writing.

Towards a Better Life: Being a Series of Epistles, or Declamations. Univ. of California Pr. 1966 $25.00 pap. $6.95

Terms for Order. Ed. by Stanley Edgar Hyman and Barbara Karmiller, Indiana Univ. Pr. 1964 pap. $4.95

Language as Symbolic Action: Essays on Life, Literature, and Method. Univ. of California Pr. 1966 $35.00 pap. $10.95

Dramatism and Development. Clark Univ. Pr. 1972 $3.00

Books about Burke

Frank, Armin Paul. *Kenneth Burke. Twayne's U.S. Authors Ser.* Irvington lib. bdg. 1969 $15.95

White, Hayden, and Margaret Brose, eds. *Representing Kenneth Burke: Selected Papers from the English Institute*. Johns Hopkins Univ. Pr. 1983 $14.50

BURTON, ROBERT. 1577–1640

Burton is remembered chiefly as the author of *The Anatomy of Melancholy*, intended as a medical treatise but regarded usually as the repository of an immense amount of quotation from widely varied works—the Bible, Greek and Latin classics, the Elizabethan writers. It was an undistinguished work, and yet became and has remained a true classic: admired for its serio-comic style, its erudition, its humane attempt to relieve the malcontent.

The book is in three parts: 1, the causes and symptoms of melancholy; 2, its cure; and 3, melancholy inspired by love and by religion. H. J. Gottlieb, in *Burton's Knowledge of English Poetry* (o.p.), observed that if all English literature were lost, it would be possible to reconstruct most of the major writers from Burton's quotations and allusions.

BOOK BY BURTON

The Anatomy of Melancholy. 1621. Ed. by A. R. Shilleto, AMS Pr. 3 vols. repr. of 1893 ed. $87.50; *Eng. Experience Ser.* Walter J. Johnson repr. of 1621 ed. 1971 $72.00; ed. by Holbrook Jackson, Random (Vintage) 1977 pap. $9.95

BOOK ABOUT BURTON

Babb, Lawrence. *Sanity in Bedlam: A Study of Robert Burton's Anatomy of Melancholy.* Greenwood repr. of 1960 ed. 1977 lib. bdg. $18.75. A study that attempts to define Burton's "aims, methods, beliefs, and accomplishments"; examines some changes in the five editions.

CARLYLE, THOMAS. 1795–1881

Carlyle, though an erratic student at Edinburgh University, read widely in the classics, mathematics, Newtonian physics, history, and philosophy. He acquired a thorough knowledge of German, and his earliest works were a life of Schiller for *The London Magazine* and a translation of *Wilhelm Meister.* His favorite style was vivid, majestic, and dramatic; his favorite devices were pathos, satire, and denunciation. He often coined a word when he needed one. His philosophical *Sartor Resartus* and his essays on *Heroes and Hero-Worship* and *Past and Present* are perhaps better known to the general reader than are his histories. In his essays, deeply influenced by the German romantics, Carlyle revolted against the rationalism of the eighteenth century, gradually espousing the glories of enlightened despotism, in which the "heroes" ruled the less intelligent. His *French Revolution* (1837) history brought him great contemporary acclaim.

BOOKS BY CARLYLE

Works of Thomas Carlyle. Ed. by H. D. Traill, AMS Pr. 30 vols. repr. of 1899 ed. $1,200.00

A Carlyle Reader. Ed. by G. B. Tennyson, Cambridge Univ. Pr. 1984 $44.50 pap. $9.95

Selected Writings. Ed. by Alan Shelston, *Penguin Eng. Lib. Ser.* 1980 pap. $4.95

Letters of Thomas Carlyle, 1826–1836. Ed. by Charles E. Norton, *Select Bibliographies Repr. Ser.* Ayer 2 vols. repr. of 1888 ed. $48.50; Richard West 2 vols. repr. of 1888 ed. $45.00

The Letters of Thomas Carlyle to His Brother Alexander, with Related Family Letters. Ed. by Edwin W. Marrs, Jr., Harvard Univ. Pr. 1968 $40.00

Montaigne: And Other Essays, Chiefly Biographical. Essay Index Repr. Ser. Ayer repr. of 1897 ed. $23.00

Sartor Resartus. 1837. Arden Lib. repr. of 1921 ed. 1981 lib. bdg. $20.00

Sartor Resartus and On Heroes and Hero-Worship. Biblio Dist. (Everyman's) repr. of 1908 ed. 1967 $11.95 pap. $3.50

The Nigger Question (and *The Negro Question*). Ed. by Eugene R. August, *Crofts Class. Ser.* Harlan Davidson text ed. 1971 $5.95 pap. $1.25

On Heroes, Hero-Worship and the Heroic in History. 1841. Ed. by Carl Niemeyer, Univ. of Nebraska Pr. (Bison) 1966 pap. $6.95
Past and Present. 1843. Ed. by Edwin Mims, Arden Lib. repr. of 1918 ed. 1981 lib. bdg. $20.00; Biblio Dist. repr. of 1912 ed. 1976 $8.95; ed. by Richard D. Altick, *Gotham Lib.* New York Univ. Pr. 1977 $9.50
Reminiscences. Ed. by James A. Froude, Darby repr. of 1881 ed. 1983 lib. bdg. $30.00; Richard West 2 vols. repr. of 1881 ed. $21.50; ed. by James A. Froude, Scholarly 2 vols. repr. of 1881 ed. 1972 $29.00

BOOKS ABOUT CARLYLE

Kaplan, Fred. *Thomas Carlyle: A Biography.* Cornell Univ. Pr. 1983 $35.00
Lehman, B. H. *Carlyle's Theory of the Hero.* AMS Pr. repr. of 1928 ed. $17.25. A classic study of its sources, history, and appearance in Carlyle's writings.
Neff, Emery. *Carlyle and Mill.* Octagon 1964 lib. bdg. $26.00. An examination of a famous friendship.
Perry, Bliss. *Thomas Carlyle: How to Know Him.* Folcroft repr. of 1915 ed. 1977 $27.50; Norwood repr. of 1915 ed. 1978 $30.00; Richard West repr. of 1915 ed. 1973 $25.00

CHESTERTON, G(ILBERT) K(EITH). 1874–1936

Chesterton was Hilaire Belloc's devoted friend and ally in literary pursuits. He was a humorist, a historian, a literary critic, and an ardent Catholic. His essays combine these qualifications most successfully. As a critic he wrote several noteworthy literary studies, among them *Robert Browning* (1903) and *George Bernard Shaw* (1909). His *Victorian Age in Literature* (1913, o.p.) was once a standard work. In the Father Brown detective stories, Chesterton created a character popular with mystery fans. *The Father Brown Omnibus* has been in print continuously for 50 years.

BOOKS BY CHESTERTON

Defendant. Essay Index Repr. Ser. Ayer repr. of 1901 ed. $12.25
Robert Browning. Richard West repr. of 1903 ed. 1973 $20.00
Varied Types. Essay Index Repr. Ser. Ayer repr. of 1903 ed. $17.00
Heretics. Essay Index Repr. Ser. Ayer repr. of 1905 ed. $19.00
All Things Considered. Essay Index Repr. Ser. Ayer repr. of 1908 ed. $19.00; Dufour 1969 $12.95; Folcroft repr. of 1915 ed. 1978 lib. bdg. $20.00
George Bernard Shaw. Arden Lib. repr. of 1909 ed. 1978 $25.00
Five Types. Essay Index Repr. Ser. Ayer repr. of 1911 ed. $12.25
Wit and Wisdom of G. K. Chesterton. Folcroft repr. of 1911 ed. 1980 lib. bdg. $30.00
Miscellany of Men. Essay Index Repr. Ser. Ayer repr. of 1912 ed. $21.00; intro. by D. E. Collins, Dufour repr. 1969 $12.95; Folcroft 1973 lib. bdg. $25.00; Scholarly repr. of 1927 ed. 1972 $20.00
Utopia of Usurers, and Other Essays. Essay Index Repr. Ser. Ayer repr. of 1917 ed. $15.00
Do We Agree?: A Debate. Arden repr. of 1928 ed. 1978 lib. bdg. $10.00; Folcroft repr. lib. bdg. $10.00; Haskell repr. of 1928 ed. 1969 lib. bdg. $39.95
Generally Speaking. Essay Index Repr. Ser. Ayer repr. of 1929 ed. $19.00
G. K. C. as M. C.: Being a Collection of Thirty-seven Introductions. Essay Index Repr. Ser. Ayer repr. of 1929 ed. $16.00
Come to Think of It. Essay Index Repr. Ser. Ayer repr. of 1931 ed. $18.00

All Is Grist: A Book of Essays. Essay Index Repr. Ser. Ayer repr. of 1932 ed. $17.00;
    Scholarly repr. of 1932 ed. 1971 $15.00
Sidelights of New London and Newer York, and Other Essays. Essay Index Repr. Ser.
    Ayer repr. of 1932 ed. 1968 $16.00
All I Survey. Essay Index Repr. Ser. Ayer repr. of 1933 ed. $20.00
As I Was Saying. Essay Index Repr. Ser. Ayer repr. of 1936 ed. $17.00; Folcroft 1973
    lib. bdg. $20.00
Autobiography. Arden Lib. repr. of 1936 ed. 1978 lib. bdg. $30.00
The Man Who Was Chesterton. Ed. by Raymond T. Bond, *Essay Index Repr. Ser.* Ayer
    repr. of 1937 ed. $42.00. Essays, stories, poems, and other writings.
End of the Armistice. Essay Index Repr. Ser. Ayer repr. of 1940 ed. $17.00
Lunacy and Letters. Ed. by Dorothy Collins, *Essay Index Repr. Ser.* Ayer repr. of 1958
    ed. $15.00. Contains 38 nonpolitical light essays, some rich in fantasy, from the
    Daily News, 1901–12. Edited by Chesterton's literary executor.
The Father Brown Omnibus. Dodd 1983 $14.95

BOOK ABOUT CHESTERTON

Evans, Maurice. *G. K. Chesterton.* Haskell repr. of 1939 ed. 1972 $39.95

COWLEY, MALCOLM. 1898–

Malcolm Cowley, critic, poet, editor, and translator, has long been an influential figure in American letters. The son of a Pittsburgh physician, Cowley studied at Harvard and the University of Montpellier, "starved" in
Greenwich Village ("and that's no figure of speech"), and lived in France,
where he met the Dada crowd and worked on two expatriate magazines, *Se-
cession* and *Broom.* From 1929 to 1944 he was associate editor of *The New
Republic.* His book *The Faulkner-Cowley File: Letters and Memories, 1944–
1962* documents his early recognition of WILLIAM FAULKNER. *The Portable
Faulkner* was published at Cowley's instigation and under his editorship in
1946, when all 17 of Faulkner's books were out of print. Its publication had
a profound effect—virtually creating Faulkner's literary revival.

BOOKS BY COWLEY

The Portable Faulkner. 1946. *Viking Portable Lib.* Penguin rev. ed. 1981 $14.95
Exile's Return: A Literary Odyssey of the 1920's. 1934. Penguin 1976 pap. $6.95; Peter
    Smith 1983 $11.75. Personal memories of the "lost generation."
Think Back on Us: A Contemporary Chronicle of the 1930's. Ed. by Henry Dan Piper,
    Southern Illinois Univ. Pr. 1967 $19.95
Many-Windowed House: Collected Essays on American Writers and American Writing.
    Ed. by Henry Dan Piper, Southern Illinois Univ. Pr. 1970 $14.95 1973 pap. $6.95
The Faulkner-Cowley File: Letters and Memories, 1944–1962. Penguin 1978 pap. $3.95
And I Worked at the Writer's Trade: Chapters of Literary History, 1918–1978. Penguin
    1979 pap. $5.95; Viking 1978 $12.50
The Dream of the Golden Mountains: Remembering the 1930's. Penguin 1981 pap.
    $5.95; Viking 1980 $14.95
A Second Flowering: Works and Days of the Lost Generation. Penguin 1980 pap. $5.95;
    Viking 1973 $10.95. Includes Hemingway, Fitzgerald, Dos Passos, Cummings,
    Wilder, Faulkner, Wolfe, and Hart Crane.
The View from Eighty. Penguin 1982 pap. $4.95; Viking 1980 $6.95

DE MAN, PAUL. 1919–1983

Born and educated in Europe, De Man's critical essays of the 1950s are chiefly indebted to the existential philosophy of Jean-Paul Sartre. Moving to Harvard from Europe in the early 1960s, he gradually developed the view that the operations of language, especially devices like metaphor and irony, subvert a text's apparent statement. Literature differed from other kinds of language in its awareness of this fact, in its recognition of its own "fictional" status. Other kinds of writers, he argued, struggle endlessly to fix their meaning in words, which despite their efforts endlessly give rise to varying understanding. The whole point of literature, on the other hand, is to create exactly this endless stream of reading, re-reading, and interpretation. De Man's critical position came to be called "deconstruction," and is strikingly similar to the views of the prominent French philosopher Jacques Derrida (see Vol. 4). His essays are difficult and closely argued, but penetrating and widely influential.

Books by De Man

Allegories of Reading: Figural Language in Rousseau, Nietzsche, Rilke, and Proust. Yale Univ. Pr. 1979 $30.00 pap. $8.95
Blindness and Insight: Essays in the Rhetoric of Contemporary Criticism. Theory and History of Lit. Ser. Univ. of Minnesota Pr. 2d rev. ed. 1983 $29.50 pap. $12.95. Essays on American and European critics and issues.
The Rhetoric of Romanticism. Columbia Univ. Pr. 1984 $22.50

DE QUINCEY, THOMAS. 1785–1859

De Quincey is now best known for his masterful *Confessions of an English Opium Eater*, written for *Blackwood's Magazine* in 1822 and much later enlarged by retrospection. He began taking opium at Oxford for relief from a toothache and fought the addiction, with occasional success, for more than 20 years. His life and works are marked by contrast: He was born to a patrimony, but lost it; he had immense intellectual gifts (he could read Greek at 15 without study and could translate and interpret the German romanticists), but would not submit to disciplined study for an Oxford degree. His own experiences and reminiscences formed the major subject of his essays; even in literary criticism he contrived to interweave biographical details obtained from personal knowledge. His *Reminiscences of the English Lake Poets* (o.p.) reveals a sharp and unique view of the great romantic poets of his day.

Books by De Quincey

Collected Writings. Ed. by David Masson, AMS Pr. 14 vols. repr. of 1889–90 ed. $315.00; *Eng. Literary Reference Ser.* Johnson Repr. 14 vols. repr. of 1889–90 ed. 1969 $540.00
Confessions of an English Opium Eater. 1822. Ed. by Althea Hayter. *Penguin Eng. Lib. Ser.* 1971 pap. $3.50; Biblio Dist. (Everyman's) repr. of 1907 ed. 1978 $7.95
English Mail-Coach and Other Essays. Biblio Dist. (Everyman's) repr. of 1912 ed. 1970 $7.95

BOOK ABOUT DE QUINCEY

Jordan, John E. *Thomas De Quincey: Literary Critic.* Gordian repr. of 1952 ed. 1973 $15.00

ELIOT, T(HOMAS) S(TEARNS). 1888–1965 (NOBEL PRIZE 1948)

T. S. Eliot's influence on aesthetic criticism was almost as great as on modern poetry. His importance in both disciplines depends upon his double endowment of a sense of language and structure and his most fundamental belief as an artist: the necessary union of intellect and emotion. "The consummate art" of the finest philosophic prose style of our language, he felt, is that "in which acute intellect and passionate feeling preserve a classic balance." His earlier critical writings were published in the time of disintegration and disillusion, when there were "no publicly acceptable structural principles, no current literary conventions." They embody his own search as a poet for material and principles. He pointed out writers who should have special significance—the Jacobean dramatists, DONNE and the metaphysical poets, DANTE (see Vol. 2) and BAUDELAIRE (see Vol. 2). He felt that the greatest art is "impersonal, in the sense that personal emotion, personal experience is extended and completed in something impersonal, not in the sense of something divorced from personal experience and passion." Eliot's Harvard doctoral thesis, *Knowledge and Experience in the Philosophy of F. H. Bradley* (1916), sheds interesting light for scholars on the roots of Eliot's poetry and criticism. Eliot did not confine his criticism to poetry, but considered some of the main cultural, religious, and political problems of his day. (See also Chapter 7 in this volume.)

BOOKS BY ELIOT

Selected Prose. Ed. by Frank Kermode, Farrar 1975 $10.95 pap. $4.95

The Sacred Wood: Essays on Poetry and Criticism. 1920. Methuen 7th ed. 1960 pap. $10.95

Selected Essays. 1932. Harcourt rev. ed. 1950 $19.95. Essays, 1917–1932, including "The Sacred Wood," "For Lancelot Andrews," "Dante," and others.

The Use of Poetry and the Use of Criticism: Studies in the Relation of Criticism to Poetry in England. 1933. Faber repr. 1985 pap. $3.95; Barnes & Noble repr. of 1964 ed. 2d ed. 1975 pap. $6.75

Elizabethan Essays. Gordon 1973 lib. bdg. $69.95; Haskell repr. of 1934 ed. 1969 lib. bdg. $39.95

Points of View. Ed. by John Hayward, Hyperion Pr. repr. of 1941 ed. 1979 $14.50

On Poetry and Poets. Octagon repr. of 1957 ed. 1975 lib. bdg. $21.50. Contains 16 critical essays, including "The Frontiers of Criticism."

Christianity and Culture. Harcourt (Harvest Bks.) 1960 pap. $5.95. Two essays: "The Idea of a Christian Society" and "Notes towards the Definition of Culture."

To Criticize the Critic. Octagon repr. of 1965 ed. 1980 lib. bdg. $19.50. Contains 12 essays, including "From Poe to Valery," "Reflections on Vers Libre," and "Ezra Pound: His Metric and Poetry."

Criticism in America: Its Function and Status. Gordon 1973 lib. bdg. $69.95; Haskell repr. of 1924 ed. 1972 lib. bdg. $39.95

The Classics and the Man of Letters. Haskell 1974 lib. bdg. $39.95

The Literary Criticism of T. S. Eliot: New Essays. Ed. by David Newton-DeMolina, Longwood Pr. 1977 $36.00

EMERSON, RALPH WALDO. 1803–1882

The American essay began with Emerson's *Nature*, published in 1836. This essay exemplifies both Emerson's fundamental vision of the beauty of nature and his method of composition, which relied heavily upon the journals he began keeping while still a student at Harvard. Many of his published essays are revisions of lectures he developed from journal entries. Though essentially without a formal unity, Emerson's essays reveal firm, consistent, philosophical commitments to the dignity of human life and to self-reliance. He led the transcendentalist movement in New England, which began as a revolt against Unitarianism, but owed much to the personal attitudes of Emerson. Though he was a minister's son and trained in the Unitarian ministry, Emerson eschewed established religion and embraced spiritual intuition. From 1840 to 1844, Emerson was editor, with Thoreau and Margaret Fuller, of *The Dial*, a transcendentalist magazine concerned with literature, philosophy, and religion. Annual bibliographies, scholarly articles, interpretations, and facsimiles of Emerson's manuscripts appear in the *Emerson Society Quarterly*, established in 1955. (See also Chapter 8 in this volume.)

Books by Emerson

Complete Works. Ed. by Edward W. Emerson, AMS Pr. 12 vols. repr. of 1903–04 ed. $348.00

Collected Works. Ed. by Alfred E. Ferguson and others, Harvard Univ. Pr. 3 vols. 1979–83 ea. $22.50–$27.50

Works. Richard West 5 vols. $50.00

Selected Writings. Ed. by Brooks Atkinson, Modern Lib. 1981 pap. $3.95; ed. by William H. Gilman, New Amer. Lib. (Signet Class.) pap. $3.95

The Portable Emerson. 1946. Ed. by Carl Bode and Malcolm Cowley, Penguin new ed. 1981 pap. $7.95

Essays. Biblio Dist. (Everyman's) 1980 $9.95 pap. $4.95

Essays of Emerson. Ed. by Robert E. Spiller, Washington Square Pr. pap. $3.95

Selected Essays. Ed. by Larzar Ziff, *Penguin Amer. Lib. Ser.* 1982 pap. $3.95

Essays and Essays. Brown Bk. 1975 pap. $4.00

Essays and Lectures. Ed. by Joel Porte, Lib. of Amer. 1983 $27.50

Five Essays on Man and Nature. Ed. by Robert E. Spiller, *Crofts Class. Ser.* Harlan Davidson 1954 pap. $3.50

Letters. Ed. by R. L. Rusk, Columbia Univ. Pr. 6 vols. 1939 $200.00. Contains 2,313 letters not previously published.

Uncollected Lectures. Ed. by Clarence Ghodes, Folcroft 1973 lib. bdg. $10.00

Early Lectures. Ed. by Robert E. Spiller, Wallace E. Williams, and Stephen E. Whicher, Harvard Univ. Pr. (Belknap Pr.) 3 vols. 1964–72 ea. $27.50–$32.50

Emerson's Literary Criticism. Ed. by Eric W. Carlson, Univ. of Nebraska Pr. 1979 $21.50

English Traits. 1856. Ed. by Howard Mumford Jones, Harvard Univ. Pr. 1966 $16.50

Journals and Miscellaneous Notebooks of Ralph Waldo Emerson. Ed. by W. H. Gilman and others, Harvard Univ. Pr. (Belknap Pr.) 16 vols. 1960–82 ea. $30.00–$40.00

Books about Emerson

Paul, Sherman. *Emerson's Angle of Vision: Man and Nature in American Experience.* AMS Pr. repr. of 1952 ed. $33.50. An attempt to evaluate the transitions in his speculative outlook.

Porte, Joel. *Emerson: Prospect and Retrospect.* Harvard Univ. Pr. 1982 text ed. $16.50 pap. $5.95

——. *Emerson and Thoreau: Transcendentalists in Conflict.* AMS Pr. repr. of 1966 ed. $31.50. The first major study of their intellectual differences.

——. *Representative Man: Ralph Waldo Emerson in His Time.* Oxford 1979 $25.00

FIEDLER, LESLIE A(ARON). 1917–

Fiedler, a literary critic and professor of English at the State University of New York, Buffalo, since 1965, has (according to Saul Maloff in the *N.Y. Times*) "a voice like that of no one else: swashbuckling, hectoring, raucous, calculatedly outrageous—and, at his best, brilliant, wonderfully suggestive, not in the way of most criticism but in the way of imaginative literature." Fiedler's well-known preoccupation with social and psychological issues emerged with *Love and Death in the American Novel*, a major critical text of the 1960s. In this book he argues that American writing has been shaped by an inability to portray mature sexual relationships and by an underlying fear of death. He admonishes critics, teachers, and readers of literature to connect text and context—to consider a poem, for example, as the sum of many contexts, including its genre, the other works of the author, the other works of his time, and so forth. Fiedler's notions of moral ambiguity echo Arnold's focus on art as criticism of life, but with an energy and style peculiar to himself. He depends a lot on generalizations (usually unexpected), making his critical remarks reflect broader considerations.

Books by Fiedler

A Fiedler Reader. Stein & Day 1977 pap. $6.95

Collected Essays. Stein & Day 2 vols. 1971 ea. $12.50

An End to Innocence. 1955. Stein & Day 1972 pap. $4.95. Essays on culture and politics, some reprinted from *Commentary* and *Partisan Review.*

Love and Death in the American Novel. 1960. Stein & Day rev. ed. 1975 pap. $12.95

No! In Thunder: Essays on Myth and Literature. 1960. Stein & Day 1972 pap. $4.95

Cross the Border—Close the Gap. Stein & Day pap. $2.95

Freaks: Myths and Images of the Secret Self. Simon & Schuster (Touchstone Bks.) 1984 pap. $9.95

The Return of the Vanishing American. Stein & Day pap. $2.95. Explores the American Western from its classic form to the cowboy's descendant, the hippie.

To the Gentiles. Stein & Day 1972 pap. $2.95

What Was Literature? Class Culture and Society. Simon & Schuster (Touchstone Bks.) 1984 pap. $6.95

FISH, STANLEY. 1938–

Fish is the most prominent of the recent critics who have focused attention on the reader and the reader's response to a literary work. In his earlier writings, he emphasized the way readers form expectations about what will come next in a work—how a sentence will end, a character act, a plot turn out. The author, he argued, played on and especially against these expectations, producing new and unexpected outcomes. More recently, he has argued that readers create the meaning of a work on the basis of codes or ways of reading they have learned from an "interpretive community" (their teachers in English classes, for instance). The reader will think the work simply "means" what he thinks it does, but in fact, the "meaning" is a product of his own socially determined activity. Fish has argued his views with clarity, verve, and polemic vigor in a series of books and essays on literature from the Renaissance onward.

Books by Fish

Surprised by Sin: The Reader in Paradise Lost. Univ. of California Pr. 1971 pap. $8.95. Milton's epic lures the reader into "sinful" expectations, then subverts them to impel the growth of religious and moral insight.

Self-Consuming Artifacts: The Experience of Seventeenth-Century Literature. Univ. of California Pr. 1973 pap. $9.95. Analyzes literary works as subverting readers' expectations.

The Living Temple: George Herbert and Catechizing. Univ. of California Pr. 1978 $24.50. Analyzes the seventeenth-century poet in the light of Fish's theories.

Is There a Text in This Class? The Authority of Interpretive Communities. Harvard Univ. Pr. text ed. 1980 $25.00 1982 pap. $8.95. Collects 15 years of essays, showing Fish's evolution from formalist reader-response to "interpretive communities" theory.

FISHER, M(ARY) F(RANCES) K(ENNEDY). 1908–

Fisher has been admired by two generations of epicures for her elegant, graceful, civilized, and splendidly informed essays on food and France. She attended Occidental College, the University of California at Los Angeles, and the University of Dijon, but studied the delights around her with more enthusiasm. Dijon, indeed, was crucial to her experience, since it was there that she learned "how to study, how to think"—and presumably how to eat as well. She has written recipes interspersed with reminiscences about food and the places she has eaten it in *The Gastronomical Me* (o.p.) and *Serve It Forth* (o.p.). She is the highly respected editor and translator of Brillat-Savarin's *Physiology of Taste* (o.p.), a work of great influence. She is also responsible for the remarkable Time-Life volume on cooking of provincial France. *Among Friends*, her account of an Episcopalian childhood in a Quaker town (Whittier, California), contains both her philosophy and her experience. She reveals her precocious interest in food and cookery and her inescapable journalistic heritage in a series of essays for the *New Yorker* included in *As They Were*. Her essays are contemplative and deeply committed to the mysterious as part of life.

Books by Fisher

As They Were. Knopf 1982 $13.95
Among Friends. North Point Pr. 1983 pap. $10.00

FRYE, NORTHROP. 1912–

Frye's interest is in the human imagination and its power to create patterns or shapes that guide our individual and social lives and our interaction with nature. These patterns are "myths" or "archetypes," and the entire mass of literature is a vast treasure house of patterns, sometimes in disguised or "displaced" form. The critic's job is to provide a precise and comprehensive classification of the forms of literature. He thus educates and liberates our imaginations from the narrow range of our own present-day culture and shows both the limited myths that organize our immediate society and the much larger range of myths that can be seen throughout human history.

BOOKS BY FRYE

Anatomy of Criticism. Princeton Univ. Pr. 1957 $36.00 pap. $7.95. His magnum opus, a comprehensive system embracing the varieties of literature.
Fables of Identity: Studies in Poetic Mythology. Harcourt 1963 pap. $5.95
The Well-Tempered Critic. Indiana Univ. Pr. (Midland Bks.) 1963 pap. $2.95
The Educated Imagination. Indiana Univ. Pr. 1964 pap. $5.95
The Return of Eden: Five Essays on Milton's Epics. 1965. Univ. of Toronto Pr. 1975 $15.00
A Natural Perspective. Harcourt 1969 pap. $4.95
The Bush Garden: Essays on the Canadian Imagination. Univ. of Toronto Pr. 1971 pap. $6.95
The Critical Path: An Essay on the Social Context of Literary Criticism. Indiana Univ. Pr. 1971 $17.50 pap. $5.95
The Secular Scripture: A Study of the Structure of Romance. Harvard Univ. Pr. 1976 $15.00 pap. $5.95
Spiritus Mundi: Essays on Literature, Myth, and Society. Indiana Univ. Pr. 1976 $20.00 pap. $7.95
Northrop Frye on Culture and Literature: A Collection of Review Essays. Ed. by Robert D. Denham, Univ. of Chicago Pr. lib. bdg. 1978 $17.50 pap. $5.50
Creation and Recreation. Univ. of Toronto Pr. 1980 pap. $6.50
The Great Code: The Bible and Literature. Harcourt 1981 $14.95 pap. $5.95
Divisions on a Ground: Essays on Canadian Culture. Ed. by James Polk, Univ. of Toronto Pr. 1982 $19.95
A Study of English Romanticism. Univ. of Chicago Pr. 1983 pap. $5.95

BOOKS ABOUT FRYE

Cook, Eleanor, and others, eds. *Centre and Labyrinth: Essays in Honour of Northrop Frye.* Univ. of Toronto Pr. 1982 $30.00
Denham, Robert D. *Northrop Frye: An Enumerative Bibliography. Author Bibliographies Ser.* Scarecrow Pr. 1974 $16.50
———. *Northrop Frye and Critical Method.* Pennsylvania State Univ. Pr. text ed. 1978 $23.75
Krieger, Murray, ed. *Northrop Frye in Modern Criticism: Selected Papers from the English Institute.* AMS Pr. repr. of 1966 ed. consult publisher for information.

GASS, WILLIAM. 1924–

Gass is Distinguished University Professor in Humanities at Washington University, St. Louis, where he teaches literature, philosophy, and writing courses. His broad background in aesthetics and philosophy began at Cornell, where he wrote *A Philosophical Investigation of Metaphor* (o.p.) and observed Ludwig Wittgenstein, "the most important intellectual experience of [his] life." Gass considers himself a prose stylist, rather than a pure novelist or critic. He further explains that his fiction is first made of words and then of characters, themes, and ideas. His first novel, *Omensetter's Luck* (1966), was described by Richard Gilman as "the most important work of fiction by an American in this literary generation." His fiction and short stories have recently given way to complex essays on aesthetic principles of language and intense, original philosophical speculation in *Fiction and the Figures of Life* (1970), which describes his critical doctrine, and *On Being Blue*, a metaphysical meditation. His emphasis on words does not preclude a highly developed sensuality that animates and enlivens his writings: "Willie Master's Lonesome Wife," an essay/novella, utilizes some innovative manipulation of typeface and linguistic features to produce a desired effect.

Books by Gass

On Being Blue: A Philosophical Inquiry. Godine 1976 $10.00 1978 pap. $6.95
Omensetter's Luck. New Amer. Lib. (Plume) pap. $5.95
Fiction and the Figures of Life. Godine 1978 pap. $7.95
The World within the Word. Knopf 1978 $10.00; Godine 1979 pap. $8.95
The Habitations of the Word: Essays. Simon & Schuster 1984 $16.95; Touchstone
  Bks. 1985 pap. $8.95

GOULD, STEPHEN JAY. 1941–

Gould, a paleontologist by avocation and a geologist by training, is a professor at Harvard who writes about current scientific theory in terms accessible to the ordinary intelligent reader. His major focus, on Darwin and the theory of evolution, has produced many "fruitful analogies between fields" of science and one loud, ongoing controversy. In 1972 Gould coauthored *Punctuated Equilibria* (o.p.) with Niles Eldredge (of the American Museum of Natural History), which suggested a reassessment of Darwin's theory of new species evolution. In short, he made it apparent that gradual development or evolution was "more a product of Western thought than a fact of nature." Gould has taken his expert opinion into legal history: as a key figure in the Arkansas trial that established that state's creationist law as unconstitutional. He insists that evolution was neither planned nor guided but composed of "odd arrangements and funny solutions . . . paths that a sensible God would never tread." His popular column in *Natural History*, "This View of Life," calls our attention to science and society, to history and the media, in humanistic, learned, and concrete language. His *Mismeasure of Man*, which attacks intelligence testing as reductive and dogmatic, won the National Book Critics Circle Award in 1982.

Books by Gould

Ever Since Darwin: Reflections in Natural History. Norton 1977 $14.95 1979 pap.
  $4.95

Ontogeny and Phylogeny. Harvard Univ. Pr. (Belknap Pr.) 1977 $25.00 1985 pap.
    $8.95
The Panda's Thumb: More Reflections in Natural History. Norton 1980 $15.95 1982
    pap. $4.95
The Mismeasure of Man. Norton 1981 $14.95 1983 pap. $5.95
Hen's Teeth and Horse's Toes: Further Reflections in Natural History. Norton 1983
    $15.50 1984 pap. $5.95

HARTMAN, GEOFFREY. 1929–

One of the subtlest modern readers of poetry, Hartman's gift is not only a
sensitive ear for sound pattern and nuances of imagery but even more a
powerful capacity to enter sympathetically into the poet's own feeling for
his poem and for his situation in the history of poetry. Hartman's essays on
English romantic poetry are unsurpassed. Recently, he has added discussions of a wide range of contemporary approaches to literature.

BOOKS BY HARTMAN

Wordsworth's Poetry: 1787–1814. 1964. Yale Univ. Pr. rev. ed. 1967 pap. $11.95
The Fate of Reading and Other Essays. Midway Repr. Ser. Univ. of Chicago Pr. repr. of
    1975 ed. text ed. 1984 pap. $9.00
Akiba's Children. Iron Mountain Pr. 1978 $12.50. Original poems.
Criticism in the Wilderness: The Study of Literature Today. Yale Univ. Pr. 1980 $30.00
    pap. $8.95. Survey of contemporary criticism, particularly in the context of
    American culture.
Saving the Text: Literature/Derrida/Philosophy. Johns Hopkins Univ. Pr. text ed. 1982
    $18.50 pap. $5.95. A sympathetic study of Derrida followed by reflections on lan-
    guage and literature.
Easy Pieces. Columbia Univ. Pr. 1985 $20.00

HAZLITT, WILLIAM. 1778–1830

Hazlitt, who wished to be a portrait painter but was forced by economic
circumstances to become a journalist, had his early literary tastes guided
by Coleridge, Wordsworth, and Lamb. His political convictions gave him
violent prejudices, made him quarrel with these three and other friends,
and marred his essays with many digressions. He was a great admirer of Napoleon, and his longest work is a biography of his hero. Most of his essays
combine a loose association of ideas with rapt comparison. He wanted to
balance reason and feeling: "To feel what is good and give reasons for the
faith that is in me." And though his passionate commitment to liberal
causes made his personal preferences occasionally unsound, his judgment of
literature in general seems to have been excellent—formed by what Keats
described as "his depth of taste."

BOOKS BY HAZLITT

Works. Ed. by Percival P. Howe, AMS Pr. 21 vols. repr. of 1934 ed. $630.00. The stan-
    dard centenary edition.
Selected Essays. Ed. by John R. Nabholtz, *Crofts Class. Ser.* Harlan Davidson text ed.
    1970 pap. $1.95
Selected Writings. Ed. by William Blythe, Penguin 1982 pap. $5.95

The Hazlitt Sampler: Selections from His Familiar, Literary and Critical Essays. Ed. by Hershel M. Sikes, Peter Smith $11.25
Hazlitt on Theater: Selections from the View of the English Stage and Criticisms and Dramatic Essays. Ed. by William Archer and Robert Lowe, intro. by William Archer, Hyperion Pr. repr. of 1957 ed. 1980 $20.75
The Round Table: A Collection of Essays and Characters of Shakespeare's Plays. 1817. Biblio Dist. (Everyman's) 1957 $9.95. Mostly by Hazlitt, but with ten contributions by Leigh Hunt.
Lectures on the English Poets. 1818. Ed. by William Hazlitt, Jr., Russell repr. of 1841 ed. 3d ed. 1968 $10.00
Lectures on the English Comic Writers. Russell repr. of 1819 ed. 1969 $10.00. Lectures delivered at the Surry Institution.
The Spirit of the Age or Contemporary Portraits: Coleridge, Scott, Byron, Wordsworth. 1825. Darby repr. of 1904 ed. 1983 lib. bdg. $20.00
Criticisms on Art. Folcroft repr. of 1856 ed. $45.00
Sketches and Essays. Darby repr. of 1903 ed. 1983 lib. bdg. $20.00
Table Talk: 1821–22. Folcroft repr. of 1906 ed. lib. bdg. $30.00

BOOKS ABOUT HAZLITT

Kinnard, John. *William Hazlitt: Critic of Power.* Columbia Univ. Pr. 1978 $31.50
Wardle, Ralph Martin. *Hazlitt.* Univ. of Nebraska Pr. 1971 $31.50. Includes bibliographic references.

HOLLAND, NORMAN H. 1927–

The leading American psychoanalytic critic, Holland's early criticism focused on the mind's dynamic functioning both in the creation and reading of poetry. Poems, he argued, aroused powerful wishes, fears, and fantasies, but also shaped them into meaning and coherence, thus protecting or defending us against them. More recently, he has claimed that each individual reader's character, established in infancy and dominant throughout life, interacts in complex ways with the themes and structures in a literary work. He has tested this theory in psychoanalytically oriented reports of the responses of actual readers.

BOOKS BY HOLLAND

Psychoanalysis and Shakespeare. Octagon repr. of 1964 ed. lib. bdg. 1976 $27.50
Five Readers Reading. Yale Univ. Pr. 1975 $26.00. Psychoanalytic reports on five experienced readers' responses to poems.
The Dynamics of Literary Response. Norton Lib. 1975 pap. $6.95. Psychoanalytic approach to reading literature.
Laughing: A Psychology of Humor. Cornell Univ. Pr. 1982 $19.95
The I. Yale Univ. Pr. 1985 $30.00

HOLMES, OLIVER WENDELL. 1809–1894

Holmes has a unique place in American letters. His animated series of essays, which first appeared in the *Atlantic Monthly* as a serial and later in book form in 1858—under the title *The Autocrat of the Breakfast Table*—brought him widespread attention. He has been compared with all the great essayists from MONTAIGNE (see Vol. 2) to Lamb, but his compositions are closer to conversational than to formal prose. Later volumes—*The Professor at the Breakfast Table, The Poet at the Breakfast Table,* and *Over the Teacups*—extend the autocrat's delightfully egotistical talks, mainly of Boston and New England, in which Holmes was by turns brilliantly witty and extremely serious. His sprightly conversational style set the pattern for the modern humor columnist. He was a devoted physician, professor of anatomy at Dartmouth, Parkman professor of anatomy and physiology at Harvard, briefly dean of Harvard's Medical School, and admired lecturer on both science and literature. His three "medicated" novels (undistinguished as literary documents) study that "mysterious borderland which lies between physiology and psychology" and demonstrate that Holmes was rather advanced in his conception of the causes and progress of neuroses and mental disease.

BOOKS BY HOLMES

The Complete Works. Scholarly 13 vols. repr. of 1892 ed. 1972 $490.00
The Autocrat of the Breakfast Table. Arden Lib. repr. of 1858 ed. 1977 lib. bdg. $20.00
Over the Teacups. Scholarly repr. of 1892 ed. 1968 $39.00
The Poet at the Breakfast Table. Scholarly repr. of the 1895 ed. 1968 $18.00
The Professor at the Breakfast Table. Scholarly repr. of 1899 ed. 1968 $18.00

BOOK ABOUT HOLMES

Small, Miriam R. *Oliver Wendell Holmes. Twayne's U.S. Authors Ser.* G. K. Hall 1962 lib. bdg. $10.95; *Twayne's U.S. Authors Ser.* New College & Univ. Pr. 1963 pap. $3.45. Includes chronology of Holmes's life and selected bibliography.

HOWE, IRVING. 1920–

A "democratic socialist," editor of the radical journal *Dissent,* and a regular contributor to *The New Republic,* Howe is professor of English at Hunter College. His first book, *Sherwood Anderson,* made a substantial impression on his contemporaries and firmly established his reputation as a critic. He has written several volumes of essays on literary topics—some of these with an emphasis on political commitments—all informed by a sensitive critical intellect. He feels that the fundamental problem with modern culture is that we're looking for meaning of life outside of it. He insists that moderation threatens our social order as much as radicalism because it is "passive, indifferent and atomized." His valuable introduction to *The Idea of the Modern in Literature and the Arts* reveals an uncomfortable awareness of the difficulties of modernism and a deep dissatisfaction with the functioning critic. He wants criticism to form our tastes, to come to the defense of literacy, and to confirm the ideal of individual imagination.

BOOKS BY HOWE

A World More Attractive: A View of Modern Literature and Politics. Essay Index Repr. Ser. 1950–63. Ayer repr. of 1963 ed. $18.00. Essays 1950–63.
Sherwood Anderson. Stanford Univ. Pr. 1951 $25.00 pap. $7.95
Politics and the Novel. Essay Index Repr. Ser. Ayer repr. of 1957 ed. $18.00; Horizon 1977 pap. $5.95. Essays on Stendhal, Dostoyevsky, Conrad, Malraux, and others.

The Decline of the New: A Collection of Essays on Modern Writers and Their Books. Horizon Pr. 1970 pap. $5.95
The Idea of the Modern in Literature and the Arts. 1971. Horizon Pr. 1977 pap. $5.95
Beyond the New Left. Horizon Pr. 1972 pap. $5.95
Celebrations and Attacks: Thirty Years of Literary and Cultural Commentary. Horizon Pr. 1978 $14.95; Harcourt (Harvest Bks.) 1980 pap. $4.95
World of Our Fathers. Pocket Bks. 1978 pap. $6.95; Simon & Schuster (Touchstone Bks.) 1983 pap. $12.95
Beyond the Welfare State. Schocken 1982 $17.95 pap. $8.95
A Margin of Hope: An Intellectual Autobiography. Harcourt 1982 $14.95

JAMES, HENRY. 1843–1916

James was best known for his novels, but he also wrote occasional essays, literary criticism, aesthetic criticism, sketches for the *New York Tribune*, portraits of other novelists and writers, and sufficient letters of merit to fill six volumes. His notebooks (o.p.), edited by F. O. Matthiessen and Kenneth B. Murdock, constitute a major document in the theory and practice of literary composition. His fine autobiography (1956, o.p.), edited by F. W. Dupee, consists of three books originally published separately: *A Small Boy and Others* (1913) and *Notes of a Son and Brother* (1914), which relate his childhood in a family blessed with moderate wealth and great understanding, and *The Middle Years* (1917). He was a consummate craftsman—devoted to ideals of art, aesthetics, and manners and determined to exemplify them in his own work. He wrote a formidable sentence: It may be argued that simply to read with comprehension a novel by James would immensely improve one's grasp of English syntax. (See also Chapter 13 in this volume.)

BOOKS BY JAMES

Notes and Reviews. Essay Index Repr. Ser. Ayer repr. of 1921 ed. 1968 $16.00
The Letters of Henry James. Ed. by Leon Edel, Harvard Univ. Pr. (Belknap Pr.) 4 vols. 1974–84 ea. $25.00–$30.00
Letters. Ed. by Percy Lubbock, Octagon 2 vols. 1969 lib. bdg. $63.00
The Art of the Novel: Critical Prefaces. 1934. Ed. by R. P. Blackmur, Northeastern Univ. Pr. text ed. 1984 pap. $9.95. A collection of the prefaces written for the New York edition of his *Complete Novels and Tales.*
Literary Reviews and Essays on American, English and French Literature. Ed. by Albert Mordell, AMS Pr. repr. of 1957 ed. $17.50; Grove 1979 pap. $4.95; New College & Univ. Pr. 1957 pap. $9.95
Parisian Sketches: Letters to the New York Tribune, 1875–1876. Ed. by Leon Edel and Ilse Dusoir Lind, Greenwood repr. of 1957 ed. 1978 lib. bdg. $21.25
Transatlantic Sketches. Essay Index Repr. Ser. Ayer repr. of 1875 ed. $21.00
French Poets and Novelists. 1878. Folcroft 1973 lib. bdg. $30.00; Gordon lib. bdg. $59.95; Richard West repr. of 1893 ed. 1980 lib. bdg. $30.00
Hawthorne. 1879. Ed. by John Morley, AMS Pr. repr. of 1887 ed. $12.50; Folcroft repr. of 1879 ed. lib. bdg. $30.00
Essays in London and Elsewhere. Essay Index Repr. Ser. Ayer repr. of 1893 ed. $18.00
Views and Reviews. AMS Pr. repr. $15.00; *Essay Index Repr. Ser.* Ayer repr. of 1908 ed. $16.00

The American Scene. 1907. Ed. by Leon Edel, Indiana Univ. Pr. 1968 $15.00 pap.
   $8.95
Within the Rim, and Other Essays, 1914–15. Essay Index Repr. Ser. Ayer repr. of 1918
   ed. $15.00
The Art of Travel. Ed. by Morton Zabel, *Essay Index Repr. Ser.* Ayer 1958 $32.00
Italian Hours: Travel Essays. Greenwood repr. of 1959 ed. 1977 lib. bdg. $21.75;
   Grove 1979 pap. $4.95
The Theory of Fiction: Henry James. Ed. by James E. Miller, Univ. of Nebraska Pr. (Bi-
   son) 1972 pap. $8.50. Excerpts and selections from the prefaces and essays orga-
   nized topically by the editor.
Selected Literary Criticism. Ed. by Morris Shapira, Cambridge Univ. Pr. 1981 pap.
   $17.95; Greenwood repr. of 1964 ed. 1978 lib. bdg. $27.50
Literary Criticism. Ed. by Leon Edel and Mark Wilson, Lib. of Amer. 1984 $27.50

JAMESON, FREDRIC.

Jameson's lucid and penetrating expositions of structuralism in *The
Prison-House of Language* and of the varieties of Marxism in *Marxism and
Form* have given him a wide audience in current theory. While he speaks always as a Marxist, Jameson explicitly attends to the various ways we read
and interpret works of literature in an effort to absorb their merits into his
own analyses and to show that a Marxist approach to the work in its historical totality is the more fundamental and comprehensive account.

BOOKS BY JAMESON

*The Prison-House of Language: A Critical Account of Structuralism and Russian For-
   malism. Princeton Essays in Lit. Ser.* 1972 pap. $8.50
Marxism and Form: Twentieth-Century Dialectical Theories of Literature. Princeton
   Univ. Pr. 1974 pap. $9.95
Fables of Aggression: Wyndham Lewis, the Modernist as Fascist. Univ. of California
   Pr. 1979 $22.50 pap. $5.95
Sartre: The Origins of a Style. Columbia Univ. Pr. 1984 $32.00 pap. $8.95
The Political Unconscious: Narrative as a Socially Symbolic Act. Cornell Univ. Pr.
   1981 $29.95 pap. $8.95. An important and widely cited book.

BOOK ABOUT JAMESON

Dowling, William C., and Althusser Jameson. *Marx: An Introduction to "The Political
   Unconscious."* Cornell Univ. Pr. 1984 $22.50 pap. $6.95

KAZIN, ALFRED. 1915–

Kazin, a literary critic and professor of English literature, established his
own critical reputation in the mid-1940s with *On Native Grounds*, a study of
American literature. He started work on it at the suggestion of Carl Van
Doren in 1939 while, he explains, "half-heartedly doing a master's essay at
Columbia on Gibbon and wondering what would ever become of me or of
the maddening age." His more recent *Bright Book of American Life* is both a
recapitulation of modernism and an evaluation of American writers who
have achieved prominence since 1945. Modernism, a favorite topic of Kazin,
denotes a literary revolution marked by spontaneity and individuality but
which was lacking in precisely the mass culture appeal necessary to its sur-

vival. *Contemporaries* includes reflective essays on travel, five essays on Freud, and some very perceptive essays on literary and political matters. The final section, "The Critic's Task," concerns itself with the critic's function within a popular and an academic context and with critical theory and principles. *Starting Out in the Thirties* describes Kazin's early years with *The New Republic* as book reviewer and evaluates his contemporaries—Malcolm Cowley, MARY MCCARTHY, Philip Rahv, Granville Hicks, and others—in a period when the depression and radical political thought, pro and con, deeply affected literary production.

BOOKS BY KAZIN

On Native Grounds: An Interpretation of Modern American Prose Literature. 1942. Harcourt 1983 pap. $9.95
A Walker in the City. 1951. Harcourt 1969 pap. $3.95. Autobiographical memories and reflections.
The Inmost Leaf: A Selection of Essays. Greenwood repr. of 1955 ed. lib. bdg. $17.50; Harcourt 1979 pap. $4.95
Contemporaries, from the Nineteenth Century to the Present. 1962. Horizon Pr. rev. ed. 1981 pap. $9.95
Starting Out in the Thirties. 1965. Random (Vintage) 1980 pap. $4.95. Sequel to *A Walker in the City.*
Bright Book of American Life: American Novelists and Storytellers from Hemingway to Mailer. Little-Atlantic 1973 $9.95; Univ. of Notre Dame Pr. text ed. 1980 pap. $6.95
New York Jew. Knopf 1978 $12.95; Random (Vintage) 1979 pap. $2.95
An American Procession. Knopf 1984 $18.95

KERMODE, FRANK. 1919–

Kermode has a sophisticated awareness of more abstruse currents in contemporary literary theory, but speaks in a language that remains accessible to the ordinary educated reader. His important work on narrative explores the various devices literature uses to shape experience, while always recognizing the tentative status of the achieved forms. More recently, he has stressed the ways literary works themselves, like our experience, are complex and opaque, marked by gaps, contradictions, and indeterminacies, which invite our interpretation, but also frustrate it.

BOOKS BY KERMODE

The Romantic Image. Routledge & Kegan 1957 o.p.
Puzzles and Epiphanies: Essays and Reviews, 1958–1961. Routledge & Kegan 1963 o.p.
The Sense of an Ending: Studies in the Theory of Fiction. Oxford 1967 pap. $8.95. A study of our sense of time and how novels end.
Continuities. Random House 1968 o.p.
Shakespeare, Spenser, Donne: Renaissance Essays. Viking 1971 o.p.
The Genesis of Secrecy: On the Interpretation of Narrative. Harvard Univ. Pr. text ed. 1979 $14.00 pap. $5.95. Insights into narrative through a reading of the Gospel of Mark.
The Art of Telling: Essays on Fiction. Harvard Univ. Pr. 1983 $15.00

The Classic: Literary Images of Permanence and Change. Harvard Univ. Pr. text ed. 1983 pap. $5.95; Viking 1975 $13.95
Forms of Attention. Fwd. by Frank Lentricchia, Univ. of Chicago Pr. 1985 $9.95. Account and critique of recent critical theory.

LAMB, CHARLES. 1775–1834

When Lamb's *Essays of Elia* was first published in 1823, he had already published his *Works*—including minor verse, a sentimental novel, an Elizabethan tragedy, extensive commentaries on Shakespeare's plays, and two distinguished critical essays—and spent more than 20 years caring devotedly for his periodically insane sister, Mary. With this considerable literary and personal experience, it is not surprising that his essays should be polished and easy, full of erudition and personal reminiscences. In the familiar essay, he employed all his acute observations of life and of London, and fully justified his years of patient and occasionally inspired letter writing. Lamb was an intimate friend of both Coleridge and Wordsworth, but he was unpersuaded by claims of the superiority of nature or the advantage of political agitation. The pseudonym "Elia" was intended to protect John, his brother, who was still clerk in the South-Sea House about which Lamb wrote his mostly autobiographical accounts.

BOOKS BY LAMB

The Works of Charles and Mary Lamb. 1903–05. Ed. by E. V. Lucas, Scholarly 7 vols. repr. 1970 $350.00
The Portable Charles Lamb. Ed. by John Mason Brown, *Viking Portable Lib.* Penguin 1980 pap. $7.95. Includes letters, poems, and essays, arranged to show various aspects of Lamb's character and interests.
The Life, Letters and Writings of Charles Lamb. Ed. by Percy Fitzgerald, Ayer 6 vols. repr. of 1895 ed. $175.00
Essays of Elia (and *Last Essays of Elia*). 1823, 1833. Biblio Dist. repr. of 1906 ed. 1978 $9.95
Selected Essays. Ed. by John R. Nabholtz, *Crofts Class. Ser.* Harlan Davidson text ed. 1967 pap. $1.25
Lamb as Critic. Ed. by Roy Park, Univ. of Nebraska Pr. 1980 $25.95
Lamb's Criticism: Selection from the Literary Criticism of Charles Lamb. Ed. by E. M. Tillyard, Greenwood repr. of 1923 ed. lib. bdg. $18.75

MACAULAY, THOMAS BABINGTON, 1st baron. 1800–1859

The grouping of Macaulay's essays according to the classification of Cotter Morison in his monograph of Macaulay—as English History, Foreign History, Literary Criticism—has been followed strictly in the Everyman's edition, less strictly in other collections. It has been hard to live down the persistent influence of some of Macaulay's essays. His strongly biased remarks (and he was not beyond conscious misstatements)—on Addison, Bacon, BYRON, DRYDEN, WALPOLE, and others—made and unmade reputations. Since even his basest opinions were uttered in the purest English prose, Macaulay's reputation as a scholar and a historian flourished. Trained in law, he became a member of Parliament and rose to the peerage in 1857.

He held a number of important cabinet posts; but the effects of his sweeping educational reform while in India are his most enduring contribution to the Whig government. His chief work is his *History of England* (1849–61). (See also Volume 3, Chapter 9.)

Books by Macaulay

Selected Writings. Ed. by John Clive and Thomas Pinney, Univ. of Chicago Pr. 1972 $25.00 1973 pap. $4.25

Critical and Historical Essays. 1843. Biblio Dist. (Everyman's) 2 vols. repr. of 1907 ed. 1966 ea. $9.95

Lays of Ancient Rome and Miscellaneous Essays and Poems. 1954. Biblio Dist. (Everyman's) 1976 $12.95

Book about Macaulay

Roberts, Sidney C. *Lord Macaulay: The Pre-Eminent Victorian.* 1927. Folcroft 1973 $8.50

MACDONALD, DWIGHT. 1906–1982

MacDonald believed thoroughly that "a people which loses contact with its past becomes culturally psychotic." In his younger years, he went through the stages of being "a Trotskyist, a pacifist and an anarchist," but his interests in mature years shifted from the political to the literary because he concluded that he could "do more about the latter than about the former." He has always been willing to amend his plans: after his graduation from Yale in 1928, a brief interlude on the executive training squad of R. H. Macy convinced him that his talents were literary. He apprenticed as an associate editor at *Fortune* and as an editor at *Partisan Review* before founding his own journal, *Politics* (1944–49), as a mouthpiece for his political philosophy. He joined the staff of the *New Yorker* in 1951 and also wrote widely popular movie reviews for *Esquire*—these last more interested in mass culture, a sociological phenomenon, than in politics.

Books by MacDonald

The Responsibility of Peoples and Other Essays in Political Criticism. Greenwood repr. of 1957 ed. 1974 lib. bdg. $15.00. A collection of essays in political criticism, many of which first appeared in the magazine *Politics.*

Against the American Grain: Essays on the Effects of Mass Culture. Da Capo repr. of 1962 ed. 1983 pap. $9.95

On Movies. Da Capo repr. of 1969 ed. 1981 pap. $9.95. Collected articles and reviews annotated from the viewpoint of 1969.

MENCKEN, H(ENRY) L(OUIS). 1880–1956

The great Baltimore iconoclast, lexicographer, and newspaperman made his *American Mercury* a famous battleground for everything it discussed in the 1920s. In apprenticeship, he began as a contentious local reporter, eventually became an editor, a war correspondent, and finally literary critic for *The Smart Set* in 1908. Mencken's collaboration with George Jean Nathan began at *The Smart Set* and survived the first few years of the *Mercury*. The

N.Y. Times described Mencken's prolific writings as "a great stream of literally millions of words of reporting, editorials, essays, commentary, articles
and books, all of it bearing the unmistakable stamp of individuality possessed by a master craftsman who was also a man of honor, of intellectual
curiosity, of humanity and of superb wit." He was wildly popular (and un-
popular) and widely influential. In 1950 he received the National Institute
and American Academy of Arts and Letters Gold Medal.

BOOKS BY MENCKEN

A Mencken Chrestomathy. Knopf 1949 $17.95. A selection from his out-of-print books,
  magazine articles, and newspaper pieces.
The Vintage Mencken. Ed. by Alistair Cooke, Random (Vintage) 1955 pap. $3.95
Prejudices: A Selection. Ed. by James T. Farrell, Random (Vintage) 1958 pap. $4.95
A Carnival of Buncombe: Writings on Politics. 1956. Intro. by Malcolm Moos, Green-
  wood 1983 lib. bdg. $35.00; intro. by Malcolm Moos, fwd. by Joseph Epstein,
  Univ. of Chicago Pr. 1984 $10.95
The Bathtub Hoax and Other Blasts and Bravos. Ed. by Robert S. McHugh, Octagon
  repr. of 1958 ed. 1976 lib. bdg. $24.00. *Chicago Tribune* columns in book form.
The American Scene: A Reader. Ed. by Huntington Cairns, Knopf 1965 $20.00; Ran-
  dom (Vintage) 1982 pap. $6.95
H. L. Mencken on Music. Ed. by Louis Cheslock, Schirmer Bks. repr. of 1916 ed. 1975
  pap. $3.95. A selection of his writings on music, together with an account of his
  musical life and a history of the Saturday Night Club.
Book of Burlesques. Scholarly repr. of 1920 ed. 1971 $39.00
Happy Days, 1880–1892. AMS Pr. repr. of 1940 ed. $31.00
Newspaper Days, 1899–1906. AMS Pr. repr. of 1941 ed. $29.50
Heathen Days, 1890–1936. AMS Pr. repr. of 1943 ed. $29.50
A Choice of Days. Ed. by Edward L. Galligan, Knopf 1980 $12.95; Random (Vintage)
  1981 pap. $4.95

BOOKS ABOUT MENCKEN

Bode, Carl. *Mencken.* Southern Illinois Univ. Pr. 2d ed. 1973 pap. $8.95
Nolte, William H. *H. L. Mencken: Literary Critic.* Wesleyan Univ. Pr. 1968 lib. bdg.
  $17.50; Univ. of Washington Pr. 1967 pap. $5.95

ONG, WALTER J. 1912–

Following the ideas of a number of cultural historians and students of
communications and media, Ong writes dazzling essays on the impact on
culture of the media of presentation and especially the importance of the
shift from an oral or manuscript-based culture in antiquity and the Middle
Ages to a culture based on books and printing after the Renaissance (and,
more recently, on film, radio, television, and computers).

BOOKS BY ONG

In the Human Grain. Macmillan 1967 $9.95
The Presence of the Word: Some Prolegomena for Cultural and Religious History. Univ.
  of Minnesota Pr. repr. of 1967 ed. 1981 pap. $8.95
*Rhetoric, Romance, and Technology: Studies in the Interaction of Expression and Cul-
  ture.* Cornell Univ. Pr. 1971 $27.50

Fighting for Life: Contest, Sexuality, and Consciousness. Cornell Univ. Pr. 1981 $19.95
Interfaces of the Word: Studies in the Evolution of Consciousness and Culture. Cornell
    Univ. Pr. 1982 $24.50 pap. $9.95
Orality and Literacy: The Technologizing of the World. Methuen 1982 $18.95 pap.
    $8.95

PATER, WALTER. 1839–1894

It is typical that Pater, to whom the origin of the aesthetic movement can
in part be traced, never assumed an active role in its development. He was
a stylist of immoderately acute sensitivity who sought for the right word as
laboriously as Flaubert did for "le mot juste." At a time when the intellectual world was regularly divided by controversy, Pater remained apart
from either social or political involvements. He seems to have done very little at all; he was an academic who traveled rarely, meeting with few people
and fewer stimulations outside Oxford. Yet his works and his attitudes
greatly influenced younger artists and critics of his time, especially Oscar
Wilde. His essays, which first appeared in periodicals, explored philosophy,
literature, and the fine arts, advancing "life for its own sake" much as Wilde
would argue "art for art's sake." Pater's *Marius the Epicurean*, generally regarded more as dogma than romance, reveals a strong sensuous attachment
to the inducements of beauty and the indulgence of passions.

BOOKS BY PATER

Works. Johnson Repr. 10 vols. repr. of 1910 ed. $195.00
Essays. Porter 1978 $24.50
Letters. Ed. by Lawrence Evans, Oxford 1970 $12.95
Marius the Epicurean. Ed. by Robert L. Wolff, Garland repr. of 1885 ed. 1975 lib.
    bdg. $66.00
The Renaissance. 1873. Folcroft repr. of 1917 ed. 1977 lib. bdg. $30.00; Richard West
    repr. $25.00; Academy Chicago 1977 pap. $5.95; *Studies in Art and Poetry,* ed. by
    Donald L. Hill, Univ. of California Pr. 1980 $42.00. The volume that established
    his reputation, particularly the essay on Leonardo da Vinci.
Appreciations: With an Essay on Style. Folcroft repr. of 1889 ed. 1978 lib. bdg. $30.00;
    Norwood repr. of 1924 ed. 1980 lib. bdg. $25.00; Richard West repr. of 1889 ea.
    1973 $25.00
Plato and Platonism. 1893. Greenwood repr. of 1910 ed. $15.50; Richard West repr. of
    1910 ed. $30.00. Lectures on aesthetic appreciation.
Greek Studies: A Series of Essays. Ed. by Charles L. Shadwell, Arden Lib. repr. of
    1895 ed. 1977 lib. bdg. $35.00
Essays from 'The Guardian.' 1896. *Essay Index Repr. Ser.* Ayer repr. of 1901 ed. $17.00
Miscellaneous Studies: Series of Essays. Arden Lib. repr. of 1913 ed. 1977 lib. bdg.
    $20.00; Norwood repr. of 1910 ed. 1979 lib. bdg. $25.00
Sketches and Reviews. Arden Lib. repr. of 1919 ed. 1978 lib. bdg. $20.00; *Essay Index
    Repr. Ser.* Ayer repr. of 1919 ed. $17.00; Folcroft repr. of 1919 ed. lib. bdg.
    $20.00; Porter 1978 $14.50
Imaginary Portraits. AMS Pr. repr. of 1924 ed. $10.00; Arden Lib. repr. of 1924 ed.
    1978 $25.00; Century Bookbindery repr. of 1910 ed. 1982 lib. bdg. $30.00; Nor-
    wood repr. of 1907 ed. 1979 lib. bdg. $20.00

BOOKS ABOUT PATER

Benson, Arthur C. *Walter Pater.* Gale repr. of 1906 ed. 1968 $35.00
Child, Ruth C. *The Aesthetic of Walter Pater.* Arden Lib. repr. of 1940 ed. 1978 $20.00;
    Folcroft repr. of 1940 ed. 1972 $20.00; Octagon repr. of 1940 ed. 1970 $17.00
Crinkley, Richmond. *Walter Pater: Humanist.* Univ. Pr. of Kentucky 1970 $18.00

PERELMAN, S(IDNEY) J(OSEPH). 1904–1979

S. J. Perelman—called the king of the "dementia praecox field" by Robert Benchley—was a prolific humorist and satirist at the *New Yorker* for almost half a century. His contributions had a surrealistic quality in style and in subject that elicited from Dorothy Parker the judgment that he had "a disciplined eye and a wild mind" and "a magnificent disregard" for his reader. His raillery was aimed at popular fiction, motion pictures, advertising, and similar features of our transient culture. In his preferred form, a short drama, Perelman excelled in the unconventional, the concentrated, the sophisticated in humor.

BOOKS BY PERELMAN

Crazy Like a Fox. 1944. Random (Vintage) 1973 pap. $3.95. Contains 46 short pieces.
The Most of S. J. Perelman. 1958. Simon & Schuster 1962 pap. $3.25
Rising Gorge. 1961. Simon & Schuster 1969 pap. $1.95
The Last Laugh. Simon & Schuster (Touchstone Bks.) 1982 pap. $4.95
Eastward Ha! Simon & Schuster (Touchstone Bks.) 1983 pap. $5.95
Westward Ha! Da Capo 1984 pap. $7.95

QUILLER-COUCH, SIR ARTHUR (THOMAS). 1863–1944

Sir Arthur Quiller-Couch ("Q"), a Cornishman, became a professor of English literature at Cambridge in 1912. His legacy includes the immensely important anthologies that he edited for Oxford University Press—*English Verse* (1900), *English Prose* (1923), *English Ballads,* and *Victorian Verse*—and nearly 50 books of essays, criticism, fiction, and poetry. He left unfinished a "lushly romantic" nineteenth-century version of the legend of Tristan and Iseult (which was completed by Daphne du Maurier and published as *Castle D'or*), but finished Stevenson's *St. Ives,* which had lacked a conclusion. His essays have an informal but nonetheless academic manner.

BOOKS BY QUILLER-COUCH

Adventures in Criticism. Gordon $59.95; Richard West repr. of 1896 ed. $10.95; Scholarly repr. of 1896 ed. 1969 $29.00; Telegraph Bks. repr. of 1896 ed. 1981 lib. bdg.
    $30.00. Includes Robinson Crusoe, Charles Reade, Henry Kingsley, and George Moore.
Studies in Literature. 1919. Richard West 1973 $30.00
Charles Dickens and Other Victorians. Kraus repr. of 1925 ed. 1968 $25.00; Richard
    West repr. of 1925 ed. 1973 $35.00
The Poet as a Citizen and Other Papers. 1934. AMS Pr. repr. of 1935 ed. $11.00

SIDNEY, SIR PHILIP. 1554–1586

To his fellow Elizabethans, Sidney was the perfect embodiment of the gentleman—a patron of the arts, a brave soldier, a gallant courtier, a notable scholar, and a fine poet. To later generations, he was remembered chiefly as a poet. But he has an important place in the history of literary criticism, as the author of the earliest major work in English in that field: *The Defense of Poesy* (also entitled *An Apology for Poetry*). Published after his death, it seems to have been a response to a narrow puritanical attack on poetry called *The School of Abuse* by Stephen Gosson. Sidney follows the classical view that poetry both teaches and delights; and establishes, with rigorous logic, the superiority of the poet to the philosopher (the poet is more concrete) and to the historian (the poet is more universal).

BOOK BY SIDNEY

An Apology for Poetry. 1595. Richard West repr. 1868 ed. $12.50. Walter J. Johnson 1971 $13.00; ed. by Forrest Robinson, Bobbs 1970 pap. $5.99; (with title *Defense of Poetry*), ed. by J. A. Van Dorsten, Oxford 1966 pap. $4.95; ed. by Lewis Soens, Univ. of Nebraska Pr. 1970 $10.95

SMITH, LOGAN PEARSALL. 1865–1946

Smith, an eminent Quaker expatriate living in England, was very active in the Society for Pure English, for which he wrote a number of tracts. He claimed to have known only interesting people—and he knew many. Bernard Berenson and Bertrand Russell were his brothers-in-law. The once popular *Trivia* and its sequels *More Trivia, Afterthoughts,* and *Last Words* are now, regrettably, out of print. *Reperusals and Re-Collections* is the last of this group. They consist of paragraph essays—a "new" prose form, very simple and very subtle. The author himself called the essays "pieces of moral prose, pensées, reflections, meditations, observations, dealing with the place and habits of men in nature and society." He added that it was "the prose of leisure, bearing no marks of economic necessity." *Milton and His Modern Critics* is a defense of MILTON against the attacks of T. S. Eliot and EZRA POUND.

BOOKS BY SMITH

The English Language. Century Bookbindery repr. of 1912 ed. 1982 lib. bdg. $20.00; Folcroft 1930 lib. bdg. $12.50; Telegraph Bks. repr. 1982 lib. bdg. $20.00
Words and Idioms: Studies in the English Language. Gale repr. of 1925 ed. 1971 $50.00
On Reading Shakespeare. Somerset repr. of 1933 ed. $29.00
Reperusals and Re-Collections. Essay Index Repr. Ser. Ayer repr. of 1937 ed. 1968 $20.00
Milton and His Modern Critics. Shoe String (Archon) repr. of 1941 ed. 1967 $13.50
A Chime of Words: The Letters of Logan Pearsall Smith. Ed. by Edwin Tribble, fwd. by John Russell, Ticknor & Fields 1984 $22.50

SONTAG, SUSAN. 1933–

Sontag, an influential cultural critic with a Harvard master's degree in philosophy, is noted for taking radical positions and venturing outrageous interpretations. Proclaiming a "new sensibility," she supported the cause of pop art and underground films. Her reputation as a formidable critic has been established by numerous reviews, essays, and articles in the *New York Review of Books,* the *N.Y. Times, Harper's,* and other periodicals. *Against Interpretation* includes her controversial essay "Notes on Camp," first published in *Partisan Review.* The title of the book introduces her argument against what she sees as the distortion of an original work by the countless critics who bend it to their own interpretations. "The aim of all commentary on art," she writes, "should be to make works of art—and, by analogy, our own experience—more, rather than less, real to us." She has a mature modernist sensibility, but manages to depict the avant-garde in language accessible to any reader. She has lectured extensively around the United States and has taught philosophy at Harvard, Sarah Lawrence, and Columbia. She is a frequent and popular television discussion personality, particularly on contemporary issues of illness or feminism.

BOOKS BY SONTAG

A Susan Sontag Reader. Farrar 1982 $17.95; Random (Vintage) 1983 pap. $6.95
Against Interpretation. 1966. Octagon repr. of 1978 lib. bdg. $20.50. A selection of critical writings, 1961–65, on modern novels, films, and theater. A nominee for the 1967 National Book Award.
Styles of Radical Will. 1969. Farrar $10.00; Dell (Delta Bks.) 1978 pap. $5.95
Illness as Metaphor. 1978. Farrar $5.95; Random (Vintage) 1979 pap. $3.95
Under the Sign of Saturn. Farrar 1980 $10.95

STEELE, SIR RICHARD. 1672–1729

Steele was born in the same year as Joseph Addison, whom he knew at Charterhouse School and at Oxford. In 1709 he began the first of a series of periodicals that established the characteristics of the "periodical essay." This essay form, which was short and usually addressed personal topics, evolved primarily from journalistic sources and for journalistic purposes. Nevertheless, the essays appearing in *The Tatler* (from 1709) and *The Spectator* (from 1711) exerted a tremendous influence. Addison, who was a frequent contributor to both periodicals, displayed insight and elegance in his 42 numbers of *The Tatler;* Steele, with less elegance and wit, produced 188 and showed a warmth and sympathy that many readers preferred to Addison's cool intelligence. Steele's best-known play, *The Conscious Lovers* (1722), retreats from the artifice and aristocratic notions of Restoration drama, promoting instead a sound middle-class gentility.

BOOKS BY STEELE

The Tatler. Ed. by Lewis Gibbs, Biblio Dist. (Everyman's) repr. of 1953 ed. 1968 $9.95
The Englishman: A Political Journal. Ed. by Rae Blanchard, Arden Lib. repr. of 1955 ed. 1981 lib. bdg. $85.00. Started in 1713, censuring the Tory ministry.

Tracts and Pamphlets. Ed. by Rae Blanchard, Octagon 1966 lib. bdg. $46.00
The Conscious Lovers. Ed. by Shirley S. Kenney, Univ. of Nebraska Pr. (Bison) 1968 $10.95. pap. $4.95

BOOKS BY STEELE AND ADDISON

The Spectator. 1711–14. Biblio Dist. (Everyman's) 4 vols. repr. of 1945 ed. 1979 ea. $14.95
Selections from The Tatler and The Spectator. Ed. by Robert J. Allen, Holt 2d ed. text ed. 1970 pap. $11.95
Critical Essays from The Spectator. Ed. by Donald F. Bond, Oxford 1970 pap. $5.95. Contains the most important critical essays, grouped by topic.
Selected Essays from The Tatler, The Spectator, and The Guardian. Ed. by Daniel McDonald, Irvington repr. of 1973 ed. text ed. pap. $19.95
The Coverley Papers from The Spectator. 1943. Scholarly repr. 1980 lib. bdg. $29.00

STEINER, GEORGE. 1929–

Son of a Jewish father who left Vienna in 1924, Steiner was brought up in France and came to the United States in 1940. After a period as a Rhodes Scholar at Oxford, he worked for the London *Economist.* Since 1974, he has been professor of English and comparative literature at the University of Geneva. Though he commands respect—and occasionally awe at his astonishing polymathic proficiency—from critics and academics in America and abroad, he belongs to no critical "school" (though he calls himself a radical humanist), nor is his writing "academic" in the strict sense. He is seeking, he says, a "philosophy of language" that can help rescue people from the cheapening torrent of words with which they are assaulted by Marshall McLuhan's "media" and from a diminution of intellectual, political, and humane values that threaten us with the silence of total ruin. In *After Babel* he defends precisely those simple contextual linguistic relationships that modern language studies ignore or dismiss. In this "bestial" age, Steiner mourns for the idealism and literacy which were lost in World War II and the Holocaust.

BOOKS BY STEINER

George Steiner: A Reader. Oxford 1984 $25.00
The Death of Tragedy. Oxford repr. of 1961 ed. 1980 pap. $8.95
Language and Silence: Essays on Language, Literature and the Inhuman. 1967. Atheneum text ed. 1970 pap. $7.95
Extraterritorial: Papers on Literature and the Language Revolution. Atheneum text ed. 1971 pap. $3.95
In Bluebeard's Castle: Some Notes toward the Redefinition of Culture. Yale Univ. Pr. 1971 pap. $7.95
After Babel: Aspects of Language and Translation. Oxford 1975 pap. $10.95
On Difficulty and Other Essays. Oxford 1978 $19.95 pap. $9.95
Antigones. Oxford 1984 $29.95

STEVENSON, ROBERT LOUIS. 1850–1894

Stevenson was a Scotsman who settled with his beloved American bride in California in 1880. Many of his essays are based upon the events in his travels—to California across the plains, through France and Belgium by donkey and canoe, and to Samoa and the South Seas. His travel sketches show "his fine eye for color and vivid impressions, that sort of sensitivity that was to add so much to the popularity of his fiction." He also produced periodical essays for *Scribner's* magazine, and a number of short stories. His style recalls Lamb: Both were acute observers, sentimental moralists, devoted to letter writing. *Virginibus Puerisque* (1881) ("Concerning Maidens and Youth") is an essay on love, marriage, and the conduct of life. It exemplifies the manner in which Stevenson gracefully introduced ethical and moral concerns into his essays. (See also Chapter 11 in this volume.)

BOOKS BY STEVENSON

Works. AMS Pr. 26 vols. repr. of 1923 ed. $1,040.00; Richard West 10 vols. repr. $300.00

Selected Writings. Ed. by Saxe Commins, *Essay Index Repr. Ser.* Ayer repr. of 1947 ed. $42.50

Essays. Intro. by William L. Phelps, Folcroft repr. of 1892 ed. 1978 lib. bdg. $15.00

Vailima Letters: Being Correspondence Addressed to Sidney Colvin, Nov. 1890–Oct. 1894. Greenwood 2 vols. repr. of 1895 ed. lib. bdg. $22.50; Scholarly 2 vols. repr. of 1894 ed. 1983 lib. bdg. $17.00

Memories and Portraits. 1887. Scholarly repr. of 1900 ed. 1969 $24.00

The Amateur Emigrant, from the Clyde to Sandy Hook, across the Plains, the Silverado Squatters and Four Essays on California. Ed. by Sidney Colvin, Greenwood 4 vols. repr. of 1911 ed. lib. bdg. $68.25

An Inland Voyage, Travels with a Donkey in the Cevennes, The Silverado Squatters. Biblio Dist. (Everyman's) repr. of 1925 ed. 1978 $12.95 1984 pap. $5.95

The Mind of Robert Louis Stevenson. Ed. by Roger Ricklefs, *Essay Index Repr. Ser.* Ayer repr. of 1963 ed. $17.00

From Scotland to Silverado. Ed. by James D. Hart, Harvard Univ. Pr. 1966 $20.00 pap. $7.95

TATE, ALLEN. 1899–1979

Tate began his literary career in 1922 as an editor of *The Fugitive,* a magazine of southern poets and critics, many of them associated with Vanderbilt University. As editor and in his own works Tate advocated regionalism, explaining that "only a return to the provinces, to the small self-contained centers of life, will put the all-destroying abstraction America safely to rest." In 1943 he held the chair of poetry in the Library of Congress. At the same time, he was editing (1944–47) another important journal of literary criticism, *Sewanee Review.* Tate claims to be "on record as a casual essayist of whom little consistency can be expected." Nevertheless, as editor of *The Fugitive* and the *Sewanee Review* he had a dramatic impact on the availability and evaluation of poets and prose writers. He made significant contributions in modern poetry and modern literary criticism. His poetry, usually identified as "modern metaphysical," he described as "gradually circling round a subject, threatening it and using the ultimate violence upon it." As a critic, he is generally placed with the "new" or formalist critics, though he adds a strong strain of religious humanism, reflected by his conversion in 1950 to Roman Catholicism. (See also Chapter 9 in this volume.)

BOOKS BY TATE

Reactionary Essays on Poetry and Ideas. Essay Index Repr. Ser. Ayer repr. of 1936 ed. 1968 $18.00

Reason in Madness: Critical Essays. Essay Index Repr. Ser. Ayer repr. of 1941 ed. 1968 $19.00

Recent American Poetry and Poetic Criticism. Folcroft repr. of 1943 ed. lib. bdg. $10.00

On the Limits of Poetry: 1928–1948. Essay Index Repr. Ser. Ayer repr. of 1948 ed. $23.00

Hovering Fly and Other Essays. Essay Index Repr. Ser. Ayer repr. of 1949 ed. 1968 $16.00

Forlorn Demon. Essay Index Repr. Ser. Ayer repr. of 1953 ed. $16.00

Memoirs and Opinions: 1926–1974 (Essays of Four Decades). 1969. Ohio Univ. Pr. (Swallow) 1975 $12.95

THOMAS, LEWIS. 1913–

Thomas, a practicing physician who began in pediatrics at Johns Hopkins and pursued interests in immunology and pediatric research as chief executive officer at the Sloan-Kettering Center in New York City, writes more about medical discoveries than about their application. He deepens the apparent dichotomy by focusing in his essays on the importance of man's place in the biological universe. He professes deep skepticism about what he calls the "engineering approach" to scientific research as deadening to the "imagination and intuition of individual scientists." His series of columns for the *New England Journal of Medicine* (from 1971), entitled "Note of a Biology Watcher," pursues his interests and prejudices in layperson's terms. These columns have been called the best short essays in English today. *Lives of a Cell,* which received the National Book Award in 1975, includes a tribute to the Biological Lab in Woods Hole, Massachusetts, where Thomas has found "if the air is right, the science will come in its own season, like pure honey." He has written with passionate conviction about drug addiction and the bureaucratic abuses that threaten to overwhelm consistent medical care in New York City hospitals.

BOOKS BY THOMAS

The Lives of a Cell: Notes of a Biology Watcher. Bantam 1975 pap. $3.95; Penguin 1978 $3.95; Viking 1974 $10.95

The Medusa and the Snail: More Notes of a Biology Watcher. Viking 1979 $10.95

Late Night Thoughts on Listening to Mahler's Ninth Symphony. Viking 1983 $12.95

The Youngest Science: Notes of a Medicine Watcher. Bantam 1984 pap. $6.95; Viking 1983 $14.75

THOREAU, HENRY DAVID. 1817–1862

Thoreau described himself as a mystic, a transcendentalist, and a natural philosopher. He is a writer of essays about nature—not of facts about nature but of his ideas and emotions in the presence of nature. His wish to understand nature led him to Walden Pond, where he lived from 1845 to 1847 in a cabin of his own construction. Though he was an educated man with a Harvard degree, fluent in ancient Greek and modern German, he preferred to study nature by living at Walden "a life of simplicity, independence, magnanimity, and trust." His journal entries from 1837 to 1861 form the basis for most of Thoreau's published works. Thoreau believed that each man should live according to his conscience, willing to oppose the majority if necessary. An early proponent of nonviolent resistance, he was jailed briefly for refusing to pay his poll tax to support the Mexican War. His essay *On Civil Disobedience*, which came from this period of passive resistance, was acknowledged by Gandhi (who read it in a South African jail) as the basis for his campaign to free India. Martin Luther King, Jr., attributed to Thoreau and Gandhi the inspiration for his leadership in the civil rights movement in the United States. When Thoreau died in 1862, the second year of the Civil War, he was little known beyond a small circle of friends and admirers; and only two volumes of his writings had been published—*A Week on the Concord and Merrimack Rivers* and *Walden*. Emerson lamented, "The country knows not yet, or in the least part, how great a son it has lost." But in the twentieth century Thoreau, the "poet-naturalist," has become spokesman not only for the transcendentalists, the naturalists, and the dissidents, but for the heritage and tradition of New England.

BOOKS BY THOREAU

Selected Works. Intro. by Walter Harding, *Cambridge Eds. Ser.* Houghton Mifflin 1975 $22.50

Selected Writings. Ed. by Lewis Leary, *Crofts Class. Ser.* Harlan Davidson text ed. 1958 pap. $3.95

The Portable Thoreau. 1947. Ed. by Carl Bode, *Viking Portable Lib.* Penguin rev. ed. 1977 pap. $7.95

Correspondence. Ed. by Carl Bode and Walter Harding, Greenwood repr. of 1958 ed. 1974 lib. bdg. $40.25

The Journal of Henry D. Thoreau. 1837–1861. Ed. by Bradford Torrey and Francis H. Allen, fwd. by Walter Harding, Dover 14 vols. in 2 repr. of 1906 ed. 1963 ea. $40.00; Gibbs M. Smith 14 vols. repr. of 1906 ed. 1984 $145.00

In the Woods and Fields of Concord: Selections from the Journals of Henry David Thoreau. Ed. by Walter Harding, Gibbs M. Smith 1982 pap. $6.95

The River. Ed. by Dudley C. Lunt, New College & Univ. Pr. 1963 pap. $5.95. Selections from his journal.

Civil Disobedience (Resistance to Civil Government). 1849. Ed. by Edmund R. Brown, Branden pap. $3.00

A Week on the Concord and Merrimack Rivers. 1849. Crowell 1972 pap. $4.95; ed. by Carl Hoyde, Princeton Univ. Pr. 1980 $36.00

Walden, or Life in the Woods. 1854. Ed. by F. B. Sanborn, AMS Pr. 2 vols. repr. of 1909 ed. $58.50; ed. by Walter Harding, Irvington text ed. $29.50 pap. $14.95; Peter Pauper 1966 $9.95; Crowell 1972 pap. $4.95; Buccaneer Bks. repr. of 1983 $17.95; ed. by Lyndon J. Shanley, Princeton Univ. Pr. 1971 $27.50

Walden and Civil Disobedience. Harper pap. $1.50; ed. by Sherman Paul, Houghton Mifflin (Riverside Eds.) 1960 pap. $5.95; Macmillan (Collier Bks.) 1962 pap.

$3.95; New Amer. Lib. (Signet Class.) 1973 pap. $1.75; ed. by Thomas Owen, *Norton Critical Eds.* text ed. 1966 pap. $6.95; *Penguin Amer. Lib. Ser.* 1983 pap. $2.95; ed. by Norman H. Pearson, Holt text ed. 1948 pap. $10.95

Walden and Other Writings. Ed. by Joseph Wood Krutch, Bantam 1971 pap. $2.50; ed. by Brooks Atkinson, Modern Lib. new ed. 1981 pap. $3.95; ed. by W. Howarth, Random 1981 pap. $3.95

Excursions. 1863. Peter Smith $11.25

The Maine Woods. 1864. Crowell 1972 pap. $4.95; ed. by Joseph J. Moldenhauer, Princeton Univ. Pr. 1972 $30.00 pap. $8.95. Includes three autobiographical accounts of trips to Maine.

Cape Cod. 1865. Crowell 1972 pap. $4.95; Little, Brown 1985 $29.45

H. D. Thoreau: A Writer's Journal. Ed. by Laurence Stapleton, Dover 1960 pap. $5.00

The Natural History Essays. Gibbs M. Smith 1980 pap. $4.95

BOOKS ABOUT THOREAU

Harding, Walter, and Michael Meyer. *The New Thoreau Handbook.* New York Univ. Pr. rev. ed. 1980 $30.00 pap. $15.00. A useful volume that attempts to summarize the known facts about Thoreau's life, his works, sources, and fame.

Krutch, Joseph Wood. *Henry David Thoreau.* Greenwood repr. of 1948 ed. 1973 lib. bdg. $22.55; Morrow 1974 pap. $4.75. "A nearly perfect fusing of biography and critical study" (*New Yorker*).

Ruland, Richard. *Twentieth-Century Interpretations of Walden.* Prentice-Hall (Spectrum Bks.) 1968 pap. $9.95

THURBER, JAMES. 1894–1961

In 1927 Thurber, at the urging of his friend E. B. White, joined the staff of the *New Yorker.* He continued to contribute his highly individual pieces and those strange, pathological pen-and-ink drawings of "huge, resigned dogs, the determined and sometimes frightening women, the globular men who try so hard to think so unsuccessfully"—for a lifetime. The period from 1925, when the *New Yorker* was founded, until 1951 and the death of its creator-editor, Harold Ross, was described by Thurber in delicious and absorbing detail in *The Years with Ross* (1959). Of his two great talents, Thurber preferred to think of himself primarily as a writer, illustrating his own books. He published "fables" in the style of AESOP (see Vol. 2) and LA FONTAINE (see Vol. 2)—usually with a "barbed tip of contemporary significance"—children's books, several plays (two Broadway hits, one successful musical revue), and endless satires and parodies in short stories or full-length works. "The Secret Life of Walter Mitty," included in *My World—and Welcome to It,* is probably his best-known story and continues to be frequently anthologized. T. S. Eliot described his work as "a form of humor which is also a way of saying something serious."

BOOKS BY THURBER

(and E. B. White). *Is Sex Necessary? or Why You Feel the Way You Do.* 1929. Harper 1984 pap. $4.76

My Life and Hard Times. Ed. by John P. Hutchens, Harper repr. of 1933 ed. 1973 pap. $3.37

My World—and Welcome to It. 1942. Harcourt (Harvest Bks.) 1983 pap. $4.95; River-
city Pr. repr. lib. bdg. $16.30
The Thurber Carnival. 1945. Harper pap. $6.68; Modern Lib. 1957 $6.95
*The Beast in Me and Other Animals: A Collection of Pieces and Drawings about Human
Beings and Less Alarming Creatures.* Harcourt (Harvest Bks.) repr. of 1948 ed.
1978 pap. $5.95; Rivercity Pr. repr. lib. bdg. $18.95
Thurber Country. 1953. Simon & Schuster (Touchstone Bks.) 1982 pap. $7.95
*Thurber Dogs: A Collection of the Master's Dogs, Written and Drawn, Real and Imagi-
nary, Living and Long Ago.* 1955. Simon & Schuster 1963 pap. $2.95
The Years with Ross. Penguin 1984 pap. $6.95

Books about Thurber

Morsberger, Robert E. *James Thurber. Twayne's U.S. Authors Ser.* New College &
Univ. Pr. 1964 $13.95 pap. $5.95
Tobias, Richard C. *The Art of James Thurber.* Ohio Univ. Pr. 1969 $13.50

TRILLIN, CALVIN MARSHALL. 1935–

Trillin personifies the great tradition of the journal essayist. He received a
degree from Yale in 1957 and shortly after became a reporter and writer for
Time. He joined the *New Yorker* staff in 1963 and began a column for the *Nation,* called "Variations," in 1978. His skillful balance of marked journalistic
instincts with mature social consciousness has been much admired: Melvin
Maddocks remarked that "there is a world of difference, he reminds us, between taking life seriously and taking seriously one's opinions about it." His
essays, which range in topic from the civil rights movement to undiscovered but distinguished eateries in middle America, demonstrate a genuine sense of perspective about the things he sees and writes about. He
makes something interesting out of his observations without making the observations more important than their subject. He can be polite and fastidi-
ous and very funny—expressing lyrical enthusiasm about barbequed ribs at
Arthur Bryant's or mild skepticism about the fashion for enduring marriage.

Books by Trillin

Alice, Let's Eat: Further Adventures of a Happy Eater. Random (Vintage) 1979 pap.
$3.50
American Fried: Adventures of a Happy Eater. Random (Vintage) 1979 pap. $3.95
Floater. Ticknor & Fields 1980 o.p.
Uncivil Liberties. Ticknor & Fields 1982 o.p.
Killings. Ticknor & Fields 1984 $14.95; *Penguin Nonfiction Ser.* 1985 pap. $6.95
Third Helpings. Penguin 1984 pap. $4.95; Ticknor & Fields 1983 $12.95

TRILLING, LIONEL. 1905–1975

Trilling has exerted a wide influence upon literature and criticism: as university professor at Columbia, where he taught English literature, and in
his long association with *Partisan Review, Kenyon Review,* and the Kenyon
School of English (now the School of Letters, Indiana University). He considered himself a true "liberal"—having a "vision of a general enlargement of

[individual] freedom and rational direction in human life." Even liberalism, as a critical mode, Trilling insisted was simply one of several ways of organizing the complexity of life; but it can reveal "variousness and possibility" just as literature, its subject, does. Trilling was viewed as a genteel moralist, but never would settle for mere simplification in literary analysis even if it led to understanding.

BOOKS BY TRILLING

The Liberal Imagination: Essays on Literature and Society. 1950. Harcourt 1979 $10.00

The Opposing Self: Nine Essays in Criticism. 1955. Harcourt 1979 $10.95 pap. $3.95. Romantic image of the self in Keats, Jane Austen, Wordsworth, Tolstoy, Dickens, Flaubert, Howells, Henry James, and George Orwell.

Sincerity and Authenticity: Six Lectures. Harvard Univ. Pr. 1972 pap. $5.95; Harcourt repr. of 1972 ed. 1980 ed. $12.95. The Charles Eliot Norton Lectures for 1969–70.

Beyond Culture. Harcourt 1979 $10.95 pap. $4.95

Last Decade: Essays and Reviews, 1965–1975. Ed. by Diana Trilling, Harcourt 1979 $9.95 1981 pap. $7.95

Speaking of Literature and Society. Ed. by Diana Trilling, Harcourt 1980 $17.95

Prefaces to the Experience of Literature. Harcourt 1981 $12.95 pap. $8.95

WHITE, E(LWYN) B(ROOKS). 1899–1985

E. B. White was educated at Cornell and served as a private in World War I. After several years as a journalist, he joined the staff of the *New Yorker*, then in its infancy. For 11 years he wrote most of the "Talk of the Town" columns. He retired to a saltwater farm in Maine, where he wrote essays regularly for *Harper's Magazine* under the title "One Man's Meat." He received several prizes: in 1960, the gold medal of the American Academy of Arts and Letters; in 1963, the Presidential Medal of Freedom, the nation's highest civilian award (he was honored along with Thornton Wilder and Edmund Wilson). His verse is original and witty but with serious undertones. His friend, the late James Thurber, described him as "a poet who loves to live half-hidden from the eye." Two books have become children's classics: *Stuart Little* (1945), about a mouse born into a human family, and *Charlotte's Web* (1952), about a spider who befriends a lonely pig.

BOOKS BY WHITE

One Man's Meat. 1942. Harper 1982 $14.37 1983 pap. $8.61

The Second Tree from the Corner. 1954. Harper 1984 $16.30 1979 pap. $4.95. Pieces written over 20 years that the author thought would stand the test of time.

Essays. Harper 1977 $14.37 1979 pap. $7.64

WILLIAMS, RAYMOND. 1921–

In Williams, literary criticism is inseparable from a wider cultural criticism, which ultimately serves the intent of transforming capitalism into a more just, classless society. Yet Williams is not doctrinaire: he studies fiction, drama, and popular culture for the insight they give us into society's "structures of feeling," views about the world held so deeply and unconsciously that they are never questioned. He seeks illumination both of past societies and of the origins of our own, always against the background of humankind's striving for a just social order. For many, he is the exemplary cultural critic of our era.

Books by Williams

The Long Revolution. Columbia Univ. Pr. repr. of 1960 ed. 1984 $25.00 pap. $10.00; Greenwood repr. of 1961 ed. lib. bdg. 1975 $22.75
Modern Tragedy. Stanford Univ. Pr. 1966 pap. $5.95
Drama from Ibsen to Brecht. Oxford 1969 o.p.
The Country and the City. Oxford 1975 pap. $8.95
Keywords: A Vocabulary of Culture and Society. Oxford 1976 pap. $8.95
Marxism and Literature. Oxford (Galaxy Bks.) text ed. 1977 pap. $6.95
Politics and Letters: Interviews with New Left Review. Schocken 1979 $27.50 pap. $9.50
Problems in Materialism and Culture: Selected Essays. Schocken 1981 pap. $8.75
The Sociology of Culture. Schocken 1982 pap. $7.95
Culture and Society, 1780–1950. Columbia Univ. Pr. 1983 $39.00 pap. $7.95
The English Novel: From Dickens to Lawrence. Merrimack 1984 pap. $8.95
The Year Two Thousand. Pantheon 1984 $16.45 pap. $8.95
Writing in Society. Schocken 1984 $27.50 pap. $9.50. Essays developing his theory of "cultural materialism" and examining contemporary critical schools and literary works.

WILSON, EDMUND. 1895–1972

Wilson roamed the world and read widely in many languages. He was a journalist for leading literary periodicals: *Vanity Fair*, where he was briefly managing editor; *The New Republic*, where he was associate editor for five years; and the *New Yorker*, where he was book reviewer in the 1940s. These varied experiences were typical of Wilson's range of interest and ability. Eternally productive and endlessly readable, he conquered American literature in countless essays. If he is idiosyncratic and lacks a rigid mold, that probably contributes to his success as a literary critic—since he was not committed to interpretation in the straitjacket of some popular approach or dogma. His critical position suits his cosmopolitan background—historical and sociological considerations prevail. He went through a brief Marxist period and experimented with Freudian criticism. *Axel's Castle*, a penetrating analysis of the symbolist writer, has exerted a great influence in contemporary literary criticism. Its dedication, to Christian Gauss of Princeton, reads: "It was principally from you that I acquired . . . my idea of what literary criticism ought to be—a history of man's ideas and imaginings in the setting of the conditions which have shaped them." His volume of satiric short stories, *Memoirs of Hecate County*, with its frankly erotic passages, was the subject of court cases in a less tolerant decade than the present one. It was his own favorite among his writings, but he complained that those who like his other work tend to disregard it.

BOOKS BY WILSON

Letters on Literature and Politics, 1912–1972. Ed. by Elena Wilson, Farrar 1977 $20.00 pap. $8.95

The Portable Edmund Wilson. Ed. by Lewis M. Dabney, Penguin 1983 $6.95

The Forties: From Notebooks and Diaries of the Period. Ed. by Leon Edel, Farrar 1983 $17.95 pap. $9.95

Axel's Castle. 1931. Norton 1984 pap. $6.95. A study in the imaginative literature of 1870–1930.

American Jitters: A Year of the Slump. Essay Index Repr. Ser. Ayer repr. of 1932 ed. $16.25

The Triple Thinkers: Twelve Essays on Literary Subjects. Farrar 1976 pap. $3.95; Octagonn repr. of 1938 ed. 1976 ed. lib. bdg. $19.00

To the Finland Station. Farrar repr. of 1940 ed. 1972 $15.00 pap. $10.95. A study in the writing and acting of history.

The Shock of Recognition. 1943. Octagon repr. of 1974 ed. lib. bdg. $75.00. A valuable collection of American literary documents, edited by Wilson.

Memoirs of Hecate County. Octagon repr. of 1946 ed. 1966 $29.00

O Canada: An American's Notes on Canadian Culture. Octagon repr. of 1966 ed. 1976 lib. bdg. $18.00

American Earthquake: A Documentary of the Jazz Age, the Great Depression and the New Deal. Farrar 1979 pap. $7.95; Octagon 1971 lib. bdg. $34.50. Essays from periodicals.

The Devils and Canon Barham: Essays on Poets, Novelists and Monsters. Fwd. by Leon Edel, Farrar 1973 $7.95

The Twenties: From Notebooks and Diaries of the Period. Ed. by Leon Edel, Farrar 1975 $10.00 pap. $6.95

Patriotic Gore: Studies in the Literature of the American Civil War. Farrar 1977 pap. $7.95; fwd. by C. Vann Woodward, Northeastern Univ. Pr. text ed. 1984 pap. $13.50; Oxford 1962 $35.00. Excellent discussions of the lives and works of some 30 persons.

The Thirties: From Notebooks and Diaries of the Period. Ed. by Leon Edel, Farrar 1980 $15.00; Washington Square Pr. 1982 pap. $6.95

The Triple Thinkers and The Wound and the Bow: A Combined Volume. Fwd. by Frank Kermode, Northeastern Univ. Pr. 1984 pap. $11.95. Altogether 19 essays on literary subjects and critical theory.

WOOLF, VIRGINIA. 1882–1941

[SEE Chapter 12 in this volume.]

CHAPTER 17

Literary Biography and Autobiography

Frederick R. Karl

> You have found out exactly what I was trying to do when you compare it [Woolf's biography of Roger Fry] to a piece of music. It's odd, for I'm not regularly musical, but I always think of my books as music before I write them. And especially with the life of Roger—there was such a mass of detail that the only way I could hold it together was by abstracting it into themes. I did try to state them in the first chapter, and then to bring in developments and variations, and then to make them all heard together and end by bringing back the first theme in the last chapter.
> —VIRGINIA WOOLF to Mrs. R. C. Trevelyan, September 4, 1940

In making these remarks to Mrs. R. C. Trevelyan (September 4, 1940), Virginia Woolf touched on several problems inherent in the writing of literary biography. Her subject, Roger Fry, was a well-known painter, but he was also the author of several creative, critical works and himself something of a biographer, of Cézanne and Bellini. In any event, Woolf chose to write a literary biography, and her problems in doing so are those created by that particular endeavor. The writing of literary biography takes on dilemmas and decisions unique to the genre.

Woolf mentions the "mass of detail" and the need to "hold it together." In one respect, the work of Roger Fry—his writing as well as his paintings—is his autobiography; and it is the biographer's job to penetrate those autobiographical works and create order, which the subject may not have perceived. For Woolf, the main decision was how to blend together so much detail, and, in her case, also, how to disguise details that she did not wish to publicize (i.e., Fry's long-term affair with Woolf's married sister, Vanessa). She had the obligation to sift through all relevant documents, read Fry's books, of course, select what she needed of her own perceptions of Fry, block out personal feelings and take a position about her subject, and, somehow, justify whatever she was doing in every line and paragraph.

What makes good literary biography? Primarily, the essential element is one few can achieve: to capture the imagination, the essence or substance, of the subject. Woolf chose to attempt this task through musical form. Other biographers may do so through a psychological or even psychoanalytic recreation of the subject's mind and imagination, or through critical perception, which is another form of reconstruction. Whatever the precise method, or blending of methods, the biographer must integrate the life, so that we comprehend how that author wrote those books, poems, or plays, or committed those acts and behaved in that way. All biography must achieve this, literary and otherwise, but the literary biographer has an additional task: to penetrate the avalanche of words pouring from his or her subject and to create a particular order. That order will provide a road into the subject's imagination. It will be based on various insights—psychological, historical, sociological, personal and sexual, broadly cultural. These are the elements and modes we have in mind when we speak of literary biography. More than any other kind of biography, it must pursue two goals: the recreation of broad contexts and the trenchant integration of imaginative materials.

Other kinds of biography and autobiography have their own integrity and literary value. Their subject may be figures from other fields of achievement, from composers to generals, from painters to financial tycoons and public figures. Some of them may also have written books and autobiographies. (One thinks of Ulysses Simpson Grant's *Personal Memoirs,* whose incisiveness may steal the biographer's thunder.) But their achievements are primarily in other forms. These biographies appear elsewhere in *The Reader's Adviser.* For biographical works in the field of authorship generally, the reader is referred to Chapter 3 in this volume. What follows will be examples of biography of writers in which the biography can be considered literature and not merely the source of information about the subject. Autobiography forms its own subgenre.

GENERAL WORKS ON LITERARY BIOGRAPHY

Aaron, Daniel, ed. *Studies in Biography. Harvard Eng. Studies* text ed. 1978 $16.00 pap. $5.95. Some good general essays on biographical problems and theories, along with individual essays on literary subjects: Boswell, Carlyle, and Emerson, among others.

Altick, Richard D. *Lives and Letters: A History of Literary Biographies in England and America.* Greenwood repr. of 1965 ed. 1979 lib. bdg. $32.50. Altick's book is a general guide to literary biographical writing, with emphasis on theories and trends. The reader's attention is also directed to Altick's *The Scholar Adventurers.*

Bowen, Catherine. *Biography: The Craft and the Calling.* Greenwood repr. of 1969 ed. 1978 lib. bdg. $22.50. The well-known biographer has written a "how-to" guide for present and future biographers.

Clifford, James L. *From Puzzles to Portraits: Problems of a Literary Biographer.* Univ. of North Carolina Pr. 1970 o.p. A pioneering book in dealing with biographical problems.

Cockshut, A. O. *Truth to Life: The Art of Biography in the Nineteenth Century.* Harcourt 1974 $7.50. Studies of six major biographies: Froude's Carlyle, Ward's Newman, Morley's Gladstone, Stanley's Arnold, Smiles' *Lives of the Engineers,* Trevelyan's Macaulay.

Edel, Leon. *Literary Biography.* Indiana Univ. Pr. 1973 o.p. Having grown out of Edel's Alexander Lectures at the University of Toronto in 1956, this is the first book to deal fully with literary biography as an art form.

————. *Stuff of Sleep and Dreams: Experiments in Literary Psychology.* Avon 1983 pap. $4.95; Harper 1982 $19.95. Edel pursues psychological and psychoanalytical readings of several writers and their careers: Joyce, Eliot, Auden, Woolf, and others.

————. *Writing Lives: Principia Biographica.* Norton 1984 $15.95. Edel here is concerned with what he calls the New Biography, which he finds in myth, archives, narrative forms, and the question of transference or the writer's emotional involvement with his subject. This is an updating of *Literary Biography*, plus six new chapters.

Ellmann, Richard. *Golden Codgers: Biographical Speculations.* Oxford 1973 $19.95 pap. $5.95. Ellmann relates problems that beset present-day biographers; essays on general literary biography and sleuthing in George Eliot, Wilde, Gide, Joyce, T. S. Eliot, and Edwardian literature.

Kendall, Paul M. *The Art of Biography.* Ed. by Robin W. Winks, *History and Historiography Ser.* Folcroft repr. of 1965 ed. lib. bdg. $40.00; Garland 1985 lib. bdg. $20.00. A study mainly of biographical theory. Kendall deals with different types of the genre at different times, among them interpretive biography, the biography of recollection, the several-volumed work, and the relationship between author and work.

Petrie, Dennis W. *Ultimately Fiction: Design in Modern American Literary Biography.* Purdue Univ. Pr. 1981 $10.95. Petrie discusses how aesthetic truth can be incorporated into historical truth in the biographical process. Essays on Edwin Millhauser's *The Life and Death of an American Writer, 1943–1954*, then on Blotner's Faulkner, Turnbull's Fitzgerald, Swanberg's Dreiser, and Edel's James.

Shaw, Thomas Shuler. *Composite Index to Profile Sketches in the New Yorker Magazine, 1925–1970.* Faxon 1972 o.p.

Strout, Cushing. *The Veracious Imagination: Essays on American History, Literature, and Biography.* Wesleyan Univ. Pr. 1981 $19.50. Essays on American history, literature, and biography as they cross each other, with some biographical theory on literary figures: Ellison, Mailer, Doctorow, and others.

Veninga, James F., ed. *The Biographer's Gift: Life, Histories, and Humanism.* Texas A & M Univ. Pr. 1983 $11.50. Discussion about the connection between humanism and biography, with some relevance to literary biography in particular.

Weintraub, Stanley. *Biography and Truth. Composition and Rhetoric Ser.* Bobbs 1967 pap. $2.50. Problems in literary biography are linked to the need to extract the truth from an individual life.

GENERAL WORKS ON LITERARY AUTOBIOGRAPHY

By its very nature, literary autobiography (as distinct from other kinds of autobiography) is far rarer than literary biography. The latter requires that a professional author research a subject and become familiar with it, but literary autobiography requires not only a writer's creative temperament but a life of sufficient interest or variety to sustain self-examination. It is, in reality, a different enterprise, in that it requires personal achievement and confession, whereas literary biography demands objectivity, a critical and historical acumen. When the "he" or "she" of biography becomes the "I" of autobiography, even the sense of historical and present time alters from something outside to an inside phenomenon.

Bruss, Elizabeth W. *Autobiographical Acts: The Changing Situation of a Literary Genre*. Johns Hopkins Univ. Pr. 1977 $15.00

Clark, Arthur. *Autobiography: Its Genesis and Phases*. Folcroft 1935 lib. bdg. $10.00

Cockshut A. O. *The Art of Autobiography in Nineteenth and Twentieth Century England*. Yale Univ. Pr. 1984 $20.00

Delaney, Paul. *British Autobiography in the Seventeenth Century*. Routledge & Kegan 1969 o.p.

Misch, Georg. *A History of Autobiography in Antiquity*. Greenwood 2 vols. repr. of 1950 ed. 1974 lib. bdg. $30.50

Olney, James. *Autobiography: Essays Theoretical and Critical*. Princeton Univ. Pr. 1980 $36.00 pap. $12.50. Recommended are essays by Louis A. Renza, "The Veto of the Imagination: A Theory of Autobiography"; Roger Rosenblatt, "Black Autobiography: Life as the Death Weapon"; Jean Starobinski, "The Style of Autobiography"; and the introductory essay by Olney, "Autobiography and the Cultural Moment: A Thematic, Historical, and Bibliographical Introduction."

――――. *Metaphors of Self: The Meaning of Autobiography*. Princeton Univ. Pr. 1972 $36.00 pap. $9.95. An important work, with application to several varieties of autobiography. Olney wrote that "the most fruitful approach to the subject of autobiography, I believe, is to consider it neither as a formal nor as an historical matter, which would be to separate it from the writer's life and his personality, but rather to see it in relation to the vital impulse to order that has always caused man to create and that, in the end, determines both the nature and the form of what he creates."

Pascal, Roy. *Design and Truth in Autobiography*. Ed. by Robin W. Wicks, *History and Historiography Ser*. Garland 1985 lib. bdg. $20.00

Spacks, Patricia M. *Imagining a Self*. Harvard Univ. Pr. 1976 $22.50

Spengemann, William C. *The Forms of Autobiography: Episodes in the History of a Literary Genre*. Yale Univ. Pr. 1980 $26.50 pap. $7.95

BIOGRAPHIES IN SERIES

The following series are of different quality and length. Some, like the Twayne group, provide sufficient biographical data, although not interpretively. Others, like the Columbia Essays and the Minnesota Pamphlets, are more critically oriented and offer only the barest biographical information. The reader should also consult the quarterly *Biography*, which offers a little of everything: brief biographies, interpretation, and bibliographies. (See also Chapter 3 in this volume.)

British Book Council. *Writers and Their Work*. Ed. by Bonamy Dobrée and Geoffrey Bullough, British Bk. Ctr. Two hundred twenty-six monographs on English-language authors. Begun in 1950, each monograph has a biocritical essay and bibliography. These are brief introductions to the writers and the biographical information is not intended to be complete.

Bucknell University Press. *Irish Writers Series*. 1971–to date. pap. ea. $1.95. Projected at 25 pamphlets. Like the British Book Council series, these intend no more than a brief introduction, with sketchy biographical information.

Columbia University Press. *Columbia Essays on Modern Writers*. 74 vols. pap. ea. $1.50. These pamphlets achieve a good balance of criticism and biography in brief format. The biographical information is standard, reaching for high points of the author's life and publications.

Gale Research Company. *Contemporary Authors.* 125 vols. Brief entries, which include biographical data, career chronology, and writings. Also has "sidelights," including reviews and commentary.

G. K. Hall. *Twayne's United States Authors Series* 348 vols.; *Twayne's English Authors Series* 288 vols.; and *Twayne's World Authors Series* 563 vols. Many of the hardbacks are eventually reprinted in paper by New College and University Press at varying prices. For some authors in all three series, the Twayne studies are the sole source of biographical information we have. In this respect, they are valuable. In terms of criticism and interpretation, they are uneven, on occasion misleading. The books tend to be of uniform length, about 50,000 to 60,000 words; for more important writers this can be restricting.

University of Minnesota. *Pamphlets on American Writers Series.* 1959–to date. 103 vols. pap. ea. $1.25. Among the editors are William Van O'Connor, Allen Tate, Robert Penn Warren, and Leonard Ungar. A series of brief pamphlets that provide critical appraisals, perfunctory biographical information, and bibliographies.

SELECTED LIST OF LITERARY BIOGRAPHIES

Bell, Quentin. *Virginia Woolf: A Biography.* Harcourt repr. of 1972 ed. 1974 pap. $9.95. The first attempt at a full biography, by her nephew.

Chute, Marchette. *Ben Jonson of Westminster.* Dutton 1953 o.p.

———. *Geoffrey Chaucer of England.* 1946. Dutton 1951 o.p.

———. *Shakespeare of London.* 1949. Dutton 1950 pap. $8.95

———. *Two Gentle Men: The Lives of George Herbert and Robert Herrick.* Dutton 1959 $6.95

Crocker, Lester G. *Jean-Jacques Rousseau.* Macmillan 2 vols. 1968–73 o.p. A sensitive, detailed psychoanalytical biography written with narrative skill and critical insight.

Day, Douglas. *Malcolm Lowry.* Oxford 1973 $22.50 1984 pap. $9.95. A balanced, judicious study of an enigmatic and difficult novelist.

Flexner, Eleanor. 1972. *Mary Wollstonecraft.* Penguin 1973 pap. o.p.

Fruman, Norman. *Coleridge: The Damaged Archangel.* Braziller 1971 $12.50

Furbank P. N. *E. M. Forster: A Life.* Harcourt 1981 pap. $8.95

Gérin, Winifred. *Charlotte Brontë: The Evolution of Genius.* Oxford 1967 $26.95 pap. $8.95

———. *Emily Brontë.* Oxford 1972 $26.95 pap. $8.95

Haight, Gordon S. *George Eliot: A Biography.* 1968. Oxford 1976 pap. $8.95. The definitive biography, which should be read along with Haight's nine-volume edition of Eliot's *Letters.*

Hildesheimer, Wolfgang. *Marbot: A Biography.* Trans. by Patricia Crampton, Braziller 1983 $16.50. The biography of a man who never existed, but who is resurrected with all the standard biographical techniques.

Holroyd, Michael. *Lytton Strachey and the Bloomsbury Group, His Work, Their Influence.* Penguin 2 vols. o.p. A masterly evocation of the entire period and group.

Johnson, Edgar. *Charles Dickens: His Tragedy and Triumph.* Viking (Richard Seaver) 1977 $19.95

Kaplan, Fred. *Thomas Carlyle: A Biography.* Cornell Univ. Pr. 1983 $35.00. Kaplan's definitive study should be read with Froude's classic biography.

Karl, Frederick R. *Joseph Conrad: The Three Lives.* Farrar 1979 $25.00 pap. $14.95. A complex weaving together of Conrad's three lives as Pole, seaman, and writer. Considered to be the definitive biography, replacing Jocelyn Baines's *Joseph Conrad,* and to be read along with the emerging edition of *Conrad's Letters* under the general editorship of Frederick R. Karl.

Millgate, Michael. *Thomas Hardy: A Biography.* Random 1982 $25.00

Mizener, Arthur. *The Saddest Story: A Biography of Ford Madox Ford.* World 1971 o.p.

Painter, George D. *Marcel Proust: A Biography.* Random 2 vols. 1978 pap. ea. $4.95

Sartre, Jean-Paul. *Baudelaire.* French & European Publications pap. $3.95; trans. by Martin Turnell, New Directions 1950 pap. $6.95

———. *Saint Genet: Actor and Martyr.* Braziller 1963 $8.50. An ingenious biographical exposition that combines narrative of a life with the argument that any revulsion we may feel toward Genet and his works results from the reader's guilt as a consequence of his complicity in the intolerance of the society that shaped Genet.

Schoenbaum, S. *William Shakespeare: A Compact Documentary Life.* Oxford 1977 $22.50 pap. $9.95. Abridged edition of *William Shakespeare: A Documentary Life.* Schoenbaum's documentary life of Shakespeare is the standard biography.

Starkie, Enid. *Arthur Rimbaud.* Greenwood repr. of 1968 ed. 1978 lib. bdg. $42.50; New Directions rev. ed. repr. 1968 pap. $9.95

———. *Baudelaire.* New Directions 1958 o.p.

———. *Flaubert.* Atheneum 2 vols. 1967–71 o.p.

Symons, A. J. *Quest for Corvo: An Experiment in Biography.* 1934. Michigan State Univ. Pr. 1955 o.p.; Penguin 1979 o.p. A biography in the form of the biographer's search for the facts about his subject—a model for later writers who used the device.

Tharp, Louise Hall. *The Appletons of Beacon Hill.* Little, Brown 1973 o.p.

———. *The Peabody Sisters of Salem.* Little, Brown 1950 o.p. Two Peabody sisters married to Nathaniel Hawthorne and Horace Mann.

Ward, Wilfred P. *Life of John Henry, Based on His Private Journals and Correspondence.* Richard West 2 vols. repr. of 1912 ed. $50.00

Weintraub, Stanley. *Private Shaw and Public Shaw: A Dual Portrait of Lawrence of Arabia and G. B. S.* Braziller 1963 o.p.

———. *Shaw: An Autobiography.* McKay (Weybright & Talley) 2 vols. 1969–70 o.p.

———. *Whistler: A Biography.* McKay (Weybright & Talley) 1974 o.p.

SELECTED LIST OF LITERARY AUTOBIOGRAPHIES

Baldwin, James. *Notes of a Native Son. Modern Class. Ser.* Bantam 1971 pap. $2.95; Beacon 1984 pap. $6.95; Doubleday $7.95. A sensitive and powerful autobiography, written at 31 by a black novelist and essayist.

Carrington, Dora. *Carrington: Letters and Extracts from Her Diaries.* Ed. by David Garnett, Holt 1971 o.p. The self-revealing writings of the child-woman camp-follower of the Bloomsbury set, who committed suicide following Lytton Strachey's death.

Dos Passos, John. *The Fourteenth Chronicle: Letters and Diaries of John Dos Passos.* Ed. by Townsend Ludington, Gambit 1973 o.p. "... an indispensable cyclorama of the belle epoque in which Dos Passos memorably flourished" (Carlos Baker).

Gorky, Maxim (Aleksei Maksimovich Peshkov). *Autobiography of Maxim Gorky*. Ed. by Isidor Schneider, Citadel Pr. repr. of 1949 ed. 1969 pap. $5.95
——. *Ilya's Childhood and Children*. Ed. by G. A. Birkett, Irvington repr. text ed. 1966 pap. $1.75
——. *My Childhood. Soviet Authors' Lib*. Beekman 1975 $11.95; ed. by Ronald Wilks, *Penguin Class. Ser*. 1966 pap. $3.95
Greene, Graham. *A Sort of Life*. 1971 Washington Square Pr. 1982 pap. $2.95
Morrell, Ottoline. *Memoirs of Lady Ottoline Morrell: A Study in Friendship, 1873–1915*. Ed. by Robert Fathorne-Hardy, Knopf 1975 o.p. "By [1914] she had made her various homes the meeting places of the outstanding young writers and artists of England and the Continent . . . . Lady Ottoline's life is a perfect picture of a pleasant, civilized life in England from the 1890's to World War II" (*LJ*). She was a friend of Leonard and Virginia Woolf, Bertrand Russell, Lord David Cecil, D. H. Lawrence, and many more of the European illustrious.
Nabokov, Vladimir. *Speak Memory: An Autobiography Revisited*. 1966. Putnam (Perigee) 1970 $7.95. A revised edition of the cosmopolitan novelist's earlier memoir *Conclusive Evidence* (o.p.).
Nicolson, Harold G. *Harold Nicolson: Diaries and Letters, 1930–1939*. Ed. by Nigel Nicolson, Atheneum 1966 o.p. A brilliant evocation, by a biographer as well as an insider, of the intellectual and cultural atmosphere of London in the last decades of the primacy of the British Empire, but now seen as marred by the editor's reticence, in sexual matters, with respect to Nicolson, his wife, and their friends.
Pritchett, Victor Sawdon. *A Cab at the Door: A Memoir*. Random 1968 $8.95 pap. $1.95. The British critic and novelist evokes his childhood and early maturity with cinematic recall.
——. *Midnight Oil*. 1972. Random (Vintage) 1973 pap. $3.95. A sequel to *A Cab at the Door*, describing the years 1921–50.
Rousseau, Jean-Jacques. *Confessions*. 1781–88. French & European Publications 1962 pap. $14.95; ed. by John M. Cohen, *Class. Ser*. Penguin 1953 pap. $5.95.
Russell, Bertrand. *Autobiography of Bertrand Russell*. Allen & Unwin 3 vols. 1967–81 ea. $17.95 *Unwin Pap. Ser*. 1978 $7.95
Woolf, Virginia. *The Diary of Virginia Woolf*. Ed. by Anne O. Bell and Andrew McNeillie, Harcourt 5 vols. vol. 2 (1978) $12.95 vol. 3 (1980) $15.95 vol. 4 (1982) $19.95 vol. 5 (1984) $19.95. Volume 1 is o.p. The *Diary*, along with the six-volume edition of the Woolf *Letters*, has proven an invaluable source of material about the writer and her artistic milieu. No study of the Bloomsbury or World War I period is complete without recourse to these 11 volumes.

CLASSIC BIOGRAPHERS: A SELECTION

BOSWELL, JAMES. 1740–1795, and JOHNSON, SAMUEL. 1709–1784

These two figures create their own category—the greatest of literary biographers and, very possibly, the greatest of subjects. Boswell's biography of Johnson was—until Leon Edel's five volumes on HENRY JAMES—the longest biography in the English language. It is the standard for all those that followed.

Boswell has had many editors. The edition by Birbeck Hill is usually considered the best because of its exhaustive annotations. The Roger Ingpen Bicentenary edition (o.p.) contains 112 illustrations and is a particularly striking one. The most considerable of all editions is the Temple Bar edition by Clement Shorter. It contains prefaces by, among others, Aleyn Lyell Reade, Gilbert K. Chesterton, A. Edward Newton, John Drinkwater, Chauncey Brewster Tinker, and R. B. Adam.

Frederick A. Pottle, Sterling Professor of English Emeritus at Yale University, is the editor of the new Yale University Press edition of *The Private Papers of James Boswell*, published by McGraw-Hill. The *Private Papers of James Boswell from Malahide Castle*, from the collection of Lt.-Col. Ralph Heywood Isham, ed. by Frederick Pottle, is now out of print, but the *Index* to the *Private Papers*, also edited by Pottle and others, is still available. Between 1925 and 1948, several caches of Boswell manuscripts, journals, and letters were discovered at Malahide and Fettercairn. These discoveries gave us first the *Tour of the Hebrides* and then the *London Journal*, which Boswell wrote in 1762 and 1763, when, at age 23, he came to London to be commissioned in the Guards. When that fell through, Boswell met and attached himself to Johnson.

Chauncey Brewster Tinker, the great Yale University teacher and scholar who made the Malahide discovery of these papers (supposedly to have been destroyed), died in 1963. Tinker was keeper of Yale's rare book collection, of which the *Private Papers* are now a part.

Second only to Boswell among contemporary writers on Dr. Johnson is his friend, Hester Lynch Piozzi, known usually as Mrs. Thrale (1741–1821). During a 20-year friendship, Johnson was a frequent guest in the home of the Thrales and accompanied them to Wales in 1774 and to France in 1775. After the death of Henry Thrale, Hester married an Italian musician, Gabriel Piozzi. She wrote verse, as well as the *Anecdotes of Dr. Johnson*. Her important diary is *Thraliana: The Diary of Mrs. Hester Lynch Thrale (Later Mrs. Piozzi) 1776–1809*, ed. by Katharine C. Balderston, now out of print. From 1784 to 1787, Mrs. Piozzi and her husband toured Europe. Her impressions of the trip are recorded in *Observations and Reflections Made in the Course of a Journey through France, Italy, and Germany*, at once a travelogue and a source book on eighteenth-century customs and mores.

Two significant works about Johnson and Boswell, now out of print, are Sir John Hawkins's *Life of Samuel Johnson* and Hesketh Pearson's *Johnson and Boswell: The Story of Their Lives*.

BOOKS BY BOSWELL

Life of Johnson Together with Boswell's Journal of a Tour to the Hebrides and Johnson's Diary of a Journey into North Wales. Ed. by Birbeck Hill, rev. & enl. by L. F. Powell, Oxford 1934–50 vols. 1–4 $189.00 vols. 5–6 2d ed. 1965 $70.00

Life of Samuel Johnson. 1791. Intro. by S. C. Roberts, Biblio Dist. (Everyman's) 2 vols. in 1 repr. of 1976 ed. 1978 $17.95; ed. by R. W. Chapman and Chauncey B. Tinker, *Oxford Stand. Authors Ser.* 1953 o.p.; intro. by B. Evans, *Modern Lib. College Ed. Ser.* Random 1964 text ed. pap. $3.95

Boswell's Life of Samuel Johnson. Ed. by Frank Brady, New Amer. Lib. (Signet Class.) abr. ed. repr. 1981 pap. $3.50

Everybody's Boswell: Being the Life of Samuel Johnson. Ed. by Frank Morley, ill. by E. H. Shepard, Ohio Univ. Pr. abr. ed. 1981 $24.95

The Private Papers of James Boswell. Ed. by Frederick A. Pottle and others, McGraw-Hill 1950–to date. The following titles have been published to date:

Boswell's London Journal, 1762–1763. Ed. by Frederick A. Pottle, pref. by Christopher Morley, 1950 pap. $6.95. Here first published from the original manuscript.

Boswell in Holland, 1763–1764. Ed. by Frederick A. Pottle, 1952 o.p. Includes his correspondence with Belle de Zuylen (Zélide).

Boswell on the Grand Tour: Germany and Switzerland, 1764. Ed. by Frederick A. Pottle, 1953 o.p.

Boswell on the Grand Tour: Italy, Corsica, and France, 1765–1766. Ed. by Frank Brady and Frederick A. Pottle, 1955 o.p.

Boswell in Search of a Wife, 1766–1769. Ed. by Frank Brady and Frederick A. Pottle, 1956 o.p. "Most entertaining since the first sensational 'London Journal.' It has every ingredient to make it popular—a succession of amorous adventures, scenes of high comedy in Boswell's most artful manner, long conversations with Samuel Johnson, and even a conventional happy ending" (*N.Y. Times*).

Boswell for the Defense, 1769–1774. Ed. by William K. Wimsatt and Frederick A. Pottle, 1962 o.p. This volume "records his marital ups and downs, his drinking bouts and occasional wenching, and his unsuccessful defense of John Reid a sheep-stealer, who, unfortunately for James's peace of mind, was executed" (*LJ*).

The Journal of a Tour to the Hebrides with Samuel Johnson. Ed. by Frederick A. Pottle, 1962 o.p. A reprint of the 1936 Viking edition by Professor Pottle and Charles H. Bennett with a new introduction, new illustrations, and a supplement based on the documents recovered since 1936.

Ominous Years, 1774–1776. Ed. by C. A. Ryskamp and Frederick A. Pottle, 1963 o.p. The eighth volume in this distinguished series covers 20 months of indecisiveness, hypochondria, self-delusions, and downright despair, with ample Johnsoniana and other records of a busy, frenetic London.

Correspondence of James Boswell and John Johnston of Grange. Ed. by Ralph S. Walker, 1966 o.p. This work, which covers the years 1759–86, is Volume 1 of the planned 40-volume series of the *Private Papers of James Boswell*, research edition, "designed chiefly for scholars and libraries." John Johnston was "Boswell's alter ego, his 'constant resort in moments of distress' " (*LJ*).

Boswell in Extremes, 1776–1778. Ed. by Charles M. Weis and Frederick A. Pottle, 1970 o.p.

The Portable Johnson and Boswell. Ed. by Louis Kronenberger, *Viking Portable Lib.* 1947 o.p. Contains substantial selections from the *Life* and from *Journal of a Tour to the Hebrides.*

The Journal of a Tour to Corsica and Memoirs of Pascal Paoli. Folcroft repr. of 1951 ed. 1975 o.p.

Journal of a Tour to the Hebrides. 1773. Ed. by Lawrence F. Powell, Biblio Dist. (Everyman's) repr. of 1958 ed. 1979 $9.95; *Oxford Stand. Authors Ser.* 1930 pap. $6.95.

BOOKS BY JOHNSON

Works of Samuel Johnson. Ed. by Francis P. Walesby, AMS Pr. 11 vols. repr. of 1825 ed. ea. $32.50 set $357.50.

Johnson: Selected Writings. Ed. by R. T. Davies, Northwestern Univ. Pr. 1965 $18.95; ed. by Patrick Cruttwell, Penguin 1982 pap. $5.95; Scholars' Facsimiles 1977 $30.00

Selected Letters of Samuel Johnson. Intro. by R. W. Chapman, AMS Pr. repr. 1925 $23.00

Dr. Johnson: His Life in Letters. Ed. by David Littlejohn, Prentice-Hall 1965 o.p.

A Johnson Reader. Ed. by Edward L. McAdam, Jr., and George Milne, Pantheon 1964 o.p.

The Critical Opinions of Samuel Johnson. Comp. by Joseph Epes Brown, Russell repr. of 1926 ed. 1961 $12.50

Selected Essays from the Rambler, Adventurer and Idler. Ed. by Walter J. Bate, Yale Univ. Pr. *Works of Samuel Johnson Ser.* 1968 $45.00 pap. $7.95

The Poems of Samuel Johnson. Ed. by David N. Smith and Edward L. McAdam, rev. by J. D. Fleeman, *Oxford Eng. Texts Ser.* 2d ed. 1974 $37.95. The first complete edition of the poems, with valuable notes.

Samuel Johnson: The Complete English Poems. Ed. by J. D. Fleeman, *Eng. Poets Ser.* Yale Univ. Pr. 1982 text ed. $22.00 pap. $7.95

Rasselas, Poems and Selected Prose. Ed. by Bertrand H. Bronson, *Rinehart Ed.* Holt 3d ed. 1971 pap. text ed. $13.95

Dictionary of the English Language: In Which the Words Are Deduced from Their Originals and Illustrated in Their Different Significations by Examples from the Best Writers. Adler's 2 vols. repr. of 1755 ed. 1968 $275.00; AMS Pr. 2 vols. repr. of 1755 ed. $100.00; pref. by Robert Burchfield, Ayer repr. of 1755 ed. 1980 $95.00; International Bk. Ctr. 2 vols. 1978 $220.00

Yale Edition of the Works of Samuel Johnson. 1958–to date. 7 vols. The following titles have been published:

Diaries, Prayers and Annals. Ed. by Edward L. McAdam, Jr., 1958 $45.00

Idler and the Adventurer. Ed. by Walter J. Bate, 1963 $50.00

Poems. Ed. by Edward L. McAdam, Jr., and George Milne, 1965 $45.00

Johnson on Shakespeare. Ed. by Arthur Sherbo, intro. by Bertrand H. Bronson; 2 vols. 1968 $80.00

Selected Essays from the Rambler, Adventurer and Idler. Ed. by Walter J. Bate, 1968 $45.00 pap. $7.95

The Rambler. Ed. by Walter J. Bate and Albrecht Strauss, 3 vols. 1969 $85.00

Journey to the Western Islands of Scotland. Ed. by Mary Lascelles, 1971 $30.00

Rasselas. Ed. by Warren Fleischauer, Barron 1977 text ed. $3.50

The History of Rasselas: Prince of Abyssinia. 1759. Folcroft repr. of 1884 ed. 1976 $50.00; ed. by Gwin J. Kolb, *Crofts Class. Ser.* Harlan Davidson 1962 text ed. pap. $3.75; ed. by J. P. Hardy, Oxford 1968 pap. $6.95; ed. by D. J. Enright, *Penguin Eng. Lib. Ser.* 1977 pap. $3.95

The Rambler. 1750–52. Ed. by S. C. Roberts, Dutton (Everyman's) o.p.

A Journey to the Western Islands of Scotland (and Boswell's *Journal of a Tour to the Hebrides*). Ed. by James Boswell, intro. by Peter Levi, Penguin 1984 pap. $6.95

Life of Johnson Together with Boswell's Journal of a Tour to the Hebrides and Johnson's Diary of a Journey into North Wales. Ed. by G. B. Hill, rev. & enl. by Lawrence F. Powell, Oxford 1934–50 vols. 1–4 $189.00 vols. 5–6 2d ed. 1965 $70.00

BOOKS ABOUT BOSWELL AND JOHNSON

Alkon, Paul K. *Samuel Johnson and Moral Discipline.* Northwestern Univ. Pr. 1967 $12.95. A study of the moral essays that Johnson wrote in the 1750s.

Bate, Walter J. *The Achievement of Samuel Johnson.* Univ. of Chicago Pr. (Phoenix Bks.) 1978 pap. $4.95
Brady, Frank. *James Boswell: The Later Years, 1769–1795.* McGraw-Hill 1984 $24.95
Halliday, F. E. *Dr. Johnson and His World.* Viking 1968 o.p. A biography with more than 150 portraits, drawings, engravings, and photographs relating to Dr. Johnson's life.
Hilles, Frederick W., ed. *New Light on Dr. Johnson: Essays on the Occasion of His 250th Birthday.* Shoe String (Archon) repr. of 1959 ed. 1967 o.p.
Krutch, Joseph W. *Samuel Johnson.* Scholarly repr. 1980 o.p.
Pottle, Frederick A. *James Boswell: The Earlier Years, 1740–1769.* McGraw-Hill 2d ed. 1984 $24.95
Quinlan, Maurice J. *Samuel Johnson: A Layman's Religion.* Univ. of Wisconsin Pr. 1964 $20.00. "The first book since 1850 to treat the aspects of Johnson's religious beliefs . . . . A fascinating examination" (*LJ*).
Sachs, Arieh. *Passionate Intelligence: Imagination and Reason in the Work of Samuel Johnson.* Johns Hopkins Univ. Pr. 1967 o.p.
Turberville, Arthur S., ed. *Johnson's England: An Account of the Life and Manners of His Age.* Oxford 2 vols. 1933 o.p.

CECIL, LORD DAVID. 1902–

A member of one of the oldest and most aristocratic families and Goldsmith Professor of English literature at Oxford University, Lord David Cecil writes mainly of literary figures of the eighteenth and nineteenth centuries.

BOOKS BY CECIL

The Stricken Deer, or The Life of Cowper. Richard West repr. of 1929 ed. $20.00
William Cowper. Folcroft repr. of 1932 ed. $10.00
Sir Walter Scott. Scholarly repr. of 1933 ed. 1971 $39.00
Jane Austen. Arden Lib. repr. of 1935 ed. 1978 lib. bdg. $15.00; Folcroft repr. of 1935 ed. lib. bdg. $10.00
Hardy the Novelist. Appel repr. of 1946 ed. o.p.
Melbourne. Power and Personality Ser. Crown (Harmony) 1979 pap. $6.95; Greenwood repr. of 1954 ed. 1971 lib. bdg. $22.50
Walter Pater: Scholar Artist. Folcroft 1955 lib. bdg. $10.00
Victorian Novelists. 1958. *Midway Repr. Ser.* Univ. of Chicago Pr. 1975 pap. $11.50
Max: A Biography of Max Beerbohm. 1965. Atheneum 1985 pap. $12.95
Visionary and Dreamer: Two Poetic Painters, Samuel Palmer and Edward Burne Jones. 1969. *Bollingen Ser.* Princeton Univ. Pr. 1970 $46.00 pap. $14.50
The Cecils of Hatfield House: An English Ruling Family. Houghton Mifflin 1973 $15.00

EDEL, (JOSEPH) LEON. 1907–

Edel has been Henry James Professor of English and American Literature at New York Universtiy and is now Citizen Professor of English Emeritus at the University of Hawaii. His *Henry James* has been considered among the finest biographies by and about an American author. Two of the volumes won the National Book Award and the Pulitzer Prize in biography. Edel has also edited James's plays and short fiction, as well as a four-volume edition of James's letters. For Edel's other contributions to biography, see his listing earlier in this chapter, under "General Works on Literary Biography." Also notable is his group biography of Bloomsbury figures in *A House of Lions*. Edel is currently editing the journals of Edmund Wilson and preparing his own autobiography.

BOOKS BY EDEL

Henry James. 1953–72. Avon 5 vols. 1978 pap. ea. $2.95

(and Edward K. Brown). *Willa Cather.* Knopf 1953 o.p. A biography completed by Edel after the death of Brown.

Henry David Thoreau. Pamphlets on Amer. Writers Ser. Univ. of Minnesota Pr. 1970 pap. $1.25

ELLMANN, RICHARD. 1918–

Richard Ellmann, American teacher and scholar, has been Goldsmith Professor of English at New College, Oxford University, since 1968. His research and writing have been primarily identified with turn-of-the-century Irish writers, especially JOYCE, YEATS, and WILDE, on whose biography he is currently working. His *James Joyce* received the National Book Award for biography. In *Ulysses on the Liffey*, a biographical-critical examination of Joyce's masterwork, the novel "is seen to work as the most complex fictional structure of all time, but, through that, it is seen to work also as a great testament to human love" (Anthony Burgess). Of *Yeats* Sean O'Faolain has said: "This is the first lucid interpretation we have had of Yeats's literary pilgrimage and poetic metabolisms. It is a masterly book, thoroughly documented, sensitive and sure-footed." Because Yeats attained literary eminence early in life and kept it so long, he became a focal center for disciples and rebels. In *Eminent Domain*, Ellmann examines the complicated interactions among selected writers who responded literarily to them. *Golden Codgers* is a volume of biographical-critical speculative essays on writers from George Eliot to T. S. Eliot.

With Ellsworth Mason, Ellmann edited *The Critical Writing of James Joyce*. He has also edited Volume 2 of the *Letters of James Joyce* and Stanislaus Joyce's *My Brother's Keeper: James Joyce's Early Years* (1958). His Wilde editions include *Oscar Wilde: A Collection of Critical Essays* and *The Artist as Critic: Critical Writings of Oscar Wilde*.

BOOKS BY ELLMANN

Yeats: The Man and the Masks. 1948. *Norton Lib.* 1978 pap. $6.95

Identity of Yeats. 1954. Oxford 2d ed. 1964 $22.50 pap. $5.95

James Joyce. 1959. Oxford 1982 pap. $14.95

Eminent Domain: Yeats among Wilde, Joyce, Eliot and Auden. Oxford 1967 o.p.

Ulysses on the Liffey. Oxford 1972 pap. $7.95

Golden Codgers: Biographical Speculations. Oxford 1973 $19.95 pap. $5.95

FROUDE, JAMES ANTHONY. 1818–1894

As friend, disciple, and literary executor of CARLYLE, Froude wrote a biography that has influenced all subsequent thought about the Victorian sage. Froude was also a theologian, historian, and novelist (*Nemesis of Faith*).

BOOKS BY FROUDE

Thomas Carlyle: A History of His Life in London 1834–1881. Richard West 2 vols. repr. of 1884 ed. $65.00; Scholarly 2 vols. repr. of 1881 ed. 1971 $59.00
Thomas Carlyle: The Making of an Historian and the Theory of the Hero in History. Amer. Class. College Pr. 2 vols. 1984 $176.50

GASKELL, MRS. ELIZABETH (CLEGHORN STEVENSON). 1810–1865

[SEE Chapter 11 in this volume.]

HARRIS, FRANK (JAMES THOMAS). 1856–1931

A controversial figure whose autobiographical writings overshadowed his efforts at biography. Of interest in the latter category are the following titles.

BOOKS BY HARRIS

The Man Shakespeare. Horizon Pr. repr. of 1909 ed. 1969 o.p.
Contemporary Portraits. 1915–23. Richard West 1973 $25.00
Oscar Wilde: His Life and Confessions. 1916. Greenwood repr. of 1959 ed. 1978 lib. bdg. $32.50; intro. by Frank MacShane and George Bernard Shaw, Horizon Pr. 1983 pap. $12.95
My Life and Loves. 1925. Ed. by John F. Gallagher, Grove 1963 pap. $4.95
Latest Contemporary Portraits. 1927. *Eng. Literary Reference Ser.* Johnson Repr. repr. of 1927 ed. 1969 $22.00; Kraus repr. of 1927 ed. $27.00

LOCKHART, JOHN GIBSON. 1794–1854

Lockhart's great work, *Memoirs of the Life of Sir Walter Scott,* is often considered next to Boswell's *Johnson* the greatest biography in English. He was SCOTT's son-in-law, editor of the prestigious *Quarterly Review* from 1825 to 1853, and the author of several novels. Lockhart's sympathy for Scott had one major disadvantage, however; he tended to whitewash or ignore the novelist's faults, something Boswell never did with Johnson.

BOOKS BY LOCKHART

Life of Robert Burns. 1828. Ed. by William S. Douglas, AMS Pr. repr. of 1892 ed. $20.00; Biblio Dist. (Everyman's) 1976 $9.95
The Life of Napoleon Bonaparte. Dutton (Everyman's) repr. of 1829 ed. o.p.
Life of Sir Walter Scott. 1837–38. AMS Pr. 10 vols. repr. of 1902 ed. 1983 $345.00; Biblio Dist. (Everyman's) repr. of 1906 ed. 1969 $8.95

BOOK ABOUT LOCKHART

Lang, Andrew. *Life and Letters of John Gibson Lockhart.* AMS Pr. 2 vols. repr. of 1897 ed. 1970. $49.50.

MAUROIS, ANDRE (pseud. of Émile Herzog). 1885–1967

Although Maurois' biographies are no longer completely reliable, he did bring a professionalism to his work, and in some of them he blended psychological insight, critical acumen, and sensitivity to complicated issues. Tremendously prolific, he was elected, in 1938, to the French Academy.

BOOKS BY MAUROIS

Ariel: The Life of Shelley. 1924. Trans. by Ella Darcy, Ungar 1957 o.p.
Aspects of Biography. 1929. Arden Lib. repr. of 1929 ed. 1977 lib. bdg. $20.00
Byron. 1930. Trans. by Hamish Miles, Arden Lib. repr. of 1930 ed. 1979 lib. bdg.
$22.50
Chateaubriand: Poet, Statesman, Lover. 1938. Trans. by Vera Fraser, Greenwood repr.
of 1938 ed. o.p.
Voltaire. 1952. Trans. by Hamish Miles, Richard West repr. of 1978 ed. lib. bdg.
$25.00
Cecil Rhodes. Shoe String (Archon) repr. of 1953 ed. 1968 o.p.
Lelia: The Life of George Sand. 1953. Trans. by Gerard Manley Hopkins, Penguin 1977
pap. $5.95
Alexandre Dumas. Trans. by Jack P. White, *Great Lives in Brief* Knopf 1955 o.p.
Titans: A Three-Generation Biography of the Dumas. Trans. by Gerard Manley Hop-
kins, Greenwood repr. of 1958 ed. 1971 lib. bdg. $27.50
Life of Sir Alexander Fleming: Discoverer of Penicillin. Trans. by Gerard Manley Hop-
kins, Dutton 1959 o.p.
Napoleon. Trans. by D. J. S. Thomson, Viking 1964 o.p.
Prometheus: The Life of Balzac. Carroll & Graf 1983 $11.95
Dickens. Richard West repr. of 1934 ed. $12.50
Points of View: From Kipling to Graham Greene. Trans. by Georges Lemaitre, Ungar
1968 o.p.

BOOK ABOUT MAUROIS

Lemaitre, Georges. *Maurois: The Writer and His Work.* Ungar rev. ed. 1968 o.p.

PEARSON, HESKETH. 1887–1964

Pearson's biographies are witty, well written, and trenchant, although
rarely profound or exhaustive.

BOOKS BY PEARSON

Doctor Darwin. 1930. Folcroft repr. of 1949 ed. lib. bdg. $35.00. A biography of Eras-
mus Darwin, early psychologist, physician, poet, and grandfather of the evolu-
tionist Charles Darwin.
Fool of Love: The Life of William Hazlitt. Scholarly repr. of 1934 ed. o.p.
The Smith of Smiths: Being the Life, Wit and Humor of Sydney Smith. Folcroft repr. of
1934 ed. lib. bdg. $40.00
Gilbert and Sullivan. Select Bibliographies Repr. Ser. Ayer repr. of 1935 ed. $19.00
The Last Actor-Managers. Bks. for Libraries 1950 o.p.
George Bernard Shaw: His Life and Personality. Atheneum 1963 o.p.
Beerbohm Tree: His Life and Laughter. Greenwood repr. of 1956 ed. 1971 o.p.
Johnson and Boswell: The Story of Their Lives. Greenwood repr. of 1959 ed. 1972 o.p.

QUENNELL, PETER (COURTNEY). 1905–

Peter Quennell has had a long and distinguished career as a biographer,
critic, and editor (of the *Cornhill Magazine* and *History Today*). He is perhaps best known for his work on BYRON and POPE.

BOOKS BY QUENNELL

Baudelaire and the Symbolists. Essay and General Lit. Index Repr. Ser. Associated Faculty Pr. repr. of 1929 ed. 1970 $19.50; *Essay Index Repr. Ser.* Ayer repr. of 1954 ed. $16.00

Byron: The Years of Fame. 1936. Shoe String (Archon) rev. ed. 1967 o.p.

Byron in Italy. Bks. for Libraries repr. of 1941 ed. 1973 o.p.

Four Portraits: Studies in the Eighteenth Century (The Profane Virtues: Four Studies of the Eighteenth Century). 1945. Arden Lib. repr. of 1946 ed. lib. bdg. $20.00

John Ruskin: The Portrait of a Prophet. British Bk. Ctr. pap. $1.95; Richard West repr. of 1949 ed. 1973 $35.00

Singular Preference: Portraits and Essays. Essay and General Lit. Index Repr. Ser. Associated Faculty Pr. repr. of 1953 ed. 1971 o.p.

Alexander Pope: The Education of Genius, 1688–1728. 1968. Stein & Day repr. 1970 pap. $6.95

Romantic England. Macmillan 1970 $11.95

Casanova in London. Stein & Day 1971 $7.95

Samuel Johnson: His Friends and Enemies. McGraw-Hill 1973 $12.95

STANLEY, ARTHUR PENRHYN. 1815–1881

Although Arthur Penrhyn Stanley made his name as a theologian—he was dean of Westminster from 1864 until his death—he was also noted as the biographer of Dr. Thomas Arnold, perhaps England's most famous schoolmaster and father of MATTHEW ARNOLD. Stanley was a pupil of Dr. Arnold's at Rugby, at the time he was trying to change the face of English public (private) education.

BOOKS BY STANLEY

The Life of Thomas Arnold, D.D., Head-Master of Rugby. Murray repr. of 1844 ed. 1904 o.p.

The Life and Correspondence of Thomas Arnold. AMS Pr. 2 vols. repr. of 1845 ed. $72.50

TREVELYAN, GEORGE OTTO. 1838–1928

Historian, politician, and member of Parliament, Trevelyan wrote his biography of Lord Macaulay from the inside, as his nephew. Like other Victorian biographers of the first rank, Trevelyan used his biography of his uncle as a way of clarifying his own political positions.

BOOK BY TREVELYAN

Life and Letters of Lord Macaulay by His Nephew. Richard West repr. of 1893 ed. lib. bdg. 1978 $40.00

CLASSIC AUTOBIOGRAPHERS: A SELECTION

ADAMS, HENRY (BROOKS). 1838–1918

The Education of Henry Adams might be called the story of an education and the recovery from it, although the writer felt that he never recovered.

The reader should contrast the earlier work, *Mont-Saint-Michel and Chartres* (privately printed 1904, published 1913), a study of thirteenth-century unity, with the *Education*, a study of twentieth-century multiplicity. It is the multiplicity of modern life, says Adams, that makes education so destructive.

Henry Adams wrote two novels, *Esther* (1884, o.p.) and the earlier cutting satire on the U.S. government, *Democracy: An American Novel* (1880). In 1905, President THEODORE ROOSEVELT (see Vol. 3) called *Democracy* "that novel which made a great furor among the educated incompetents and the pessimists generally. . . . It had a superficial and rotten cleverness, but it was essentially false, essentially mean and base, and it is amusing to read it now and see how completely events have given it the lie." (See Chapter 7 of Volume 3 for the main listing for Henry Adams.)

BOOKS BY ADAMS

Letters of Henry Adams. Ed. by Worthington C. Ford, Kraus 2 vols. repr. 1930 o.p.
A Cycle of Adams Letters, 1861–1865. Ed. by Worthington C. Ford, Kraus 2 vols. in 1 repr. of 1920 ed. o.p. A collection of letters between Adams and his family.
Henry Adams and His Friends: A Collection of His Unpublished Letters. Ed. by Harold D. Cater, Octagon repr. 1970 lib. bdg. $42.50. A collection of 650 unpublished letters to many different people, edited with a biographical and interpretive introduction by Harold Dean Cater.
The Education of Henry Adams. 1906. Ed. by Ernest Samuels, Houghton Mifflin (Riv. Eds.) 1973 pap. $7.95

BOOKS ABOUT ADAMS

Samuels, Ernest. *Henry Adams.* Harvard Univ. Pr. 4 vols. 1948–64 o.p.
Stevenson, Elizabeth. *Henry Adams: A Biography.* Octagon repr. 1977 lib. bdg. $31.50. "The fullest, finest account yet written of one of the fullest, finest Americans" (Paul Engle). It received the Bancroft Prize in 1956.

CASANOVA (or Casanova de Seingalt, Giovanni Jacopo [or Giacomo]). 1725–1798

Casanova's *Memoirs*, written in French, create an absorbing portrait of an eighteenth-century Italian—a shallow, amoral and vital man, whose private life, as he records it, was a succession of amorous adventures. His public life, also not without intrigue, was spent in the service of police, kings, and popes. At his death, Casanova was a librarian for Count Waldstein in Bohemia.

The *Memoirs* has an interesting bibliographic history. The original manuscript is owned by the Brockhaus Company in Wiesbaden, which bought it in 1820 from Carlo Angiolini, Casanova's grandnephew. The first edition in 12 volumes (an expurgated edition) was published in Germany by Brockhaus from 1822 to 1828, according to the *N.Y. Times.* "The English translation by Machen (1794, o.p.) first appeared in London in 1894 in 12 volumes. It was based on the Laforgue edition in French of 1826, generally considered the most satisfactory and complete and the one on which most [editions in English until the Trask translation] have been based. The London 1894 edition was reprinted in the U.S. in 1920. It came out again in New York in 1925 under the Aventuros imprint with the addition of [an Arthur] Symons introduction. This reappeared, privately printed, in 1930 with the 12 volumes in six" (*LJ*). The Putnam hardcover edition of Machen's translation (6 vols. 1959–61 o.p.) is reproduced by Dover in three volumes. Scholars now agree that the edition prepared by Jean Laforgue (from which Machen translated) is somewhat "truncated, bowdlerized and embellished" (*LJ*). Brockhaus, in collaboration with Plon of Paris, therefore published the original, unexpurgated manuscript in Europe, 1960–62, from which Willard Trask has made his translation. Harcourt has published the original 12 volumes in six double volumes translated by Trask. For his translation of Volumes 1 and 2, Willard Trask received the 1967 National Book Award "in recognition of the lucidity, tact and *joie de vivre* with which he has rendered into contemporary English the first two volumes of the 'History of My Life.' While remaining loyal to both the tempo and spirit of the original French, Mr. Trask has written a version in an English fully contemporary yet remarkably Italian in sensibility. With admirable restraint and refinement, he has conveyed the zest and sensuous delight of the original." The complicated story of the first posthumous publication of the work and subsequent editions in German, French, English and other languages is told in Trask's introduction to Volumes 1 and 2.

BOOKS BY CASANOVA

Memoirs. Ed. by Leonard L. Levinson, Macmillan (Collier Bks.) o.p.
Giacomo Casanova: History of My Life. Trans. with an intro. by Willard Trask, Harcourt 12 vols. 1966–71 ea. $10.00

BOOK ABOUT CASANOVA

Ellis, Havelock. *Casanova: An Appreciation*. Branden o.p.

CHESTERFIELD (PHILIP DORMER STANHOPE), 4th Earl of. 1694–1773

An English statesman, celebrated wit and conversationalist, Lord Chesterfield achieved lasting fame through his letters to his natural son and to his adopted godson. The brilliant *Letters to His Son*, first published by his widow in 1774, was written to acquaint the boy with, and encourage him to acquire, the manners and standards of a man of the world. The letters are "shrewd and exquisitely phrased observations, witty, elegant, cynical." The similar *Letters to His Godson* (o.p.), of which 236 are extant, was not published until 1890. Chesterfield was an intimate of POPE and SWIFT and corresponded with VOLTAIRE (see Vol. 2). As the patron of Samuel Johnson, he provoked Johnson's famous letter of rebuke after his belated praise of Johnson's *Dictionary*, which he had ignored in prospectus since 1747.

BOOKS BY CHESTERFIELD

Letters. Ed. by Bonamy Dobrée, AMS Pr. 6 vols. repr. of 1932 ed. o.p.
Letters to His Son. 1774. Dutton (Everyman's) o.p.

BOOK ABOUT CHESTERFIELD

Shellabarger, Samuel. *Lord Chesterfield and His World*. Biblo & Tannen repr. of 1951 ed. 1971 $15.00

EVELYN, JOHN. 1620–1706

As the diary of a devout and honorable gentleman of scholarly attainment and exemplary character, Evelyn's diary is in sharp contrast to that of his friend and contemporary Pepys. Evelyn was far more self-righteous and less likable than Pepys. His journals cover the eras of the Civil War, the Commonwealth, and the reign of Charles II, a period of 56 years. "It has been Evelyn's misfortune always to be thought of with Pepys," writes D. W. Brogan in the *N.Y. Times*, when the real parallel is "not with Pepys but with such French contemporaries as Madame de Sevigne and the Duc de Saint-Simon . . . . Except that they were friends, both Fellows of the Royal Society, contemporary witnesses, Evelyn and Pepys are not really to be linked together. This scholarly country gentleman, so much more a high Anglican than a passionate royalist, is very different from Pepys, the climbing bureaucrat of bourgeois Dissenting origin who had to swim for his life in the turbulent seas of the Restoration. So readers of this magnificent (and highly readable) edition [by E. S. de Beer] must begin by not expecting the same kind of entertainment they get from Pepys."

BOOK BY EVELYN

The Diary of John Evelyn. Ed. by William Bray, pref. by George W. Russell, Richard West 2 vols. repr. of 1907 ed. $40.00; ed. by William Bray, Biblio Dist. (Everyman's) 2 vols. in 1 repr. of 1952 ed. 1973 $9.95; ed. by John Bowle, Oxford 1983 $37.50

GIDE, ANDRE (PAUL GUILLAUME). 1869–1951. (NOBEL PRIZE 1947)

Gide was awarded the Nobel Prize in 1947 for the "extensive and artistically important authorship in which he exposed the problems and conditions of mankind." In that year, too, the first volume of his *Journals* was published in English.

BOOKS BY GIDE

Journals. Trans. with an intro. by Justin O'Brien, 1947–51. Random (Vintage) 2 vols. abr. ed. 1956 pap. vol. 1 $1.65 vol. 2 $1.95. Originally published by Knopf in four volumes.

So Be It, or The Chips Are Down. Trans. with an intro. by Justin O'Brien, Knopf 1959 $3.95. Informal journal of random reflections.

The Correspondence of André Gide and Edmund Gosse, 1904–1928. Ed. by Linette F. Brugmans, *New York Univ. Studies in Romance Languages and Lit.* Greenwood repr. of 1959 ed. 1977 lib. bdg. $22.50. Although temperamentally different and separated by age and by language, the English critic Gosse shared with Gide a profound regard for French literature.

Self-Portraits: The Gide-Valery Letters. Ed. by Robert Mallet, trans. by June Guieharnaud, Univ. of Chicago Pr. 1966 o.p.

MONTAGU, LADY MARY WORTLEY. 1689–1762

Lady Mary, one of the first of independent Western women, was noted in the eighteenth century as a wit, as a poet, and for her sparkling letters. Misunderstood in her own time and later, she quarreled with her friends POPE and SWIFT and was bitterly attacked by them. She finally left her husband and country to live in Italy (1739–61) and from there wrote letters to her daughter, the Countess of Bute. She continued, however, to write to her husband, and they apparently remained on friendly, if only epistolary, terms. Halsband's scholarly and definitive biography (see below) contains a series of hitherto unpublished love letters from her to Count Algarotti, the eminent Italian man of letters and friend of VOLTAIRE (see Vol. 2). Of *The Complete Letters, Vol. 3, SR* said: "It is exemplary in every respect: the text has been meticulously prepared, the notes are helpful yet tactfully concise, the index and supplementary apparatus most useful."

BOOKS BY MONTAGU

The Complete Letters. Ed. by Robert Halsband, Oxford 3 vols. 1965–67 o.p.
Letters and Works of Lady Mary Wortley Montagu. Ed. by Lord Wharncliffe, AMS Pr. 2 vols. repr. of 1861 ed. $55.00
Selected Letters. Ed. by Robert Halsband, St. Martin's 1971 o.p.
Letters from the Levant: During the Embassy to Constantinople, 1716–18. Eastern Europe Collection Ser. Ayer repr. of 1838 ed. 1970 $22.00

BOOK ABOUT MONTAGU

Halsband, Robert. *Life of Lady Mary Wortley Montagu.* Oxford 1956 $34.95

PEPYS, SAMUEL. 1633–1703

Pepys's candid and endlessly entertaining anecdotal diary was written in cipher and remained unreadable for more than a century after his death. Lord Grenville is credited with discovery of the key to the cipher. He gave the key to the Reverend John Smith, then a college undergraduate, who took three years to transcribe the manuscript. The Smith transcription was edited by Lord Braybrooke and first published in 1825. Braybrooke regarded the *Diary* of value only as a record of public events and expurgated the personal material as much as possible. The Braybrooke text, therefore, is not complete. A less abridged edition by the Reverend Mynors Bright appeared in 1875–79 (o.p.). The first purportedly complete and unabridged edition was by Henry B. Wheatley, based on Bright's transcription and first published in 10 volumes in the Bohn Library, 1893–1905, the ninth volume being Pepysiana. This edition was reissued as a subscription edition in 18 volumes, again on India paper in 3 volumes by Harcourt (o.p.), and was eventually published in 2 volumes by Random House, but without the Braybrooke notes.

Pepys was not a man of letters. He served 28 years in the Admiralty Department after the Restoration of the Stuarts in 1660. He was twice Secretary of the Admiralty and the foremost authority on naval matters in his time. He portrays himself candidly in his *Diary* as a "man of wide interests and varied affairs: an inveterate playgoer and a minor patron of the arts, a conscientious husband and householder, a responsible public official, and a friend (sometimes a self-acknowledged flatterer) of the great and powerful." His personal foibles and amorous adventures (in spite of his "conscientious" status as husband) have lent his journals a fascination that appears to be perennial.

The *Diary* covers only nine and one-half years and was discontinued because of failing eyesight. Pepys's later life has been studied by J. R. Tanner in his edition of *The Private Correspondence of Samuel Pepys, 1697–1703* (o.p.), *Further Correspondence of Samuel Pepys, 1662–1679* (o.p.), and *Mr. Pepys: An Introduction to His Diary with a Sketch of His Later Life.* Pepys's second diary, a journal of a trip to Tangier, 1683–84, is contained in *The Letters and Second Diary of Samuel Pepys* (o.p.). Two more diaries, dealing with the period of the so-called Popish plot, were discovered in 1935 at Magdalene College, Cambridge University, by Arthur Bryant and Francis Turner.

BOOKS BY PEPYS

The Diary of Samuel Pepys, 1660–1669. Ed. by Robert Latham and William Matthews, Univ. of California Pr. 11 vols. 1970–1983 o.p. Vols. 1–8 each represent the unabridged and unexpurgated diary of one year; Vol. 9 covers January 1668 through May 1669. The final volumes are still in print and are a companion (commentary) and an index to the previous volumes (each of which has its own index). This is the definitive edition, scrupulous in its textual readings and unexpurgated. Earlier editions include the following, each under the same title, *Diary, 1660–1669:*
    Diary. Biblio Dist. (Everyman's) 3 vols. repr. of 1953 ed. 1968–81 ea. $9.95
    Everybody's Pepys: The Diary of Samuel Pepys, 1660–1669. Ed. by O. F. Morshead, British Bk. Ctr. text ed. $16.50
    Diary of Samuel Pepys. Ed. by Henry B. Wheatley, AMS Pr. 10 vols. repr. of 1899 ed. lib. bdg. $375.00; ed. by E. H. Shepard, Peter Smith 1960 $16.25
The Illustrated Pepys: Extracts from the Diary. Ed. by Robert Latham, Univ. of California Pr. 1978 $15.95
The Letters of Samuel Pepys and His Family Circle. Ed. by H. T. Heath, Oxford 1955 o.p.
Memoirs of the Royal Navy. Haskell repr. of 1906 ed. 1969 o.p.

BOOKS ABOUT PEPYS

Barber, Richard. *Samuel Pepys Esq.* Univ. of California Pr. 1970 $16.95
Bradford, Gamaliel. *Soul of Samuel Pepys.* Associated Faculty Pr. repr. of 1924 ed. 1969 $19.50
Hunt, Percival. *Samuel Pepys in the Diary.* Greenwood repr. of 1958 ed. 1978 lib. bdg. $19.00
Lee, Sidney. *Pepys and Shakespeare.* Folcroft repr. of 1906 ed. 1974 lib. bdg. $8.50
Marburg, Clara. *Mister Pepys and Mr. Evelyn.* Folcroft repr. of 1935 ed. o.p.
McAfee, Helen. *Pepys on the Restoration Stage.* Blom 1816 o.p.
Ponsonby, Arthur. *Samuel Pepys.* Arden Lib. repr. of 1928 ed. 1982 lib. bdg. $25.00; Associated Faculty Pr. repr. of 1928 ed. 1971 $21.00; *Select Bibliographies Repr. Ser.* Ayer repr. of 1928 ed. $22.00; Folcroft 1973 lib. bdg. $20.00; Telegraph Bks. repr. of 1928 ed. 1980 lib. bdg. $20.00
Tanner, Joseph R. *Samuel Pepys and the Royal Navy.* Folcroft repr. of 1920 ed. 1974 lib. bdg. $16.50; *Eng. Lit. Ser.* Haskell repr. of 1920 ed. 1971 lib. bdg. $44.95
Taylor, Ivan E. *Samuel Pepys. Twayne's Eng. Authors Ser.* 1967 o.p.

SASSOON, SIEGFRIED (LORRAINE). 1886–1967

Siegfried Sassoon, son of Sir Alfred Sassoon of a remarkable and wealthy family of Sephardic Jews, was perhaps of recent years the third most famous of the British World War I poets, after RUPERT BROOKE, the romantic, and WILFRED OWEN, whose disillusioned poems Sassoon collected and published after Owen's death.

BOOK BY SASSOON

Memoirs of an Infantry Officer. Faber 1965 pap. $6.95; Macmillan (Collier Bks.) 1969 pap. $1.50

SITWELL, SIR OSBERT, 5th Bart. 1892–1969

The Sitwell brothers and their sister, Edith, were all literary. Their essays are rich in discussions of archaeology, architecture, painting, music, and the reverie evoked by names and places. Their culture, charm, and urbanity are recorded in Sir Osbert's reminiscences of their patrician family and estate. Begun in *Left Hand, Right Hand* (1944), they are continued in *The Scarlet Tree* (1946), which won the London Times Award in 1948. *Great Morning!* (1947) is the third volume of his autobiography. The fourth volume, *Laughter in the Next Room* (1948), covers the period from 1918 to the death of Sir George Sitwell, their remarkable and eccentric father, in 1944. It is notable for its portraits of extraordinary people in the arts whom Sir Osbert encountered in his career as a writer. The fifth and final volume, *Noble Essences* (1950), contains more brilliant reminiscences of his talented friends. In addition to *Tales My Father Taught Me* (1962), which rounds out the character of Sir George in rather a grand manner, Sir Osbert has issued his own selections of his essays under the title *Pound Wise.*

BOOK BY SITWELL

Autobiography. 5 vols. Peter Smith vol. 1 1944 o.p. Greenwood vols. 2–5 1946–50 o.p.

BOOKS ABOUT SITWELL

Fifoot, Richard. *Bibliography of Edith, Osbert and Sacheverell Sitwell.* Shoe String (Archon) 2d ed. 1971 $27.50

Fulford, Roger. *Osbert Sitwell.* British Bk. Ctr. repr. pap. $1.95

WALPOLE, HORACE, 4th Earl of Orford. 1717–1797

Walpole's charming, vivacious, and often brilliant letters (7,000 extant letters written and received) are "a monument to his writing skill as well as an invaluable picture of Georgian England." He always professed to be an amateur in literary affairs, as he amused himself with printing on his private printing press at his Strawberry Hill estate, where he printed many of the first editions of his own works and THOMAS GRAY's *Odes.*

Wilmarth Sheldon Lewis, a remarkably dedicated—and independently wealthy—scholar, who kept the Yale Walpole project going since its start in 1933, has told his own story in an autobiography, *One Man's Education,* which is "an engaging book of reminiscences" (*LJ*). Lewis's *Collector's Progress* (1951, o.p.) is an account of his "lifelong enthusiasm for collecting which finally focused on Horace Walpole and saw its fruition in his justly famous Walpole collection" (*LJ*).

BOOKS BY WALPOLE

The Yale Edition of Horace Walpole's Correspondence. 48 vols. 1937–to date.
Selected Letters. Ed. by W. Hadley, Biblio Dist. (Everyman's) repr. of 1926 ed. 1967 $9.95
Honest Diplomat at the Hague: Private Letters, 1715–1716. Ed. by John J. Murray, *Biography Index Repr. Ser.* Ayer repr. of 1955 ed. $22.00
Memoirs of the Reign of King George Second. AMS Pr. 3 vols. repr. of 1846 ed. $115.00
Last Journals of Horace Walpole during the Reign of George Third. Ed. by Frances A. Steuart, AMS Pr. 2 vols. repr. of 1910 ed. $95.00
Memoirs of the Reign of King George Third. Ed. by Russell G. Barker, AMS Pr. 4 vols. repr. of 1894 ed. $105.00; *Select Bibliographies Repr. Ser.* Ayer 4 vols. repr. of 1894 ed. $99.00

BOOKS ABOUT WALPOLE

Judd, Gerrit P. *Horace Walpole's Memoirs.* New College & Univ. Pr. 1959 pap. $5.95
Ketton-Cremer, R. W. *Horace Walpole: A Biography.* Cornell Univ. Pr. 3d ed. 1966 o.p. "[The author] has tried to rescue Walpole from a reputation for malice, affectation and triviality, a tone set by Macaulay, and to show [him] as a 'kindlier, wiser, more consistent and straightforward man' " (*LJ*). A "delightful, admirable biography" (*South Atlantic Quarterly*).
Lewis, Wilmarth S. *Horace Walpole.* National Gallery of Art o.p. The facts of Walpole's life plus many anecdotes distilled from 35 years of scholarly enthusiasm by the editor of the famous Yale edition of Walpole's correspondence.
Plumb, J. H. *Sir Robert Walpole.* Kelley 2 vols. 1961 o.p.
Smith, Warren Hunting. *Horace Walpole, Writer, Politician, and Connoisseur.* Yale Univ. Pr. 1967 o.p. Nineteen essays by Walpolian scholars throughout the world. Scholarly in its appeal but important for the first-published material it contains.

WOOLF, LEONARD. 1880–1969

Woolf's most visibly lasting accomplishment will probably be the volumes of his autobiography.

BOOKS BY WOOLF

Sowing: An Autobiography of the Years 1880 to 1904. Harcourt 1975 o.p.
Growing: An Autobiography of the Years 1904 to 1911. Harcourt 1975 o.p.
Beginning Again: An Autobiography of the Years 1911 to 1918. Harcourt 1975 o.p.
Downhill All the Way: An Autobiography of the Years 1919 to 1939. Harcourt 1975 o.p.
The Journey Not the Arrival Matters: An Autobiography of the Years 1939 to 1969. Harcourt 1975 o.p.

Name Index

In addition to authors, this index includes the names of persons mentioned in connection with titles of books written, whether they appear in introductory essays, general bibliographies at the beginnings of chapters, discussions under main headings, or "Books About" sections. Persons mentioned in passing—to indicate friendships, relationships, and so on—are generally not indexed. Editors are not indexed unless there is no specific author given; such books include anthologies, bibliographies, yearbooks, and the like. Translators, writers of introductions, forewords, afterwords, etc., are not indexed except for those instances where the translator seems as closely attached to a title as the real author, e.g., FitzGerald's translation of the *Rubáiyát of Omar Khayyám*. Main name headings appear in boldface as do the page numbers on which the main entries appear.

Title Index

Titles of all books discussed in *The Reader's Adviser* are indexed here, except broad generic titles such as "Complete Works," "Selections," "Poems," "Correspondence." Also omitted is any title listed with a main-entry author that includes that author's name, e.g., *Collected Prose of T. S. Eliot*, and titles under "Books About," e.g., *Eliot's Early Years* by Lyndall Gordon. The only exception to this is Shakespeare (Volume 2), where all works by and about him are indexed. To locate all titles by and about a main-entry author, the user should refer to the Name Index for the author's primary listing (given in boldface). Whenever the name of a main-entry author is part of a title indexed here, the page reference is to a section other than the primary listing. In general, subtitles are omitted. When two or more identical titles by different authors appear, the last name of each author is given in parentheses following the title.

Subject Index

This index provides detailed, multiple-approach access to the subject content of the volume, employing the subject headings as entry terms. Arrangement is alphabetical. Where subjects involve both literary forms and national literatures, entries are grouped first by form and then by country. Collective terms for authors are included, e.g., *Biographers, Dramatists, Economists, Poets,* but the reader is reminded to use the Name Index to locate individual writers. Reflecting the general coverage of Volume 1, entries refer to American and British works unless stated otherwise.